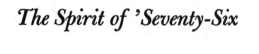

The Spirit of 'Seventy-Six

The Spirit
of
'Seventy-Six

THE STORY OF THE AMERICAN REVOLUTION
AS TOLD BY PARTICIPANTS

EDITED BY

Henry Steele Commager

AND

Richard B. Morris

CASTLE BOOKS

This edition published in 2002 by
CASTLE BOOKS

A division of Book Sales, Inc.
114 Northfield Avenue
Edison, New Jersey 08837

This edition published by arrangement with and permission of

HarperCollins Publishers, Inc.
10 East 53rd Street
New York, New York 10022

Library of Congress Catalog Card Number: 67-11325

ISBN: 0-7858-1463-9

Printed in the United States of America

This new edition is inscribed to
CASS CANFIELD
with admiration and affection

Table of Contents

(Names of authors are indicated by italics)

CHAPTER ONE: THE FIERCE SPIRIT OF RESISTANCE . . 1

List of Illustrations

List of Maps

Preface to the One-Volume Edition

The imminence of the American Revolution's bicentennial observances gives special point to the issuance of this one-volume edition of *The Spirit of 'Seventy-Six*, which presents the complete text of the original edition but in a more compact format. That forthcoming anniversary should underscore the central role the War for Independence has played in the shaping of our political tradition. It should serve to remind Americans that from the start their ancestors displayed a high level of tolerance for change, experimentation, and innovation, a conviction that progress could be achieved by enlightened self-government, and a deep-seated attachment to freedom. To those critics in other parts of the world who view America as being captive to a counterrevolutionary temper, the anniversary should serve as a needed corrective as well as a reminder, too, that America set off the chain reaction of revolutions that have continued at an accelerated pace from 1776 down to our own time.

HENRY STEELE COMMAGER
RICHARD B. MORRIS

Introduction

"WHO SHALL WRITE the history of the American Revolution?" asked John Adams in 1815. "Who can write it? Who will ever be able to write it?" If that task seemed formidable to one who had lived through every moment of it, who had known all the great actors in the turbulent drama, and who had kept the most compendious records, how shall it seem to us today when the actors have long since left the stage, when the flickering light of camp-fires, the whiff of grapeshot and the sound of oratory are merely words on crumbling paper?

The very phrase, the American Revolution, conjures up for us images familiar and heroic: Captain Parker mustering his little band on Lexington Common, Warren and Putnam in the thick of the fight on Bunker's Hill, Washington crossing the ice-floed Delaware, bloody footprints on the snow of Valley Forge, John Paul Jones closing with the *Serapis*, Nathan Hale beneath the gallows, Clark's riflemen wading the swollen waters of the Wabash, Morgan smashing Tarleton at Cowpens, the "world turned upside down" at Yorktown, and many others. This is as it should be, for these things have gone into American memory, and into the making of the American character.

Yet, needless to say, the Revolution was not all fighting; indeed the fighting, though essential, was perhaps not the most important part of it. No large armies were ever engaged on either side; there were comparatively few pitched battles; battle casualties were small; and much of the fighting was what we would now call guerrilla warfare. John Adams saw "the real American Revolution" as a "radical change in the principles, opinions, sentiments and affections of the people," and thought it was, above all, "in the minds and hearts of the people." The Revolution was, indeed, a wonderfully complex event, and historians are still exploring its labyrinthine complexities and philosophers its ultimate meaning. The Revolution was a war for political independence—the first great struggle to achieve independence from an imperial connection in modern times—and as such its impact was world-wide. It ushered in an era of revolutions on the European continent, in Latin America, and eventually in Asia and Africa—an era that is still with us. It was the birth of a nation—a nation different in its creation and in its character from the nations of the Old World, and one which was destined to fix the character of much of modern nationalism. It was the formulation of new principles of the relation of men to government, and of the relation of colonies to mother country. It was a series of far-reaching democratic reforms, the inauguration of effective self-government and of social and economic equality.

These are sweeping and abstract concepts; the Revolution was, too, many things that are simple and concrete. It was the Continental Congress debating the Suffolk Resolves; it was Jefferson writing the Declaration of Independence; it was the towns of Massachusetts drawing up the first state constitution; it was the confiscation of Tory estates and their redistribution to Patriots; it was Franklin at the Court of Versailles; it was the breaking of the Indian power on the northern and the southern borderlands; it was Jefferson and Madison toppling the Established Church in Virginia; it was the winning of the West and the settlement of the West; it was Tom Paine and Joel Barlow and Philip Freneau and the beginnings of American literature.

The Revolution was both a war for independence and a civil war. Unlike the War for Southern Independence, however, it was fought not between great sections of the country, but in each state and county and village, where brother opposed brother and father fought against son. Yet it was not a class war, not in the sense in which so many European revolutions were to be class wars. Both rich and poor fought on the Patriot side—large landowners like Washington and Jefferson, the Livingstons, the Schuylers, and the Van Rensselaers; affluent merchants like John Hancock and the Browns of Providence; men of affairs like Robert Morris of Pennsylvania and Henry Laurens of South Carolina; and, along with these, attorneys, clergymen, shopkeepers, farmers, mechanics, apprentices and fishermen. And the Loyalists, too, included large numbers from these very same groups and classes.

Unlike most later revolutions, but like the American Civil War, the War for Independence was distinguished by its concern for and emphasis upon legality. The Americans fought for the rights of Englishmen, as they believed them to be guaranteed by the British Constitution, and for the rights of man as they understood them to be guaranteed by Nature and Nature's God. That this was not a far-fetched or wholly partisan view is clear from the enthusiasm with which it was endorsed by many of the most distinguished British statesmen. Men like Chatham, Burke and Fox asserted, at the time, that the Americans were the champions of English liberties, and throughout the nineteenth century this view was accepted by historians like William E. Lecky, John Richard Green and George Otto Trevelyan.

There was, to be sure, a seamier side to the Revolution—tarring and feathering, lynching, the repudiation of debts and the confiscation of Tory estates, the vindictive persecution of inoffensive Loyalists. But there was no systematic Terror, no Thermidor, no mailed fist, and if the Revolution often seemed wanton and cruel to its victims it was, by comparison with the French, the Russian or the Spanish revolutions of later years, an almost decorous affair. The explanation is not hard to seek. From beginning to end the Revolution was led by an elite, not only benevolent and enlightened, but prosperous and conservative. Washington, John Adams, James Wilson, Hamilton, Jefferson, Franklin, Laurens—these and others like them constituted perhaps the most conservative, respectable and disinterested revolutionary agitators that any revolution ever confessed. These leaders—most of them trained to the law—insisted that the Revolution be managed in an orderly and lawful fashion and that the war be fought according to rules prevailing in civilized nations. They deprecated alike fanaticism and lawlessness, and it is a curious commentary on the American temperament that the eloquent and devoted Tom Paine was distrusted almost as much as the odious Benedict Arnold.

This legalism is prophetic of the America that was to develop in the course of the next century. Nothing is more interesting, indeed, than to detect the emergence, even this early, and in abnormal circumstances, of traits of character we have come to think of as American. The American who emerges from these pages is already—as St. John de Crèvecoeur wrote at the time—a new man. He is independent; he is impatient of discipline; he hopelessly mixes up military, economic and social activities. He is equalitarian, and has little patience with those who claim to be his superiors. He is ambitious and avaricious, and much given to speculation and to getting ahead. He is literate, takes an active part in the business of politics, and carries into camp the habits of self-government. He does not like fighting for its own sake, but fights well when he has to; he has little use for the military hierarchy, and bucks like a colt against taking orders. He is ingenious and practical; prefers a stone wall to an open field, and a timely retreat to a foolhardy advance. He is young and tough, survives hardships and diseases that would wipe out his more vulnerable descendants; he lives simply and unaffectedly. He is on the whole cheerful and good-humored, decent and honest; commits few crimes against persons (unless they are Indians) and, unless our sources deceive us by prudish silence, has a relatively high standard of sexual morality. He is vaguely religious, and already certain that there is a benign Providence whose chief concern is with him and his country.

Had the American Revolution been merely two wars—one against Britain and another to decide who would rule at home—it would still have constituted a formidable challenge to those who would write its history. But in addition the Revolution was a part, and a major part, of a world war. It was fought within sight of the cliffs of Dover, at Gibraltar, off the Cape of Good Hope, and along the Coromandel Coast. It was waged in the British Parliament as well as in the Continental Congress. Its objectives were pursued as relentlessly in Paris and Madrid as on Lake Champlain or the Delaware. And, in one way or another, it drew a large part of Europe into the conflict: thirty thousand German mercenaries, for example, an army and a navy from France, volunteers from most countries of northern Europe, and the Courts of Berlin and Copenhagen, the Hague and St. Petersburg. A roll call which includes Lafayette, Rochambeau, Fersen, von Steuben, Pulaski and Kosciusko, on the one side, and Knyphausen, André, La Corne, Breymann and Riedesel on the other, proclaims eloquently the international character of the war.

In the eighteenth century, even more than today, soldiers accepted the principle later immortalized by Alfred, Lord Tennyson: "Their's not to reason why, their's but to do and die." That was certainly true of the British soldiers who fought in America and, even more glaringly, of the German mercenaries who fought alongside them. The reader will look in vain for any ideology in the British accounts of the war, for any realization that more was at stake than military victory over upstart rebels. Even British statesmen—with the exception of the handful who championed the American cause—

rarely rose to any notion more exalted than that of punishing rebellion, preserving colonies and vindicating privilege. But from the beginning the Americans were conscious of and self-conscious about what they were doing, and
throughout the war their fighting was justified by moral and ideological
considerations. It was a "decent respect to the opinions of mankind" that
persuaded her leaders to set forth the causes that impelled them to separation;
what other people or nation had ever bothered with the opinions of mankind? And from beginning to end the Americans appealed to the judgment
of posterity, confident that posterity would approve of what they were doing. "We esteem ourselves bound by obligations of respect to the rest of the
world to make known the justice of our cause," said the Congress at the very
outset of the struggle. "I am well aware of the toil and blood and treasure
that it will cost us to maintain this declaration and support and defend these
States," wrote John Adams of the Declaration of Independence; "I can see
that the end is more than worth all the means, and that posterity will triumph
in that day's transactions." In the last of his *Crisis* papers Tom Paine observed
that "to see it in our power to make a world happy—to teach mankind the art
of being so—to exhibit, on the theatre of the universe, a character hitherto
unknown—and to have, as it were, a new creation intrusted to our hands, are
honors that command reflection and can neither be too highly estimated nor
too greatly received." Down in aristocratic Charleston, Judge Drayton
echoed the sentiment: "Thus has suddenly arisen in the world a new empire . . . and bids fair, by the blessing of God, to be the most glorious of any
upon record. America hails Europe, Asia and Africa. She proffers peace and
plenty." And Washington, in his last wartime circular to the States, reminded his fellow countrymen that "with our fate will the destiny of unborn
Millions be involved." The Americans, in short, did not conceive of their
struggle as a selfish or parochial one. They fought not for themselves alone,
but for all mankind; not for the rewards of the moment, but for the illimit-
able future. It is this that gives more than dramatic or even patriotic interest
to what they said and what they did.

No participant in the American Revolution was more conscious of the
challenge it offered to the historian than John Adams. He recognized that
before a sound history could be written—if indeed such a history could ever
be written—it would be necessary to "search and collect all the records, pamphlets, newspapers, and even handbills"; it was an enterprise to which he
invited Hezekiah Niles and other "young men of letters in all the States,"
promising them a task both "interesting and amusing." Niles himself so far
followed Adams' suggestion as to bring out, four years later, a slender volume somewhat grandiosely called *Principles and Acts of the Revolution*; his
purpose, he said, was "to show the feelings that prevailed in the Revolution,
not to give a history of events."

A history of events was certainly a more arduous task, and clearly it could
not be done until the source material had been assembled. The first undertaking of this nature was that launched by Peter Force, a journalist and
printer who had fought in the War of 1812 and later served as mayor of
Washington. His was the most ambitious project for collecting the docu-

mentary record of the Revolutionary period that has ever been projected. He planned, in all, six extensive series of volumes; he managed to publish only nine volumes in two of the series, but each one contained the equivalent of five or six ordinary volumes. Yet this vast mountain of source material carried the story only through the year 1776. Had Secretary of State Marcy not churlishly cut off appropriations for further volumes—and had his own strength held out—Force would single-handed have given us a compilation like the *Acta Sanctorum*, the *Monumenta Germaniae Historica* or the *Jesuit Relations*.

Other historians of the early national period like the Reverend Jared Sparks and George Bancroft devoted themselves to transcribing, collecting and editing the sources of the American Revolution. The indefatigable Frank Moore—who was later to exploit the Civil War—scanned the newspapers and gleaned many intriguing if unrelated items, and garnered some of the songs and ballads of the war. An extensive compilation of the diplomatic records was carried through to completion by Francis Wharton, who so happily combined theology and international law; and at the end of the century the bibliophile Benjamin Franklin Stevens issued no less than twenty-five volumes of *Facsimiles of Manuscripts in European Archives Relating to America, 1773-1783*. More recently Edmund C. Burnett has illuminated the formal record provided in the multivolumed *Journals of the Continental Congress* by compiling eight volumes of *Letters*, private as well as official, of its members. More valuable for our purposes than any of these somewhat fragmentary collections of sources are the voluminous writings of those men known collectively, and affectionately, as the Founding Fathers. To the earlier generation of scholars who made available selections from the writings of Washington, Jefferson, Franklin, John and Samuel Adams, John Jay, Tom Paine and others, we are deeply indebted, but our sense of obligation cannot blind us to the inadequacies of these editions. Happily new editions of Franklin, John Adams, Hamilton and Madison are promised, and Julian Boyd's *Writings of Thomas Jefferson*, one of the glories of American scholarship, has already covered the whole period of the Revolution and beyond.

To tell the story of the American Revolution in the words of participants has involved extensive examination of a vast miscellany of sources hitherto discrete: letters, diaries, journals, orderly books, official records of the Congress and of state legislatures, diplomatic correspondence, local histories, Parliamentary debates, the writings of statesmen on both sides of the Atlantic, the voluminous collections and proceedings of historical societies, and many manuscript repositories. It has meant running down countless clues to discover the best account of a battle, or an account written from a new vantage point; the best report of a debate; the most authentic record of a negotiation; the most faithful reflection of an attitude or a mood. When the mountain of material was finally assembled, it required sifting and verification and winnowing until the documents were slimmed down to the dimensions of these two volumes. In that winnowing it was inevitable that some precious things would be sacrificed to the demands of space, but it is perhaps astonishing that though much was taken, much abides.

The source material for the history of the American Revolution differs strikingly from that available for the history of the American Civil War. For one thing, though military participation was as general in all kinds of society, literary participation was not. In the Civil War every soldier, Union and Confederate alike, seemed to carry a notebook in his knapsack and to spend his ample spare time keeping a journal or indicting long letters to family and friends. Not so during the Revolution. The literary contribution from the privates of this war is meager. In the Civil War the best accounts came from privates or minor officers—a Chauncey Cook, a Jenkins Lloyd Jones, an Augustus Buell, a Frank Haskell, a John S. Wise. But in the Revolution those who played the leading political and military roles played, too, the leading literary roles: Washington, Franklin, Jefferson, Hamilton, John Adams, Ethan Allen, George Rogers Clark, Nathanael Greene and their associates. And what is true for the Americans is doubly true for the British and their German allies, where illiteracy was all but universal in the rank and file.

Another and striking difference between the reporting of the Revolution and of later wars is in the place of the newspaper. The Revolution had no Bull Run Russell, no George Alfred Townsend, no Frank Vizetelly. Local news was often ignored by newspaper printers because nobody in the community was presumed to know what had happened. Events were normally covered not by reporters, but by letters, addressed either to the editor or the printer or to leading figures in public life. Major political letters and essays often saw the light of day in the columns of newspapers, but seldom if ever great reporting. Newspaper accounts, then, furnish only a small portion of the story which the participants relate in these pages. The best of the American are garnered in Force's *Archives*, or in Moore's *Diary of the American Revolution;* the best British reports are to be found in Dodsley's famous *Annual Register*, and are probably from the gifted pen of Edmund Burke.

Happily this inadequacy is more than compensated by the richness of other sources, and particularly of the correspondence of that group we call The Fathers. It was an age of great letter-writing—the greatest in our history (and probably in English as well); an age when letter-writing was not so much an art as second nature. The astonishing thing is not only that men like Washington and Franklin, Hamilton and Jefferson, Adams and Jay wrote so well but that they found time to write so much so well. It is at once an exhilarating and a sobering thought that the writings of this single generation of the Fathers outweighs, qualitatively, and almost quantitatively, the writings of all the leading public men of our history in the century and a half since their day.

Their letters bear on every page the imprint of strong personalities; they are the letters of men who were ardent, opinionated, obstinate, brave, imaginative and eloquent. Above all, they are the letters of men who were untroubled by doubts and misgivings, who were sure of themselves and of the cause for which they fought. They could be refreshingly indiscreet, to our delight if not to that of their contemporaries: "A certain great man is most damnably deficient," wrote General Charles Lee of Washington. A Congressman could give even a General a dressing-down; thus Thomas Burke told General John Sullivan after Brandywine that he was "an officer whose evil conduct was forever productive of misfortunes to the army." Many a contemporary suffered from the sharp tongue and sharper pen of John Adams. "A certain great fortune and piddling genius," he wrote of poor John Dickinson, "has given a silly cast to our whole doings." Or consider Franklin, after enormous provocation from the exasperating Arthur Lee, explaining that he had "omitted answering some of your letters, particularly your angry ones, in which you, with very magisterial airs, schooled and documented me, as if I had been one of your domestics." Bluntest of all, when occasion merited it, was Washington himself. To General Heath, after the fiasco of Fort Independence, he wrote: "Your summons, as you did not attempt to fulfill your threat, was not only idle but farcical." To Joseph Reed he exploded, from his camp in Cambridge, that "such a dearth of public spirit, and want of virtue, such stock-jobbing and fertility in all the low arts to obtain advantages of one kind or another in this great change of military arrangement, I never saw before and pray God I may never be witness to again." And of the hapless General Conway, Washington wrote, "He is capable of all the malignity of detraction, and all the meanness of intrigue to gratify the absurd resentment of disappointed vanity, or to answer the purposes of personal aggrandizement and promote the interests of faction."

Another quality that gives these letters vitality and excitement is the courage, even the bravura, that animated their authors. "This is the most magnificent movement of all," wrote young John Adams of the destruction of the tea. Whether or not Ethan Allen actually called for Ticonderoga's surrender "in the name of Jehovah and the Continental Congress" the remark was perfectly in character with the man, as was the answer that John Paul Jones gave to the captain of the *Serapis*, "I have not yet begun to fight"; and James Mugford's dying words to his crew, "Don't give up the ship! You will beat them off!" So Benedict Arnold after the bloody repulse before Quebec, "I am in the way of my duty, and know no fear." So, too, Colonel McIntosh's reply to Colonel Fuser's demand for the surrender of Fort Morris, "Come and take it." Even the women expressed something of this sense of defiance; when a redcoat pointed his musket at nurse Sarah Tarrant of Salem, she cried, "Fire if you have the courage, but I doubt it." Alas, the women are but poorly represented in these pages. Except for a few, like the sprightly Mercy Warren or the devoted Abigail Adams, they were not much given to letters, or what they wrote was not salvaged for posterity.

It was an age of magnificent oratory, and the echoes of some of the more memorable speeches can be caught in these pages. From the first stirring appeals in the Continental Congress down to Washington's moving rebuke to the authors of the Newburgh Resolves, oratory quickened the spirit of resistance and inspired loyalty to the Patriot cause. "Gentlemen may cry, 'Peace! peace!' but there is no peace," warned Patrick Henry, and "the next gale that blew from the north" brought news of Lexington. Or listen to the mighty Edmund Burke. "An Englishman," he said, "is the unfittest person on earth to argue another Englishman into slavery." Burke could be scorching as well as defiant; note his burlesque of Burgoyne's proclamation threatening the Americans with Indian warfare: "My tender-hearted hyenas go forth." Or listen to the boyish Marquis of Granby on American taxation: "I disavow the whole system. It is commenced in iniquity, it is pursued with resentment; and it can terminate in nothing but blood. Under whatsoever shape in futurity it may be revived ... it shall from me meet the most constant, determined and invariable opposition." Or, finally, hearken to Washington at Newburgh: "Let me conjure you, in the name of our common country, as you value your own sacred honor, as you respect the rights of humanity, as you regard the military and national character of America, to express your utmost horror and detestation of the man who wishes, under any specious pretenses, to overturn the liberties of our country."

Here, then, is the story of the American Revolution as its participants told it or wrote it. It is not the whole story—that would be impossible—nor is it even the story of the whole war. To a large degree the record as we present it here is a fortuitous one: editors are not, after all, free agents, but must content themselves with what is available. It was a literate and a literary generation, but there are, nevertheless, jagged gaps in the record: men busy fighting a war did not always find time to record it. What would we not give for Sam Adams' account of the most famous of all Tea Parties; for Washington's account of the passage of the Delaware; for Jefferson's story—contemporary, not retrospective—of the writing of the Great Declaration; for Morgan's story of his victory at Cowpens! Yet the military record is, on the whole, rich and full. Far more serious are the gaps in the nonmilitary record. It is shocking that so few of the doctors—Benjamin Rush is almost the only exception—left a record of the medical and surgical history of the war. We have no right to expect too much of the story of espionage and counterespionage, but what would we not give for the inner story of the baffling James Rivington, or for a circumstantial account of his change of allegiance from the pen of the gifted Benjamin Thompson, Count Rumford! There are scores of prison narratives, but almost all of them melodramatic; there are—in the orders of Washington and his generals—hundreds of items on discipline, but nobody thought to discuss the problem as a whole. And what of the many other things we would know about: the commissary, the services of supply, arms and ammunition, transportation, finance and currency, morale; the evidence on all these is meager, disjointed and prosaic.

The situation with respect to the British side of the war is nothing less than deplorable. The melancholy fact is that, except in realms of high debate, the British themselves fail us. There are some magnificent speeches in Parliament; but aside from the narratives of a Sergeant Lamb, a Frederick Mackenzie, an Ambrose Serle and a few others, who wrote not too condescendingly about the fighting, the literary record is feeble. The explanation for this is a bit baffling. It is partly that the English were preoccupied with so many other matters; partly that the war was fought by professional soldiers and these were not much given to literature; partly that proportionately far fewer Englishmen were involved than Americans. And let it not be forgotten that though Britain boasted far more men of letters than America, the general level of literacy was substantially lower than in America.

We have tried to present most aspects of the war, the political, the diplomatic, the social and economic, the intellectual and cultural as well as the military and naval; and we have tried to let the British present their own case as fairly as possible. There are of course many omissions, dictated by space: readers who may regret gaps and deformities can console themselves with the thought that these hurt the editors more than they hurt the readers. One major omission is deliberate: the story of the movement toward a closer union. The reader will look in vain here for the writing of the Articles of Confederation, for the many proposals to revise and repair those Articles; or for the evolution of the policies that culminated in the Ordinances of 1784, 1785 and 1787. The explanation of this is simple: the story is much too large and too important to be compressed within the limits of a chapter, and has been reserved, therefore, for a subsequent volume.

The source material is presented as it has come to us; needless to say, it has not always come in virginal form. We have taken few liberties with the text, and those only which scholarly opinion in general approves: we have broken up solid pages of print into paragraphs; spelled out abbreviations; inserted essential punctuation, and occasionally corrected (rather than modernized) spelling where necessary to clarity and understanding. Aside from these minor changes, the misspellings, the flouting of grammar and syntax, are as they were first written down with quill pen on paper. It should not be necessary to add that as we have not attempted to correct minor matters of spelling and punctuation, so we have not sought to correct major matters of fact or interpretation. If we were to attempt to correct every analysis of tactics, every report of casualties, every legal argument, every interpretation of character, the editorial notes would far outstrip the text. Quite aside from this, errors, misconceptions and misinterpretations are themselves an essential part of the record.

Much is said in these two volumes about the powerful forces which were arrayed against the Patriots, about their enemies, external and internal, about their divisions and squabbles, the ravages of selfishness and self-interest, of vanity and greed, which thwarted the Patriot efforts both on the military and on the home fronts. How, then, did it happen that the Patriots did win, and against overwhelming odds? We shall not attempt here a consideration of causation in history, or even an evaluation of the importance of such matters as French assistance, British blunders, or geography. Fundamentally the answer to the question about American victory is to be found in the phrase, commonly assigned to Jefferson, which provides the title for these volumes. The Patriots won because the Spirit of 'Seventy-Six was kept alive in the hearts of common soldiers and commissioned officers and a few dedicated generals and statesmen until the British recognized the impossibility of subduing such a people and acquiesced in their independence.

There is, too, in much of the writing of the Revolution a strain of loftiness, a nobility, a style and spirit of greatness. No man exemplified that spirit better than Washington, who looms large in these pages as an indispensable symbol of selfless patriotism and integrity. We see him quickening the Pa-

triot cause in Virginia on the eve of the crisis, taking command of a rabble
in arms at Cambridge and forcing the British out of Boston, outwitted but
undismayed at Long Island, delivering lightning blows at Trenton and Princeton, faltering momentarily at Brandywine and Germantown, standing fast
through the ordeal of Valley Forge and, the next winter, of Morristown,
holding out against jealousy and stupidity and rashness in Congress and in
the army, and in the end, by the sheer power of determination and force
of personality, keeping the army in being until the day of deliverance at
Yorktown. His was the Spirit of 'Seventy-Six, a spirit most eloquently captured by Thomas Paine's first *Crisis* paper: "These are the times that try
men's souls. The summer soldier and the sunshine patriot will shrink from
the service of their country. But he who stands it now deserves the love
and thanks of man and woman."

In these pages we meet some who did not shrink, who marched with
Arnold in that memorable journey to Quebec, who walked with bloody feet
at Princeton, or waded the icy waters of the Wabash on the march to Vincennes, or suffered in the *Jersey* prison ship at New York, or fought with
Marion along the Pedee or died at Cowpens or Eutaw Springs, so that their
children and their children's children could be free. For they knew, as did the
Athenians of old, that "the price of happiness is freedom, and the price of
freedom a brave heart." They knew, with John Adams, that "freedom is a
counterbalance for poverty, discord and war." They made it possible for
Washington to say, in that Inaugural Address which ended one era and
ushered in another: "The preservation of the sacred fire of liberty, and the
destiny of the republican model of government, are justly considered as
deeply, perhaps as finally, staked on the experiment entrusted to the hands of
the American people."

HENRY STEELE COMMAGER
RICHARD B. MORRIS

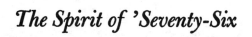

The Spirit of 'Seventy-Six

CHAPTER ONE

The Fierce Spirit of Resistance

WE MUST *begin somewhere and, notwithstanding John Adams' insistence that the Revolution was in the hearts and minds of men and began with the first plantation in America, we must begin with some decisive act. It is not difficult to find that act: the Boston Tea Party. Earlier issues and conflicts had agitated and even exacerbated relations between the colonies and the mother country—the Stamp Act, the Townshend Acts, the seizure of the sloop* Liberty, *the Boston Massacre, the burning of the* Gaspée—*but none of these precipitated an open break. That came over what appeared to be a less serious issue, and one lacking in those constitutional overtones so dear to the American patriots—the Act of Parliament of May 10, 1773, permitting the East India Company to export tea to the colonies with remission of ordinary British duties and with the assurance of a virtual monopoly on the retail sale. It was a clever plan. The Americans would get their tea cheaper than ever before; the company would be rescued from financial ruin; and the principle of a tax—that "peppercorn of principle"—would be vindicated. "It was no purpose making objections, for the King would have it so," said Lord North.*

The East India Company promptly took advantage of the new law by shipping half a million pounds of tea to a picked group of agents in Boston, New York, Philadelphia and Charleston. It was the danger of this monopoly rather than the tax itself—only 3 pence to the pound—that aroused resentment in the colonies. In Charleston the tea was landed but placed in government warehouses and allowed to rot; in Philadelphia, New York and elsewhere the ships were not permitted to land their offensive cargoes. Only in Boston did the authorities, egged on by the stubborn Hutchinson, persist in the attempt to land the tea. It was to prevent this that Samuel Adams, Hancock, Warren, Revere and other leaders of the Massachusetts radicals organized the Boston Tea Party.

It was the end of November 1773 when the first ship bearing tea sailed into Boston harbor—the Dartmouth; *she was shortly followed by two others. "The flame is kindled, and like lightning it catches from soul to soul," wrote Abigail Adams to her husband John. Boston erupted into public meetings and private conferences; "the town is as furious as it was in the time of the Stamp Act," said Governor Hutchinson. Two mass meetings resolved that the ships must*

I

return to England without payment of duty. This Governor Hutchinson refused to permit, and the issue was joined.

I. MOHAWK INDIANS SPILL TEA IN BOSTON HARBOR

December 16, 1773, is one of the fateful days of American history. All day long the people of Boston and surrounding towns, "merchants, yeomen, gentlemen" to the number of 7,000 (it was said), swarmed down to the wharves to look at the three ships, their holds big with history, or milled around the crooked streets of the old town, or gazed into the windows of the Green Dragon Tavern, meeting place of the radicals, or thronged into the Old South Meeting House to listen to their leaders discuss what was to be done if Governor Hutchinson and Captain Rotch proved obdurate. In the afternoon young Josiah Quincy—with John Adams he had defended British soldiers tried for murder at the time of the "massacre"—spoke to the motion that the people of Boston should not suffer the tea to land; we give here a brief extract of that speech as recalled later by the Reverend William Gordon, self-appointed historian of the Revolution.

When Captain Rotch gave his final answer that "if called upon by the proper officers he should attempt, for his own security, to land the tea," there was a war whoop and "prodigious shouting"; the meeting broke up; the crowd poured down to Griffin's wharf; and three bands of Mohawk Indians—or were they Narragansett?—went quietly on board the three ships and threw overboard 342 chests of tea.

We give here an excerpt from Josiah Quincy's speech; a contemporary ballad; an account by the merchant John Andrews, whom we shall meet again; a suspiciously circumstantial account dictated many years later by one of the survivors, George Hewes; and Governor Hutchinson's sedate statement, written twenty years later but bearing all the marks of authenticity which we associate with his judicious mind.

1. Josiah Quincy, Jr., Exhorts the Bostonians to Firmness

In Old South Meeting House, to the motion that the people of Boston should not suffer the tea to land.

December 16, 1773

It is not, Mr. Moderator, the spirit that vapors within these walls that must stand us in stead. The exertions of this day will call forth events which will make a very different spirit necessary for our salvation. Whoever supposes that shouts and hosannas will terminate the trials of the day entertains a childish fancy. We must be grossly ignorant of the importance and value of the prize for which we contend; we must be equally ignorant of the power of those who have combined against us; we must be blind to that malice, inveteracy and insatiable revenge which actuate our enemies, public and private, abroad and in our bosom, to hope that we shall end this controversy without the sharpest conflicts, to flatter ourselves that popular resolves, popular harangues, popular acclamations and popular vapor will vanquish our foes. Let us consider the issue. Let us look to the end. Let us weigh and consider before

we advance to those measures which must bring on the most trying and terrific struggle this country ever saw.

    —FROTHINGHAM, *Rise of the Republic of the United States*, pp. 306-307.

2. RALLYING SONG OF THE TEA PARTY

1773

Rally, Mohawks! bring out your axes,
And tell King George we'll pay no taxes
    On his foreign tea;
His threats are vain, and vain to think
To force our girls and wives to drink
    His vile Bohea!
Then rally, boys, and hasten on
To meet our chiefs at the Green Dragon.

Our Warren's there and bold Revere,
With hands to do, and words to cheer,
    For liberty and laws;
Our country's "braves" and firm defenders
Shall ne'er be left by true North-Enders
    Fighting Freedom's cause!
Then rally, boys, and hasten on
To meet our chiefs at the Green Dragon.

    —Goss, *Life of Colonel Paul Revere*, I, 128n.

3. "YOU'D HAVE THOUGHT THE INHABITANTS OF THE INFERNAL REGIONS HAD BROKE LOOSE"

John Andrews to William Barrell, merchant of Philadelphia.

                             Boston, December 18, 1773

    However precarious our situation may be, yet *such* is the present calm
composure of the people that a stranger would hardly think that ten thousand
pounds sterling of the East India Company's tea was destroyed the night, or
rather the evening before last, yet it's a serious truth; and if yours, together
with the other Southern provinces, should rest satisfied with *their* quota being
stored, poor Boston will feel the whole weight of ministerial vengeance. However, it's the opinion of most people that we stand an equal chance now
whether troops are sent in consequence of it or not; whereas, had it been
stored, we should inevitably have had them to enforce the sale of it.

    The affair was transacted with greatest regularity and despatch. Mr.
Rotch, finding he exposed himself not only to the loss of his ship but for the
value of the tea, in case he sent her back with it *without a clearance from the
custom house*, as the Admiral kept a ship in readiness to make a seizure of it
whenever it should sail under *those circumstances*, therefore declined complying with his former promises and absolutely declared his vessel should not
carry it without a *proper* clearance could be procured or he to be indemnified
for the value of her: when a general muster was assembled, from this and all
the neighboring towns, to the number of five or six thousand, at 10 o'clock

Thursday morning in the Old South Meeting House, where they passed a *unanimous* vote that the tea should go out of the harbour that afternoon, and sent a committee with Mr. Rotch to the Custom house to *demand* a clearance, which the collector told them was not in his power to give, without the duties being first paid. They then sent Mr. Rotch to Milton to ask a pass from the Governor, who sent for answer that "consistent with the rules of government and his duty to the King he could not grant one without they produced a previous clearance from the office."

By the time he returned with this message the candles were light in the house, and upon reading it, such prodigious shouts were made that induced me, while drinking tea at home, to go out and know the cause of it. The house was so crowded I could get no farther than the porch, when I found the moderator was just declaring the meeting to be *dissolved*, which caused another general shout, out doors and in, and three cheers. What with that, and the consequent noise of breaking up the meeting, you'd thought that the inhabitants of the infernal regions had broke loose. For my part, I went contentedly home and finished my tea, but was soon informed what was going forward: but still not crediting it without ocular demonstration, I went and was *satisfied*.

They mustered, I'm told, upon Fort Hill, to the number of about two hundred, and proceeded, two by two, to Griffin's wharf, where Hall, Bruce and Coffin lay, each with 114 chests of the *ill-fated* article on board; the two former with *only* that article, but the latter, arrived at the wharf only the day before, was freighted with a large quantity of other goods, which they took the *greatest* care not to injure in the least, and before *nine* o'clock in the evening, every chest from on board the three vessels was knocked to pieces and flung over the sides. They say the actors were *Indians* from *Narragansett*. Whether they were or not, to a transient observer they appeared as *such*, being cloathed in blankets with the heads muffled, and copper-colored countenances, being each armed with a hatchet or axe, and pair pistols, nor was their *dialect* different from what I conceive these geniusses to speak, as their jargon was unintelligible to all but themselves. . . .

Should not have troubled you with this, by this post, hadn't I thought you would be glad of a more particular account of so *important a transaction* than you could have obtained by common report; and if it affords my brother but a *temporary* amusement, I shall be more than repaid for the trouble of writing it. . . .

—ANDREWS, "Letters," *Mass. Hist. Soc. Proc.*, VIII, 325-326.

4. "No Attempt Was Made to Resist Us"

[1834]

Recollections of George Hewes.

The tea destroyed was contained in three ships, lying near each other at what was called at that time Griffin's wharf, and were surrounded by armed ships of war, the commanders of which had publicly declared that if the rebels, as they were pleased to style the Bostonians, should not withdraw their opposition to the landing of the tea before a certain day, the 17th day of

December, 1773, they should on that day force it on shore, under the cover of their cannon's mouth. On the day preceding the seventeenth, there was a meeting of the citizens of the county of Suffolk, convened at one of the churches in Boston, for the purpose of consulting on what measures might be considered expedient to prevent the landing of the tea, or secure the people from the collection of the duty. At that meeting a committee was appointed to wait on Governor Hutchinson, and request him to inform them whether he would take any measures to satisfy the people on the object of the meeting. To the first application of this committee, the Governor told them he would give them a definite answer by five o'clock in the afternoon. At the hour appointed, the committee again repaired to the Governor's house, and on inquiry found he had gone to his country seat at Milton, a distance of about six miles. When the committee returned and informed the meeting of the absence of the Governor, there was a confused murmur among the members, and the meeting was immediately dissolved, many of them crying out, "Let every man do his duty, and be true to his country"; and there was a general huzza for Griffin's wharf.

It was now evening, and I immediately dressed myself in the costume of an Indian, equipped with a small hatchet, which I and my associates denominated the tomahawk, with which, and a club, after having painted my face and hands with coal dust in the shop of a blacksmith, I repaired to Griffin's wharf, where the ships lay that contained the tea. When I first appeared in the street after being thus disguised, I fell in with many who were dressed, equipped and painted as I was, and who fell in with me and marched in order to the place of our destination.

When we arrived at the wharf, there were three of our number who assumed an authority to direct our operations, to which we readily submitted. They divided us into three parties, for the purpose of boarding the three ships which contained the tea at the same time. The name of him who commanded the division to which I was assigned was Leonard Pitt. The names of the other commanders I never knew. We were immediately ordered by the respective commanders to board all the ships at the same time, which we promptly obeyed. The commander of the division to which I belonged, as soon as we were on board the ship, appointed me boatswain, and ordered me to go to the captain and demand of him the keys to the hatches and a dozen candles. I made the demand accordingly, and the captain promptly replied, and delivered the articles; but requested me at the same time to do no damage to the ship or rigging. We then were ordered by our commander to open the hatches and take out all the chests of tea and throw them overboard, and we immediately proceeded to execute his orders, first cutting and splitting the chests with our tomahawks, so as thoroughly to expose them to the effects of the water.

In about three hours from the time we went on board, we had thus broken and thrown overboard every tea chest to be found in the ship, while those in the other ships were disposing of the tea in the same way, at the same time. We were surrounded by British armed ships, but no attempt was made to resist us.

We then quietly retired to our several places of residence, without having any conversation with each other, or taking any measures to discover who were our associates; nor do I recollect of our having had the knowledge of the name of a single individual concerned in that affair, except that of Leonard Pitt, the commander of my division, whom I have mentioned. There appeared to be an understanding that each individual should volunteer his services, keep his own secret, and risk the consequence for himself. No disorder took place during that transaction, and it was observed at that time that the stillest night ensued that Boston had enjoyed for many months.

During the time we were throwing the tea overboard, there were several attempts made by some of the citizens of Boston and its vicinity to carry off small quantities of it for their family use. To effect that object, they would watch their opportunity to snatch up a handful from the deck, where it became plentifully scattered, and put it into their pockets. One Captain O'Connor, whom I well knew, came on board for that purpose, and when he supposed he was not noticed, filled his pockets, and also the lining of his coat. But I had detected him and gave information to the captain of what he was doing. We were ordered to take him into custody, and just as he was stepping from the vessel, I seized him by the skirt of his coat, and in attempting to pull him back, I tore it off; but, springing forward, by a rapid effort he made his escape. He had, however, to run a gauntlet through the crowd upon the wharf, each one, as he passed, giving him a kick or a stroke.

Another attempt was made to save a little tea from the ruins of the cargo by a tall, aged man who wore a large cocked hat and white wig, which was fashionable at that time. He had slightly slipped a little into his pocket, but being detected, they seized him and, taking his hat and wig from his head, threw them, together with the tea, of which they had emptied his pockets, into the water. In consideration of his advanced age, he was permitted to escape, with now and then a slight kick.

The next morning, after we had cleared the ships of the tea, it was discovered that very considerable quantities of it were floating upon the surface of the water; and to prevent the possibility of any of its being saved for use, a number of small boats were manned by sailors and citizens, who rowed them into those parts of the harbor wherever the tea was visible, and by beating it with oars and paddles so thoroughly drenched it as to render its entire destruction inevitable.

—[Hawkes,] *A Retrospect of the Boston Tea-Party,* pp. 39-41.

5. Hutchinson Preserves the Constitution Rather Than the Tea

The people were summoned, by notifications posted in different quarters, to meet at the tree of liberty, to hear the resignation of the consignees of the tea, which was then daily expected. The consignees also, by a letter left at one of their houses, were required to attend at the same time at their peril. The people met, but, the consignees not appearing, a committee was appointed to acquaint them at one of their warehouses where they had met that, as they had neglected to attend, the people thought themselves warranted to consider them as their enemies. They treated the message with contempt, and the people, many of whom had followed the committee, forced open the doors of the warehouse and attempted to enter a room in which the consignees, with some of their friends, were shut up; but, meeting with resistance, they soon after dispersed, and the body of the people who remained at the tree, upon the return of their committee, dispersed also. This seems to have been intended only as an intimation to the consignees of what they had to expect.

Two days after, what was called a "legal" meeting of the inhabitants was held in Faneuil Hall. Here the resolves which had been passed by the people of Philadelphia were first adopted; and then a further resolve passed that the inhabitants of the town, by all means in their power, will prevent the sale of the teas exported by the East India Company, and that they justly expect no merchant will, on any pretence whatever, import any tea liable to the duty. Committees were also appointed to wait on the several persons to whom the teas were consigned, and in the name of the town to request them from a regard to their characters, and to the peace and good order of the town, immediately to resign their trust. Each of the consignees gave an answer of the same import, that, as they were not yet acquainted with the terms upon which the teas were consigned to them, they were not able to give a definite answer to the request of the town. The answers were all voted to be daringly affrontive to the town, and the meeting was immediately after dissolved.

Three vessels were expected every hour with the teas. The consignees were afraid of exposing themselves and their bondsmen to damages, which might arise from a refusal or neglect to execute their trust; on the other hand, they were anxiously concerned for their personal safety, and made their application to the governor. He foresaw that this would prove a more difficult affair than any which had preceded it since he had been in the chair. The controversies with the council and house had a tendency to deprive him of the esteem and favour of the people; but he had not been apprehensive of injury to his person. He was now to encounter with bodies of the people collected together, and a great proportion of them the lowest part of the people, from whom, when there is no power to restrain them, acts of violence are to be expected. He knew that the council would give him no aid. . . . He had no expectations of being able to protect the persons of the consignees or the property under their care. He considered that, if the ships came into the harbour above the castle, they could not pass by it again without a permit under his hand, and that his granting such permit would be more than he should be able to justify. He therefore advised to their anchoring without the castle, and their waiting for orders; and this advice was approved of by the consignees, and by the owner of the ship first expected, if not by the owners of the other ships; and orders were given to the pilots accordingly.

All design of riots and acts of violence had been disclaimed by the conductors of measures for preventing the tea from being landed. A great number of rioters assembled, notwithstanding, before the house of Mr. Clarke, one of the consignees, in the evening, and attempted to force their way in, broke the windows to pieces, and otherwise damaged it, so as to cause the occupiers to remove out of it. One of the consignees fired with ball upon the mob from one of the windows, soon after which the rioters dispersed. . . .

On Sunday one of the ships with the tea arrived, and anchored below the castle. Notification in a form* proper to inflame the people was posted up, calling upon them to assemble; and while the governor and council were sitting on the Monday in the council chamber, and known to be consulting upon means for preserving the peace of the town, several thousands, inhabitants of Boston and other towns, were assembled in a publick meeting-house at a small distance, in direct opposition and defiance. The council, when they had considered the exception which the governor had made, ordered a recommitment of the report; but it was returned without any material alteration, all advice to secure the tea upon its being landed being expressly refused, because such advice would be a measure for procuring payment of the duty. Three or four of the council in the debate appeared to disapprove of the report, but, when the question was put, it passed unanimously; and the last and senior councilor, though he had argued very strongly against it, gave his voice for it, adding that it would not do for him to be alone. The council advised the governor's calling upon the magistrates to meet, and to take necessary care for the preservation of the peace; which advice being complied with, the people, in a few hours after, passed a vote, which they caused to be printed, declaring that "the conduct of Governor Hutchinson, in requiring the justices of peace in the town to meet and use their endeavours to suppress routs, riots, etc., carried a designed reflection upon the people there met together, and was solely calculated to serve the views of administration." The council, declining any further advice, were dismissed; the people continued together, in possession of all the power of government, for any purpose they thought fit. . . .

The governor, seeing the powers of government thus taken out of the hands of the legally established authority, could not justify a total silence, though he knew he could say nothing which would check the usurpers. He sent the sheriff with a proclamation to be read in the meeting, bearing testimony against it as an unlawful assembly, and requiring the moderator and the people present forthwith to separate at their peril. The sheriff desired leave to read the directions he had received from the governor, which was granted; but the reading of the proclamation was opposed, until Mr. Adams signified his acquiescence. Being read, a general hiss followed, and then a question whether they would surcease all further proceedings, as the governor required, which was determined in the negative, *nemine contradicente.* . . .

As a permit or pass was always required at the castle for all vessels except small coasters, and there were several men of war in the harbour, which it was supposed would stop the ship from proceeding any other way, the destruction of the tea was considered as necessary to prevent payment of the duty. A demand was made from the collector, in form, of a clearance for the ship, which he could not grant until the goods which were imported, and regularly entered, were landed, and the duties paid or secured; and the like demand of a

---

* "Friends! brethren! countrymen!—That worst of plagues, the detested tea, shipped for this port by the East India Company, is now arrived in this harbour—the hour of destruction or manly opposition to the machinations of tyranny stare you in the face. Every friend to his country, to himself, and posterity, is now called upon to meet at Faneuil Hall, at nine o'clock *this day,* at which time the bells will ring, to make an united and successful resistance to this last, worst, and most destructive measure of administration."

permit was made of the naval officer, with whom blank permits were intrusted by the governor, to be filled up and delivered to such vessels only as had been cleared at the custom-house, and, therefore, in this case was refused. It was expected that in twenty days after the arrival of the tea a demand of the duty would be made by the collector, and the ship or goods be seized; which would occasion additional difficulties.

Another meeting of the body was, therefore, called, in order to inquire the reason of the delay in sending the ship back to England. The people came into Boston from the adjacent towns within twenty miles, from some, more, from others, less, as they were affected; and, as soon as they were assembled [December 14, 1773], enjoined the owner of the ship, at his peril, to demand of the collector of the customs a clearance for the ship, and appointed ten of their number a committee to accompany him; and adjourned for two days to receive the report.

Being reassembled and informed by the owner that a clearance was refused, he was then enjoined immediately to apply to the governor for a pass by the castle. He made an apology to the governor for coming upon such an errand, having been compelled to it; and received an answer that no pass ever had been, or lawfully could be, given to any vessel which had not first been cleared at the custom-house, and that, upon his producing a clearance, such pass would immediately be given by the naval officer. The governor inquired of him whether he did not apprehend his ship in danger from the people, and offered him a letter to Admiral Montagu, desiring him to afford all necessary protection. He said he had been advised to remove his vessel under the stern of the admiral's ship, but, among other reasons for not doing it, mentioned his fears of the rage of the people; that his concern was not for his ship, which he did not believe was in danger, but he could not tell what would be the fate of the tea on board. He declined taking any letter to the admiral, and returned to the people. The governor was unable to judge what would be the next step. The secretary had informed him that a principal leader of the people had declared, in the hearing of the deputy secretary, that, if the governor should refuse a pass, he would demand it himself, at the head of one hundred and fifty men, etc.; and he was not without apprehensions of a further application. But he was relieved from his suspense, the same evening, by intelligence from town of the total destruction of the tea.

It was not expected that the governor would comply with the demand; and, before it was possible for the owner of the ship to return from the country with an answer, about fifty men had prepared themselves and passed by the house where the people were assembled to the wharf where the vessels lay, being covered with blankets and making the appearance of Indians. The body of the people remained until they had received the governor's answer; and then, after it had been observed to them that, everything else in their power having been done, it now remained to proceed in the only way left, and that, the owner of the ship having behaved like a man of honour, no injury ought to be offered to his person or property, the meeting was declared to be dissolved, and the body of the people repaired to the wharf and surrounded the immediate actors, as a guard and security, until they had finished their work. In two or three hours they hoisted out of the holds of the ships three hundred and forty-two chests of tea and emptied them into the sea. . . .

This was the boldest stroke which had yet been struck in America. The people in all parts of the province shewed more or less concern at the expected consequences. They were, however, at a distance; something might intervene to divert them. Besides, the thing was done: there was no way of nullifying it. Their leaders feared no consequences. To engage the people in some desperate measure had long been their plan. They never discovered more concern than when the people were quiet upon the repeal of an act of Parliament, or upon concessions made or assurances given; and never more satisfaction than when government had taken any new measures, or appeared to be inclined to them, tending, or which might be improved, to irritate and disturb the people. They had nothing to fear for themselves. They had gone too far to recede. If the colonies were subject to the supreme authority and laws of Great Britain, their offences, long since, had been of the highest nature. Their all depended upon attaining to the object which first engaged them. There was no way of attaining to it but by involving the body of the people in the same circumstances they were in themselves. And it is certain that ever after this time an opinion was easily instilled, and was continually increasing, that the body of the people had also gone too far to recede, and that an open and general revolt must be the consequence; and it was not long before actual preparations were visibly making for it in most parts of the province.

—HUTCHINSON, *History of Massachusetts-Bay*, III, 423-440 *passim*.

II. PARLIAMENT PUNISHES THE BOSTONIANS

"This," wrote young John Adams in his Diary, "is the most significant movement of all. There is a dignity, a majesty, a sublimity, in this last effort of the patriots that I greatly admire. This destruction of the tea is so bold, so daring, so firm, intrepid and inflexible, and it must have important consequences, and so lasting that I cannot but consider it as an epocha in history."

As usual John Adams was right. The destruction of the tea did indeed have important consequences. Americans generally applauded the boldness of the Bostonians, though even among them there were yet voices of disapprobation; but in Britain the reaction was sharp and violent. Parliament met on March 7 in an angry mood, and Lord North, reflecting faithfully George III's determination to make an example of the wicked Americans, asked for a series of acts to punish the Bostonians: the notorious Intolerable Acts. The first of these, the Boston Port Bill, laid before Parliament March 14, precipitated a debate which was to continue for seven years. The friends of America—Chatham, Burke, Conway, Johnstone, Fox and their followers—had eloquence and logic on their side, but Lord North had numbers. The act closing the port of Boston passed the Commons March 25 and received the royal assent a week later. North followed it with a series of other acts: the Massachusetts Government Act, the Administration of Justice Act, the Quartering Act and—in a somewhat different category—the Quebec Act. Taken together these were named, by Patriots, the Intolerable Acts.

We give here some excerpts of the debates in the Commons, and two let-ters from William Lee (brother of the more famous Richard Henry Lee, Arthur Lee and Francis Lightfoot Lee of Virginia) who at the time served as alderman of the city of London, the only American ever to hold that office.

1. THE FATEFUL DEBATE

A. LORD NORTH CALLS FOR SWIFT PUNISHMENT

Debate in the Commons on the Boston Port Bill, March 14, 1774.

. . . As soon as the House had resumed its former tranquillity, his Majesty's speech of the 7th instant was read. Upon which, Lord North rose. He said it contained two propositions: the one to enable his Majesty to put an end to the present disturbances in America, the other to secure the just dependence of the colonies on the crown of Great Britain. His lordship observed that the present disorders originated in Boston, in the province of Massachusetts Bay; and hoped that the method he should propose to the House would be adopted. He should confine himself particularly to those disturbances which had been created since the 1st of December. He said that it was impossible for our com-merce to be safe whilst it continued in the harbour of Boston, and it was highly necessary that some port or other should be found for the landing of our mer-chandize where our laws would give full protection; he therefore hoped that the removal of the custom-house officers from the town of Boston would be thought a necessary step; and that the consequence of that would produce one other proposition, which would be the preventing any shipping from en-deavouring to land their wares and merchandize there by blocking up the use of that harbour; he said he should move for leave to bring in a bill for those two purposes.

He observed that this was the third time the officers of the customs had been prevented from doing their duty in the harbour of Boston; he thought the inhabitants of the town of Boston deserved punishment. He said, Perhaps it may be objected that some few individuals may suffer on this account who ought not; but where the authority of a town had been, as it were, asleep and inactive, it was no new thing for the whole town to be fined for such neglect: he instanced the city of London in King Charles the Second's time, when Dr. Lamb was killed by unknown persons, the city was fined for such; and the case of Edinburgh, in Captain Porteous's affair, when a fine was set upon the whole; and also at Glasgow, when the house of Mr. Campbell was pulled down, part of the revenue of that town was sequestered to make good the damage.

He observed that Boston did not stand in so fair a light as either of the three before mentioned places, for that Boston had been upwards of seven years in riot and confusion, and associations had been held against receiving British merchandize so long ago. He observed that proceedings were openly carried on in the beginning of last November, to the 17th of December, denying the force or efficacy of the laws of this country to be exerted in the harbour of Boston; that during the above time there was not the least interposition offered by the inhabitants of the town; that at their public meetings they had regularly given orders for nightly watches to be appointed, consisting of a large body of persons, which were to prevent the landing of the tea. As the merchandize of Great Britain, this surely was highly criminal, and a direct opposition to the execution of an act of parliament; and as the tea belonging to the India Company had remained twenty days in the harbour without a clearance, they were afraid lest it should be seized by the custom-house officers, and by that means landed; they therefore destroyed it on the 20th day. That this appeared to be a violent and outrageous proceeding done to our fellow subjects by a set of people who could not, in any shape, claim more than the natural privilege of trading with their fellow-subjects. That Boston had been the ringleader in all riots, and had at all times shewn a desire of seeing the laws of Great Britain attempted in vain in the colony of Massachusetts Bay.

—Cobbett, *Parliamentary History of England,* XVII, 1163-1165.

B. MR. VAN ARGUES THAT BOSTON OUGHT TO BE KNOCKED ABOUT THE EARS

Debate in the Commons on the Boston Port Bill, March 23, 1774.

Lord North said: The test of the Bostonians will not be the indemnification of the East India Company alone; it will remain in the breast of the King not to restore the port until peace and obedience shall be observed in the port of Boston. I am ready to admit a clause to secure those wharfs and quays which are now in use, to see the same when the port shall be restored.

He observed, he had been charged with changing his opinion; that the declaration which he had made tended chiefly to the punishment of the Bostonians, and that the Bill particularly adhered to the views of making the India Company satisfaction. He believed the House would do him the justice to say that he had declared both those measures to be his intention at the first setting out of the business, as well as to restore the trade to a proper footing; that he hoped he had never deviated from them, notwithstanding what the hon. gentleman [Mr. Fox] had charged him with; that he should never be ashamed, at any time, to give up his opinion to better judgement.

Mr. Van said he agreed to the flagitiousness of the offence in the Americans, and therefore was of opinion that the town of Boston ought to be knocked about their ears and destroyed. *Delenda est Carthago.* Said he, I am of opinion you will never meet with that proper obedience to the laws of this country until you have destroyed that nest of locusts.

—Cobbett, *Parliamentary History of England,* XVII, 1178.

C. LORD GEORGE GERMAIN: "PUT AN END TO THEIR TOWN MEETINGS"

Debate in the Commons on the bill for regulating the government of Massachusetts Bay, March 28, 1774.

Lord George Germain said: I could have wished that the noble lord, when he was forming this scheme of salvation to this country, would have at least considered that there were other parts of the internal government necessary to be put under some regulation. I mean particularly the internal government of the province of Massachusetts Bay. I wish to see the council of that country on the same footing as other colonies. There is a degree of absurdity, at present, in the election of the council. I cannot, Sir, disagree with the noble lord, nor can I think he will do a better thing than to put an end to their town meetings. I would not have men of a mercantile cast every day collecting themselves together and debating about political matters; I would have them follow their occupations as merchants, and not consider themselves as ministers of that country. I would also wish that all corporate powers might be given to certain people in every town, in the same manner that corporations are formed here; I should then expect to see some subordination, some authority and order. I do not know by what power those are to be formed, but I wish that they may be formed by some. . . .

I would wish to bring the constitution of America as similar to our own as possible. I would wish to see the council of that country similar to a House of Lords in this. I would wish to see chancery suits determined by a court of chancery, and not by the assembly of that province. At present, their assembly is a downright clog upon all the proceedings of the governor, and the council are continually thwarting and opposing any proposition he may make for the security and welfare of that government. You have, Sir, no government, no governor; the whole are the proceedings of a tumultuous and riotous rabble, who ought, if they had the least prudence, to follow their mercantile employment and not trouble themselves with politics and government, which they do not understand.

We are told by some gentlemen, Oh! do not break the charter; do not take away their rights that are granted to them by the predecessors of the crown. Whoever, Sir, wishes to preserve such charters without a due correction and regulation; whoever, Sir, wishes for such subjects, I wish them no worse than to govern them. Put this people, Sir, upon a free footing of government; do not let us be every day asserting our rights by words, and they denying our authority and preventing the execution of our laws. Let us, Sir, persevere in refining that government which cannot support itself, and proceed on in the manner we have begun, and I make no doubt but, by a manly and steady perseverance, things may be restored from a state of anarchy and confusion to peace, quietude and due obedience to the laws of this country.

—COBBETT, *Parliamentary History of England*, XVII, 1195-1196.

D. "WE MUST RISK SOMETHING; IF WE DO NOT IT IS ALL OVER": LORD NORTH

Debate on the bill for regulating the government of Massachusetts Bay, April 22, 1774.

Lord North said: . . . Gentlemen say, Let the colony come to your bar and be heard in their defence; though it is not likely that they will come, when they deny your authority in every instance. Can we remain in this situation long? We must effectually take some measure to correct and amend the defects of that government. I have heard so many different opinions in regard to our conduct in America, I hardly know how to answer them. The hon. gentleman who spoke last formerly blamed the tame and insipid conduct of government; now he condemns this measure as harsh and severe. The Americans have tarred and feathered your subjects, plundered your merchants, burnt your ships, denied all obedience to your laws and authority; yet so clement and so long forbearing has our conduct been that it is incumbent on us now to take a different course. Whatever may be the consequence, we must risk something; if we do not, all is over. The measure now proposed is nothing more than taking the election of counsellors out of the hands of those people who are continually acting in defiance and resistance of your laws.

It has also been said by gentlemen, Send for the Americans to your bar—give them redress a twelvemonth hence. Surely, Sir, this cannot be the language that is to give effectual relief to America; it is not, I say again, political convenience, it is political necessity that urges this measure. If this is not the proper method, shew me any other which is preferable, and I will postpone it.

—COBBETT, *Parliamentary History of England*, XVII, 1280-1281.

E. CHARLES JAMES FOX: "CONSIDER WHETHER IT IS MORE PROPER TO GOVERN BY FORCE OR BY MANAGEMENT"

Debate in the Commons on the bill for regulating the government of Massachusetts Bay, May 2, 1774.

Mr. Charles Fox said: I take this to be the question, whether America is to be governed by force or management? I never could conceive that the Americans could be taxed without their consent. Just as the House of Commons stands to the House of Lords with regard to taxation and legislation, so stands America with Great Britain. There is not an American but who must reject and resist the principle and right of our taxing them. The question, then, is shortly this: Whether we ought to govern America on these principles? Can this country gain strength by keeping up such a dispute as this? Tell me when America is to be taxed, so as to relieve the burthens of this country. I look upon this measure to be in effect taking away their charter; if their charter is to be taken away, for God's sake let it be taken away by law, and not by a legislative coercion. But I cannot conceive that any law whatever, while their charter continues, will make them think that you have a right to tax them. If a system of force is to be established, there is no provision for that in this Bill; it does not go far enough; if it is to induce them by fair means, it goes too far. The only method by which the Americans will ever think they are attached to this country will be by laying aside the right of taxing. I consider this Bill as a Bill of pains and penalties, for it begins with a crime and ends with a punishment; but I wish gentlemen would consider whether it is more proper to govern by military force or by management.

—COBBETT, *Parliamentary History of England*, XVII, 1313.

F. EDMUND BURKE: "A GREAT MANY RED COATS WILL NEVER GOVERN AMERICA"

Debate in the Commons on the bill for regulating the government of Massachusetts Bay, May 2, 1774.

Mr. Edmund Burke said: The question that is before you is a great one; it is no less than the proscription of provinces, and cities, and nations, upon their trial. Except that when the saints of God are to judge the world, I do not know one of greater importance. . . .

If you govern America at all, Sir, it must be by an army; but the Bill before us carries with it the force of that army; and I am of opinion they never will consent without force being used.

I have to protest against this Bill because you refuse to hear the parties aggrieved. Consider what you are doing when you are taking the trial over the Atlantic seas, 3,000 miles to Great Britain; witnesses may be subpoenaed, and called upon by the prisoner, as many as he pleases. Let me, for God's sake, wish that gentlemen would think a little more that a fair trial may be had in America; and that while the King appoints the judge, there is a degree of fairness that people should the jury.

Repeal, Sir, the Act which gave rise to this disturbance; this will be the remedy to bring peace and quietness and restore authority; but a great black book and a great many red coats will never be able to govern it. It is true, the Americans cannot resist the force of this country, but it will cause wranglings, scuffling and discontent. Such remedies as the foregoing will create disturbances that can never be quieted.

—COBBETT, *Parliamentary History of England,* XVII, 1314-1315.

2. "THE INTENTION OF THIS ACT IS TOTALLY TO ANNIHILATE BOSTON"

William Lee to Richard Henry Lee.

London, 17 March 1774

My dear Brother:

I must give you a little dissertation on Politics. The American business engages at present the whole attention of every one here, from the King to the shopkeeper. The inclosed paper will give you a sketch of the bill that is to be brought into the House of Commons to-morrow respecting Boston, but I am told by several members (for none but members are admitted when American affairs are on the carpet) that Lord North said, in the bill some alteration of the charter of the Massachusetts Bay would be introduced, and declared that the punishment of Boston was intended as an example to all the other Colonies, who should be treated in the same manner whenever they dared to resist the shackles which the King is determined they shall wear (perhaps the last sentiment was not conveyed in my words, but the meaning was truly the same), but that it was necessary and prudent to punish one Colony at a time, and Boston being the foremost in asserting their rights, it was proper to begin with it first. This you may be assured is the language of every ministerial scoundrel. The intention of this act is totally to annihilate the town of Boston, which will most effectually be done, if the people there permit it to be carried into execution. Lord North, Dartmouth and, some say, Lord Mansfield have been against these measures; but the King with his usual obstinacy and tyrannical disposition is determined, if it be possible, to inslave you all; the Bedford Party, Lord Temple and the remnant of the Grenville Party, Lord Suffolk and Wedderburne, wish the same as well as to make their court to the King, so that Lords North and Dartmouth have been over ruled in the cabinet, where the whole business is settled, and Parliament made the instrument when it is thought convenient; for the mode of business is quite changed in this country from what it was formerly. Neither King nor Minister ever do anything wrong, because Parliament is very ready to sanctify what the King or Minister determines to be right.

These violent measures would never have been attempted (for there is not a more certain truth in nature than that tyrants are always cowards) but upon the following principles or reasons: from the conduct of the Bostonians in admitting the troops in 1768 to land and be quartered in the town without any resistance—though they had an act of Parliament in their favor, and after they had made the world believe by a great deal of blustering, and everybody here firmly expected, they would proceed to extremities, in so much that the stocks here fell upon it, as if war had been actually declared against France or Spain—the King and his friends, as they are called, think there will be no resistance now. Secondly, they believe that the other Colonies will look on quietly and see Boston destroyed.

In both these conjectures I flatter myself they will be mistaken. The people of Boston seem to me to have been preparing for such a stroke for some time: I think they are now provided, and the less they talk the more I expect they will do, especially as they know the European powers are ready at any moment to give them any assistance they want. As to the second reason, I cannot believe the other Colonies will not interfere, and that very warmly. Everything at present seems to me to be very properly situated in N. York, Pennsylvania and So. Carolina, and if the Virginia Assembly does but stir in the business, I have no doubt there will be a perfect union among all the Colonies, which is indeed more absolutely necessary now than at any time before, as the attack is intended against the whole, and I am of opinion it will check the sanguinary spirit of your enemies here, if they find the Colonies are firm and closely united. Indeed, it is evident you have no alternative but to resist united and most probably be free, or to submit and be slaves at once.

The plan I leave to you. You have many friends here upon principle, as you will perceive from the inclosed printed letter to Lord North, signed E. B., which is supposed to be Edmund Burke's, who is the mouth of the Rockingham Party; which should be reprinted in all the American papers. Write me often, especially from your Assembly.

—FORD, ed., *Letters of William Lee*, I, 81-85.

3. "A SETTLED PLAN TO SUBVERT THE CONSTITUTION OF THIS COUNTRY"

William Lee to Richard Henry Lee.

London, 10 September 1774

My dear Brother:

I have perused your letter to our brother, Arthur Lee, as he is absent on a tour to Italy. I find from a letter of our brother, Francis Lightfoot Lee, an idea has been entertained in Virginia of paying for the East India Company's tea destroyed at Boston; I cannot think such a measure will be adopted at the Congress. In my judgment it is totally wrong and cannot be supported on any principle of Policy or Justice; my reasons for this opinion are too numerous to be set down here, especially as they can be of little use, since the measure must be fully canvassed before this gets to hand; . . . I will give some hints of what in my opinion ought to be your conduct.

A settled plan is laid to subvert the liberties and constitution of this country, as well as that of America. You are personally obnoxious to the King and his Junto, as having shown more spirit in support of your rights than the people of this country, who are immersed in riches, luxury and dissipation.

Therefore, every nerve will be exerted to subdue your spirit, and make you first bow your necks to the yoke, which will prove a useful example to the people at home. The plan is deeply laid by the King, Lords Bute, Mansfield and Wedderburne; for which purpose they employ the most useful tools in the kingdom: Lord North, a tyrant from principle, cunning, treacherous and persevering, a perfect adept; and his brother-in-law, Lord Dartmouth, who will whine, preach and cry, while he is preparing privately a dagger to stab you to the heart. Under this direction, the several acts against Boston, the Massachusetts Bay and Quebec act, have passed the last sessions; to enforce them soldiers and ships of war have already been sent to Boston, and many more will follow on the least occasion. General Carleton, the ablest officer in the British service, is sent to his Government of Quebec, to embody 30,000 Roman Catholics there. The Ministers have offered to General Amherst the command in chief of America, and to General Sir William Draper, the government of New York. General Amherst has not yet agreed to accept, but has it now in consideration. Amherst, Gage, Carleton and Draper are to be employed against you.

From these facts it is evident that open war is intended against you, provided the people here sit still, and the question is, how are you to oppose it? In my opinion every method is lawfully warrantable. As the first blow is struck by the Ministry, and every tie of allegiance is broken by the Quebec Act, which is absolutely a dissolution of this Government, the compact between the King and the people is totally done away with. The people of New England have been prudently providing for the worst event, lately having two entire vessels, privately loaded with arms and ammunitions from Scotland, with twice as many small arms and double the amount of powder that was usual, shipt from hence. I wish every Colony had been as provident, but I do not find that they have. However, let us consider what peaceable steps should be first pursued, that your last efforts may be warrantable in the eyes of God and Man. . . .

—FORD, ed., *Letters of William Lee*, I, 87-90.

III. INTOLERABLE ACTS UNITE THE COLONIES

The Boston Port Bill received the royal signature the last day of March, 1774, but was not to go into effect until the first of June; in the interval, it was hoped, the Americans would come to their senses. Instead the Bostonians greeted the Act with defiance. "Should Europe empty all her force we'll meet her in array," wrote the Patriot Joseph Warren, soon to die at Bunker's Hill; while Sam Adams, who bore some responsibility for the crisis, assured Arthur Lee over in London that the people of Boston would "sustain the shock with dignity and . . . gloriously defeat the designs of their enemies." From New England towns and then from all the colonies came a ground swell of defiance and support. A thousand people assembled in Farmington, Connecticut, resolved that "we are the sons of freedom," and "till time shall be no more, that godlike virtue shall blazon our hemisphere." Patriots in Baltimore sent encouragement and pledged themselves to stop all trade with the mother country; New Hampshire inaugurated resistance; Jersey spoke for suspension of trade; South Carolina resolved that "the whole continent must be animated with one great soul and all Americans must resolve to stand by one another even unto the position of death."

Virginia, the largest colony, was of crucial importance. There Jefferson, Henry, Richard Henry Lee and Francis Lightfoot Lee, convinced of "the necessity of arousing our people from the lethargy into which they had fallen," cooked up a resolution—as Jefferson put it—calling for a general day of prayer; this was duly passed. Three days later 89 members of the Burgesses resolved that an attack on one colony was an attack on all, and on May 31 the Burgesses concluded a nonimportation agreement. And the freeholders of Albemarle County drew up a series of resolutions, drafted by Jefferson, which stated among other things that "no other legislature whatever can rightly exercise authority over them" except the one of their own choosing. More important was the steady drift of George Washington toward the patriot cause. Rich, respectable, conservative and moderate, Washington found himself as outraged by the Intolerable Acts as Sam Adams or Thomas Jefferson. "Shall we supinely sit and see one province after another fall a prey to despotism?" he rhetorically asked his friend Bryan Fairfax who, like Galloway in Pennsylvania, looked with alarm on the rapid course of events. Washington's own answer—"we must assert our rights or submit to every imposition that can be heaped upon us"—was big with significance for the future of America.

1. "Free America"

Ascribed to Joseph Warren, 1774.

> That seat of science, Athens,
>   And earth's proud mistress, Rome;
> Where now are all their glories?
>   We scarce can find a tomb.
> Then guard your rights, Americans,
>   Nor stoop to lawless sway;
> Oppose, oppose, oppose, oppose,
>   For North America.
>
> We led fair Freedom hither,
>   And lo, the desert smiled!
> A paradise of pleasure
>   Was opened in the wild!
> Your harvest, bold Americans,
>   No power shall snatch away!
> Huzza, huzza, huzza, huzza,
>   For free America.
>
> Torn from a world of tyrants,
>   Beneath this western sky,
> We formed a new dominion,
>   A land of liberty:

The world shall own we're masters here;
  Then hasten on the day:
Huzza, huzza, huzza, huzza,
  For free America. . . .

Lift up your hands, ye heroes,
  And swear with proud disdain,
The wretch that would ensnare you
  Shall lay his snares in vain:
Should Europe empty all her force,
  We'll meet her in array,
And fight and shout, and shout and fight
  For North America.

Some future day shall crown us
  The masters of the main,
Our fleets shall speak in thunder
  To England, France and Spain;
And the nations over the ocean spread
  Shall tremble and obey
The sons, the sons, the sons, the sons
  Of brave America. . . .

—STEDMAN AND HUTCHINSON, *Library of American Literature*, III, 256-257.

2. "FRUSTRATE THE DIABOLICAL DESIGNS OF OUR ENEMIES"

Samuel Adams to Arthur Lee.

Boston, May 18, 1774

My Dear Sir: The edict of the British Parliament, commonly called the Boston Port Act, came safely to my hand. For flagrant injustice and barbarity, one might search in vain among the archives of Constantinople to find a match for it. But what else could have been expected from a Parliament too long under the dictates and controul of an Administration which seems to be totally lost to all sense and feeling of morality, and governed by passion, cruelty and revenge?

For us to reason against *such* an Act would be idleness. Our business is to find means to evade its malignant design. The inhabitants view it not with astonishment, but with indignation. They discover the utmost contempt of the framers of it; while they are yet disposed to consider the body of the nation (though represented by such a Parliament) in the character they have sustained heretofore, humane and generous. They resent the behaviour of the merchants in London—those, I mean, who receive their bread from them—in infamously deserting their cause at the time of extremity. They can easily believe that the industrious manufacturers, whose time is wholly spent in their various employments, are misled and imposed upon by such miscreants as have ungratefully devoted themselves to an abandoned Ministry, not regarding the ruin of those who have been their best benefactors. But the inhabitants of this town must and will look to their own safety, which they see does not consist in a servile compliance with the ignominious terms of this barbarous edict. Though the means of preserving their liberties should distress and even ruin the British manufacturers, they are resolved (but with reluctance) to try the experiment. To this they are impelled by motives of self-preservation. They feel humanely for those who must suffer, but, being innocent, are not the objects of their revenge. They have already called upon their sister Colonies (as you will see by the enclosed note) who not only feel for them as fellow-citizens, but look upon them as suffering the stroke of Ministerial vengeance in the common cause of America; that cause which the Colonists have pledged themselves to each other not to give up.

In the meantime, I trust in God this devoted town will sustain the shock with dignity; and, supported by their brethren, will gloriously defeat the designs of their common enemies. Calmness, courage and unanimity prevail. While they are resolved not tamely to submit, they will, by refraining from any acts of violence, avoid the snare that they discover to be laid for them by posting regiments so near them.

I heartily thank you for your spirited exertions. Use means for the preservation of your health. Our warmest gratitude is due to Lords Camden and Shelburne. Our dependence is upon the wisdom of the few of the British nobility. We suspect studied insult in the appointment of the person who is Commander-in-chief of the troops in America to be our Governour; and I think there appears to be in it more than a design to insult upon any specious pretence. We will endeavour, by circumspection and sound prudence, to frustrate the diabolical designs of our enemies.

                    —FORCE, *American Archives*, 4th Series, I, 332-333.

3. "WE ARE THE SONS OF FREEDOM"

Proceedings of Farmington, Connecticut, on the Boston Port Act, May 19, 1774.

Early in the morning was found the following handbill, posted up in various parts of the town, viz:

> To pass through the fire at six o'clock this evening, in honour to the immortal goddess of Liberty, the late infamous Act of the British Parliament for farther distressing the American Colonies; the place of execution will be the public parade, where all Sons of Liberty are desired to attend.

Accordingly, a very numerous and respectable body were assembled of near one thousand people, when a huge pole, just forty-five feet high, was erected and consecrated to the shrine of liberty; after which the Act of Parliament for blocking up the Boston harbour was read aloud, sentenced to the flames and executed by the hands of the common hangman; then the following resolves were passed, *nem. con.:*

1ST. That it is the greatest dignity, interest and happiness of every American to be united with our parent State, while our liberties are duly secured, maintained and supported by our rightful Sovereign, whose person we greatly revere; whose government, while duly administered, we are ready with our lives and properties to support.

2D. That the present ministry, being instigated by the devil and led on by their wicked and corrupt hearts, have a design to take away our liberties and properties and to enslave us forever.

3D. That the late Act which their malice hath caused to be passed in Parliament, for blocking up the port of Boston, is unjust, illegal and oppressive; and that we and every American are sharers in the insults offered to the town of Boston.

4TH. That those pimps and parasites who dared to advise their master to such detestable measures be held in utter abhorrence by us and every American, and their names loaded with the curses of all succeeding generations.

5TH. That we scorn the chains of slavery; we despise every attempt to rivet them upon us; we are the sons of freedom and resolved that, till time shall be no more, godlike virtue shall blazon our hemisphere.

—FORCE, *American Archives*, 4th Series, I, 336.

4. PHILADELPHIA RALLIES TO THE AID OF BOSTON

Pennsylvania Resolutions on the Boston Port Act.

Philadelphia, June 20, 1774

At a very large and respectable meeting of the freeholders and freemen of the city and county of Philadelphia, on June 18, 1774. Thomas Willing, John Dickinson, chairmen.

I. Resolved, That the act of parliament for shutting up the port of Boston is unconstitutional, oppressive to the inhabitants of that town, dangerous to the liberties of the British colonies, and therefore, considering our brethren at Boston as suffering in the common cause of America:

II. That a congress of deputies from the several colonies in North America is the most probable and proper mode of procuring relief for our suffering brethren, obtaining redress of American grievances, securing our rights and liberties, and re-establishing peace and harmony between Great Britain and these colonies, on a constitutional foundation.

III. That a large and respectable committee be immediately appointed for the city and county of Philadelphia, to correspond with the sister colonies and with the several counties in this province, in order that all may unite in promoting and endeavoring to attain the great and valuable ends mentioned in the foregoing resolution.

IV. That the committee nominated by this meeting shall consult together, and on mature deliberation determine what is the most proper mode of collecting the sense of this province, and appointing deputies for the same, to attend a general congress, and having determined thereupon, shall take such measures as by them shall be judged most expedient, for procuring this province to be represented at the said congress in the best manner that can be devised for promoting the public welfare.

V. That the committee be instructed immediately to set on foot a subscription for the relief of such poor inhabitants of the town of Boston as may be deprived of their means of subsistence. . . .

VI. That the committee consist of forty-three persons. . . .
—NILES, ed., *Principles and Acts of the Revolution*, p. 180.

5. VIRGINIA FALLS INTO LINE

Resolution of the House of Burgesses, Tuesday, May 24.

This House, being deeply impressed with Apprehension of the great Dangers to be derived to British America, from the hostile Invasion of the City of Boston, . . . whose Commerce and Harbour are on the 1st Day of June next to be stopped by an armed Force, deem it highly necessary that the said first Day of June be set apart by the Members of this House as a Day of Fasting, Humiliation, and Prayer, devoutly to implore the divine Interposition for averting the heavy Calamity, which threatens Destruction to our civil Rights, and the Evils of civil War; to give us one Heart and one Mind firmly to oppose, by all just and proper Means, every Injury to American Rights, and that the Minds of his Majesty and his Parliament may be inspired from above with Wisdom, Moderation, and Justice, to remove from the loyal People of America all Cause of Danger from a continued Pursuit of Measures pregnant with their Ruin.

Ordered, therefore, that the Members of this House do attend in their Places at the Hour of ten in the Forenoon, on the said 1st Day of June next, in Order to proceed with the Speaker and the Mace to the Church in this City for the Purposes aforesaid, and that the Reverend Mr. Price be appointed to read Prayers, and the Reverend Mr. Gwatkin to preach a Sermon suitable to the Occasion.

—BOYD, ed., *Papers of Thomas Jefferson*, I, 105-106.

6. JEFFERSON ARGUES THAT PARLIAMENT HAS NO AUTHORITY

Resolutions of freeholders of Albemarle County, Virginia.

July 26, 1774

At a meeting of the Freeholders of the County of Albemarle, assembled in their collective body, at the Court House of the said County, on the 26th of July, 1774:

Resolved, That the inhabitants of the Several States of British America are subject to the laws which they adopted at their first settlement, and to such others as have been since made by their respective Legislatures, duly constituted and appointed with their own consent. That no other Legislature whatever can rightly exercise authority over them; and that these privileges they hold as the common rights of mankind, confirmed by the political constitutions they have respectively assumed, and also by several charters of compact from the Crown.

Resolved, That these their natural and legal rights have in frequent instances been invaded by the Parliament of Great Britain and particularly that they were so by an act lately passed to take away the trade of the inhabitants of the town of Boston, in the province of Massachusetts Bay; that all such assumptions of unlawful power are dangerous to the right of the British empire in general, and should be considered as its common cause, and that we will ever be ready to join with our fellow-subjects in every part of the same, in executing all those rightful powers which God has given us, for the re-establishment and guaranteeing such their constitutional rights, when, where, and by whomsoever invaded.

It is the opinion of this meeting, that the most eligible means of effecting these purposes, will be to put an immediate stop to all imports from Great Britain, . . . and to all exports thereto, after the first day of October, 1775; and immediately to discontinue all commercial intercourse with every part of the British Empire which shall not in like manner break off their commerce with Great Britain.

It is the opinion of this meeting, that we immediately cease to import all commodities from every part of the world, which are subjected by the British Parliament to the payment of duties in America.

It is the opinion of this meeting, that these measures should be pursued until a repeal be obtained of the Act for blocking up the harbour of Boston; of the Acts prohibiting or restraining internal manufactures in America; of the Acts imposing on any commodities duties to be paid in America; and of the Act laying restrictions on the American trade; and that on such repeal it will be reasonable to grant to our brethren of Great Britain such privileges in commerce as may amply compensate their fraternal assistance, past and future.

Resolved, However, that this meeting do submit these their opinions to the Convention of Deputies from the several counties of this Colony, and appointed to be held at Williamsburg on the first day of August next, and also to the General Congress of Deputies from the several American States, when and wheresoever held; and that they will concur in these or any other measures which such Convention or such Congress shall adopt as most expedient for the American good; and we do appoint Thomas Jefferson and John Walker our Deputies to act for this county at the said Convention, and instruct them to conform themselves to these our Resolutions and Opinions.

—Ford, ed., *Writings of Jefferson*, I, 418.

7. Washington Takes His Stand Against British Tyranny

A. "god only knows what is to become of us"

George Washington to George William Fairfax.

Williamsburg, June 10, 1774

. . . Our Assembly met at this place the 4th. Ulto. according to Proragation, and dissolved the 26th. for entering into a resolve of which the Inclosd is a Copy, and which the Govr. thought reflected too much upon his Majesty, and the British Parliament to pass over unnoticed; this Dissolution was as sudden as unexpected for there were other resolves of a much more spirited nature ready to be offerd to the House wch. would have been unanimously adopted respecting the Boston Port Bill as it is calld but were withheld till the Important business of the Country could be gone through. As the case stands the assembly sat In 22 days for nothing. . . .

The day after this Event the Members convend themselves at the Raleigh Tavern and enterd into the Inclosd Association which being followed two days after by an Express from Boston accompanied by the Sentiments of some

Meetings in our Sister Colonies to the Northwd. the proceedings mentiond in the Inclos'd Papers were had thereupon and a general meeting requested of all the late Representatives in this City on the first of August when it is hopd, and expected that some vigorous (and effectual) measures will be effectually adopted to obtain that justice which is denied to our Petitions and Remonstrances (and Prayers); in short the Ministry may rely on it that Americans will never be tax'd without their own consent that the cause of Boston the despotick Measures in respect to it I mean now is and ever will be considerd as the cause of America (not that we approve their conduct in destroyg. the Tea) and that we shall not suffer ourselves to be sacrificed by piece meals though god only knows what is to become of us, threatned as we are with so many hoverg. evils as hang over us at present; having a cruel and blood thirsty Enemy upon our Backs, the Indians, between whom and our Frontier Inhabitants many Skirmishes have happnd, and with whom a general War is inevitable whilst those from whom we have a right to seek protection are endeavouring by every piece of Art and despotism to fix the Shackles of Slavery upon us.

—FITZPATRICK, ed., *Writings of Washington*, III, 223-224.

B. "SHALL WE WHINE AND CRY FOR RELIEF WHEN WE HAVE ALREADY TRIED IT IN VAIN?"

George Washington to Bryan Fairfax.

Mount Vernon, July 20, 1774

... The conduct of the Boston people could not justify the rigor of their measures, unless there had been a requisition of payment and refusal of it; nor did that measure require an act to deprive the government of Massachusetts Bay of their charter, or to exempt offenders from trial in the place where offences were committed, as there was not, nor could not be, a single instance produced to manifest the necessity of it. Are not all these things self evident proofs of a fixed and uniform plan to tax us? If we want further proofs, do not all the debates in the House of Commons serve to confirm this? And has not General Gage's conduct since his arrival, (in stopping the address of his Council, and publishing a proclamation more becoming a Turkish bashaw, than an English governor, declaring it treason to associate in any manner by which the commerce of Great Britain is to be affected,) exhibited an unexampled testimony of the most despotic system of tyranny, that ever was practised in a free government? In short, what further proofs are wanted to satisfy one of the designs of the ministry, than their own acts, which are uniform and plainly tending to the same point, nay, if I mistake not, avowedly to fix the right of taxation? What hope then from petitioning, when they tell us, that now or never is the time to fix the matter? Shall we, after this, whine and cry for relief, when we have already tried it in vain? Or shall we supinely sit and see one province after another fall a prey to despotism? If I was in any doubt, as to the right which the Parliament of Great Britain had to tax us without our consent, I should most heartily coincide with you in opinion, that to petition, and petition only, is the proper method to apply for relief; because we should then be asking a favor, and not claiming a right, which, by the law of nature and our constitution, we are, in my opinion, indubitably entitled to. I should even think it criminal to go further than this, under such an idea; but none such I have. I think the Parliament of Great Britain hath no more right to put their hands into my pocket, without my consent, than I have to put my hands into yours for money; and this being already urged to them in a firm, but decent manner, by all the colonies, what reason is there to expect any thing from their justice?

—FITZPATRICK, ed., *Writings of Washington*, III, 232-233.

C. "THE CRISIS IS ARRIVED WHEN WE MUST ASSERT OUR RIGHTS"

George Washington to Bryan Fairfax.

Mount Vernon, August 24, 1774

... In truth, persuaded as I am, that you have read all the political pieces, which compose a large share of the *Gazette* at this time, I should think it, but for your request, a piece of inexcusable arrogance in me, to make the least essay towards a change in your political opinions; for I am sure I have no new lights to throw upon the subject, or any other arguments to offer in support of my own doctrine, than what you have seen; and could only in general add, that an innate spirit of freedom first told me, that the measures, which administration hath for some time been, and now are most violently pursuing, are repugnant to every principle of natural justice; whilst much abler heads than my own hath fully convinced me, that it is not only repugnant to natural right, but subversive of the laws and constitution of Great Britain itself, in the establishment of which some of the best blood in the kingdom hath been spilt. Satisfied, then, that the acts of a British Parliament are no longer governed by the principles of justice, that it is trampling upon the valuable rights of Americans, confirmed to them by charter and constitution they themselves boast of, and convinced beyond the smallest doubt, that these measures are the result of deliberation, and attempted to be carried into execution by the hand of power, is it a time to trifle, or risk our cause upon petitions, which with difficulty obtain access, and afterwards are thrown by with the utmost contempt? Or should we, because heretofore unsuspicious of design, and then unwilling to enter into disputes with the mother country, go on to bear more, and forbear to enumerate our just causes of complaint? For my own part, I shall not undertake to say where the line between Great Britain and the colonies should be drawn; but I am clearly of opinion, that one ought to be drawn, and our rights clearly ascertained. I could wish, I own, that the dispute had been left to posterity to determine, but the crisis is arrived when we must assert our rights, or submit to every imposition, that can be heaped upon us, till custom and use shall make us as tame and abject slaves, as the blacks we rule over with such arbitrary sway....

—FITZPATRICK, ed., *Writings of Washington*, III, 240-242.

IV. BOSTON BELEAGUERED AND SAVED

The Boston Port Bill went into effect June 1; it closed the port of Boston not only to overseas trade, but even to coastal shipping. The fateful day was observed with fasting and prayer; public buildings were draped in black, and church bells tolled from morning to night. Soon regiments of redcoats turned the town into a garrison. By November 1774, 11 regiments were quartered in the city. Meantime thousands of the inhabitants fled to the country or near-by towns; trade was at a standstill; stores closed; property fell in value, and only British expenditures kept up the economic life of the town.

Hutchinson had been permitted to return to England and General Gage was acting governor. It was Gage who had hoped to bring Boston to her knees by this Draconian program. But the Massachusetts House resolved that the city should be succored, and the town itself broadcast an appeal for aid. "I find," wrote Gage in surprise, "that they have some warm friends in New York and Philadelphia." They had, indeed, and elsewhere too. Soon food and supplies were pouring in from all the colonies: flour, fish, sheep, beef cattle, pork, grain, rice, provisions of all kinds. "In God's name," said the Tory preacher Samuel Seabury, "are not the people of Boston able to relieve their own poor? Must they go begging from Nova Scotia to Georgia to support a few poor people whom their perverseness and ill conduct have thrown into distress?"

By trying to isolate Boston the British government had made the city a martyr and contributed greatly to unifying colonial sentiment in her behalf.

The best description of Boston during these difficult months comes from the pen of the Whig merchant, John Andrews, who stayed in the beleaguered city to guard his property and his mercantile business. In his letters to William Barrell, who kept a store in Philadelphia, we can read the story of hard times, of the flood of aid, of frequent brushes between soldiers and inhabitants, of mounting discontent, and of the crisis which threatened to explode into open war. The most dangerous of these came the first week of September. General Gage had sent out a small force to seize a store of gunpowder at Quarry Hill, in Charlestown; news of the expedition flew like fire from town to town, growing as it spread into monstrous tales of pillage and rapine. Within twenty-four hours 4,000 minutemen marched on Boston—a number larger than the army Gage commanded—and during the next day or two, thousands more straggled in: the total number was rumored to be around 20,000. When it became clear that the rumor was false, the minutemen drifted home again. The lesson was lost on the purblind Gage—who made the same mistake eight months later—but not on the members of the Continental Congress, even then gathering in the City of Brotherly Love.

1. John Andrews Describes the Sufferings and the Heroism of Boston

To William Barrell.

May 18th, 1774

Imagine to yourself the horror painted in the faces of a string of slaves condemned by the Inquisition to perpetual drudgery at the oar! Such is the dejection imprinted on every countenance we meet in this once happy, but now totally ruined town.

Yes, Bill, nothing will save us but an entire stoppage of trade, both to England and the West Indies, throughout the continent: and that must be determined as speedily as absolutely. The least hesitancy on your part *to the southerd*, and the matter is over; we must acknowledge and ask forgiveness for all past offences, whether we have been guilty of any or no; give up the point so long contested, and acknowledge the right of Parliament to d——n us whenever they please; and to add to all this, we must pay for an article unjustly forced upon us with a sole view to pick our pockets (not that I would by any means justify the destruction of that article). When that is done, where are we? Why, in much the same situation as before, without one flattering hope of relief: entirely dependant on the will of an arbitrary Minister, who'd sacrifice the Kingdom to gratify a cursed revenge. A more convincing proof we can't have than in the present Act for blocking up our Port, which could not have been more severely and strongly expressed if all the Devils in the infernal regions had had a hand in the draughting it.

Shall endeavor to content myself to stay here till I see what turn affairs will take. If to my liking, well; if not, shall look out for some other place of residence, as I sincerely believe they intend to put their threats in execution; which is, to make the town a desolate wilderness, and the grass to grow in our streets.

Our Militia was yesterday mustered for the reception of General Gage, who was proclaimed Governor amid the acclamations of the people. He expressed himself as sensible of the unwelcome errand he came upon, but as a servant of the Crown he was obliged to see the Act put in execution; but would do all in his power to serve us. Whether they were only words of course or not, can't say; am a little doubtful. There was an elegant entertainment provided for him at Faneuil Hall, and after a number of toasts gave by him, in which the prosperity of the town of Boston was included, he gave "Governor Hutchinson," which was received by a general hiss. Such is the detestation in which that tool of tyrants is held among us. . . . The damned *arch traitor*, as he is called, is very much chagrined at being superseded, as it's only last Thursday when he gave orders for repairs to his houses in town and country, and upon the workman's suggestions that he would be succeeded soon, he said it was like many other reports that prevailed, for that he had all the satisfaction he could wish for or expect from home, and every part of his conduct was entirely approved of, and left to his option whether to enjoy the Government or go to England. But now a guilty conscience has induced him to take refuge at the Castle.

It's reported here that your Government, as well as New York, is to be changed and removed, the one to Burlington and the other to Amboy, with requisitions made upon both, and more particularly upon Rhode Island.

June 12th, 1774

If my last was in a desponding stile, I'm sure I have much more reason to be so now; as ought else than poverty and distress stare us in the face. . . . Animosities run higher than ever, each party charging the other as bringing ruin upon their country; that unless some expediency is adopted to get the Port open by paying for the tea (which seems to be the only one) am afraid we shall experience the worst of evils, *a civil war*, which God avert!

The trading part promised themselves a general compliance with the tenor of the Act . . . but . . . those who have governed the town for years past and were in a great measure the authors of all our evils by their injudicious conduct are grown more obstinate than ever, and seem determined to bring total destruction upon us: which may be sufficiently evinced by all their conduct. They not only intend to deprive us of trade in future, but render us utterly incapable of contributing that assistance which will be absolutely necessary for the support of the indigent the approaching fall and winter, by their *cruel* endeavors to stop the *little* inland trade we expected.

Our wharfs are intirely deserted; not a topsail vessel to be seen either there or in the harbour, save the ships of war and transport, the latter of which land their passengers in this town tomorrow. Four regiments are already arrived, and four more are expected. How they are to be disposed of, can't say. It's gave out that if the General Court don't provide barracks for them, they are to be quartered on the inhabitants in the fall: if so, am determined not to stay in it. The executors of the Act seem to strain points beyond what was ever intended, for they make all the vessels, both with grain and wood, entirely unload at Marblehead before they'll permit them to come in here, which conduct, in regard to the article of wood, has already greatly enhanced the price, and the masters say they won't come at all, if they are to be always put to such trouble, as they are obliged to hire another vessel to unload into, and then to return it back again, as they have no wharves to admit of their landing it on. Nor will they suffer any article of merchandize to be brought or carried over Charles River ferry, [so] that we are obliged to pay for 28 miles land carriage to get our goods from Marblehead or Salem.

Could fill up a number of sheets to enumerate all our difficulties.

September 2nd, 1774

The country people, being vastly more vigilant and spirited than the town, did not fail to visit Brattle and Sewall's house last evening, but not finding either of 'em at home, they quietly went off. But a report having prevailed through the country (by reason of the seizure of the powder yesterday) that the same game had been played here, and the inhabitants disarmed, has raised such a spirit as will require the utmost prudence to allay; for they are in arms at all quarters, being determined to see us redressed.

At eight o'clock this morning there were about three thousand under their regular leaders at Cambridge common, and continually increasing; had left their arms at a little distance, when Judge Lee and Danforth waited upon 'em, and gave them the fullest assurances that they had resigned their seats at the board and would not act in any capacity whatever that was disagreeable to the people.

Lieutenant Governor Oliver is come to town and Brattle is gone to the Castle, which, I believe, is the only place of safety for him in the province.

Four or five expresses have come down to Charlestown and here, to acquaint us that between Sudbury and this, above ten thousand men are in arms, and are continually coming down from the country back: that their determination is to collect about forty or fifty thousand by night (which they are sure of accomplishing) when they intend to fling in about fifteen thousand by the way of the Neck, and as many more over the ferry: when once got possession, to come in like locusts and rid the town of every soldier. But such a scheme is so big with mischief and calamity that the committee of correspondence, selectmen and every prudent man in the town of Charlestown set off to appease 'em early in the morning; and the committee of correspondence from this town also went at the same time. Since which, accounts have been so alarming that between ten and eleven o'clock the selectmen set out from here, to try what they could do to satisfy and disperse 'em.

Ruthy set out this morning for Hingham, in company with my mother, Mr. Breck and Ben. Am rejoiced that she is out of the way, just at this time.

A guard of soldiers is set upon the powder house at the back of the Common, so that people are debarred from selling their own property; and the guard upon the Neck is doubled, as well as that the whole battalions have had new flints, etc., delivered out to them. . . .

September 25th, 1774

. . . The example of our *worthy* brethren of New York in not letting their vessels for Government service, as well as that their carpenters would not engage in any work for 'em, has induced the country people to think seriously whether they were right in supplying with timber, joice and straw for the barracks here. They accordingly met and determined in the negative; sent committees to the several contractors to let them know if they supplied any further they would incur the resentment of the *whole* country; and at the same time signified to our committee of correspondence that they did not think it eligible for the workmen here to go on with building barracks or preparing houses for the reception of the troops, as we might possibly, by persisting, not only incur blame from our sister colonies, but essentially affect the union now subsisting between town and country; which circumstance caused the committee to get together Saturday P.M., when they passed a vote that it was not prudent for the workmen to go on with the frames, etc., nor in any shape to contribute towards the accomodation of the soldiery, as they might themselves give offence to their country brethren.

The purport of which coming to the Governor, he sent his compliments to the selectmen, and begged their attendance at six o'clock this evening, when he requested of them that they would not take any measures to prevent the workmen from going on with the barracks.

They replied it was not in their power to influence *the country*, and it lay principally with *them* whether the workmen should proceed or not: that they themselves were disposed to have the barracks go on, as they conceived it much more for the benefit of the town (if the soldiery must be here) to have them kept together, rather than to be *scattered* over the town, as in *that case* it would be a very difficult matter to keep them in order.

The Governor seemed a great deal worried about the affair, and am told that in the course of the conversation he expressed himself thus—"Good G—d! for G—d's sake, Gentlemen! they have got two months work to do, and the soldiers ought to be in barracks in one. Do consider, Gentlemen!"

Thus the tables are in *some* measure turned. Formerly they solicited the

Governor, but now it seems he solicits them. A pretty good mess for Sunday, Bill, don't you think it is?

October 1, 1774

It's common for the soldiers to fire at a target fixed in the stream at the bottom of the common. A countryman stood by a few days ago, and laughed very heartily at a whole regiment's firing, and not one being able to hit it. The officer observed him, and asked why he laughed.

"Perhaps you'll be affronted if I tell you," replied the countryman.

No, he would not, he said.

"*Why then,*" says he, "I laugh to see how awkward they fire. Why, I'll be bount I hit it ten times running."

"Ah! will you?" replied the officer. "Come try. Soldiers, go and bring five of the best guns, and load 'em for this honest man."

"Why, you need not bring so many: let me have any one that comes to hand," replied the other, "but I chuse to load *myself*." He accordingly loaded, and asked the officer where he should fire. He replied, "To the right,"—when he pulled tricker, and drove the ball as near the right as possible. The officer was amazed—and said he could not do it again, as that was only by chance.

He loaded again. "Where shall I fire?"

"*To the left,*"—when he performed as well as before.

"Come! Once more," says the officer.

He prepared the third time. "Where shall I fire *naow?*"

"*In the center.*"

He took aim, and the ball went as exact in the middle as possible. The officers as well as soldiers stared, and thought the Devil was in the man. "Why," says the countryman, "I'll tell you *naow.* I have got a *boy* at home that will toss up an apple and shoot out all the seeds as it's coming down."

The country towns, in general, have chose their own officers and muster for exercise once a week at least—when the parson as well as the squire stands in the ranks with a firelock. In particular at Marblehead, they turn out three or four times a week, when Col. Lee as well as the clergymen there are not ashamed to appear in the ranks, to be taught the manual exercise in particular.

One more anecdote, and I'll close this barren day. When the 59th Regiment came from Salem and were drawn up on each side the Neck, a remarkable tall countryman, near eight feet high, struted between 'em at the head of his waggon, looking *very* sly and contemptuously on one side and t'other, which attracted the notice of the whole regiment.

"Ay, ay," says he, "you don't know what *boys* we have got in the country. I am near nine feet high, and one of the smallest among 'em"—which caused much merriment to the spectators, as well as surprise to the soldiers.

Indeed, Bill! were I to tell you of all the jokes and wittisisms of the country people, I would have little else to do.

January 21st, 1775

Last evening a number of drunken officers attacked the town house watch between eleven and 12 o'clock, when the assistance of the New Boston watch was called, and a general battle ensued; some wounded on both sides. A party from the main guard was brought up with their captain together with another party from the Governor's. Had it not been for the prudence of two officers that were sober, the captain of the main guard would have acted a second tragedy to the 5th March, as he was much disguised with liquor and would have ordered the guard to fire on the watch had he not been restrained. His name is Gore, being a captain in the 5th or Earl Peircy's Regiment. He was degraded not long since for some misdemeanour.

This afternoon there was a general squabble between the butchers in the market and a number of soldiers. It first began by a soldier's tripping up the heals of a fisherman who was walking through the market with a piece of beef in his hands. A guard from the 47th barracks appered and carried off the soldiers, together with one butcher who was most active, the officer taking him by the collar. He was able to have crushed the officer, but was advised to be quiet. Young Ned Gray insisted on it that he should not be carried into the guard house, upon which many hard words passed between him and the captain of the guard. However, Gray prevailed, and they carried the man into Miss Foster's store close by the barracks, from whence the officer dismissed him after finding upon deliberation that his conduct was not justifiable—and seemed to be much afraid lest the butcher should take advantage of him by law or complaint.

—ANDREWS, "Letters," *Mass. Hist. Soc. Proc.*, VIII, 327-396 *passim.*

2. ALL AMERICA RALLIES TO THE AID OF BELEAGUERED BOSTON

A. WINDHAM, CONNECTICUT

To the Committee of Correspondence, Boston.

28th June, 1774

Gentlemen,

'Tis with pity, mixed with indignation, that we have beheld the cruel and unmanly attacks made by the British Parliament on the loyal and patriotic Town of Boston, who seem destined to feel the force of ministerial wrath, the whole weight of parliamentary vengeance levelled at them in a manner so replete with cruelty and injustice as must strike every heart with horror, and fill every breast with rage that is not entirely void of every sentiment of honor and justice and callous to all the common feelings of humanity. But when we consider the cause of all these calamities, that it is nothing less, on your part, than a strict adherence to the fundamental principles of the Constitution, which, when attacked, you dared openly to assert and vindicate, and stand foremost in the glorious cause of Liberty, in which you are contending not only for your own, but ours and the common rights of every American; when we reflect that it is this for which you are suffering such horrid cruelties, for which your streets have been stained with blood, and for which you now feel the horrors of a military government, we are overwhelmed with a conflict of tumultuous passions, and filled with that manly ardor which bids us join you hand in hand and suffer with you in the common cause; nay, even, if the sad exigence of affairs should ever require it, to determine, in defence of every thing for which life is worth enjoying, to meet that death which will be glorious and infinitely preferable to a life dragged on in that low, servile state which is evidently planned for us, and which nothing less than the most heroic fortitude and the highest exertions of every civil and Christian virtue can prevent.

Give us leave, therefore, gentlemen, to entreat, to beg, to conjure you, by everything that is dear, by everything that is sacred, by the venerable names of our pious forefathers, who suffered, who bled in the defence of Liberty, not to desert the cause at this trying crisis, but to use your utmost influence in pursuing and persevering in every measure which may have a tendency to produce the desired effect.

. . . As a testimony of our commiseration of your misfortunes, the Town, on the 23d instant, at a legal and very full meeting, unanimously chose a committee to procure subscriptions for your present relief. Accordingly, we have procured a small flock of sheep, which at this season are not so good as we could wish, but are the best we had, and the people of this Town were almost unanimous in contributing to this purpose.

B. BALTIMORE, MARYLAND

To Committee of Correspondence in the Town of Boston.

Aug. 4, 1774

Gentlemen,

By order of the Committee of Correspondence for this Town, we have shipped on board the sloop *America*, Perkins Allen, master, three thousand bushels of corn, twenty barrels of rye flour, two barrels of pork and twenty barrels of bread, for the relief of our brethren, the distressed inhabitants of your Town, being in virtue of a subscription raised by the inhabitants of Baltimore Town, on that account.

In the bill of lading for said articles is also included one thousand bushels of corn, which we have purchased and shipped for the same account, on the strength of a subscription now making by the inhabitants of Annapolis, which a gentleman of their Committee has assured us should be paid to us when their collections are made. As there was spare room in the vessel, we were glad of an opportunity of furthering to you a part of their benevolent intentions. We flatter ourselves the good people of this Province, who have in general discovered a hearty disposition to sympathy in your grievances, will generously contribute, according to their articles, to maintain and support every sufferer in your and their common cause. If we can be in the least instrumental in furthering any contributions made in favor of your inhabitants, it will give us the most sincere pleasure and some opportunity of exercising the grateful sense of many obligations which, as individuals, we are under to many good people of your Province. We are, with the highest respect,

Gentlemen, your most humble servants,

SAM'L AND ROB'T PURVIANCE

C. BROOKLYN IN POMFRET, CONNECTICUT

To Samuel Adams, Esq., Chairman to the Committee of Correspondence.

August 11, 1774

Gentlemen,

With our hearts deeply impressed with the feelings of humanity towards our near and dear brethren of Boston, who are now suffering under a ministerial, revengeful hand, and at the same time full of gratitude to the patriotic inhabitants for the noble stand which they have made against all oppressive innovations, and with unfeigned love for all British America, who must, if Boston is subjugated, alternately fall a prey to ministerial ambition, send you one hundred and twenty-five sheep, as a present from the inhabitants of the parish of Brooklyn, hoping thereby you may be enabled to stand more firm (if possible) in the glorious cause in which you are embarked, notwithstanding the repeated, unheard of daring attacks which the British Parliament are making upon the rights which you ought to enjoy as English-born subjects; and if so, we shall of consequence contribute our mite towards the salvation of British America, which is all our ambition.

In zeal in our country's cause, we are exceeded by none; but our abilities and opportunities do not admit of our being of that weight in the American scale as we would to God we were.

We mean, in the first place, to attempt to appease the fire (raised by your committing the India tea to the watery element as a merited oblation to Neptune) of an ambitious and vindictive minister, by the blood of rams and of lambs; if that do not answer the end, we are ready to march in the van and to sprinkle the American altars with our hearts blood, if occasion should be.

The latent seeds of destruction which are implanted in the constitution of almost every state or empire have grown in England, in these last nine years, with amazing rapidity, and now are mature for harvest; and ere long we shall see reapers flocking from all parts of Europe, who will sweep their fields with the besom of destruction. This thought occasions a cloud of melancholy to arise in the breast of every descendant from Britain, which is only dissipated by the pleasing prospect every American has before him! Here we have an unbounded, fertile country, worth contending for with blood! Here bribery and corruption, which are certain forebodings of a speedy dissolution, are as yet only known by names. To us, ere long, Britain's glory will be transferred, where it will shine with accumulated brilliancy.

We cannot but rejoice with you on account of the union and firmness of the Continent. The public virtue now exhibited by the Americans exceeds all of its kind that can be produced in the annals of the Greeks and Romans. Behold them from North to South, from East to West, striving to comfort the Town of Boston, both by publishing their sentiments in regard to the present tyrannical administration, and by supporting their poor with provision, who, otherwise, in this present stagnation of business, would have reduced the opulent to a state of penury and despair in a short time.

You are held up as a spectacle to the whole world. All Christendom are longing to see the event of the American contest. And do, most noble citizens, play your part manfully, of which, we make no doubt, your names are either to be held in eternal veneration or execration. If you stand out, your names cannot be too much applauded by all Europe and all future generations, which is the hearty desire and wish of us, who are, with utmost respect, your most obedient and humble servants.

> Israel Putnam, [*et al.*], *Committee of Correspondence for the Parish of Brooklyn*

D. KINGSTON, NEW HAMPSHIRE

To the Overseers of the Town of Boston.

Sept. 14th., 1774

Gentlemen,

The inhabitants of Kingston, in the Province of New Hampshire, see with deep concern the unhappy misunderstanding and disagreement that now subsists between Great Britain and these American Colonies, being fully sensible the happiness of both countries depend on an union, harmony and agreement to be established between them on a just, equitable and permanent foundation. But when we consider the new, arbitrary and unjust claims of our brethren in Great Britain to levy taxes upon us at their sovereign will and pleasure, and to make laws to bind us in all cases whatsoever, we view and consider ourselves and our posterity under the operations of these claims as absolute slaves; for what is a slave but one who is bound in all cases whatsoever by the will and command of another? And we look on the late unjust, cruel, hostile and tyrannical Acts of the British Parliament, respecting the Massachusetts Bay in general, and the Town of Boston in particular, as consequences of these unreighteous claims, and from them clearly see what the whole continent has to expect under their operation. . . .

We wish the Town of Boston wisdom and prudence to conduct them in these trying and critical times, and that their struggle for liberty may be crowned with abundant success. We look on the cause in which you are engaged as a common cause, and that we and our posterity are equally interested with you in the event. We beg leave to assure that this Town will readily assist the Town of Boston to the utmost of their ability, in every prudent measure that may be taken for regaining their just rights and privileges from all unjust invaders. We heartily sympathize with the poor of the Town of Boston under their present distress, and as an earnest of our readiness to assist you, this Town have contributed and sent by the bearers hereof, one hundred sheep as a present for their relief, to be disposed of for their use in such way and manner as you shall think best.

We are, in behalf of the donors, Your most obedient humble servants,

> Jacob Hooke, [*et al.*]

E. ESSEX COUNTY, VIRGINIA

John Hancock, Esq., or the Overseers of the Poor of the Town of Boston.

Sept. 19th, 1774

Gentlemen:

This serves to inform you that we have consigned to you, by the schooner *Sally*, James Perkins, master, one thousand and eighty-seven bushels of Indian corn, for the use of our suffering brethren in your Town, it being a part only of the contribution by the people in this County for their relief. The remainder, amounting to four or five hundred bushels, shall come by the first opportunity. We can venture to assure you that the Virginians are warmly disposed to assist them, and hope for their steady and prudent perseverance in the common cause of our country, from whence only we can hope for a happy termination of our distresses. We pray God for an happy issue to our virtuous struggles, and we beg leave to assure you that we have the most sincere regard for our northward brethren, and are,

Gentlemen, your most obedient servants,

JOHN UPSHAW, [*et al.*]

F. DURHAM, NEW HAMPSHIRE

Nov. 21st, 1774

Gentlemen,

We take pleasure in transmitting to you, by Mr. Scammel, a few cattle, with a small sum of money, which a number of persons in this place, tenderly sympathizing with our suffering brethren in Boston, have contributed towards their support. With this, or soon after, you will receive the donations of a number in Lee, a parish lately set off from this Town, and in a few days those of Dover, Newmarket and other adjacent Towns. What you herewith receive comes not from the opulent, but mostly from the industrious yeomanry in this parish. We have but a few persons of affluent fortunes among us, but those have most cheerfully contributed to the relief of the distressed in your metropolis.

This is considered by us, not as a gift or an act of charity, but of justice, as a small part of what we are in duty bound to communicate to those truly noble and patriotic advocates of American freedom who are bravely standing in the gap between us and slavery, defending the common interests of a whole continent and gloriously struggling in the cause of Liberty. Upon you the eyes of all America are fixed. Upon your invincible patience, fortitude and resolution (under God) depends all that is dear to them and their prosperity. May that superintendent gracious Being, whose ears are ever open to the cry of the oppressed, in answer to the incessant prayers of his people defend our just cause, turn the counsels of our enemies into foolishness, deliver us from the hands of our oppressors, and make those very measures, by which they are endeavoring to compass our destruction, the means of fixing our invaluable rights and privileges upon a more firm and lasting basis. . . .

JOHN ADAMS

JOHN SULLIVAN   *Committee*

—"Correspondence between a committee of the town of Boston and contributors of donations for the relief of the sufferers of the Boston Port Bill," *Mass. Hist. Soc. Coll.*, 4th Series, IV, 4-6, 38-40, 50-52, 75-76, 81-82, 83, 144-145, 251.

3. A BRITISH OFFICER COMPLAINS OF BOREDOM AND DISORDER

1775, Jany. 1st. Nothing remarkable but the drunkenness among the soldiers, which is now got to a very great pitch; owing to the cheapness of the liquor, a man may get drunk for a copper or two. Still a hard frost. . . .

12th. The frost is broke up and today it rains and thaws. Gaming having got to a very great length among many of the officers, the Genl. lately expressed his disapprobation of a club they have instituted for that purpose; but finding that of no effect, he has set on foot a subscription for a card assembly, which will be very reasonable, as there are rules that no person is to play for above a certain sum; a number of people have subscribed; they call it the Anti-Gambling-Club. I fancy the Genl. is trying to shame the other club, but I don't believe he will succeed, as it's very rare seeing a person alter who is once entered into that way, unless it is by being incapable of continuing it, which I dare say will be the case of many of them before the winter is over.

On the 9th inst. Govr. Wentworth issued a proclamation couched in the most spirited terms, accusing those people who had forcibly entered the Castle of William and Mary at Portsmouth and taken from thence barrels of powder, cannon and small arms, of treason and rebellion; and exhorting all His Majesty's loyal subjects in that Province to exert themselves in the detection of those high offenders, and to use every means of bringing them to a punishment equal to their crimes. Yesterday evening was a ball by subscription; seven of each corps was the number fixed, and the ladies were invited by the managers; this scheme was proposed by Mrs. G——e and carried into execution by her favorites, by which she enjoyed a dance and an opportunity of seeing her friends at no expense. . . .

14th. Cards sent from the Loyal Society of the Blue and Orange to Genls. Gage and Haldiman, Brigadiers Earl Percy, Pigott and Jones, and to the Adml., inviting them to dine with the Society on the Queen's Birthday. Ordered this day that for the future the troops are to receive 4 days salt provision and 3 days fresh, all except the marines and regimental hospitals. We have been fortunate in having only fresh for so long a time; the troops in America used always to have salt before this time. . . .

21st. Last night there was a riot in King Street in consequence of an officer having been insulted by the watchmen, which has frequently happened, as those people suppose from their employment that they may do it with impunity; the contrary, however, they experienced last night. A number of officers as well as townsmen were assembled, and in consequence of the watch having brandished their hooks and other weapons, several officers drew their swords and wounds were given on both sides, some officers slightly; one of the watch lost a nose, another a thumb, besides many others by the points of swords, but less conspicuous than those above mentioned. A court of enquiry is ordered to set next Monday, consisting of five field officers, to enquire into the circumstances of the riot. . . .

March 6th. This day an oration was delivered by Dr. Warren, a notorious Whig, at the great South Meeting opposite the Governor's House; it was in commemoration of what they term the Massacre on the 5th of March, 1770. It was known for some days that this was to be delivered; accordingly a great number of officers assembled at it, when after he had finished 'a most seditious, inflammatory harangue, John Hancock stood up and made a short speech in the same strain, at the end of which some of the officers cried out, "Fie! Fie!" which being mistaken for the cry of fire an alarm immediately ensued, which filled the people with such consternation that they were getting out as fast as they could by the doors and windows. It was imagined that there would have been a riot, which if there had would in all probability have proved fatal to Hancock, Adams, Warren and the rest of those villains, as they were all up in the pulpit together, and the meeting was crowded with officers and seaman in such a manner that they could not have escaped; however, it luckily did not turn out so. It would indeed have been a pity for them to have made their exit in that way, as I hope we shall have the pleasure before long of seeing them do it by the hands of the hangman. The General, hearing there was to be a procession at night upon the same occasion, sent for the selectmen and told them that they had better not have any such thing, as most likely it would produce a disturbance, from which if any bad consequences ensued he would make them answerable; this put a stop to it and they did not put it in execution; the General in case they should had ordered all the regts. to be in readiness to turn out at a moment's warning, and strengthened some of the guards. . . .

March 30th. The 1st Brigade marched into the country at 6 o'clock in the morning; it alarmed the people a good deal. Expresses were sent to every town near; at Watertown about 9 miles off, they got 2 pieces of cannon to the bridge and loaded 'em, but nobody would stay to fire them; at Cambridge they were so alarmed that they pulled up the bridge. However, they were quit for their fears, for after marching about the country for five hours we returned peaceably home. . . .

—DANA, ed., "Diary of a British Officer,"
Atlantic Monthly, XXXIX, 394-398.

CHAPTER TWO

Congress Asserts the Rights of Americans

SHORTLY AFTER *the occupation of Boston by the redcoats, in July 1774, Ezra Stiles of New Haven wrote prophetically that "if oppression proceeds, despotism may force an annual congress; and a public spirit of enterprise may originate in an American Magna Charta and Bill of Rights, supported by such intrepid and persevering importunity as even sovereignty may hereafter judge it not wise to withstand. There will be a Runnymede in America." The first Continental Congress was not a Runnymede, but the second was, so the future President of Yale College was right, as usual.*

A congress of the American states was very much in the minds of the Patriot leaders; it was less than ten years, after all, since the Stamp Act Congress had organized successful resistance to obnoxious Parliamentary acts. As early as May 17, 1774, the freemen of Providence recommended an intercolonial convention to consider the rights of Americans; and a number of other communities quickly endorsed this proposal, some of them in order to fend off more drastic measures. Again, as back in the days of the Stamp Act crisis, it was the action of Virginia and of Massachusetts that proved decisive. On May 27, 89 Burgesses, among them Washington, Jefferson, Randolph, Pendleton and Henry, met in the Raleigh Tavern at Williamsburg, announced that the cause of one colony was the cause of all, and called for a general congress. On June 17 Samuel Adams moved in the Massachusetts House to call a congress of all the colonies at Philadelphia on the first day of September next; the resolution was passed with but eleven negative votes, and Governor Gage promptly dissolved the House.

Massachusetts selected James Bowdoin, Thomas Cushing, Robert Treat Paine and the "brace of Adamses" to represent her at the first Continental Congress. John Adams, the youngest of the delegates, proved the most important; certainly for our purposes he is, for we rely on him for the most interesting and perceptive account of the Congress. Not quite forty, Adams had already developed most of those traits of character which were to distinguish him throughout a long life of public and literary service: passionate devotion to duty, self-conscious rectitude and a deep suspicion of the rectitude of others, immense learning allied with immense industry, pedantry, agonized introspection, faith in liberty and distrust of the ability of ordinary men to exercise it, indefatigable literary energy, and a style at once idiosyncratic, muscular and luminous. In his letters to his friend and counselor, James Warren (husband to the redoubtable Mercy Otis), and in his justly famous Diary, Adams debated the issues of the forthcoming Congress, and etched, sometimes in acid, portraits of his fellow members.

I. UNION FOR RESISTANCE

1. VIRGINIA: "AN ATTACK ON ONE COLONY IS AN ATTACK ON ALL"

May 27, 1774

... We are further clearly of opinion, that an attack, made on one of our sister colonies, to compel submission to arbitrary taxes, is an attack made on all British America, and threatens ruin to the rights of all, unless the united wisdom of the whole be applied. And for this purpose it is recommended to the committee of correspondence, that they communicate, with their several corresponding committees, on the expediency of appointing deputies from the several colonies of British America, to meet in general Congress, at such place annually as shall be thought most convenient; there to deliberate on those general measures which the united interests of America may from time to time require.

—BOYD, ed., *Papers of Thomas Jefferson*, I, 108.

2. MASSACHUSETTS ACTS

In the House of Representatives, June 17, 1774

This House having duly considered, and being deeply affected with the unhappy differences which have long subsisted and are increasing between Great Britain and the American Colonies, do resolve, that a meeting of Committees from the several Colonies on this Continent is highly expedient and necessary, to consult upon the present state of the Colonies and the miseries to which they are and must be reduced by the operation of certain Acts of Parliament respecting America; and to deliberate and determine upon wise and proper measures to be by them recommended to all the Colonies for the recovery and establishment of their just rights and liberties, civil and religious, and the restoration of union and harmony between Great Britain and the Colonies, most ardently desired by all good men.

Therefore resolved, That the Honourable James Bowdoin, Esq., the Honourable Thomas Cushing, Esq., Mr. Samuel Adams, John Adams and Robert Treat Paine be ... appointed a Committee ... for the purposes aforesaid ... to meet in the City of Philadelphia ... on the first day of September next....

—FORCE, *American Archives*, 4th Series, I, 421.

3. "IT WILL BE A NURSERY OF AMERICAN STATESMEN"

John Adams to James Warren.

Ipswich, 25 June 1774

The principal topic was the enterprise to Philadelphia. I view the assembly that is to be there as I do the court of Areopagus, the council of the Amphictyons, a conclave, a sanhedrin, a divan, I know not what. I suppose you sent me there to school. I thank you for thinking me an apt scholar, or capable of learning. For my own part, I am at a loss, totally at a loss, what to do when we get there; but I hope to be there taught.

It is to be a school of political prophets, I suppose, a nursery of American statesmen. May it thrive and prosper and flourish, and from this fountain may there issue streams which shall gladden all the cities and towns in North America forever! I am for making it annual, and for sending an entire new set every year, that all the principal geniuses may go to the university in rotation, that we may have politicians in plenty. Our great complaint is the scarcity of men fit to govern such mighty interests as are clashing in the present contest. A scarcity indeed! For who is sufficient for these things? Our policy must be to improve every opportunity and means for forming our people, and preparing leaders for them in the grand march of politics. We must make our children travel. You and I have too many cares and occupations, and therefore we must recommend it to Mrs. Warren, and her friend Mrs. Adams, to teach our sons the divine science of the politics; and to be frank, I suspect they understand it better than we do.

There is one ugly reflection. Brutus and Cassius were conquered and slain. Hampden died in the field, Sidney on the scaffold, Harrington in jail, etc. This is cold comfort. Politics are an ordeal path among red-hot ploughshares. Who, then, would be a politician for the pleasure of running about barefoot among them? Yet somebody must. And I think those whose characters, circumstances, educations, etc., call them, ought to follow.

Yet I do not think that one or a few men are under any moral obligation to sacrifice for themselves and families all the pleasures, profits and prospects of life, while others for whose benefit this is to be done lie idle, enjoying all the sweets of society, accumulating wealth in abundance, and laying foundations for opulent and powerful families for many generations. No. I think the arduous duties of the times ought to be discharged in rotation, and I never will engage more in politics but upon this system. . . .

—ADAMS, ed., *Works of John Adams*, IX, 338-339.

4. "WHAT AVAILS PRUDENCE, WISDOM, FORTITUDE, WITHOUT LEGIONS?"

John Adams to James Warren.

Braintree, July 17, 1774

Among many other agreeable things which occurred to me on my return from my eastern circuit, I found your letter of the fourteenth instant. Your sentiments always inspire and animate me; but never more upon any occasion than on this. I believe with you that the confidence of the people in the Congress is so great that they will support its decisions as far as possible. And, indeed, it may well be expected that many men of sound judgment will be of that assembly. But what avails prudence, wisdom, policy, fortitude, integrity, without power, without legions? When Demosthenes (God forgive the vanity of recollecting his example!) went ambassador from Athens to the other states of Greece, to excite a confederacy against Philip, he did not go to propose a non-importation or non-consumption agreement!

You "presume the greater part of the number will be masters in politicks," "prophets replete with the true spirit of prophecy." I hope it will be so. But

I must say I am not one of those masters. I must be a scholar. I feel my own insufficiency for this important business. I confess myself ignorant of the characters which compose the Court of Great Britain as well as of the people who compose the nation; at least I have not that minute and accurate knowledge of either which an American senator ought to have of both. I have not that knowledge of the commerce of the several Colonies, nor even of my own Province, which may be necessary.

In short, as compiehensive knowledge of arts and sciences, especially of law and history, of geography, commerce, war and of life, is necessary for an American statesman at this time as was ever necessary for a British or a Roman senator, or a British or Roman general.

Our New England educations are quite unequal to the production of such great characters.

There is one point in which most men seem to be agreed, viz—that it is in our power so to distress the commercial and manufacturing interests in G. Britain as to make them rise up and become importunate petitioners for us to the King, Parliament and Ministry. But others deny this. Some of the higher Tories say that all we can do of this kind will be despised—ridiculed—and that they can live longer without us than we can without them. That the distresses we can occasion would be of but a few individuals and the clamours or miseries of these will be disregarded as trifling considerations in comparison of the loss of the obedience of the Colonies, etc., etc., etc.

That nothing short of such distresses as should produce convulsions would effect any thing at all.

However, I have no faith in these doctrines. The national debts and taxes are so excessive that it seems to me impossible the people should bear the loss of so great a part of their trade.

But what do you think of a non-exportation to Great Britain? Is it expedient to advise to a general non-exportation? Will not such a measure hurt ourselves? What will be the consequence? Must not fish, rice, wheat, tobacco, etc., etc., etc., perish on our hands, or must not thousands of families perish who once lived by raising and producing those commodities in America?

Your maxim, that we have nothing to expect from their justice but everything to hope from their fears, I have ever thought is just as "any of Solomon"; but I confess I have grown more scrupulous of late than ever—more disposed to discuss, examine and minutely weigh every political position than usual. I have employed the best force of my understanding in considering this apophthegm; and the result is that we have indeed nothing to expect from their justice. The Ministry, the beggarly prostituted voters, high and low, have no principles of public virtue on which we can depend, and they are interested to plunder us. But I am not so clear that we have everything to hope from their fears. They are a gallant brave high-spirited people still; and if any means can be found to make the chastisement of the Colonies popular, a Minister, who means nothing by serving in a public station but to make a fortune in wealth and titles, may push a measure to dreadful extremities.

—*Warren-Adams Letters*, I, 29-31.

5. JOSEPH HAWLEY URGES JOHN ADAMS TO KEEP IN THE BACKGROUND

Northampton, July 25, 1774

... You cannot, Sir, but be fully apprised that a good issue of the Congress depends a good deal on the harmony, good understanding, and I had almost said brotherly love, of its members; and everything tending to beget and improve such mutual affection, and indeed to cement the body, ought to be practiced; and every thing in the least tending to create disgust or strangeness, coldness, or so much as indifference, carefully avoided. Now there is an opinion which does in some degree obtain in the other colonies, that the Massachusetts gentlemen, and especially of the town of Boston, do affect to dictate and take the lead in continental measures; that we are apt, from an inward vanity and self-conceit, to assume big and haughty airs. Whether this opinion has any foundation in fact, I am not certain. Our own tories propagate it, if they did not at first suggest it. Now I pray that every thing in the conduct and behaviour of our gentlemen which might tend to beget or strengthen such an opinion, might be most carefully avoided.

It is highly probable, in my opinion, that you will meet gentlemen from several of the other colonies fully equal to yourselves or any of you in their knowledge of Great Britain, the colonies, law, history, government, commerce, etc. I know some of the gentlemen of Connecticut are very sensible, ingenious, solid men. Who will go from New York, I have not heard, but I know there are very able men there; and by what we from time to time see in the public papers, and what our assembly and committees have received from the assemblies and committees of the more southern colonies, we must be satisfied that they have men of as much sense and literature as any we can or ever could boast of. But enough of this sort, and I ask pardon that I have said so much of it.

Another thing I beg leave just to hint—that it is very likely that you may meet divers gentlemen in Congress who are of Dutch, or Scotch, or Irish extract. Many more there are in those southern colonies of those descents than in these New England colonies, and many of them very worthy, learned men. *Quaere*, therefore, whether prudence would not direct that every thing should be very cautiously avoided which could give any the least umbrage, disgust or affront to any of such pedigree. For as of every nation and blood, he that feareth God and worketh righteousness is accepted of Him, so they ought to be of us. Small things may have important effects in such a business. That which disparages our family ancestors or nation is apt to stick by us, if cast up in comparison, and their blood you will find as warm as ours. ...

—ADAMS, ed., *Works of John Adams*, IX, 344-345.

6. ON TO PHILADELPHIA

From the Diary of John Adams.

August 10, 1774, Wednesday. The committee for the Congress took their departure from Boston, from Mr. Cushing's house, and rode to Coolidge's, where they dined in company with a large number of gentlemen, who went out and prepared an entertainment for them at that place. A most kindly and affectionate meeting we had, and about four in the afternoon we took our leave of them, amidst the kind wishes and fervent prayers of every man in the company for our health and success. This scene was truly affecting, beyond all description affecting. I lodged at Colonel Buck's. . . .

16. Tuesday. This morning, Dr. Eliot Rawson, Mr. Alsop, Mr. Mortimer and others, the committee of correspondence, Mr. Henshaw and many other gentlemen came to pay their respects to us, and to assure us that they thought we had their all in our hands, and that they would abide by whatever should be determined on, even to a total stoppage of trade to Europe and the West Indies. . . .

At four we made for New Haven. Seven miles out of town, at a tavern, we met a great number of carriages and of horsemen who had come out to meet us. The sheriff of the county and constable of the town and the justices of peace were in the train. As we were coming, we met others to the amount of I know not what number, but a very great one. As we came into the town, all the bells in town were set to ringing, and the people, men, women and children, were crowding at the doors and windows as if it was to see a coronation. At nine o'clock the cannon were fired, about a dozen guns, I think.

These expressions of respect to us are intended as demonstrations of the sympathy of this people with the Massachusetts Bay and its capital, and to show their expectations from the Congress and their determination to carry into execution whatever shall be agreed upon. No governor of a province, nor general of an army, was ever treated with so much ceremony and assiduity as we have been throughout the whole colony of Connecticut, hitherto, but especially all the way from Hartford to New Haven inclusively.

Nothing shows to me the spirit of the town of New Haven in a stronger point of light than the politeness of Mr. Ingersoll, Judge of Admiralty for the Pennsylvanian Middle District, who came over with his neighbors this evening and made his compliments very respectfully to Tom Cushing, Sam Adams, John Adams and Bob Paine. The numbers of gentlemen who have waited on us from Hartford to this place, the heat of the weather and the shortness of the time have made it impossible for me to learn their names.

17. Wednesday. At New Haven. We are told here that New York is now well united and very firm. This morning, Roger Sherman, Esquire, one of the delegates for Connecticut, came to see us at the tavern, Isaac Bears's. He is between fifty and sixty, a solid, sensible man. He said he read Mr. Otis's *Rights*, etc., in 1764, and thought that he had conceded away the rights of America. He thought the reverse of the declaratory act was true, namely, that the Parliament of Great Britain had authority to make laws for America in no case whatever. He would have been very willing that Massachusetts should have rescinded that part of their Circular Letter where they allow Parliament to be the supreme Legislative over the Colonies in any case. . . .

20. Saturday. . . . We breakfasted at Day's, and arrived in the city of New York at ten o'clock, at Hull's, a tavern, the sign the Bunch of Grapes. We rode by several very elegant country seats before we came to the city. This city will be a subject of much speculation to me. From Hull's we went to private lodgings at Mr. Tobias Stoutenberg's, in King Street, very near the City Hall one way, and the French Church the other. Mr. McDougall and Mr. Platt came to see us. Mr. Platt asked us to dinner next Monday. Mr. McDougall staid longer and talked a good deal. He is a very sensible man, and an open one. He has none of the mean cunning which disgraces so many of my countrymen. He offers to wait on us this afternoon to see the city. . . .

22. *Monday.* This morning we took Mr. McDougall into our coach, and rode three miles out of town to Mr. Morin Scott's to breakfast—a very pleasant ride. Mr. Scott has an elegant seat there, with Hudson's River just behind his house, and a rural prospect all around him. Mr. Scott, his lady and daughter, and her husband, Mr. Litchfield, were dressed to receive us. We sat in a fine airy entry till called into a front room to breakfast. A more elegant breakfast I never saw—rich plate, a very large silver coffee-pot, a very large silver tea-pot, napkins of the very finest materials, toast, and bread and butter in great perfection. After breakfast a plate of beautiful peaches, another of pears, and another of plums, and a muskmelon were placed on the table. . . .

Mr. McDougall gave a caution to avoid every expression here which looked like an allusion to the last appeal. He says there is a powerful party here who are intimidated by fears of a civil war, and they have been induced to acquiesce by assurances that there was no danger, and that a peaceful cessation of commerce would effect relief. Another party, he says, are intimidated lest the levelling spirit of the New England Colonies should propagate itself into New York. Another party are prompted by Episcopalian prejudices against New England. Another party are merchants largely concerned in navigation, and therefore afraid of non-importation, non-consumption and non-exportation agreements. Another party are those who are looking up to Government for favors.

About eleven o'clock, four of the delegates for the city and county of New York came to make their compliments to us—Mr. Duane, Mr. Livingston, Mr. Low and Mr. Alsop. Mr. Livingston is a downright, straightforward man. Mr. Alsop is a soft, sweet man. Mr. Duane has a sly, surveying eye, a little squint-eyed; between forty and forty-five, I should guess; very sensible, I think, and very artful. He says their private correspondence and their agent's letters, Mr. Burke, are that the nation is against us; that we cannot depend upon any support of any kind from thence; that the merchants are very much against us; that their pride is touched, and what they call rights, by our turning away their ships from our ports. A question arose whether it was a prerogative of the Crown at common law to license wharves. I thought it was by statutes at home, which were never extended to America before the Boston Port Bill. Mr. Duane was of my opinion. Mr. Livingston thought it was a prerogative of the Crown at common law; said it had been so understood here; that all the public wharves in this town were by charter from the Governor. He questioned whether the officers of the customs were obliged to attend any wharves but licensed ones.

Mr. Morin Scott called upon us at our lodgings and politely insisted upon our taking a seat in his chariot to Mr. Platt's. We accepted the invitation, and, when we came there, were shown into as elegant a chamber as ever I saw— the furniture as rich and splendid as any of Mr. Boylston's. Mr. Low, Mr.

Peter Vanbrugh Livingston, Mr. Philip Livingston, Dr. Treat, a brother of the minister, and Mr. McDougall, Mr. Scott and Mr. Litchfield dined with us and spent the afternoon.

P. V. Livingston is a sensible man and a gentleman. He has been in trade, is rich, and now lives upon his income. Phil. Livingston is a great, rough, rapid mortal. There is no holding any conversation with him. He blusters away; says if England should turn us adrift, we should instantly go to civil wars among ourselves, to determine which Colony should govern all the rest; seems to dread New England, the levelling spirit, etc. Hints were thrown out of the Goths and Vandals; mention was made of our hanging the Quakers, etc. I told him the very existence of the Colony was at that time at stake—surrounded with Indians at war, against whom they could not have defended the Colony if the Quakers had been permitted to go on.

23. Tuesday.... Went to the Coffee House and saw the Virginia Paper; the spirit of the people is prodigious; their resolutions are really grand. We then went to Mr. Peter Vanbrugh Livingston's, where, at three o'clock, we dined with Scott, McDougall, Philip Livingston, Mr. Thomas Smith and a young gentleman, son of Mr. Peter Livingston. Smith and young Livingston seem to be modest, decent and sensible men.

The way we have been in, of breakfasting, dining, drinking coffee, etc., about the city, is very disagreeable on some accounts. Although it introduces us to the acquaintance of many respectable people here, yet it hinders us from seeing the college, the churches, the printers' offices and booksellers' shops, and many other things which we should choose to see.

With all the opulence and splendor of this city, there is very little good breeding to be found. We have been treated with an assiduous respect; but I have not seen one real gentleman, one well-bred man, since I came to town. At their entertainments there is no conversation that is agreeable; there is no modesty, no attention to one another. They talk very loud, very fast, and all together. If they ask you a question, before you can utter three words of your answer they will break out upon you again, and talk away.

—ADAMS, ed., *Works of John Adams,* II, 340-353, *passim.*

II. THE FIRST CONGRESS DEBATES
THE RIGHTS OF AMERICANS

Fifty-five delegates to the first Continental Congress met in Philadelphia September 5, 1774, and set in force motions which eventuated in American independence. Dr. Johnson called them "zealots of anarchy" and "dictators of sedition," while Lord Chatham described the body as "the most honourable assembly of statesmen since those of ancient Greeks and Romans, in the most virtuous times." Actually the Congress was a distinguished group of men, most of them long associated with resistance against the new policy inaugurated in 1764. Massachusetts sent the two Adamses and Bowdoin; Connecticut, Roger Sherman; from New York came John Jay and Philip Livingston; and from New Jersey another Livingston, William. Pennsylvania's delegation included Joseph Galloway, who eventually threw in his lot with the Loyalists, and John Dickinson, "penman of the Revolution." From Delaware came Caesar Rodney, from Maryland Samuel Chase, and from South Carolina two Rutledges and Christopher Gadsden. The Virginia delegation was the most illustrious of all: George Washington, Richard Henry Lee, Peyton Randolph, Richard Bland, Edmund Pendleton and Patrick Henry; Randolph was chosen President of the Congress. Here, as John Adams said, "are fortunes, abilities, learning, eloquence, acuteness, equal to any I ever met with in my life."

It is John Adams who has given us not only sketches of the members and of social life in the pleasant little city of Philadelphia, but the record of the debate as well, and if he tended to give undue prominence to John Adams, that can perhaps be forgiven. In the beginning the Congress seemed pretty evenly divided between the radicals, who wanted action, and the moderates—Adams called them "trimmers and timeservers"—who preferred petitions. The radicals seized the initiative and held it. They won two initial victories: the choice of Carpenter's Hall, rather than the State House, as the meeting place, and the election of the Philadelphia radical, Charles Thomson, as secretary. Then came a decisive test.

Hard on the heels of Gage's expedition to seize gunpowder on Quarry Hill, outside Boston, delegates from every town and district of Suffolk County, which included Boston and environs, met at Woodward's Tavern in Dedham, and there, on September 9, passed a series of resolutions which had been drawn up by Joseph Warren. Riding night and day, Paul Revere, who gallops through the Revolution like a centaur, brought these Suffolk Resolves to Philadelphia on the seventeenth. There was a sharp debate; then Congress adopted them and thereby endorsed them. "This was one of the happiest days of my life," wrote John Adams. "In Congress we had generous, noble sentiments and manly eloquence. This day convinced me that America will support Massachusetts or perish with her."

What elated Adams, alarmed the conservatives. Their leader was Joseph Galloway, a rich Philadelphia merchant and lawyer long active in colonial politics, speaker of the Pennsylvania Assembly, and a man of parts. On September 28 Galloway introduced his famous Plan of Union, a plan designed to give the American colonies something like dominion status in the empire. "Among all the difficulties in the way of effective and united action in 1774," wrote John Adams, "no more alarming one happened than the plan presented by Mr. Joseph Galloway." After a sharp tussle the plan was defeated by a vote of six to five, and subsequently expunged from the minutes of the Congress. We give here not the plan itself, but Benjamin Franklin's droll comment on it. Galloway drifted into loyalism, joined Howe when that general occupied Philadelphia, and departed for the mother country where he became the leading spokesman for the Loyalist position.

With the Galloway Plan out of the way, Congress settled down to business and endorsed in rapid succession a series of notable state papers. On October 14 came the Declaration and Resolves, which included a declaration of the rights of the colonies. Four days later Congress adopted the Association which has some claim to be considered the first true American union: it provided for nonimportation, nonconsumption and a cessation of slave trade. Other papers included an Address to the People of Great Britain, *drafted by young John Jay of New York; an* Address to the Inhabitants of Quebec, *and a* Petition to the King, *both largely the work of Dickinson.*

What authority did the Congress have to pass these far-reaching acts and resolutions? It is a question that has intrigued the historian and the political theorist from that day to this. A writer in the Essex Gazette *answered the question with infectious simplicity: "The American Congress derives all its power, wisdom and justice, not from scrawls of parchment signed by kings, but from the people. . . . A freeman in honoring and obeying the Congress honors and obeys himself. The least deviation from the resolves of the Congress will be treason." But a Tory asked,*

> *Could the Inquisition, Venice, Rome or Japan*
> *Have devised so horrid, so wicked a Plan?*

Within a few months assemblies, conventions, or town and county meetings of eleven colonies had approved or ratified the proceedings of the Congress. The New York Assembly rejected ratification; that of Georgia did not get a chance to act on it.

1. JOHN ADAMS LIMNS MEMBERS OF THE FIRST CONTINENTAL CONGRESS

September 1, 1774. Thursday. We dined at Friend Collins's, Stephen Collins's, with Governor Hopkins, Governor Ward, Mr. Galloway, Mr. Rhoades, etc. In the evening, all the gentlemen of the Congress who were arrived in town met at Smith's, the new city tavern, and spent the evening together. Twenty-five members were come. Virginia, North Carolina, Maryland and the city of New York were not arrived. Mr. William Livingston, from the Jerseys, lately of New York, was there. He is a plain man, tall, black, wears his hair; nothing elegant or genteel about him. They say he is no public speaker, but very sensible and learned, and a ready writer. Mr. Rutledge, the elder, was there, but his appearance is not very promising. There is no keenness in his eye, no depth in his countenance; nothing of the profound, sagacious, brilliant or sparkling in his first appearance.

Yesterday we removed our lodgings to the house of Miss Jane Port, in Arch Street, about half way between Front Street and Second Street. I find that there is a tribe of people here exactly like the tribe in Massachusetts of Hutchinsonian Addressers. There is, indeed, a set in every colony. We have seen the revolutions of their sentiments. Their opinions have undergone as many changes as the moon. At the time of the Stamp Act, and just before it, they professed to be against the parliamentary claim of right to tax Americans, to be friends to our constitutions, our charter, etc. Bernard was privately, secretly, endeavoring to procure an alteration of our charter. But he concealed his designs until his letters were detected. Hutchinson professed to be a staunch friend to liberty and to our charter until his letters were detected. A great number of good people thought him a good man, and a sincere friend to the Congregational interest in religion, and to our charter privileges. They went on with this Machiavelian dissimulation until those letters were detected. After that, they waited until the Boston Port Bill was passed, and then, thinking the people must submit immediately and that Lord North would carry his whole system triumphantly, they threw off the mask. Dr. Smith, Mr. Galloway, Mr. Vaughan and others in this town are now just where the Hutchinsonian faction were in the year 1764, when we were endeavoring to obtain a repeal of the Stamp Act.

2. Friday. Dined at Mr. Thomas Mifflin's, with Mr. Lynch, Mr. Middleton and the two Rutledges with their ladies. The two Rutledges are good lawyers. Governor Hopkins and Governor Ward were in company. Mr. Lynch gave us a sentiment: "The brave Dantzickers, who declare they will be free in the face of the greatest monarch in Europe." We were very sociable and happy. After coffee we went to the tavern, where we were introduced to Peyton Randolph, Esquire, Speaker of Virginia, Colonel Harrison, Richard Henry Lee, Esquire, and Colonel Bland. Randolph is a large, well-looking man; Lee is a tall, spare man; Bland is a learned, bookish man.

These gentlemen from Virginia appear to be the most spirited and consistent of any. Harrison said he would have come on foot rather than not come. Bland said he would have gone, upon this occasion, if it had been to Jericho.

3. Saturday. Breakfasted at Dr. Shippen's; Dr. Witherspoon was there. Col. R. H. Lee lodges there; he is a masterly man. This Mr. Lee is a brother of the sheriff of London, and of Dr. Arthur Lee, and of Mrs. Shippen; they are all sensible and deep thinkers. Lee is for making the repeal of every revenue law, the Boston Port Bill, the bill for altering the Massachusetts constitution, and the Quebec Bill, and the removal of all the troops, the end of the Congress, and an abstinence from all dutied articles, the means—rum, molasses, sugar, tea, wine, fruits, etc. He is absolutely certain that the same ship which carries home the resolution will bring back the redress. If we were to suppose that any time would intervene, he should be for exceptions. He thinks we should inform his Majesty that we never can be happy while the Lords Bute, Mansfield and North are his confidants and counsellors. He took his pen and attempted a calculation of the numbers of people represented by the Congress, which he made about two millions two hundred thousand; and of the revenue, now actually raised, which he made eighty thousand pounds sterling. He would not allow Lord North to have great abilities; he had seen no symptoms of them; his whole administration had been blunder. He said the opposition had been so feeble and incompetent hitherto that it was time to make vigorous exertions.

Mrs. Shippen is a religious and a reasoning lady. She said she had often thought that the people of Boston could not have behaved through their trials with so much prudence and firmness at the same time, if they had not been influenced by a superior power. Mr. Lee thinks that to strike at the Navigation Acts would unite every man in Britain against us, because the kingdom could not exist without them, and the advantages they derive from these regulations and restrictions of our trade are an ample compensation for all the protection they have offered us, or will afford us. Dr. Witherspoon enters with great spirit into the American cause. He seems as hearty a friend as any of the natives, an animated Son of Liberty. This forenoon, Mr. Caesar Rodney of the lower counties on Delaware River, two Mr. Tilghmans from

Maryland were introduced to us. We went with Mr. William Barrell to his store, and drank punch, and eat dried smoked sprats with him; read the papers and our letters from Boston; dined with Mr. Joseph Reed, the lawyer, with Mrs. Deberdt and Mrs. Reed, Mr. Willing, Mr. Thomas Smith, Mr. Dehart, etc.; spent the evening at Mr. Mifflin's, with Lee and Harrison from Virginia, the two Rutledges, Dr. Witherspoon, Dr. Shippen, Dr. Steptoe and another gentleman; an elegant supper, and we drank sentiments till eleven o'clock. Lee and Harrison were very high. Lee had dined with Mr. Dickinson and drank Burgundy the whole afternoon.

Harrison gave us for a sentiment, "A constitutional death to the Lords Bute, Mansfield and North." Paine gave us, "May the collision of British flint and American steel produce that spark of liberty which shall illumine the latest posterity." "Wisdom to Britain, and firmness to the Colonies; may Britain be wise, and America free." "The friends of America throughout the world." "Union of the Colonies." "Unanimity to the Congress." "May the result of the Congress answer the expectations of the people." "Union of Britain and the Colonies on a constitutional foundation," and many other such toasts.

Young Rutledge told me he studied three years at the Temple. He thinks this a great distinction; says he took a volume of notes which J. Quincy transcribed; says that young gentlemen ought to travel early, because that freedom and ease of behavior which is so necessary cannot be acquired but in early life. This Rutledge is young, sprightly, but not deep; he has the most indistinct, inarticulate way of speaking; speaks through his nose; a wretched speaker in conversation. How he will shine in public, I don't yet know. He seems good-natured, though conceited. His lady is with him, in bad health. His brother still maintains the air of reserve, design and cunning, like Duane and Galloway and Bob Auchmuty.

Caesar Rodney is the oddest-looking man in the world; he is tall, thin and slender as a reed, pale; his face is not bigger than a large apple, yet there is sense and fire, spirit, wit and humor in his countenance. He made himself very merry with Ruggles and his pretended scruples and timidities at the last Congress. Mr. Reed told us at dinner that he never saw greater joy than he saw in London when the news arrived that the non-importation agreement was broke. They were universally shaking hands and congratulating each other. . . .

—ADAMS, ed., *Works of John Adams*, II, 361-364.

2. HENRY: "ALL AMERICA IS THROWN INTO ONE MASS"

Notes of John Adams on the debates in the Continental Congress.

September 5, 1774

Mr. [Patrick] Henry. Government is dissolved. Fleets and armies and the present state of things show that government is dissolved. Where are your landmarks, your boundaries of Colonies? We are in a state of nature, sir. I did propose that a scale should be laid down; that part of North America which was once Massachusetts Bay, and that part which was once Virginia, ought to be considered as having a weight. Will not people complain? Ten thousand Virginians have not outweighed one thousand others.

I will submit, however; I am determined to submit if I am overruled.

A worthy gentleman (ego) near me seemed to admit the necessity of obtaining a more adequate representation.

I hope future ages will quote our proceedings with applause. It is one of the great duties of the democratical part of the constitution to keep itself pure. It is known in my Province that some other Colonies are not so numerous or rich as they are. I am for giving all the satisfaction in my power.

The distinctions between Virginians, Pennsylvanians, New Yorkers and New Englanders are no more. I am not a Virginian, but an American.

Slaves are to be thrown out of the question, and if the freemen can be represented according to their numbers, I am satisfied.

Mr. Lynch. I differ in one point from the gentleman from Virginia, that is, in thinking that numbers only ought to determine the weight of Colonies. I think that property ought to be considered, and that it ought to be a compound of numbers and property that should determine the weight of the Colonies.

I think it cannot be now settled.

Mr. Rutledge. We have no legal authority; and obedience to our determinations will only follow the reasonableness, the apparent utility and necessity of the measures we adopt. We have no coercive or legislative authority. Our constituents are bound only in honor to observe our determinations.

Governor Ward. There are a great number of counties in Virginia very unequal in point of wealth and numbers, yet each has a right to send two members.

Mr. Lee. But one reason which prevails with me, and that is, that we are not at this time provided with proper materials. I am afraid we are not.

Mr. Gadsden. I can't see any way of voting, but by Colonies.

Colonel Bland. I agree with the gentleman (ego) who spoke near me, that we are not at present provided with materials to ascertain the importance of each Colony. The question is whether the rights and liberties of America shall be contended for or given up to arbitrary powers.

Mr. Pendleton. If the committee should find themselves unable to ascertain the weight of the Colonies by their numbers and property, they will report this, and this will lay the foundation for the Congress to take some other steps to procure evidence of numbers and property at some future time.

Mr. Henry. I agree that authentic accounts cannot be had, if by authenticity is meant attestations of officers of the Crown.

I go upon the supposition that government is at an end. All distinctions are thrown down. All America is thrown into one mass. We must aim at the minutiae of rectitude.

Mr. Jay. Could I suppose that we came to frame an American constitution, instead of endeavoring to correct the faults in an old one—I can't yet think that all government is at an end. The measure of arbitrary power is not full, and I think it must run over before we undertake to frame a new constitution.

To the virtue, spirit and abilities of Virginia, we owe much. I should always, therefore, from inclination as well as justice, be for giving Virginia its full weight.

I am not clear that we ought not to be bound by a majority, though ever so small, but I only mentioned it as a matter of danger, worthy of consideration.

—ADAMS, ed., *Works of John Adams*, II, 366-368.

3. THE RIGHTS OF AMERICANS

Notes of John Adams.

September 8, [1774]

In the Committee for stating rights, grievances and means of redress.

Colonel Lee. The rights are built on a fourfold foundation: on nature, on the British constitution, on charters, and on immemorial usage. The Navigation Act, a capital violation.

Mr. Jay. It is necessary to recur to the law of nature and the British constitution to ascertain our rights. The constitution of Great Britain will not apply to some of the charter rights.

A mother country surcharged with inhabitants, they have a right to emigrate. It may be said, if we leave our country, we cannot leave our allegiance. But there is no allegiance without protection, and emigrants have a right to erect what government they please.

Mr. J. Rutledge. Emigrants would not have a right to set up what constitution they please. A subject could not alienate his allegiance.

Lee. Can't see why we should not lay our rights upon the broadest bottom, the ground of nature. Our ancestors found here no government.

Mr. Pendleton. Consider how far we have a right to interfere with regard to the Canada constitution. If the majority of the people there should be pleased with the new constitution, would not the people of America and of England have a right to oppose it, and prevent such a constitution being established in our neighborhood?

Lee. It is contended that the Crown had no right to grant such charters as it has to the Colonies, and, therefore, we shall rest our rights on a feeble foundation if we rest them only on charters; nor will it weaken our objections to the Canada bill.

Mr. Rutledge. Our claims, I think, are well founded on the British constitution, and not on the law of nature.

Colonel Dyer. Part of the country within the Canada bill is a conquered country, and part not. It is said to be a rule that the King can give a conquered country what law he pleases.

Mr. Jay. I can't think the British constitution inseparably attached to the person of every subject. Whence did the constitution derive its authority? from compact; might not that authority be given up by compact?

Mr. William Livingston. A corporation cannot make a corporation; charter governments have done it. King can't appoint a person to make a justice of peace; all governors do it. Therefore it will not do for America to rest wholly on the laws of England.

Mr. Sherman. The ministry contend that the Colonies are only like corporations in England, and therefore subordinate to the legislature of the kingdom. The Colonies not bound to the King or Crown by the act of settlement, but by their consent to it. There is no other legislative over the Colonies but their respective assemblies.

The Colonies adopt the common law, not as the common law, but as the highest reason.

Mr. Duane. Upon the whole, for grounding our rights on the laws and constitution of the country from whence we sprung, and charters, without recurring to the law of nature; because this will be a feeble support. Charters are compacts between the Crown and the people, and I think on this foundation the charter governments stand firm.

England is governed by a limited monarchy and free constitution. Privileges of Englishmen were inherent, their birthright and inheritance, and cannot be deprived of them without their consent.

Objection: that all the rights of Englishmen will make us independent. I hope a line may be drawn to obviate this objection.

James was against Parliament interfering with the Colonies. In the reign of Charles II the sentiments of the Crown seem to have been changed. The Navigation Act was made; Massachusetts denied the authority, but made a law to enforce it in the Colony.

Lee. Life, and liberty which is necessary for the security of life, cannot be given up when we enter into society.

Mr. Rutledge. The first emigrants could not be considered as in a state of nature; they had no right to elect a new king.

Mr. Jay. I have always withheld my assent from the position that every subject discovering land (does it) for the state to which he belongs.

Mr. Galloway. I never could find the rights of Americans in the distinction between taxation and legislation, nor in the distinction between laws for revenue and for the regulation of trade. I have looked for our rights in the law of nature, but could not find them in a state of nature, but always in a state of political society.

I have looked for them in the constitution of the English government, and there found them. We may draw them from this source securely.

Power results from the real property of the society. The states of Greece, Macedon, Rome were founded on this plan. None but landholders could vote in the comitia or stand for offices.

English constitution founded on the same principle. Among the Saxons, the landholders were obliged to attend, and shared among them the power. In the Norman period, the same. When the landholders could not all attend, the representatives of the freeholders came in. Before the reign of Henry IV an attempt was made to give the tenants *in capite* a right to vote. Magna Charta—archbishops, bishops, abbots, earls and barons, and tenants *in capite* held all the lands in England.

It is of the essence of the English constitution that no laws shall be binding but such as are made by the consent of the proprietors in England.

How, then, did it stand with our ancestors when they came over here? They could not be bound by any laws made by the British Parliament, excepting those made before. I never could see any reason to allow that we are bound to any law made since, nor could I ever make any distinction between the sorts of law.

I have ever thought we might reduce our rights to one—an exemption from all laws made by British Parliament since the emigration of our ancestors. It follows, therefore, that all the acts of Parliament made since are violations of our rights.

These claims are all defensible upon the principles even of our enemies—Lord North himself, when he shall inform himself of the true principles of the constitution, etc.

I am well aware that my arguments tend to an independency of the Colonies, and militate against the maxims that there must be some absolute power to draw together all the wills and strength of the empire.

—ADAMS, ed., *Works of John Adams*, II, 370-373.

4. DELEGATES FROM SUFFOLK COUNTY DEFY THE POWER OF BRITAIN

THE SUFFOLK RESOLVES
(drafted by Joseph Warren)

Whereas the power but not the justice, the vengeance but not the wisdom of Great-Britain, which of old persecuted, scourged, and exiled our fugitive parents from their native shores, now pursues us, their guiltless children, with unrelenting severity: And *whereas*, this, then savage and uncultivated desart, was purchased by the toil and treasure, or acquired by the blood and valor of those our venerable progenitors; to us they bequeathed the dearbought inheritance, to our care and protection they consigned it, and the most sacred obligations are upon us to transmit the glorious purchase, unfettered by power, unclogged with shackles, to our innocent and beloved offspring. . . . If we arrest the hand which would ransack our pockets, if we disarm the parricide which points the dagger to our bosoms, if we nobly defeat that fatal edict which proclaims a power to frame laws for us in all cases whatsoever, thereby entailing the endless and numberless curses of slavery upon us, our heirs and their heirs forever; if we successfully resist that unparalleled usurpation of unconstitutional power, whereby our capital is robbed of the means of life; whereby the streets of Boston are thronged with military executioners; whereby our coasts are lined and harbours crouded with ships of war; whereby the charter of the colony, that sacred barrier against the encroachments of tyranny, is mutilated and, in effect, annihilated; whereby a murderous law is framed to shelter villains from the hands of justice; whereby the unalienable and inestimable inheritance, which we derived from nature, the constitution of Britain, and the privileges warranted to us in the charter of the province, is totally wrecked, annulled, and vacated, posterity will acknowledge that virtue which preserved them free and happy; and while we enjoy the rewards and blessings of the faithful, the torrent of panegyrists will roll our reputations to that latest period, when the streams of time shall be absorbed in the abyss of eternity.

Therefore, we have resolved, and do resolve: . . .

3. That the late acts of the British parliament for blocking up the harbour of Boston, for altering the established form of government in this colony, and for screening the most flagitious violators of the laws of the province from a legal trial, are gross infractions of those rights to which we are justly entitled by the laws of nature, the British constitution, and the charter of the province.

4. That no obedience is due from this province to either or any part of the acts above-mentioned, but that they be rejected as the attempts of a wicked administration to enslave America. . . .

7. That it be recommended to the collectors of taxes, constables and all other officers, who have public monies in their hands, to retain the same, and not to make any payment thereof to the provincial county treasurer until the civil government of the province is placed upon a constitutional foundation, or until it shall otherwise be ordered by the proposed provincial Congress. . . .

10. That the late act of parliament for establishing the Roman Catholic religion and the French laws in that extensive country, now called Canada, is dangerous in an extreme degree to the Protestant religion and to the civil rights and liberties of all America; and, therefore, as men and Protestant Christians we are indispensably obliged to take all proper measures for our security.

11. That whereas our enemies have flattered themselves that they shall make an easy prey of this numerous, brave and hardy people, from an apprehension that they are unacquainted with military discipline; we, therefore, for the honour, defence and security of this county and province, advise, as it has been recommended to take away all commissions from the officers of the militia, that those who now hold commissions, or such other persons, be elected in each town as officers in the militia, as shall be judged of sufficient capacity for that purpose, and who have evidenced themselves the inflexible friends to the rights of the people; and that the inhabitants of those towns and districts, who are qualified, do use their utmost diligence to acquaint themselves with the art of war as soon as possible, and do, for that purpose, appear under arms at least once every week. . . .

14. That until our rights are fully restored to us, we will, to the utmost of our power, and we recommend the same to the other counties, to withhold all commercial intercourse with Great-Britain, Ireland, and the West-Indies, and abstain from the consumption of British merchandise and manufactures, and especially of East-India teas and piece goods, with such additions, alterations, and exceptions only, as the General Congress of the colonies may agree to. . . .

—*Journals of the Continental Congress*, I, 31-36.

5. The Continental Congress Endorses the Suffolk Resolves

Saturday, September 18, 1774

The Congress, taking the foregoing into consideration,

Resolved unan., That this assembly deeply feels the suffering of their countrymen in the Massachusetts-Bay, under the operation of the late unjust, cruel and oppressive acts of the British Parliament—that they most thoroughly approve the wisdom and fortitude with which opposition to these wicked ministerial measures has hitherto been conducted, and they earnestly recommend to their brethren a perseverance in the same firm and temperate conduct as expressed in the resolutions determined upon at a meeting of the delegates for the county of Suffolk on Tuesday, the 6th instant, trusting that the effect[s] of the united efforts of North America in their behalf will carry such conviction to the British nation of the unwise, unjust and ruinous policy of the present administration as quickly to introduce better men and wiser measures. . . .

—Journals of the Continental Congress, I, 39.

6. FRANKLIN DEPRECATES THE GALLOWAY PLAN

Benjamin Franklin to Joseph Galloway.

London, Feb. 25, 1775

Dear Friend,

In my last per Falconer I mentioned to you my showing your Plan of Union to Lords Chatham and Camden. I now hear that you had sent it to Lord Dartmouth. Lord Gower I believe alluded to it, when in the House he censured the Congress severely, as first resolving to receive a Plan for uniting the Colonies to the Mother Country, and afterwards rejecting it and ordering their first Resolution to be erased out of their minutes. Permit me to hint to you that it is whispered here by ministerial people that yourself and Mr. Jay of New York are friends to their measures and give them private intelligence of the views of the popular or country party in America. I do not believe this; but I thought it a duty of friendship to acquaint you with the report.

I have not heard what objections were made to the plan in the Congress, nor would I make more than this one, that, when I consider the extream corruption prevalent among all orders of men in this old rotten State, and the glorious publick virtue so predominant in our rising country, I cannot but apprehend more mischief than benefit from a closer union. I fear they will drag us after them in all the plundering wars which their desperate circumstances, injustice and rapacity may prompt them to undertake; and their wide-wasting prodigality and profusion is a gulph that will swallow up every aid we may distress ourselves to afford them.

Here numberless and needless places, enormous salaries, pensions, perquisites, bribes, groundless quarrels, foolish expeditions, false accounts or no accounts, contracts and jobbs devour all revenue, and produce continual necessity in the midst of natural plenty. I apprehend, therefore, that to unite us intimately will only be to corrupt and poison us also. It seems like Mezentius's coupling and binding together the dead and the living.

> "*tormenti genus, et sanie taboque fluentes,*
> *Complexu in misero, longa sic morte necabat.*"

However, I would try any thing, and bear any thing that can be borne with safety to our just liberties, rather than engage in a war with such near relations, unless compelled to it by dire necessity in our own defence. . . .

—SMYTH, ed., Writings of Franklin, VI, 311-312.

III. THE DECLARATION OF RIGHTS

1. JOHN ADAMS DRAFTS THE DECLARATION

From the Autobiography.   [1804]

After some days of general discussion, two committees were appointed of twelve members each, one from each state, Georgia not having yet come in. The first committee was instructed to prepare a bill of rights, as it was called, or a declaration of the rights of the Colonies; the second, a list of infringements or violations of those rights. Congress was pleased to appoint me on the first committee, as the member for Massachusetts.

It would be endless to attempt even an abridgement of the discussions in this committee, which met regularly every morning for many days successively, till it became an object of jealousy to all the other members of Congress. It was, indeed, very much against my judgment that the committee was so soon appointed, as I wished to hear all the great topics handled in Congress at large in the first place. They were very deliberately considered and debated in the committee, however. The two points which labored the most were:

1. Whether we should recur to the law of nature, as well as to the British constitution and our American charters and grants. Mr. Galloway and Mr. Duane were for excluding the law of nature. I was very strenuous for retaining and insisting on it, as a resource to which we might be driven by Parliament much sooner than we were aware.

2. The other great question was, what authority we should concede to Parliament; whether we should deny the authority of Parliament in all cases; whether we should allow any authority to it in our internal affairs; or whether we should allow it to regulate the trade of the empire with or without any restrictions. These discussions spun into great length, and nothing was decided. After many fruitless essays, the committee determined to appoint a sub-committee to make a draught of a set of articles that might be laid in writing before the grand committee, and become the foundation of a more regular debate and final decision. I was appointed on the sub-committee, in which, after going over the ground again, a set of articles were drawn and debated one by one. After several days deliberation, we agreed upon all the articles excepting one, and that was the authority of Parliament, which was indeed the essence of the whole controversy; some were for a flat denial of all authority; others for denying the power of taxation only; some for denying internal but admitting external, taxation. After a multitude of motions had been made, discussed, negatived, it seemed as if we should never agree upon any thing.

Mr. John Rutledge of South Carolina, one of the committee, addressing himself to me, was pleased to say, "Adams, we must agree upon something; you appear to be as familiar with the subject as any of us, and I like your expressions—'*the necessity of the case*' and '*excluding all ideas of taxation, external and internal.*' I have a great opinion of that same idea of the necessity of the case, and I am determined against all taxation for revenue. Come, take the pen and see if you can't produce something that will unite us."

Some others of the committee seconding Mr. Rutledge, I took a sheet of paper and drew up an article. When it was read, I believe not one of the committee was fully satisfied with it; but they all soon acknowledged that there was no hope of hitting on any thing in which we could all agree with more satisfaction. All therefore agreed to this, and upon this depended the union of the Colonies. . . .

Another long debate ensued, especially on this article, and various changes and modifications of it were attempted, but none adopted.

—ADAMS, ed., *Works of John Adams*, II, 373-375.

2. DECLARATION AND RESOLVES OF THE FIRST CONGRESS

October 14, 1774

That the inhabitants of the English Colonies in North America, by the immutable laws of nature, the principles of the English constitution, and the several charters or compacts, have the following Rights:

Resolved, N. C. D.

1. That they are entitled to life, liberty, and property, and they have never ceded to any sovereign power whatever, a right to dispose of either without their consent.

2. That our ancestors, who first settled these colonies, were at the time of their emigration from the mother country, entitled to all the rights, liberties, and immunities of free and natural-born subjects within the realm of England.

3. That by such emigration they by no means forfeited, surrendered, or lost any of those rights, but that they were, and their descendants now are entitled to the exercise and enjoyment of all such of them, as their local and other circumstances enable them to exercise and enjoy.

4. That the foundation of English liberty, and of all free government, is a right in the people to participate in their legislative council: and as the English colonists are not represented, and from their local and other circumstances, cannot properly be represented in the British parliament, they are entitled to a free and exclusive power of legislation in their several provincial legislatures, where their right of representation can alone be preserved, in all cases of taxation and internal polity, subject only to the negative of their sovereign, in such manner as has been heretofore used and accustomed. But, from the necessity of the case, and a regard to the mutual interest of both countries, we cheerfully consent to the operation of such acts of the British parliament, as are bona fide restrained to the regulation of our external commerce, for the purpose of securing the commercial advantages of the whole empire to the mother country, and the commercial benefits of its respective members excluding every idea of taxation, internal or external, for raising a revenue on the subjects in America without their consent.

5. That the respective colonies are entitled to the common law of England, and more especially to the great and inestimable privilege of being tried by their peers of the vicinage, according to the course of that law.

6. That they are entitled to the benefit of such of the English statutes, as existed at the time of their colonization; and which they have, by experience, respectively found to be applicable to their several local and other circumstances.

7. That these, his majesty's colonies, are likewise entitled to all the im-

munities and privileges granted and confirmed to them by royal charters, or secured by their several codes of provincial laws.

8. That they have a right peaceably to assemble, consider of their grievances, and petition the King; and that all prosecutions, prohibitory proclamations, and commitments for the same, are illegal.

9. That the keeping a standing army in these colonies, in times of peace, without the consent of the legislature of that colony in which such army is kept, is against law.

10. It is indispensably necessary to good government, and rendered essential by the English constitution, that the constituent branches of the legislature be independent of each other; that, therefore, the exercise of legislative power in several colonies, by a council appointed during pleasure, by the crown, is unconstitutional, dangerous, and destructive to the freedom of American legislation.

—Journals of the Continental Congress, I, 67-70.

CHAPTER THREE

The War Begins

IN ONE SENSE *it is doubtless true that nobody, in 1775, wanted war; in another sense it is almost equally clear that both the Americans and the British were aching for a showdown. The quarrel between the colonies and the mother country, or between the more intransigent elements in them, had dragged on so long that patience was worn thin, and some kind of explosion was almost inevitable. All the summer and fall of 1774 and into the winter, the redcoats occupied Boston, sallying out from time to time to show their strength, but mostly wondering whether they were an occupying army or a besieged garrison. And all during these months Patriots trained and drilled, collected powder and stores, voiced their sympathy with the Bostonians and their contempt for the British, and carried on a ceaseless propaganda which cast the Bostonians in the role of martyrs and the British in the role of tyrants and banditti. Though it was against the Bostonians that the Intolerable Acts were chiefly directed, the British were not clever enough to localize the conflict, but with astonishing shortsightedness persuaded all the colonies to make the cause of Boston their own. And they made clear, too, that they had no solution except force. The Continental Congress made equally clear that Americans were not to be intimidated—the adoption of the Suffolk Resolves settled that. Even more outrageous, from the British point of view, was the success of the Association. This organization, to which every colony but Georgia acceded, was dedicated to nonintercourse with the mother country as well as a discontinuance of the slave trade. Under its terms the Continental Congress —itself an extralegal body—authorized the creation of Committees of Safety to enforce the nonimportation and nonconsumption agreements, and these were speedily set up in most of the colonies. Moderates opposed them, with some success, in New York and Philadelphia, but on the whole they commanded cooperation and obedience. English importations into New York, for example, which had reached £437,937 in 1774, fell to £1,228 the following year! No wonder merchants in Leeds, Manchester, Birmingham, Glasgow and other manufacturing towns petitioned Parliament to abandon their policy of coercion.*

To these petitions Lord North and the King turned a deaf ear. American resistance merely stiffened their determination to bring Massachusetts to her knees. On November 18 George III wrote Lord North that "New England governments are in a state of rebellion, blows must decide."

Thereafter intimidation rather than persuasion, repression·rather than conciliation, became the formal policy. General Gage, inclined to be easy-going, hardened his heart and will. Speaking of the Patriot leaders, he declared that "*until they are sent home prisoners, I fear we shall have no peace*," and the expedition to seize the stores at Concord was also designed to apprehend Hancock and Adams. Soon Gage was calling for reinforcements. "*If you think ten thousand men sufficient, send twenty*," he wrote to Lord Barrington, and in December requested "*a sufficient force to command the country by marching into it.*" To make all this official, so to speak, Massachusetts was proclaimed in a state of rebellion on February 9, 1775, and in April not only the Bay Colony but five other colonies were cut off from trade with Europe and from the North Atlantic fisheries. That was punishment with a vengeance!

It would have been a miracle had all this not exploded into violence, and there was no miracle. It was a dress rehearsal for violence in September 1774, when militiamen gathered threateningly outside Cambridge. There was a little prologue in Salem in February, when Colonel Leslie marched up to the bridge and then marched back again. Then, because Gage had learned nothing from these two warnings, or because he chose to disregard them, came the fateful expedition to Lexington and Concord, and the war was on.

It was not really clear at the time that Lexington and Concord meant war. The moderates in the Second Continental Congress, which met less than a month after Lexington, still hoped for reconciliation, as did the moderates in Parliament, and not until the following August were the colonies formally proclaimed in a state of rebellion. Could the fighting have been isolated at Boston, war might still have been avoided, but British intransigence combined with American determination to spread it. The impetus for the attack on Fort Ticonderoga came from New England, to be sure—from the Massachusetts Committee of Safety and the Green Mountain boys of Vermont—but the attack was significant because it marked the beginning of offensive rather than merely defensive action by the Americans, and because it spread the fighting into New York, then striving to remain neutral. And that spring, too, Virginians took the road, mildly and hesitatingly, to rebellion. There Lord Dunmore was even more obtuse than Gage; not content with dissolving the Burgesses and seizing the gunpowder in Williamsburg, he went to the extremes of inciting Negro slaves to rebel against their masters, and firing the little metropolis of Norfolk.

˙I. WILL THE AMERICANS FIGHT?

The freemen of Massachusetts had bared their teeth, as it were, in September 1774 when they gathered, 20,000 strong, to resist and overawe General Gage. And, in adopting the Suffolk Resolves, the Continental Congress had put the stamp of approval on their conduct. All through the winter of 1774-1775 the training of militia, the making of arms and munitions, the organization for defense, and for offense too, went forward. And, as a contemporary observed, "*sedition flowed copiously from the pulpits.*" Early in February 1775 the second Provincial Congress of Massachusetts charged its Committee

*of Safety to make preparation for war, and appointed general officers for the
as yet nonexistent army.*

*Did the British, did Gage, read aright the signs of the times? Nothing is
more revealing than the general contempt in which British soldiers and statesmen, who should have known better, held the Americans. Lord Jeffrey Amherst said that with 5,000 men he could march from one end of the colonies
to the other without opposition, and Franklin heard one General Clarke boast
that with but a thousand Grenadiers he would undertake to march from
Maine to Georgia and geld all the males, some by force and the rest by a little
coaxing! And in the course of the debate on cutting off New England from
the fisheries, the Earl of Sandwich—again in Franklin's hearing—assured the
House that the Americans were raw, undisciplined and cowardly. Major
Pitcairn, who originally shared this view, soon learned better. But Captain
Evelyn could write his father in Ireland that "the rebels are the most absolute
cowards on the face of the earth."*

1. "Blows Must Decide"

The King to Lord North.

Queens House Novr. 18th, 1774

I am not sorry that the line of conduct seems now chalked out, which the
enclosed dispatches thoroughly justify; the New England governments are
in a state of rebellion, blows must decide whether they are to be subject to
this country or independent.

—Donne, ed., *Correspondence of George III with Lord North*, I, 214-215.

2. "Raw, Undisciplined, Cowardly"

In the House of Commons.

February 10, 1775

The Earl of Sandwich. The noble Lord mentions the impracticability of
conquering America; I cannot think the noble Lord can be serious on this
matter. Suppose the Colonies do abound in men, what does that signify?
They are raw, undisciplined, cowardly men. I wish instead of forty or fifty
thousand of these *brave* fellows they would produce in the field at least two
hundred thousand; the more the better, the easier would be the conquest;
if they did not run away, they would starve themselves into compliance with
our measures. . . . Are these the men to fright us from the post of honour?
Believe me, my Lords, the very sound of a cannon would carry them off . . .
as fast as their feet could carry them. This is too trifling a part of the argument to detain your Lordships any longer.

—Force, *American Archives*, 4th Series, I, 1682-1683.

3. "I Mean to Seize Them All and Send Them to England"

Major John Pitcairn to the Earl of Sandwich.

Boston, 14th February, 1775

My Lord—I have taken the liberty to write twice to your Lordship before
this, since I came here: one letter I sent by Colonel Prescott, the other by the
packet from New York.

I think many of the people of this country begin to think they have gone too far. The behaviour of the New York people will have a very good effect: the General thinks he sees it already, and all the friends to Government are of opinion that vigorous measures at present would soon put an end to this rebellion. The deluded people are made believe that they are invincible. A very impudent publication, lately come out, asserts that they are an over-match for all Europe in their own country. When this army is ordered to act against them, they will soon be convinced that they are very insignificant when opposed to regular troops. I have sent your Lordship enclosed with this the newspaper with the late resolves of the Provincial Congress; impudent enough they are. . . .

I often march out with our battalion six or seven miles into the country. The people swear at us sometimes, but that does us no harm. I often wish to have orders to march to Cambridge and seize those impudent rascals that have the assurance to make such resolves. They sometimes do not know what to think of us; for we march into the town where they are all assembled, but we have no orders to do what I wish to do, and what I think may easily be done— I mean to seize them all and send them to England.

I have sent your Lordship some of the publications of this country. There is one I am sorry I can't get: it is called "What do you think of the Congress now?" If I can get it before the ship sails, I shall certainly send it.

—BARNES & OWEN, eds., *Private Papers of the Earl of Sandwich*, I, 57-59.

4. "WHAT FOOLS YOU ARE TO RESIST THE POWER OF GREAT BRITAIN!"

Major John Pitcairn to the Earl of Sandwich.

Boston, 4th March, 1775

. . . Orders are anxiously expected from England to chastise those very bad people. The General had some of the Great Whigs, as they are called here, with him two days ago, when he took that opportunity of telling them, and swore to it by the living God, that if there was a single man of the King's troops killed in any of their towns he would burn it to the ground. "What fools you are," said he, "to pretend to resist the power of Great Britain; she maintained last war three hundred thousand men, and will do the same now rather than suffer the ungrateful people of this country to continue in their rebellion." This behaviour of the General's gives great satisfaction to the friends of Government. I am satisfied that one active campaign, a smart action, and burning two or three of their towns, will set everything to rights. Nothing now, I am afraid, but this will ever convince those foolish bad people that England is in earnest. What a sad misfortune it was to this country, the repealing the Stamp Act; every friend to Government here asserts in the strongest terms that this had been the cause of all their misfortunes. . . .

—BARNES & OWENS, eds., *Private Papers of the Earl of Sandwich*, I, 59.

II. COLONEL LESLIE'S EXPEDITION TO SALEM

Though Gage never expressed himself contemptuously toward the Americans, he did in the end adopt a contemptuous view: "They will be lyons whilst we are lambs, but if we take the resolute part they will undoubtedly prove very meek." As if to try out this theory, on February 26 he ordered Colonel Leslie to Salem to seize some stores and cannon which the Patriots had collected there. This Salem expedition, which might have been the opening battle of the war, turned out to be an opéra bouffe. *Early on the morning of the twenty-sixth Leslie sailed with 240 men for Marblehead; after disembarking there, he marched on the ancient town of Salem, only to be denied passage over the drawbridge by the unterrified townspeople.*

What happened is told in the accounts by Mrs. Story and William Gavett, and celebrated in the mock heroics of John Trumbull. What is fascinating is that we hear, in this first episode of the war, the notes of "The World Turned Upside Down," and that we hear, too, in the shrill voice of nurse Sarah Tarrant the original version of what was much later to emerge as the story of Barbara Frietchie.

1. COLONEL LESLIE IS TURNED BACK AT SALEM BRIDGE

William Gavett's account.

February 1775

On Sunday, 26 Feb'y, 1775, my father came home from church rather sooner than usual, which attracted my notice, and said to my mother, "The reg'lars are come and are marching as fast as they can towards the Northfields bridge"; and looking towards her with a very solemn face, remarked, "I don't know what will be the consequence but something very serious, and I wish you to keep the children home." I looked out of the window just at this time and saw the troops passing the house. My father then stepped out and stood at the foot of the yard looking into the street. While there our minister Mr. Barnard came along and took my father by the arm, and they walked down towards the bridge beside the troops. My father was very intimate with Mr. Barnard, but was not a deacon of his church. . . .

Colonel David Mason had received tidings of the approach of the British troops and ran into the North Church, which was contiguous to his dwelling, during service in the afternoon, and cried out, at the top of his voice, "The reg'lars are coming after the guns and are now near Malloon's Mills!" One David Boyce, a Quaker who lived near the church, was instantly out with his team to assist in carrying the guns out of the reach of the troops, and they were conveyed to the neighborhood of what was then called Buffum's Hill, to the northwest of the road leading to Danvers. . . . My father looked in between the platoons . . . to see if he could recognize any of the soldiers who had been stationed at Fort William on the Neck, many of whom were known to him, but he could discover no familiar faces—was blackguarded by the soldiers for his inquisitiveness, who asked him, with oaths, what he was looking after. The northern leaf of the draw was hoisted when the troops approached the bridge, which prevented them from going any further.

Their commander, Col. Leslie . . . then remarked to Capt. [John] Felt, or in his hearing, that he should be obliged to fire upon the people on the northern side of the bridge if they did not lower the leaf. Captain Felt told him if the troops did fire they would all be dead men, or words to that effect. It was understood afterwards that if the troops fired upon the people, Felt intended to grapple with Col. Leslie and jump into the river, for, said he, "I would willingly be drowned myself to be the death of one Englishman." . . .

The people soon began scuttling two gondolas which lay on the western side of the bridge, and the troops also got into them to prevent it. One Joseph Whicher, the foreman in Col. Sprague's distillery, was at work scuttling the colonel's gondola, and the soldiers ordered him to desist, and threatened to stab him with their bayonets if he did not—whereupon he opened his breast and dared them to strike. They pricked his breast so as to draw blood. . . .

It was a very cold day, and the soldiers were without any overcoats, and shivered excessively and shewed signs of being cold. Many of the inhabitants climbed upon the leaf of the draw and blackguarded the troops. Among them was a man who cried out as loud as possible, "Soldiers, red-jackets, lobster-coats, cowards, *damnation to your government!*" The inhabitants rebuked him for it and requested nothing should be done to irritate the troops. Colonel Leslie now spoke to Mr. Barnard, probably observing by his canonical dress that he was a clergyman, and said, "I will get over this bridge before I return to Boston, if I stay here till next autumn." Mr. Barnard replied, he prayed to Heaven there might be no collision, or words of a similar import. Then the colonel remarked, he should burst into the stores of William West and Eben Bickford and make barracks of them for his troops until he could obtain a passage; and turning to Captain Felt, said, "By God! I will not be defeated"; to which Captain Felt replied, "You must acknowledge you have already been baffled."

In the course of the debate between Colonel Leslie and the inhabitants, the colonel remarked that he was upon the King's Highway and would not be prevented passing over the bridge.

Old Mr. James Barr, an Englishman and a man of much nerve, then replied to him: "It is *not* the King's Highway; it is a road built by the owners of the lots on the other side, and no king, country or town has anything to do with it."

The colonel replied, "There may be two words to that."

And Mr. Barr rejoined, "Egad, I think that will be the best way for you to conclude the King has nothing to do with it."

Then the colonel asked Captain Felt if he had any authority to order the leaf of the draw to be lowered, and Captain Felt replied there was no authority in the case, but there might be some influence. Colonel Leslie then promised, if they would allow him to pass over the bridge, he would march but fifty rods and return immediately, without troubling or disturbing anything. Captain Felt was at first unwilling to allow the troops to pass over on any terms, but at length consented, and requested to have the leaf lowered. In this he was joined by Mr. Barnard and Colonel Pickering, and the leaf was lowered down. The troops then passed over and marched the distance agreed upon without violating their pledge, then wheeled and marched back again, and continued their march through North Street in the direction of Marblehead.

A nurse named Sarah Tarrant, in one of the houses near the termination of their route, in Northfields, placed herself at the open window and called out to them: "Go home and tell your master he has sent you on a fool's errand and broken the peace of our Sabbath. What," said she, "do you think we were born in the woods, to be frightened by owls?" One of the soldiers pointed his musket at her, and she exclaimed, "Fire if you have the courage, but I doubt it."

—GAVETT, "Account of the Affair at North Bridge,"
Essex Institute Proc., I, 126-128.

2. COLONEL LESLIE RETREATS: "THE WORLD TURNED UPSIDE DOWN"

Account dictated by the mother of Justice Joseph Story.

In the year 1774 some of the most influential men in the colonies received information that Gov. Gage had received orders and was determined to disarm the colonists by seizing their arms and ammunition. Many persons who were friendly to Great Britain were determined to resist all acts of usurpation and tyranny on the part of the Crown. They did not believe the Governor would attempt to enforce this order, but were very watchful and jealous of every movement made by him.

Some Tories in Salem gave Gov. Gage notice that there were some cannon and military stores in a certain place in Salem which they pointed out and described. On the 26 February, 1775, the Governor ordered from Castle William Lieut.-Col. Leslie with the 64th Regiment in a transport, to land at Marblehead, and from thence to march to Salem and seize the cannon and munitions of war. His orders were peremptory—he landed his troops upon Marblehead Neck in a very quiet manner, expecting not to be discovered or his movements suspected in such an obscure spot; but he little knew the jealous watchfulness of the Americans. By the time their feet touched the land, a man went into the town of Marblehead who saw them land, and the alarm was immediately given by a dozen men running to the door of the new meetinghouse and beating the alarm signal agreed upon, and crying out, "To arms, to arms!" A person on the watch saw the soldiers come out of the Neck lane in single file, form upon Burbier's plain and then march to Salem, playing "Yankee Doodle". . . . After the draw was lowered, Col. Leslie and his men passed over and advanced upon the road the number of paces agreed upon, wheeled about, the music playing the old-fashioned tune of "The World's Turned Upside Down," and marched to Marblehead Neck, whence they embarked.

—STORY, "Account Dictated," *Essex Institute Proc.*, I, 134-135.

3. LESLIE LOST NO TIME OR MEN

1775
Through Salem straight, without delay,
The bold battalion took its way;
Marched o'er a bridge, in open sight
Of several Yankees armed for fight;

Then, without loss of time or men,
Veered round for Boston back again,
And found so well their projects thrive
That every soul got home alive.

—TRUMBULL, *M'Fingal*, pp. 59-60.

III. THE MIDNIGHT RIDE OF PAUL REVERE

Thanks largely to Longfellow, no episode in the history of the Revolution is more familiar than that of the midnight ride of Paul Revere. Although Revere was not the only messenger to sound the alarm—William Dawes, for example, was across the narrow neck even before Revere shoved off by boat —it is more than the accident of a poetic name that has assured him fame. He was a man of parts: a skillful engraver, a master silversmith, an ardent Patriot, friend to the Adamses and Hancock and Warren. He had been one of the Mohawks who boarded the Dartmouth; *and then he had carried the news of the Tea Party to near-by towns; as official courier of the Provincial Congress he had carried the Suffolk Resolves to Philadelphia and gone on many another errand.*

The immediate background of Lexington and Concord is, in a way, a comedy of espionage. General Gage had decided to seize military stores at Concord as early as April 15; thanks to an elaborate system of intelligence, the Patriots had wind of this at once, and on the morning of the sixteenth Revere was off to spread the alarm. Gage, in turn, knew that the Patriots had been alerted. It was on his return from Concord on the sixteenth that Revere made the famous agreement for a signal from the steeple of the North Church: one if by land and two if by sea. Gage had determined on the night of the eighteenth for his expedition. Late that night—before the grenadiers were under way—Dr. Warren sent William Dawes across the Boston Neck to Cambridge and Lexington, and arranged for Revere to be rowed over to Charlestown and there mount and spread the alarm. Revere later wrote two accounts of this famous ride, a rather short one in 1783, and a longer one, in a letter to Dr. Jeremy Belknap, in 1798. It is from this second and more circumstantial version that we take our excerpt.

Revere continued to serve as a courier and in many other capacities as well. He seemed to have a special talent for associating himself with historic events: he designed the official seal for the new nation; engraved the first Continental money; cast, in his foundry, the spikes and copper accessories for "Old Ironsides"; and made the copper plate for the dome of the Boston State House, and for the boilers of Robert Fulton's steam ferryboats.

Two by Water and One by Land

Paul Revere to Dr. Jeremy Belknap.

[1798]

In the fall of 1774 and winter of 1775, I was one of upwards of thirty, chiefly mechanics, who formed ourselves into a committee for the purpose of watching the movements of the British soldiers, and gaining every intelligence of the movements of the Tories. We held our meetings at the Green Dragon tavern. We were so careful that our meetings should be kept secret that every time we met, every person swore upon the Bible that they would not discover any of our transactions but to Messrs. Hancock, Adams, Doctors Warren, Church and one or two more.

. . . In the winter, towards the spring, we frequently took turns, two and two, to watch the soldiers by patrolling the streets all night. The Saturday night preceding the 19th of April, about 12 o'clock at night, the boats belonging to the transports were all launched and carried under the sterns of the men-of-war. (They had been previously hauled up and repaired.) We likewise found that the grenadiers and light infantry were all taken off duty.

From these movements we expected something serious was to be transacted. On Tuesday evening, the 18th, it was observed that a number of soldiers were marching towards the bottom of the Common. About 10 o'clock, Dr. Warren sent in great haste for me and begged that I would immediately set off for Lexington, where Messrs. Hancock and Adams were, and acquaint them of the movement, and that it was thought they were the objects.

When I got to Dr. Warren's house, I found he had sent an express by land to Lexington—a Mr. William Daws. The Sunday before, by desire of Dr. Warren, I had been to Lexington, to Messrs. Hancock and Adams, who were at the Rev. Mr. Clark's. I returned at night through Charlestown; there I agreed with a Colonel Conant and some other gentlemen that if the British went out by water, we would show two lanthorns in the North Church steeple; and if by land, one, as a signal; for we were apprehensive it would be difficult to cross the Charles River or get over Boston Neck. I left Dr. Warren, called upon a friend and desired him to make the signals.

I then went home, took my boots and surtout, went to the north part of the town, where I had kept a boat; two friends rowed me across Charles River, a little to the eastward where the *Somerset* man-of-war lay. It was then young flood, the ship was winding, and the moon was rising. They landed me on the Charlestown side. When I got into town, I met Colonel Conant and several others; they said they had seen our signals. I told them what was acting, and went to get me a horse; I got a horse of Deacon Larkin. While the horse was preparing, Richard Devens, Esq., who was one of the Committee of Safety, came to me and told me that he came down the road from Lexington after sundown that evening; that he met ten British officers, all well mounted, and armed, going up the road.

I set off upon a very good horse; it was then about eleven o'clock and very pleasant. After I had passed Charlestown Neck . . . I saw two men on horseback under a tree. When I got near them, I discovered they were British officers. One tried to get ahead of me, and the other to take me. I turned my horse very quick and galloped towards Charlestown Neck, and then pushed for the Medford Road. The one who chased me, endeavoring to cut me off, got into a clay pond near where Mr. Russell's Tavern is now built. I got clear of him, and went through Medford, over the bridge and up to Menotomy. In Medford, I awaked the captain of the minute men; and after that, I alarmed almost every house, till I got to Lexington. I found Messrs. Hancock and Adams at the Rev. Mr. Clark's; I told them my errand and enquired for Mr. Daws; they said he had not been there; I related the story of the two officers, and supposed that he must have been stopped, as he ought to have been there before me.

After I had been there about half an hour, Mr. Daws came; we refreshed ourselves, and set off for Concord. We were overtaken by a young Dr. Prescott, whom we found to be a high Son of Liberty. I told them of the ten officers that Mr. Devens met, and that it was probable we might be stopped before we got to Concord; for I supposed that after night they divided themselves, and that two of them had fixed themselves in such passages as were most likely to stop any intelligence going to Concord. I likewise mentioned that we had better alarm all the inhabitants till we got to Concord. The young doctor much approved of it and said he would stop with either of us, for the people between that and Concord knew him and would give the more credit to what we said.

We had got nearly half way. Mr. Daws and the doctor stopped to alarm the people of a house. I was about one hundred rods ahead when I saw two men in nearly the same situation as those officers were near Charlestown. I called for the doctor and Mr. Daws to come up. In an instant I was surrounded by four. They had placed themselves in a straight road that inclined each way; they had taken down a pair of bars on the north side of the road, and two of them were under a tree in the pasture. The doctor being foremost, he came up and we tried to get past them; but they being armed with pistols and swords, they forced us into the pasture. The doctor jumped his horse over a low stone wall and got to Concord.

I observed a wood at a small distance and made for that. When I got there, out started six officers on horseback and ordered me to dismount. One of them, who appeared to have the command, examined me, where I came from and what my name was. I told him. He asked me if I was an express. I answered in the affirmative. He demanded what time I left Boston. I told him, and added that their troops had catched aground in passing the river, and that there would be five hundred Americans there in a short time, for I had alarmed the country all the way up. He immediately rode towards those who stopped us, when all five of them came down upon a full gallop. One of them, whom I afterwards found to be a Major Mitchel, of the 5th Regiment, clapped his pistol to my head, called me by name and told me he was going to ask me some questions, and if I did not give him true answers, he would blow my brains out. He then asked me similar questions to those above. He then ordered me to mount my horse, after searching me for arms. He then ordered them to advance and to lead me in front. When we got to the road, they turned down towards Lexington. When we had got about one mile, the major rode up to the officer that was leading me, and told him to give me to the sergeant. As soon as he took me, the major ordered him, if I attempted to run, or anybody insulted them, to blow my brains out.

We rode till we got near Lexington meeting-house, when the militia fired a volley of guns, which appeared to alarm them very much. The major inquired of me how far it was to Cambridge, and if there were any other road.

After some consultation, the major rode up to the sergeant and asked if his horse was tired. He answered him he was—he was a sergeant of grenadiers and had a small horse. "Then," said he, "take that man's horse." I dismounted, and the sergeant mounted my horse, when they all rode towards Lexington meeting-house.

I went across the burying-ground and some pastures and came to the Rev. Mr. Clark's house, where I found Messrs. Hancock and Adams. I told them of my treatment, and they concluded to go from that house towards Woburn. I went with them and a Mr. Lowell, who was a clerk to Mr. Hancock.

When we got to the house where they intended to stop, Mr. Lowell and myself returned to Mr. Clark's, to find what was going on. When we got there, an elderly man came in; he said he had just come from the tavern, that a man had come from Boston who said there were no British troops coming. Mr. Lowell and myself went towards the tavern, when we met a man on a full gallop, who told us the troops were coming up the rocks. We afterwards met another, who said they were close by. Mr. Lowell asked me to go to the tavern with him, to get a trunk of papers belonging to Mr. Hancock. We went up chamber, and while we were getting the trunk, we saw the British very near, upon a full march. We hurried towards Mr. Clark's house. In our way we passed through the militia. There were about fifty. When we had got about one hundred yards from the meeting-house, the British troops appeared on both sides of the meeting-house. In their front was an officer on horseback. They made a short halt; *when I saw, and heard, a gun fired*, which appeared to be a pistol. Then I could distinguish two guns, and then a continual roar of musketry; when we made off with the trunk.

—REVERE, "Letter," *Mass. Hist. Soc. Proc.*, XVI, 371-374.

IV. A TOWN CALLED LEXINGTON

The purpose of Colonel Francis Smith's expedition was twofold: to apprehend John Hancock and Samuel Adams, reputed to be in Lexington, and to seize arms and military provisions in Concord, six miles west. Even before the redcoats had crossed the Charles the alarm was out, and all during the night there were a tolling of bells and firing of guns which proclaimed that the countryside was aroused. Revere and Dawes reached Lexington a little after midnight, found the two statesmen at the parsonage of the Reverend Jonas Clark—his wife was Hancock's cousin—and persuaded them to seek safety in flight.

"What a glorious morning this is!" said Sam Adams to Hancock as they made their way across the meadows, and added, "I mean for America."

At the same time the town bell tolled the alarm, and Captain John Parker and about 70 militiamen rolled out of their beds and assembled on the little triangular village green. As nothing happened the militiamen retired to their homes, or to the Buckman Tavern, with the warning to be on the alert, while Revere and Dawes pushed on toward Concord.

Just before dawn, at about four o'clock, the drums beat the alarm, and once again the militiamen straggled to the common—somewhere between 50 and 70 of them altogether. This time it was the real thing: there was a tramp of feet and English voices barking orders, and out of the dark and the morning mist came the redcoats, six companies of them under Major John Pitcairn. Captain Parker said to his men, "Don't fire unless fired upon. But if they want a war let it begin here"—that, at least, is the way his grandson Theodore Parker heard it. There was a cry, "Disperse, ye rebels!" a pistol shot, two musket shots and a roll of musketry, and the war was on.

The literature of Lexington is voluminous and unsatisfactory. Though Fortescue, the historian of the British Army, says that the question "Who fired the first shot?" is "really of trifling importance," it was not thought trifling at the time. Each side hurried to collect testimonials—a better term than evidence—and as the Americans were more favorably situated here they won the battle of words—and of propaganda. We give here seven accounts, three British and four American, and we give them in order of appearance, as it were. First is an account of the expedition written on April 19 by a British officer, probably Lieutenant John Barker of the King's Own; second, a letter from John Adams—who was not a participant—written the same day; third, a letter from General Gage, brushing the whole thing off as a minor nuisance; fourth, an almost contemporary letter from a seaman, probably John Crozier, master of the Empress of Russia, *to his friend Dr. Rogers, of the British Navy; fifth, a semiofficial account of both Lexington and Concord by the ubiquitous Reverend William Gordon of near-by Roxbury, who fancied himself the historian of the Revolution; sixth, the anniversary sermon by the Reverend Jonas Clark who had been an eyewitness of the fray and who had collected testimony during the year; and finally a deposition made half a century later by one of the participants, Sylvanus Wood.*

Interestingly enough, the American account of Lexington and Concord reached England before the British. Horace Walpole read it, and on June 5 wrote his friend Sir Horace Mann: "So here is this fatal war commenced!

> *The child that is unborn shall rue*
> *The hunting of that day!"*

1. "From Beginning to End Ill Planned and Ill Executed"

Account presumably by Lieutenant John Barker of the King's Own.

1775, April 19th. Last night between 10 and 11 o'clock all the Grenadiers and Light Infantry of the army, making about 600 men (under the command of Lt. Col. Smith of the 10th and Major Pitcairn of the Marines), embarked and were landed upon the opposite shore on Cambridge Marsh; few but the commanding officers knew what expedition we were going upon. After getting over the marsh, where we were wet up to the knees, we were halted in a dirty road and stood there till two o'clock in the morning, waiting for provisions to be brought from the boats and to be divided, and which most of the men threw away, having carried some with 'em. At 2 o'clock we began our march by wading through a very long ford up to our middles. After going a few miles we took 3 or 4 people who were going off to give intelligence.

About 5 miles on this side of a town called Lexington, which lay in our road, we heard there were some hundreds of people collected together intending to oppose us and stop our going on. At 5 o'clock we arrived there and saw a number of people, I believe between 2 and 300, formed in a common in the middle of the town. We still continued advancing, keeping prepared against an attack tho' without intending to attack them; but on our coming near them they fired one or two shots, upon which our men without any orders rushed in upon them, fired and put 'em to flight. Several of them were killed, we could not tell how many because they were got behind walls and into the woods. We had a man of the 10th Light Infantry wounded, nobody else hurt. We then formed on the common, but with some difficulty, the men were so wild they could hear no orders.

We waited a considerable time there, and at length proceeded on our way to Concord, which we then learnt was our destination, in order to destroy a magazine of stores collected there. We met with no interruption till within a mile or two of the town, where the country people had occupied a hill which commanded the road. The Light Infantry were ordered away to the right and ascended the height in one line, upon which the Yankies quitted it without firing, which they did likewise for one or two more successively. They then crossed the river beyond the town, and we marched into the town after taking possession of a hill with a Liberty Pole on it and a flag flying, which was cut down. The Yankies had the hill but left it to us. We expected they would have made a stand there, but they did not chuse it.

While the Grenadiers remained in the town, destroying 3 pieces of cannon, several gun carriages and about 100 barrels of flour with harness and other things, the Light companies were detached beyond the river to examine some houses for more stores. One of these companies was left at the bridge, another on a hill ¼ of a mile from that; the other 3 went forward 2 or 3 miles to seek for some cannon which had been there but had been taken away that morning. During this time the people were gathering together in great numbers and, taking advantage of our scattered disposition, seemed as if they were going to cut off the communication with the bridge, upon which the two companies joined and went to the bridge to support that company. The three companies drew up in the road the far side the bridge and the Rebels on the hill above, covered by a wall; in that situation they remained a long time, very near an hour, the three companies expecting to be attacked by the Rebels, who were about 1000 strong. Captn. Lawrie, who commanded these three companies, sent to Col. Smith begging he would send more troops to his assistance and informing him of his situation. The Colonel ordered 2 or 3 companies, but put himself at their head, by which means stopt 'em from being time enough, for being a very fat heavy man he would not have reached the bridge in half an hour, tho' it was not half a mile to it.

In the mean time the Rebels marched into the road and were coming down upon us when Captn. Lawrie made his men retire to this side the bridge (which by the bye he ought to have done at first, and then he would have had time to make a good disposition, but at this time he had not, for the Rebels were got so near him that his people were obliged to form the best way they could). As soon as they were over the bridge the three companies got one

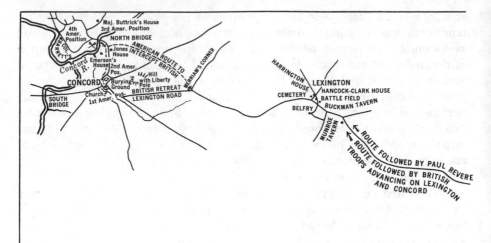

**BOSTON,
LEXINGTON AND CONCORD**

behind the other so that only the front one could fire. The Rebels when they got near the bridge halted and fronted, filling the road from the top to the bottom. The fire soon began from a dropping shot on our side, when they and the front company fired almost at the same instant, there being nobody to support the front company. The others not firing, the whole were forced to quit the bridge and return toward Concord. Some of the Grenadiers met 'em in the road and then advanced to meet the Rebels, who had got this side the bridge and on a good height, but seeing the manoeuvre they thought proper to retire again over the bridge. The whole then went into Concord, drew up in the town and waited for the 3 companies that were gone on, which arrived in about an hour. Four officers of 8 who were at the bridge were wounded; 3 men killed; 1 sergt. and several men wounded.

After getting as good conveniences for the wounded as we could, and having done the business we were sent upon, we set out upon our return. Before the whole had quitted the town we were fired on from houses and behind trees, and before we had gone ½ a mile we were fired on from all sides, but mostly from the rear, where people had hid themselves in houses till we had passed, and then fired. The country was an amazing strong one, full of hills, woods, stone walls, etc., which the Rebels did not fail to take advantage of, for they were all lined with people who kept an incessant fire upon us, as we did too upon them, but not with the same advantage, for they were so concealed there was hardly any seeing them. In this way we marched between 9 and 10 miles, their numbers increasing from all parts, while ours was reduced by deaths, wounds and fatigue; and we were totally surrounded with such an incessant fire as it's impossible to conceive; our ammunition was likewise near expended.

In this critical situation we perceived the 1st Brigade coming to our assistance: it consisted of the 4th, 23rd and 47th Regiments, and the battalion of Marines, with two field pieces, 6-pounders. We had been flattered ever since the morning with expectations of the Brigade coming out, but at this time had given up all hopes of it, as it was so late. I since heard it was owing to a mistake of the orders, or the Brigade would have been with us 2 hours sooner. As soon as the Rebels saw this reinforcement, and tasted the field pieces, they retired, and we formed on a rising ground and rested ourselves a little while, which was extremely necessary for our men, who were almost exhausted with fatigue.

In about ½ an hour we marched again, and, some of the Brigade taking the flanking parties, we marched pretty quiet for about 2 miles. They then began to pepper us again from the same sort of places, but at rather a greater distance. We were now obliged to force almost every house in the road, for the Rebels had taken possession of them and galled us exceedingly; but they suffered for their temerity, for all that were found in the houses were put to death.

When we got to Menotomy there was a very heavy fire; after that we took the short cut into the Charles Town road, very luckily for us too, for the Rebels, thinking we should endeavour to return by Cambridge, had broken down the bridge and had a great number of men to line the road and to receive us there. However, we threw them and went on to Charles Town without any great interruption. We got there between 7 and 8 oclock at night, took possession of the hill above the town, and waited for the boats to carry us over, which came some time after. The Rebels did not chuse to follow us to the hill, as they must have fought us on open ground and that they did not like. The piquets of the army were sent over to Charles Town and 200 of the 64th to keep that ground; they threw up a work to secure themselves, and we embarked and got home very late in the night. . . .

Thus ended this expedition, which from the beginning to end was as ill planned and ill executed as it was possible to be. Had we not idled away three hours on Cambridge Marsh waiting for provisions that were not wanted, we should have had no interruption at Lexington, but by our stay the country people had got intelligence and time to assemble. We should have reached Concord soon after day break, before they could have heard of us, by which we should have destroyed more cannon and stores, which they had had time enough to convey away before our arrival. We might also have got easier back and not been so much harassed, as they would not have had time to assemble so many people; even the people of Salem and Marblehead, above 20 miles off, had intelligence and time enough to march and meet us on our return; they met us somewhere about Menotomy, but they lost a good many for their pains. . . .

Thus for a few trifling stores the Grenadiers and Light Infantry had a march of about 50 miles (going and returning) through an enemy's country, and in all human probability must every man have been cut off if the Brigade had not fortunately come to their assistance; for when the Brigade joined us there were very few men had any ammunition left, and so fatigued that we could not keep flanking parties out, so that we must soon have laid down our arms or been picked off by the Rebels at their pleasure.

—DANA, ed., "Diary of a British Officer,"
Atlantic Monthly, XXXIX, 398-401 *passim*.

2. "A SCENE THE MOST SHOCKING NEW ENGLAND EVER BEHELD"

John Adams to William Barrell.

April 19, [1775]

Yesterday produced a scene the most shocking New England ever beheld. Last Saturday P.M. orders were sent to the several regiments quartered here not to let their Grenadiers or Light Infantry do any duty till further orders, upon which the inhabitants conjectured that some secret expedition was on foot, and being on the look out, they observed those bodies upon the move between ten and eleven o'clock the evening before last, observing a perfect silence in their march towards a point opposite Phip's farm, where [boats?] were in waiting that conveyed 'em over.

The men appointed to alarm the country upon such occasions got over by stealth as early as they [could] and took their different routs. The first advice we had was about eight o'clock in the morning, when it was reported that the troops had fired upon and killed five men in Lexington—previous to which an officer came express to his Excellency Governor Gage, when between eight and nine o'clock a brigade marched out under the command of Earl Piercy, consisting of the Marines, the Welch Fusileers, the 4th Regiment, the 47th, and two field pieces.

About twelve o'clock it was gave out by the general's aide camps that no person was killed, and that a single gun had not been fired, which report was variously believed—but between one and two, certain accounts came that eight were killed outright and fourteen wounded of the inhabitants of Lexington—who had about forty men drawn out early in the morning near the meeting house to exercise. The party of the Light Infantry and Grenadiers, to the number of about eight hundred, came up to them and ordered them to disperse. The commander of 'em replied that they were only innocently amusing themselves with exercise, that they had not any ammunition with 'em, and therefore should not molest or disturb them. Which answer not satisfying, the troops fired upon and killed three or four, the others took to their heels and the troops continued to fire. A few took refuge in the meeting, when the soldiers shoved up the windows and pointed their guns in and killed three there. Thus much is best account I can learn of the beginning of this fatal day.

You must naturally suppose that such a piece would rouse the country (allowed the report to be true). The troops continued their march to Concord, entered the town, and refreshed themselves in the meeting and town house. In the latter place they found some ammunition and stores belonging to the country, which they found they could not bring away by reason that the country people had occupied all the posts around 'em. They therefore set fire to the house, which the people extinguished. They set fire a second time, which brought on a general engagement at about eleven o'clock. The troops took two pieces [of] cannon from the peasants, but their numbers increasing they soon regained 'em, and the troops were obliged to retreat towards town.

About noon they were joined by the other brigade under Earl Piercy, when another very *warm* engagement came on at Lexington, which the troops could not stand; therefore were obliged to continue their retreat, which they did with the bravery becoming British soldiers—but the country were in a manner desperate, not regarding their cannon (any more) in the least, and followed 'em till seven in the evening, by which time they got into Charlestown, when they left off the pursuit, least they might injure the inhabitants.

I stood upon the hills in town and saw the engagement very plain. It was very bloody for seven hours. It's conjectured that one half the soldiers at least were killed.

The last brigade was sent over the ferry in the evening to secure their retreat—where they are this morning entrenching themselves upon Bunker's Hill [to] get a safe retreat to this town. It's impossible to learn any particulars, as the communication between town and country is at present broken off. They were till ten o'clock last night bringing over their wounded, several of which are since [dead], two officers in particular.

When I reflect and consider that the fight was between those whose parents but a few generations ago were brothers, I shudder at the thought, and there's no knowing where our calamities will end.

—ADAMS, "Letter," *Mass. Hist. Soc. Proc.*, VIII, 403-405.

3. "NOTHING BUT AN AFFAIR THAT HAPPENED HERE ON THE NINETEENTH"

Thomas Gage to Lord Barrington, Secretary of War.

Boston, April 22, 1775

... I have now nothing to trouble your Lordship with, but of an affair that happened here on the 19th instant. I have intelligence of a large quantity of military stores being collected at Concord, for the avowed purpose of supplying a body of troops to act in opposition to his Majesty's Government, I gott the Grenadiers and Light Infantry out of town, under the command of Lieutenant Colonel Smith of the 10th Regiment, and Major Pitcairne of the Marines, with as much secrecy as possible, on the 18th at night, and with orders to destroy the said military stores, and supported them the next morning by eight companys of the 4th, the same number of the 23d, 47th and Marines under the command of Lord Percy. It appears from the firing of alarm guns and ringing of bells that the march of Lieutenant Colonel Smith was discovered, and he was opposed by a body of men within six miles of Concord; some few of whom first began to fire upon his advanced companys, which brought on a fire from the troops that dispersed the body opposed to them, and they proceeded to Concord, where they destroyed all the military stores they could find.

On the return of the troops, they were attacked from all quarters where any cover was to be found, from whence it was practicable to annoy them; and they were so fatigued with their march that it was with difficulty they could keep out their flanking partys to remove the enemy at a distance, so that they were at length a good deal pressed. Lord Percy then arrived oppertunely to their assistance with his brigade and two pieces of cannon. And notwithstanding a continual skirmish for the space of fifteen miles, receiving fire from every hill, fence, house, barn, etc., His Lordship kept the enemy off and brought the troops to Charles Town, from whence they were ferryed over to Boston.

Too much praise cannot be given to Lord Percy for his remarkable activity and conduct during the whole day. Lieutenant Col. Smith and Major Pitcairne did everything men could do, as did all the officers in general, and the men behaved with their usual intrepidity.

—CARTER, ed., *Correspondence of Gage*, II, 673-674.

4. "THE FATIGUE OUR PEOPLE PASSED THROUGH CAN HARDLY BE BELIEVED"

John Crozier (?) to Dr. Rogers.

Empress of Russia, Boston, April 23, 1775

... On the 18th instant between 11 and 12 o'clock at night I conducted all the boats of the fleet (as well men a war as transports) to the back part of Boston, where I received the Granadiers and Light Infantry amounting to 850 officers and men and landed them on a point of marsh or mudland which is overflowed with the last quarter flood; this service, I presume to say, was performed with secrecy and quietness, having oars muffled and every necessary precaution taken, but the watchful inhabitants whose houses are intermixed with the soldiers barracks heard the troops arms and from thence concluded that something was going on, tho they could not conceive how or where directed. In consequence of this conception, a light was shown at the top of a church stiple directing those in the country to be on their guard.

The intention of this expedition was to distroy some guns and provision which were collected near Concord, a town 20 miles from where the troops were landed. Colonel Smith, a gallant old officer, commanded this detachment and performed the above service. A firelock was snapt over a wall by one of the country people but did not go off. The next who pulled his triger wounded one of the Light Infantry company of General Hodgsons of the Kings Own. The fire then commenced and fell heavy on our troops, the militia having posted them selves behind walls, in houses and woods and had possession of almost every eminence or rising ground which commanded the long vale through which the King's troops were under the disagreeable necessity of passing in their return.

Colonel Smith was wounded early in the action and must have been cut off with all those he commanded had not Earl Percy come to his relief with the First Brigade; on the appearance of it our almost conquered Granadiers and Light Infantry gave three cheers and renewed the defence with more spirits.

Lord Percys courage and good conduct on this occasion must do him immortal honour. Upon taking the command he ordered the King's Own to flank on the right, and the 27th on the left, the Royal Welsh Fuseliers to defend the rear, and in this manner retreated for at least 11 miles before he reached Charlestown—for they could not cross at Cambridge where the bridge is, they haveing tore it up, and filled the town and houses with armed men to prevent his passage; our loss in this small essay ammounts to 250 killed, wounded and missing. And we are at present cept up in Boston, they being in possession of Roxbury, a little village just before our lines with the Royal and Rebel centenels within musquet shot of each other.

The fatigue which our people passed through the day which I have described can hardly be believed, having marched at least 45 miles and the Light Companys perhaps 60. A most amiable young man of General Hodgsons's fell that day, his name Knight, brother to Knight of the 43 who was with us at Jamaica.

The enthuseastic zeal with which those people have behaved must convince every reasonable man what a difficult and unpleasant task General Gage has before him. Even weamin had firelocks. One was seen to fire a blunder bus between her father and husband, from their windows; there they three with an infant child soon suffered the fury of the day. In another house which was long defended by 8 resolute fellows the Grenadiers at last got possession when, after having run their bayonets into 7, the 8th continued to abuse them with all the moat like roge [rage] of a true Cromwellian, and but a moment before he quitted this world applyed such epethets as I must leave unmentioned. God of his infinite mercy be pleased to restore peace and unanimity to those countrys again, for I never did nor can think that arms will enforce obedience. . . .

The number of the country people who fired on our troops might be about 5 thousand, ranged along from Concord to Charlestown, but not less than 20 thousand were that day under arms and on the march to join the others. Their loss we find to be nearly on a footing with our own.

Three days have now passed without communication with the country; three more will reduce this town to a most unpleasant situation; for there dependence for provision was from day to day on supply from the country; that ceasing you may conceive the consequences. Preparations are now making on both sides the Neck for attacking and defending. The Hampshire and Connecticut Militia have joined so that Rebel army are now numerous. Collins is well and stationed between Charles Town and the end of this town to assist in the defence. The General and Earl Percy shall have the perusal of your letter. . . .

—TYLER, ed., "Account of Lexington," *William & Mary Quarterly*, 3rd Series, X, No. 1, 104-107.

5. "You Damned Rebels, Lay Down Your Arms!"

The Reverend William Gordon of Roxbury to a gentleman in England.

May 17, 1775

My Dear Sir: . . . On the first of the night, when it was very dark, the detachment, consisting of all the Grenadiers and Light Infantry, the flower of the army, to the amount of eight hundred or better, officers included, the companies having been filled up, and several of the inimical torified natives repaired to the boats and got into them just as the moon rose, crossed the water, landed on Cambridge side, took through a private way to avoid discovery, and therefore had to go through some places up to their thighs in water. They made a quick march of it to Lexington about thirteen miles from Charlestown, and got there by half an hour after four.

Here I must pause again, to acquaint you that in the morning of the 19th, before we had breakfasted, between eight and nine, the whole neighbourhood was in alarm; the minute-men (so called from their having agreed to turn out at a minute's warning) were collecting together; we had an account that the Regulars had killed six of our men at Lexington; the country was in an uproar; another detachment was coming out of Boston, and I was desired to take care of myself and partner. . . .

Soon after the affair, knowing what untruths are propagated by each party in matters of this nature, I concluded that I would ride to Concord, inquire for myself and not rest upon the depositions that might be taken by others. Accordingly I went last week. . . .

Before Major Pitcairn arrived at Lexington signal guns had been fired, and the bells had been rung to give the alarm; but let not the sound of bells lead you to think of a ring of bells like what you hear in England; for they are only small-sized bells (one in a parish), just sufficient to notify to the people the time for attending worship, etc. Lexington being alarmed, the train band or Militia and the alarm men (consisting of the aged and others exempted from turning out, excepting upon an alarm) repaired in general to the common, close in with the meeting-house, the usual place of parade; and there were present when the roll was called over about one hundred and thirty of both, as I was told by Mr. Daniel Harrington, clerk to the company, who further said that the night being chilly, so as to make it uncomfortable being upon the parade, they having received no certain intelligence of the Regulars being upon their march, and being waiting for the same, the men were dismissed, to appear again at the beat of drum. Some who lived near went home, others to the publick house at the corner of the common.

Upon information being received, about half an hour after, that the troops were not far off, the remains of the company who were at hand collected together, to the amount of about sixty or seventy, by the time the Regulars appeared, but were chiefly in a confused state, only a few of them being drawn up, which accounts for other witnesses making the number less, about thirty. There were present as spectators about forty more, scarce any of whom had arms. . . .

The simple truth I take to be this, which I received from one of the prisoners at Concord in free conversation, one James Marr, a native of Aberdeen, in Scotland. . . . They were met by three men on horseback before they got to the meeting-house a good way; an officer bid them stop; to which it was answered, "You had better turn back, for you shall not enter the town"; when the said three persons rode back again, and at some distance one of them offered to fire, but the piece flashed in the pan without going off. I asked Marr whether he could tell if the piece was designed at the soldiers, or to give an alarm. He could not say which. The said Marr further declared that when they and the others were advanced, Major Pitcairn said to the Lexington

Company (which by the by was the only one there), "Stop, you rebels!" and he supposed that the design was to take away their arms; but upon seeing the Regulars they dispersed, and a firing commenced, but who fired first he could not say. . . .

I shall not trouble you with more particulars, but give you the substance as it lies in my own mind, collected from the persons whom I examined for my own satisfaction. The Lexington Company upon seeing the troops, and being of themselves so unequal a match for them, were deliberating for a few moments what they should do, when several dispersing of their own heads, the captain soon ordered the rest to disperse for their own safety. Before the order was given, three or four of the regular officers, seeing the company as they came up on the rising ground on this side the meeting, rode forward one or more round the meeting-house, leaving it on the right hand, and so came upon them that way. Upon coming up one cried out, "You damned rebels, lay down your arms"; another, "Stop, you rebels"; a third, "Disperse, you rebels," etc. Major Pitcairn, I suppose, thinking himself justified by Parliamentary authority to consider them as rebels, perceiving that they did not actually lay down their arms, observing that the generality were getting off, while a few continued in their military position, and apprehending there could be no great hurt in killing a few such Yankees, which might probably, according to the notions that had been instilled into him by the tory party of the Americans being poltrons, end all the contest, gave the command to fire, then fired his own pistol, and so set the whole affair agoing.

—Force, *American Archives*, 4th Series, II, 625-629.

6. "Fire! By God, Fire!"

From a sermon by the Reverend Jonas Clark,
pastor of the church in Lexington.

April 19, 1776

Between the hours of twelve and one, on the morning of the nineteenth of April, we received intelligence, by express, from the Honorable Joseph Warren, Esq., at Boston, "that a large body of the king's troops (supposed to be a brigade of about 12 or 1500) were embarked in boats from Boston, and gone over to land on Lechmere's Point (so called) in Cambridge; and that it was shrewdly suspected that they were ordered to seize and destroy the stores belonging to the colony, then deposited at Concord." . . .

Upon this intelligence, as also upon information of the conduct of the officers as above-mentioned, the militia of this town were alarmed and ordered to meet on the usual place of parade; not with any design of commencing hostilities upon the king's troops, but to consult what might be done for our own and the people's safety; and also to be ready for whatever service providence might call us out to, upon this alarming occasion, in case overt acts of violence or open hostilities should be committed by this mercenary band of armed and blood-thirsty oppressors. . . .

The militia met according to order and waited the return of the messengers, that they might order their measures as occasion should require. Between 3 and 4 o'clock, one of the expresses returned, informing that there was no appearance of the troops on the roads either from Cambridge or Charles-town; and that it was supposed that the movements in the army the evening before were only a feint to alarm the people. Upon this, therefore, the militia company were dismissed for the present, but with orders to be within call of the drum—waiting the return of the other messenger, who was expected in about an hour, or sooner, if any discovery should be made of the motions of the troops. But he was prevented by their silent and sudden arrival at the place where he was waiting for intelligence. So that, after all this precaution, we had no notice of their approach till the brigade was actually in the town and upon a quick march within about a mile and a quarter of the meeting house and place of parade.

However, the commanding officer thought best to call the company to-gether, not with any design of opposing so superior a force, much less of commencing hostilities, but only with a view to determine what to do, when and where to meet, and to dismiss and disperse.

Accordingly, about half an hour after four o'clock, alarm guns were fired, and the drums beat to arms, and the militia were collecting together. Some, to the number of about 50 or 60, or possibly more, were on the parade, others were coming towards it. In the mean time, the troops having thus stolen a march upon us and, to prevent any intelligence of their approach, having seized and held prisoners several persons whom they met unarmed upon the road, seemed to come determined for murder and bloodshed—and that whether provoked to it or not! When within about half a quarter of a mile of the meeting-house, they halted, and the command was given to prime and load; which being done, they marched on till they came up to the east end of said meeting-house, in sight of our militia (collecting as aforesaid) who were about 12 or 13 rods distant.

Immediately upon their appearing so suddenly and so nigh, Capt. Parker, who commanded the militia company, ordered the men to disperse and take care of themselves, and not to fire. Upon this, our men dispersed—but many of them not so speedily as they might have done, not having the most distant idea of such brutal barbarity and more than savage cruelty from the troops of a British king, as they immediately experienced! For, no sooner did they come in sight of our company, but one of them, supposed to be an officer of rank, was heard to say to the troops, "Damn them! We will have them!" Upon which the troops shouted aloud, huzza'd, and rushed furiously towards our men.

About the same time, three officers (supposed to be Col. Smith, Major Pitcairn and another officer) advanced on horse back to the front of the body, and coming within 5 or 6 rods of the militia, one of them cried out, "Ye vil-lains, ye Rebels, disperse! Damn you, disperse!"—or words to this effect. One of them (whether the same or not is not easily determined) said, "Lay down your arms! Damn you, why don't you lay down your arms?" The second of these officers, about this time, fired a pistol towards the militia as they were dispersing. The foremost, who was within a few yards of our men, brandish-ing his sword and then pointing towards them, with a loud voice said to the troops, "Fire! By God, fire!"—which was instantly followed by a discharge of arms from the said troops, succeeded by a very heavy and close fire upon our party, dispersing, so long as any of them were within reach. Eight were left dead upon the ground! Ten were wounded. The rest of the company, through divine goodness, were (to a miracle) preserved unhurt in this murderous action! . . .

One circumstance more before the brigade quitted Lexington, I beg leave to mention, as what may give a further specimen of the spirit and character of the officers and men of this body of troops. After the militia company were dispersed and the firing ceased, the troops drew up and formed in a body on the common, fired a volley and gave three huzzas, by way of triumph and as expressive of the joy of victory and glory of conquest! Of this transaction, I was a witness, having, at that time, a fair view of their motions and being at the distance of not more than 70 or 80 rods from them.

—HUDSON, *History of Lexington*, I, 527-529, 530.

7. "PARKER FORMED US IN SINGLE FILE"

A minuteman's account of Lexington.

I, Sylvanus Wood, of Woburn, in the county of Middlesex, and commonwealth of Massachusetts, aged seventy-four years, do testify and say that on the morning of the 19th of April, 1775, I was an inhabitant of Woburn, living with Deacon Obadiah Kendall; that about an hour before the break of day on said morning, I heard the Lexington bell ring, and fearing there was difficulty there, I immediately arose, took my gun and, with Robert Douglass, went in haste to Lexington, which was about three miles distant.

When I arrived there, I inquired of Captain Parker, the commander of the Lexington company, what was the news. Parker told me he did not know what to believe, for a man had come up about half an hour before and informed him that the British troops were not on the road. But while we were talking, a messenger came up and told the captain that the British troops were within half a mile. Parker immediately turned to his drummer, William Diman, and ordered him to beat to arms, which was done. Captain Parker then asked me if I would parade with his company. I told him I would. Parker then asked me if the young man with me would parade. I spoke to Douglass, and he said he would follow the captain and me.

By this time many of the company had gathered around the captain at the hearing of the drum, where we stood, which was about half way between the meeting-house and Buckman's tavern. Parker says to his men, "Every man of you, who is equipped, follow me; and those of you who are not equipped, go into the meeting-house and furnish yourselves from the magazine, and immediately join the company." Parker led those of us who were equipped to the north end of Lexington Common, near the Bedford Road, and formed us in single file. I was stationed about in the centre of the company. While we were standing, I left my place and went from one end of the company to the other and counted every man who was paraded, and the whole number was thirty-eight, and no more.

Just as I had finished and got back to my place, I perceived the British troops had arrived on the spot between the meeting-house and Buckman's, near where Captain Parker stood when he first led off his men. The British troops immediately wheeled so as to cut off those who had gone into the meeting-house. The British troops approached us rapidly in platoons, with a general officer on horseback at their head. The officer came up to within about two rods of the centre of the company, where I stood, the first platoon being about three rods distant. They there halted. The officer then swung his sword, and said, "Lay down your arms, you damned rebels, or you are all dead men. Fire!" Some guns were fired by the British at us from the first platoon, but no person was killed or hurt, being probably charged only with powder.

Just at this time, Captain Parker ordered every man to take care of himself. The company immediately dispersed; and while the company was dispersing and leaping over the wall, the second platoon of the British fired and killed some of our men. There was not a gun fired by any of Captain Parker's company, within my knowledge. I was so situated that I must have known it, had any thing of the kind taken place before a total dispersion of our company. I have been intimately acquainted with the inhabitants of Lexington, and particularly with those of Captain Parker's company, and, with one exception, I have never heard any of them say or pretend that there was any firing at the British from Parker's company, or any individual in it, until within a year or two. One member of the company told me, many years since, that, after Parker's company had dispersed, and he was at some distance, he gave them "the guts of his gun." . . .

SYLVANUS WOOD

Middlesex, ss., June 17, 1826.—Then the above-named Sylvanus Wood personally appeared, and subscribed and made oath to the foregoing affidavit. Before me,

NATHAN BROOKS,
Justice of the Peace.
—DAWSON, *Battles of the United States*, I, 22-23.

V. CONCORD

After Lexington, Concord. By the time Major Pitcairn was ready to move on, Colonel Smith had brought up the rest of his forces, and the reinforced column pushed into Concord, swept aside American resistance and destroyed such stores as they could find. But by now the countryside was thoroughly aroused, and minutemen were pouring into Concord from every near-by town and village and farm. How the Americans held the North Bridge; how they counterattacked and drove the exhausted redcoats pell-mell down the road toward Boston; how the British were rescued, at Lexington, by a strong relief column under Lord Percy; how they tramped sullenly back to Boston, while the Americans shot at them from behind stone walls, trees and houses; how they finally reached haven with casualties of 250 and retired to lick their wounds—all this is so familiar it has become part of American legend.

The story of Concord is told here by the Reverend William Emerson, grandfather of the more famous Emerson who wrote "Concord Bridge." The account of the retreat comes fresh from the diary of Lieutenant Frederick Mackenzie of the Royal Welsh Fusiliers, one of the liveliest and most perceptive of British diarists. Lord Percy's brief account is an official report. Captain Evelyn's letter is included more for what it tells of the British military mentality than of Concord.

1. WILLIAM EMERSON DESCRIBES THE STAND AT CONCORD BRIDGE

1775, 19 April. This morning, between 1 and 2 o'clock, we were alarmed by the ringing of the bell, and upon examination found that the troops, to the number of 800, had stole their march from Boston, in boats and barges, from the bottom of the Common over to a point in Cambridge, near to Inman's farm, and were at Lexington Meeting-house, half an hour before sunrise, where they had fired upon a body of our men, and (as we afterward heard) had killed several.

This intelligence was brought us at first by Dr. Samuel Prescott, who narrowly escaped the guard that were sent before on horses, purposely to prevent all posts and messengers from giving us timely information. He, by the help of a very fleet horse, crossing several walls and fences, arrived at Concord at the time above mentioned; when several posts were immediately despatched, that returning confirmed the account of the regulars' arrival at Lexington, and that they were on their way to Concord.

Upon this, a number of our minute men belonging to this town, and Acton and Lyncoln, with several others that were in readiness, marched out to meet them, while the alarm company were preparing to receive them in the town. Capt. Minot, who commanded them, thought it proper to take possession of the hill above the meeting-house, as the most advantageous situation. No sooner had our men gained it than we were met by the companies that were sent out to meet the troops, who informed us that they were just upon us, and that we must retreat, as their number was more than treble ours.

We then retreated from the hill near the Liberty Pole and took a new post back of the town upon an eminence, where we formed into two battalions and waited the arrival of the enemy. Scarcely had we formed before we saw the British troops at the distance of a quarter of a mile, glittering in arms, advancing towards us with the greatest celerity. Some were for making a stand, notwithstanding the superiority of their number; but others more prudent thought best to retreat till our strength should be equal to the enemy's by recruits from neighboring towns that were continually coming to our assistance.

Accordingly we retreated over the bridge, when the troops came into the town, set fire to several carriages for the artillery, destroyed 60 barrels flour, rifled several houses, took possession of the town-house, destroyed 500 lb. of balls, set a guard of 100 men at the North Bridge, and sent up a party to the house of Col. Barrett, where they were in expectation of finding a quantity of warlike stores. But these were happily secured just before their arrival, by transportation into the woods and other by-places.

In the meantime, the guard set by the enemy to secure the pass at the North Bridge were alarmed by the approach of our people, who had retreated, as mentioned before, and were now advancing with special orders not to fire upon the troops unless fired upon. These orders were so punctually observed that we received the fire of the enemy in three several and separate discharges of their pieces before it was returned by our commanding officer; the firing then soon became general for several minutes, in which skirmish two were killed on each side, and several of the enemy wounded.

It may here be observed, by the way, that we were the more cautious to prevent beginning a rupture with the King's troops, as we were then uncertain what had happened at Lexington, and knew [not?] that they had begun the quarrel there by first firing upon our people and killing eight men upon the spot.

The three companies of troops soon quitted their post at the bridge and retreated in the greatest disorder and confusion to the main body, who were soon upon the march to meet them. For half an hour, the enemy, by their marches and countermarches, discovered great fickleness and inconstancy of mind, sometimes advancing, sometimes returning to their former posts; till at length they quitted the town and retreated by the way they came. In the meantime, a party of our men (150) took the back way through the Great Fields into the east quarter and had placed themselves to advantage, lying in ambush behind walls, fences and buildings, ready to fire upo the enemy on their retreat.

—EMERSON, Diary, in R. W. Emerson, *Miscellanies*, 91 ff.

2. GENERAL PERCY TO THE RESCUE!

From the diary of Lieutenant Frederick Mackenzie.

19 April. At 7 o'clock this morning a brigade order was received by our regiment, dated at 6 o'clock, for the 1st Brigade to assemble at ½ past 7 on the grand parade. We accordingly assembled the regiment with the utmost expedition, and with the 4th and 47th were on the parade at the hour appointed, with one days provisions. By some mistake the Marines did not receive the order until the other regiments of the brigade were assembled, by which means it was half past 8 o'clock before the brigade was ready to march. Here we understood that we were to march out of town to support the troops that went out last night.

A quarter before 9, we marched in the following order: advanced guard of a captain and 50 men; 2 six-pounders, 4th Regiment, 47th Regiment, 1st Battalion of Marines, 23rd Regiment or Royal Welch Fusiliers; rear guard of a captain and 50 men; the whole under the command of Brigadier General Earl Percy. We went out of Boston by the Neck and marched thro' Roxbury, Cambridge and Menotomy, towards Lexington. In all the places we marched through, and in the houses on the road, few or no people were to be seen; and the houses were in general shut up.

When we arrived near Lexington, some persons who came from Concord informed that the Grenadiers and Light Infantry were at that place, and that some persons had been killed and wounded by them early in the morning at Lexington. As we pursued our march, about 2 o'clock we heard some straggling shots fired about a mile in our front. As we advanced we heard the firing plainer and more frequent, and at half after 2, being near the church at Lexington, and the fire encreasing, we were ordered to form the line, which was immediately done by extending on each side of the road, but by reason of the stone walls and other obstructions it was not formed in so regular a manner as it should have been. The Grenadiers and Light Infantry were at this time retiring towards Lexington, fired upon by the Rebels, who took every advantage the face of the country afforded them. As soon as the Grenadiers and Light Infantry perceived the 1st Brigade drawn up for their support, they shouted repeatedly, and the firing ceased for a short time.

The ground we first formed upon was something elevated and commanded a view of that before us for about a mile, where it was terminated by some pretty high grounds covered with wood. The village of Lexington lay between both parties. We could observe a considerable number of the Rebels, but they were much scattered, and not above 50 of them to be seen in a body in any place. Many lay concealed behind the stone walls and fences. They appeared most numerous in the road near the church, and in a wood in the front, and on the left flank of the line where our regiment was posted. A few cannon shot were fired at those on and near the road, which dispersed them.

The flank companies now retired and formed behind the brigade, which was soon fired upon by the Rebels most advanced. A brisk fire was returned, but without much effect. As there was a piece of open morassy ground in front of the left of our regiment, it would have been difficult to have passed it under the fire of the Rebels from behind the trees and walls on the other side. Indeed no part of the brigade was ordered to advance; we therefore drew up near the morass, in expectation of orders how to act, sending an officer for one of the 6-pounders. During this time the Rebels endeavored to gain our flanks, and crept into the covered ground on either side and as close as they could in front, firing now and then in perfect security. We also advanced a few of our best marksmen who fired at those who shewed themselves.

About ¼ past 3, Earl Percy having come to a resolution of returning to Boston, and having made his disposition for that purpose, our regiment received orders to form the rear guard. We immediately lined the walls and other cover in our front with some marksmen, and retired from the right of companies by files to the high ground a small distance in our rear, where we again formed in line, and remained in that position for near half an hour, during which time the flank companies and the other regiments of the brigade began their march in one column on the road towards Cambridge.

As the country for many miles round Boston and in the neighbourhood of Lexington and Concord had by this time had notice of what was doing, as well by the firing as from expresses which had been [sent] from Boston and the adjacent places in all directions, numbers of armed men on foot and on horseback were continually coming from all parts guided by the fire, and before the column had advanced a mile on the road, we were fired at from all quarters, but particularly from the houses on the roadside, and the adjacent stone walls. Several of the troops were killed and wounded in this way, and the soldiers were so enraged at suffering from an unseen enemy that they forced open many of the houses from which the fire proceeded, and put to death all those found in them. Those houses would certainly have been burnt had any fire been found in them, or had there been time to kindle any; but only three or four near where we first formed suffered in this way.

As the troops drew nearer to Cambridge the number and fire of the Rebels increased, and altho they did not shew themselves openly in a body in any part, except on the road in our rear, our men threw away their fire very inconsiderately and without being certain of its effect; this emboldened them and induced them to draw nearer, but whenever a cannon shot was fired at any considerable number, they instantly dispersed.

Our regiment, having formed the rear guard for near 7 miles and expended a great part of its ammunition, was then relieved by the Marines which was the next battalion in the column. . . .

During the whole of the march from Lexington the Rebels kept an incessant irregular fire from all points at the column, which was the more galling as our flanking parties, which at first were placed at sufficient distances to cover the march of it, were at last, from the different obstructions they occasionally met with, obliged to keep almost close to it. Our men had very few opportunities of getting good shots at the Rebels, as they hardly ever fired but under cover of a stone wall, from behind a tree, or out of a house; and the moment they had fired they lay down out of sight until they had loaded again or the column had passed. In the road indeed in our rear, they were most numerous and came on pretty close, frequently calling out, "King Hancock forever!"

Many of them were killed in the houses on the road side from whence they fired; in some of them 7 or 8 men were destroyed. Some houses were forced open in which no person could be discovered, but when the column had passed, numbers sallied out from some place in which they had lain concealed, fired at the rear guard, and augmented the number which followed us. If we had had time to set fire to those houses many Rebels must have perished in them, but as night drew on Lord Percy thought it best to continue the march. Many houses were plundered by the soldiers, notwithstanding the efforts of the officers to prevent it. I have no doubt this inflamed the Rebels, and made many of them follow us farther than they would otherwise have done. By all accounts some soldiers who staid too long in the houses were killed in the very act of plundering by those who lay concealed in them. We brought in about ten prisoners, some of whom were taken in arms. One or two more were killed on the march, while prisoners, by the fire of their own people.

Few or no women or children were to be seen throughout the day. As the country had undoubted intelligence that some troops were to march out, and the Rebels were probably determined to attack them, it is generally supposed they had previously removed their families from the neighbourhood. . . .

—MACKENZIE, *Diary*, I, 19-22.

3. "Not a Stone Wall Whence the Rebels Did Not Fire upon Us"

Hugh, Earl Percy to Governor Gage.

Boston, 20 April, 1775

Sir—In obedience to your Excellency's orders I marched yesterday morning at 9 o'clock, with the First Brigade and 2 field-pieces, in order to cover the retreat of the Grenadiers and Light Infantry, on their return from the expedition to Concord.

As all the houses were shut up and there was not the appearance of a single inhabitant, I could get no intelligence concerning them till I had passed Menotomy, when I was informed that the Rebels had attacked His Majesty's troops, who were retiring, overpowered by numbers, greatly exhausted and fatigued, and having expended almost all their ammunition. And about 2 o'clock I met them retiring through the town of Lexington.

I immediately ordered the 2 fieldpieces to fire at the Rebels, and drew up the brigade on a height. The shot from the cannon had the desired effect and stopped the Rebels for a little time, who immediately dispersed and endeavoured to surround us, being very numerous. As it began now to grow pretty late, and we had 15 miles to retire, and only our 36 rounds, I ordered the Grenadiers and Light Infantry to move off first, and covered them with my brigade, sending out very strong flanking parties, which were absolutely necessary, as there was not a stone-wall or house, though before in appearance evacuated, from whence the Rebels did not fire upon us.

As soon as they saw us begin to retire, they pressed very much upon our rear-guard, which for that reason I relieved every now and then. In this manner we retired for 15 miles under an incessant fire all round us, till we arrived at Charlestown between 7 and 8 in the even, very much fatigued with a march of above 30 miles, and having expended almost all our ammunition.

We had the misfortune of losing a good many men in the retreat, tho' nothing like the number which, from many circumstances, I have reason to believe were killed of the Rebels.

His Majesty's troops during the whole of the affair behaved with their usual intrepidity and spirit. Nor were they a little exasperated at the cruelty and barbarity of the Rebels who scalped and cut off the ears of some of the wounded men who fell into their hands.

—Bolton, ed., *Letters of Hugh, Earl Percy*, pp. 49-51.

4. "The Most Absolute Cowards on the Face of the Earth"

Captain W. G. Evelyn of the "King's Own" to the Reverend Doctor Evelyn, his father, at Trim, Ireland.

Boston, April 23rd, 1775

My Dear Sir—It is impossible but you must hear an account, and probably a most exaggerated one, of the little fracas that happened here a few days ago, between us and the Yankey scoundrels. Our bickerings and heartburnings, as might naturally be expected, came at length to blows, and both sides have lost some men. Were you not to hear from me on the occasion, you might imagine I was hurt; at least, you expect from me some account of the affair. The rebels, you know, have of a long time been making preparations as if to frighten us, though we always imagined they were too great cowards ever to presume to do it; but though they are the most absolute cowards on the face of the earth, yet they are just now worked up to such a degree of enthusiasm and madness that they are easily persuaded the Lord is to assist them in whatever they undertake, and that they must be invincible. . . .

The loss of the rebels cannot be ascertained, but we have reason to think several hundreds were killed. Our regiment had four or five men killed, and about twenty-four wounded. Of the whole, about seventy killed, and 150 wounded; among which last were several officers. . . .

—SCULL, ed., *Memoir and Letters of Captain Evelyn,* pp. 53-55.

VI. SOUNDING THE ALARM

The minutemen who had rallied at Lexington and Concord and harassed the British all the way back to Boston were courageous but neither efficient nor resourceful. They were fresh, they outnumbered the British two to one, they were not encumbered with accouterments or baggage; they enjoyed all the advantages of fighting from behind shelter. Yet they exacted comparatively few casualties: almost 4,000 militiamen, firing all day long, managed to score less than 300 hits! Had they at any time organized a force to break the British column in two, or had they even managed to throw up road blocks, they might well have destroyed or captured the enemy. Lord Percy's achievement in bringing back the expedition almost intact was a brilliant one.

When the British stumbled into Charlestown, in the evening of the nineteenth, they were not only exhausted but defeated. The defeat, as it turned out, was not so much military as political and moral. For Lexington and Concord was what the Patriots had been waiting for. The British had taken the offensive; the British had fired the first shot. Not only this but the British had been guilty of atrocities to boot—arson and pillage and rapine and murder. All this the Americans alleged, and doubtless believed. We think of propaganda as a modern development, but there is very little that our generation could teach the Patriots of 1775 about propaganda. The Massachusetts Committee of Safety hurried its version over to England, and broadcast it throughout the colonies. Never before had news traveled so fast. Israel Bissel, a regular postrider, was off on the morning of the nineteenth with the stirring tale; that noon—so legend has it—he reached Worcester, and his horse fell dead. The next day he was in New London. Then on to New Haven, and by the twenty-third he had reached New York. Within a few hours he rode on through New Jersey and reached Philadelphia the next day. Other couriers sped the news to New Hampshire, to western Massachusetts, to the Hudson Valley and the Hampshire Grants.

Couriers carried not only news of the fateful day, but appeals for help.

"We conjure you by all that is sacred"—so read the appeals to the towns of Massachusetts, to Connecticut, to the Providence Plantations, and all the way south. The appeals were scarcely necessary. Already the minutemen were on their way to Cambridge, and even before the provincial legislatures or the committees of safety had acted, the army outside Boston had grown by thousands. A New Hampshire contingent marched 55 miles in 18 hours, reaching Cambridge by sunrise of the twenty-first; Benedict Arnold, erstwhile druggist and merchant, led his company from New Haven without delay and arrived April 29. Ezra Stiles—later President of Yale—tells us how the news reached Providence, and how the Plantations responded. Meantime Massachusetts voted to call for an army of 30,000; Connecticut provided for 6,000; New Hampshire added another 2,000; Rhode Island sent three regiments. And back in England the Lords gravely argued the impossibility of raising soldiers in Britain, and the necessity of recruiting from Russia or the Germanies.

Everywhere the news of Lexington and Concord strengthened the hands and fired the hearts of the Patriots. In reluctant New York the radicals seized British military stores and organized to place the colony alongside its sisters. A letter from an anonymous lady of Philadelphia describes how that city responded to the challenge. In Charleston the Provincial Congress promptly raised two regiments of infantry and a third of rangers, and voted £140,000 in bills of credit for the forthcoming contest. Even little frontier Georgia joined in by raising a liberty pole on the King's birthday and sending a shipment of rice to the Bostonians.

"A general rebellion throughout America is coming on suddenly and swiftly," wrote Governor Wright of Georgia. It was, indeed, but Gage and Howe were blind to the significance of it. They still thought that a little firmness would settle the whole matter. General Howe, who reached Boston late in May, wrote that things would not improve until the American armies should be roughly dealt with; he had no doubt of his ability to get rough. General Gage persisted in thinking that he could somehow win back the Americans— all but Hancock and Sam Adams, anyway, who were forever damned. And back in England King George, who had said that blows would decide, had nothing now to recommend but more blows.

1. ISRAEL BISSEL CARRIES THE NEWS OF LEXINGTON AND CONCORD

Alarm sent by Committee of Watertown, Massachusetts.

April 19, 1775
Wednesday Morning near 11 O'clock

To all friends of American liberty, be it known that this morning before break of day, a brigade, consisting of about 1000 or 1200 men, landed at Phipp's farm at Cambridge and marched to Lexington, where they found a company of our militia in arms, upon whom they fired without any provocation and killed 6 men and wounded 4 others. By an express from Boston we find another brigade are now upon their march from Boston supposed to be about 1000. The bearer Israel Bissel is charged to alarm the country quite to

Connecticut, and all persons are desired to furnish him with fresh horses, as they may be needed. I have spoken with several who have seen the dead and wounded.

J PALMER, one of the Committee of Safety

Forwarded from Worcester April 19th 1775.

Brooklyn ....Thursday 11 O'clock.
Norwich ....4 o'clock.
New London ....7 O'clock.
Lynne ....Friday morning 1 O'clock.
Say Brook ....4 O'clock.
Shillingsworth ....7 O'clock.
E Guilford ....8 o'clock.
Guilford ....10 o'clock.
Bradford [Branford] ....12 o'clock.
New Haven ....April 21st.
Rec'd and forwarded on certain intelligence.
Fairfield ....April 22nd 8 o'clock.

Thursday 3 o'clock Afternoon

Since the above received the following by second express:
Sir

I am this moment informed by express from Woodstock, taken from the mouth of the express that arrived there 2 o'clock afternoon, that the contest between the First Brigade that marched on Concord was still continuing this morning at the town of Lexington, to which brigade had retreated.

That another brigade said to be the Second, mentioned in the letter of this morning, had landed with a quantity of artilery, at the place where the First did. The Provincials were determined to prevent the two brigades from joining their strength if possible, and remain in great need of succor.

—N.B. The Regulars, when in Concord, burnt the court house, took 2 pieces of cannon, which they rendered useless and began to take up Concord Bridge, on which Capt. ——— (who with many on both sides were soon killed) made an attack on the King's troops, when they retreated to Lexington.

I am, Sir

EB WILLIAMS

Col Obadiah, Canterbury

P.S. Mr. McFarland of Plainfield, Mass., has just returned from Boston by way of Providence, who conversed with an express from Lexington, who further informs that 4000 of our troops had surrounded the First Brigade who were on a hill in Lexington. That the action continued and there were about 50 of our men killed and 150 Regulars as near as they could determine when the express came away. It will be expedient for every man to go who is fit and willing.

New York Committee Chamber,
4 o'clock, 23rd April, 1775, P.M.

Received the within by express and forward by express to N. Brunswick with directions to stop at Elizabeth Town and acquaint the Committee there with the foregoing particulars.

by order

J Low, *Chairman*

The Committee at New Brunswick are ordered to forward this to Philadelphia.

—BOUDINOT, *Journal or Historical Recollections*, pp. 1-2.

2. THE MASSACHUSETTS COMMITTEE OF SAFETY APPEALS FOR HELP

Committee of Safety to the Several Towns in Massachusetts.

Cambridge, April 28, 1775

Gentlemen: The barbarous murders committed on our innocent brethren on Wednesday the 19th instant have made it absolutely necessary that we immediately raise an army to defend our wives and children from the butchering hands of an inhuman soldiery, who, incensed at the obstacles they met with in their bloody progress, and enraged at being repulsed from the field of slaughter, will, without doubt, take the first opportunity in their power to ravage this devoted country with fire and sword. We conjure, therefore, by all that is dear, by all that is sacred, that you give all assistance possible in forming the army. Our all is at stake. Death and devastation are the certain consequences of delay; every moment is infinitely precious; an hour lost may deluge your country in blood and entail perpetual slavery upon the few of your posterity who may survive the carnage. We beg and entreat, as you will answer it to your country, to your own conscience, and, above all, to God himself, that you will hasten and encourage, by all possible means, the enlistment of men to form the army, and send them forward to head quarters at Cambridge, with that expedition which the vast importance and instant urgency of the affair demands.

—FORCE, *American Archives*, 4th Series, II, 433.

3. "THE WAY IS OPEN AND CLEAR NOW FOR THE AMERICANS"

Diary of Dr. Ezra Stiles.

April 20. At eight o'clock this morning an express arrived in town from Providence, with the following letter:

"Providence, April 19, 1775
"10 o'clock at night

"Sir

"This evening intelligence hath been received that about twelve hundred of the Regulars have proceeded from Boston towards Concord, and having fired upon and killed a number of the inhabitants of Lexington, are now actually engaged in butchering and destroying our brethren there in the most inhuman manner, that the inhabitants oppose them with zeal and courage and numbers have already fallen on both sides. Reinforcements were at ten o'clock under motion from Boston, and the Provincials were alarmed and mustering as fast as possible. It appears necessary therefore that we immediately make some provision for their assistance, . . . We shall impatiently wait your arrival as numbers are ready and wait only orders to proceed.

"The countrys friend and yours,

"S. HOPKINS

"To Major General Potter."

Upon receipt of this news the town was thrown into alarm, and all went into preparation. The Governor issued warrants for calling the Assembly to meet at Providence next Saturday. Gen. Potter (who lives at Bristol) set off this morning, with numbers from Bristol and Warren. None have marched from Newport to-day, tho' Col. Dayton tells me this afternoon that there are five hundred armed and ready to march, waiting only the Governors orders. The Tories have, in order to intimidate, circulated thro' the town that Capt Wallace, of the *Rose* man o' war, insolently says he will fire upon the town and lay it in ashes, if any march from hence. This intimidates some people. They are training, exercising and preparing all day.

It is said that the Regulars, coming up with about 30 minute men exercising at Lexington, ordered them to lay down their arms—that upon refusal, the Regulars dastardly fired upon them and killed six—that the others returned the fire and killed some of the Regulars. But of this there is no certainty. Gov. Hopkins does not inform the basis of his intelligence—dont even date his letter. And it is not known whether the troops marched to Lexington yesterday morning, or before. It is probable the whole country is thrown into the same alarm as last September. The good Lord direct and overrule all for his Glory and the good of his Chosen. It is happy that the troops have given the first blow—the way is open and clear now for the Americans. If they will but tarry out of Boston a few days, I doubt not the Americans will give a good account of them. But I fear their cowardice has made them instantly return to Boston.

All that I rely upon in this news is that they have marched to Lexington and killed a few men. I am not a little apprehensive that it may prove only another false alarm, designedly excited by our people to prevent the troops from marching out of Boston into the country.

[*April*] *21.* This has been a day of universal anxiety and solicitude in town. All business is laid aside. Various have been the reports from different parts. From all which I collect that on Wednesday 19th inst about 1500 troops went, early in the morning before day, in boats from Boston by water, and landed about Cambridge, and proceeded by a quick march to Concord and there destroyed about 50 barrels of flour and spiked up some cannon; and then returned thro' Lexington to Charlestown, and so passed over to Boston the evening of the same day; that the country was alarmed, and about 300 minute men attacked them at Lexington, when a number were killed on both sides. That these 300 harassed them in the return and again attacked them between Cambridge and Charlestown; when more were slain on both sides. The number slain said to be about 80 Regulars and 40 Provincials. An express left Cambridge yesterday and came to Providence about eleven o'clock this forenoon, and the news reached Newport at five o'clock this afternoon, informing that yesterday there were assembled 16 or seventeen thousand Provincials of which 7000 were at Cambridge, 4000 at Charlestown and 4000 at Roxbury. Col. Ward wrote to Providence to stay the further accession of troops as they had more than a sufficiency assembled. Col. Putnam was marching from Connecticut with a body of forces from that Colony. This is the state of the news to-day. None marched from Newport, nor from Providence.

[*April*] 22. This day brings further confirmation of the news yesterday, but no new intelligence. It is remarkable that 19th inst, the day of the march from Boston to Concord and commencement of actual hostilities, was the day of the anniversary fast thro' Connecticut. We do indeed hear that Gen. Gage having sent a vessel to take off his 100 men sent to Marshfield, the minute men of the neighboring towns assembled to prevent and secure the soldiers from being carried off. And that a great light was seen from Providence in the direction of Marshfield, which is 60 miles off, supposed to be the firing of that town. But this I do not credit. That light was seen from Newport by the watch last night. But Marshfield is a dispersed settlement. The supposition is in no wise credible. Tho probably the party is secured—for things are becoming more and more serious every day.

The Governor of North Carolina in a speech to his Assembly now sitting inveighed against the last Congress, and against sending delegates to the present. But the Assembly gave him a warm reply, have approved their delegates, and stand firm in the Cause of Liberty.

—DEXTER, ed., *Literary Diary of Ezra Stiles*, I, 535-538.

4. "Nothing Is Heard Now but the Trumpet and Drum"

From a lady of Philadelphia to Captain S——, a British officer in Boston.

Sir—We received a letter from you—wherein you let Mr. S. know that you had written after the battle of Lexington, particularly to me—knowing my martial spirit—that I would delight to read the exploits of heroes. Surely, my friend, you must mean the New England heroes, as they alone performed exploits worthy fame—while the regulars, vastly superior in numbers, were obliged to retreat with a rapidity unequalled, except by the French at the battle of Minden. Indeed, General Gage gives them their due praise in his letter home, where he says Lord Percy was remarkable for his activity. You will not, I hope, take offence at any expression that, in the warmth of my heart, should escape me, when I assure you that though we consider you as a public enemy, we regard you as a private friend; and while we detest the cause you are fighting for, we wish well to your own personal interest and safety. Thus far by way of apology. As to the martial spirit you suppose me to possess, you are greatly mistaken. I tremble at the thoughts of war; but of all wars, a civil one: our all is at stake; and we are called upon by every tie that is dear and sacred to exert the spirit that Heaven has given us in this righteous struggle for liberty.

I will tell you what I have done. My only brother I have sent to the camp with my prayers and blessings; I hope he will not disgrace me; I am confident he will behave with honor and emulate the great examples he has before him; and had I twenty sons and brothers they should go. I have retrenched every superfluous expense in my table and family; tea I have not drank since last Christmas, nor bought a new cap or gown since your defeat at Lexington, and what I never did before, have learnt to knit, and am now making stockings of American wool for my servants, and this way do I throw in my mite to the public good. I know this, that as free I can die but once, but as a slave I shall not be worthy of life.

I have the pleasure to assure you that these are the sentiments of all my sister Americans. They have sacrificed both assemblies, parties of pleasure, tea drinking and finery to that great spirit of patriotism that actuates all ranks and degrees of people throughout this extensive continent. If these are the sentiments of females, what must glow in the breasts of our husbands, brothers and sons? They are as with one heart determined to die or be free.

It is not a quibble in politics, a science which few understand, which we are contending for; it is this plain truth, which the most ignorant peasant knows, and is clear to the weakest capacity, that no man has a right to take their money without their consent. The supposition is ridiculous and absurd, as none but highwaymen and robbers attempt it. Can you, my friend, reconcile it with your own good sense, that a body of men in Great Britain, who have little intercourse with America, and of course know nothing of us, nor are supposed to see or feel the misery they would inflict upon us, shall invest themselves with a power to command our lives and properties, at all times and in all cases whatsoever? You say you are no politician. Oh, sir, it requires no Machivelian head to develop this, and to discover this tyranny and oppression. It is written with a sun beam. Every one will see and know it because it will make them feel, and we shall be unworthy of the blessings of Heaven, if we ever submit to it.

All ranks of men amongst us are in arms. Nothing is heard now in our streets but the trumpet and drum; and the universal cry is "Americans, to arms!" All your friends are officers: there are Captain S. D., Lieut. B. and Captain J. S. We have five regiments in the city and country of Philadelphia, complete in arms and uniforms, and very expert at the military manoeuvres. We have companies of light-horse, light infantry, grenadiers, riflemen and Indians, several companies of artillery, and some excellent brass cannon and field pieces. Add to this that every county in Pennsylvania and the Delaware government can send two thousand men to the field. Heaven seems to smile on us, for in the memory of man never were known such quantities of flax, and sheep without number.

We are making powder fast and do not want for ammunition. In short, we want for nothing but ships of war to defend us, which we could procure by making alliances: but such is our attachment to Great Britain that we sincerely wish for reconciliation, and cannot bear the thoughts of throwing off all dependence on her, which such a step would assuredly lead to. The God of mercy will, I hope, open the eyes of our king that he may see, while in seeking our destruction, he will go near to complete his own. It is my ardent prayer that the effusion of blood may be stopped. We hope yet to see you in

this city, a friend to the liberties of America, which will give infinite satisfaction to

Your sincere friend,   C. S.

—NILES, *Principles and Acts of the Revolution*, pp. 116-117.

5. GAGE PROMISES TO PARDON ALL REBELS EXCEPT SAMUEL ADAMS AND JOHN HANCOCK

Proclamation by Governor Gage.

June 12, 1775

Whereas, the infatuated multitude, who have long suffered themselves to
be conducted by certain well known incendiaries and traitors, in a fatal pro-
gression of crimes against the constitutional authority of the State, have at
length proceeded to avowed Rebellion; and the good effects which were
expected to arise from the patience and lenity of the King's Government have
been often frustrated, and are now rendered hopeless, by the influence of the
same evil counsels; it only remains for those who are invested with supreme
rule, as well for the punishment of the guilty, as the protection of the well-
affected, to prove they do not bear the sword in vain.

. . . A number of armed persons, to the amount of many thousands, assembled on the 19th of April last, and from behind walls and lurking holes,
attacked a detachment of the King's Troops, who, not suspecting so consummate an act of frenzy, unprepared for vengeance, and willing to decline it,
made use of their arms only in their own defence. Since that period, the
rebels, deriving confidence from impunity, have added insult to outrage; have
repeatedly fired upon the King's ships and subjects with cannon and small-
arms; have possessed the roads and other communications by which the Town
of Boston was supplied with provisions; and with a preposterous parade of
military arrangement they affected to hold the army besieged; while part of
their body made daily and indiscriminate invasions upon private property,
and, with a wantonness of cruelty ever incident to lawless tumult, carry
depredation and distress wherever they turn their steps. The actions of the
19th of April are of such notoriety as must baffle all attempts to contradict
them, and the flames of buildings and other property from the islands and
adjacent country, for some weeks past, spread a melancholy confirmation of
the subsequent assertions.

In this exigency of complicated calamities, I avail myself of the last effort
within the bounds of my duty to spare the effusion of blood; to offer, and I do
hereby, in His Majesty's name, offer and promise his most gracious pardon
to all persons who shall forthwith lay down their arms and return to their
duties of peaceable subjects, excepting only from the benefit of such pardon
Samuel Adams and *John Hancock*, whose offences are of too flagitious a nature to admit of any other consideration than that of condign punishment.

And to the end that no person within the limits of this offered mercy may
plead ignorance of the consequences of refusing it, I, by these presents, proclaim not only the persons above named and excepted, but also all their adherents, associates and abetters (meaning to comprehend in those terms, all
and every person and persons, of what class, denomination or description

soever) who have appeared in arms against the King's Government and shall not lay down the same as afore-mentioned; and likewise all such as shall so take arms after the date hereof, or who shall in any wise protect or conceal such offenders, or assist them with money, provisions, cattle, arms, ammunition, carriages or any other necessary for subsistence or offence, or shall hold secret correspondence with them by letter, message, single or otherwise, to be Rebels and Traitors, and as such to be treated.

—Force, *American Archives*, 4th Series, II, 967-970.

6. King George: "When Once These Rebels Have Felt a Smart Blow"

George III to Lord Sandwich.

Kew, 1st July, 1775

Your letter accompanying those received from Major Pitcairn is just arrived: that officer's conduct seems highly praiseworthy. I am of his opinion that when once these rebels have felt a smart blow, they will submit; and no situation can ever change my fixed resolution, either to bring the colonies to a due obedience to the legislature of the mother country or to cast them off!

—Barnes & Owen, eds., *Private Papers of Earl of Sandwich*, I, 63.

VII. TICONDEROGA

The First Continental Congress had authorized defensive but not offensive operations; certainly Lexington and Concord, and even the siege of Boston, could come under this authorization. But it is not clear that after Lexington the Americans cared to make such a distinction. In any event less than a month passed before they took the offensive.

As the American forces closed in around Boston, it became obvious that they lacked the artillery for effective action against the fortifications which the British had erected. At this juncture it occurred to several officers—Benedict Arnold among them—that there were cannon to be had for the taking at Fort Ticonderoga on Lake Champlain. The Massachusetts Committee of Safety directed Arnold to raise a small force in western Massachusetts and capture Ticonderoga. Meantime the same idea had occurred to several members of the Connecticut Committee of Safety—Colonel Samuel Parsons, Silas Deane and others. Acting on their own, they authorized various soldiers, among them Ethan Allen of Vermont (then called the New Hampshire Grants) and Captain Edward Mott, to raise a force (preferably in Massachusetts and Vermont) and move on Ticonderoga. Early in May these expeditions converged on Lake Champlain—Allen and the Connecticut officers with perhaps 200 or 300 followers, Arnold with none. There was a tussle for command; neither commander would give way, and they sensibly agreed to share the command. On the night of May 9, Allen and Arnold with a force of some 83 men crossed Lake Champlain, and at dawn of the tenth surprised and captured the fort without a shot. The haul included over a hundred cannon and substantial military stores. Arnold went on to seize Crown Point, a few miles north; then, with characteristic energy, he commandeered the one British ship on the lake, sailed it to St. Johns and captured that outpost just beyond the Canadian border. Thus at the very beginning of the war the Americans, by a combination of luck and foresight, were astride the strategic military road to Canada.

1. Captain Mott Raises Volunteers to Attack Ticonderoga

From the journal of Captain Edward Mott of Connecticut.

Preston [Conn.], Friday, 28th April, 1775. Set out for Hartford, where I arrived the same day. Saw Christopher Leffingwell, Esq., who inquired of me about the situation of the people of Boston. When I had gave him an account, he asked me how they could be relieved, and where I thought we could get artillery and stores. I told him I knew not, except we went and took possession of Ticonderoga and Crown Point, which I thought might be done by surprise with a small number of men. Mr. Leffingwell left me, and in a short time came to me again and brought with him Samuel H. Parsons and Silas Deane, Esqrs., when he asked me if I would undertake such an expedition as we had talked of before. I told him I would.

They told me they wished I had been there one day sooner; that they had been on such a plan, and that they had sent off Messrs. Noah Phelps and Bernard Romans, who they had supplied with £300 in cash from the Treasury, and ordered them to draw for more if they should need; that said Phelps and Romans were gone by the way of Salisbury, where they would make a stop; they expected a small number of men would join them; and if I would go after them, they would give me an order or letter to them to join with them and to have my voice with them in conducting the affair and laying out the money; and also that I might take five or six men with me.

On which, I took with me Mr. Jeremiah Halsey, Mr. Epaphras Bull, Mr. Wm. Nichols, Mr. Elijah Babcock, and John Bigelow joined me; and Saturday the 29th April, in the afternoon, we set out on said expedition.

That night arrived at Smith's in New Hartford: stayed that night. The next day, being Sunday the 30th April, on our way to Salisbury . . . ; and the next day, having augmented our company to the number of sixteen in the whole, we concluded it was not best to add any more, as we meant to keep our business a secret and ride through the country unarmed till we came to the New Settlements on the Grants. We arrived at Mr. Dewey's in Sheffield and there we sent off Mr. Jer. Halsey and Capt. John Stephens to go to Albany in order to discover the temper of the people in that place, and to return and inform us as soon as possible.

That night we arrived at Col. Easton's in Pittsfield, where we fell in company with John Brown Esq. who had been at Canada and Ticonderoga about a month before; on which we concluded to make known our business to Col. Easton and said Brown, and to take their advice on the same. I was advised by Messrs. Deane, Leffingwell and Parsons, at Hartford, not to raise our men till we came to the N. Hampshire Grants, lest we should be discovered by having too long a march through the country. But when we advised with said Easton and Brown, they advised us that as there was a great scarcity of provisions in the Grants, and as the people were generally poor, it would be difficult to get a sufficient number of men there; therefore we had better raise a number of men sooner. Said Easton and Brown concluded to go with us, and Easton said he would assist me in raising some men in his regiment. We then concluded for me to go with Col. Easton to Jericho and Williamstown to raise men, and the rest of us to go forward to Bennington and see if they could purchase provisions there. We raised 24 men in Jericho and 15 in Williamstown, and got them equipped ready to march. Then Col. Easton and I set out for Bennington.

That evening we met with an express from our people informing us that they had seen a man directly from Ticonderoga, and that he informed them that they were reinforced at Ticonderoga and were repairing the garrison and were every way on their guard; therefore it was best for us to dismiss the men we had raised and proceed no further, as we should not succeed. I asked who the man was, where he belonged and where he was going, but could get no account; on which I ordered that the men should not be dismissed but that we would proceed.

The next day I arrived at Bennington. There overtook our people. . . . I inquired why they sent back to me to dismiss the expedition when neither our men from Albany nor the reconnoitering party were returned. They said they did not think that we should succeed. I told them that fellow they saw knew nothing about the garrison; that I had seen him since and had examined him strictly, and that he was a lying fellow and had not been at the fort. I told them with the two hundred men that we proposed to raise I was not afraid to go round the fort in open light; if it was re-inforced with five hundred men, they would not follow us out into the woods; that the accounts we had would not do to go back with and tell in Hartford.

While on this discourse, Mr. Halsey and Stephens came back from Albany and both agreed with me that it was best to go forward; after which Mr. Halsey and Mr. Bull both declared that they would not go back for no story, till they had seen the fort themselves. On which it was concluded that we should proceed; and as provisions were very scarce on the Grants, we sent Capt. Stephens and Mr. Hewitt to Albany New City to purchase provisions and send to us as soon as they could; and Mr. Romans left us and joined no more; we were all glad, as he had been a trouble to us all the time he was with us.

Then we proceeded to raise the men as fast as possible, and sent forward men on whom we could depend, to waylay the roads that lead from those places we were raising men in to Fort Edward, Lake George, Skenesborough, Ticonderoga or Crown Point—with orders to take up all those who were passing from either of those garrisons and send to us to be examined, and that all who were passing towards those garrisons from us should be stopped, so that no intelligence should go from us to the garrisons. And on Sunday night the seventh of May, we all arrived at Cassel Town, the place where we had appointed for the men all to meet; and on Monday the 8th of May, the Committee all got together to conclude in what method we would proceed in order to accomplish our design—of which Committee I was Chairman.

And after debating on the different methods to proceed, and in what manner to retreat in case of a repulse, we resolved and voted that we would proceed in the following manner, viz: that a party of thirty men, under the command of Capt. Herrick, should, the next day in the afternoon, take into custody Major Skene and his party and boats; and that the rest of the men, which consisted of about 140, should go through Shoreham to the Lake, opposite to Ticonderoga; and that a part of the men that went to Skenesborough should, in the night following, go down the Lake by Ticonderoga in the boats to Shoreham, in order to carry men across the Lake to Ticonderoga. We also sent Capt. Douglas to go to Crown Point and see if he could not agree with his brother-in-law, who lived there, to hire the king's boats on some stratagem, and send up the Lake from there to assist in carrying over our men. It was further agreed that Col. Ethan Allen should have the command of the party that should go against Ticonderoga, agreeable to my promise made to the men when I engaged them to go, that they should be commanded by their own officers.

In the evening after, the party that was to go to Skenesborough was drafted out, and Col. Allen was gone to Mr. Wessells, in Shoreham, to meet some men who were to come in there, having received his orders, at what time he must be ready and must take possession of the garrison of Ticonderoga—the whole plan being settled by a vote of the Committee.

In the evening Col. Arnold came to us with his orders and demanded the command of our people, as he said we had no proper orders. We told him we could not surrender the command to him, as our people were raised on condition that they would be commanded by their own officers. He persisted in his demand, and the next morning he proceeded forward to overtake Col. Allen. I was then with the party that was going to Skenesborough, a mile and a half distance from the other party. When Col. Arnold went after Col. Allen, the whole party followed him, for fear he should prevail on Col. Allen to resign the command, and left all the provisions, so that I, with Capt. Phelps and Babcock, was obliged to leave the party that I was with, and go with the packhorses with the provisions, and could not overtake them till the first division had crossed the Lake. We followed them as soon as the boats got back, and when we got over they were in possession of the fort. We entered the fort immediately, and soon got the Regular troops under guard and their arms all in our possession. This was done on Wednesday the 10th of May.
—Mott, Journal, *Conn. Hist. Soc. Coll.*, I, 165-172.

2. "Mr. Allen's Orders Were from the Province of Connecticut"

From the report of Lieutenant Jocelyn Feltham of the British garrison at Ticonderoga to General Gage.

New York, 11th June, 1775

. . . Capt. Delaplace having in the course of the winter applied to Gen. Carleton for a reinforcement, as he had reason to suspect some attack from some circumstances that happened in his neighbourhood, Gen. Carleton was pleased to order a detachment of a subaltern and 20 men to be sent in two or three separate parties, the first party of which was sent as a crew along with Major Dunbar who left Canada about the 12th April. I being the first subaltern on command was ordered down with 10 men in a few days more, to give up to Capt. Delaplace with whom Lt. Wadman was to remain, having received orders from the regiment some time before to join there. As he was not arrived when I came I had orders to wait until he did. I was 12 days there before he came, which was about an hour after the fort was surprized.

I had not lain in the fort on my arrival, having left the only tolerable rooms there were for Mr. Wadman if he arrived with his family, but being unwell, had lain in the fort for two or three nights preceding the 10th May, on which morning about half an hour after three in my sleep I was awakened by numbers of shrieks and the words "No quarter, no quarter!" from a number of armed rabble. I jumped up, about which time I heard the noise continue in the area of the fort. I ran undressed to knock at Capt. Delaplace's door and to receive his orders or wake him. The door was fast. The room I lay in being close to Capt. Delaplace's, I stept back, put on my coat and waist coat and returned to his room, there being no possibility of getting to the men, as there were numbers of the rioters on the bastions of the wing of the fort on which the door of my room and back door of Capt. Delaplace's room led. With great difficulty I got into his room, being pursued, from which there there was a door down by-stairs into the area of the fort. I asked Capt. Delaplace, who was now just up, what I should do, and offered to force my way if possible to our men.

On opening this door, the bottom of the stairs was filled with the rioters and many were forcing their way up, knowing the commanding officer lived there, as they had broke open the lower rooms where the officers live in winter and could not find them there. From the top of the stairs I endeavoured to make them hear me, but it was impossible. On making a signal not to come up the stairs, they stopped and proclaimed silence among themselves. I then addressed them, but in a stile not agreeable to them I asked them a number of questions, expecting to amuse them till our people fired, which I must certainly own I thought would have been the case.

After asking them the most material questions I could think, viz., by what authority they entered His Majesty's fort, who were the leaders, what their intent, etc., etc., I was informed by one Ethan Allen and one Benedict Arnold that they had a joint command, Arnold informing me he came from instructions received from the congress at Cambridge, which he afterwards shewed me. Mr. Allen told me his orders were from the province of Connecticut and that he must have immediate possession of the fort and all the effects of George the Third (those were his words), Mr. Allen insisting on this with a drawn sword over my head and numbers of his followers' firelocks presented at me, alledging I was commanding officer and to give up the fort, and if it was not complied with, or that there was a single gun fired in the fort, neither man, woman or child should be left alive in the fort. Mr. Arnold begged it in a genteel manner but without success. It was owing to him they were prevented getting into Capt. Delaplace's room, after they found I did not command.

Capt. Delaplace, being now dressed, came out, when after talking to him some time, they put me back into the room. They placed two sentrys on me and took Capt. Delaplace down stairs. They also placed sentrys at the back door.

From the beginning of the noise till half an hour after this I never saw a soldier, tho' I heard a great noise in their rooms and can not account otherwise than that they must have been seized in their beds before I got on the stairs, or at the first coming in, which must be the case as Allen wounded one of the guard on his struggling with him in the guard room immediately after his entrance into the fort. When I did see our men they were drawn up without arms, which were all put into one room over which they placed sentrys and allotted one to each soldier.

Their strength at first coming—that is, the number they had ferried over in the night—amounted to about 90, but from their entrance and shouting they were constantly landing men till about 10 o'clock when I suppose there were about 300, and by the next morning at least another 100, who I suppose were waiting the event and came now to join in the plunder which was most rigidly performed as to liquors, provisions, etc., whether belonging to His Majesty or private property.

About noon on the 10th May, our men were sent to the landing at Lake George, and sent over next day, then marched by Albany to Hartford in Connecticut where they arrived on the 22d.

—FRENCH, *Taking of Ticonderoga*, pp. 42-45.

3. "IN THE NAME OF JEHOVAH AND THE CONTINENTAL CONGRESS"

From the narrative of Colonel Ethan Allen, first published in March 1779.

Ever since I arrived to a state of manhood and acquainted myself with the general history of mankind, I have felt a sincere passion for liberty. The history of nations doomed to perpetual slavery, in consequence of yielding up to tyrants their natural born liberties, I read with a sort of philosophical horror; so that the first systematical and bloody attempt at Lexington to enslave America thoroughly electrified my mind and fully determined me to take part with my country.

And while I was wishing for an opportunity to signalize myself in its behalf, directions were privately sent to me from the then colony (now state) of Connecticut to raise the Green Mountain Boys, and (if possible) with them to surprise and take the fortress Ticonderoga. This enterprise I cheerfully undertook; and, after first guarding all the several passes that led thither, to cut off all intelligence between the garrison and the country, made a forced march from Bennington and arrived at the lake opposite to Ticonderoga on the evening of the ninth day of May, 1775, with two hundred and thirty valiant Green Mountain Boys; and it was with the utmost difficulty that I procured boats to cross the lake. However, I landed eighty-three men near the garrison, and sent the boats back for the rear guard commanded by Col. Seth Warner. But the day began to dawn, and I found myself under a necessity to attack the fort before the rear could cross the lake; and, as it was viewed hazardous, I harangued the officers and soldiers in the manner following:

"Friends and fellow soldiers, you have, for a number of years past, been a scourge and terror to arbitrary power. Your valour has been famed abroad and acknowledged, as appears by the advice and orders to me (from the general assembly of Connecticut) to surprise and take the garrison now before us. I now propose to advance before you and in person conduct you through the wicket-gate; for we must this morning either quit our pretensions to valour, or possess ourselves of this fortress in a few minutes; and, in as much as it is a desperate attempt (which none but the bravest of men dare undertake), I do not urge it on any contrary to his will. You that will undertake voluntarily, poise your firelocks!"

The men being (at this time) drawn up in three ranks, each poised his firelock. I ordered them to face to the right, and, at the head of the centre-file, marched them immediately to the wicket gate aforesaid, where I found a centry posted, who instantly snapped his fusees at me. I ran immediately toward him, and he retreated through the covered way into the parade within the garrison, gave a halloo and ran under a bomb-proof. My party who followed me into the fort, I formed on the parade in such a manner as to face the two barracks which faced each other. The garrison being asleep (except the centries), we gave three huzzas which greatly surprised them. One of the centries made a pass at one of my officers with a charged bayonet and slightly wounded him. My first thought was to kill him with my sword; but, in an instant, altered the design and fury of the blow to a slight cut on the side of the head; upon which he dropped his gun and asked quarter, which I readily granted him, and demanded of him the place where the commanding officer kept. He shewed me a pair of stairs in the front of a barrack, on the west part of the garrison, which led up to a second story in said barrack, to which I immediately repaired, and ordered the commander (Capt. Delaplace) to come forth instantly, or I would sacrifice the whole garrison; at which the captain came immediately to the door with his breeches in his hand, when I ordered him to deliver to me the fort instantly, who asked me by what authority I demanded it; I answered, "In the name of the great Jehovah and the Continental Congress."

The authority of the Congress being very little known at that time, he began to speak again; but I interrupted him and, with my drawn sword over his head, again demanded an immediate surrender of the garrison; to which he then complied, and ordered his men to be forthwith paraded without arms, as he had given up the garrison. In the mean time some of my officers had given orders, and in consequence thereof, sundry of the barrack doors were beat down, and about one third of the garrison imprisoned, which consisted of the said commander, a Lieut. Feltham, a conductor of artillery, a gunner, two serjeants and forty-four rank and file; about one hundred pieces of cannon, one 13-inch mortar and a number of swivels.

This surprise was carried into execution in the gray of the morning of the 10th day of May, 1775. The sun seemed to rise that morning with a superior lustre; and Ticonderoga and its dependencies smiled on its conquerors, who tossed about the flowing bowl and wished success to Congress and the liberty and freedom of America. . . . Col. Warner with the rear guard crossed the lake and joined me early in the morning, whom I sent off without loss of time, with about one hundred men, to take possession of Crown Point, which was garrisoned with a serjeant and twelve men; which he took possession of the same day, as also upwards of one hundred pieces of cannon.

But one thing now remained to be done to make ourselves complete masters of Lake Champlain: This was to possess ourselves of a sloop of war, which was then laying at St. John's; to effect which, it was agreed in a council of war to arm and man out a certain schooner, which lay at South Bay, and that Capt. (now General) Arnold should command her, and that I should command the batteaux. The necessary preparations being made, we set sail from Ticonderoga in quest of the sloop, which was much larger and carried more guns and heavier metal than the schooner.

General Arnold, with the schooner sailing faster than the batteaux, arrived at St. John's and by surprise possessed himself of the sloop before I could arrive with the batteaux. He also made prisoners of a serjeant and twelve men, who were garrisoned at that place. It is worthy [of] remark that as soon as General Arnold had secured the prisoners on board and had made preparation for sailing, the wind which but a few hours before was fresh in the south and well served to carry us to St. John's, now shifted and came fresh from the north; and in about one hour's time General Arnold sailed with the prize and schooner for Ticonderoga. When I met him with my party, within a few miles of St. John's, he saluted me with a discharge of cannon, which I returned with a volley of small arms. This being repeated three times, I went on board the sloop with my party, where several loyal Congress healths were drank.

We were now masters of Lake Champlain and the garrisons depending thereon.

—ALLEN, *Narrative*, pp. 5-11.

4. COLONEL ALLEN IS "ENTIRELY UNACQUAINTED WITH MILITARY SERVICE"

Colonel Benedict Arnold's report on the capture of Ticonderoga to the Massachusetts Committee of Safety.

Ticonderoga, May 11, 1775

Gentlemen:—I wrote you yesterday that, arriving in the vicinity of this place, I found one hundred and fifty men collected at the instance of some gentlemen from Connecticut (designed on the same errand on which I came), headed by Colonel Ethan Allen, and that I had joined them, not thinking proper to wait the arrival of the troops I had engaged on the road, but to attempt the fort by surprise; that we had taken the fort at four o'clock yesterday morning without opposition and had made prisoners one captain, one lieutenant and forty-odd privates and subalterns, and that we found the fort in a most ruinous condition and not worth repairing; that a party of fifty men were gone to Crown Point, and that I intended to follow with as many men to seize the sloop, etc., and that I intended to keep possession here until I had farther advice from you.

On and before our taking possession here I had agreed with Colonel Allen to issue farther orders jointly, until I could raise a sufficient number of men to relieve his people; on which plan we proceeded when I wrote you yesterday: since which, Colonel Allen, finding he had the ascendency over his people, positively insisted I should have no command, as I had forbid the soldiers plundering and destroying private property. The power is now taken out of my hands, and I am not consulted, nor have I a voice in any matters.

There is here at present near one hundred men, who are in the greatest confusion and anarchy, destroying and plundering private property, committing every enormity and paying no attention to public service. The party I advised were gone to Crown Point are returned, having met with head winds; and that expedition and taking the sloop (mounted with six guns) is entirely laid aside. There is not the least regularity among the troops, but every thing is governed by whim and caprice—the soldiers threatening to leave the garrison on the least affront. Most of them must return home soon, as their families are suffering. Under our present situation, I believe one hundred men would retake the fortress, and there seems no prospect of things being in a better situation.

I have therefore thought proper to send an express advising you of the state of affairs, not doubting you will take the matter into your serious consideration and order a number of troops to join those I have coming on here; or that you will appoint some other person to take the command of them and this place, as you shall think most proper. Colonel Allen is a proper man to head his own wild people, but entirely unacquainted with military service; and as I am the only person who has been legally authorized to take possession of this place, I am determined to insist on my right, and I think it my duty to remain here against all opposition until I have farther orders.

I cannot comply with your orders in regard to the cannon, etc., for want of men. I have wrote to the Governor and General Assembly of Connecticut, advising them of my appointment and giving them an exact detail of matters as they stand at present. I should be extremely glad to be honorably acquitted of my commission, and that a proper person might be appointed in my room. But, as I have, in consequence of my orders from you, gentlemen, been the first person who entered and took possession of the fort, I shall keep it, at every hazard, until I have further advice and orders from you and the General Assembly of Connecticut.

—DAWSON, *Battles of the United States*, I, 38-39.

VIII. VIRGINIA TAKES THE ROAD TO REVOLUTION

Virginia and Massachusetts had from the beginning taken the lead in opposition to the new British policy inaugurated by the Proclamation line of 1763 and the Stamp Act; it was entirely proper that Virginia should be the first colony to range herself alongside Massachusetts in the crisis of 1774-75. As early as January 1774 a committee of planters of Fairfax County—including George Washington and George Mason—moved to tighten Virginia's defenses by strengthening the militia. They resolved somewhat pharisaically "that a well regulated militia is the natural strength and only stable security of a free government, and that such militia will relieve our mother country from any expense in our protection and defence, will obviate the pretence of a necessity of taxing us on that account, and render it unnecessary to keep standing armies among us." On March 20, 1775, a convention met at Richmond, in accordance with recommendations of the First Continental Congress, to take up the whole question of colonial relations with the mother country. Its deliberations were, for the most part, innocuous, but on March 23 it took up, in the spirit of the Fairfax County resolutions, a proposal that the "colony be immediately put into a posture of defense." It was on this resolution that Patrick Henry made the famous speech which has come down to us largely in the form remembered or imagined by William Wirt. "The next gale that sweeps from the north will bring to our ears the clash of resounding arms"— it was almost too prophetic to be true! But if it is not good history it is good historical legend. The resolutions, in any event, were passed and Virginia ranged herself behind the Continental Congress—and selected delegates to the next one.

Alarmed by this display of defiance, Governor Dunmore, on the night of April 20, directed a small body of marines to seize the gunpowder in Williamsburg. Had it not been that the Virginians were moderate, and Dunmore without an army, another Concord might have ensued. The Virginians gathered in arms—hundreds of them—and threatened to recapture the powder. Dunmore—not for the first or the last time—lost his head. "The whole country can easily be made a solitude," he threatened, "and by the living God if an insult is offered to me or to those who have obeyed my orders, I will declare freedom to the slaves and lay the town in ashes!" When he had cooled off, however, he paid for the powder, and then—to show that he was not to be frightened—he outlawed Patrick Henry just as he was about to set off for the Second Continental Congress.

Meantime the Conciliatory Plan which Lord North pushed through Parliament in February reached the colonies, and early in June Dunmore convened the Burgesses to listen to its terms. By them Parliament would "forbear" to lay any but regulatory taxes upon any American colony which through its own assembly taxed itself for the support of defence and civil government. Yet even as the Burgesses were discussing them, the Governor, once again frightened, took refuge on the warship Fowey, in the York River. Not surprisingly the Burgesses rejected the North plan and adopted a series of resolutions, drafted by Jefferson, setting forth their unity with the other colonies.

There ensued some months of desultory skirmishing which came to a head in November when Dunmore outraged Virginia sentiment by proclaiming martial law and promising freedom to Negro slaves who joined the royal cause. When the militia leader William Woodford moved his meager forces toward the port of Norfolk, Dunmore decided to take the offensive. At Great Bridge the redcoats—led by the same Colonel Leslie who had been turned back at Salem—suffered a stunning defeat and withdrew to their ships lying in Norfolk harbor. There, for some weeks, Dunmore glowered and sulked; in January he decided that the situation had become intolerable, and turned his naval guns on the hapless town. With some connivance from the Patriots, Norfolk was destroyed. Dunmore's desperate act did not harm the Patriots, but it did irreparable harm to the Virginia Loyalists—most of them located in Norfolk—forfeited the last chance of accommodation with the moderates, and provided invaluable material for Patriot propaganda.

Some two months after the affair at Great Bridge, Governor Martin of North Carolina organized a Tory expedition from his floating capitol, the sloop of war Scorpion. *Under Donald McDonald, Loyalist leader of the Scots clans of the colony, the Loyalists tried to fight their way through to the coast. The North Carolina militia under Colonel James Moore met them at Moore's Creek Bridge. Shouting "King George and the Broadswords" the Highlanders in plaids and kilts rushed the bridge but were cut down and fled in confusion; no less than 850 of them were captured, the largest haul of prisoners so far. This victory led to the termination of royal government in North Carolina.*

We give here Patrick Henry's speech—or alleged speech; an account of the removal of the powder; some paragraphs from Jefferson's memorable resolutions on the Conciliatory Plan; Dunmore's proclamation promising freedom to the slaves; a contemporary letter telling how the Virginians prepared for war; Colonel Woodford's account of the affair at Great Bridge; two accounts of the burning of Norfolk; and Colonel Moore's own report on the battle at Moore's Creek Bridge.

1. "Gentlemen May Cry 'Peace! Peace!' but There Is No Peace"

Patrick Henry's speech in the Virginia Convention, March 23, 1775, as reported by William Wirt.

Mr. President: It is natural to man to indulge in the illusions of hope. We are apt to shut our eyes against a painful truth—and listen to the song of that syren, till she transforms us into beasts. Is this the part of wise men, engaged in a great and arduous struggle for liberty? Are we disposed to be of the number of those who, having eyes, see not, and having ears, hear not, the things which so nearly concern their temporal salvation? For my part, whatever anguish of spirit it may cost, I am willing to know the whole truth; to know the worst, and to provide for it.

I have but one lamp by which my feet are guided; and that is the lamp of experience. I know of no way of judging of the future but by the past. And judging by the past, I wish to know what there has been in the conduct of the British ministry for the last ten years, to justify those hopes with which gentlemen have been pleased to solace themselves and the house? Is it that insidious smile with which our petition has been lately received? Trust it not, sir; it will prove a snare to your feet. Suffer not yourselves to be betrayed with a kiss. Ask yourselves how this gracious reception of our petition comports with those warlike preparations which cover our waters and darken our land. Are fleets and armies necessary to a work of love and reconciliation? Have we shown ourselves so unwilling to be reconciled that force must be called in to win back our love? Let us not deceive ourselves, sir. These are the implements of war and subjugation—the last arguments to which kings resort. I ask gentlemen, sir, what means this martial array, if its purpose be not to force us to submission? Can gentlemen assign any other possible motive for it? Has Great Britain any enemy in this quarter of the world, to call for all this accumulation of navies and armies? No, sir, she has none. They are meant for us: they can be meant for no other. They are sent over to bind and rivet upon us those chains which the British ministry have been so long forging. And what have we to oppose to them? Shall we try argument? Sir, we have been trying that for the last ten years. Have we anything new to offer upon the subject? Nothing. We have held the subject up in every light of which it is capable; but it has been all in vain. Shall we resort to entreaty and humble supplication? What terms shall we find which have not been already exhausted? Let us not, I beseech you, sir, deceive ourselves longer.

Sir, we have done everything that could be done to avert the storm which is now coming on. We have petitioned—we have remonstrated—we have supplicated—we have prostrated ourselves before the throne, and have implored its interposition to arrest the tyrannical hands of the ministry and parliament. Our petitions have been slighted; our remonstrances have produced additional violence and insult; our supplications have been disregarded; and we have been spurned, with contempt, from the foot of the throne. In vain, after these things, may we indulge the fond hope of peace and reconciliation. There is no longer any room for hope. If we wish to be free—if we mean to preserve inviolate those inestimable privileges for which we have been so long contending—if we mean not basely to abandon the noble struggle in which we have been so long engaged, and which we have pledged ourselves never to abandon until the glorious object of our contest shall be obtained—we must fight!—I repeat it, sir, we must fight! An appeal to arms and to the God of Hosts is all that is left us!

They tell us, sir, that we are weak—unable to cope with so formidable an adversary. But when shall we be stronger? Will it be the next week or the next year? Will it be when we are totally disarmed, and when a British guard shall be stationed in every house? Shall we gather strength by irresolution and inaction? Shall we acquire the means of effectual resistance by lying supinely on our backs, and hugging the delusive phantom of hope, until our enemies shall have bound us hand and foot? Sir, we are not weak, if we make a proper use of those means which the God of nature hath placed in our power. Three millions of people, armed in the holy cause of liberty, and in such a country as that which we possess, are invincible by any force which our enemy can send against us. Besides, sir, we shall not fight our battles alone. There is a just God who presides over the destinies of nations; and who will raise up friends to fight our battles for us. The battle, sir, is not to the strong alone; it is to the vigilant, the active, the brave. Besides, sir, we have no election. If we were base enough to desire it, it is now too late to retire from the contest. There is no retreat but in submission and slavery! Our chains are forged. Their clanking may be heard on the plains of Boston! The war is inevitable —and let it come! I repeat it, sir, let it come!

It is in vain, sir, to extenuate the matter. Gentlemen may cry, "Peace! peace!"—but there is no peace. The war is actually begun! The next gale that sweeps from the north will bring to our ears the clash of resounding arms! Our brethren are already in the field! Why stand we here idle? What is it that gentlemen wish? What would they have? Is life so dear, or peace so sweet, as to be purchased at the price of chains and slavery? Forbid it, Almighty God! I know not what course others may take; but as for me, give me liberty or give me death!

—WIRT, *Life of Henry*, pp. 120-123.

2. VIRGINIANS PROTEST THE REMOVAL OF THE POWDER

Williamsburgh, Virginia, April 21, 1775

This morning, between three and four o'clock, all the gunpowder in the magazine, to the amount, as we hear, of about twenty barrels, was carried off in his Excellency the Governour's wagon, escorted by Captain Collins and a detachment of marines from the armed schooner *Magdalen*, now lying at Burwell's Ferry, and lodged on board that vessel. As soon as the news of this manoeuvre took wind, the whole city was alarmed and much exasperated; and numbers got themselves in readiness to repair to the Palace to demand from the Governour a restoration of what they so justly supposed was deposited in this magazine for the country's defence. However, as some gentlemen represented the propriety of remonstrating to the Governour upon this occasion in a decent and respectful manner, the Common Hall assembled, who, after deliberating some time, waited upon his Excellency with the following Address, which was presented by the Honourable Peyton Randolph, Esquire, Recorder of this city, and is as follows: . . .

My Lord: We, His Majesty's dutiful and loyal subjects, the Mayor, Recorder, Aldermen, and Common Council of the City of Williamsburgh, in Common Hall assembled, humbly beg leave to represent to your Excellency that the inhabitants of this city were this morning exceedingly alarmed by a report that a large quantity of gunpowder was, in the preceding night, while they were sleeping in their beds, removed from the publick magazine in this city, and conveyed under an escort of marines on board one of His Majesty's armed vessels lying at a ferry on James River.

We beg leave to represent to your Excellency that as this magazine was erected at the publick expense of this Colony, and appropriated to the safe-keeping of such munition as should be lodged from time to time, for the protection and security of the country, by arming thereout such of the militia as might be necessary in case of invasions and insurrections, they humbly conceive it to be the only proper repository to be resorted to in times of imminent danger.

We farther beg leave to inform your Excellency that from various reports at present prevailing in different parts of the country, we have too much reason to believe that some wicked and designing persons have instilled the most diabolical notions into the minds of our slaves, and that, therefore, the utmost attention to our internal security is become the more necessary.

The circumstances of this city, my Lord, we consider as peculiar and critical. The inhabitants, from the situation of the magazine in the middle of their city, have for a long tract of time been exposed to all those dangers which have happened in many countries from explosions and other accidents. They have, from time to time, thought it incumbent on them to guard the magazine. For their security, they have for some time past judged it necessary to keep strong patrols on foot. In their present circumstances, then, to have the chief and necessary means of their defence removed cannot but be extremely alarming.

Considering ourselves as guardians of the city, we therefore humbly desire to be informed by your Excellency upon what motives and for what particular purpose the powder has been carried off in such a manner: and we earnestly entreat your Excellency to order it to be immediately returned to the magazine.

To which His Excellency returned this oral answer:

That hearing of an insurrection in a neighbouring county, he had removed the powder from the magazine, where he did not think it secure, to a place where it would be in perfect security; and that, upon his word and honour, whenever it was wanted on any insurrection, it should be delivered in half an hour. That he had removed it in the night time to prevent any alarm; and that Captain Collins had his express commands for the part he had acted. He was surprised to hear the people were under arms on this occasion, and that he should not think it prudent to put powder into their hands in such a situation.

—FORCE, *American Archives*, 4th Series, II, 371-372.

3. VIRGINIA REJECTS NORTH'S CONCILIATORY OVERTURES

Thomas Jefferson's Virginia Resolutions.

June 10, 1775

Resolved . . . That wishing nothing so sincerely as the perpetual continuance of that brotherly love which we bear to our fellow subjects of Great Britain . . . we were pleased to receive his Lordship's notification that a benevolent tender had at length been made by the British House of Commons towards bringing to a good end our unhappy disputes with the Mother Country; that next to the possession of liberty, we should consider such Reconciliation the greatest of all human blessings. With these dispositions we entered into consideration of that Resolution: we examined it minutely; we viewed it in every point of light in which we were able to place it; and with pain and disappointment we must ultimately declare it only changes the form of oppression, without lightening its burthen. That we cannot close with the terms of that Resolution for these Reasons:

Because the British Parliament has no right to intermeddle with the support of civil government in the Colonies. . . .

Because to render perpetual our exemption from an unjust taxation, we must saddle ourselves with a perpetual tax adequate to the expectations and subject to the disposal of Parliament alone. . . .

Because on our undertaking to grant money as is proposed, the Commons only resolve to forbear levying pecuniary taxes on us; still leaving unrepealed their several Acts passed for the purposes of restraining the trade and altering the form of Government of the Eastern Colonies; . . .

Because at the very time of requiring from us grants of Money they are making disposition to invade us with large Armaments. . . .

Because on our agreeing to contribute our proportion towards the common defence, they do not propose to lay open to us a free trade with all the world; . . .

Because the proposition now made to us involves the interest of all the other Colonies. . . .

—BOYD, ed., *Papers of Thomas Jefferson*, I, 170-172.

4. FREEDOM FOR NEGROES WHO JOIN THE ROYAL CAUSE: LORD DUNMORE

Proclamation by John, Earl of Dunmore.

Off Norfolk, November 7, 1775

As I have ever entertained hopes that an accommodation might have taken place between Great Britain and this Colony, without being compelled by my duty to this most disagreeable, but now absolutely necessary step, rendered so by a body of armed men, unlawfully assembled, firing on His Majesty's Tenders; and the formation of an Army, and that Army now on their march to attack His Majesty's Troops, and destroy the well-disposed subjects of this Colony: To defeat such treasonable purposes, and that all such traitors and their abettors may be brought to justice, and that the peace and good order of this Colony may be again restored, which the ordinary course of the civil law is unable to effect, I have thought fit to issue this my Proclamation, hereby declaring, that until the aforesaid good purposes can be obtained, I do, in virtue of the power and authority to me given by His Majesty, determine to execute martial law, and cause the same to be executed throughout this Colony. And to the end that peace and good order may the sooner be restored, I do require every person capable of bearing arms to resort to His Majesty's standard, or be looked upon as traitors to His Majesty's crown and Government, and thereby become liable to the penalty the law inflicts upon such offences—such as forfeiture of life, confiscation of lands, etc., etc.: and I do hereby further declare all indented servants, Negroes or others, (appertaining to Rebels) free, that are able and willing to bear arms, they joining His Majesty's Troops as soon as may be, for the more speedily reducing this Colony to a proper sense of their duty to His Majesty's crown and dignity. I do further order and require all His Majesty's liege subjects to retain their quit-rents, or any other taxes due, or that may become due, in their own custody, till such time as peace may be again restored to this, at present, most unhappy Country, or demanded of them for their former salutary purposes, by officers properly authorized to receive the same.

Given under my hand, on board the Ship *William*, off Norfolk, the 7th day of November, in the sixteenth year of His Majesty's reign.

DUNMORE

God Save the King!
—FORCE, *American Archives*, 4th Series, III, 1385.

5. VIRGINIA PREPARES FOR WAR

Extract from a letter from Virginia, Rappahannock River, as printed in the *Morning Chronicle and London Advertiser*, August 21, 1775.

July 1, 1775

. . . It would really surprise you to see the preparations making for our defence, all persons arming themselves, and independent companies, from 100 to 150 men in every county of Virginia, well equipped and daily endeavouring to instruct themselves in the art of war, in order [to] oppose any forces that shall be sent here; this has been the case ever since the battle of Boston, and I can positively affirm that in a few days an army of at least 7 or 8 thousand well-disciplined men might be got together (well armed) for the protection of this country; and, from the best information I can get, the Northern Colonies have forces far superior to this country, so that you may depend there will be many most bloody battles before the Americans will give up their liberties.

I am afraid the scheme of Parliament will be the ruin of the British constitution, for should they at last reduce the Americans (which I much doubt), I am sure that it will so weaken the British power that they must become a prey to some other nation, for I am sure that America never will submit while there are a sufficient number of its inhabitants left as will make the appearance of an army, so that the King will have but few subjects left here, and those few, perhaps, not well attached to his person.

When you traded here you well knew it to be the ambition of the people of this country to endeavour who should be best dressed with the British manufactures, but they are now quite on the contrary extreme, for their glory now is to dress in their own manufacture, for you may be well assured that many people, who a few years ago would not wear a shirt of less value than 2s. 6d. or 3s. sterling per yard, now put on a cotton shirt of their own manufacture, and the example is daily followed by all ranks of people here: you may see from this how scandalous our G[overnor] has been in informing the ministry that we could not subsist more than one or two years without the assistance of the British manufactory. I hope he and every such ——— who has been the cause of the present disturbances will be brought to condign punishment. Instead of our fields being planted with tobacco, as usual, they are now flourishing with cotton and flax, and our pastures well stored with sheep; so I think there will not be the least danger of our suffering for want of clothes. I heartily wish you and your family all happiness, and I pray God that the disputes now subsisting between the Colonies and Britain may be speedily settled for the interest of both, . . .

—WILLARD, ed., *Letters on the American Revolution*, pp. 157-158.

6. "A Second Bunker's Hill . . . We Kept Our Post"

Colonel William Woodford to the Virginia Convention.

Great-Bridge, December 10, 1775

A servant belonging to Major Marshall, who deserted the other night from Colonel Scott's party, has completely taken his Lordship in. Lieutenant Batut, who is wounded and at present my prisoner, informs me that this fellow told them not more than three hundred shirt-men were here, and that imprudent man caught at the bait, despatching Captain Leslie with all the regulars (about two hundred) who arrived at the bridge about three o'clock in the morning, joined about three hundred black and white slaves, laid planks upon the bridge, and crossed just after our reveille had beat; and lucky time for us, and, you will say, rather an improper season for them to make their push, when, of course all our men must be under arms. The above lieutenant commanded the advanced party, and Captain Fordyce, of the Grenadiers, led the van with his company, who, for coolness and bravery, deserved a better fate, as well as the brave fellows who fell with him, who behaved like heroes. They marched up to our breastwork with fixed bayonets, and perhaps a hotter fire never happened or a greater carnage, for the number of troops. None of the blacks, etc., in the rear, with Captain Leslie, advanced further than the bridge.

I have the pleasure to inform you that the victory was complete, and that most of their dead and wounded, with two pieces of cannon, were carried off under cover of their guns from the fort. We buried twelve besides the captain (him with all the military honours due to his rank), and have prisoners Lieutenant Batut and sixteen privates, all wounded; thirty-five stands of arms and accoutrements, three officers' fusils, powder, ball and cartridges, with sundry other things, have likewise fallen into our hands.

This was a second Bunker's Hill affair, in miniature, with this difference, that we kept our post and had only one man wounded in the hand.

—Force, *American Archives*, 4th Series, IV, 228.

7. "The Detested Town of Norfolk Is No More"

From the journal of a midshipman on board His Majesty's ship *Otter*.

December 9th.—Our troops, with about sixty townsmen from Norfolk, and a detachment of sailors from the ships, among whom I had the honor to march, set out from Norfolk to attack, once more, the rebels at Great Bridge, who had been lodged there some time, and had erected a breastwork opposite to our fort, upon their side of the river. We arrived at the fort half an hour after three in the morning, and, after refreshing ourselves, prepared to attack the rebels in their intrenchments.

Captain Squire, ever ready to assist my lord in the public cause, had sent his gunners and men to manage two pieces of cannon, who were in the front, and ordered to begin the attack. But how can it be supposed that, with two hundred men, we could force a strong intrenchment, defended by at least two thousand? Yet this was attempted, and we marched up to their works with the intrepidity of lions. But alas! we retreated with much fewer brave fellows than we took out. Their fire was so heavy that had we not retreated as we did, we should every one have been cut off. Figure to yourself a strong breastwork built across a causeway, on which six men only could advance abreast; a large swamp almost surrounded them, at the back of which were two small breastworks to flank us in our attack on their intrenchments. Under these disadvantages it was impossible to succeed; yet our men were so enraged that all the entreaties and scarcely the threats of their officers could prevail on them to retreat, which at last they did. .... We set out on our return for Norfolk about seven o'clock in the evening, at which place we arrived at twelve, and the soldiers were embarked on board vessels prepared for that purpose.

December 14th.—The rebels, having now nothing to obstruct their passage, arrived and took possession of Norfolk, and in the evening saluted us with a volley of small arms; . . . the next morning, I was sent on shore to their commander to inform him that if another shot was fired at the *Otter*, they must expect the town to be knocked about their ears.

January 9th.—The detested town of Norfolk is no more! Its destruction happened on New Year's Day. About four o'clock in the afternoon the signal was given from the *Liverpool*, when a dreadful cannonading began from the three ships, which lasted till it was too hot for the rebels to stand on their wharves. Our boats now landed, and set fire to the town in several places. It burned fiercely all night, and the next day; nor are the flames yet extinguished; but no more of Norfolk remains than about twelve houses which have escaped the flames.

—DAWSON, *Battles of the United States*, I, 126-127.

8. THE BRITISH FIRE NORFOLK

Colonel Robert Howe of the North Carolina troops to the Virginia Convention.

Norfolk, January 2, 1776

The cannonade of the town began about a quarter after three yesterday, from upwards of one hundred pieces of cannon, and continued till near ten at night, without intermission; it then abated a little, and continued till two this morning. Under cover of their guns they landed and set fire to the town in several places near the water, though our men strove to prevent them all in their power; but the houses near the water being chiefly of wood, they took fire immediately, and the fire spread with amazing rapidity. It is now become general, and the whole town will, I doubt not, be consumed in a day or two. Expecting that the fire would throw us into confusion, they frequently landed, and were every time repulsed, I imagine with loss, but with what loss I cannot tell; the burning of the town has made several avenues which yesterday they had not, so that they may now fire with greater effect; the tide is now rising, and we expect at high water another cannonade.

I have only to wish it may be ineffectual as the last; for we have not one man killed, and but a few wounded. I cannot enter into the melancholy consideration of the women and children running through a crowd of shot to get out of the town, some of them with children at their breasts; a few have, I hear, been killed. Does it not call for vengeance, both from God and man?

It is but justice to inform you that I had the pleasure to find every officer ready to execute orders at a moment's warning, and that the men behaved with steadiness and spirit. Colonel Stevens went down at my command and headed some men near the water, where he engaged a party who had landed, with a spirit and conduct of a good officer. Of my friend, Colonel Woodford, it is almost needless to speak, but I cannot avoid expressing that I received from him every assistance which conduct and spirit could give me.

—FORCE, *American Archives*, 4th Series, IV, 538.

9. THE AFFAIR AT MOORE'S CREEK BRIDGE

General James Moore to the North Carolina Provincial Council.

Wilmington [N. C.], March 2, 1776

... Just when I was prepared to march I received an express from Colonel Caswell, informing that the Tories had raised a flat which had been sunk in Black River, about five miles above him, and by erecting a bridge, had passed it with their whole army.

I then determined, as the last expedient, to proceed immediately in boats down the Northwest River to Dollison's Landing, about sixty miles from them; and to take possession of Moore's Creek Bridge, about ten miles from them, at the same time acquainting Colonel Caswell of my intentions, and recommending him to retreat to Moore's Creek Bridge, if possible; but if not, to follow on in their rear.

The next day, by four o'clock, we arrived at Dollison's Landing; but as we could not possibly march that night, for want of horses for the artillery, I dispatched an express to Moore's Creek Bridge, to learn the situation of affairs there, and was informed that Colonel Lillington, who had the day before taken his stand at the bridge, was that afternoon reinforced by Colonel Caswell, and that they had raised a small breastwork and destroyed a part of the bridge.

The next morning (the 27th) at break of day an alarm gun was fired; immediately after which, scarcely allowing our people a moment to prepare, the Tory army, with Captain Macleod at their head, made their attack on Colonel Caswell and Colonel Lillington, and, finding a small intrenchment next the bridge on our side empty, concluded that our people had abandoned their post, and in the most furious manner advanced within thirty paces of our breastwork and artillery, where they met a very proper reception. Captain Macleod and Captain Campbell fell within a few paces of the breastwork, the former of whom received upwards of twenty balls through his body; and in a very few minutes their whole army was put to flight and most shamefully abandoned their general, who was next day taken prisoner.

The loss of the enemy in this action, from the best accounts we have been able to learn, is about thirty killed and wounded; but as numbers of them must have fallen into the creek, besides many more that were carried off, I suppose their loss may be estimated at about fifty. We had only two wounded, one of which died this day.

Thus, sir, I have the pleasure to inform you, has most happily terminated a very dangerous insurrection and will, I trust, put an effectual check to Toryism in this country.

—DAWSON, *Battles of the United States,* I, 131-132.

CHAPTER FOUR

Bunker's Hill

IN HIS *bombastic proclamation of June 12, 1775, General Gage had charged, among many other foolish things, that "the rebels . . . with a preposterous parade of military arrangement, affected to hold the army besieged." The arrangements may have been preposterous, but the siege was more than an affectation; it was real. A straggling American army (if it is proper to use that term) of some 7,000 or 8,000 men stretched in a great semicircle from the Mystic River on the north, through Cambridge and Roxbury, to Dorchester. Confined on their narrow peninsula were some 4,000 British—their numbers were augmented by reinforcements that came in during the spring months. For all his rodomontade Gage was not eager to renew hostilities after Concord, but the failure of Lord North's conciliatory plan left him, in the end, no alternative. Besides, on May 25 the Cerberus had sailed into Boston harbor with no less than three new major generals who came, after all, to fight: Sir William Howe, the Whig general who disapproved of the war; the American-born Sir Henry Clinton; and General John Burgoyne who had distinguished himself by his virulent attacks on Clive in the House, and by his bold forays into dramatic literature. All three came with some reputation and high ambition and found America the graveyard of both.*

General Gage knew that his position was precarious. He was hemmed in by land, and on sea supported only fortuitously by the incredible Admiral Graves who did not think it proper to take the offensive. He realized that American command either of Dorchester Heights to the south, or of Charlestown, across the bay, would make Boston untenable, and early in June decided to seize both strategic points. American intelligence, which was all but unfailing, got wind of this plan, and on June 15 the Committee of Public Safety called for the occupation of Bunker's Hill on Charlestown peninsula. During the night of the sixteenth about 1,600 Americans, under the command of Colonel William Prescott and General Israel Putnam, moved quietly onto the peninsula, and dug in on the little hill nearest Boston which came to be called Breed's Hill. Thus, as on the Concord expedition, Gage forfeited the initiative. He knew that he had to dislodge the Americans, or expose Boston to attack, and to this task he addressed himself with admirable energy. But energy was almost the only virtue which he did display. Instead of taking the obvious course of cutting the Americans off at the narrow neck of the peninsula, or the equally obvious (if more difficult) course of bombarding their positions from the sea, he chose to launch a frontal attack. In the end he drove the Americans from both Breed's Hill and Bunker's Hill, but it was one of the costliest victories in British military annals.

Neither side could take much satisfaction in Bunker's Hill, but the American failures were more serious than the British. From beginning to end the American battle had been a series of miscalculations and frustrations. There was no unified command, and indeed some question as to who was actually in command; less than one fifth the available forces were brought into action; reinforcements failed to come up or, coming up, fled; Bunker's Hill would have been a much stronger position than Breed's Hill; the lack of powder and the failure to bring up new supplies during the day were inexcusable. Yet most of these can be charged to inexperience. Gage could plead no such excuse. His strategy was clear. Pride and folly dictated the direct attack—contempt for the Americans which ought to have vanished with Concord, pride in the invulnerability of British arms.

I. THE SIEGE OF BOSTON

1. "Our Situation Here Is Beyond Description"

Peter Oliver, who here laments the pass to which the folly of American radicals and Ministerial extremists had brought the country, was the son of the Chief Justice Oliver who as one of the "Mandamus Councillors" incurred the particular enmity of the Patriots. After the outbreak of hostilities he took refuge in Boston, and eventually left with Howe for Halifax, and England.

Peter Oliver to his brother.

Boston, June 1st, 1775

Dear Brother,

We learn by the *Cerberus* man-of-war, which arrived last Thursday the 25th of May, that you have done with the thoughts of coming to Boston at present, which rejoices your friends.

I received yours dated at Bath, and am much obliged to you.

Our situation here, without any exaggeration, is beyond description almost; it is such as eye has not seen nor ear heard, nor hath it ever entered into the heart of man to conceive Boston ever to arrive at.

We are besieged this moment with 10 or 15000 men, from Roxbury to Cambridge; their rebell sentrys within call of the troops' sentrys on the Neck. We are every hour expecting an attack by land or water. All marketing from the country stopt ever since the battle. Fire and slaughter hourly threatened, and not out of danger from some of the inhabitants within, of setting the town of [on] fire. All the interest the Judge and I ound [owned] in Middleborough exposed to the ravage of a set of robbers, Mr. Conant at the head of them. Poor Jenny and Phoebe, and children, we can't hear of, or get any word to; whether they are all living or not, or whether the works and buildings are left standing is rather a doubt with me, for we have heard since the battle that a number set out to destroy and burn our interest, but that the selectmen interposed and saved them.

You seem in England to be entirely ignorant of the temper of our people.

They are as much determined from Florida to Hallifax to oppose you at home, do what you will, as I hear the Ministry are determined to pursue their plan. I am in no doubt but you will be able to conquer America at last, but a horrid bloody scene will be opened here as never was in New England before. What comfort or satisfaction do you think we take now, or can take, when the dreadful scene opens?

Your wife is in Plymouth, yet we can't get any intelligence of her, good or bad.

It is said by the rebels at Roxbury that Col. Watson has given his quota to support the people.

Good God! Do thou avert the impending calamity that threatens this former happy land, and turn the hearts of those deluded wretches from the power of sin and Satan to thy unerring precepts, and then, and then only, shall we be once more a happy people favoured of Heaven. . . .

O tempora! O mores! Yrs as usual,

PETER OLIVER, JUNR.

—HUTCHINSON, ed., *Diary and Letters of Thomas Hutchinson*, I, 458-460.

2. GENERAL GAGE CONFESSES THAT ALL WARLIKE PREPARATIONS ARE WANTING

This letter was written the day General Gage issued his pompous proclamation outlawing Hancock and Samuel Adams, and should be read against the background of that state paper. Clearly General Gage was not nearly so sure of himself as he sounded, and clearly, too, his patience with the Americans had come to an end.

General Gage to Lord North.

Boston, 12 June 1775

The situation these wretches have taken in forming the blockade of this town is judicious and strong, being well intrenched where the situation requires it and with cannon. Their numbers are great, exclusive of every inhabitant armed coming in to join that part of their army that may be attacked; upon the alarm being given, they come far and near, and the longer the action lasts, the greater their numbers grow. Their mode of engaging is (like all other inhabitants of a strong country) by getting behind fences and every sort of covering, firing from thence; then retire and load under cover and return to the charge; or take another situation from whence they fire. The country for 30 miles round is amazingly well situated for their manner of fighting, being covered with woods and small stone wall inclosures, exceedingly uneven and much cutt with ravins. . . .

In our present state all warlike preparations are wanting. No survey of the adjacent country, no proper boats for landing troops, not a sufficient number of horses for the artillery nor for regimental baggage. No forage, either hay or corn of any consequence—no waggons or harness for horses, except some prepared by Colonel Cleveland for the artillery.

No fascines or pickets. The military chest att the lowest ebb, about three or four thousand only remaining, which goes fast for the subsistence of the troops.

The rebellious colonys will supply nothing. Some of these articles will, I hope, be furnished from Quebec, but unless Government enters heartily into the wants here by immediately sending all the supplys wanting, particularly for the winter, the army will do them little service. Flatbottom boats are much wanted. Our intelligence is so scanty that what we gett from the inland country for the most part is sent to the general by the Rebels. Very few or no spies; we are therefore intirely ignorant of what they are about in the neighborhood. . . .

—FORTESCUE, ed., *Correspondence of King George*, III, 215-216.

3. "A SITUATION TOO GREAT FOR HIS TALENTS"

Lord George Germain who, as Lord Sackville, had been declared "unfit to serve his majesty in any military capacity whatsoever" because of his misconduct in battle during the Seven Years' War, was rehabilitated by George III and appointed in 1775 to the post of Secretary of State for the Colonies. Although he contributed more than his fair share to losing the colonies, he was never backward in criticizing others for their failures. He was at outs with Sir Guy Carleton; had not spoken to Lord Howe for seventeen years; and had no use for Gage. This harsh judgment came after the fiasco of Lexington and Concord; after Bunker's Hill Gage was recalled.

Lord George Germain to Lord Suffolk.

June 16 or 17, 1775

. . . The particulars of the skirmish surprized me very much, as I had no conception the loss of the troops could have been so great when everybody agrees that the men behaved with proper spirit. The disposition I fear was originally defective, and the manner of opposing an enemy that avoids facing you in the open field is totally different from what young officers learn from the common discipline of the army. Mr. Braddock first suffered in the last war by a surprise from the Indians, and his little army was sacrifized without seeing an enemy and, by keeping together and firing in bodys, could neither defend themselves nor annoy their opponents. Another discipline was then established and all our light troops in America were taught to separate and secure themselves by trees, walls or hedges, and became so formidable both to the Indians and Canadians that they were victorious upon all occasions, and ever protected the main body of the army from surprize or insult. Nobody understands that discipline so well as General Howe, who had the command of the light troops, and who will, I am persuaded, teach the present army to be as formidable as that he formerly acted with.

Your Lordship wishes me to write freely. I must then lament that General Gage, with all his good qualitys, finds himself in a situation of too great importance for his talents. The conduct of such a war requires more than common abilities, the distance from the seat of Government necessarily leaves much to the discretion and the resources of the general, and I doubt whether Mr. Gage will venture to take a single step beyond the letter of his instructions, or whether the troops have that opinion of him as to march with confidence of success under his command. This consideration, however, makes taking every measure for immediately increasing your forces the more necessary, and what your Lordship mentions of sending more small ships of war is the surest method of bringing the rebellious part of that continent to reason, for I have no conception, when the trade is effectually stopped, that the numbers of distressed people will not combine in favour of Government, and shake off the power of those factious leaders who have been the authors of the present confusion. . . .

—GR. BRIT. HIST. MSS. COMM., *Stopford-Sackville Manuscripts*, II, 2.

II. BUNKER'S HILL: THE AMERICAN VERSION

The story of Bunker's Hill begins on June 15 when the Committee of Safety got wind of Gage's plan to occupy both Dorchester Heights and the heights on Charlestown peninsula. The next day the Americans moved to forestall the enemy. Acting on orders from General Artemas Ward, Colonel Prescott of Pepperell rounded up his own regiment, elements of other Massachusetts militia regiments, a small contingent of Connecticut troops, and Captain Gridley's company of artillery which boasted two fieldpieces. After a prayer service conducted by President Langdon of Harvard College, this miscellaneous body crossed over Charlestown Neck, and moved out to the tip of the peninsula where they proceeded to throw up defenses on the little knoll later known as Breed's Hill. Early sunrise on June 17 discovered entrenchments of five or six feet on Breed's Hill, a straggling fence along the base of Bunker's Hill, and activity everywhere on the peninsula. The British first attempted to oust the Americans by a smart bombardment from the sea, but with little effect. The ships then turned their guns on the little town nestling below the two hills, and soon reduced Charlestown to ashes; fortunately most of its inhabitants had already fled to the American lines, so the only damage was to property.

Bunker's Hill—as it came to be called—was an altogether greater battle than Lexington or Concord, but the literature dealing with it is not so voluminous. We give here half a dozen narratives of the battle by American hands. Amos Farnsworth, who introduces the story, was a corporal in the Massachusetts militia, from near-by Groton. Peter Brown, who tells us of the labors of the night of the sixteenth, was a clerk in Colonel Prescott's regiment who, notwithstanding his youth, wrote a lively style. Captain John Chester was one of the Connecticut men who were hurried over to reinforce the hard-pressed soldiers on the afternoon of the day of battle. The brief account by Colonel Prescott, though written some two months after the battle, is of particular interest. For though Prescott was not the ranking officer on the field—both Israel Putnam and Joseph Warren outranked him—he was nevertheless in actual command of the fighting. Of him Daniel Webster later said: "From the first breaking of the ground to the retreat, he acted the most important part; and if it were proper to give the battle a name, from any distinguished agent in it, it should be called Prescott's battle." It is not without interest that

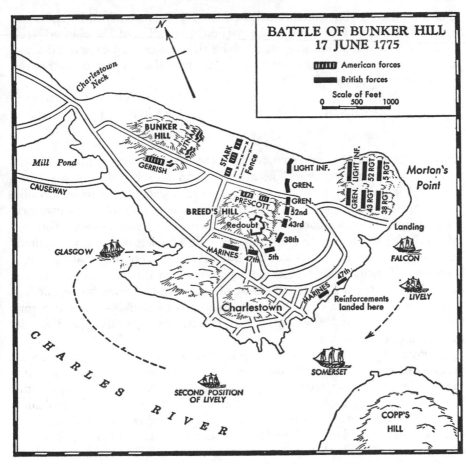

BATTLE OF BUNKER HILL
17 JUNE 1775

American forces
British forces

Scale of Feet
0   500   1000

From The Encyclopedia of American History   *Courtesy of Harper & Brothers*
by Richard B. Morris

Colonel Prescott was the grandfather of the historian of The Conquest of
Mexico *and* The Conquest of Peru.

*Shortly after the battle the Committee of Safety appointed the Reverend
Peter Thacher and two others to write up an official account. Dr. Thacher—
who had witnessed the fight from the near-by Mystic River—wrote the narrative, which was then rushed over to Arthur Lee in London; this version is
taken from a manuscript in the American Antiquarian Society. As a kind of
appendix we include an item on the burning of Charlestown—a letter by
an eyewitness.*

1. THE COMMITTEE OF SAFETY CALLS FOR THE OCCUPATION OF BUNKER'S HILL

Cambridge, June 15, 1775

Whereas, it appears of importance to the safety of this colony that possession of the hill called Bunker's Hill, in Charlestown, be securely kept and
defended; and also, some one hill or hills on Dorchester Neck be likewise secured; therefore, *resolved,* unanimously, that it be recommended to the coun-

cil of war that the above mentioned Bunker's Hill be maintained by sufficient forces being posted there; and as the particular situation of Dorchester Neck is unknown to this committee, they advise that the council of war take and pursue such steps, respecting the same, as to them shall appear to be for the security of this colony.

BENJA. WHITE, *Chairman*
—FROTHINGHAM, *History of the Siege of Boston*, pp. 116-117.

2. "WE WARE OVERPOWERED BY NUMBERS"

Diary of Amos Farnsworth, a corporal in the Massachusetts militia.

Friday June 16. Nothing done in the forenoon; in the afternoon we had orders to be redy to march. At six agreable to orders our regiment preadid and about sun-set we was drawn up and herd prayers; and about dusk marched for Bunkers Hill under command of our own Col Prescott. Just before we turned out of the rode to go up Bunkers-Hill, Charlestown, we was halted; and about sixty men was taken out of our batallion to go into Charlestown, I being one of them. Capt Nutten heded us down to the town house; we sot our centres by the waterside; the most of us got in the town house but had orders not to shut our eyes. Our men marched to Bunker-Hill and begun thair intrenchment and careed it on with the utmost viger all night. Early in the morning I joined them.

Saturday June 17. The enemy appeared to be much alarmed on Saturday morning when thay discovered our operations and immediately began a heavy cannonading from a batery on Corps-Hill, Boston, and from the ships in the harbour. We with little loss continued to carry on our works till 1 o'clock when we discovered a large body of the enemy crossing Charles-River from Boston. Thay landed on a point of land about a mile eastward of our intrenchment and immediately disposed thair army for an attack, previous to which thay set fire to the town of Charlestown. It is supposed that the enemy intended to attack us under the cover of the smoke from the burning houses, the wind favouring them in such a design; while on the other side their army was extending northward towards Mistick-River with an apparant design of surrounding our men in the works, and of cutting of[f] any assistance intended for our relief. Thay ware however in some measure counteracted in this design, and drew their army into closer order.

As the enemy approached, our men was not only exposed to the attack of a very numerous musketry, but to the heavy fire of the battery on Corps-Hill, 4 or 5 men of war, several armed boats or floating batteries in Mistick-River, and a number of field pieces. Notwithstanding we within the intrenchment, and at a breast work without, sustained the enemy's attacks with great bravery and resolution, kiled and wounded great numbers, and repulsed them several times; and after bearing, for about 2 hours, as sever and heavy a fire as perhaps ever was known, and many having fired away all their ammunition, and having no reinforsement, althoe thare was a great boddy of men nie by, we ware over-powered by numbers and obliged to leave the intrenchment, retreating about sunset to a small distance over Charlestown Neck.

N.B. I did not leave the intrenchment untill the enemy got in. I then retreated ten or fifteen rods; then I receved a wound in my rite arm, the bawl gowing through a little below my elbow breaking the little shel bone. Another bawl struk my back, taking a piece of skin about as big as a penny. But I got to Cambridge that night. The town of Charlestown supposed to contain about 300 dwelling-houses, a great number of which ware large and elegant, besides 150 or 200 other buildings, are almost all laid in ashes by the barbarity and wanton cruelty of that infernal villain Thomas Gage.

Oh, the goodness of God in preserving my life althoe thay fell on my right hand and on my left! O, may this act of deliverance of thine, Oh God, lead me never to distrust the[e]; but may I ever trust in the[e] and put confodence in no arm of flesh! I was in great pane the first night with my wound.

—FARNSWORTH, "Diary," *Mass. Hist. Soc. Proc.*, 2nd Series, XII, 83-84.

3. PETER BROWN CONCLUDES THAT "GOD FOUGHT OUR BATTLE FOR US"

Peter Brown to his mother.

Cambridge, June 28, 1775

Frydy the 16th of June we were ordered to parade at 6 o'clock with one day's provisions and blankets ready for a march somewhere, but we did not know where. So we readly and cheerfully obeyed, the whole that was called for, which was these three, Col. Prescotts, Frys and Nicksons regiments. . . . About 9 o'clock at night we marched down on to Charlestown Hill against Cox Hill in Boston where we entrenched, and made a fort of about ten rod long and eight wide, with a breast work of about 8 more. We worked there undiscovered till about 5 in the morn and then we saw our danger, being against 8 ships of the line and all Boston fortified against us.

The danger we were in made us think there was treachery, and that we were brot there to be all slain, and I must and will venture to say that there was treachery, oversight or presumption in the conduct of our officers. And about half after 5 in the morn, we not having above half the fort done, they began to fire, I suppose as soon as they had orders, pretty briskly a few minutes, and then stopt, and then again to the number of about 20 or more. They killed one of us, and then they ceased till about 11 o'clock and then they began pretty brisk again; and that caused some of our young country people to desert, apprehending the danger in a clearer manner than the rest, who were more diligent in digging and fortifying ourselves against them. We began to be almost beat out, being tired by our labour and having no sleep the night before, but little victuals, no drink but rum. . . .

They fired very earm [warm] from Boston and from on board till about 2 o'clock, when they began to fire from the ships in ferry way, and from the ship that lay in the river against the Neck to stop our reinforcements, which they did in some measure. One cannon cut off 3 men in two on the neck of land. Our officers sent time after time after the cannons from Cambridge in the morning and could get but four, the captain of which fired but a few times and then swang his hat round three times to the enemy, then ceased to fire. It being about 3 o'clock, there was a little cessation of the cannons roaring. Come to look, there was a matter of 40 barges full of Regulars coming over to us: it is supposed there were about 3000 of them and about 700 of us left not deserted, besides 500 reinforcements that could not get so night [nigh] to us as to do any good hardly till the[y] saw that we must all be cut off, or some of them, and then they advanced. When our officers saw that the Regulars would land, they ordered the artillery to go out of the fort and prevent their landing if possible, from which the artillery captain took his pieces and went right off home to Cambridge fast as he could, for which he is now confined and we expect will be shot for it.

But the enemy landed and fronted before us and formed themselves in an oblong square, so as to surround us, which they did in part, and after they were well formed they advanced towards us in order to swallow us up, but they found a choaky mouthful of us, tho' we could do nothing with our small arms as yet for distance, and had but two cannon and nary gunner. And they from Boston and from the ships a-firing and throwing bombs keeping us down till they got almost round us. But God in mercy to us fought our battle for us and altho' we were but few and so were suffered to be defeated by them, we were preserved in a most wonderful manner far beyond expectation, to admiration, for out of our regiment there was about 37 killed, 4 or 5 taken captive, and about 47 wounded. . . .

If we should be called into action again I hope to have courage and strength to act my part valiantly in defence of our liberties and our country, trusting in him who hath yet kept me and hath covered my head in the day of battle, and tho' we have lost 4 of our company and our Lieutenant's thigh broke and he taken captive by the cruel enemies of America, I was not suffered to be toutched altho' I was in the fort till the Regulars came in and I jumped over the walls, and ran for about half a mile where balls flew like hailstones and cannons roared like thunder.

Your dutiful Son

Peter Brown

—Dexter, ed., *Literary Diary of Ezra Stiles*, I, 595-596.

4. "I Waited Not but Ran and Hasted to My Company"

Captain John Chester to the Reverend Joseph Fish of Stonington, Connecticut.

Camp at Cambridge, July 22, 1775

Rev. and Much Respected Sir:

. . . I shall endeavor, as far as my time and business will permit, to give you, sir, the particulars of the battle of Charlestown. . . .

As to my own concern in it, with that of my company, would inform that one subaltern, one sergeant and thirty privates were draughted out over night to intrench. They tarried, and fought till the retreat. Just after dinner on Saturday, 17th ult., I was walking out from my lodgings, quite calm and composed, and all at once the drums beat to arms, and bells rang, and a great noise in Cambridge. Capt. Putnam came by on full gallop. "What is the matter?" says I.

"Have you not heard?"

"No."

"Why, the regulars are landing at Charlestown," says he, "and Father says you must all meet and march immediately to Bunker Hill to oppose the enemy."

I waited not, but ran and got my arms and ammunition, and hasted to my company (who were in the church for barracks) and found them nearly ready to march. We soon marched, with our frocks and trowsers on over our other clothes (for our company is in uniform wholly blue, turned up with red), for we were loath to expose ourselves by our dress, and down we marched. I imagined we arrived at the hill near the close of the battle. When we arrived there was not a company with us in any kind of order, although, when we first set out, perhaps three regiments were by our side and near us; but here they were scattered, some behind rocks and hay-cocks, and thirty men, perhaps, behind an apple-tree, and frequently twenty men round a wounded man, retreating, when not more than three or four could touch him to advantage. Others were retreating, seemingly without any excuse, and some said they had left the fort with leave of the officers, because they had been all night and day on fatigue, without sleep, victuals or drink; and some said they had no officers to head them, which, indeed, seemed to be the case.

At last I met with a considerable company who were going off rank and file. I called to the officer that led them, and asked why he retreated. He made me no answer. I halted my men, and told him if he went on it should be at his peril. He still seemed regardless of me. I then ordered my men to make ready. They immediately cocked, and declared if I ordered they would fire. Upon that they stopped short, tried to excuse themselves; but I could not tarry to hear him, but ordered him forward, and he complied.

We were then very soon in the heat of action. Before we reached the summit of Bunker Hill, and while we were going over the Neck, we were in imminent danger from the cannon-shot, which buzzed around us like hail. The musquetry began before we passed the Neck; and when we were on the top of the hill, and during our descent to the foot of it on the south, the small as well as cannon shot were incessantly whistling by us. We joined our army on the right of the centre, just by a poor stone fence, two or three feet high, and very thin, so that the bullets came through. Here we lost our regularity, as every company had done before us, and fought as they did, every man loading and firing as fast as he could. As near as I could guess, we fought standing about six minutes, my officers and men think. . . .

—FROTHINGHAM, *History of the Siege of Boston*, pp. 389-391.

5. "Our Ammunition Being Nearly Exhausted, We Was Obliged to Retreat"

Colonel William Prescott to John Adams.

Camp at Cambridge, Aug. 25, 1775

. . . On the 16th June, in the evening, I received orders to march to Breed's Hill in Charlestown, with a party of about one thousand men, consisting of three hundred of my own regiment, Colonel Bridge and Lieut. Brickett, with a detachment of theirs, and two hundred Connecticut forces, commanded by Captain Knowlton. We arrived at the spot, the lines were drawn by the engineer, and we began the intrenchment about twelve o'clock; and plying the work with all possible expedition till just before sunrising, when the enemy began a very heavy cannonading and bombardment. In the interim the engineer forsook me. Having thrown up a small redoubt, found it necessary to draw a line about twenty rods in length from the fort northerly, under a very warm fire from the enemy's artillery. About this time, the above field officers, being indisposed, could render me but little service, and the most of the men under their command deserted the party.

The enemy continuing an incessant fire with their artillery, about two o'clock in the afternoon on the 17th, the enemy began to land a north-easterly point from the fort, and I ordered the train, with two field-pieces, to go and oppose them, and the Connecticut forces to support them; but the train marched a different course, and I believe those sent to their support followed, as I suppose, to Bunker's Hill. Another party of the enemy landed and fired the town. There was a party of Hampshire, in conjunction with some other forces, lined a fence at the distance of three score rods back of the fort, partly to the north.

About an hour after the enemy landed, they began to march to the attack in three columns. I commanded my Lieutenant-Col. Robinson and Major Woods, each with a detachment, to flank the enemy, who, I have reason to think, behaved with prudence and courage. I was now left with perhaps one hundred and fifty men in the fort. The enemy advanced and fired very hotly on the fort, and meeting with a warm reception, there was a very smart firing on both sides. After a considerable time, finding our ammunition was almost spent, I commanded a cessation till the enemy advanced within thirty yards, when we gave them such a hot fire that they were obliged to retire nearly one hundred and fifty yards before they could rally and come up again to the attack.

Our ammunition being nearly exhausted, could keep up only a scattering fire. The enemy, being numerous, surrounded our little fort, began to mount our lines and enter the fort with their bayonets. We was obliged to retreat through them, while they kept up as hot a fire as it was possible for them to make. We, having very few bayonets, could make no resistence. We kept the fort about one hour and twenty minutes after the attack with small arms. . . .

—Frothingham, *History of the Siege of Boston*, pp. 395-396.

6. The Americans Are Driven from Their Redoubt: Peter Thacher

Eyewitness narrative prepared about two weeks
after the Battle of Bunker Hill.

In consequence of undoubted information received from Boston by the commanders of the Continental Army at Cambridge that Genl Gage with a part of his troops purposed the next day to take possession of Bunker's Hill, a promontory just at the entrance of the peninsula of Charlestown, they determined with the advice of the Committee of Safety of the Massachusetts Province to send a party who might erect some fortifications upon the hill and prevent this design.

Accordingly on the 16th of June, orders were issued that a party of about one thousand men should that evening march to Charlestown and entrench upon the hill. About 9 o clock in the evening the detachment marched upon the design to Breed's hill situated on the further part of the peninsula next to Boston, for by a mistake of orders this hill was marked out for the entrenchment instead of the other. As there were many things necessary to be done preparatory to the entrenchments being thrown up which could not be done before lest the enemy should observe them, it was nearly twelve o clock before the work was entered upon, for the clocks in Boston were heard to strike about 10 minutes after the men first took their tools into their hands. The work was carried on in every animation and success so that by the dawn of the day they had nearly completed a small redoubt about eight rods square.

At this time an heavy fire began from 3 men of war, a number of floating batteries and from a fortification of the enemys on Cops hill in Boston directly opposite to our little redoubt. These kept up an incessant shower of shot and bombs, by which one man pretty soon fell. Not discouraged by the melancholly fate of their companion, the soldiers laboured indefatigably till they had thrown up a small breastwork extending from the north side of the redoubt . . . to the bottom of the hill but were prevented by the intolerable fire of the enemy from completing them whol[ly] in such a manner as to make them defensible.

Having laboured thus between 12 and 1 o'clock a number of boats and barges filled with soldiers were observed approaching towards Charlestown. These landed their troops at a place called Moretons Point, situated a little to the eastward of our works. The brigade formed upon their landing tho they were something galled by the fire of two small field pieces which we had placed at the end of the intrenchments. They stood thus formed till a second brigade arrived from Boston to join them.

Having sent out large flank guards in order to surround them they began a very slow march towards our lines. At this instant flames and smoke were seen to arise in large clouds from the town of Charlestown [which] had been set on fire from some of the enemys batterys with a design to favour their attack upon our lines by the smoke which they imagined would have been blown directly that way and thence covered them in their attack, but the wind changing at this instant it was carried another way.

The provincials in the redoubt and the lines reserved their fire till the enemy had come within about 10 or 12 yards and then discharged at once upon them. The fire threw their body into very great confusion, and all of them after having kept a fire for some time retreated in very great disorder down to the point where they landed, and there some of them even into their boats.

At this time their officers were observed by spectators on the opposite shore to come there and then use the most passionate gestures and even to push forward the men with their swords. At length by their exertions the troops were again rallied and marched up to the entrenchments. The Americans reserved their fire and a second time put the regulars to flight who once more retreated in precipitation to their boats.

The same or greater exertions were now again observed to be made by their officers, and having formed once more they brought some cannon to bear in such a manner as to rake the inside of the breastwork, and having drove the provincials thence into the redoubt they determined now, it appeared, to make a decisive effort. The fire from the ships and batteries as well as from the cannon in front of their army was redoubled. Innumerable bombs were sent into the fort. The officers behind the army of the regulars were observed to goad forward their men with renewed exertion. The breastwork on the side of the entrenchment without the redoubt was abandoned, the ammunition of the provincials was expended, the enemy advanced on three sides of the fort at once and scaled the walls.

Can it be wondered at then that the word was given to retreat? But even this was not done till the redoubt was half filled with regulars, and the provincials had for some time kept up an engagement with the but ends of their muskets which unfortunately were not fixed with bayonets. . . .

With very great signs of exultation the British troops again took possession of the hill whither they had fled after their retreat from Concord, and it was expected that they would have prosecuted the advantage which they had gained by marching immediately to Cambridge which was then indeed in an almost defenceless state; they did not however do this, but kept firing with their cannon from the hill and from their ships and batteries across the Neck. The wonder which was excited and the conduct of them soon ceased when a certain account arrived from Boston that of 3 thousand who marched out on the expedition, no less than 1500, among which were 92 commission officers, were killed and wounded, a more severe blow than the British troops had ever before met with in proportion to the number who were engaged, and the time the engagement lasted from the first fire of the musketry to the last was exactly an hour and an half.

—THACHER, "Narrative," *Historical Magazine*, 2nd Series, III, 382-384.

7. "IT WAS A PRETTY TOWN BUT NOW IT IS NOTHING BUT A HEAP OF RUINS"

Part of a letter from Boston, brought by the *Cerberus*.

Boston, June 23, 1775

. . . An account of the action at Buncker's Hill, at the back of Charlestown, you will have in General Gage's and General Howe's letters. I will only tell you that General Howe was sent out with two thousand five hundred men, or better, to dislodge a body of our troops on Buncker's Hill. When the troops had begun their march, the ships threw carcases into Charlestown and have burned it entirely. It was a pretty town! but now there is not one house left standing! It is nothing but a heap of ruins. Let this dispute end which way it will, though you can never conquer us, this once fair and opulent province is ruined! All America will revenge our cause.

On the first attack your troops gave way; they did not expect so heavy a fire. General Howe rallied them; for near a minute he was quite alone; his aid de camp was killed at his side. The officers brought up the men and suffered for their temerity. General Clinton with another corps presently followed. General Putnam, who had not quite 4000 Connecticut men, thought the whole army was coming and without the least disorder, or even pursued a single step, left Buncker's Hill and went to another hill, about half a mile further, where he has remained ever since, without the least disturbance. If the mercenaries had offered to march a yard after him, General Ward, with his New England men, was ready to give a good account of them. . . .

Believe me you cannot succeed in this mad and wicked attempt to conquer. Every hill will be disputed with you, and every inch of ground. Two more such actions will destroy your army. . . .

—WILLARD, ed., *Letters on the American Revolution*, pp. 143-144.

III. BUNKER'S HILL: THE BRITISH VERSION

The best American accounts of Bunker's Hill come from the pens of ordinary soldiers like Private Peter Brown or Corporal Amos Farnsworth, or from civilian onlookers; it is characteristic that the British accounts should be written by officers like Generals Gage, Howe and Burgoyne and Lord Rawdon. Other differences, too, reflect what we may begin to call national characteristics. The American accounts are informal, almost inchoate; they mirror the disorganized, haphazard character of the American fighting, with its curious mixture of audacity and ineptitude, heroism and cowardice. The British accounts have about them a formal literary quality: they seem (what in effect they were) like reports back home designed to reach the papers or to be used in Parliament. The Americans were, technically, defeated and driven from the peninsula, but their narratives confess no sense of defeat or despair, rather of pride and resolution; the British, who carried the day, sound a uniform note of astonishment, indignation and distress.

It was, indeed, a Pyrrhic victory. Altogether British casualties were about 1,150 out of a total of about 2,500 men engaged, while the Americans lost perhaps 400 out of a total of 1,500 or 1,600. "The loss we have sustained," wrote General Gage, "is greater than we can bear." Certainly it was greater than his reputation could bear. Soon his subordinate Burgoyne was writing of him that "he was an officer totally unsuited for the command," and in October he was recalled, never to fight again.

We give here six British accounts to match the American. First is a letter by Francis, Lord Rawdon, who was in the thick of the fight. He later had a long and distinguished career in the Napoleonic Wars and in India. As with so many of the British officers (he was Irish, and raised a regiment of Volunteers of Ireland in Philadelphia) one feels that he would have preferred a clear-cut defeat at the hands of social equals to this dubious victory over social inferiors! It is interesting to note that Rawdon, like all the other British narrators, finds it necessary greatly to exaggerate American numbers in order to account for the large disparity in casualties, and the fact that only want of powder saved the British from destruction.

Our second account comes from General Sir William Howe who distinguished himself by personal bravery though not by tactical genius in the battle, and who found it intolerable that the Americans should fight in their way rather than in approved European style. After Gage's recall, Howe succeeded to the command—and did no better than his predecessor. "Gentle-

man Johnny" Burgoyne did not have the satisfaction of getting into the thick of the fight, but he did manage to give us the best literary description of the battle that has come down to us. General Gage, whose letter to Lord Barrington is somewhat livelier than his official report, called the engagement a success, but added that "small armies can't afford such losses"; he had no word of criticism for his own strategy or Howe's tactics. There follows an account by an anonymous British officer highly critical of the mismanagement of the whole affair and particularly of Howe's part in it; it was later used at the Inquiry which the Howe brothers called for. We conclude with an outburst of ill-temper from Ann Hulton, Loyalist sister of the commissioner of customs in Boston.

1. "OUR MEN ADVANCED WITH INFINITE SPIRIT"

Francis, Lord Rawdon to his uncle, Francis, tenth Earl of Huntingdon.

Camp on the heights of Charlestown. 1775, June 20, Tues.

I have the pleasure, my dearest Lord, to inform you that we have at length given the rebels a signal defeat. On Saturday last, the 17th of this month, a large party of them were observed at work on the hills above Charlestown, throwing up a battery which would, if perfected, have probably destroyed the greatest part of Boston. The men-of-war in the harbour could not elevate their guns sufficiently to bear upon it, for which reason four twenty-four-pounders were ordered from the artillery park to play upon it. They struck it several times, but being at a great distance, and the work of an extraordinary thickness and solidity, they could make no impression on it.

About noon the Grenadiers (in which corps I am), the Light Infantry and the Second Brigade, in all about 2,400 men, were ordered to embark under the command of General Howe. The shipping kept up so warm a cannonade on the coast that we landed without opposition within half a mile of Charlestown, which the fire from the vessels had forced the rebels to abandon. The work we had seen from Boston was upon the heights just above this town, but upon approaching it we perceived that it was continued quite to the bottom of the hill on the side where we landed. We had halted for some time till our cannon came up, during which time we perceived great numbers of the enemy marching into their works. Our cannon fired upon the entrenchment for some time, but it was so strong that our balls had no effect upon it, and their men kept so close behind it that they were in no danger.

Our men at last grew impatient, and all crying out, "Push on! push on!" advanced with infinite spirit to attack the work with their small arms. As soon as the rebels perceived this, they rose up and poured in so heavy a fire upon us that the oldest officers say they never saw a sharper action. They kept up this fire till we were within ten yards of them; nay, they even knocked down my captain, close beside me, after we had got into the ditch of the entrenchment. Nothing, however, could long resist the courage of our men. The rebels were obliged to abandon the post, but continued a running fight from one fence, or wall, to another, till we entirely drove them off the peninsula of Charlestown. The night coming on we threw up a kind of breast-work and stood to our arms all night, but they did not attack us. We have now fortified our camp, and are in daily expectation of having another brush with them.

Their army consisted of above 6,000 men, a force which, situated as they were, should have kept off five times our number. Our loss is very great. There are above sixty officers killed and wounded, and men in proportion. The rebels had above ninety killed on the spot, besides wounded and prisoners. General Putnam, who commanded them (and is a very brave fellow), was shot through the thigh, but got off. The famous Doctor Warren, the greatest incendiary in all America, was killed on the spot. Only eleven of our Grenadier company are left; other companies have suffered even more. I received no hurt of any kind, but a ball passed through a close cap which I had made in imitation of the foreign travelling caps and wore for convenience sake, for we no longer think of appearances at present. I was everywhere in the thickest of the fire and flatter myself that I behaved as you could wish.

—Gr. Brit. Hist. Mss. Comm., *Hastings Manuscripts*, III, 154-155.

2. General Howe Concludes That "Success Was Too Dearly Bought"

Sir William Howe (probably to the British Adjutant General).

Camp upon the Heights of Charlestown, June 22 and 24

. . . The troops were no sooner ashore than it was instantly perceived the enemy were very strongly posted, the redoubt upon their right being large and full of men with cannon. To the right of the redoubt they had troops in the houses of Charles Town, about 200 yards distant from the redoubt, the intermediate space not occupied, being exposed to the cannon of the Boston side battery.

From the left of the redoubt, they had a line cannon-proof, about 80 yards in length; and from thence to their left, close upon the Mystic River, they had a breast work made with strong railing taken from the fences and stuffed with hay, which effectually secured those behind it from musquettry. This breast work about 300 yards in extent—they had made the whole in the night of the 16th.

As a specimen of our knowledge of service, the centrys on the Boston side had heard the Rebels at work all night without making any other report of it, except mentioning it in conversation in the morning. The first knowledge the General had of it was by hearing one of the ships firing at the workmen, and going to see what occasioned the firing. Their works when we landed were crowded with men, about 500 yards from us.

From the appearance of their situation and numbers, and seeing that they were pouring in all the strength they could collect, I sent to General Gage to desire a reinforcement, which he immediately complied with, the remaining Light Companies and Grenadiers, with the 47th Battalion and 1st of the Marines landing soon after. Our strength being then about 2200 rank and file, with six field pieces, two light 12-pounders and two howitzers, we begun the attack (the troops in two lines, with Pigott upon the left) by a sharp cannonade, the line moving slowly and frequently halting to give time for the artillery to fire.

The Light Companies upon the right were ordered to keep along the beach to attack the left point of the enemy's breast work, which being carried, they were to attack them in flank. The Grenadiers being directed to attack the enemy's left in front, supported by the 5th and 52d, their orders were executed by the Grenadiers and 2 battalions with a laudable perseverance, but not with the greatest share of discipline, for as soon as the order with which they set forward to the attack with bayonets was checked by a difficulty they met with in getting over some very high fences of strong railing, under a heavy fire, well kept up by the Rebels, they began firing, and by crowding fell into disorder, and in this state the 2d line mixt with them. The Light Infantry at the same time being repulsed, there was *a moment that I never felt before,* but by the gallantry of the officers it was all recovered and the attack carried.

Upon the left, Pigott met with the same obstruction from the fences, and also had the troops in the houses to combat with, before he could proceed to assail the redoubt, or to turn it to his left, but the town being set on fire by order at this critical time by a carcass from the battery on the Boston side, Pigott was relieved from his enemies in that quarter, and at the 2d onset he carried the redoubt in the handsomest manner, tho' it was most obstinately defended to the last. Thirty of the Rebels not having time to get away were killed with bayonets in it. The little man is worthy of Our Master's favour.

But I now come to the fatal consequences of this action—92 officers killed and wounded—a most dreadful account. I have lost my aid de camp Sherwin, who was shot thro' the body and died the next day. Our friend Abercrombie is also gone—he had only a flesh wound, but is said to have been in a very bad habit of body. The General's returns will give you the particulars of what I call this unhappy day. I freely confess to you, when I look to the consequences of it, in the loss of so many brave officers, I do it with horror. The success is too dearly bought. Our killed, serjeants and rank and file, about 160; 300 wounded and in hospital, with as many more incapable of present duty. The Rebels left near 100 killed and 30 wounded, but I have this morning learnt from a deserter from them that they had 300 killed and a great number wounded.

We took five pieces of cannon, and their numbers are said to have been near 6000, but I do not suppose they had more than between 4 and 5000 engaged.

The corps remained upon their arms the night of the action, where we are now encamped in a strong situation, with redoubts commanding the isthmus in our front, the enemy being in two corps about one mile and a half distant from us and both well entrenched; the principal body being upon a height called Summer Hill commanding the way from thence to Cambridge; the other called Winter Hill upon the road to Midford (or Mystich) on the side of Roxbury—they are also entrenched and have artillery at all their posts.

Entre nous, I have heard a bird sing that we can do no more this campaign than endeavour to preserve the town of Boston, which it is supposed the Rebels mean to destroy by fire or sword or both—and it is my opinion, with the strength we shall have collected here upon the arrival of the 4 battalions last from Ireland (one of which, with Bailey of the 23d, came in the day before yesterday), that we must not risk the endangering the loss of Boston—tho' should anything offer in our favour, I should hope we may not let pass the opportunity.

The intentions of these wretches are to fortify every post in our way; wait to be attacked at every one, having their rear secure, destroying as many of us as they can before they set out to their next strong situation, and, in this defensive mode (the whole country coming into them upon every action), they must in the end get the better of our small numbers. We can not (as the General tells us) muster more now than 3400 rank and file for duty, including the Marines and the three last regiments from Ireland.

—FORTESCUE, ed., *Correspondence of King George*, III, 220-224.

3. GENERAL BURGOYNE CALLS IT A DAY OF GLORY

To Lord Stanley.

Boston, June 25, 1775

. . . It was absolutely necessary we should make ourselves masters of these heights, and we proposed to begin with Dorchester, because, from the particular situation of batteries and shipping, . . . it would evidently be effected without any considerable loss. Every thing was accordingly disposed; my two colleagues and myself (who, by the by, have never differed one jot of military sentiment) had, in concert with General Gage, formed the plan. Howe was to land the transports on the Point; Clinton in the centre; and I was to cannonade from the causeway or the Neck: each to take advantage of circumstances. The operations must have been very easy; this was to have been executed on the 18th.

On the 17th, at dawn of day, we found the enemy had pushed intrenchments with great diligence during the night, on the heights of Charlestown, and we evidently saw that every hour gave them fresh strength; it therefore became necessary to alter our plan and attack on that side. Howe, as second in command, was detached with about two thousand men, and landed on the outward side of the peninsula, covered with shipping, without opposition; he was to advance from thence up the hill which was over Charlestown, where the strength of the enemy lay; he had under him Brigadier-General Pigot. Clinton and myself took our stand (for we had not any fixed post) in a large battery directly opposite to Charlestown, and commanded it, and also reaching the heights above it, and thereby facilitating Howe's attack.

Howe's disposition was exceedingly soldierlike; in my opinion it was perfect. As his first arm advanced up the hill they met with a thousand impediments from strong fences, and were much exposed. They were also exceedingly hurt by musketry from Charlestown, though Clinton and I did not perceive it until Howe sent us word by a boat and desired us to set fire to the town, which was immediately done; we threw a parcel of shells, and the whole was instantly in flames; our battery afterwards kept an incessant fire on the heights; it was seconded by a number of frigates, floating batteries and one ship-of-the-line.

And now ensued one of the greatest scenes of war that can be conceived: if we look to the height, Howe's corps, ascending the hill in the face of intrenchments, and in a very disadvantageous ground, was much engaged; to the left the enemy pouring in fresh troops by thousands, over the land; and in the arm of the sea our ships and floating batteries cannonading them; straight before us a large and noble town in one great blaze—the church-steeples, being timber, were great pyramids of fire above the rest; behind us, the church-steeples and heights of our own camp covered with spectators of the rest of our army which was engaged; the hills round the country covered with spectators; the enemy all in anxious suspense; the roar of cannon, mortars and musketry; the crash of churches, ships upon the stocks, and whole streets falling together, to fill the ear; the storm of the redoubts, with the objects above described, to fill the eye; and the reflection that, perhaps, a defeat was a final loss to the British Empire in America, to fill the mind—made the whole picture, and a complication of horrour and importance, beyond any thing that ever came to my lot to be witness to.

I much lament Tom's absence; it was a sight for a young soldier that the longest service may not furnish again; and had he been with me he would likewise have been out of danger; for, except for two cannon balls that went a hundred yards over our heads, we were not in any part of the direction of the enemy's shot.

A moment of the day was critical: Howe's left were staggered; two battalions had been sent to re-enforce them, but we perceived them on the beach seeming in embarrassment what way to march. Clinton then, next for business, took the part without waiting for orders, to throw himself into a boat to head them; he arrived in time to be of service; the day ended with glory, and the success was most important, considering the ascendancy it gave the Regular troops; but the loss was uncommon in officers for the numbers engaged. . . .

—FORCE, *American Archives*, 4th Series, II, 1094-1095.

4. GENERAL GAGE: "THE LOSS IS GREATER THAN WE CAN BEAR"

To Lord Barrington, Secretary of State for War.

Boston, June 26, 1775

My Lord: You will receive an account of some success against the Rebels, but attended with a long list of killed and wounded on our side; so many of the latter that the hospital has hardly hands sufficient to take care of them. These people shew a spirit and conduct against us they never shewed against the French, and every body has judged of them from their formed appearance and behaviour when joyned with the Kings forces in the last war; which has led many into great mistakes.

They are now spirited up by a rage and enthousiasm as great as ever people were possessed of, and you must proceed in earnest or give the business up. A small body acting in one spot will not avail. You must have large armys, making divertions on different sides, to divide their force.

The loss we have sustained is greater than we can bear. Small armys cant afford such losses, especially when the advantage gained tends to little more than the gaining of a post—a material one indeed, as our own security depended on it. The troops are sent out too late, the Rebels were at least two months before-hand with us, and your Lordship would be astonished to see the tract of country they have entrenched and fortifyed; their number is great, so many hands have been employed.

We are here, to use a common expression, taking the bull by the horns, attacking the enemy in their strong parts. I wish this cursed place was burned. The only use is its harbour, which may be said to be material; but in all other respects it is the worst place either to act offensively from, or defencively. I have before wrote your Lordship my opinion that a large army must at length be employed to reduce these people, and mentioned the hiring of foreign troops. I fear it must come to that, or else to avoid a land war and make use only of your fleet. I dont find one province in appearance better disposed than another, tho' I think if this army was in New York, that we should find many friends, and be able to raise forces in that province on the side of Government. . . .

—CARTER, ed., *Correspondence of Gage*, II, 686-687.

5. "TOO GREAT A CONFIDENCE OCCASIONED THE DREADFUL LOSS"

Letter of a British officer.

Boston, July 5, 1775

We have lost 1000 men killed and wounded. We burned Charlestown during the engagement, as the rebels from it exceedingly galled our left. Major Pitcairn was killed from it. Too great a confidence in ourselves, which is always dangerous, occasioned this dreadful loss. "Let us take the bull by the horns" was the phrase of some great men among us, as we marched on. We went to battle without even reconnoitering the position of the enemy. Had we only wanted to drive them from their ground, without the loss of a man, the *Cymetry* transport, which drew little water and mounted 18 nine-pounders, could have been towed up Mystic Channel and brought to within musket-shot of their left flank, which was quite naked, and she could have lain water-borne at the lowest ebb tide; or one of our covered boats, musket-proof, carrying a heavy piece of cannon, might have been rowed close in, and one charge on their uncovered flank would have dislodged them in a moment. Had we intended to have taken the whole rebel army prisoners, we needed only have landed in their rear and occupied the high ground above Bunker's hill. By this movement we shut them up in the peninsula as in a bag, their rear exposed to the fire of our cannon and if we pleased our musquetry. In short, they must have surrendered instantly or been blown to pieces.

But from an absurd and destructive confidence, carelessness or ignorance, we have lost a thousand of our best men and officers and have given the rebels great matter of triumph by showing them what mischief they can do us. They were not followed, though Clinton proposed it. Their deserters since tell us that not a man would have remained at Cambridge, had but a single regiment been seen coming along the Neck.

Had we seen and rejected all the advantages I have mentioned above, even our manner of attacking in front was ruinous. In advancing, not a shot should have been fired, as it retarded the troops, whose movement should have been as rapid as possible. They should not have been brought up in line, but in columns with light infantry in the intervals, to keep up a smart fire against the top of the breastwork. If this had been done, their works would have been carried in three minutes, with not a tenth part of our present loss. We should have been forced to retire, if Gen. Clinton had not come up with a reinforcement of 5 or 600 men. This re-established the left under Pigot and saved our honour.

The wretched blunder of the over-sized balls sprung from the dotage of an officer of rank in that corps, who spends his whole time in dallying with the schoolmaster's daughters. God knows he is old enough—he is no Sampson—yet he must have his Dalilah.

Another circumstance equally true and astonishing is that Gen. Gage had undoubted intelligence early in May that the rebels intended to possess Bunker's hill; yet no step was taken to secure that important post, though it commanded all the north part of the town. He likewise had an exact return of the corps that composed the rebel army then investing the town; of every piece of cannon they possessed; of their intended lines of blockade; and of the numbers expected and on their march from the other provinces.

We are all wrong at the head. My mind cannot help dwelling upon our cursed mistakes. Such ill conduct at the first out-set argues a gross ignorance of the most common rules of the profession, and gives us, for the future, anxious forebodings. I have lost some of those I most valued. This madness or ignorance nothing can excuse. The brave men's lives were wantonly thrown away. Our conductor as much murdered them as if he had cut their throats himself on Boston Common. Had he fallen, ought we to have regretted him?   —*Detail and Conduct of the American War*, pp. 13-15.

6. Gentlemen Fall by the Hands of Despicable Wretches: Ann Hulton

Boston, June 20, 1775

...From the heights of this place we have a view of the whole town, the harbor and country round for a great extent, and last Saturday I was a spectator of a most awful scene my eyes ever beheld.

On the morning of the 17th it was observed that the rebels had thrown up a breastwork and were preparing to open a battery upon the heights above Charlestown, from whence they might incommode the shipping and destroy the north part of Boston. Immediately a cannonading began from the battery in the north part of the town and the ships of war on those works and on the enemy wherever they could be discovered within reach of their guns.

Soon after eleven o'clock the grenadiers, light infantry, marines and two battalions marched out of their encampments and embarked in boats, and before high water were landed on a point of land to the eastward of Charlestown, and they immediately took post on a little eminence. Great was our trepidation lest they should be attacked by superior numbers before they could be all assembled and properly prepared, but more boats arrived, and the whole advanced, some on the other side, round the hill where the battery was erected, and some through part of Charlestown.

On that side of the hill which was not visible from Boston, it seems very strong lines were thrown up and were occupied by many thousands of the rebels. The troops advanced with great ardor towards the intrenchments, but were much galled in the assault, both from the artillery and the small arms, and many brave officers and men were killed and wounded. As soon as they got to the intrenchments, the rebels fled, and many of them were killed in the trenches and in their flight. The marines, in marching through part of Charlestown, were fired at from the houses, and there fell their brave commander, Major Pitcairn. His son was likewise wounded. Hearing his father was killed, he cried out, "I have lost my father"; immediately the corps returned, "We have lost our father." How glorious to die with such an epitaph!

Upon the firing from the houses, the town was immediately set in flames, and at four o'clock we saw the fire and the sword, all the horrors of war raging. The town was burning all night; the rebels sheltered themselves in the adjacent hills and the neighborhood of Cambridge, and the army possessed themselves of Charlestown Neck. We were exulting in seeing the flight of our enemies, but in an hour or two we had occasion to mourn and lament. Dear was the purchase of our safety! In the evening the streets were filled with the wounded and the dying; the sight of which, with the lamentations of the women and children over their husbands and fathers, pierced one to the soul. We were now every moment hearing of some officer or other of our friends and acquaintance who had fallen in our defence and in supporting the honor of our country. . . .

The rebels have occupied a hill about a mile from Charlestown Neck; they are very numerous, and have thrown up intrenchments, and are raising a redoubt on the higher part, whilst the ships and troops cannonade them wherever they can reach them. In the same manner, on the other side of Boston Neck, on the high ground above Roxbury meeting [house], the rebels are intrenching and raising a battery. Such is our present situation.

In this army are many of noble family, many very respectable, virtuous and amiable characters, and it grieves one that gentlemen, brave British soldiers, should fall by the hands of such despicable wretches as compose the banditti of the country; amongst whom there is not one that has the least pretension to be called a gentleman. They are a most rude, depraved, degenerate race, and it is a mortification to us that they speak English and can trace themselves from that stock.

Since Adams went to Philadelphia, one Warren, a rascally patriot and apothecary of this town, has had the lead in the Provincial Congress. He signed commissions and acted as President. This fellow happily was killed, in coming out of the trenches the other day, where he had commanded and spirited the people, etc., to defend the lines, which, he assured them, were impregnable. You may judge what the herd must be when such a one is their leader. Here it is only justice to say that there are many worthy people in this province, but that the chief of them are now in Boston, and that amongst the gentlemen of the Council particularly are many respectable and worthy characters.

—HULTON, *Letters of a Loyalist Lady*, pp. 97-100.

CHAPTER FIVE

The Battle for Boston

AFTER THE *battle of Bunker's Hill, Gage was just about where he had been before: weakened by heavy casualties and hemmed in by an American army that seemed to grow constantly in strength. This was, in fact, an illusion; had Gage seized the offensive at once after the battle of June 17 he might well have driven the Americans from their lines. For the Americans were disorganized, and lacked powder, ammunition and supplies. And while Gage did not have the strength for a frontal attack he did control the coastal waters and might well have flanked the Americans by sea.*

In July however the American cause took a dramatic turn for the better. Just a month after the Second Continental Congress met in Philadelphia it took the army outside Boston under its wing, and appointed George Washington commander in chief. It was an act second in importance only to the Declaration of Independence the following year.

When, early in July, Washington arrived in Cambridge to take command (not, apparently, under the "Washington" elm) of the forces there, he was appalled at what he found. Though the American forces numbered some 16,000 or 17,000, there was no real army, no unified command, no proper discipline, no adequate commissary, no provision for military supplies, and no money. Worst of all, most of the soldiers had enlisted for short terms only, and insisted on going home when their time was up. Washington's first task was not to fight, but to create an army capable of fighting. To this task he addressed himself with inexhaustible energy, with firmness, and with a patience that sometimes wore thin. Gradually, over the months, he got long-term enlistments, stiffened discipline, built barracks, accumulated supplies, weeded out incompetent officers, pried some money loose from the Congress, and whipped the army together into a fighting force.

Fortunately that summer and fall the British had no stomach for the offensive. Bunker's Hill had been a shock; reinforcements came in slowly; Admiral Graves was not to be relied on. In September Gage was recalled, and Howe appointed to the command, but the new general showed no more energy or initiative than his predecessor. Steadily through the fall and winter months disease, desertion and demoralization took their toll. Reinforcements poured in, but presented an additional burden on the inadequate supply of food, fuel and medicines rather than new strength. The Navy made sporadic displays of force, but without substantial results: in October there was an inglorious attack on Bristol, Rhode Island, to get sheep and cattle; Falmouth,

Maine, was gratuitously burned; and throughout the winter there was a series of skirmishes on the islands in the bay, mostly inconclusive.

During December the American army was in danger of total disintegration, but a new army was recruited and drilled and whipped into shape; by January 10, 1776, there were some 8,200 men on the rolls, and by March the number had increased to about 16,000. Washington wished to take the offensive, or at least to draw Howe out for a fight, but the shortage of powder and of guns frustrated this plan. Late in January, Henry Knox brought in 45 cannon and 16 mortars which he had hauled across the snow from Lake Champlain; the supply of powder improved, and Washington felt strong enough to act. To his brother-in-law Burwell Bassett he wrote that "we are preparing to take possession of a post which will, it is generally thought, bring on a rumpus between us and the enemy." The post was Dorchester Heights.

On March 4 General John Thomas with 2,000 men moved onto Dorchester Heights and threw up prefabricated defenses. It was Bunker's Hill over again, only this time the Americans held all the advantages—and this time there was a new commanding general. Howe decided to counterattack at once, but bad weather intervened, and when the weather cleared, it was too late. When on March 16 Washington fortified Foster's Hill (or Nook's Hill) commanding Boston, Howe saw that the game was up, and next morning he abandoned the city which the British had held so long. Ten days later the whole army sailed for Halifax, taking with them more than a thousand hapless Loyalists.

Thus, eleven months after the opening of hostilities, the battle for Boston came to an end. Confronted by colonial intransigence, the British had chosen to be tough, and their policy of toughness had brought them disaster everywhere. They had been defeated along the road from Concord to Boston, defeated again at Bunker's Hill—that was now clear—and finally forced out of Boston. New York was in the hands of the Americans, and so too Ticonderoga and Crown Point, and Dunmore had been forced to flee Virginia. After only one year of fighting the British had been ousted from their colonies. And meantime the Americans had moved steadily toward independence. They had created state governments that carried on all the ordinary business of government; they had cemented a political union; they had organized and maintained an army; they had inspired an American party in Parliament, and in Britain; they had excited the sympathy and the timid aid of France. And in Jefferson, in Franklin, in John Adams, in John Jay, and in Washington they had found leaders far more capable than those who directed the destinies of Britain at this crisis.

I. WASHINGTON IS APPOINTED TO THE COMMAND OF THE AMERICAN ARMY

The Second Continental Congress met in Philadelphia on May 10, 1775; it took members a month to get around to the pressing military problems presented by the fighting around Boston. Early in June the Congress com-

*mitted itself to some kind of responsibility for the armies besieging Boston,
and on June 15 it took a step which was to prove decisive. On motion from
John Adams it unanimously appointed George Washington "to command
all the continental forces." The reasons for the choice of Washington were
obvious and compelling. Of all Americans he had the most lustrous military
reputation; he was from Virginia and both Adamses thought it desirable to
play down the New England role by electing a Southerner to the chief command; he was rich and aristocratic; a moderate but indubitably a Patriot, he
had a bearing and a character that inspired confidence. It is suggestive that
no other name was proposed or even considered (except perhaps by Hancock
himself); it is interesting that the usually jaundiced John Adams could write
to his wife Abigail of "the modest and virtuous, the amiable, generous, and
brave George Washington."*

*Washington accepted the command in a speech of simplicity and mod-
esty; and with a characteristic gesture he added that he would refuse any
compensation above his expenses; throughout the war he held rigorously to
this decision.*

*At the same time Congress pushed ahead with a more elaborate military
establishment. Four major generals were named: Artemas Ward, then commanding the New England troops before Boston; Charles Lee, an adventurer
and soldier of fortune who had fought in both the British and Polish armies,
and who capitalized on his inflated reputation by holding Congress up for a
total of some £11,000 in payment of debts and other obligations; Philip
Schuyler of New York who, like Washington, had a military reputation from
the French and Indian War, vast estates, aristocratic connections and a zeal
for liberty, but who lacked Washington's military competence; and finally
Connecticut's hero, the ancient but still active General Israel Putnam.*

*Washington left Philadelphia on June 23 and arrived in Cambridge ten
days later. There he was met by a delegation from the Massachusetts Provincial Congress with an address apologizing for the condition of the army.
"The hurry with which it was necessarily collected and the many disadvantages arising from a suspension of government," they said, accounted for
much of the difficulty. And the General would also please to remember that
the greatest part of the soldiers "have never before seen service; and although
naturally brave and of good understanding, yet, for want of experience in
military life, have but little knowledge of divers things most essential to the
preservation of health and even life." Washington set himself at once to the
task of making good these deficiencies, and within three weeks was able to
write to General Schuyler—then on duty in New York—that "Confusion and
Disorder reigned in every Department. . . . However we mend every Day,
and I flatter myself that in a little Time we shall work up these raw materials into good stuff."*

1. John Adams Nominates George Washington

From his Autobiography.

   . . . Mr. Hancock himself had an ambition to be appointed commander-
in-chief. Whether he thought an election a compliment due to him, and

intended to have the honor of declining it, or whether he would have accepted, I know not. To the compliment he had some pretensions, for, at that time, his exertions, sacrifices and general merits in the cause of his country had been incomparably greater than those of Colonel Washington. But the delicacy of his health, and his entire want of experience in actual service, though an excellent militia officer, were decisive objections to him in my mind. In canvassing this subject, out of doors, I found too that even among the delegates of Virginia there were difficulties. The apostolical reasonings among themselves, which should be greatest, were not less energetic among the saints of the ancient dominion than they were among us of New England. In several conversations, I found more than one very cool about the appointment of Washington, and particularly Mr. Pendleton was very clear and full against it.

Full of anxieties concerning these confusions, and apprehending daily that we should hear very distressing news from Boston, I walked with Mr. Samuel Adams in the State House yard, for a little exercise and fresh air, before the hour of Congress, and there represented to him the various dangers that surrounded us. He agreed to them all, but said, "What shall we do?" I answered him that he knew I had taken great pains to get our colleagues to agree upon some plan, that we might be unanimous; but he knew that they would pledge themselves to nothing; but I was determined to take a step which should compel them and all the other members of Congress to declare themselves for or against something. "I am determined this morning to make a direct motion that Congress should adopt the army before Boston, and appoint Colonel Washington commander of it." Mr. Adams seemed to think very seriously of it, but said nothing.

Accordingly, when Congress had assembled, I rose in my place, and in as short a speech as the subject would admit, represented the state of the Colonies, the uncertainty in the minds of the people, their great expectation and anxiety, the distresses of the army, the danger of its dissolution, the difficulty of collecting another, and the probability that the British army would take advantage of our delays, march out of Boston, and spread desolation as far as they could go. I concluded with a motion, in form, that Congress would adopt the army at Cambridge, and appoint a General; that though this was not the proper time to nominate a General, yet, as I had reason to believe this was a point of the greatest difficulty, I had no hesitation to declare that I had but one gentleman in my mind for that important command, and that was a gentleman from Virginia who was among us and very well known to all of us, a gentleman whose skill and experience as an officer, whose independent fortune, great talents, and excellent universal character would command the approbation of all America, and unite the cordial exertions of all the Colonies better than any other person in the Union.

Mr. Washington, who happened to sit near the door, as soon as he heard me allude to him, from his usual modesty darted into the library-room. Mr. Hancock—who was our President, which gave me an opportunity to observe his countenance while I was speaking on the state of the Colonies, the army at Cambridge, and the enemy—heard me with visible pleasure; but when I came to describe Washington for the commander, I never remarked a more sudden and striking change of countenance. Mortification and resentment were expressed as forcibly as his face could exhibit them. Mr. Samuel Adams seconded the motion, and that did not soften the President's physiognomy at all.

The subject came under debate, and several gentlemen declared themselves against the appointment of Mr. Washington, not on account of any personal objection against him, but because the army were all from New England, had a General of their own, appeared to be satisfied with him, and had proved themselves able to imprison the British army in Boston, which was all they expected or desired at that time. Mr. Pendleton, of Virginia, Mr. Sherman, of Connecticut, were very explicit in declaring this opinion; Mr. Cushing and several others more faintly expressed their opposition, and their fears of discontents in the army and in New England. Mr. Paine expressed a great opinion of General Ward and a strong friendship for him, having been his classmate at college, or at least his contemporary; but gave no opinion upon the question.

The subject was postponed to a future day. In the mean time, pains were taken out of doors to obtain a unanimity, and the voices were generally so clearly in favor of Washington that the dissentient members were persuaded to withdraw their opposition, and Mr. Washington was nominated, I believe by Mr. Thomas Johnson of Maryland, unanimously elected, and the army adopted.

–ADAMS, ed., *Works of John Adams*, II, 415-418.

2. "I Do Not Think Myself Equal to the Command"

[June 16, 1775]

Mr. President: Tho' I am truly sensible of the high Honour done me in this Appointment, yet I feel great distress from a consciousness that my abilities and Military experience may not be equal to the extensive and important Trust: However as the Congress desires I will enter upon the momentous duty, and exert every power I Possess In their Service for the Support of the glorious Cause: I beg they will accept my most cordial thanks for this distinguished testimony of their Approbation.

But lest some unlucky event should happen unfavourable to my reputation, I beg it may be remembered by every Gentleman in the room, that I this day declare with the utmost sincerity, I do not think myself equal to the Command I am honoured with.

As to pay, Sir, I beg leave to Assure the Congress that as no pecuniary consideration could have tempted me to have accepted this Arduous employment, (at the expence of my domestic ease and happiness) I do not wish to make any proffit from it: I will keep an exact Account of my expences; those I doubt not they will discharge and that is all I desire.

GEORGE WASHINGTON
–FITZPATRICK, ed., *Writings of Washington*, III, 292-293.

3. "A Kind of Destiny Has Thrown Me upon This Service"

George Washington to Martha Washington.

Philadelphia, June 18, 1775

My Dearest:

I am now set down to write to you on a subject which fills me with inexpressible concern, and this concern is greatly aggravated and increased, when I reflect upon the uneasiness I know it will give you. It has been determined in Congress, that the whole army raised for the defence of the American cause shall be put under my care, and that it is necessary for me to proceed immediately to Boston to take upon me the command of it.

You may believe me, my dear Patsy, when I assure you, in the most solemn manner that, so far from seeking this appointment, I have used every endeavor in my power to avoid it, not only from my unwillingness to part with you and the family, but from a consciousness of its being a trust too great for my capacity, and that I should enjoy more real happiness in one month with you at home, than I have the most distant prospect of finding abroad, if my stay were to be seven times seven years. But as it has been a kind of destiny, that has thrown me upon this service, I shall hope that my undertaking it is designed to answer some good purpose. You might, and I suppose did perceive, from the tenor of my letters, that I was apprehensive I could not avoid this appointment, as I did not pretend to intimate when I should return. That was the case. It was utterly out of my power to refuse this appointment, without exposing my character to such censures, as would have reflected dishonor upon myself, and given pain to my friends. This, I am sure, could not, and ought not, to be pleasing to you, and must have lessened me considerably in my own esteem. I shall rely, therefore, confidently on that Providence, which has heretofore preserved and been bountiful to me, not doubting but that I shall return safe to you in the fall. I shall feel no pain from the toil or the danger of the campaign; my unhappiness will flow from the uneasiness I know you will feel from being left alone. I therefore beg, that you will summon your whole fortitude, and pass your time as agreeably as possible. Nothing will give me so much sincere satisfaction as to hear this, and to hear it from your own pen. My earnest and ardent desire is, that you would pursue any plan that is most likely to produce content, and a tolerable degree of tranquillity; as it must add greatly to my uneasy feelings to hear, that you are dissatisfied or complaining at what I really could not avoid.

As life is always uncertain, and common prudence dictates to every man the necessity of settling his temporal concerns, while it is in his power, and while the mind is calm and undisturbed, I have, since I came to this place (for I had not time to do it before I left home) got Colonel Pendleton to draft a will for me, by the directions I gave him, which will I now enclose. The provision made for you in case of my death will, I hope, be agreeable.

I shall add nothing more, as I have several letters to write, but to desire that you will remember me to your friends, and to assure you that I am with the most unfeigned regard, my dear Patsy, your affectionate, &c.

—FITZPATRICK, ed., *Writings of Washington*, III, 293-295.

4. ADAM'S FALL: THE TRIP TO CAMBRIDGE

1775

When Congress sent great Washington
    All clothed in power and breeches,
To meet old Britain's warlike sons
    And make some rebel speeches;

'Twas then he took his gloomy way
    Astride his dapple donkeys,
And travelled well, both night and day,
    Until he reached the Yankees.

Away from camp, 'bout three miles off,
    From Lily he dismounted,
His sergeant brushed his sun-burnt wig
    While he the specie counted.

All prinkéd up in *full* bag-wig,
    The shaking notwithstanding,
In leathers tight, oh glorious sight!
    He reached the Yankee landing.

The women ran, the darkeys too;
    And all the bells, they tolléd;
For Britain's son, by Doodle doo,
    We're sure to be consoléd. . . .

Full many a child went into camp,
    All dressed in homespun kersey,
To see the greatest rebel scamp
    That ever crossed o'er Jersey. . . .

Upon a stump, he placed himself,
    Great Washington did he,
And through the nose of lawyer Close
    Proclaimed great Liberty.

The patriot brave, the patriot fair,
    From fervor had grown thinner,
So off they marched, with patriot zeal,
    And took a patriot dinner.

—MOORE, ed., *Songs and Ballads*, pp. 99-102.

5. WASHINGTON SURVEYS THE CONDITION OF THE ARMY

To his brother John Augustine Washington.

Camp at Cambridge, July 27, 1775

On the 2nd Inst. I arrived at this place, after passing through a great deal of delightful Country, covered with grass, (although the Season has been dry) in a very different manner to what our Lands in Virginia are.

I found a mixed multitude of People here, under very little discipline, order, or Government. I found the enemy in possession of a place called Bunker's Hill, on Charles Town Neck, strongly Intrenched, and Fortifying themselves; I found part of our Army on two Hills, (called Winter and Prospect Hills) about a Mile and a quarter from the enemy on Bunker's Hill, in a very insecure state; I found another part of the Army at this Village; and a third part at Roxbury, guarding the Entrance in and out of Boston.

My whole time, since I came here, has been Imployed in throwing up Lines of Defence at these three several places; to secure, in the first Instance, our own Troops from any attempts of the Enemy; and, in the next, to cut off all Communication between their troops and the Country; For to do this, and to prevent them from penetrating into the Country with Fire and Sword, and to harass them if they do, is all that is expected of me; and if effected, must totally overthrow the designs of Administration, as the whole Force of Great Britain in the Town and Harbour of Boston can answer no other end than to sink her under the disgrace and weight of the expense. Their Force, including Marines, Tories, &c., are computed, from the best accounts I can get, at about 12,000 Men; ours, including Sick absent, &c., at about 16,000; but then we have a Cemi Circle of Eight or Nine Miles, to guard to every part of which we are obliged to be equally attentive; whilst they, situated as it were in the Center of the Cemicircle, can bend their whole Force (having the entire command of the Water), against any one part of it with equal facility; This renders our Situation not very agreeable, though necessary; however, by incessant labour (Sundays not excepted), we are in a much better posture of defence than when I first came. . . .

The Enemy are sickly, and scarce of Fresh provisions. Beef, which is chiefly got by slaughtering their Milch Cows in Boston, sells from one shilling to 18d. Sterling per lb.; and that it may not get cheaper, or more plenty, I have drove all the Stock, within a considerable distance of this place, back into the Country, out of the Way of the Men of war's Boats; In short, I have, and shall continue to do, every thing in my power to distress them. The Transports are all arrived and their whole Reinforcement is Landed, so that I can see no reason why they should not, if they ever attempt it, come boldly out and put the matter to Issue at once; if they think themselves not strong enough to do this, they surely will carry their Arms (having Ships of War and Transports ready) to some other part of the Continent, or relinquish the dispute; the last of which the Ministry, unless compelled, will never agree to do. Our Works, and those of the Enemy are so near and quite open between that we see every thing that each other is doing. I recollect nothing more worth mentioning. I shall therefore conclude with my best wishes, and love to my Sister and Family, and Compliments to any enquiring Friends, your most affectionate brother.

—FITZPATRICK, ed., *Writings of Washington*, III, 371-373.

II. BOSTON UNDER SIEGE

No other city in America had suffered so much from the quarrel with the mother country as Boston. Troops had been quartered there in 1768, and in 1770 had perpetrated the famous "massacre"; it had been the scene of the most giddy of many "tea parties"; it had been singled out for punishment and perhaps destruction by the Intolerable Acts. Now, after Lexington and Concord, it was an occupied city and a city besieged. Many of its inhabitants had fled the city at the commencement of hostilities, and during the summer Gage permitted others to go. By July its population had declined from 17,000 to less than 7,000 civilians.

Not all of those who remained behind were Loyalists. Some stayed because they had no other place to go; others—like John Andrews—to take care of their property or their business; still others for personal or professional reasons. When Howe finally sailed away in March only about 1,000 Loyalists went with him—a small fraction of the remaining population. Meantime those who chose to stay on in the city suffered all the hardships of the siege and of exposure to the enemy. They endured shortages of food and fuel; they were exposed to the somewhat moderate dangers of bombardment and fire; their property was exposed to the ravages of a soldiery not too particular about distinctions between Loyalists and Rebels.

We give here two accounts from the pens of men who lived through the siege: the inveterate letter writer John Andrews, and Deacon Timothy Newell of the Brattle Street Church; one comment from the ever-vivacious Abigail Adams; one letter from an anonymous British officer whose opinions were equally contemptuous of American ladies and American soldiers; and a ballad which enjoyed wide—and perhaps undeserved—popularity in American camps at the time.

1. "PORK AND BEANS ONE DAY AND BEANS AND PORK ANOTHER"

John Andrews to William Barrell.

June 1, 1775

Your favor of the 2nd May per post came to hand but a few days since. You earnestly request my writing you by *every* post, at which time you did not consider the embarrassments we are under in town, and that a letter cannot pass without being liable to the inspection of both parties, unless by water. I wrote you by Breck, as well as by Mr. Prince, which letters I presume you have received. If my brother can get a pass to go out, shall give him this to forward, if possible, without inspection. Its hard to stay cooped up here and feed upon salt provissions, more especially without one's wife, Bill, but at the same time would not wish to have her here under the present disagreable circumstances—though I find an absolute necessity to be here myself, as the soldiery think they have a license to plunder every one's house and store who leaves the town, of which they have given convincing proofs already. And the wanton destruction of property at the late fire makes the duty, in my mind, more incumbent on me.

We have now and then a carcase offered for sale in the market, which formerly we would not have picked up in the street; but bad as it is, it readily sells for eight pence lawful money per lb., and a quarter of lamb when it makes its appearance, which is rarely once a week, sells for a dollar, weighing only three or three and a half pounds. To such shifts has the necessity of the times drove us; wood not scarcely to be got at twenty two shillings a cord. Was it not for a triffle of salt provissions that we have, 'twould be impossible for us to live. Pork and beans one day, and beans and pork another, and fish when we can catch it. Am necessitated to submit to such living or risque the little all I have in the world, which consists in my stock of goods and furniture to the amount of between two and three thousand sterling, as it's said without scruple that those who leave the town forfeit all the effects they leave behind. Whether they hold it up as *only* a means to detain people or not, I cant say—but in regard to slaves their actions have been consistant with the doctrine, however absurd. It has so far availed as to influence many to stay, who would otherways have gone.

—ANDREWS, "Letters," *Mass. Hist. Soc. Proc.*, VIII, 405-408.

2. TIMOTHY NEWELL DESCRIBES LIFE UNDER BRITISH OCCUPATION

From his Journal.

10th July [*1775*]. Provincials last night attacked the centinels at the lines, and burnt Brown's shop.

12th. Two men of war made a heavy fire on Long Island. The Provincials last night in 65 whale boats and 500 men went over to Long Island and took off 31 head of cattle, with a number of sheep and quantity of hay, and likewise seized on and brought off fourteen of the King's mowers with the family belonging to the island. The next day they returned again and set fire to the mansion house and barn, etc.—this within sight of the man of war, who kept up a constant fire on them.

14th. Last night was awoke by the discharge of cannon on the lines. Master James Lovell, Master Leach, John Hunt, have been imprisoned some time past—all they know why it is so is they are charged with free speaking on the public measures; Dorrington, his son and daughter and the nurse for blowing up fires in the evening—they are charged with giving signals in this way to the army without.

20th. Mr. Carpenter was taken by the night patrole. Upon examination he had swam over to Dorchester and back again, was tried here that day and sentence of death passed on him and to be executed the next day—his coffin brot into the gaol yard, his halter bought and he dressed as criminals are before execution. Sentence was respited and a few days after was pardoned.

23d. The Castle, it is publicly talked, will be dismantled. This evening many guns fired at and from the man of war at N. Boston. Ten or twelve transports it is said sailed this day with 150 soldiers upon a secret expedition for provisions.

August 1st. This week passed tolerably quiet. Last night at half past 12 oclock was awoke with a heavy firing from a man of war at the Provincials on Phip's farm. From the lines at Charlestown and Boston it appeared as if a general attack was made. The firing continued till 6 oclock. The George Tavern was burnt by the Regulars and the house at the light house by the Provincials (about 300) who took about 30 soldiers and a number of carpenters. This morning half past 4 oclock awoke with cannonade and small arms from Charlestown which lasted till eleven oclock after that.

Very trying scenes.

This day was invited by two gentlemen to dine upon *rats*. The whole of this day till sunset a constant fire up Mistic River from the lines and out centinels at Charlestown and the Provincials from Mount Prospect.

4th. John Gill imprisoned, charged with printing sedition, treason and rebellion.

6th. Skirmishing up Mistic River, upon which the Provincials and they had a skirmish, many shots exchanged but nothing decisive.

15th. Cannonade from the lines most of this afternoon on both sides. The General's fleet of transports arrived from their cruise, having taken from the islands of Gardners, etc., about two thousand sheep, one hundred and ten oxen, butter, eggs, etc., etc.

16th. Cannonade from both lines.

17th. Cannonade again.

19th. Ditto. A 42-pounder split on the lines, killed a bombardier and wounded one or two men.

20th to 25th. Daily firing from the lines and from the centinels on both sides.

27th Sabbath. Cannonading from the lines at Charlestown on new works— a nearer approach, also much firing of small arms.

29th. Several bombs from ditto on ditto in the night.

30th. Ditto. In the night ditto. Bombarding from the lines on Bunkers Hill.

1st Sept. Ditto. Almost constant firing from the centinels at each other. New works arise upon the Neck by the Provincials who approach very near.

11th. Sept. A serjent and 5 men taken by the Provincials at Dorchester.

12th. Went in a boat to relieve a lad blown off in a canoe.

17th. [*Oct*.] Two floating batteries from the Provincials from Cambridge River fired a number of cannon into the camp at the Common; the shot went thro houses by the Lamb Tavern, etc. A deserter who came in this morning says one of the cannon split and killed and wounded several. 5 or 6 hats, a waistcoat and part of a boat came on shore at the bottom of the Common.

25th. Several nights past the whole army was ordered not to undress. The cannon all loaded with grape shot from a full apprehension the Provincials would make an attack upon the town. The streets paraded all night by the Light Horse.

27th. The spacious Old South Meeting House taken possession of by the Light Horse 17th Regiment of Dragoons commanded by Lieut. Col. Samuel Birch. The pulpit, pews and seats all cut to pieces and carried off in the most savage manner as can be expressed, and destined for a riding school. The beautiful carved pew with the silk furniture of Deacon Hubbard's was taken down and carried to ——'s house by an officer and made a hog stye. The above was effected by the solicitation of General Burgoyne.

30th. A soldier, one of the Light-Horse men, was hanged at the head of their camp for attempting to desert. Proclamation issued by General Howe for the inhabitants to sign an Association to take arms, etc.

November 4th. A Proclamation issued for people to give in their names to go out of town, but before the time limited expired a stop was put to it. This like others of the kind seems only designed to continue the vexation of the people.

9th. Several companies of Regulars from Charlestown went over to Phip's farm to take a number of cattle feeding there. The Provincials came upon them and soon drove them on board boats after an engagement. It is said several are wounded and none killed, but they supposed many of the Provincials killed.

16th. Many people turned out of their houses for the troops to enter. The keys of our meeting house cellars demanded of me by Major Sheriff by order of General Howe. Houses, fences, trees, etc., pulled down and carried off for fuel. My wharf and barn pulled down by order of General Robinson. Beef, mutton, pork at 1/6 pr. pound, geese 14/, fowls 6/8. L[awful] M[oney].

19th. A large ship arrived from Plymouth in England with every kind of provisions dead and alive, hogs, sheep, fowls, ducks, eggs, mince meat, etc, ginger-bread, etc. *Memorandum* 25 regiments of Kings troops now in this distressed town.

24th. November. A transport ship carried about 400 of our inhabitants to Point Shirley. One poor Dutch woman attempted to carry with her about 60 dollars. Morrison the deserter seized them and carried them to the town major. Ten dollars was stopped by him.

—NEWELL, "Journal," *Mass. Hist. Soc. Coll.*, 4th Series, I, 264-266, 269-270.

3. "THE PRESENT STATE IS THAT OF THE MOST ABJECT SLAVES"

Abigail Adams to John Adams.

Braintree, 5 July, 1775

I should have been more particular, but I thought you knew every thing that passed here. The present state of the inhabitants of Boston is that of the most abject slaves, under the most cruel and despotic of tyrants. Among many instances I could mention, let me relate one. Upon the 17th of June, printed handbills were posted up at the corners of the streets and upon houses, forbidding any inhabitants to go upon their houses, or upon any eminence, on pain of death; the inhabitants dared not to look out of their houses, nor to be heard or seen to ask a question. Our prisoners were brought over to the Long Wharf, and there lay all night, without any care of their wounds or any resting-place but the pavements, until the next day, when they exchanged it for the jail, since which we hear they are civilly treated.

Their living cannot be good, as they can have no fresh provisions; their beef, we hear, is all gone, and their own wounded men die very fast, so that they have a report that the bullets were poisoned. Fish they cannot have, they have rendered it so difficult to procure; and the admiral is such a villain as to oblige every fishing schooner to pay a dollar every time it goes out. The money that has been paid for passes is incredible. Some have been given ten, twenty, thirty and forty dollars, to get out with a small proportion of their things. It is reported and believed that they have taken up a number of persons and committed them to jail, we know not for what in particular. Master Lovell is confined in the dungeon; a son of Mr. Edes is in jail, and one Wilburt, a ship carpenter, is now upon trial for his life. God alone knows to what length these wretches will go, and I hope restrain their malice.

I would not have you be distressed about me. Danger, they say, makes people valiant. Hitherto I have been distressed, but not dismayed. I have felt for my country and her sons, and have bled with them and for them. Not all the havoc and devastation they have made has wounded me like the death of Warren. We want him in the Senate; we want him in his profession; we want him in the field. We mourn for the citizen, the senator, the physician, and the warrior. May we have others raised up in his room.

—ADAMS, ed., *Letters of Mrs. Adams*, I, 48-49.

4. "As to Their Taking up Arms, It Is Mere Bullying"

Letter from an officer in the British Army.

Boston, November 22, 1775

According to my promise I write to you on my arrival here. The troops are just put into quarters. The workmen at Boston were so mulish that the General was obliged to send to Nova Scotia for carpenters and bricklayers to fit up barracks for our accommodation. The country is very plentiful, and all sorts of provisions cheaper than in London, tho' much risen from such a number of people being got together. The inhabitants of this province retain the religious and civil principles brought over by their forefathers, in the reign of King Charles I, and are at least an hundred years behind hand with the people of England in every refinement. With the most austere show of devotion, they are destitute of every principle or religion of common honesty, and are reckoned the most arrant cheats and hypocrites on the whole continent of America. The women are very handsome, but, like old mother Eve, very frail. Our camp has been as well supplied in that way since we have been on Boston common, as if our tents were pitched on Blackheath.

As to what you hear of their taking up arms to resist the force of England, it is mere bullying, and will go no further than words: whenever it comes to blows, he that can run fastest will think himself best off. Believe me, any two regiments here ought to be decimated, if they did not beat in the field the whole force of the Massachusetts Province; for tho' they are numerous, they are but a mob without order or discipline, and very aukward at handling their arms. If you have ever seen a train-band colonel marching his regiment from Ludgate-hill to the Artillery-Ground, in them you have an epitome of the discipline of an American army.

We expect to pass the winter very quietly. The Saints here begin to relish the money we spend among them, and I believe, notwithstanding all their noise, would be very sorry to part with us.

—WILLARD, ed., *Letters on the American Revolution*, pp. 14-16.

5. THE IRISHMAN'S EPISTLE TO THE TROOPS IN BOSTON

1775

By my faith, but I think ye're all makers of bulls,
With your brains in your breeches, your ——— in your skulls.
Get home with your muskets, and put up your swords,
And look in your books for the meaning of words.
You see now, my honeys, how much you're mistaken,
For Concord by discord can never be beaten.

How brave ye went out with your muskets all bright,
And thought to be-frighten the folks with the sight;
But when you got there how they powdered your pums,
And all the way home how they peppered your ———,
And is it not, honeys, a comical crack,
To be proud in the face, and be shot in the back?

How come ye to think, now, they did not know how
To be after their firelocks as smartly as you?
Why, you see now, my honeys, 'tis nothing at all
But to pull at the trigger, and pop goes the ball.

And what have you got now with all your designing,
But a town without victuals to sit down and dine in;
And to look on the ground like a parcel of noodles,
And sing how the Yankees have beaten the Doodles.
I'm sure if you're wise you'll make peace for dinner,
For fighting and fasting will soon make ye thinner.

—MOORE, ed., *Songs and Ballads*, pp. 92-93.

III. CREATING AN AMERICAN ARMY

Washington could write his friend Schuyler on July 28 that "confusion and disorder reigned in every department," and also that "we mend every day." As the summer wore on it was the confusion and disorder that made the sharpest impression and excited the most passionate observation, though it was perhaps the mending that was ultimately the most important. The problems that confronted Washington when he took command appeared well-nigh insuperable. The army was not an army in any accepted sense of the word, but an agglomeration of forces still technically under state control, and even paid and supplied (after a fashion) by the states; the soldiers were not soldiers in the eighteenth-century sense of the word, but a haphazard collection of volunteers, skillful enough in the use of musket or rifle, but almost wholly without experience or training, disrespectful of officers, fiercely resentful of discipline, ignorant of the rules of hygiene, wasteful and disorderly.

Almost everything was wanting—muskets, powder, lead, blankets, food, medi-
cine, tents, tools and—of course—money.

We give here a potpourri of description and commentary on conditions
in the American camps. The first is from the pen of an anonymous British
officer and describes conditions between Lexington and Bunker's Hill; the
second from the same Reverend William Emerson to whom we owe one
of the best accounts of Concord. The third and most circumstantial picture
is drawn by the gifted young Benjamin Thompson of Woburn, Massachu-
setts, and Concord, New Hampshire. A protégé of Governor Wentworth—
who made him a major in the New Hampshire Provincial Regiment at
twenty—Thompson had at first wavered between the Patriot and Royal
causes and then—probably because he got better terms—thrown in his lot with
the British. Though as commander of a regiment in the South and on Long
Island he later inflicted a good deal of damage on the Americans, and then
lived the rest of his life abroad (as Count Rumford of the Holy Roman Em-
pire), he provided in his will for a chair of physics at Harvard College. A
final letter describes some of the difficulties Washington experienced with
the riflemen from Pennsylvania and Virginia—good soldiers, but better suited
to frontier warfare against the Indians than to the discipline of an army camp.

1. "A Drunken, Canting, Lying, Praying Rabble"

Letter from a surgeon of one of His Majesty's ships at Boston.

May 26, 1775

My curiosity led me to make use of the privilege of my profession to
visit the New-England camp, and some as acquaintances in it who had formerly been my fellow-students at Edinburgh. Among others I saw ——— who
attends a number of those that were wounded on the 19th of April. I did not
think it fair to ask him the particulars of that day, as we are on different
sides; but he assured their loss greatly exceeds that of the regulars.

There is a large body of them in arms near the town of Boston. Their
camp and quarters are plentifully supplied with all sorts of provisions, and
the roads are crouded with carts and carriages, bringing them rum, cyder,
etc., from the neighbouring towns, for without New-England rum, a New-
England army could not be kept together; they could neither fight nor say
their prayers, one with another; they drink at least a bottle of it a man a day.
I had the honour to see several of their great generals, and among the rest,
General Judadiah Pribble: He is a stout looking old fellow, seems to be
turned of 70.

This army, which you will hear so much said, and see so much wrote
about, is truly nothing but a drunken, canting, lying, praying, hypocritical
rabble, without order, subjection, discipline, or cleanliness; and must fall to
pieces of itself in the course of three months, notwithstanding every endeavour of their leaders, teachers, and preachers, though the last are the most
canting, hypocritical, lying scoundrels that this or any other country ever
afforded. You are mistaken, if you think they are Presbyterian; they are
Congregationists, divided and subdivided into a variety of distinctions, the

descendants of Oliver Cromwell's army, who truly inherit the spirit which was the occasion of so much bloodshed in your country from the year 1642 till the Restoration, but these people are happily placed at a distance from you, and though they may occasion a little expence of men and money before they are reduced to order, yet they cannot extend the calamities of war to your island. They have not been hitherto the least molested since the affair at Lexington. Time has been given for their passions to subside, but I do not suppose that the General's patience will continue much longer; he is at present confined to the town of Boston, and all supplies from the country stopped, and both the navy and the army live upon salt provisions of that sort; I am well informed, there are nine months provisions in the town.

—Willard, ed., *Letters on the American Revolution*, pp. 119-121.

2. The Reverend William Emerson Describes Conditions in the American Camp

To his wife.

July 17, 1775

'Tis also very diverting to walk among the camps. They are as different in their form as the owners are in their dress; and every tent is a portraiture of the temper and taste of the persons that incamp in it. Some are made of boards, some of sailcloth, and some partly of one and partly of the other. Others are made of stone and turf, and others again of birch and other brush. Some are thrown up in a hurry and look as if they could not help it—mere necessity—others are curiously wrought with doors and windows done with wreaths and withes in the manner of a basket. Some are your proper tents and marquees, and look like the regular camp of the enemy. These are the Rhode-Islanders, who are furnished with tent equipage from among ourselves and every thing in the most exact English taste. However I think that the great variety of the American camp is, upon the whole, rather a beauty than a blemish to the army. . . .

There is a great overturning in camp as to order and regularity. New lords new laws. The Generals Washington and Lee are upon the lines every day. New orders from his Excellency are read to the respective regiments every morning after prayers. The strictest government is taking place, and great distinction is made between officers and soldiers. Everyone is made to know his place and keep it, or be tied up and receive not 1000 but thirty or forty lashes according to his crime. Thousands are at work every day from four till eleven o'clock in the morning. It is surprising how much work has been done.

—French, *First Year of the American Revolution*, pp. 300-301.

3. The American Soldiers Are Dirty, Nasty, Insubordinate and Quarrelsome

Observations by Benjamin Thompson (afterward Count Rumford).

Boston, November 4, 1775

. . . The army in general is not very badly accoutered, but most wretchedly clothed, and as dirty a set of mortals as ever disgraced the name of a soldier. They have had no clothes of any sort provided for them by the Congress (except the detachment of 1,133 that are gone to Canada under Col. Arnold, who had each of them a new coat and a linen frock served out to them before they set out), tho' the army in general, and the Massachusetts forces in particular, had encouragement of having coats given them by way of bounty for inlisting. And the neglect of the Congress to fulfill their promise in this respect has been the source of not a little uneasiness among the soldiers.

They have no women in the camp to do washing for the men, and they in general not being used to doing things of this sort, and thinking it rather a disparagement to them, choose rather to let their linen, etc., rot upon their backs than to be at the trouble of cleaning 'em themselves. And to this nasty way of life, and to the change of their diet from milk, vegetables, etc., to living almost intirely upon flesh, must be attributed those putrid, malignant and infectious disorders which broke out among them soon after their taking the field, and which have prevailed with unabating fury during the whole summer.

The leading men among them (with their usual art and cunning) have been indefatigable in their endeavors to conceal the real state of the army in this respect, and to convince the world that the soldiers were tolerably healthy. But the contrary has been apparent, even to a demonstration, to every person that had but the smallest acquaintance with their camp. And so great was the prevalence of these disorders in the month of July that out of 4,207 men who were stationed upon Prospect Hill no more than 2,227 were returned fit for duty.

The mortality among them must have been very great, and to this in a great measure must be attributed the present weakness of their regiments; many of which were much stronger when they came into the field. But the number of soldiers that have died in the camp is comparatively small to those vast numbers that have gone off in the interior parts of the country. For immediately upon being taken down with these disorders they have in general been carried back into the country to their own homes, where they have not only died themselves, but by spreading the infection among their relatives and friends have introduced such a general mortality throughout New England as was never known since its first planting. Great numbers have been carried off in all parts of the country. Some towns 'tis said have lost near one-third of their inhabitants; and there is scarce a village but has suffered more or less from the raging virulence of these dreadful disorders. . . .

The soldiers in general are most heartily sick of the service, and I believe it would be with the utmost difficulty that they could be prevailed upon to serve another campaign. The Continental Congress are very sensible of this, and have lately sent a committee to the camp to consult with the general officers upon some method of raising the necessary forces to serve during the winter season, as the greatest part of the army that is now in the field is to be disbanded upon the last day of December.

Whether they will be successful in their endeavours to persuade the soldiers to re-inlist or not, I cannot say, but am rather inclined to think that they will. For as they are men possessed of every species of cunning and artifice, and as their political existence depends upon the existence of the army, they will leave no stone unturned to accomplish their designs.

Notwithstanding the indefatigable indeavours of Mr. Washington and the other generals, and particularly of Adjutant General Gates, to arrange and discipline the army, yet any tolerable degree of order and subordination is what they are totally unacquainted with in the rebel camp. And the doctrines of independence and levellism have been so effectually sown throughout the country, and so universally imbibed by all ranks of men, that I apprehend it will be with the greatest difficulty that the inferior officers and soldiers will be ever brought to any tolerable degree of subjection to the commands of their superiors.

Many of their leading men are not insensible of this, and I have often heard them lament that the existence of that very spirit which induced the common people to take up arms and resist the authority of Great Britain, should induce them to resist the authority of their own officers, and by that means effectually prevent their ever making good soldiers.

Another great reason why it is impossible to introduce a proper degree of subordination in the rebel army is the great degree of equality as to birth, fortune and education that universally prevails among them. For men cannot bear to be commanded by others that are their superiors in nothing but in having had the good fortune to get a superior commission, for which perhaps they stood equally fair. And in addition to this, the officers and men are not only in general very nearly upon a par as to birth, fortune, etc., but in particular regiments are most commonly neighbours and acquaintances, and as such can with less patience submit to that degree of absolute submission and subordination which is necessary to form a well-disciplined corps.

Another reason why the army can never be well united and regulated is the disagreement and jealousies between the different troops from the different Colonies; which must never fail to create disaffection and uneasiness among them. The Massachusetts forces already complain very loudly of the partiality of the General to the Virginians, and have even gone so far as to tax him with taking pleasure in bringing their officers to court martials, and having them cashiered that he may fill their places with his friends from that quarter. The gentlemen from the Southern Colonies, in their turn, complain of the enormous proportion of New England officers in the army, and particularly of those belonging to the province of Massachusetts Bay, and say, as the cause is now become a common one, and the experience is general, they ought to have an equal chance for command with their neighbours.

Thus have these jealousies and uneasiness already begun which I think cannot fail to increase and grow every day more and more interesting, and if they do not finally destroy the very existence of the army (which I think they bid very fair to do), yet must unavoidably render it much less formidable than it otherways might have been.

Of all useless sets of men that ever incumbered an army, surely the boasted riflemen are certainly the most so. When they came to the camp

they had every liberty and indulgence allowed them that they could possibly wish for. They had more pay than any other soldiers; did no duty; were under no restraint from the commands of their officers, but went when and where they pleased, without being subject to be stopped or examined by any one, and did almost intirely as they pleased in every respect whatever. But they have not answered the end for which they were designed in any one article whatever. For instead of being the best marksmen in the world, and picking off every regular that was to be seen, there is scarsely a regiment in camp but can produce men that can beat them at shooting, and the army is now universally convinced that the continual fire which they kept up by the week and month together has had no other effect than to waste their ammunition and convince the King's troops that they are not really so formidable adversaries as they would wish to be thought. . . .
—GR. BRIT. HIST. MSS. COMM., *Stopford-Sackville Manuscripts*, II, 15-18.

4. THE VIRGINIA REGIMENT OF RIFLEMEN MUTINY OUT OF BOREDOM

Jesse Lukens to Mr. John Shaw, Jr.

Prospect Hill, Sept. 13, 1775

. . . Our camp is separate from all others about 100 yards—all our courts martial and duty was separate—we were excused from all working parties, camp guards, and camp duty. This indulgence, together with the remissness of discipline and care in our young officers, had rendered the men rather insolent for good soldiers. They had twice before broke open our guard house and released their companions who were confined there for small crimes, and once when an offender was brought to the post to be whipped, it was with the utmost difficulty they were kept from rescuing him in the presence of all their officers—they openly damned them and behaved with great insolence. However the colonel was pleased to pardon the man and all remained quiet.

But on Sunday last, the adjutant having confined a serjeant for neglect of duty and murmuring, the men began again and threatened to take him out. The adjutant, being a man of spirit, seized the principal mutineer and put him in also, and coming to report the matter to the colonel, where we, all sitting down after dinner, were alarmed with a huzzaing and upon going out found they had broke open the guard house and taken the man out. The colonel and lieutenant colonel with several of the officers and friends seized the fellow from amongst them and ordered a guard to take him to Cambridge at the Main Guard, which was done without any violent opposition, but in about 20 minutes 32 of Capt. Ross's company with their loaded rifles swore by God they would go to the Main Guard and release the man or lose their lives, and set off as hard as they could run—it was in vain to attempt stopping them.

We stayed in camp and kept the others quiet—sent word to General Washington, who reinforced the guard to 500 men with fixed bayonets and loaded pieces. Col. Hitchcock's regiment (being the one next us) was ordered under arms and some part of General Green's brigade (as the generals were determined to subdue by force the mutineers and did not know how far it might spread in our battalion). Generals Washington, Lee and Green came immediately, and our 32 mutineers who had gone about half a mile towards Cambridge and taken possession of a hill and woods, beginning to be frightened at their proceedings, were not so hardened but upon the General's ordering them to ground their arms they did it immediately. The General then ordered another of our company's (Capt. Nagles) to surround them with their loaded guns, which was immediately done and did the company great honor. However, to convince our people (as I suppose, mind) that it did not altogether depend upon themselves, he ordered two of the ring leaders to be bound. I was glad to find our men all true and ready to do their duty except these 32 rascals—26 were conveyed to the Quarter Guard on Prospect Hill and 6 of the principals to the Main Guard.

You cannot conceive what disgrace we are all in and how much the General is chagrined that only one regiment should come from the South and that set so infamous an example: and in order that idleness shall not be a further bane to us, the general orders on Monday were "That Col. Thompson's regiment shall be upon all parties of fatigue (working parties) and do all other camp duty with any other regiment."

The men have since been tried by a general court martial and convicted of mutiny and were only fined 20s each for the use of the hospital—too small a punishment for so base a crime and mitigated no doubt on account of their having come so far to serve the cause and its being the first crime. The men are returned to their camp, seem exceedingly sorry for their misbehavior and promise amendment.

This will, I hope, awaken the attention of our officers to their duty (for to their remissness I charge our whole disgrace) and the men being employed will yet no doubt do honor to their provinces, for this much I can say for them: that upon every alarm it was impossible for men to behave with more readiness or attend better to their duty; it is only in the camp that we cut a poor figure. Tomorrow morning or some time in the day may perhaps restore our honor, if we behave in the day of battle as well as I hope we shall; you must know that this is a conjecture of my own and founded on no better materials than a poor unexperienced judgement.

—Lukens, "Letter," *American Historical Record*, I, 547-548.

IV. HOLDING THE ARMY TOGETHER

Undoubtedly the most difficult and vexatious of the many problems that confronted General Washington was the elementary one of holding the army together. Most of the soldiers had enlisted only until the end of the year, and the terms of enlistment of the Connecticut militia ran out on December 10, 1775. Some of the soldiers sought to anticipate their freedom by going home early; many of those who did leave took their muskets with them. Notwithstanding the most moving appeals from Washington and others, few of those whose time was up were willing to re-enlist. During

*December the army seemed to melt away, and Washington was fearful that
the British would learn of his predicament and seize the offensive—as indeed
they should have done. In January 1776 things took a turn for the better.
Of the 7,000 or so due to go home, almost half finally re-enlisted, an example
of patriotism which it would have been difficult to match in Britain at that
time. On January 1 Washington flew the first Continental flag; there is some
dispute about its pattern, but all agree that it contained thirteen red and white
stripes. During January vacancies were filled up by re-enlistments and by
new contingents that poured in not only from the New England states but
from the states to the south, and the army increased to over 10,000 effectives.*

*We give quotations from a diary and general orders that illuminate the
problem of discipline and re-enlistment, and second a group of extracts from
the letters of General Washington, chiefly to his quondam secretary, Joseph
Reed of Philadelphia. Washington is not ordinarily thought of as a historian,
but no other participant in the war contributed so much or so well to the
historical records as he did.*

1. Simeon Lyman Refuses to Be Terrified into Re-Enlistment

From the journal of a Connecticut soldier.

Wednesday, November 29th, [*1775*]. In the morning the whole regiment
was ordered to parade before the genera[l's] door, and they formed a hollow
square, and the general came in and made a speech to us, and then those that
would stay till January must follow the fifers and colors, and the captains
turned out and they marched round the company several times, and there
was about a 100 soldiers turned out. The most of them had listed to stay
another year, and they was led down to the colonel's and treated, and the rest
was dismissed to return to their tents again, and I washed my clothes, and
about sunset we went out and chose 2 corporals, and then they brought 2
bottles of brandy and they drinked it, and then they was dismissed.

Thursday, 30th. About 12 o'clock they fired about 10 cannon to salute.
In the afternoon we was ordered out to see who would stay 3 weeks longer,
and there was but three that would stay and they had listed to stay another
year, and they dismissed them.

December, Friday, 1st. We was ordered to parade before the general's
door, the whole regiment, and General Lee and General Solivan came out,
and those that would not stay 4 days longer after their enlistments was out
they was ordered to turn out, and there was about 3 quarters turned out, and
we was ordered to form a hollow square, and General Lee came in and the
first words was "Men, I do not know what to call you; [you] are the worst
of all creatures," and flung and curst and swore at us, and said if we would
not stay he would order us to go on Bunker Hill and if we would not go he
would order the riflemen to fire at us, and they talked they would take our
guns and take our names down, and our lieutenants begged of us to stay and
we went and joined the rest, and they got about 10 of their guns, and the
men was marched off, and the general said that they should go to the work

house and be confined, and they agreed to stay the four days, and they gave them a dram, and the colonel told us that he would give us another the next morning, and we was dismissed. There was one that was a mind to have one of his mates turn out with him, and the general see him and he catched his gun out of his hands and struck him on the head and ordered him to be put under guard.

Saturday, 2d. I was on quarter guard in the morning. They was paraded before the colonel's door and he gave us a dram, and then they read some new orders to us and they said that we must not go out of our brigade without a written pass from our captain, and before night there was a paper set up on the general's door not to let the soldiers have any victual if they would not stay 3 weeks longer, and they said that they was 50 miles in the country, and some was mad and said they would not stay the 4 days, and the paper was took down as soon as it was dark, and another put up that General Lee was a fool and if he had not come here we should not know it. The sentries fired at each other all day by spells, and at night our guard took 4 of their horses, and the mortar piece that our men took from the regulars was brought to Cambridge. It was 13 inches across. They brought several chests of small arms, and General Put[nam] dashed a bottle on it and called it the royal congress.

Sunday, 3d. It was my turn to cook, and at night we had orders that if we would stay till 10th we should have a written pass, and we felt a good deal better for it.

Monday, 4th. I wrote a letter and drawed off the advertisement that was sat up to keep us from having anything on the road. . . .

Saturday, 9th. The whole regiment was ordered out on the parade, and we was ordered to stand three deep, and the captains was in the front and the luten and the sergeants in the rear, and the general came round the whole, and we all made a salute to him, and then we was ordered to march down before the general's door, and those that was agoing to stay another year should march out and front the regiments, and they was dismissed to go to their tents, and the officers was ordered to view our arms, and then we was dismissed and we came home, and then we was ordered to turn [in] our guns and ammunition and our guns was to be priced, and orders was that all that was not well might march off, and those that had sent for horses and hey (no others) sot off, and when it came night we had orders to go on Plowd Hill and handle the lances all night, and they all said they would not go, and they did not get one.

Sunday, 10th. In the morning we was ordered to parade before the general's door, and we was counted off and dismissed, and we we[nt] to the luten and he gave us a dram, and then we marched off to Cambridg and I see the brass mortar piece, and then we marched to Watertown and then to Waltham and then to Western, then to Sutbury. There we stayed all night and I got a good supper and lay in a good bed. We traveled 15 miles and it was wet and sloppy and it rained all night.

—LYMAN, "Journal," *Conn. Hist. Soc. Coll.*, VII, 128-131.

2. The Connecticut Troops Depart

GENERAL ORDERS

Head Quarters, Cambridge, December 3, 1775
Parole Sawbridge. Countersign Hartley.

It is with surprise and Astonishment The General learns, that notwith-standing the Information that was communicated to the Connecticut Troops, of the Relief being ordered to supply their places, by the 10th of this month; that many of them have taken their Army with them and gone off, not only without leave, but contrary to express Orders; this is therefore to inform those who remain, that the General has sent an Express to the Governor of Connecticut, with the names of such men as have left the Camp, in Order, that they may be dealt with, in a manner suited to the Ignominy of their behaviour. The General also informs those who remain, that it is necessary for them to obtain a written discharge, from the Commanding Officer of the Regt. they belong to, when they are dismissed on the 10th Instant; that they may be distinguished from, and not treated, as Deserters.

The Colonels and commanding Officers of the Connecticut Regiments, are to give in the Names of all those of their respective regiments, for the purpose above mentioned.

—Fitzpatrick, ed., *Writings of Washington*, IV, 138-139.

3. General Washington Describes Conditions in the American Army

To the New York Legislature.

Camp at Cambridge, August 8, 1775
Gentlemen: It must give great concern to any Considerate Mind that, when this whole Continent, at vast expense of Blood and Treasure, is endeavouring to Establish Liberties on the most secure and Solid Foundations, not only by a laudable Opposition of Force to Force, but by denying itself the usual advantages of Trade; there are men among us so basely sordid as to Counteract all our Exertions, for the sake of a little Gain. You cannot but have heard that the Distresses of the Ministerial Troops for fresh Provisions and many other Necessaries, at Boston, were very great; It is a Policy, Justi-fiable by all the Laws of War, to endeavour to increase them; Desertions, Discouragement, and a Dissatisfaction with the Service, besides weakening their strength, are some of the Natural Consequences of such a Situation; and, if continued, might afford the fairest Hope of Success, without further Effu-sion of human Blood. A vessel cleared lately out of New York for St. Croix, with fresh Provisions, and other Articles, has just gone into Boston, instead of pursuing her Voyage to the West Indies; I have endeavoured to discover the Name of the Captain or Owner, but, as yet, without success. . . . I make no doubt you will be able to discover and expose the Villain. And if you could fall upon some effectual Measures, to prevent the like in future, it would be doing a Signal Service to our Common Country.

To Lund Washington.

Camp at Cambridge, August 20, 1775

... The People of this government have obtained a Character which they by no means deserved; their officers generally speaking are the most indifferent kind of People I ever saw. I have already broke one Colo. and five Captains for Cowardice and for drawing more Pay and Provisions than they had Men in their Companies; there is two more Colos. now under arrest, and to be tried for the same offences; in short they are by no means such Troops, in any respect, as you are led to believe of them from the accts. which are published, but I need not make myself Enemies among them by this declaration, although it is consistent with truth. I dare say the Men would fight very well (if properly Officered) although they are an exceeding dirty and nasty people; had they been properly conducted at Bunkers Hill . . . or those that were there properly supported, the Regulars would have met with a shameful defeat, and a much more considerable loss than they did . . . ; it was for their behaviour on that occasion that the above Officers were broke, for I never spared one that was accused of Cowardice but brot 'em to immediate Tryal. . . .

To Richard Henry Lee.

Camp at Cambridge, August 29, 1775

... As we have now nearly compleated our Lines of Defence, we [have] nothing more, in my opinion, to fear from the Enemy, provided we can keep our men to their duty and make them watchful and vigilant; but it is among the most difficult tasks I ever undertook in my life to induce these people to believe that there is, or can be, danger till the Bayonet is pushed at their Breasts; not that it proceeds from any uncommon prowess, but rather from an unaccountable kind of stupidity in the lower class of these people which, believe me, prevails but too generally among the officers of the Massachusetts part of the Army who are nearly of the same kidney with the Privates, and adds not a little to my difficulties; as there is no such thing as getting of officers of this stamp to exert themselves in carrying orders into execution—to curry favor with the men (by whom they were chosen, and on whose smiles possibly they may think they may again rely) seems to be one of the principal objects of their attention. . . .

There has been so many great, and capital errors, and abuses to rectify— so many examples to make—and so little Inclination in the officers of inferior Rank to contribute their aid to accomplish this work, that my life has been nothing else (since I came here) but one continued round of annoyance and fatigue; in short no pecuniary recompense could induce me to undergo what I have, especially as I expect, by shewing so little countenance to irregularities and publick abuses, to render myself very obnoxious to a greater part of these People.

To the President of Congress.

Camp at Cambridge, September 21, 1775

... It gives me great Pain to be obliged to sollicit the Attention of the Hon. Congress to the State of the Army, in Terms which imply the Slightest

Apprehension of being neglected: But my Situation is inexpressibly distressing to see the Winter fast approaching upon a naked Army, the time of their Service within a few Weeks of expiring, and no Provision yet made for such important Events. Added to this the Military Chest is totally exhausted. The Paymaster has not a single Dollar in Hand. The Commissary General assures me he has strained his Credit to the utmost for the Subsistence of the Army:— The Quarter Master General is precisely in the same situation, and the greater part of the Army in a State not far from mutiny, upon the Deduction from their stated Allowance. I know not to whom to impute this Failure, but I am of opinion, if the Evil is not immediately remedied and more Punctuality observed in the future, the Army must absolutely break up.

To Joseph Reed.

Cambridge, November 28, 1775

. . . What an astonishing thing it is that those who are employed to sign the Continental bills should not be able, or inclined, to do it as fast as they are wanted. They will prove the destruction of the army, if they are not more attentive and diligent. Such a dearth of public spirit, and want of virtue, such stock-jobbing, and fertility in all the low arts to obtain advantages of one kind or another, in this great change of military arrangement, I never saw before, and pray God I may never be witness to again. What will be the ultimate end of these manoeuvres is beyond my scan. I tremble at the prospect. We have been till this time enlisting about three thousand five hundred men. To engage these I have been obliged to allow furloughs as far as fifty men a regiment, and the Officers I am persuaded indulge as many more. The Connecticut troops will not be prevailed upon to stay longer than their term (saving those who have enlisted for the next campaign, and mostly on furlough), and such a dirty, mercenary spirit pervades the whole, that I should not be at all surprised at any disaster that may happen. In short, after the last of this month our lines will be so weakened, that the minutemen and militia must be called in for their defence; these, being under no kind of government themselves, will destroy the little subordination I have been laboring to establish, and run me into one evil whilst I am endeavoring to avoid another; but the lesser must be chosen. Could I have foreseen what I have, and am likely to experience, no consideration upon earth should have induced me to accept this command. A regiment or any subordinate department would have been accompanied with ten times the satisfaction, and perhaps the honor.

To Joseph Reed.

Cambridge, January 4, 1776

. . . It is easier to conceive than to describe the situation of my mind for some time past, and my feelings under our present circumstances. Search the vast volumes of history through, and I much question whether a case similar to ours is to be found; to wit, to maintain a post against the flower of the British troops for six months together, without ———, and at the end of them to have one army disbanded and another to raise within the same distance of a reinforced enemy. It is too much to attempt. What may be the final issue of the last manoeuvre, time only can tell. I wish this month was well over our heads. The same desire of retiring into a chimney-corner seized the troops of New Hampshire, Rhode Island, and Massachusetts, (so soon as their time expired,) as had worked upon those of Connecticut, notwithstanding many of them made a tender of their services to continue, till the lines could be sufficiently strengthened. We are now left with a good deal less than half raised regiments, and about five thousand militia, who only stand ingaged to the middle of this month; when, according to custom, they will depart, let the necessity of their stay be never so urgent. Thus it is, that for more than two months past, I have scarcely immerged from one difficulty before I have plunged into another. How it will end, God in his great goodness will direct. I am thankful for his protection to this time. We are told that we shall soon get the army completed, but I have been told so many things which have never come to pass, that I distrust every thing. . . .

To Joseph Reed.

Cambridge, February 10, 1776

. . . I know the unhappy predicament I stand in; I know that much is expected of me; I know, that without men, without arms, without ammunition, without any thing fit for the accommodation of a soldier, little is to be done; and, which is mortifying, I know, that I cannot stand justified to the world without exposing my own weakness, and injuring the cause, by declaring my wants, which I am determined not to do, further than unavoidable necessity brings every man acquainted with them.

If, under these disadvantages, I am able to keep above water, (as it were) in the esteem of mankind, I shall feel myself happy; but if, from the unknown peculiarity of my circumstances, I suffer in the opinion of the world, I shall not think you take the freedom of a friend, if you conceal the reflections that may be cast upon my conduct. My own situation feels so irksome to me at times, that, if I did not consult the public good, more than my own tranquillity, I should long ere this have put every thing to the cast of a Dye. So far from my having an army of twenty thousand men well armed &c., I have been here with less than one half of it, including sick, furloughed, and on command, and those neither armed nor clothed, as they should be. In short, my situation has been such, that I have been obliged to use art to conceal it from my own officers. The Congress, as you observe, expect, I believe, that I should do more than others,—for whilst they compel me to enlist men without a bounty, they give 40 dollars to others, which will, I expect, put a stand to our enlistments; for notwithstanding all the publick virtue which is ascrib'd to these people, there is no nation under the sun, (that I ever came across) pay greater adoration to money than they do. I am pleas'd to find that your Battalions are cloathed and look well, and that they are filing off for Canada. I wish I could say that the troops here had altered much in Dress or appearance. Our regiments are little more than half compleat, and recruiting nearly at a stand. In all my letters I fail not the mention of Tents, and now perceive that notice is taken of yr. application. I have been convinced, by General Howe's conduct, that he has either been very ignorant of our situation (which I do not believe) or that he has received positive orders (which, I think, is natural to conclude) not to put anything to the hazard till his reinforcements arrive; otherwise there has been time since the first of December, that we must have fought like men to have maintained these Lines, so great is their extent. . . .

    —FITZPATRICK, ed., *Writings of Washington*, III, 407, 433, 450-454, 512; IV, 124-125, 211-212, 319-320.

V. THE BRITISH IN BOSTON ARE FRUSTRATED AND BORED

Gage should have abandoned Boston after the flight from Concord, and certainly after Bunker's Hill, but there were persuasive reasons why neither he nor his successor felt that they could do so. They did not want to appear to be driven out by the Americans: neither their pride nor their government would have stood for that. They did not have enough shipping to transport the army and the governmental and Loyalist dependents, along with accumulated supplies and material of war. And, perhaps most important of all, they did not have anywhere to go. So, notwithstanding the fact that strategically Boston was no longer of any value to them, and that by allowing themselves to be besieged they tied up the largest army and naval forces available to suppress the rebellion, they hung on.

Boston was not a very pleasant city for an occupying army, and both officers and men seem to have had a dull time of it, though it did have the advantage of being comparatively safe. Officers consoled themselves with amateur dramatics, and a riding academy in the Old South Church and—if we are to trust one letter writer—with complaisant Boston girls; the privates did not have even these consolations. The whole army suffered from scurvy and from smallpox which "raged in the streets and cantonments." Almost everything that the army needed, except fish, had to be brought in from England, Canada or the West Indies at some risk and great expense: food, clothing, medicines, ammunition, fodder. At first the army used whatever wood was available for fuel; they tore down the houses that still stood in Charlestown, old houses in Boston, barns, fences, even the steeple of the Old North Church, and they cut down many fine trees, including the famous Liberty Elm, which had been a rallying place for the Sons of Liberty. After this supply was exhausted, they depended on the mother country for coal, as for other supplies. Bad fortune attended this as so many other operations of George III's government. A prodigious quantity of supplies was shipped from Britain: 5,000 oxen, 14,000 sheep, 10,000 butts of beer, oats, hay, flour and other necessities, but the transports were delayed, the food rotted, the flour mildewed, half the animals died; when the fleet neared American waters it was scattered by storm, some of the ships driven to the West Indies, others picked up by American privateers; in the end only a fraction of the provisions reached Boston.

1. "They Grow Daily More Bold"

Boston, July 25, 1775

As far as I can guess from a matter not perfectly known, we at present are worse off than the rebels. In point of numbers they so far surpass us that we are like a few children in the midst of a large crowd. Trusting to this superiority, they grow daily more and more bold, menacing us most insolently; and we fear when the days shorten and dark nights come on, they'll put some of their threats in execution, unless other reinforcements and a fleet of war arrive soon. They know our situation, as well as we do ourselves, from the villains that are left in town, who acquaint them with all our proceedings, making signals by night with gunpowder, and at day, out of church steeples. About three weeks ago three fellows were taken out of one of the latter, who confess they had been so employed for seven days. Another was caught last week swimming over to the rebels with one of their General's passes in his pocket. He will be hanged in a day or two. Since we have been here we have been reinforced by four regiments; but many of the men are ill with fluxes, occasioned by the bad water which they got on landing, and the want of fresh provisions.

No action has happened since the 17th of June; a few shot have been exchanged by scouting parties: one morning they beat in our advanced guard, and burnt the guard-house; and on the 19th instant they set fire to the light house and one of our men of war lying but a mile from it; as it was calm we could not get at them, their whale-boats, in which they made their escape, out-rowing any of our boats, and a small island lying between them and the ship prevented her firing on them. They took from the light-house a six-pounder and a swivel.

—Willard, ed., *Letters on the American Revolution*, pp. 174-175.

2. The British Entertain Themselves with Amateur Theatricals

From the Narrative Journal of Lieutenant Martin Hunter of the British Light Infantry.

I was appointed Lieutenant in Orders next day [after the battle of Bunker's Hill], very vain of my promotion, and a few days after removed to the Light Infantry Company. About a month after the action I was taken ill, brought on by eating green apples, and obliged to go to Boston; and I am very certain I should not have recovered if it had not been for General Grant's good soup. He was so good as [to] send me a basin every day. Fresh meat was not then to be had for love or money. I was indebted to Captain Brown of the 52nd, who was the General's brigade-major, for this mark of the General's favour. Captain Symes of the 52nd was also very good to me. He regularly sent me milk from Charlestown every morning. The scarcity of meat at this time was so great that Lord Percy killed a foal, had it roasted, and invited a party to dinner, and Major Musgrave's fat mare was stolen, killed, and sold in the market for beef.

Redoubts were made on Charlestown Heights, and the troops remained in camp some time after the ground was white with snow. Broke up camp, and the regiment ordered into quarters at Boston. A strong detachment, of a field-officer and three hundred men, were left in the redoubt. This detachment was relieved from Boston every fortnight.

Plays were acted twice every week by the officers and some of the Boston ladies. Miss Sally Fletcher acted the part of Zara. She was a very pretty girl and did it very well. A farce called "The Blockade of Boston," written, I believe, by General Burgoyne, was acted. The enemy knew the night it was to be performed and made an attack on the mill at Charlestown at the very hour that the farce began. I happened to be on duty in the redoubt at Charlestown that night. The enemy came along the mill-dam and surprised a sergeant's guard that was posted at the mill. Some shots were fired, and we all immediately turned out and manned the works. A shot was fired by one of our advanced sentries, and instantly the firing commenced in the redoubt, and it was a considerable time before it could be stopped. Not a man of the enemy was within three miles of us, and the party that came along the mill-dam had effected their object and carried off the sergeant's guard. However, our firing caused a general alarm at Boston, and all the troops got under arms.

An orderly sergeant that was standing outside the playhouse door heard the firing and immediately ran into the playhouse, got upon the stage and cried, "Turn out! Turn out! They are hard at it, hammer and tongs." The whole audience thought that the sergeant was acting a part in the farce, and that he did it so well that there was a general clap, and such a noise that he could not be heard for a considerable time. When the clapping was over he again cried, "What the deuce are you all about? If you won't believe me, by Jasus, you need only go to the door, and there you will see and hear both!" If it was the intention of the enemy to put a stop to the farce for that night they certainly succeeded, as all the officers immediately left the playhouse and joined their regiments.

The detachment at Charlestown was relieved three days after, and we returned to Boston.

—HUNTER, *Journal*, pp. 12-14.

3. "NOTHING IS TO BE SEEN BUT DISTRACTIONS AND MELANCHOLY"

Letter sent to England by an officer at Boston.

Boston, August 18, 1775

In my last of the preceding month I informed you of my resolution to resign my commission. Since that time I have made no less than three applications to the generals for that purpose; but all the answer I can obtain is that my request shall be considered of; if it is complied with, be assured that it will be followed by 20 or 30 more, no less a number of brave, honest brother officers having declared their abhorrence of the inhuman service we are upon, and of the shocking outrages that have been committed.

The discontent of our army, occasioned by a scarcity of provisions, the dreadful mortality that has crept into it, and the advancement, insolence and self-sufficiency of a number of Scotch officers, is inconceivable. This very day several common soldiers were reprimanded, and threatened with the most exemplary punishment, for swearing they ought to be commanded by Englishmen, and that they would not sacrifice their lives in an attempt to butcher their friends and fellow subjects for any interested North Briton upon earth. This is the first instance of the kind; but as there is a general murmur, and too much room for complaint, it is likely to be productive of very serious consequences.

Boston, the metropolis of North America (where we now are, and have been so long cooped up) may very justly be termed the grave of England and the slaughter house of America. Nothing is to be heard in it but execrations and clamour; nothing is to be seen but distractions and melancholy, disease and death. The soldiery, and inhabitants likewise, I am sure have done sufficient penance here for the sins of their whole lives. The latter are all ruined; many that were worth 16 or 20 thousand pounds have not a sixpence left; and if any one of them in the anguish of his heart, or the bitterness of his soul, dares mutter any thing like resentment for the loss of his fortune, a distressed family or a murdered friend, he is immediately thrown into a loathsome prison.

If we hear a gun fired upon the Neck, we are all under arms in a moment, and tremble least the Provincials should force their way into the town and put us all to the sword for our cruelty at Lexington and setting fire to the large, ancient and flourishing town of Charlestown. Certainly our conduct at both places was alike inhuman and unjustifiable; and if heaven punishes us for it, it is no more than we deserve.

With regard to diet, we are obliged to live on salt beef and salt pork, much the greater part of which is as hard as wood, as lean as carion, and as rusty as the devil. Could we have good beer, it would, in some measure, prevent their pernicious effects and alleviate the hardships we labour under; but that is impossible, our only beverage being new rum or spruce liquor, which soon throws us into the bloody flux and runs us off our legs in a few days, and has made the remains of our famished army look like so many regiments of skeletons. Could you view our hospitals and see how fast we drop off, your very heart would bleed within you. Thirty bodies are frequently thrown into a trench at a time, like those of so many dogs, no bell being suffered to toll upon the occasion.

But the glorious expedition we are upon is approved of by an all-wise, all-merciful Ministry; and therefore all must be right. Your news-writers, indeed, have had the modesty to assert that we are in high spirits, and want for nothing; but unless we have a speedy supply of English flour, sheep, oxen, coals, potatoes, porter, cloaths, etc., we shall perish for want of them; and when the Ministry hire transports for sending the various articles I have enumerated, the nation will know what credit is to be given to their pensioned scribes and political observation writers. 'Tis well for our generals that we have no where to run to; for could the men desert, I am of opinion that they would soon be left by themselves; but situated as we are, we must unavoidably live and die together.

We have often endeavoured to fall upon the Provincials by surprize; but their vigilance has as constantly frustrated our design. I am glad of it, and sincerely wish, with you, that an obstinate, bloody minded Junto might be brought to repentance; for it is much more reasonable that a few desperadoes should be hung up, *ad terrorem*, for an example to posterity, than that the common rights of mankind should be violated, and thousands of innocent people should perish.

—WILLARD, *Letters on the American Revolution*, pp. 189-192.

VI. THE BRITISH NAVY INEFFECTIVELY HARASSES THE AMERICANS

Meantime what was the Navy doing? That Britain ruled the waves, nobody would deny, yet the British failed egregiously to get any benefit out of their naval superiority. In part this was because Admiral Graves preferred writing dispatches to fighting battles, and was in any event reluctant to assume the offensive without specific orders. In part it was because the First Lord of the Admiralty, Lord Sandwich, was perhaps the most corrupt man in British public life, and as inefficient as he was corrupt. But a large part of the explanation is much simpler: there was nothing much that the Navy could do. There was as yet no American Navy to fight; the hundreds of whale and fishing boats, upon which the Americans depended for their operations in Boston harbor and surrounding waters, were far too small, too swift and too elusive for the guns of the British men-of-war. The Navy could, of course, punish American coastal towns, and beginning in October it proceeded to undertake this, but in a desultory manner. Thus, though half a dozen towns had been marked out for destruction, only Falmouth—now Portland—was actually destroyed. Even when Graves was recalled and replaced by Vice-Admiral Molyneux Shuldham, conditions did not improve; the new vice-admiral's record of bad luck continued to pursue him in American waters.

We give here General Burgoyne's outburst on the futility of the Navy; Admiral Graves's own defense—written some time later and to be taken at a substantial discount; and accounts of the attacks on Bristol, Rhode Island, and Falmouth, Maine.

1. "WHAT THE ADMIRAL IS *Not* DOING"

General Burgoyne to Lord George Germain.

Boston, Aug. 20, 1775

... It may perhaps be asked in England what is the Admiral doing? I wish I was able to answer that question satisfactorily. But I can only say what he is *not* doing.

That he is *not* supplying the troops with sheep and oxen, the dinners of the best of us bear the meagre testimony; the want of broth in the hospitals bears a more melancholy one.

He is *not* defending his own flocks and herds, for the enemy has repeatedly and in the most insulting manner plundered his own appropriated islands.

He is *not* defending the other islands in the harbour, for the enemy landed in force, burned the lighthouse at noonday, and killed and took a party of marines almost under the guns of two or three men-of-war.

He is *not* employing his ships to keep up communication and intelligence with the servants and friends of Government at different parts of the continent, for I do not believe General Gage has received a letter from any correspondents out of Boston these six weeks.

He is surely intent upon greater objects, you will think: supporting in material points the dignity and terror of the British flag, and where a number of botes have been built for the rebels, privateers fitted out, prizes carried in, the King's armed vessels sunk, the crews made prisoners, the officers killed, he is doubtless enforcing instant restitution and reparation by the voice of his cannon and laying the towns in ashes which refuse his terms. Alas! he is *not!* The British thunder is diverted or controlled by pitiful attentions and Quaker-like scruples, and under such influence insult and impunity, like righteousness and peace, have kissed each other.

I should have hesitated in giving an account that may appear invidious, had not the facts been too notorious to expose me to that censure, and my feelings in this great cause too sensible to observe them without some impatience. Upon the whole when the supineness of this department is added to the diffidence of the other, and the defects of Quartermaster General, Adjutant General, Secretaries and commissaries are superadded to both, they will make altogether a mass of insufficiency that I am afraid would counteract and disappoint the ablest counsels in the world.

—GR. BRIT. HIST. MSS. COMM., *9th Report*, III, 81.

2. ADMIRAL GRAVES EXHAUSTS EVERY RESOURCE TO ANNOY THE REBELS

Written in his own defense.

The Admiral was intent upon employing the small force which he had in the most effectual manner for the King's service. He assisted the army with convoys, seamen for their transports, and open boats for their outposts, almost to the disabling of the squadron; for sailors were not now to be procured, and the complements still remaining upon the lowest peace-establishment, a few desertions or a moderate sickness reduced them below the power of acting with any good effect. And what a situation was the Admiral's! Wholly uncertain with respect to the future measures of Administration towards the Colonies; in a very great want of all naval stores, as well as of artificers; on an enemy's coast with winter approaching, when navigation is holden by the Americans themselves to be no longer practicable, and yet the critical situation both of the fleet and army such that his few tattered cruizers must at all hazards be kept out to protect and conduct into port the precarious supplies expected from England, as what alone could enable us to maintain ourselves at Boston; and to sum up all, no accounts, no directions, no orders from home.

However, under all these disadvantages, the Admiral zealously continued to exert every power and exhaust every resource to annoy the Rebels, and to cover our beleaguered army.

—FRENCH, *First Year of the American Revolution*, pp. 538-539.

3. Bristol Buys Off a Bombardment

Extract of a letter from Bristol, in the *New York Gazette*, October 23, 1775.

October 8, 1775

Yesterday afternoon appeared in sight of Bristol Harbor a very formidable fleet, consisting of sixteen sail, viz.: three men-of-war, one bomb ketch and other armed vessels, all of which, excepting the *Glasgow*, which ran ashore at Papaquash Point, drew up in a line of battle from one end of the town to the other. Soon after they had moored, a barge came from the *Rose* to the head of a wharf, with the lieutenant who asked if there were any gentlemen on the wharf? William Bradford, being present, answered yes, whereupon the lieutenant informed him Captain Wallace had a demand to make on the town and desired that two or three of the principal men or magistrates of the town would go on board his ship within an hour and hear his proposals; otherwise hostilities would be commenced against the town.

The above gentleman replied, as a magistrate, that, in his opinion, Captain Wallace was under a greater obligation to come ashore and make his demands known to the town than for the magistrates to go on board his ship to hear them; and added that if Captain Wallace would come to the head of the wharf the next morning, he should be treated as a gentleman, and the town would consider of his demands. With this answer the lieutenant returned on board the *Rose*.

The inhabitants, being made acquainted with the above association, repaired to the wharf and waited with the utmost impatience for a reply from Captain Wallace, till an hour had expired, when the whole fleet began a most heavy cannonading, and the bomb vessel to bombard and heave shells and carcases into the town; which continued without intermission an hour and a half.

In the mean time, Colonel Potter, in the hottest of the fire, went upon the head of the wharf, hailed the *Rose*, went on board and requested a cessation of hostilities till the inhabitants might choose a committee to go on board and treat with Captain Wallace; which request was complied with; and six hours were allowed for the above purpose. Colonel Potter returned and made a report to the committee of inspection, who chose a select committee to hear Captain Wallace's demands, which, after they had gone on board, Captain Wallace informed them were a supply of two hundred sheep and thirty fat cattle. This demand, the committee replied, it was impossible to comply with; for the country people had been in and driven off their stock, saving a few sheep and some milch cows.

After some hours had expired during the negotiation without coming to any agreement, Captain Wallace told them: "I have this one proposal to make: if you will promise to supply me with forty sheep, at or before twelve o'clock, I will assure you that another gun shall not be discharged."

The committee, seeing themselves reduced to the distressing alternative, either to supply their most inveterate enemy with provisions or to devote to the flames the town, with all the goods, besides near one hundred sick persons who could not be removed without the utmost hazard of their lives—I

say, seeing themselves reduced to this dreadful dilemma of two evils, reluctantly chose the least, by agreeing to supply them with forty sheep at the
time appointed, which was punctually performed. . . .

What equally challenges our admiration and gratitude to God is that no
more lives were lost, or persons hurt, by such an incessant and hot fire; the
streets being full of men, women and children the whole time. The shrieks of
the women, the cries of the children and groans of the sick would have extorted a tear from even the eye of a Nero.

–MOORE, *Diary of the American Revolution*, I, 148-150.

4. THE BOMBARDMENT OF BRISTOL, RHODE ISLAND

1775

October, 'twas the seventh day,
As I have heard the people say,
Wallace—his name be ever curs't—
Came on our harbour just at dusk,

And there his ship did safely moor
And quickly sent his barge ashore,
With orders that should not be broke,
Or that we might expect a smoke,

Demanding that our magistrates
Should quickly come on board his ship
And let him have some sheep and cattle
Or that they might expect a battle.

At eight o'clock by signal given,
Our peaceful atmosphere was riven;
Women with children in their arms
With doleful cries ran to the farms.

With all their firing and their skill
They did not any person kill,
Neither was any person hurt
Except the Reverend Parson Burt.

And he was not killed by a ball,
As judged by jurors one and all,
But being in a sickly state,
He frightened fell, which proved his fate.

Another truth to you I'll tell
That you may see they levelled well,
For aiming for to kill the people,
They fired their shot into a steeple.

They firéd low, they firéd high,
The women scream, the children cry,
And all their firing and their racket
Shot off the topmast of a packet!

–MUNRO, *History of Bristol, Rhode Island*, pp. 205-206.

5. THE BRITISH BURN FALMOUTH

A. "ORDERS TO EXECUTE A JUST PUNISHMENT ON THE TOWN"

To the People of Falmouth.

Canceau, Falmouth, Oct. 16, 1775

After so many premeditated attacks on the legal prerogatives of the best of Sovereigns, after the repeated instances you have experienced in Britain's long forbearance of the rod of correction, and the merciful and paternal extension of her hands to embrace you, again and again, have been regarded as vain and nugatory; and in place of a dutiful and grateful return to your King and parent state, you have been guilty of the most unpardonable rebellion, supported by the ambition of a set of designing men, whose insidious deeds have cruelly imposed on the credulity of their fellow-creatures, and at last have brought the whole into the same dilemma, which leads me to feel not a little the woes of the innocent of them, in particular on the present occasion, from my having it in orders to execute a just punishment on the Town of Falmouth. In the name of which authority, I previously warned you to remove without delay the human species out of the said Town, for which purpose I give you the time of two hours; at the period of which, a red pendant will be hoisted at the main topgallant mast head, with a gun. But should your imprudence lead you to show the least resistance, you will in that case free me of that humanity so strongly pointed out in my orders, as well as in my inclination. I also observe that all those who did, on a former occasion, fly to the King's ship under my command for protection, that the same door is now open and ready to receive them. . . .

H. MOWAT, *Captain*
—FORCE, *American Archives*, 4th Series, III, 154.

B. "ALL THE COMPACT PART OF THE TOWN IS GONE"

January 15, 1776

Report by the Selectmen of Falmouth on the Destruction.

It was about 9 o'clock on Wednesday, being the 18th of October, that the firing began from all the . . . vessels, with all possible briskness, discharging on every part of the town which lay on a regular descent toward the harbour an horrible shower of balls, from three to nine pounds weight, bombs, carcasses, live shells, grape-shot and musket-balls. The firing lasted, without many minutes cessation, until about six o'clock P.M., during which time several parties came ashore and set buildings on fire by hand. Parties of our people, and others from the neighboring towns, ran down to oppose them, and it is thought killed several. One officer, after he fell, was stripped of a neat pair of pistols, his flask and cockade. Through the goodness of God no life was lost on our side, and only one man wounded. . . . Had no opposition been made, we do not believe they would have left one building standing; and more opposition would have been made had not the people's attention been taken up in securing their effects. Besides, it was very unfortunate that our companies of sea-coast men were put under the direction of a committee; for they did not, and we suppose could not, get together in the hurry of affairs, and therefore could give no authoritative directions.

As near as we can judge, about three-quarters of the buildings, reckoning according to their value, are consumed, consisting of about 130 dwelling-houses, many of which held two or three families apiece, besides barns, and almost every store and warehouse in town. St. Paul's Church, a large new building, with the bell; a very elegant and costly new court-house, not quite finished; a fine engine, almost new; the old town house and the publick library, were all consumed. But one or two wharves have escaped the flames; and every vessel in the harbour, of any considerable bigness, was burnt, excepting two, which the enemy carried away with them. The warning given was so short that but few teams could be procured to remove the goods out; much was caried out by hand; but, as far as we can learn, not much more than half of the moveables were saved out of the buildings that were burnt. All the compact part of the town is gone; and among the hundred dwelling-houses that are standing, there are but few good buildings, and those damaged with balls passing through them or bombs bursting. . . .

ENOCH FREEMAN [*et al*], *Selectmen of the Town of Falmouth*
—FORCE, *American Archives*, 4th Series, III, 1172-1173.

C. "THE SAME DESOLATION IS MEDITATED UPON ALL THE TOWNS ON THE COAST"

George Washington to the President of the Continental Congress.

Camp at Cambridge, Oct. 24, 1775

Sir: My conjecture of the destination of the late squadron from Boston in my last has been unhappily verified by an outrage exceeding in barbarity and cruelty every hostile act practiced among civilized nations. I have enclosed the account given me by Mr. Jones, a gentleman of the Town of Falmouth, of the destruction of that . . . village. . . . The orders shown by the Captain for this horrid procedure by which it appears the same desolation is meditated upon all the Towns on the coast, made it my duty to communicate it as quickly and extensively as possible. As Portsmouth was the next place to which he proposed to go, General Sullivan was permitted to go up and give them his assistance and advice, to ward off the blow. I flatter myself the like event will not happen there, as they have a fortification of some strength, and a vessel has arrived at a place called Sheepscut, with one thousand five hundred pounds of powder. . . .

—FORCE, *American Archives*, 4th Series, III, 1151.

VII. BOSTON REDEEMED

All through the winter the two armies watched each other across the narrow necks of Boston and Charlestown peninsulas, both growing stronger, yet neither strong enough to take the offensive. General Howe had replaced Gage, Admiral Shuldham supplanted the inept Graves, and the British forces had grown to some 7,000 or 8,000, but they still stood on the defensive. What else, after all, could they do? By now the Americans were firmly entrenched, and even if, at great cost, the British had broken through the American lines they would have gained nothing. As General Burgoyne wrote to an English friend, "Look, my Lord, upon the country near Boston—it is all fortification. Driven from one hill you will see the enemy retrenched upon the next and every step we move must be the slow step of a siege." Washington, whose army was being built up to 16,000, was eager to fight, but he, too, was stopped by considerations of matériel. Over 2,000 of his men lacked muskets; there were never more than nine or ten rounds of ammunition per man; and there were not enough cannon for an effective bombardment of Boston or advancing British lines. Yet with every day Washington grew more impatient. He knew that Howe would withdraw from the city at the earliest feasible moment, and he was eager to force him to give battle, not only in order to inflict losses on him, but to stiffen American morale. In January he submitted to his council of war "the indispensable necessity of making a Bold attempt to conquer the Ministerial Troops before they can be reinforced in the spring," but found no support.

Then late in January the picture changed. Colonel Knox, the stout and amiable Boston bookseller who had become colonel of artillery, brought 43 cannon and 14 mortars from Ticonderoga over the mountains to Framingham, on January 25, and in the course of the next month these were brought into the American lines. At the same time powder and ammunition stocks were built up to the point where Washington felt he could afford a bombardment and an attack.

Now Washington prepared to force the issue. The British held Charlestown peninsula, but with unpardonable folly they had failed to seize and fortify Dorchester Heights to the south of Boston. Washington took advantage of this oversight—if it can be called that. On March 2 he opened a heavy bombardment on Boston Neck, and on the evening of March 4 General John Thomas, with a picked force of 2,000 men, moved onto Dorchester Heights. Washington knew that he would have to have some kind of fortifications for his men by next morning, and as the ground was frozen they could not dig in as they had on Breed's Hill. With characteristic ingenuity they had prefabricated their entrenchments. During the previous weeks they had constructed portable timber frames which could be filled with hay, and barrels to fill with dirt and stones. When General Thomas moved onto the Heights he was accompanied by 350 oxcarts loaded with these materials. Working feverishly through the night, the American advance forces threw up their timber wall, cut down fruit trees to form an abatis in front of the timber, and in front of these placed their stone-filled barrels, useful in defense and dangerous on offense. It was, said the British Engineer Archibald Robertson, "a most astonishing night's work, and must have employed from 15 to 20,000 men."

Howe found himself in the predicament that had faced Gage back in June. Like Gage he decided to attack at once. But as the British surveyed the American position on Dorchester Heights, almost impregnable with entrenchments and artillery, and manned now by some 4,000 men, they came to realize that an attack might well be suicidal. What, then, to do? Happily fate intervened; that night a storm of hurricane proportions blew up, making it quite impossible to transport troops to the beaches below Dorchester Heights, and by the time the storm had spent itself the American position really was impregnable. Howe rightly concluded that he had no choice but to pull out. There was a tacit agreement on both sides not to damage the city while preparations for evacuation went forward. On St. Patrick's Day, March 17, the British sailed away—some 10,000 soldiers and sailors, and about 1,000 Loyalist refugees. "The last trump," said Washington, "could not have struck them with greater consternation." For ten days the fleet lingered in Nantasket Roads, then sailed for Halifax. The battle for Boston was over.

We are fortunate in having a number of vivid accounts of this last chapter of the siege of Boston. Knox himself tells of the hauling of the cannon from Lake Champlain; Samuel Webb of Connecticut describes the preparations for the offensive. Colonel Stuart, son of former Prime Minister Bute, makes clear the hopelessness of the British position, as does Sir William Howe, himself so largely responsible for that hopelessness. The ubiquitous Reverend William Gordon, already planning to write a history of the war, tells the whole story of the attack from the beginning of the bombardment to the final evacuation. And finally Deacon Newell of the Brattle Street Church, who had endured so many indignities, celebrates in his journal the deliverance of his city.

1. Transporting the Ticonderoga Cannon to Boston

Journal of Henry Knox of the Continental Army.

January 1st to the 4th [1776]. Employed in getting holes cut in the different crossing places in the river in order to strengthen the ice. This day, the 4th, arrived a brass 24-pounder and a small mortar. I this day sent a letter to Genl Washington, one to Brig Genl Gates, also one to Capt Baylor and one to my lovely Lucy.

In the afternoon much alarmed by hearing that one of the heaviest cannon had fallen in to the river at Half Moon Ferry. This Genl Schuyler came and informed me just as I was going to sit down to dinner. I immediately set out for a slay and went up to the Half Moon where I reached at dusk, and not hearing of the others and fearing that they would meet the same fate, I sent off an express to Sloss's ferry, about 7 miles distant, with a letter to Mr. Schuyler informing him of my excessive surprize at the careless manner in which he carried the cannon over, without taking those precautions which by his instructions he was bound to have done and by no means to attempt crossing where he was untill I came. The express returned and informed that they had all got safely over. I then sent off another express to Mr. Swartz to cross at Sloss's, as the ice was so much stronger there than at Half Moon, the usual place of crossing. . . .

Sunday Jan 7th Albany. The cannon, which the night before last came over at Sloss's ferry, we attempted to get over the ferry here, which we effected excepting the last, which fell into the river notwithstanding the precautions we took, and in its fall broke all the ice for 14 feet around it. This was a misfortune as it retarded the dispatch which I wished to use in this business. We pushed the 10 sleds on, which got over safe, and then I went to getting the drowned cannon out, which we partly effected, but by reason of the nights coming could not do it entirely.

8th. Went on the ice about 8 o'clock in the morning and proceeded so cautiously that before night we got over three sleds and were so lucky as to get the cannon out of the river, owing to the assistance the good people of the city of Albany gave, in return for which we christened her—*The Albany*.

The 9th. Got several spare slays, also some spare string of horses, in case of any accident. After taking my leave of General Schuyler and some other of my friends in Albany, I sat out from there about twelve o'clock and went as far as Claverac, about 9 miles beyond Kinderhook. I first saw all the cannon set out from the ferry opposite Albany.

10th. Reached No. 1, after having climbed mountains from which we might almost have seen all the kingdoms of earth.

11th. Went 12 miles thro' the Green Woods to Blanford. It appeared to me almost a miracle that people with heavy loads should be able to get up and down such hills as are here, with any thing of heavy loads. *11th.* At Blanford we overtook the first division who had tarried here untill we came up, and refused going any further, on account that there was no snow beyond five or six miles further in which space there was the tremendous Glasgow or West-field Mountain to go down. But after about three hours persuasion, I hiring two teams of oxen, they agreed to go.

—Knox, "Diary," *New-England Historical and Genealogical Register,*
XXX, 324-325.

2. The Balance of Forces in the Siege of Boston

From the Journal of Lieutenant Samuel Webb of the Continental Army.

March 1, 1776. Our affairs growing now to a critical situation, I can no longer neglect minuteing the daily occurrances and manoevers of our army, and that of our enemy, which has been besieged and close blockaded by land ever since the 19th of April last—by an army which they have called a set of poltroons and cowards—in which they must have altered their sentiments or they would have ventured an attempt to raise the siege.

The greatest preparations are now makeing to approach our enemies with an endeavour to rout them from their garrison—for while the sea is open to them they will get supplied with provisions—and they are in hourly expectation of large reinforcements from England. Their garrison at present amount to about 6000 effective men. Boston being a peninsula they are fortifyed in the strongest manner possible; even the strong fortifications of Gibralter is said not to equall them. They have cut a canal thro' the Neck, by which Boston is now an island.

On the south and west sides they are strongly fortified by a chain of forts both on the ridge of hills running the whole length of the town, and below all round the waters edge. On the north and east sides lie a number of ships of war, which sufficiently prevent our attempting to penetrate in that way, having no naval force equal to that lying in the harbour. Opposite the north east of the town lies Noddle Island, which at low water you can get on to from the main at Chelsea. This point runs in bluff and looks over the shiping not more than 400 yards distance, nor exceeding 600 to the thick settled part of the town.

Directly east of the old fortification gates on the south part of the town lies Dorchester Point, which commands the south part of the town and is at least 600 yards within their outer lines on the Neck next Roxbury. A strong battery erected on this point would enable us to cut off the communication between the town and their outworks on the Neck, at the same time annoy the ships and town. Neither of these two posts are taken possession, owing, on the side of the enemy, to want of a proper number of men to garrison them, and on ours powder and artillery to maintain them, but having lately been supplied with some of both these necessary articles, we are now making preparations to take possession of both, by erecting great number of facines, gabions, pressing hay, etc. etc.

Our commander-in-chief is determined to loose no time in putting into execution this plan, for should the enemy be enabled by reinforcements to maintain these posts they would enlarge their limits greatly by which means have it in their power frequently to make excursions into the country adjoining and lay waste with fire and sword our villages, farms, houses, etc. The enemy seem equally sensible of the importance of these two posts, and 'tis said their commander has swore if we brake ground on either he will sally on us—if he was sure of looseing two thirds of his army. This is what we wish for, trusting (through the assistance of Heaven) this would be a means of rescueing from their hands our capital and many of our friends, who are now confined there contrary to the solemn compact made between Genl. Gage and them.

Should they sally on us, we have a prospect of makeing them to take to their ships and flee; in this case we fear the loss of the town by their seting fire to it, but this is trifeling in comparison to the loss of our valuable privileges, which may God preserve us in the enjoyment of. The enemy are erecting two batteries on Mount Whoredom, against ours on Lechmores Point, and the one on Cobble-Hill known by the name of Putnam's Impregnable Battery. . . .

Our worthy commander in chief (in orders a day or two past) has in the most pathetic terms told the soldiery that on our present conduct depends the salvation of America; that in all probability e'er long we shall be called to the field of battle; that he is confident his troops will behave as deserves the cause we are contending for; but that in all army's their are those who would flee before a much smaller number, and that should any such be found sculking or retreating before the enemy without orders, they must expect instant death by way of example to others.

—WEBB, *Correspondence and Journals,* I, 129-132.

3. WASHINGTON SEIZES THE HEIGHTS OF DORCHESTER

The Reverend William Gordon to Samuel Wilson.

Jamaica Plain, April 6, 1776

Our brave and sensible commander in chief his Excellency Gen'l Washington, having laid his plan for seizing and fortifying Dorchester hills that overlook the town, . . . applied to the New England governments . . . for a reinforcement of some thousands for two months, ending with the last of

March, which was accordingly sent. Our troops were busied in making fascines and in getting every other matter in readiness. A battle was expected and ardently wished for, whenever we should possess the hills. It was urged by some to go on so as that the engagement might happen on the 5th of March, the day on which the unarmed mob was fired upon at Boston by Capt. Preston's men. It was accordingly concluded to enter upon the work the 4th at night.

In the mean time to amuse the enemy, our bomb batteries being finished on Cambridge and Roxbury side, a few shells were thrown into town Saturday night March the third; till then it was not believed that we had so many warlike instruments, but we had sent to Ticonderoga and had brought over the lakes, while froze sufficient to bear, cannon, mortars and howittzs, to the amount of fifty and better; shells we got from the king's store at N. York. On the Lord's day night more shells were thrown, besides firing a number of cannon into the town. The Monday night it was repeated and increased considerably; but not one of our friends in town was hurt; about half a dozen soldiers lost their limbs.

All things being ready, as soon as the evening admitted of it, the undertaking went forward. The covering party consisting of 800 men led the way; then the carts with the entrenching tools; after that the main working body under Gen'l Thomas consisting of about 1200; a train of more than 300 carts loaded with fascines, presst hay, in bundles of seven or eight hundred, etc., closed the procession. Every one knew his place and business; the covering party when upon the ground divided, half went to the point next to Boston, the other to that next to the Castle. All possible silence was observed. The wind lay so as to carry what noise could not be avoided, by driving the stakes and picking against the frozen ground (for the frost was still more than a foot thick, about a foot and a half) to carry, I say, what noise could not be avoided into the harbour between the town and the castle, so as not to be heard and regarded by such as had no suspicion of what we were after, especially as there was a continued cannonade on both sides. Many of the carts made three trips, some four.

Gen'l Thomas told me that he pulled out his watch and found that by ten o'clock at night, they had got two forts, one upon each hill, sufficient to defend them from small arms and grape shot. The men continued working with the utmost spirit, till relieved the Tuesday morning about three. The neighbouring militia had been called in for three days to guard against accidents, and were in by twelve at night, some before, in the evening. The night was remarkably mild, a finer for working could not have been taken out of the whole 365. It was hazy below so that our people could not be seen, tho' it was a bright moon light night above on the hills.

When the ministerialists discovered in the morning early what we had been after, they were astonished upon seeing what we had done. Gen'l How was seen to scratch his head and heard to say by those that were about him that he did not know what he should do, that the provincials (he likely called them by some other name) had done more work in one night than his whole army would have done in six months. In this strong manner did he express his surprise. He soon called a council of war and determined upon attempting to dislodge our people (the Admiral having informed him that if we possessed those heights he could not keep one of his Majesty's ships in the harbour).

Spectators in abundance, Yours among the rest, were looking out upon the adjacent hills for a bloody battle. The wharf was thronged with soldiers, while numbers were going on board vessels; the provincials rejoiced at seeing it, clapped their hands and wished for the expected attack.

Gen. Washington said to those that were at hand, "Remember it is the fifth of March, and avenge the death of your brethren!" It was immediately asked what the General said by those that were not near enough to hear, and as soon answered; and so from one to another thro' all the troops, which added fresh fuel to the martial fire before kindled. . . .

The tide was turned, and the day too far spent to admit of the regulars coming out and attacking on the fifth of March. They would have been under great disadvantages had they landed after high water, at the point next to the town. Gen'l How proposed attacking therefore the next morning very early. . . .

I came home early, finding nothing could be done that evening; and being fatigued with riding forward and backward, and the exercise of body and mind natural to such a peculiar state of things, and designing to be up by day break and down in view of what might be going on, I went to bed about eight. I expected that the men of war would get as near to Dorchester hills as possible, that the next morning at day break a most heavy cannonade would begin; and I thought it probable that the regulars would land under cover of it, and proceed to attack the provincials. But when I heard in the night how amazingly strong the wind blew (for it was such a storm as scarce any one remembered to have heard) and how it rained towards morning, I concluded that the ships could not stir, and pleased myself with the reflection that the Lord might be working deliverance for us and preventing the effusion of human blood.

The event proved that it was so. The storm hindered the attack; and it was so given out afterward, in general orders by Gen. How as appears by one of the orderly books that fell into our hands. Immediately orders were given to prepare for embarking the troops, that the town might be speedily evacuated. The Tories were thunder-struck, and terribly dejected. All was hurry and confusion: the soldiers working like horses night and day, getting on board what they could as fast as possible. On the 17th of March in the morning they evacuated the town.

—Gordon, "Letter," *Mass. Hist. Soc. Proc.*, LX, 361-364.

4. General Howe Justifies His Decision to Evacuate Boston

To the Earl of Dartmouth.

On Board His Majesty's Ship *Chatham*,
Nantasket Road, March 21, 1776

My Lord:—It is with great regret I am obliged to inform your lordship that after all my struggles to supply the army with provisions from the Southern provinces and the West Indies, from whence none of the vessels have yet returned, and after an anxious expectation of more transports to convey the troops, stores, civil officers, inhabitants, and effects, the enemy, by taking possession of and fortifying the commanding heights on Dorchester Neck, in order to force the ships, by their cannon, to quit the harbor, has reduced me to the necessity either of exposing the army to the greatest distresses by remaining in Boston, or of withdrawing from it under such straitened circumstances.

The importance of preserving this force, when it could no longer act to advantage, did not leave any room to doubt of the propriety of its removal; and since my determination, taken on the 7th instant, I have exerted every expedient to accomplish the arduous task, which was executed on the 17th following, in the forenoon, without the least molestation from the rebels, the transports having been previously watered, and fitted for sea in every respect, excepting the article of provisions, in the view of complying with His Majesty's commands for a movement from Boston, as soon as I might be enabled to effect it. . . .

The rebels, about the latter end of January, erected new works and batteries on a point of land opposite to West Boston, at a place known by the name of Phipps's Farm, which, laying under cover of their strongest posts, and so situated as to be supported by their whole force from Cambridge, was not to be prevented; soon afterwards the militia of the country was called in, and, having intelligence that the enemy intended to possess themselves of Dorchester Neck, I ordered a detachment from Castle William, on the 13th of February, under the command of Lieutenant-colonel Leslie, and one composed of grenadiers and light-infantry from Boston, commanded by Major Musgrave, to pass over the ice, with directions to destroy the houses and every kind of cover whatever upon that peninsula, which was executed, and six of the enemy's guard made prisoners.

On the 2d instant [March], at night, the rebels began a cannonade upon the town from Roxbury and Phipps's Farm, and threw some shells from both places, without doing any personal damage, and but little to the buildings; the same was repeated on the evenings of the 3d and 4th, by which only six men were wounded; the fire being returned from our batteries, but at such a distance as to be very uncertain in the execution.

It was discovered on the 5th, in the morning, that the enemy had thrown up three very extensive works, with strong abatis round them, on the commanding hill on Dorchester Neck, which must have been the employment of at least twelve thousand men in a situation so critical. I determined upon an immediate attack, with all the force I could transport. The ardor of the troops encouraged me in this hazardous enterprise; regiments were expeditiously embarked on board transports to fall down the harbor, and flat-boats were to receive other troops, making the whole two thousand four hundred men, to rendezvous at Castle William, from whence the descent was to be made, on the night of the 5th, but the wind unfortunately coming contrary and blowing very hard, the ships were not able to get to their destination, and this circumstance also making it impossible to employ the boats, the attempt became impracticable.

The weather continuing boisterous the next day and night, gave the enemy time to improve their works, to bring up their cannon, and to put themselves into such a state of defence that I could promise myself little success by attacking them under all the disadvantages I had to encounter; wherefore I judged it most advisable to prepare for the evacuation of the town, upon the assurance of one month's provision from Admiral Shuldham, who, in this emergency, as he has on every other occasion, offered all the assistance he could afford.

A thousand difficulties arose on account of the disproportion of transports for the conveyance of the troops, the well-affected inhabitants, their most valuable property, and the quantity of military stores to be carried away; however, as the enemy gave no interruption but during the nights, and that inconsiderable, I found the whole in readiness to depart on the 14th, if the wind had favored, and assisted by the abilities and assiduity of Captains Reynar and Montagu, of His Majesty's ships *Chatham* and *Fowey*, who superintended the embarkation, and by the alacrity of the officers under them, this operation was effected on the 17th, and the rear guard embarked at nine o'clock in the morning, without the least loss, irregularity, or accident. Such military stores as could not be taken on board were destroyed, and the utmost expedition is now using to get ready for sea in the best state our circumstances will allow; the admiral leaving all the ships-of-war he can spare from the convoy for the security and protection of such vessels as may be bound for Boston.

Every provision my situation would afford has been made for the accommodation of the inhabitants and the preservation of their effects; all the woolen goods, also, that I could find room for, belonging to those who chose to stay behind, the want of which is more distressing to the enemy than any other article whatever, have been shipped; inventories of them taken in the best manner possible, and put under the charge of proper persons, in order to be hereafter stored. The demolition of the castle has been effectually executed, and an armed ship is sent by the admiral, express, to advise the different governors on the continent of this removal. . . .

—DAWSON, *Battles of the United States*, I, 94-95.

5. THE BRITISH EVACUATE BOSTON

Colonel Charles Stuart to Lord Bute.

Halifax, April 28, 1776

. . . Nothing particular happened till Feb; we took a few prizes, and the enemy were more than equally successful in this point.

About the middle of Feb. we were informed that the Rebels had a quantity of fascines and entrenching tools on Dorchester Neck for the purpose of throwing up works. Deserters informed the General that the enemy intended to bombard the town, and preparations were made to hinder their work. A battery of four 32-pounders was made on Shoredon Hill and another strong one at Boston's Point. The Rebels at the same time made a battery within point-blank cannon shot of our lines, and with such caution that we could not discover that it was intended for a battery.

On the 3rd March at 9 oclock at even they began a pretty hot cannonade and bombardment. Their shells were thrown in an excellent direction, they took effect near the centre of the town, and tore several houses to pieces; the cannon was usually well fired, one shot killed 8 men of the 22nd Regt. and houses were pierced through and through with balls they fired from Phipps's Farm. Our lines were raked from the new battery they had made and tho' we returned shot and shell, I am very, very sorry to say with not quite so much judgement.

The bombardment continued for five nights, and a nobler scene it was impossible to behold: sheets of fire seemed to come from our batteries; some of the shells crossed one another in the air, and then bursting looked beautiful. The inhabitants were in a horrid situation, particularly the women who were several times drove from their houses by shot, and crying for protection.

On the 8th or 9th March, I forget which, they ceased firing, and at daybreak next morning we perceived two posts upon the highest hills of Dorchester peninsula, that appeared more like majick than the work of human beings. They were each of them near 200 ft. long on the side next the town, and seemed to be strong cases of packed hay about 10 ft. high with an abattis of vast thickness round both. We discovered near 6000 people, most of them at work; they opened embrasures before 9 oclock and about 2 oclock had made a ditch and connected the two hills by a breastwork.

We fired a few shots, but the position was too strong to be affected; the General therefore determined to attack it. A quantity of artillery and three regiments immediately embarked under the command of General Jones, the Grenadiers, Lt. Infantry, and other regts. amounting in all to 2500 men commanded by General Howe, Lord Percy and General Robertson.

Brigadier Jones was to have staid with the three regts. aboard ship until he was joined by Gen. Howe at 9 oclock at night, when the whole was to have gone in boats and landed. God knows whether it was a fortunate circumstance or not, but at any rate so high a wind arose that it was impossible for the boats to take to sea.

The next day the General assembled the field officers and acquainted us that the intended attack had failed through the inclemency of the weather, that he had consulted the engineers, who declared that the works had been so strengthened as to render any present attack very doubtful, and that should the enemy augment their works upon that peninsula from such a commanding height we should inevitably be drove from the town.

He also told us that there was no more than 6 weeks' provisions in the garrison, which obliged him to go to Halifax instead of to New York.

The principal citizens, on hearing that the town was to be evacuated, came to General Howe, and requested that the town might not be burnt; the General made answer that if the enemy molested him in his retreat he would certainly burn it; if not, he would leave the town standing.

This was made known by a flag of truce to the Rebels; in consequence of which we made our retreat unmolested.

We sailed soon after under convoy of the Admiral to this place. From a scarcity of transports we were crowded with two regts. in each ship and nothing could be more horrid. . . .

—WORTLEY, ed., *Correspondence of Bute and Stuart*, pp. 76-79.

6. "THUS WAS THIS UNHAPPY TOWN RELIEVED"

Journal of Timothy Newell, a selectman of Boston.

[*March*] *17th Lord's day.* This morning at 3 o'clock, the troops began to move—guards, chevaux de freze, crow feet strewed in the streets to prevent being pursued. They all embarked at about 9 oclock and the whole fleet came to sail. Every vessel which they did not carry off, they rendered unfit for use. Not even a boat left to cross the river.

Thus was this unhappy distressed town (through a manifest interposition of divine providence) relieved from a set of men whose unparralleled wickedness, profanity, debauchery and cruelty is inexpressible, enduring a siege from the 19th April 1775 to the 17th March 1776. Immediately upon the fleet's sailing the Select Men set off through the lines to Roxbury to acquaint General Washington of the evacuation of the town. After sending a message Major Ward, aid to General Ward, came to us at the lines and soon after the General himself, who received us in the most polite and affectionate manner, and permitted us to pass to Watertown to acquaint the Council of this happy event. The General immediately ordered a detachment of 2000 troops to take possession of the town under the command of General Putnam who the next day began their works in fortifying Forthill, etc., for the better security of the town. A number of loaded shells with trains of powder covered with straw were found in houses left by the Regulars near the fortifycation.

—NEWELL, "Journal," *Mass. Hist. Soc. Coll.*, 4th Series, I, 274-276.

CHAPTER SIX

The Canadian Campaigns

FOR AMERICANS, Canada was the ignis fatuus of the Revolution. In 1759 the fate of the continent had been decided on the Plains of Abraham, before Quebec, and many Americans were convinced that history would repeat itself. But how would history go about repeating itself? Would Americans now play the role that the British had played, and wrest Canada from its masters by military force? Or would Canada—which was after all a "conquered" province, and overwhelmingly French—throw off the imperial ties and bind herself to the American states?

This was, at first, the official position. Surely the Canadians resented British tyranny just as keenly as other Americans! Surely they would see that their future was inextricably tied to the future of the rest of the continent! Surely they could be won over by persuasion, by kind words, by logic! On June 1, 1775, Congress formally resolved that there should be no expedition against Canada, and soon it was discussing the Commission which would be sent up to spread the gospel of freedom. And the Articles of Confederation—drafted as early as 1776 but not approved until 1777—contained the provision that "Canada, acceding to this confederation, shall be admitted into . . . the union, but no other colony shall be admitted . . . unless . . . by nine states."

But on this matter as on so many others, Congress was inconsistent. Benedict Arnold, thirsting for action and for glory, was convinced that Canada could be conquered that very summer, and that he was the man to do it. So was Ethan Allen. In unison, though not in harmony, they had taken Ticonderoga, and Arnold had gone on to St. Johns, in Quebec, and captured it; now they were persuaded that they could do it again. Somehow they convinced the Congress, too, for on June 27 Congress reversed itself and voted "that if General Schuyler finds it practicable and that it will not be disagreeable to the Canadians, he shall immediately take possession of St. Johns, Montreal, and any other parts of the country."

This seemed to leave out Arnold and Allen, but did not in fact do so; it was never easy to leave them out. Allen shortly joined General Schuyler's miscellaneous forces gathering at Crown Point, and as for Arnold, he had already persuaded Washington to send him off on a rival invasion—through Maine and to Quebec.

General Schuyler—he had been appointed one of the four major generals *under Washington, and in command in New York—did find an expedition to Canada practicable, and on July 18 reached Ticonderoga and began to organize such forces as he had, or could collect, for an offensive against Montreal. A month later the dashing and resourceful young Richard Montgomery arrived to be second in command; when Schuyler fell sick the command of the expedition passed to Montgomery. "Not a moment is to be lost," wrote Washington, but two months were lost before the expedition really accomplished anything. Finally St. Johns fell; then Montreal; then Montgomery prepared to march on Quebec, join forces with Arnold, reduce the ancient fortress, attach the fourteenth colony firmly to the other thirteen, and win the war in Canada.*

Alas, everything went wrong. With superhuman courage and energy Arnold brought his forces through the wilderness of Maine and to the St. Lawrence. Montgomery joined him before Quebec, but the able British commander, General Guy Carleton, had reached the city first, somehow brought together a defensive force, strengthened the fortifications, and made the place well-nigh impregnable. There was an attack; Montgomery was killed, Arnold wounded, the American forces slaughtered or scattered. The great expedition turned into a fiasco and then a tragedy. Congress rushed reinforcements, but the British sent over stronger reinforcements. The Americans retreated; their retreat turned into a rout; they were decimated by smallpox and other diseases; what finally staggered into Ticonderoga and Crown Point was the wreck of an army.

Carleton was ready to turn the tables, to drive down along the Richelieu, Lake Champlain, Lake George to Albany and then down the Hudson, to cut off New England, to end the war as Montgomery and Arnold had hoped to end the war. He had been Arnold's nemesis; now the tables were turned, and Arnold—with the help of Nature and the weather—stopped him. Canada was not conquered, and was not to be conquered, but at least it was not to be the instrument of the destruction of the American cause.

We give here five chapters in the history of the Canadian campaigns: the Schuyler-Montgomery attack on St. Johns and Montreal; Arnold's heroic expediton through Maine and to Quebec; the assault on Quebec and its repulse; the agonized retreat from Quebec to Montreal to Chambly to Ticonderoga; the final and decisive fight on the waters of Lake Champlain, and the end of the counterattack.

I. THE BEGINNING: THE CAPTURE OF ST. JOHNS AND MONTREAL

The obvious approach to Quebec is by water up Lake Champlain and (in so far as rapids will allow) along the Richelieu River to the St. Lawrence. That is the route Abercromby took in '58 and Amherst in '59—though they didn't get very far; it is the route that Burgoyne used in '77—he got pretty far, but not far enough. When Congress decided on a Canadian expedition after all, it entrusted it, of necessity, to the commander in chief in New York, General Philip Schuyler. There was no particular reason why Schuyler should have been made a major general, and he proved to be an unlucky choice. Partly he had little of the kind of drive that Arnold, for example, had; partly he was sick; and partly he had no stomach for the expedition anyway. That he had difficulties is clear—who, in that day, didn't? It is equally clear that he made the most of them. Fortunately for the American cause General Montgomery joined him in mid-August. Montgomery had just the qualities that Schuyler lacked: energy, high spirits, resourcefulness and experience. Schuyler retired to Albany and Montgomery took command. There was a slow advance up the lake and the Richelieu, then a ridiculous two-month siege of the feebly held post at St. Johns. The ubiquitous Ethan Allen was there; impetuous as always, he decided to capture Montreal on his own, and was himself captured instead. Within a week the straggling army had reached Montreal. General Guy Carleton put up a show of resistance, but he had only 150 militia. He escaped, and made his way to Quebec; Montreal fell, without a struggle, on November 13. Precious weeks had been wasted, but the first stage of the campaign was crowned with success.

1. General Schuyler Finds Nonchalance Prevailing at Ticonderoga

General Philip Schuyler to General Washington.

Ticonderoga, July 18, 1775

. . . You will expect that I should say something about this place and the troops here. Not one earthly thing for offence or defence has been done; *the commanding officer had no orders, he only came to re-enforce the garrison, and he expected the General!* But this, my dear General, as well as what follows in this paragraph, I pray may be *entre nous*, for reasons I need not suggest. About ten o'clock last night I arrived at the landing place, the north end of Lake George, a post occupied by a captain and one hundred men. A sentinel, on being informed I was in the boat, quitted his post to go and awake the guard, consisting of three men, in which he had no success. I walked up and came to another, a sergeant's guard. Here the sentinel challenged, but suffered me to come up to him, the whole guard, like the first, in the soundest sleep. With a pen-knife only I could have cut off both guards, and then have set fire to the block-house, destroyed the stores, and starved the people here. At this post I have pointedly recommended vigilance and care, as all the stores from Fort George must necessarily be landed there. But I hope to get the better of this inattention. The officers and men are all good looking people, and decent in their deportment, and I really believe will make good soldiers as soon as I can get the better of this *nonchalance* of theirs. Bravery, I believe, they are far from wanting. As soon as I am a little settled, I shall do myself the honour to send you a return of my strength both on land and water.

I enclose your Excellency a copy of a letter from Colonel Johnson, with a copy of an examination of a person lately from Canada, contradictory of the accounts I gave you in my last from Saratoga. You will perceive that he is gone to Canada. I hope Carleton, if he should be able to procure a body of

Indians, will not be in a hurry to pay us a visit. I wish to be a little more decently prepared to receive him, in doing which, be assured I shall lose no time. . . .

—FORCE, *American Archives*, 4th Series, II, 1685.

2. AMERICAN AGENTS STIR UP DISCONTENT AMONG THE CANADIANS

Journal of Thomas Ainslie, Collector of Customs of the Port of Quebec.

In June the Canadian peasants began to shew a disposition little to be expected from a conquered people who had been treated with so much lenity by Government. The agents and friends of the Congress had not been idle— by word and by writing they had poisoned their minds—they were brought to believe that the Minister had laid a plan to enslave them, and to make them the instruments of enslaving all the neighbouring provinces, that they would be continually at war, far removed from their wives and families. Armed strangers had appeared in some of the parishes below Quebec; they disappeared suddenly: nobody knew their business—it was conjectured that they came to learn the sentiments of the country people, and the state of Quebec. Those who knew with what facility the hunters of New England can traverse the woods had apprehensions that the rebels might send parties from their back settlements to harass us near Quebec, in the absence of Gen. Carleton, who was up the country to oppose their entry into Canada by way of St. Johns. Woodsmen may enter this province by more ways than one—by the Chaudiere and by St. Francis, rivers taking their rise in the mountains between Canada and New England; these passes are well known to the back settlers in Massachusetts and in New Hampshire. There is a third still easier than the two mentioned, by St. Johns River in Nova Scotia and Madawaska River over the carrying place to Kamouraska on the River St. Laurence about an hundred miles below Quebec. . . .

The agents for the Congress in this country represented to that body that nothing was to be apprehended from the Canadians in their present temper of mind, that so far from opposing the Continental troops, they would receive them with open arms, nay that perhaps great numbers would join them, for that they appeared to be thoroughly tinctured with the true spirit of rebellion, thanks to the never ceasing labours of the malcontents in this Province. . . .

They drew the most hideous pictures of the distresses and miseries that would be entailed on the present race, and on their latest posterity if the Quebec Act should take place. From the impressions made by these seditious people, the Canadians look upon the Rebels as their best friends, and are ready to receive them as the asserters of their rights and liberties.

Some of these Grumbletonians are friends to the Constitution but are highly incensed against the Quebec bill.

They see with pain that their malice has contributed to incline the Canadians to throw off their allegiance—they meant to stir them up to a general application for a repeal of the act, not to rebellion.

—AINSLIE, "Journal," pp. 12-13.

3. The Americans Lay Siege to St. Johns

Samuel Mott of Connecticut to Governor Jonathan Trumbull.

Camp before St. John's, October 6, 1775

Ever since the 17th of last month we have laid siege to this place; it is a very difficult place to come at, as it is almost surrounded with sunken swamps and marshy ground; many small occurrences have happened during the siege, which I cannot recapitulate. The enemy, it is thought, have fired six hundred bomb-shells, besides numbers of cannon-shot, and showers of grape-shot; but we have lost but about a dozen men by them all. They played very severely on us when we were erecting our batteries. I was for three days successively where the shot and shells came, and the grape-shot rattled around me like hail; but a good God has preserved me. . . .

Colonel Allen has been very serviceable in bringing in the Canadians and Indians; but being encouraged by some others, he has, rather contrary to his own judgment, crossed the river, about five miles below Montreal, with only about thirty New-England men and seventy Canadian friends, one hundred in the whole; and intended to augment his number of Canadians, and, if possible, get possession of Montreal; but he was the next morning met by St. Luke La Corne, with about four hundred Regulars and French Tories. They overpowered Allen, and he is either killed or taken, with about twenty of his men, (which was a severe stroke to us); he, however, made some havock; he stood his ground firing till they surrounded him, although his men forsook him. The Town-Major of Montreal, with some other of the most potent Tories, were killed in the engagement.

On the 3d instant there was a severe engagement between the French Whigs on one side, and the French Tories and Regulars on the other side, at Chambly, about thirteen miles from this place. The Tory party had the advantage, as they fired about fifty cannon-shot on our Whigs, when they had only small arms to defend with. They lost several men on each side. The Whigs maintained their ground. In short, it is a melancholy prospect to see that all Canada is in one continued scene of war and bloodshed. If we don't carry our point, we have brought Canada into the most deplorable situation possible to conceive, as those people who have taken arms in our favour, with their wives and children, will be left to cruelty without mercy, and any of our army will hardly escape with safety. It is amazing to me that the Colonies should have so little sense of the importance of this expedition as not to give us a good large army, well furnished, in due season, which indeed would have nearly settled the controversy; but we have never yet been two thousand strong, exclusive of our friends of Canada, although we assume to ourselves all the airs of a potent army. . . .

I have been present with the General at a Congress and treaty with the Indians, where the heads of all the seven nations of Canada were present; and matters were conducted with great solemnity and to the mutual satisfaction of all.

Yesterday St. Luke La Corne (that arch devil incarnate), who has butchered hundreds, men, women and children, of our Colonies in the late war in the most inhuman manner, who has ever been a head and leader of the Canadians and all the Indians, now finding that, notwithstanding all his wiles and falsehoods, the Indians and more than half the Canadians are become friendly to us, he has now sent a message to us, desiring a conference with us. The General has agreed to a conference, to be held at La Prairie to-morrow: Major Brown and the aid-de-camp on our side, and that wretch, St. Luke, with the principal leaders of the Tory faction of Montreal, on the other side. It is a very delicate embassy, and the consequences will better manifest the event than it can be guessed. The Indians of all the tribes, and the Canadians who join us, have all learned English enough to say "Liberty" and "Bostonian," and all call themselves Yankee. The Indians boast much of it, and will smite on their breasts, saying, "Me Yankee."

It is very grievous to me that General Schuyler is not here; I had a very good understanding with him, and a good agreement in all the modes of prosecuting the expedition; but to my sorrow and the embarrassment of the service, there is not that good understanding as I could wish now. General Montgomery's chief confidant is one Col. Campbell, a Scotchman, who has been an officer in the Regulars and is now Deputy Quartermaster-General, and is very profane. I should be very sorry to inform your Honour that there is scarcely a word heard from head-quarters without some oaths and curses on every occasion; but I value myself on the righteousness of the cause, and hope in God for success. I have no great opinion of Montgomery's generalship, although I believe him to be a man of courage; that is but a small (though essential) qualification of a general.

For all the pretensions of New-York, there has not been one head colonel of a regiment seen in the army this year; and out of their three thousand five hundred men, we have never had more than six hundred down here, until within these four days there have come down between two and three hundred more. I recollect nothing more material. The firing goes on now pretty briskly. The enemy are very strongly fortified. The event of each day can only be told or even guessed at the close of it.

—FORCE, American Archives, 4th Series, III, 972-974.

4. ST. JOHNS FALLS: "A FATAL STAB TO THE FOES OF FREEDOM"

Letter of an officer of the New York troops in Canada.

St. John's, November 3, 1775

I have the pleasure to inform you that I had the honour of marching into and taking possession of this fortress, at the head of my company, and about two hundred men from the different corps of which our army is composed, about nine o'clock this morning, when the garrison, consisting of about six hundred men, marched out and grounded their arms on the plains to the westward of the fort (agreeable to the terms of the enclosed capitulation), and were immediately embarked in batteaus for Captain Mead's encampment, and from thence to be sent under guard, as speedily as possible, for Ticonderoga, Connecticut, or any other place which the Continental Congress may direct. I most sincerely congratulate you on this most fortunate event, which, in my opinion, will be a most fatal stab to the hellish machinations of the foes of freedom, as it will facilitate the reduction of Canada and secure the Canadians in our favour.

We have taken in the fort a considerable quantity of military stores; among which are seventeen pieces of excellent brass artillery, two of them twenty-four pounders, the rest of them field-pieces, two royal howitzers, several mortars, cohorns, and a considerable number of iron cannon. There were in the garrison about five hundred regular troops; the rest were composed of Canadian volunteers, among whom are many of their noblesse; who, I believe, are (from appearance) on the stool of repentance. And as you may be fond of knowing how we have proceeded in carrying on the siege of this place . . . , I will give you a detail of the particular operations. . . .

On Saturday, the 28th ultimo, the main body of the army decamped from the south, and marched to the north side of the fort, under the command of General Wooster. We were joined in the evening by General Montgomery, and the same night we began to throw up a breastwork (on an eminence which entirely commanded the enemy's works) in order to erect a battery of cannon and mortars; this battery they kept continually pelting at with grapeshot and shells, but without doing us the least injury, until Wednesday morning, when we opened our battery, consisting of three twelve and one nine-pounders, three mortars, and as many cohorns, with which we kept an almost incessant blaze on them [the] great part of the day, and likewise from our battery on the east side of the river, which the enemy returned with the greatest spirit.

Late in the afternoon I received a message from General Montgomery, ordering me to cease firing till further orders; these orders were extremely disagreeable to me, when I saw some of my men bleeding before my eyes, and dying with the wounds which they had received. On our ceasing to fire, the General ordered a parley to be beat, and sent in an officer to demand a surrender of the fort. Two officers soon after returned with him, and were led blindfold through the camp to the General's tent, where a pretty long conference was held, and they promised the General an answer from the commanding officer next morning, which promise was complied with. The answer imported that if they should receive no relief within four days, he would then send in some proposals. The General replied that he must have an explicit answer next morning, and the garrison must remain prisoners of war, at all events; and that if they had any intention to renew hostilities, they need only signify it by firing a gun as a signal. This, though very unpalatable, they were at length obliged to digest, as you see by the capitulation.

—Force, *American Archives*, 4th Series, III, 1343.

5. Montreal Is Captured: "The Troops Came as Friends"

Journal of Benjamin Trumbull, chaplain with the
First Connecticut Regiment.

Saturday November 11th 1775. This morning is cold and sower; the ground is white with snow, and it rains and snows, bids fair for a tempestuous season. . . .

Seing that the regiment were not like to march and looking upon it important that the General should know our situation, at a quarter after 11 o'clock I determined to march forward for Le Praire [La Prairie] and began my march with two soldiers for my pilots. I arrived at Le Praire 18 miles from St. John's just as it began to be dark. I marched the whole of the day in mud and water sometimes midleg high and in general over shoe, carried a small pack, a case of pistols by my side, with my gun, cartouch box, etc. The whole day was stormy; it rained and snowed till about sunset, when the snow and rain ceased and the wind blew up raw and cold at north west. Under our feet was snow and ice and water, over our heads clouds, snow and rain; before us the mountains appeared all white with snow and ice. It was remarkable to see the Americans after almost infinite fatigues and hardships marching on at this advanced season, badly clothed and badly provided for, to Montreal, pressing on to new seiges and new conquests. This day the entrenching tools came on and in the afternoon Colonel Ward with that part of General Woosters regiment which had been left behind began his march for Le Praire. I was very wet and weary, got into a small warm room, dried my feet and clothes and had a comfortable night.

This day the generals who arrived at Lepraire on Wednesday the 8th instant passed the River St. Lawrence about nine miles from Montreal and landed on St. Pauls Island. The field pieces and light artilery came up the night before, the evening of the 10th instant. A considerable part of the army passed the river with them and landed without opposition. Of the Connecticut troops, part of General Woosters regiment and Colonel Waterbury's went over on this first embarkation: there were not boats for the other troops.

Lords Day November 12 was a cold blustering day, wind at northwest, cloudy and sower, difficult passing the river on account of the wind and current which is rapid and strong. Colonel Ward comes in to day with his part, and the troops which had crossed the river, with the generals. Marched into the subarbs of Montreal and encamped just without the city.

Monday November 13. The generals marched into the city just at evening. The citizens before their entrance proposed terms of capitulation, but the generals observed that they had no right to any capitulation; that they had no men to defend them, no artilery or any means of defence; that the troops came not as enemies but as friends to protect them, and as they pretended to be affraid that the troops would plunder them, they assured them that they should not be plundered but should be safe in their persons and estates. . . .

Tuesday November 14th 1775. . . . Governor Carlton on Saturday evening, when our men were marching into the confines of the city, left it with his regulars amounting to about 80 in number, with some Canadians who had entered into the measures of the Ministry, fell down the river with eleven ships and vessels. . . . Before his departure he destroyed most of the bataux belonging to the King distributed among the nobless, and one way or other conveyed away almost the whole of the Kings stores, and spiked all the canon they left and filled them with balls, etc. Some houses which had been built for the Kings service they damaged, braking out the windows and sashes, taring up the floors, etc. Orders were given by General Prescot to burn them, but on the application of some gentlemen of the town representing that it would expose the whole town to be consumed in one general conflagration, he declared that such a thing as burning said houses had never entered into his heart, and enquired who had given such orders; they told him General Prescot. He however countermanded the orders. General Carlton is said to have some humanity; disavows his having ever set the savages on the Americans. The harsh and inhumane things which have been done this way are rather ascribed to General Prescot, St. Luke La-Corn, Capt. Frasier and others of their character and the nobless.

—TRUMBULL, "Journal," *Conn. Hist. Soc. Coll.,* VII, 162-166.

II. ARNOLD LEADS AN EXPEDITION TO QUEBEC

The attack on Canada was to be a two-pronged affair or, as we might say now, a pincer operation. As the left wing of the American forces swung on to Montreal, an east wing was to drive through Maine to the St. Lawrence; the two were to converge on the fortress of Quebec. Benedict Arnold had already proved himself a man of action, and Washington made him a colonel and authorized him to lead an expedition to Quebec. The new colonel raised a force of about a thousand men, most of them woodsmen and frontiersmen, from the armies around Cambridge; among them were young Aaron Burr and the famous Daniel Morgan who had fought under Washington in the French and Indian War. According to tradition young Burr was accompanied by an Indian maiden named Jacataqua, one of the female camp followers of the campaign, an "Abenaki Queen with golden thighs." Whether authentic or not, the story is in keeping with Burr's later career. The high-spirited little army went by boat to the mouth of the Kennebec, and by September 24 had reached the rapids above what is now Augusta. The going along the Kennebec was not too hard; the real hardship came with the long portage along the Dead River and to Lake Megantic, and on along the Chaudière.

The hardship, the misery, the valor of that march is sufficiently described in our accounts so that it need not be celebrated here: those who want the full story of this wonderful expedition will turn to Kenneth Roberts' March to Quebec. *One of the most wonderful things about it is that so many simple, hungry, sick, miserable men had time to keep journals. We quote from two of them. Abner Stocking was a twenty-two-year-old private in Captain Hanchet's Connecticut company; his own journal was evidently copied, in part, from the journals of his friends, but is no less authentic for that. Dr. Isaac Senter, another twenty-two-year-older, was a physician from Rhode Island. He had joined up with the army before Cambridge, where he served as surgeon, and volunteered for this expedition; his is probably the best of the journals. He lived through not only the Canadian but other campaigns, and after the war achieved some fame as a physician in Newport.*

1. "OUR FATIGUES SEEMED DAILY TO INCREASE"

Journal of Abner Stocking, a private in Arnold's army.

Sept. 13. 1775. All things being in readiness for our departure, we set out from Cambridge, near Boston, on the 13th Sept. at sunset, and encamped

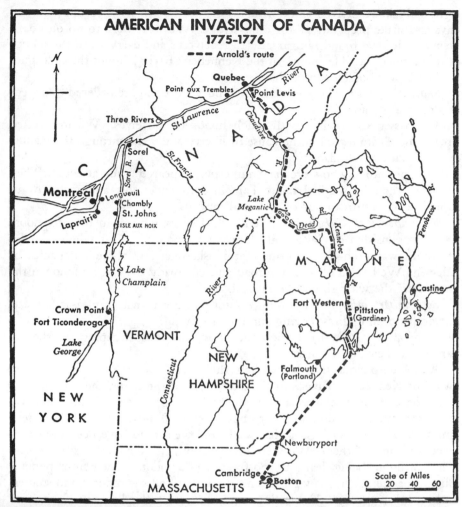

AMERICAN INVASION OF CANADA
1775-1776

From *The American Revolution*
by *John Richard Alden*

Courtesy of Harper & Brothers

at Mistick at eight o'clock at night. We were all in high spirits, intending to endure with fortitude all the fatigues and hardships that we might meet with in our march to Quebec.

September 14th. This morning we began our march at 5 o'clock and at sunset encamped at Danvers, a place twenty miles distant from Mistick.

The weather through the day was very sultry and hot for the season of the year. The country through which we passed appeared barren and but thinly inhabited.

September 15th. This morning we marched very early, and encamped at night within five miles of Newbury Port. The inhabitants who visited us in our encampment expressed many good wishes for our success in our intended enterprise.

September 16th. Zealous in the cause, and not knowing the hardships and distresses we were to encounter, we as usual began our march very early. At eight o'clock we arrived at Newbury Port where we were to tarry several days and make preparations for our voyage. We were here to go on board vessels which we found lying ready to receive us and carry us to the mouth of the Kennebeck. The mouth of the Kennebeck River is about thirty leagues to the eastward of Newbury Port.

September 17th. We are still in Newbury Port and are ordered to appear at a general review.

We passed the review with much honor to ourselves. We manifested great zeal and animation in the cause of liberty and went through the manual exercise with much alacrity.

The spectators, who were very numerous, appeared much affected. They probably thought we had many hardships to encounter and many of us should never return to our parents and families.

September 18th. We this day embarked at six o'clock in the afternoon. Our fleet consisted of eleven sail, sloops and schooners. Our whole number of troops was 1100—11 companies of musketmen and three companies of riflemen. We hauled off into the road and got ready to weigh anchor in the morning if the wind should be favorable.

September 19th. This morning we got under way with a pleasant breeze, our drums beating, fifes playing and colours flying.

Many pretty girls stood upon the shore, I suppose weeping for the departure of their sweethearts.

At eleven o'clock this day we left the entrance of the harbor and bore away for Kennebeck River. In the latter part of the night, there came on a thick fog and our fleet was separated. At break of day we found ourselves in a most dangerous situation, very near a reef of rocks. The rocks indeed appeared on all sides of us, so that we feared we should have been dashed to pieces on some of them. We were brought into this deplorable situation by means of liquor being dealt out too freely to our pilots. Their intemperance much endangered their own lives and the lives of all the officers and soldiers on board; but through the blessing of God we all arrived safe in Kennebeck River.

September 20. This day was very pleasant, and with a gentle breeze we sailed and rowed 30 miles up the Kennebeck River. By the evening tide we floated within six miles of Fort Western, where we were obliged to leave our sloops and take to our bateaus.

September 21. This day we arrived at Fort Western, where we tarried until the 25th in order to make farther preparation for our voyage up the river, and our march through the wilderness. . . .

September 25th. Early this morning, we embarked on board our batteaus and proceeded on our way. We labored hard through the day and found ourselves at night but about 7 miles from the place of our departure. The current began to be swift. We encamped at night by the edge of a cornfield and fared very sumptuously.

September 26th. This day we started very early and made our encampment at evening 4 miles below Fort Halifax. We began to experience great difficulty from the increasing rapidity of the current, and the water becoming shoal.

September 27th. This day we carried our batteaus and baggage round Ticonnick Falls. The land carriage was only about 40 rods. After launching in again and getting our provisions and baggage on board, we pushed against the stream on our way about three miles.

September 28th. This day we proceeded 8 miles but with great difficulty. The stream was in some places very rapid and shoal, and in others so deep that those who dragged the boats were obliged to nearly swim. We encountered these hardships and fatigues with great courage and perseverance from the zeal we felt in the cause. When night came on, wet and fatigued as we were, we had to encamp on the cold ground. It was at this time that we inclined to think of the comfortable accommodations we had left at home.

September 29th. This day we arrived to the second carrying place, called Skowhegan Falls. Though this was only 60 rods over, it occasioned much delay and great fatigue. We had to ascend a ragged rock, near on 100 feet in height and almost perpendicular. Though it seemed as though we could hardly ascend it without any burden, we succeeded in dragging our batteaus and baggage up it.

September 30th. After getting over the carrying place, we found the water more still. We proceeded 5 miles and at sundown encamped in a most delightful wood, where I thought I could have spent some time agreeably in solitude, in contemplating the works of nature. The forest was stripped of its verdure, but still appeared to me beautiful. I thought that though we were in a thick wilderness, uninhabited by human beings, yet we were as much in the immediate presence of our divine protector as when in the crowded city.

October 1st. This day we proceeded with unusual perseverance, but as the water was exceedingly rapid, we could advance but slowly. It was but a small part of the way that any thing could be done by rowing or setting. While one took the batteau by the bow, another kept hold of the stern to keep her from upsetting or filling with water. Thus our fatigues seemed daily to encrease. But what we most dreaded was the frost and cold from which we began to suffer considerably.

October 2d. This day we carried over Norridgewock Falls, one mile and a quarter. At night we encamped at a place formerly inhabited by the natives and afterwards by the French and Indians; the former had erected a mass house for their devotions, but had deserted it at the time the New England forces made great slaughter among them in the French war. A few inhabitants were now living here, who rendered us some assistance. The temple of worship contained some curiosities, such as crosses, etc. We took up our lodgings here for the night and were much pleased with our accommodations. The place had the appearance of once having been the residence of a considerable number of inhabitants.

October 3d. Having had some better refreshment than usual, we pushed on our way with increased resolution. We had now taken leave of the last inhabitants. The remainder of our route was to be through a trackless wilderness. We now entered a doleful barren woods; the timber mostly pine and hemlock—some thick patches of spruce and fir, and some groves of sugar-maple.

—STOCKING, "Journal," *Magazine of History*, Extra No. 75, pp. 9-13.

2. DR. ISAAC SENTER DESCRIBES THE MISERIES AND STARVATION OF THE MARCH

Tuesday, October 24th, [*1775*]. Approaching necessity now obliged us to double our diligence. Three miles only had we proceeded ere we came to a troublesome water-fall in the river, distant half a mile. Not more than the last mentioned distance before we were brought up by another, distance the same. As the number of falls increased, the water became consequently more rapid. The heights of land upon each side of the river, which had hitherto been inconsiderable, now became prodigiously mountainous, closing as it were up the river with an aspect of an immense heighth. The river was now become very narrow, and such a horrid current as rendered it impossible to proceed in any other method than by hauling the batteaux up by the bushes, painters, etc.

Here we met several boats returning loaded with invalids, and lamentable stories of the inaccessibleness of the river, and the impracticability of any further progress into the country; among which was Mr. Jackson . . . , complaining of the gout most severely, joined to all the terrors of approaching famine. I was now exhorted in the most pathetic terms to return, on pain of famishing upon contrary conduct, and the army were all returning except a few who were many miles forward with Col. Arnold. However his elocution did not prevail; I therefore bid him adieu and proceeded.

Not far had I proceeded before I discovered several wrecks of batteaux belonging to the front division of riflemen, etc., with an increased velocity of the water. A direful howling wilderness, not describable. With much labour and difficulty I arrived with the principal part of my baggage (leaving the batteaux made fast) to the encampment. Two miles from thence I met the informants last mentioned, where were Col. Greene's division, etc., waiting for the remainder of the army to come up, that they might get some provisions, ere they advanced any further. Upon enquiry I found them almost destitute of any eatable whatever, except a few *candles*, which were used for supper, and breakfast the next morning, by boiling them in water gruel, etc.

Wednesday, 25. Every prospect of distress now came thundering on with a twofold rapidity. A storm of snow had covered the ground of nigh six inches deep, attended with very severe weather. We now waited in anxious expectation for Col. Enos' division to come up, in order that we might have a recruit of provisions ere we could start off the ground. An express was ordered both up and down the river, the one up the river in quest of Col. Arnold, that he might be informed of the state of the army, many of whom were now entirely destitute of any sustenance. The colonel had left previous orders for the two divisions, viz.: Greene's and Enos', to come to an adjustment of the provisions, send back any who were indisposed, either in body or mind, and pursue him with the others immediately. The other express went down the river to desire Col. Enos and officers to attend in consultation. They accordingly came up before noon, when a council of war was ordered. Here sat a number of grimacers—melancholy aspects who had been preaching to their men the doctrine of impenetrability and non-perseverance. Col. Enos in the chair. The matter was debated upon the expediency of proceeding on for Quebec. The party against going urging the impossibility, averring the whole provisions, when averaged, would not support the army five days.

The arrangements of men and provisions being made at Fort Western, in such a manner as to proceed with the greater expedition. For this end it was thought necessary that Capt. Morgan's company with a few pioneers should advance in the first division, Col. Greene's in the second, and Enos, with Capt. Colbourn's company of artificers, to bring up the rear. The advantage of the arrangement was very conspicuous, as the rear division would not only have the roads cut, rivers cleared passible for boats, etc., but stages of encampments formed and the bough huts remaining for the rear. The men being thus arranged, the provisions were distributed according to the supposed difficulty or facility attending the different dispositions. Many of the first companies took only two or three barrels of flour with several of bread, most in a small proportion, while the companies in the last division had not less than fourteen of flour and ten of bread. The bread, as mentioned before, was condemned in consequence of the leaky casks, therefore the proportion of bread being much greater in the first division, their loss was consequently the greater.

These hints being premised, I now proceed to the determination of the council of war. After debating upon the state of the army with respect to provisions, there was found very little in the division then encamped at the falls (which I shall name *Hydrophobus*). The other companies not being come up, either through fear that they should be obliged to come to a divider, or to shew their disapprobation of proceeding any further. The question being put whether all to return, or only part, the majority were for part only returning. . . .

According to Col. Arnold's recommendation the invalids were allowed to return, as also the timorous. One batteau only for each company to proceed, in order to carry the military stores, medicines, etc, . . . The officers who were for going forward requested the division of the provisions, and that it was necessary they should have the far greater quantity in proportion to the number of men, as the supposed distance that they had to go ere they arrived into the inhabitants was greater than what they had come, after leaving the Cenebec inhabitants. To this the returning party (being predetermined) would not consent. . . . To compel them to a just division we were not in a situation, as being the weakest party. Expostulations and entreaties had hitherto been fruitless. Col. Enos, who more immediately commanded the division of *returners*, was called upon to give positive orders for a small quantity, if no more. He replied that his men were out of his power, and that they had determined to keep their possessed quantity whether they went back or forward. They finally concluded to spare 2½ barrels of flour, if determined to pursue our destination. . . .

Thus circumstanced, we were left the alternative of accepting their small pittance, and proceed or return. The former was adopted, with a determined resolution to go through or die. Received it, put it on board of our boats, quit the few tents we were in possession of, with all other camp equipage, took each man to his duds on his back, bid them adieu, and away—passed the river, passed over falls and encamped.

Thursday, 26th. We were now within 154 computed miles of the Canadian inhabitants; every man made the best of his way to the Chaudière pond, the place of rendezvous for all the forward party except Col. Arnold. Passed three carrying places on the river. Passed over several rocky mountains and monstrous precipices, to appearance inaccessible; fired with more than Hannibalian enthusiasm, American Alps nor Pyrenees were obstacles. Passed a pond which the river ran through, lodged on a promontory of another. Only Jack Wright was in company. Came to us in the night Maj. Ogden, volunteer, who being lost spied our fire, and came on shore in his boat in which were military stores, etc.

Friday, 27th. Our bill of fare for last night and this morning consisted of the jawbone of a swine destitute of any covering. This we boiled in a quantity of water, that with a little thickening constituted our sumptuous eating. For covering, the atmosphere only, except a blanket. . . .

Saturday, 28th. A letter per express from General Arnold, at 4 o'clock, P. M., requesting as speedy a procedure as possible. That one of his expresses (Jackquith) had returned from the Canadian inhabitants, informing of their amicable disposition towards us, that he had received their pledge of friendship in a loaf of bread, etc. By this time our men were all arrived, embodied, and the glad tidings promulgated among them, to the unspeakable joy of the whole camp. In consequence of this news we were ordered to be in motion immediately. The provisions were ordered into one fund, in order that every man might be acquainted with what he had to depend upon to carry him into the inhabitants, computed at about a hundred miles. Upon a division of the provisions there [were] five pints per man. Pork, though the only meat, was not properly divisible, as the whole amount would not have been an ounce per man. The officers in general were generous enough to dispense with [it] for the better satisfaction and encouragement of the soldiers. Decamped this evening and marched a mile and a half.

Sunday, 29th. Not less than 14 days had our detachment been upon half allowance ere yesterday's division took place. That several of the men devoured the whole of their flour the last evening, determined (as they expressed it) to have a full meal, letting the morrow look out for itself. The ground being overflowed with water before the little stream emptied into the Chaudière, it was thought best by the majority to go to the southeast of the stream upon the higher land and so pass round the lake; however, there were three or four companies proceeded down the stream as far as they could, then leaving it to the southward, and taking the north-westerly shore round the lake. While Col. Greene and most of his officers including myself took our course N. E. and by E. for the Chaudière. Deluded by a pretended pilot, we found our error ere night closed upon us.

From the first appearance of daylight this morn we picked up our small affairs and beat a march. Not long had we marched this course before we came into a spruce and cedar swamp and arrived at a small pond at 11 o'clock, through the most execrable bogmire, impenetrable *Pluxus* of shrubs, imaginable. This pond we pursued till coming to an outlet rivulet, [which] we followed to a lake much larger than the first, and notwithstanding the most confident assertions of our pilot, we pursued this pond the most of the day, but no Chaudière. . . . This day's march was computed at eighteen miles. Capt. Morgan's company, with seven batteaux, followed the 7 mile stream, with a purpose of passing the south lake, which they effected. These old woodsmen had resolutely persevered in carrying that number of boats over the mountains, with an intent to still preserve a certain quantity of the military stores, which by no other means could be conveyed any further than the Chaudière.

Monday, 30th. . . . This was the third day we had been in search of the Chaudière, who were only seven computed miles distant the 28th inst. Nor were we possessed of any certainty that our course would bring us either to the lake or river, not knowing the point it lay from where we started. However we came to a resolution to continue it. In this state of uncertainty we wandered through hideous swamps and mountainous precipices, with the conjoint addition of cold, wet and hunger, not to mention our fatigue—with the terrible apprehension of famishing in this desert. The pretended pilot was not less frightened than many of the rest; added to that the severe execrations he received, from the front of the army to the rear, made his office not a little disagreeable.

Several of the men towards evening were ready to give up any thoughts of ever arriving at the desired haven. Hunger and fatigue had so much the ascendancy over many of the poor fellows, added to their despair of arrival, that some of them were left in the river, nor were heard of afterwards. In turn with Col. Greene, I carried the compass the greater part of this day. In this condition we proceeded with as little knowledge of where we were or where we should get to, as if we had been in the unknown interior of Africa, or the deserts of Arabia.

Just as the sun was departing, we brought a pond or lake, which finally proved to be Chaudière, and soon the small footpath made by the other division of the army, whose choice turned to their account. Our arrival here was succeeded with three huzzas, and then came to our encampment.

Tuesday, 31. The appearance of daylight roused us as usual, and we had advanced with all possible speed till about 11 o'clock, ere we saw the Chaudière River, which we last night imagined within a mile. Animated afresh with the sight of a stream, which we very well knew would conduct us into the inhabitants if our strength continued, we proceeded with renewed vigour. The emptying of the Chaudière is beautiful, and formed a very agreeable ascent, though the stream is somewhat rapid. The land was now much descending, yet very difficult travelling. The spruce, cedar and hemlock were the chief growth of the earth, and these were in tolerable plenty, almost impenetrably so in many places.

We now began to discover the wrecked batteaux of those who conducted the ammunition, etc. These were seven in number, who followed the seven mile stream into the Chaudière lake, river, etc., and soon came to an encampment, where I found Capt. Morgan and most of the boatmen who were wrecked upon a fall in the river, losing every thing except their lives, which they all saved by swimming, except one of Morgan's riflemen. This was the first man drowned in all the dangers we were exposed to, and the third [lost] by casualties, except some lost in the wilderness, the number unknown. At this encampment was Lieut. McCleland, of Morgan's company, almost expiring with a violent *peripneumonia*. Necessaries were distributed as much as possible, with two lads of the company in charge of him. Nor was this poor fellow the only one left sick upon this river. Life depending upon a vigorous push for the inhabitants, and that did not admit of any stay for any person; nor could the two lads have been prevailed upon had not provisions been dealt out sufficient to conduct them to the inhabitants, with the promising to send them relief as soon as possible from the settlements.

In this general wreck my medicine box suffered the fate of the rest, with a set of capital instruments, etc. Though little was to be feared from either my chirurgical apparatus or physical portions, I had, however, a few necessaries in that way in my knapsack, etc., with a lancet in my pocket, which enabled me at least to comply with the Sangradoine method.

Continued our march about five miles further.

Wednesday, Nov. 1st. Our greatest luxuries now consisted in a little water, stiffened with flour, in imitation of shoemakers' paste, which was christened with the name of Lillipu. Instead of the diarrhea, which tried our men most shockingly in the former part of our march, the reverse was now the complaint, which continued for many days. We had now arrived, as we thought, to almost the zenith of distress. Several had been entirely destitute of either meat or bread for many days. These chiefly consisted of those who devoured their provision immediately, and a number who were in the boats. The voracious disposition many of us had now arrived at rendered almost any thing admissible. Clean and unclean were forms now little in use. In company was a poor dog [who had] hitherto lived through all the tribulations, became a prey for the sustenance of the assassinators. This poor animal was instantly devoured, without leaving any vestige of the sacrifice. Nor did the shaving soap, pomatum, and even the lip salve, leather of their shoes, cartridge boxes, etc., share any better fate. Passed several poor fellows, truly commiserating [them].

Thursday, 2d. Long ere this necessity had obliged us to dismiss all our encamping equipage, excepting a small light tin kettle among a number; but nothing to cut our wood, etc. According to our strength and spirits, we were scattered up and down the river at the distance of perhaps twenty miles. Not more than eight miles had we marched when a vision of horned cattle, four-footed beasts, etc., rode and drove by animals resembling Plato's two footed featherless ones. Upon a nigher approach our vision proved real! Exclamations of joy, echoes of gladness resounded from front to rear with a [*Te Deum*]. Three horned cattle, two horses, eighteen Canadians and one American. A heifer was chosen as victim to our wants, slain and divided accordingly. Each man was restricted to one pound of beef. Soon arrived two more Canadians in b[irch] canoes, ladened with a coarse kind of meal, mutton, tobacco, etc. Each man drew likewise a pint of this provender. The mutton was destined for the sick. They proceeded up the river in order to the rear's partaking of the same benediction. We sat down, eat our rations, blessed our stars, and thought it luxury. Upon a general computation we marched from 20 to 30 miles per day. Twenty miles only from this to the settlements. Lodged at the great falls this night.

—Senter, "Journal," *Magazine of History*, Extra No. 42, pp. 25-37.

3. Colonel Arnold Celebrates the Heroism of His March to Quebec

Colonel Benedict Arnold, probably to General Schuyler.

Pointe Aux Trembles, November 27, 1775

. . . Thus in about eight weeks we completed a march of near six hundred miles, not to be paralleled in history; the men having with the greatest fortitude and perseverance hauled their batteaux up rapid streams, being obliged to wade almost the whole way, near 180 miles, carried them on their shoulders near forty miles, over hills, swamps and bogs almost impenetrable, and to their knees in mire; being often obliged to cross three or four times with their baggage. Short of provisions, part of the detachment disheartened and gone back; famine staring us in the face; an enemy's country and uncertainty ahead. Notwithstanding all these obstacles, the officers and men, inspired and fired with the love of liberty and their country, pushed on with a fortitude superior to every obstacle, and most of them had not one day's provision for a week.

I have thus given you a short but imperfect sketch of our march. The night we crossed the St. Lawrence, found it impossible to get our ladders over, and the enemy being apprised of our coming, we found it impracticable to attack them without too great a risk; we therefore invested the town and cut off their communication with the country. We continued in this situation until the 20th, having often attempted to draw out the garrison in vain. On a strict scrutiny into our ammunition, found many of our cartridges (which to appearance were good) inserviceable and not ten rounds each for the men, who were almost naked, bare footed and much fatigued; and as the garrison was daily increasing and nearly double our numbers, we thought it prudent to retire to this place and wait the arrival of Gen. Montgomery, with artillery, clothing, etc., who to our great joy has this morning joined us with about 300 men. We propose immediately investing the town and make no doubt in a few days to bring Gov. Carlton to terms. You will excuse the incorrectness of my letter and believe me with the greatest esteem.

—Arnold, "Letters," *Maine Hist. Soc. Coll.*, I, 383-385.

III. THE FATEFUL ASSAULT ON QUEBEC

Not until November 9 did Arnold's emaciated and ragged band reach the banks of the St. Lawrence, and as yet Montgomery had not come up from Montreal. The delay was fatal. Quebec had been defended by only a handful of men, but its leaders were indomitable. Colonel Allan Maclean brought in his regiment of Royal Highland Emigrants; the governor of the city, Hector Cramahé, raised 500 soldiers; another 300 were drawn from the ships in the harbor; eventually Maclean—and after him Carleton—commanded a force of over 1,700. Arnold had only 700 or so, and Montgomery brought another 300. More to the point, he brought warm clothing for the freezing veterans of the Maine woods, and cannon and ammunition. Arnold tried to bluff the fortress into surrender, but without effect. He tried to hammer it into submission, but his cannon could not batter down the fortifications. If Quebec was to fall it would have to fall to assault. The plans were carefully laid. The assault would have to be a surprise, which meant nighttime and, preferably, a snowstorm—a gamble as risky for the Americans as for the French and British defenders. Arnold and Montgomery divided their forces, Arnold tried to attack from the north, or Charles River side, Montgomery from the west and south, the St. Lawrence side. The desperate assault was launched in a blinding blizzard early in the morning of the first day of the year. Almost from the beginning everything went wrong. Montgomery was killed; Arnold was wounded; the attack disintegrated. The Americans lost perhaps 60 men killed but over 400 prisoners; the defenders lost only 18 killed and wounded. Arnold drew off to lick his wounds; he breathed defiance; he vowed to renew the attack.

Among those who contribute to our account of the disaster, nothing is known of Major Henry Caldwell, or of Thomas Ainslie except that he was a literary collector of customs for the port of Quebec. John Henry was a seventeen-year-old member of Arnold's army; his journal was dictated many years later.

1. Montgomery Joins Arnold Before Quebec

General Richard Montgomery to General Schuyler.

Heights of Abraham, Dec. 5, 1775

I have been this evening favoured with yours of the 19th ult., and return to you many thanks for your warm congratulations. Nothing shall be wanting on my part to reap the advantage of our good fortune. The season has proved so favourable as to enable me to join Colonel Arnold at Point-aux-Trembles, where I arrived with the vessels Mr. Prescott made us a present of. They carried the few troops, about three hundred, which were equipped for a winter campaign, with the artillery, etc. Colonel Livingston is on his way, with some part of his regiment of Canadians.

Mr. Carleton, who is I suppose ashamed to show himself in England, is now in town, and puts on the show of defence. The works of Quebeck are extremely extensive, and very incapable of being defended.

His garrison consists of Maclean's banditti, the sailors from the frigates and other vessels laid up, together with the citizens obliged to take up arms, most of whom are impatient of the fatigues of a siege, and wish to see matters accommodated amicably. I propose amusing Mr. Carleton with a formal attack, erecting batteries, etc., but mean to assault the works, I believe, towards the lower town, which is the weakest part. I have this day written to Mr. Carleton, and also to the inhabitants, which I hope will have some effect. I shall be very sorry to be reduced to this mode of attack, because I know the melancholy consequences, but the approaching severe season, and the weakness of the garrison, together with the nature of the works, point it out too strong to be passed by.

I find Colonel Arnold's corps an exceeding fine one, inured to fatigue, and well accustomed to cannon shot (at Cambridge). There is a style of discipline among them much superior to what I have been used to see this campaign. He himself is active, intelligent and enterprising. Fortune often baffles the sanguine expectations of poor mortals. I am not intoxicated with the favours I have received at her hands, but I do think there is a fair prospect of success.

The Governour has been so kind as to send out of town many of our friends who refused to do military duty; among them several very intelligent men, capable of doing me considerable service. One of them, a Mr. Antill, I have appointed chief engineer, Mr. Mott and all his suite having returned home. Be so good as to show Congress the necessity I was under of clothing the troops, to induce them to stay and undertake this service at such an inclement season. . . .

With a year's clothing of the 7th and 26th, I have relieved the distresses of Arnold's corps, and forwarded the clothing of some other corps. The greatest part of that clothing is a fair prize, except such as immediately belonged to the prisoners taken on board; they must be paid for theirs, as it was their own property. We shall have more time hereafter to settle this affair. Should there be any reason to apprehend an effort next spring to regain Canada, I would not wish to see less than ten thousand men ordered here. The Canadians will be our friends as long as we are able to maintain our ground, but they must not be depended upon, especially for defensive operations. The great distance from any support or relief renders it in my opinion absolutely necessary to make the most formidable preparations for the security of this important Province. What advantages the country below Quebeck affords for defence I cannot yet assert, but the rapids of Richlieu, some miles above, may be defended against all the navy and all the military force of Great Britain, by such a body of troops as I have mentioned, provided with sufficient artillery, row-gallies, and proper vessels fitted for fire-ships.

—Force, *American Archives*, 4th Series, IV, 188-189.

2. The Death of Montgomery

Journal of Abner Stocking.

Between four and five in the morning [of Jan. 1] the signal was given; and the several divisions moved to the assault, under a violent storm of snow.

The plan was so well concerted that from the side of the River St. Lawrence along the fortified front round to the bason, every part seemed equally threatened. Montgomery, at the head of the New York troops, advanced along the St. Lawrence by the way of Aunce de Mère, under Cape Diamond. The first barrier to be surmounted on this side was at the Pot-Ash. It was defended by a battery in which were mounted a few pieces of artillery, about two hundred paces in front of which was a block-house and picket. The guard placed at the block-house, being chiefly Canadians, having given a random and harmless fire, threw away their arms and fled in confusion to the barrier.

Unfortunately, the difficulties of the route rendered it impossible for Montgomery instantly to avail himself of this first impression. Cape Diamond, around which he was to make his way, presents a precipice, the foot of which is washed by the river, where enormous and rugged masses of ice had been piled on each other, so as to render the way almost impassable. Along the scanty path leading under the projecting rocks of the precipice, the Americans pressed forward in a narrow file, until they reached the block-house and picket. Montgomery, who was himself in front, assisted with his own hands to cut down or pull up the pickets, and open a passage for his troops; but the excessive roughness and difficulty of the way had so lengthened his line of march that he found it absolutely necessary to halt a few minutes in order to collect a force with which he might venture to proceed. Having reassembled about two hundred men, whom he encouraged alike by his voice and his example, he advanced boldly and rapidly at their head to force the barrier. One or two persons had now ventured to return to the battery, and, seizing a slow-match standing by one of the guns, discharged the piece, when the American front was within forty paces of it. This single accidental fire was a fatal one. The general with Captains M'Pherson and Cheeseman, two valuable young officers near his person, the first of whom was his aid, together with his orderly sergeant and a private, were killed on the spot. The loss of their general, in whom their confidence had been so justly placed, discouraged the troops; and Colonel Campbell, on whom the command devolved but who did not partake of that spirit of heroism which had animated their departed chief, made no attempt to prosecute the enterprise. This whole division retired precipitately from the action and left the garrison at leisure, after recovering from the consternation into which they had been thrown, to direct their undivided force against Arnold.

—STOCKING, "Journal," *Magazine of History*, Extra No. 75, pp. 26-30.

3. MAJOR CALDWELL TELLS HOW ARNOLD'S ATTACK WAS FRUSTRATED

Letter probably written by Major Henry Caldwell of the British Army to General James Murray.

Sloop-of-War *Hunter*, June 15, 1776

The 31st of December about five o'clock in the morning we were alarmed at our picket by Capt. Fraser, who was captain of the main guard and, returning from his rounds, told us that there was a brisk firing kept up at Cape

Diamond. The morning was dark, and at that time a drizzling kind of snow falling. McLean (who was second in command in the garrison, and who really, to do him justice, was indefatigable in the pains he took) begged that I would take part of my corps to Cape Diamond, and if I found it a false attack (as we both supposed it to be), after leaving the necessary reinforcements there, I might return with the rest. I accordingly went there, found the enemy firing at a distance, saw there was nothing serious intended, and after ordering a proper disposition to be made, proceeded to Port Louis. . . .

I hastened, with what expedition I could, by the back of the Hotel Dieu, in the Lower Town, and on my way passed by the picket drawn up under the field officer of the day, who was Major Cox, formerly of the 47th and now Lieut.-Governor of Gaspé. I got him to allow me to take your friend Nairne, with a subaltern and thirty men, and then proceeded to the Lower Town, where I found things, though not in a good way, yet not desperate. The enemy had got in at the Sault-au-Matelot, but, neglecting to push on, as they should have done, were stopped at the second barrier which our people got shut just as I arrived. It was so placed as to shut up the street of the Sault-au-Matelot from any communications with the rest of the Lower Town. As I was coming up, I found our people, the Canadians especially, shy of advancing towards the barrier, and was obliged to exert myself a good deal. To do old Voyer, their colonel, justice, though he is no great officer, yet he did not show any want of spirit. However, my coming up with Nairne and a lieutenant, with fifty seamen, gave our people new spirits.

I posted people in the different houses that commanded the street of Sault-au-Matelot; some in the house where Levy, the Jew, formerly lived, others at Lymeburner's. The officers of the Fusileers I posted in the street with fixed bayonets, ready to receive the enemy in case they got on our side of the barrier. They had, on their side of it, fixed some ladders, and then another to our side as it were to come down by, that was useful to us. I ordered it to be pulled away and fixed it to the window in the gable end of a house towards us, the front of which commanded the street of the Sault-au-Matelot and their side of the barrier.

Then I sent Captain Nairne and Dambourges, an officer also of McLean's corps, with a party of their people. Nairne and Dambourges entered the window with a great deal of spirit and got into the house on that side, just as the enemy was entering it by the front door. But Nairne soon disloged them with his bayonets, driving them into the street; nor did they approach the barrier afterwards. They however kept up a brisk fire from back windows of the houses they had occupied in Sault-au-Matelot Street on our people in Lymeburner's house, on his wharf, and the street adjacent, from one of their houses.

I had a narrow escape, for going at day-break to reconnoitre on the wharf under them, just as they took post there, they asked, "Who is there?"

At first I thought they might have been some of Nairne's people, who I knew were next door to them, and answered, "A friend—who are you?"

They answered, "Captain Morgan's company."

I told them to have good heart for they would soon be in the town, and immediately got behind a pile of boards beside me, not above ten or twelve yards from them, and escaped.

Their fire, however, a good deal slackened towards nine o'clock, especially after I brought a 9-pounder on Lymeburner's wharf to bear upon them, the first shot of which killed one of their men and wounded another. I then called out to Nairne in their hearing, so that he should let me know when he heard firing on the other side; our General had sent 500 men to hem the enemy in on that side; they soon after began to give themselves up and surrender to Nairne, who sent them through the window to us. They then began to crowd in in such numbers that we opened the barrier, and they all gave themselves up on that side, while the party that made the sortie were busy in the same manner on the other side of the post, and which had delayed so long from coming up in taking and sending in by Palace Gate some straggling prisoners; but they had not a shot fired at them, and just arrived on that end of the post, the enemy surprised at the time [by] the officer I sent to take possession of our old post, [who] arrived with a small party, supported by Nairne with 100 men.

Thus ended our attack on that side, in which the enemy had about 20 men killed, upwards of 40 men wounded, and about 400 made prisoners. Had they acted with more spirit, they might have pushed in at first and possessed themselves of the whole of Lower Town, and let their friends in at the other side, before our people had time to have recovered from a certain degree of panic, which seized them on the first news of the post being surprised.

　　—Literary Historical Society of Quebec, *Manuscripts Relating to the Early History of Canada*, 2nd Series, V, 9-13.

4. "It Was Apparent That We Must Surrender"

Account of John Henry, Pennsylvania private in Arnold's army.

It was not until the night of the thirty-first of December, 1775, that such kind of weather ensued as was considered favorable for the assault. The forepart of the night was admirably enlightened by a luminous moon. Many of us, officers as well as privates, had dispersed in various directions among the farm and tippling houses of the vicinity. We well knew the signal for rallying. This was no other than a snow-storm. About twelve o'clock P.M., the heaven was overcast. We repaired to quarters. By two o'clock we were accoutred and began our march. The storm was outrageous, and the cold wind extremely biting. In this northern country the snow is blown horizontally into the faces of travelers on most occasions—this was our case.

January 1st. When we came to Craig's house, near Palace Gate, a horrible roar of cannon took place, and a ringing of all the bells of the city, which are very numerous and of all sizes. Arnold, heading the forlorn hope, advanced perhaps one hundred yards before the main body. After these followed Lamb's artillerists. Morgan's company led in the secondary part of the column of infantry. [Captain] Smith's followed, headed by Steele, the captain, from particular causes, being absent. Hendrick's company succeeded, and the eastern men, so far as known to me, followed in due order. The snow was deeper than in the fields, because of the nature of the ground. The path made by Arnold, Lamb and Morgan was almost imperceptible because of the falling snow; covering the locks of our guns with the lappets of our coats, holding down our heads (for it was impossible to bear up our faces against the imperious storm of wind and snow), we ran along the foot of the hill in single file. Along the first of our run, from Palace Gate, for several hundred paces, there stood a range of insulated buildings which seemed to be store-houses; we passed these quickly in single file, pretty wide apart. The interstices were from thirty to fifty yards. In these intervals we received a tremendous fire of musketry from the ramparts above us. Here we lost some brave men, when powerless to return the salutes we received, as the enemy was covered by his impregnable defences. They were even sightless to us; we could see nothing but the blaze from the muzzles of their muskets.

A number of vessels of various sizes lay along the beach, moored by their hawsers or cables to the houses. Pacing after my leader, Lieutenant Steele, at a great rate, one of these ropes took me under the chin and cast me headlong down a declivity of at least fifteen feet. The place appeared to be either a dry dock or a sawpit. My descent was terrible; gun and all was involved in a great depth of snow. Most unluckily, however, one of my knees received a violent contusion on a piece of scraggy ice, which was covered by the snow. On like occasions we can scarce expect, in the hurry of attack, that our intimates should attend to any other than their own concerns. Mine went from me, regardless of my fate. Scrabbling out of the cavity, without assistance, divesting my person and gun of the snow, and limping into the line, it was attempted to assume a station and preserve it. These were none of my friends —they knew me not. We had not gone twenty yards in my hobbling gait before I was thrown out and compelled to await the arrival of a chasm in the line, where a new place might be obtained. Men in affairs such as this seem in the main to lose the compassionate feeling and are averse from being dislodged from their original stations.

We proceeded rapidly, exposed to a long line of fire from the garrison, for now we were unprotected by any buildings. The fire had slackened in a small degree. The enemy had been partly called off to resist the general and strengthen the party opposed to Arnold in our front.

Now we saw Colonel Arnold returning, wounded in the leg and supported by two gentlemen. . . . Arnold called to the troops in a cheering voice as we passed, urging us forward, yet it was observable among the soldiery, with whom it was my misfortune to be now placed, that the colonel's retiring damped their spirits. A cant term, "We are sold," was repeatedly heard in many parts throughout the line.

Thus proceeding enfiladed by an animated but lessened fire, we came to the first barrier, where Arnold had been wounded in the onset. This contest had lasted but a few minutes and was somewhat severe, but the energy of our men prevailed. The embrasures were entered when the enemy were discharging their guns. The guard, consisting of thirty persons, were either taken or fled, leaving their arms behind them.

At this time it was discovered that our guns were useless, because of the dampness. The snow, which lodged in our fleecy coats, was melted by the warmth of our bodies. Thence came that disaster. Many of the party, knowing the circumstance, threw aside their own and seized the British arms. These were not only elegant, but were such as befitted the hand of a real soldier. It was said that ten thousand stand of such arms had been received from England in the previous summer for arming the Canadian militia. Those people were loath to bear them in opposition to our rights.

From the first barrier to the second, there was a circular course along the sides of houses, and partly through a street, probably of three hundred yards or more. This second barrier was erected across and near the mouth of a narrow street, adjacent to the foot of the hill, which opened into a larger, leading soon into the main body of the lower town. Here it was that the most serious contention took place; this became the bone of strife.

The admirable Montgomery by this time (though it was unknown to us) was no more; yet we expected momentarily to join him. The firing on that side of the fortress ceased, his division fell under the command of a Colonel Campbell of the New York line, a worthless chief who retreated without making an effort in pursuance of the general's original plans. The inevitable consequence was that the whole of the forces on that side of the city, and those who were opposed to the dastardly persons employed to make the false attacks, embodied and came down to oppose our division.

Here was sharp shooting. We were on the disadvantageous side of the barrier for such a purpose. Confined in a narrow street hardly more than twenty feet wide, and on the lower ground, scarcely a ball, well aimed or otherwise, but must take effect upon us. Morgan, Hendricks, Steele, Humphreys and a crowd of every class of the army had gathered into the narrow pass, attempting to surmount the barrier, which was about twelve or more feet high and so strongly constructed that nothing but artillery could effectuate its destruction.

There was a construction fifteen or twenty yards within the barrier, upon a rising ground, the cannon of which much overtopped the height of the barrier; hence we were assailed by grape shot in abundance. This erection we called the platform. Again, within the barrier, and close in to it, were two ranges of musketeers, armed with musket and bayonet, ready to receive those who might venture the dangerous leap. Add to all this that the enemy occupied the upper chambers of the houses, in the interior of the barrier, on both sides of the street, from the windows of which we became fair marks. The enemy having the advantage of the ground in front, a vast superiority of numbers [and] dry and better arms gave them an irresistible power in so narrow a space.

Humphreys, upon a mound which was speedily erected, attended by many brave men, attempted to scale the barrier, but was compelled to retreat by the formidable phalanx of bayonets within and the weight of fire from the platform and the buildings. Morgan, brave to temerity, stormed and raged; Hendricks, Steele, Nichols, Humphreys, equally brave, were sedate, though under a tremendous fire. The platform, which was within our view,

was evacuated by the accuracy of our fire, and few persons dared venture there again.

Now it was that the necessity of the occupancy of the houses, on our side of the barrier, became apparent. Orders were given by Morgan to that effect. We entered—this was near daylight. The houses were a shelter from which we could fire with much accuracy. Yet even here some valuable lives were lost. Hendricks, when aiming his rifle at some prominent person, died by a straggling ball through his heart. He staggered a few feet backwards and fell upon a bed, where he instantly expired. He was an ornament of our little society. The amiable Humphreys died by a like kind of wound, but it was in the street, before we entered the buildings. Many other brave men fell at this place; among these were Lieutenant Cooper, of Connecticut, and perhaps fifty or sixty non-commissioned officers and privates. The wounded were numerous, and many of them dangerously so. Captain Lamb, of the York artillerists, had nearly one half of his face carried away by a grape or canister shot. My friend Steele lost three of his fingers as he was presenting his gun to fire; Captain Hubbard and Lieutenant Fisdle were also among the wounded. When we reflect upon the whole of the dangers at this barricade, and the formidable force that came to annoy us, it is a matter of surprise that so many should escape death and wounding as did.

All hope of success having vanished, a retreat was contemplated, but hesitation, uncertainty and a lassitude of mind, which generally takes place in the affairs of men when we fail in a project upon which we have attached much expectation, now followed. That moment was foolishly lost when such a movement might have been made with tolerable success. Captain Laws, at the head of two hundred men, issuing from Palace Gate, most fairly and handsomely cooped us up. Many of the men, aware of the consequences, and all our Indians and Canadians (except Natanis and another) escaped across the ice which covered the bay of St. Charles, before the arrival of Captain Laws. This was a dangerous and desperate adventure, but worth while the undertaking, in avoidance of our subsequent sufferings. Its desperateness consisted in running two miles across shoal ice, thrown up by the high tides of this latitude—and its danger in the meeting with air holes, deceptively covered by the bed of snow.

. . . About nine o'clock, A.M., it was apparent to all of us that we must surrender. It was done.

HENRY, *Account of Arnold's Campaign Against Quebec*, pp. 107-115.

5. BENEDICT ARNOLD BOASTS THAT HE WILL NOT LEAVE QUEBEC

Colonel Benedict Arnold to Hannah Arnold.

Camp before Quebeck, January 6, 1776

Before this reaches you I make no doubt you will have heard of our misfortune of the 31st ultimo and will be anxious for my safety. I should have wrote you before, but a continual hurry of business has prevented me. The command of the army, by the death of my truly great and good friend, General Montgomery, devolved on me; a task, I find, too heavy under my present circumstances.

I received a wound by a ball through my left leg, at the time I had gained the first battery at the lower town, which, by the loss of blood, rendered me very weak. As soon as the main body came up, with some assistance I returned to the hospital, near a mile, on foot, being obliged to draw one leg after me, and a great part of the way under the continual fire of the enemy from the walls, at no greater distance than fifty yards. I providentially escaped, though several were shot down at my side.

I soon learned the death of our general, who attacked the town at the side opposite to me; he behaved heroically; marched up in the face of their cannon and, when he had nearly gained the pass, received the fatal shot, or the town would have been ours. This occasioned the disaster that afterwards happened to my detachment, which, after the general's defeat, had the whole garrison to encounter, under every disadvantage of ground, etc., etc. To return was impossible, as the route was within fifty yards and exposed to the fire of the whole garrison, who had brought several pieces out of one of the gates, which our people would have been obliged to pass. In this situation, they maintained their ground near three hours, but, being overpowered with numbers, were obliged to lay down their arms; about three hundred, including Captain Lamb, of New-York, and part of the train, were taken prisoners and, as near as I can judge, about sixty killed and wounded. Captain Oswald is among the prisoners; he was with me in a selected party of about twenty-five, who attacked the first battery, behaved gallantly and gained much honour. The prisoners are treated politely and supplied with every thing the garrison affords. Governour Carleton sent to let me know that the soldiers' baggage, if I pleased, might be sent to them, which I shall immediately send.

Though the enemy are now double our number, they have made no attempt to come out. We are as well prepared to receive them as we can possibly be in our present situation, divided at a distance of two miles. I expect General Wooster from Montreal in a few days with a reinforcement. I hope we shall be properly supported with troops by the Congress. I have no thoughts of leaving this proud town until I first enter it in triumph.

My wound has been exceeding painful, but is now easy, and the surgeons assure me will be well in eight weeks. I know you will be anxious for me. That Providence which has carried me through so many dangers is still my protection. I am in the way of my duty and know no fear.

　　　　　　—Force, *American Archives*, 4th Series, IV, 589-590.

6. "Thus Was Quebec Freed from a Swarm of Misguided People"

Journal of Thomas Ainslie.

May 6th, [*1776*]. There was frost last night with a gentle breeze at N. E. About 4 o'clock this morning guns were heard at a distance—we heard repeated reports nearer and nearer.

A woman came early to Palace Gate and informed the sentry that Mr. Thomas with his reinforcement was arrived and that Mr. Wooster was gone off, that they all appear in confusion, loading all the carts they can find with baggage, arms, etc.

About 6 oclock a vessel appeared turning Point Levy to the inconceivable joy of all who saw her. The news soon reached every pillow in town; people half dressed ran down to the Grand Battery to feast their eyes with the sight of a ship of war displaying the Union flag.

She made signals of friendship and proved to be the *Surprize* frigate commanded by Capt. Lindsay; part of the 29th Regiment with the marines belonging to that ship were immediately landed. The *Isis* and Sloop *Martin* arrived the same tide; their marines were also landed. The whole made about 200.

The drums beat to arms; the different corps assembled on the Parade.

It was there proposed that the volunteers of the British and Canadian militia should join the troops and sailors to engage the Rebels on the plains; to their credit be it said that almost to a man both corps were anxious to be led to action.

The general at the head of about 800 men marched out at 12 oclock; the little army extended itself quite across the plains, making a fine appearance. The Rebels saw us very formidable.

A few shots were exchanged by our advanced party and the rear guard of the enemy; their balls whistled over us without hurting a man. They fled most precipitately as soon as our field pieces began to play on their guard houses and advanced posts. They left cannon, mortars, field pieces, muskets and even their cloaths behind them. As we pursued them we found the road strewed with arms, cartridges, cloaths, bread, pork, etc.

Their confusion was so great, their panic so violent, that they left orderly books and papers, which for their own credit should not have left. Look whatsoever way one would, he saw men flying and loaden carts driving full speed.

We took possession of their General Hospital and of a guard house two miles beyond it; of Holland house, Mr. Dupres', etc. There and at Sillerie we found provisions and artillery stores.

We returned to town about 4 oclock. The *Surprize* and *Martin* sailed up the river to destroy the enemy craft. A guard was posted at the General Hospital in the evening. . . .

May 7. Party's are detached all around. The Rebels abandoned the *Gaspey* on the approach of our ships; she was half prepared as a fire ship. We found two other vessels without any body on board.

The frigates fired on bateaus full of runaways; the turning of the tide unfortunately forced them to come to an anchor, and the bateaus rowed close to shore and got off.

To lighten their boats they inhumanly threw out many of their sick men upon the beach. Some of them expired before our parties could get to their relief; those objects of compassion whom we found alive were sent to the General Hospital.

Thus was the country round Quebec freed from a swarm of misguided people, led by designing men, enemies to the libertys of their country, under the specious title of the Assertors of American Rights.

—AINSLIE, *Journal*, pp. 82-84.

IV. THE ARMY IN RETREAT

Notwithstanding his disastrous defeat, Arnold refused to retreat, but hung grimly on in the hope that reinforcements might enable him to renew the attack. Sure enough the reinforcements began to trickle in, and by May there were probably 7,000 Americans in Canada—and, in addition, the three commissioners, Benjamin Franklin, Charles Carroll of Carrollton and Samuel Chase, whose mission to win the affections of the habitants, *hopefully authorized by a deluded Congress, was as desperate as had been Arnold's attack. But as fast as the American army was built up, it seemed to melt away—partly due to desertion, but chiefly to smallpox. And at the same time the British, too, were pouring in reinforcements. When in May the British fleet sailed down the St. Lawrence and up to Quebec, it was clear that the game was up. Arnold had already been supplanted by the feeble General David Wooster, and had withdrawn to Montreal. The morale of the Americans went to pieces, and a substantial force surrendered at "The Cedars," a small post some forty miles above Montreal, almost without firing a shot. All through May and June they retreated, along the St. Lawrence, down the Richelieu, back to their own country. As they fled, their situation got increasingly desperate. The ravages of smallpox spread, and so, too, other diseases. Even Crown Point was abandoned, and eventually the pitiful remnants of the army found refuge at Fort Ticonderoga.*

Of our chroniclers we have met Dr. Senter before. John Lacey was a Pennsylvania captain. All we know of young Charles Cushing is that he was from Massachusetts. General John Sullivan was a New Hampshireman who had won some small reputation for courage and enterprise during the fighting around Boston. A member of the Second Continental Congress, he was commissioned brigadier general; took charge of the army on its retreat from Canada; fought with Washington in New York and in the Pennsylvania campaign; and later took command of an expedition into the Indian country. After the war he was three times governor of his state. His military career was far stormier than his political.

1. THE COWARDLY SURRENDER AT THE CEDARS

Report of Committee of Congress to consider General Arnold's Cartel after The Cedars.

In Congress, July 10, 1776

The Committee find that a party of three hundred and ninety Continental troops, under the command of Colonel Bedel, was posted at the Cedars, about forty-three miles above Montreal; that they had there formed some works of defence, the greater part of them picketed lines, the rest a breastwork, with two field-pieces mounted.

That on Wednesday the 15th of May, Colonel Bedel received intelligence that a party of the enemy, consisting of about six hundred regulars, Canadians and Indians, were on the way to attack his post, and were within nine miles of it; that Colonel Bedel thereon set out himself for Montreal, to procure a reinforcement, whereupon the command at the Cedars devolved on Major Butterfield.

That on Thursday, a reinforcement, under the command of Major Sherburne, marched from Montreal for the Cedars, while a larger detachment should be getting ready to proceed thither with Brigadier-General Arnold.

That on Friday the 19th, the enemy, under the command of Captain Forster, invested the post at the Cedars, and for two days kept up a loose, scattering fire; that Major Butterfield, from the very first, proposed to surrender the post, and refused repeated solicitations from his officers and men to permit them to sally out on the enemy.

That on Sunday afternoon, a flag being sent in by the enemy, Major Butterfield agreed to surrender the fort and garrison to Captain Forster, capitulating with him (whether verbally or in writing, does not appear) that the garrison should not be put into the hands of the savages, and that their baggage should not be plundered.

That, at the time of the surrender, the enemy consisted of about forty regulars, one hundred Canadians and five hundred Indians, and had no cannon. The garrison had sustained no injury from the fire, but the having one man wounded; they had twenty rounds of cartridges a man, thirty rounds for one field-piece, and five for another, half a barrel of gunpowder, fifteen pounds of musket ball, and provisions sufficient to have lasted them twenty or thirty days. Major Butterfield knew that a reinforcement was on its way, and, moreover, was so near the main body of the army that he could not doubt of being supported by that.

That immediately on the surrender, the garrison was put into the custody of the savages, who plundered them of their baggage and even stripped them of their clothes.

That Major Sherburne having landed on Monday the 20th, at Quinze Chiens, about nine miles from the Cedars, and marched on with his party, consisting then of one hundred men, to within four miles thereof, was there attacked by about five hundred of the enemy; that he maintained his ground about one hour, and then, being constrained to retreat, performed the same in good order, receiving and returning a constant fire for about forty minutes; when the enemy finding means to post advanced parties in such a manner as to intercept their further retreat, they also were made prisoners of war.

That they were immediately put into the custody of the savages, carried to where Major Butterfield and his party were, and stripped of their baggage and wearing apparel. That two of them were put to death that evening; four or five others at different times afterwards—one of whom was of those who surrendered on capitulation at the Cedars, and was killed on the eighth day after that surrender. That one was first shot and, while retaining life and sensation, was roasted, as was related by one of his companions now in possession of the savages, who himself saw the fact; and that several others, being worn down by famine and cruelty, were exposed on an island, naked and perishing with cold and hunger. . . .

That, on Sunday the 26th, the prisoners were carried to Quinze Chiens, when it was discovered that General Arnold was approaching, and making dispositions to attack them.

That Captain Forster, having desired Major Sherburne to attend a flag which he was about to send to General Arnold for confirmation of the Cartel, carried him into the council of the Indians, then sitting, who told him that it was a mercy never before shown in their wars, that they had put to death so few of the prisoners; but that he must expect, and so inform General Arnold, that they should certainly kill every man who should thereafter fall into their hands. That Captain Forster joined in desiring that this bloody message should be delivered to General Arnold, and moreover, that he should be notified that if he rejected cartel and attacked him, every man of the prisoners should be put to instant death.

That General Arnold was extremely averse from entering into any agreement, and was at length induced to do it by no other motive than that of saving the prisoners from cruel and inhuman death, threatened in such terms as left no doubt it was to be perpetrated, and that he did in the end conclude it, after several flags received from Captain Forster, and a relinquishment by him of the unequal article, restraining our soldiers from again bearing arms. . . .

                              —FORCE, *American Archives*, 5th Series, I, 158-161.

2. GENERAL SULLIVAN FINDS THAT NO ONE THING IS RIGHT

General John Sullivan to John Hancock, President of the Congress.

                                        St. Johns, June 1, 1776

I must beg leave to inform Congress that I arrived here last evening with my brigade except Col. Draytons and part of Col. Waines regiment, the former of which was by order of General Schuyler sent to Tryon County. The latter I hear are detained at New York I know not for what length of time. Upon my arrival I was informed that General Thomas was down with the small pox without the least prospect of a recovery. General Worster [Wooster] is here with his baggage, returning to Connecticut, by means of which the command devolves upon me.

I have done every thing I possibly could in the time to get information of the true state of affairs—and can in a word inform you that no one thing is right. Every thing is in the utmost confusion and almost every one frightened at they know not what. The report is that General Carlton has advanced to Three Rivers and the ships are coming up the River St. Lawrence. Other persons who have come from eighty miles below Quebeck declare that there is no appearance of men or ships on this side that city, and for my own part I am fully convinced that the latter report is true. However that may be, I am surprized that an army should live in continual fear of and even retreat before an enemy which no person among them has seen. I think they might at least have ventured some persons in whom they could confide to view them from the neighbouring heighths and give some account of their numbers and movements, but nothing of this kind is done.

I shall set out early tomorrow for Montreal and will proceed till I can find with certainty where the enemy is and what they are about. I find the lower and some of the higher class of French people in our favour and fear much that we are about to leave them. . . .

I am extremely sorry to inform you that from the officers whose business it was to give Congress the true state of matters, Congress has not, as I believe, received any thing like it. This I conclude from the repeated letters sent to Gen. Washington giving the most favourable accounts and promising a speedy reduction of Quebeck, when there was not even a probability of it and the army with which this was to be done had dwindled into a mobb without even the form of order or regularity. The consequence of which we have experienced by the infamous retreat from Quebeck and the still more scandalous surrender of the post at the Cedars. . . .

I find no proper commissary appointed and the publick stores left to the mercies of searjeants and other persons who are guilty of every kind of fraud. The regiments sent here are torn and divided into numerous parts scattered from one end of the country to another. This method, besides its being highly impolitick, will ever prevent the officers from making proper returns of their men and naturally destroys that subordination which ever ought to be kept up in an army.

—HAMMOND, ed., *Letters and Papers of Sullivan*, I, 212-214.

3. DR. SENTER DESCRIBES THE ABANDONMENT OF MONTREAL

[January 1776]

The first stand we endeavoured to make was at Point de Shambo [Deschambault], 45 miles from Quebec, but not being able to collect provisions sufficient, were obliged to abandon it and proceed up along. The poor inhabitants, seeing we were abandoning their country, were in the utmost dilemma, expecting as many as had been aiding us every way to be sacrificed to the barbarity of those whose severity they had long felt, though under the specious pretence of civil government, which, in fact, had been in essence nothing but an arrogant military one. No provisions could be obtained but by force of arms. No conveniences for ferrying our troops over the rivers emptying in upon either side of the St. Lawrence, except a canoe or two, and these were rare. By reason of the spring flood which in this country is amazing in many low places, the army were obliged to travel a great distance round them, as the river had overflowed its banks in many places to the distance of several miles. In this perplexed situation we however arrived at Sorel, about forty miles below Montreal, where we made a stand and collected our whole force, which was not very formidable, notwithstanding several new recruits had by this time arrived.

The small-pox still very rife in the army—new troops few of them who had had it—I was ordered by Gen. Thomas, who commanded, to repair to Montreal and erect an hospital for their reception, as well by the natural way as inoculation. I accordingly made application to General Arnold, then commanding in the city, and obtained a fine capacious house belonging to the East India Company. It was convenient for nigh six hundred. I generally inoculated a regiment at a class, who had it so favourable as to be able to do garrison duty during the whole time.

About this time an action happened up above Montreal at the Cedars, nine miles from hence, between Major Shereburne and party, and a number of savages, with one company of regular troops. Shereburne and the chief of his party were taken, some few killed, etc.

We were now betwixt the two armies of the foe, under every embarassment possible, no quantity of ammunition, no provisions but obtained by force of arms. Sorel, a low, unhealthy place at the entrance of the River Chamblee into the St. Lawrence, flat and almost upon a water level. Land the highest some distance back of our fortifications. Works might easily be raised entirely overlooking ours. A number of men about this time detached to attack the advanced guard at the "Three Rivers." These proved unsuccessful, and Gen. Thompson with the chief of the division were killed and captured. Fortune and the country seemed jointly against us. Our principal fortifications [were] not tenable against an equal number if attacked by land. Our prospect was still gloomy. A committee from Congress had been in Montreal for some time with a view of giving the money currency, but it answered no purpose. Gen. Thomas caught the natural small-pox, sickened at Sorel, was carried to Chamblee and died. Soon after this General Sullivan arrived and took the command. Wooster went to Montreal, and Arnold to Chamblee. Enemy drawing upon us from every quarter, assimilating the savages.

Our army, weakened by the small-pox, and in fine every movement against the enemy unsuccessful, a retreat was ordered to St. John's. The troops accordingly evacuated Montreal the 9th of June.

—SENTER, "Journal," *Magazine of History*, Extra No. 42, pp. 58-59.

4. DEFEAT AT TROIS RIVIÈRES AND THE FLIGHT FROM CANADA

Memoirs of John Lacey of Pennsylvania, a captain in the Continental Army.

June 8th. Last night Gen. Sullivan received a letter from Gen. Thompson advising him that he proposed to attack the enemy at the Three Rivers by surprise, with his whole body this morning. The river at this place was very wide, called Lake Sent Peters. The armey was to cross over in batteaus, land above the Three Rivers and attack the enemy at daylight. Early in the morning we heard firing down the river, which we supposed to be the attack on the enemy according to Gen. Thompson's letter. It was, however, broaken and at intervils, not like a general charge. We waited all this day in suspence without a word of inteligence from the armey.

On the morning of the 9th we again heard the report of cannon, tho singly, and soon discontinued. About 10 o'clock A.M. the batteaus of the armey came in sight. In great anxiety we all hastned to the edge of the river to meet the batteaus, but was sadly mortifyed to find our armey had been defeated; that the batteaus which transported over the armey being cut off by the enemy from the troops who lost their way, [the troops] came up by detachment to the enemies batteries, were driven back, [and] finding the enemy in possession of the place where the batteaus were left, took to the woods and swamps. Major Woods, who was left in command of the batteaus and baggage, found himself cut off from the American armey and discovering two of the enemies frigates under way ordered the batteaus to push up the river. Having proceeded some distance and night coming on, he halted with an expectation to meet with our armey on their retreat, where he remained till morning. The ships of war Major Wood discovered under way the day before had entered Lake St. Peters, nearly abreast of the batteaus. Finding himself in this precarious situation he ordered those in the batteaus to proceed directly with them to the mouth of the Sorrell—about 45 miles—with all possible dispatch, thus, abandening the armey to make the best of their way through horrid swamps up the north side of the river.

On the 10th by order of Gen. Sullivan crossed the River St. Lawrence to the north side with a scout of ten riffler men and Lieut. Read, to proceed down the St. Lawrence untill we met the retreating armey. Proceeded through most horrid swamps, were almost devoured by muskeetoes of a monsterous seize and innumerable numbers; came into a very indifferent and swampy road, not meeting with a single habitation, which we followed untill after dark, when we luckely fell in with the leading detachment under Capt. Smith of the 6th Pennsylvania Regiment, with whome we returned, leaving two of our men to direct those in the rear the route to the mouth of the Sorrell. The troops being so scattered, they did not arrive untill the latter part or evening of the next day.

On the 12th of June, threw up a breast work of sand in front of our encampment, keeping a lookout for the enemy, who were duly waiting for a fair wind to their heavy vessels up the rapids into Lake St. Peters, the only obstruction in their way here, and even up to Montreall.

On the 15th a flag arrived from Gen. Carlton with letters from Gen. Thompson and Col. Ervine of the 6th Pennsylvania Regiment, who were taken prisoners, advising they were used well by Gen. Carlton. According to report our loss was upward of three hundred missing; as very few were either killed or wounded at the Three Rivers, it was presumed they were generally taken prisoners. It appeared 17 were missing from my company who, according to Lieut. Smiths account, must all be prisoners as the company never came in reach of the enemies muskets, and that the vallient Capt. Moore ran at the first fire of the enemies cannon without returning a shot, being at too great a distance for the fire of muskets to do any execution.

On the night of the 13th a council of war was held at Gen. Sullivans head quarters, at which it was decided that it was advisable for the whole of the American armey to evacuate Canada, and to . . . make a stand at Ticonderoga.

On the morning of the fourteenth orders were given to retreat. . . .

About 4 oclock on the afternoon of the 17th left St. Johns in a batteau for the Isle Aux Noix with Ensigne Varnum and Doctor Mouse, with about 25 soldiers to row the batteau, being very heavy laden with cannon ball and other baggage; did not reach that island until next morning almost weried to death—the men began to sicken very fast.

On the 19th the remainder of the armey came in batteaus and landed on the island. As the rear of the armey left Saint Johns the enemies van appeared.

On the 20th the greater part of our batteaus, with two thousand sick and invaleeds, left this island for Crown Point. . . . I chose to remain, still having good health. . . .

—LACEY, "Memoirs," *Penn. Mag. of Hist. and Biog.*, XXV, 200 ff.

5. THE ARMY RETREATS IN DISORDER TO CROWN POINT

Charles Cushing to his brother.

Camp at Crown-Point, June 13, 1776

Dear Friend and Brother: . . . We set off for Sorel with heavy hearts, none of us expecting to come back again, for General Burgoyne and all his troops were come in, our army but small in comparison to his, and if we were defeated, there would be no retreat. We got to Chambly the first day, and the next morning set off for Sorel, and before night met Colonel Greaton about twenty-three miles from the mouth of the river, who came directly from there. He informed us the army were retreating as fast as possible, that the enemy's fleet was just below them, and he ordered us to go on shore and cook some victuals, and then return back to Chambly as fast as possible. After refreshing ourselves a little, we set off about dark, and rowed all night very hard, the current running rapidly. In the morning, about seven o'clock, we got up to Chambly, when, after refreshing ourselves with a little breakfast, we were obliged to assist in getting the batteaus, cannon and other stores above the lower rapids; and then it is as much as twenty men can do to tow a loaded batteau up the river in many places.

After our party had drawn over two batteaus, two pieces of cannon and all their tents and baggage, and put them on board, we set off with three or four boats up the river. In some places the men were obliged to wade up to their middle. At dark, having got about half-way up to St. John's, we pitched our tents and lay down to rest. In the morning we proceeded to St. John's. During this fatigue, the men had but little to eat but pork and flour, and lake water to drink.

The army at Sorel brought off all their artillery and other stores and arrived safe at Chambly; and in eight hours after their departure, the enemy had come up with their fleet and taken possession of Sorel. At Chambly, General Sullivan made all the despatch possible in getting over the artillery, stores and boats, there being a large quantity of them, and not less than a hundred batteaus. We lost one or two pieces of cannon by staving the boats, and one or two more were left. The row galleys were burnt, and I think we left but little else, except four schooners that we burnt in the river.

Our army, consisting of about six thousand men, were now all retreated safely to St. John's, and the enemy at Montreal and Chambly. We then sent the sick and some of the stores to the Isle-aux-Noix, the Isle-au-Motte and Point-au-Fer, not having boats to carry the whole army and stores at once; and as soon as the boats came back, the whole army embarked and went to the Isle-aux-Noix. Here, what boats could be spared were sent to Crown-Point with sick and stores, as a great part of the army were sick, many with the small-pox, and many of those who had had it were sick with the flux. Here we were obliged to wait for boats eight days, where we could get nothing but pork and flour. The island being small, not more than one mile in length and a quarter of a mile in width, the land low, the days hot, and at night great dews, and such a number of men on so small a spot, and many of them sick—the place stunk enough to breed an infection.

At length the boats returned from Crown-Point. We were ordered to strike our tents and put all our baggage on board, and the invalids who were not able to march by land. Those of our regiment who were well, and about a thousand or more, were set over to the west side, to go by land to Point-au-Fer, about twenty-six miles. During our stay at the Isle-aux-Noix, there went a number of officers about a mile below to a house to drink spruce beer; but unfortunately were beset by a party of Indians, who killed and scalped one ensign, one captain and two privates, and took several prisoners. We heard the guns and saw the fire. A party was immediately sent to their assistance; but the enemy were gone and had left the dead stripped all to their shirts. They were brought to the Isle-aux-Noix and decently buried. They all belonged to the rifle regiment. The Indians attacked several boats on the lake that went above after some flour, killed two or three men and wounded six more; the others escaped.

About noon we marched for Point-au-Fer, and soon came where there was only an Indian path and a wet swamp, which was for a great distance almost up to our knees in mud and water. Besides this, it rained very hard all the afternoon. At dark we came out against a bay in the lake, within about six miles of Point-au-Fer. We had now nothing but the ground to lie on and the heavens to cover us; and what with the rain, sweat and mud, we had but little about us that was dry. We soon built fires and dried ourselves as well as we could, and then lay down to rest with our feet to the fire. I slept very well and got up in the morning refreshed. The weather cleared off pleasant; we got some breakfast; and about nine o'clock there came boats enough to take us all off. The remainder of the army came in batteaus from the Isle-aux-Noix, and all arrived at the Isle-au-Motte that night. We soon had boats enough to carry the whole army to Crown-Point, and, I think, nothing remarkable happened till we arrived there.

—FORCE, *American Archives*, 5th Series, I, 130-131.

6. BENEDICT ARNOLD AT ST. JOHNS: "LET US NOT FALL ALL TOGETHER"

General Arnold to General Sullivan.

Chamble [Chambly], June 13, 1776

I went to St Johns yesterday where I found every thing in the greatest confusion, not one stroke done to fortify the camp, the engineer a perfect sott, at that and this place near three thousand sick. I have given orders that the sick draw only half rations in future. I have ordered Colonel Antell to St Johns, and an abette and lines to be immediately begun to inclose the two old forts and an encampment sufficient to hold six thousand men.

I am fully of opinion not one minute ought to be lost in securing our retreat and saving our heavy cannon and baggage and provisions. The enemy will neaver attack you at Sorell; their force is doubtless much superior to ours, and we have no advice of any reinforcement. Shall we sacrafice the few men we have by endeavring to keep possession of a small part of the country which can be of little or no service to us? The junction of the Canadians with the Colonies, an object which brought us into this country, is now at an end. Let us quit them and secure our own country before it is too late. There will be more honour in making a safe retreat than hazarding a battle against such superiority which will doubtless be attended with the loss of men, artillery, etc., and the only pass to our country.

These arguments are not urged by fear for my personal safety. I am content to be the last man who quits this country and fall so that my country rise—but let us not fall all together. . . .

—HAMMOND, ed., *Letters and Papers of Sullivan*, I, 237-238.

V. ARNOLD SAVES THE AMERICAN ARMY: THE BATTLES ON LAKE CHAMPLAIN

With the collapse of the Canadian campaign, the American flank was wide open to counterattack. Had Carleton been ready, and had he moved with characteristic speed, he might have destroyed the American army in the north, and struck down the Hudson to join forces with Howe in New York. But he was taken by surprise; and it took time to bring his forces together, to provide supplies and food for them for a fall campaign. While he was organizing his offensive, the American army, decimated by disease and dissension, was getting restored to health and strength; morale was improved. By August it was 5,000 strong; there was a new commander—Horatio Gates—but then Schuyler wouldn't yield his place. By September Carleton, with a large and well-equipped army, had reached St. Johns. Unable to run the rapids there, he took his boats apart and rebuilt them below the rapids, but all this took time.

Meantime Benedict Arnold had been put in charge of naval operations on Lake Champlain. In a whirlwind of energy and a miracle of resourcefulness, he called in ships' carpenters from the coast, blacksmiths from near-by towns, and recruited sailors and marines who could man boats. He repaired some old batteaux, built a small squadron of gondolas and galleys, and prepared to do battle with Carleton's substitute for the Royal Navy. That battle came on October 11-13. Carleton's superior force swept Arnold's squadron off the lake, but Arnold inflicted heavy damage on it. And what is more to the point his challenge to Carleton required that general to lose over a month in building a navy able to overwhelm the American. That month was decisive. Carleton was not prepared for a winter campaign, and withdrew to Canada, leaving the Americans in possession of Ticonderoga.

Of Arnold's makeshift squadron Captain Mahan writes: "Never had any force, big or small, lived to better purpose, or died more gloriously. . . . That the Americans were strong enough to impose the capitulation of Saratoga was due to the invaluable year of delay secured to them by their little navy on Lake Champlain."

We need introduce only two of our four participants. John Trumbull, a son of Governor Trumbull, had served briefly as aide-de-camp to Washington, and then been assigned as adjutant to General Gates with the rank of Colonel. Shortly after the Lake Champlain campaign he resigned his commission and went to London to paint; to his familiarity with the war and his skill as a painter we owe much of our picture of the war and of its heroes. Lieutenant James Hadden was one of the soldiers who had come over in the reinforcements of May 1776; he commanded a gunboat in the battle of Valcour Island. He was later to have a long and distinguished career in the Peninsular war.

1. CROWN POINT: "I FOUND NOT AN ARMY BUT A MOB"

John Trumbull to his father, Governor of Connecticut.

Ticonderoga, July 12, 1776

Honored Sir: Since I left Albany I have not wrote you nor have I received any of yours. I arrived at this place the fourth day—and from hence went on to Crown Point soon after. At that place I found not an army, but a mob, the shattered remains of twelve or fifteen very fine battalions, ruined by sickness, fatigue and desertions and void of every idea of discipline or subordination. . . .

Last spring . . . the army was upwards of ten thousand strong. . . . We have now three thousand sick and about the same number well. This leaves near five thousand men to be accounted for. Of them the enemy have cost us perhaps one, sickness another thousand, and the others God alone knows in what manner they are disposed of!

Among the few we have remaining, there is neither order, subordination, nor harmony, the officers, as well as men, of one colony insulting and quarreling with those of another. This wretched situation of our troops induced the General Officers, in a Council of War, to determine on a retreat to this place. The post we are to occupy here is very advantageous. It is a height opposite to the old works which commands the entrance of Lakes Champlain and George. 'Tis almost inaccessible except in two places where we propose roads. The rest is surrounded by rocks and precipices. We shall easily be possessed with provisions from Skeensborough, at the head of Lake Champlain, and can easily retire that way into the country. This, without a naval superiority on the lakes, I fear we shall be obliged to do, notwithstanding the strength of our camp, unless we are very soon joined by six or eight thousand men.

How we shall maintain our naval superiority I must confess myself much at a loss. 'Tis true we build a thing *called* a gondola, perhaps as much as one in a week, but where is our rigging for them, where our guns? We have, to be sure, a great train of artillery, but they are very few of them mounted on carriages, and our materials and conveniences for mounting them are very slender.

We have carpenters, shipbuilders and mechanichs in plenty, but neither places for them to work in nor materials in that plenty we ought to have.

To oppose the enemy on the lake, we have a schooner of twelve carriage guns, a sloop of eight, two small schooners to carry four or six each and three gondolas. . . .

The enemy we find are at St. John's repairing the works at that place and building three schooners and two sloops. They have, no doubt, everything ready to their hands, the rigging made, the guns mounted, and only the wooden work to perform, in which I fear they will have advantage of us. . . .

General Sullivan has set off for New York in disgust at being superseded by General Gates, and General Gates himself is superseded by General Schuyler, on this supposition, that, as the army which he (General Gates) was ordered to command in *Canada* is now within the limits of *New York*, the command devolves on *him*, that is Schuyler. In this manner we now rest. . . .

I must beg you, Sir, to forward the militia as fast as possible; without them we are ruined. They need not fear the small pox, as the sick and infected are removed to Fort George, and they will come up by Skeensborough. Every precaution possible will be continued to prevent a further spread of this fatal disorder. . . .

—TRUMBULL, "Letters," Lloyd W. Smith Collection.

2. GENERAL ARNOLD DESCRIBES THE BATTLE OF VALCOUR BAY

To General Schuyler.

Schuyler's Island, Oct. 12, 1776

Dear General: Yesterday morning at eight o'clock, the enemy's fleet, consisting of one ship mounting sixteen guns, one snow mounting the same number, one schooner of fourteen guns, two of twelve, two sloops, a bomb-ketch and a large vessel (that did not come up), with fifteen or twenty flat-bottomed boats or gondolas, carrying one twelve or eighteen-pounder in their bows, appeared off Cumberland Head. We immediately prepared to receive them. The galleys and *Royal Savage* were ordered under way; the rest of our fleet lay at an anchor. At eleven o'clock they ran under the lee of Valcour and began the attack. The schooner, by some bad management, fell to leeward and was first attacked; one of her masts was wounded, and her rigging shot away. The captain thought prudent to run her on the point of Valcour, where all the men were saved. They boarded her, and at night set fire to her. At half-past twelve the engagement became general and very warm. Some of the enemy's ships and all her gondolas beat and rowed up within musket-shot of us. They continued a very hot fire with round and grape-shot until five o'clock, when they thought proper to retire to about six or seven hundred yards distance, and continued the fire until dark. The *Congress* and *Washington* have suffered greatly; the latter lost her first lieutenant killed, captain and master wounded. The *New-York* lost all her officers, except her captain. The *Philadelphia* was hulled in so many places that she sunk in about one hour after the engagement was over. The whole killed and wounded amounts to about sixty. The enemy landed a large number of Indians on the island and each shore, who kept an incessant fire on us, but did little damage. The enemy had, to appearance, upwards of one thousand in batteaus, prepared for boarding. We suffered much for want of seamen and gunners. I was obliged myself to point most of the guns on board the *Congress*, which I believe did good execution. The *Congress* received seven shot between wind and water, was hulled a dozen times, had her mainmast wounded in two places and her yard in one. The *Washington* was hulled a number of times, her mainmast shot through, and must have a new one. Both vessels are very leaky and want repairing.

On consulting with General Waterbury and Colonel Wigglesworth, it was thought prudent to return to Crown Point, every vessel's ammunition being nearly three-fourths spent. At seven o'clock, Colonel Wigglesworth, in the *Trumbull*, got under way, the gondolas and small vessels followed, and the *Congress* and *Washington* brought up the rear. The enemy did not attempt to molest us. Most of the fleet is this minute come to anchor. The wind is small to the southward. The enemy's fleet is under way to leeward and beating up. As soon as our leaks are stopped, the whole fleet will make the utmost despatch to Crown Point, where I beg you will send ammunition and your further orders for us. On the whole, I think we have had a very fortunate escape and have great reason to return our humble and hearty thanks to Almighty God for preserving and delivering so many of us from our more than savage enemies.

—Force, *American Archives*, 5th Series, III, 253-254.

3. The British Destroy Arnold's Fleet at Valcour Bay

Journal of Lieutenant James Hadden of the Royal Artillery.

About the 5th of October [1776] everything being ready, a fleet, consisting of one ship, two schooners, one radeau, one gondolas and 22 gun boats, proceeded from St. Johns up the Sorel River to the entrance of Lake Champlain at the Isle aux Noix, 15 miles from St. Johns. . . .

The 10th October the fleet proceeded to the southern end of Isle au Mot on the eastern side of Lake Champlain, which afterwards widens very considerably, to about 12 or 15 miles in many places. The 11th October the army arrived at Point au Fer under Gen. Burgoyne, and early in the morning the fleet proceeded under Gen. Carleton and Captain Pringle of the Navy.

A large detachment of savages under Major Carlton also moved with the fleet in their canoes, which were very regularly ranged. These canoes are made of the birch bark, and some of them brought 1500 miles down the country, several of which would contain 30 people. The savages *paddle* them across the lakes and down the rivers with great dexterity, and being very light they are carried across any breaks in the water communication; they land every night, most of which they dance and sing. In wet weather they prop up one side and lay under the canoe.

About 11 o'clock this morning one of the enemies vessels was discovered and immediately pursued into a bay on the eastern shore of the lake, where the rest of their fleet was found at an anchor in the form of a crescent between Valcour Island and the continent. Their fleet consisted of 3 row gallies, 2 schooners, 2 sloops and 8 gondolas, carrying in all 90 guns. That of the British carried only 87 pieces of ordnance, including 8 howitzers. The pursuit of this vessel was without order or regularity; the wind being fair to go down the lake enables us to overtake the vessel before she could (by tacks) get in to the rest of their fleet, but lost to us the opportunity of going in at the upper end of the island and attacking the whole at once. The vessel, which proved to be the *Royal Savage* taken by them from St. John's last year, carrying 14 guns, was run on shore and most of the men escaped on to Valcour Island, in effecting which they were fired upon by the gun boats. This firing at one object drew us all in a cluster, and four of the enemies vessels getting under weigh to support the *Royal Savage* fired upon the boats with success. An order was therefore given by the commanding officer for the boats to form across the bay: this was soon effected, tho' under the enemies whole fire and unsupported, all the King's vessels having dropped too far to leeward. This unequal combat was maintained for two hours without any aid, when the *Carlton* schooner of 14 guns 6 pairs got into the bay and immediately received the enemies whole fire which was continued without intermission for about an hour, when the boats of the fleet towed her off, and left the gun boats to maintain the conflict. This was done till the boats had expended their ammunition, when they were withdrawn. . . .

The boats were now formed between the vessels of the British fleet, just without the enemies shot, being withdrawn a little before sunset and the *Royal Savage* blown up: this last was an unnecessary measure as she might at a more leisure moment have been got off, or at all events her stores saved, and in her present position no use could be made of her by the enemy, night coming on and a determination to make a general attack early next morning.

The Rebels having no land force, the savages took post on the main and Valcour Island; thus being upon both flanks they were able to annoy them in the working of their guns; this had the effect of now and then obliging the Rebels to turn a gun that way, which danger the savages avoided by getting behind trees.

The boats having received a small supply of ammunition were unaccountably ordered to anchor under cover of a small island without the opening of the bay.

The enemy, finding their force diminished and the rest so severely handled by little more than ⅓ the British fleet, determined to withdraw towards Crown Point, and passing through our fleet about 10 o'clock at night effected it undiscovered; this the former position of the gun boats would probably have prevented. All the enemies vessels used oars and on this occasion they were muffled. This retreat did great honor to Gen. Arnold, who acted as admiral to the Rebel fleet on this occasion. The wind changing prevented the success of his attempt and, making but little way in the night, they were scarcely out of sight when their retreat was discovered at day break. The British fleet stood after them, and gained ground considerably till the violence of the wind and a great swell obliged both fleets to anchor. Towards evening the weather was more moderate and the fleet proceeded, the boats using their oars to make head against the wind. The Rebel vessels, gaining little way when under sail from the violence of a contrary wind and thinking we were at an anchor, remained so all night, and though the British fleet gained but little by a contrary conduct, that little enabled them to overtake the enemy next day when the wind proved fair. Our ship and schooners being better sailers first came up with the Rebel fleet and retarding their movements till the whole were in sight. Three of the stern-most vessels struck their coulours, in one of which was Brig. Gen. Waterbury, their second in command. Arnold ran his own vessel and 5 others on shore and set fire to them. The three foremost only escaped to Tyconderoga; as did Gen. Arnold with most of the crew's of the burnt vessels. . . .

–HADDEN, *Journal*, pp. 16-32.

4. Burgoyne Marches Up to Ticonderoga and Marches Back Again

Memoirs of John Lacey of Pennsylvania, a captain
in the Continental Army in 1776.

On the morning of the 28th of October, word was brought by our scouts and look out boats on the lakes that the enemy were approaching both by land and water. A general alarm was fired, and every one hurryed to his post. All was bustle; the whole camp presented a terrific blaze of fire arms issuing from every quarter to prepare for battle, which was momently expected to commence. Collem after collem presented their fronts along the lines, with fixed byonet, whose glissining fire arms reflecting the bright raise of the sun presented a luster from their tablits more radient than the sun itself. What mind could resist a flash like this! The sounds of the drums to arms, the reports of the alarm cannon, and the crye of the seargents to the men in hurrying them from their tents of "Turn out! Turn out!" would make even a coward brave. These were, however, the times that tryed mens souls, and here only the sunshine and summer soldier srunk [*sic*] from the expected conflict.

I will throw a vail over some names, who but the evening before bosted over a glass of grog what feats they intended to do on the approach of the enemy, now srunk with sickning apathy within the cover of their tents and markees, never appeared to head their men, leaving that task to their subalterns to perform. On finding at last the enemy had made a halt, and that this movement was only to cover a reconitering from them, they came out as boald soldiers as ever, complaining only of a little sick headake.

On the day after the before mentioned reincounter, Gen. Gates, the Commander in Chief, issued the following General Orders:

Head Quarters Oct. 29th '76.

The General returns his thanks to the Officers and Soldiers of the whole Army for the alert and spirited manner with which they proposed to face the Enemy yesterday. And particularly to the Regiments of Reed, Poor and Greaton, for the dispatch they made in crossing the Lake immediately on their being ordered to Reinforce the French lines and Redoubts.

This order is a proof of the activity and ready willingness of the troops; they were indeed in high spirits, and seme to vie with each other who should first arive at their respective alarm posts. I viewed the men and observed their countenances with pleasure to be animated and not a ray of fear depicted in the face of any of them, and am confident had the enemy made an attack at that time, they would not have dishonoured either themselves or their country. Their view, however, was otherwise, perhaps to trye us, and, to make a view of our camp, situation and strength, no doubt Gen. Burgoin, who commanded at Crown Point, was with his suit on the point of some of the mountains with glasses overlooking our encampment, fortifications and troops, and not very well liking our position and appearance, towards the close of the day the British army retired, not having came nearer to us than what we call Half Way Point, three miles from Ticondiroga, but from which we and they had a fair view of each other. As the enemy approached, our scouts and pickets retired without firing. Within supporting distance of our lines, they halted for their reception.

Nothing worth noticing after this affair took place between the enemy and our army, and on the 13th of November we received information they had evacuated Crown Point and gown over the lake toward St. Johns, giving up the further contest for the present. . . .

Here ended the Northern Campaign for the year 1776.

—LACEY, "Memoirs," *Penn. Mag. of Hist. and Biog.*, XXV, 510-12.

CHAPTER SEVEN

"A Great Empire and Little Minds"

IT IS A *commonplace that in America the Revolution was a Civil War. It is customary to add that in Britain, too, the Revolution was a civil war. The use of the same term for the two countries is, however, confusing and misleading. In the American states the Civil War was an actual war, one which employed the rifle, the bayonet, the torch and the gallows; in Britain it was a war of words and of political maneuvers. The difference in weapons and in tactics was fundamental. In America Loyalists gave aid to the enemy; in Britain the Whigs gave comfort, but no aid, to America. In America the Loyalists delayed Patriot victory; in Britain the friends of America had no perceptible influence on the course of events, and were unable even to mitigate the follies of the King and his ministers.*

British politics in the reign of George III is still very much of a battle-ground for historians. The old Whig picture of a power-mad King seeking to impose his rule on Britain and America alike, has pretty much gone by the board, and so, too, has the naïve interpretation of the King's opponents as single-minded champions of liberty. We know, now, that by his own lights George III was very much a patriot king, and if those lights were dim, it was the dimness of stupidity rather than of wickedness. We know, too, that Burke, Chatham and Shelburne were by no means ready to embrace the American view of the empire, or even of the rights of man, and that Fox, Wilkes and Grafton had another side to them than that which the Americans chose to see.

Yet there was more truth in the Whig view of the Revolution than some modern historians are prepared to concede. The folly of George III in his attitude not only toward his American subjects, but toward such men as Chatham (whom he called "a trumpet of sedition"), approached the criminal. And the devotion of a Camden, a Barré or a Fox to constitutional liberty compared favorably with that of a Jefferson, a William Livingston or an Adams. George III was not trying to establish the divine right of kings, but his policies were designed to destroy the cabinet system which had been created under Walpole, and to sponge out party lines; his methods were those of influence, intimidation and corruption, and his tools were for the most part beneath contempt. Horace Walpole was not a disinterested observer, but there is no reason to quarrel too sharply with his evaluation of the North ministry:

Lord North was a pliant tool, without system or principle; Lord George Germaine of desperate ambition and character; Wedderburn a thorough knave; Lord Sandwich a more profligate knave; Lord Gower a villain capable of any crime; Elliott, Jenkinson, Cornwall, mutes that would have fixed the bowstring round the throat of the constitution. (Last Journals, II, 5)

And for all his earlier cordiality to the American colonies, George III was wholly incapable of understanding their point of view or of presiding over the evolution of a federal empire such as Franklin and Jefferson envisioned. On the other hand Chatham and Burke, Fox and Shelburne, though they were not prepared to concede Parliamentary supremacy, were prepared to waive it, and had caught a glimpse of the possibility of transforming the old empire into a commonwealth of nations.

Opposition to the royal policies followed a curve that was closely related to the fortunes of the war itself. It appeared at once, and powerfully, with the proposal of the Intolerable Acts, mounted to a crescendo during '75 and '76, died down after the Declaration of Independence, reappeared briefly after Saratoga, all but disappeared at the time of the French alliance, and became vocal once more with the military fiascoes of 1781. This is easy to understand. While it was clear to Chatham and Burke that North's policies, if he persisted in them, would disrupt the empire, they were by no means ready to concede the inevitability of those policies. But as the royal program made its inexorable progress through Parliament, the worst forebodings of the opposition were realized, one by one. The Americans were treated as unruly children; they were punished; they were excluded from trade and from the fisheries; they were finally pronounced rebels and ousted from the empire even before they had ousted themselves! By these steps Lord North and his royal master proved that the quarrel was not subject to rational solution.

Yet while each of these steps vindicated the prophecies of the opposition, this vindication merely added to their embarrassment. It was graceful to champion the Americans while they were still, technically, loyal subjects of the King; it was difficult to do so after they had taken up arms against the King; it was desperate to do so after independence, and impossible after the French alliance. War, as always, played into the hands of government, and by winning ever larger Parliamentary majorities George III could feel that he had vindicated the constitution and his own policies even though he had lost the empire in the process.

Had the issue in Parliament been decided by eloquence, there is no doubt who would have won, for the Whigs—if we may use that loose term—had almost a monopoly on eloquence, and on logic as well. Unhappily the Ministry had the votes. Rarely in English history has so good a cause been espoused by so glorious a phalanx of Parliamentary orators: Edmund Burke, the most profound political philosopher of his day; Chatham, splendid even in decline, who had saved the empire once and was prepared to save it again; the brilliant Charles James Fox; the learned and eloquent Camden; Shelburne, farsighted and shrewd; Wilkes, a sort of Parliamentary Tom Paine; the re-

pentant Grafton; the plain but upright Rockingham; General Conway as courageous in debate as on the field of battle—these and a dozen others.

Yet notwithstanding their eloquence and their logic they were never able to influence, much less to control, the course of events. From the vote on the Intolerable Acts until the vote on Dunning's resolution of 1780, through one fatal measure after another, they were overwhelmed by the ministerial majority. Why?

The answer is twofold. First the Parliament chosen in the general election of the fall of 1774 was singularly corrupt, even by the genial standards of the eighteenth century. The King, after all, had almost a million pounds to dispose of in his civil list, and through his lieutenants, Secretary of the Treasury Robinson and Richard Rigby, Paymaster of the Forces (who drew the interest on over a million pounds of public money as his reward), he fought elections, bought seats, bailed out insolvent members, dispensed patronage and pensions, sold military offices, and in countless other ways assured himself a loyal following. He could therefore count on a substantial number of those who bothered to attend Parliament to vote the way they were bought. But at the same time there is no reason to suppose that they would have voted differently had they not been bought. By instinct and conviction as well as by interest the majority of the noble lords, the members from rotten boroughs and the country squires who made up so large a part of Parliament were thoroughly conservative and thoroughly out of sympathy with the American rebels—or with any rebels. Indeed the wonder is that members displayed as much independence as they did, and as much liberalism.

The debate over the American war raged not only in Parliament but in the nation at large. The churches took sides (dissenters tended to sympathize with the Americans) and so did the universities, with Oxford more ostentatiously loyal than Cambridge. Merchants divided, and flooded Parliament with addresses and petitions. There was a veritable war of pamphlets, some spontaneous, some commissioned. Even army and navy officers, in those easygoing days, found it possible to indulge their own private views about the justice of the war, and the highest officers in both services refused to serve in America. If the war did nothing else it stirred the English mind out of its political lethargy, dramatized the issues not only of imperial relations but of Crown and Parliament, re-established the dignity of moral issues, and proved a training ground for political talent.

We can give here only fragmentary illuminations of the English scene. We begin with the early efforts of Chatham and Burke to stave off disaster. Next are provided some samples of the petitions and counterpetitions that rained on King and Parliament, and some samples, too, from the war of pamphlets at the outbreak of the quarrel. When Parliament reconvened in October 1775 the great debate was resumed, and some of the memorable passages from that debate will be found here. The debate was by no means ended in '75 but the issues were, in a sense, decided: merely a few examples of later protests have been appended to indicate that they did continue, and in vain. Finally we relate here something of the unhappy story of the hiring of German mercenaries and the American reaction to that fateful gesture.

I. A GREAT EMPIRE AND LITTLE MINDS
GO ILL TOGETHER

Here follow excerpts from four memorable speeches on American affairs on the eve of the conflict with the colonies. The first is from an address—printed but not spoken—by the gifted Jonathan Shipley, Bishop of St. Asaph, in opposition to the Massachusetts Government Act. Not many bishops espoused the American cause, but St. Asaph had early come under the influence of Benjamin Franklin, and made himself the steadfast champion of America. "The cause of liberty and America has been greatly obliged to you," wrote Franklin to him at the end of the war. If his opposition to ministerial policy had no effect on the course of the war, it did help give respectability to the American party. Our second excerpt is from one of the speeches of William Pitt, Earl of Chatham. In January 1775 Chatham emerged from his retirement to rally Parliament against a policy he thought ruinous. On the twentieth of that month he moved to withdraw Gage's troops from Massachusetts, and it was in support of this motion that he delivered this memorable address with oft-quoted tribute to the brilliance and wisdom of the American state papers. The motion was lost 68-18. When ten days later Chatham introduced a plan for peace he rallied more support, but was voted down 61-32.

Our third excerpt is from what is doubtless the most famous speech delivered in Parliament in the course of the American Revolution: Burke's speech On Conciliation with America. *Neither Burke nor this speech needs any introduction. It is worth noting that notwithstanding the eloquence, the logic and the wit that have delighted generations of readers, the proposal itself was voted down 271-78.*

Finally we include a few paragraphs from the maiden speech of a young peer—he was only 22—who represented Cambridge University: Charles Manners, Marquis of Granby and shortly Duke of Rutland. On March 19 North had moved a bill to restrain the commerce of the Southern colonies as well as that of New England; Granby seized the occasion to declare his sentiments.

1. "BY ENSLAVING YOUR COLONIES YOU EXTINGUISH
THE FAIREST HOPES OF MANKIND"

The Bishop of St. Asaph on the Massachusetts Government Act, May 1774.

My Lords, I look upon North America as the only great nursery of freemen now left upon the face of the earth. We have seen the liberties of Poland and Sweden swept away, in the course of one year, by treachery and usurpation. The free towns of Germany are like so many dying sparks that go out one after another, and which must all be soon extinguished under the destructive greatness of their neighbours. Holland is little more than a great trading company, with luxurious manners, and an exhausted revenue. . . . Switzerland alone is free and happy within the narrow enclosure of its rocks and vallies. As for the state of this country, my Lords, I can only refer myself to your own secret thoughts. I am disposed to think and hope the best of

Public Liberty. Were I to describe her, according to my own ideas at present, I should say that she has a sickly countenance, but I trust she has a strong constitution.

But whatever may be our future fate, the greatest glory that attends this country, a greater than any other nation ever acquired, is to have formed and nursed up to such a state of happiness those Colonies whom we are now so eager to butcher. We ought to cherish them as the immortal monuments of our public justice and wisdom; as the heirs of our better days, of our old arts and manners, and of our expiring national virtues. What work of art, or power, or public utility, has ever equalled the glory of having peopled a continent without guilt or bloodshed, with a multitude of free and happy commonwealths; to have given them the best arts of life and government, and to have suffered them under the shelter of our authority, to acquire in peace the skill to use them. In comparison of this, the policy of governing by influence, and even the pride of war and victory, are dishonest tricks and poor contemptible pageantry.

We seem not to be sensible of the high and important trust which Providence has committed to our charge. The most precious remains of civil liberty that the world can now boast of are lodged in our hands; and God forbid that we should violate so sacred a deposit. By enslaving your Colonies, you not only ruin the peace, the commerce and the fortunes of both countries, but you extinguish the fairest hopes, shut up the last asylum of mankind. I think, my Lords, without being weakly superstitious, that a good man may hope that heaven will take part against the execution of a plan which seems big not only with mischief but impiety.

—FORCE, *American Archives*, 4th Series, I, 103-104.

2. CHATHAM: "YOU CANNOT BUT RESPECT THEIR CAUSE"

Debate in the Lords on the motion to withdraw General Gage's troops from Boston, January 20, 1775.

This resistance to your arbitrary system of taxation might have been forseen: it was obvious from the nature of things and of mankind; and above all from Whiggish spirit flourishing in that country. The spirit which now resists your taxation in America is the same which formerly opposed loans, benevolences and ship-money in England: the same spirit which called all England on its legs, and by the Bill of Rights vindicated the English constitution: the same spirit which established the great fundamental, essential maxim of your liberties—*that no subject of England shall be taxed but by his own consent.*

This glorious spirit of Whiggism animates three millions in America; who prefer poverty with liberty to gilded chains and sordid affluence; and who will die in defence of their rights as men, as freemen. What shall oppose this spirit, aided by the congenial flame glowing in the breasts of every Whig in England, to the amount, I hope, of double the American numbers? Ireland they have to a man. In that country, joined as it is with the cause of colonies and placed at their head, the distinction I contend for is and must be observed. This country superintends and controuls their trade and navigation; but they tax themselves. And this distinction between external and internal control is sacred and insurmountable; it is involved in the abstract nature of things. Property is private, individual, absolute. Trade is an extended and complicated consideration: it reaches as far as ships can sail or winds can blow: it is a great and various machine. To regulate the numberless movements of its several parts, and combine them into effect for the good of the whole, requires the superintending wisdom and energy of the supreme power in the empire. But this supreme power has no effect towards internal taxation; for it does not exist in that relation; there is no such thing, no such idea in this constitution, as a supreme power operating upon property. Let this distinction then remain for ever ascertained: taxation is theirs, commercial regulation is ours. As an American I would recognize to England her supreme right of regulating commerce and navigation: as an Englishman by birth and principle, I recognize to the Americans their supreme unalienable right in their property; a right which they are justified in the defence of to the last extremity. To maintain this principle is the common cause of the Whigs on the other side of the Atlantic, and on this. " 'Tis liberty to liberty engaged," that they will defend themselves, their families, and their country. In this great cause they are immoveably allied: it is the alliance of God and nature—immutable, eternal—fixed as the firmament of heaven.

To such united force, what force shall be opposed?—What, my lords?—A few regiments in America, and seventeen or eighteen thousand men at home!—The idea is too ridiculous to take up a moment of your lordships' time. Nor can such a national and principled union be resisted by the tricks of office, or ministerial manoeuvre. Laying of papers on your table, or counting numbers on a division, will not avert or postpone the hour of danger: it must arrive, my lords, unless these fatal acts are done away; it must arrive in all its horrors, and then these boastful ministers, spite of all their confidence, and all their manoeuvres, shall be forced to hide their heads. They shall be forced to a disgraceful abandonment of their present measures and principles, which they avow, but cannot defend; measures which they presume to attempt, but cannot hope to effectuate. They cannot, my lords, they cannot stir a step; they have not a move left; they are check-mated.

But it is not repealing this act of parliament, it is not repealing a piece of parchment, that can restore America to our bosom; you must repeal her fears and her resentments; and you may then hope for her love and gratitude. But now, insulted with an armed force, posted at Boston; irritated with an hostile array before her eyes, her concessions, if you could force them, would be suspicious and insecure; they will be *irato animo;* they will not be the sound honourable passions of freemen, they will be the dictates of fear, and extortions of force. But it is more than evident that you cannot force them, united as they are, to your unworthy terms of submission—it is impossible: and when I hear General Gage censured for inactivity, I must retort with indignation on those whose intemperate measures and improvident councils have betrayed him into his present situation. His situation reminds me, my lords, of the answer of a French general in the civil wars of France—Monsieur Condé opposed to Monsieur Turenne: he was asked how it happened that he did not take his adversary prisoner, as he was often very near him: "*J'ai peur qu'il ne me prenne*";—I'm afraid he'll take me.

When your lordships look at the papers transmitted us from America; when you consider their decency, firmness and wisdom, you cannot but respect their cause, and wish to make it your own. For myself, I must declare and avow that in all my reading and observation—and it has been my favourite study—I have read Thucydides, and have studied and admired the master-states of the world—that for solidity of reasoning, force of sagacity, and wisdom of conclusion, under such a complication of difficult circumstances, no nation or body of men can stand in preference to the general Congress at Philadelphia.

I trust it is obvious to your lordships that all attempts to impose servitude upon such men, to establish despotism over such a mighty continental nation must be vain, must be fatal. We shall be forced ultimately to retract; let us retract while we can, not when we must. I say we must necessarily undo these violent oppressive acts: they must be repealed—you will repeal them; I pledge myself for it, that you will in the end repeal them; I stake my reputation on it: I will consent to be taken for an idiot if they are not finally repealed. Avoid, then, this humiliating, disgraceful necessity. With a dignity becoming your exalted situation, make the first advances to concord, to peace and happiness: for that is your true dignity, to act with prudence and justice. That you should first concede is obvious, from sound and rational policy. Concession comes with better grace and more salutary effect from superior power; it reconciles superiority of power with the feelings of men; and establishes solid confidence on the foundations of affection and gratitude.

—Cobbett, *Parliamentary History of England*, XVIII, 153-156.

3. Burke Pleads for Conciliation with the Colonies

Debate in the House, March 22, 1775.

The proposition is peace. Not peace through the medium of war; not peace to be hunted through the labyrinth of intricate and endless negotiations; not peace to arise out of universal discord, fomented from principle, in all parts of the empire; not peace to depend on the juridical determination of perplexing questions, or the precise marking the shadowy boundaries of a complex government. It is simple peace; sought in its natural course, and in its ordinary haunts. It is peace sought in the spirit of peace; and laid in principles purely pacific. I propose, by removing the ground of the difference, and by restoring the former *unsuspecting confidence of the colonies in the mother country*, to give permanent satisfaction to your people; and (far from a scheme of ruling by discord) to reconcile them to each other in the same act, and by the bond of the very same interest which reconciles them to British government. . . .

I am sensible, Sir, that all which I have asserted in my detail is admitted in the gross; but that quite a different conclusion is drawn from it. America, gentlemen say, is a noble object. It is an object well worth fighting for. Certainly it is, if fighting a people be the best way of gaining them. Gentle-

men in this respect will be led to their choice of means by their complexions
and their habits. Those who understand the military art will of course have
some predilection for it. Those who wield the thunder of the state may have
more confidence in the efficacy of arms. But I confess, possibly for want of
this knowledge, my opinion is much more in favour of prudent management
than of force; considering force not as an odious, but a feeble instrument for
preserving a people so numerous, so active, so growing, so spirited as this, in
a profitable and subordinate connexion with us.

First, Sir, permit me to observe that the use of force alone is but *temporary*. It may subdue for a moment; but it does not remove the necessity of
subduing again: and a nation is not governed, which is perpetually to be
conquered. . . .

Lastly, we have no sort of *experience* in favour of force as an instrument
in the rule of our colonies. Their growth and their utility has been owing
to methods altogether different. Our ancient indulgence has been said to be
pursued to a fault. It may be so. But we know, if feeling is evidence, that
our fault was more tolerable than our attempt to mend it; and our sin far more
salutary than our penitence.

These, Sir, are my reasons for not entertaining that high opinion of untried
force, by which many gentlemen, for whose sentiments in other particulars
I have great respect, seem to be so greatly captivated. But there is still behind
a third consideration concerning this object, which serves to determine my
opinion on the sort of policy which ought to be pursued in the management
of America, even more than its population and its commerce. I mean its
temper and character.

In this character of the Americans, a love of freedom is the predominat-
ing feature which marks and distinguishes the whole: and as an ardent is
always a jealous affection, your colonies become suspicious, restive and untractable whenever they see the least attempt to wrest from them by force,
or shuffle from them by chicane, what they think the only advantage worth
living for. This fierce spirit of liberty is stronger in the English colonies
probably than in any other people of the earth. . . .

Permit me, Sir, to add another circumstance in our colonies, which contributes no mean part towards the growth and effect of this untractable
spirit. I mean their education. In no country perhaps in the world is the
law so general a study. The profession itself is numerous and powerful; and
in most provinces it takes the lead. The greater number of the deputies sent
to the congress were lawyers. But all who read, and most do read, endeavor
to obtain some smattering in that science. I have been told by an eminent
bookseller that in no branch of business, after tracts of popular devotion,
were so many books as those on the law exported to the plantations. The
colonists have now fallen into the way of printing them for their own use.
I hear that they have sold nearly as many of Blackstone's Commentaries in
America as in England. General Gage marks out this disposition very particularly in a letter on your table. He states that all the people in his government are lawyers, or smatterers in law; and that in Boston they have been en-

abled, by successful chicane, wholly to evade many parts of one of your capital penal constitutions. . . .

This study renders men acute, inquisitive, dextrous, prompt in attack, ready in defence, full of resources. In other countries, the people, more simple, and of a less mercurial cast, judge of an ill principle in government only by an actual grievance; here they anticipate the evil, and judge of the pressure of the grievance by the badness of the principle. They augur misgovernment at a distance, and snuff the approach of tyranny in every tainted breeze.

The last cause of this disobedient spirit in the colonies is hardly less powerful than the rest, as it is not merely moral, but laid deep in the natural constitution of things. Three thousand miles of ocean lie between you and them. No contrivance can prevent the effect of this distance in weakening government. Seas roll, and months pass, between the order and the execution; and the want of a speedy explanation of a single point is enough to defeat a whole system. . . .

Then, Sir, from these six capital sources: of descent; of form of government; of religion in the northern provinces; of manners in the southern; of education; of the remoteness of situation from the first mover of government; from all these causes a fierce spirit of liberty has grown up. It has grown with the growth of the people in your colonies, and increased with the increase of their wealth; a spirit that unhappily meeting with an exercise of power in England, which, however lawful, is not reconcilable to any ideas of liberty, much less with theirs, has kindled this flame that is ready to consume us. . . .

Sir, if I were capable of engaging you to an equal attention, I would state, that, as far as I am capable of discerning, there are but three ways of proceeding relative to this stubborn spirit, which prevails in your colonies and disturbs your government. These are—To change that spirit, as inconvenient, by removing the causes. To prosecute it as criminal. Or, to comply with it as necessary. . . .

To impoverish the colonies in general, and in particular to arrest the noble course of their marine enterprises, would be a more easy task. I freely confess it. We have shown a disposition to a system of this kind; a disposition even to continue the restraint after the offence; looking on ourselves as rivals to our colonies, and persuaded that of course we must gain all that they shall lose. Much mischief we may certainly do. The power inadequate to all other things is often more than sufficient for this. I do not look on the direct and immediate power of the colonies to resist our violence as very formidable. In this, however, I may be mistaken. But when I consider that we have colonies for no purpose but to be serviceable to us, it seems to my poor understanding a little preposterous to make them unserviceable, in order to keep them obedient. It is, in truth, nothing more than the old, and as I thought exploded problem of tyranny, which proposes to beggar its subjects into submission. But remember, when you have completed your system of impoverishment, that nature still proceeds in her ordinary course; that discontent will increase with misery; and that there are critical moments in the fortune of all states, when they who are too weak to contribute to your prosperity, may be strong enough to complete your ruin. *Spoliatis arma supersunt.*

The temper and character which prevail in our colonies are, I am afraid, unalterable by any human art. We cannot, I fear, falsify the pedigree of this fierce people, and persuade them that they are not sprung from a nation in whose veins the blood of freedom circulates. The language in which they would hear you tell them this tale would detect the imposition; your speech would betray you. An Englishman is the unfittest person on earth to argue another Englishman into slavery. . . .

But let us suppose all these moral difficulties got over. The ocean remains. You cannot pump this dry; and as long as it continues in its present bed, so long all the causes which weaken authority by distance will continue. "Ye gods, annihilate but space and time, and make two lovers happy!"—was a pious and passionate prayer;—but just as reasonable as many of the serious wishes of very grave and solemn politicians.

If then, Sir, it seems almost desperate to think of any alternative course for changing the moral causes (and not quite easy to remove the natural) which produce prejudices irreconcilable to the late exercise of our authority; but that the spirit infallibly will continue; and, continuing, will produce such effects as now embarrass us; the second mode under consideration is to prosecute that spirit in its overt acts, as *criminal.*

At this proposition I must pause a moment. The thing seems a great deal too big for my ideas of jurisprudence. It should seem to my way of conceiving such matters that there is a very wide difference in reason and policy between the mode of proceeding on their regular conduct of scattered individuals, or even of bands of men, who disturb order within the state, and the civil dissensions which may, from time to time, on great questions, agitate the several communities which compose a great empire. It looks to me to be narrow and pedantic to apply the ordinary ideas of criminal justice to this great public contest. I do not know the method of drawing up an indictment against a whole people. . . .

In this situation, let us seriously and coolly ponder. What is it we have got by all our menaces, which have been many and ferocious? What advantages have we derived from the penal laws we have passed, and which, for the time, have been severe and numerous? What advances have we made towards our object by the sending of a force, which, by land and sea, is no contemptible strength? Has the disorder abated? Nothing less.—When I see things in this situation, after such confident hopes, bold promises, and active exertions, I cannot, for my life, avoid a suspicion that the plan itself is not correctly right.

If then the removal of the causes of this spirit of American liberty be, for the greater part, or rather entirely, impracticable; if the ideas of criminal process be inapplicable, or if applicable, are in the highest degree inexpedient; what way yet remains? No way is open but the third and last—to comply with the American spirit as necessary; or, if you please, to submit to it as a necessary evil. . . .

The question with me is, not whether you have a right to render your people miserable; but whether it is not your interest to make them happy. It is not what a lawyer tells me I *may* do; but what humanity, reason and justice tell me I ought to do. Is a politic act the worse for being a generous one? Is no concession proper but that which is made from your want of right to keep what you grant? Or does it lessen the grace or dignity of relaxing in the exercise of an odious claim, because you have your evidence-room full of titles, and your magazines stuffed with arms to enforce them? Of what avail are they, when the reason of the thing tells me that the assertion of my title is the loss of my suit; and that I could do nothing but wound myself by the use of my own weapons? . . .

My idea, therefore, without considering whether we yield as matter of right, or grant as matter of favour, is *to admit the people of our colonies into an interest in the constitution;* and, by recording that admission in the journals of parliament, to give them as strong an assurance as the nature of the thing will admit, that we mean forever to adhere to that solemn declaration of systematic indulgence. . . .

The question now, on all this accumulated matter, is;—whether you will choose to abide by a profitable experience, or a mischievous theory; whether you choose to build on imagination, or fact; whether you prefer enjoyment, or hope; satisfaction in your subjects, or discontent? . . .

I must be deeply concerned whenever it is my misfortune to continue a difference with the majority of this House. But as the reasons for that difference are my apology for thus troubling you, suffer me to state them in a very few words. . . .

My hold of the colonies is in the close affection which grows from common names, from kindred blood, from similar privileges and equal protection. These are ties, which, though light as air, are as strong as links of iron. Let the colonies always keep the idea of their civil rights associated with your government;—they will cling and grapple with you; and no force under heaven will be of power to tear them from their allegiance. But let it be once understood that your government may be one thing, and their privileges another; that these two things may exist without any mutual relation; the cement is gone; the cohesion is loosened; and everything hastens to decay and dissolution. As long as you have the wisdom to keep the sovereign authority of this country as the sanctuary of liberty, the sacred temple consecrated to our common faith, wherever the chosen race and sons of England worship freedom, they will turn their faces towards you. . . .

Do not entertain so weak an imagination as that your registers and your bonds, your affidavits and your sufferances, your cockets and your clearances, are what form the great securities of your commerce. Do not dream that your letters of office, and your instructions, and your suspending clauses, are the things that hold together the great contexture of the mysterious whole. These things do not make your government. Dead instruments, passive tools as they are, it is the spirit of the English communion that gives all their life and efficacy to them. It is the spirit of the English constitution which, infused through the mighty mass, pervades, feeds, unites, invigorates, vivifies every part of the empire, even down to the minutest member. . . .

All this, I know well enough, will sound wild and chimerical to the profane herd of those vulgar and mechanical politicians who have no place among us; a sort of people who think that nothing exists but what is gross and material; and who therefore, far from being qualified to be directors of the great movement of empire, are not fit to turn a wheel in the machine. But to men truly initiated and rightly taught, these ruling and master principles, which, in the opinion of such men as I have mentioned, have no substantial existence, are in truth everything, and all in all. Magnanimity in politics is not seldom the truest wisdom; and a great empire and little minds go ill together. If we are conscious of our situation and glow with zeal to fill our place as becomes our station and ourselves, we ought to auspicate all our public proceedings on America with the old warning of the church, *Sursum corda!* We ought to elevate our minds to the greatness of that trust to which the order of Providence has called us. By adverting to the dignity of this high calling, our ancestors have turned a savage wilderness into a glorious empire; and have made the most extensive, and the only honourable conquests, not by destroying but by promoting the wealth, the number, the happiness of the human race. Let us get an American revenue as we have got an American empire. English privileges have made it all that it is; English privileges will make it all it can be.

—COBBETT, *Parliamentary History of England*, XVIII, 478-536 *passim.*

4. "I Disavow the Whole System"

The Marquis of Granby [Charles Manners]:

April 5, 1775

. . . As to the bill immediately the object of our consideration [the bill to restrain the trade of the Southern colonies], I think it in every respect so arbitrary, so oppressive, and so totally founded on principles of resentment that I am exceedingly happy at having this public opportunity of bearing my testimony against it, in the strongest manner I am able. In God's name, what language are you now holding out to America! Resign your property, divest yourselves of your privileges and freedom, renounce every thing that can make life comfortable, or we will destroy your commerce, we will involve your country in all the miseries of famine; and if you express the sensations of men at such harsh treatment, we will then declare you in a state of rebellion and put yourselves and your families to fire and sword. . . . You can with no more justice compel the Americans to your obedience, by the operation of the present measures, by making use of their necessities and withholding from them that commerce on which their existence depends, than a ruffian can found an equitable claim to my possessions when he forcibly enters my house and with a dagger at my throat . . . makes me seal deeds which will convey to him my estate and property. . . .

Sir, I shall not trouble this House any longer, as this matter has been so fully discussed, though I must confess that I am not sorry a debate has taken place, because I was rather desirous of making a kind of political creed, some professions of my sentiments on this important, this very serious national question. From the fullest conviction of my soul I disclaim every idea both of policy and right internally to tax America. I disavow the whole system. It is commenced in iniquity, it is pursued with resentment; and it can terminate in nothing but blood. Under whatsoever shape in futurity it may be revived, by whomsoever produced and supported, it shall from me meet the most constant, determined and invariable opposition.

—COBBETT, *Parliamentary History of England*, XVIII, 601-603.

II. THE AMERICAN WAR DIVIDES ENGLISH OPINION

It is sometimes difficult to know whether hostility to the war was inspired more by sympathy with the Americans or hostility to the King and his ministers. The Americans excited sympathy among Englishmen for a variety of reasons—because they were members of the same family; because they were championing the cause of freedom; because, if they stayed happily within the empire, they would strengthen that empire immeasurably. There was in addition a sense that the Americans were fighting the English cause in opposing the wrong-headedness of the King and his ministers; and there was a lively appreciation of the economic value of the colonies and of the cost of war.

Interestingly enough the Americans found friends not only among the opposition politicians, the merchants and the intellectuals, but in the armed services as well. Thus Lord Frederick Cavendish, who had fought bravely in the Seven Years' War and was a lieutenant general at the outbreak of the Revolution, refused to apply for a command, and sat the war out; thus, too, the famous Sir Jeffrey Amherst, commander in chief of the forces, rejected all the overtures of the King offering him active command. And General Henry Conway, scarcely less famous, not only refused to take any part in the war but opposed it at every point. Nor was the situation in the Royal Navy very different. Admiral Keppel confessed that "professional employment was the dearest object of his life [but] he would not accept it in America." When France entered the war he did consent to command the Channel Fleet. It is against this background that we read the letter of the young Earl of Effingham refusing to serve in a cause which he thought pernicious. "When the duties of a soldier and a citizen become inconsistent," he said in the Lords, "I shall always think myself obliged to sink the character of the soldier in that of the citizen." He was thanked for his stand by the Corporations of London and Dublin.

The petitions from merchants and city corporations need little explanation: we include one from the Lord Mayor and Aldermen of London not only because of the importance of the city and the eloquence of the document, but because it may have been written by the only American to serve as Alderman of London, William Lee of the far-flung Lee clan. Actually the Ministry was able to drum up more petitions than the opposition: there is an interesting item in the British budget for 1776 which reads "Commons Addresses, £13,000." The addresses from the two ancient universities did not come within this category, but there is evidence that the Ministry had to bring heavy pressure on the more liberal of the two universities, Cambridge, to wring from them a supporting address.

1. Lord Effingham Refuses to Draw His Sword Against the Americans

His resignation of his commission in the Army.

Adelphi Buildings, April 12, 1775

To Lord Barrington, Secretary at War.

My Lord,

I beg the favour of your Lordship to lay before his Majesty the peculiar embarrassment of my present function.

Your Lordship is no stranger to the conduct which I have observed in the unhappy disputes with our American colonies.

The King is too just and too generous not to believe that the votes I have given in Parliament have been given according to the dictates of my conscience. Whether I have erred or not, the course of future events must determine. In the mean time, if I were capable of such duplicity as to be any way concerned in enforcing those measures of which I have so publicly and solemnly expressed my disapprobation, I should ill deserve what I am most ambitious of obtaining, the esteem and favourable opinion of my Sovereign.

My request therefore to your Lordship is this, that after having laid those circumstances before the King, you will assure his Majesty that he has not a subject who is more ready than I am with the utmost chearfulness to sacrifice his life and fortune in support of the safety, honour, and dignity of his Majesty's crown and person. But the very same principles which have inspired me with these unalterable sentiments of duty and affection to his Majesty, will not suffer me to be instrumental in depriving any part of his people of those liberties which form the best security for their fidelity and obedience to his government. As I cannot, without reproach from my conscience, consent to bear arms against my fellow subjects in America in what, to my weak discernment, is not a clear cause; and as it seems now to be finally resolved that the 22d Regiment is to go upon American service, I desire your Lordship to lay me in the most dutiful manner at his Majesty's feet, and humbly beg that I may be permitted to retire.

Your Lordship will also be so obliging to entreat that as I waive what the custom of the service would entitle me to, the right of selling what I bought, I may be allowed to retain my rank in the Army, that whenever the envy or ambition of foreign powers should require it, I may be enabled to serve his Majesty and my country in that way in which alone I can expect to serve them with any degree of effect.

Your Lordship will easily conceive the regret and mortification I feel at being necessitated to quit the military profession, which has been that of my ancestors for many generations, to which I have been bred almost from my infancy, to which I have devoted the study of my life, and to perfect myself in which I have sought instruction and service in whatever part of the world they were to be found.

I have delayed this to the last moment, lest any wrong construction should be given to a conduct which is influenced only by the purest motives. I complain of nothing; I love my profession and course of life, in which I might be useful to the public, so long as my constitutional principles and my notions of honour permitted me to continue in it.

I have the honour to be, with great respect,

Your Lordship's most obedient,

And most humble servant,

EFFINGHAM

—ALMON, ed., *The Remembrancer*, I, 165-166.

2. THE LORD MAYOR AND ALDERMEN OF LONDON PLEAD THE CAUSE OF AMERICA

June 14, 1775

To the King's Most Excellent Majesty

The humble Address, Remonstrance, and Petition of the Lord Mayor, Aldermen, and Livery of the City of London, in Common Hall assembled:

Most Gracious Sovereign,

We your Majesty's most faithful subjects, the Lord Mayor, Aldermen, and Livery of the City of London, in Common Hall assembled, are compelled again to disturb your Majesty's repose with our complaints.

We have already expressed to your Majesty our abhorrence of the tyrannical measures pursued against our fellow-subjects in America, as well as of the men who secretely advise, and of the Ministers who execute their measures.

We desire to repeat again, that the power contended for over the Colonies, under the specious name of dignity, is to all intents and purposes, despotism; that the exercise of despotic power in any part of the empire is inconsistent with the character and safety of this country.

As we would not suffer any man, or body of men, to establish arbitrary power over us, we cannot acquiesce in any attempt to force it upon any part of our fellow-subjects; we are persuaded that by the sacred, unalterable rights of human nature, as well as by every principle of the constitution, the Americans ought to enjoy peace, liberty and safety; that whatever power invades these rights ought to be resisted; we hold such resistance, in vindication of their constitutional rights, to be their indispensable duty to God, from whom those rights are derived to themselves, who cannot be safe and happy without them; to their posterity, who have a right to claim this inheritance at their hands unviolated and unimpaired.

We have already remonstrated to your Majesty that these measures were big with all the consequences which could alarm a free and commercial people; a deep and perhaps fatal wound to commerce; the ruin of manufactures;

the diminution of the revenue, and consequent increase of taxes; the aliena-tion of the colonies, and the blood of your Majesty's subjects.

Unhappily, Sire, the worst of these apprehensions is now realized in all its horror: We have seen with equal dread and concern a civil war commenced in America by your Majesty's Commander in Chief: Will your Majesty be pleased to consider what must be the situation of your people here, who have nothing now to expect from America but Gazettes of blood and mutual lists of their slaughtered fellow-subjects.

Every moment's prosecution of this fatal war may loosen irreparably the bonds of that connection on which the glory and safety of the British Empire depend.

If anything could add to the alarm of these events, it is your Majesty's having declared your confidence in the wisdom of men a majority of whom are notoriously bribed to betray their constituents and their country. It is the misfortune of your Majesty, it is the misfortune and grief of your people, to have a Grand Council and a representative under an undue and dangerous influence; an influence, which though procured by your Ministers, is dan-gerous to your Majesty, by deceiving you, and to your people, by betraying them.

In such a situation, your petitioners are bound to declare to your Majesty, that they cannot and will not sit unconcerned; that they will exert them-selves, at every hazard, to bring those who have advised these ruinous meas-ures to the justice of this country, and of the much-injured Colonies.

We have already signified our persuasion that these evils originate in the secret advice of those who are equally enemies of your Majesty's title and to the rights of your people. Your petitioners are now compelled to say that your Throne is surrounded by men avowedly inimical to those principles on which your Majesty possesses the Crown, and this people their liberties: At a time of such difficulty and danger, public confidence is essential to your Majesty's repose, and to the preservation of your people: Such confidence cannot be obtained by Ministers and advisers who want wisdom and hold principles incompatible with freedom; nor can any hope of relief be expected from a Parliament chosen under a national delusion, insidiously raised by misrepresentations touching the true state of America, and artfully embraced by a precipitate dissolution.

Your petitioners therefore again pray and beseech your Majesty to dis-miss your present Ministers and advisers from your person and counsels for ever; to dissolve a Parliament who, by various acts of cruelty and injustice, have manifested a spirit of persecution against our brethren in America, and given their sanction to popery and arbitrary power; to put your future con-fidence in Ministers whose known and unshaken attachment to the constitu-tion, joined to their wisdom and integrity, may enable your Majesty to settle this alarming dispute upon the sure, honourable and lasting foundation of general liberty.

And a motion being made, and question put, to agree to the said Ad-dress, Remonstrance and Petition, the same was resolved in the affirmative.

—ALMON, ed., *The Remembrancer*, I, 76-77.

3. Oxford and Cambridge Support the King

Address of the Chancellor, Masters and Scholars of the University of Oxford, presented by their Chancellor, Lord North.

October 26, 1775

. . . We think ourselves obliged, by every principle of conscientious duty to our King, by every motive of love and affection to our country, to declare our utter abhorrence of those base artifices and seditious proceedings by which your Majesty's American subjects have been tempted to violate the laws, to resist the authority, and at length to rebel against the sovereignty of the British legislature.

We have observed with deep concern the pernicious tendency of that profligate licentiousness by which every part of the legislative power has of late been insulted and reviled. . . .

We now deplore the miseries into which our deluded fellow-subjects in America have been by these seducing arts betrayed; plunged, as they are, in all the horrors of a civil war, unnaturally commenced against the State which gave them birth and protection.

The magnanimity and lenity of your Majesty's disposition . . . give us just confidence to hope that when . . . your rebellious subjects shall be reduced under the power they have thus wantonly provoked, the royal mercy will be displayed in the pardon of a people who have forfeited their lives and fortunes to the justice of the State. . . .

—Force, *American Archives*, 4th Series, III, 1187.

Address of the Chancellor, Masters and Scholars of the University of Cambridge, presented to His Majesty.

November, 1775

. . . We cannot remain silent spectators of the unnatural rebellion into which many of our brethren in your Majesty's American Colonies have been unhappily seduced. We see their delusion with equal indignation and concern; we disclaim the opinions on which they proceed as destructive of the happiest Constitution that hath ever existed in the history of mankind, and subversive of all order and good government; yet we pity their infatuation, and lament the miseries which it is necessarily bringing upon them.

—Force, *American Archives*, 4th Series, III, 1631.

III. DISCONTENT IN BRITAIN

The American cause was not popular among the people generally, but neither was the war itself nor, for that matter, the King. Perhaps the best index of the unpopularity of the war was the inability of the government to raise an army. There were in all probability nearly a million men of fighting age in Britain, in 1776, but the government could neither recruit nor impress enough men to bring the army up to the quota of 55,000, and had to resort to German mercenaries. Recruiting went slowly in England, a bit better in Scotland, and very badly in Ireland. We give here three documents which illuminate this situation: a letter from a gentleman of Cork to an officer in

Boston on the difficulties of recruiting; a letter from the famous evangelist John Wesley to the Earl of Dartmouth describing the hatred for the King— a comment which contrasted sharply with Wesley's public avowals; and a report from Pierre Augustin Caron de Beaumarchais—then a French agent in London but better known as the author of The Marriage of Figaro—*to his royal master. We include, too, a broadside attack on the Tories.*

1. "Never Did the Recruiting Parties Meet Such Ill Success"

Letter to an officer in Boston.

Cork, September 8, 1775

People are much divided in their sentiments about the Americans. Placemen, pensioners, Tories and Jacobites, with some stupid, ignorant mercenary Whigs, are violent against them, but the bulk of the people of England and Ireland are strongly in their interest. . . . How this unnatural combustion will end, the Lord only knows; but one thing I know, that I wish you and my other friends were removed from a service at once so disgraceful and so dangerous. Never did the recruiting parties meet with such ill success in every part of this Kingdom as at present, so invincible is the dislike of all ranks of people to the American service. The inhabitants of Bandon, Youghall, Birr and other towns have entered into a resolution not to suffer any among them to enlist for the purpose of enslaving their American brethren. There have been no less than five parties at once in Charleville, and after stunning the town—God knows how long—with their fifes and drums, they were able to pick up only one recruit, who was under Mr. Robert's influence. Though the principal Romanists in Cork and Limerick have formed associations and offered bounties to such recruits as shall list on this occasion, yet have they very little success; for though the heads of that communion are in the interest of Government, the lower class, who have not sagacity enough to make proper distinctions, are, to a man, attached to the Americans, and say plainly the Irish ought to follow their example. Even Lord Kenmore, who on this occasion took the lead, had his recruiting party severely beat in Tralee, and their drum broke to pieces. . . . Many of the draughts that are come here to fill up the regiments ordered abroad, swear they will never draw a trigger against the Americans, among whom they have all relations; and most of the English and Irish soldiers that left this last April and May expressed so much repugnance to the service they were ordered on that I am fully persuaded, if your army was not shut up in Boston, it must suffer exceedingly by desertion. . . .

—Force, *American Archives*, 4th Series, III, 168-169.

2. "They Despise His Majesty and Hate Him with a Perfect Hatred"

The Reverend John Wesley to the Earl of Dartmouth.

Haverford West, August 23, 1775

A letter which I received . . . yesterday occasions my giving you this trouble. You told him, the administration having been assured from every part of the Kingdom, that trade was as plentiful and flourishing as ever, and the people as well employed and well satisfied.

Sir, I aver from my own personal knowledge, from the testimony of my own eyes and ears, that there cannot be a more notorious falsehood than has been palmed upon them for truth. I aver that in every part of England where I have been (and I have been east, west, north and south within these two years) trade in general is exceedingly decayed, and thousands of people are quite unemployed. Some I know to have perished for want of bread; others, I have seen creeping up and down like walking shadows. I except three or four manufacturing towns, which have suffered less than others.

I aver, 2, that the people in general all over the nation are so far from being well satisfied, that they are far more deeply dissatisfied than they appear to have been even a year or two before the Great Rebellion, and far more dangerously dissatisfied. The bulk of the people in every city, town and village where I've been, do not so much aim at the Ministry, as they usually did in the last century, but at the King himself. He is the object of their anger, contempt and malice. They heartily despise his Majesty and hate him with a perfect hatred. They wish to imbrue their hands in his blood; they are full of the spirit of murder and rebellion, and I am persuaded, should any occasion offer, thousands would be ready to act what they now speak. It is as much as ever I can do, and sometimes more than I can do, to keep this plague from infecting my own friends. And nineteen or twenty to whom I speak in defence of the King seem never to have heard a word spoken for him before. I marvel what wretches they are who abuse the credulity of the Ministry, by these florid accounts. Even where I was last, in the West Riding of Yorkshire, a tenant of Lord Dartmouth was telling me, "Sir, our tradesmen are breaking all around me, so that I know not what the end will be." Even in Leeds I had appointed to dine at a merchant's, but before I came, the bailiffs were in possession of the house. Upon my saying, "I thought Mr.—— had been in good circumstances" I was answered, "He *was* so: but the American war has ruined him."

—GR. BRIT. HIST. MSS. COMM., *Dartmouth Papers*, III, 220.

3. ENGLAND IS ON THE VERGE OF RUIN

Beaumarchais to the King of France.

September 21, 1775

I withdrew from England under the pretext of going to the country, and have come in all haste from London to Paris, in order to confer with Messieurs de Vergennes and Sartines on matters which are too important and too delicate to be intrusted to the fidelity of any courier.

Sire, England is in such a crisis, such a state of disorder within and without, that it would be almost on the point of ruin if her neighbors and rivals were themselves in a state to occupy themselves seriously about her. I will set forth faithfully the position of the English in America; I received the particulars from an inhabitant of Philadelphia, who had lately arrived from the colonies, and had just been present at a conference with the English ministers, who were thrown into the greatest trouble, and struck with terror by his recital. The Americans, determined to suffer everything rather than give way, and full of that enthusiasm for liberty which has so often rendered the little nation of Corsica redoubtable to the Genoese, have thirty-eight thousand effective men, armed and resolute, beneath the walls of Boston; they have reduced the English army to the necessity of dying of hunger in this town, or of seeking for winter quarters elsewhere, which it will do forthwith. About forty thousand men, well armed, and as determined as the former, defend the rest of the country, without these eighty thousand men having taken away a single laborer from the ground, a single workman from the manufactories. All those persons who were engaged in the fisheries, which the English have destroyed, have become soldiers, and feel that they have to avenge the ruin of their families and the liberty of their country; all those persons who took part in maritime commerce, which the English have brought to an end, have joined the fishermen to make war on their common persecutors; all the persons who worked in the harbors have increased the army of furious men, whose actions are all animated by a spirit of vengeance and hatred.

I say, sire, that such a nation must be invincible, above all, when it has at its back as much country as it can possibly require for retreating, even if the English could make themselves masters of all their seaboard, which they are far from having done. All sensible persons, then, are convinced, in England, that the English colonies are lost to the mother country, and that is also my opinion.

The open war which is taking place in America is less fatal to England than the intestine war which must yet break out in London; the bitterness between the parties has been carried to the greatest excess since the proclamation of the King of England which declares the Americans to be rebels. This absurdity, this masterpiece of madness on the part of the government, has renewed the strength of all the men of the opposition, who have united against it. A resolution has been taken to come to an open collision with the court party during the first sittings of the Parliament. It is thought that these sittings will not pass without seven or eight members of the opposition being sent to the Tower of London, and that is just the appointed time for sounding the tocsin. Lord Rochford, who has been my friend for the last fifteen years, in conversing with me, said these words, with a sigh: "*I am much afraid, sir, that the winter will not pass without some heads being brought down, either among the king's party or the opposition.*" On the other side, the Lord-mayor Wilkes, in a moment of joy and liberty, at the end of a splendid dinner, said to me publicly the following words: "The King of England has long done me the honor of hating me. For my part, I have always rendered him the justice of despising him. The time has come for deciding which of us has formed the best opinion of the other, and on which side the wind will cause heads to fall."

Lord North, who is threatened with all this, would willingly give in his resignation if he could do so with honor and safety.

—De Lomenie, *Beaumarchais*, pp. 262 ff.

IV. THE WAR OF PAMPHLETS

The American Revolution set off a literary war that enlisted some of the most skillful and fluent pens in England: the pamphlets interest us today more for their indication of literary sentiment than for their logic or their style. Dr. Johnson had long entertained most malign sentiments about the Americans, and his attack on the Americans, Taxation No Tyranny, *represented his genuine sentiments rather than a payment of indebtedness to a government which gave him a pension of £300 a year; it is perhaps relevant, however, that in his* Dictionary *he had defined a pension as "generally understood to mean pay given to a state hireling for treason to his country." Johnson's pamphlet was more widely circulated in John Wesley's popular version: "A Calm Address to our American Colonies." Boswell's friendliness to the Americans is as familiar as Johnson's hostility; we give here a few samples from the ever-famous biography. Catherine Macaulay, whose "Address" we quote here, was in her day one of the most famous of English literary figures. Author of an eight-volume* History of England, *and of dozens of smaller books and pamphlets, friend to Hume, Franklin, Turgot and others, she managed to incur at once the contempt of Dr. Johnson and John Wilkes, and was perhaps better known in her own day for her marriage—at the age of almost fifty—to a beardless youth of twenty-one. Mrs. Macaulay had many American friends, and after the war made a triumphal visit to America. Dr. Richard Price, the last of our pamphleteers, was a far more substantial figure than Mrs. Macaulay. A nonconformist clergyman, intimate of Franklin, Turgot and Shelburne, he wrote widely on questions of religion, morals, finance and politics. His "Observations" won him the freedom of the city of London, and his friendship to America an LL.D. from Yale University.*

1. DOCTOR JOHNSON HAS NO PATIENCE WITH AMERICAN ARGUMENTS

[1775]

They have tried to infect the people of England with the contagion of disloyalty. Their credit is happily not such as gives them influence proportionate to their malice. When they talk of their pretended immunities *guarrantied by the plighted faith of Government, and the most solemn compacts with English Sovereigns,* we think ourselves at liberty to inquire when the faith was plighted and the compact made; and when we can only find that King James and King Charles the First promised the settlers in Massachuset's Bay, now famous by the appellation of Bostonians, exemption from taxes for seven years, we infer with Mr. Mauduit that by this *solemn compact* they were, after the expiration of the stipulated term, liable to taxation.

When they apply to our compassion by telling us that they are to be carried from their own country to be tried for certain offences, we are not so ready to pity them as to advise them not to offend. While they are innocent they are safe.

When they tell of laws made expressly for their punishment, we answer that tumults and seditions were always punishable, and that the new law prescribes only the mode of execution.

When it is said that the whole town of Boston is distressed for a misdemeanor of a few, we wonder at their shamelessness; for we know that the town of Boston, and all the associated provinces, are now in rebellion to defend or justify the criminals.

If frauds in the imposts of Boston are tried by commission without a jury, they are tried here in the same mode; and why should the Bostonians expect from us more tenderness for them than for ourselves?

If they are condemned unheard, it is because there is no need of a trial. The crime is manifest and notorious. All trial is the investigation of something doubtful. An Italian philosopher observes that no man desires to hear what he has already seen.

If their assemblies have been suddenly dissolved, what was the reason? Their deliberations were indecent, and their intentions seditious. The power of dissolution is granted and reserved for such times of turbulence. Their best friends have been lately soliciting the King to dissolve his Parliament, to do what they so loudly complain of suffering.

That the same vengeance involves the innocent and guilty is an evil to be lamented, but human caution cannot prevent it, nor human power always redress it. To bring misery on those who have not deserved it is part of the aggregated guilt of rebellion. . . .

To what is urged of new powers granted to the Courts of Admiralty, or the extension of authority conferred on the judges, it may be answered in a few words that they have themselves made such regulations necessary; that they are established for the prevention of greater evils; at the same time, it must be observed that these powers have not been extended since the rebellion in America. . . .

When subordinate communities oppose the decrees of the general legislature with defiance thus audacious, and malignity thus acrimonious, nothing remains but to conquer or to yield; to allow their claim of independence, or to reduce them by force to submission and allegiance. . . .

On the original contrivers of mischief let an insulted nation pour out its vengeance. With whatever design they have inflamed this pernicious contest, they are themselves equally detestable. If they wish success to the Colonies, they are traitors to this country; if they wish defeat, they are traitors at once to America and England. To them and them only must be imputed the interruption of commerce, and the miseries of war, the sorrow of these that shall be ruined, and the blood of those that shall fall.

—JOHNSON, *Taxation No Tyranny*, pp. 55-87 *passim.*

2. BOSWELL AND JOHNSON DIFFER ON THE AMERICAN WAR

March 21, 1775

The doubts which, in my correspondence with him [Samuel Johnson], I had ventured to state as to the justice and wisdom of the conduct of Great Britain towards the American colonies, while I at the same time requested that he would enable me to inform myself upon that momentous subject, he had altogether disregarded; and had recently published a pamphlet, entitled

"Taxation no Tyranny; an Answer to the Resolutions and Address of the American Congress."

He had long before indulged most unfavourable sentiments of our fellow-subjects in America. For, as early as 1769, I was told by Dr. John Campbell that he had said of them, "Sir, they are a race of convicts, and ought to be thankful for anything we allow them short of hanging."

Of this performance I avoided to talk with him; for I had now formed a clear and settled opinion that the people of America were well warranted to resist a claim that their fellow-subjects in the mother-country should have the entire command of their fortunes, by taxing them without their own consent; and the extreme violence which it breathed appeared to me so unsuitable to the mildness of a Christian philosopher, and so directly opposite to the principles of peace which he had so beautifully recommended in his pamphlet respecting Falkland's Islands, that I was sorry to see him appear in so unfavourable a light. Besides, I could not perceive in it that ability of argument, or that felicity of expression, for which he was, upon other occasions, so eminent. Positive assertion, sarcastical severity, and extravagant ridicule, which he himself reprobated as a test of truth, were united in this rhapsody. . . .

September 23, 1777

. . . I unluckily entered upon the controversy concerning the right of Great Britain to tax America, and attempted to argue in favour of our fellow-subjects on the other side of the Atlantick. I insisted that America might be very well governed, and made to yield sufficient revenue by the means of *influence*, as exemplified in Ireland, while the people might be pleased with the imagination of their participating of the British constitution, by having a body of representatives, without whose consent money could not be exacted from them. Johnson could not bear my thus opposing his avowed opinion, which he had exerted himself with an extreme degree of heat to enforce; and the violent agitation into which he was thrown, while answering, or rather reprimanding me, alarmed me so that I heartily repented of my having unthinkingly introduced the subject. I myself, however, grew warm, and the change was great from the calm state of philosophical discussion in which we had a little before been pleasingly employed.

I talked of the corruption of the British Parliament, in which I alledged that any question, however unreasonable or unjust, might be carried by a venal majority; and I spoke with high admiration of the Roman Senate; and he maintained that the British Parliament was not corrupt, and that there was no occasion to corrupt its members, asserting that there was hardly ever any question in which a man might not very well vote either upon one side or the other. He said there had been none in his time except that respecting America.

Sunday, April 1, 1781

Sir Philip [Jennings Clerk] defended the Opposition to the American war ably and with temper, and I joined him. He said the majority of the nation was against the ministry. JOHNSON: "*I*, Sir, am against the ministry; but it is for having too little of that, of which Opposition thinks they have too much.

Were I minister, if any man wagged his finger against me, he should be turned out; for that which it is in the power of government to give at pleasure to one or to another should be given to the supporters of government. If you will not oppose at the expence of losing your place, your opposition will not be honest, you will feel no serious grievance; and the present opposition is only a contest to get what others have. Sir Robert Walpole acted as I would do. As to the American war, the *sense* of the nation is *with* the ministry. The majority of those who can *understand* is with it; the majority of those who can only *hear* is against it; and as those who can only hear are more numerous than those who can understand, and Opposition is always loudest, a majority of the rabble will be for Opposition."

This boisterous vivacity entertained us; but the truth in my opinion was that those who could understand the best were against the American war, as almost every man now is, when the question has been coolly considered.

—BOSWELL, *Life of Johnson*, pp. 237, 353, 455.

3. MRS. MACAULAY PROPHESIES THE RUIN OF BRITAIN

An "Address to the People of England, Scotland and Ireland on the Present Important Crisis of Affairs," by Catherine Macaulay, 1775.

It is not impossible, my fellow citizens, that after having tamely suffered the government, by a yearly increase of taxes, to beggar yourselves and your posterity, you may be led away with the wicked but delusive hope that the Ministry, when they have the power to pick the pockets of your American brethren, will have the moderation to save those of their countrymen.

If these are your thoughts, my fellow citizens, little have you studied your own natures, and the experience of all ages, which must have convinced you that the want of power is the only limitation to the exertion of human selfishness; but should you be contented to bid defiance to the warnings of common policy, should you be contented to be slaves in the hope that the Americans will bear the greater part of the burden of your enormous taxes, be assured that such an alternative will never be in your power. No. If a civil war commences between Great Britain and her Colonies, either the Mother Country, by one great exertion, may ruin both herself and America, or the Americans, by a lingering contest, will gain an independency; and in this case, all those advantages which you for some time have enjoyed by your Colonies, and advantages which have hitherto preserved you from a national bankruptcy, must for ever have an end; and whilst a new, a flourishing, and an extensive empire of freemen is established on the other side the Atlantic, you, with the loss of all those blessings you have received by the unrivalled state of your commerce, will be left to the bare possession of your foggy islands, and this under the sway of a domestic despot, or you will become the provinces of some powerful European state.

If a long succession of abused prosperity should, my friends and fellow citizens, have entirely deprived you of that virtue, the renown of which makes you even at this day respectable among all the nations of the civilized world; if neither the principles of justice or generosity have any weight with you, let me conjure you to take into consideration the interests of your safety and preservation. Suffer me again to remind you of the imminent danger of your situation: Your Ministers, by attacking the rights of all America, have effected that which the malicious policy of more judicious minds would have avoided. Your colonists, convinced that their safety depends on their harmony, are now united in one strong bond of union; nor will it be in the power of a Machiavel to take any advantage of those feuds and jealousies which formerly subsisted among them, and which exposed their liberties to more real danger than all the fleets and armies we are able to send against them. Your Ministers also, deceived by present appearances, vainly imagine, because our rivals in Europe are encouraging us to engage beyond the possibility of a retreat, that they will reject the opportunity when it offers of putting a final end to the greatness and the glory of our empire; but if, by the imprudent measures of the government the public expences increase, or the public income decrease to such a degree that the public revenue fail, and you be rendered unable to pay the interest of your debt, then will no longer be delayed the day and the hour of your destruction; then will you become an easy prey to the courts of France and Spain, who, you may depend upon it, will fall upon you as soon as they see you fairly engaged in a war with your Colonists; and, according to what is foretold you in a late publication, that conjecture will prove the latest and the uttermost of your prosperity, your peace, and in all probability of your existence as an independent state and nation.

Rouse, my countrymen! rouse from that state of guilty dissipation in which you have too long remained, and, in which, if you longer continue, you are lost for ever. Rouse! and unite in one general effort till, by your unanimous and repeated Addresses to the Throne, and to both Houses of Parliament, you draw the attention of every part of the government to their own interests, and to the dangerous state of the British empire.

—MACAULAY, "Address," *Magazine of History,*
Extra No. 114, XXIX, No. 2, 16-18.

4. DOCTOR PRICE: "BLIND RESENTMENT AND DESIRE FOR REVENGE"

[1776]

There are the following reasons which seem to make it too probable that the present conflict with America is a contest for power only, abstracted from all the advantages connected with it.

There is a love of power for its own sake inherent in human nature; and it cannot be uncharitable to suppose that the nation in general, and the cabinet in particular, are too likely to be influenced by it. What can be more flattering than to look across the Atlantic and to see in the boundless continent of America increasing MILLIONS whom we have a right to order as we please, who hold their property at our disposal, and who have no other law than our will. With what complacency have we been used to talk of them as OUR subjects? Is it not the interruption they now give to this pleasure, is it not the opposition they make to our pride, and not any injury they have done us, that is the secret spring of our present animosity against them?

I wish all in this kingdom would examine themselves carefully on this point. Perhaps they might find that they have not known what spirit they are of. Perhaps they would become sensible that it was a spirit of domination, more than a regard to the true interest of this country, that lately led so many of them, with such savage folly, to address the throne for the slaughter of their brethren in America, if they will not submit to them; and make offers of their lives and fortunes for that purpose. Indeed, I am persuaded that, were pride and the lust of dominion exterminated from every heart among us, and the humility of Christians infused in their room, this quarrel would be soon ended.

2dly. Another reason for believing that this is a contest for power only is that our ministers have frequently declared that their object is not to draw a revenue from America; and that many of those who are warmest for continuing it, represent the American trade as of no great consequence.

But what deserves particular consideration here is that this is a contest from which no advantage can possibly be derived. Not a revenue: for the provinces of America, when desolated, will afford no revenue; or if they should, the expence of subduing them and keeping them in subjection will much exceed that revenue. Not any of the advantages of trade: for it is a folly, next to insanity, to think trade can be promoted by impoverishing our customers, and fixing in their minds an everlasting abhorrence of us. It remains, therefore, that this war can have no other object than the extension of power. Miserable reflection! To sheath our swords in the bowels of our brethren, and spread misery and ruin among a happy people, for no other end than to oblige them to acknowledge our supremacy. How horrid! This is the cursed ambition that led a Caesar and an Alexander, and many other mad conquerors, to attack peaceful communities and to lay waste the earth.

But a worse principle than even this influences some among us. Pride and the love of dominion are principles hateful enough; but blind resentment and the desire of revenge are infernal principles; and these, I am afraid, have no small share at present in guiding our public conduct. One cannot help indeed being astonished at the virulence with which some speak on the present occasion against the Colonies. For what have they done? Have they crossed the ocean and invaded us? Have they attempted to take from us the fruits of our labour, and to overturn that form of government which we hold so sacred? This cannot be pretended. On the contrary. This is what we have done to them. We have transported ourselves to their peaceful retreats, and employed our fleets and armies to stop up their ports, to destroy their commerce, to seize their effects and to burn their towns. Would we but let them alone, and suffer them to enjoy in security their property and governments, instead of disturbing us, they would thank and bless us. And yet it is WE who imagine ourselves ill-used.

The truth is, we expected to find them a cowardly rabble who would lie quietly at our feet, and they have disappointed us. They have risen in their own defence and repelled force by force. They deny the plenitude of our power over them and insist on being treated as free communities. It is THIS that has provoked us; and kindled our governors into rage.

—PRICE, *Observations on the Nature of Civil Liberty*, pp. 31-33.

V. THE GREAT DEBATE OF OCTOBER 1775

On October 26, 1775, the King opened the second session of the Four-teenth Parliament with a speech from the throne that was as implacable as it was unenlightened. In both Houses supporters of the government moved the customary address of thanks; these motions set off one of the most heated debates in modern Parliamentary history—debates which fill several hundred pages of the Parliamentary History. *Most of the speakers here are familiar enough, and need no introduction. Rockingham, Grafton and Shelburne were, of course, among the most distinguished of noble lords who championed the American cause. Thirty-three lords voted against the address of thanks, but only 19 signed the notable protest entered on the Journal. Of the debaters in the House only "Governor" Johnstone and Serjeant Adair may be unfa-miliar. Johnstone had been Governor of Florida; trading on his American connections, he was later made a member of the Carlisle Commission but de-stroyed his usefulness by trying to bribe members of the Congress; on his return he switched over to the government side and was duly rewarded with command of a naval squadron. Serjeant Adair, a graduate of Peterhouse, Cam-bridge, was a follower of Wilkes and recorder of the City of London. It is appropriate to recall that Wedderburn was the man who as solicitor general poured billingsgate upon Franklin in 1774 when the latter was called before a committee of the Privy Council which investigated the release of letters writ-ten by Thomas Hutchinson criticizing affairs in Massachusetts; he was later elevated to the position of Lord Chancellor.*

1. George III: The Spirit of the British Nation Is Too High to Give Up the American Colonies

The King's Speech on Opening the Session of Parliament, October 26, 1775.
My Lords and Gentlemen:
. . . Those who have long too successfully laboured to inflame my people in America by gross misrepresentations, and to infuse into their minds a sys-tem of opinions repugnant to the true constitution of the colonies, and to their subordinate relation to Great Britain, now openly avow their revolt, hostility, and rebellion. They have raised troops, and are collecting a naval force; they have seized the public revenue, and assumed to themselves legis-lative, executive, and judicial powers, which they already exercise in the most arbitrary manner over the persons and properties of their fellow subjects. And although many of these unhappy people still retain their loyalty, and may be too wise not to see the fatal consequence of this usurpation, and wish to resist it, yet the torrent of violence has been strong enough to compel their acquiescence till a sufficient force shall appear to support them.

The authors and promoters of this desperate conspiracy have, in the con-duct of it, derived great advantage from the difference of our intention and theirs. They meant only to amuse, by vague expressions of attachment to the parent state, and the strongest protestations of loyalty to me, whilst they were preparing for a general revolt. On our part, though it was declared in your last session that a rebellion existed within the province of the Massachusetts Bay, yet even that province we wished rather to reclaim than to subdue. The resolutions of parliament breathed a spirit of moderation and forbearance; conciliatory propositions accompanied the measures taken to enforce authority, and the coercive acts were adapted to cases of criminal combinations amongst subjects not then in arms. I have acted with the same temper, anxious to prevent, if it had been possible, the effusion of the blood of my subjects, and the calamities which are inseparable from a state of war; still hoping that my people in America would have discerned the traitorous views of their leaders, and have been convinced that to be a subject of Great Britain, with all its consequences, is to be the freest member of any civil society in the known world.

The rebellious war now levied is become more general, and is manifestly carried on for the purpose of establishing an independent empire. I need not dwell upon the fatal effects of the success of such a plan. The object is too important, the spirit of the British nation too high, the resources with which God hath blessed her too numerous, to give up so many colonies which she has planted with great industry, nursed with great tenderness, encouraged with many commercial advantages, and protected and defended at much expence of blood and treasure.

It is now become the part of wisdom and (in its effects) of clemency to put a speedy end to these disorders by the most decisive exertions. For this purpose I have increased my naval establishment and greatly augmented my land forces; but in such a manner as may be the least burthensome to my kingdom.

I have also the satisfaction to inform you that I have received the most friendly offers of foreign assistance; and if I shall make any treaties in consequence thereof, they shall be laid before you. . . .

When the unhappy and deluded multitude, against whom this force will be directed, shall become sensible of their error, I shall be ready to receive the misled with tenderness and mercy. . . .

—COBBETT, *Parliamentary History of England*, XVIII, 695-697.

2. THE DEBATE IN THE LORDS

A. TWO NOBLE LORDS SUPPORT HIS MAJESTY

October 26, 1775

Viscount Dudley: . . . Having asserted the sovereign authority of the British legislature over every part of the British dominions, his Lordship contended that the present rebellion in America was fomented and supported by a desperate faction in this country; that none but the men of the worst dispositions and most pernicious designs would encourage the claims of America; and that, as they had been wrong in almost everything else, he was glad to find that they had been mistaken in their predictions relative to the distresses which the dispute with America would bring upon this nation. He had the pleasure of acquainting their lordships that he lived in the midst of a manufacturing country, in the neighbourhood of Birmingham, Wolverhampton, etc., and he could affirm, from the most authentick information collected upon the spot, that none of the direful effects, so often echoed through that House, and which it had been said would flow from the measures pursued by administration and supported by Parliament, had been yet, nor were likely to be felt.

Earl Grosvenor: said he was not used to speaking. Politicks were not in his way; but he thought the King's speech was a good speech, and as such ought to be answered in the terms moved by the noble Lord.

—FORCE, *American Archives*, 4th Series, VI, 5-6, 10.

B. THE MARQUIS OF ROCKINGHAM: "THE DREADFUL CALAMITY OF SHEDDING BRITISH BLOOD"

October 26, 1775

The Marquis of Rockingham, after enumerating the conduct of the several administrations for some years past respecting America, condemned the speech, which he called the speech of the minister, in very pointed terms; and contended that the measures recommended from the throne were big with the most portentous and ruinous consequences. His lordship moved an amendment, by inserting after the word "throne" in the first paragraph, these words:

"That we behold with the utmost concern the disorders and discontents in the British colonies rather increased than diminished by the means which have been used to suppress and allay them; a circumstance alone sufficient to give this House just reason to fear, that those means were not originally well considered, or properly adapted to answer the ends to which they were directed. . . .

"Deeply impressed with a sense of this melancholy state of the public concerns, we shall, on the fullest information we can obtain, and with the most mature deliberation we can employ, review the whole of the late proceedings, that we may be enabled to discover, as we shall be most willing to apply, the most effectual means for restoring order to the distracted affairs of the British empire, confidence to his Majesty's government, obedience, by a prudent and temperate use of its powers, to the authority of parliament, and satisfaction and happiness to all his people.

"By these means, we trust, we shall avoid any occasion for having recourse to the alarming and dangerous expedient of calling in foreign forces to the support of his Majesty's authority within his own dominions, and the still more dreadful calamity of shedding British blood by British hands."

—COBBETT, *Parliamentary History of England*, XVIII, 708-709.

C. THE DUKE OF GRAFTON: "REPEAL EVERY ACT SINCE 1763 RELATIVE TO AMERICA!"

October 26, 1775

The Duke of Grafton: . . . His general sentiments respecting America were well known; he should not therefore take up their Lordships' time in explaining them. It was true, he had supported Administration, but it was upon a general idea that means of conciliation might be devised and adopted. He expressed his ignorance of the true state of America, and asserted that he had been misled and deceived; for that reason chiefly he could not think of concurring any longer in measures of which he never really approved, but to which he lent his countenance, in expectation that, the stronger Government was, the more likely matters were to be amicably adjusted. He had a proposition which, with their Lordships' leave, he would submit to the House. He knew it could not originate with their Lordships, as it must come through the other House, because it would affect the revenue. Perhaps, said his Grace, it will not gain your approbation entirely this night; but, believe me, you will like it better to-morrow, and still better in three days hence. It will daily grow in your esteem. In a fortnight, I promise you, it will have more friends, until at length it will gain universal assent and approbation. The proposition is only this: to bring in a bill for repealing every act (I think there are thirteen) which has been passed in this country since the year 1763 relative to America. This, I will venture to assert, will answer every end; and nothing less will accomplish any effectual purpose, without scenes of ruin and destruction which I cannot think on without the utmost grief and horror. . . .

—FORCE, *American Archives*, 4th Series, VI, 5-6.

D. THE EARL OF SHELBURNE PROPHESIES RUIN

October 26, 1775

. . . It is with equal astonishment and concern, my Lords, that I perceive not the least mention made in the speech which has been this day delivered to us, of a paper the most important of any that could possibly come under the consideration of this House: I mean the last petition from the General Congress in America. How comes it that the Colonies are charged with planning independency, in the face of their explicit declaration to the contrary, contained in that petition? Who is it that presumes to put an assertion (what shall I call it, my Lords?) contrary to fact, contrary to evidence, notorious to the whole world, in that mouth from which truth alone, if unprompted, would issue? Is it their intention, by thus perpetually sounding independence in the ears of the Americans, to lead them to it, or, by treating them, upon suspicion, with every possible violence, to compel them into that which must be our ruin? For let visionary writers say what they will, it is a plain and incontestable fact that the commerce of America is the vital stream of this great empire.

A noble and reverend Lord has insinuated the petition seems to him to be conceived in terms of great art and ambiguity. I have examined it with great care; but this morning I read it repeatedly, and, to my apprehension, except a certain degree of address necessary to meet the prejudices which have been wickedly and industriously excited here, there cannot be a fairer opportunity of extricating this country from the ruinous situation in which the folly of Administration has involved us. It furnishes the fairest foundation for an honourable and advantageous accommodation. I have been long and intimately known to some gentlemen of that country, one of whom now takes a considerable share in their proceedings; and I have ever found them and their correspondents constant and earnest in the wish for conciliation, upon the terms of ancient connection. . . .

But is it possible that your Lordships should not have marked, and marked with indignation, the levity, and even ridicule, with which the noble Lord at the head of the Admiralty [The Earl of Sandwich] has treated this most solemn subject? No man who did not feel himself secure in the promise of impunity from some quarter would proclaim his mistakes in triumph and sport with the calamities of his country. It is astonishing that any one should have dared to promise impunity to such fatal errors, and a conduct so criminal: it is your Lordships' business to look to this. Should such men not only be at large unaccused, but highly trusted, adding fresh insults, misleading by fresh misinformation, and manifesting a total contempt of the publick, both here and in America? The noble Lord laughs at all propositions of conciliation; repeats his imputation of cowardice against the Americans; says the idea of rights is to be driven out of their heads by blows; and ridicules the objections to employing foreigners and papists. Is this a language, my Lords, becoming so great an officer of state? Is it decent thus to stigmatise so great a part of the empire with so base a calumny? It is impossible that noble Lord can have less intolerancy in his disposition than I have; but it does not therefore follow that I should think it a measure of no moment, or of inconsiderable danger, to arm the hands of those who are strangers to toleration, and who pant for the extirpation of the Protestant religion. By what authority is it, that the Crown has put the string of fortresses of this empire into the possession of foreign troops? I do not inquire whether it is with or against the letter of any particular law. I see it fundamentally infringing the first principles of our Government; and do not hesitate to pronounce it high treason against the Constitution. I foretell it is a measure which the indignation of the country will pursue till it is utterly condemned. . . .

My Lords, the Ministers lament that it is their task, in this American business, to support the measure of another Administration. This is some acknowledgment, at least, that the measure was wrong. Why, then, did they support it? What secret influence has compelled them to heap errors on errors, grievance upon grievance till they have shaken the Constitution to its foundation, and brought the whole empire into danger and confusion? The Americans judge from facts. They have seen a uniform lurking spirit of despotism pervade every Administration. It has prevailed over the wisest and most constitutional counsels; it has precipitated us into the most pernicious of all wars—a war with our brothers, our friends, and our fellow-subjects. It was this lurking spirit of despotism that produced the Stamp Act in 1765; that fettered the repeal of that act in 1766; that revived the principles of it in 1767; that has accumulated oppression upon oppression since, till at length it has openly established, by the Quebeck Bill, Popery and arbitrary power over half America.

—COBBETT, *Parliamentary History of England*, XVIII, 722-725.

E. PROTEST OF THE DISSENTING LORDS

October 26, 1775

The following Protest was entered:
Dissentient,

1st. Because we cannot, as Englishmen, as Christians, or as men of common humanity, consent to the prosecution of a cruel civil war, so little supported by justice, and so very fatal in its necessary consequences, as that which is now waging against our brethren and fellow-subjects in America. We have beheld, with sorrow and indignation, session after session, and notwithstanding repeated warnings of the danger, attempts made to deprive some millions of British subjects of their trade, their laws, their constitution, their mutual intercourse, and of the very food which God has given them for their subsistence. We have beheld endeavours used to enforce these impolitick severities at the point of the bayonet. . . . When we consider these things, we cannot look upon our fellow-subjects in America in any other light than that of freemen driven to resistance by acts of oppression and violence.

2dly. Because this unnatural war, thus commenced in oppression, and in the most erroneous policy, must, if persevered in, be finally ruinous in its effects. The commerce of Great Britain with America was great and increasing; the profits immense; the advantages, as a nursery of seamen, and as an inexhaustible magazine of naval stores, infinite; and the continuance of that commerce, particularly in times of war, when most wanted to support our fleets and revenues, not precarious as all foreign trade must be, but depending solely on ourselves. These valuable resources, which enable us to face the united efforts of the House of Bourbon, are actually lost to Great Britain, and irretrievably lost, unless redeemed by immediate and effectual pacification.

3dly. Because Great Britain, deprived of so valuable a part of its resources, and not animated either with motives of self-defence or with those prospects of advantage and glory which have hitherto supported this nation in all its foreign wars, may possibly find itself unable to supply the means of carrying on a civil war, at such a vast distance, in a country so peculiarly circumstanced, and under the complicated difficulties which necessarily attend it. Still less should we be able to preserve by mere force that vast continent, and that growing multitude of resolute freemen who inhabit it, even if that or any other country was worth governing against the inclination of all its inhabitants. . . .

4thly. Because we conceive the calling in foreign forces to decide domestick quarrels to be a measure both disgraceful and dangerous. . . .

5thly. Because the Ministers who are to be entrusted with the management of this war have proved themselves unequal to the task, and in every degree unworthy of publick trust. Parliament has given them every assistance they asked; no unforeseen accidents have stood in their way; no storms have disabled or delayed their operations; no foreign power hath, as yet, interfered; but notwithstanding these advantages, by their ignorance, negligence, and want of conduct, our arms have been disgraced; . . . Whether we consider its extent or its commerce, England has lost half its empire in one campaign. . . . We cannot, therefore, consent to an Address, which may deceive his Majesty and the publick into a belief of the confidence of this House in the present Ministers, who have deceived Parliament, disgraced the nation, lost the Colonies, and involved us in a civil war, against our clearest interests, and upon the most unjustifiable grounds, wantonly spilling the blood of thousands of our fellow-subjects.

EFFINGHAM, CHOLMONDELEY, DEVONSHIRE, ROCKINGHAM, KING, CHEDWORTH, RICHMOND, PORTLAND, TORRINGTON, STAMFORD, BOYLE, FITZWILLIAM, PONSONBY, CRAVEN, ARCHER, ABINGDON, SCARBOROUGH, THANET, MANCHESTER.
—FORCE, *American Archives*, 4th Series, VI, 14-16.

3. THE DEBATE IN THE COMMONS

A. MR. WEDDERBURN: "AMERICA MUST BE CONQUERED!"

Thursday, October 26, 1775

Mr. Wedderburn said: . . . Why, then, do we hesitate? Because an inconsiderable party, inconsistent in their own politicks, and always hostile to all government but their own, endeavour to obstruct our measures, and clog the wheels of Government? Let us rather second the indignant voice of the nation, which presses in from all quarters upon the Sovereign, calling loudly for vigorous measures, and for the suppression of faction. Shall we be deaf to its call? Sir, we have been too long deaf; we have too long shown our forbearance and long-suffering; faction must now be curbed, must be subdued and crushed; our thunders must go forth; America must be conquered.

Had my advice been taken (and gentlemen insinuate it is taken too much), the House must do me the justice to own that a much more powerful force than General Gage had would have been sent to America. But it is not yet, I apprehend, too late; for I am not one of those ill-boding prophets who, from every disaster, augur destructive consequences, and whose prophecies, like those of antiquity, contribute more than any other circumstance to their own completion. I hold it dastardly in the counsellor of a great and mighty empire to encourage despondence, and to be the croaking raven of future mischiefs and calamities. . . . Exert your courage in proportion to the difficulties to be surmounted; and, like your own oaks in the ocean, rise superior to the storm. Such is the language of the genuine friend of England; such, I am persuaded, is the language expected from us by a gallant nation, whose spirit, instead of being depressed, is only roused by adverse accidents. Shall we stand as a mound in the way of this torrent, which has hitherto borne down all opposition? Sir, I do not approve of that policy that would repress plebeian haughtiness, as it is called, and check that pride of empire with the idea of which the souls of our common people swell, feeling their own importance.

"Our lowest mechanicks," it has been urged, "now talk familiarly of *our* subjects." And why should they not? Feeling their own consequence, why should they not, like freemen, give free course to their thoughts? Howeve lightly this spirit may be now prized, it is what has raised England to the great and glorious state which she now occupies. Do you imagine that the allurement of six pence a day fills our armies, mounts a breach, or takes a battery of cannon? No, sir; we owe all this to the ferment of youthful blood, to the high spirit of the people, to a love of glory, and a sense of national honour. Let us cherish so noble a principle, and we shall soon feel the good effects of its operation. This principle it was that frequently humbled the pride of France, that formerly ruined the Spanish armada, and lately baffled the Bourbon confederacy; the principle, in short, that lately crushed every power that ever had the temerity to encounter your collected rage. View the state of England in Elizabeth's reign, and learn fortitude from her example. . . .

—Force, *American Archives*, 4th Series, VI, 41-42.

B. MR. JOHNSTONE: "INSTITUTIONS THAT HAVE REARED SUCH ELEVATED SPIRITS!"

October 26, 1775

Mr. Johnstone: . . . I maintain that the sense of the best and wisest men in this country are on the side of the Americans; that three to one in Ireland are on their side; that the soldiers and sailors feel an unwillingness to the service; that you never will find the same exertions of spirit in this as in other wars. I speak it to the credit of the fleet and army: they do not like to butcher men whom the greatest characters in this country consider as contending in the glorious cause of preserving those institutions which are necessary to the happiness, security and elevation of the human mind. I am well informed that four field officers in the four regiments now going from Ireland have desired leave to retire or sell out. I do not mean to say that the soldiers or sailors in America have shown any signs of cowardice; this is below their spirit: I only assert that they in general proclaim it a disagreeable service; most of the army feel it as such. That numbers have not deserted is owing to their situation.

There is a wide difference between the English officer or soldier who barely does his duty, and the general exertions of the New England army, where every man is thinking of what further service he can perform; where every soldier is a Scaevola. To a mind who loves to contemplate the glorious spirit of freedom, no spectacle can be more affecting than the action at Bunkers Hill. To see an irregular peasantry commanded by a physician, inferior in number, opposed by every circumstance of cannon and bombs that could terrify timid minds, calmly waiting the attack of the gallant Howe leading on the best troops in the world, with an excellent train of artillery, and twice repulsing those very troops who had often chased the chosen battalions of France, and at last retiring for want of ammunition, but in so respectable a manner that they were not even pursued—who can reflect on such scenes, and not adore the Constitution of Government which could breed such men! Who will not pause and examine, before he destroys institutions that have reared such elevated spirits! Who is there that can dismiss all doubts on the justice of the cause which can inspire such conscious rectitude?

The conduct of the people of New England for wisdom, courage, temperance, fortitude, and all those qualities that can command the admiration of noble minds, is not surpassed in the history of any nation under the sun. Instead of wreaking our vengeance against that Colony their heroism alone should plead their forgiveness.

—FORCE, *American Archives,* 4th Series, VI, 31.

C. JOHN WILKES: "NO PART OF THE SUBJECTS OF THIS EMPIRE WILL EVER SUBMIT TO BE SLAVES"

October 26, 1775

The Lord Mayor, Mr. Wilkes: . . . I think this war, Sir, fatal and ruinous to our country. It absolutely annihilates the only great source of our wealth, which we enjoyed unrivalled by other nations, and deprives us of the fruits of the laborious industry of near three million of subjects, which centered here. That commerce has already taken its flight, and our American merchants are now deploring the consequences of a wretched policy, which has been pursued to their destruction. It is, Sir, no less ruinous with regard to the enormous expence of the fleets and armies necessary for this nefarious undertaking, and of consequence the enormous supplies to be raised, so that we are wasting our present wealth, while we are destroying the sources of all we might have in future. An humane mind must contemplate with agony the dreadful calamities and convulsions which are the consequence of every civil war, and especially a civil war of this magnitude and extent.

I speak, Sir, as a firm friend to England and America, but still more to universal liberty and the rights of all mankind. I trust no part of the subjects of this vast empire will ever submit to be slaves. I am sure the Americans are too high-spirited to brook the idea. Your whole power, and that of your allies, if you add any, even of all the German troops, of all the ruffians from the north, whom you can hire, cannot effect so wicked a purpose. The conduct of the present administration has already wrested the sceptre of America out of the hands of our sovereign, and he has now scarcely even a postmaster left in that whole northern continent. More than half the empire is already lost, and almost all the rest in confusion and anarchy. The ministry have brought our sovereign into a more disgraceful situation than any crowned head now living. He alone has already lost, by their fatal counsels, more territory than the three great united powers of Russia, Austria and Prussia have together by a wicked confederacy robbed Poland of, and by equal acts of violence and injustice from administration.

England was never engaged in a contest of such importance to our most valuable concerns and possessions. We are fighting for the subjection, the unconditional submission, of a country infinitely more extended than our own, of which every day increases the wealth, the natural strength, the population. Should we not succeed, it will be a loss never enough to be deplored, a bosom friendship soured to hate and resentment. We shall be considered as their most implacable enemies, an eternal separation will follow, and the grandeur of the British empire pass away. Success, final success, seems to me not equivocal, not uncertain, but impossible. However we may differ among ourselves, they are perfectly united. On this side the Atlantic party-rage unhappily divides us, but one soul animates the vast northern continent of America, the general congress, and each provincial assembly. An appeal has been made to the sword; and at the close of the last campaign what have we conquered? Bunker's-hill only, and with the loss of 1,200 men. Are we to pay as dearly for the rest of America? The idea of the conquest of that immense continent is as romantic as unjust.

The Hon. gentleman who moved the Address says, "The Americans have been treated with lenity." Will facts justify this assertion? Was your Boston Port Bill a measure of lenity? Was your Fishery Bill a measure of lenity? Was your Bill for taking away the charter of the Massachusetts Bay a measure of lenity, or even justice? I omit your many other gross provocations and insults, by which the brave Americans have been driven into their present state.

He asserts that they avow a disposition to be independent. On the contrary, Sir, all the declarations, both of the late and the present congress, uniformly tend to this one object, of being put on the same footing the Americans were in the year 1763. This has been their only demand, from which they have never varied. Their daily prayers and petitions are for liberty, peace and safety. I use the words of the congress the last year. They justly expect to be put on an equal footing with the other subjects of the empire, and are willing to come into any fair agreement with you in commercial concerns. If you confine all our trade to yourselves, say they; if you make a monopoly of our commerce; if you shut all the other ports of the world against us, do not tax us likewise. If you tax us, then give us a free trade, such as you enjoy yourselves. Let us have equal advantages of commerce, all other ports open to us; then we can, and will, cheerfully, voluntarily pay taxes. You will have a free-will offering given with pleasure, not grudgingly.

It must give, Sir, every man who loves this country the deepest concern at the naming in the Address foreign troops, Hanoverians and Hessians, who are now called to interfere in our domestic quarrels, not to dwell this day on the illegality of the measure, the danger and disgrace attending foreign mercenaries. The militia, indeed, are, we are told, to be now employed, and that noble institution is at present complimented by ministers, but we know they hate the very name of a militia, and that measure is adopted only because the embodying of these forces enables administration to butcher more of our fellow subjects in America.

Sir, I disapprove not only the evil spirit of the whole Address, but likewise the wretched adulation of almost every part of it. My wish and hope therefore is that it will be rejected by the House, and that another dutiful, yet decent, manly Address will be presented to the King, praying his Majesty that he would sheath the sword, prevent the farther effusion of the blood of our fellow subjects, adopt some mode of negociation with the general congress, in compliance with their repeated petition, and thereby restore peace and harmony to this distracted empire.

—COBBETT, *Parliamentary History of England*, XVIII, 734-737.

D. CHARLES JAMES FOX: "ALEXANDER NEVER GAINED MORE IN ONE CAMPAIGN
THAN THE NOBLE LORD HAS LOST"

October 26, 1775

Mr. Fox described Lord North as the blundering pilot who had brought
the nation into its present difficulties. Administration, he said, exult at having
brought us into this dilemma. They have reason to triumph. Lord Chatham,
the king of Prussia, nay, Alexander the Great, never gained more in one
campaign than the noble lord has lost—he has lost a whole continent. Although he thought the Americans had gone too far, and were not justifiable
in what they had done, yet they were more justifiable for resisting than they
would have been had they submitted to the tyrannical acts of a British parliament—that when the question was whether a people ought to submit to
slavery or aim at freedom by a spirited resistance, the alternative which must
strike every Englishman was the choice of the latter. . . .

—COBBETT, *Parliamentary History of England*, XVIII, 769.

E. MR. SERJEANT ADAIR: "WE CANNOT CONQUER AMERICA"

October 27, 1775

Mr. Serjeant Adair: . . . The war in which we are engaged is, of all others,
in its nature the most ruinous and destructive. Whatever may be the event,
we must be the sufferers; for such is the unhappy nature of the contest that the
losses and mischiefs of both sides must ultimately fall upon us. Whose treasures will be exhausted by the expence? Whose commerce will be ruined and
destroyed? The blood of whose subjects will be spilt but those of the British
empire?

If such are the present effects of this war, the event must be still more
fatal to this kingdom. Let us consider it, Sir, upon either supposition of success or disappointment, of conquest or defeat. The present situation of the
colonies, their union, their conduct, their enthusiastic spirit of liberty, and
the fatal experience of the last campaign, has fully convinced every man,
even the most sanguine, that we cannot expect bloodless laurels or an easy
conquest. We must lay our accounts for the most alarming and dangerous
resistance; and if a full exertion of all the powers and resources of this kingdom, which I am far from thinking the most probable event, should at length,
after a long and obstinate contest, in which both sides will be almost equally
exhausted, prevail over every effort of liberty, reduce the colonies to a forced
submission, and complete the conquest of America—in what respect shall we
be gainers by such a conquest? What shall we acquire at such an expence but
the empty assertion of an unprofitable sovereignty over desolated provinces,
or a few miserable slaves? Instead of those flourishing dominions, the wealth
and commerce of which has rendered us the greatest nation in the world, we
shall find ourselves possessed of a vast territory, which, drained of the sources
from whence that greatness flowed, that communicated itself so plentifully
to us, will be not only useless and unprofitable, but burthensome and destructive; acquired by violence and force, it cannot be preserved but by the same
means; and our acknowledged revenues must be still further drained by the

constant expence of fleets and armies to support our unjust authority and to defend from foreign invasion those provinces which we shall have deprived of the means of defending themselves. These, Sir, are the happy consequences that we may expect from the most prosperous success.

But suppose for a moment the event should be different; suppose the extent and natural advantages of their country, their distance from us, that union which our measures have produced, and above all that ardour of liberty, that enthusiastic and desperate spirit, which our injustice and oppression have excited, should carry the Americans through the dreadful struggle with success and enable them in the end to baffle and defeat the utmost exertions of their infatuated and deluded country. In the course and event of such a struggle, is it possible to suppose that America will not follow the dangerous example which we are going to set her of having recourse to foreign assistance; that in the future establishment of her commerce, she will not give the preference to any nation in Europe over that which has attempted to enslave and destroy her and has not desisted from the unnatural attempt till after the utmost, though ineffectual, exertion of all her power and resources? In what situation will Great Britain then find herself? Her colonies will not only be totally lost to her, but, at least as to the benefits of their commerce, thrown into the hands of other powers, most probably her natural enemies. Reduced to her insular dominions; curtailed in her commerce; the principal source of her wealth and naval power transferred into the hands of her enemies; her blood and treasures exhausted; her revenues lessened; oppressed with an enormous debt, and debilitated with unsuccessful exertions; she will lose her power and consequence in the system of Europe, and be exposed almost a defenceless prey to the first neighbour who shall chuse to invade her.

These, Sir, are the consequences which must ensue from the measures we are now called upon to approve and support. Whether they are followed by defeat or success, they will, almost with equal certainty, destroy the power, the glory, the happiness of this once great and flourishing empire. It is my opinion that we cannot conquer America; I have not a doubt that we cannot acquire or maintain a beneficial sovereignty over her by violence and force.

Sir, I could not be easy in my own mind without entering the strongest and most public protestations against measures which appear to me to be fraught with the destruction of this mighty empire. I wash my hands of the blood of my fellow subjects; and shall at least have this satisfaction, amidst the impending calamities of the public, not only to think that I have not contributed to, but that I have done all in my power to oppose and avert the ruin of my country.

—Cobbett, *Parliamentary History of England*, XVIII, 787-791.

VI. GEORGE III HIRES MERCENARIES

In the Seven Years' War, said the Earl of Shelburne, Britain was able to raise an army of 300,000 men; now she cannot find 50,000 soldiers. The explanation he found in the war itself, for "in a worthy cause we can get soldiers enough." King George tried to prove the cause worthy by raising soldiers in Hanover: he sent 4000 of his own troops to Gibraltar and Minorca and replaced them with loyal Hanoverians. He took another 4000 soldiers out of Ireland, and replaced them, too, with mercenaries. But this was of little help. He tried to hire soldiers from Empress Catherine of Russia, but his overtures were rejected and, he wrote, "not in so genteel a manner as I should have thought might have been expected from Her; She has not had the Civility to answer in her own hand." Then the King tried to hire the so-called Scotch Brigade from the Dutch, but again without success. Finally he turned to the German principalities, long an arsenal for other people's armies. Frederick the Great of Prussia would have none of it, but the other princes—in Burke's wonderful phrase—"snuffed the cadaverous taint of lucrative war." The Prince of Brunswick-Lüneburg, brother-in-law to George III, was ready to sell 4300 men for £160,000. The Prince of Hanau, who had 74 children to support, wanted to get in on a good thing, and so did the Landgrave of Hesse-Cassel with reputedly 100 children to maintain. Out of a population of some 300,000 this ruler managed to provide almost 20,000 mercenaries—for some £3,000,000. Altogether Britain obtained some 30,000 German mercenaries, at a total cost of £4,700,000; of these 30,000 some 12,000 were killed, or stayed in America.

The hiring of German mercenaries seemed even to some of the British a dirty business. To make the matter worse, however, the Ministry had struck a thoroughly bad bargain with the German princes. The treaties—to preserve appearances they took the form of treaties of reciprocity—excited heated criticism when they were introduced into Parliament, but were nevertheless voted by 252-88 in the Commons and 100-32 in the Lords.

We give here a small group of miscellaneous documents on the Hessians: the rejection of British overtures by the Dutch; the King's treaty with the Prince of Hesse-Cassel with some criticism and some defense; a handbill—probably written by Thomas Jefferson—designed to induce the Hessians to desert; and a typically Franklinesque satire on the sale of the Hessians.

1. The Dutch Refuse to Lend Troops to Britain

Opinion of Johan Derk van der Capellen on request of the King of Great Britain for the loan of the Scotch Brigade.

December 16, 1775

Honourable and Mighty Gentlemen: . . . This brings me to my last observation. Though not as principals, yet as auxiliaries, our troops would be employed towards suppressing (what some please to call) a rebellion in the American colonies; for which purpose I would rather see janizaries hired than troops of a free State. In what an odious light must this unnatural civil war appear to all Europe, a war in which even savages . . . refuse to engage; more odious, still, would it appear for a people to take a part therein who were themselves once slaves, bore that hateful name, but at last had spirit to fight themselves free. But, above all, it must appear superlatively detestable to me, who think the Americans worthy of every man's esteem and look upon them as a brave people, defending in a becoming, manly and religious manner those rights which, as men, they derive from God, not from the legislature of Great Britain. Their mode of proceeding will, I hope, serve as an example to every nation deprived, by any means, of its privileges, yet fortunate enough in being able to make suitable efforts towards retaining or regaining them. . . .

—FORCE, *American Archives*, 4th Series, IV, 285-286.

2. KING GEORGE HIRES HESSIAN MERCENARIES

A. TREATY WITH THE PRINCE OF HESSE-CASSEL

Be it known to all whom it may concern that his Majesty the King of Great Britain, having judged proper to accept a body of infantry of the troops of his Most Serene Highness the Hereditary Prince of Hesse Cassel, reigning Count of Hanau, etc., to be employed in the service of Great Britain, the high contracting parties . . . have agreed upon the following articles:

Art. I. The said Most Serene Prince yields to his Britannick Majesty a body of infantry of six hundred and sixty men, which shall be at the entire disposition of the King of Great Britain.

Art. II. The Most Serene Prince engages to equip completely this corps; and that it shall be ready to march the 20th of the month of March next, at farthest. The said corps shall pass in review before his Majesty's Commissary at Hanau, if that can be done, or at some other place as opportunity shall offer.

Art. III. The Most Serene Prince engages to furnish the recruits annually necessary. These recruits shall be delivered to his Britannick Majesty's Commissary, disciplined and completely equipped. . . .

Art. VIII. There shall be paid to his Most Serene Highness, under the title of levy money, for each foot soldier thirty crowns Banco—the crown reckoned at fifty-three sols of Holland. . . .

Art. IX. According to custom, three wounded men shall be reckoned as one killed. A man killed shall be paid for at the rate of the levy money. If it shall happen that any company of the corps should be entirely ruined or destroyed, the King will pay the expense of the necessary recruits to reestablish this corps. . . .

Art. XII. His Britannick Majesty will grant to the Most Serene Prince, during all the time that this body of troops shall be in the pay of his Majesty, an annual subsidy of twenty-five thousand and fifty crowns Banco. . . .

Done at Hanau, the 5th of February, 1776.

WILLIAM FAUCITT,
FREDERICK BARON DE MALSBOURG

—FORCE, *American Archives*, 4th Series, VI, 276-277.

B. LORD NORTH JUSTIFIES THE HIRING OF MERCENARIES

February 29, 1776

Lord North [Introducing a Treaty with the Landgrave of Hesse] urged the necessity of the measure, and the great effects he expected from it. He said, no questions could arise upon it but three, all of which were too plain to require much elucidation: Whether the troops proposed to be hired were wanted? whether the terms on which they were procured were advantageous? and whether the force was such as might be deemed fully adequate to effect the operations for which it was intended?

As to the first point, he said that reducing America to a proper constitutional state of obedience being the great object of Parliament, the best and most speedy means of effecting so desirable a purpose was the motive which induced Administration to adopt the measure, because men could be readier had, and upon much cheaper terms in this way, than we could possibly recruit them at home. On the second, he observed, that not only in the view of comparative cheapness with home levies, but as referring to former times, the present troops would cost us less than (taking all the circumstances together) we could have expected. And, lastly, that the force which this measure would enable us to send to America would be such as, in all human probability, would compel that country to agree to terms of submission, perhaps without any further effusion of blood.

—FORCE, *American Archives*, 4th Series, VI, 277.

C. "A COMPOUND OF THE MOST SOLEMN MOCKERY, FALLACY AND GROSS IMPOSITION"

March 5, 1776

Lord Camden: . . . As for the treaties now on your Lordships' table, and the proposed effect of the present motion, I shall beg your Lordships' indulgence for a few words. If I understand them right, they contain an agreement with the Landgrave of Hesse, Duke of Brunswick, and Prince of Hanau, for a certain number of troops for specifick sums of money, accompanied by subsequent conditions of a double subsidy to be paid, in case the war should be terminated in a shorter time than that usually fixed for the existence of subsidiary treaties. To give this bargain the appearance of what it really is not, the whole is stuffed up with pompous expressions of alliance, founded in reciprocal support and common interest; as if these petty States were really concerned in the event of the present contest between this country and America.

Now, my Lords, I would appeal to any of your Lordships if the whole of this transaction be not a compound of the most solemn mockery, fallacy and gross imposition that was ever attempted to be put on a House of Parliament. Is there one of your Lordships who does not perceive most clearly that the whole is a mere mercenary bargain for the hire of troops on one side, and the sale of human blood on the other; and that the devoted wretches thus purchased for slaughter are mere mercenaries, in the worst sense of the word? . . . The history of all ages and nations prove the fatal effects of calling in foreign auxiliaries, but more particularly mere mercenaries, to fight their battles; and my memory hardly furnishes me with a single instance of conquest over any great state or empire, in which the conquerors were not first introduced into the country as friends and allies. This general truth, my Lords, I allow, does not directly apply to the present treaties; but the principle, were the national imbecility such as your Lordships heard it described to be this day really just, ought to create cause of great and serious alarm to every one of your Lordships. I cannot better express my disapprobation of employing foreigners, particularly to fight our domestick quarrels, than by quoting the opinion of that great man, Sir Walter Raleigh. In his *History of the World,* he says "that they are seditious, unfaithful, disobedient, devourers and destroyers of all places and countries whither they are drawn, as being held by no other bond but their own commodity. Yea, that which is most fearful among such hirelings is, that they have often, and in time of greatest extremity, not only refused to fight in the defence of those who have entertained them, but revolted to the contrary part, to the utter ruin of those Princes and States who have trusted them."

—FORCE, *American Archives,* 4th Series, VI, 310-311.

3. CONGRESS TRIES TO SEDUCE THE HESSIANS FROM THEIR ALLIANCE

August 14, 1776

Whereas it has been the wise policy of these states to extend the protection of their laws to all those who should settle among them, of whatever nation or religion they might be, and to admit them to a participation of the benefits of civil and religious freedom; and the benevolence of this practice, as well as its salutary effects, have rendered it worthy of being continued in future times.

And whereas his Britannic majesty, in order to destroy our freedom and happiness, has commenced against us a cruel and unprovoked war; and, unable to engage Britons sufficient to execute his sanguinary measures, has applied for aid to certain foreign princes, who are in the habit of selling the blood of their people for money, and from them has procured and transported hither considerable numbers of foreigners.

And it is conceived, that such foreigners, if apprised of the practice of these states, would chuse to accept of lands, liberty, safety and a communion of good laws, and mild government, in a country where many of their friends and relations are already happily settled, rather than continue exposed to the toils and dangers of a long and bloody war, waged against a people, guilty of no other crime than that of refusing to exchange freedom for slavery; and that they will do this the more especially when they reflect that after they shall have violated every Christian and moral precept by invading and attempting to destroy those who have never injured them or their country, their only reward, if they escape death and captivity, will be a return to the despotism of their prince, to be by him again sold to do the drudgery of some other enemy to the rights of mankind.

And whereas the parliament of Great Britain have thought fit, by a late act, not merely to invite our troops to desert our service, but to direct a compulsion of our people, taken at sea, to serve against their country:

Resolved, Therefore, that these states will receive all such foreigners who shall leave the armies of his Britannic majesty in America and shall chuse to become members of any of these states; that they shall be protected in the free exercise of their respective religions, and be invested with the rights, privileges and immunities of natives, as established by the laws of these states;

and, moreover, that this Congress will provide, for every such person, 50 acres of unappropriated lands in some of these states, to be held by him and his heirs in absolute property.

—Journals of the Continental Congress, V, 653-655.

4. FRANKLIN WRITES A SATIRE ON THE SALE OF THE HESSIANS

From the Count de Schaumbergh to the Baron Hohendorf,
Commanding the Hessian Troops in America.

Rome, February 18, 1777

Monsieur Le Baron:—On my return from Naples, I received at Rome your letter of the 27th December of last year. I have learned with unspeakable pleasure the courage our troops exhibited at Trenton, and you cannot imagine my joy on being told that of the 1,950 Hessians engaged in the fight but 345 escaped. There were just 1,605 men killed, and I cannot sufficiently commend your prudence in sending an exact list of the dead to my minister in London. This precaution was the more necessary as the report sent to the English ministry does not give but 1,455 dead. This would make 483,450 florins instead of 643,500 which I am entitled to demand under our convention. You will comprehend the prejudice which such an error would work in my finances, and I do not doubt you will take the necessary pains to prove that Lord North's list is false and yours correct.

The court of London objects that there were a hundred wounded who ought not to be included in the list, nor paid for as dead; but I trust you will not overlook my instructions to you on quitting Cassel, and that you will not have tried by human succor to recall the life of the unfortunates whose days could not be lengthened but by the loss of a leg or an arm. That would be making them a pernicious present, and I am sure they would rather die than live in a condition no longer fit for my service. I do not mean by this that you should assassinate them; we should be humane, my dear Baron, but you may insinuate to the surgeons with entire propriety that a crippled man is a reproach to their profession, and that there is no wiser course than to let every one of them die when he ceases to be fit to fight.

I am about to send you some new recruits. Don't economize them. Remember glory before all things. Glory is true wealth. There is nothing degrades the soldier like the love of money. He must care only for honour and reputation, but his reputation must be acquired in the midst of dangers. A battle gained without costing the conqueror any blood is an inglorious success, while the conquered cover themselves with glory by perishing with their arms in their hands. Do you remember that of the 300 Lacedaemonians who defended the defile of Thermopylae, not one returned? How happy should I be could I say the same of my brave Hessians!

It is true that their king, Leonidas, perished with them: but things have changed, and it is no longer the custom for princes of the empire to go and fight in America for a cause with which they have no concern. And besides, to whom should they pay the thirty guineas per man if I did not stay in Europe to receive them? Then, it is necessary also that I be ready to send recruits to replace the men you lose. For this purpose I must return to Hesse.

It is true, grown men are becoming scarce there, but I will send you boys. Besides, the scarcer the commodity the higher the price. I am assured that the women and little girls have begun to till our lands, and they get on not badly. You did right to send back to Europe that Dr. Crumerus who was so successful in curing dysentery. Don't bother with a man who is subject to looseness of the bowels. That disease makes bad soldiers. One coward will do more mischief in an engagement than ten brave men will do good. Better that they burst in their barracks than fly in a battle and tarnish the glory of our arms. Besides, you know that they pay me as killed for all who die from disease, and I don't get a farthing for runaways.

My trip to Italy, which has cost me enormously, makes it desirable that there should be a great mortality among them. You will therefore promise promotion to all who expose themselves; you will exhort them to seek glory in the midst of dangers; you will say to Major Maundorff that I am not at all content with his saving the 345 men who escaped the massacre of Trenton. Through the whole campaign he has not had ten men killed in consequence of his orders. Finally, let it be your principal object to prolong the war and avoid a decisive engagement on either side, for I have made arrangements for a grand Italian opera, and I do not wish to be obliged to give it up. Meantime I pray God, my dear Baron de Hohendorf, to have you in his holy and gracious keeping.

—SMYTH, ed., Writings of Franklin, VII, 27-29.

CHAPTER EIGHT

The Great Declaration

WRITING OF *the Declaration of Independence, the embittered Governor Hutchinson alleged that some American leaders had been working for independence ever since the days of the Stamp Act. Late in life John Adams appeared to give support to this theory. The Revolution, he assured his old friend Thomas McKean of Pennsylvania, "was in the minds of the people, and in the union of the colonies, both of which were accomplished before hostilities commenced." But at almost the same time he was assuring another friend that while there had always been a desire for independence from Parliament, there had never been any desire for independence from the Crown before the crisis of 1775-1776. "For my part," he wrote, "there was not a moment during the Revolution when I would not have given everything I ever possessed for a restoration to the state of things before the contest began."*

Though there is some exaggeration in this, the evidence is conclusive that it was a "restoration to the state of things before the contest began" that almost all Americans wanted. In March 1775 Benjamin Franklin could assure Lord Chatham that "he had never heard in any conversation from any person drunk or sober the least expression of a wish for a separation or hint that such a thing would be advantageous to America." According to the Maryland clergyman, Jonathan Boucher, George Washington on his way to Philadelphia in the spring of 1776 asserted that "if I ever heard of his joining in any such measures [as independence] I had his leave to set him down for everything wicked." The Loyalist Boucher is not wholly reliable, yet a few weeks later Washington himself was assuring the New York Provincial Congress that "every exertion of my worthy colleagues and myself will be equally extended to the re-establishment of peace and harmony between the Mother Country and these Colonies." Nor can we doubt the authenticity of that report by James Hogg from the short-lived colony of Transylvania that as late as October 1775 both Samuel and John Adams regarded anything looking to independence as an impropriety.

Few things about the history of the American Revolution are more impressive than the slowness with which feeling in favor of independence matured, and the reluctance of the great majority of Americans to contemplate the necessity or the inevitability of a final separation. Far from being those rash, headstrong and violent demagogues that Hutchinson described, that Germain denounced, that King George imagined, the leaders of the American Revolution were prudent, cautious and judicious. There were exceptions, to

*be sure, and it is doubtless true that there were radicals in every colony work-
ing for independence as early as 1775: Sam Adams and Joseph Hawley, Patrick
Henry and Richard Henry Lee, Thomas Jefferson and William Henry Drayton, to name but a few of the more prominent. But the great majority of
those who voted independence and ultimately won it were not, at the beginning, separatists.*

*Even Lexington and Concord and Bunker's Hill, even the creation of a
Continental Army and the appointment of a Continental commander, did not
bring about a revolution in American attitude. The Second Continental Congress might proclaim the necessity of taking up arms, create an army and a
navy, authorize privateers, open negotiations (after a fashion) with France,
and launch an attack on Canada, but it still petitioned for reconciliation. And
even after George III had cavalierly rejected the petition and proclaimed the
colonies in a state of rebellion, their spokesmen in Philadelphia hesitated, debated, and indulged in wishful thinking that somehow the cup of independence
might be dashed from their lips.*

*The decisive change in sentiment can be dated from the publication of that
remarkable pamphlet,* Common Sense, *written by the gifted Thomas Paine,
newly arrived from England. Published early in January 1776, it was speedily
republished in most of the cities of the colonies, and within a few weeks its
influence was felt everywhere. "Thousands," wrote the South Carolina historian Ramsay, "were converted by it and were led to long for a separation
from the mother country." Some, indeed, heard Paine's words as sounding
brass and tinkling cymbals, but to most he spoke with the tongue of angels.
In any event the common sense of Paine's arguments appealed alike to the
man at the plow and in the street, the soldier in camp and the statesman at
his desk in the Continental Congress in Philadelphia.*

*By early spring of 1776 the trend for independence was beginning to ac-
celerate as two things became increasingly clear: that the mother country had
no intention of acquiescing in American demands without intolerable reservations; and that the colonies could, in fact, if united and helped by France, win
a contest of arms. In any event February and March saw an upsurge of revolutionary sentiment and activity. In rapid succession the Continental Congress
authorized privateers, and armed them; placed an embargo on trade with
Britain and the West Indies; sent Silas Deane to France to win financial and
other support; instructed the colonies to disarm all unfriendly persons; and
opened the ports of America to all nations except Britain.*

*Meantime sentiment for independence was growing rapidly in the states—
a term which we must use now instead of "colonies." Late in March, South
Carolina adopted a constitution which implied a condition of independence;
on April 12 North Carolina instructed her delegation in Congress that they
might concur with others in a declaration of independence; and early in May
Rhode Island fell into line. Now, indeed, as John Adams wrote exultantly,
every day independence rolled in like a torrent. May 15 was perhaps the
decisive day: on that day Virginia, the most populous and most powerful of
the states, voted for independence, and Congress formally instructed the
states to form their own independent governments.*

Now it was only a question of time. New England and the South had both swung over to independence; only the Middle States held back. Under the leadership of such men as Dickinson and Wilson of Pennsylvania, Duane and Jay of New York, Carter Braxton of Virginia and Edward Rutledge of South Carolina, and a handful of others, the moderates gathered themselves for a last stand. When on June 7 Richard Henry Lee introduced his famous resolution looking to independence, they were strong enough to win a postponement of the vote, but that was, in reality, their last show of strength. On July 1 the ever-vacillating John Dickinson tried to stem the tide, but in vain; the next day independence was voted without a dissenting voice.

Meantime a committee of five had "prepared a declaration in conformity to" the resolution of independence: with admirable prescience this committee assigned the task to young Thomas Jefferson, freshly arrived from Virginia. Jefferson's Declaration, not too seriously changed by the committee, was submitted to the Congress on June 28, debated on the second, third and fourth of July, and passed on that now famous day. It was signed, in a desultory fashion, during the following weeks.

No one, not even Jefferson, played a larger role in bringing thirteen reluctant colonies to a declaration of independence than stanch John Adams, and no one rejoiced more deeply when this "greatest question which ever was debated in America" was decided. And it was Adams who in a moment of exultation pronounced the perfect apothegm on the events of the day of independence:

> *I am well aware of the toil and blood and treasure it will cost us to maintain this declaration and support and defend these States. Yet through all the gloom I can see the rays of ravishing light and glory. I can see that the end is more than worth all the means, and that posterity will triumph in that day's transactions.*

I. BENJAMIN RUSH LIMNS SOME OF THE FOUNDING FATHERS

Benjamin Rush was only thirty when the Revolutionary War broke out, but as with so many other young men of his day, he had already achieved position and fame. At the age of twenty-one he had sailed for Edinburgh to study medicine at that famous center, and while abroad had learned not only science but philosophy, and had come under the influence of Dr. Franklin. Back in Philadelphia he rose rapidly to eminence: professor at the College of Philadelphia, leading physician, member of the American Philosophical Society, zealous reformer and ardent Patriot. He early became an advocate of independence, encouraged Tom Paine to write Common Sense, and was elected to the Continental Congress where he had the good fortune to be one of the "signers." In 1777 he became surgeon general of the armies of the Middle Department, and we shall meet him again, enthusiastic, passionate, quarrelsome. Rush knew everybody, and took everybody's measure, not always judiciously. These sketches were written about 1800.

[1800]

SAMUEL ADAMS. He was near sixty years of age when he took his seat in Congress, but possessed all the vigor of mind of a young man of five and twenty. He was a republican in principle and manners. He once acknowledged to me "that the independance of the United States upon Great Britain had been the first wish of his heart seven years before the war." About the same time he said to me "if it were revealed to him that 999 Americans out of 1000 would perish in a war for liberty, he would vote for that war, rather than see his country enslaved. The survivors in such a war, though few (he said), would propagate a nation of freemen." He abhorred a standing army, and used to say that they were the "shoeblacks of Society." He dreaded the undue influence of an individual in a Republic, and once said to me, "Let us beware of continental and State great men." He loved simplicity and economy in the administration of government, and despised the appeals which are made to the eyes and ears of the common people in order to govern them. He considered national happiness and the public patronage of religion as inseperably connected; and so great was his regard for public worship, as the means of promoting religion, that he constantly attended divine service in the German church in York town while the Congress sat there, when there was no service in their chappel, although he was ignorant of the German language. His morals were irreproachable, and even ambition and avarice, the usual vices of politicians, seemed to have no place in his breast. He seldom spoke in Congress, but was active in preparing and doing business out of doors. In some parts of his conduct I have thought he discovered more of the prejudices of a Massachusetts man than the liberal sentiments of a citizen of the United States. His abilities were considerable, and his knowledge extensive and correct upon Revolutionary subjects, and both friends and enemies agree in viewing him as one of the most active instruments of the American Revolution.

JOHN ADAMS. He was a distant relation of Saml. Adams, but possessed another species of character. He had been educated a lawyer, and stood high in his profession in his native state. He was a most sensible and forcible speaker. Every member of Congress in 1776 acknowledged him to be the first man in the House. Dr. Brownson (of Georgia) used to say when he spoke, he fancied an angel was let down from heaven to illumine the Congress. He saw the whole of a subject at a single glance, and by a happy union of the powers of reasoning and persuasion often succeeded in carrying measures which were at first sight of an unpopular nature. His replies to reflections upon himself, or upon the New England States, were replete with the most poignant humor or satyre. I sat next to him while Genl. Sullivan was delivering a request to Congress from Lord Howe for an interview with a committee of the House in their private capacities, after the defeat of the American Army on Long Island on the 26th of August 1776. Mr. Adams, under a sudden impression of the design, and dread of the consequences of the measure, whispered to me a wish "that the first ball that had been fired on the day of the defeat of our army, had gone through his head." When he rose to speak against the proposed interview, he called Genl. Sullivan "a decoy duck, whom Lord Howe has sent among us to seduce us into a renunciation of our independence." In a debate in which Mr. C—— insinuated the New England troops as the principal cause of the failure of the expedition into Canada in 1775 [actually 1776], he said "the cause of the failure of that expedition was chiefly to be ascribed to the impudence of the gentleman from Maryland who has fomented jealousies and quarrels between the troops from the New England and Southern States in his visit to Canada, and (said Mr. Adams) if he were now penetrated, as he ought to be, with a sense of his improper and wicked conduct, he would fall down upon his knees upon this floor, and ask our forgiveness. He would afterwards retire with shame, and spend the remainder of his life in sackcloth and ashes, deploring the mischief he has done his country." He was equally fearless of men, and of the consequences of a bold assertion of his opinion in all his speeches. . . .

He was a stranger to dissimulation, and appeared to be more jealous of his reputation for integrity than for talents or knowledge. He was strictly moral, and at all times respectful to Religion. In speaking of the probable issue of the war he said to me in Baltimore in the winter of 1777, "We shall succeed in our struggle, provided we repent of our sins, and forsake them," and then added, "I will see it out, or go to heaven in its ruins." He possessed more learning probably, both ancient and modern, than any man who subscribed the Declaration of Independance. His reading was various. Even the old English poets were familiar to him. He once told me he had read all Bolingbroke's works with great attention. He admired nothing in them but the stile, and to acquire it, he said he had when a young man transcribed his "Idea of a Patriot King." When he went to Holland to negociate a treaty with that country, he left a blank in Congress. . . .

ELBRIDGE GERRY. He was a respectable young merchant, of a liberal education and considerable knowledge. He was slow in his perceptions and in his manner of doing business, and stammering in his speech, but he knew and embraced truth when he saw it. He had no local or state prejudices. Every part of his conduct in 1775, 1776 and 1777 indicated him to be a sensible, upright man, and a genuine friend to republican forms of government.

ROGER SHEARMAN [SHERMAN]. A plain man of slender education. He taught himself mathematicks, and afterwards acquired some property and a good deal of reputation by making almanacks. He was so regular in business and so democratic in his principles that he was called by one of his friends "a republican machine." Patrick Henry asked him in 1774 why the people of Connecticut were more zealous in the cause of liberty than the people of other States; he answered "because we have more to lose than any of them." "What is that?" said Mr. Henry. "Our beloved charter," replied Mr. Sherman. He was not less distinguished for his piety than his patriotism. He once objected to a motion for Congress sitting on a Sunday upon an occasion which he thought did not require it, and gave as a reason for his objection a regard of the commands of his Maker. Upon hearing of the defeat of the American army on Long Island, where they were entrenched and fortified by a chain of hills, he said to me in coming out of Congress, "Truly in vain is salvation hoped for from the hills, and from the multitude of mountains" ('Jeremiah iii, 23).

GEORGE CLYMER. A cool, firm, consistent Republican who loved liberty and government with an equal affection. Under the appearance of manners that were cold and indolent, he concealed a mind that was always warm and active towards the interests of his country. He was well informed in history ancient and modern, and frequently displayed flashes of wit and humor in conversation. His style in writing was simple, correct and sometimes eloquent. "The mould in which this man's mind was cast (to use the words of Lord Peterborough when speaking of Wm. Law) was seldom used."

JAMES WILSON. An eminent lawyer and a great and enlightened statesman. He had been educated for a clergyman in Scotland, and was a profound and accurate scholar. He spoke often in Congress, and his eloquence was of the most commanding kind. He reasoned, declaimed and persuaded according to circumstances with equal effect. His mind, while he spoke, was one blaze of light. Not a word ever fell from his lips out of time, or out of place, nor could a word be taken from or added to his speeches without injuring them. He rendered great and essential services to his country in every stage of the Revolution.

THOMAS JEFFERSON. He possessed a genius of the first order. It was universal in its objects. He was not less distinguished for his political than his mathematical and philosophical knowledge. The objects of his benevolence were as extensive as those of his knowledge. He was not only the friend of his country, but of all nations and religions. While Congress were deliberating upon the measure of sending Commissioners to France I asked him what he thought of being one of them. He said "he would go to hell to serve his country." He was afterwards elected a Commissioner, but declined at that time on account of the sickness of his wife. He seldom spoke in Congress.

ARTHUR MIDDLETON. A man of a cynical temper, but of upright intentions towards his country. He had been educated in England and was a critical Latin and Greek scholar. He read Horace and other classicks during his recess from Congress. He spoke frequently, and always with asperity or personalities. He disliked business, and when put upon the Committee of Accounts he refused to serve and gave as a reason for it that "he hated accounts, that he did not even keep his own accounts, and that he knew nothing about them."

CHARLES THOMPSON. A man of great learning and general knowledge, at all times a genuine Republican, and in the evening of his life a sincere Christian. He was the intimate friend of John Dickinson. He was once told in my presence that he ought to write a history of the Revolution. "No," said he, "I ought not, for I should contradict all the histories of the great events of the Revolution, and shew by my account of men, motives and measures, that we are wholly indebted to the agency of providence for its successful issue. Let the world admire the supposed wisdom and valor of our great men. Perhaps they may adopt the qualities that have been ascribed to them, and thus good may be done. I shall not undeceive future generations."

GENERAL CHARLES LEE. His character was a medley of opposite and contradicting qualities. He loved and admired public virtue, but was addicted to many private vices. He was obscene, profane, and at times impious in his conversation. His avarice discovered itself in every transaction of his life. He studied singularity and eccentricity in his dress, appetite, accommodations, stile in writing, speaking, and swearing. Even his will partook of this weakness in his character. He had many successive intimates, whom he called friends, but he appeared to have no affection for any thing human. A troop of dogs which he permitted to follow him every where seemed to engross his whole heart. He despised prudence, and used to call it "a rascally virtue." With these vices and oddities, he was sincere, and no one ever detected him in a lye, or even in an equivocation. He likewise possessed courage, which he evinced in many battles and duels in different parts of the world. His genius was considerable, and his attainments great in classical learning and in modern languages. He was eloquent and at times witty and brilliant in conversation. He was useful in the beginning of the war by inspiring our citizens with military ideas and lessening in our soldiers their superstitious fear of the valor and discipline of the British army. When he heard of the sentence of the court martial which suspended him from his command, he said "Oh, that I were a dog, that I might not call man my brother!"

—CORNER, ed., *Autobiography of Benjamin Rush*, pp. 139-156 *passim*.

II. DEFIANCE OR RECONCILIATION

On May 10, 1775, the Second Continental Congress formally opened in the State House in Philadelphia. Most of the members who drifted in that week or the next were veterans of the First Congress, but there were some very important additions: Benjamin Franklin and James Wilson from Pennsylvania, John Hancock—shortly to be chosen President—from Massachusetts, George Clinton and Philip Schuyler from New York, and, in time, Thomas Jefferson from Virginia. One gratifying addition was a delegate from the frontier colony of Georgia which had not been represented in the First Congress. "There never appeared more perfect unanimity among any sett of men," wrote the enthusiastic Richard Henry Lee, but within a short time unanimity gave way to dissension. There was however (or appeared to be) unanimity on the appointment of Washington to the chief command, and at least an appearance of agreement on the addresses, proclamations and petitions that streamed out from the State House during these early weeks.

But differences of opinion over the fundamental question of separation or reconciliation were deep, and grew deeper with the swift rush of events. What is most interesting is that these differences were not merely between radicals like John Adams or Jefferson and conservatives like Dickinson or Wilson; they were differences in the hearts and minds of individuals. Men seemingly as far apart in their views as John Adams and John Dickinson found themselves equally torn by doubts and misgivings. We can see this best in the two documents from which we take extracts: the Declaration of the Causes and Necessity of Taking Up Arms, *and the so-called* Olive Branch Petition *to the King; it is revealing that the same man, John Dickinson, helped draft the first and wrote the second, and that John Adams signed both. And it is suggestive, too, that though Adams thought Dickinson had given a "silly cast" to the business of the Congress, he himself was by no means ready to embrace representatives from the upstart colony of Transylvania who had defied the Crown and assumed independence. And as late as August 25—two months after he had helped write the Declaration—Jefferson could assure his kinsman John Randolph that he was "looking with fondness towards a reconciliation with Great Britain."*

Actually it was George III who did more to help members of Congress make up their minds than the maneuvers of the Adamses or the eloquence of a Jefferson. The Olive Branch Petition, which Congress passed July 8, 1775, was entrusted, to Richard Penn, descendant of William Penn, whose loyalty could not be suspect; he was to present it to Lord Dartmouth who, in turn, was to pass it on to the King. But with characteristic stubbornness, George III refused to receive it. "The King and his Cabinet," said Lord Suffolk, "are determined to listen to nothing from the illegal congress, to treat with the colonies only one by one, and in no event to recognize them in any form of association." No wonder the French ambassador wrote home to Vergennes that "these people appear to me in a delirium."

While Americans waited for an answer, sentiment for reconciliation grew. Had there been any encouragement from the mother country, it might have crystallized into policy. But on November 1 the Congress heard not only of the rejection of the petition, but that the King had proclaimed the colonies in a state of rebellion. That day, too, brought word that the King was planning to hire German mercenaries, and that the British navy had wantonly burned the town of Falmouth. After all this it was hard to think of reconciliation.

We present here excerpts from the Declaration of the Causes and Necessity of Taking Up Arms—*a document written jointly by Jefferson and Dickinson—and from the* Olive Branch Petition; *John Adams' unfortunate letter castigating Dickinson; the Royal Proclamation of Rebellion; and some instructions from Pennsylvania which suggest how strong was loyal sentiment in that and other colonies.*

1. "Our Cause Is Just. Our Union Is Perfect"

DECLARATION OF THE CAUSES AND NECESSITY OF TAKING UP ARMS

July 6, 1775

... We are reduced to the alternative of chusing an unconditional submission to the tyranny of irritated ministers, or resistence by force. The latter is our choice. We have counted the cost of this contest, and find nothing so dreadful as voluntary slavery. Honour, justice, and humanity forbid us tamely to surrender that freedom which we received from our gallant ancestors, and which our innocent posterity have a right to receive from us. We cannot endure the infamy and guilt of resigning succeeding generations to that wretchedness which inevitably awaits them, if we basely entail hereditary bondage upon them.

Our cause is just. Our union is perfect. Our internal resources are great, and, if necessary, foreign assistance is undoubtedly attainable. We gratefully acknowledge, as signal instances of the Divine favour towards us, that his Providence would not permit us to be called into this severe controversy, until we were grown up to our present strength, had been previously exercised in warlike operation, and possessed of the means of defending ourselves. With hearts fortified with these animating reflections, we most solemnly, before God and the world, declare that, exerting the utmost energy of those powers which our beneficent Creator hath graciously bestowed upon us, the arms we have been compelled by our enemies to assume, we will, in defiance of every hazard, with unabating firmness and perseverance, employ for the preservation of our liberties; being with one mind resolved to die freemen rather than to live slaves.

Lest this declaration should disquiet the minds of our friends and fellow-subjects in any part of the empire, we assure them that we mean not to dissolve that union which has so long and so happily subsisted between us, and which we sincerely wish to see restored. Necessity has not yet driven us into that desperate measure, nor induced us to excite any other nation to war against them. We have not raised armies with ambitious designs of separating from Great-Britain, and establishing independent states. We fight not for glory or for conquest. We exhibit to mankind the remarkable spectacle of a people attacked by unprovoked enemies, without any imputation or even suspicion of offenses. . . .

With an humble confidence in the mercies of the supreme and impartial Judge and Ruler of the Universe, we most devoutly implore his divine goodness to protect us happily through this great conflict, to dispose our adversaries to reconciliation on reasonable terms, and thereby to relieve the empire from the calamities of civil war.

By order of Congress
John Hancock, *President*
—Journals of the Continental Congress, II, 140 ff.

2. Congress Sends an Olive Branch Petition

To the King's Most Excellent Majesty.

July 8, 1775

Most Gracious Sovereign: We, your Majesty's faithful subjects in the Colonies of. . . .

Attached to your Majesty's person, family, and government, with all devotion that principle and affection can inspire; connected with Great Britain by the strongest ties that can unite societies, and deploring every event that tends in any degree to weaken them, we solemnly assure your Majesty, that we not only most ardently desire the former harmony between her and these Colonies may be restored, but that a concord may be established between them upon so firm a basis as to perpetuate its blessings, uninterrupted by any future dissensions to succeeding generations in both countries, and to transmit your Majesty's name to posterity, adorned with that signal and lasting glory that has attended the memory of those illustrious personages, whose virtues and abilities have extricated states from dangerous convulsions, and by securing happiness to others have erected the most noble and durable monuments to their own fame.

We therefore beseech your Majesty, that your royal authority and influence may be graciously interposed to procure us relief from our afflicting fears and jealousies, occasioned by the system before-mentioned, and to settle peace through every part of our Dominions, with all humility submitting to your Majesty's wise consideration, whether it may not be expedient, for facilitating those important purposes, that your Majesty be pleased to direct some mode, by which the united applications of your faithful Colonists to the Throne, in pursuance of their common counsels may be improved into a happy and permanent reconciliation; and that, in the meantime, measures may be taken for preventing the further destruction of the lives of your Majesty's subjects; and that such statutes as more immediately distress any of your Majesty's Colonies may be repealed. . . .

—FORCE, *American Archives*, 4th Series, II, 1870-1871.

3. "MR. DICKINSON GIVES A SILLY CAST TO OUR DOINGS"

From the Diary of John Adams.

I took my hat, and went out of the door of Congress Hall. Mr. Dickinson observed me and darted out after me. He broke out upon me in a most abrupt and extraordinary manner: in as violent a passion as he was capable of feeling, and with an air, countenance and gestures as rough and haughty as if I had been a school-boy and he the master. He vociferated, "What is the reason, Mr. Adams, that you New England men oppose our measures of reconciliation? There, now, is Sullivan, in a long harangue, following you in a determined opposition to our petition to the King. Look ye! if you don't concur with us in our pacific system, I and a number of us will break off from you and New England, and we will carry on the opposition by ourselves in our own way." I own I was shocked with this magisterial salutation. . . .

The more I reflected on Mr. Dickinson's rude lecture in the State House yard, the more I was vexed with it; and the determination of Congress in favor of the petition did not allay the irritation. . . . I took my pen and wrote a very few lines to my wife, and about an equal number to General James Warren. Irritated with the unpoliteness of Mr. Dickinson and more mortified with his success in Congress, I wrote something like what has been published, but not exactly.

John Adams to James Warren.

Philadelphia, 24 July 1775

Dear Sir: I am determined to write freely to you this time. A certain great fortune and piddling genius whose fame has been trumpeted so loudly has given a silly cast to our whole doings. We are between hawk and buzzard. We ought to have had in our hands a month ago the whole legislative, executive and judicial of the whole continent, and have completely modelled a constitution; to have raised a naval power and opened all our ports wide; to have arrested every friend of government on the continent and held them as hostages for the poor victims in Boston, and then opened the door as wide as possible for peace and reconciliation. After this, they might have petitioned, negotiated, addressed, etc., if they would. Is all this extravagant? Is it wild? Is it not the soundest policy? . . .

—ADAMS, ed., *Works of John Adams*, II, 410, 411.

4. George III Proclaims the Americans in a State of Rebellion

August 23, 1775

Whereas many of our subjects in divers parts of our Colonies and Plantations in North America, misled by dangerous and ill designing men, and forgetting the allegiance which they owe to the power that has protected and supported them; after various disorderly acts committed in disturbance of the publick peace, to the obstruction of lawful commerce, and to the oppression of our loyal subjects carrying on the same; have at length proceeded to open and avowed rebellion, by arraying themselves in a hostile manner, to withstand the execution of the law, and traitorously preparing, ordering and levying war against us: And whereas, there is reason to apprehend that such rebellion hath been much promoted and encouraged by the traitorous correspondence, counsels and comfort of divers wicked and desperate persons within this realm: To the end therefore, that none of our subjects may neglect or violate their duty through ignorance thereof, or through any doubt of the protection which the law will afford to their loyalty and zeal, we have thought fit, by and with the advice of our Privy Council, to issue our Royal Proclamation, hereby declaring, that not only all our Officers, civil and military, are obliged to exert their utmost endeavours to suppress such rebellion, and to bring the traitors to justice, but that all our subjects of this Realm, and the dominions thereunto belonging, are bound by law to be aiding and assisting in the suppression of such rebellion, and to disclose and make known all traitorous conspiracies and attempts against us, our crown and dignity; and we do accordingly strictly charge and command all our Officers, as well civil as military, and all others our obedient and loyal subjects, to use their utmost endeavours to withstand and suppress such rebellion, and to disclose and make known all treasons and traitorous conspiracies which they shall know to be against us, our crown and dignity; and for that purpose, that they transmit to one of our principal Secretaries of State, or other proper officer, due and full information of all persons who shall be found carrying on correspondence with, or in any manner or degree aiding or abetting the persons now in open arms and rebellion against our Government, within any of our Colonies and Plantations in North America, in order to bring to condign punishment the authors, perpetrators, and abetters of such traitorous designs.

Given at our Court at St. James's the twenty-third day of August, one thousand seven hundred and seventy-five, in the fifteenth year of our reign.

God save the King.

—Force, American Archives, 4th Series, III, 240-241.

5. Pennsylvania Instructs Against Independence

In the Assembly, November 9, 1775

The trust reposed in you is of such a nature and the modes of executing it may be so diversified in the course of your deliberations that it is scarcely possible to give you particular instructions respecting it.

We, therefore, in general direct that you, or any four of you, meet in Congress the delegates of the several colonies now assembled in this city and any such delegates as may meet in Congress next year; that you consult together on the present critical and alarming state of public affairs; that you exert your utmost endeavours to agree upon and recommend such measures as you shall judge to afford the best prospect of obtaining redress of American grievances, and restoring that union and harmony between Great Britain and the colonies so essential to the welfare and happiness of both countries.

Though the oppressive measures of the British Parliament and administration have compelled us to resist their violence by force of arms, yet we strictly enjoin you that you, in behalf of this colony, dissent from and utterly reject any propositions, should such be made, that may cause or lead to a separation from our mother country or a change of the form of this government.

You are directed to make report of your proceedings to this House.

—*Pennsylvania Archives*, 8th Series, VIII, 352-353.

III. THE TURN OF THE TIDE

The rejection of the Olive Branch Petition and the Proclamation of Rebellion persuaded many wavering Americans that separation was inevitable, and after November 1775 expressions of defiance more and more drowned out those voices calling for reconciliation. Doubtless the most important single influence in bringing about a change in popular sentiment was the publication, in January 1776, of Common Sense, *"by an Englishman." The author was indeed an Englishman, scarcely a year out of England when he penned his remarkable pamphlet. Thomas Paine had arrived in Philadelphia the end of November 1774, and with characteristic impetuosity had thrown himself at once into the struggle for American rights, and made the American cause his own. As he himself wrote later, "When the country into which I had just set my foot was set on fire about my ears, it was time to stir. Those who had been long settled had something to defend; those who had just come had something to pursue; and the call and the concern was equal and universal. For in a country wherein all men were once adventurers, the difference of a few years in their arrival could make none in their rights."*

An inveterate champion of the poor and the oppressed, Paine had written an essay pleading the cause of the Negro slave; this caught the attention of the versatile Benjamin Rush who urged the essayist to put his talents to a larger task—that of pleading the cause of independence itself. Nothing pleased Paine more, and the pamphlet, which Rush christened Common Sense, *was published on January 9, 1776. Soon it was being reprinted everywhere in the colonies, in Boston and Salem, in Providence and Newport, in New York and in Charleston, and, with suitable omissions, in London itself; soon it was translated into German, into Dutch, into French. It caught the popular fancy as nothing before or since; it sold by the thousand; within three months, according to Paine, it had sold 120,000 copies; no other modern book has enjoyed a comparable sale, or a comparable influence, not* Uncle Tom's Cabin, *not* Progress and Poverty. *It was, as Moses Coit Tyler wrote, "precisely fitted to the hour, to the spot, to the passions of men. . . . It brushes away the tangles and cobwebs of technical debate, and flashes common sense upon the situation.*

*It was meant for plain men, in desperate danger, and desperately in earnest."
Above all it presented arguments elementary and to be understood by all, in
language that could be read by all; it appealed to the widespread popular sense
of Americanism, of separation, of equalitarianism; it appealed to passion and
to prejudice as well as to reason.*

The influence of Common Sense *was prodigious, and from all parts of the
country came testimony of the revolution it was working in the minds and
hearts of Americans. "I beg leave to let you know that I have read* Common
Sense," *wrote Major Hawley to Elbridge Gerry, "and that every sentiment
has sunk into my well prepared heart." Charles Lee wrote to Washington that
"I never saw such a masterly, irresistible performance. . . . I own myself convinced by the arguments of the necessity of separation." And Washington
himself wrote with characteristic reserve, that "I find* Common Sense *is working a powerful change in the minds of men."*

*We give here early expressions of sentiment for independence from
Thomas Jefferson and General Nathanael Greene—expressions which could be
matched in every colony; Benjamin Rush's account of how* Common Sense
*came to be written; a series of excerpts from the pamphlet itself; and—as if to
justify John Adams' ungenerous reflection that though it "probably converted
some" it turned others away from independence—an outburst of dissent from
that old curmudgeon, Landon Carter of Virginia.*

1. "Power to Declare and Assert a Separation"

Thomas Jefferson to John Randolph.

Philadelphia, November 29, 1775

Dear Sir: . . . It is an immense misfortune to the whole Empire, to have a
King of such a disposition at such a time. We are told, and every thing proves
it true, that he is the bitterest enemy we have. His Minister is able, and that
satisfies me that ignorance or wickedness somewhere controls him. In an
earlier part of this contest, our petitions told him, that from our King there
was but one appeal. The admonition was despised, and that appeal forced on
us. To undo his Empire, he has but one more truth to learn: that, after Colonies have drawn the sword, there is but one step more they can take. That
step is now pressed upon us, by the measures adopted, as if they were afraid
we would not take it.

Believe me, dear Sir, there is not in the British Empire a man who more
cordially loves a union with Great Britain than I do. But, by the *God* that
made me, I will cease to exist before I yield to a connection on such terms as
the British Parliament propose; and in this I think I speak the sentiments of
America. We want neither inducement nor power, to declare and assert a
separation. It is will alone which is wanting, and that is growing apace, under
the fostering hand of our King. One bloody campaign will probably decide,
everlastingly, our future course; I am sorry to find a bloody campaign is decided on. If our winds and waters should not combine to rescue their shores
from slavery, and General Howe's re-enforcement should arrive in safety, we
have hopes he will be inspirited to come out of Boston and take another drub-

bing; and we must drub him soundly, before the sceptred tyrant will know we are not mere brutes, to crouch under his hand, and kiss the rod with which he deigns to scourge us.

Yours, &c.,

THOMAS JEFFERSON

—FORCE, *American Archives*, 4th Series, III, 1706-1707.

2. GENERAL GREENE SAYS THE TIME FOR DELIBERATION IS OVER

Nathanael Greene to Samuel Ward, Member of the Congress from Rhode Island.

Camp on Prospect Hill, January 4, 1776

Dear Sir. . . . I am now to open my mind a little more freely. It hath been said that Canada in the late war was conquered in Germany. Who knows but that Britain may be in the present controversy! I take it for granted that France and Spain have made overtures to the Congress. Let us embrace them as brothers. We want not their land force in America: their navy we do. Their commerce will be mutually beneficial; they will doubtless pay the expense of their fleet, as it will be employed in protecting their own trade. Their military stores we want amazingly. Those will be articles of commerce. The Elector of Hanover has ordered his German troops to relieve the garrisons of Gibraltar and Port-Mahon; France will of consequence attack and subdue Hanover with little trouble. This will bring on a very severe war in Germany and turn Great Britain's attention that way. This may prevent immense expense and innumerable calamities in America.

Permit me, then, to recommend from the sincerity of my heart, ready at all times to bleed in my country's cause, a declaration of independence; and call upon the world, and the great God who governs it, to witness the necessity, propriety and rectitude thereof.

My worthy friend, the interests of mankind hang upon that truly worthy body of which you are a member. You stand the representatives not of America only, but of the whole world; the friends of liberty, and the supporters of the rights of Human Nature.

How will posterity, millions yet unborn, bless the memory of those brave patriots who are now hastening the consummation of Freedom, Truth and Religion! But want of decision renders wisdom in council insignificant, as want of power hath prevented us here from destroying the mercenary troops now in Boston. . . . How can we, then, startle at the idea of expense, when our whole property, our dearest connexions, our liberty, nay! life itself is at stake? Let us, therefore, act like men inspired with a resolution that nothing but the frowns of Heaven shall conquer us. It is no time for deliberation; the hour is swiftly rolling on when the plains of America will be deluged with human blood. Resolves, declarations and all the parade of heroism in words will not obtain a victory. Arms and ammunition are as necessary as men and must be had at the expense of everything short of Britain's claims. . . .

—FORCE, *American Archives*, 4th Series, IV, 572.

3. Dr. Rush Stands Godfather to *Common Sense*

[1800]

About the year 1774 a certain Thomas Paine arrived in Philadelphia from England with a letter of recommendation from Dr. Franklin. . . . In one of my visits to Mr. Aitken's bookstore I met with Mr. Paine, and was introduced to him by Mr. Aitken. His conversation became at once interesting. I asked him to visit me, which he did a few days afterwards. Our subjects of conversation were political. I perceived with pleasure that he had realized the independence of the American colonies upon Great Britain, and that he considered the measure as necessary to bring the war to a speedy and successful issue.

I had before this interview put some thoughts upon paper upon this subject, and was preparing an address to the inhabitants of the colonies upon it. But I had hesitated as to the time, and I shuddered at the prospect of the consequence of its not being well received. I mentioned the subject to Mr. Paine, and asked him what he thought of writing a pamphlet upon it. I suggested to him that he had nothing to fear from the popular odium to which such a publication might expose him, for he could live anywhere, but that my profession and connections, which tied me to Philadelphia where a great majority of the citizens and some of my friends were hostile to a separation of our country from Great Britain, forbade me to come forward as a pioneer in that important controversy. He readily assented to the proposal, and from time to time he called at my house and read to me every chapter of the proposed pamphlet as he composed it. I recollect being charmed with a sentence in it which by accident, or perhaps by design, was not published. It was as follows: "Nothing can be conceived of more absurd than three millions of people flocking to the American shore every time a vessel arrives from England, to know what portion of liberty they shall enjoy."

When Mr. Paine had finished his pamphlet, I advised him to shew it to Dr. Franklin, Mr. Rittenhouse and Saml. Adams, all of whom I knew were decided friends to American independence. I mention these facts to refute a report that Mr. Paine was assisted in composing his pamphlet by one or more of the above gentlemen. They never saw it till it was written, and then only by my advice. I gave it at his request the title of "Common Sense."

—Corner, ed., *Autobiography of Benjamin Rush*, pp. 113-114.

4. *Common Sense*

Some writers have so confounded society with government as to leave little or no distinction between them; whereas they are not only different, but have different origins. Society is produced by our wants and government by our wickedness; the former promotes our happiness *positively* by uniting our affections, the latter *negatively* by restraining our vices. The one encourages intercourse, the other creates distinctions. The first is a patron, the last a punisher.

Society in every state is a blessing, but government, even in its best state, is but a necessary evil; in its worst state an intolerable one; for when we suffer or are exposed to the same miseries *by a government*, which we might expect in a country *without government*, our calamity is heightened by reflecting that we furnish the means by which we suffer. Government, like dress, is the badge of lost innocence; the palaces of kings are built upon the ruins of the bowers of paradise. For were the impulses of conscience clear, uniform, and irresistibly obeyed, man would need no other lawgiver; but that not being the case, he finds it necessary to surrender up a part of his property to furnish means for the protection of the rest; and this he is induced to do by the same prudence which in every other case advises him out of two evils to choose the least. *Wherefore*, security being the true design and end of government, it unanswerably follows that whatever *form* thereof appears most likely to ensure it to us, with the least expense and greatest benefit, is preferable to all others. . . .

But there is another and greater distinction for which no truly natural or religious reason can be assigned, and that is the distinction of men into *kings* and *subjects*. Male and female are the distinctions of nature, good and bad the distinctions of heaven; but how a race of men came into the world so exalted above the rest, and distinguished like some new species, is worth inquiring into, and whether they are the means of happiness or of misery to mankind.

In the early ages of the world, according to the Scripture chronology there were no kings; the consequence of which was there were no wars; it is the pride of kings which throws mankind into confusion. Holland without a king hath enjoyed more peace for this last century than any of the monarchical governments in Europe. Antiquity favors the same remark; for the quiet and rural lives of the first patriarchs have a happy something in them, which vanishes when we come to the history of Jewish royalty.

Government by kings was first introduced into the world by the heathens, from whom the children of Israel copied the custom. It was the most prosperous invention the Devil ever set on foot for the promotion of idolatry. The heathens paid divine honors to their deceased kings, and the Christian world has improved on the plan by doing the same to their living ones. How impious is the title of sacred Majesty applied to a worm, who in the midst of his splendor is crumbling into dust!

As the exalting one man so greatly above the rest cannot be justified on the equal rights of nature, so neither can it be defended on the authority of Scripture; for the will of the Almighty, as declared by Gideon and the prophet Samuel, expressly disapproves of government by kings. . . .

To the evil of monarchy we have added that of hereditary succession; and as the first is a degradation and lessening of ourselves, so the second, claimed as a matter of right, is an insult and imposition on posterity. For all men being originally equals, no *one* by *birth* could have a right to set up his own family in perpetual preference to all others forever, and though himself might deserve *some* decent degree of honors of his contemporaries, yet his descendants might be far too unworthy to inherit them. One of the strongest natural proofs of the folly of hereditary right in kings, is that nature disapproves it, otherwise she would not so frequently turn it into ridicule by giving mankind an *ass for a lion*.

... Most wise men in their private sentiments have ever treated hereditary right with contempt; yet it is one of those evils which when once established is not easily removed; many submit from fear, others from superstition, and the most powerful part shares with the king the plunder of the rest.

This is supposing the present race of kings in the world to have had an honorable origin; whereas it is more than probable that, could we take off the dark covering of antiquity and trace them to their first rise, we should find the first of them nothing better than the principal ruffian of some restless gang, whose savage manners of pre-eminence in subtility obtained him the title of chief among plunderers; and who by increasing in power, and extending his depredations, overawed the quiet and defenseless to purchase their safety by frequent contributions. Yet his electors could have no idea of giving hereditary right to his descendants, because such a perpetual exclusion of themselves was incompatible with the free and unrestrained principles they professed to live by. Wherefore, hereditary succession in the early ages of monarchy could not take place as a matter of claim, but as something casual or complemental; but as few or no records were extant in those days, and traditionary history stuffed with fables, it was very easy, after the lapse of a few generations, to trump up some superstitious tale conveniently timed, Mahomet-like, to cram hereditary right down the throats of the vulgar. Perhaps the disorders which threatened, or seemed to threaten, on the decease of a leader and the choice of a new one (for elections among ruffians could not be very orderly) induced many at first to favor hereditary pretensions; by which means it happened, as it hath happened since, that what at first was submitted to as a convenience was afterwards claimed as a right.

England, since the conquest, hath known some few good monarchs, but groaned beneath a much larger number of bad ones; yet no man in his senses can say that their claim under William the Conqueror is a very honorable one. A French bastard, landing with an armed banditti and establishing himself king of England against the consent of the natives, is in plain terms a very paltry rascally original. It certainly hath no divinity in it. However it is needless to spend much time in exposing the folly of hereditary right; if there are any so weak as to believe it, let them promiscuously worship the Ass and the Lion, and welcome. I shall neither copy their humility, nor disturb their devotion. ...

The nearer any government approaches to a republic, the less business there is for a king. It is somewhat difficult to find a proper name for the government of England. Sir William Meredith calls it a republic; but in its present state it is unworthy of the name, because the corrupt influence of the crown, by having all the places in its disposal, hath so effectually swallowed up the power, and eaten out the virtue of the House of Commons (the republican part in the constitution) that the government of England is nearly as monarchical as that of France or Spain. Men fall out with names without understanding them. For 'tis the republican and not the monarchical part of the constitution of England which Englishmen glory in, viz. the liberty of choosing a house of commons from out of their own body—and it is easy to see that when republican virtues fail, slavery ensues. Why is the constitution of England sickly but because monarchy hath poisoned the republic, the crown has engrossed the commons?

In England a king hath little more to do than to make war and give away places; which in plain terms is to improverish the nation and set it together by the ears. A pretty business indeed for a man to be allowed eight hundred thousand sterling a year for, and worshipped into the bargain! Of more worth is one honest man to society, and in the sight of God, than all the crowned ruffians that ever lived. . . .

The sun never shined on a cause of greater worth. 'Tis not the affair of a city, a county, a province, or a kingdom; but of a continent—of at least one-eighth part of the habitable globe. 'Tis not the concern of a day, a year, or an age; posterity are virtually involved in the contest, and will be more or less affected even to the end of time by the proceedings now. Now is the seed-time of continental union, faith, and honor. The least fracture now will be like a name engraved with the point of a pin on the tender rind of a young oak; the wound would enlarge with the tree, and posterity read it in full grown characters.

By referring the matter from argument to arms, a new era for politics is struck—a new method of thinking has arisen. All plans, proposals, etc. prior to the nineteenth of April, i.e. to the commencement of hostilities, are like the almanacks of the last year; which though proper then, are superseded and useless now. Whatever was advanced by the advocates on either side of the question then, terminated in one and the same point, viz. a union with Great Britain; the only difference between the parties was the method of effecting it; the one proposing force, the other friendship; but it has so far happened that the first has failed, and the second has withdrawn her influence.

As much has been said of the advantages of reconciliation, which, like an agreeable dream, has passed away and left us as we were, it is but right that we should examine the contrary side of the argument, and inquire into some of the many material injuries which these colonies sustain, and always will sustain, by being connected with and dependent on Great Britain. To examine that connection and dependence on the principles of nature and common sense; to see what we have to trust to, if separated, and what we are to expect, if dependent.

I have heard it asserted by some, that as America has flourished under her former connection with Great Britain, the same connection is necessary towards her future happiness, and will always have the same effect. Nothing can be more fallacious than this kind of argument. We may as well assert that because a child has thrived upon milk, it is never to have meat, or that the first twenty years of our lives is to become a precedent for the next twenty. But even this is admitting more than is true; for I answer roundly that America would have flourished as much, and probably much more, had no European power taken any notice of her. The commerce by which she hath enriched herself are the necessaries of life, and will always have a market while eating is the custom of Europe. . . .

But Britain is the parent country, say some. Then the more shame upon her conduct. Even brutes do not devour their young, nor savages make war upon their families; wherefore, the assertion, if true, turns to her reproach; but it happens not to be true, or only partly so, and the phrase *parent* or *mother country* hath been jesuitically adopted by the king and his parasites, with a low papistical design of gaining an unfair bias on the credulous weakness of our minds. Europe, and not England, is the parent country of America. This new world hath been the asylum for the persecuted lovers of civil and religious liberty from *every part* of Europe. Hither have they fled, not from the tender embraces of the mother, but from the cruelty of the monster; and it is so far true of England, that the same tyranny which drove the first emigrants from home pursues their descendants still. . . .

I challenge the warmest advocate for reconciliation to show a single advantage that this continent can reap by being connected with Great Britain. I repeat the challenge, not a single advantage is derived. Our corn will fetch its price in any market in Europe, and our imported goods must be paid for, buy them where we will.

But the injuries and disadvantages which we sustain by that connection are without number; and our duty to mankind at large, as well as to ourselves, instruct us to renounce the alliance: because any submission to, or dependence on, Great Britain, tends directly to involve this continent in European wars and quarrels, and set us at variance with nations who would otherwise seek our friendship, and against whom we have neither anger nor complaint. As Europe is our market for trade, we ought to form no partial connection with any part of it. 'Tis the true interest of America to steer clear of European contentions, which she never can do while by her dependence on Britain she is made the makeweight in the scale of British politics.

Europe is too thickly planted with kingdoms to be long at peace, an whenever a war breaks out between England and any foreign power, the trade of America goes to ruin, *because of her connection with Britain.* The next war may not turn out like the last, and should it not, the advocates for reconciliation now will be wishing for separation then, because neutrality in that case would be a safer convoy than a man of war. Everything that is right or reasonable pleads for separation. The blood of the slain, the weeping voice of nature cries, *'Tis time to part.* Even the distance at which the Almighty hath placed England and America is a strong and natural proof that the authority of the one over the other was never the design of heaven. . . .

It is repugnant to reason, to the universal order of things, to all examples from former ages, to suppose that this continent can long remain subject to any external power. The most sanguine in Britain doth not think so. The utmost stretch of human wisdom cannot, at this time, compass a plan, short of separation, which can promise the continent even a year's security. Reconciliation is *now* a fallacious dream. Nature has deserted the connection, and art cannot supply her place. For, as Milton wisely expresses, "Never can true reconcilement grow where wounds of deadly hate have pierced so deep." ...

As to government matters, it is not in the power of Britain to do this continent justice: the business of it will soon be too weighty and intricate to be managed with any tolerable degree of convenience by a power so distant from us, and so very ignorant of us; for if they cannot conquer us they cannot govern us. To be always running three or four thousand miles with a tale or a petition, waiting four or five months for an answer, which, when obtained, requires five or six more to explain it in, will in a few years be looked upon as folly and childishness. There was a time when it was proper, and there is a proper time for it to cease.

Small islands not capable of protecting themselves are the proper objects for government to take under their care; but there is something absurd in supposing a continent to be perpetually governed by an island. In no instance hath nature made the satellite larger than its primary planet; and as England and America, with respect to each other, reverse the common order of nature, it is evident that they belong to different systems. England to Europe: America to itself.

I am not induced by motives of pride, party, or resentment to espouse the doctrine of separation and independence; I am clearly, positively, and conscientiously persuaded that 'tis the true interest of this continent to be so; that everything short of *that* is mere patchwork, that it can afford no lasting felicity—that it is leaving the sword to our children, and shrinking back at a time when a little more, a little further, would have rendered this continent the glory of the earth. ...

To talk of friendship with those in whom our reason forbids us to have faith, and our affections wounded through a thousand pores instruct us to detest, is madness and folly. Every day wears out the little remains of kindred between us and them; and can there be any reason to hope that as the relationship expires the affection will increase, or that we shall agree better when we have ten times more and greater concerns to quarrel over than ever?

Ye that tell us of harmony and reconciliation, can ye restore to us the time that is past? Can ye give to prostitution its former innocence? Neither can ye reconcile Britain and America. The last cord now is broken, the people of England are presenting addresses against us. There are injuries which nature cannot forgive; she would cease to be nature if she did. As well can the lover forgive the ravisher of his mistress, as the continent forgive the murderers of Britain. The Almighty hath implanted in us these inextinguishable feelings for good and wise purposes. They are the guardians of his image in our hearts. They distinguish us from the herd of common animals. The social compact would dissolve, and justice be extirpated from the earth, or have only a casual existence, were we callous to the touches of affection. The robber and the murderer would often escape unpunished, did not the injuries which our tempers sustain, provoke us into justice.

O ye that love mankind! Ye that dare oppose not only the tyranny but the tyrant, stand forth! Every spot of the old world is overrun with oppression. Freedom hath been hunted round the globe. Asia and Africa have long expelled her. Europe regards her like a stranger, and England hath given her warning to depart. O receive the fugitive, and prepare in time an asylum for mankind!

—PAINE, *Common Sense, passim.*

5. COLONEL CARTER CALLS IT "RASCALLY AND NONSENSICAL"

Diary of Colonel Landon Carter.

14 Wednesday, February, 1776. I see the Philadelphia pamphlet called *Common Sense* is much advertised in Philadelphia, and it is pretended to be written by an Englishman. If true, it is really much to be suspected of its secret intentions to fix an ill impression that the Americans are resolved not to be reconciled. And, indeed, that matter is encouraged under the most absurd arguments in the world. But I do suppose it to be the concealed topic of even some in the Congress, though they have so repeatedly contradicted, and though they have so severely reprehended Dr. Cooper some time ago, who actually charged them with a design of independency. I have written an answer to the Extracts published by Purdie, but as I do understand by the advertizements, though it is said to be in great demand, the new edition is to contain many additions, I would wait to see what they are; for the present impression of it is quite scandalous and disgraces the American cause much; which, as it is reasonably imagined to be supported by almighty mercy, I would not have its original justice, constitutional freedom, in the least sullied. . . .

24 Saturday, February, 1776. I was at Col. Tayloe's yesterday. Jones was there. At first he introduced the pamphlet called *Common Sense*, of Philadelphia production, as a most incomparable performance. I replied it was as rascally and nonsensical as possible, for it was only a sophisticated attempt to throw all men out of principles, and I showed him several parts, and it was as much the random of a despot as anything could be, for it declared every man a damned scoundrel that didn't think as he did, a coward and sycophant; and, after reducing mankind to mere brutish nature, that of an implacable and unforgiving temper, it tells us it is that image of God at first implanted in us. Just as if he who said "Father, forgive them," etc., in his expiring moments, intended to instance himself on the cross as an example of unforgiveness. This man writes for independency, and is under the necessity of stating an independence in man at his creation, when it is evident he must be a social being. . . .

29 Friday, March, 1776. . . . This R. H. is a prodigious admirer, if not partly a writer in the pamphlet *Common Sense*, which is so violent for an independency as to call every man who is not as absurdly implacable as he is a damned rascal and sycophant, that is, a coward. I could not help expressing my detestation at so brutish an author, who must, from the very appellation, be a tyrant in his own heart and, to be sure, a very fit person to head an aristocratic power which must generate from this independency reduced into ever so formal a republican show, and this, no doubt, the lowest in oratory has sunk deep in his own mind. But if Landon will go to town, I will write by him and strive to disappoint these artists, even in revenge.

I was yesterday told that one Robinson, from Philadelphia, has told somebody that independency was thrice proposed in the Congress, but it was each time thrown out by a vast majority; and that to the northward nine-tenths of the people are violently against it. What an opprobrium must this be to these gentlemen of the Congress who not only denied their tendency to independency when they were charged with it by writers, but have over and over again told the whole British world that they only desired to be re-instated as they were in 1763!

13 Saturday, April 1776. . . . I begin now more and more to see that the pamphlet called *Common Sense*, supporting independency, is written by a member of the Congress; for every now and then, when it is answered to the northward, some one or another, perhaps member of the same club, is sure to threaten those who write against it with the terrors of disuniting the Colonies and offending the majesty of the people of particular places. This is comical. *Common Sense* has no uneasiness of this sort, though he offends against even sense and truth and even against his own position—nay, though he advances new and dangerous doctrines to the peace and happiness of every society. And yet the creature boasts that he is not or has not been answered.

—CARTER, "Diary," *William & Mary Quarterly,* XVI, 149-152, 258-264.

IV. INDEPENDENCE LIKE A TORRENT

By spring of 1776 the current was flowing swiftly toward independence. Washington's victory before Boston explained, in part, the new note of confidence, and so, too, the public reaction to Common Sense. *But most important, in all probability, was the growing realization that the policy of George III left the colonists no feasible alternative. In any event after mid-February Congress took one decisive step after another. On February 18 it authorized privateers; on February 26 it placed an embargo on exports to Britain and the British West Indies; on March 3 it sent Silas Deane to France to negotiate for aid, and instructed him to assure Vergennes "that there was a great appearance that the colonies would come to a total separation"; on March 14 it voted to disarm all Loyalists; on April 6 it opened American ports to the trade of all nations except Britain.*

Perhaps even more important was the swift change of sentiment in the states. Almost everywhere, except in the Middle States, the radicals succeeded in getting control of the machinery of government, and committing their states to independence. As early as March 26 South Carolina adopted a constitution which by implication, at least, repudiated the royal tie. On April 12 North Carolina took the bold step of instructing her delegates to support independence, and early in May Rhode Island followed her lead.

Virginia and Massachusetts had precipitated the issue with the mother country; now at last both embraced the logical conclusion of their policies and their arguments, and committed themselves to independence. On May 10 the Provisional Congress of Massachusetts voted, with characteristic concern for democratic processes, to sound out opinion in the towns on the question of independence. All through May and June the freemen of Massachusetts met in their town meetings, solemnly debated the great question, and voted for independence. Here and there was heard a dissenting or a cautious voice, but on the whole it was clear that in Massachusetts public opinion was well ahead of official opinion on this issue.

Even more important was the decision in Virginia. There by his short-sighted and uncompromising tactics, Lord Dunmore had antagonized almost all moderates and waverers, and when a Convention met at Williamsburg on May 6, support for independence was well-nigh unanimous. The question was not, in fact, whether the Convention would vote for separation, but how it would do so: by independent act, or by instructing delegates in Congress to act with other states. Curiously enough it was the moderate Edmund Pendle-ton who proposed to move decisively for independence, and the fiery Patrick Henry who now wanted to wait on the action of sister states and on foreign aid. On May 15 Pendleton's resolution calling on the Congress to vote inde-pendence passed unanimously. That night the old capital was illuminated while enthusiastic Patriots rang bells, fired salutes, hauled down the British flag and raised a "Union Flag of the American States."

The Virginia Resolutions did not reach Philadelphia until May 27, but meantime Congress itself had taken a step which John Adams, at least, thought decisive. Early in May, Adams, now hot for action, had introduced a resolution instructing every colony to adopt such government "as shall best conduce to the happiness and safety of their constituents in particular, and America in general." This resolution was adopted on May 10; five days later—just as Virginia was acting—Congress adopted a preamble to the resolution which was a sort of trial run on independence. So at least said Adams who wrote exul-tantly to his wife that "Great Britain has at last driven America to the last step, a complete separation from her; a total absolute independence, not only of her Parliament, but of her Crown, for such is the amount of the resolve."

1. "Let Us under God Trust Our Cause to the Sword"

Samuel Adams to James Warren.

Philadelphia, April 16, 1776

My Dear Sir,—I have not yet congratulated you on the unexpected and happy change of our affairs in the removal of the Rebel army from Boston. Our worthy friend Major Hawley in his letter to me declines giving me joy on this occasion. He thinks it best to put off the ceremony till the Congress shall proclaim Independency. In my opinion, however, it becomes us to rejoyce and religiously to acknowledge the goodness of the Supreme Being who in this instance hath signally appeared for us. Our countrymen are too wise to suffer this favorable event to put them off their guard. They will fortify the harbour of Boston, still defend the sea coasts and keep the military spirit universally alive.

I perfectly agree with the Major in his opinion of the necessity of pro-claiming Independency. The salvation of this country depends upon its being done speedily. I am anxious to have it done. Every day's delay trys my patience. I can give you not the least color of a reason why it is not done. We are told that Commissioners are coming out to offer us such terms of reconciliation as we may with safety accept of. Why then should we shut the door? This is all amusement. I am exceedingly disgusted when I hear it mentioned. Experience should teach us to pay no regard to it. We know that it has been the constant practice of the King and his junto ever since this struggle began to endeavor to make us believe their designs were pacifick, while they have been meditating the most destructive plans, and they insult our understandings by attempting thus to impose upon us even while they are putting these plans into execution.

Can the King repeal or dispense with Acts of Parliament? Would he repeal the detestable Acts which we have complained of, if it was in his power? Did he ever show a disposition to do acts of justice and redress the grievances of his subjects? Why then do gentlemen expect it? They do not scruple to own that he is a tyrant; are they then willing to be his slaves and dependent upon a nation so lost to all sense of liberty and virtue as to enable and encourage him to act the tyrant? This has been done by the British nation against the remonstrances of common honesty and common sense. They are now doing it and will continue to do it, until we break the band of connection and publickly avow an independence.

It is folly for us to suffer ourselves any longer to be amused. Reconciliation upon reasonable terms is no part of their plan: the only alternative is independence or slavery. Their designs still are as they ever have been to subjugate us. Our unalterable resolution should be to be free. They have attempted to subdue us by force, but God be praised! in vain. Their arts may be more dangerous than their arms. Let us then renounce all treaty with them upon any score but that of total separation, and under God trust our cause to our swords.

One of our moderate prudent Whigs would be startled at what I now write—I do not correspond with such kind of men. You know I never overmuch admired them. Their moderation has brought us to this pass, and if they were to be regarded, they would continue the conflict a century. There are such moderate men here, but their principles are daily going out of fashion. The child Independence is now struggling for birth. I trust that in a short time it will be brought forth and in spite of Pharaoh all America shall hail the dignified stranger.

—Warren-Adams Letters, I, 224-225.

2. "For God's Sake Let There Be a Full Revolution"

Joseph Hawley to Elbridge Gerry.

Watertown, May 1, 1776

My Dear Sir,

The tories dread a declaration of independency and a course of conduct on that plan more than death. They console themselves with a belief that the southern colonies will not accede to it. My hand and heart is full of it. There will be no abiding union without it. When the colonies come to be pressed with taxes they will divide and crumble to pieces. Will a government stand on recommendations? They will not. Can we subsist, and support our trading people without trade? It appears more and more every day in the country and the army that we cannot. Nay, without a real continental government our army will overrun us, and people will by and by, sooner than you may be aware of, call for their old constitutions, and as they did in England after Cromwell's death, call in Charles the Second. For God's sake let there be a full revolution, or all has been done in vain. Independence and a well planned continental government will save us. God bless you. Amen and amen. J.H.

—AUSTIN, *Life of Elbridge Gerry*, pp. 175-176.

3. "EVERY DAY ROLLS IN UPON US INDEPENDENCE LIKE A TORRENT"

John Adams to James Warren.

May 20, 1776

My Dear Sir,—Every post and every day rolls in upon us Independence like a torrent. The delegates from Georgia made their appearance this day in Congress with unlimited powers and these gentlemen themselves are very firm. South Carolina has erected her government and given her delegates ample powers, and they are firm enough. North Carolina have given theirs full powers, after repealing an instruction given last August against Confederation and Independence. This days post has brought a multitude of letters from Virginia, all of which breath the same spirit. They agree they shall institute a government—all are agreed in this they say. Here are four Colonies to the southward who are perfectly agreed now with the four to the northward. Five in the middle are not yet quite so ripe; but they are very near it. I expect that New York will come to a fresh election of delegates in the course of this week, give them full powers, and determine to institute a government.

The Convention of New Jersey is about meeting and will assume a government.

Pennsylvania Assembly meets this day and it is said will repeal their instruction to their delegates which has made them so exceedingly obnoxious to America in general, and their own constituents in particular.

We have had an entertaining maneuvre this morning in the State House yard. The Committee of the City summoned a meeting at nine o'clock in the State House yard to consider of the Resolve of Congress of the fifteenth instant. The weather was very rainy, and the meeting was in the open air like the Comitia of the Romans, a stage was erected *extempore* for the moderator and the few orators to ascend——Col. Roberdeau was the Moderator; Col. McKean, Col. Cadwallader and Col. Matlack the principal orators. It was the very first town meeting I ever saw in Philadelphia and it was conducted with great order, decency and propriety.

The first step taken was this: the Moderator produced the Resolve of Congress of the 15th inst. and read it with a loud stentorian voice that might be heard a quarter of a mile. "Whereas his Brittanic Majesty, etc." As soon as this was read, the multitude, several thousands, some say, tho so wett, rended the welkin with three cheers, hatts flying as usual, etc.

Then a number of resolutions were produced, and moved, and determined with great unanimity. These resolutions I will send you as soon as published. The drift of the whole was that the Assembly was not a body properly constituted, authorized, and qualified to carry the resolve for instituting a new government into execution and therefore that a Convention should be called. And at last they voted to support and defend the measure of a Convention, at the utmost hazard and at all events, etc.

The Delaware Government, generally, is of the same opinion with the best Americans, very orthodox in their faith and very exemplary in their practice. Maryland remains to be mentioned. That is so eccentric a Colony—sometimes so hot, sometimes so cold; now so high, then so low—that I know not what to say about it or to expect from it. I have often wished it could exchange places with Halifax. When they get agoing I expect some wild extravagant flight or other from it. To be sure they must go beyond every body else when they begin to go.

Thus I have rambled through the continent, and you will perceive by this state of it, that we can't be very remote from the most decisive measures and the most critical events. What do you think must be my sensations when I see the Congress now daily passing resolutions which I most earnestly pressed for against wind and tide twelve months ago? and which I have not omitted to labour for a month together from that time to this? What do you think must be my reflections when I see the Farmer Dickinson himself now confessing the falsehood of all his prophecies, and the truth of mine, and confessing himself now for instituting governments, forming a Continental Constitution, making alliances with foreigners, opening ports and all that—and confessing that the defence of the Colonies and preparations for defence have been neglected, in consequence of fond delusive hopes and deceitfull expectations?

I assure you this is no gratification of my vanity.

The gloomy prospect of carnage and devastation that now presents itself in every part of the continent, and which has been in the most express and decisive, nay dogmatical terms foretold by me a thousand times, is too affecting to give me pleasure. It moves my keenest indignation. Yet I dare not hint at these things for I hate to give pain to gentlemen whom I believe sufficiently punished by their own reflections.

                                        —*Warren-Adams Letters,* I, 249-251.

4. Will the Towns Support Independence?

Massachusetts House of Representatives to the Towns.

                                                        May 10, 1776

Resolved, As the opinion of this House that the inhabitants of each Town in this Colony ought, in full meeting warned for that purpose, to advise the person or persons who shall be chosen to represent them in the next General Court whether that, if the honourable Congress should, for the safety of the said Colony, declare them independent of the Kingdom of Great Britain, they, the said inhabitants, will solemnly engage, with their lives and fortunes, to support them in the measure.

                              —Force, *American Archives,* 4th Series, VI, 420.

5. Massachusetts Town Meetings Call for Independence

A. malden declares why independence is necessary

At a legal meeting of the inhabitants of the town of Malden (Mass.), May 27, 1776, it was voted unanimously that the following instructions be given to their representative, viz. to Mr. Ezra Sargeant.

Sir—A resolution of the hon. house of representatives, calling upon the several towns in this colony to express their minds in respect to the important question of American independence, is the occasion of our now instructing you. The time was, sir, when we loved the king and the people of Great Britain with an affection truly filial; we felt ourselves interested in their glory; we shared in their joys and sorrows; we cheerfully poured the fruit of all our labours into the lap of our mother country, and without reluctance expended our blood and our treasure in their cause.

These were our sentiments toward Great Britain while she continued to act the part of a parent state; we felt ourselves happy in our connection with her, nor wished it to be dissolved; but our sentiments are altered, it is now the ardent wish of our soul that America may become a free and independent state.

A sense of unprovoked injuries will arouse the resentment of the most peaceful. Such injuries these colonies have received from Britain. Unjustifiable claims have been made by the king and his minions to tax us without our consent; these claims have been prosecuted in a manner cruel and unjust to the highest degree. The frantic policy of administration hath induced them to send fleets and armies to America; that, by depriving us of our trade, and cutting the throats of our brethren, they might awe us into submission, and erect a system of despotism in America, which should so far enlarge the influence of the crown as to enable it to rivet their shackles upon the people of Great Britain.

This plan was brought to a crisis upon the ever memorable nineteenth of April. We remember the fatal day! the expiring groans of our countrymen yet vibrate on our ears! and we now behold the flames of their peaceful dwellings ascending to Heaven! we hear their blood crying to us from the ground for vengeance! charging us, as we value the peace of their names, to have no further connection with—who can unfeelingly hear of the slaughter of—and composedly sleep with their blood upon his soul. The manner in which the war has been prosecuted hath confirmed us in these sentiments; piracy and murder, robbery and breach of faith, have been conspicuous in the conduct of the king's troops: defenceless towns have been attacked and destroyed: the ruins of Charlestown, which are daily in our view, daily reminds us of this: the cries of the widow and the orphan demand our attention; they demand that the hand of pity should wipe the tear from their eye, and that the sword of their country should avenge their wrongs. We long entertained hope that the spirit of the British nation would once more induce them to assert their own and our rights, and bring to condign punishment the elevated villains who have trampled upon the sacred rights of men and affronted the majesty of the people. We hoped in vain; they have lost their love of freedom, they have lost their spirit of just resentment; we therefore renounce with disdain our connexion with a kingdom of slaves; we bid a final adieu to Britain.

Could an accommodation now be effected, we have reason to think that it would be fatal to the liberties of America; we should soon catch the contagion of venality and dissipation, which hath led Britains to lawless domination. Were we placed in the situation we were in 1763; were the powers of appointing to offices, and commanding the militia, in the hands of governors, our arts, trade and manufactures would be cramped; nay, more than this, the life of every man who has been active in the cause of his country would be endangered.

For these reasons, as well as many others which might be produced, we are confirmed in the opinion that the present age would be deficient in their duty to God, their posterity and themselves, if they do not establish an American republic. This is the only form of government which we wish to see established; for we can never be willingly subject to any other King than he who, being possessed of infinite wisdom, goodness and rectitude, is alone fit to possess unlimited power.

—Massachusetts Archives, CLVI, 101.

B. scituate freemen pledge their lives to independence

Instructions to Nathan Cushing, Esqr., Representative of the Town of Scituate.

June 4th, 1776

The Inhabitants of this Town being called together on the recommendation of our General Assembly to Signify our minds on the great point of Independence on Great-Britain, think fit to Instruct you on that head.

The Ministry of that Kingdom, having formed a design of Subjecting the Colonies to a distant, external and absolute power in all Cases whatsoever, wherein the Colonies have not, nor in the nature of things can have any share by Representation, have, for a course of years past, exerted their utmost Art and Endeavours to put the same plan, so destructive to both Countries, into Execution. But finding it, through the noble and virtuous opposition of the Sons of Freedom, impracticable by means of mere political Artifice and Corruption, they have at length had a fatal Recourse to a Standing Army, so repugnant to the nature of a free Government, to fire and Sword, to Bloodshed and Devastation, calling in the aid of foreign Troops, as well as endeavouring to stir up the Savages of the wilderness to exercise their barbarities upon us, being determined, by all appearances, if practicable, to extirpate the Americans from the face of the Earth, unless they tamely resign the Rights of humanity, and to repeople this once happy Country with the ready Sons of Vassalage, if such can be found.

We therefor, Apprehending such a subjection utterly inconsistant with the just rights and blessings of Society, unanimously Instruct you to endeavour that our Delegates in Congress be informed, in case that Representative Body of the Continent should think fit to declare the Colonies Independant of Great

Britain, of our readiness and determination to assist with our Lives and Fortunes in Support of that, we apprehend, necessary Measure.
—MASSACHUSETTS ARCHIVES, CLVI, 103.

C. NATICK FINDS IMPROPRIETY IN COLONIAL SUBORDINATION

At a Meeting of the Town of Natick, June 20th, 1776
. . . It was unanimously voted that in consideration of the many Acts of
the brittish Parliament passed at diverse Sessions of the same within about 13
years past, relating to said Colonies especially those within the two or three
last years, by which every Idea of Moderation, Justice, Humanity and Christianity are intirely laid aside and those principles and measures adopted and
pursued which would disgrace the most uninlightened and uncivilized Tribe
of aboriginal natives in the most interior parts of this extensive continent—And
also in consideration of the glaring Impropriety, Incapacity and fatal Tendency of any State whatever at the Distance of 3000 Miles to legislate for these
colonies, which at the same Time are so numerous, so knowing and capable
of Legislating, or to have a negative upon those Laws which they in their
respective assemblies, and by their united Representatives in general Congress
shall from Time to Time enact and establish for themselves—and upon diverse
other considerations, which for Brevity sake we omit to mention—We the
Inhabitants of Natick in Town Meeting assembled Do hereby declare . . . that
should the honorable continental Congress declare these American Colonies
independent of the Kingdom of Great Brittain we will with our Lives and
fortunes join with the other Inhabitants of this Colony and with those of the
other Colonies in supporting them in said Measure which we look upon to be
both important and necessary and which, if we may be permitted to suggest
our opinion, the sooner it is come into we shall have fewer Difficulties to
conflict with and the grand objects of peace, Liberty and Safety will be more
likely speedily to be restored and established in our once happy land.
—MASSACHUSETTS ARCHIVES, CLVI, 113.

6. VIRGINIA RESOLVES FOR INDEPENDENCE

In Convention, May the 15th 1776
Present One Hundred and Twelve Members
Forasmuch as all the endeavours of the United Colonies by the most decent
representations and petitions to the king and parliament of Great Britain to
restore peace and security to America under the British government and a
re-union with that people upon just and liberal terms instead of a redress of
grievances have produced from an imperious and vindictive administration
increased insult, oppression and a vigorous attempt to effect our total destruction. By a late act, all these colonies are declared to be in rebellion and out
of the protection of the British crown, our properties subjected to confiscation, our people, when captivated, compelled to join in the murder and
plunder of their relations and countrymen, and all former rapine and oppression of Americans declared legal and just. Fleets and armies are raised, and
the aid of foreign troops engaged to assist these destructive purposes. The
king's representative in this colony hath not only withheld all the powers of

government from operating for our safety, but, having retired on board an armed ship, is carrying on a piratical and savage war against us, tempting our slaves by every artifice to resort to him, and training and employing them against their masters. In this state of extreme danger, we have no alternative left but an abject submission to the will of those over-bearing tyrants, or a total separation from the crown and government of Great Britain, uniting and exerting the strength of all America for defence, and forming alliances with foreign powers for commerce and aid in war:

Wherefore, appealing to the SEARCHER OF HEARTS for the sincerity of former declarations, expressing our desire to preserve the connection with that nation, and that we are driven from that inclination by their wicked councils, and the eternal laws of self-preservation:

RESOLVED unanimously, that the delegates appointed to represent this colony in General Congress be instructed to propose to that respectable body to declare the United Colonies free and independent states, absolved from all allegiance to, or dependence upon, the crown or parliament of Great Britain; and that they give the assent of this colony to such declaration, and to whatever measures may be thought proper and necessary by the Congress for forming foreign alliances and a confederation of the colonies, at such time, and in such manner, as to them shall seem best; *Provided,* that the power of forming government for, and the regulations of the internal concerns of each colony, be left to the respective colonial legislatures.

RESOLVED unanimously, that a committee be appointed to prepare a *Declaration of Rights*, and such a plan of government as will be most likely to maintain peace and order in this colony, and secure substantial and equal liberty to the people.

JOHN TAXEWELL   EDMD. PENDLETON P.
Clerk of the Convention
                —BOYD, ed., *Papers of Thomas Jefferson*, I, 290-291.

7. RECOMMENDATIONS BY THE CONGRESS TO ESTABLISH NEW GOVERNMENTS

In Congress, May 15, 1776

Whereas his Britannick Majesty, in conjunction with the Lords and Commons of Great Britain, has, by a late act of Parliament, excluded the inhabitants of these United Colonies from the protection of his Crown: And *whereas* no answer whatever to the humble petition of the Colonies for redress of grievances and reconciliation with Great Britain has been, or is likely to be, given; but the whole force of that Kingdom, aided by foreign mercenaries, is to be exerted for the destruction of the good people of these Colonies: And *whereas* it appears absolutely irreconciliable to reason and good conscience for the people of these colonies now to take the oaths and affirmations necessary for the support of any Government under the Crown of Great Britain; and it is necessary that the exercise of every kind of authority under the said Crown should be totally suppressed, and all the powers of Government exerted under the authority of the people of the Colonies, for the preservation of internal peace, virtue, and good order, as well as for the defence of their lives, liberties and properties, against the hostile invasions and cruel depredations of their enemies: Therefore

Resolved, That it be recommended to the respective Assemblies and Conventions of the United Colonies, where no Government sufficient to the exigencies of their affairs has been hitherto established, to adopt such Government as shall, in the opinion of the Representatives of the People, best conduce to the happiness and safety of their constituents in particular and America in general.

By Order of Congress, JOHN HANCOCK, *President*
—FORCE, *American Archives,* 4th Series, VI, 466.

V. THE FINAL DEBATE

On June 7 Richard Henry Lee of Virginia introduced the momentous resolution calling for a declaration of independence, foreign alliances, and a confederation of the American states. This bold proposal precipitated a warm debate which made clear that though the majority of the delegations in Congress were ready for independence, the Middle States "were not yet ripe for bidding adieu to the British connection." It was therefore agreed to postpone action for three weeks; meantime a committee was appointed to draft the necessary declaration. The three-week delay was fatal to the temporizers. On June 14 both Delaware and Connecticut instructed for independence; the next day New Hampshire followed. On that day, too, New Jersey ousted the Loyalist Governor Franklin, and a few days later sent a new delegation to the Congress, authorized to vote independence. And on June 28 Maryland swung into line. The barrier of the Middle Colonies had been broken.

The first day of July, Congress took up the first Lee resolution. There was a stirring debate; Dickinson spoke eloquently for delay; Adams and—apparently—Richard Henry Lee urged the necessity of action. The vote that day disappointed the radicals. South Carolina, surprisingly enough, voted against independence, and so did Pennsylvania; Delaware was divided, and New York, then in the throes of reorganizing itself, refrained from action. Nine to four was not a satisfactory vote for so momentous an issue. That night saw the radicals working with herculean energy to intimidate the intransigents and convert the moderates. Riding all night, Caesar Rodney covered the eighty miles between Dover and Philadelphia in time to swing the vote of Delaware to independence. The delegates from South Carolina changed their minds. Two Pennsylvania dissidents, Dickinson and Robert Morris, stayed away, James Wilson changed his mind, or his vote, and Pennsylvania moved at last into the ranks of independence. That left only New York, and New York courteously refrained from casting a vote. So on July 2 the Congress could vote unanimously for independence. The decree had indeed gone forth.

John Adams and Jefferson are the best historians of independence, and here as in the next section we allow them to tell the story. Jefferson's record of the great debate of June 1776 is, according to Julian Boyd, "the best single source of information concerning the movement toward independence." Just when it was written we do not know, but possibly in the late summer or early fall of 1776, and certainly not later than the end of the war. Its authenticity is, in any event, beyond dispute. Unhappily Jefferson, usually a voluminous and a magnificent letter writer, appears to have written very few letters during June, and those of a purely routine character; happily John Adams, equally voluminous and perhaps more entertaining, sent out a stream of letters which tell us something of what was happening and a great deal about that irresistible figure, John Adams.

1. RICHARD HENRY LEE INTRODUCES SOME FATEFUL RESOLUTIONS

June 7, 1776

RESOLVED, That these United Colonies are, and of right ought to be, free and independent States, that they are absolved from all allegiance to the British Crown, and that all political connection between them and the State of Great Britain is, and ought to be totally dissolved.

That it is expedient forthwith to take the most effectual measures for forming foreign Alliances.

That a plan of confederation be prepared and transmitted to the respective Colonies for their consideration and approbation.

—*Journals of the Continental Congress, V, 425.*

2. "THE SENSIBLE PART OF THE HOUSE OPPOSED THE MOTION"

Edward Rutledge to John Jay.

June 8, 1776

The Congress sat till 7 o'clock this evening in consequence of a motion of Richard Henry Lee's rendering ourselves a free and independent state. The sensible part of the house opposed the motion—they had no objection to forming a scheme of a treaty which they would send to France by proper persons and uniting this continent by a confederacy. They saw no wisdom in a declaration of independence, nor any other purpose to be enforced by it but placing ourselves in the power of those with whom we mean to treat, giving our enemy notice of our intentions before we had taken any steps to execute them and thereby enabling them to counteract us in our intentions and rendering ourselves ridiculous in the eyes of foreign powers by attempting to bring them into an union with us before we had united with each other. For daily experience evinces that the inhabitants of every colony consider themselves at liberty to do as they please upon almost every occasion. And a man must have the impudence of a New Englander to propose in our present disjointed state any treaty (honourable to us) to a nation now at peace. No reason could be assigned for pressing into this measure but the reason of every madman, a show of our spirit.

The event, however, was that the question was postponed; it is to be renewed on Monday when I mean to move that it should be postponed for 3 weeks or months. In the meantime, the plan of confederation and the scheme of treaty may go on. I don't know whether I shall succeed in this motion; I think not, it is at least doubtful. However, I must do what is right in my own eyes, and consequences must take care of themselves.

I wish you had been here. The whole argument was sustained on one side by Robert Livingston, James Wilson, John Dickinson and myself and by the power of all New England, Virginia and Georgia at the other.

—BURNETT, *Letters of Members of the Continental Congress*, I, 476-477.

3. JEFFERSON RECORDS THE GREAT DEBATE OVER INDEPENDENCE

Notes of Proceedings in the Continental Congress.

June 7 to August 1, 1776

Friday, June 7, 1776, the Delegates from Virginia moved in obedience to instructions from their constituents that the Congress should declare that these United colonies are & of right ought to be free & independent states, that they are absolved from all allegiance to the British crown, and that all political connection between them and the state of Great Britain is & ought to be totally dissolved; that measures should be immediately taken for procuring the assistance of foreign powers, and a Confederation be formed to bind the colonies more closely together.

The house being obliged to attend at that time to some other business, the proposition was referred to the next day when the members were ordered to attend punctually at ten o'clock.

Saturday June 8, they proceeded to take it into consideration and referred it to a committee of the whole, into which they immediately resolved themselves, and passed that day & Monday the 10th in debating on the subject.

It was argued by Wilson, Robert R. Livingston, E. Rutledge, Dickinson and others:

That tho' they were friends to the measures themselves, and saw the impossibility that we should ever again be united with Gr. Britain, yet they were against adopting them at this time:

That the conduct we had formerly observed was wise & proper now, of deferring to take any capital step till the voice of the people drove us into it:

That they were our power, & without them our declarations could not be carried into effect:

That the people of the middle colonies (Maryland, Delaware, Pennsylva., the Jersies & N. York) were not yet ripe for bidding adieu to British connection but that they were fast ripening & in a short time would join in the general voice of America:

That the resolution entered into by this house on the 15th of May for suppressing the exercise of all powers derived from the crown, had shewn, by the ferment into which it had thrown these middle colonies, that they had not yet accomodated their minds to a separation from the mother country:

That some of them had expressly forbidden their delegates to consent to such a declaration, and others had given no instructions, & consequently no powers, to give such consent:

That if the delegates of any particular colony had no power to declare such colony independent, certain they were the others could not declare it for them; the colonies as yet being perfectly independent of each other:

That the assembly of Pennsylvania was now sitting above stairs, their convention would sit within a few days, the convention of New York was now sitting, & those of the Jersies and Delaware counties would meet on the Monday following & it was probable these bodies would take up the question of Independence & would declare to their delegates the voice of their state:

That if such a declaration should now be agreed to, these delegates must retire & possibly their colonies might secede from the Union:

That such a secession would weaken us more than could be compensated by any foreign alliance:

That in the event of such a division, foreign powers would either refuse to join themselves to our fortunes, or having us so much in their power as that desperate declaration would place us, they would insist on terms proportionably more hard & prejudicial:

That we had little reason to expect an alliance with those to whom alone as yet we had cast our eyes:

That France & Spain had reason to be jealous of that rising power which would one day certainly strip them of all their American possessions:

That it was more likely they should form a connection with the British court, who, if they should find themselves unable otherwise to extricate themselves from their difficulties, would agree to a partition of our territories, restoring Canada to France, & the Floridas to Spain, to accomplish for themselves a recovery of these colonies:

That it would not be long before we should receive certain information of the disposition of the French court, from the agent whom we had sent to Paris for that purpose:

That if this disposition should be favorable, by waiting the event of the present campaign, which we all hope would be successful, we should have reason to expect an alliance on better terms:

That this would in fact work no delay of any effectual aid from such ally, as, from the advance of the season & distance of our situation, it was impossible we could receive any assistance during this campaign:

That it was prudent to fix among ourselves the terms on which we would form an alliance, before we declared we would form one at all events:

And that if these were agreed on & our Declaration of Independence ready by the time our Ambassadour should be prepared to sail, it would be as well, as to go into that Declaration at this day:

On the other side it was urged by J. Adams, Wythe and others:

That no gentleman had argued against the policy of the right of separation from Britain, nor had supposed it possible we should ever renew our connection: that they had only opposed it's being now declared:

That the question was not whether, by a declaration of independence, we should make ourselves what we are not; but whether we should declare a fact which already exists:

That as to the people or parliament of England, we had alwais been independent of them, their restraints on our trade deriving efficacy from our acquiescence only & not from any rights they possessed of imposing them, & that so far our connection had been federal only, & was now dissolved by the commencement of hostilities:

That as to the king, we had bound to him by allegiance, but that this bond was now dissolved by his assent to the late act of parliament, by which he declares us out of his protection; and by his levying war on us, a fact which had long ago proved us out of his protection; it being a certain position in law that allegiance & protection are reciprocal, the one ceasing when the other is withdrawn:

That James the IId. never declared the people of England out of his protection yet his action proved it & parliament declared it:

No delegates then can be denied, or ever want, a power of declaring an existent truth:

That the delegates from the Delaware counties having declared their constituents ready to join, there are only two colonies, Pennsylvania & Maryland whose delegates are absolutely tied up, and that these had by their instructions only reserved a right of confirming or rejecting the measure:

That the instructions from Pennsylvania might be accounted for from the times in which they were drawn, near a twelvemonth ago, since which the face of affairs has totally changed:

That within that time it had become apparent that Britain was determined to accept nothing less than a carte blanche, and that the king's answer to the Lord Mayor, Alderman & common council of London, which had come to hand four days ago, must have satisfied every one of this point:

That the people wait for us to lead the way:

That they are in favour of the measure, tho' the instructions given by some of their *representatives* are not:

That the voice of the representatives is not alwais consonant with the voice of the people, and that this is remarkably the case in these middle colonies:

That the effect of the resolution of the 15th. of May has proved this, which, raising the murmurs of some in t! colonies of Pennsylvania & Maryland, called forth the opposing voice of the freer part of the people, & proved them to be the majority, even in these colonies:

That the backwardness of these two colonies might be ascribed partly to the influence of proprietary power & connections, & partly to their having not yet been attacked by the enemy:

That these causes were not likely to be soon removed, as there seemed no probability that the enemy would make either of these the seat of this summer's war:

That it would be in vain to wait either weeks or months for perfect unanimity, since it was impossible that all men should ever become of one sentiment on any question:

That the conduct of some colonies from the beginning of this contest, had given reason to suspect it was their settled policy to keep in the rear of the confederacy, that their particular prospect might be better even in the worst event:

That therefore it was necessary for those colonies who had thrown themselves forward & hazarded all from the beginning, to come forward now also, and put all again to their own hazard;

That the history of the Dutch revolution, of whom three states only confederated at first proved that a secession of some colonies would not be so dangerous as some apprehended:

That a declaration of Independence alone could render it consistent with European delicacy for European powers to treat with us, or even to receive an Ambassador from us:

That till this they would not receive our vessels into their ports, nor acknowledge the adjudications of our courts of Admiralty to be legitimate, in cases of capture of British vessels:

That tho' France & Spain may be jealous of our rising power, they must think it will be much more formidable with the addition of Great Britain; and will therefore see it their interest to prevent a coalition; but should they refuse, we shall be but where we are; whereas without trying we shall never know whether they will aid us or not:

That the present campaign may be unsuccessful, & therefore we had better propose an alliance while our affairs wear a hopeful aspect:

That to wait the event of this campaign will certainly work delay, because during this summer France may assist us effectually by cutting off those supplies of provisions from England & Ireland on which the enemy's armies here are to depend; or by setting in motion the great power they have collected in the West Indies, & calling our enemy to the defence of the possessions they have there:

That it would be idle to lose time in settling the terms of alliance, till we had first determined we would enter into alliance:

That it is necessary to lose no time in opening a trade for our people, who will want clothes, and will want money too for the paiment of taxes:

And that the only misfortune is that we did not enter into alliance with France six months sooner, as besides opening their ports for the vent of our last year's produce, they might have marched an army into Germany and prevented the petty princes there from selling their unhappy subjects to subdue us.

—Boyd, ed., *Papers of Thomas Jefferson*, I, 309 ff.

4. "The Decree Is Gone Forth"

John Adams to Patrick Henry.

Philadelphia, June 3, 1776

My Dear Sir,—

. . . The dons, the bashaws, the grandees, the patricians, the sachems, the nabobs, call them by what names you please, sigh and groan and fret, and sometimes stamp and foam and curse, but all in vain. The decree is gone forth, and it cannot be recalled, that a more equal liberty than has prevailed in other parts of the earth must be established in America. The exuberance of pride which has produced an insolent domination in a few, a very few, opulent, monopolizing families, will be brought down nearer to the confines of reason and moderation than they have been used to. This is all the evil which they themselves will endure. It will do them good in this world, and in every other. For pride was not made for man, only as a tormentor.

—Adams, ed., *Works of John Adams*, IX, 387-388.

5. "A Revolution the Most Complete and Remarkable in History"

John Adams to William Cushing.

Philadelphia, June 9, 1776

... It would give me great pleasure to ride this eastern circuit with you, and prate before you at the bar, as I used to do. But I am destined to another fate, to drudgery of the most wasting, exhausting, consuming kind that I ever went through in my whole life. Objects of the most stupendous magnitude, and measures in which the lives and liberties of millions yet unborn are intimately interested, are now before us. We are in the very midst of a revolution the most complete, unexpected and remarkable of any in the history of nations. A few important subjects must be dispatched before I can return to my family. Every colony must be induced to institute a perfect government. All the colonies must confederate together in some solemn band of union. The Congress must declare the colonies free and independent States, and ambassadors must be sent abroad to foreign courts to solicit their acknowledgement of us as sovereign States, and to form with them, at least with some of them, commercial treaties of friendship and alliance. When these things are once completed, I shall think that I have answered the end of my creation, and sing my *nunc dimittis*, return to my farm, family, ride circuits, plead law, or judge causes, just which you please.

—Adams, ed., *Works of John Adams*, IX, 391.

6. "It Is Universally Acknowledged We Must Be Independent"

John Adams to John Winthrop.

Philadelphia, June 23, 1776

Your favor of June 1st is before me. It is now universally acknowledged that we are and must be independent. But still, objections are made to a declaration of it. It is said that such a declaration will arouse and unite Great Britain. But are they not already aroused and united, as much as they will be? Will not such a declaration arouse and unite the friends of liberty, the few who are left, in opposition to the present system? It is also said that such a declaration will put us in the power of foreign States; that France will take advantage of us when they see we cannot recede, and demand severe terms of us; that she, and Spain too, will rejoice to see Britain and America wasting each other. But this reasoning has no weight with me, because I am not for soliciting any political connection, or military assistance, or indeed naval, from France. I wish for nothing but commerce, a mere marine treaty with them. And this they will never grant until we make the declaration, and this, I think, they cannot refuse, after we have made it.

The advantages which will result from such a declaration are, in my opinion, very numerous and very great. After that event the colonies will hesitate no longer to complete their governments. They will establish tests, and ascertain the criminality of toryism. The presses will produce no more seditious or traitorous speculations. Slanders upon public men and measures will be lessened. The legislatures of the colonies will exert themselves to manufacture saltpetre, sulphur, powder, arms, cannon, mortars, clothing, and every thing necessary for the support of life. Our civil governments will feel a vigor hitherto unknown. Our military operations by sea and land will be conducted with greater spirit. Privateers will swarm in vast numbers. Foreigners will then exert themselves to supply us with what we want. A foreign court will not disdain to treat with us upon equal terms. Nay farther, in my opinion, such a declaration, instead of uniting the people of Great Britain against us, will raise such a storm against the measures of administration as will obstruct the war, and throw the kingdom into confusion.

A committee is appointed to prepare a confederation of the colonies, ascertaining the terms and ends of the compact and the limits of the Continental Constitution; and another committee is appointed to draw up a declaration that these colonies are free and independent States. And other committees are appointed for other purposes, as important. These committees will report in a week or two, and then the last finishing strokes will be given to the politics of this revolution. Nothing after that will remain but war. . . .

—ADAMS, *Works of John Adams*, IX, 409-410.

7. "A Bloody Conflict We Are Destined to Endure"

John Adams to Samuel Chase of Annapolis, Maryland.

Philadelphia, July 1, 1776

Your favor by the post this morning gave me much pleasure, but the generous and unanimous vote of your Convention gave me much more. It was brought into Congress this morning, just as we were entering on the great debate. That debate took up the most of the day, but it was an idle mispence of time, for nothing was said but what had been repeated and hackneyed in that room before, a hundred times, for six months past. In the committee of the whole, the question was carried in the affirmative, and reported to the house. A colony desired it to be postponed until to-morrow. Then it will pass by a great majority; perhaps with almost unanimity. Yet I cannot promise this. Because one or two gentlemen may possibly be found, who will vote point-blank against the known and declared sense of their constituents. Maryland, however, I have the pleasure to inform you, behaved well, Paca, generously and nobly. . . .

If you imagine that I expect this declaration will ward off calamities from this country, you are much mistaken. A bloody conflict we are destined to endure. This has been my opinion from the beginning. You will certainly remember my declared opinion was, at the first Congress, when we found that we could not agree upon an immediate non-exportation, that the contest would not be settled without bloodshed; and that if hostilities should once commence, they would terminate in an incurable animosity between the two countries. Every political event since the nineteenth of April, 1775, has confirmed me in this opinion. If you imagine that I flatter myself with happiness and halcyon days after a separation from Great Britain, you are mistaken again. I do not expect that our new government will be so quiet as I could wish, nor that happy harmony, confidence and affection between the colonies, that every good American ought to study, labor, and pray for, for a long time.

But freedom is a counterbalance for poverty, discord and war and more.

It is your hard lot and mine to be called into life at such a time. Yet even these times have their pleasures.

—ADAMS, ed., *Works of John Adams*, IX, 415-416.

8. JOHN ADAMS CARRIES THE DAY

From his Autobiography.

Friday, June 28, 1776. A new delegation appeared from New Jersey. Mr. William Livingston and all others who had hitherto resisted independence were left out. Richard Stockton, Francis Hopkinson and Dr. John Witherspoon were new members.

Monday, July 1. A resolution of the Convention of Maryland, passed the 28th of June, was laid before Congress, and read, as follows:

"That the instructions given to their deputies in December last be recalled, and the restriction therein contained, removed; and that their deputies to be authorized and empowered to concur with the other United Colonies, or a majority of them, in declaring the United Colonies free and independent States; in forming a compact between them, and in making foreign alliances, etc." . . .

I am not able to recollect whether it was on this or some preceding day that the greatest and most solemn debate was had on the question of independence. The subject had been in contemplation for more than a year, and frequent discussions had been had concerning it. At one time and another all the arguments for it and against it had been exhausted and were become familiar. I expected no more would be said in public, but that the question would be put and decided. Mr. Dickinson, however, was determined to bear his testimony against it with more formality. He had prepared himself apparently with great labor and ardent zeal, and in a speech of great length, and with all his eloquence, he combined together all that had before been written in pamphlets and newspapers, and all that had from time to time been said in Congress by himself and others. He conducted the debate not only with great ingenuity and eloquence, but with equal politeness and candor, and was answered in the same spirit.

No member rose to answer him, and after waiting some time in hopes that some one less obnoxious than myself, who had been all along for a year before, and still was, represented and believed to be the author of all the mischief, would move, I determined to speak.

It has been said by some of our historians that I began by an invocation to the god of eloquence. This is a misrepresentation. Nothing so puerile as this fell from me. I began by saying that this was the first time of my life that I had ever wished for the talents and eloquence of the ancient orators of Greece and Rome, for I was very sure that none of them ever had before him a question of more importance to his country and to the world. They would probably, upon less occasions than this, have begun by solemn invocations to their divinities for assistance; but the question before me appeared so simple that I had confidence enough in the plain understanding and common sense that had been given me to believe that I could answer, to the satisfaction of the House, all the arguments which had been produced, notwithstanding the abilities which had been displayed, and the eloquence with which they had been enforced.

Mr. Dickinson, some years afterwards, published his speech. I had made no preparation beforehand and never committed any minutes of mine to writing. But if I had a copy of Mr. Dickinson's before me, I would now, after nine and twenty years have elapsed, endeavor to recollect mine.

Before the final question was put, the new delegates from New Jersey came in, and Mr. Stockton, Dr. Witherspoon and Mr. Hopkinson, very respectable characters, expressed a great desire to hear the arguments. All was silence; no one would speak; all eyes were turned upon me.

Mr. Edward Rutledge came to me and said, laughing, "Nobody will speak but you upon this subject. You have all the topics so ready that you must satisfy the gentlemen from New Jersey."

I answered him, laughing, that it had so much the air of exhibiting like an actor or gladiator, for the entertainment of the audience, that I was ashamed to repeat what I had said twenty times before, and I thought nothing new could be advanced by me. The New Jersey gentlemen, however, still insisting on hearing at least a recapitulation of the arguments, and no other gentleman being willing to speak, I summed up the reasons, objections and answers in as concise a manner as I could, till at length the Jersey gentlemen said they were fully satisfied and ready for the question, which was then put and determined in the affirmative.

—ADAMS, ed., *Works of John Adams*, III, 53-58.

9. "I ARRIVED IN TIME TO GIVE MY VOICE FOR INDEPENDENCE"

Caesar Rodney to Thomas Rodney.

Philadelphia, July the 4th, 1776

Sir:

I arrived in Congress (tho detained by thunder and rain) time enough to give my voice in the matter of Independence. It is determined by the Thirteen United Colonies, without even one decenting Colony. We have now got through with the whole of the Declaration, and ordered it to be printed, so that you will soon have the pleasure of seeing it. Hand-bills of it will be printed, and sent to the armies, cities, county towns, etc. To be published or rather proclaimed in form. Don't neglect to attend closely and carefully to my harvest and you'l oblige Yours, etc.   CAESAR RODNEY

—BURNETT, *Letters of Members of the Continental Congress*, I, 528.

VI. THE GREAT DECLARATION

When on June 10 the Congress voted to postpone consideration of Lee's resolution for independence for three weeks, it appointed a committee to draft a declaration of independence, and to this committee named Thomas Jefferson, Benjamin Franklin, John Adams, Robert Livingston and Roger Sherman. This committee, in turn, delegated the task to Jefferson. Just thirty-three years old at the time, Jefferson was one of the youngest members of the Congress, and one of the newest, but already well known. He had written the Summary View, *thought by some the best statement of the Amer-*

ican case; he had drafted the answer to Lord North's proposal for reconcilia-
tion, and contributed a large, possibly a major, part to the Declaration of the
Causes and Necessity of Taking Up Arms.

Considering how articulate and literary were the members of the com-
mittee—Jefferson, Franklin and Adams wrote incessantly—we know tantaliz-
ingly little about the actual drafting of this memorable document. There is no
strictly contemporary account, and Jefferson himself, though he found time
to write about almost everything else, never found time to give a really cir-
cumstantial account of this chapter of his life. Yet it is possible to reconstruct,
from such documents as we do have, part of the story. We know, for exam-
ple, that Jefferson wrote the Declaration in two weeks, for it was worked
over by the committee and submitted to the Congress on June 28. We know
that he wrote it at his desk (still preserved) in the second-floor parlor of the
house of a young German bricklayer named Graff, and that he "turned neither
to book nor pamphlet" but drew on his store of political philosophy. We
know a good deal about the alterations by Franklin and Adams, and by the
Congress, most of them verbal, but one at least substantial—the omission of the
diatribe against slavery and the slave trade. But whatever is still uncertain and
unclear about the drafting of the Declaration, one thing is beyond dispute,
that the Declaration as we know it was the product of the mind and pen of
Thomas Jefferson.

Congress debated Jefferson's draft of the Declaration on the afternoon of
the second, on the third and part of the fourth of July, and then adopted it
"unanimously"—though New York did not vote, and New York's representa-
tive on the committee, Robert Livingston, did not sign. There was a formal
"signing" on August 2, and some desultory signing thereafter, and eventually
fifty-five Americans assured immortality for themselves by putting their sig-
natures on the document, but an impenetrable cloud conceals the actual his-
tory of the signing.

We include here five documents, or groups of documents. First is Jeffer-
son's account of the writing of the Declaration, written shortly after the
event, brief and inconclusive. Then come three accounts written almost half
a century later. The first is from the pungent pen of John Adams in reply to
an inquiry from Jefferson's inveterate enemy Timothy Pickering who wanted
to make a Fourth of July speech showing that Jefferson was not really very
important. Adams's phrase "the Frankfort advice" refers to a meeting at
Frankfort with members of the Pennsylvania delegation who urged the Mas-
sachusetts men to keep themselves in the background and let Virginia take
the lead. The second and third are by Jefferson himself, one of them setting
Pickering and Adams right on details, the other recalling the broad philo-
sophical background of the Declaration. Third comes Jefferson's "Rough
Draft" as reconstructed by the Jeffersonian scholar, Julian Boyd; it is, says
Dr. Boyd, "the most extraordinarily interesting document in American
history." We have given here only the preamble and the controversial para-
graph on slavery. Fourth is the Declaration itself, in its final form. And finally
a group of letters and accounts which suggest something of the exultation and
jubilation that greeted the decision for independence.

1. "The Committee Desired Me to Draw the Declaration"

Jefferson's own account.

It appearing in the course of these debates that the colonies of New York, New Jersey, Pennsylvania, Delaware, Maryland & South Carolina were not yet matured for falling from the parent stem, but that they were fast advancing to that state, it was thought most prudent to wait a while for them, and to postpone the final decisions to July 1, but that this might occasion as little delay as possible a committee was appointed to prepare a declaration of independence. the Commee. were J. Adams, Dr. Franklin, Roger Sherman, Robert R. Livingston & myself. committees were also appointed at the same time to prepare a plan of confederation for the colonies, and to state the terms proper to be proposed for foreign alliance.

the committee for drawing the declaration of Independence desired me to do it. it was accordingly done and being approved by them, I reported it to the house on Friday the 28th. of June when it was read and ordered to lie on the table.

on Monday the 1st. of July the house resolved itself into a commee. of the whole & resumed the consideration of the original motion made by the delegates of Virginia, which being again debated through the day, was carried in the affirmative by the votes of N. Hampshire, Connecticut, Massachusets, Rhode Island, N. Jersey, Maryland, Virginia, N. Carolina, & Georgia. S. Carolina and Pennsylvania voted against it. Delaware having but two members present, they were divided: the delegates for New York declared they were for it themselves, & were assured their constituents were for it, but that their instructions having been drawn near a twelvemonth before, when reconciliation was still the general object, they were enjoined by them to do nothing which should impede that object. they therefore thought themselves not justifiable in voting on either side, and asked leave to withdraw from the question, which was given them.

the Commee. rose & reported their resolution to the house. Mr. Rutledge of S. Carolina then requested the determination might be put off to the next day, as he believed his collegues, tho' they disapproved of the resolution, would then join in it for the sake of unanimity. the ultimate question whether the house would agree to the resolution of the committee was accordingly postponed to the next day [July 2], when it was again moved and S. Carolina concurred in voting for it. in the mean time a third member had come post from the Delaware counties and turned the vote of that colony in favor of the resolution. members of a different sentiment attending that morning from Pennsylvania also, their vote was changed, so that the whole 12 colonies who were authorized to vote at all, gave their voices for it: and within a few days the convention of N. York approved of it and thus supplied the void occasioned by the withdrawing of their delegates from the vote.

Congress proceeded the same day [July 2] to consider the declaration of Independence, which had been reported & laid on the table the Friday preceding, and on Monday referred to a commee. of the whole. the pusillanimous idea that we had friends in England worth keeping terms with, still haunted the minds of many. for this reason those passages which conveyed censures on the people of England were struck out, lest they should give them offense. the clause too, reprobating the enslaving the inhabitants of Africa, was struck out in complaisance to South Carolina & Georgia, who had never attempted to restrain the importation of slaves and who on the contrary still wished to continue it. our Northern brethren also I believe felt a little tender under those censures; for tho' their people have very few slaves themselves yet they had been pretty considerable carriers of them to others. The debates having taken up the greater parts of the 2d. 3d. & 4th. days of July were, in the evening of the last closed. the declaration was reported by the commee., agreed to by the house, and signed by every member present except Mr. Dickinson.

—BOYD, ed., *Papers of Thomas Jefferson*, I, 309-315.

2. JOHN ADAMS PLACES VIRGINIA AT THE HEAD OF EVERYTHING

To Timothy Pickering.

August 6, 1822

You inquire why so young a man as Mr. Jefferson was placed at the head of the committee for preparing a Declaration of Independence? I answer: It was the Frankfort advice to place Virginia at the head of everything. Mr. Richard Henry Lee might be gone to Virginia, to his sick family, for aught I know, but that was not the reason for Mr. Jefferson's appointment. There were three committees appointed at the same time, one for the Declaration of Independence, another for preparing articles of confederation, and another for preparing a treaty to be proposed to France. Mr. Lee was chosen for the Committee of Confederation, and it was not thought convenient that the same person should be upon both. Mr. Jefferson came into Congress in June, 1775, and brought with him a reputation for literature, science, and a happy talent of composition. Writings of his were handed about, remarkable for the peculiar felicity of expression. Though a silent member in Congress, he was so prompt, frank, explicit and decisive upon committees and in conversation—not even Samuel Adams was more so—that he soon seized upon my heart; and upon this occasion I gave him my vote, and did all in my power to procure the votes of others. I think he had one more vote than any other, and that placed him at the head of the committee. I had the next highest number, and that placed me the second. The committee met, discussed the subject, and then appointed Mr. Jefferson and me to make the draught, I suppose because we were the two first on the list.

The sub-committee met. Jefferson proposed to me to make the draught. I said, "I will not."
"You should do it."
"Oh! no."
"Why will you not? You ought to do it."
"I will not."
"Why?"
"Reason enough."
"What can be your reasons?"
"Reason first—You are a Virginian, and a Virginian ought to appear at the

head of this business. Reason second—I am obnoxious, suspected and unpopular. You are very much otherwise. Reason third—You can write ten times better than I can."

"Well," said Jefferson, "if you are decided, I will do as well as I can."

"Very well. When you have drawn it up, we will have a meeting."

A meeting we accordingly had, and conned the paper over. I was delighted with its high tone and the flights of oratory with which it abounded, especially that concerning Negro slavery, which, though I knew his Southern brethren would never suffer to pass in Congress, I certainly never would oppose. There were other expressions which I would not have inserted, if I had drawn it up, particularly that which called the King tyrant. I thought this too personal; for I never believed George to be a tyrant in disposition and in nature; I always believed him to be deceived by his courtiers on both sides of the Atlantic, and, in his official capacity only, cruel. I thought the expression too passionate, and too much like scolding, for so grave and solemn a document; but as Franklin and Sherman were to inspect it afterwards, I thought it would not become me to strike it out. I consented to report it, and do not now remember that I made or suggested a single alteration.

We reported it to the committee of five. It was read, and I do not remember that Franklin or Sherman criticized any thing. We were all in haste. Congress was impatient, and the instrument was reported, as I believe, in Jefferson's handwriting, as he first drew it. Congress cut off about a quarter of it, as I expected they would; but they obliterated some of the best of it, and left all that was exceptionable, if any thing in it was. I have long wondered that the original draught has not been published. I suppose the reason is the vehement philippic against Negro slavery.

As you justly observe, there is not an idea in it but what had been hackneyed in Congress for two years before. The substance of it is contained in the declaration of rights and the violation of those rights, in the Journals of Congress, in 1774. Indeed, the essence of it is contained in a pamphlet, voted and printed by the town of Boston, before the first Congress met, composed by James Otis, as I suppose, in one of his lucid intervals, and pruned and polished by Samuel Adams.

—ADAMS, ed., *Works of John Adams*, II, 513-514n.

3. "I Turned to Neither Book nor Pamphlet"

Thomas Jefferson to James Madison.

Monticello, August 30, 1823

Dear Sir, . . . The committee of five met; no such thing as a sub-committee was proposed, but they unanimously pressed on myself alone to undertake the draught. I consented; I drew it; but before I reported it to the committee, I communicated it *separately* to Dr. Franklin and Mr. Adams, requesting their corrections, because they were the two members of whose judgments and amendments I wished most to have the benefit before presenting it to the committee. . . . Their alterations were two or three only, and merely verbal. I then wrote a fair copy, reported it to the committee, and from them, unaltered, to

Congress. This personal communication and consultation with Mr. Adams, he has misremembered into the actings of a sub-committee.

Pickering's observations, and Mr. Adams' in addition, "that it contained no new ideas, that it is a common-place compilation, its sentiments hacknied in Congress for two years before, and its essence contained in Otis's pamphlet" may all be true. Of that I am not to be the judge. Richard Henry Lee charged it as copied from Locke's treatise on government. Otis' pamphlet I never saw and whether I had gathered my ideas from reading or reflection I do not know. I only know that I turned to neither book nor pamphlet while writing it. I did not consider it as any part of my charge to invent new ideas altogether, and to offer no sentiment which had ever been expressed before. Had Mr. Adams been so restrained, Congress would have lost the benefit of his bold and impressive advocations of the rights of Revolution. For no man's confident and fervid addresses, more than Mr. Adams', encouraged and supported us through the difficulties surrounding us, which, like the ceaseless action of gravity weighed on us by night and by day. Yet on the same ground, we may ask what of these elevated thoughts was new, or can be affirmed never before to have entered the conceptions of man?

Whether, also, the sentiments of Independence, and the reasons for declaring it, which make so great a portion of the instrument, had been hackneyed in Congress for two years before the 4th of July '76, or this dictum also of Mr. Adams be another slip of memory, let history say. This, however, I will say for Mr. Adams, that he supported the Declaration with zeal and ability, fighting fearlessly for every word of it. As to myself, I thought it a duty to be, on that occasion, a passive auditor of the opinions of others, more impartial judges than I could be, of its merits or demerits. During the debate I was sitting by Doctor Franklin, and he observed that I was writhing a little under the acrimonious criticisms of some of its parts; and it was on that occasion, that by way of comfort, he told me the story of John Thompson, the hatter, and his new sign.

—Ford, ed., *Writings of Jefferson*, X, 266-268.

4. "It Was Intended to Be an Expression of the American Mind"

Thomas Jefferson to Henry Lee.

Monticello, May 8, 1825

... With respect to our rights, and the acts of the British government contravening those rights, there was but one opinion on this side of the water. All American whigs thought alike on these subjects. When forced, therefore, to resort to arms for redress, an appeal to the tribunal of the world was deemed proper for our justification. This was the object of the Declaration of Independence. Not to find out new principles, or new arguments, never before thought of, not merely to say things which had never been said before; but to place before mankind the common sense of the subject, in terms so plain and firm as to command their assent, and to justify ourselves in the independent stand we are compelled to take. Neither aiming at originality of principle or sentiment, nor yet copied from any particular and previous writing, it was intended to be an expression of the American mind, and to give to that expression the proper tone and spirit called for by the occasion. All its authority rests then on the harmonizing sentiments of the day, whether expressed in conversation, in letters, printed essays, or in the elementary books of public right, as Aristotle, Cicero, Locke, Sidney, etc. . . .

—Ford, ed., *Writings of Jefferson*, X, 344-345.

5. Jefferson's Rough Draft of the Declaration

A Declaration of the Representatives of the United States of America, in General Congress assembled.

When in the course of human events it becomes necessary for a people to advance from that subordination in which they have hitherto remained, and to assume among the powers of the earth the equal and independant station to which the laws of nature and of nature's god entitle them, a decent respect to the opinions of mankind requires that they should declare the causes which impel them to the change.

We hold these truths to be sacred and undeniable; that all men are created equal and independant, that from that equal creation they derive rights inherent and inalienable, among which are the preservation of life, and liberty and the pursuit of happiness; that to secure these ends, governments are instituted among men, deriving their just powers from the consent of the governed; that whenever any form of government shall become destructive of these ends, it is the right of the people to alter or to abolish it, and to institute new government, laying it's foundation on such principles and organising it's powers in such form, as to them shall seem most likely to effect their safety and happiness. prudence indeed will dictate that governments long established should not be changed for light and transient causes: and accordingly all experience hath shewn that mankind are more disposed to suffer while evils are sufferable, than to right themselves by abolishing the forms to which they are accustomed. but when a long train of abuses and usurpations, begun at a distinguished period, and pursuing invariably the same object, evinces a design to subject them to arbitrary power, it is their right, it is their duty, to throw off such government and to provide new guards for their future security. such has been the patient sufferance of these colonies; and such is now the necessity which constrains them to expunge their former systems of government. the history of his present majesty, is a history of unremitting injuries and usurpations, among which no one fact stands single or solitary to contradict the uniform tenor of the rest, all of which have in direct object the establishment of an absolute tyranny over these states. to prove this, let facts be submitted to a candid world, for the truth of which we pledge a faith yet unsullied by falsehood. . . .

6. The Clause Reprobating the Enslaving the Inhabitants of Africa

. . . he has waged cruel war against human nature itself, violating it's most sacred rights of life & liberty in the persons of a distant people who never offended him, captivating & carrying them into slavery in another hemisphere, or to incur miserable death in their transportation thither. This piratical warfare, the opprobrium of *infidel* powers, is the warfare of the CHRISTIAN king of Great Britain, determined to keep open a market where MEN should be bought and sold, he has prostituted his negative for suppressing every legislative attempt to prohibit or to restrain this execrable commerce: and that this assemblage of horrors might want no fact of distinguished die, he is now exciting those very people to rise in arms among us, and to purchase that liberty of which *he* has deprived them, by murdering the people upon whom he also obtruded them; thus paying off former crimes committed against the *liberties* of one people, with crimes which he urges them to commit against the *lives* of another.

—BOYD, *The Declaration of Independence*, pp. 19-21.

7. THE DECLARATION OF INDEPENDENCE

In Congress, July 4, 1776
THE UNANIMOUS DECLARATION OF THE THIRTEEN
UNITED STATES OF AMERICA

When in the Course of human events, it becomes necessary for one people to dissolve the political bands which have connected them with another, and to assume among the Powers of the earth, the separate and equal station to which the Laws of Nature and of Nature's God entitle them, a decent respect to the opinions of mankind requires that they should declare the causes which impel them to the separation.

We hold these truths to be self-evident, that all men are created equal, that they are endowed by their Creator with certain unalienable Rights, that among these are Life, Liberty and the pursuit of Happiness. That to secure these rights, Governments are instituted among Men, deriving their just powers from the consent of the governed, That whenever any Form of Government becomes destructive of these ends, it is the Right of the People to alter or to abolish it, and to institute new Government, laying its foundation on such principles and organizing its powers in such form, as to them shall seem most likely to effect their Safety and Happiness. Prudence, indeed, will dictate that Governments long established should not be changed for light and transient causes; and accordingly all experience hath shown, that mankind are more disposed to suffer, while evils are sufferable, than to right themselves by abolishing the forms to which they are accustomed. But when a long train of abuses and usurpations, pursuing invariably the same Object evinces a design to reduce them under absolute Despotism, it is their right, it is their duty, to throw off such Government, and to provide new Guards for their future security.—Such has been the patient sufferance of these Colonies; and such is now the necessity which constrains them to alter their former Systems of Government. The history of the present King of Great Britain is a history of repeated injuries and usurpations, all having in direct object the establishment of an absolute Tyranny over these States. To prove this, let Facts be submitted to a candid world.

He has refused his Assent to Laws, the most wholesome and necessary for the public good.

He has forbidden his Governors to pass Laws of immediate and pressing importance, unless suspended in their operation till his Assent should be obtained; and when so suspended, he has utterly neglected to attend to them.

He has refused to pass other Laws for the accommodation of large districts of people, unless those people would relinquish the right of Representation in the Legislature, a right inestimable to them and formidable to tyrants only.

He has called together legislative bodies at places unusual, uncomfortable, and distant from the depository of their Public Records, for the sole purpose of fatiguing them into compliance with his measures.

He has dissolved Representative Houses repeatedly, for opposing with manly firmness his invasions on the rights of the people.

He has refused for a long time, after such dissolutions, to cause others to be elected; whereby the Legislative Powers, incapable of Annihilation, have returned to the People at large for their exercise; the State remaining in the mean time exposed to all the dangers of invasion from without, and convulsions within.

He has endeavoured to prevent the population of these States; for that purpose obstructing the Laws of Naturalization of Foreigners; refusing to pass others to encourage their migration hither, and raising the conditions of new Appropriations of Lands.

He has obstructed the Administration of Justice, by refusing his Assent to Laws for establishing Judiciary Powers.

He has made Judges dependent on his Will alone, for the tenure of their offices, and the amount and payment of their salaries.

He has erected a multitude of New Offices, and sent hither swarms of Officers to harass our People, and eat out their substance.

He has kept among us, in times of peace, Standing Armies without the Consent of our legislature.

He has affected to render the Military independent of and superior to the Civil Power.

He has combined with others to subject us to a jurisdiction foreign to our constitution, and unacknowledged by our laws; giving his Assent to their acts of pretended legislation:

For quartering large bodies of armed troops among us:

For protecting them, by a mock Trial, from Punishment for any Murders which they should commit on the Inhabitants of these States:

For cutting off our Trade with all parts of the world:

For imposing taxes on us without our Consent:

For depriving us in many cases, of the benefits of Trial by Jury:

For transporting us beyond Seas to be tried for pretended offences:

For abolishing the free System of English Laws in a neighbouring Province, establishing therein an Arbitrary government, and enlarging its Boundaries so as to render it at once an example and fit instrument for introducing the same absolute rule into these Colonies:

For taking away our Charters, abolishing our most valuable Laws, and altering fundamentally the Forms of our Governments.

For suspending our own Legislature, and declaring themselves invested with Power to legislate for us in all cases whatsoever.

He has abdicated Government here, by declaring us out of his Protection and waging War against us.

He has plundered our seas, ravaged our Coasts, burnt our towns, and destroyed the lives of our people.

He is at this time transporting large armies of foreign mercenaries to compleat the works of death, desolation and tyranny, already begun with circumstances of Cruelty & perfidy scarcely paralleled in the most barbarous ages, and totally unworthy the Head of a civilized nation.

He has constrained our fellow Citizens taken Captive on the high Seas to bear Arms against their Country, to become the executioners of their friends and Brethren, or to fall themselves by their Hands.

He has excited domestic insurrections amongst us, and has endeavoured to bring on the inhabitants of our frontiers, the merciless Indian Savages, whose known rule of warfare, is an undistinguished destruction of all ages, sexes and conditions.

In every stage of these Oppressions We have Petitioned for Redress in the most humble terms: Our repeated Petitions have been answered only by repeated injury. A Prince, whose character is thus marked by every act which may define a Tyrant, is unfit to be the ruler of a free People.

Nor have We been wanting in attention to our Brittish brethren. We have warned them from time to time of attempts by their legislature to extend an unwarrantable jurisdiction over us. We have reminded them of the circumstances of our emigration and settlement here. We have appealed to their native justice and magnanimity, and we have conjured them by the ties of our common kindred to disavow these usurpations, which would inevitably interrupt our connections and correspondence. They too have been deaf to the voice of justice and of consanguinity. We must, therefore, acquiesce in the necessity, which denounces our Separation, and hold them, as we hold the rest of mankind, Enemies in War, in Peace Friends.

We, therefore, the Representatives of the united States of America, in General Congress, Assembled, appealing to the Supreme Judge of the world for the rectitude of our intentions, do, in the Name and by Authority of the good People of these Colonies, solemnly publish and declare, That these United Colonies are, and of Right ought to be Free and Independent States; that they are Absolved from all Allegiance to the British Crown, and that all political connection between them and the State of Great Britain, is and ought to be totally dissolved; and that as Free and Independent States, they have full Power to levy War, conclude Peace, contract Alliances, establish Commerce, and to do all other Acts and Things which Independent States may of right do. And for the support of this Declaration, with a firm reliance on the Protection of Divine Providence, we mutually pledge to each other our Lives, our Fortunes and our sacred Honor.

JOHN HANCOCK

New Hampshire
JOSIAH BARTLETT,
WM. WHIPPLE,
MATTHEW THORNTON.
Massachusetts-Bay
SAML. ADAMS,
JOHN ADAMS,
ROBT. TREAT PAINE,
ELBRIDGE GERRY.
Rhode Island
STEP. HOPKINS,
WILLIAM ELLERY.
Connecticut
ROGER SHERMAN,
SAM'EL HUNTINGTON,
WM. WILLIAMS,
OLIVER WOLCOTT.
Georgia
BUTTON GWINNETT,
LYMAN HALL,
GEO. WALTON.
Maryland
SAMUEL CHASE,
WM. PACA,
THOS. STONE,
CHARLES CARROLL of Carrollton.
Virginia
GEORGE WYTHE,
RICHARD HENRY LEE,
TH. JEFFERSON,
BENJA. HARRISON,
THS. NELSON, JR.,
FRANCIS LIGHTFOOT LEE,
CARTER BRAXTON.

New York
WM. FLOYD,
PHIL. LIVINGSTON,
FRANS. LEWIS,
LEWIS MORRIS.
Pennsylvania
ROBT. MORRIS,
BENJAMIN RUSH,
BENJA. FRANKLIN,
JOHN MORTON,
GEO. CLYMER,
JAS. SMITH,
GEO. TAYLOR,
JAMES WILSON,
GEO. ROSS.
Delaware
CAESAR RODNEY,
GEO. READ,
THO. M'KEAN.
North Carolina
WM. HOOPER,
JOSEPH HEWES,
JOHN PENN.
South Carolina
EDWARD RUTLEDGE,
THOS. HEYWARD, JUNR.,
THOMAS LYNCH, JUNR.,
ARTHUR MIDDLETON.
New Jersey
RICHD. STOCKTON,
JNO. WITHERSPOON,
FRAS. HOPKINSON,
JOHN HART,
ABRA. CLARK.

—THORPE, ed., *Federal and State Constitutions*, I, 3 ff.

8. "A GREATER QUESTION NEVER WILL BE DECIDED AMONG MEN"

John Adams to Abigail Adams.

Philadelphia, 3 July, 1776

... Yesterday the greatest question was decided which ever was debated in America, and a greater, perhaps, never was nor will be decided among men. A resolution was passed without one dissenting colony, "that these United Colonies are, and of right ought to be, free and independent States, and as such they have, and of right ought to have, full power to make war, conclude peace, establish commerce, and to do all other acts and things which other States may rightfully do." You will see in a few days a Declaration setting forth the causes which have impelled us to this mighty revolution, and the reasons which will justify it in the sight of God and man. A plan of confederation will be taken up in a few days.

When I look back to the year 1761, and recollect the argument concerning writs of assistance in the superior court, which I have hitherto considered as the commencement of this controversy between Great Britain and America, and run through the whole period from that time to this, and recollect the series of political events, the chain of causes and effects, I am surprised at the suddenness as well as greatness of this revolution. Britain has been filled with folly, and America with wisdom. At least, this is my judgment. Time must determine. It is the will of Heaven that the two countries should be sundered forever. It may be the will of Heaven that America shall suffer calamities still more wasting, and distress yet more dreadful. If this is to be the case, it will have this good effect at least. It will inspire us with many virtues which we have not, and correct many errors, follies and vices which threaten to disturb, dishonor and destroy us. The furnace of affliction produces refinement, in States as well as individuals. And the new governments we are assuming in every part will require a purification from our vices, and an augmentation of our virtues, or they will be no blessings. The people will have unbounded power, and the people are extremely addicted to corruption and venality, as well as the great. But I must submit all my hopes and fears to an overruling Providence, in which, unfashionable as the faith may be, I firmly believe.

—ADAMS, ed., *Works of John Adams*, IX, 418.

9. "THROUGH ALL THE GLOOM RAYS OF RAVISHING LIGHT AND GLORY"

John Adams to Abigail Adams.

3 July 1776

The second day of July, 1776, will be the most memorable epocha in the history of America. I am apt to believe that it will be celebrated by succeeding generations as the great anniversary festival. It ought to be commemorated as the day of deliverance, by solemn acts of devotion to God Almighty. It ought to be solemnized with pomp and parade, with shows, games, sports, guns, bells, bonfires and illuminations, from one end of this continent to the other, from this time forward, forevermore.

You will think me transported with enthusiasm, but I am not. I am well aware of the toil, and blood, and treasure, that it will cost us to maintain this declaration, and support and defend these States. Yet, through all the gloom, I can see the rays of ravishing light and glory. I can see that the end is more than worth all the means, and that posterity will triumph in that day's transaction, even although we should rue it, which I trust in God we shall not.

—ADAMS, ed., *Works of John Adams*, IX, 420.

10. "THE BELLS RANG ALL DAY AND ALMOST ALL NIGHT"

John Adams to Samuel Chase.

Philadelphia, 9 July, 1776

Yours of the 5th came to me the 8th. You will see by this post that the river is passed, and the bridge cut away. The Declaration was yesterday published and proclaimed from that awful stage in the State-house yard; by whom, do you think? By the Committee of Safety, the Committee of Inspection, and a great crowd of people. Three cheers rended the welkin. The battalions paraded on the Common, and gave us the *feu de joie*, notwithstanding the scarcity of powder. The bells rang all day and almost all night. Even the chimers chimed away. The election for the city was carried on, amidst all this flurry, with the utmost decency and order. Who are chosen, I cannot say; but the list was Franklin, Rittenhouse, Owen Biddle, Cannon, Schlosser, Matlack and Kuhl. Thus you see the effect of men of fortune acting against the sense of the people!

As soon as an American seal is prepared, I conjecture the Declarations will be subscribed by all the members, which will give you the opportunity you wish for, of transmitting your name among the votaries of independence.

—ADAMS, ed., *Works of John Adams*, IX, 420-421.

11. "THUS THE CONGRESS HAVE TIED A GORDIAN KNOT"

From the Diary of Ezra Stiles.

July 13, 1776. Mr. Channing returned from Newport and brought the Congresses Declaration of INDEPENDENCY dated at Philadelphia the fourth day of July instant. This I read at noon, and for the first time realized Independency. Thus the CONGRESS have tied a Gordian knot, which the Parliament will find they can neither cut nor untie. The *thirteen united Colonies* now rise into an *Independent Republic* among the kingdoms, states and empires on earth. May the Supreme and Omnipotent Lord of the Monarchical Republic of the immense Universe shower down his blessings upon it, and ever keep it under his holy protection! And have I lived to see such an important and astonishing revolution? Scotch policy transfused thro' the collective body of the ruling powers in Great Britain; and their violent, oppressive and haughty measures have weaned and alienated the affections of three millions of people, and dismembered them from a once beloved parent state. Cursed be that arbitrary policy! Let it never poison the United States of America!

—DEXTER, ed., *Literary Diary of Ezra Stiles*, II, 23-24.

12. SAVANNAH BURIES GEORGE III AND CELEBRATES INDEPENDENCE

Savannah, in Georgia, August 10, 1776

. . . His Excellency, the President, and the Honourable the Council met in the Council chamber, and read the Declaration. They then proceeded to the square before the Assembly House, and read it likewise before a great concourse of people, when the Grenadier and Light Infantry Companies fired a general volley. After this they proceeded in the following procession to the Liberty Pole: the Grenadiers in front; the Provost-Marshall on horseback, with his sword drawn; the Secretary with the Declaration; his Excellency the President; the Honourable the Council and Gentlemen; then the Light Infantry and the rest of the Militia of the town and district of Savannah. At the Liberty Pole they were met by the Georgia Battalion who, after reading of the Declaration, discharged their field-pieces and fired in platoons.

Upon this they proceeded to the Battery at the Trustees garden, where the Declaration was read for the last time, and cannon of the Battery discharged. His Excellency and Council, Colonel Lachlan McIntosh, and other gentlemen, with the Militia, dined under the Cedar Trees, and cheerfully drank to the United Free and Independent States of America. In the evening the town was illuminated, and there was exhibited a very solemn funeral procession, attended by the Grenadier and Light Infantry Companies, and other Militia, with their drums muffled and fifes, and a greater number of people than ever appeared on any occasion before in this Province, when George III was interred before the Court-House, in the following manner:

For as much as George III, of Great Britain, hath most flagrantly violated his coronation oath and trampled upon the constitution of our country and the sacred rights of mankind, we therefore commit his political existence to the ground, corruption to corruption, tyranny to the grave, and oppression to eternal infamy, in sure and certain hope that he will never obtain a resurrection to rule again over these United States of America. But my friends and fellow-citizens, let us not be sorry as men without hope for tyrants that thus depart; rather let us remember America is free and independent; that she is, and will be, with the blessing of the Almighty, great among the nations of the earth. Let this encourage us in well-doing to fight for our rights and privileges, for our wives and children, for all that is near and dear unto us. May God give us his blessing, and let all the people say Amen!

–Force, *American Archives*, 5th Series, I, 882.

13. "The Almighty Has Made Choice of the Present Generation"

Judge William Henry Drayton's Charge to the Grand Jury.

Charleston, S. C., Oct. 15, 1776

It is but to glance an eye over the historic page to be assured that the duration of empire is limited by the Almighty decree. Empires have their rise to a zenith—and their declension to a dissolution. The years of a man, nay the hours of the insect on the bank of the Hypanis that lives but a day, epitomize the advance and decay of the strength and duration of dominion! One common fate awaits all things upon earth—a thousand causes accelerate or delay their perfection or ruin. To look a little into remote times, we see that, from the most contemptible origin upon record, Rome became the most powerful state the sun ever saw: The world bowed before her imperial Fasces! Yet, having run through all the vicissitudes of dominion, her course was finished. Her empire was dissolved, that the separated members of it might arise to run through similar revolutions.

Great Britain was a part of this mighty empire. But, being dissolved from it, in her turn she also extended her dominion—arrived at, and passed her zenith. Three and thirty years numbered the illustrious days of the Roman greatness. Eight years measure the duration of the British grandeur in meridian lustre! How few are the days of true glory. The extent of the Roman period is from their complete conquest of Italy, which gave them a place whereon to stand, that they might shake the world, to the original cause of their declension, their introduction of Asiatic luxury. The British period is from the year 1758, when they victoriously pursued their enemies into every quarter of the globe, to the immediate cause of their decline—their injustice displayed by the stamp act. In short, like the Roman empire, Great Britain in her constitution of government, contained a poison to bring on her decay, and in each case, this poison was drawn into a ruinous operation by the riches and luxuries of the east.

Thus, by natural causes and common effects, the American states are become dissolved from the British dominion. And is it to be wondered at that Britain has experienced the invariable fate of empire! We are not surprised when we see youth or age yield to the common lot of humanity. Nay, to repine that, in our day, America is dissolved from the British state, is impiously to question the unerring wisdom of Providence. The Almighty setteth up, and he casteth down: He breaks the sceptre, and transfers the dominion: He has made choice of the present generation to erect the American empire. Thankful as we are, and ought to be, for an appointment of the kind, the most illustrious that ever was, let each individual exert himself in this important operation directed by Jehovah himself. From a short retrospect, it is evident the work was not the present design of man.

—NILES, *Principles and Acts of the Revolution*, pp. 336-337.

CHAPTER NINE

The Loyalists

WHEN JOHN ADAMS *was in Holland, in 1780, trying to win support to the American cause, he solemnly assured one inquirer that not one twentieth of the American people were tainted with loyalism. Writing in 1815, in a more objective mood (if Adams can ever be accused of objectivity), he put the situation differently. "If I were called upon to calculate the divisions among the people of America I should say that full one-third were averse to the revolution. . . . An opposite third conceived a hatred of the English and gave themselves up to an enthusiastic gratitude to France. The middle third, comprising principally the yeomanry, the soundest part of the nation, and always averse to war, were rather lukewarm both to England and France; and sometimes stragglers from them, and sometimes the whole body, united with the first or the last third, according to circumstances." Other estimates at the time differed as widely as those of Adams at different times. While most Patriots asserted that the Americans were well-nigh unanimous in their devotion to liberty and independence, the Loyalist Joseph Galloway confidently testified that four fifths of all Americans were, or wanted to be, loyal to the King!*

These differences of opinion and assertion are not hard to understand, for the estimates turn not so much on evidence as on semantics and the subjective interpretation of the evidence. How define the terms "Patriot" and Loyalist"? If by Patriot we mean only those who were ready to fight for the new nation, then Adams' one third is too high; after all, a free population of only 2,000,000 could not put over 25,000 men in the field at once, and a rich and fertile land allowed its soldiers to freeze and to starve. If by Loyalist we mean only those who were actively loyal, and whose loyalty carried them into exile or into British ranks, then again Adams' estimate is too large. But if the term Loyalist be stretched to cover not only those who were actively loyal, but those who were against independence and war, and tried to hold aloof, then the figure of one third is clearly too small. Two things are apparent: that there was always a substantial portion of the American population which had no enthusiasm for either the rebellion or its suppression, and that the number and zeal of Patriots and Loyalists alike changed constantly with the varying fortunes of the war.

The situation has other dimensions as well. To some extent, and for some purposes, the Revolution was a class conflict, a war, if not between the "haves" and the "have-nots," then between the "ins" and the "outs." While it is possible to discern fairly clear social and economic patterns of loyalism and rebellion in any one state, it is almost impossible to generalize these for all the states. Thus while on the whole the landed gentry of New York were Loyalists (with such notable exceptions as the Van Rensselaers, the Livingstons, and the Schuylers!), this was not true of the landed gentry of Virginia; while the small farmers of Massachusetts were Patriots, this was not true of the small farmers of upstate New York or upcountry North Carolina; while most Loyalists were Anglicans, in Pennsylvania it was the Quakers and in the Carolinas the dissenters who more commonly joined the Royal ranks. In so far as the Revolution involved not only the question of home rule, but the question who should rule at home, it tended to identify radicalism with patriotism, and conservatism with loyalism. Much of loyalism in Pennsylvania, for example, reflected the long-standing quarrel between the Quakers and the Scots-Irish; the "Loyalists" who fought at Moore's Creek Bridge in 1776, and at King's Mountain later, were not fighting for King George but against the low-country planters who had punished them at the time of the Regulator uprising; and no one has ever succeeded in unraveling the tangled strands of patriotism, state pride, self-seeking, war, speculation and diplomacy, which the Allen brothers of Vermont wove during these years.

Loyalism had both a geographical and a class pattern, and both were opaque. It was stronger in the Middle States than in New England, stronger in the lower South than in the upper, strongest of all in New York—which the British held through most of the war. It was weakest in Massachusetts and Connecticut, and in Virginia, the oldest colonies, with the longest traditions and habits of self-government. A fairly accurate indication of geographical distribution is provided by the statistics of compensation to Loyalists granted by the British government at the close of the war. Of those receiving compensation 941 were from New York, 321 from South Carolina, 226 from Massachusetts, 208 from New Jersey, 148 from Pennsylvania, 140 from Virginia, 135 from North Carolina, and 129 from Georgia.

Loyalism had something of a class pattern as well. In a broad way it can be said that rich merchants, large landowners, Anglican clergymen, professional men, and officials tended to be loyal. But there are so many exceptions that the generalization is not very helpful: thus great landowners like Washington in Virginia and Willie Jones in North Carolina were Patriots; so were lawyers like Adams and Jefferson and professional men like Benjamin Rush and Doctor Warren, and many of the leading merchants of Boston, Philadelphia and Charleston. In a broad way it can be said that the small farmers, seamen, fishermen and dissenters were Patriots, but the small farmers of upstate New York and upcountry North Carolina provided many supporters to the Crown, the Quakers were mostly loyal, and John Wesley used his influence to keep his American followers faithful to the mother country.

Perhaps the best indication of the strength and tenacity of loyalism can be read in the figures (we cannot say statistics) of those who left the American states for new homes in Britain or Canada during and after the war. Altogether the Loyalist exodus withdrew some 75,000 to 80,000 from the American population—roughly one out of every 30 white families. It was a loss the new nation could ill afford.

At the very outset of the conflict the Loyalists formulated an elaborate rationale for their position—one which should appeal to those who find the Unionist arguments of 1861 convincing. But they were far more than a vocal minority; they were a fighting minority as well. From the beginning many of them took an active part in the war. Loyalists did most of the fighting in upcountry North and South Carolina; Loyalists harried the northern frontier, and with Brant's Indians perpetrated the Wyoming and Cherry Valley massacres; Loyalists helped the British regulars hold New York and Long Island. Loyalists provided, too, many Royal regiments: the Tory Rangers, Tarleton's Legion, Rawdon's Volunteers, St. Leger's Loyal Greens, the Pennsylvania Loyalists and many others; it has been estimated that altogether some 30,000 Loyalists at one time or another wore the British uniform. Yet though the British permitted themselves to be bemused by the phantom of great Loyalist armies, they did next to nothing to organize, support, maintain and reward Loyalist military co-operation.

It is no wonder that many Americans regarded the Loyalists with a loathing which they never felt for the British regulars, nor that they treated them with incomparably greater severity. They took for granted that they would have to fight the British, but to many of them it seemed monstrous that they should have to fight fellow Americans as well. Then, too, the rules of war of necessity applied to the fighting between British and American armies, but no rules of war protected the hapless Loyalists who were, in the eyes of the Americans, not formal opponents but renegades and traitors. "If America fails," observed a committee of the Congress in 1776, with palpable exaggeration, "it will be owing to such divisions more than to the force of our enemies." At the beginning there were efforts to win over the Loyalists by reason, or by social and economic pressures, but these mild methods speedily gave way to harsher ones: whipping, coats of tar and feathers, fines, confiscation of property, banishment, and—on paper at least—death. These rancorous measures had the support of Washington, Governor Livingston and Gouverneur Morris, men otherwise moderate and judicious. The Loyalists, in turn, met bitterness with bitterness and savagery with savagery, especially in the border warfare along the great frontier arc from upper New York around to Kentucky and down to South Carolina and Georgia.

A thousand or more Loyalists sailed to Halifax and eventually to England in 1776, and all through the war others made their painful way to the mother country, until not only London but provincial cities like Bristol had their little refugee colonies. Most of these exiles were dependent on British bounty, and few of them were happy in England. The British, in turn, did not quite know what to do with these American refugees who (with the conspicuous exception of Benjamin Thompson, later Count Rumford) were too old to fight, too poor to go into business, too unsophisticated to fit into the government, and too embittered to give sound advice. Most of them suffered the fate of such refugees at all times: they were men without a country.

Happily neither the Americans nor the English were good haters, and the passions of war evaporated quickly after the Treaty of Paris. If few states restored Loyalist property (as they were morally though perhaps not

*legally bound to do) most of them did repeal their punitive legislation.
Within a short time a good many quondam Loyalists—like the inimitable
Samuel Curwen—found it possible to return to their old homes and resume
their old ways of life.*

I. THE LOYALISTS ARGUE THEIR CAUSE

*In a sense the Loyalist argument was more logical, as it was certainly more
natural, than the Patriot, for Loyalists had merely to defend the old tried and
true system that had functioned for 150 years, while the Patriots had to justify
a revolution. Almost everything was on the side of maintaining the status
quo: loyalty to King and Empire, desire for peace, fear of change, and sentiment. To most Americans loyalty to George III was as natural as is loyalty
to Elizabeth II to Canadians today. And very few Americans—anyway outside
Boston—actually felt the heavy hand of tyranny about which demagogues
like Sam Adams and Tom Paine so furiously declaimed. Nor was the alternative of independence anything which respectable folk could contemplate
without distress. Was it not ridiculous to suppose that a handful of colonials
could successfully oppose the most powerful empire on the globe? Was it not
absurd to think that thirteen independent colonies could be welded together
into a single nation? And was it not downright frightening to contemplate
rule not by the statesmen who had ruled so well in the past, but by fire-
brands and demagogues who were preaching doctrines of democracy and
equality?*

*So the Loyalists reasoned, and to many thoughtful men at the time their
reasoning seemed sound. The literary argument of the Loyalists has been so
luminously explored by Moses Coit Tyler in his magisterial* Literary History
of the Revolution *that we need not rehearse it here. We can present only a
few brief excerpts from that argument. First is a small segment of the* Westchester Farmer, *the Reverend Samuel Seabury's reply to Alexander Hamilton's* Full Vindication of the Measures of Congress; *Hamilton, in turn, replied
to Seabury with another pamphlet, the* Farmer Refuted. *Seabury, a zealous
Anglican minister and an ardent pamphleteer, attached himself to the Royal
cause once the war was under way, and was duly rewarded with a chaplaincy
in one of the King's regiments, and a D.D. from Oxford University; after the
war he served as first bishop of the Episcopal Church in America. Our second selection, from the pen of young Peter Van Schaack, illustrates well the
mental and spiritual travail through which many upright Americans went in
this crisis. Talented beyond most of his contemporaries, married into one of
the first families of the province of New York, and active in the prerevolu-
tionary agitation for American rights, Van Schaack was one of those who
championed the American cause but drew back in alarm from independence.
He tried to remain neutral, and for a time succeeded, but in 1778 he went into
exile in England and stayed there throughout the war. When in 1784, however, the New York legislature restored his citizenship he gladly came home
and settled for the rest of his life in Kinderhook. Something of the hard lot of*

*the neutral, exposed to the hostility and ravages of both sides, is told in the
diary of James Allen of Philadelphia.*

1. The Reverend Samuel Seabury Argues the Cause of Great Britain

December 24, 1774

In answer to Alexander Hamilton.

... Do you think, Sir, that Great Britain is like an old, wrinkled, withered,
worn-out hag, whom every jackanapes that truants along the streets may
insult with impunity? You will find her a vigorous matron, just approaching
a green old age; and with spirit and strength sufficient to chastise her unduti-
ful and rebellious children. Your measures have as yet produced none of the
effects you looked for: Great Britain is not as yet intimidated; she has already
a considerable fleet and army in America; more ships and troops are expected
in the spring; every appearance indicates a design in her to support her claim
with vigour. You may call it *infatuation, madness, frantic extravagance*, to
hazard so small a number of troops as she can spare against the thousands of
New England. Should the dreadful contest once begin—— But God forbid!
Save, heavenly Father! O save my country from perdition!

Consider, Sir, is it right to risk the valuable blessings of property, liberty
and life, to the single chance of war? Of the worst kind of war—a civil war?
a civil war founded on rebellion? Without ever attempting the peaceable
mode of accommodation? Without ever asking a redress of our complaints
from the only power on earth who can redress them? When disputes happen
between nations independent of each other, they first attempt to settle them
by their ambassadors; they seldom run hastily to war till they have tried what
can be done by treaty and mediation. I would make many more concessions
to a parent than were justly due to him, rather than engage with him in a duel.
But we are rushing into a war with our parent state without offering the
least concession; without even deigning to propose an accommodation. You,
Sir, have employed your pen, and exerted your abilities, in vindicating and
recommending measures which you know must, if persisted in, have a direct
tendency to produce and accelerate this dreadful event. The congress also
foresaw the horrid tragedy that must be acted in America, should their measures be generally adopted; why else did they advise us "to extend our views
to *mournful* events," and be in *all* "respects prepared for *every* contingency?"

May God forgive *them*, but may he confound *their* devices; and may he
give *you* repentance and a better mind!

—Seabury, *Letters of a Westchester Farmer*, pp. 140-141.

2. A New York Moderate Weighs Loyalty Against Rebellion

From the journal of Peter Van Schaack.

January, 1776, at Kinderhook

The only foundation of all legitimate governments is certainly a compact
between the rulers and the people, containing mutual conditions, and equally
obligatory on both the contracting parties. No question can therefore exist,
at this enlightened day, about the lawfulness of resistance, in cases of gross

and palpable infractions on the part of the governing power. It is impossible, however, clearly to ascertain every case which shall effect a dissolution of this contract; for these, though always tacitly implied, are never expressly declared, in any form of government.

As a man is bound by the sacred ties of conscience to yield obedience to every act of the legislature so long as the government exists, so, on the other hand, he owes it to the cause of liberty to resist the invasion of those rights which, being inherent and unalienable, could not be surrendered at the institution of the civil society of which he is a member. In times of civil commotions, therefore, an investigation of those rights which will necessarily infer an inquiry into the nature of government, becomes the indispensable duty of every man.

There are perhaps few questions relating to government of more difficulty than that at present subsisting between Great Britain and the Colonies. It originated about the *degree* of subordination we owe to the British Parliament, but by a rapid progress it seems now to be whether we are members of the empire or not. In this view, the principles of Mr. Locke and other advocates for the rights of mankind are little to the purpose. His treatise throughout presupposes rulers and subjects of the *same state*, and upon a supposition that we are members of the empire, his reasonings, if not inapplicable, will be found rather to militate against our claims; for he holds the necessity of a *supreme power*, and the necessary existence of *one legislature* only in every society, in the strongest terms.

Here arises the doubt: if we are parts of the same state, we cannot complain of a *usurpation*, unless in a qualified sense, but we must found our resistance upon an *undue and oppressive* exercise of a power we recognize. In short, our reasonings must resolve into one or the other of the following three grounds, and our right of resistance must be founded upon either the first or third of them; for either, first, we owe no obedience to any acts of Parliament; or, secondly, we are bound by all acts to which British subjects in Great Britain would, if passed with respect to them, owe obedience; or, thirdly, we are subordinate in a certain degree, or, in other words, certain acts may be valid in Britain which are not so here.

Upon the first point I am exceedingly clear in my mind, for I consider the Colonies as members of the British empire, and subordinate to the Parliament. But, with regard to the second and third, I am not so clear. The necessity of a supreme power in every state strikes me very forcibly; at the same time, I foresee the destructive consequences of a right in Parliament to bind us in all cases whatsoever. To obviate the ill effects of either extreme, some middle way should be found out, by which the benefits to the empire should be secured arising from the doctrine of a supreme power, while the abuses of that power to the prejudice of the colonists should be guarded against; and this, I hope, will be the happy effect of the present struggle.

The basis of such a compact must be the securing to the Americans the essential rights of Britons, but so modified as shall best consist with the general benefit of the *whole*. If upon such a compact we cannot possess the specific privileges of the inhabitants of Great Britain (as for instance a representation in Parliament we cannot), this must not be an obstacle; for there is certainly a point in which the general good of the whole, with the least possible disadvantage to every part, does centre, though it may be difficult to discern it, and every *individual* part must give way to the *general good*. . . .

It may be said that these principles terminate in passive obedience: far from it. I perceive that several of the acts exceed those bounds which, of right, ought to circumscribe the Parliament. But my difficulty arises from this, that, taking the whole of the acts complained of together, they do not, I think, manifest a system of slavery, but may fairly be imputed to human frailty and the difficulty of the subject. Most of them seem to have sprung out of particular occasions, and are unconnected with each other, and some of them are precisely of the nature of other acts made before the commencement of his present Majesty's reign, which is the era when the supposed design of subjugating the colonies began. If these acts have exceeded what is and ought to be declared to be the line of right, and thus we have been sufferers in *some respects* by the undefined state of the subject, it will also, I think, appear from such a union, when established, if past transactions are to be measured by the standard hereafter to be fixed, that *we* have hitherto been deficient in other respects, and derived *benefit* from the same unsettled state.

In short, I think those acts may have been passed without a preconcerted plan of enslaving us, and it appears to me that the more favorable construction ought ever to be put on the conduct of our rulers. I cannot therefore think the government *dissolved;* and as long as the society lasts, the power that every individual gave the society when he entered into it can never revert to the individuals again, but will always remain in the community.

If it be asked how we come to be subject to the authority of the British Parliament, I answer, by the same compact which entitles us to the benefits of the British constitution and its laws; and that we derive advantage even from some kind of subordination, whatever the degree of it should be, is evident, because, without such a controlling common umpire, the colonies must become independent states, which would be introductive of anarchy and confusion among ourselves.

Some kind of dependence being then, in my idea, necessary for our own happiness, I would choose to see a claim made of a constitution which shall concede this point, as, before that is done by us and rejected by the mother country, I cannot see any principle of regard for my country which will authorize me in taking up arms, as absolute *dependence* and *independence* are two extremes which I would avoid; for, should we succeed in the latter, we shall still be in a sea of uncertainty and have to fight among ourselves for that constitution we aim at.

There are many very weighty reasons besides the above to restrain a man from taking up arms, but some of them are of too delicate a nature to be put upon paper; however, it may be proper to mention what does *not* restrain *me*. It is not from apprehension of the consequences should America be subdued, or the hopes of any favor from government, both which I disclaim; nor is it from any disparagement of the cause my countrymen are engaged in, or a desire of obstructing the present measures.

I am fully convinced that men of the greatest abilities and the soundest integrity have taken parts in this war with America, and their measures should have a fair trial. But this is too serious a matter, implicitly to yield to the authority of any characters, however respectable. Every man must exercise his own reason and judge for himself; "for he that appeals to Heaven must be sure that he has right on his side," according to Mr. Locke. It is a question of morality and religion, in which a man cannot conscientiously take an active part without being convinced in his own mind of the justice of the cause; for obedience while government exists being clear on the one hand, the dissolution of the government must be equally so, to justify an appeal to arms; and whatever disagreeable consequences may follow from dissenting from the general voice, yet I cannot but remember that I am to render an account of my conduct before a more awful tribunal, where no man can be justified who stands accused by his own conscience of taking part in measures which, through the distress and bloodshed of his fellow-creatures, may precipitate his country into ruin.

—Van Schaack, *Life of Peter Van Schaack*, pp. 54-58.

3. James Allen of Philadelphia Finds It Hard to Be Neutral

October 15, 1777 . . . Gen Washington has issued orders to take the blankets, shoes, stockings, etc., of private families for the use of the army. This, together with the licentiousness, plundering, stealing and impressing of the military, will sink this country to perdition. Misery begins to wear her ghastliest form; it is impossible to endure it. Three fourths of my income arises from my estate in Philadelphia, from which I am cut off. My rents here being paid in continental money, which is now depreciated as 6 to 1 and I obliged to pay in all articles four fold—in some, as butter, meat, cheese, etc., nine fold—ruin can't be very distant.

The prevailing idea now is that no man has any property in what the publick has use for, and it is seldom they ask the owner; so wanton is this species of oppression called pressing that if they could by fair means get anything by a little trouble, they chuse to take private property by violence if somewhat nearer at hand. This I have seen in many instances, and felt in my own case. When the hospital and publick works were erected in this little town [Northampton, Pennsylvania], I offered to supply them with wood at a reasonable rate, to avoid being plundered; yet they have hitherto gone on cutting my timber, burning my fences and taking bricks from me, rather than employ some of the many idle men they have in cutting wood.

The militia who occasionally assemble here, and have now met for near a month, plunder without ceremony all who do not turn out in militia; horses, waggons, cows, turkeys are daily brought into town. Yesterday a farmer sold me his whole brood of turkeys and fowls on receiving information that a neighbour, with whom he had a law suit 3 years ago, had informed the militia, who were setting out to take them away. It is probable they will soon plunder me of them, as every night they steal my poultry. The officers of militia never think of punishing them, neither are they able or disposed to do it. It is a fine time to gratify low private revenge, and few opportunities are lost.

My tenants whose rents are due in sterling often pay off arrears of 6 or 7 years in continental money at the old exchange, and yet I dare not object, tho' I am as much robbed of my property as if it was taken out of my drawer.
—ALLEN, "Diary," *Penn. Mag. of Hist. and Biog.*, IX, 295-296.

II. THE RUTH OF CIVIL WAR

The very strength of loyalism in America condemned it to persecution. Had the Loyalists been few in number, weak and disorganized, the Patriots might have ignored them, or have contented themselves with making sure that they could do no harm. But they were numerous and powerful, strong enough at times to take the offensive against the Patriots and endanger the success of the Revolution. It was not, therefore, surprising that even before Independence the Patriots moved to frustrate, intimidate, punish and, if possible, wipe out loyalism. In the fall of 1774 the Provincial Congress of Massachusetts denounced Loyalists as "infamous betrayers of their country," and the Continental Congress in setting up the Association called for a "committee in every county, city and town . . . to observe the conduct of all persons touching this association . . . to the end that all foes to the rights of British America may be publicly known and universally contemned as enemies of American liberty."

It was in fact these self-constituted committees of safety—often the successors of the earlier committees of correspondence and the Liberty Boys—that were the instruments for intimidating Loyalists. Such groups could not be easily controlled, nor was there any assurance that they would operate with a nice regard for justice, or that they would not, on occasion, confuse loyalism with conservatism or Anglicanism, or use their extralegal authority to indulge personal or class grudges. Most of the early violence—breaking windows, whipping, tarring and feathering—was perpetrated by members of these committees and their friends and hangers-on.

Very soon, however, the provincial legislatures gave at least an appearance of legality to the proceedings of these committees. State after state passed test laws, required ostentatious proof of devotion to the Patriot cause, and imposed penalties against loyalism, active and passive alike. In a broad way these laws limited freedom of speech and freedom of movement, disfranchised, suppressed, quarantined or banished Tories, and made adhering to George III a crime punishable by confiscation of property and, in extreme and aggravated cases, by death.

The treatment of the Loyalists was harsh, but harshness has almost always characterized the treatment of those who were on the wrong, or losing, side of a revolution. From the point of view of the Patriots, the Loyalists were traitors and therefore worse than open enemies. Nor can the judicious historian deny that the Patriots had considerable justification for their attitude and their actions. Loyalists were numerous enough to be dangerous; they did in fact give aid to the enemy; many were spies and informers, many more sold food and supplies to the British; thousands fought in the British ranks.

And it cannot fairly be said that Americans were more severe in their treatment of Tories than the British had been in their treatment of the Scots after Culloden, for example, or of the Irish after a long series of uprisings, or than the Austrians had been in their punishment of Italians who rebelled against their rule, or the French in their treatment of other Frenchmen who were not sufficiently extreme in their revolutionary zeal. The administration of the loyalty and security programs in our own day should make us more understanding of the enormously difficult problems that confronted the Patriots during the Revolution.

Indeed what is perhaps most impressive about this melancholy chapter is not the severity but the relative mildness of the Patriots. There was violence, to be sure, but little bloodshed and few authenticated cases of loss of life. Thus while the Pennsylvania "Blacklist" of Loyalists guilty of high treason contained 490 names, only a handful of these were punished, and only two finally hanged. While the New York Committee to Detect Conspiracies tried some 1,000 Loyalist "traitors," over 600 of these were released on bail, and few actually punished. Far more open to criticism is the ruthlessness with which some states applied the policy of confiscation of Tory estates, and it is hard not to suspect that here covetousness rather than patriotism dictated zeal. New York, Pennsylvania, Virginia, North Carolina and other states confiscated large Tory estates. Some of these properties were large and were ultimately acquired by small farmers. Thus Tories unwittingly made their contribution to American economic democracy. Other confiscated holdings were relatively small and were picked up by speculators with ready cash or by neighboring farmers capitalizing on the misfortunes of former friends. As was to be expected, Patriot "insiders" not infrequently profited in such dealings, but it must be borne in mind that the objective of such confiscation measures was to raise cash for the hard-pressed states and to punish notorious Tories, not to bring about economic leveling.

We present here a series of accounts of the mistreatment of Loyalists, from Massachusetts to South Carolina. First an inspirational document which suggests something of how widespread was the net with which to catch Tories—an appeal, rather late in the day, to greed and hatred. All the rest of the documents date from the outbreak of the conflict. Our first witness, Ann Hulton, it will be remembered, was the sister of the Commissioner of Customs of Boston; next come two accounts of the sufferings of Connecticut Loyalists, Dr. Beebe of East Haddam and the Reverend Samuel Peters of Hebron. Third we give a lively picture of conditions in Wilmington, North Carolina, as seen through the highly prejudiced eyes of Janet Schaw, another sister of a Royal official. Captain Alexander Graydon of Pennsylvania is one of the best historians of the Revolution in that state, and this story of the trials of Dr. Kearsley is a familiar one. Lord Campbell's letter to the "good" Lord Dartmouth suggests that Negro slaves suspected of treason fared worse than white Loyalists or traitors. All the misdeeds which the Loyalists relate here were perpetrated by mobs. We include also a sample of what might be called legal—or at least quasi-legal—intimidation: punishment for subversion as provided by committees of safety.

1. "The Tories! The Tories Will Yet Be the Ruin of You!"

Appeal to the Inhabitants of Philadelphia, 1779.

Rouse, America! Your danger is great—great from a quarter where you least expect it. The Tories, the Tories will yet be the ruin of you! 'Tis high time they were separated from among you. They are now busy engaged in undermining your liberties. They have a thousand ways of doing it, and they make use of them all. Who were the occasion of this war? The Tories. Who persuaded the tyrant of Britain to prosecute it in a manner before unknown to civilized nations, and shocking even to barbarians? The Tories! Who prevailed on the savages of the wilderness to join the standard of the enemy? The Tories! . . . Who advised and who assisted in burning your towns, ravaging your country and violating the chastity of your women? The Tories! Who are the occasion that thousands of you now mourn the loss of your dearest connections? The Tories. Who have always counteracted the endeavors of Congress to secure the liberties of this country? The Tories! . . . Who take the oaths of allegiance to the States one day and break them the next? The Tories! Who prevent your battalions from being filled? The Tories! Who dissuade from entering the army? The Tories! Who persuade those who have enlisted to desert? The Tories! Who harbor those who do desert? The Tories!

In short, who wish to see us conquered, to see us slaves, to see us hewers of wood and drawers of water? The Tories!

—Moore, *Diary of the American Revolution*, II, 166.

2. "The Unhappy Wretch Still Cried: 'Curse All Traitors!'"

Ann Hulton to Mrs. Lightbody.

Boston, January 31, 1774

. . . But the most shocking cruelty was exercised a few nights ago, upon a poor old man, a tidesman, one Malcolm. He is reckoned creasy, a quarrel was picked with him, he was afterward taken and tarred and feathered. Theres no law that knows a punishment for the greatest crimes beyond what this is of cruel torture. And this instance exceeds any other before it. He was stript stark naked, one of the severest cold nights this winter, his body covered all over with tar, then with feathers, his arm dislocated in tearing off his cloaths. He was dragged in a cart with thousands attending, some beating him with clubs and knocking him out of the cart, then in again. They gave him several severe whippings, at different parts of the town. This spectacle of horror and sportive cruelty was exhibited for about five hours.

The unhappy wretch they say behaved with the greatest intrepidity and fortitude all the while. Before he was taken, [he] defended himself a long time against numbers, and afterwards when under torture they demanded of him to curse his masters, the King, Governor, etc., which they could not make him do, but he still cried, "Curse all traitors!" They brought him to the gallows and put a rope about his neck, saying they would hang him. He said he wished they would, but that they could not, for God was above the Devil.

The doctors say that it is impossible this poor creature can live. They say his flesh comes off his back in stakes.

It is the second time he has been tarred and feathered and this is looked upon more to intimidate the judges and others than a spite to the unhappy victim tho' they owe him a grudge for some things particularly. He was with Govr. Tryon in the battle with the Regulators and the Governor has declared that he was of great servise to him in that affair, by his undaunted spirit encountering the greatest dangers.

Govr. Tryon had sent him a gift of ten guineas just before this inhuman treatment. He has a wife and family and an aged father and mother who, they say, saw the spectacle which no indifferent person can mention without horror.

These few instances amongst many serve to shew the abject state of government and the licentiousness and barbarism of the times. There's no majestrate that dare or will act to suppress the outrages. No person is secure. There are many objects pointed at, at this time, and when once marked out for vengeance, their ruin is certain.

The judges have only a weeks time allowed them to consider whether they will take the salaries from the Crown or no. Govr. Hutchinson is going to England as soon as the season will permit.

We are under no apprehension at present on our own account but we can't look upon our safety secure for long.

—HULTON, *Letters of a Loyalist Lady*, pp. 70-72.

3. "THE NEW FASHION DRESS OF TAR AND FEATHERS"

Joseph Spencer to Governor Trumbull.

East Haddam, [Connecticut], September 14, 1774

Honoured Sir: Doctor Beebe, who will deliver this, will wait on your Honour in hopes of the favour of your Honour's advice with respect to an unhappy affair that concerns himself. The zeal of people here, in general, runs very high for what is called Liberty; and there being a few amongst us that don't agree with the rest, who are called Tories, many people here have thought proper to visit the Tories and demand some satisfaction with relation to their principles and practices; and they have accordingly visited several in this society, and I think they have, except Doctor Beebe, given them satisfaction. They have, a large number of them, visited the Doctor this week, and he refused to say any thing that gave satisfaction, and the people have been so rough with him as to give him the new fashion dress of tar and feathers; and he thinks himself extremely abused, and has been desirous that I would grant surety of the peace against a few of them, but I declined; he seems to think he is obliged, in duty, to prosecute some of them; but, however, has finally applied to your Honour for advice as to the necessity or expediency of his prosecuting in this case.

I hope also, myself, to have your Honour's advice as to my duty with respect to signing a precept for the Doctor in this case. I believe if one should be granted, it will not be executed to any advantage without force from abroad to govern our people; for although these rough measures lately taken place with us are contrary to my mind, yet I am not able to prevent it at present.

I am, honoured sir, your Honour's most obedient and humble servant,
JOSEPH SPENCER
—FORCE, *American Archives*, 4th Series, I, 787.

4. THE MOBS CRY: "DOWN WITH THE CHURCH, THE RAGS OF POPERY!"

The Reverend Samuel Peters to the Reverend Doctor Achmuty of New York.

Boston, October 1, 1774

Reverend Sir: The riots and mobs that have attended me and my house, set on by the Governour of Connecticut, have compelled me to take up my abode here; and the clergy of Connecticut must fall a sacrifice, with the several churches, very soon to the rage of the puritan nobility, if the old serpent, that dragon, is not bound. Yesterday I waited on his Excellency, the Admiral, etc., Doctor Canner, Mr. Troutbeck, Doctor Byles, etc. I am soon to sail for England; I shall stand in great need of your letters, and the letters of the clergy of New-York; direct to Mr. Rice Williams, woollen draper, in London, where I shall put up. Judge Achmuty, etc., etc., will do all things reasonable for the neighbouring charter; necessity calls for such friendship, as the head is sick and the heart faint, and spiritual iniquity rides in high places with halberts, pistols and swords. See the Proclamation I send you by my nephew, and their pious Sabbath day, the 4th of last month, when the preachers and magistrates left the pulpits, etc., for the gun and drum, and set off for Boston, cursing the King and Lord North, General Gage, the Bishops and their cursed Curates, and the Church of England. And for my telling the church people not to take up arms, etc., it being high treason, etc., the Sons of Liberty have almost killed one of my church, tarred and feathered two, abused others; and on the sixth day destroyed my windows, and rent my clothes, even my gown, etc., crying out, "Down with the church, the rags of Popery," etc. Their rebellion is obvious; treason is common; and robbery is their daily diversion; the Lord deliver us from anarchy! The bounds of New-York may directly extend to Connecticut River, Boston meet them, and New-Hampshire take the Province of Maine, and Rhode Island be swallowed up as Dathan. Pray lose no time, nor fear worse times than attend,

Reverend sir, your very humble servant,
SAMUEL PETERS
—FORCE, *American Archives*, 4th Series, I, 716.

5. JANET SCHAW SEES THE OBEDIENT SONS OF BRITANNIA INSULTED

Wilmington, North Carolina, [June 1775]

Good heavens, what a scene this town is! Surely you folks at home have adopted the old maxim of King Charles: "Make friends of your foes, leave friends to shift for themselves."

We came down in the morning in time for the review, which the heat made as terrible to the spectators as to the soldiers, or what you please to call them. They had certainly fainted under it, had not the constant draughts of grog supported them. Their exercise was that of bush-fighting, but it appeared so confused and so perfectly different from any thing I ever saw,

I cannot say whether they performed it well or not; but this I know, that they were heated with rum till capable of committing the most shocking outrages. We stood in the balcony of Doctor Cobham's house and they were reviewed on a field mostly covered with what are called here scrubby oaks, which are only a little better than brushwood. They at last however assembled on the plain field, and I must really laugh while I recollect their figures: 2000 men in their shirts and trousers, preceded by a very ill beat-drum and a fiddler, who was also in his shirt with a long sword and a cue at his hair, who played with all his might. They made indeed a most unmartial appearance. But the worst figure there can shoot from behind a bush and kill even a General Wolfe.

Before the review was over, I heard a cry of tar and feather. I was ready to faint at the idea of this dreadful operation. I would have gladly quitted the balcony, but was so much afraid the victim was one of my friends that I was not able to move; and he indeed proved to be one, tho' in a humble station. For it was Mr. Neilson's poor English groom. You can hardly conceive what I felt when I saw him dragged forward, poor devil, frighted out of his wits. However at the request of some of the officers, who had been Neilson's friends, his punishment was changed into that of mounting on a table and begging pardon for having smiled at the regiment. He was then drummed and fiddled out of town, with a strict prohibition of ever being seen in it again.

One might have expected that, tho' I had been imprudent all my life, the present occasion might have inspired me with some degree of caution, and yet I can tell you I had almost incurred the poor groom's fate from my own folly. Several of the officers came up to dine, amongst others Colonel Howe, who with less ceremony than might have been expected from his general politeness stept into an apartment adjoining the hall and took up a book I had been reading, which he brought open in his hand into the company. I was piqued at his freedom, and reproved him with a half compliment to his general good breeding. He owned his fault and with much gallantry promised to submit to whatever punishment I would inflict. You shall only, said I, read aloud a few pages which I will point out, and I am sure you will do Shakespear justice. He bowed and took the book, but no sooner observed that I had turned up for him that part of Henry the fourth where Falstaff describes his company, than he coloured like scarlet. I saw he made the application instantly; however he read it thro', tho' not with the vivacity he generally speaks; however he recovered himself and, coming close up to me, whispered, "You will certainly get yourself tarred and feathered; shall I apply to be executioner?"

I am going to seal this up. Adieu.

I closed my last packet at Doctor Cobham's after the review, and as I hoped to hear of some method of getting it sent to you, stayed, tho' Miss Rutherford was obliged to go home. As soon as she was gone, I went into the town, the entry of which I found closed up by a detachment of the soldiers; but as the officer immediately made way for me, I took no further notice of it, but advanced to the middle of the street, where I found a number of the first people in town standing together, who (to use Milton's phrase) seemed much impassioned. As most of them were my acquaintances, I stopped to speak to them, but they with one voice begged me for heaven's sake to get off the street, making me observe they were prisoners, adding that every avenue of the town was shut up, and that in all human probability some scene would be acted very unfit for me to witness. I could not take the friendly advice, for I became unable to move and absolutely petrified with horror.

Observing however an officer with whom I had just dined, I beckoned him to me. He came, but with no very agreeable look, and on my asking him what was the matter, he presented a paper he had folded in his hand. "If you will persuade them to sign this they are at liberty," said he, "but till then must remain under this guard, as they must suffer the penalties they have justly incurred."

"And we will suffer every thing," replied one of them, "before we abjure our king, our country and our principles. This, ladies," said he turning to me, who was now joined by several ladies, "is what they call their Test, but by what authority this gentleman forces it on us, we are yet to learn."

"There is my authority," pointing to the soldiers with the most insolent air; "dispute it, if you can."

Oh Britannia, what are you doing, while your true obedient sons are thus insulted by their unlawful brethren; are they also forgot by their natural parents?

—ANDREWS, ed., *Journal of a Lady of Quality*, pp. 189-192.

6. How Philadelphians Dealt with Tories

Memoirs of Alexander Graydon.

August, 1775

Among the disaffected in Philadelphia, Doctor Kearsley was pre-eminently ardent and rash. An extremely zealous Loyalist, and impetuous in his temper, he had given much umbrage to the whigs; and if I am not mistaken, he had been detected in some hostile machinations. Hence he was deemed a proper subject for the fashionable punishment of tarring, feathering and carting. He was seized at his own door by a party of the militia, and, in the attempt to resist them, received a wound in his hand from a bayonet. Being overpowered, he was placed in a cart provided for the purpose, and amidst a multitude of boys and idlers, paraded through the streets to the tune of the rogue's march. I happened to be at the coffee-house when the concourse arrived there. They made a halt, while the Doctor, foaming with rage and indignation, without his hat, his wig dishevelled and bloody from his wounded hand, stood up in the cart and called for a bowl of punch. It was quickly handed to him; when so vehement was his thirst that he drained it of its contents before he took it from his lips.

What were the feelings of others on this lawless proceeding, I know not, but mine, I must confess, revolted at the spectacle. I was shocked at seeing a lately respected citizen so cruelly vilified, and was imprudent enough to say that, had I been a magistrate, I would, at every hazard, have interposed my authority in suppression of the outrage. But this was not the only instance which convinced me that I wanted nerves for a revolutionist. It must be admitted, however, that the conduct of the populace was marked by a lenity which peculiarly distinguished the cradle of our republicanism. Tar and feathers had been dispensed with, and excepting the injury he had received in his hand, no sort of violence was offered by the mob to their victim. But to a man of high spirit, as the Doctor was, the indignity in its lightest form was sufficient to madden him: it probably had this effect, since his conduct became so extremely outrageous that it was thought necessary to confine him. From the city he was soon after removed to Carlisle, where he died during the war.

A few days after the carting of Mr. Kearsley, Mr. Isaac Hunt, the attorney, was treated in the same manner, but he managed the matter much better than his precursor. Instead of braving his conductors like the Doctor, Mr. Hunt was a pattern of meekness and humility; and at every halt that was made, he rose and expressed his acknowledgments to the crowd for their forbearance and civility. After a parade of an hour or two, he was set down at his own door, as uninjured in body as in mind. He soon after removed to one of the islands—if I mistake not, to Barbadoes—where, it was understood, he took orders.

Not long after these occurrences, Major Skene of the British Army ventured to show himself in Philadelphia. Whatever might have been his inducement to the measure, it was deemed expedient by the newly constituted authorities to have him arrested and secured. A guard was accordingly placed over him at his lodgings at the city tavern. The officer to whose charge he was especially committed was Mr. Francis Wade, the brewer, an Irishman of distinguished zeal in the cause, and one who was supposed to possess talents peculiarly befitting him for the task of curbing the spirit of a haughty Briton, which Skene undoubtedly was.

I well recollect the day that the guard was paraded to escort him out of the city on his way to some other station. An immense crowd of spectators stood before the door of his quarters, and lined the street through which he was to pass. The weather being warm, the window sashes of his apartment were raised, and Skene, with his bottle of wine upon the table, having just finished his dinner, roared out in the voice of a Stentor, "*God save great George our king!*" Had the spirit of seventy-five in any degree resembled the spirit of Jacobinism, to which it has been unjustly compared, this bravado would unquestionably have brought the Major to the *lamp-post*, and set his head upon a pike; but as, fortunately for him, it did not, he was suffered to proceed with his song, and the auditory seemed more generally amused than offended.

—GRAYDON, *Memoirs of His Own Time*, pp. 126-128.

7. "A Poor Man Was Tarred and Feathered Ten Times"

Lord William Campbell to Lord Dartmouth.

Charlestown [S. C.], August 19, 1775

. . . This is a very disagreeable subject for me to dwell on, but my duty requires I should represent the true state of this Province, and of my unfortunate vicinage of N. Carolina, and Georgia, which is equally neglected, equally abandoned. Your Lordship will, I am sure, excuse my warmth when I acquaint that yesterday under colour of law they hanged and burned an unfortunate wretch, a free Negro of considerable property, one of the most valuable and useful men in his way in the Province, on suspicion of instigating an insurrection, for which I am convinced there was not the least ground.

I could not save him, my Lord! the very reflection harrows my soul! I have only the comfort to think I left no means untried to preserve him.

They have now dipt their hands in blood. God Almighty knows where it will end, but I am determined to remain till the last extremity in hope to promote the King's service, tho my familys being here adds not a little to my distress.

Another act of barbarity, tho happily of not so tragical a nature, was committed a few days ago on a poor man, the gunner of Fort Johnson, who for expressing his loyalty was tarred and feathered 10 or 12 times, in different parts of the town, and otherwise treated with great cruelty, stopping him at the doors of those Crown officers who were most obnoxious; and the mob so grossly insullted Mr. Milligan, in particular, who is surgeon to the forts and garrisons in this Province, that he was under a necessity of taking refuge on board the King's ship till the packet boat sails.

—Gr. Brit. Hist. Mss. Comm., *Dartmouth Papers*, II, 354.

8. Tar and Feathers Make Thomas Randolph Repent

From the records of the Committee of Safety.

New York, December 28, 1775

The 6th of December, at Quibbletown, Middlesex County, Piscataway Township, New-Jersey, Thomas Randolph, cooper, who had publickly proved himself an enemy to his country, by reviling and using his utmost endeavours to oppose the proceedings of the Continental and Provincial Conventions and Committees, in defence of their rights and liberties; and he, being judged a person of not consequence enough for a severer punishment, was ordered to be stripped naked, well coated with tar and feathers, and carried in a wagon publickly round the town; which punishment was accordingly inflicted. And as he soon became duly sensible of his offence, for which he earnestly begged pardon, and promised to atone, as far as he was able, by a contrary behaviour for the future, he was released, and suffered to return to his house in less than half an hour. The whole was conducted with that regularity and decorum that ought to be observed in all publick punishments.

—Force, *American Archives*, 4th Series, IV, 203.

III. THE PROPRIETY AND LEGALITY OF LOYALTY OATHS

Most of the provincial assemblies had recourse to loyalty oaths at an early stage in the controversy with the mother country. The Massachusetts Provincial Congress, for example, required a special loyalty test for the "Governours and Instructors" of Harvard College. Many Loyalists managed to evade the requirement; many others, doubtless, took it under duress; here and there some refused to take it on principle, and their arguments against the legality and justice of the special loyalty oath are of lively interest to us today.

Even before the Declaration of Independence, Rhode Island passed a test act which provided that any male inhabitant over sixteen years of age "suspected of being inimical to the United American Colonies" might be summoned before a member of the Assembly and required to subscribe to an oath of loyalty. In July 1776 additional acts provided a fine of £100 on any person who persisted in acknowledging George III, and forfeiture of the right to vote and other rights of citizenship. No sooner were these acts on the law books than officers of the Rhode Island Brigade presented the Assembly with a list of 77 inhabitants of Newport suspected of being Loyalists. Among these were four Jews. They were promptly called before the Assembly and according to its proceedings,

> *Rabbi Isaac de Abraham Touro appeared and refused to sign the test as he had not been naturalized and it is against his Religious Principles and likewise he is a subject to the States of Holland. Isaac Hart refused to sign the test until it was required of all alike. Meyer Pollock refused to sign because it was contrary to the custom of Jews.*

But it was the fourth, Moses M. Hays, who raised the issue of principle most elaborately. We give here the report of the Committee on Suspected Persons on his appearance before it, and his own petition to the Assembly.

No less interesting is the argument formulated by Peter Van Schaack, whom we have already met earlier in this chapter. Persuasive as it was, it was not accepted; yet the New York authorities permitted Van Schaack to live on at Kinderhook, on parole, and to leave the next year for England.

It should be added that loyalty oaths were also imposed by the British military authorities, and that such an oath was reputed to have been taken under duress by Richard Stockton, a Signer, when he was captured by the British.

1. Moses Hays Refuses to Take a Loyalty Oath

[July 1, 1776]

Report of the Rhode Island Committee on Suspected Persons.

He refused to sign the Test and called for his accusers. He was then told there was a number present whom he saw there. He likewise called for his accusation which was read.

"I have and ever shall hold the strongest principles and attachments to the just rights and privileges of this my native land, and ever have and shall conform to the rules and acts of this government and pay as I always have my proportion of its exigencies. I always have asserted my sentiments in favor of America and confess the war on its part just.

"I decline subscribing the Test at present from these principles: first, that I deny ever being inimical to my country and call for my accusers and proof of conviction. Second, that I am an Israelite and am not allowed the liberty of a vote, or voice in common with the rest of the voters though consistent with the Constitution and the other Colonies. Thirdly, because the Test is not general and consequently subject to many glaring inconveniences. Fourthly, Continental Congress nor the General Assembly of this nor the Legislatures of the other Colonies have never in this contest taken any notice or countenance respecting the society of Israelites to which I belong. When any rule, order or directions is made by the Congress or General Assembly I shall to the utmost of my power adhere to the same."

To the Honorable the General Assembly of Rhode Island Now Sitting at New Port:

New Port, July 17, 1776

Moses M. Hays of New Port begs leave humbly to represent to your honors that he hath ever been warmly and zealously attacht to the rights and liberties of the colonies and ever uniformly conducted himself consistant with the rest of the good and friendly people of these colonies, and always despised inimicall principles, and as farr as one person can testify for another, numbers of creditable persons can testify. Yet on the 12th inst. was cited by the sheriff to appear at the court house on that same day at 2 o'clock in the afternoon when I attended accordingly, and being called was informed by your honorable speaker that an information had been lodged against me among a number of persons of being inimicall to the country (Mr. Sears, Mr. Fowler and Mr. Geo. Wanton and some officers present). I denied and do still deny holding or entertaining such principles, and desired to know my accusers and accusations.

I was answered by Mr. Bowles reading a paper purporting to be a complaint from the officers that there were many suspected inimicall persons in town and naming them; desired they might be called on. And no other allegations appearing against me I declined signing the Test then for reasons I gave in writing, which will no doubt be laid before your honors and trust they will appear justifiable.

I ask of your Honors the rights and privileges due other free citizens when I conform to everything generally done and acted and again implore that the justice of your Honors may interfere in my behalf and will give me leave again to call for the cause and my accusation of inimicalty, that I may have an opportunity of vindication before your Honors. I am with great respect

Your Honors most obedient and humble servant,

M. M. HAYS

—GENERAL ASSEMBLY PAPERS, Revolutionary War, "Suspected Persons," p. 14, Rhode Island State Archives.

2. THE TEST OATH IS ILLEGAL AND ILLOGICAL

Peter Van Schaack to the Provincial Convention.

Kinderhook, 25th January, 1777

Gentlemen:

I am now about setting out, conformably to the sentence of your Committee, to make the town of Boston my prison, to which I am condemned by them unheard, upon a charge of maintaining an equivocal neutrality in the present struggles. How far the punishment of banishment for this can be justified, either by the practice of other nations or upon those principles on which alone legitimate governments are founded, and how far it answers those ends, which alone make punishments a lawful exercise of power, I shall not at present inquire; but as it implies that your committee considers me as a subject of your State, it behooves me, gentlemen, "to address you with that freedom which can never give offence to the representatives of a free people."

When I appeared before the Albany committee, I refused to answer the question whether I considered myself as a subject of Great Britain or of the State of New York, because I perceived the dilemma in which it would involve me, of either bringing punishment on myself, in consequence of my own declaration, or of taking an oath which, if I had been never so clear respecting the propositions it contains under the circumstances it was offered to me, and in my present situation I should not have taken.

The reasons peculiar to myself I shall not urge; but, supposing the independency of this State to be clearly established, I conceive it is premature to tender an oath of allegiance before the government to which it imposes subjection, the time it is to take place of the present exceptionable one, and who are to be the rulers, as well as the mode of their appointment in future, are known; . . .

But, gentlemen, admitting there was never so clear a majority in favor of independency, and who were convinced that they were absolved from their allegiance, and admitting that you are now vested with powers to form a new government by the suffrages of a majority of the people of this State; permit me to observe that those who are of different sentiments, be they never so few, are not absolutely concluded in point of right thereby. The question whether a government is dissolved and the people released from their allegiance is, in my opinion, a question of morality as well as religion, in which *every man* must judge, as he must answer for himself; and this idea is fairly held up to the public in your late address, wherein you declare "that every individual must one day answer for the part he now acts." If he must *answer* for the part he acts, which certainly presupposes the right of private judgement, he can never be justifiable in the sight of God or man if he acts against the light of his own conviction. In such a case no majority, however respectable, can decide for him.

But, admitting that a man is never so clear about the dissolution of the old government, I hold it that every *individual* has still a right to choose the State of which he will become a member; for before he surrenders any part of his natural liberty, he has a right to know what security he will have for the enjoyment of the residue, and "men being by nature free, equal and independent," the subjection of any one to the political power of a State can arise only from "his own consent." I speak of the formation of society and of a man's initiating himself therein, so as to make himself a member of it; for I admit that when once the society *is* formed, the majority of its members undoubtedly conclude the rest.

Upon these principles, I hold it that you cannot justly put me to the alternative of choosing to be a subject of Great Britain, or of this State, because should I deny subjection to Great Britain, it would not follow that I must necessarily be a member of the State of New York; on the contrary, I should still hold that I had a right, by the "immutable laws of nature," to choose any other State of which I would become a member. And, gentlemen, if you think me so dangerous a man as that my liberty at home is incompatible with the public safety, I now claim it at your hands as my right that you permit me to remove from your State into any other I may prefer, in which case I reserve to myself the power of disposing my property by sale or otherwise. . . .

If my principles are ill-founded, or misapplied, I shall readily retract my errors when pointed out; but if they are founded on the immutable laws of nature and the sacred rights of mankind, if they are such as are generally acknowledged by writers of the greatest eminence, and if they are necessarily connected with the same principles on which the American opposition is justified, I trust they will readily be admitted by you, though urged by an extra-judicial way, but are clearly connected with my defence, on a charge which has been thought of importance enough to subject me to banishment from my native place. . . .

—Van Schaack, *Life of Peter Van Schaack*, pp. 71-76.

IV. THE RISING TIDE OF FURY

After the Declaration of Independence not only the popular but what might be called the official attitude toward Tories became increasingly virulent. The most interesting thing about this collection of letters is not the extreme severity of the opinions expressed, but the dignity and distinction of those who were prepared to be so ruthless. Hawley and Sam Adams were, from the beginning, implacable in their devotion to independence and their hatred of loyalism; but Patrick Henry had wavered a bit on independence; Gouverneur Morris, like his colleagues Jay and Duane, had wavered and temporized; and Governor Livingston, though an ardent Patriot, was an aristocrat and a gentleman. This particular letter of his concerned an appeal by the Loyalist Philip Schuyler, member of a family as famous as Livingston's, to return to his New Jersey home.

1. Major Hawley Wants Death for All Tories

Joseph Hawley to Elbridge Gerry.

Northampton, July 17, 1776

Dear Sir: I have often said that I supposed a Declaration of Independence would be accompanied with a declaration of high treason. Most certainly it must immediately, and without the least delay, follow it. Can we subsist —did any State ever subsist, without exterminating traitors? I never desire to see high treason extended here further than it is now extended in Britain. But an act of high treason we must have instantly. The Colonies have long suffered inexpressibly for want of it. No one thing made the Declaration of Independence indispensably necessary more than cutting off traitors. It is amazingly wonderful that, having no capital punishment for our intestine enemies, we have not been utterly ruined before now. For God's sake, let us not run such risks a day longer! It appears to me, sir, that high treason ought to be the same in all the United States, saving to the legislature of each Colony or State the right of attainting individuals by act or bill of attainder. The present times show most clearly the wisdom and sound policy of the common law in that doctrine, or part thereof, which consists in attainting by an act of the whole legislature. Our Tories (be sure the learned of them) knew very well the absurdity of punishing as high treason any acts or deeds in favour of the Government of the King of Great Britain, so long as we all allowed him to be King of the Colonies.

Dear Sir, this matter admits of no delay; and when the act declaratory of high treason is passed, the strongest recommendation for a strict execution of it, I humbly conceive, ought to accompany it. Our whole cause is every moment in amazing danger for want of it. The common understanding of the people, like unerring instinct, has long declared this; and from the clear discerning which they have had of it, they have been long in agonies about it. They expect that effectual care will now be taken for the general safety, and that all those who shall be convicted of endeavouring, by overt act, to destroy the State, shall be cut off from the earth.

—FORCE, *American Archives*, 5th Series, I, 403-404.

2. "REVOLUTIONS ARE SELDOM ACHIEVED WITHOUT CALAMITY"

Gouverneur Morris to his mother [a Loyalist].

December 19, 1776

I am sorry it is not in my power to see you at present. I know it is your wish that I were removed from public affairs; indeed, as far as relates to my own ease and enjoyments, I wish so too. But I know it is the duty of every good citizen or man to preserve that post in which by a superior order he is placed. Where the happiness of a considerable part of our fellow creatures is deeply concerned, we soon feel the insignificancy of an individual. And whatever lot that individual shall experience, while a conscious rectitude of conduct inspires and supports him, though he may be unfortunate, he cannot be miserable.

What may be the event of the present war, it is not in man to determine. Great revolutions of empire are seldom achieved without much human calamity; but the worst which can happen is to fall on the last bleak mountain of America, and he who dies there, in defence of the injured rights of mankind, is happier than his conqueror, more beloved of mankind, more applauded by his own heart.

—SPARKS, *Life of Gouverneur Morris*, I, 22.

3. MORE IS TO BE FEARED FROM THE LOYALISTS THAN THE BRITISH!

Samuel Adams to James Warren.

Baltimore, February 16, 1777

My Dear Sir,—A few days ago a small expedition was made by the authority of this State aided by a detachment of Continental Regulars, to suppress the Tories in the Counties of Somerset and Worcester on the Eastern Shore of Chessepeak, where they are numerous and have arisen to a great pitch of violence. We this day have a rumour that one of their principals, a Doctor Cheyney, is taken and we hope to hear of the business being effectually done, very soon. In my opinion, much more is to be apprehended from the secret machinations of these rascally people than from the open violence of British and Hessian soldiers, whose success has been in a great measure owing to the aid they have received from them.

You know that the Tories in America have always acted upon one system. Their head quarters used to be at Boston—more lately at Philadelphia. They have continually embarrassed the publick councils there and afforded intelligence, advice and assistance to General Howe. Their influence is extended throughout the United States. Boston has its full share of them, and yet I do not hear that measures have been taken to suppress them. On the contrary, I am informed that the citizens are grown so polite as to treat them with tokens of civility and respect. Can a man take fire into his bosom and not be burned? Your Massachusetts Tories communicate with the enemy in Britain as well as New York. They give and receive intelligence, from whence they early form a judgment of their measures. I am told they discovered an air of insolent tryumph in their countenances, and saucily enjoyed the success of Howe's forces in Jersey before it happened.

Indeed, my friend, if measures are not soon taken, and the most vigorous ones, to root out these pernicious weeds, it will be in vain for America to persevere in this generous struggle for the publick liberty. . . .

—*Warren-Adams Letters*, I, 291-292.

4. GOVERNOR PATRICK HENRY EXERCISES POWERS NOT GIVEN BY LAW

To Benjamin Harrison, Speaker of the House of Delegates.

May 25, 1779

Sir: A certain Zechariah Snead was detected going secretly to the British flag vessels, and, being examined and found to lay under very strong suspicions of disaffection, has been ordered to gaol. A few days ago, a person calling her self Letitia Fitzgerald appeared in this city; her husband, she pretends, is the eldest son of the Duke of Leinster, was apprehended in the Nansemond County and was under examination for treasonable practices, when the enemy entered Suffolk and released him. A great variety of circumstances concur to induce a belief that this is a dangerous woman, and that she came hither with some wicked intention. She was therefore sent to gaol also.

The Executive having in these two instances exercised a power not expressly given them by law, I take this method of informing the legislature of it, and have only to add that apprehension for the public safety is the sole reason for the proceeding.

I am, Sir, Your most humble servant,

P. HENRY

—WIRT, *Life of Henry*, III, 242.

5. GOVERNOR LIVINGSTON NEVER WANTS THE LOYALISTS BACK

William Livingston to Robert Livingston.

Trenton, April 22, 1782

Dear Brother,

I have just now received your letter of the 12th instant, desiring my passport for Mr. Philip Schuyler to come from New York to Second River, and for the two Miss Schuylers to go thither and fetch him. I am persuaded that I need use no arguments to convince either you, or Sister Livingston, of the particular pleasure it would give me to oblige her in any request that was consistent with my duty to this State to grant. But the present is not in that predicament. I have never given any permission for a person to return into this State who had voluntarily left our lines to go into those of the enemy, as I am informed this gentleman has done. Such people have had an opportunity to make their election. They have made it. They must abide by the event of their choice; and we do not want them back again. Nor have I ever granted a permission for their relations living amongst us, to visit them in the enemys lines. This rule I have inviolably adhered to, in opposition to the warmest solicitations of my nearest connections, having in similar cases refused the applications of Lady Stirling, Sister Alida Hoffman, and the children of Mrs. Van Horne.

I am sensible that in particular instances the rule might be counter acted without public detriment, and probably in the case in question the readmission of Mr Schuyler would not prove injurious to the State. But the precedent would be pernicious, and once established no one in like circumstances could be refused without the imputation of partiality; and the fatal consequences that would attend an universal indulgence are too obvious to require an illustration. My relations, I am sure, would not wish me to adopt a measure that would either be prejudicial to the country on the one hand, or expose my administration on the other to be branded with the reproach of partiality to individuals.

I hope, however, that this will not prevent Sister from prosecuting her purpose of coming into New-Jersey to see her friends and relations, who, I dare say, will be glad to see her; and I believe none more so than my family at Elizabeth Town. If she inquires about the proper rout as she comes on, I believe she will be in no danger from the enemy. . . .

I doubt whether we shall have a peace this summer, as the ultra-atlantic blockheads will probably try another campaign, which will only redound to our advantage by bringing them so much the lower, and the winter I suppose will be consumed in negotiation. But next spring I believe we must have it, as the people of England, among many other reasons that inspire that hope, are turning Liberty Boys in shoals, and are determined, whether the royal fool will hear or not, to beseige his throne with petitions and remonstrances against the farther prosecution of the war. Scotland itself, even the land of rebellion and loyalty, is running into associations and committees and drawing the most spirited remonstrances for putting an immediate period to the American war, in order to prevent the utter ruin of Great Britain. What think you of Congress now! Rivington owes me one of his ears; and I suppose Governor Clinton claims the other; and as the fellow has but two the public may take his head.

I am your affectionate brother and humble servant,

WIL: LIVINGSTON

—ROBINSON & LEDER, eds., "Governor Livingston,"
William & Mary Quarterly, 3rd Series, XIII, 396-397.

V. TORY DEFIANCE

Loyalists took the offensive not only in military but in verbal battle. We have already seen something of the Loyalist argument; we present here a few examples of what might be called Loyalist defiance. The letters speak for themselves; it is sufficient that we introduce, here, the speakers. Peter Oliver —already an old man when the conflict with the mother country broke out— was a distinguished member of one of the Bay Colony's distinguished families. A graduate of Harvard College, he had been appointed chief justice of the colony in 1771; a member of the Hutchinson circle, he was a councillor and then a "mandamus" councillor, who enjoyed the distinction of impeachment by an outraged General Court. Oliver sailed with Gage to England where Oxford promptly gave him a degree of Doctor of Civil Laws. Jonathan Sewall (or, as he later spelled it, Sewell) is best known to us through the Diary of John Adams. A graduate of Harvard College, he was for long intimate with Adams, who counted him his closest friend. Personal resentment against the General Court apparently turned Sewall from his earlier ardent attachment to the colonial cause; he attached himself to the Hutchinson-Oliver group, was made attorney general, and like Oliver sailed for England in 1775 where he eventually settled in Bristol. Adams said of him that "he possessed a lively wit, a pleasing humor, brilliant imagination, a great subtlety of reasoning and an insinuating eloquence."

Jacob Duché was an Anglican preacher who found revolutionary violence and separation from England not to his taste. Member of an old Philadelphia family, brother-in-law to Francis Hopkinson, he had studied at Cambridge University and formed sentimental ties to England. At the beginning of the Revolutionary struggle, however, Duché was an ardent and eloquent Patriot, and chaplain to the Continental Congress. When Howe captured Philadelphia he promptly put the Reverend Mr. Duché in jail, and there, apparently, Duché experienced a change of mind or of heart. This famous letter was the product of that change. Ostracized for his apostasy, Duché left for England in December 1777, but his heart was in America, and he never reconciled himself to his exile. Not until 1792 did Pennsylvania permit him to return to his old home. Still inclined to sudden conversions, he was at the end of his life converted to Swedenborgianism.

Jonathan Odell, like Jacob Duché, was an Anglican clergyman who, curiously enough, had served in his day as a surgeon in the British Army. On the outbreak of the war he took refuge with the British in New York where he was made army chaplain, secretary to General Carleton, and served as a go-between in negotiations between André and Arnold. This indictment

of Washington was part of a longer poem, "The American Times," published
in Rivington's Royal Gazette. Odell departed with the British at the end of
the war, and lived out his life in New Brunswick.

1. PETER OLIVER POINTS OUT THAT HEAVEN PUNISHES ALL REBELS
To Polly Hutchinson, his sister-in-law.

Boston, May 26th, 1775

My Dear Polly,—

The only satisfaction that absent friends can receive from each other is
by intercourse in an epistolary way. This intercourse hath been interrupted
by the Sons of Anarchy, and is like to be a short time to come, but I have great
reason to think not much longer, for yesterday arrived three approved generals—Howe, Clinton and Burgoyne, who are to be followed (and who are
expected in a few days) by 5 or 6000 troops from Ireland, with a regiment of
horse; so that we shall have here 13 or 14000 well disciplined troops, when
the campaign will be opened by 5 as fine general officers as perhaps are in
the King's service. They expected in England that we were in a much better
situation than we are, or more would have been sent. But I can assure you
from the best and undoubted authority that the English nation were never
more united than they are now against the Americans; and that force of ships,
men and mony are now devoted to support the dignity of Great Britain; and
I have good reason to think that when the news of the late battle arrives,
which I suppose is now arrived in England, that we shall have this summer
20 or 30 thousand over, and somebody must pay for them.

What miseries must attend a conquest or no conquest! They plunder the
properties of all the friends of Government, and the public must pay for
them. They boast of their numbers, but their numbers grow tired: they say
their leaders have deceived them, and they are uneasy. A person who hath
been active for years past in the defection sent to me to-day to intercede for
him, and is almost distracted; another of the like stamp sent to me to get his
house excepted from the ravages of the troops when they go out, but he is
fled himself out of the Province.

I feel the miseries which impend over my country: may Heaven avert
them by the people's being convinced of the horrid crime of rebellion, before
it is too late! The God of Order may punish a community for a time with
their own disorders, but it is incompatible with the rectitude of the Divine
Nature to suffer anarchy to prevail. Observe, my dear, the course of Providence: the first and grand incendiary is now marked out as a madman; Moli-
neaux is supposed to have died an unnatural death; Mr. Bowdoin is not far
from dying; Pitts not likely to continue long; Denny, it is said, is ill with a
mortification in his leg; Hancock is thought to be ruined in his large fortune;
Lee, of Marblehead, is dead, and after the battle was frighted, and continued
so till he died; I am informed that Hawley has guards about him to prevent
his injuring himself. . . .

Yours Affectionately,
PETER OLIVER

—HUTCHINSON, ed., *Diary and Letters of Thomas Hutchinson*, I, 457-458.

2. A MASSACHUSETTS LOYALIST BIDS HIS AMERICAN FRIENDS TREMBLE

Jonathan Sewall to John Foxcroft.

London, March 14, 1775

Dear Johnny,

Don't be frightened at seeing a letter from an old tory friend, lest it should come under the inspection of your high and mighty committees, as I suppose will be the case in your *free* and independent *state*. I hereby declare I have never received a line from you since I left Cambridge, August 31, 1774, excepting one while I was at Boston relative to two gowns which Molly H. stole from my wife, of which I desired you to make enquiry, and this is the first scrip I have attempted to you since the said date, so that you can't be charged with holding a correspondence with me. Thus much to prevent any mistakes which might expose you to the perils of tarring and feathering, Simsbury mines, a gaol or a galows.

I presume it can give no offence to committees, congresses, parsons, or generals that I embrace a favourable, or rather a *possible* opportunity of *advising* you that I am yet in the land of the living, though very probably they may all be offended at the fact; but to ease their gall-bladders a little, I assure you and them, I hope in God I shall not live to see the day when America shall become independent of Great Britain. I suppose by this time you have entered so thoroughly into their mad scheme that it will afford you no pleasure to hear your quondam friends on this side of the Atlantic are well. However, I will mortify you by assuring you they are all in good health and spirits, and government has liberally supplied the wants of all the tory refugees who needed its assistance; and none here entertains the penumbra of a doubt how the game will end. No more does pious, frank, single-eyed, conscientious Dr. Elliot, you will say. Aye, I have seen his letters and compared them with two or three conversations he had with me between Charlestown Ferry and the college, not long before my flight. Well, duplicity may be justified on some principles for aught I know; but I don't like it. . . .

I should like to take one peep at my house, but I suppose I should not know it again. *Sic transit gloria mundi.* I shan't break my heart about it. Every dog they say has his day, and I doubt not I shall have mine. Ah, my old friend, could you form a just idea of the immense wealth and power of the British nation, you would tremble at the foolish audacity of your pigmy states. Another summer will bring you all over to my opinion. I feel for the miseries hastening on my countrymen, but they must thank their own folly. God bless and carry you safe through!

—AUSTIN, *Life of Elbridge Gerry*, I, 270-272.

3. WASHINGTON IMPLORED TO LEAD THE COLONIES BACK TO BRITAIN

The Reverend Jacob Duché to George Washington.

Philadelphia, October 8, 1777

. . . And now, my dear Sir, suffer me in the language of truth and real affection to address myself to you. All the world must be convinced that you are engaged in the service of your country from motives perfectly disinterested. You risked every thing that was dear to you. You abandoned all those sweets of domestic life of which your affluent fortune gave you the uninter-rupted enjoyment. But had you? could you have had the least idea of matters being carried to such a dangerous extremity as they are now? Your most intimate friends at that time shuddered at the thoughts of a separation from the mother country; and I took it for granted that your sentiments coincided with theirs. What have been the consequences of this rash and violent measure? A degeneracy of representation—confusion of counsels—blunders without number. The most respectable characters have withdrawn themselves, and are succeeded by a great majority of illiberal and violent men.

Take an impartial view of the present Congress, and what can you expect from them? Your feelings must be greatly hurt by the representation from your native province. You have no longer a Randolph, a Bland, or a Braxton; . . . Characters now present themselves whose minds can never mingle with your own. Your Harrison alone remains, and he disgusted with his unworthy associates. As to those of my own province, some of them are so obscure that their very names never met my ears before, and others have only been dis-tinguished for the weakness of their understandings and the violence of their tempers. One alone I except from the general charge. . . .

From the New England Provinces can you find one that as a gentleman you could wish to associate with? unless the soft and mild address of Mr. Hancock can atone for his want of every other qualification necessary for the station he fills. Bankrupts, attorneys, and men of desperate fortunes are his colleagues.

Maryland no longer sends a Tilghman and a Protestant Carroll. Carolina has lost its Lynch, and the elder Middleton has retired.

Are the dregs of a Congress then still to influence a mind like yours? These are not the men you engaged to serve. These are not the men that America has chosen to represent her now. Most of them were elected by a little low faction, and the few gentlemen that are among them now well known to be upon the balance and looking up to your hand alone to move the beam. 'Tis you, Sir, and you alone that supports the present Congress. Of this you must be fully sensible. Long before they left Philadelphia, their dignity and con-sequence was gone. What must it be now, since their precipitate retreat? . . .

After this view of Congress, turn to your army. The whole world knows that its very existence depends upon you, that your death or captivity dis-perses it in a moment, and that there is not a man on that side of the question in America, capable of succeeding you. As to the army itself, what have you to expect from them? Have they not frequently abandoned even yourself in the hour of extremity? Have you, can you have, the least confidence in a set of undisciplined men and officers, many of whom have been taken from the lowest of the people, without principle and without courage? Take away those that surround your person, how few are there that you can ask to sit at your table?

Turn to your little navy—of *that little*, what is *left?* Of the Delaware fleet, part are taken, the rest must soon surrender. Of those in the other Provinces, some taken, one or two at sea, and others lying unmanned and unrigged in their harbours.

And now where are your resources? O, my dear Sir! how sadly have you been abused by a faction void of truth and void of tenderness to you and your country! They have amused you with hopes of a declaration of war on the part of France. Believe me from the best authority, it was a fiction from the first. . . .

From your friends in England, you have nothing to expect. Their numbers are diminished to a cipher. The spirit of the whole nation is in full activity against you. A few sounding names among the nobility, though perpetually rung in your ears, are said to be without character, without influence. Disappointed ambition, I am told, has made them desperate, and they only wish to make the deluded Americans instruments of their revenge. All orders and ranks of men in Great Britain are now unanimous, and determined to risk their all on the contest. Trade and manufactures are found to flourish; and new channels are continually opening, that will, perhaps, more than supply the old. In a word, your harbours are blocked up, your cities fall one after another, fortress after fortress, battle after battle is lost. A British army, after having passed almost unmolested through a vast extent of country, have possessed themselves with ease of the capital of America. How unequal the contest now! How fruitless the expense of blood!

Under so many discourageing circumstances, can virtue, can honour, can the love of your country prompt you to persevere? Humanity itself (and sure I am humanity is no stranger to your breast) calls upon you to desist. Your army must perish for want of common necessaries, or thousands of innocent families must perish to support them. Wherever they encamp the country must be impoverished. Wherever they march the troops of Britain will pursue, and must complete the devastation which America herself has begun.

Perhaps it may be said that "it is better to die than to be slaves." This, indeed, is a splendid maxim in theory; and, perhaps, in some instances, may be found experimentally true. But where there is the least probability of any happy accommodation, surely wisdom and humanity call for some sacrifices to be made to prevent inevitable destruction. You will know that there is but one invincible bar to such an accommodation; could this be removed, other obstacles might readily be overcome. 'Tis to you, and you alone, your bleeding country looks, and calls aloud for this sacrifice. Your arm alone has strength sufficient to remove this bar. May Heaven inspire you with the glorious resolution of exerting this strength at so interesting a crisis, and thus immortalizing yourself as a friend and guardian of your country.

Your penetrating eye needs not more explicit language to discern my meaning. With that prudence and delicacy, therefore, of which I know you to be possessed, represent to Congress the indispensable necessity of rescinding the hasty and ill-advised Declaration of Independency. Recommend, and you have an undoubted right to recommend, an immediate cessation of hostilities. Let the controversy be taken up where that Declaration left it, and where Lord Howe certainly expected to find it. Let men of clear and impartial characters, in or out of Congress, liberal in their sentiments, heretofore independent in their fortunes (and some such may surely be found in

America), be appointed to confer with His Majesty's Commissioners. Let them, if they please, prepare some well-digested constitutional plan, to lay before them as the commencement of a negotiation. When they have gone thus far, I am confident that the most happy consequences will ensue. Unanimity will immediately take place through the different Provinces. Thousands who are now ardently wishing and praying for such a measure will step forth and declare themselves the zealous advocates of constitutional liberty, and millions will bless the Hero that left the field of war to decide this most important contest with the weapons of wisdom and humanity. . . .

Your most obedient and
Sincere friend and servant
JACOB DUCHÉ

—GRAYDON, Memoirs of His Own Time, p. 429 ff.

4. "HEAR THY INDICTMENT, WASHINGTON . . ."

Jonathan Odell

Hear thy indictment, Washington, at large;
Attend and listen to the solemn charge:
Thou hast supported an atrocious cause
Against thy King, thy country, and the laws;
Committed perjury, encouraged lies,
Forced conscience, broken the most sacred ties;
Myriads of wives and daughters at thy hand
Their slaughtered husbands, slaughtered sons, demand;
That pastures hear no more the lowing kine,
That towns are desolate, all—all is thine;
The frequent sacrilege that pained my sight,
The blasphemies my pen abhors to write,
Innumerable crimes on thee must fall—
For thou maintainest, thou defendest, all. . .

What could when half-way up the hill to fame,
Induce thee to go back and link with shame?
Was it ambition, vanity, or spite
That prompted thee with Congress to unite;
Or did all three within thy bosom roll,
"Thou heart of hero with a traitor's soul"?
Go, wretched author of thy country's grief,
Patron of villainy, of villains chief;
Seek with thy cursèd crew the central gloom,
Ere truth's avenging sword begin thy doom;
Or sudden vengeance of celestial dart
Precipitate thee with augmented smart.

—SARGENT, ed., Loyalist Poetry, pp. 10-12.

VI. LOYALISTS IN EXILE

A romantic aura commonly clings to the exiles from a lost cause—the Huguenots who found refuge in Holland and England, the Stuarts in France, the aristocratic refugees from the French Revolution who scattered about the courts and capitals of Europe—but the Loyalists who found refuge in London or in Canada during and after the American Revolution did not have a very romantic time of it. As we have already seen, many of the distinguished opponents of independence followed Governor Hutchinson to England in 1775 and 1776, and others drifted over in the course of the war. Nova Scotia, too, had its quota of distinguished Loyalists, but most of those who went there, or to Upper Canada, were of the plainer sort. Many of the exiles in London and the provincial towns were men of education, much given to writing letters and keeping diaries, and it is possible for us to reconstruct their lives abroad with some authenticity.

Perhaps the best of the diaries is that kept by the Salem judge, Samuel Curwen. A graduate of Harvard College, he had taken part in the expedition against Louisbourg, then been appointed customs officer and, eventually, judge of the vice-admiralty court. His official position and his temperament inclined him to conservatism, and he was one of the supporters of Governor Hutchinson. With the outbreak of war, he departed first for Philadelphia, then for London. Fortunately for us he kept a diary and preserved his letters; these give us vivid pictures of the American group in London and tell us that few of them—certainly not Curwen himself—were ever happy in exile.

Many of those who fled to England were men of property, but they were rarely able to take any property with them; most of them therefore found themselves with fairly high standards of living and no means to maintain them. Inevitably they became pensioners of the British government. Curwen himself received a meager pension of £100, but as he had thoughtfully left his wife in Salem, he was able to manage with this. Not so most of the others, who clamored for pensions, offices, half pay and other perquisites, and often received them.

Indeed, a good part of the energies of the Americans in exile went to persuading the British government to compensate them for the injuries they had suffered. And the government was, on the whole, generous, though few of the Loyalists thought so. Colonial officials were usually given jobs back in England, or put on pension; those who had served in the army were put on half pay; preachers were assigned to parishes in the country or the provincial towns. But what about compensation for losses—which, often considerable, were invariably exaggerated in the telling? Some 5,000 Loyalists eventually submitted claims for compensation; these claims totaled well over £10,000,000. The Crown established a commission to inquire into these claims; the commission, working with admirable impartiality and thoroughness, held hearings in London, Montreal, Quebec, Halifax, and even New York, and eventually made awards totaling some £3,000,000. In addition pensions for loss of office went to 204 Loyalists, to the sum of almost £26,000 annually, and annual allowances to another 588 who had lost no property but had other claims on the bounty of the British government.

Far more important were the arrangements made for the refugees who fled to Canada—Nova Scotia, New Brunswick and Upper Canada or Ontario. Here the British government was not only generous but farsighted.

It granted 500 acres of land to heads of families, and 300 acres to single men; set aside 2,000 acres in each township to the support of religion and 1,000 acres to the support of schools; provided rations, fuel, clothing and other forms of assistance for a period of years. Altogether the government gave some 3,000,000 acres of land to the United Empire Loyalists, as they came to be called, and spent some $9,000,000 on resettling them.

We give here some extracts from the diary and letters of Samuel Curwen, and a letter from David Colden, son of the famous Cadwallader, of New York, describing his efforts to obtain compensation from the government. He died a few weeks after writing this letter, but his claim was eventually settled by an outright award of £2,720, with £880 to his son and £460 to each daughter.

1. A Massachusetts Loyalist Eats Out His Heart in Exile

From the diary of Samuel Curwen.

Philadelphia, May 4, 1775. Since the late unhappy affairs at Concord and Lexington, finding the spirit of the people to rise on every fresh alarm (which has been almost hourly) and their tempers to get more and more soured and malevolent against all moderate men, whom they see fit to reproach as enemies of their country by the name of Tories, among whom I am unhappily (although unjustly) ranked, and unable longer to bear their undeserved reproaches and menaces hourly denounced against myself and others, I think it a duty I owe myself to withdraw for awhile from the storm which, to my foreboding mind, is approaching. Having in vain endeavored to persuade my wife to accompany me—her apprehensions of danger from an incensed soldiery, a people licentious and enthusiastically mad and broken loose from all the restraints of law or religion being less terrible to her than a short passage on the ocean—and being moreover encouraged by her, I left my late peaceful home (in my sixtieth year) in search of personal security and those rights which, by the laws of God, I ought to have enjoyed undisturbed there, and embarked at Beverly on board the schooner *Lively*, Captain Johnson, bound hither, on Sunday, the 23d ultimo, and have just arrived, hoping to find an asylum amongst Quakers and Dutchmen, who, I presume, from former experience, have too great a regard for ease and property to sacrifice either, at this time of doubtful disputation, on the altar of an unknown goddess, or rather doubtful divinity.

My fellow-passengers were Andrew Cabot and his wife and child, and Andrew Dodge. My townsman, Benjamin Goodhue, was kind enough to come on board, and having made my kinsman and correspondent, Samuel Smith, acquainted with my arrival, he was pleased to come on board also, and his first salutation, "We will protect you, though a Tory," embarrassed me not a little; but soon recovering my surprise, we fell into a friendly conversation, and he taking me to his house, I dined with his family and their minister, Mr. Sproat, suffering some mortification in the case of truth.

After an invitation to make his house my home during my stay here, which I did not accept, I took leave and went in pursuit of lodgings, and on enquiring at several houses, ascertained they were full, or for particular reasons would not take me; and so many refused as made it fearful whether, like Cain, I had not a discouraging mark upon me or a strong feature of Toryism. The whole city appears to be deep in congressional principles, and inveterate against "Hutchinsonian Addressers." Happily we at length arrived at one Mrs. Swords', a widow lady, in Chestnut-street, with whom I found quarters, rendered more agreeable by S. Waterhouse's company, who also lodges here....

May 6, 1775. Saw Pelatiah Webster, who, at the instance of Mr. Goodhue, treats me civilly. Having had several intimations that my residence here would be unpleasant, if allowed at all, when it shall be known that I am what is called "an Addresser," . . . I have . . . consulted the few friends I think it worth while to advise with, and, on the result, am determined to proceed to London in the vessel in which I came here.

On the credit of Samuel Smith and Sons, I have, with their assistance, procured flour to freight a vessel.

May 7, 1775, Sunday. Dr. Franklin arrived last night, which was announced by ringing of bells, to the great joy of the city. I cannot but promise myself some good, as his knowledge and experience must have influence in the approaching Congress, which will, I doubt not, listen to his judgment. He is, it is said, to return to England again soon, at Lord Chatham's instance, who tells him he must be on the spot at the opening of Parliament.

May 9, 1775. Dined with Stephen Collins; passed the evening at Joseph Reed's, in company with Col. Washington (a fine figure, and of a most easy and agreeable address), Richard Henry Lee and Col. Harrison, three of the Virginia delegates. Besides Mr. and Mrs. Reed were Mrs. Deberdt, Dr. Shippen and Thomas Smith. I staid till twelve o'clock, the conversation being chiefly on the most feasible and prudent method of stopping up the channel of the Delaware to prevent the coming up of any large ships to the city. I could not see the least disposition to accomodate matters.

Col. Caswell and Mr. Hewes, the North Carolina delegates, arrived this day, and are at our lodgings....

May 12, 1775. Sent my baggage on board the *Lively;* received a letter from Stephen Collins to Mr. Neat, of London; paid my respects to Mrs. Deberdt, and received a letter to her son. Received my invoice of flour from Samuel Smith and Sons. Mr. Startin presented me with an open letter on Wilkinson and Co., Birmingham, and Mr. Reed and lady gave me letters to their brother, Dennis Deberdt, London. From post-office took Rivington's two last newspapers, and received from the publishers all the present week's Philadelphia papers. Messrs. Lee and Webster took leave, and with my fellow-passenger, Mr. Webster's son Pelatiah, I went on board the *Lively.*

May 16, 1775. Spoke Capt. Waterman in a schooner from Nantucket, who brought me a letter from Nathan Goodale, stating that his family, Mr. Pynchon's and Mr. Orne's had arrived there, to which I replied....

London, July 4. Arrived at the New England Coffee-House, Threadneedle-street, at 7 o'clock, P.M., July 5. Met my townsman and friend,

Benjamin Pickman, which rejoiced me; we walked to Westminster Hall; in Chancery saw Sir Thomas Sewell, Master of the Rolls, sitting with his hat on; at Common Pleas saw Judge Blackstone and Sergeant Glynn; and the King's Bench, Lord Mansfield and Mr. Sergeant Wedderburne. Lord Mansfield's manner is like the late Judge Dudley's, of Massachusetts. His peering eyes denote a penetration and comprehension peculiarly his own. Mr. Wedderburne spoke, but at no great length.

July 9, 1775. Went to Old Jewry Meeting-house, where I met Gov. Hutchinson, his son and daughter—a cordial reception and invitation to visit him. Mr. Isaac Smith and Mr. Deberdt sat in the pew next me.

To Rev. Thomas Barnard, Salem.

London, 22d July, 1775

Dear Sir:

The dissipation, self-forgetfulness and vicious indulgences of every kind which characterize this metropolis are not to be wondered at. The temptations are too great for that degree of philosophy and religion ordinarily possessed by the bulk of mankind. The unbounded riches of many afford the means of every species of luxury, which (thank God) our part of America is ignorant of; and the example of the wealthy and great is contagious.

From the diary again.

April 1, A.M. [1776]. At Gov. Hutchinson's; he was alone, reading a new pamphlet entitled "An Inquiry whether Great Britain or America is most in fault." I accepted an invitation to return to dinner. Taking leave for the present, I departed, walking through the palace and park to Mr. Bliss's lodgings, where I met Judge Sewall, Mr. Oxnard and Mr. Smith; returned to the Governor's, with whom only young Oliver and myself dined.

From thence, in passing through Leicester-Square, I called in at Mr. Copley's to see Mr. Clarke and the family, who kindly pressed my staying to tea; and in the mean time amused myself by seeing his performances in painting. He was then at work on a family-piece containing himself, Mr. Clarke, his wife and four children, of all of whom I observed a very striking likeness. At tea was present Mr. West, a Philadelphian, a most masterly hand in historic painting; author of the well known and applauded piece, now in print, called "West's Death of Wolfe," and taken from his painting. He is now at work on a piece called the "Death of Stephen," for the King, and for which he is to have one thousand pounds. Mr. West is the King's history-painter, and was kind enough to put me into a way of obtaining a sight of the Queen's palace, which he tells me contains, except Houghton Hall, the finest collection of capital paintings of any house in England.

Returned with Mr. Clarke, who was going to see his son Jonathan, sick. . . .

[*April 3, 1776.*] Went with Mr. Clarke to procure more convenient lodgings for his sick son, which we found, as recommended by Dr. Pitcairn, in Cross-street, in what is called the Queen's House, said to be a place of

Elizabeth's, on a small scale, low, and in the taste of the sixteenth century. The remains of the porter's lodge at the bottom of the garden, in a peculiar style, are yet seen. In one of the lower rooms is a painting on the windows, with the date of 1588. . . .

May 4. Called on my friend Browne, who had sent a message last evening by Mr. Pickman to invite his three countrymen to his lodgings. Col. Browne acquainted me with some facts relative to the unfortunate abandonment of Boston by the King's troops; which after all has the appearance of being forced. Would to God this ill-judged, unnatural quarrel was ended, but I fear thousands of useful innocents must be sacrificed to the wickedness, pride and folly of unprincipled men. Many of our countrymen called during our stay.

To Dr. Charles Russell, Antigua.

London, June 10, 1776

Dear Sir:

I congratulate you on your retreat from the land of oppression and tyranny; for, surely, greater never appeared since the days of Nimrod. I sincerely wish well to my native country, and am of opinion that the happiness of it depends on restraining the violences and outrages of profligate and unprincipled men, who run riot against all the laws of justice, truth and religion. Sad and deplorable is the condition of those few that, like Abdiel amidst hostile bands of fallen spirits, retain their primitive loyalty. So strangely unprosperous hitherto have been the measures of administration in America that the active Provincials have taken courage, and accomplished what in contemplation would have appeared morally impossible.

Gen. Burgoyne sailed from hence ten weeks ago for Canada with four thousand Brunswickers and seven or eight regiments; Lord Howe, in the *Eagle,* about a month since, and the first division of Hessians, consisting of eight or ten thousand, about a fortnight before him. Gen. Howe, his brother, with nine thousand, was at Halifax the beginning of April. The second division ('tis said) will sail this week, consisting of four thousand, which completes the whole number of foreign troops. The whole of the regular army on the Continent will not be short of forty thousand men.

It is surprising what little seeming effect the loss of American orders has on the manufactories; they have been in full employ ever since the dispute arose; stocks are not one jot lessened, the people in general little moved by it; business and amusement so totally engross all ranks and orders here that Administration finds no difficulty on the score to pursue their plans. The general disapprobation of that folly of independence which America now evidently aims at makes it a difficult part for her friends to act.

By letters from Salem to the 16th April I find they were in a quiet state there, and hugging themselves in the fatal error that Government had abandoned the design of reducing them to obedience. Six vessels laden with refugees are arrived from Halifax, amongst whom are R. Lechmere, I. Vassal, Col. Oliver, Treasurer Gray, etc. Those who bring property here may do well enough, but for those who expect reimbursement for losses, or supply for present support, will find to their cost the hand of charity very cold; the latter may be kept from starving, and beyond that their hopes are vain. "Blessed is he (saith Pope) that expecteth nothing, for he shall never be disappointed"; nor a more interesting truth was ever uttered.

I find my finances so visibly lessening that I wish I could remove from this expensive country (being heartily tired of it) and, old as I am, would gladly enter into a business connection anywhere consistently with decency and integrity, which I would fain preserve. The use of the property I left behind me I fear I shall never be the better for; little did I expect from affluence to be reduced to such rigid economy as prudence now exacts. To beg is a meanness I wish never to be reduced to, and to starve is stupid; one comfort, as I am fast declining into the vale of life: my miseries cannot probably be of long continuance.

With great esteem; etc.

S. CURWEN

—CURWEN, *Journal and Letters*, pp. 25-63 *passim.*

2. BRITAIN ECONOMIZES ON THE LOYALISTS

Samuel Curwen to the Reverend Isaac Smith.

London, February 14, 1783

Dear Sir: . . . This day I went to the Treasury to inquire about my allowance, and to my comfort found it stood as at first. A few are raised, some struck off, more lessened. Of those that have come to my knowledge, Gov. Oliver's is lessened £100, out of £300; Mr. Williams, who has married a fortune here, is struck off; Harrison Gray, with a wife and two children, struck off; his brother Lewis lessened to £50; D. Ingersoll reduced from £200 to £100; Samuel H. Sparhawk, from £150 to £80; Benjamin Gridley from £150 to £100; Thomas Danforth's, Samuel Sewall's, Samuel Porter's, Peter Johonnot's, G. Brinley's, Edward Oxnard's and mine continue as at first; Chandler's raised £50; Samuel Fitch's £20; Col. Morrow's £50; one whose name I forget is sunk from £100 to £30; and many names and sums totally forgotten. On the whole, it is said the sum paid last year to refugees, amounting to near £80,000, is now shrunk by the late reform to £38,000; and if the Commissioners act on the same frugal plan respecting the petitioners whose cases will probably soon be considered, I very much doubt whether the sum of last year's expenditures under this head, including all their additional allowances, will not exceed this year's.

This is the great, the important day on which the preliminaries are to undergo a most critical and severe discussion, and will determine the fate of Lord Shelburne's Administration; news unluckily for it has arrived that the Government of Virginia has declared they will pay no regard to any remonstrances, or request, or requisition respecting Refugees, which manifests the fatality of the preliminary article recommending the same.

Your faithful friend,

S. CURWEN

—CURWEN, *Journal and Letters*, pp. 404-405.

3. LOYALISTS DEVOTE THEMSELVES TO ALLOWANCES AND COMPENSATION

David Colden to his wife.

London, June 27, 1784

My dearest Nancey,

I had the pleasure to write to you from Falmouth, by a packett then waiting for a wind, which I hope would give you very early intelligence of our safe arrival there, in 21 days from Sandy Hook. . . .

I have a well furnished parlour, bed room and what they call a powdering room for dressing in, for which I pay a guinea a week. I board myself; the maid of the house dresses my victuals, goes to market for me, and sets the table; so that I have little use for a servant, and have not yet got one.

I have already had the pleasure to see almost all my American acquaintance, and shall find employment for some time in returning their visits. As yet I have been wholly occupied in receiving visits, and in pursuing the first step that is taken by all my distressed fellow sufferers; I mean the applications to obtain something for my present support. What will be my success I do not yet know. My friends encourage me to have good hopes; but it is much more difficult to obtain the largest allowance of £200 a year, now, than it was some time agoe. When I have accomplished this part of my business, I shall then endeavour to get the examination of my claim for compensation brought on as soon as possible.

When this is done I shall perhaps be able to indulge myself in what is ever nearest my heart. I mean the contemplation of a plan for geting you and my dear dear daughters settled with me somewhere. At present I can say nothing to you on the subject with any more certainty than when I was in America. But be assured, my dear Nancey, this great and astonishing part of the world has nothing in it that can abate the extream anxiety I feel to be with you and my children.

I have not yet been out to look at any one of the great or wonderfull things that are to be seen in this city. I have had a glance at some of them in passing, but as I am obliged to go about in a coach (both because I have not, as you know, breath to walk, and if I had, would never find my way), I have not been able to make the least observation on any thing.

Cad has already seen St James's—the Kings and Prince of Wales's stables—Kensington Gardens—Westminster Abbey and many other places. He is happy in having the two Ludlows, McWaltons son, and other Yorkers who go about with him. Sandy Hamilton is much grown, and only that he is too much the man, is much improved. His father looks very well, and lives as if flush of money; yet he has got nothing from Govt and his friends are as much at a loss as we used to be to know how he manages. Antill has got as much added to his half pay as makes him £200 a year. He tells me he has wrote for Peggy, but—— Yesterday I dined and passed the evening at Captn Doughlass's—they live in a genteel stile; she in a thriving way. Susan Middleton grows up too stout, and does not get rid of her red face, which is a great loss to her, but she is a pleasant, unaffected girl. Mrs Douglass never looked better. Bob Auchmuty was there; he was among my first visitants. He intends going to Halifax this season. Jack Middleton has called several times, and is very friendly to Cad. I am surprised to think how many of my friends have found me out in so short a time! Even Mr Patterson, who lives in the city not less than three miles from me, was here yesterday, and told Cad he would carry him to see many places. He has got so much added to his half pay as makes him up £160 a year with which he appears well satisfied. Which is the case with very few of the poor folks from America that I have seen. Many of them have got no allowance yet; and I shall probably be as far forward in my application as those who were much earlier here. My worthy friend Judge Ludlow gives me that full share of his kindest attention on which I had an undoubted reliance. Even his matters are not so determined that he can say when [he] will leave this country, or where he will go to—the probability at present is to Nova Scotia, and that he may go there this season. I shall push hard not to be left behind. James Delancey will sail in two or three weeks to Halifax, by whom I shall write to our friends in that part of the world. James has been very attentive to me—and the old Genl affectionately kind.

Supposeing, my dear Nancey, that you are still mistress at Spring Hill, I must put you in mind of disposing of all the old iron, plow shears, harrow teeth, tire of cart wheels, etc., etc. They can be conveyed privatly to Tom, and besides paying his acct. will produce something for you. Send the steel mill to Mr Ustick, if he will take it. I owe him for some seed wheat. Sell the iron bound waggon; L. Laurence will assist you in it. As to beds, beding, and the kitchen furniture you have left, you had best not part with any of it: should we settle either in Nova Scotia or Canada, you cannot any way be supplied as well as by bringing it with you. You will not, my dear, however flatter yourself that there is any probability of our geting together before next spring, for if I should get to Nova Scotia this fall, it must be too late to bring you there. It is indeed quite too early for me to say any thing on this subject, but it so occupies my heart and head that I am induced to communicate even my present thoughts about it. . . .

Tell my friends and neighbors, and all who ever think of me, that I daily think of them with a warm heart and sincere good will. If I have time I will write a line to my girls; I know it will make them happy; never had parent the happiness of children more at heart than I have theirs. God bless and protect you all!

I am my dear Nancey's most affect.
DAVID COLDEN
—Manuscript Division, N. Y. Public Lib.

VII. THE RETURN OF THE NATIVES

Many of those who were forced into exile counted themselves foes of independence but friends to America. Whatever their distaste for the leveling principles of the Americans, they discovered, when they arrived in England, that they were even less at home in the aristocratic and corrupt upper-class circles of the mother country than in the homespun society of the colonies. Even a man like Hutchinson never ceased to think fondly of his home land—Massachusetts Bay—or to speak affectionately of it. Many—we will never know how many—managed to make their peace with the American authorities, and their neighbors, and return to their native shores. We give here what may perhaps be regarded as a happy ending to a melancholy tale: the return of Samuel Curwen and of Peter Van Schaack to their old homes.

1. SAMUEL CURWEN COMES HOME

Samuel Curwen to William Pynchon.

London, November 28, 1783

Dear Sir:

However unfavorable to my wishes the result of the American Assemblies may be, I shall be gratified by receiving the earliest advices. Capt. Nathaniel West brings me a message from the principal merchants and citizens of Salem, prospering and encouraging my return; which instance of moderation I view as an honor to the town and respectful to myself, and I wish to return my thanks through you. It affords me pleasure, and I would cheerfully accept the offer; but should the popular dislike rise against me, especially if cooperating with governmental resolves, to what a plight should I be reduced, being at present (but for how long is a painful uncertainty) on the British Government list for £100 a year (a competency for a single person exercising strict economy), to surrender this precarious allowance without public assurances of personal security.

It would be little short of madness, should the popular rage combine with the public decisions to prevent our future residence; deprived of all assistance, and even the last refuge of the wretched, hope here, expelled there. Imagine to yourself the distress of an old man, without health, under such adverse circumstances, and you will advise me to wait with resignation till the several Assemblies shall have taken decisive measures on congressional recommendation, agreeably to the Provisional Treaty, if that body shall deem it prudent to conform to what their Commissioners have agreed to.

But enough of this. One of your Massachusetts public ministers, Mr. John Adams, is here in all the pride of American independence; by Mr. Gorham I am told he uttered to him the following speech, that "together with the war he had buried all animosity against the absentees." Though he is of a rigid temper and a thorough-paced Republican, candor obliges me to give him credit for the humanity of the sentiment, being spoken in private and to one of his own party, and probably without an intention to be published abroad.

In a conversation with my informant, he further replied that he chose to consider himself as a plain American Republican; his garb plain, without a sword, which is carrying his transatlantic ideas, I fear, a little too far. Should he have the curiosity, or his public character render it expedient, to attend at a royal levee, or at a drawing-room at St. James's on a Court day, I hope he will not deserve and meet with as mortifying a repulse as our late Chancellor, Lord Thurlow, at the Court of Versailles, whose surly pertinacity in wearing a bob-wig occasioned his being refused admittance into the

King's presence. However frivolous a part of dress soever a sword may appear to one of Mr. Adams's scholar-like turn, he is by this time, I fancy, too well acquainted with the etiquette of Courts to neglect so necessary an appendage, without which no one can find admittance out of the clerical line.

I have nothing further to add but my ardent wishes for an increase of the health and happiness of yourself and family; for I am truly,

Your friend,
S. Curwen

From the diary.

July 10, 1784. To the Treasury; found the American door besieged by a score of mendicants like myself, waiting their turns. Though I thought my early attendance would have entitled me to No. 1, I was glad to stand No. 21. So great was the crowd that I was more than once about to depart and leave them.

July 28, 1784. Took leave at lodgings 107 Bishopgate-street within and proceeded to the ship *Union*, lying at Irongate, where I propose to abide till my arrival at Gravesend. Paid twenty guineas in part for my passage money. From henceforth I bid an everlasting farewell to London. . . .

Sept. 25. Arrived at Boston, and at half past three o'clock landed at the end of Long Wharf, after an absence of nine years and five months, occasioned by a lamented civil war, excited by ambitious, selfish men here and in England, to the disgrace, dishonor, distress and disparagement of these extensive territories. By plunder and rapine some few have accumulated wealth, but many more are greatly injured in their circumstances; some have to lament over the wreck of their departed wealth and estates, of which pitiable number I am; my affairs having sunk into irretrievable ruin.

—Curwen, *Journal and Letters*, pp. 393, 412, 413, 415.

2. "John Jay Did Not Cease a Friend to Peter Van Schaack"

John Jay to Peter Van Schaack.

Paris, September 17, 1782

Doctor Franklin sent me this morning your letter of the 11 August last. I thank you for it. Aptitude to change in anything never made a part of my disposition, and I hope makes no part of my character. In the course of the present troubles I have adhered to certain fixed principles, and faithfully obeyed their dictates, without regarding the consequences of such conduct to my friends, my family or myself; all of whom, however dreadful the thought, I have been ready to sacrifice if necessary to the public objects in contest.

Believe me, my heart has nevertheless been, on more than one occasion, afflicted by the execution of what I thought and still think was my duty. I felt very sensibly for you and for others, but as society can regard only the political propriety of men's conduct, and not the moral propriety of their motives to it, I could only lament your unavoidably becoming classed with many whose morality was convenience, and whose politics changed with the aspect of public affairs. My regard for you as a good old friend continued, notwithstanding. God knows that inclination never had a share in any proceedings of mine against you; from such thorns no man could expect to gather grapes, and the only consolation that can grow in their unkindly shade is a consciousness of doing one's duty and the reflection that, as on the one hand I have uniformly preferred the public's weal to my friends and connections, so on the other I have never been urged by private resentments to injure a single individual. Your judgment and consequently your conscience differed from mine on a very important question; but though as an independent American I considered all who were not for us, and you among the rest, as against us, yet be assured that John Jay did not cease to be a friend to Peter Van Schaack. No one can serve two masters. Either Britain was right and America wrong, or America right and Britain wrong. They who thought Britain right were bound to support her, and America had a just claim to the services of those who approved her cause. Hence it became our duty to take one side or the other, and no man is to be blamed for preferring the one which his reason recommended as the most just and virtuous.

Several of our countrymen indeed left and took arms against us, not from any such principles, but from the most dishonourable of human motives. Their conduct has been of a piece with their inducements, for they have far outstripped savages in perfidy and cruelty. Against these men every American must set his face and steel his heart. There are others of them, though not many, who, I believe, opposed us because they thought they could not conscientiously go with us. To such of them as have behaved with humanity I wish every species of prosperity that may consist with the good of my country.

You see how naturally I slide into the habit of writing as freely as I used to speak to you. Ah! my friend, if ever I see New York again, I expect to meet with "the shade of many a departed joy"; my heart bleeds to think of it. Where and how are your children? Whenever, as a private friend, it may be in my power to do good to either, tell me; while I have a loaf, you and they may freely partake of it. Don't let this idea hurt you. If your circumstances are easy, I rejoice; if not, let me take off some of their rougher edges.

Mrs. Jay is obliged by your remembrance, and presents you her compliments. The health of us both is but delicate. Our little girl has been very ill, but is now well. My best wishes always attend you, and be assured that, notwithstanding many political changes,

I remain, dear Peter,

Your affectionate friend and servant,

JOHN JAY

—JAY, *Correspondence and Public Papers*, II, 343-345.

3. "MY HEART WARMS UP WHEN OUR COUNTRY IS THE SUBJECT"

Peter Van Schaack to John Jay.

London, October 15, 1782

I will not attempt to describe my feelings upon perusal of your very friendly letter. I consider it as a perfect picture, in which I can trace every well-known feature of your character. Your unreserved commemoration of our old friendship, and assurance of its continuance; your kind inquiries into the situation of me and my children, and generous offers with respect to both them and myself; and your pathetic allusion to the melancholy scenes you will meet upon your return to New York, melted my heart; and every idea of party distinction or political competition vanished in an instant.

The line you have drawn between your political character and your private friendships is so strongly marked, and will be so strictly attended by me, that I hope our correspondence will not end here. Be assured that were I arraigned at the bar, and you my judge, I should expect to stand or fall only by the merits of my cause.

With respect to the great contest in which, unfortunately, I differed from others of my valuable friends as well as yourself, I can say with the most sacred regard to truth, I was actuated by no motive unfriendly to my country, nor by any consideration of a personal private nature. Men's hearts are not always known, even to themselves; but believe me that I spared no pains in examining into all the secret recesses of mine. I can say, too, that my wishes were to have gone with you. The very appearance (and in my view of things it was appearance only) of taking part against my country distressed me in the extreme. Could it be for the sake of Great Britain that I could wish to sacrifice the welfare of my native country? My attachment to her (great indeed it was) was founded in the relation she stood in to America, and the happiness which I conceived America derived from it; nor did it appear to me, from anything that had happened, that the connexion was dissolved. Upon the whole, as even in a doubtful case I would rather be the patient sufferer than run the risk of being the active aggressor; and as I should rather be even a figure for the hand of scorn to point its slow and moving finger at than to destroy the peace of my own mind, I concluded, rather that to support a cause I could not approve, to bear distress that might result from the part I took; and if America is happier for the revolution, I declare solemnly that I shall rejoice that the side I was on was the unsuccessful one.

You, my dear sir, will excuse my saying thus much on a subject so interesting to all that is dear to me in life. My heart warms up whenever our country (I must call it my country) is the subject; and in my separation from it, "I have dragged at each remove a lengthening chain." . . .

—JAY, *Correspondence and Public Papers*, II, 354-355.

CHAPTER TEN

The Struggle for Democracy at Home

THE AMERICAN REVOLUTION *has a twofold character. It was a war for independence which led to the breakup of the Old Empire and the emergence of a new nation in the New World. It was an internal revolution, which provided the occasion and the impetus for far-reaching changes in government, economy and society. In terms now familiar, it solved the problem of home rule in the empire, and raised the problem of who should rule at home.*

This chapter addresses itself to the important but rarely dramatic story of the internal changes that accompanied the war itself. Some of those changes were an almost inevitable product of the war. To some extent they came of their own accord; to some extent they were planned or contrived. For the most part they were a combination of fortuity and contrivance, for wise and farsighted leaders took advantage of processes of change and tried to channel them into what they thought were the right paths.

The Revolutionary War, like almost all wars, brought its own far-reaching changes, and this even without any deliberate revolutionary program. The destruction of royal governments required the establishment of new American governments, and it was clear that this provided an opportunity to establish them on sound foundations: every state but Connecticut and Rhode Island seized this opportunity. The war, too, revived American titles to western lands, and opened up vast areas to settlement on what were, almost of necessity, liberal terms. It dispossessed tens of thousands of Tories, provided the occasion for the confiscation of royal and proprietary lands and of Loyalist estates, and even of debts owed to British merchants. Thus the Irish poet Tom Moore could sneer at

> *Those vaunted demagogues who nobly rose*
> *From England's debtors to be England's foes,*
> *Who could their monarch in their purse forget*
> *And break allegiance but to cancel debt.*

All this brought with it a redistribution of existing wealth, and the creation of new sources of wealth. And war itself, then as always, stirred up and metamorphosed society and economy. It threw men of different colonies and different classes together. It brought in tens of thousands of British, thousands of French and German soldiers and sailors, who contributed something to the wealth, something to the habits, and something even to the stock of the Americans. It put a premium on talent rather than on wealth or family; created innumerable vacancies in government, church and business, and filled those vacancies with new men; loosened men from habitual loyalties and attached them to new ideas and institutions.

This was all in what might be called the ordinary course of wartime history. But more was involved in the internal revolution than this. It was difficult to justify a war on the basis of the philosophy of the Declaration of Independence and not feel some compulsion to apply that philosophy to domestic concerns. All men, said the Continental Congress, were created equal, and endowed with inalienable rights, including life, liberty and happiness. Governments exist to secure men in these rights—it is for this reason that they are established. These sentiments—Jefferson called them self-evident truths—commanded the support of Patriot leaders and presumably of the American people generally. They were not the doctrines of a closet-philosophy, but had consequences. It is with some of these consequences, institutional or intellectual, that we are concerned here.

The obvious place for Americans to begin was in the making of governments. The passing of royal authority necessitated the establishment of independent state governments, and after the Congressional Resolution of May 15, 1776, all the states—except Connecticut and Rhode Island, which were content with their colonial charters—proceeded to refashion their governments, carrying out, with different degrees of thoroughness, the political principle that government derives its authority from below. The most far-reaching consequence of the Revolution internally is this institutionalization of the principle that men make government. The method was the constitutional convention; its product was new state constitutions.

Those constitutions inevitably covered wide ground, and provided an opportunity, again, to apply some of the more urgent principles of the Revolutionary philosophy. The first constitution, that of Virginia, was drafted by a leading political philosopher, George Mason, and contained a Bill of Rights which soon became a model for other states, here and abroad. The new constitutions, and their bills of rights, did away with many of the built-in privileges that had been part of the royal and proprietary governments, toppled Church establishments, introduced sweeping reforms in the organization and structure of government, and less sweeping changes in suffrage and representation; and furnished an opportunity for the expression of pious sentiments about such matters as democracy, education and slavery. In some states these sentiments were translated into legislation or into unofficial practices.

It would, of course, be misleading to present the Revolution as a social revolution in the sense of the French Revolution, or of the Russian Revolution of our own time. It would be equally misleading to omit this chapter of our history, or to minimize its importance. It must be confessed, however, that it does not lend itself eagerly to narrative presentation. Most of the material that illuminates social and economic changes is formal and elaborate, rather than informal and personal. It is explicit in constitutions, laws, proclamations and similar documents which cannot be called vivacious, rather than implicit in personal accounts. There was, it seems, but little awareness of what was going on and little temptation to describe it. Here, as in so many chapters, we are grateful for the combination of philosophical insight, practical energy, and literary affluence in Thomas Jefferson and John Adams.

The richest material tells the story of constitution making. Another group of documents, far less elaborate, illuminates the story of religious free-dom; a third suggests something of the criticism of and assault on slavery; and a fourth touches on some new departures in education—mostly on paper. We include, in addition, a few miscellaneous papers touching on social changes and on that process of democratization which was eventually to be of immense importance.

I. ALL POWER IS IN THE PEOPLE

Although the Declaration of Independence propounded a revolutionary and explosive philosophy, at the time its arguments excited little attention and almost no opposition. Even the Loyalists, unalterably opposed to independ-ence and often embittered or outraged by American egalitarianism, had little to say in criticism of the philosophical argument set forth in the Declaration. We may assume, then, that what Jefferson announced was, indeed, the com-mon sense of the matter, and that when he wrote that "I did not consider it as any part of my charge to invent new ideas" he in a sense accepted the imputation that his ideas were familiar and commonplace.

It is fascinating to see how, during these Revolutionary years, Americans took both the ideas and the practices of democracy in their stride; how they took for granted that the source of all authority was in the people and that men had an indubitable right to alter, or abolish, governments, and to institute new governments. This was not, after all, so surprising. Nature, or history, is always aping art, and the methods of making government which Locke and Rousseau imagined to belong to some golden age of the past, and which mod-ern sociologists assert belong only to the imagination, had been familiar practice in America since the days of the Mayflower Compact and the Funda-mental Orders of Connecticut.

We give here a handful of documents which present, in dramatic form, this instinctive habit of making government by democratic processes. First there is a letter from Richard Henderson, founder of the Transylvania Colony in what is now Kentucky, describing the habits of freedom that obtain among Americans, and after it comes, quite logically, Henderson's address to the delegates who had gathered together to draw up a compact of government. In May 1775 Henderson had called a convention of representatives from the four little settlements of Boonsboro, Harrodsburg, Boiling Springs and St. Asaph's Station. After listening to Henderson's eloquent words the delegates accepted the constitution which he had written vesting authority largely in the Transylvania Company. Even when these and other newcomers revolted against the Transylvania Company the next year, they followed in their re-volt the democratic procedure which Henderson had advised.

The notion that government of necessity derives its authority from the consent of the governed was widespread and contagious. We give here three expressions of it from three different societies: first, the "mechanicks" of New York who argued that authority to create a constitution had to come from "the inhabitants at large"; second, the freeholders of a town in Connecticut, who argued that the town should elect, directly, its representative to the Con-tinental Congress; third, the frontier town of Hanover, New Hampshire—

torn by the rival claims of New Hampshire and Vermont—which argued the absurdity of government by a legislature which held over from before independence. Finally we have Samuel Adams' declaration of faith in the democratic processes as recalled by a traveling Frenchman, the Marquis de Chastellux.

1. AMERICANS "FREE AS THEIR OWN THOUGHTS"

Richard Henderson to Cunningham Corbett, a Glasgow merchant.

Bladensburgh, July 30, 1774

Dear Sir: . . . You know something of the disposition that rules the people here. As you go northward, they are not less zealous, but more steady. And it is to be wished that those who attempt to give law to this country had correspondents among that set of men whom we call the country gentlemen of America, to correct the advices which they receive from other quarters. These men have ideas of liberty resembling the old English ideas. They have always hitherto been, as King Alfred said the English ought to be, *free as their own thoughts.* Indeed, even our commonality have never been used to stand in awe of rank and station. They are a well-informed, reasoning commonality too, perhaps the most of any on earth, because of the free intercourse between man and man that prevails in America: their free access to courts of law, as parties and jurors, where they hear the rights of the subject nobly debated; their frequent and free elections, which give occasion for candidates to scan each other's principles and conduct before the tribunal of the people, together with the freedom and general circulation of newspapers, and the eagerness and leisure of the people to read them, or to listen to those who do.

In such a country it is plain that the sentiments of the ablest patriots soon become the general sentiments. Our ancestors, say they, with a view of enlarging, not of diminishing the rights of their posterity, emigrated to a waste country, then useless, stipulating allegiance to the Crown, and coincidence of laws with those of England, and reserving all the rights of Englishmen, especially exemption from taxes, unless they should tax themselves. This contract was solemnly ratified in the face of the world by charters. England breaks the contract, claims a right of taxation, and sends an army to enforce it. If a contract, say they, must bind both parties, or else neither party, and she breaks loose, now, are we bound? . . .

—FORCE, *American Archives*, 4th Series, III, 54-55.

2. "ALL POWER IS ORIGINALLY IN THE PEOPLE"

Richard Henderson's address to the Transylvania delegates.

23 May, 1775

Mr. Chairman, and Gentlemen of the Convention:

You are called and assembled at this time for a noble and an honourable purpose—a purpose, however ridiculous or idle it may appear at first view to superficial minds, yet is of the most solid consequence; and if prudence, firmness and wisdom are suffered to influence your councils and direct your conduct, the peace and harmony of thousands may be expected to result from your deliberations; in short, you are about a work of the utmost importance to the well-being of this country in general, in which the interest and security of each and every individual is inseparably connected; for that State is truly sickly, politically speaking, whose laws or edicts are not careful, equally, of the different members, and most distant branches, which constitute the one united whole. Nay, it is not only a solecism in politics, but an insult to common sense, to attempt the happiness of any community, or composing laws for their benefit, without securing to each individual his full proportion of advantage arising out of the general mass; thereby making his interest (that most powerful incentive to the actions of mankind) the consequence of obedience. This, at once, not only gives force and energy to legislation, but as justice is and must be eternally the same, so your laws, founded in wisdom, will gather strength by time, and find an advocate in every wise and well-disposed person.

You, perhaps, are fixing the palladium, or placing the first cornerstone of an edifice, the height and magnificence of whose superstructure is now in the womb of futurity, and can only become great and glorious in proportion to the excellence of its foundation. These considerations, gentlemen, will no doubt animate and inspire you with sentiments worthy of the grandeur of the subject.

Our peculiar circumstances in this remote country, surrounded on all sides with difficulties, and equally subject to one common danger, which threatens our common overthrow, must, I think, in their effects, secure to us an union of interests, and consequently that harmony in opinion, so essential to the forming good, wise and wholesome laws.

If any doubt remain amongst you with respect to the forces or efficacy of whatever laws you now or hereafter make, be pleased to consider that all power is originally in the people; therefore, make it their interest by impartial and beneficial laws, and you may be sure of their inclination to see them enforced. For it is not to be supposed that a people, anxious and desirous of having laws made, who approve of the method of choosing Delegates or Representatives to meet in General Convention for that purpose, can want the necessary and concomitant virtue to carry them into execution.

Nay, gentlemen, for argument's sake, let us set virtue, for a moment, out of the question, and see how the matter will then stand. You must admit that it is, and ever will be, the interest of a large majority that the laws should be esteemed and held sacred. If so, surely this large majority can never want inclination or power to give sanction and efficacy to those very laws which advance their interest and secure their property.

And now, Mr. Chairman and gentlemen of the Convention, as it is indispensably necessary that laws should be composed for the regulation of our conduct—as we have a right to make such laws without giving offence to Great Britain, or any of the American Colonies—without disturbing the repose of any society or community under Heaven—if it is probable, nay, certain, that the laws may derive force and efficacy from our mutual consent, and that consent resulting from our own virtue, interest and convenience, nothing remains but to set about the business immediately, and let the event determine the wisdom of the undertaking.

Among the many objects that must present themselves for your consideration, the first in order must, from its importance, be that of establishing courts of justice and tribunals, for the punishment of such as may offend against the laws you are about to make. As this law will be the chief cornerstone in the ground work or basis of our Constitution, let us, in a particular manner, recommend the most dispassionate attention, while you take for your guide as much of the spirit and genius of the laws of England as can be interwoven with those of this country. We are all Englishmen, or what amounts to the same; ourselves and our fathers have, for many generations, experienced the invaluable blessings of that most excellent Constitution, and surely we cannot want motives to copy from so noble an original.

Many things, no doubt, crowd upon your minds, and seem equally to demand your attention. But next to that of restraining vice and immorality, surely nothing can be of more importance than establishing some plain and easy method of recovery of debts, and determining matters of dispute with respect to property, contracts, torts, injuries, etc. These things are so essential, that if not strictly attended to, our name will become odious abroad, and our peace of short and precarious duration. It would give honest and disinterested persons cause to suspect that there was some colourable reason, at least for the unworthy and scandalous assertions, together with the groundless insinuations contained in an infamous and scurrilous libel lately printed and published, concerning the settlement of this country. . . .

I have not the least doubt, gentlemen, but that your conduct, in this Convention will manifest the honest and laudable intentions of the present adventurers, whilst a conscious blush confounds the wilful calumniators and officious detractors of our infant and, as yet, little community.

Next to the establishment of courts or tribunals, as well for the punishment of publick offenders as the recovering of just debts, that of establishing and regulating a militia seems of the greatest importance. It is apparent that, without some wise institution respecting our mutual defence, the different towns or settlements are, every day, exposed to the most imminent danger, and liable to be destroyed at the mere will of the savage Indians.

Nothing, I am persuaded, but their entire ignorance of our weakness and want of order has, hitherto, preserved us from the destructive and rapacious hands of cruelty, and given us an opportunity, at this time, of forming secure, defensive plans, to be supported and carried into execution by the authority and sanction of a well digested law.

There are sundry other things highly worthy your consideration, and demand redress, such as the wanton destruction of our game, the only support of life amongst many of us, and for want of which the country would be abandoned ere tomorrow, and scarcely a probability remain of its ever becoming the habitation of any Christian people. This, together with the practice of many foreigners who make a business of hunting in our country, killing, driving off and lessening the number of wild cattle and other game, whilst the value of the skins and furs is appropriated to the benefit of persons not concerned or interested in our settlements. These are evils, I say, that I am convinced cannot escape your notice and attention.

Mr. Chairman and Gentlemen of the Convention, you may assure yourselves that this new-born country is an object of the most particular attention of the Proprietors here on the spot, as well as those on the other side of the mountains, and that they will most cheerfully concur in every measure which can, in the most distant and remote degree, promote its happiness or contribute to its grandeur.

—SAUNDERS, ed., *Colonial Records of North Carolina*, IX, 1268-1271.

3. "EVERY MAN IS A CO-LEGISLATOR WITH ALL THE OTHERS"

Address of the Mechanicks of New York City to the Delegates to the Congress of New York.

Mechanicks' Hall, June 14, 1776

Elected Delegates: With due confidence in the declaration which you lately made to the Chairman of our General Committee that you are, at all times, ready and willing to attend to every request of your "constituents or any part of them"; we, the Mechanicks in Union, though a very inconsiderable part of your constituents, beg leave to represent that one of the clauses in your Resolve respecting the establishment of a new form of Government is erroneously construed, and for that reason may serve the most dangerous purposes; for it is well known how indefatigable the emissaries of the British Government are in the pursuit of every scheme which is likely to bring disgrace upon our ruler, and ruin upon us all. At the same time we cheerfully acknowledge that the genuine spirit of liberty which animates the other parts of that Resolve, did not permit us to interpret it in any other sense than that which is the most obvious, and likewise the most favourable to the natural rights of man.

We could not, we never can, believe you intended that the future delegates or yourselves should be vested with the power of framing a new Constitution for this Colony, and that its inhabitants at large should not exercise the right which God has given them, in common with all men, to judge whether it be consistent with their interest to accept or reject a Constitution framed for that State of which they are members. This is the birthright of every man, to whatever state he may belong. There he is, or ought to be, by inalienable right, a co-legislator with all the other members of that community. Conscious of our own want of abilities, we are, alas! but too sensible that every individual is not qualified for assisting in the framing of a Constitution. But that share of common sense which the Almighty has bountifully distributed amongst mankind in general, is sufficient to quicken every one's feeling, and enable him to judge rightly what degree of safety and what advantages he is likely to enjoy, or be deprived of, under any Constitution proposed to him.

For this reason, should a preposterous confidence in the abilities and integrity of our future Delegates delude us into measures which might imply a renunciation of our inalienable right to ratify our laws, we believe that your wisdom, your patriotism, your own interest, nay, your ambition itself, would urge you to exert all the powers of persuasion you possess, and try every method which, in your opinion, would deter us from perpetrating that impious and frantick act of self-destruction; for as it would precipitate us into a state of absolute slavery, the lawful power which till now you have received from your constitutents to be exercised over a free people, would be annihilated by that unnatural act. It might probably accelerate our political death; but it must immediately cause your own. . . .

Signed by order of the Committee: Malcolm McEuen, Chairman

—Force, *American Archives*, 4th Series, VI, 895.

4. Delegates to Congress Must Be Elected by All Freeholders

Instructions to their Representatives, voted by the freemen of a town in Connecticut, at their annual meeting in September 1776.

Gentlemen: Although we repose the highest confidence in your zeal for the publick weal and particular attention to the true interests of your constituents, yet we think it our duty to manifest to you our sentiments respecting a matter which we hope may come under the consideration of the honourable General Assembly of the State of Connecticut the ensuing session, and in our apprehension is of the utmost importance to the people of this State, viz: The mode of electing Delegates to represent this State in the General Congress of America.

The exigency of publick affairs have heretofore seemed to require that they should be nominated and appointed by the General Assembly, which has been done to general satisfaction. America is now declared independent, and is forming into an empire unconnected with any other part of the globe. We think it a duty we owe ourselves and posterity to guard our rights and privileges on every quarter, lest a precedent, founded at first in necessity or accident, should be in time construed to deprive us of one privilege which we deem essential to the preservation of all the rest.

The power of electing Representatives, who, with others, are entrusted with power to declare war and make peace, to form alliances with foreign nations, and to make laws for an extensive empire, (we conceive) can be lodged nowhere in so safe hands as that of the whole body of freeholders in a State. Bribery and corruption, intrigue and undue influence, is much more easily practised upon a few than many; although we have the highest value for our own General Assembly, whose members have heretofore been governed and directed by the most laudable of principles, the love of their country's welfare, yet we are not sure that in all future times the same attention will be paid to the true interest of their constituents, or the same principle be the ruling motive of action; and we must declare to you that we think it a right which unalienably belongs to the freeholders of this State to elect members to represent them in the General Congress of America, and a right and power which posterity cannot be deprived of by any previous or present obligation to others.

We do, therefore, as part of the freeholders of this State, enjoin it upon you as our Representatives in General Assembly, to use your utmost influence that the Assembly do order and direct that such election of Delegates to represent this State in General Congress, be annually made by the freeholders, or freemen at large, and not by their Representatives in General Assembly.

—Force, *American Archives*, 5th Series, II, 113-114.

5. "ALL POWER ORIGINATES FROM THE PEOPLE"

To the Freeholders and Inhabitants of New Hampshire.

January 30, 1777

... We proceed to observe that the declaration of independency made the antecedent form of government to be of necessity null and void; and by that act the people of the different colonies slid back into a state of nature, and in that condition they were to begin anew. But has it been so in the government of New Hampshire? I ask how shall we know that independency has been proclaimed, if we only consult the civil economy of this state? In fact, we have no other sign of it but the bare declaration of the Congress. I ask again, what advantage independency has been of to this government, since it had the same legislature before as after the declaration? Think on these matters; and though it is now late, yet that very consideration proves the necessity of dissolving soon the present unconstitutional legislature, and planting the seed anew.

But if it be still asserted that the legislative constitution is founded on independency, it will prove, if anything, that this very constitution established independency itself, before it was proclaimed by the congress. All power originates from the people. A state of independency before a plan of government is formed, supposes the whole right to be vested in them who by a full representation are to rear a new fabric. But it has not been so in the present case; for this very assembly, which was in being before the declaration of independency, has dictated the regulations that took place afterwards. The grossest absurdity, which will appear in one word, [is], viz., the legislature over the people before independency was unconstitutional and deprived them of their rights, yet this very unconstitutional legislature has marked out their liberties for them in the state of independency. As much as to say, an unconstitutional body have made a constitutional one. Would to God that you might carefully weigh these matters, and that every one would measure them by the feelings in his own mind!

There has been for some time a dispute among you as to the right of each incorporated town to a distinct representation. But that it is just seems so plain from the nature of the thing and what has been wrote upon the subject, that there remains but little room for objection. The chief argument now made use of is that if every small incorporated town is represented distinctly, it will be a great expense to the people. The absurdity of this will appear in a few words. ...

Should any, in the character of a Committee or otherwise, endeavor to compound matters with the people in the aggrieved towns, as an impartial writer I conjure you strenuously to adhere to these two important articles:

1. That you give not up an ace of the rights that the *smallest* town has to a distinct representation, if incorporated—the bare number of individuals being, in this case, out of the question.

2ndly. That as the present assembly is unconstitutional, being the same, virtually, as before the declaration of independency, they do dissolve themselves, after having notified each corporate town to form a new body that may fix on a plan of government, which can be the only proper seal of your concurrence in independency. Thus you will act a consistent part, and secure your palace from being pilfered within while you are filling up the breaches that are made without.

—CHASE, *History of Dartmouth College*, I, 431-433.

6. SAMUEL ADAMS EXPLAINS HOW AMERICANS MAKE GOVERNMENT

Marquis de Chastellux' recollections, 1780-1782.

... From this subject we passed to a more interesting one: the form of government which should be given to each state; for it is only on account of the future that it is necessary to take a retrospect of the past. The revolution has taken place, and the republic is beginning; it is an infant newly born, the question is how to nourish and rear it to maturity. I expressed to Mr. Adams some anxiety for the foundations on which the new constitutions are formed, and particularly on that of Massachusetts. Every citizen, said I, every man who pays taxes, has a right to vote in the election of representatives who form the legislative body, and who may be called the sovereign power. All this is very well for the present moment, because every citizen is pretty equally at his ease, or may be so in a short time, but the success of commerce, and even of agriculture, will introduce riches amongst you, and riches will produce inequality of fortunes, and of property. Now, wherever this inequality exists, the real force will invariably be on the side of property; for that if the influence in government be not proportioned to that property, there will always be a contrariety, a combat between the form of government and its natural tendency, the right will be on the one side, and the power on the other; the balance then can only exist between the two equally dangerous extremes of aristocracy and anarchy. Besides, the ideal worth of men must ever be comparative: an individual without property is a discontented citizen, when the state is poor; place a rich man near him, he dwindles into a clown. What will result then one day from vesting the right of election in this class of citizens? The source of civil broils, or corruption, perhaps both at the same time.

The following was pretty nearly the answer of Mr. Adams: I am very sensible of the force of your objections; we are not what we should be, we should labour rather for the future than for the present moment. I build a country house, and have infant children; I ought doubtless to construct their apartments with an eye to the time in which they shall be grown up and married: but we have not neglected this precaution.

In the first place, I must inform you that this new constitution was proposed and agreed to in the most legitimate manner of which there is any example since the days of Lycurgus. A committee chosen from the members of the legislative body, then existing, and which might be considered as a provisional government, was named to prepare a new code of laws. As soon as it was prepared, each county or district was required to name a committee to examine this plan: it was recommended to them to send it back at the expiration of a certain time, with their observations. These observations having been discussed by the committee, and the necessary alterations made, the plan was sent back to each particular committee. When they had all approved it, they received orders to communicate it to the people at large, and to demand their suffrages. If two-thirds of the voters approved it, it was to have the force of law, and be regarded as the work of the people themselves; of two and twenty thousand suffrages, a much greater proportion than two-thirds was in favour of the new constitution.

Now these were the principles on which it was established: a state is never free but when each citizen is bound by no law whatever that he has not approved of, either by himself, or by his representatives; but to represent another man, it is necessary to have been elected by him; every citizen therefore should have a part in elections.

On the other hand, it would be in vain for the people to possess the right of electing representatives, were they restrained in the choice of them to a particular class; it is necessary therefore not to require too much property as a qualification for the *representative of the people*. Accordingly the house of representatives which form the legislative body, and the true *sovereign*, are the people themselves represented by their delegates.

Thus far the government is purely democratical; but it is the permanent and enlightened will of the people which should constitute law, and not the passions and sallies to which they are too subject. It is necessary to moderate their first emotions, and bring them to the test of enquiry and reflection. This is the important business entrusted with the governor and senate, who represent with us the negative power, vested in England in the upper-house, and even in the crown, with this difference only, that in our new constitution the senate has a right to reject a law, and the governor to suspend the promulgation, and return it for a reconsideration; but these forms complied with, if, after this fresh examination, the people persist in their resolution, and there is then not, as before, a mere majority, but two-thirds of the suffrages in favour of the law, the governor and senate are compelled to give it their sanction. Thus this power moderates without destroying the authority of the people, and such is the organization of our republic as to prevent the springs from breaking by too rapid a movement, without ever stopping them entirely.

Now, it is here we have given all its weight to property. A man must have a pretty considerable property to vote for a member of the senate; he must have a more considerable one to make himself eligible. Thus the democracy is pure and entirely in the assembly, which represents the *sovereign;* and the aristocracy, or, if you will, the *optimacy*, is to be found only in the moderating power, where it is the more necessary as men never watch more carefully over the state than when they have a great interest in its destiny.

As to the power of commanding armies, it ought neither to be vested in a great nor even in a small number of men: the governor alone can employ the forces by sea and land according to the necessity; but the land forces will consist only in the militia, which, as it is composed of the people themselves, can never act against the people.

—CHASTELLUX, *Travels in North America*, I, 268 ff.

II. MASSACHUSETTS REALIZES THE THEORIES
OF THE WISEST WRITERS

The period of the American Revolution was remarkably creative, and nowhere more so than in the realm of political institutions. Out of it came the modern federal system, the written constitution, a new colonial system, judicial review and, in a sense, the modern political party. And out of it came the fundamental institution of modern democracy, the constitutional convention. It is the fundamental institution of democracy because it provides a constitutional method for abolishing government and instituting new government on the basis of consent.

Government, Jefferson had said, derives its authority from the consent of the governed, and whenever it becomes destructive of the ends for which it is created it is the right of the people to alter or abolish it and to institute new governments. Congress endorsed and public opinion applauded this argument. But was it not an invitation to perpetual warfare? Jefferson himself was fearful of its logical consequences, and hastened to add that prudence would dictate that governments be not overthrown for light and transient causes. But that did not really meet the problem, for when were men who thought they suffered ever prudent?

The American Revolution itself was a violent revolution. How could men have revolution without violence? How could they legalize revolution? The answer: the constitutional convention.

If an institution is ever the lengthened shadow of one man, then the constitutional convention is the lengthened shadow of John Adams. Yet what he wrote and said, others thought; and resolutions such as those from the towns of Concord and Pittsfield, in Massachusetts, indicate how widespread and deep was the understanding of sound political principles at the time. Yet it was, indubitably, Adams who raised, who agitated, and who worried this question until in the end his colleagues "heard him with more patience" and even began "to ask him civil questions." That he was ready with his answers, he himself testifies; we can forgive his vanity the more easily as we recognize that his were the right answers. In any event Congress followed his lead in advising the states how to go about the business of setting up state governments. And it was in Massachusetts that the process was carried out with the most scrupulous respect to sound political principles.

The process can be followed in some detail. On September 17, 1776, the Massachusetts House asked the towns to vote whether they would authorize it to draw up a new constitution. To this inquiry Concord and Pittsfield replied with statements of the principles that should govern constitution making. The Assembly did not, however, proceed with constitution making, but appointed a committee to draw up a constitution. This committee reported in December 1777, and the next year a convention met, accepted this draft, and submitted it to the towns. It lacked a Bill of Rights, and other necessary features, and was defeated by the resounding vote of 9,972 to 2,083. The next year the General Court, in a chastened mood, took up once again the task of constitution making. Again it asked the people to authorize a convention, which was done. It is worthy of note that all freemen over 21 were entitled to vote on this issue. The convention, which met the following year, had a distinguished membership, including Sam Adams, Hancock, Bowdoin, Parsons and others. Happily John Adams had just come home from France, and was able to guide the deliberations of the convention and, eventually, to draft the constitution. This second try was submitted to the towns and accepted. Thus, said Adams, Massachusetts had "realized the theories of the wisest writers." Thus, wrote Thomas Dawes, "the people of Massachusetts have reduced to practice a wonderful theory. A numerous people have convened in a state of nature, and like our ideas of the patriarchs, have deputed a few fathers of the land to draw up for them a glorious covenant."

New Hampshire speedily adopted the Massachusetts institution of the constitutional convention, and eventually all the other states did the same. From the time of the French and Spanish-American revolutions down to our own day the constitutional convention has spread throughout the globe.

1. How to Glide Insensibly from an Old Government to a New

John Adams to Mercy Warren.

April 16, 1776

. . . I know of no researches in any of the sciences more ingenious than those which have been made after the best forms of government, nor can there be a more agreeable employment to a benevolent heart. The time is now approaching when the Colonies will find themselves under a necessity of engaging in earnest in this great and indispensable work. I have ever thought it the most difficult and dangerous part of the business Americans have to do in this mighty contest, to contrive some method for the Colonies to glide insensibly from under the old government into a peaceable and contented submission to new ones. It is a long time since this opinion was conceived, and it has never been out of my mind. My constant endeavour has been to convince gentlemen of the necessity of turning their thoughts to these subjects. At present, the sense of this necessity seems to be general, and measures are taking which must terminate in a compleat revolution. There is danger of convulsions, but, I hope, not great ones.

The form of government which you admire, when its principles are pure is admirable; indeed, it is productive of every thing which is great and excellent among men. But its principles are as easily destroyed as human nature is corrupted. Such a government is only to be supported by pure religion or austere morals. Public virtue cannot exist in a nation without private, and public virtue is the only foundation of republics. There must be a positive passion for the public good, the public interest, honour, power and glory, established in the minds of the people, or there can be no republican government, nor any real liberty: and this public passion must be superiour to all private passions. Men must be ready, they must pride themselves and be happy to sacrifice their private pleasures, passions and interests, nay, their private friendships and dearest connections, when they stand in competition with the rights of society.

Is there in the world a nation which deserves this character? There have been several, but they are no more. Our dear Americans perhaps have as much of it as any nation now existing, and New England perhaps has more than the rest of America. But I have seen all along my life such selfishness and littleness even in New England that I sometimes tremble to think that, altho we are engaged in the best cause that ever employed the human heart, yet the prospect of success is doubtful not for want of power or of wisdom but of virtue.

—*Warren-Adams Letters*, I, 221-222.

2. JOHN ADAMS EXPLAINS HOW TO SET UP STATE GOVERNMENTS

From the Autobiography.

On Friday, June 2d, 1775,

"The President laid before Congress a letter from the Provincial Convention of Massachusetts Bay, dated May 16th, which was read, setting forth the difficulties they labor under for want of a regular form of government, and as they and the other Colonies are now compelled to raise an army to defend themselves from the butcheries and devastations of their implacable enemies, which renders it still more necessary to have a regular established government, requesting the Congress to favor them with explicit advice respecting the taking up and exercising the powers of civil government, and declaring their readiness to submit to such a general plan as the Congress may direct for the Colonies, or make it their great study to establish such a form of government there as shall not only promote their advantage, but the union and interest of all America." *(Journals of Congress)*

This subject had engaged much of my attention before I left Massachusetts, and had been frequently the subject of conversation between me and many of my friends—Dr. Winthrop, Dr. Cooper, Colonel Otis, the two Warrens, Major Hawley and others, besides my colleagues in Congress—and lay with great weight upon my mind, as the most difficult and dangerous business that we had to do (for from the beginning, I always expected we should have more difficulty and danger in our attempts to govern ourselves, and in our negotiations and connections with foreign powers, than from all the fleets and armies of Great Britain).

It lay, therefore, with great weight upon my mind, and when this letter was read, I embraced the opportunity to open myself in Congress, and most earnestly to entreat the serious attention of all the members, and of all the continent, to the measures which the times demanded. For my part, I thought there was great wisdom in the adage, "When the sword is drawn, throw away the scabbard." Whether we threw it away voluntarily or not, it was useless now, and would be useless forever. The pride of Britain, flushed with late triumphs and conquests, their infinite contempt of all the power of America, with an insolent, arbitrary Scotch faction, with a Bute and Mansfield at their head for a ministry, we might depend upon it, would force us to call forth every energy and resource of the country to seek the friendship of England's enemies, and we had no rational hope but from the *Ratio ultima regum et rerum publicarum.*

These efforts could not be made without government, and as I supposed no man would think of consolidating this vast continent under one national government, we should probably, after the example of the Greeks, the Dutch and the Swiss, form a confederacy of states, each of which must have a separate government. That the case of Massachusetts was the most urgent, but that it could not be long before every other Colony must follow her example. That with a view to this subject, I had looked into the ancient and modern confederacies for examples, but they all appeared to me to have been huddled up in a hurry by a few chiefs. But we had a people of more intelligence, curiosity and enterprise, who must be all consulted, and we must realize the theories of the wisest writers, and invite the people to erect the whole building with their own hands, upon the broadest foundation. That this could be done only by conventions of representatives chosen by the people in the several colonies, in the most exact proportions. That it was my opinion that Congress ought now to recommend to the people of every Colony to call such conventions immediately, and set up governments of their own, under their own authority; for the people were the source of all authority and original of all power.

These were new, strange and terrible doctrines to the greatest part of the members, but not a very small number heard them with apparent pleasure, and none more than Mr. John Rutledge, of South Carolina, and Mr. John Sullivan, of New Hampshire. . . .

On Wednesday, October 18th, 1775, the delegates from New Hampshire laid before the Congress a part of the instructions delivered to them by their Colony, in these words:

"We would have you immediately use your utmost endeavors to obtain advice and direction of the Congress with respect to a method for our administering justice, and regulating our civil police. We press you not to delay this matter, as its being done speedily will probably prevent the greatest confusion among us."

This instruction might have been obtained by Mr. Langdon or Mr. Whipple, but I always supposed it was General Sullivan who suggested the measures because he left Congress with a stronger impression upon his mind of the importance of it than I ever observed in either of the others. Be this, however, as it may have been, I embraced with joy the opportunity of haranguing on the subject at large and urging Congress to resolve on a general recommendation to all the States to call conventions and institute regular governments. I reasoned from various topics, many of which, perhaps, I could not now recollect. . . .

Although the opposition was still inveterate, many members of Congress began to hear me with more patience, and some began to ask me civil questions. "How can the people institute governments?"

My answer was, "By conventions of representatives, freely, fairly and proportionably chosen."

"When the convention has fabricated a government, or a constitution rather, how do we know the people will submit to it?"

"If there is any doubt of that, the convention may send out their project of a constitution to the people in their several towns, counties or districts, and the people may make the acceptance of it their own act."

"But the people know nothing about constitutions."

"I believe you are much mistaken in that supposition; if you are not, they will not oppose a plan prepared by their own chosen friends; but I believe that in every considerable portion of the people, there will be found some men who will understand the subject as well as their representatives, and these will assist in enlightening the rest."

"But what plan of government would you advise?"

"A plan as nearly resembling the government under which we were born, and have lived, as the circumstances of the country will admit. Kings we never had among us. Nobles we never had. Nothing hereditary ever existed in the country; nor will the country require or admit of any such thing. But governors and councils we have always had, as well as representatives. A legislature in three branches ought to be preserved, and independent judges."

"Where and how will you get your governors and councils?"

"By elections."

"How—who shall elect?"

"The representatives of the people in a convention will be the best qualified to contrive a mode." . . .

Friday, May 10, 1776. Congress resumed the consideration of the resolution reported from the committee of the whole, and the same was agreed as follows:

"*Resolved,* That it be recommended to the respective assemblies and conventions of the United Colonies, where no government sufficient to the exigencies of their affairs hath been hitherto established, to adopt such government as shall, in the opinion of the representatives of the people, best conduce to the happiness and safety of their constituents in particular, and America in general. . . ."

This resolution I considered as an epocha, a decisive event. It was a measure which I had invariably pursued for a whole year, and contended for, through a scene and a series of anxiety, labor, study, argument and obloquy, which was then little known, and is now forgotten by all but Dr. Rush and a very few who, like him, survive. Millions of curses were poured out upon me for these exertions and for these triumphs over them, by many who, whatever their pretences may have been, have never forgotten, nor cordially forgiven me. By these I mean, not the Tories, for from them I received always more candor, but a class of people who thought proper and convenient to themselves to go along with the public opinion in appearance, though in their hearts they detested it. Although they might think the public opinion was right, in general, in its difference with Great Britain, yet they secretly regretted the separation, and, above all things, the connection with France. Such a party has always existed, and was the final ruin of the federal administration, as will hereafter very plainly appear. . . .

—ADAMS, ed., *Works of John Adams*, III, 13-16, 18-20, 44-45.

3. STATE MAKING IN MASSACHUSETTS

A. WHO MAY ENACT A CONSTITUTION?

In the House of Representatives, September 17th, 1776.

Resolved, That it be recommended to the male inhabitants of each town in this State, being free and twenty-one years of age or upwards, that they assemble as soon as they can in Town-Meeting, upon reasonable previous warning to be therefore given, according to law; and that in such Meeting, they consider and determine whether they will give their consent that the present House of Representatives of this State of the Massachusetts-Bay in New-England, together with the Council, if they consent in one Body with the House, and by equal voice, should consult, agree on, and enact such a Constitution and form of government for this State, as the said House of Representatives and Council as aforesaid, on the fullest and most mature deliberation, shall judge will most conduce to the safety, peace and happiness of this State, in all after successions and generations; and if they would direct that the same be made public for the inspection and perusal of the inhabitants, before the ratification thereof by the Assembly. . . .

J. WARREN, *Speaker*
—MASSACHUSETTS ARCHIVES, CLXI, 180.

B. "GOD HAS NOW OPENED A DOOR"

Vote of Petersham Town Meeting, on forming a Constitution.

September 27, 1776

The question being put, whether this Town will consent that the present General Court shall form a Constitution of Government agreeable to their resolve of the 17th instant, and it passed in the negative, unanimously. Also unanimously voted, that the following draft be lodged in the Secretary's office, as the sense of this Town respecting that matter, agreeable to the resolve aforesaid.

The inhabitants, in order to express their mind respecting the forming a Constitution of Government for this State, would humbly show, that it is their opinion that it will be of little avail for this people to shed their blood and spend their treasure in opposing foreign tyranny, if, after all, we should fix a basis of Government partial, unsafe, and not fit for the enjoyment of free and virtuous men. We think that God, in his providence, has now opened a door, possibly the only one that this State will ever have, for the laying a foundation for its prosperity, peace and glory. A Constitution of Government, one levied on the laws of the people, cannot easily be altered (especially for the better), as the craftiness of designing men, if any errours are suffered to be fixed in its foundation in their favour, it will be next to impossible to remove them; therefore, in so momentous and important a matter, we would be willing to set out fair, and on the most likely ground to obtain the prize.

If we may be allowed to speak our minds freely, we apprehend that the present General Court of this State are not in a situation most likely to effect this great work to advantage, nor do we believe that when all the towns who have not sent a member, may have sent as many as the late law will allow them, that they will be in a proper situation for so great and important a business; for while the mercantile towns swarm with Representatives, the freehold interest of the country (in which we presume there is the most safety) have neglected to choose such a number as the late regulation entitles them; and the late resolve of Court does not empower any town who have a right to choose a number and have elected but one, to make any addition; and further, a late General Court having taken it upon them in a thin House, uninstructed and without consulting the people, materially to alter the fundamental principles of representation, and as we apprehend much for the worse, most sensibly affects us. . . .

—FORCE, *American Archives*, 5th Series, II, 576-577.

C. ASHFIELD READS A CONSTITUTIONAL LESSON TO THE GENERAL COURT

To the Honorabel House of Representatives of the State of the Massachusetts Bay in New England Assembled for the Good of this State Having Referred your Resolve of September the 17, 1776 Directing the Several Towns to Call A Meting for the Spesal pirpos of Causing thair Vots or Resolves to be Returned to the Secretarys Office of this State, the Town After having Ben Previously Warned, Met on thusda 26th of September instant and After Debating the Matur Ajurned to October the 4, 1776. Then Met and in the Fullest and most mature Dilibrate Maner Came Into the folowing Resolves

Viz 1 Voted that it is our mind that we should have the forme of Sivil Goverment Set up for the good of this Stat.

   2 Voted that the Presant Reprasentatives of the Peopel shall forme the Constitution Exclusive of the Counsel for the Good of this State and Returne it to the Sevarale Towns for their Exceptanc Before the Ratifycation thairof

   3 Voted that we will take the Law of God for the foundation of the forme of our Goverment, for as the Old Laws that we have Ben Ruled by under the British Constitution have Proved Inefectual to Secuer us from the more then Savige Crualty of tiranical Opreseans and Sense the God of Nature hath Enabeled us to Brake that yoke of Bondage we think our Selves Bound in Duty to God and our Country to Opose the Least Apearanc of them Old Tiranical Laws taking Place again

   4 Voted that it is our Opinniun that we Do not want any Goviner but the Goviner of the univarse, and under him a States Ginaral to Consult with the wrest of the united States for the good of the whole

   5 Voted that it is our opinian that Each Town is Invested with a Native Athority to Chuse A Comitte or Number of Juges Consisting of A Number of wise understanding and Prudant Men that Sall Jug and Detarmin all Cases betwixt Man and Man, Setel Intesttate Estats and Colect all Debts that have Ben Contracted, or may be Contracted within their Limits and all contravarsies what Soever Except in the

case of Murdor and then it will be Necesary to Call in Eleven men from Eleven Nabouring Towns that Shall be Cose for that Porpos Anuly to Joge and Condemn Such Moderrers

6 Voted that it is our opinion that the Town Clark shal Register all Deads within the Leminits of Said Town

7 Voted that it our opinan that the Asembelly of this Stat Consist of one Colecttive body the Members of which body shall Anually be Alected

8 Voted that we Do Not Want any Laws Made to Govern in Eclasastics Afairs fairmly Believeng the Divine Law to be sufficant and that by which we and all Our Religion affairs ought to Governed by

9 Voted that it is our opinion that the Representitive of this State Be Payed out of the Publick Treshuour of this State which monies Shall be Colected of the whole State

10 Voted that it is ower Opinion that all acts Pased by the Gineral Cort of this State Respecting the Several Towns Be Sent to the Sevarale Towns for their acceptants Before they shall be in force.

Ashfield October 4th: 1776

A tru copy Test

Aaron Lyon Clark P T

—Massachusetts Archives, CLXI, 131.

D. NEW SALEM REJECTS THE PROPOSED CONSTITUTION OF 1778

New Salem, May the 19th, 1778

To the Honorable House of Representatives of the State of Massachusetts Bay. Gentlemen agreeable to your Resolve We have meet and Carfully Examiand the New form for a constetution and unanimasly Disaproved of it. The No Present at said meeting being, 74 - - - - -

Because We conceive that there are some things contained *in it* that are Injures to the Rights of a free People——

1ly Because there is two Branches Proposed to make the Legaslative authority When we conceive that one Branch will *answer* all the Porposes of Good Government much Better then two.

2ly Because in said constetution mens worth of money seems to be Pointed out as Qualifycations But we think where the Great Auther of Natur hath furnished a man to the satisfaction of the Electors and he Legaly chosen he aught to have a *seat* and voice in any socity of men or to serve in any office whatever.

3ly Because said constetution as we conceive admitts of three times to Numeras a house since one third part the Number would Dispatch *Business* with Greater Briefness and be Less Burdensome to the State.

4ly Because the Eases method for the People Setteling their one civel Cases is Not Pointed out in this Constetution we conceive that it Would be more for the well Being of the People to have authority *in* Each town to settle their one civel affairs. - - - - -

5ly Because said Constetution Deprives the People of their just Rights of chusing their Civel and Military officers (viz) *Justices* Captains and Sub-boltons etc. - - - - -

6ly Because Said Constetution maks no Provision against Extravagences In Sallarys Pencions and fees we conceive that No Sallary ought to be granted Nor pencion Given or fee seet with a Less Majority then four to one.

BENJA. SOUTHWICK JUR

UR.L. PUTNAM   *Selectmen*

JOHN KING

—MASSACHUSETTS ARCHIVES, CLXI, 366.

4. MASSACHUSETTS FINALLY GETS A CONSTITUTION

A. MILTON WANTS AMENDMENTS

At a Legal Town Meeting Held in Milton on the 22d day of May 1780

The Committee appointed by the Town to take into consideration a Constitution or Frame of Government, Agreed upon by the Delegates of the People of the State of Massachusetts-Bay, Reported as follows Viz.

Gentlemen, we your Constituents having thoroughly considered the Constitution, or Frame of Government offered by the Convention, to the People of this State; are of opinion that it is in General exceedingly well calculated to promote the Peace, Freedom, and Prosperity of this State.

—Notwithstanding we would submit a few amendments to the consideration of the Convention.

In the 16th Art. in the Declaration of Rights after "the Liberty of the Press" we would have inserted these words, Viz, *and the Liberty of Speech as it respects Publick men in their Publick conduct,*

For unless *this* Liberty of Speech is granted, we are apprehensive it may be dangerous in some future time, even in Publick Town Meetings, to speak the truth of weak, or wicked Rulers—and thus the most regular, peaceable and effectual method of calling the servants of the People to account, and of reducing them to private life, may be in a great measure prevented,

And in the 7th Art. in the 2d Chap. we would have a clause inserted giving power to the Governor, in the recess of the General Court, to order the Militia or Navy to the Assistance of any Neighbouring State invaded, or threatned with immediate invasion.

Many reasons might be offered to support this amendment, but it is sufficient to say that the 3d Art. in the Confederation oblieges us to afford such assistance, and in the recess of the General Court, it cannot be done, but by the Governor.

And in the 2d Chapter, 4th Sec. and 1st Art. we would have the service of the Commissary General limited to five years.

For we apprehend every person largely entrusted with Publick property, ought to be often shifted—by that means their accounts will be much likelier to be critically examined and fairly adjusted, and the property of the People be better ascertained and secured.

In the 4th Chapt. we propose that no person shall be chosen a member of Congress unless he be an Inhabitant of this State, and possessed of a considerable real Property—the Estate adequate to the important trust, we mean not precisely to determine, but have the same to be affixed by the convention as their wisdom shall dictate.

In the 7th Art. in the 6th Chapt. we propose that the Writ of Habeas corpus shall never be suspended but in times of war, or threatned Invasion, and then for a time not exceeding six months, for we cannot conceive of any possible advantage arising to the Community by the Legislature suspending this Writ in times of publick Tranquility, But Injury may accrue to individuals, by a suspension thereof. And in times of War, or threatned Invasion six months is fully sufficient for any Legislature to ascertain the precise crime, and to procure the evidence against any Individual, in order to bring him for Trial.

Then the following Questions were put, and Voted as follows, Viz.

Question. If you will accept of the said Constitution as proposed to be amended, and do direct your Delegates to move in Convention for the same be pleased to manifest it,   yeas 111   nays 0

Question. If your Delegates cannot obtain all, or any of the aforesaid alterations, will you accept of said Constitution as reported by the Convention; if you will be pleased to manifest it.   yeas 110   nays 1

Question. Should any other amendments or propositions be made, that appear agreeable to two thirds of the Voters throughout the State, Do you instruct your Delegates to join in confirming the same, If you do be pleased to manifest it,   yeas 110   nays 1

Question. Should the Constitution be made agreeable to two thirds of the Voters, as aforesaid, do you impower your Delegates to use their discretion in Convention in fixing the time when this Constitution, or Frame of Government shall take place, If you do be pleased to manifest it   yeas 111   nays 0

Attest AMARIAH BLAKE *Town Clerk*

—MASSACHUSETTS ARCHIVES, CCLXXVII, 73.

B. WEST SPRINGFIELD IS CONTENT WITH ONE AMENDMENT

West Springfield, June 2, 1780

Gentlemen

The Town of Wt. Springfield having convened in a legal Meeting to consider the Constitution or Frame of Government, agreed upon by the Convention of this State and by them proposed to the People for their Approbation, Rejection, or Amendment, having had the same repeatedly read, proceeded to a Discussion of the several Articles therein contained, and have unanimously voted to approve of all the several Articles except these following, viz. the third Article in the Bill of Rights. . . . The Meeting then voted to choose a Committee to state Objections. The Committee took the Matter under Consideration and reported as follows, viz.

1st Because we conceive Religion or the Worship of God to be an unalienable Right inherent in every Individual, that we of Right cannot invest The Legislature with Authority to institute the Worship of God at stated Times and Seasons this being at all Times a Matter between God and Individuals and must be a Matter of our Choice. 2. Because we conceive that if the Legislature may be impowered to oblige all the Citizens to attend on the public Worship of God at stated Times and Seasons they may prohibit the Worship of God at any other Time. *If the Legislature may institue publick Worship they may* also define what that Worship shall be and so the Right of private Judgment will be at an End. 3. Because we conceive the Religion of the Gospel was fully instituted by it's Divine Author; (it is therefore repugnant to the Rules of Christianity for the Legislature to interfere otherwise than to defend the Citizens in the free Exercise of their own religious Professions and Sentiments) And consequently the Interposition of the Civil Authority is not necessary to the Religion of the Gospel which has always flourished most without it and therefore the Good of Society would be promoted by leaving the Christian Religion to the Care of the Great Head of the Church who has promisd his Presence with it to the End of the World. Instead of promoting Religion and the consequent Good of Society we fear it will produce Law Suits, Bitterness and Ill-Will among the citizens of of the Commonwealth.

—Massachusetts Archives, CCLXXVI, 71.

C. john adams' town accepts—with reservations

The Comtee of the Town of Braintree, "*for taking into Consideration the Form of Government*" etc., having attended that Service, Report the following alterations, and additions, as being, in their opinion, of considerable importance, They also observed Several others, such as *may*, instead of *shall*; *Judge*, instead of *Justice*, etc, which being of smaller moment, are not particularly mentioned. Tho' the following are, in the Opinion of your Comtee, of great importance, and such as they wish to take place, yet, being impressed with the necessity of having a new, and better, form of Governmt than the present; they also Report, as their Opinion, that 'tis better to accept the new Constitution, without any alteration, than to remain any longer under the present; Provided, there be possitive provision made, for having another Convention within a short space of time, and so from time to time, at regular and reasonable distances from *each other, for Revision of the then Constitution.*

Preamble

a. instead of, "*safety and tranquility, their natural rights, and the blessing of life*": say *in greater safety and tranquility, all those rights, properties, and blessings of life, for the secure enjoyment of which, they enter into civil society.*

The Reason. Men, when they enter into civil society, relinquish some of their natural rights, in order to their more secure enjoyment of the remainder.

At a Meeting of the Town of Braintree, on adjournment, on the 5th of June 1780. Then Voted, that the new Constitution, with the alterations and amendments made by their Comtee, be accepted. Ninety-five voted in favor of it, but none appeared against it.

Braintree June 5th 1780

To the Sec y of the Convention.

DANL ARNOLD

STEPHEN PENNIMAN   *Selectmen*

—MASSACHUSETTS ARCHIVES, CCLXXVII, 63.

III. TWO BILLS OF RIGHTS

Americans had long been familiar with bills of rights. They took for granted that they enjoyed all the rights and privileges of Englishmen, and assumed that these included the rights asserted in Magna Charta, the Petition of Right and the great Bill of Rights of 1689. More to the point, they had long been accustomed to their own bills of rights, though not under that precise name: thus the Maryland Act for the Liberties of the People of 1639; the Massachusetts Body of Liberties of 1641; the Plantation Agreement of the Narragansett Plantations; the Fundamental Laws of West Jersey of 1676; and the Pennsylvania Charter of Privileges of 1701. In the light of this long experience it was not surprising that when Americans came to draw up the constitutions for their states they included bills of rights. The most famous of the American bills of rights are doubtless those of Virginia and Massachusetts. The first was drafted almost entirely by George Mason of Gunston Hall, a leading figure in the Virginia enlightenment; the second by John Adams. The Virginia bill of rights served as a model for those of other American states, and had some influence abroad, especially in France.

1. THE VIRGINIA DECLARATION OF RIGHTS

May 15, 1776

A declaration of rights made by the representatives of the good people of Virginia, assembled in full and free convention; which rights do pertain to them and their posterity, as the basis and foundation of government.

SECTION 1. That all men are by nature equally free and independent and have certain inherent rights, of which, when they enter into a state of society, they cannot, by any compact, deprive or divest their posterity; namely, the enjoyment of life and liberty, with the means of acquiring and possessing property, and pursuing and obtaining happiness and safety.

SEC. 2. That all power is vested in, and consequently derived from, the people; that magistrates are their trustees and servants and at all times amenable to them.

SEC. 3. That government is or ought to be instituted for the common benefit, protection, and security of the people, nation, or community; of all the various modes and forms of government, that is best which is capable of producing the greatest degree of happiness and safety and is most effectually secured against the danger of maladministration; and that, when any government shall be found inadequate or contrary to these purposes, a majority of the community hath an indubitable, inalienable, and indefeasible right to reform, alter, or abolish it, in such manner as shall be judged most conducive to the public weal.

SEC. 4. That no man, or set of men, are entitled to exclusive or separate emoluments or privileges from the community, but in consideration of public services; which, not being descendible, neither ought the offices of magistrate, legislator, or judge to be hereditary.

SEC. 5. That the legislative and executive powers of the state should be separate and distinct from the judiciary; and that the members of the two first may be restrained from oppression, by feeling and participating the burdens of the people, they should, at fixed periods, be reduced to a private station, return into that body from which they were originally taken, and the vacancies be supplied by frequent, certain, and regular elections, in which all, or any part, of the former members, to be again eligible, or ineligible, as the laws shall direct.

SEC. 6. That elections of members to serve as representatives of the people, in assembly, ought to be free; and that all men, having sufficient evidence of permanent common interest with, and attachment to, the community, have the right of suffrage and cannot be taxed or deprived of their property for public uses without their own consent, or that of their representatives so elected, nor bound by any law to which they have not, in like manner, assented for the public good.

SEC. 7. That all power of suspending laws, or the execution of laws, by any authority, without consent of the representatives of the people, is injurious to their rights and ought not to be exercised.

SEC. 8. That in all capital or criminal prosecutions a man hath a right to demand the cause and nature of his accusation, to be confronted with the accusers and witnesses, to call for evidence in his favor, and to a speedy trial by an impartial jury of twelve men of his vicinage, without whose unanimous consent he cannot be found guilty; nor can he be compelled to give evidence against himself; that no man be deprived of his liberty, except by the law of the land or the judgment of his peers.

SEC. 9. That excessive bail ought not to be required, nor excessive fines imposed, nor cruel and unusual punishments inflicted.

SEC. 10. That general warrants, whereby an officer or messenger may be commanded to search suspected places without evidence of a fact committed, or to seize any person or persons not named, or whose offense is not particularly described and supported by evidence, are grievous and oppressive and ought not to be granted.

SEC. 11. That in controversies respecting property, and in suits between man and man, the ancient trial by jury is preferable to any other and ought to be held sacred.

SEC. 12. That the freedom of the press is one of the great bulwarks of liberty and can never be restrained but by despotic governments.

SEC. 13. That a well-regulated militia, composed of the body of the people, trained to arms, is the proper, natural, and safe defense of a free state;

that standing armies, in time of peace, should be avoided as dangerous to liberty; and that in all cases the military should be under strict subordination to, and governed by, the civil power.

Sec. 14. That the people have a right to uniform government; and, therefore, that no government separate from or independent of the government of Virginia ought to be erected or established within the limits thereof.

Sec. 15. That no free government, or the blessings of liberty, can be preserved to any people, but by a firm adherence to justice, moderation, temperance, frugality, and virtue, and by frequent recurrence to fundamental principles.

Sec. 16. That religion, or the duty which we owe to our Creator and the manner of discharging it, can be directed only by reason and conviction, not by force or violence; and therefore all men are equally entitled to the free exercise of religion, according to the dictates of conscience; and that it is the mutual duty of all to practice Christian forbearance, love, and charity toward each other.   —Hening, *Statutes at Large of Virginia*, IX, 110.

2. Massachusetts Bill of Rights
1780

The end of the institution, maintenance, and administration of government, is to secure the existence of the body-politic, to protect it, and to furnish the individuals who compose it with the power of enjoying in safety and tranquillity their natural rights, and the blessings of life: and whenever these great objects are not obtained, the people have a right to alter the government, and to take measures necessary for their safety, prosperity and happiness.

The body-politic is formed by a voluntary association of individuals; it is a social compact by which the whole people covenants with each citizen and each citizen with the whole people that all shall be governed by certain laws for the common good. It is the duty of the people, therefore, in framing a constitution of government, to provide for an equitable mode of making laws, as well as for an impartial interpretation and a faithful execution of them; that every man may, at all times, find his security in them.

We, therefore, the people of Massachusetts, acknowledging, with grateful hearts, the goodness of the great Legislator of the universe, in affording us, in the course of His Providence, an opportunity, deliberately and peaceably, without fraud, violence, or surprise, of entering into an original, explicit, and solemn compact with each other; and of forming a new constitution of civil government, for ourselves and posterity; and devoutly imploring His direction in so interesting a design, do agree upon, ordain, and establish, the following Declaration of Rights, and Frame of Government, as the Constitution of the Commonwealth of Massachusetts.

Part the First
A Declaration of the Rights of the Inhabitants of the Commonwealth of Massachusetts

Article I. All men are born free and equal, and have certain natural, essential, and unalienable rights; among which may be reckoned the right of enjoying and defending their lives and liberties; that of acquiring, possessing, and protecting property; in fine, that of seeking and obtaining their safety and happiness.

II. It is the right as well as the duty of all men in society, publicly, and at stated seasons, to worship the Supreme Being, the great Creator and Pre-server of the universe. And no subject shall be hurt, molested, or restrained, in his person, liberty, or estate, for worshipping God in the manner and sea-son most agreeable to the dictates of his own conscience; or for his religious profession of sentiments; provided he doth not disturb the public peace, or obstruct others in their religious worship. . . .

As the happiness of a people and the good order and preservation of civil government essentially depend upon piety, religion, and morality, and as these cannot be generally diffused through a community but by the institu-tion of the public worship of God and of public instructions, in piety, re-ligion, and morality. Therefore to promote their happiness and secure the good order and preservation of their government, the people of this com-monwealth have a right to invest their legislature with power to authorize and require, and the legislature shall from time to time authorize and re-quire, the several towns . . . and other bodies-politic or religious societies, to make suitable provision, at their own expense, for the institution of the public worship of God and the support and maintenance of public Protestant teachers of piety, religion, and morality. . . .

And the people of this commonwealth . . . do invest their legislature with authority to enjoin upon all the subjects an attendance upon the instructions of the public teachers aforesaid. . . .

And every denomination of Christians, demeaning themselves peaceably and as good subjects of the commonwealth, shall be equally under the pro-tection of the law; and no subordination of any one sect or denomination to another shall ever be established by law.

IV. The people of this commonwealth have the sole and exclusive right of governing themselves, as a free, sovereign, and independent State, and do, and forever hereafter shall, exercise and enjoy every power, jurisdiction, and right, which is not, or may not hereafter be, by them expressly delegated to the United States of America, in Congress assembled.

V. All power residing originally in the people, and being derived from them, the several magistrates and officers of government, vested with au-thority, whether legislative, executive, or judicial, are their substitutes and agents, and are at all times accountable to them. . . .

VII. Government is instituted for the common good, for the protection, safety, prosperity, and happiness of the people and not for the profit, honor or private interest of any one man, family, or class of men: therefore the people alone have an incontestible unalienable, and indefeasible right to in-stitute government; and to reform, alter, or totally change the same, when their protection, safety, prosperity, and happiness require it.

VIII. In order to prevent those who are vested with authority from be-coming oppressors, the people have a right, at such periods and in such manner as they shall establish by their frame of government, to cause their public officers to return to private life; and to fill up vacant places by certain and regular elections and appointments. . . .

X. Each individual of the society has a right to be protected by it in the enjoyment of his life, liberty, and property. . . . No part of the property of any individual can, with justice, be taken from him, or applied to public uses, without his own consent, or that of the representative body of the people. . . . And whenever the public exigencies require that the property of any individual should be appropriated to public uses, he shall receive a reasonable compensation therefor. . . .

XII. No subject shall be held to answer for any crimes or offence, until the same is fully and plainly . . . described to him; or be compelled to accuse, or furnish evidence against himself. And every subject shall have a right to produce all proofs that may be favorable to him; to meet the witnesses against him face to face, and to be fully heard in his defence by himself, or his counsel, at his election. And no subject shall be arrested, . . . or deprived of his life, liberty or estate, but by the judgment of his peers, or the law of the land.

And the legislature shall not make any law that shall subject any person to a capital or infamous punishment, excepting for the government of the army and navy, without trial by jury. . . .

XIV. Every subject has a right to be secure from all unreasonable searches, and seizures, of his person, his houses, his papers, and all his possessions. . . . And no warrant ought to be issued but in cases, and with the formalities prescribed by the laws.

XV. In all controversies concerning property, and in all suits between two or more persons, . . . the parties have a right to a trial by jury; and this method of procedure shall be held sacred. . . .

XVI. The liberty of the press is essential to the security of freedom in a state it ought not, therefore, to be restricted in this commonwealth.

XVII. The people have a right to keep and to bear arms for the common defence. And as, in time of peace, armies are dangerous to liberty, they ought not to be maintained without the consent of the legislature; and the military power shall always be held in an exact subordination to the civil authority, and be governed by it.

XVIII. A frequent recurrence to the fundamental principles of the constitution, and a constant adherence to those of piety, justice, moderation, temperance, industry and frugality, are absolutely necessary to preserve the advantages of liberty, and to maintain a free government. The people ought, consequently, to have a particular attention to all those principles, in the choice of their officers and representatives: and they have a right to require of their lawgivers and magistrates an exact and constant observance of them, in the formation and execution of the laws necessary for the good administration of the commonwealth.

XIX. The people have a right, in an orderly and peaceable manner to assemble to consult upon the common good; give instructions to their representatives, and to request of the legislative body, by the way of addresses, petitions, or remonstrances, redress of the wrongs done them, and of the grievances they suffer. . . .

XXIV. Laws made to punish for actions done before the existence of such laws, and which have not been declared crimes by preceding laws, are unjust, oppressive, and inconsistent with the fundamental principles of a free government. . . .

XXIX. It is essential to the preservation of the rights of every individual, his life, liberty, property, and character, that there be an impartial interpretation of the laws, and administration of justice. It is the right of every citizen to be tried by judges as free, impartial, and independent as the lot of humanity will admit. It is, therefore, not only the best policy, but for the security of the rights of the people, and of every citizen, that the judges of the supreme judicial court should hold their offices as long as they behave themselves well; and that they should have honorable salaries ascertained and established by standing laws.

XXX. In the government of this commonwealth, the legislative department shall never exercise the executive and judicial powers, or either of them: the executive shall never exercise the legislative and judicial powers, or either of them: the judicial shall never exercise the legislative and executive powers, or either of them: to the end it may be the government of laws and not of men.

—THORPE, *Federal and State Constitutions*, III, 1888-1893.

IV. FREEDOM EMBRACES RELIGION AS WELL AS POLITICS

When the Revolution broke out, the Anglican Church was the established church in every colony from Maryland south; the Congregational Church enjoyed special privileges in Massachusetts, Connecticut and New Hampshire, and the Anglican and the Dutch Reformed in parts of New York. In all of these colonies the dissenters—in the South perhaps a majority of the population—were discriminated against in various ways. The Revolution wrecked the establishment in Maryland and North Carolina, and jolted it badly in South Carolina and Georgia. It was in Virginia that the issue of religious freedom and an establishment was debated and fought out most thoroughly. Here the establishment was thoroughly entrenched, and here even some of the dissenters had no objection to state support of religion as long as their denominations enjoyed some of the support. The Constitution of 1776 declared that "all men are equally entitled to the free exercise of religion," but not until 1779 was the Church disestablished, and it required another seven years before the legislature was prepared to enact Jefferson's Statute for Religious Freedom. Jefferson characterized this fight—with some exaggeration—as "the severest contest in which I have ever been engaged," and regarded its successful outcome as one of the three most important achievements of his life.

The new constitutions of the Middle States embodied the principle of religious freedom and equality as a matter of course—though even in liberal Pennsylvania members of the Assembly were required to take an oath that they were orthodox Protestant Christians. Religious liberty and equality already obtained in Vermont and Rhode Island; elsewhere in New England the privileged position of the Congregational Church was strengthened by the Revolution. These states instituted, or continued, a sort of quasi establishment according to which everyone had to pay a religious tax either to the Congregational Church of the parish where he resided, or to some other recognized and organized church. Quakers and Baptists protested against this illiberal arrangement even before independence, and we give here John Adams' account of a meeting with prominent Quakers—one which clearly embarrassed him—and a petition of Massachusetts Baptists for exemption from what they considered illiberal and illegal taxation.

1. Quakers Protest the Illiberality of Massachusetts

John Adams' account of a Philadelphia conference.

October 1774

Governor Hopkins and Governor Ward, of Rhode Island, came to our lodgings and said to us that President Manning, of Rhode Island College, and Mr. Backus, of Massachusetts, were in town, and had conversed with some gentlemen in Philadelphia who wished to communicate to us a little business, and wished we would meet them at six in the evening at Carpenters' Hall. Whether they explained their affairs more particularly to any of my colleagues, I know not; but I had no idea of the design. We all went at the hour, and to my great surprise found the hall almost full of people, and a great number of Quakers seated at a long table with their broad brimmed beavers on their heads. We were invited to seats among them, and informed that they had received complaints from some Anabaptists and some Friends in Massachusetts against certain laws of that province, restrictive of the liberty of conscience, and some instances were mentioned in the General Court, and in the courts of justice, in which Friends and Baptists had been grievously oppressed. I know not how my colleagues felt, but I own I was greatly surprised and somewhat indignant, being, like my friend Chase, of a temper naturally quick and warm, at seeing our State and her delegates thus summoned before a self-created tribunal, which was neither legal nor constitutional.

Israel Pemberton, a Quaker of large property and more intrigue, began to speak, and said that Congress were here endeavoring to form a union of the Colonies; but there were difficulties in the way, and none of more importance than liberty of conscience. The laws of New England, and particularly of Massachusetts, were inconsistent with it, for they not only compelled men to pay to the building of churches and support of ministers, but to go to some known religious assembly on first days, etc., and that he and his friends were desirous of engaging us to assure them that our State would repeal all those laws, and place things as they were in Pennsylvania.

A suspicion instantly arose in my mind, which I have ever believed to have been well founded, that this artful Jesuit, for I had been apprised before of his character, was endeavoring to avail himself of this opportunity to break up the Congress, or at least to withdraw the Quakers and the governing part of Pennsylvania from us; for, at that time, by means of a most unequal representation, the Quakers had a majority in their House of Assembly, and, by consequence, the whole power of the State in their hands. I arose and spoke in answer to him. The substance of what I said was that we had no authority to bind our constituents to any such proposals; that the laws of Massachusetts were the most mild and equitable establishment of religion that was known in the world; if indeed they could be called an establishment; that it would be in vain for us to enter into any conferences on such a subject, for we knew beforehand our constituents would disavow all we could do or say for the satisfaction of those who invited us to this meeting. That the people of Massachusetts were as religious and conscientious as the people of Pennsylvania; that their conscience dictated to them that it was their duty to support those laws, and therefore the very liberty of conscience, which Mr. Pemberton invoked, would demand indulgence for the tender consciences of the people of Massachusetts, and allow them to preserve their laws; that, it might be depended on, this was a point that could not be carried; that I would not deceive them by insinuating the faintest hope, for I knew they might as well turn the heavenly bodies out of their annual and diurnal courses, as the people of Massachusetts at the present day from their meeting-house and Sunday laws.

Pemberton made no reply but this: "Oh! sir, pray don't urge liberty of conscience in favor of such laws!"

If I had known the particular complaints which were to be alleged, and if Pemberton had not broken irregularly into the midst of things, it might have been better, perhaps, to have postponed this declaration. However, the gentlemen proceeded and stated the particular cases of oppression, which were alleged in our general and executive courts. It happened that Mr. Cushing and Mr. Samuel Adams had been present in the General Court when the petitions had been under deliberation, and they explained the whole so clearly that every reasonable man must have been satisfied. Mr. Paine and I had been concerned at the bar in every action in the executive courts which was complained of, and we explained them all to the entire satisfaction of impartial men, and showed that there had been no oppression or injustice in any of them.

—Hovey, *Memoir of Life and Times of the Rev. Isaac Backus,* pp. 349-351.

2. Bay State Baptists Claim Exemption from Illegal Taxation

To the honorable Congress of the Massachusetts province, convened at Cambridge, November 22, 1774.

Honored Gentlemen: At a time when all America are alarmed at the open and violent attempts that have been made against their liberties, it affords great cause of joy and thankfulness to see the colonies so happily united to defend their rights; and particularly that their late Continental Congress have been directed into measures so wise and salutary for obtaining relief and securing our future liberties; and who have wisely extended their regards to the rights and freedom of the poor Africans. Since then the law of equity has prevailed so far, we hope that it will move this honorable assembly to pay a just regard to their English neighbors and brethren at home.

It seems that the two main rights which all America are contending for at this day, are—Not to be taxed where they are not represented, and—To have their causes tried by unbiased judges. And the Baptist churches in this province as heartily unite with their countrymen in this cause as any denomination in the land; and are as ready to exert all their abilities to defend it. Yet only because they have thought it to be their duty to claim an equal title to these rights with their neighbors, they have repeatedly been accused of evil attempts against the general welfare of the colony; therefore, we have thought it expedient to lay a brief statement of the case before this assembly.

. . . When our churches understood that the Congress at Philadelphia was designed, not only to seek present relief, but also to lay a foundation for the future welfare of our country, they desired me to repair to that city and, with the best advice I could obtain, to try if something could not be done to obtain and secure full religious liberty to our denomination with others. I proceeded accordingly and, with a number of gentlemen and friends, had a conference with the honored delegates of this province upon this subject; but one of them repeatedly declared that he believed this attempt proceeded from the enemies of America; the injustice of which inflection, let facts declare.

The Baptists at Montague took advice of a lawyer, and endeavored to comply with your law, according to his direction; yet they were taxed and strained upon; they sued for relief in your courts, which was so far from helping them that it took away one hundred and fifteen dollars more. The Baptists in Haverhill took the same method; but the case was turned against them, which cost them about three hundred dollars. . . . The Baptists in Warwick complied with your law, yet were taxed to the parish minister; and for it eighteen of them were imprisoned about forty miles from home, in the extremity of last winter; and when our General Court were addressed upon it, they afforded no help. The Baptists in Chelmsford complied with your law, yet they were taxed; and three of them were imprisoned in January, 1773; and when they sued for recompense, their case was shifted off from court to court, till it has cost them above a hundred dollars; and when the Superior Court, at Charlestown, last April, were constrained to give Nathan Crosby his case, as having been taxed and imprisoned unlawfully, yet they gave him but three pounds damages and costs of court; and at the same time judged that the constable who carried him to prison should recover costs of Crosby for his so doing. If this is unbiased judgment, we know not what bias means. Must we be blamed for not lying still, and thus let our countrymen trample upon our rights, and deny us that very liberty that they are ready to take up arms to defend for themselves? You profess to exempt us from taxes to your worship, and yet tax us every year. Great complaints have been made about a tax which the British Parliament laid upon paper; but you require a paper tax of us annually.

That which has made the greatest noise is a tax of three pence a pound upon tea; but your law of last June laid a tax of the same sum every year upon the Baptists in each parish, as they would expect to defend themselves against a greater one. And only because the Baptists in Middleboro' have refused to pay that little tax, we hear that the first parish in said town have this fall voted to lay a greater tax upon us. All America are alarmed at the tea tax; though, if they please, they can avoid it by not buying the tea; but we have no such liberty. We must either pay the little tax, or else your people appear, even in this time of extremity, determined to lay the great one upon us. But these lines are to let you know that we are determined not to pay either of them; not only upon your principle of not being taxed where we are not represented, but also because we dare not render that homage to any earthly power which I and many of my brethren are fully convinced belongs only to God. We cannot give in the certificates you require without implicitly allowing to men that authority which we believe in our consciences belongs only to God. Here, therefore, we claim charter rights, liberty of conscience. And if any still deny it to us, they must answer it to Him who has said, "With what measure ye mete, it shall be measured to you again."

If any ask what we would have, we answer: Only allow us freely to enjoy the religious liberty that they do in Boston, and we ask no more.

We remain hearty friends to our country, and ready to do all in our power for its general welfare.

Isaac Backus
Agent for the Baptist Churches in this Province.
By advice of their Committee.

Boston, December 2, 1774
　　　—Hovey, *Memoir of Life and Times of the Rev. Isaac Backus,*
　　　pp. 215-216, 218, 219-221.

3. "Remove All Religious as Well as Civil Bondage"

October 24, 1776

To the Honourable the General Assembly of Virginia

The Memorial of the Presbytery of Hanover humbly represents:

. . . It is well known that in the frontier counties, which are justly supposed to contain a fifth part of the inhabitants of Virginia, the dissenters have borne the heavy burdens of purchasing glebes, building churches, and supporting the established clergy where there are very few Episcopalians, either to assist in bearing the expense, or to reap the advantage; and that throughout the other parts of the country, there are also many thousands of zealous friends and defenders of our State, who, besides the invidious and disadvantageous restrictions to which they have been subjected, annually pay large taxes to support an establishment from which their consciences and principles oblige them to dissent: all of which are confessedly so many violations of their natural rights; and in their consequences, a restraint upon freedom of inquiry and private judgment.

In this enlightened age, and in a land where all, of every denomination, are united in the most strenuous efforts to be free, we hope and expect that our representatives will cheerfully concur in removing every species of religious, as well as civil bondage. Certain it is that every argument for civil liberty gains additional strength when applied to liberty in the concerns of religion; and there is no argument in favour of establishing the Christian religion but what may be pleaded, with equal propriety, for establishing the tenets of Mahomed by those who believe the Alcoran; or, if this be not true, it is at least impossible for the magistrate to adjudge the right of preference among the various sects that profess the Christian faith without erecting a chair of infallibility, which would lead us back to the church of Rome.

—FOOTE, *Sketches of Virginia*, pp. 328 ff.

4. VIRGINIA DISSENTERS ARE FREED FROM THE ESTABLISHMENT

The Reverend Caleb Wallace to the Reverend James Caldwell.

April 8, 1777

Our Bill of Rights declares that all men are equally entitled to the free exercise of religion according to the dictates of conscience, etc. Yet in some subsequent Acts it is manifest that our Assembly designed to continue the old Church Establishment. This, and some petitions which were circulated through various parts of the country in behalf of dignified Episcopacy, gave a general alarm to the people of dissenting principles, and the common cry was, if this is continued, what great advantage shall we derive from being independent of Great Britain? And is it not as bad for our Assembly to violate their own Declaration of Rights as for the British Parliament to break our Charter? The Baptists circulated a counter petition which was signed by above 10,000, chiefly freeholders. Our Transalpian Presbyterians were much chagrined with what they understood was like to be publickly done, and with what was said and done in a more private way against dissenters; and indeed many dissenters in every part of the country were unwilling any longer to bear the burden of an establishment.

These circumstances induced our Presbytery to take the lead and prepare a memorial on the subject to be presented to our House at the session last fall, and as none of the members who were older in the ministry and better qualified could undertake it, the Presbytery appointed me their deputy, which obliged me to make the case a popular study, which indeed I had done for some time before, and to attend the General Assembly 6 or 8 weeks. The result was the Assembly passed an act exempting dissenters for all time to come from supporting the Church of England, declaring all penal and persecuting laws against any mode of worship, etc., null and void, for the present left all denominations to support their clergy by voluntary contributions, reserving the consideration of a general assessment for the support of religion (as they phrase it) to a future session. . . .

—WIRT, *Life of Henry*, I, 493-495.

5. VIRGINIA STATUTE OF RELIGIOUS FREEDOM

An Act for establishing Religious Freedom, January 16, 1786

I. WHEREAS Almighty God hath created the mind free; that all attempts to influence it by temporal punishments or burthens, or by civil incapacitations, tend only to beget habits of hypocrisy and meanness, and are a departure from the plan of the Holy author of our religion, who being Lord both of body and mind, yet chose not to propagate it by coercions on either, as was in his Almighty power to do; that the impious presumption of legislators and rulers, civil as well as ecclesiastical, who being themselves but fallible and uninspired men, have assumed dominion over the faith of others, setting up their own opinions and modes of thinking as the only true and infallible, and as such endeavouring to impose them on others, hath established and maintained false religions over the greatest part of the world, and through all time; that to compel a man to furnish contributions of money for the propagation of opinions which he disbelieves, is sinful and tyrannical; that even the forcing him to support this or that teacher of his own religious persuasion, is depriving him of the comfortable liberty of giving his contributions to the particular pastor whose morals he would make his pattern, and whose powers he feels most persuasive to righteousness, and is withdrawing from the ministry those temporary rewards, which proceeding from an approbation of their personal conduct, are an additional incitement to earnest and unremitting labours for the instruction of mankind; that our civil rights have no dependence on our religious opinions, any more than our opinions in physics or geometry; that therefore the proscribing any citizen as unworthy the public confidence by laying upon him an incapacity of being called to offices of trust and emolument, unless he profess or renounce this or that religious opinion, is depriving him injuriously of those privileges and advantages to which in common with his fellow-citizens he has a natural right; that it tends only to corrupt the principles of that religion it is meant to encourage, by bribing with a monopoly of worldly honours and emoluments, those who will externally profess and conform to it; that though indeed these are criminal who do not withstand such temptation, yet neither are those innocent who lay the bait in their way; that to suffer the civil magistrate to intrude his powers into the field of opinion, and to restrain the profession or propagation of principles on supposition of their ill tendency, is a dangerous fallacy, which at once destroys all religious liberty, because he being of course judge of that tendency will make his opinions the rule of judgment, and approve or condemn the sentiments of others only as they shall square with or differ from his own; that it is time enough for the rightful purposes of civil government, for its officers to interfere when principles break out into overt acts against peace and good order; and finally, that truth is great and will prevail if left to herself, that she is the proper and sufficient antagonist to error, and has nothing to fear from the conflict, unless by human interposition disarmed of her natural weapons, free argument and debate, errors ceasing to be dangerous when it is permitted freely to contradict them.

II. *Be it enacted by the General Assembly*, that no man shall be compelled to frequent or support any religious worship, place or ministry whatsoever, nor shall be enforced, restrained, molested, or burthened in his body or goods, nor shall otherwise suffer on account of his religious opinions or belief; but that all men shall be free to profess, and by argument to maintain, their opinion in matters of religion, and that the same shall in no wise diminish, enlarge or affect their civil capacities.

III. And though we well know that this assembly, elected by the people for the ordinary purposes of legislation only, have no power to restrain the acts of succeeding assemblies, constituted with powers equal to our own, and that therefore to declare this act to be irrevocable would be of no effect in law; yet as we are free to declare, and do declare, that the rights hereby asserted are of the natural rights of mankind, and that if any act shall hereafter be passed to repeal the present, or to narrow its operation, such act will be an infringement of natural right.

—HENING, ed., *Statutes at Large of Virginia*, XII, 84 ff.

V. HOW RECONCILE FREEDOM TO SLAVERY?

When the ill-tempered Dr. Johnson had jeered at American "slave-drivers" prating of "liberty," the thrust had struck home, for the paradox to which he referred was indeed an embarrassing one. "All men are created equal," wrote Jefferson—who was himself a slaveholder—and slaveholders from almost every state in the new nation had endorsed the sentiment. Did it mean that they recognized slavery as a wrong, as in violent conflict with the ideals of the Declaration and the objectives of the Revolution? If so, what did they propose to do to resolve the paradox?

There can be little doubt that when Jefferson wrote that all men were created equal he was thinking of white men. Yet there were those in the American states who were prepared to apply the principle to blacks as well as whites. As early as 1774 Rhode Island provided that hereafter all slaves brought into the colony should be free, and related this decision to the larger struggle for liberty:

> *Whereas [so read the resolution] the inhabitants of America are generally engaged in the preservation of their own rights and liberties, among which that of personal freedom must be considered as the greatest, and as those who are desirous of enjoying all the advantages of liberty themselves should be willing to extend personal liberty to others . . .*

The Constitution of Vermont (not admitted as a state until 1791) abolished slavery outright. In Massachusetts the Supreme Court held that the provision of the Constitution declaring all men free and equal meant just what it said. Pennsylvania provided for gradual emancipation after 1780, and Connecticut and Rhode Island for gradual emancipation after 1784.

The problem was incomparably more difficult in the South, where slaves constituted a large part of the population: probably 200,000 in Virginia, and 100,000 in South Carolina. Yet even here the leaders did what they could to mitigate slavery, and some of them, at least, confessed their awareness that slavery was irreconcilable with professions of freedom. The Continental Congress had tried to outlaw the slave trade in 1774; Delaware prohibited it in 1776, Virginia in 1778, and Maryland in 1783, while North and South Carolina placed somewhat ineffective restrictions upon it.

Emancipation was far more difficult, especially in the South. Here proposals for even gradual emancipation were defeated, and manumission laws adopted in a most gingerly fashion. Jefferson's original proposal of 1784 to outlaw slavery in the western territory—from the Great Lakes to the Gulf—

was defeated by the close vote of 7 to 6, but the Northwest Ordinance of 1787 did decree freedom in the territory north of the Ohio.

1. "A Time Will Come to Abolish This Lamentable Evil"

Patrick Henry to Robert Pleasants.

Hanover, January 18, 1773

Dear Sir: I take this opportunity to acknowledge the receipt of Anthony Benezet's book against the slave trade. I thank you for it. It is not a little surprising that the professors of Christianity, whose chief excellence consists in softening the human heart and in cherishing and improving its finer feelings, should encourage a practice so totally repugnant to the first impressions of right and wrong. What adds to the wonder is that this abominable practice has been introduced in the most enlightened ages. Times that seem to have pretensions to boast of high improvements in the arts and sciences, and refined morality, have brought into general use, and guarded by many laws, a species of violence and tyranny which our more rude and barbarous, but more honest ancestors detested. Is it not amazing that at a time when the rights of humanity are defined and understood with precision, in a country, above all others, fond of liberty, that in such an age and in such a country we find men professing a religion the most humane, mild, gentle and generous, adopting a principle as repugnant to humanity as it is inconsistent with the Bible, and destructive to liberty? Every thinking, honest man rejects it in speculation; how few in practice from conscientious motives!

Would anyone believe I am the master of slaves of my own purchase! I am drawn along by the general inconvenience of living here without them. I will not, I cannot justify it. However culpable my conduct, I will so far pay my devoir to virtue as to own the excellence and rectitude of her precepts, and lament my want of conformity to them.

I believe a time will come when an opportunity will be offered to abolish this lamentable evil. Everything we do is to improve it, if it happens in our day; if not, let us transmit to our descendents, together with our slaves, a pity for their unhappy lot and an abhorrence of slavery. If we cannot reduce this wished-for reformation to practice, let us treat the unhappy victims with lenity. It is the furthest advance we can make toward justice. It is a debt we owe to the purity of our religion, to show that it is at variance with that law which warrants slavery.

I know not when to stop. I could say many things on the subject, a serious view of which gives a gloomy perspective to future times.

—Wirt, Life of Henry, I, 152-153.

2. To Vindicate Slavery Is to Condemn the American Cause

Robert Pleasants to Patrick Henry.

Curles, 3rd mo. 28, 1777

Respected Friend; A knowledge of thy sentiments, a remembrance of former favors, and thy present exalted station induceth me to offer a few hints to thy consideration, which being, I apprehend, of great importance, may not be unworthy a serious thought at some leisure moment. It is in respect to slavery, of which thou art not altogether a stranger to mine, as well as some others of our friends sentiments, and perhaps too thou may have been informed that some of us from a full conviction of the injustice, and an apprehension of duty, have been induced to embrace the present favorable juncture, when the representatives of the people have nobly declared *all men equally free,* to manumit divers of our Negroes; and propose, without any desire to offend or thereby to injure any person, to invest more of them with the same inestimable priviledge. . . .

Indeed few, very few, are now so insensible of the injustice of holding our fellow men in bondage as to undertake to vindicate it; nor can it be done, in my apprehension, without condemning the present measures in America; for if less injury offered to ourselves from the mother country can justify the expense of so much blood and treasure, how can we impose with propriety absolute slavery on others? It hath often appeared to me as if this very matter was one, if not the principal cause of our present troubles, and that we ought first to have cleansed our own hands before we could consistently oppose the measures of others tending to the same purpose; and I firmly believe the doing this justice to the injured Africans would be an acceptable offering to him who "rules in the Kingdoms of men," and "giveth wisdom to the wise, and knowledge to those who have understanding," and for a purpose too of His own glory; and happy will it be for us if we apply our talents accordingly; for such it is that are often made a blessing to themselves, to their posterity, and to mankind in general. But if on the contrary we seek our own glory and present interest by forbidden means, how can we expect peace here, or happiness hereafter? O may we, therefore, "break off our sins by righteousness, and our iniquities by showing mercy to the poor, if haply it may be a lengthening of our tranquillity!"

The Declaration of Rights is indeed noble, and I can but wish and hope thy great abilities and interest may be exerted towards a full and clear explanation and confirmation thereof; for, without that, the present struggle for liberty, if successful, would be but partial, and instead of abolishing, might lay the foundation of greater imposition and tyranny to our posterity than any we have yet known; and considering the uncertainty of future events, and all human foresight, the immediate posterity of those now in power might be effected by such partiality, as well as others whose grievances might remain unredressed.

It would therefore become the interest, as well as duty, of a wise and virtuous legislature, in forming a government, to establish a general, uniform and constant liberty, as well civil as religious; for this end, I just propose to drop a hint, which hath appeared to me as likely to accomplish the great and wise end of a general freedom, without the dangers and inconveniences which some apprehend from a present total abolition of slavery, as any thing that hath occurred to me, and perhaps might be as generally approved; which is to enact that all children of slaves to be born in future be absolutely free at the usual ages of 18 and 21, and that such who are convinced of the injustice of keeping slaves, and willing to give up the property which the law hath invested them with, may under certain regulations (so as not at an age to become chargable, or from other impediments obnoxious to the community) have free liberty to do it.

By such a law I apprehend the children would be educated with proper notions of freedom, and be better fitted for the enjoyment of it than many now are; the state secured from intestine enemies and convulsions (which some think would attend a total immediate discharge), its true interest promoted, in proportion to the number of free-men interested in its peace and prosperity, and, above all, to do that justice to others which we contend for and claim as the unalterable birthright of every man.

—Wirt, *Life of Henry*, III, 49-51.

3. Tom Paine Calls for an End to Slavery

From the *Pennsylvania Journal and The Weekly Advertiser*.

March 8, 1775

The chief design of this paper is not to disprove [slavery], which many have sufficiently done; but to entreat Americans to consider:

1. With what consistency or decency they complain so loudly of attempts to enslave them, while they hold so many hundred thousands in slavery; and annually enslave many thousands more, without any pretence of authority, or claim upon them?

2. How just, how suitable to our crime is the punishment with which providence threatens us? We have enslaved multitudes, and shed much innocent blood in doing it; and now we are threatened with the same. And while other evils are confessed and bewailed, why not this especially, and publicly; than which no other vice has brought so much guilt on the land?

3. Whether, then, all ought not immediately to discontinue and renounce it, with grief and abhorrence? Should not every society bear testimony against it, and account obstinate persisters in it bad men, enemies to their country, and exclude them from fellowship; as they often do for much lesser faults?

4. The great question may be—what should be done with those who are enslaved already? To turn the old and infirm free would be injustice and cruelty; they who enjoyed the labors of their better days should keep and treat them humanely. As to the rest, let prudent men, with the assistance of legislatures, determine what is practicable for masters, and best for them. Perhaps some could give them lands upon reasonable rent; some, employing them in their labor still, might give them some reasonable allowances for it; so as all may have some property, and fruits of their labors at their own disposal, and be encouraged to industry; the family may live together, and enjoy the natural satisfaction of exercising relative affections and duties, with civil protection and other advantages, like fellow men. Perhaps they may sometime form useful barrier settlements on the frontiers. Then they may become interested in the public welfare, and assist in promoting it; instead of being dangerous, as now they are, should any enemy promise them a better condition. . . .

These are the sentiments of justice and humanity

—Conway, ed., *The Writings of Paine*, I, 7-9.

4. HENRY LAURENS CONFESSES HIS HATRED OF SLAVERY

Henry Laurens to John Laurens.

Charleston, S. C., 14th August, 1776

My Negroes, all to a man, are strongly attached to me; hitherto not one of them has attempted to desert; on the contrary, those who are more exposed hold themselves always ready to fly from the enemy in case of a sudden descent. Many hundreds of that colour have been stolen and decoyed by the servants of King George the Third. Captains of British ships of war and noble lords have busied themselves in such inglorious pilferage, to the disgrace of their master and disgrace of their cause. These Negroes were first enslaved by the English; acts of parliament have established the slave trade in favour of the home-residing English, and almost totally prohibited the Americans from reaping any share of it. Men of war, forts, castles, governors, companies and committees are employed and authorized by the English parliament to protect, regulate and extend the slave trade. Negroes are brought by Englishmen and sold as slaves to Americans. Bristol, Liverpool, Manchester, Birmingham, etc., etc., live upon the slave trade. The British parliament now employ their men-of-war to steal those Negroes from the Americans to whom they had sold them, pretending to set the poor wretches free, but basely trepan and sell them into tenfold worse slavery in the West Indies, where probably they will become the property of Englishmen again, and of some who sit in parliament. What meanness! What complicated wickedness appears in this scene! O England, how changed! How fallen!

You know, my dear son, I abhor slavery. I was born in a country where slavery had been established by British kings and parliaments, as well as by the laws of that country ages before my existence. I found the Christian religion and slavery growing under the same authority and cultivation. I nevertheless disliked it. In former days there was no combating the prejudices of men supported by interest; the day I hope is approaching when, from principles of gratitude as well as justice, every man will strive to be foremost in showing his readiness to comply with the golden rule.

Not less than twenty thousand pounds sterling would all my Negroes produce if sold at public auction tomorrow. I am not the man who enslaved them; they are indebted to Englishmen for that favour; nevertheless I am devising means for manumitting many of them, and for cutting off the entail of slavery. Great powers oppose me—the laws and customs of my country, my own and the avarice of my countrymen. What will my children say if I deprive them of so much estate? These are difficulties, but not insuperable. I will do as much as I can in my time, and leave the rest to a better hand.

—MOORE, ed., *Materials for History*, pp. 19-21.

5. EMANCIPATION IN PENNSYLVANIA—1780

Preamble to the act passed by the Pennsylvania Assembly, March 1, 1780.

When we contemplate our abhorrence of that condition to which the arms and tyranny of Great Britain were exerted to reduce us, when we look back on the variety of dangers to which we have been exposed, and how miraculously our wants in many instances have been supplied, and our deliverances wrought, when even hope and human fortitude have become unequal to the conflict, we are unavoidably led to a serious and grateful sense of the manifold blessings which we have undeservedly received from the hand of that Being from whom every good and perfect gift cometh.

Impressed with these ideas, we conceive that it is our duty, and we rejoice that it is in our power, to extend a portion of that freedom to others which has been extended to us, and release them from the state of thralldom to which we ourselves were tyrannically doomed, and from which we have now every prospect of being delivered. It is not for us to inquire why, in the creation of mankind, the inhabitants of the several parts of the earth were distinguished by a difference in feature or complexion. It is sufficient to know that all are the work of the Almighty Hand. We find in the distribution of the human species, that the most fertile as well as the most barren parts of the earth are inhabited by men of complexions different from ours, and from each other; from whence we may reasonably as well as religiously infer that He who placed them in their various situations has extended equally his care and protection to all, and that it becomes not us to counteract His mercies.

We esteem it a peculiar blessing granted to us that we are enabled this day to add one more step to universal civilization by removing, as much as possible, the sorrows of those who have lived in undeserved bondage, and from which, by the assumed authority of the kings of Great Britain, no effectual legal relief could be obtained. Weaned, by a long course of experience, from those narrow prejudices and partialities we had imbibed, we find our hearts enlarged with kindness and benevolence toward men of all conditions and nations, and we conceive ourselves at this particular period particularly called upon by the blessings which we have received, to manifest the sincerity of our profession, and to give a substantial proof of our gratitude. . . .

—MITCHELL and FLANDERS, *Statutes at Large of Pennsylvania*, X, 67-68.

6. MASSACHUSETTS PUTS AN END TO SLAVERY—1783

The position of slavery in Massachusetts had been a dubious one for some time even before the Revolution; the Revolution itself dealt a deathblow to slavery. In 1776 the clause of the Body of Liberties allowing enslavement of "lawful captives taken in just wars" was repealed as far as concerned Negroes taken on the high seas. The first article of the Bill of Rights of the Massachusetts Constitution of 1780 provided that "All men are born free and equal." In 1783 the case of Commonwealth v. Nathaniel Jennison came before the court. Jennison, indicted for assault on Quock Walker, defended his behavior on the ground that Walker was his slave. The court, speaking through the Chief Justice who was soon to be appointed to the first United States Supreme Court, ruled that under the provision of the Constitution of Massachusetts slavery was abolished in Massachusetts.

CUSHING, C. J.: As to the doctrine of slavery and the right of Christians to hold Africans in perpetual servitude, and sell and treat them as we do our horses and cattle, that (it is true) has been heretofore countenanced by the Province Laws formerly, but nowhere is it expressly enacted or established. It has been a usage—a usage which took its origin from the practice of some of the European nations, and the regulations of the British government respecting the then Colonies, for the benefit of trade and wealth. But whatever sentiments have formerly prevailed in this particular or slid in upon us by the example of others, a different idea has taken place with the people of America, more favorable to the natural rights of mankind, and to that natural, innate desire of Liberty, which the Heaven (without regard to color, complexion, or shape of noses-features) has inspired all the human race. And upon this ground our Constitution of Government, by which the people of this Commonwealth have solemnly bound themselves, sets out with declaring that all men are born free and equal—and that every subject is entitled to liberty, and to have it guarded by the laws, as well as life and property—and in short is totally repugnant to the idea of being born slaves. This being the case, I think the idea of slavery is inconsistent with our own conduct and Constitution; and that there can be no such thing as perpetual servitude of a rational creature, unless his liberty is forfeited by some criminal conduct or given up by personal consent or contract. . . .

—Mass. Hist. Soc., *Proceedings* (1873-75), p. 293.

VI. AUSTERITY, MORALITY AND EQUALITY

In part because the Revolution was fought against a King, a Court, an aristocracy, and in part because its ultimate success demanded sacrifice, it was accompanied by appeals for simplicity, virtue and morality. Such appeals, to be sure, accompany every war, and more often than not are purely verbal gestures that need not be taken seriously by the historian. We give here a few examples of the attempt to encourage, or to legislate, virtue: a Virginia resolution against gambling and profanity; a letter from the Spartan Sam Adams warning against levity; and an early tirade against titles from the pen of that indefatigable leveler, Tom Paine. It would be naïve to suppose that Americans generally accommodated themselves to the views expressed here, but not to conclude that these were widely accepted.

1. VIRGINIA SEEKS TO OUTLAW GAMING AND SWEARING

Resolution of the Virginia Convention.

June 25, 1776

WHEREAS gaming, at best, is but an idle amusement, when carried to excess is the parent of avarice, dissipation, profaneness, and every other passion which can debase the human mind, and is therefore forbidden by the Continental Association, as more peculiarly improper at this time, when our important struggle for liberty and freedom renders the practice of the most rigid virtue necessary to sustain us under and carry us through the conflict; that this pernicious and destructive vice may not prevail among the officers and soldiers of our Army, the morals of the youth therein preserved from corruption, and they restored, untainted, to their worthy parents, who have cheerfully spared them from their domestick endearments to the assistance and protection of their country:

Resolved, unanimously, That it be earnestly recommended to the General or Commanding officer of the Continental Troops in this Colony, to take such steps as to him shall appear most proper for preventing profane swearing, all manner of gaming, as well as every other vice and immorality among the officers and soldiers under his command; and that it be, and is, hereby declared to all who are or may be candidates for offices, civil or military, in the pay of this Colony, that the practice of gaming and profane swearing will ever be considered as an exclusion from all publick offices or employments. . . .

                    —FORCE, *American Archives*, 4th Series, VI, 1590.

2. MAY WE NEVER BE GIVEN TO THE FOLLY OF PARADE!

Samuel Adams to Elbridge Gerry.

                                        Philadelphia, November 27, 1780

More, in my opinion, is to be done than conquering our British enemies, in order to establish the liberties of our country on a solid basis. Human nature, I am afraid, is too much debased to relish the republican principles in which the new government of the commonwealth of Massachusetts appears to be founded. Mankind is prone enough to political idolatry; and may it not be added that the former government—I mean the last charter—being calculated to make servile men rather than free citizens, the minds of many of our countrymen have been inured to a cringing obsequiousness, too deeply wrought into habit to be easily eradicated? Such a temper is widely different from that just reverence which every virtuous citizen will show to the upright magistrate. If my fears on this head are ill grounded, I hope I shall be excused. They proceed from a cordial affection for that country, to the service of which I have devoted the greatest part of my life.

May Heaven inspire the present rulers with wisdom and sound understanding! In all probability they will stamp the character of the people. It is natural for a sensible observer to form an estimate of the people from an opinion of the men whom they set up for their legislators and magistrates. And besides, if we look into the history of governours, we shall find that their principles and manners have always had a mighty influence on the people. Should vanity and foppery ever be the ruling taste among the great, the body of the people would be in danger of catching the distemper, and the ridiculous maxims of the one would become fashionable among the other.

I pray God, we may never be addicted to levity and the folly of parade. Pomp and show serve very well to promote the purposes of European and Asiatic grandeur, in countries where the mystery of iniquity is carried to the highest pitch, and millions are tame enough to believe that they are born only to be subservient to the capricious will of a single great man, or a few! It requires council and sound judgement to render our country secure in a flourishing condition. If men of wisdom and knowledge, of moderation and temperance, of patience, fortitude and perseverance, of sobriety and true republican simplicity of manners, of zeal for the honour of the Supreme Being and the welfare of the commonwealth, if men possessed of these and other excellent qualities are chosen to fill the seats of government, we may expect that our affairs will rest on a solid and permanent foundation.

—AUSTIN, *Life of Elbridge Gerry*, pp. 361-362.

3. TOM PAINE: "THE FREEMAN SEES THROUGH THE MAGIC OF A TITLE"

From *Pennsylvania Magazine*, May 1775.

When I reflect on the pompous titles bestowed on unworthy men, I feel an indignity that instructs me to despise the absurdity. The *Honorable* plunderer of his country, or the *Right Honorable* murderer of mankind, create such a contrast of ideas as exhibit a monster rather than a man. Virtue is inflamed at the violation, and sober reason calls it nonsense.

Dignities and high sounding names have different effects on different beholders. The lustre of the *Star* and the title of *My Lord* overawe the superstitious vulgar, and forbid them to inquire into the character of the possessor: Nay more, they are, as it were, bewitched to admire in the great the vices they would honestly condemn in themselves. This sacrifice of common sense is the certain badge which distinguishes slavery from freedom; for when men yield up the privilege of thinking, the last shadow of liberty quits the horizon.

But the reasonable freeman sees through the magic of a title, and examines the man before he approves him. To him the honors of the worthless serve to write their masters' vices in capitals, and their stars shine to no other end than to read them by. The possessors of undue honors are themselves sensible of this; for when their repeated guilt renders their persons unsafe, they disown their rank, and, like glowworms, extinguish themselves into common reptiles, to avoid discovery. Thus Jeffries sunk into a fisherman, and his master escaped in the habit of a peasant.

Modesty forbids men, separately or collectively, to assume titles. But as all honors, even that of kings, originated from the public, the public may justly be called the fountain of true honor. And it is with much pleasure I have heard the title of *Honorable* applied to a body of men, who, nobly disregarding private ease and interest for public welfare, have justly merited the address of the The Honorable Continental Congress.

VOX POPULI

—CONWAY, ed., *The Writings of Paine*, II, 33-34.

VII. EDUCATION FOR A FREE PEOPLE

War brought the notion that political independence should be accompanied by intellectual. "America must be as independent in literature as she is in politics," declaimed Noah Webster and, a short time later, he called upon Americans to "unshackle your minds, and act like independent beings. You have an empire to raise and support by your exertions and a national character to establish and extend by your wisdom and virtue."

During the Revolution the constitutions of Massachusetts, Pennsylvania, North Carolina, Georgia and Vermont specifically recognized public responsibility for the education of the young. A number of academies and colleges were established, at least on paper: the Phillips Andover and Exeter academies in 1778 and 1781; Hampden Sydney College in 1782; and Dickinson College in 1783; half a dozen others came in the years of the Confederation. Yet on the whole, of course, education suffered during the war; schools were closed, teachers lost to the profession; libraries and scientific apparatus scattered; young people drawn off to warlike or other pursuits.

Perhaps the most interesting developments in the realm of education during the war years are of opinion or principle. Thus the recognition of an obligation to provide schools for all the young; the emphasis on the practical and the suspicion of classical education; hostility to study abroad and readiness to provide substitutes at home; and the feeble beginnings of American grammars, histories and other textbooks supposedly suitable for American youth.

We give here Jefferson's plan for education in Virginia embodied in a bill presented to the Virginia legislature in 1779, but not acted on; the Georgia provision for the creation of a state university; and Jefferson's touching reminder to the great scientist Rittenhouse that the community of learning and science takes precedence over the demands of politics.

1. Jefferson Proposes a Revolution in Education for Virginia

1781

... This bill proposes to lay off every county into small districts of five or six miles square, called hundreds, and in each of them to establish a school for teaching reading, writing and arithmetic. The tutor to be supported by the hundred, and every person in it entitled to send their children three years gratis, and as much longer as they please, paying for it. These schools to be under a visitor who is annually to choose the boy, of best genius in the school, of those whose parents are too poor to give them further education, and to send him forward to one of the grammar schools, of which twenty are proposed to be erected in different parts of the country, for teaching Greek, Latin, Geography, and the higher branches of numerical arithmetic. Of the boys thus sent in one year, trial is to be made at the grammar schools one or two years, and the best genius of the whole selected, and continued six years, and the residue dismissed. By this means twenty of the best geniusses will be raked from the rubbish annually, and be instructed, at the public expense, so far as the grammar schools go. At the end of six years' instruction, one half are to be discontinued (from among whom the grammar schools will probably be supplied with future masters); and the other half, who are to be chosen for the superiority of their parts and disposition, are to be sent and continued three years in the study of such sciences as they shall choose, at William and Mary college, the plan of which is proposed to be enlarged, as will be hereafter explained, and extended to all the useful sciences. The ultimate result of the whole scheme of education would be the teaching all the children of the state reading, writing, and common arithmetic; turning out ten annually of superior genius, well taught in Greek, Latin, Geography, and the higher branches of arithmetic; turning out ten others annually, of still superior parts, who to those branches of learning shall have added such of the sciences as their genius shall have led them to; the furnishing to the wealthier part of the people convenient schools at which their children may be educated at their own expense. The general objects of this law are to provide an education adapted to the years, to the capacity, and the condition of every one, and directed to their freedom and happiness. . . .

Every government degenerates when trusted to the rulers of the people alone. The people themselves therefore are its only safe depositories; and to render even them safe, their minds must be improved to a certain degree. This indeed is not all that is necessary, though it be essentially necessary. An amendment of our constitution must here come in aid of the public education. The influence over government must be shared among all the people. If every individual which composes their mass participates of the ultimate authority, the government will be safe; because the corrupting the whole mass will exceed any private sources of wealth; and public ones cannot be provided but by levies on the people. . . .

Lastly, it is proposed by a bill . . . to begin a public library and gallery, by laying out a certain sum annually in books, paintings, and statues.
—JEFFERSON, *Notes on Virginia*, answer to Query XIV.

2. GEORGIA PROVIDES FOR A STATE UNIVERSITY

January 27, 1785

An Act for the more full and complete establishment of a public seat of learning in this State

As it is the distinguishing happiness of free governments that civil order should be the result of choice, and not necessity, and the common wishes of the people become the laws of the land, their public property, and even existence, very much depends upon suitably forming the minds and morals of their citizens. Where the minds of the people in general are viciously disposed and unprincipled, and their conduct disorderly, a free government will be attended with greater confusion, and with evils more horrid than the wild uncultivated state of nature: It can only be happy where the public principles and opinions are properly directed, and their manners regulated. This is an influence beyond the sketch of laws and punishments, and can be claimed only by religion and education. It should therefore be among the first objects of those who wish well to the national prosperity, to encourage and support the principles of religion and morality, and early to place the youth under the forming hand of society, that by instruction they may be moulded to the love of virtue and good order. Sending them abroad to other countries for their education will not answer these purposes, is too humiliating an acknowledgment of the ignorance or inferiority of our own, and will always be the cause of so great foreign attachments that upon principles of policy it is not admissible.

This country in times of our common danger and distress found such security in the principles and abilities which wise regulations had before established in the minds of our countrymen, that our present happiness, joined to pleasing prospects, should conspire to make us feel ourselves under the strongest obligation to form the youth, the rising hope of our land, to render the glorious and essential services to our country. . . .
—WATKINS, *Digest of the Laws of Georgia*, pp. 299 ff.

3. "The World Has Never Had a Ryttenhouse Before"

Jefferson to David Rittenhouse.

Monticello in Albemarle, Virginia, July 19, 1778

Writing to a philosopher, I may hope to be pardoned for intruding some thoughts of my own, tho' they relate to him personally. Your time for two years past has, I believe, been principally employed in the civil government of your country. Tho' I have been aware of the authority our cause would acquire with the world from it's being known that yourself and Doctr. Franklin were zealous friends to it, and am myself duly impressed with a sense of the arduousness of government, and the obligation those are under who are able to conduct it, yet I am also satisfied there is an order of geniusses above that obligation, and therefore exempted from it. No body can conceive that nature ever intended to throw away a Newton upon the occupations of a crown. It would have been a prodigality for which even the conduct of providence might have been arraigned, had he been by birth annexed to what was so far below him. Cooperating with nature in her ordinary oeconomy, we should dispose of and employ the geniusses of men according to their several orders and degrees. I doubt not there are in your country many persons equal to the task of conducting government: but you should consider that the world has but one Ryttenhouse, and that it never had one before. The amazing mechanical representation of the solar system which you conceived and executed, has never been surpassed by any but the work of which it is a copy. Are those powers then, which being intended for the erudition of the world, like air and light, the world's common property, to be taken from their proper pursuit to do the commonplace drudgery of governing a single state, a work which may be executed by men of an ordinary stature, such as are always and every where to be found? Without having ascended mount Sina for inspiration, I can pronounce that the precept, in the decalogue of the vulgar, that they shall not make to themselves "the likeness of any thing that is in the heavens above" is reversed for you, and that you will fulfill the highest purposes of your creation by employing yourself in the perpetual breach of that inhibition. For my own country in particular you must remember something like a promise that it should be adorned with one of them. The taking of your city by the enemy has hitherto prevented the proposition from being made and approved by our legislature.

The zeal of a true Whig in science must excuse the hazarding these free thoughts, which flow from a desire of promoting the diffusion of knowledge and of your fame, and from one who can assure you truly that he is with much sincerity & esteem Your most obedt. & most humble servt.,

Th. Jefferson

—Boyd, ed., *Papers of Thomas Jefferson*, II, 202-203.

VIII. WILL THE REVOLUTION WIPE OUT
CLASS DISTINCTIONS?

After the Civil War it was commonly said, in the South, that the bottom rail was on the top. The Revolution was not a social revolution in which the upper classes were swept away, their places and their property taken by the lower; indeed in the America of the 1770's the very term "upper" and "lower" class are misleading. Yet there was class consciousness: merchants, clergy, planters did constitute a class of "betters," and workingmen, fishermen, indentured servants and others—men like John Adams' horsejockey—did belong to the "lower orders." All of this was in a state of change, and the Revolution speeded up the process. Some respectable folks lamented the change, others merely its speed. Conservatives, who were often quite as ardent Patriots as the radicals, looked with misgivings on some manifestations of the leveling which accompanied the war; others on some of the political experiments, a unicameral legislature, for example, or manhood suffrage. The reaction of the Loyalists to the social pretensions of some of the Patriots can be read in the sentiments which John Trumbull puts into the mouth of his Loyalist caricature, Squire M'Fingal. Of our commentators, William Hooper, a leader of the Revolutionary movement in North Carolina and a signer of the Declaration was fundamentally conservative; the same might be said for John Adams, and even for young John Trumbull.

In no state was the internal revolution carried further than in Pennsylvania where a radical-dominated Convention wrote a democratic constitution, giving the vote to every freeman twenty-one years of age who paid public taxes, and providing for a unicameral legislature. Torn by dissension, religious differences, and opposing interests, the Whig aristocracy had yielded their leadership of the Revolutionary movement to the radicals. The latter, instead of submitting the Constitution to the people for ratification, imposed upon the voters as a condition of voting an oath to support the new constitution. The conservatives were highly critical of the behavior of the radicals. To them it was a portent of social leveling. Robert Proud, historian of Pennsylvania, castigated the Convention in verse which is included in this section.

1. "Is the Revolution Fought for the Benefit of Debtors?"

From the Diary of John Adams.

[The fall of 1775]

An event of the most trifling nature in appearance, and fit only to excite laughter in other times, struck me into a profound reverie, if not a fit of melancholy. I met a man who had sometimes been my client, and sometimes I had been against him. He, though a common horse-jockey, was sometimes in the right, and I had commonly been successful in his favor in our courts of law. He was always in the law, and had been sued in many actions at almost every court.

As soon as he saw me, he came up to me, and his first salutation to me was: "Oh, Mr. Adams, what great things have you and your colleagues done for us! We can never be grateful enough to you. There are no Courts of Justice now in this Province, and I hope there never will be another."

Is this the object for which I have been contending? said I to myself, for I rode along without any answer to this wretch. Are these the sentiments of such people, and how many of them are there in the country? Half the nation, for what I know; for half the nation are debtors, if not more, and these have been, in all countries, the sentiments of debtors. If the power of the country should get into such hands, and there is great danger that it will, to what purpose have we sacrificed our time, health, and every thing else? Surely we must guard against this spirit and these principles, or we shall repent of all our conduct. . . .

—Adams, ed., *Works of John Adams*, II, 420-421.

2. A Pennsylvanian Warns of the Cruelty of the "Servile Sway"

Robert Proud, [1776]

Of all the plagues that scourge the human race,
None can be worse than *upstarts*, when in place;
Their pow'r to shew, no action they forbear,
They tyrannize o'er all, while all they fear.
No savage rage, no rav'nous beast of prey
Exceeds the cruelty of *Servile Sway!*

As if the foot to be the head inclined,
Or body should aspire to rule the mind;
As when the power of fire, of air and flood,
In proper bounds, support the common good;
But when they break the bound to them assigned,
They most pernicious are to human kind;
So are those men, whose duty's to obey,
When they usurp the rule, and bear the sway.

In order God has wisely ranged the whole,
And animates that order, as the Soul;
In due gradation ev'ry rank must be,
Some high, some low, but all in their degree:
This law in ev'ry flock and herd we find,
In ev'ry living thing of ev'ry kind;
Their Chief precedes, as in the fields they stray,
The rest in *order* follow and obey.

Much more in men this *order* ought to dwell,
As they in rank and reason do excel;
A state the nearest to the Bless'd above,
Where all degrees in beauteous order move:
Which those who violate are sure to be
The tools of woeful infelicity!

Ev'n so are men, far worse than beasts of prey
When those *usurp the rule*, who should obey;
In *self-security* weak mortals find
The will of God is thus to scourge mankind.

—Proud, "On the Violation of Established and Lawful Order, Rule or Government Applied to the Present Times in Pennsa. in 1776," *Pennsylvania Magazine*, XIII (1889), 435-436.

3. The Tyranny of a Unicameral Legislature

William Hooper, delegate from North Carolina to the Continental Congress, to the Congress at Halifax.

Philadelphia, October 26, 1776

Honoured Sir:

... A single branch of legislation is a many headed monster which without any check must soon defeat the very purposes for which it was created, and its members become a tyranny dreadful in proportion to the numbers which compose it; and, possessed of power uncontrolled, would soon exercise it to put themselves free from the restraint of those who made them, and to make their own political existence perpetual. The consultations of large bodies are likewise less correct and perfect than those where a few only are concerned. The people at large have generally just objects in their pursuit but often fall short in the means made use of to obtain them. A warmth of zeal may lead them into errors which a more cool, dispassionate enquiry may discover and rectify.

This points out the necessity of another branch of legislation at least, which may be a refinement of the first choice of the people at large, selected for their wisdom, remarkable integrity, or that weight which arises from property and gives independence and impartiality to the human mind. For my own part I once thought it would be wise to adopt a double check as in the British Constitution, but from the abuses which power in the hand of an individual is liable to, and the unreasonableness that an individual should abrogate at pleasure the acts of the Representatives of the people, refined by a second body whom we may call, for fashion's sake, Counsellors, and as they are a kind of barrier for the people's rights against the encroachment of their delegates, I am now convinced that a third branch of legislation is at least unnecessary. But for the sake of execution we must have a magistrate solely executive, and with aid of his Council (I mean a Privy Council) let him have such executive powers as may give energy to government.

Pennsylvania adopted the visionary system of a single branch. The people soon saw the monster the Convention had framed for them with horror, and with one accord stifled it in its cradle before it had begun its outrages. ...

—Saunders, ed., *Colonial Records of North Carolina*, X, 867-868.

4. Too Much Revolution in Georgia

John Wereat to Henry Laurens.

Savannah, August 30th, 1777

My Dear Sir:

... I now begin to tremble for the fate that awaits this devoted country; honesty, integrity and love of justice, being the declared and avowed principles of any man, are crimes sufficient to secure him the hateful name of tory, and to hold him up to the resentment of the people as an enemy to his country. I think I told you some time ago that I thought the augmentation of the present representation under our present circumstances a great evil; every day's experience convinces me that it is so, and it requires no great degree of prescience to declare that Georgia cannot exist as a separate state twelve months longer, without the immediate interposition of Congress.

I told you in a former letter how the laws that this country are to be ruled by were framed and agreed upon at a nightly meeting in a tavern. This, though dangerous in its consequences, is but a part of the evil. We have now another nocturnal society established, who have arrogated to themselves the name of *The Liberty Society*. The business of this cabal, as far as I am capable of judging, seems to be principally intended to poison the minds of the people throughout the state, and to set them at enmity with every man who is not of their party. They, or the leaders of them, seem to be void of every sentiment of honour, and truth is a stranger to their proceedings; they bellow *liberty*, but take every method in their power to deprive the best part of the community of even the shadow of it. Those wretches appear to me to have a manifest intention to destroy the reputation of their neighbours, in order to raise themselves fortunes and political fame upon the ruins of the real friends of their country, and the American cause. . . .

—Moore, ed., *Materials for History*, pp. 39-40.

5. M'Fingal Jeers at the Pretensions of the Patriots

[1782]

While every clown that tills the plains,
Though bankrupt in estate and brains,
By this new light transformed to traitor,
Forsakes his plough to turn dictator,
Starts an haranguing chief of Whigs,
And drags you by the ears, like pigs,
All bluster, armed with factious licence,
New-born at once to politicians.
Each leather-aproned dunce, grown wise,
Presents his forward face t'advise,
And tattered legislators meet,
From every workshop through the street.
His goose the tailor finds new use in,
To patch and turn the Constitution;
The blacksmith comes with sledge and grate
To iron-bind the wheels of state;
The quack forbears his patients' souse,
To purge the Council and the House;
The tinker quits his moulds and doxies,
To cast assembly-men and proxies.
From dunghills deep of blackest hue,
Your dirt-bred patriots spring to view,
To wealth and power and honors rise,
Like new-winged maggots changed to flies,
And fluttering round in high parade,
Strut in the robe, or gay cockade.

—John Trumbull, *M'Fingal.*

CHAPTER ELEVEN

The Battle for New York

WITH THE FAILURE *to put down the rebellion in New England the British determined to strike at two centers of loyalism, South Carolina and New York. Defeated in their expectations of quick victory in the South in an abbreviated campaign which will be treated subsequently, the government for a time concentrated its strategic operations in the Middle States.*

New York City was the first center of such operations. Its magnificent harbor could accommodate the British fleet. He who controlled the Hudson could divide the colonies. The British strategic plan provided that General Howe was to move his heavily reinforced army from Halifax and, after occupying the city, spread control northward along the Hudson. A Canadian expedition under Carleton would push southward and join Howe at Albany. Having driven a wedge between New England and the South, the former region could be proceeded against at leisure and the back of insurgency would be broken. But the New York campaign failed, in part as a result of bad over-all planning and miscalculation, in part from military incompetence, in part from the politico-military character of the mission of the brothers Howe, the admiral and the general. Coming over in the dual role of conquerors and conciliators, the Howes, originally sympathetic to the colonial cause, hoped to persuade the Patriots to lay down their arms despite the adoption of the Declaration of Independence. By the fall of '76 they were disabused of the likelihood of a negotiated settlement, but they had lost precious time.

In addition to the brothers Howe the action around New York propels to the center of the stage such notable military personages as the cautious and suspicious Sir Henry Clinton; the dashing Major General Charles, Lord Cornwallis; and the able Lieutenant General Baron Wilhelm von Knyphausen, the sixty-year-old commander of the Hessians. On the Patriot side it throws the spotlight on that colorful if incompetent veteran Indian fighter from Connecticut, Israel Putnam; the hard-drinking and hard-fighting Jerseyite, General William Alexander, who as Lord Stirling claimed a lapsed Scottish earldom; and the controversial fighting Irishman from New Hampshire, John Sullivan.

The excerpts in this chapter relate the story of the preparation for war in New York, the arrival of the British naval and military forces, the great amphibious landing on Long Island and the ensuing battle, Washington's withdrawal to New York, the battle for Manhattan, the retreat to White Plains, and the fall of Fort Washington, the last Patriot stronghold on Manhattan Island.

I. THE REDCOATS BRING WAR TO THE MIDDLE STATES

In the spring of '76 no Patriot leader could have confidently predicted just where the British would strike and what, if any, general plan of campaign they would soon divulge. Nevertheless, after the British evacuated Boston, Washington considered New York vital to any successful defense against invasion. William Alexander, Lord Stirling, was for a time in command of New York after General Charles Lee's departure for the South early in 1776. Control of New York City and the Hudson River would, according to Washington, give the British "an easy pass to Canada." Impressing on Stirling the "vast importance" of holding the city, Washington began to dispatch troops there on March 18. Heath's, Sullivan's, Greene's and Spencer's brigades were sent, with Israel Putnam in general command. When the army assembled, the Virginians were properly shocked at the democratic practices among the New England militia, the existence of nepotism and the poor morale. So deep was the spirit of sectionalism within the army that Washington was impelled to issue a general order appealing for unity in the ranks. Meantime, the man power of the city was called up to build fortifications, the woodlands of the rich Loyalists were leveled, and the city's mansions used as barracks. "Oh, the houses of New York, if you could see the insides of them!" lamented a New York resident. As always, the huge army attracted prostitutes along with the usual variety of camp followers.

1. "For God's Sake Do Not Delay!" Stirling Pleads

Lord Stirling to Samuel Tucker, President of the Committee of Safety of the Province of New Jersey.

Elizabeth Town, March 23, 1776

I have just received the enclosed letters from General Washington and Brigadier General Thompson. From them you will see the necessity of every province contiguous to New York exerting themselves in sending troops to that place [to] assist in fortifying and defending it, and also fortifying and defending such parts of this province as are most liable and likely to be invaded, with an attention to the latter.

I came over from New York yesterday in order to view the grounds on the Heights [of] Bergen Neck and the Kills Van Kull, and Staten Island; I was prevented by the bad weather in proceeding [as] far in this work as I could have wished; but on the whole I think that the militia of the counties of Bergen and Middlesex should be immediately employed in fortifying Amboy, Elizabeth Town Point, the·Kills and Bergen Neck with Poules Hook. I shall communicate my plan to Brigadier General Livingston and shall return to New York tomorrow morning. I will be here again in a day or two, and bring some assistant [eng]ineer's with me in order to lay out such works as General Thompson on my report approves of.

In the mean time I hope your Committee of Safety will without delay direct the militia before mentioned to be employed in the way above suggested, and also to direct the militia of the interiour counties to march either to the succour of New York or of the most exposed parts of this province as may be found necessary. There is a resolution of Congress passed a few days ago that such militia of this province as are called upon for the service of fortifying and defending New York shall receive pay agreeable to the establishment [of] the Continental troops of the Middle Departments and as these works proposed in New Jersey are with view to the same point, I make not the least [doubt] but the troops employed on them will be put on the same footing. . . . But for Gods sake do not at this critical moment suffer any delay in your directions for the m[ovement] of the militia from the interiour counties, nor [for] the employment of the others in the works of defence which may be found necessary.

—STIRLING PAPERS, New York Hist. Soc., IV, No. 85.

2. THE CHARACTER OF THE AMERICAN ARMY

Memoirs of Captain Alexander Graydon.

A considerable portion of our motley army had already assembled in New York and its vicinity. The troops were chiefly from the eastern provinces; those from the southern, with the exception of Hand's, Magaw's and our regiment, had not yet come on. The appearance of things was not much calculated to excite sanguine expectations in the mind of a sober observer. Great numbers of people were indeed to be seen, and those who are not accustomed to the sight of bodies under arms are always prone to exaggerate them. But this propensity to swell the mass had not an equal tendency to convert it into soldiery; and the irregularity, want of discipline, bad arms and defective equipment in all respects of this multitudinous assemblage gave no favourable impression of its prowess.

The materials of which the eastern battalions were composed were apparently the same as those of which I had seen so unpromising a specimen at Lake George. I speak particularly of the officers, who were in no single respect distinguishable from their men, other than in the coloured cockades, which, for this very purpose, had been prescribed in general orders; a different colour being assigned to the officers of each grade. So far from aiming at a deportment which might raise them above their privates, and thence prompt them to due respect and obedience to their commands, the object was, by humility, to preserve the existing blessing of equality: an illustrious instance of which was given by Colonel Putnam, the chief engineer of the army, and no less a personage than the nephew of the major-general of that name.

"What," says a person meeting him one day with a piece of meat in his hand, "carrying home your rations yourself, Colonel?"

"Yes," says he, "and I do it to set the officers a good example."

But if any aristocratic tendencies had been really discovered by the colonel among his countrymen, requiring this wholesome example, they must have been of recent origin, and the effects of southern contamination, since I have been credibly informed that it was no unusual thing in the army before Boston for a colonel to make drummers and fifers of his sons, thereby not only being enabled to form a very snug, economical mess, but to aid also considerably the revenue of the family chest. In short, it appeared that the sordid spirit of gain was the vital principle of this greater part of the army.

—GRAYDON, *Memoirs of His Own Time*, pp. 147-148.

3. "Let All Distinctions of Nations and Provinces Be Lost"

General Orders from George Washington.

Head Quarters, New York, August 1, 1776

It is with great concern, the General understands, that Jealousies &c. are arisen among the troops from the different Provinces, of reflections frequently thrown out, which can only tend to irritate each other, and injure the noble cause in which we are engaged, and which we ought to support with one hand and one heart. The General most earnestly entreats the officers, and soldiers, to consider the consequences; that they can no way assist our cruel enemies more effectually, than making division among ourselves; That the Honor and Success of the army, and the safety of our bleeding Country, depends upon harmony and good agreement with each other; That the Provinces are all United to oppose the common enemy, and all distinctions sunk in the name of an American; to make this honorable, and preserve the Liberty of our Country, ought to be our only emulation, and he will be the best Soldier, and the best Patriot, who contributes most to this glorious work, whatever his Station, or from whatever part of the Continent, he may come.

Let all distinctions of Nations, Countries, and Provinces, therefore be lost in the generous contest, who shall behave with the most Courage against the enemy, and the most kindness and good humour to each other—If there are any officers, or soldiers, so lost to virtue and a love of their Country as to continue in such practices after this order; The General assures them, and is directed by Congress to declare, to the whole Army, that such persons shall be severely punished and dismissed the service with disgrace.

—Fitzpatrick, ed., *Writings of Washington*, V, 361-362.

4. Hell's Work and the Problem of Whores

Colonel Loammi Baldwin to his wife, Mary, of Woburn, Massachusetts.

North River, New York, June 12, 1776

My Dear: This are with my warmest affections and sincere love to you, duty and regards to your honored parents, love to brothers and sisters. Hoping this will find you all in good health as they leave me. A better note of health I never enjoyed, blessed be God for it! I want much to see you but do not expect to enjoy that pleasure and Happiness unless you should come to York where, General Heath says, it is probable we shall remain during the sumer and the army have augmented to 25,000 men.

We are in dayly expectation of the enimy. Our works go on well. His Excellency returned from Congress about five days ago, but nothing very material of his business has transpired.

The army continues healthy. The inhabitants of the holy ground has brought some of the officers and a number of the soldiers into dificulty. The whores (by information) continue their imploy which is become very lucrative. Their unparalleled conduct is a sufficient antidote against any desires that a person can have that has one spark of modesty or virtue left in him and the last attum [*sic*] must certainly be lost before he can associate himself with these bitchfoxly jades, jills, haggs, strums, prostitutes and all these multiplyed into one another and then their full character not displayed.

Perhaps you will call me censorious and exclaim too much upon bare reports when I say that I was never within the doors of nor 'changed a word with any of them except in the execution of my duty as officer of the day in going the grand round with my guard of escort, have broke up the knots of men and women fighting, pulling caps, swearing, crying "Murder" etc—hurried them off to the Provost dungeon by half dozens, there let them lay mixed till next day. Then some are punished and sum get off clear—Hell's work.

—BALDWIN PAPERS, Houghton Library, Harvard University.

II. THE EVE OF BATTLE

The arrival of British men-of-war in lower New York Bay toward the end of June put the American army on the alert. General William Howe disembarked some 10,000 men on Staten Island, a landing that was unopposed. His brother, Admiral Lord Richard Howe, followed with a strong fleet and some 150 transports on July 12. Throughout the summer reinforcements continued to reach Staten Island. Admiral Sir Peter Parker's battered fleet brought Generals Henry Clinton and Lord Cornwallis, after their defeat at Charleston, and Commodore Hotham brought Guards and Hessians on August 12. In all, the invading army numbered 32,000, about 9,000 of whom were German mercenaries.

1. THE BRITISH FLEET HAS ARRIVED—"HURRY ON THE MILITIA!"

Journal of Samuel Blachley Webb, aide-de-camp to Washington.

29 June [*1776*].—This morning at 9 o'clock, we discovered our signals hoisted on Staten Island, signifying the appearance of a fleet. At 2 o'clock P.M. an express arrived, informing a fleet of more than one hundred square rigged vessels had arrived and anchored in the Hook. This is the fleet which we forced to evacuate Boston, and went on to Halifax last March, where they have been waiting for reinforcements, and have now arrived here with a view of puting their cursed plans into execution. But Heaven, *we hope and trust*, will frustrate their cruel designs. A warm and bloody campaign is the least we may expect. May God grant us victory and success over them is our most fervent prayer. Expresses are this day gone to Connecticut, the Jerseys, etc., to hurry on the militia.

July 1st.—By express from Long Island, we are informed that the whole fleet weighed anchor and came from Sandy Hook, over under the Long Island shore, and anchored about half a mile from the shore—which leads us to think they mean a descent upon the island this night. A reinforcement of 500 men were sent over at 9 o'clock this evening to reinforce the troops on Long Island under General Green. We have also received intelligence that our cruisers on the back of Long Island have taken and carried in one of the enemie's fleet laden with intrenching tools.

New York, July 2d.—Att 9 o'clock this morning the whole army was under arms at their several alarm posts, occasioned by five large men of war coursing up through the narrows. We supposed them coursing on to attack our forts. Never did I see men more chearfull; they seem to wish the enemies approach. They came up to the watering place, about five miles above the narrows, and came to. Their tenders took three or four of our small craft plying between this and the Jersey shore. Att 6 o'clock P.M. about 50 of the fleet followed and anchored with the others. Orders that the whole army lie on their arms and be at their alarm posts before the dawning of the day. A warm campaign, in all probability, will soon ensue. Relying on the justice of our cause, and puting our confidence in the Supreme Being, at the same time exerting our every nerve, we trust the design of our enemies will be frustrated.

—WEBB, *Correspondence and Journals*, I, 150-152.

2. BRITISH TROOPS LAND UNOPPOSED ON STATEN ISLAND

Diary of Archibald Robertson, captain-lieutenant in the Royal Engineers.

July 2nd [1776]

Weighed anchor at 10 morning and stood for the Narrows, the tide just on the turn against us and a light breeze. At 11 the tide turned and becoming allmost calm and the wind ahead the transports fell into great confusion, all dropping upon one another without steerage way which obliged us to come to an anchor. Some of the ships within 7 or 800 yards of Long Island. We observed a good many of the Rebels in motion on shore. They fired musquetry at the nearest ships without effect. About 12 the ships nearest were ordered to drop down with the tide. Lucky for us the Rebels had no cannon here or we must have suffered a good deal. The *Phoenix, Greyhound* and *Rose* men of war got about 4 or 5 miles ahead and brought too. About ¼ past one the *Phoenix* made the signal for preparing to land. It rained smartly, and the 1st division of transports got under way with the first of the flood tide, and about 9 we got up to the watering place on Staaten Island where the 3 men of war had hauled close inshore, the General on board the *Greyhound*, and the Grenadiers and Light Infantry under Earl Percy. Generals Robertson and Leslie landed immediately without opposition, the inhabitants wellcoming them ashore. They lay near the landing place all night.

—LYDENBERG, ed., *Diaries and Sketches of Robertson*, pp. 86-87.

3. NEW YORK BOMBARDED

Diary of the Reverend Mr. Shewkirk of the Moravian Church of New York.

Friday [July] 12th [1776]

A few more ships came in through the Narrows, and it was reported that the great fleet from England began to arrive. In the afternoon about 3 o'clock there was unexpectedly a smart firing. Two men of war, with some tenders, came up. They fired from all the batteries, but did little execution. The wind and tide being in their favor, the ships sailed fast up the North River, and soon were out of sight. When they came this side of Trinity Church, they began to fire smartly. The balls and bullets went through several houses between here and Greenwich. Six men were killed, either some or all by ill-managing the cannons, though it is said that a couple were killed by the ship's firing; one man's leg was broke, etc. The six were put this evening into one grave on the Bowling Green. The smoke of the firing drew over our street like a cloud, and the air was filled with the smell of the powder.

This affair caused a great fright in the city. Women and children and some with their bundles came from the lower parts, and walked to the Bowery, which was lined with people. Mother Bosler had been brought down into their cellar. Phil. Sypher's, with their child, which was sick, came again to our house. Not long after this affair was over, the fleet below fired a salute, Admiral Howe coming in from England.

—JOHNSTON, *Campaign of 1776*, II, 110-111.

4. "The Villainy and Madness of These Deluded People"

Journal of Ambrose Serle, secretary to Lord Richard Howe.

Friday, July 12th, 1776

This morning, the sun shining bright, we had a beautiful prospect of the coast of New Jersey at about 5 or 6 miles distance. The land was cleared in many places, and the woods were interspersed with houses, which being covered with white shingles appeared very plainly all along the shore. We passed Sandy Hook in the afternoon, and about 6 o'clock arrived safe off the east side of Staten Island. The country on both sides was highly picturesque and agreeable.

Nothing could exceed the joy that appeared throughout the fleet and army upon our arrival. We were saluted by all the ships of war in the harbour, by the cheers of the sailors all along the ships, and by those of the soldiers on the shore. A finer scene could not be exhibited, both of country, ships and men, all heightened by one of the brightest days that can be imagined. What added to their pleasure was that this very day about noon the *Phoenix* of 40 guns and the *Rose* of 20, with three tenders, forced their passage up the river in defiance of all their vaunted batteries, and got safe above the town, which will much intercept the provisions of the Rebels. We heard the canonade, and saw the smoke at a distance.

As soon as we came to anchor, Admiral Shuldham came on board, and soon after Genl. Howe, with several officers of their respective departments. By them we learnt the deplorable situation of His Majesty's faithful subjects; that they were hunted after and shot at in the woods and swamps, to which they had fled for these four months to avoid the savage fury of the Rebels; that many of them were forced to take up arms and join their forces; and that deserters and others flocked to the King's army continually. We also heared that the Congress had now announced the Colonies to be INDEPENDENT STATES, with several other articles of intelligence that proclaim the villainy and the madness of these deluded people. Where we anchored was in full view of New York, and of the Rebels' head quarters under Washington, who is now made their generalissimo with full powers.

—SERLE, *American Journal*, pp. 28-30.

5. "Fair Nymphs of This Isle Are in Wonderful Tribulation"

Francis, Lord Rawdon, to Francis, tenth Earl of Huntingdon.

Staten Island, near New York, August 5, 1776

We are just arrived here, my dearest Lord, after a very pleasant passage. Your letter of April 4th met me as soon as I set foot on shore. The company my letter from Virginia found you in is certainly the pleasantest in the world. Though I have neither a yellow damask drawing-room nor Constantia cape, I cultivate the acquaintance in a tent with Madeira, and *after all* there is but little difference.

The fair nymphs of this isle are in wonderful tribulation, as the fresh meat our men have got here has made them as riotous as satyrs. A girl cannot step into the bushes to pluck a rose without running the most imminent risk of being ravished, and they are so little accustomed to these vigorous methods that they don't bear them with the proper resignation, and of consequence we have most entertaining courts-martial every day.

To the southward they behaved much better in these cases, if I may judge from a woman who having been forced by seven of our men, [came] to make a complaint to me "not of their usage," she said; "No, thank God, she despised that," but of their having taken an old prayer book for which she had a particular affection.

A girl on this island made a complaint the other day to Lord Percy of her being deflowered, as she said, by some grenadiers. Lord Percy asked her how she knew them to be grenadiers, as it happened in the dark. "Oh, good God," cried she, "they could be nothing else, and if your Lordship will examine I am sure you will find it so."

All the English troops are encamped, or in cantonment, upon this island, as healthy and spirited a body of men as ever took the field. Several transports with Highlanders have been taken by the rebel privateers; the rest are all arrived, and are so enraged against the Yankees for some insults offered to their captive comrades that I think the first corps of psalm-singers who come in the way of their broad swords will be in a very awkward situation. Should my grandmother want any cherubins to adorn a new chapel, I dare say the Highlander would supply her with heads of the elect for that purpose at a cheap rate; but my grandmother will probably change sides when she hears that the Hessians sing hymns as loud as the Yankees, though it must be owned they have not the godly twang through the nose which distinguishes the faithful.

Some of the Hessians are arrived and long much to have a brush with the rebels, of whom they have a most despicable opinion. They are good troops but in point of men nothing equal to ours.

Some of the Guards are arrived, but not yet landed. Everybody seems to have formed a most favourable opinion of them. The desire they have shown to come upon service has pleased the line exceedingly and it will be their own faults if they do not keep this tide of applause in their favour.

I imagine that we shall very soon come to action, and I do not doubt but the consequence will be fatal to the rebels. An army composed as theirs is cannot bear the frown of adversity. General Carlton's successes in Canada have dispirited them exceedingly: their situation is critical, with his victorious army in their rear whilst they have such a force as ours in front. They have mustered all their troops to meet us and have entrenched themselves every where, but they will not be trifling obstacles that will stop a body of men so keen for service as ours are. I speak always with due submission to the goddess Nemesis, but I think she owes the Americans a *croc-en-jambe*, and when she pays it, I flatter myself she will do it effectually. Every measure, indeed, which can ensure success seems to have been taken on our side, and though I do not by any means deny the powerful influence of your deity, Fortune, upon all human affairs, I think there are certain precautions which have wonderful efficacy in deciding the event of every undertaking.

I am still with General Clinton. . . .

—Gr. Brit. Hist. Mss. Comm., *Hastings Manuscripts*, III, 179-180.

6. General Putnam Clamps the Cork Down on the Madeira

Narrative of a Continental private, thought to be James Sullivan Martin.

The soldiers at New-York had an idea that the enemy, when they took possession of the town, would make a general seizure of all property that could be of use to them as military or commissary stores. Hence they imagined that it was no injury to supply themselves when they thought they could do so with impunity, which was the cause of my having any hand in the transaction I am going to relate. Whether the reader will attribute it to levity, necessity or roguery, I am not able to say; perhaps to one or the other of them; it may be, to all.

I was stationed in Stone-Street, near the southwest angle of the city. Directly opposite to my quarters was a wine cellar; there were in the cellar at this time several pipes of Madeira wine. By some means the soldiers had "smelt it out." Some of them had, at mid-day, taken the iron grating from a window in the back yard, and one had entered the cellar and, by means of a powder-horn divested of its bottom, had supplied himself with wine, and was helping his comrades through the window with a "delicious draught," when the owner of the wine, having discovered what they were about, very wisely, as it seemed, came into the street and opened an outer door to the cellar in open view of every passenger. The soldiers quickly filled the cellar, when he, to save his property, proposed to sell it at what he called a cheap rate—I think, a dollar a gallon. In one corner of the cellar lay a large pile of oil flasks, holding from half a gallon to a gallon each; they were empty and not very savory neither, as they had lain there till the oil which adhered to the sides and bottoms had become quite rancid. While the owner was drawing for his purchasers on one side of the cellar, behind him on the other side another set of purchasers were drawing for themselves, filling those flasks. As it appeared to have a brisk sale, especially in the latter case, I concluded I would take a flask amongst the rest, which I accordingly did, and conveyed it in safety to my room, and went back into the street to see the end.

The owner of the wine soon found out what was going forward on his premises, and began remonstrating, but he preached to the wind. Finding that he could effect nothing with them, he went to Gen. Putnam's quarters, which was not more than three or four rods off. The General immediately repaired in person to the field of action. The soldiers getting word of his approach hurried out into the street, when he, mounting himself upon the doorsteps of my quarters, began "harangueing the multitude," threatening to hang every mother's son of them. Whether he was to be the hangman or not, he did not say; but I took every word he said for gospel, and expected nothing else but to be hanged before the morrow night. I sincerely wished him hanged and out of the way, for fixing himself upon the steps of our door; but he soon ended his discourse and came down from his rostrum, and the soldiers dispersed, no doubt much edified.

I got home as soon as the General had left the coast clear, took a draught of the wine, and then flung the flask and the remainder of the wine out of my window, from the third story, into the water cistern in the back yard, where it remains to this day for aught I know. However, I might have kept it if I had not been in too much haste to free myself from being hanged by General Putnam, or by his order. I never heard any thing further about the wine or being hanged about it; he doubtless forgot it.

—MARTIN (?), *Narrative*, pp. 15-18.

III. THE HOWES' FIRST ATTEMPTS AT CONCILIATION

Before coming to America the Howe brothers had been named by King George as peace commissioners acting under authority of Parliament. They were empowered to pardon and protect those Americans who returned to their allegiance, but had no authority to negotiate with any colony until all the revolutionary armies and congresses had been dissolved. Members of the opposition Whig bloc and friendly to the colonies, the Howes put out preliminary feelers to Washington. The American commander designated Colonels Henry Knox and Joseph Reed and Lieutenant Colonel Samuel Webb, an aide, to meet the officer coming into the harbor under a flag of truce, but not to accept any letter which was not properly addressed to him as commander in chief of the American forces. Were it not that the issues were so portentous, the negotiations might have been more suited to opéra bouffe. Colonel Reed, Washington's confidant, had been untiring in his efforts to bring about conciliation with the mother country.

1. "GEORGE WASHINGTON, ESQ." IS NOT AT HOME

Colonel Henry Knox to his wife Lucy.

July 15, 1776

Lord Howe yesterday sent a flag of truce up to the city. They came within about four miles of the city and were met by some of Colonel Tupper's people, who detained them until his Excellency's pleasure should be known. Accordingly, Colonel Reed and myself went down in the barge to receive the message. When we came to them, the officer, who was, I believe, captain of the *Eagle* man-of-war, rose up and bowed, keeping his hat off: "I have a letter, sir, from Lord Howe to Mr. Washington."

"Sir," says Colonel Reed, "we have no person in our army with that address."

"Sir," says the officer, "will you look at the address?" He took out of his pocket a letter which was thus addressed:

"George Washington, Esq., New York
"Howe."

"No, sir," says Colonel Reed, "I cannot receive that letter."

"I am very sorry," says the officer, "and so will be Lord Howe, that any error in the superscription should prevent the letter being received by *General Washington.*"

"Why, sir," says Colonel Reed, "I must obey orders."

"Oh, yes, sir, you must obey orders, to be sure."

Then, after giving him a letter from Colonel Campbell to General Howe, and some other letters from prisoners to their friends, we stood off, having saluted and bowed to each other. After we had got a little way, the officer put about his barge and stood for us and asked by what particular title he chose to be addressed.

Colonel Reed said, "You are sensible, sir, of the rank of General Washington in our army?"

"Yes, sir, we are. I am sure my Lord Howe will lament exceedingly this affair, as the letter is quite of a civil nature, and not a military one. He laments exceedingly that he was not here a little sooner"; which we suppose to allude to the Declaration of Independence; upon which we bowed and parted in the most genteel terms imaginable.

—BROOKS, *Henry Knox*, p. 58.

2. WASHINGTON REFUSES TO NEGOTIATE

Colonel Henry Knox to his wife Lucy.

July 22, 1776

On Saturday I wrote you we had a capital flag of truce, no less than the adjutant-general of General Howe's army. He had an interview with General Washington at our house. The purport of his message was, in very elegant, polite strains, to endeavour to persuade General Washington to receive a letter directed to George Washington, Esq., etc., etc. In the course of his talk every other word was, "May it please your Excellency," "If your Excellency so pleases"; in short, no person could pay more respect than the said adjutant-general, whose name is Colonel Paterson, a person we do not know. He said the "etc., etc." implied everything. "It does so," said the General, "and anything." He said Lord and General Howe lamented exceedingly that any errors in the direction should interrupt that frequent intercourse between the two armies which might be necessary in the course of the service. That Lord Howe had come out with great powers. The General said he had heard that Lord Howe had come out with very great powers to pardon, but he had come to the wrong place; the Americans had not offended, therefore they needed no pardon. This confused him.

After a considerable deal of talk about the good disposition of Lord and General Howe, he asked, "Has your Excellency no particular commands with which you would please to honour me to Lord and General Howe?"

"Nothing, sir, but my particular compliments to both"—a good answer.

General Washington was very handsomely dressed and made a most elegant appearance. Colonel Paterson appeared awe-struck, as if he was before something supernatural. Indeed I don't wonder at it. He was before a very great man indeed. We had a cold collation provided, in which I lamented most exceedingly the absence of my Lucy. The General's servants did it tolerably well, though Mr. Adjutant-general disappointed us. As it grew late, he even excused himself from drinking one glass of wine. He said Lord Howe and General Howe would wait for him, as they were to dine on board the *Eagle* man-of-war; he took his leave and went off.

—BROOKS, Henry Knox, p. 59.

IV. THE BATTLE OF LONG ISLAND BEGINS

As the crucial hour approached, both sides seemed singularly optimistic about the outcome. The British were in a holiday mood despite their late humiliation in Boston and their more recent repulse at Charleston. Writing from his headquarters in New York to the officers and soldiers of the Pennsylvania Associators, Washington declared on August 8: "The fate of our country depends in all human probability on the exertion of a few weeks." This was a strange miscalculation by Washington, who normally took a realistic view of military matters.

There was a great storm the night of August 21. As soon as it was over the British amphibious operation pushed ahead efficiently. On the morning of August 22, Howe's forces under cover of the guns of the British ships disembarked on Long Island in the vicinity of the Narrows. In a few hours 15,000 troops were landed without opposition, and were reinforced three days later by General Philip von Heister's German division.

Opposing the 20,000 invading troops was an army of under 8,000, mostly raw militia and about half of them outside the defense works in Brooklyn. Because of his illness General Nathanael Greene turned his command over to General John Sullivan, a strenuous but vain and certainly inferior officer who was in hot water throughout the war. On the twenty-third Sullivan reported success in a minor skirmish, adding: "These things argue well for us, and I hope are so many preludes to a general victory." The next day Washington superseded him in the command by Israel Putnam, whose courage was matched by his stupidity and inexperience. In fact, Putnam never really exercised the command conferred on him. Our first chronicler, one of the best-known diarists of the period, died of dysentery six weeks after recording the entry below.

1. STORM AND ALARM AS THE BRITISH LAND

Journal of Philip Vickers Fithian, chaplain with the New Jersey militia.

August 22, 1776

We had last night a most terrible storm of wind, thunder and lightening! So violent as I have not seen since about this time in August 1773. We expect it must have damaged the shipping. It has done a little injury in the harbour tho not so much as from a most furious sudden wind, lasting an hour and a half, might be expected! These two days past many of the ships have gone out. And this morning, before seven, thirteen weighed and went out. It is said by express those which went yesterday were fitted with troups.

Several hundred men are making a breastwork still along the river only as

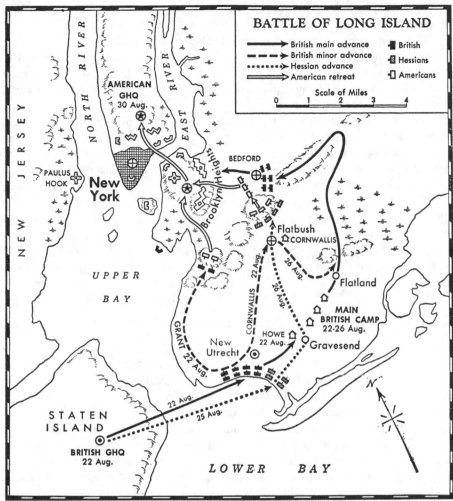

From **The Encyclopedia of American History**
by *Richard B. Morris*

Courtesy of Harper & Brothers

a defence from musquetry. It runs close by our lodging so that we shall have only to step into the trench, load, fire, etc!

Crack! Crack! An alarm from Red-Hook. Crack! Crack! Crack! The alarm repeated from Cobble-Hill. Orders are given for the drums to beat *to arms*. The enemy have been landing for some time down at the Narrows, and, it is said, have now ashore several thousand. The battalions of riffle-men stationed there, on the enemy's landing, left their camp and came up the island, setting on fire, all the way, the stacks of grain; this is the first degree of ravage occasioned by this unworthy and unchristian assault of our enemies that I have been witness to.

Every battalion, for the present, was ordered to repair to its proper alarm-post. Ours, however, soon had orders to enter Fort-Box. I equipt myself for an action with my gun, canteen, knapsack, blanket, and with the regiment entered the fort and waited for further orders.

Three battalions were ordered off immediately to intercept them and annoy their march.

The alarm guns were fired a little before twelve o'clock.

Before four two brigades were over from New-York, the greater number of which marched on to meet the enemy. Generals Sullivan and Green rode on to gain some intelligence of their place and numbers. Word soon came back that they are within a few miles.

Our battalion all turned out and made a formidable piquet round our little fortification, in order to retard the approach of the enemy and hinder their surrounding us, especially their horse. The men work with vigor; a sense of necessity and the security of life are strong springs to industry.

About eight in the evening the generals returned into camp, and inform that the enemy have made a halt at Flat-Bush, about four miles distance—that the several battalions advanced are in ambush and otherways arranged to annoy them—and that our battalions, after the guards are taken out, may repair to quarters til two in the morning, when all without fail are to be at their post. No officer or soldier is to take off his clothes, and all are to lye on their arms.

—FITHIAN, *Journal*, pp. 214-216.

2. THE BRITISH DISEMBARK IN A HOLIDAY MOOD

Journal of Ambrose Serle, secretary to Lord Richard Howe.

Thursday, [August] 22d, 1776

Early this morning the English troops, the Highlanders and Preston's Light Horse, landed on Long Island. The disembarkation was effected upon the flat shore, near Gravesend, without the least resistance; the inhuman Rebels contenting themselves with burning as much of the people's corn as they could (tho' the great rains which fell last night very happily prevented much of their design), with driving off their cattle as far as their time would permit, and doing as much injury to the inhabitants, who are generally well disposed, as they possibly could. The soldiers and sailors seemed as merry as in a holiday, and regaled themselves with the fine apples, which hung every where upon the trees in a great abundance. After the landing was pretty well effected, I went with two or three gentlemen on shore to Mr. De Nuys's house, opposite the Narrows, whose family were rejoiced at the deliverance from the tyranny they had so long undergone from the Rebels. It was really diverting to see sailors and apples tumbling from the trees together.

The General pushed on to his post, and was joined by great numbers of the people. Every thing relative to the disembarkation was conducted in admirable order, and succeeded beyond our most sanguine wishes.

The island seems extremely fertile, and the country rather flat. There were some fine cattle still remaining; and proper precautions were taken to prevent our people from plundering. . . .

In a word, the disembarkation of about 15,000 troops, upon a fine beach, their forming upon the adjacent plain, a fleet of above 300 ships and vessels with their sails spread open to dry, the sun shining clear upon them, the green hills and meadows after the rain, and the calm surface of the water upon the contiguous sea and up the sound, exhibited one of the finest and most picturesque scenes that the imagination can fancy or the eye behold. Add to all this the vast importance of the business and of the motions of the day, and the mind feels itself wonderfully engaged by the variety and greatness of the objects; but finds, or should find, in the midst of all, that there is no assurance or dependence in these things, but in Him only who saveth by many or by few, and who giveth the victory when and where and how He pleaseth. In this frame a man may be disappointed of his present wish, but not of his hope or future expectation. He may err in his judgment, but he is right in his heart.

—SERLE, *American Journal*, pp. 71-74.

3. "LET THEM COME ON AS SOON AS THEY DARE!"

Colonel William Douglas of Connecticut to his wife.

New York, August 23, 1776

I have only time to acquaint you that I am well, as I hope this may find you. The enemy landed yesterday at Gravesend about nine miles from our lines. Our flying parties are anoying of them all the while. We have reinforced our selves and I hope will be able to make a good stand. We expect the fleat up every tide if the wind serves. Our fire ships in the North River behaved manfully, have burnt one of their tenders. The rest of the enemy left the river the first opportunity afterward. Our Connecticut Militia have come in bravely. Twelve regiments were on the Grand Perade at one time yesterday. Almost one half of this grand army now consists of Connecticut troops. The Militia are a fine set of men. I'm fully of the opinion that if the enemy attempt to carry this citty by storm it will cost them very deer. They may burn it, but they cant take it, and it is of no service to them to destroy it.

Night before last we had a most terrible thunderstorm. One capt., two lieuts. of the first battalion of York troops were killed with lightning in one place. Also two men in two different places. The wind and wether has been remarkeable in our favour for this sometime past, has brought on our troops and kept back the enemy and we begin to shew like a formadable army and I hope that the same kind Providence that has wonderfully carried us thus far will shew his power in bringing us off victorious, and take to himself the glory.

Satterday the 24th. Our men had yesterday two small brushes with the enemy on Long Island. Have repulsed them both times. As yet things look well on our side. A few days now will detirmine the work is begun. Our troops are rally in high sperits and it is a general voice, Let them come on as soon as they can, or dare! There has been a heavey clashing of arms on Long Island this morning but I have not yet heard the consequence.

—DOUGLAS, "Letters," *N. Y. Hist. Soc. Quarterly Bulletin*, XIII, 81.

V. SULLIVAN LEAVES THE BACK DOOR OPEN

General Howe had experienced enough of bloody frontal attacks at Bunker's Hill and wanted no more of them. To divert the Americans from his main move, the British commander dispatched General James Grant toward

Gravesend to attack the defender's right wing under Stirling, and Von Heis-
ter was ordered to bombard the center of the line held by Colonel Edward
Hand. But the main move was a night flanking march to get around in the
rear of Sullivan's left. Guided by a Tory farmer, Sir Henry Clinton moved
up from Flatlands during the night of the twenty-sixth, arrived at the stra-
tegic Jamaica Pass which he found undefended, and swung down the Jamaica
Road toward Bedford. The Americans were outflanked. In view of the lack
of clear intelligence of the British moves during the confusing night and day
that followed, it might be unfair to place all the blame on Sullivan, but his sub-
ordinate, the Pennsylvanian, Colonel Samuel Miles, was the immediate scape-
goat. The debacle was followed by the customary military post-mortems.

1. GENERAL PARSONS BLAMES IT ON COLONEL MILES

Brigadier General Samuel Parsons to John Adams.

Morrisania, October 8, 1776

... To give you a clear idea of the matter [the Battle of Long Island], I must trouble you with a description of that part of the country where the enemy landed and encamped, and the intervening lands between that and our lines.

From the point of land which forms the east side of the Narrows, runs a ridge of hills about N. E. in length about 5 or 6 miles, covered with a thick wood, which terminate in a small rising land near Jamaica; through these hills are three passes only, one near the Narrows, one on the road called the Flatbush Road and one called the Bedford Road, being a cross road from Bedford to Flatbush which lies on the southerly side of these hills; these passes are through the mountains or hills, easily defensible, being very narrow and the lands high and mountainous on each side. These are the only roads which can be passed from the south side the hill to our lines, except a road leading around the easterly end of the hills to Jamaica. On each of these roads were placed a guard of 800 men, and east of them in the wood was placed Col Miles with his battalion to watch the motion of the enemy on that part, with orders to keep a party constantly reconnoitering to and across the Jamaica Road. The sentinels were so placed as to keep a constant communication between the three guards on the three roads. South of these hills lies a large plain extending from the North River easterly to Rockaway Bay perhaps 5 miles and southerly to the sound bounded on the south by the Sound and on the north by the hills. Those hills were from two or three miles and a half from our lines. The enemy landed on this plain and extended their camp from the river to Flatbush perhaps 3 or 4 miles.

On the day of the surprise I was on duty, and at the first dawn of the day the guards from the west road near the Narrows came to my quarters and informed me the enemy were advancing in great numbers by that road. I soon found it true and that the whole guard had fled without firing a gun; these (by way of retaliation I must tell you) were all New Yorkers and Pennsylvanians; I found by fair daylight the enemy were through the woods and descending the hill on the north side, on which with 20 of my fugitive guard, being all I could collect, I took post on a height in their front at about half a mile's distance—which halted their column and gave time for Lord Sterling with his forces to come up; thus much for the west road.

On the east next Jamaica Col. Miles suffered the enemy to march not less than 6 miles till they came near two miles in rear of the guards before he discovered and gave notice of their approach. This also was in the night and the guard kept by Pennsylvanians altogether—the New England and New Jersey troops being in the other two roads through which the enemy did not attempt to pass.

We were surprised—our principal barrier lost by that surprise, but as far as the cover of the night is an excuse we have it. The landing of the troops could not be prevented at the distance of 6 or 7 miles from our lines; on a plain under the cannon of the ships, just in view of the shore. Our unequal numbers would not admit attacking them on the plain when landed.

—JOHNSTON, *Campaign of 1776*, II, 35-36.

2. COLONEL MILES BLAMES IT ON SULLIVAN

On the landing of the British army on Long Island, I was ordered over with my rifle regiment to watch their motions. I marched near to the village of Flat Bush, where the Highlanders then lay, but they moved the next day to Gen'l Howe's camp, and their place was supplied by the Hessians. I lay here within cannon shot of the Hessian camp for four days without receiving a single order from Gen'l Sullivan, who commanded on Long Island, out of the lines. The day before the action he came to the camp, and I then told him the situation of the British army; that Gen'l Howe, with the main body, lay on my left, about a mile and a half or two miles, and I was convinced when the army moved that Gen'l Howe would fall into the Jamaica road, and I hoped there were troops there to watch them.

Notwithstanding this information, which indeed he might have obtained from his own observation, if he had attended to his duty as a general ought to have done, no steps were taken, but there was a small redoubt in front of the village which seemed to take up the whole of his attention, and where he stayed until the principal part of the British army had gotten between him and the lines, by which means he was made prisoner as well as myself. If Gen'l Sullivan had taken the requisite precaution, and given his orders agreeably to the attention of the Commander-in-Chief, there would have been few if any prisoners taken on the 27th of August, 1776.

. . . I will here state my position and conduct. I lay directly in front of the village of Flat Bush, but on the left of the road leading to New York, where the Hessians were encamped. We were so near each other that their shells they sometimes fired went many rods beyond my camp.

The main body of the enemy, under the immediate command of Gen'l Howe, lay about 2 miles to my left, and General Grant, with another body of British troops, lay about four miles on my right. There were several small bodies of Americans dispersed to my right, but not a man to my left, although the main body of the enemy lay to my left, of which I had given General Sullivan notice. This was our situation on the 26th of August.

About one o'clock at night Gen. Grant, on the right, and Gen. Howe, on my left, began their march, and by daylight Grant had got within a mile of our entrenchments, and Gen. Howe had got into the Jamaica road about two miles from our lines. The Hessians kept their position until 7 in the morning. As soon as they moved the firing began at our redoubt. I immediately marched towards where firing was, but had not proceeded more than 1 or 200 yards until I was stopped by Colonel Wyllys, who told me that I could not pass on; that we were to defend a road that lead from Flatbush road to the Jamaica road. Col. Wyllys being a Continental, and I a State commission, he was considered a senior officer and I was obliged to submit; but I told him I was convinced the main body of the enemy would take the Jamaica road, that there was no probability of their coming along the road he was then guarding, and if he would not let me proceed to where the firing was, I would return and endeavor to get into the Jamaica road before Gen. Howe. To this he consented, and I immediately made a retrograde march, and after marching nearly two miles, the whole distance through woods, I arrived within sight of the Jamaica road, and to my great mortification I saw the main body of the enemy in full march between me and our lines, and the baggage guard just coming into the road.

A thought struck me of attacking the baggage guard, and, if possible, to cut my way through them and proceed to Hell Gate to cross the Sound. I, however, ordered the men to remain quite still (I had then but the first battalion with me, for, the second being some distance in the rear, I directed Major Williams, who was on horseback, to return and order Lt. Col. Brodhead to push on by the left of the enemy and endeavor get into our lines that way, and happily they succeeded, but had to wade a mill dam by which a few were drowned) and I took the adjutant with me and crept as near the road as I thought prudent, to try and ascertain the number of the baggage guard, and I saw a grenadier stepping into the woods. I got a tree between him and me until he came near, and I took him prisoner and examined him. I found that there was a whole brigade with the baggage, commanded by a general officer.

I immediately returned to the battalion and called a council of the officers and laid three propositions before them: *1st*, to attack the baggage guard and endeavor to cut our way through them and proceed to Hell Gate and so cross the Sound; *2nd*, to lay where we were until the whole had passed us and then proceed to Hell Gate; or, *3d*, to endeavor to force our way through the enemy's flank guards into our line at Brooklyn. The first was thought a dangerous and useless attempt as the enemy was so superior in force. The 2nd I thought the most eligible, for it was evident that adopting either of the other propositions we must lose a number of men without affecting the enemy materially, as we had so small a force, not more than 230 men. This was, however, objected to, under the idea that we should be blamed for not fighting at all, and perhaps charged with cowardice, which would be worse than death itself.

The 3d proposition was therefore adopted, and we immediately began our march, but had not proceeded more than half a mile until we fell in with a body of 7 or 800 light infantry, which we attacked without any hesitation, but their superiority of numbers encouraged them to march up with their bayonets, which we could not withstand, having none ourselves. I therefore ordered the troops to push on towards our lines. I remained on the ground myself until they had all passed me (the enemy were then within less than 20 yards of us), and by this means I came into the rear instead of the front of my command.

We had proceeded but a short distance before we were again engaged with a superior body of the enemy, and here we lost a number of men, but took Major Moncrieffe, their commanding officer, prisoner, but he was a Scotch prize, for Ensign Brodhead, who took him and had him in possession for some hours, was obliged to surrender himself. Finding that the enemy had possession of the ground between us and our lines, and that it was impossible to cut our way through as a body, I directed the men to make the best of their way as well as they could; some few got in safe, but there were 159 taken prisoners. I was myself entirely cut off from our lines and therefore endeavored to conceal myself, with a few men who would not leave me. I hoped to remain until night, when I intended to try to get to Hell Gate and cross the Sound; but about 3 o'clock in the afternoon was discovered by a party of Hessians and obliged to surrender. Thus ended the career of that day.

—MILES, "Journal," *Pennsylvania Archives*, 2nd Series, I, 520-522.

VI. STIRLING MAKES A GALLANT STAND

Fragments of Sullivan's forces broke through the enemy's lines, but a large portion were killed, wounded or taken prisoner. To occupy the Americans during the main British move on the left, General Grant attacked Stirling on the American right. There a gallant defense was put up by Smallwood's Marylands and Haslet's Delawares. Colonel John Haslet of the Delaware battalion reported how the Delaware men drew up on the side of a hill, standing more than four hours "in close array, their colours flying, the enemy's artillery playing on them all the while, not daring to advance and attack them, though six times their number and nearly surrounding them." They finally on orders retreated through a marsh and over a creek, bringing off twenty-three prisoners. In the course of the fierce attack and counterattack Grant was killed and Lord Stirling made prisoner.

1. THE ATTACK ON CORNWALLIS FAILS

Lord Stirling to George Washington.

Eagle, August 29, 1776

I have now an opportunity of informing you of what has happened to me since I had last the pleasure of seeing you. About three o'clock in the morning of the 27th, I was called up and informed by General Putnam that the enemy were advancing by the road from Flatbush to the Red Lion, and ordered me to march with the two regiments nearest at hand to meet them;

these happened to be Haslet's and Smallwood's, with which I accordingly marched, and was on the road to the Narrows just as daylight began to appear.

We proceeded to within half a mile of the Red Lion, and there met Colonel Atlee, with his regiment, who informed me that the enemy were in sight; indeed, I then saw their front between us and the Red Lion. I desired Colonel Atlee to place his regiment on the left of the road, and to wait their coming up, when I went to form the two regiments I had brought with me, along a ridge from the road up to a piece of wood on the top of the hill. This was done instantly, upon very advantageous ground. Our opponents advanced and were fired upon in the road by Atlee's, who, after two or three rounds, retreated to the wood on my left and there formed. By this time Kichline's riflemen arrived; part of them I placed along a hedge, under the front of the hill, and the rest in the front of the wood.

The troops opposed to me were two brigades of four regiments each, under the command of General Grant, who advanced their light troops to within one hundred and fifty yards of our right front and took possession of an orchard there, and some hedges that extended towards our left; this brought on an exchange of fire between those troops and our riflemen, which continued for about two hours, and then ceased by those light troops retiring to their main body.

In the mean time, Captain Carpenter brought up two field-pieces, which were placed on the side of the hill, so as to command the road and the only approach for some hundred yards. On the part of General Grant there were two field-pieces: one howitz advanced to within three hundred yards of the front of our right, and a like detachment of artillery to the front of our left, on a rising ground, at about six hundred yards' distance. One of their brigades formed in two lines opposite to our right, and the others extended in one line to top of the hills in front of our left.

In this position we stood, cannonading one another, till near eleven o'clock, when I found that General Howe, with the main body of the army, was between me and our lines, and saw that the only chance of escaping being all made prisoners was to pass the creek near the Yellow Mills; and in order to render this the more practicable, I found it absolutely necessary to attack a body of troops commanded by Lord Cornwallis, posted at the house near the Upper Mills. This I instantly did, with about half of Smallwood's, first ordering all the other troops to make the best of their way through the creek. We continued the attack a considerable time, the men having been rallied and the attack renewed five or six several times, and were on the point of driving Lord Cornwallis from his station, but large succors arriving rendered it impossible to do more than provide for safety. I endeavored to get in between that house and Fort Box, but on attempting it, I found a considerable body of troops in my front, and several in pursuit of me on the right and left, and a constant firing on me. I immediately turned the point of a hill which covered me from their fire, and I was soon out of the reach of my pursuers. I soon found it would be in vain to attempt to make my escape, and therefore went to surrender myself to General de Heister, commander-in-chief of the Hessians.

—DAWSON, *Battles of the United States*, I, 151-152.

2. The American Stand on Stirling's Left

Journal of Colonel Samuel J. Atlee, commanding a Pennsylvania battalion.

August 27, 1776

... I then received orders from Lord Stirling to advance with my battalion and oppose the enemy's passing a morass or swamp at the foot of a fine rising ground, upon which they were first discovered, and thereby give time to our brigade to form upon the heights. This order I immediately obeyed, notwithstanding we must be exposed, without any kind of cover, to the great fire of the enemy's musketry and field pieces, charged with round and grape shot, and finely situated upon the eminence above mentioned, having the entire command of the ground I was ordered to occupy. My battalion, although new and never before having the opportunity of facing an enemy, sustained their fire until the brigade had formed; but finding we could not possibly prevent their crossing the swamp, I ordered my detachment to file off to the left and take post in a wood upon the left of the brigade. Here I looked upon myself advantageously situated and might be enabled, upon the advance of the enemy, to give him a warm reception. In this affair I lost but one soldier, shot with a grape shot through his throat. I had not taken post in the above mentioned wood but a few minutes when I received a reinforcement of two companies of the Delawares, under Captain Stedman, with orders from Lord Stirling to file off further to the left and prevent, if possible, a body of the enemy observed advancing to flank the brigade.

The enemy's troops by this time had passed the swamp and formed in line of battle opposite ours. A heavy fire, as well from small arms as artillery, ensued, with very little damage on our side; what the enemy sustained we could not judge. Upon filing off to the left, according to the orders I had received, I espied at the distance of about three hundred yards a hill of clear ground, which I judged to be a proper situation to oppose the troops ordered to flank us, and which I determined, if possible, to gain before them. At the foot of this hill a few of Huntington's Connecticut Regiment, that had been upon the picket, joined me. In order to gain and secure the hill, I ordered the troops to wheel to the right and march up the hill abreast. When within about forty yards of the summit, we very unexpectedly received a very heavy fire from the enemy taken post there before us, notwithstanding the forced march I made.

The enemy's situation was so very advantageous, the back of the hill where they had taken post being formed by nature into a breast-work, that, had they directed their fire properly or been marksmen, they must have cut off the greatest part of my detachment, I having, before I advanced [up] the hill, posted a part of my small number along the skirt of a wood upon my right, and left a guard at the foot of the hill to prevent my being surrounded and my retreat to the brigade in case of necessity being cut off, the enemy being vastly superior in numbers, their detachment consisting of the Twenty-Third and Forty-Fourth Regiments and part of the Seventeenth.

Upon receiving the above heavy fire, which continued very warm and they secure behind the hill, a small halt was made, and the detachment fell

back a few paces. Here Capt. Stedman, with all the Delawares except the
Lieutenants Stewart and Harney with about sixteen privates, left me and drew
after them some of my own. The remainder, after recovering a little from
this, their first shock, I ordered to advance, at the same time desiring them to
preserve their fire and aim aright. They immediately, with the resolution of
veteran soldiers, obeyed the order. The enemy, finding their opponents fast
advancing and determined to dispute the ground with them, fled with precipitation, leaving behind them twelve killed upon the spot and a lieutenant
and four privates wounded. In this engagement I lost my worthy friend and
Lieutenant-Colonel (Parry) shot through the head, who fell without a groan,
fighting in defence of his much injured country. In the midst of the action
I ordered four soldiers to carry him as speedily as possible within the lines at
Brookline. . . .

I fully expected, as did most of my officers, that the strength of the
British army was advancing in this quarter to our lines. But how greatly were
we deceived when intelligence was received by some scattering soldiers that
the right wing and centre of the army, amongst which were the Hessians,
were advancing to surround us. This we were soon convinced of by an exceeding heavy fire in our rear. No troops having been posted to oppose the
march of this grand body of the enemy's army but Colonel Miles's two battalions of rifles, Colonel Willis's battalion of Connecticut, and a part of Lutz
and Kiechlien's battalions of the Pennsylvania Flying-Camp, I once more sent
my adjutant to Lord Stirling, to acquaint him with the last success obtained
by my party, and to request his further orders; but receiving no answer, the
adjutant not returning, and waiting near three quarters of an hour for the
enemy, they not approaching in front but those in the rear drawing near, I
thought it most prudent to join the brigade, where I might be of more advantage than in my present situation. . . .

How great was my surprise I leave any one to judge when, upon coming
to the ground occupied by our troops, to find it evacuated and the troops gone
off without my receiving the least intelligence of the movement or order what
to do, although I had so shortly before sent my adjutant to the general for
that purpose. The general must have known, by my continuing in my post
at the hill, I must, with all my party, inevitably fall a sacrifice to the enemy.
An opportunity yet afforded, with risking the lives of some of us, of getting
off. But perceiving a body of the enemy advancing, which proved to be the
English Grenadiers, under Lieutenant-Colonel Monckton, to fall upon the
rear of our brigade, which I could see at a distance, I ordered my party once
more to advance and support a few brave fellows, endeavoring to prevent, but
without success, the destruction of their countrymen. The timely assistance
of a number often tried, and as often victorious, encouraged those already
engaged and obliged the enemy to quit the ground they had gained and retire
to a fence lined with trees. Here we kept up a close fire, until the brigade had
retreated out of our sight, when, not being able, through the weakness of my
party already greatly fatigued and once more destitute of ammunition, to
break through the enemy, and finding my retreat after the brigade cut off, I

filed off to the right, to endeavour, if possible, to escape through that quarter. . . .

After marching about half a mile to the right, I fell in with General Parsons and a small number by him collected. In consultation with the general it was determined to break through the enemy, who were here within a little way of us, and endeavour to make up the island. I then pushed off, with such of the officers and soldiers that were willing to run this hazard. What became of General Parsons I know not, never having seen him since. . . .

I imagined that if I could cross the Flatbush road, I could then make my escape by Hell-Gate, but coming to the road found it everywhere strictly guarded. After trying the road in several places, both to the right and left, and finding no passage, we retired to an eminence about sixty perches from the road, to consult whether best to conceal ourselves in the adjacent swamps or divide into small parties, when we espied a party of Hessians who had discovered and were endeavouring to surround us. The opinion we had formed of these troops determined us to run any risk rather than fall into their hands; and finding after all our struggles no prospect of escaping, we determined to throw ourselves into the mercy of a battalion of Highlanders posted upon an eminence near the Flatbush road, not far from where we had last sat. This we did about five o'clock in the afternoon to the number of twenty-three, thereby escaping the pursuit of a party of Hessians who came to the Highlanders immediately after our surrender. . . .

Thus ended this most unfortunate 27th of August, 1776, during which myself and my detachment underwent great fatigue and escaped death in a variety of instances. And I am happy to reflect that during the whole of this perilous day, one and all, to the utmost of their powers and abilities, exerted themselves in performing their several duties, for which I shall ever retain a grateful sense, and do, for and in behalf of my country, return to them my sincere acknowledgments, as I flatter myself, under God, they were the means of twice preserving the brigade from being cut to pieces: first in preventing the troops in which Grant bore a command from falling upon the left flank; and lastly, in so bravely attacking the Grenadiers, where Monckton commanded, and thereby preventing the destruction of the rear. In the first Grant fell, in the latter was Monckton wounded.

—FORCE, *American Archives*, 5th Series, I, 1251-1255.

3. "GOOD GOD! WHAT BRAVE FELLOWS I MUST THIS DAY LOSE!"

Letter of an unknown Patriot soldier.

New York, September 1, 1776

Last Monday we went over to L. I., and about midnight were alarmed by some of our scouting parties, who advised us that the enemy were coming up the island with several field-pieces. Upon which near 3,000 men were ordered out, chiefly of Marylanders and Pennsylvanians, to attack them on their march. About sunrise we came up with a large body of them. The Delaware and Maryland battalions made one part. Col. Atlee, with his battalion, a little before us, had taken post in an orchard and behind a barn; and on the approach of the enemy, he gave them a very severe fire for a considerable time, till they were near surrounding him, when he retreated to the woods. The enemy then advanced to us, when Lord Stirling, who commanded, immediately drew up in a line and offered them battle in the true English taste. The British then advanced within about 300 yards of us and began a very heavy fire from ther cannon and mortars: for both the balls and shells flew very fast, now and then taking off a head.

Our men stood it amazingly well, not even one showed a disposition to shrink. Our orders were not to fire till the enemy came within 50 yards of us; but when they perceived we stood their fire so coolly and resolutely, they declined coming any nearer, though treble our number.

In this situation we stood from sunrise till 12 o'clock, the enemy firing on us the chief part of the time, when the main body of British, by a route we never dreamed of, had surrounded us and driven within the lines, or scattered in the woods, all our men except the Delaware and Maryland battalions, who were standing at bay with double their number. Thus situated, we were ordered to attempt a retreat by fighting our way through the enemy, who had posted themselves and nearly filled every road and field between us and our lines. We had not retreated a quarter of a mile before we were fired on by an advanced party of the enemy and those in the rear playing their artillery on us.

Our men fought with more than Roman valor. We forced the advanced party which first attacked us to give way, through which opening we got a passage down to the side of a marsh, seldom before waded over, which we passed, and then swam a narrow river, all the while exposed to the enemy's fire. Capts. Ramsay's and Scott's companies were in front and sustained the first fire of the enemy, when hardly a man fell. The whole of the right wing of our battalion, thinking it impossible to march through the marsh, attempted to force their way through the woods, where they, almost to a man, were killed or taken.

... Most of our generals, on a high hill in the lines, viewed us with glasses as we were retreating, and saw the enemy we had to pass through, though we could not. Many thought we would surrender in a body without firing. When we began the attack, Gen. Washington wrung his hands and cried out, "Good God! what brave fellows I must this day lose!" Major Guest commanded the Maryland battalion (the col. and lt. col. being both at York). Capts. Adams and Lucas were sick. The Major, Capt. Ramsay and Lt. Plunket were foremost and within 100 yards of the enemy's muzzles when they were fired on by the enemy, who were chiefly under cover of an orchard, save a few that showed themselves and pretended to give up, clubbing their firelocks till we came within 40 yards, when they immediately presented and blazed in our faces; they entirely overshot us and killed some men away behind in the rear.

I had the satisfaction of dropping one the first fire. I was so near I could not miss. I discharged my rifle 7 times that day.

—Onderdonk, *Revolutionary Incidents*, pp. 147-148.

4. A Common Soldier Has a Snuff of Gunpowder

Narrative of a Continental private.

I remained in New-York two or three months, in which time several things occurred, but so trifling that I shall not mention them. When, sometime in the latter part of August, I was ordered upon a fatigue party, we had scarcely reached the grand parade when I saw our sergeant-major directing his course up Broadway toward us in rather an unusual step for him. He soon arrived and informed us, and then the commanding officer of the party, that he had orders to take off all belonging to our regiment and march us to our quarters, as the regiment was ordered to Long-Island, the British having landed in force there. Although this was not unexpected to me, yet it gave me rather a disagreeable feeling, as I was pretty well assured I should have to snuff a little gunpowder. However I kept my cogitations to myself, went to my quarters, packed up my clothes, and got myself in readiness for the expedition as soon as possible. I then went to the top of the house where I had a full view of that part of the island; I distinctly saw the smoke of the field-artillery, but the distance and the unfavorableness of the wind prevented my hearing their report, at least but faintly.

The horrors of battle there presented themselves to my mind in all their hideousness. I must come to it now, thought I—well, I will endeavor to do my duty as well as I am able and leave the event with Providence. We were soon ordered to our regimental parade, from which, as soon as the regiment was formed, we were marched off for the ferry. At the lower end of the street were placed several casks of sea-bread, made, I believe, of canel and peas-meal, nearly hard enough for musket flints; the casks were unheaded and each man was allowed to take as many as he could as he marched by. As my good luck would have it, there was a momentary halt made; I improved the opportunity thus offered me, as every good soldier should upon all important occasions, to get as many of the biscuit as I possibly could. No one said any thing to me, and I filled my bosom, and took as many as I could hold in my hand, a dozen or more in all, and when we arrived at the ferry-stairs I stowed them away in my knapsack.

We quickly embarked on board of the boats. As each boat started, three cheers were given by those on board, which was returned by the numerous spectators who thronged the wharves; they all wished us good luck apparently; although it was, with most of them, perhaps nothing more than ceremony. We soon landed at Brooklyn, upon the island, marched up the ascent from the ferry to the plain.

We now began to meet the wounded men, another sight I was unacquainted with, some with broken legs and some with broken heads. The sight of these a little daunted me and made me think of home, but the sight and thought vanished together. We marched a short distance when we halted to refresh ourselves. Whether we had any other victuals besides the hard bread I do not remember, but I remember my gnawing at them; they were hard enough to break the teeth of a rat. One of the soldiers complaining of thirst to his officer, "Look at that man," said he, pointing to me; "he is not thirsty,

I will warrant it." I felt a little elevated to be stiled a man. While resting here, which was not more than twenty minutes or half an hour, the Americans and British were warmly engaged within sight of us.

What were the feelings of most or all the young soldiers at this time I know not, but I know what were mine; but let mine or theirs be what they might, I saw a lieutenant who appeared to have feelings not very enviable. Whether he was actuated by fear or the canteen I cannot determine now; I thought it fear at the time, for he ran round among the men of his company, snivelling and blubbering, praying each one if he had aught against him, or if *he* had injured any one, that they would forgive him, declaring at the same time that he, from his heart, forgave them if they had offended him, and I gave him full credit for his assertion, for had he been at the gallows with a halter about his neck, he could not have shown more fear or penitence. A fine soldier you are, I thought, a fine officer, an exemplary man for young soldiers! I would have then suffered anything short of death rather than have made such an exhibition of myself; but, as the poet says,

> "Fear does things so like a witch
> 'Tis hard to distinguish which is which."

The officers of the new levies wore cockades of different colours to distinguish them from the standing forces, as they were called; the field officers wore red, the captains white, and the subaltern officers green. While we were resting here our lieutenant-colonel and major (our colonel not being with us) took their cockades from their hats; being asked the reason, the lieutenant-colonel replied that he was willing to risk his life in the cause of his country, but was unwilling to stand a particular mark for the enemy to fire at. He was a fine officer and a brave soldier.

We were called upon to fall in and proceed. We had not gone far, about half a mile, when I heard one in the rear ask another where his musket was. I looked around and saw one of the soldiers stemming off without his gun, having left it where we last halted; he was inspecting his side as if undetermined whether he had it or not; he then fell out of the ranks to go in search of it. One of the company, who had brought it on (wishing to see how far he would go before he missed it), gave it to him. The reader will naturally enough conclude that he was a brave soldier. Well, he was a brave fellow for all this accident, and received two severe wounds by musket balls while fearlessly fighting for his country at the battle of White Plains. So true is the proverb, "A singed cat may make a good mouser." Stranger things may happen.

We overtook a small party of the artillery here dragging a heavy twelve-pounder upon a field carriage, sinking half way to the naves in the sandy soil. They plead hard for some of us to assist them to get in their piece; our officers, however, paid no attention to their entreaties, but pressed forward towards a creek, where a large party of Americans and British were engaged. By the time we arrived, the enemy had driven our men into the creek, or rather mill-pond (the tide being up), where such as could swim got across; those that could not swim, and could not procure anything to buoy them up, sunk. The British, having several fieldpieces stationed by a brick house, were pouring the cannister and grape upon the Americans like a shower of hail. They would doubtless have done them much more damage than they did but for the twelve-pounder mentioned above; the men, having gotten it within sufficient distance to reach them, and opening a fire upon them, soon obliged them to shift their quarters.

There was in this action a regiment of Maryland troops (volunteers), all young gentlemen. When they came out of the water and mud to us, looking like water rats, it was a truly pitiful sight. Many of them were killed in the pond, and more were drowned. Some of us went into the water after the fall of the tide and took out a number of corpses and a great many arms that were sunk in the pond and creek.

—MARTIN(?), *Narrative*, pp. 18-21.

5. "WE HAVE GIVEN THE REBELS A D——D CRUSH"

Extract of a letter from an officer in General Frazier's battalion.

September 3, 1776

Rejoice, my friend, that we have given the Rebels a d——d crush. We landed on Long-Island the 22d ult., without opposition. On the 27th we had a very warm action, in which the Scots regiments behaved with the greatest bravery and carried the day after an obstinate resistance on the Rebel side. But we flanked and overpowered them with numbers. The Hessians and our brave Highlanders gave no quarters; and it was a fine sight to see with what alacrity they despatched the Rebels with their bayonets after we had surrounded them so that they could not resist. Multitudes were drowned and suffocated in morasses—a proper punishment for all Rebels. Our battalion outmarched all the rest, and was always first up with the Rebel fugitives. A fellow they call Lord Stirling, one of their generals, with two others, is prisoner, and a great many of their officers, men, artillery, and stores. It was a glorious achievement, my friend, and will immortalize us and crush Rebel colonies. Our loss was nothing. We took care to tell the Hessians that the Rebels had resolved to give no quarters to them in particular, which made them fight desperately and put all to death that fell into their hands. You know all stratagems are lawful in war, especially against such vile enemies to their King and country. The island is all ours, and we shall soon take New-York, for the Rebels dare not look us in the face. I expect the affair will be over this campaign, and we shall all return covered with American laurels and have the cream of American lands allotted us for our services.

—FORCE, *American Archives*, 5th Series, I, 1259-1260.

VII. THE WITHDRAWAL TO NEW YORK

After the rout of Sullivan's forces and the capture of Lord Stirling, Howe, with a caution and deliberation that were to become legendary, failed to press his advantage and assault the Brooklyn entrenchments forthwith. He waited until the next day, and thereby threw away the victory. The next day it was too late. Having placed a goodly portion of the main American army on an island where they could be completely sealed off by the British fleet, Washington became alert to the peril and during the night of August 29-30 he man-

aged a masterly withdrawal of Putnam's entire force to New York City. The British victory on Long Island however, though sweeping was indecisive. The Americans suffered some 1,500 casualties at a cost to Howe of only 400 of his own men. But the main American army was still a fighting force.

1. The American Forces Must Be Moved Across the East River

John Morin Scott, Brigadier General from New York, to John Jay, member of the Congress from New York.

New York, September 6, 1776

I shall begin with our retreat from Long Island. For previous to that event the convention was so near the scene of action that they must have been acquainted with every occurrence. I was summoned to a council of war at Mr. Philip Livingston's house on Thursday, 29th ult., never having had reason to expect a proposition for a retreat till it was mentioned. Upon my arrival at the lines on the Tuesday morning before, and just after the enemy, by beating General Sullivan and Lord Stirling, had gained the Heights which in their nature appear to have been more defensible than the lines were, it was obvious to me we could not maintain them for any long time, should the enemy approach us regularly. They were unfinished in several places when I arrived there, and we were obliged hastily to finish them, and you may imagine with very little perfection, particularly across the main road, the most likely for the approach of the enemys heavy artillery.

In this place three of my battalions were placed, the centre of the line in ground so low that the rising ground immediately without it would have put it in the power of a man at 40 yards distance to fire under my horse's belly whenever he pleased. You may judge of our situation, subject to almost incessant rains, without baggage or tents and almost without victuals or drink; and in some part of the lines the men standing up to their middles in water. The enemy were evidently incircling us from water to water with intent to hem us in upon a small neck of land. In this situation they had as perfect a command of the island except the small neck on which we were posted as they now have.

Thus things stood when the retreat was suddenly proposed. I as suddenly objected to it from an aversion to giving the enemy a single inch of ground. But [I] was soon convinced by the unanswerable reasons for it. They were these: Invested by an enemy of about double our number from water to water, scant in almost every necessary of life and without covering and liable every moment to have the communication between us and the city cut off by the entrance of the frigates into the East River between (late) Governor's Island and Long Island; which General McDougall assured us from his own nautic experience was very feasible. In such a situation, we should have been reduced to the alternative of desperately attempting to cut our way [through] a vastly superior enemy with the certain loss of a valuable stock of artiller[y] and artillery stores which the government had been collecting with great pains, or by famine and fatigue been made an easy prey to the enemy. In either case the campaign would have ended in the total ruin of our army. The resolution therefore to retreat was unanimous and tho formed late in the day was executed the following night with unexpected success.

—JAY, *Correspondence and Public Papers*, I, 79-80.

2. COLONEL TALLMADGE RECALLS THE ANXIOUS NIGHT OF AUGUST 29

Account by Benjamin Tallmadge of Connecticut.

This was the first time in my life that I had witnessed the awful scene of a battle [Long Island], when man was engaged to destroy his fellow-man. I well remember my sensations on the occasion, for they were solemn beyond description, and very hardly could I bring my mind to be willing to attempt the life of a fellow-creature. Our army having retired behind their intrenchment, which extended from Vanbrunt's Mills on the west to the East River, flanked occasionally by redoubts, the British army took their position, in full array, directly in front of our position. Our intrenchment was so weak that it is most wonderful the British general did not attempt to storm it soon after the battle in which his troops had been victorious.

Gen. Washington was so fully aware of the perilous situation of this division of his army that he immediately convened a council of war, at which the propriety of retiring to New York was decided on. After sustaining incessant fatigue and constant watchfulness for two days and nights, attended by heavy rain, exposed every moment to an attack from a vastly superior force in front, and to be cut off from the possibility of a retreat to New York by the fleet which might enter the East River, on the night of the 29th of August Gen. Washington commenced recrossing his troops from Brooklyn to New York.

To move so large a body of troops, with all their necessary appendages, across a river a full mile wide, with a rapid current, in the face of a victorious, well disciplined army nearly three times as numerous as his own, and a fleet capable of stopping the navigation so that not one boat could have passed over, seemed to present most formidable obstacles. But in face of these difficulties, the Commander-in-Chief so arranged his business that on the evening of the 29th, by 10 o'clock, the troops began to retire from the lines in such a manner that no chasm was made in the lines, but as one regiment left their station on guard, the remaining troops moved to the right and left and filled up the vacancies, while Gen. Washington took his station at the ferry and superintended the embarkation of the troops.

It was one of the most anxious, busy nights that I ever recollect, and being the third in which hardly any of us had closed our eyes in sleep, we were all greatly fatigued. As the dawn of the next day approached, those of us who remained in the trenches became very anxious for our own safety, and when the dawn appeared there were several regiments still on duty. At this time a very dense fog began to rise, and it seemed to settle in a peculiar manner over both encampments. I recollect this peculiar providential occurrence perfectly well; and so very dense was the atmosphere that I could scarcely discern a man at six yards' distance.

When the sun rose we had just received orders to leave the lines, but before we reached the ferry, the Commander-in-Chief sent one of his aids to order the regiment to repair again to their former station on the lines. Col. Chester immediately faced to the right about and returned, where we tarried until the sun had risen, but the fog remained as dense as ever. Finally, the second order arrived for the regiment to retire, and we very joyfully bid those trenches a long adieu. When we reached Brooklyn ferry, the boats had not returned from their last trip, but they very soon appeared and took the whole regiment over to New York; and I think I saw Gen. Washington on the ferry stairs when I stepped into one of the last boats that received the troops. I left my horse tied to a post at the ferry.

The troops having now all safely reached New York, and the fog continuing as thick as ever, I began to think of my favorite horse and requested leave of volunteers to go with me, and guiding the boat myself, I obtained my horse and got off some distance into the river before the enemy appeared in Brooklyn.

As soon as they reached the ferry we were saluted merrily from their musketry, and finally by their field pieces; but we returned in safety. In the history of warfare I do not recollect a more fortunate retreat. After all, the providential appearance of the fog saved a part of our army from being captured, and certainly myself, among others who formed the rear guard. Gen. Washington has never received the credit which was due to him for this wise and most fortunate measure.

—TALLMADGE, *Memoir*, pp. 11-14.

3. "GOOD GOD! GENERAL MIFFLIN, I AM AFRAID YOU HAVE RUINED US"

Account by General Edward Hand.

In the evening of the 29th of August, 1776, with several other commanding officers of corps, I received orders to attend Major-General Mifflin. When assembled, General Mifflin informed us that in consequence of the determination of a board of general officers, the evacuation of Long Island, where we then were, was to be attempted that night; that the commander-in-chief had honored him with the command of the covering party, and that our corps were to be employed in that service. He then assigned us our several stations, which we were to occupy as soon as it was dark, and pointed out Brooklyn Church as an alarm-post to which the whole were to repair and unitedly oppose the enemy in case they discovered our movements and made an attack in consequence. My regiment was posted in a redoubt on the left and in the lines on the right of the great road below Brooklyn Church. Captain Henry Miller commanded in the redoubt. Part of a regiment of the flying camp of the State of New York were, in the beginning of the night, posted near me; they showed so much uneasiness at their situation that I petitioned General Mifflin to suffer them to march off, lest they might communicate the panic with which they were seized to my people. The general granted my request, and they marched off accordingly.

After that, nothing remarkable happened at my post till about two o'clock in the morning, when Alexander Scammell, since adjutant general, who that day acted as aid-de-camp to the commander-in-chief, came from the left, inquiring for General Mifflin, who happened to be with me at the time. Scammell told him that the boats were waiting, and the commander-in-chief anxious for the arrival of the troops at the ferry. General Mifflin said he thought he must be mistaken, that he did not imagine the General could mean the troops he immediately commanded. Scammell replied he was not mistaken, adding that he came from the extreme left, had ordered all the troops he had met to march; that in consequence they were then in motion, and that he would go on and give the same orders. General Mifflin then ordered me to call my advance picquets and sentinels, to collect and form my regiment, and to march as soon as possible, and quitted me.

Having marched into the great road leading to the church, I fell in with the troops returning from the left of the lines. Having arrived at the church, I halted to take up my camp equipage, which, in the course of the night, I had carried there by a small party. General Mifflin came up at the instant and asked the reason of the halt. I told him, and he seemed very much displeased, and exclaimed: "D——n your pots and kettles! I wish the devil had them! March on!"

I obeyed, but had not gone far before I perceived the front had halted, and hastening to inquire the cause, I met the commander-in-chief, who perceived me and said: "Is not that Colonel Hand?" I answered in the affirmative. His Excellency said he was surprised at me in particular; that he did not expect I would have abandoned my post. I answered that I had not abandoned it; that I had marched by order of my immediate commanding officer. He said it was impossible. I told him I hoped, if I could satisfy him I had the orders of General Mifflin, he would not think me particularly to blame. He said he undoubtedly would not.

General Mifflin just then coming up, and asking what the matter was, His Excellency said: "Good God! General Mifflin, I am afraid you have ruined us by so unseasonably withdrawing the troops from the lines."

General Mifflin replied with some warmth: "I did it by your order."

His Excellency declared it could not be.

General Mifflin swore: "By God, I did," and asked: "Did Scammell act as an aid-de-camp for the day, or did he not?"

His Excellency acknowledged he did.

"Then," said Mifflin, "I had orders through him."

The General replied it was a dreadful mistake, and informed him that matters were in much confusion at the ferry, and, unless we could resume our posts before the enemy discovered we had left them, in all probability the most disagreeable consequences would follow. We immediately returned, and had the good fortune to recover our former stations and keep them for some hours longer without the enemy perceiving what was going forward.

—HAND PAPERS, *Pennsylvania Archives*, 2nd Series, X, 308-309.

4. THE BRITISH LOOK ACROSS AT THE PROMISED LAND

Journal of Sir George Collier, Commander of the *Rainbow*.

The enemy's loss in killed and wounded, in the different skirmishes on Long Island, was about 4,000 men. Amongst the prisoners were two of their generals—one named Sullivan, who had been bred a lawyer; the other calling himself Lord Stirling. About 6,000 rebels, commanded by old Gates, fled across the water, who might all have been taken prisoners, had our troops been *suffered* to push on, or even if the men-of-war had proceeded to attack the batteries, as by getting into the East River they would have prevented boats from passing. Washington's army, with this reinforcement, amounted to 11,000 men; ours was at least double that number. As fresh reinforcements from Staten Island had joined the general, the men-of-war had moved gradually up as the troops advanced, and when the latter got to the margin of the East River (which was about half a mile across), the ships anchored just out of gunshot of the batteries of New York.

The having to deal with a generous, merciful, *forbearing* enemy, who would take no unfair *advantages*, must surely have been highly satisfactory to General Washington, and he was certainly very deficient in not expressing his gratitude to General Howe for his *kind* behaviour towards him. Far from taking the rash resolution of *hastily passing* over the East River after Gates and *crushing at once* a frightened, trembling enemy, he generously gave them time to recover from their panic, to throw up *fresh works*, to make new arrangements, and to recover from the torpid state the rebellion appeared in from its late shock.

For *many succeeding* days did our brave veterans, consisting of twenty-two thousand men, stand on the banks of the East River, like Moses on Mount Pisgah, looking at their promised land, little more than half a mile distant. The rebel's standards waved insolently in the air from many different quarters of New York. The British troops could scarcely contain their indignation at the sight and at their own *inactivity;* the officers were *displeased and amazed,* not being able to account for the strange delay. Gates fled across the river on the 29th August. The *Rainbow* (with Sir George Collier) went to sea from thence on another service on the 8th September, at which time the royal army still remained on the *same spot* inactive, and without making any motions whatever. . . .

—COLLIER, "Journal," *Long Island Hist. Soc. Memoirs,*
II (1869), 413-414.

VIII. THE FUTILE MISSION OF THE HOWES: THE NEGOTIATIONS WITH MEMBERS OF CONGRESS

In his unpublished memoirs Allen McLane, a dashing American cavalry officer, observed that "if independence had not been declared before the battle of the 27th, it is the opinion of the writer that it would not have been declared." This opinion was obviously held by Sir William Howe, who felt that the Americans after the rout on Long Island might now be ready to sit down at the table and adjust their grievances, and who, in the order of priorities, placed conciliation ahead of decisive victory on the field of battle.

Delaying precious weeks before crossing over to Manhattan in pursuit of Washington, Sir William and his brother, Lord Richard, sought out members of the rebel Congress. That their efforts were foredoomed to failure should have been apparent from Benjamin Franklin's crushing reply on July 20. Nevertheless, Congress felt that the possibility of conciliation should at least be explored. It dispatched three committeemen—Franklin, John Adams and Rutledge—to Staten Island, who, after hearing out Lord Howe, reported to Congress that the admiral's authority did not go beyond extending pardons and making recommendations to the Ministry. "We apprehended any expectation from the effects of such a power would have been too uncertain and precarious to be relied on by America, had she still continued in her state of dependence," they concluded.

1. "Injuries Have Extinguished Every Spark of Affection"

Benjamin Franklin to Lord Howe.

Philadelphia, 20 July, 1776

My Lord:—I received safe the letters your lordship so kindly forwarded to me, and beg you to accept my thanks.

The official despatches, to which you refer me, contain nothing more than what we had seen in the act of Parliament, viz., offers of pardon upon submission, which I am sorry to find, as it must give your lordship pain to be sent so far on so hopeless a business. Directing pardons to be offered the colonies, who are the very parties injured, expresses indeed that opinion of our ignorance, baseness, and insensibility, which your uninformed and proud nation has long been pleased to entertain of us; but it can have no other effect than that of increasing our resentment.

It is impossible we should think of submission to a government that has with the most wanton barbarity and cruelty burnt our defenceless towns in the midst of winter, excited the savages to massacre our farmers, and our slaves to murder their masters, and is even now bringing foreign mercenaries to deluge our settlements with blood. These atrocious injuries have extinguished every remaining spark of affection for that parent country we once held so dear; but, were it possible for *us* to forget and forgive them, it is not possible for *you* (I mean the British nation) to forgive the people you have so heavily injured. You can never confide again in those as fellow-subjects, and permit them to enjoy equal freedom, to whom you know you have given such just cause of lasting enmity. And this must impel you, were we again under your government, to endeavor the breaking of our spirit by the severest tyranny, and obstructing, by every means in your power, our growing strength and prosperity.

But your lordship mentions "the king's paternal solicitude for promoting the establishment of lasting *peace* and union with the colonies." If by peace is here meant a peace to be entered into between Britain and America, as distinct states now at war, and his Majesty has given your lordship powers to treat with us of such a peace, I may venture to say, though without authority, that I think a treaty for that purpose not yet quite impracticable, before we enter into foreign alliances. But I am persuaded you have no such powers. Your nation, though, by punishing those American governors who have created and fomented the discord, rebuilding our burnt towns, and repairing as far as possible the mischiefs done us, might yet recover a great share of our regard and the greatest part of our growing commerce, with all the advantage of that additional strength to be derived from a friendship with us; but I know too well her abounding pride and deficient wisdom, to believe she will ever take such salutary measures. Her fondness for conquest, as a warlike nation, her lust of dominion as an ambitious one, and her thirst for a gainful monopoly as a commercial one (none of them legitimate causes of war), will all join to hide from her eyes every view of her true interests, and continually goad her on in those ruinous distant expeditions, as destructive both of lives and treasure, that must prove as pernicious to her in the end as the crusades formerly were to most of the nations of Europe.

I have not the vanity, my lord, to think of intimidating by thus predicting the effects of this war; for I know it will in England have the fate of all my former predictions, not to be believed till the event shall verify it.

Long did I endeavor, with unfeigned and unwearied zeal, to preserve from breaking that fine and noble china vase, the British empire; for I knew that, being once broken, the separate parts could not retain even their share of the strength or value that existed in the whole, and that a perfect reunion of those parts could scarce ever be hoped for. Your Lordship may possibly remember the tears of joy that wet my cheek, when, at your good sister's in London, you once gave me expectations that a reconciliation might soon take place. I had the misfortune to find those expectations disappointed, and to be treated as the cause of the mischief I was laboring to prevent. My consolation under that groundless and malevolent treatment was that I retained the friendship of many wise and good men in that country, and, among the rest, some share in the regard of Lord Howe.

The well-founded esteem and, permit me to say, affection, which I shall always have for your lordship, makes it painful to me to see you engaged in conducting a war, the great ground of which, as expressed in your letter, is "the necessity of preventing the American trade from passing into foreign channels." To me it seems that neither the obtaining or retaining of any trade, how valuable soever, is an object for which men may justly spill each other's blood; that the true and sure means of extending and securing commerce is the goodness and cheapness of commodities; and that the profit of no trade can ever be equal to the expense of compelling it, and of holding it, by fleets and armies.

I consider this war against us, therefore, as both unjust and unwise; and I am persuaded that cool, dispassionate posterity will condemn to infamy those who advised it; and that even success will not save from some degree of dishonor those who voluntarily engaged to conduct it. I know your great motive in coming hither was the hope of being instrumental in a reconciliation; and I believe, when you find *that* impossible on any terms given you to propose, you will relinquish so odious a command, and return to a more honorable private station.

With the greatest and most sincere respect, I have the honor to be, my Lord, your Lordship's most obedient humble servant, . . .

—Bigelow, ed., *Works of Franklin*, VI, 23-27.

2. LORD HOWE STATES THE CASE FOR SUBMISSION

Notes of Henry Strachey, secretary to Lord Howe, with his interpolations in parentheses.

September 11, 1776

Lord Howe received the gentlemen on the beach—Dr. Franklin introduced Mr. Adams and Mr. Rutledge—Lord Howe very politely expressed the sense he entertained of the confidence they had placed in him by thus putting themselves in his hands——

A general and immaterial conversation from the beach to the house—the Hessian guard saluted, as they passed——

A cold dinner was on the table—dined—the Hessian colonel present—immediately after dinner he retired.

Lord Howe informed them it was long since he had entertained an opinion that the differences between the two countries might be accommodated to the satisfaction of both—that he was known to be a well wisher to America—particularly to the Province of Massachusetts Bay, which had endeared itself to him by the very high honors it had bestowed upon the memory of his eldest brother—that his going out as Commissioner from the King had been early mentioned, but that afterwards for some time he had heard no more of it—that an idea had then arisen of sending several Commissioners, to which he had objected—that his wish was to go out singly and with a Civil Commission only, in which case his plan was to have gone immediately to Philadelphia—that he had even objected to his brother's being on the Commission, from the delicacy of the situation and his desire to take upon himself all the reproach that might be the consequence of it—that it was however thought necessary that the general should be joined in the Commission for reasons which he explained (having their hands upon the two services)—and that he, Lord Howe, should also have the naval command, in which he had acquiesced—that he had hoped to reach America before the army had moved, and did not doubt but if their disposition had been the same as expressed in their Petition to the King, he should have been able to have brought about an accommodation to the satisfaction of both countries—that he thought the Petition was a sufficient basis to confer upon—that it contained matter which with candour and discussion might be wrought into a plan of permanency—that the Address to the People, which accompanied the Petition to His Majesty, tended to destroy the good effects that might otherwise have been hoped for from the Petition—that he had however still flattered himself that upon the grounds of the Petition he should be able to do some good——

[Mr. Rutledge mentioned (by way of answer to Lord Howe's remark upon that point) that their Petition to the King contained all which they thought was proper to be addressed to His Majesty—that the other matters which could not come under the head of a Petition, and therefore could not with propriety be inserted, were put into the Address to the People, which was only calculated to shew them the importance of America to Great Britain—

and that the Petition to the King was by all of them meant to be respectful.]

That they themselves had changed the ground since he left England by their Declaration of Independency, which, if it could not be got over, precluded him from all treaty, as they must know, and he had explicitly said so in his letter to Dr. Franklin, that he had not, nor did he expect ever to have, powers to consider the Colonies in the light of Independent States—that they must also be sensible that he could not confer with them as a Congress—that he could not acknowledge that body which was not acknowledged by the King, whose delegate he was; neither, for the same reason, could he confer with these gentlemen as a Committee of the Congress—that if they would not lay aside that distinction, it would be improper for him to proceed—that he thought it an unessential form, which might for the present lie dormant—that they must give him leave to consider them merely as gentlemen of great ability and influence in the country—and that they were now met to converse together upon the subject of differences, and to try if any outline could be drawn to put a stop to the calamities of war, and to bring forward some plan that might be satisfactory both to America and to England. He desired them to consider the delicacy of his situation—the reproach he was liable to, if he should be understood by any step of his to acknowledge or to treat with the Congress—that he hoped they would not by any implication commit him upon that point—that he was rather going beyond his powers in the present meeting——

[Dr. Franklin said, "You may depend upon our taking care of that, my Lord."]

That he thought the idea of a Congress might easily be thrown out of the question at present, for that if matters could be so settled that the King's government should be re-established, the Congress would of course cease to exist, and if they meant such accommodation, they must see how unnecessary and useless it was to stand upon that form which they knew they were to give up upon the restoration of legal government——

[Dr. Franklin said that His Lordship might consider the gentlemen present in any view he thought proper—that they were also at liberty to consider themselves in their real character—there was no necessity on this occasion to distinguish between the Congress and individuals—and that the conversation might be held as amongst friends.

The two other gentlemen assented, in very few words, to what the Doctor had said.]

Lord Howe then proceeded—that on his arrival in this country he had thought it expedient to issue a Declaration, which they had done him the honor to comment upon—that he had endeavored to couch it in such terms as would be the least exceptionable—that he had concluded they must have judged he had not expressed in it all he had to say, though enough, he thought, to bring on a discussion which might lead the way to accommodation—that their Declaration of Independency had since rendered him the more cautious of opening himself—that it was absolutely impossible for him to treat, or confer, upon that ground, or to admit the idea in the smallest degree—that he flattered himself if that were given up, there was still room for him to effect the King's purposes—that his Majesty's most earnest desire was to make his American subjects happy, to cause a reform in whatever affected the freedom of their legislation, and to concur with his Parliament in the redress of any real grievances—that his powers were, generally, to restore peace and grant pardons, to attend to complaints and representations, and to confer upon means of establishing a re-union upon terms honorable and advantageous to the colonies as well as to Great Britain—that they knew we expected aid from America—that the dispute seemed to be only concerning the mode of obtaining it——

[Doctor Franklin here said, "*That* we never refused, *upon requisition.*"]

Lord Howe continued—that their money was the smallest consideration—that America could produce more solid advantages to Great Britain—that it was her commerce, her strength, her men, that we chiefly wanted——

[Here Dr. Franklin said with rather a sneering laugh, "Ay, my Lord, we have a pretty considerable manufactory of men"—alluding as it should seem to their numerous army. Marginal notation of Lord Howe: "No—to their increasing population."]

Lord Howe continued: "It is desirable to put a stop to these ruinous extremities, as well for the sake of our country as yours—when an American falls, England feels it. Is there no way of treading back this step of Independency, and opening the door to a full discussion?"

Lord Howe concluded with saying that having thus opened to them the general purport of the Commisson, and the King's disposition to a permanent peace, he must stop to hear what they might chuse to observe.

Dr. Franklin said he supposed His Lordship had seen the Resolution of the Congress which had sent them hither—that the Resolution contained the whole of their Commission—that if this conversation was productive of no immediate good effect, it might be of service at a future time—that America had considered the Prohibitory Act as the answer to her Petition to the King—forces had been sent out, and towns destroyed—that they could not expect happiness now under the *domination* of Great Britain—that all former attachment was *obliterated*—that America could not return again to the domination of Great Britain, and therefore imagined that Great Britain meant to rest it upon force—the other gentlemen will deliver their sentiments——

Mr. Adams said that he had no objection to Lord Howe's considering him, on the present occasion, merely as a private gentleman, or in any character except that of a British subject—that the Resolution of the Congress to declare the Independency was not taken up upon their own authority—that they had been instructed so to do by *all* the Colonies—and that it was not in their power to treat otherwise than as independent States. He mentioned warmly his own determination not to depart from the idea of Independency, and spoke in the common way of the power of the Crown, which was comprehended in the ideal power of Lords and Commons.

Mr. Rutledge began by saying he had been one of the oldest Members of the Congress—that he had been one from the beginning—that he thought it was worth the consideration of Great Britain whether she would not receive greater advantages by an alliance with the Colonies as independent States than she had ever hitherto done—that she might still enjoy *a great share* of the commerce—that she would have their raw materials for her manufactures—that they could protect the West India Islands much more effectively and more easily than she can—that they could assist her in the Newfoundland trade—that he was glad this conversation had happened, as it would be the occasion of opening to Great Britain the consideration of the advantages she might derive from America by an alliance with her as an independent State, before anything is settled with other foreign powers—that it was impossible the people should consent to come again under the English government—he could answer for South Carolina—that government had been very oppressive—that the Crown officers had claimed privilege and confined people upon pretense of a breach of privilege—that they had at last taken the government into their own hands—that the people were now settled and happy under that government and would not (even if they, the Congress, could desire it) return to the King's government——

Lord Howe said that if such were their sentiments, he could only lament it was not in his power to bring about the accommodation he wished—that he had not authority, nor did he expect he ever should have, to treat with the Colonies as States independent of the Crown of Great Britain—and that he was sorry the gentlemen had had the trouble of coming so far, to so little purpose—that if the Colonies would not give up the system of Independency, it was impossible for him to enter into any negociation——

Dr. Franklin observed that it would take as much time for them to refer to and get an answer from their constituents as it would the Commissioners to get fresh instructions from home, which he supposed might be done in about 3 months——

Lord Howe replied it was in vain to think of his receiving instructions to treat upon that ground——

After a little pause, Dr. Franklin suddenly said, "Well, my Lord, as America is to expect nothing but upon total unconditional submission——"

[Lord Howe interrupted the Doctor at the word submission—said that Great Britain did not require unconditional submission, that he thought what he had already said to them proved the contrary, and desired the gentlemen would not go away with such an idea——

Memorandum—Perhaps Dr. Franklin meant submission to the Crown, in opposition to their Principle of Independency.]

"—And Your Lordship has no proposition to make us, give me leave to ask whether, if we should make propositions to Great Britain (not that I know or am authorized to say we shall), you would receive and transmit them."

Lord Howe said he did not know that he could avoid receiving any papers that might be put into his hands—seemed rather doubtful about the propriety of transmitting home, but did not say that he would decline it.

—Ford, ed., "Howe's Commission to Pacify the Colonies,"
Atlantic Monthly, LXXVII, 759-762.

3. John Adams Learns That He Is Marked Out for Punishment

From the Autobiography.

Monday, September 9, 1776

There were a few circumstances which appear neither in the Journals of Congress nor in my letters, which may be thought by some worth preserving. Lord Howe had sent over an officer as a hostage for our security. I said to Dr. Franklin, it would be childish in us to depend upon such a pledge, and insisted on taking him over with us and keeping our surety on the same side of the water with us. My colleagues exulted in the proposition and agreed to it instantly. We told the officer, if he held himself under our direction, he must go back with us. He bowed assent, and we all embarked in his lordship's barge. As we approached the shore, his lordship, observing us, came down to the water's edge to receive us, and, looking at the officer, he said, "Gentlemen, you make me a very high compliment, and you may depend upon it I will consider it as the most sacred of things." We walked up to the house between lines of guards of grenadiers, looking fierce as ten Furies, and making all the grimaces, and gestures, and motions of their muskets, with bayonets fixed, which, I suppose, military etiquette requires, but which we neither understood nor regarded.

The house had been the habitation of military guards and was as dirty as a stable; but his lordship had prepared a large handsome room by spreading a carpet of moss and green sprigs from bushes and shrubs in the neighborhood, till he had made it not only wholesome, but romantically elegant; and he entertained us with good claret, good bread, cold ham, tongues and mutton. . . .

Two or three circumstances which are omitted in this report and, indeed, not thought worth notice in any of my private letters, I afterwards found circulated in Europe, and oftener repeated than any other part of this whole transaction. Lord Howe was profuse in his expressions of gratitude to the state of Massachusetts for erecting a marble monument in Westminster Abbey to his elder brother, Lord Howe, who was killed in America in the last French war, saying, "he esteemed that honor to his family *above all things in this world*. That such was his gratitude and affection to this country, on that account, that he felt for America as for a brother, and, if America should fall, he should feel and lament it like the loss of a brother."

Dr. Franklin, with an easy air and a collected countenance, a bow, a smile and all that *naïveté* which sometimes appeared in his conversation and is often observed in his writings, replied, "My Lord, we will do our utmost endeavors to save your lordship that mortification."

His lordship appeared to feel this with more sensibility than I could expect; but he only returned, "I suppose you will endeavor to give us employment in Europe." To this observation, not a word, nor a look, from which he could draw any inference, escaped any of the committee.

Another circumstance, of no more importance than the former, was so much celebrated in Europe that it has often reminded me of the question of Phocion to his fellow-citizens, when something he had said in public was received by the people of Athens with clamorous applause: "Have I said any foolish thing?" When his lordship observed to us that he could not confer with us as members of Congress or public characters, but only as private persons and British subjects, Mr. John Adams answered somewhat quickly, "Your lordship may consider me in what light you please, and, indeed, I should be willing to consider myself, for a few moments, in any character which would be agreeable to your lordship, *except that of a British subject.*"

His lordship, at these words, turned to Dr. Franklin and Mr. Rutledge and said, "Mr. Adams is a decided character," with so much gravity and solemnity that I now believe it meant more than either of my colleagues, or myself, understood at the time.

In our report to Congress, we supposed that the commissioners, Lord and General Howe, had, by their commission, power to except from pardon all that they should think proper; but I was informed in England afterwards that a number were expressly excepted, by name, from pardon, by the Privy Council, and that John Adams was one of them, and that this list of exceptions was given as an instruction to the two Howes with their commission. When I was afterwards a minister plenipotentiary at the Court of St. James, the king and the ministry were often insulted, ridiculed and reproached in the newspapers for having conducted themselves with so much folly as to be reduced to the humiliating necessity of receiving, as an ambassador, a man who stood recorded by the Privy Council as a rebel expressly excepted from pardon.

If this is true, it will account for his lordship's gloomy denunciation of me as "a decided character."

—ADAMS, ed., *Works of John Adams*, III, 77-80.

IX. AWAITING THE ATTACK

To Nicholas Cresswell, an English traveler in New York, it was inconceivable that the British could be beaten or halted by an undisciplined mob such as the American army appeared to be. Washington and his staff shared something of this pessimism. General Greene, John Jay and other Patriots urged that Washington burn New York to prevent it from serving as winter headquarters for the British or as garrison and refuge for the Loyalists who swarmed into it. Washington was unable to obtain authorization from the Congress for so drastic an act, and decided that he must pull most of his forces out of the city and off Manhattan Island.

1. GREENE URGES WASHINGTON TO BURN NEW YORK CITY

Nathanael Greene to George Washington.

Kingsbridge, New-York Island, September 5, 1776

The critical situation which the army is in, will, I hope, sufficiently apologize for my troubling your Excellency with this letter. The sentiments are dictated, I am sure, by an honest mind—a mind which feels deeply interested in the salvation of this country, and for the honour and reputation of the General under whom he serves.

The object under consideration is whether a general and speedy retreat from this island is necessary or not. To me it appears the only eligible plan to oppose the enemy successfully and secure ourselves from disgrace. I think we have no object on this side of King's Bridge. Our troops are now so scattered that one part may be cut off before the others can come to their support. In this situation, suppose the enemy should run up the North River several ships of force and a number of transports at the same time, and effect a landing between the town and middle division of the army; another party from Long-Island should land right opposite; these two parties form a line across the island, and entrench themselves. The two flanks of this line could be easily supported by the shipping; the center, fortified with the redoubts, would render it very difficult if not impossible to cut our way through.

At the time the enemy are executing this movement or manoeuvre, they will be able to make sufficient diversions, if not real lodgments, to render it impossible for the centre and upper divisions of the army to afford any assistance here. Should this event take place (and by the by, I don't think it very improbable), your Excellency will be reduced to that situation which every prudent general would wish to avoid—that is, of being obliged to fight the enemy to a disadvantage, or submit.

It has been agreed that the city of New-York would not be tenable if the enemy got possession of Long-Island and Governour's Island. They are now in possession of both these places. Notwithstanding, I think we might hold it for some time, but the annoyance must be so great as to render it an unfit place to quarter troops in. If we should hold it, we must hold it to a great disadvantage.

The city and island of New-York are no objects for us; we are not to bring them into competition with the general interests of America. Part of the army already has met with a defeat; the country is struck with a panick; any capital loss at this time may ruin the cause. 'Tis our business to study to avoid any considerable misfortune, and to take post where the enemy will be obliged to fight us, and not we them.

The sacrifice of the vast property of New-York and the suburbs I hope has no influence upon your Excellency's measures. Remember the King of France. When Charles the Fifth, Emperor of Germany, invaded his kingdom, he laid whole provinces waste, and by that policy he starved and ruined Charles' army and defeated him without fighting a battle. Two-thirds of the property of the city of New-York and the suburbs belongs to the Tories. We have no very great reason to run any considerable risk for its defence. If we attempt to hold the city and island, and should not be able finally, we shall be wasting time unnecessarily and betray a defect of judgment, if no worse misfortune attend it.

I give it as my opinion that a general and speedy retreat is absolutely necessary, and that the honour and interest of America require it. I would burn the city and suburbs, and that for the following reasons: If the enemy gets possession of the city, we never can recover the possession without a superior naval force to theirs; it will deprive the enemy of an opportunity of barracking their whole army together, which, if they could do, would be a very great security. It will deprive them of a general market; the price of things would prove a temptation to our people to supply them for the sake of grain, in direct violation of the laws of their country.

All these advantages would result from the destruction of the city, and not one benefit can arise to us from its preservation that I can conceive of. If the city once gets into the enemy's hands, it will be at their mercy either to save or destroy it, after they have made what use of it they think proper. . . .

—Force, *American Archives*, 5th Series, II, 182-183.

2. "Between Hawk and Buzzard"

Joseph Reed, Washington's Adjutant General, to his wife.

New York, September 6, 1776

I have wrote you twice this week but whether my letters can reach you or not I dont know—I hope they do, as they will serve to keep up your spirits in our critical situation. We are still here in a posture somewhat awkward; we think (at least I do) that we cannot stay and yet we do not know how to go—so that we may be properly said to be between hawk and buzzard.

To attempt a description of all the circumstances which attend us would take more time than I can spare nor would it give you any great consolation. Our comfort is that the season is far advanced, and if a sacrifice of us can save the cause of America there will be time to collect another army before spring and the country be preserved. The councils of the Congress seem to be dark and intricate and very badly calculated to raise or continue an army from which substantial benefit can be derived.

My sensations are too acute and forebodings too strong for such a service, tho I do not find my spirits sink under difficulties but rather rise. I sometimes think my mind a very particular one. It rises when those of others fall and suffers by anticipating the apprehended evil. To use the modern phrase, I have made it up for whatever may happen and feel no other concern than what arises from reflections on you and our dear little folks. And even these I get rid of as soon as possible for it can only unfit me for duty without doing you any service. It is impossible under such circumstances not to have and feel some dependence on Providence. . . .

When I look around and see how few of the numbers who talked so largely of death and honour [are] around me, and those who are here are those from whom it could least be expected, such as the Tilghmans, etc., I am lost in wonder and surprize. Some of our Philadelphia gentlemen who came over on visits, upon the first cannon shot went off in a most violent hurry. Your noisy Sons of Liberty I find are the quietest on the field. . . . The motions of the enemy are very dark and mysterious. Such another surprize would do us much mischief.

I send enclosed a list of such officers as have sent out for their baggage and are certainly prisoners—I suppose there are others whom we shall hear of. I am glad Atlee is safe because every body allows he behaved well. An engagement or even an expectation of one gives a wonderful insight into the characters of men . . . but we are young soldiers——

—Reed Papers, IV, 57, N. Y. Hist. Soc.

3. "If My Countrymen Are Beaten by These Ragamuffins!"

Journal of Nicholas Cresswell.

New York, Saturday, September 7th, 1776. Left Newark. Crossed Passihack or Second River, then Hackensack River, then North River at Powlershook Ferry. River about 1½ miles wide. Landed in New York about nine o'clock, when one Collins, an Irish merchant, and myself rambled about the town till three in the afternoon before we could get anything for breakfast. At length we found a little Dutch tippling house and persuaded the old woman to get us something to eat. It was a stew of pork bones and cabbage so full of garlic, nothing but necessity would have compelled me to eat it; my companion would not taste another mouthful. Nothing to be got here. All the inhabitants are moved out. The town full of soldiers. Viewing the town and fortifications and contriving means to effect my escape, but despair of it, the rivers are too well guarded. . . .

Newark, New Jersey—Sunday, September 8th, 1776. Left New York early this morning. Crossed the North River to Powlershook. While we waited for the stage, viewed the *Sleber* fortifications here. They are made of earth, but what number of guns or what size I cannot tell. No admittance into the fort. The troops stationed here are Yankee men, the nastiest devils in creation. It would be impossible for any human creature whose organs of smelling was more delicate than that of a hog to live one day under the lee of this camp, such a complication of stinks. Saw a Yankee put a pint of molasses into about a gallon of mutton broth. The army here is numerous, but ragged, dirty, sickly and ill-disciplined. If my countrymen are beaten by these ragamuffins I shall be much surprized. Their fleet is large and it is said their army is numerous. New York must fall into their hands, their batteries on Long Island command the town. Heard a smart cannonade crossing the ferry this morning, supposed to be at Hellgate. The fleet is within 2 miles of the town. Got to Newark to dinner. Great scarcity of provisions, the roads full of soldiers. Very uneasy. Must be obliged to go into Canada or stay in this d––d country.

—Cresswell, *Journal*, pp. 157-159.

4. Washington Explains the Decision to Abandon New York

To the President of Congress.

New York, Head Quarters, September 8, 1776

It is now extremely obvious, from all Intelligence, from their movements and every other circumstance, that having landed their whole Army on Long-Island, (except about 4000, on Staten-Island) they mean to enclose us on the Island of New-York by taking post in our Rear, while the Shipping effectually secure the Front, and thus either by cutting off our communication with the Country, oblige us to fight them on their own Terms, or surrender at discretion, or by a brilliant Stroke endeavour to cut this Army in pieces and secure the Collection of Arms and Stores which they well know we shall not be soon able to replace.

Having therefore their System unfolded to us, it became an important consideration how it could be most successfully opposed. On every side there is a Choice of difficulties and every Measure on our part (however painful the reflection is from experience) to be formed with some Apprehension that all our Troops will not do their duty.

In deliberating on this Question it was impossible to forget, that History, our own experience, the advice of our ablest Friends in Europe, the fears of the Enemy, and even the Declarations of Congress demonstrate, that on our Side the War should be defensive. It has even been called a War of Posts. That we should on all occasions avoid a general Action, or put anything to the Risque, unless compelled by a necessity, into which we ought never to be drawn.

The Arguments on which such a System was founded were deemed unanswerable and experience has given her sanction. With these views, and being fully persuaded that it would be presumption to draw out our Young Troops into open ground, against their Superiors both in number and Discipline; I have never spared the Spade and Pick Axe; I confess I have not found that readiness to defend even strong Posts, at all hazards, which is necessary to derive the greatest benefit from them. The honor of making a brave defence does not seem to be a sufficient stimulus, when the success is very doubtful, and the falling into the Enemy's hands probable. But I doubt not this will be gradually attained.

We are now in a strong Post, but not an Impregnable one, nay acknowledged by every man of Judgment to be untenable, unless the Enemy will make the Attack upon Lines, when they can avoid it and their Movements indicate that they mean to do so. To draw the whole Army together in order to arrange the defence proportionate to the extent of Lines and works, would leave the Country open to an Approach, and put the fate of this Army and its Stores on the hazard of making a successful defence in the City, or the Issue of an Engagement out of it. On the other hand to abandon a City, which has been by some deemed defensible and on whose Works much Labour has been bestowed, has a tendency to dispirit the Troops and enfeeble our Cause. It has also been considered as the Key to the Northern Country. But as to this I am fully of opinion, that by Establishing of strong posts at Mount Washington on the upper part of this Island and on the Jersey side opposite to it, with the Assistance of the Obstructions already made and which may be improved in the Water, that not only the navigation of Hudson's River but an easier and better communication, may be effectually secured between the Northern and Southern States. This I believe every one acquainted with the situation of the Country will readily agree to, and will appear evident to those who have an Opportunity of recuring to good maps. These and the many other consequences, which will be involved in the determination of our next measure, have given our Minds full employ and led every one to form a Judgement as the various objects presented themselves to his view. . . .

I am sensible a retreating Army is incircled with difficulties, that the declining an Engagement subjects a General to reproach and that the common Cause may be in some measure affected by the discouragements which it throws over the minds of many; nor am I insensible of the contrary effects, if a brilliant stroke could be made with any Probability of success, especially after our loss upon Long-Island: but when the fate of America may be at stake on the Issue; when the Wisdom of cooler moments and experienced Men have decided that we should protract the War if Possible; I cannot think it safe or wise to adopt a different System, when the season for Action draws so near a close. That the Enemy mean to Winter in New-York there can be no doubt; that with such an Armament they can drive us out is equally clear. The Congress having resolved, that it should not be destroyed, nothing seems to remain but to determine the time of their taking Possession.

It is our Interest and wish to prolong it, as much as possible, provided the delay does not affect our further measures.

—FITZPATRICK, ed., *Writings of Washington*, VI, 27-32.

X. THE EAST RIVER CROSSING AND THE KIP'S BAY ROUT

Anticipating Washington's withdrawal from New York, Howe determined to trap the American army by another flanking move. While the fleet was to bombard the city's front and right flank, the army was to cross over from the present site of Astoria, turn Washington's left flank, cut off his communications, and force him to surrender.

On the eve of the attack, September 13, Howe issued the following order:

> *An attack upon the enemy being shortly intended, the soldiers are reminded of their evident superiority on the 27th August, by charging the rebels with their bayonets even in woods where they had thought themselves invincible.*
>
> *The General therefore recommends to the troops an entire dependence upon their bayonets, with which they will ever command that success which their bravery so well deserves.* (General Howe's Orderly Book, Lloyd W. Smith Collection.)

The crossing began on the evening of the fourteenth. Soon after, under cover of ten warships, Sir Henry Clinton embarked at the mouth of Newtown Creek and landed his men at Kip's Bay, now 34th Street and the East River. The panic-stricken militia were put to rout and the fugitives were pursued to Murray Hill. According to venerated if dubious tradition Howe lingered for nearly two hours at the residence of Mrs. Murray to enjoy her Madeira, and Putnam, at the sacrifice of baggage, stores and most of his artillery, escaped to the American defense line on Harlem Heights.

1. THE BRITISH PLAN TO SEAL OFF WASHINGTON'S FORCES

Diary of Captain Frederick Mackenzie, of the Royal Welsh Fusiliers.

September 9, 1776

Everything indicates that we shall soon attempt something decisive against the Rebels, but considering the nature of the shore at Hellgate, and rapidity of the tides and variety of eddies there, I do not suppose the landing will be made in that place. It appears probable that the erecting batteries against the enemy's works at Hellgate, and making so much demonstration there, is intended to draw their attention from some other point, for owing to the situation and construction of their principal work, it is extremely difficult to destroy it effectually.

The Rebels appeared at first to intend confining the defence of New York Island to that part of it near Kingsbridge, but as by so doing we should have had no chance of destroying or capturing any considerable number of them, it was perhaps thought proper to give them some confidence and induce them to remain and defend New York, and by so doing, give us an opportunity of cutting off a considerable part of their army, which their situation on a long narrow island, without the means of crossing either of the rivers, makes them liable to. They now therefore appear as if they intend to keep possession of New York and prevent our landing. Tis supposed they have not less than 4000 men between Hellgate and New York, with a considerable quantity of artillery.

It is supposed we shall land somewhere about Haerlem, and by taking a position across the island, which is narrow in that part, endeavor to cut off all that part of the rebel army between us and New York, for if some ships go up the North River at the same time it will be almost impossible for any of them to escape. The island in that part affords some very advantageous positions, which would enable us to prevent those near New York from escaping to Kingsbridge, or receiving any assistance from thence. The destruction or capture of a considerable part of the rebel army in this manner would be attended with numerous advantages, as it would impress the remainder with a dread of being surrounded and cut off in every place where they took post, would encrease their discontent, and probably be the means of breaking up the whole of their army, and reducing the Colonies to submission.

It is in our power at any time to drive them from New York and take possession of it, but if we attacked them there, they might set fire to it and once more slip out of our hands. It is of very material consequence to prevent them from burning the town, which will no doubt afford quarters to a considerable part of our army during the ensuing winter, and be made the principal depot of stores, and harbour for our shipping.

—MACKENZIE, *Diary*, I, 41-42.

2. "The British Were Always about Their Deviltry"

Narrative of a Continental private.

One evening, while lying here, we heard a heavy cannonade at the city and before dark saw four of the enemy's ships that had passed the town and were coming up the East River; they anchored just below us. These ships were the *Phoenix*, of forty-four guns; the *Roebuck*, of forty-four; the *Rose*, of thirty-two; and another, the name of which I have forgotten. Half of our regiment was sent off under the command of our major to man something that were called "lines," although they were nothing more than a ditch dug along on the bank of the river, with the dirt thrown out towards the water. They staid in these lines during the night, and returned to camp in the morning unmolested.

The other half of the regiment went the next night, under the command of the lieut. colonel, upon the like errand. We arrived at the lines about dark, and were ordered to leave our packs in a copse wood, under a guard, and go into the lines without them; what was the cause of this piece of *wise* policy I never knew; but I knew the effects of it, which was that I never saw my knapsack from that day to this; nor did any of the rest of our party, unless they came across them by accident in our retreat. We "manned the lines," and lay quite as unmolested, during the whole night, as Samson did the half of his in the city of Gaza, and upon about as foolish a business, though there was some difference in our getting away; we did not go off in so much triumph quite as he did. We had a chain of sentinels quite up the river, for four or five miles in length. At an interval of every half hour they passed the watchword to each other—"all is well." I heard the British on board their shipping answer, "We will alter your tune before to-morrow night"—and they were as good as their word for once.

It was quite a dark night, and at daybreak the first thing that "saluted our eyes" was all the four ships at anchor, with springs upon their cables, and within musket shot of us. The *Phoenix* lying a little quartering and her stern towards me, I could read her name as distinctly as though I had been directly under her stern. What is the meaning of all this? thought I; what is coming forward now? They appeared to be very busy on shipboard, but we lay still and showed our good breeding by not interfering with them, as they were strangers, and we knew not but they were bashful withal. As soon as it was fairly light, we saw their boats coming out of a creek or cove, on the Long-Island side of the water, filled with British soldiers. When they came to the edge of the tide, they formed their boats in line. They continued to augment their forces from the island until they appeared like a large clover field in full bloom.

And now was coming on the famous Kipp's Bay affair, which has been criticised so much by the historians of the Revolution. I was there, and will give a true statement of all that *I* saw during that day.

It was a Sabbath morning, the day in which the British were always employed about their deviltry, if possible; because, they said, they had the prayers of the church on that day. We lay very quiet in our ditch, waiting their motions, till the sun was an hour or two high; we heard a cannonade at the city, but our attention was drawn toward our own guests. But they being a little dilatory in their operations, I stepped into an old warehouse which stood close by me, with the door open, inviting me in, and sat down upon a stool; the floor was strewed with papers which had in some former period been used in the concerns of the house, but were then lying in "woful confusion." I was very demurely perusing these papers when all of a sudden there came such a peal of thunder from the British shipping that I thought my head would go with the sound. I made a frog's leap for the ditch, and lay as still as I possibly could, and began to consider which part of my carcass was to go first.

The British played their parts well; indeed, they had nothing to hinder them. We kept the lines till they were almost levelled upon us, when our officers, seeing we could make no resistance, and no orders coming from any superior officer, and that we must soon be entirely exposed to the rake of their guns, gave the order to leave the lines. In retreating, we had to cross a level clear spot of ground, forty or fifty rods wide, exposed to the whole of the enemy's fire; and they gave it to us in prime order; the grape shot and langrage flew merrily, which served to quicken our motions.

When I had gotten a little out of the reach of their combustibles, I found myself in company with one who was a neighbour of mine when at home, and one other man belonging to our regiment; where the rest of them were I knew not. We went into a house by the highway, in which were two women and some small children, all crying most bitterly; we asked the women if they had any spirits in the house; they placed a case bottle of rum upon the table and bid us help ourselves. We each of us drank a glass and, bidding them good bye, betook ourselves to the highway again. . . .

—MARTIN(?), *Narrative*, pp. 25-28.

3. MISTRESS MURRAY'S MADEIRA SAVES PUTNAM'S ARMY

Journal of James Thacher, surgeon with the Continental army.

September 20, 1776

When retreating from New York, Major General Putnam, at the head of three thousand five hundred Continental troops, was in the rear and the last that left the city. In order to avoid any of the enemy that might be advancing in the direct road to the city, he made choice of a road parallel with and contiguous to the North River, till he could arrive at a certain angle, whence another road would conduct him in such a direction as that he might form a junction with our army. It so happened that a body of eight thousand British and Hessians were at the same moment advancing on the road, which would have brought them in immediate contact with General Putnam, before he could have reached the turn into the other road.

Most fortunately, the British generals, seeing no prospect of engaging our troops, halted their own, and repaired to the house of Mr. Robert Murray, a Quaker and a friend of our cause; Mrs. Murray treated them with cake and wine, and they were induced to tarry two hours or more, Governor Tryon frequently joking her about her American friends. By this happy incident General Putnam, by continuing his march, escaped a rencounter with a greatly superior force, which must have proved fatal to his whole party. One half-hour, it is said, would have been sufficient for the enemy to have secured the road at the turn, and entirely cut off General Putnam's retreat. It has since become almost a common saying among our officers that Mrs. Murray saved this part of the American army.

—THACHER, *Military Journal*, pp. 70-71.

4. "THE DASTARDLY BEHAVIOUR OF THE REBELS SINKS BELOW REMARK"

Journal of Ambrose Serle, secretary to Lord Howe.

Sunday, 15th. Septr.

This morning about 7 o'clock, the *Renown* of 50 guns, Capt. Banks, the *Repulse* of 32 guns, Capt. Davis, and the *Pearl* of 32 guns, Capt. Wilkinson, with the schooner, Lieut. Brown, sailed up the North River. The morning was fine the tide flowed, and there was a fresh breeze. The Rebels began their canonade as furiously as they could, but apparently with very little effect, as their guns were but poorly served. The ships, as these were the grand batteries of the enemy, returned a heavy fire and struck the walls of the batteries and the sods of earth which the Rebels had raised, very frequently. What other damage our people did them, we as yet know not; but 'tis observed that, except for beating down particular structures, or clearing the way for other operations, cannon have but a very small or precarious effect. The great business is always accomplished by the minor implements of war.

About a quarter before 9, the ships came to an anchor in the North River, in view of the fleet, at about 4 or 5 miles distance above it, and beyond the principal works of the enemy.

A transport, during the affair upon the North River, went up the East River and joined the other ships, almost without molestation.

The whole scene was awful and grand; I might say beautiful, but for the melancholy seriousness which must attend every circumstance where the lives of men, even the basest malefactors, are at stake. The hills, the woods, the river, the town, the ships and pillars of smoke, all heightened by a most clear and delightful morning, furnished the finest landscape that either art and nature combined could draw, or the imagination conceive.

After this affair had subsided for a little while, a most tremendous discharge of cannon from the ships began (as was concerted) in the East River, in order to cover the landing of the troops upon New York Island. So terrible and so incessant a roar of guns few even in the army and navy had ever heard before. Above 70 large pieces of cannon were in play, together with swivels and small arms from the ships, while the batteries added to the uproar upon the land.

The Rebels were apparently frightened away by the horrid din, and deserted the town and all their works in the utmost precipitation. The King's forces took possession of the place, incredible as it may seem, without the loss of a man. Nothing could equal the expressions of joy shewn by the inhabitants upon the arrival of the King's officers among them. They even carried some of them upon their shoulders about the streets, and behaved in all respects, women as well as men, like overjoyed bedlamites. One thing is worth remarking: a woman pulled down the Rebel standard upon the fort, and a woman hoisted up in its stead His Majesty's flag, after trampling the other under foot with the most contemptuous indignation. I first espied both circumstances from the ship, and could not help paying the first congratulations to Lord H. upon the occasion.

The spirit and activity of the troops and seamen were unequalled: Every man pressed to be foremost, consistent with order, and to court distinction. The dastardly behaviour of the Rebels, on the other hand, sinks below remark. The ground where our people landed was far from being advantageous; the tide rapid; the current unequal; the shore shallow; and themselves obliged to march up on ground where these poltroons had been at work to entrench themselves for several months. Providentially, the wind coming in with a fine breeze from the S. W. which it had not done before since we have been here, and which was the most favorable circumstance our people could have desired, enabled the boats to carry over the forces almost in a direct line, and return in like manner for the second division, notwithstanding the rapidity of the current. Thus this town and its environs, which these blustering gentlemen had taken such wonderful pains to fortify, were given up in two or three hours without any defence or the least appearance of a manly resistance.

In the evening the Admiral ordered up the *Mercury* of 24, and the *Fowey* of 20 guns, to lie close to the town, to prevent the transport boats from going on shore and plundering, which many of them appeared very ready to do.
—SERLE, *American Journal*, pp. 103-105.

5. A YANKEE CHAPLAIN DEFENDS THE AMERICAN TROOPS AT KIP'S BAY

Journal of Benjamin Trumbull, chaplain with the First Connecticut Regiment.
September, 1776

A little after day light on Sunday morning September 15 two ships of the line and three frigates drew up near the shore within musket shot of the lines and entrenchments and came to anchor there in a proper situation to fire most furiously upon our lines. In this situation they lay entirely quiet till about 10 o'clock. During this time boats were passing from the island to the ships and men put on board, and about 100 boats full of men came out of New Town Creek and made towards the shore.

When things were thus prepared, the ships about 10 o'clock, after firing a signal gun, began from the mouths of near an 100 canon a most furious canonade on the lines, which soon levelled them almost with the ground in some places, and buried our men who were in the lines almost under sand and sods of earth, and made such a dust and smoke that there was no possibility of firing on the enemy to any advantage, and then not without the utmost hazzard. While the canon poured in such a tremendous fire on the lines the ships from their round tops kept up a smart fire with swivels loaded with grape shot which they were able to fire almost into the entrenchments, they were so near.

The boats all this time kept out of the reach of the musquetry and finally, turning off to the left a little north of the lines in the smoke of the ships, made good their landing without receiving any anoyance from our troops. They soon marched up to the main road and formed across it and on the hills above our troops in order to cut off their retreat.

The Continental troops now left the lines, and there being no general orders given how to form them that they might support each other in a general attack, or any disposition made for it, they attempted an escape round the enemy in the best manner they could, and generally made their escape.

Colonels Selden, Hart and Tompson were taken with Major Porter and Brigadier Major Wyllys, and an 150 or 200 men were either killed or taken. Some canon, tents, flower and a great deal of baggage fell into the enemies hands. This on the whole was an unfortunate day to the American States. The loss was owing principally to a want of wagons and horses to remove the guns and baggage, and to the situation of the troops left behind, and the neglect in the officers in not forming some proper plan of defence.

The army was principally called off to the northward and had been in a state of retreat from the city for some days. All the field pieces had been removed out of the town and most of the artilery companies. And though few canon had been left in the forts to keep up the farce of defence and op- position, yet there was not one that could anoy the shiping or be brought on to the assistance of the infantry. They could [not] see nor expect any as- sistance from the troops above as they were all retreating. Officers and men had expected that their retreat would be cut off unless they could fight their way through them, which they thought very dangerous and precarious. In such a situation it was not reasonable to expect that they would make any vigorous stand.

The men were blamed for retreating and even flying in these circum- stances, but I imagine the fault was principally in the general officers in not disposing of things so as to give the men a rational prospect of defence and a safe retreat should they engage the enemy. And it is probable many lives were saved, and much [loss] to the army prevented, in their coming off as they did, tho' it was not honourable. It is admirable that so few men are lost.

—TRUMBULL, "Journal," *Conn. Hist. Soc. Coll.,* VII, 193-195.

6. "GOOD GOD, HAVE I GOT SUCH TROOPS AS THOSE!"

General George Weedon to John Page, President of the Virginia Council.
Head Quarters at Morris's Heights 10 miles above York
September 20, 1776

Since my last we have evacuated New York, a step that was found abso- lutely necessary for the preservation of the army, as we held it on very pre- carious terms, and might have been attended with the worst of consequences at this time, the General not haveing an army that he could depend upon, and so circumstanced from the situation of the place that a safe retreat could not be made had the enemy have landed above us, which was easy to effect.

We should have got of[f] all the stores and troops on Sunday night, but believe the enemy suspected a thing of the sort, and early on Sunday morn- ing sent several frigates up the East and North Rivers, and landed two con- siderable armies near the same time on the shores of each. General Putnam commanded in York, and had time to bring the troops out whilst our batteries amused the shipping. Two brigades of northern troops were to oppose their landing, and engage them. They run of[f] without fireing a gun, tho' Gen- eral Washington was himself present, and all he, his aide de camps and other general officers could do, they were not to be rallied till they had got some miles.

The General was so exasperated that he struck several officers in their flight, three times dashed his hatt on the ground, and at last exclaimed, "Good God, have I got such troops as those!" It was with difficulty his friends could get him to quit the field, so great was his emotions. He however got of[f] safe, and all the troops as you may think. Nothing was left in York but about 700 barrels of flower and some old corne of little consequence. . . .

—Weedon Papers, Chicago Historical Soc.

XI. THE BRITISH REPULSE AT HARLEM HEIGHTS

After the rout at Kip's Bay, Washington consolidated his lines behind fortified Harlem Heights. His defense in depth comprised a triple line of entrenchments extending across Manhattan. Observing the enemy's light troops incautiously advancing to the high ground opposite the American camp just north of Manhattanville, Washington ordered Colonel Thomas Knowlton, a hero of Bunker's Hill, and Major Andrew Leitch to get in their rear, while the British would be diverted by a feigned direct attack. A perfect plan partially miscarried when the firing on the front started before Knowlton and Leitch could get completely around the enemy's flank. The British were driven back from a wood to a buckwheat field, present site of Barnard College at 116th Street and Broadway, and thence retreated to what is now 110th Street. Washington declined to follow up the victory when he learned that Cornwallis had come up with reinforcements. But for the first time in the New York campaign the British had retreated, and, as George Clinton, shortly to become governor of New York, who participated in the engagement observed, they were "mortified." "If I only had a pair of pistols," he wrote a friend, "I am sure I would at least have shot a puppy of an officer I found slinking off in the heat of the action."

1. THE ENGLISH FOX HUNTERS SOUND THEIR BUGLES

Adjutant General Joseph Reed to his wife.

Heights near Kingsbridge, September 17, 1776

Just after I had sealed my letter and sent it away, an account came that the enemy were advancing upon us in three large columns. We have so many false reports that I desired the General to permit me to go and discover what truth there was in the account. I accordingly went down to our most advanced guard and while I was talking with the officer, the enemy's advanced guard fired upon us at a small distance. Our men behaved well, stood and returned the fire till, overpowered by numbers, they were obliged to retreat. The enemy advanced upon us very fast. I had not quitted a house 5 minutes before they were in possession of it.

Finding how things were going I went over to the General to get some support for the brave fellows who had behaved so well. By the time I got to him the enemy appeared in open view and in the most insulting manner sounded their bugle horns as is usual after a fox chase. I never felt such a sensation before; it seemed to crown our disgrace.

The General was prevailed on to order over a party to attack them, and as I had been upon the ground which no one else had, it fell to me to conduct them. An unhappy movement was made by a regiment of ours which had been ordered to amuse them while those I was with expected to take them in the rear. But being diverted by this the Virginia regiment, with which I was, went another course; finding there was no stopping them, I went with them the new way—and in a few minutes our brave fellows mounted up the rocks and attacked them; then they ran in turn. Each party sent in more succours so that at last it became a very considerable engagement and men fell on every side.

However, our troops still pressed on, drove the enemy above a mile and a half till the General ordered them to give over the pursuit, fearing the whole of the enemy's army would advance upon them; they retreated in very good order and I assure you it has given another face of things in our army. The men have recovered their spirits and feel a confidence which before they had quite lost. We have several prisoners and have buried a considerable number of their dead. Our own loss is also considerable. The Virginia major (Leech) who went up first with me was wounded with 3 shott in less than 3 minutes. But our greatest loss was a brave officer from Connecticut whose name and spirit ought to be immortalized, one Col Knowlton. I assisted him off and when gasping in the agonies of death all his inquiry was if we had drove the enemy.

Be not alarmed, my dear creature, when I tell you the horse I rode received a shot just behind his fore shoulder. It happened to be [one] taken from a number on the hill. Tho' [many fell] round me, thank God I was not struck [by] a single ball, and I have the great happiness [to know] that I have by getting the General to [direct a] reinforcement to go over contributed in [some way] to the benefit which may result from this [action]. When I speak of its importance I do not mean that I think the enemy have suffered a loss which will affect their operations—but it has given spirits to our men that I hope they will now look the enemy in the face with confidence. But alas our situation here must soon be a very distressing one if we do not receive much relief in the articles of stores, provision, forage, etc. The demands of a large army are very great and we are in a very doubtful condition on this head.

—Reed Papers, IV, 59, N. Y. Hist. Soc.

2. "The Virginia and Maryland Troops Bear the Palm"

Lieutenant Colonel Tench Tilghman to his father.

Headquarters at Col. Morris's House, September 19, 1776

I wrote you a few lines since we removed to this place. On Monday last we had a pretty smart skirmish with the British troops which was brought on in the following manner. The General rode down to our farthest lines, and when he came near them heard a firing which he was informed was between our scouts and the out guards of the enemy. When our men came in they informed the General that there were a party of about 300 behind a woody hill, tho' they only showed a very small party to us. Upon this the General laid a plan for attacking them in the rear and cutting off their retreat, which was to be effected in the following manner.

Major Leitch, with three companies of Colonel Weedon's Virginia regiment, and Colonel Knowlton, with his Rangers, were to steal round while a party were to march towards them and seem as if they intended to attack in front, but not to make any real attack till they saw our men fairly in their rear.

The bait took as to one part; as soon as they saw our party in front the enemy ran down the hill and took possession of some fences and bushes and began to fire at them, but at too great a distance to do much execution. Unluckily Colonel Knowlton and Major Leitch began their attack too soon; it was rather in flank than in rear. The action now grew warm. Major Leitch was wounded early in the engagement and Colonel Knowlton soon after, the latter mortally; he was one of the bravest and best officers in the army. Their men notwithstanding persisted with the greatest bravery.

The General finding they wanted support ordered over part of Colonel Griffiths's and part of Colonel Richardson's Maryland regiments; these troops tho' young charged with as much bravery as I can conceive; they gave two fires and then rushed right forward which drove the enemy from the wood into a buckwheat field, from whence they retreated. The General, fearing (as we afterwards found) that a large body was coming up to support them, sent me over to bring our men off. They gave a hurra and left the field in good order.

We had about 40 wounded and very few killed. A serjeant who deserted says their accounts were 89 wounded and 8 killed, but in the latter he is mistaken for we have buried more than double that number. We find their force was much more considerable than we imagined when the General ordered the attack. It consisted of the 2d Battalion of Light Infantry, a battalion of the Royal Highlanders and 3 companies of Hessian rifle men.

The prisoners we took told us they expected our men would have run away as they did the day before, but that they were never more surprised than to see us advancing to attack them. The Virginia and Maryland troops bear the palm. They are well officered and behave with as much regularity as possible, while the Eastern people are plundering everything that comes in their way. An ensign is to be tried for marauding to-day; the General will execute him if he can get a court martial to convict him.

I like our post here exceedingly; I think if we give it up it is our own faults.

—Tilghman, *Memoir*, pp. 138-139.

3. "Upon the Whole They Got Cursedly Thrashed"

General George Weedon to John Page, President of the Virginia Council.
Head Quarters at Morris's Heights 10 miles above York,
September 20th, 1776

. . . The enemy, elated at this piece of sucess, formed next morning and advanced in three columns. A disposition was made at this place to check them, in which your 3d Virginia Regiment made part. I was ordered to defend a pass at a val[l]ey that divides those hights from New York and the country below. The brave Major Leitch was detached with 3 rifle companies commanded by Captains Thornton, West and Ashby to flank the enemy that were then makeing for it. I soon got engaged, as did the major and his party. How we behaved it does not become me to say. Let it suffice to tell you that we had the Generals thanks in publick orders for our conduct. We were reinforced by some Maryland troops and others who behaved well. The poor major received three balls through his body before he quitted the field, and so lucky are their direction that I am in hopes he will do well. At present he is in a fair way.

I lost with his party and my own three killed and 12 wounded. The other cores that joined us lost in proportion. The enemies loss was at first supposed to be 97, but a deserter that came in today makes them to have lost between 2 and 3 hundred. This is partly confirmed by an old countryman to whose barn they carried their wounded. He declares they had at one time 97 wounded that was brought in, and that night sent it to their main army in waggons, several of which the deserter says is since dead. Upon the whole they got cursedly thrashed and have since declaired they did not think the Virginians had got up.

We are now very near neighbours, and view each other every hour in the day. The two armies lay within two miles of each other and a general action is every hour expected. I am more easy in my mind since we have got elbow room, and had the army first thrown up lines here it would have saved vast labour and expence. Indeed, I could wish we were three miles further back yet, as it's not our business to run any risque of being surrounded, an advantage that this country affords the enemy by the number of navigable rivers and creeks that make into it, and in many places do not leave the land more than a mile or two [wide]. . . .

—Weedon Papers, Chicago Historical Soc.

XII. NEW YORK IN FLAMES: THE GREAT FIRE OF SEPTEMBER 20

A goodly portion of what Washington was helpless to defend went up in flames and smoke in the night of September 20, 1776. The fire broke out in a wooden house on a wharf near Whitehall Slip and was spread rapidly by a stiff breeze from the south. The American troops had carted away all the church bells for conversion into cannon, so that alarms could not be quickly sounded. Fire companies were undermanned and disorganized and engines and pumps out of order. A shift of wind about 2 A.M. of the twenty-first confined the fire to an area between Broadway and the North River, but the destruction of 493 houses was a major disaster for the British, who were now confronted with the problem of finding quarters for the army and housing for returning Tories.

The British command, which had hoped to seize New York intact for its headquarters, was infuriated. The Tory New York Mercury called the fire an "atrocious deed, which in guilt and villainy is not inferior to the Gunpowder Plot." Ambrose Serle, Howe's secretary, charged that "the New England people" were "at the bottom of this plot," and Howe himself asserted that the "wretches . . . succeeded too well." If there was sabotage, it was unauthorized by the American commander, but, as Washington put it, "Providence, or some good honest fellow, has done more for us than we were disposed to do for ourselves."

1. A British Officer Sees the Fire as "Designedly Set"

Diary of Captain Frederick Mackenzie.

20th Sept—A little after 12 o'clock last night a most dreadful fire broke out in New York, in three different places in the south and windward part of the town. The alarm was soon given, but unfortunately there was a brisk wind at south, which spread the flames with such irresistible rapidity that, notwithstanding every assistance was given which the present circumstances admitted, it was impossible to check its progress till about 11 this day, when by preventing it from crossing the Broad-way at the north part of the town, it was stopped from spreading any further that way, and about 12 it was so far got under that there was no danger of its extending beyond those houses which were then on fire. It broke out first near the Exchange, and burnt all the houses on the west side of Broad Street, almost as far as the City Hall, and from thence all those in Beaver Street, and almost every house on the west side of the town between the Broad way and the North River, as far as the College, amounting in the whole to about 600 houses, besides several churches, particularly Trinity Church, the principal one in town.

On its first appearance two regiments of the 5th Brigade went into town, and some time after, a great number of seamen from the fleet were sent on shore under proper officers by order of Lord Howe, to give assistance. About daybreak the Brigade of Guards came in from camp, but from the absence of the regular firemen, the bad state of the engines, a want of buckets, and a scarcity of water, the efforts of the troops and seamen, tho' very great, could not prevent the fire from spreading in the manner it did. The first notice I had of it was from the sentry at Genl Smith's quarters at Mr Elliott's house, who called me up about 10 clock and said New York was on fire; on going to the window I observed an immense column of fire and smoke, and went and called Genl Smith, who said he would follow me into town as soon as possible. I dressed myself immediately and ran into town, a distance of two miles, but when I got there the fire had got to such a head there seemed to be no hopes of stopping it, and those who were present did little more than look on and lament the misfortune. As soon as buckets and water could be got, the seamen and the troops, assisted by some of the inhabitants, did what they could to arrest its progress, but the fresh wind and the combustible nature of the materials of which almost all the houses were built, rendered all their efforts vain.

From a variety of circumstances which occurred it is beyond a doubt that the town was designedly set on fire, either by some of those fellows who concealed themselves in it since the 15th instant, or by some villains left behind for the purpose. Some of them were caught by the soldiers in the very act of setting fire to the inside of empty houses at a distance from the fire; many were detected with matches and combustibles under their clothes, and combustibles were found in several houses. One villain who abused and cut a woman who was employed in bringing water to the engines, and who was found cutting the handles of the fire buckets, was hung up by the heels on the spot by the seamen. One or two others who were found in houses with fire brands in their hands were put to death by the enraged soldiery and thrown into the flames. There is no doubt however that the flames were communicated to several houses by means of the burning flakes of the shingles, which, being light, were carried by the wind to some distance and falling on the roofs of houses covered with shingles (which is most generally the case at New York) and whose inhabitants were either absent or inattentive, kindled the fire anew. The Trinity Church, a very handsome, ancient building, was perceived to be on fire long before the fire reached the adjacent houses, and as it stood at some distance from any house, little doubt remained that it was set on fire wilfully.

During the time the Rebels were in possession of the town, many of them were heard to say they would burn it, sooner than it should become a nest for Tories—and several inhabitants who were most violently attached to the Rebel cause have been heard to declare they would set fire to their own houses sooner than they should be occupied by the King's troops.

No assistance could be sent from the army till after daybreak, as the general was apprehensive the Rebels had some design of attacking the army.

It is almost impossible to conceive a scene of more horror and distress than the above. The sick, the aged, women, and children half naked were seen going they knew not where, and taking refuge in houses which were at a distance from the fire, but from whence they were in several instances driven a second and even a third time by the devouring element, and at last in a state of despair laying themselves down on the Common. The terror was encreased by the horrid noise of the burning and falling houses, the pulling down of such wooden buildings as served to conduct the fire (in which the soldiers and seamen were particularly active and useful), the rattling of above 100 waggons, sent in from the army and which were constantly employed in conveying to the Common such goods and effects as could be saved. The confused voices of so many men, the shrieks and cries of the women and children, the seeing the fire break out unexpectedly in places at a distance, which manifested a design of totally destroying the city, with numberless other circumstances of private misery and distress, made this one of the most tremendous and affecting scenes I ever beheld.

The appearance of the Trinity Church, when completely in flames, was a very grand sight, for the spire being entirely framed of wood and covered with shingles, a lofty pyramid of fire appeared, and as soon as the shingles were burnt away the frame appeared with every separate piece of timber burning, until the principal timbers were burnt through, when the whole fell with a great noise.

—MACKENZIE, *Diary*, I, 58-61.

2. "SOME WICKED INCENDIARIES HAD A HAND IN THIS"

Diary of the Reverend Mr. Shewkirk.

Saturday [*Sept.*] *21st.*—In the first hour of the day, soon after midnight, the whole city was alarmed by a dreadful fire. Br. Shewkirk, who was alone in the chapel-house, was not a little struck when he saw the whole air red and thought it to be very near; but going into the street, he found that it was in the low west end of the town, and went thither. When he came down the Broad Way, he met with Sister Sykes and her children. She was almost spent carrying the child, and a large bundle besides. He took the bundle and went back with them, and let them in to our house; when he left them and returned with their prentice to the fire, taking some buckets along. The fire was then in the lower part of Broad Street, Stone Street, etc. It spread so violently that all what was done was but of little effect; if one was in one street and looked about, it broke out already again in another street above; and thus it raged all the night and till about noon. The wind was pretty high from south-east and drove the flames to the northwest.

It broke out about White Hall; destroyed a part of Broad Street, Stone Street, Beaver Street, the Broadway, and then the streets going to the North River, and all along the North River as far as the King's College. Great pains was taken to save Trinity Church, the oldest and largest of the English churches, but in vain; it was destroyed, as also the old Lutheran church; and St. Paul's, at the upper end of the Broadway, escaped very narrowly.

Some of our families brought off their goods to our house. Bro. Shewkirk had the pleasure to be a comfort to our neighbors, who were much frightened the fire might come this way; and indeed, if the wind had shifted to the west as it had the appearance a couple of times, the whole city might have been destroyed. The corner house of our street, going to the Broadway, catched already; Bro. Shewkirk ordered our long ladder, and the others to be fetched out of our burying ground; which were of service in carrying the water up to the roof of said house in buckets; and by the industry of all the people the fire was put out. Several of our people have sustained considerable loss: Sister Kilburn has lost two houses; Pell's three houses; Jacobson one, and Widow Zoeller her's; and others have lost a part of their goods; as Lepper, Eastman, etc.

There are great reasons to suspect that some wicked incendiaries had a hand in this dreadful fire, which has consumed the fourth part of the city; several persons have been apprehended; moreover there were few hands of the inhabitants to assist; the bells being carried off, no timely alarm was given; the engines were out of order; the fire company broke; and also no proper order and directions, etc.; all of which contributed to the spreading of the flames.

—JOHNSTON, *Campaign of 1776*, II, 118-119.

3. "THE WRETCHES SUCCEEDED TOO WELL"

Sir William Howe to Lord George Germain.

York Island, September 23, 1776

My Lord: Between the 20th and 21st instant, at midnight, a most horrid attempt was made by a number of wretches to burn the town of New York, in which they succeeded too well, having set it on fire in several places with matches and combustibles that had been prepared with great art and ingenuity. Many were detected in the fact, and some killed upon the spot by the enraged troops in garrison; and had it not been for the exertions of Major-General Robertson, the officers under his command in the town and the brigade of Guards detached from the camp, the whole must infallibly have been consumed, as the night was extremely windy.

The destruction is computed to be about one-quarter of the town; and we have reason to suspect there are villains still lurking there, ready to finish the work they had begun, one person, escaping the pursuit of a sentinel the following night, having declared he would again set fire to the town the first opportunity. The strictest search is making after these incendiaries, and the most effectual measures taken to guard against the preparation of their villainous and wicked designs.

—FORCE, *American Archives*, 5th Series, II, 462.

XIII. THE MARTYRDOM OF NATHAN HALE

Under the date of September 22, 1776, Howe's Orderly Book contains a laconic entry: "A spy from the enemy by his own full confession, apprehended last night, was executed this day at 11 o'clock in front of the Artillery Park." The spy was young Nathan Hale, who, after Harlem Heights, had volunteered to go on a mission to secure intelligence about British troop movements in and around New York City. Apprehended on Long Island, and identified as an American officer, reputedly by his own cousin Samuel Hale, he was brought to the city the day after the fire, interrogated by General Howe, summarily turned over to the provost marshal, and hanged somewhere in the neighborhood of the present site of Grand Central Terminal. This curt account of the tragic incident is in a contemporary paper:

> This day, one Hale, in New York, on suspicion of being a spy was taken up and dragged without ceremony to the execution post, and hung up. General Washington has since sent in a flag, supposed to be on that account.

Nothing here about Hale's immortal last words, which seem to have been first recorded in the Essex Journal *of Newburyport, Massachusetts, which reported on February 13, 1777, that Hale had declared on the gallows: "If he had ten thousand lives, he would lay them all down, if called to it, in defence of his injured, bleeding country." But it is to the memoirs of William Hull, who was to surrender Detroit to the British in the War of 1812, that we are indebted for the commonly accepted last words as recorded by Hull's daughter, Maria Hull Campbell. A contemporary ballad, probably the best to come out of the war, commemorated Hale's mission, arrest and execution.*

1. A BRITISH CAPTAIN SEES HALE DIE LIKE A HERO

Diary of Captain Frederick Mackenzie.

Sept. 22. A person named Nathaniel Hales, a lieutenant in the Rebel army and a native of Connecticut, was apprehended as a spy last night upon Long Island; and having this day made a full and free confession to the Commander in Chief of his being employed by Mr Washington in that capacity, he was hanged at 11 o'clock in front of the park of artillery. He was about 24 years of age, and had been educated at the College of Newhaven in Connecticut. He behaved with great composure and resolution, saying he thought it the duty of every good officer to obey any orders given him by his Commander in Chief; and desired the spectators to be at all times prepared to meet death in whatever shape it might appear.

—MACKENZIE, *Diary*, I, 61-62.

2. "I Only Regret That I Have But One Life to Lose for My Country"

From the manuscript memoirs of Captain William Hull of Connecticut.

In a few days an officer came to our camp, under a flag of truce, and informed Hamilton, then a captain of artillery, but afterwards the aid of General Washington, that Captain Hale had been arrested within the British lines, condemned as a spy, and executed that morning.

I learned the melancholy particulars from this officer, who was present at his execution and seemed touched by the circumstances attending it.

He said that Captain Hale had passed through their army, both of Long Island and York Island. That he had procured sketches of the fortifications, and made memoranda of their number and different positions. When apprehended, he was taken before Sir William Howe, and these papers, found concealed about his person, betrayed his intentions. He at once declared his name, his rank in the American army, and his object in coming within the British lines.

Sir William Howe, without the form of a trial, gave orders for his execution the following morning. He was placed in the custody of the Provost Marshal, who was a refugee and hardened to human suffering and every softening sentiment of the heart. Captain Hale, alone, without sympathy or support, save that from above, on the near approach of death asked for a clergyman to attend him. It was refused. He then requested a Bible; that too was refused by his inhuman jailer.

"On the morning of his execution," continued the officer, "my station was near the fatal spot, and I requested the Provost Marshal to permit the prisoner to sit in my marquee, while he was making the necessary preparations. Captain Hale entered: he was calm, and bore himself with gentle dignity, in the consciousness of rectitude and high intentions. He asked for writing materials, which I furnished him: he wrote two letters, one to his mother and one to a brother officer." He was shortly after summoned to the gallows. But a few persons were around him, yet his characteristic dying words were remembered. He said, "I only regret that I have but one life to lose for my country."

—CAMPBELL, *General William Hull*, pp. 37-38.

3. Ballad of Nathan Hale
[1776]

The breezes went steadily thro' the tall pines,
    A-saying "oh! hu-ush!" a-saying "oh! hu-ush!"
As stilly stole by a bold legion of horse,
    For Hale in the bush, for Hale in the bush.

"Keep still!" said the thrush as she nestled her young,
  In a nest by the road; in a nest by the road.
"For the tyrants are near, and with them appear
  What bodes us no good, what bodes us no good."

The brave captain heard it, and thought of his home,
  In a cot by the brook; in a cot by the brook.
With mother and sister and memories dear,
  He so gaily forsook; he so gaily forsook.

Cooling shades of the night were coming apace,
  The tattoo had beat; the tattoo had beat.
The noble one sprang from his dark lurking place
  To make his retreat; to make his retreat.

He warily trod on the dry rustling leaves,
  As he passed through the wood; as he passed through the wood;
And silently gained his rude launch on the shore,
  As she played with the flood; as she played with the flood....

The guards of the camp, on that dark, dreary night,
  Had a murderous will; had a murderous will.
They took him and bore him afar from the shore,
  To a hut on the hill; to a hut on the hill.

No mother was there, nor a friend who could cheer,
  In that little stone cell; in that little stone cell.
But he trusted in love, from his father above.
  In his heart, all was well; in his heart, all was well.

An ominous owl with his solemn bass voice,
  Sat moaning hard by; sat moaning hard by.
"The tyrant's proud minions most gladly rejoice,
  "For he must soon die; for he must soon die."

The brave fellow told them, no thing he restrained—
  The cruel gen'ral; the cruel gen'ral—
His errand from camp, of the ends to be gained,
  And said that was all; and said that was all.

They took him and bound him and bore him away,
  Down the hill's grassy side; down the hill's grassy side.
'Twas there the base hirelings, in royal array,
  His cause did deride; his cause did deride.

Five minutes were given, short moments, no more,
  For him to repent; for him to repent;
He prayed for his mother, he asked not another.
  To Heaven he went; to Heaven he went.

The faith of a martyr, the tragedy shewed,
　　As he trod the last stage; as he trod the last stage.
And Britons will shudder at gallant Hale's blood,
　　As his words do presage; as his words do presage.

"Thou pale king of terrors, thou life's gloomy foe,
　　Go frighten the slave, go frighten the slave;
Tell tyrants, to you their allegiance they owe
　　No fears for the brave; no fears for the brave."
　　　　　　　　—MOORE, ed., *Songs and Ballads*, pp. 131-133.

XIV. AWAITING HOWE'S NEXT MOVE

The army was riddled with plunderers, drifters and fair-weather soldiers. Washington's solution: Better pay and more prestige for officers, long-term enlistments for privates, no dependence upon the militia. Rather a standing army than "inevitable ruin." Meantime, distrust of Washington among the officers was deepening. As Colonel Haslet of the Delaware battalion put it in a letter of September 4 to Caesar Rodney, the Delaware Patriot leader: "Would to Heaven General Lee were here is the language of officers and men." Washington himself confessed to being in an "unhappy, divided" state of mind.

While a reorganization of the army was exigent, Washington had to make the necessary moves with such forces as he had in anticipation of Howe's next attack. Although a Westchester landing seemed imminent, Washington yielded to a general council and divided the American forces to be prepared for alternative attack plans by the British. It was indeed a time of desperation. "We are hellishly frightened," Gouverneur Morris wrote to Robert R. Livingston on October 8, adding, "but don't say a word of that for we shall get our spirits again." That very same day the British Captain Frederick Mackenzie noted in his diary that the rebels were about to make their last stand.

1. CHARGES OF INDISCRIMINATE PLUNDERING BY THE PATRIOTS

Lewis Morris, Jr., to his father, Lewis Morris, the Signer.

New York, September 6, 1776

Dear Sir,

　. . . When I received your letter I was at the bridge looking for a sloop to carry some furniture to the Fish Kill, which I believe I shall send off next day after to-morrow. From your letter I believed you were acquainted with Mamma's moving up to Harrison's Purchase with her family where she has carried a great deal of furniture and all her linnen and wearing apparel, and therefore your position of moveing her to Philadelphia will be attended with many obstacles, for she can neither bring cloaths sufficient for the family nor utensils to keep house, as most of the carts and waggons are pressed in the service; however I shall set off in the morning to propose the scheme and if she approves of it, I shall spare neither time nor trouble in effecting of it.

　I wish you had sent me a duplicate of your letter by Billy, for the post office is moved up to Dobes's Ferry and shall be at a loss what to do with the stocks till I receive it, and if I send it is ten to one if I get it and perhaps I may be upon the wing for it for these two or three days. I assure you, Sir, your affairs at Morrisania, however secure you may think they may be, are in a very critical situation; in all probability they may be in possession of the enemy in a little time; for from their manoeuvre Westchester County is their object, and let me whisper to you a secret from my suspicions and the appearance of theirs: We are retreating to King's Bridge; if so, Morrisania will fall of course.

I wish you was home to assist me; you have a great deal at stake which I hope I shall be able to secure. There is a regiment at Morrisania, and your own house is made a barrack of, that is for the officers, and there are troops all about us which makes it impossible to prosecute the business of the farm— and besides they press your horses; the two coaches horses were pressed this afternoon which Colonel Shee has returned, and I believe unless speedily secured your breeding mares will come next. . . . Your fat cattle are in the hands of the commissary. . . . Colonel Hand's regiment plunder every body in Westchester County indiscriminately, even yourself have not escaped. Montrasseurs Island they plundered and committed the most unwarrantable destruction upon it; fifty dozen of bottles were broke in the cellar, the paper tore from the rooms and every pane of glass broke to pieces. His furniture and cloaths were brought over to Morrisania and sold at publick auction. Jimmy Delancey, Oliver and John, after giving their parole, are gone off to the enemy and their house is plundered. Mrs. Wilkins is upon Long Island with her husband and her house is plundered and hers and Mrs. Moncriefe's cloathes were sold at vendue. Seabury has likewise eloped, and Mrs. Wilkins has very industriously propagated that you had fled to France. Such brimstones will certainly meet with their desert. Give my love to all, and believe me to be

Your dutiful son,
L. Morris

—Morris, "Letters," *N. Y. Hist. Soc. Coll.*, VIII, 440-443.

2. "The Army Is Now Only a Receptacle for Ragamuffins"

Major General Henry Knox to his brother.

Heights of Harlem, 8 Miles from New York, Sept. 23d, 1776

The general is as worthy a man as breathes, but he cannot do every thing nor be everywhere. He wants good assistants. There is a radical evil in our army—the lack of officers. We ought to have men of merit in the most extensive and unlimited sense of the word. Instead of which, the bulk of the officers of the army are a parcel of ignorant, stupid men, who might make tolerable soldiers, but are bad officers; and until Congress forms an establishment to induce men proper for the purpose to leave ther usual employments and enter the service, it is ten to one they will be beat till they are heartily tired of it. We ought to have academies, in which the whole theory of the art of war shall be taught, and every other encouragement possible given to draw persons into the army that may give a lustre to our arms. As the army now stands, it is only a receptacle for ragamuffins. You will observe, I am chagrined, not more so than at any other time since I've been in the army; but many late affairs, of which I've been an eye-witness, have so totally sickened me that unless some very different mode of conduct is observed in the formation of the new army, I shall not think myself obliged by either the laws of God or nature to risk my reputation on so cobweb a foundation. . . .

—DRAKE, *Henry Knox*, pp. 31-32.

3. "WE ARE NOW ON THE EVE OF ANOTHER DISSOLUTION OF OUR ARMY"

George Washington to John Hancock.

   Colonel Morris's, on the Heights of Harlem, September 24, 1776

 Sir: From the hours alloted to Sleep, I will borrow a few Moments to convey my thoughts on sundry important matters to Congress. I shall offer them, with that sincerity which ought to characterize a man of candour; and with the freedom which may be used in giving useful information, without incurring the imputation of presumption.

 We are now, as it were, upon the eve of another dissolution of our Army; the remembrance of the difficulties which happened upon that occasion last year, the consequences which might have followed the change, if proper advantages had been taken by the Enemy; added to a knowledge of the present temper and Situation of the Troops, reflect but a very gloomy prospect upon the appearance of things now, and satisfie me, beyond the possibility of doubt, that unless some speedy, and effectual measures are adopted by Congress, our cause will be lost.

 It is in vain to expect, that any (or more than a trifling) part of this Army will again engage in the Service on the encouragement offered by Congress. When Men find that their Townsmen and Companions are receiving 20, 30, and more dollars, for a few Months Service, (which is truely the case) it cannot be expected; without using compulsion; and to force them into the Service would answer no valuable purpose. When Men are irritated, and the Passions inflamed, they fly hastely and chearfully to Arms; but after the first emotions are over, to expect, among such People, as compose the bulk of the Army, that they are influenced by any other principles than those of Interest, is to look for what never did, and I fear never will happen; the Congress will deceive themselves therefore if they expect it.

 A Soldier reasoned with upon the goodness of the cause he is engaged in, and the inestimable rights he is contending for, hears you with patience, and acknowledges the truth of your observations, but adds, that it is of no more Importance to him than others. The Officer makes you the same reply, with this further remark, that his pay will not support him, and he cannot ruin himself and Family to serve his Country, when every Member of the community is equally Interested, and benefitted by his Labours. The few therefore, who act upon Principles of disinterestedness, are, comparatively speaking, no more than a drop in the Ocean.

 It becomes evidently clear then, that as this Contest is not likely to be the Work of a day; as the War must be carried on systematically, and to do it, you must have good Officers, there are, in my Judgment, no other possible means to obtain them but by establishing your Army upon a permanent footing; and giving your Officers good pay; this will induce Gentlemen, and Men of Character to engage; and till the bulk of your Officers are composed of such persons as are actuated by Principles of honour, and a spirit of enter-prize, you have little to expect from them.—They ought to have such allow-ances as will enable them to live like, and support the Characters of Gentle-men; and not be driven by a scanty pittance to the low, and dirty arts which many of them practice, to filch the Publick of more than the difference of pay would amount to upon an ample allowe. besides, something is due to the Man who puts his life in his hand, hazards his health, and forsakes the Sweets of domestick enjoyments. Why a Captn. in the Continental Service should re-ceive no more than 5/. Curry per day, for performing the same duties that an officer of the same Rank in the British Service receives 10/. Sterlg. for, I never could conceive; especially when the latter is provided with every necessity he requires, upon the best terms, and the former can scarce procure them, at any Rate. There is nothing that gives a Man consequence, and renders him fit for Command, like a support that renders him Independent of every body but the State he Serves.

With respect to the Men, nothing but a good bounty can obtain them upon a permanent establishment; and for no shorter time than the continuance of the War, ought they to be engaged; as Facts incontestibly prove, that the difficulty, and cost of Inlistments, increase with time. When the Army was first raised at Cambridge, I am persuaded the Men might have been got with-out a bounty for the War: after this, they began to see that the Contest was not likely to end so speedily as was immagined, and to feel their consequence, by remarking, that to get the Militia In, in the course of last year, many Towns were induced to give them a bounty.

Foreseeing the Evils resulting from this, and the destructive consequences which unavoidably would follow short Inlistments, I took the Liberty in a long Letter, written by myself (date not now recollected, as my Letter Book is not here) to recommend the Inlistments for and during the War; assigning such Reasons for it, as experience has since convinced me were well founded. At that time twenty Dollars would, I am persuaded, have engaged the Men for this term. But it will not do to look back, and if the present opportunity is slip'd, I am perswaded that twelve months more will Increase our difficulties fourfold. I shall therefore take the freedom of giving it as my opinion, that a good Bounty be immediately offered, aided by the proffer of at least 100, or 150 Acres of Land and a suit of Cloaths and Blanket, to each non-Comd. Officer and Soldier; as I have good authority for saying, that however high the Men's pay may appear, it is barely sufficient in the present scarcity and dearness of all kinds of goods, to keep them in Cloaths, much less afford support to their Families.

If this encouragement then is given to the Men, and such Pay allowed the Officers as will induce Gentlemen of Character and liberal Sentiments to en-gage; and proper care and precaution used in the nomination (having more regard to the Characters of Persons, than the Number of Men they can Inlist) we should in a little time have an Army able to cope with any that can be opposed to it, as there are excellent Materials to form one out of: but while the only merit an Officer possesses is his ability to raise Men; while those Men consider, and treat him as an equal; and (in the Character of an Officer) regard him no more than a broomstick, being mixed together as one common herd; no order nor no discipline can prevail; nor will the Officer ever meet with the respect which is essentially necessary to due subordination.

To place any dependance upon Militia, is, assuredly, resting upon a broken staff. Men just dragged from the tender Scenes of domestick life, unaccustomed to the din of Arms; totally unacquainted with every kind of Military skill, which being followed by a want of confidence in themselves, when opposed to Troops regularly trained, disciplined, and appointed, superior in knowledge, and superior in Arms, makes them timid, and ready to fly from their own shadows. Besides, the sudden change in their manner of living, (particularly in their lodging) brings on sickness in many; impatience in all, and such an unconquerable desire of returning to their respective homes that it not only produces shameful, and scandalous Desertions among themselves, but infuses the like spirit in others. Again, Men accustomed to unbounded freedom, and no control, cannot brook the Restraint which is indispensably necessary to the good order and Government of an Army; without which, licentiousness, and every kind of disorder triumphantly reign. To bring Men to a proper degree of Subordination, is not the work of a day, a Month or even a year; and unhappily for us, and the cause we are Engaged in, the little discipline I have been labouring to establish in the Army under my immediate Command, is in a manner done away by having such a mixture of Troops as have been called together within these few Months.

Relaxed, and unfit, as our Rules and Regulations of War are, for the Government of an Army, the Militia (those properly so called, for of these we have two sorts, the Six Months Men and those sent in as a temporary aid) do not think themselves subject to 'em, and therefore take liberties, which the Soldier is punished for; This creates jealousy; jealousy begets dissatisfaction; and these by degrees ripen into Mutiny; keeping the whole Army in a confused, and disordered State; rendering the time of those who wish to see regularity and good Order prevail more unhappy than Words can describe. Besides this, such repeated changes take place, that all arrangement is set at nought, and the constant fluctuation of things, deranges every plan. . . .

These Sir, Congress may be assured, are but a small part of the Inconveniences which might be enumerated and attributed to Militia; but there is one that merits particular attention, and that is the expence. Certain I am, that it would be cheaper to keep 50 or 100,000 Men in constant pay than to depend upon half the number, and supply the other half occasionally by Militia. The time the latter is in pay before and after they are in Camp, assembling and Marching; the waste of Ammunition; the consumption of Stores, which in spite of every Resolution, and requisition of Congress they must be furnished with, or sent home, added to other incidental expenses consequent upon their coming, and conduct in Camp, surpasses all Idea, and destroys every kind of regularity and oeconomy which you could establish among fixed and Settled Troops; and will, in my opinion prove (if the scheme is adhered to) the Ruin of our Cause.

The Jealousies of a standing Army, and the Evils to be apprehended from one, are remote; and in my judgment, situated and circumstanced as we are, not at all to be dreaded; but the consequence of wanting one, according to my Ideas, formed from the present view of things, is certain, and inevitable Ruin; for if I was called upon to declare upon Oath, whether the Militia have been most serviceable or hurtful upon the whole; I should subscribe to the latter. I do not mean by this however to arraign the Conduct of Congress, in so doing I should equally condemn my own measures, (if I did not my judgment); but experience, which is the best criterion to work by, so fully, clearly, and decisively reprobates the practice of trusting to Militia, that no Man who regards order, regularity, and oeconomy; or who has any regard for his own honour, Character, or peace of Mind, will risk them upon this Issue. . . .

Another matter highly worthy of attention, is, that other Rules and Regulations may be adopted for the Government of the Army than those now in existence, otherwise the Army, but for the name, might as well be disbanded. For the most atrocious offences, (one or two Instances only excepted) a Man receives no more than 39 Lashes; and these perhaps (thro' the collusion of the Officer who is to see it inflicted), are given in such a manner as to become rather a matter of sport than punishment; but when inflicted as they ought, many hardened fellows who have been the Subjects, have declared that for a bottle of Rum they would undergo a Second operation; It is evident therefore that this punishment is inadequate to many Crimes it is assigned to, as a proof of it, thirty and 40 Soldiers will desert at a time; and of late, a practice prevail . . . of the most alarming nature; and which will, if it cannot be checked, prove fatal both to the Country and Army; I mean the infamous practice of Plundering, for, under the Idea of Tory property, or property which may fall into the hands of the Enemy, no Man is secure in his effects, and scarcely in his Person; for in order to get at them, we have several Instances of People being frightened out of their Houses under pretence of those Houses being ordered to be burnt, and this is done with a view of seizing the Goods; nay, in order that the villainy may be more effectually concealed, some Houses have actually been burnt to cover the theft.

I have with some others, used my utmost endeavours to stop this horrid practice, but under the present lust after plunder, and want of Laws to punish Offenders, I might almost as well attempt to remove Mount Atlas. —I have ordered instant corporal Punishment upon every Man who passes our Lines, or is seen with Plunder, that the Offenders might be punished for disobedience of Orders; and Inclose you the proceedings of a Court Martial held upon an Officer, who with a Party of Men had robbd a House a little beyond our Lines of a number of valuable goods; among which (to shew that nothing escapes) were four large Pier looking Glasses, Women's Cloaths, and other Articles which one would think, could be of no earthly use to him. He was met by a Major of Brigade who ordered him to return the Goods, as taken contrary to Genl. Orders, which he not only peremptorily refused to do, but drew up his Party and swore he would defend them at the hazard of his Life; on which I ordered him to be arrested, and tryed for Plundering, Disobedience of Orders, and Mutiny; for the result, I refer to the Proceedings of the Court;

whose judgment appeared so exceedingly extraordinary, that I ordered a Reconsideration of the matter, upon which, and with the Assistance of fresh
evidence, they made Shift to Cashier him. . . .

> —FITZPATRICK, ed., *Writings of Washington*, VI, 106-115.

4. THE FATAL DECISION TO HOLD FORT WASHINGTON

From the memoirs of Major General William Heath of the Continental Army.

> September 16, 1776

It now became an object of high importance to calculate, if possible,
where the British would make their next attempt; and here the general officers
were divided in opinion. A part of them imagined that the British would first
endeavour to make themselves masters of the whole of New-York Island, and
that, therefore, the reduction of Fort Washington and its dependencies would
be their object. Others supposed that they would make a landing either at
Morrisania, Hunt's or Frog's Point, which eventually would produce as certain a reduction of the works on the island, with very little loss to the British.
It was therefore determined in council to guard against both; and for this
purpose 10,000 men were to be retained on the island, at and near Fort Washington. Our General's division was to be augmented to 10,000 men, and a
floating bridge was to be thrown across Haarlem Creek, that these two bodies
might communicate with and support each other, as circumstances might require; and Maj.-Gen. Greene was to command the flying camp on the Jersey
side of the Hudson, which was to consist of 5000. The different arrangements
took place accordingly.

> —HEATH, *Memoirs*, p. 53.

XV. THE RETREAT TO WHITE PLAINS

*Howe's next moves—or his failure to make them—cost him the war. It
took him two months after the Battle of Long Island to move less than thirty
miles to reach White Plains. Deciding to circumvent Washington rather
than risk a frontal attack, Howe, under cover of fog, embarked his main
army during the night of October 12 and landed an advance force at Throg's
Neck, a peninsula on what is now the Bronx. Washington had already anticipated this move. A small detachment of Pennsylvania riflemen posted behind
a woodpile threw the British back in confusion. To cross the creek and
marsh at this point and in the face of increasing opposition seemed hazardous
to Howe, who embarked his troops once more and landed three miles east at
Pell's Point.*

*Howe's landing on Westchester imperiled Washington's main army. Ac-
cordingly the American general and his staff decided to retreat to White
Plains, then a completely isolated country spot remote from military supplies.
The main American move began on October 18. Meantime, Colonel John
Glover of Marblehead, whose men had ferried the American army back to
Manhattan from Brooklyn Heights and who was a leading exponent of am-
phibious warfare, fought a valiant delaying action against the British about a
mile from their landing place at Pell's Point, and Haslet attempted a surprise*

attack on a corps of Tories under the redoubtable Ranger, Robert Rogers, at Mamaroneck, and took 36 prisoners ahead with him to White Plains.

1. THE BRITISH ALMOST MEET DISASTER AT HELL GATE

Diary of Captain Frederick Mackenzie.

October 23, 1776 . . . Some of the captains of the navy who attended for the regulating of the boats and vessels when they went through Hellgate with the army the morning of the 12th instant, have since declared that it was a most hazardous enterprize to go through a channel of that dangerous nature with such a fleet, and before it was daylight. What made it still more dangerous was that an unexpected fog came on early in the morning, which prevented them in a great degree from seeing the boat and buoys which had been previously fixed to mark the proper channel. It was too late when the fog came on to postpone the movement; the troops and everything necessary were embarked, and the wind and tide answered exactly; therefore notwithstanding the hazard it could not be delayed.

I dare say at the moment the army began to move the general and admiral would have compounded for the loss of one or two hundred men. Fortune, however, favored the bold:—only one boat, having on board an officer and 25 artillery men and three 6-pounders was sunk. All but four men and the guns were saved, which was more than could have been expected. Everything else got safe through that dangerous passage, where at all times, except at high and low water, the tide runs with the utmost rapidity, forming dreadful whirlpools, and at half tide roaring over the masses of rocks which project into, or rear up their broken heads in the middle of the channel. In one place if the stream catches a boat or vessel, it is drawn into a kind of whirlpool or eddy, where it is carried round several times with great violence, and then, if not sucked in, is thrown on the adjacent rocks and dashed to pieces. One boat with a detachment of Grenadiers was caught into this place, and after some turns round was thrown upon the shore, but fortunately the men got out safe, and soon after got into another boat and followed the army.

This passage is thought extremely dangerous by those who are best acquainted with it, and who take every advantage of winds, tides and other circumstances. When I was formerly quartered at New York, I frequently went out as far as Hellgate to see vessels go through, especially when there were any which carried topsails, and the pilots were generally under much apprehension when they had such vessels under their charge. Those men were in the utmost astonishment to see ships of war of 44 guns, frigates, transports full of troops, horses and waggons, and flat boats with troops and artillery, attempting and accomplishing so difficult an undertaking with such a trifling loss. To any other nation the obstacles would have seemed insurmountable.

Since the army went through, I have frequently seen large transports go through stern foremost, with all sails set and filled, the strength of the tide overcoming the power of the wind upon the sails. Some officers of the Navy say this is the safest way, as the ship has better and more certain steerage.

—MACKENZIE, *Diary*, I, 84-86.

2. At Pelham: "A Pretty Close Fire Which Checked Them"

Memoirs of Major General William Heath.

[*October*] *18th.*—The regiment at West Chester causeway had been relieved by another. The officer on command there, this morning, sent up an
express to our General, informing him that the British were opening up an
embrasure in their work at the end of the causeway, and that he apprehended
they intended, under a cannonade from this, to attempt to pass. Our General
ordered one of his aids to gallop his horse to the officer commanding the
brigade, near Valentine's, the nearest to West Chester, and order him to form
his brigade instantly. Arriving, himself, by the time the brigade was formed,
he ordered the officer to march with the utmost expedition to the head of the
causeway, to reinforce the troops there; himself moving on with them.

When the troops had advanced to about half the way between the head
of the creek and the post at the head of the causeway, another express met
him, informing him that the whole British army were in motion and seemed
to be moving towards the pass at the head of the creek. Upon this, the brigade
was ordered to halt, the whole to prime and load, and the rear regiment to
file off by the left, and march briskly to reinforce the Americans at the pass,
at the head of the creek.

At this instant, Gen. Washington came up and, having inquired of our
General the state of things, ordered him to return immediately and have his
division formed ready for action, and to take such a position as might appear
best calculated to oppose the enemy, should they attempt to land another
body of troops on Morrisania, which he thought not improbable. Our General immediately obeyed the order.

The wind was now fresh at south-west. The British crossed to the other
side of Frog's Neck, embarked on board their boats, crossed over the cove,
landed on Pell's Neck, and moved briskly upwards. Three or four of the
American regiments advanced towards them, and took a good position behind
a stone fence. When the British had advanced sufficiently near, they gave
them a pretty close fire, which checked them, and even obliged them to fall
back; but being immediately supported, they returned vigorously to the
charge. The action was sharp for a short time; but the Americans were soon
obliged to give way to superior force. . . .

—HEATH, *Memoirs*, pp. 64-65.

3. A Marblehead Hero Longs for General Lee at Pelham

Letter from Colonel John Glover.

Mile Square, October 22, 1776

You no doubt heard the enemy landed all their army on Frog's Point the
11th instant, leaving only twelve hundred men in York, and there remained
until the 18th, which was Friday.

I arose early in the morning and went on the hill with my glass, and discovered a number of ships in the Sound under way; in a very short time saw
the boats, upwards of two hundred sail, all manned and formed in four grand
divisions. I immediately sent off Major Lee express to General Lee, who was

about three miles distant, and without waiting his orders, turned out the brigade I have the honour to command, and very luckily for us I did, as it turned out afterwards, the enemy having stole a march one and a half miles on us. I marched down to oppose their landing with about seven hundred and fifty men and three field-pieces, but had not gone more than half the distance before I met their advanced guard, about thirty men; upon which I detached a captain's guard of fifty men to meet them, while I could dispose of the main body to advantage.

This plan succeeded very well, as you will hereafter see. The enemy had the advantage of us, being posted on an eminence which commanded the ground we had to march over. However, I did the best I could and disposed of my little party to the best of my judgment. . . .

This disposed of, I rode forward—(oh! the anxiety of mind I was then in for the fate of the day—the lives of seven hundred and fifty men immediately at hazard, and under God their preservation entirely depended on their being well disposed of; besides this, my country, my honour, my own life, and every thing that was dear, appeared at that critical moment to be at stake. I would have given a thousand worlds to have had General Lee or some other experienced officer present, to direct or at least to approve of what I had done —looked around, but could see none, they all being three miles from me, and the action came on so sudden it was out of their power to be with me)—to the advance guard, and ordered them to advance, who did, within fifty yards, and received their fire without the loss of a man; we returned it and fell[ed] four of them, and kept the ground till we exchanged five rounds.

Their body being much larger than mine, and having two men killed and several wounded, which weakened my party, the enemy pushing forward not more than thirty yards distant, I ordered a retreat, which was masterly well done by the captain that commanded the party. The enemy gave a shout and advanced; Colonel Reed's, laying under cover of a stone wall undiscovered till they came within thirty yards, then rose up and gave them the whole charge; the enemy broke and retreated for the main body to come up.

In this situation we remained about an hour and a half, when they appeared about four thousand, with seven pieces of artillery; they now advanced, keeping up a constant fire of artillery; we kept our post under cover of the stone wall before mentoned till they came within fifty yards of us, rose up and gave them the whole charge of the battalion; they halted and returned the fire with showers of musketry and cannon balls. We exchanged seven rounds at this post, retreated, and formed in the rear of Colonel Shepherd and on his left; they then shouted and pushed on till they came on Shepherd, posted behind a fine double stone wall; he rose up and fired by grand divisions, by which he kept up a constant fire and maintained his part till he exchanged seventeen rounds with them, and caused them to retreat several times, once in particular so far that a soldier of Colonel Shepherd's leaped over the wall and took a hat and canteen off of a captain that lay dead on the ground they retreated from.

However, their body being so much larger than ours, we were, for the preservation of our men, forced to retreat. . . . The enemy halted, and played away their artillery at us, and we at them, till night, without any damage on our side, and but very little on theirs. At dark we came off, and marched about three miles, leading to Dobb's Ferry, after fighting all day without victuals or drink, laying as a picket all night, the heavens over us and the earth under us, which was all we had, having left our baggage at the old encampment we left in the morning. The next morning marched over to Mile Square. I had eight men killed and thirteen wounded, among which was Colonel Shepherd, a brave officer.

—Force, *American Archives*, 5th Series, II, 1188-1189.

XVI. HOWE'S FUTILE STROKE AT WHITE PLAINS

As late as October 26, Captain Frederick Mackenzie of the Royal Welsh Fusiliers recorded in his diary that "the cautious conduct of General Howe in all the operations of this campaign is generally approved of." The bitter fruits of that caution were to be evident in the next few critical weeks.

Howe waited at New Rochelle until October 22, when he was reinforced by Hessians under Knyphausen, again giving Washington time to build up his position at White Plains. On the morning of the twenty-eighth the opposing armies, each about 13,000 strong, confronted each other. Washington's forces held entrenchments on hilly ground in the village of White Plains. His left rested on a millpond; his right on a bend in the Bronx River, which protected his flank and rear. Again Howe avoided a frontal attack, but sent his main forces to seize Chatterton's Hill, a steep unfortified point across the Bronx River. When the British advanced they met a withering fire from young Captain Alexander Hamilton's artillery. But when the Hessians came up on the right, General McDougall, exposed to heavy fire in front and flank, was forced to retreat across the stream to White Plains. Howe won the hill, but let victory slip from his grasp. Again he waited for reinforcements before attacking. A storm further delayed his operations, and Washington was able to pull back his forces north to New Castle, with the main American army intact.

1. "Gentlemen, We Have Other Business than Reconnoitring"

Major General William Heath's account.

October 27th.—In the forenoon a heavy cannonade was heard towards Fort Washington. Thirteen Hessians and two or three British soldiers were sent in on this day. From the American camp to the west-south-west, there appeared to be a very commanding height, worthy of attention. The Commander in Chief ordered the General Officers who were off duty to attend him to reconnoitre this ground on this morning. When arrived at the ground, although very commanding, it did not appear so much so as other grounds to the north and almost parallel with the left of the army, as it was then formed.

"Yonder," says Major-Gen. Lee, pointing to the grounds just mentioned, "is the ground we ought to occupy."

"Let us go and view it," replied the Commander in Chief.

When on the way, a light-horseman came up in full gallop, his horse almost out of breath, and addressed Gen. Washington: "The British are on the camp, sir."

The General observed: "Gentlemen, we have now other business than reconnoitring," putting his horse in full gallop for the camp, and followed by the other officers.

When arrived at head-quarters, the Adjutant-General Re[e]d, who had remained at camp, informed the Commander in Chief that the guards had been all beat in, and the whole American army were now at their respective posts, in order of battle. The Commander in Chief turned round to the officers and only said, "Gentlemen, you will repair to your respective posts, and do the best you can."

Our General, on arriving at his own division, found them all in the lines; and, from the height of his post, found that the first attack was directed against the Americans on Chatterton's Hill. The little river Bronx, which ran between the American right and this hill, after running round its north side, turned and ran down on the east and south-east.

—HEATH, Memoirs, pp. 68-71.

2. THE FIGHT FOR CHATTERTON'S HILL

Colonel John Haslet to Caesar Rodney.

November 12, 1776

I received his Excellency's orders to take possession of the hill [Chatterton's Hill] beyond our lines, and the command of the Militia regiments there posted; which was done. We had not been many minutes on the ground when the cannonade began, and the second shot wounded a militia-man in the thigh, upon which the whole regiment broke and fled immediately, and were not rallied without much difficulty. Soon after, General McDougall's brigade took post behind us. Some of our officers expressed much apprehension from the fire of our friends so posted. On my application to the general, he ordered us to the right, formed his own brigade on the left, and ordered Brooks's Massachusetts Militia still farther to the right, behind a stone fence.

The troops being thus disposed, I went up to the top of the hill, in front of our troops, accompanied by Major McDonough, to reconnoitre the enemy, I plainly perceived them marching to the White-Plain, in eight columns, and stop in the wheat-fields a considerable time. I saw their General Officers on horse back assemble in council, and soon their whole body face about and in one continued column march to the hill opposite to our right. I then applied to General McDougall again to vary his disposition, and advised him to order my regiment farther onward, and replace it with Colonel Smallwood's, or order the colonel forward, for there was no dependence to be placed on the Militia. The latter measure was adopted.

On my seeing the enemy's march to the creek begin in a column of their main body, and urging the necessity of bringing our field-pieces immediately forward to bear upon them, the general ordered one, and that so poorly appointed, that myself was forced to assist in dragging it along the rear of the regiment. While so employed, a cannon-ball struck the carriage, and scattered the shot about, a wad of tow blazing in the middle. The artillerymen fled. One alone was prevailed upon to tread out the blaze and collect the shot. The few that returned made not more than two discharges, when they retreated with the field-piece.

At this time the Maryland battalion was warmly engaged, and the enemy ascending the hill. The cannonade from twelve or fifteen pieces, well served, kept up a continual peal of reiterated thunder. The Militia regiment behind the fence fled in confusion, without more than a random, scattering fire. Colonel Smallwood in a quarter of an hour afterwards gave way also. The rest of General McDougall's brigade never came up to the scene of action. Part of the first three Delaware companies also retreated in disorder, but not till after several were wounded and killed. The left of the regiment took post behind a fence on the top of the hill with most of the officers, and twice repulsed the Light Troops and Horse of the enemy; but seeing ourselves deserted on all hands, and the continued column of the enemy advancing, we also retired. Covering the retreat of our party, and forming at the foot of the hill, we marched into camp in the rear of the body sent to reinforce us.

—RODNEY, *Letters*, pp. 142-143.

XVII. THE FALL OF FORT WASHINGTON

Admitting to 150 killed and wounded in the joint British-Hessian attack on Chatterton Hill, Archibald Robertson of the Royal Engineers noted in his diary under the date of October 28: "This day General Knipphausen advanced toward King's Bridge. Fort Independence, etc., taken possession of." On November 5 Howe left White Plains for Dobbs Ferry, toward which his army was already moving. "The design of this manoeuvre is a matter of much conjecture," Washington reported to Congress. The Americans actually expected Howe to cross into Jersey or to move up the Hudson. He did neither.

Why he changed his whole plan of campaign and decided to move south against Fort Washington on Manhattan Island is now clear. An American traitor, William Demont, an ensign in Magaw's 5th Pennsylvania, deserted and turned over the plans of that fort to the British. Conclusive evidence of this treachery is found in the contemporary diary kept by the British officer, Captain Mackenzie, and in a letter from the turncoat himself which was not published until a hundred years after the event.

The damage had been done, but as Alexander Graydon later observed, intelligence about the fort might readily have been obtained "from hundreds in New York" who had "a perfect knowledge of the ground we occupied." Standing near the northern end of Manhattan, Fort Washington was no longer tenable and should have been abandoned, especially after two British ships of 44 guns each and a 20-gun frigate had passed by the obstructions placed across the river to block the fleet. Washington advised Nathanael Greene to evacuate the fort but left the decision to his subordinate. Greene advised him: "I cannot conceive the garrison to be in any great danger." Against his better judgment Washington permitted Greene to retain the garrison there. The Rhode Island anchorsmith and ex-Quaker, whose judgment cost the Americans 2,900 troops, one of the major blunders of the war, was

George Washington at Princeton. Portrait by Charles Willson Peale *(The Pennsylvania Academy of the Fine Arts)*

Samuel Adams. Portrait by John Singleton Copley   (*Museum of Fine Arts, Boston*)

Paul Revere. Portrait by John Singleton Copley (*Museum of Fine Arts, Boston*)

John Adams. Portrait by Charles Willson Peale   (*Independence National Historical Park Collection*)

THREE PATRIOT LEADERS

Bostonians in Distress.   A contemporary London cartoon depicts the effect on Boston of the closing of the port. The Bostonians are caged like felons and left to starve, saved only by codfish sent from Marblehead and gifts from many other towns.   (*Library of Congress*)

The Bostonians Paying The Excise-man or Tarring and Feathering.   A London cartoon showing what happened to John Malcomb, a Tory exciseman who collected the Tea Tax in Boston in 1774.   (*Library of Congress*)

Battle of Lexington (*The New-York Historical Society*)

Retreat from Concord. Engraving by James Smillie from a painting by Chappel

Death of Joseph Warren as the British carry Breed's Hill Redoubt. Painting by John Trumbull   (*Library of Congress*)

Bunker's Hill, or America's Head Dress.   A contemporary cartoon   (*Library of Congress*)

BRITISH WAR LORDS IN AMERICA

Sir William Howe (*Emmet Collection, New York Library*)

Lord Richard Howe (*The New-York Historical Society*)

FRENCH ALLIES IN AMERICA

Rochambeau (*Musée Bonnat, Bayonne, France*)

Comte de Grasse

Battle of Long Island: Retreat of Americans under Lord Stirling across Gowanus Creek.
Engraving by James Smillie from a painting by Chappel

The great fire of New York, September 20-21, 1776. Engraved by André Basset

The landing of the British troops in the Jerseys, November 20, 1776.   Water color attributed to Lord Rawdon

Clinton tells Burgoyne he will "try something"

Undated letter of late July or early August, 1777, from Sir Henry Clinton to General John Burgoyne informing him of Howe's move on Philadelphia. When the letter is covered by an hourglass-shaped mask, sent by separate messenger, the following message is disclosed. "Sir W. Howe is gone to the Chesapeak bay with the greatest part of the Army. I hear he is landed but am not certain. I am left to command here with too small a force to make any effectual diversion in your favour. I shall try something at any rate. It may be of use to you. I own to you I think Sir W.'s move just at this time the worst he could take." (*Clinton Papers, William L. Clements Library, Ann Arbor, Michigan*)

Benedict Arnold wounded leading the attack on Breymann's Redoubt at Bemis Heights. Engraving of original painting by Chappel

Burgoyne's surrender at Saratoga. Currier lithograph of original painting by John Trumbull in the Capitol at Washington (*Library of Congress*)

Signing the Declaration of Independence (*Library of Congress*)

Qualifying for a Campaign (Library of Congress)

the youngest of Washington's brigadiers. He still had much to learn, but he was fast to learn it and ended the war as an outstanding military figure.

Washington, who saw the battle of Fort Washington from the heights of Morrisania, tried to prepare an escape route for the besieged garrison and urged Magaw to hold out until nightfall, but the commander, finding his position untenable, personally surrendered to the Hessian Knyphausen. This was a tribute to Hessian accomplishments that day, for, along with two Highland regiments, the German troops had broken the back of the defense, charging up the hillside on the north and east side of the American works while Lord Percy's troops attacked the strong lines overlooking Harlem. The Hessians were reputed to have given no quarter.

The British lost 458 killed and wounded but took 2,800 prisoners. It was one of the costliest capitulations of the entire war. The numbers of the captured were swollen by troops who had been defending outlying areas and were forced by two British crossings of the Harlem River and naval movements to retire behind the fortifications.

1. A Traitor Reveals the Plans of Fort Washington

Diary of Captain Frederick Mackenzie.

3rd November. General Knyphausen, with six Hessian battalions which had taken post on the heights near Kingsbridge lately, passed over to this island yesterday, without a shot being fired at him, and encamped on the high grounds near Fort Washington. This movement completely cuts off all communication between the Rebel troops on this island, and those under Genl. Washington. . . .

In the several attacks lately made on the Rebels by the troops under Genl. Howe, very few prisoners have been taken. The soldiers generally made use of their bayonets. The 17th Dragoons are said to have behaved remarkably well, and to have taken several batteries. Preparations have been making for some time past by the Barrack Master General in New York for the reception of such troops as may be quartered there during the ensuing winter. Many of the public buildings have been and others are fitting up for hospitals; such as the College, the Bridewell, the Workhouse, the new hospital, and some of the meeting houses and churches. . . .

The first object at present is the reduction of Fort Washington, and thereby the complete possession of this island: after which Genl. Howe will probably detach a considerable part of the army to the southward, where operations may be carried on with advantage during the winter, or else penetrate into Jersey and endeavor to enlarge the quarters of the army in a province abounding with provisions, fuel and other necessary supplies. The extension of our quarters will also give the Loyalists an opportunity of declaring themselves, and circumscribe the resources of the enemy.

A man named Diamond, who says he was Ensign and Adjutant and acted as Major of Brigade in the Rebel Army, deserted yesterday from their advanced post. He says the Rebels remaining on this island amount to about 2000 men, who, if they are obliged to abandon their advanced works, are to retire into Fort Washington and defend it to the last extremity, having therein two months provisions, many cannon and plenty of ammunition. He says there are great dissentions in the Rebel Army, everybody finding fault with the mode of proceeding, and the inferior officers, even ensigns, insisting that, in such a cause, every man has a right to assist in council and to give his opinion. They are much distressed for clothing. The people from the Southern Colonies declare they will not go into New England, and the others that they will not march to the southward. If this account is true in any degree, they must soon go to pieces.

—MACKENZIE, *Diary*, I, 94-96.

2. A TRAITOR OWNS: "I SACRIFICED ALL I WAS WORTH"

William Demont to the Reverend Dr. Peters.

London, January 16, 1792

... On the 2nd of November 1776 I sacrificed all I was worth in the world to the service of my King and country, and joined the then Lord Percy, brought in with me the plans of Fort Washington, by which plans that fortress was taken by his Majesty's troops the 16 instant, together with 2700 prisoners and stores and ammunition to the amount of 1800 pounds. At the same time I may with justice affirm, from my knowledge of the works I saved the lives of many of his Majesty's subjects. These, Sir, are facts well known to every General Officer which was there.

—DEMONT, "Letter," *Mag. of Am. Hist.*

3. THE FALL OF THE OUTER DEFENSES

Alexander Graydon's account.

At ten o'clock in the morning, a large body of the enemy appeared on Haerlem plains, preceded by their field pieces, and advanced with their whole body towards a rocky point of the height, which skirted the plains in a southern direction from the first line, and at a considerable distance from it—and, commencing a brisk fire on the small work constructed there, drove out the party which held it, consisting of twenty men, and took possession of it, the men retiring with the picket guard to the first line. The enemy, having gained the heights, advanced in column on open ground towards the first line; whilst a party of their troops pushed forward and took possession of a small unoccupied work in front of the first line; from whence they opened their fire with some field pieces and a howitzer, upon the line, but without effect. When the column came within proper distance, a fire from the six-pounder was directed against it; on which, the whole column inclined to their left and took post behind a piece of woods, where they remained. As it was suspected that they would make an attempt on the right of the line, under cover of the wood, that part was strengthened.

Things remained in this position for about an hour and a half, during which interval General Washington, with Generals Putnam, Greene, Mercer and other principal officers, came over the North River from Fort Lee and crossed the island to Morris's house; whence they viewed the position of our troops and the operations of the enemy in that quarter. Having remained there a sufficient time to observe the arrangement that had been made for the defence of that part of the island, they retired by the way they came, and returned to Fort Lee, without making any change in the disposition of the troops or communicating any new orders. It is a fact not generally known that the British troops took possession of the very spot on which the Commander-in-chief, and the general officers with him, had stood, in fifteen minutes after they left it.

Colonel Rawlings was some time late in the morning attacked by the Hessians, whom he fought with great gallantry and effect, as they were climbing the heights, until the arms of the riflemen became useless from the foulness they contracted from the frequent repetition of their fire. From this incident, and the great superiority of the enemy, Colonel Rawlings was obliged to retire into the fort. The enemy, having gained the heights, immediately pushed forward towards the fort and took post behind a large store-house within a small distance of it.

But to return to what passed at the first line towards New York. Intelligence having been received by Colonel Cadwalader that the enemy were coming down Haerlem River in boats to land in his rear, he detached Captain Lenox with fifty men to oppose them, and, on farther information, a hundred more, with Captains Edwards and Tudor. This force, with the addition of about the same number from Fort Washington, arrived on the heights near Morris's house, early enough to fire on the enemy in their boats, which was done with such effect that about ninety were killed and wounded. The great superiority, however, of the enemy (their numbers amounting to about eight hundred men) prevailed over the bravery and good conduct of our troops, who, with some loss, retired to Fort Washington.

This body of the enemy immediately advanced and took possession of the grounds in advance of and a little below Morris's house, where some soldiers' huts had been left standing, not far from the second line. This position of the enemy being observed, it was expected they would march down and take possession of the second line (which, from the want of men, was entirely without defence) and thereby place the troops in the first line between two fires. This important movement did not, however, take place, owing, as was afterwards learned, to the apprehension they entertained that the enclosed bastions concealed therein a number of men whose fire would greatly annoy them. They hesitated; and this being perceived from the delay that took place, Colonel Cadwalader, to avoid the fatal consequences that must have resulted from the expected movement, immediately resolved to retire to the fort with the troops under his command; and as the measure required promptness and activity, he sent orders to the right and left of the line to move off towards Fort Washington, on the signal being given; which, after a proper interval of time, being made, the whole was put in motion (those on the left retiring obliquely towards the centre of the second line) past the second line, and when they came opposite to the body of the enemy posted at the huts, received their fire, which was returned in an irregular manner; and, pursuing the road which led to the fort, under the heights by the North River, arrived there with little or no loss.

The militia under Colonel Baxter, posted on Haerlem River, were attacked by the British guards and light infantry, who landed on the island of New

York, protected by the fire from the work on the heights on the opposite side of the river. A short contest ensued; but our troops, overpowered by numbers, and leaving behind them Colonel Baxter who was killed by a British officer as he was bravely encouraging his men, retired to the fort. The guards and light infantry then crossed the island to the heights on the North River, a little below the fort, under which Colonel Cadwalader with his party, but a few minutes before, had passed in his way to the fort.

—GRAYDON, Memoirs of His Own Time, pp. 191-202.

4. "THUS THE HESSIANS TOOK POSSESSION OF THE FORT"

Journal of John Reuber, Hessian soldier in the regiment of Colonel Johann Rall.

17 November, in the morning before day-break, all the regiments and corps were assembled, the Hessians on the right wing at the north haven; the English troops upon the left wing at the south haven. When it was now day and the Americans perceived us, but nothing more very plainly, at once these two ships of war, on both sides, made their master-strokes upon the fort, and we began at the same time on the land with cannon, and all the regiments marched forward up the hill and were obliged to creep along up the rocks, one falling down alive, another being shot dead. We were obliged to drag ourselves by the beech-tree bushes up the height where we could not really stand.

At last, however, we got about on the top of the hill where there were trees and great stones. We had a hard time of it there together. Because they now had no idea of yielding, Col. Rall gave the word of command, thus: "All that are my grenadiers, march forwards!" All the drummers struck up the march, the hautboy-players blew. At once all that were yet alive shouted, "Hurrah!" Immediately all were mingled together, Americans and Hessians. There was no more firing, but all ran forward pell-mell upon the fortress.

Before we came up, the Americans had a trench about the fortress, as soon as we were within which, the order came to halt. Then the Americans had a mind to run out through us, but then came the command: "Hold! you are all prisoners of war." The fort was at once demanded by Gen. V. Kniphausen. The Rebels were allowed two hours for capitulating; when they were expired, the fort was surrendered to General V. Kniphausen with all the munitions of war and provisions belonging thereto within and without the fort; all guns and arms were to be laid down, and when all this was done, Rall's regiment and the old Lossberg, being made to form into two lines facing each other, they were required to march out between the two regiments and deposit their guns and other weapons.

Then came the English and took them to New York into custody, and when the first transport was off, the second marched out of the citadel and was as strong as the first, and they also were conducted to New York into confinement. And when all this was got through with, it was night. Thus the Hessians took possession of the fort, and the rest marched again round to Kingsbridge into our old camp we had before stopped so long. Then came the order that the fort should be called Fort Kniphausen.

—JOHNSTON, Battle of Harlem Heights, pp. 229-231.

CHAPTER TWELVE

"Bagging the Fox"

THE TITLE OF *this chapter comes from a nonchalant boast of Cornwallis that he would catch Washington in New Jersey as a hunter bags a fox. That proved easier said than done. The British strategy after the fall of Fort Washington was to trap the main Patriot army, which under the Fabian tactics of its commander had fallen back toward Philadelphia and held a thin line on the Delaware River. Then with lightning counterpunches at Trenton and Princeton Washington turned the tide of battle in the Jerseys and saved his army, which was to make its winter quarters in the hills around Morristown.*

As we have already seen, Carleton had failed to push down from the North to Albany. The grand pincer operation had fizzled out, for, aside from New York City, Howe had little to show for his gigantic effort. In fact it could be persuasively argued that the Jersey campaign was a turning point in the war. Washington's main army had been saved and Patriot morale had been in large part restored.

The campaign in the Jerseys brings to the fore a number of personalities, among them the flashy and talented Cornet Banastre Tarleton of the British Light Dragoons, destined to become Britain's most formidable cavalry officer, and the willful and unstable Charles Lee, a former British army officer, who held the rank of major general and until the Jersey campaign enjoyed an inflated reputation. That so vacuous and untrustworthy a character as Lee could be seriously considered by many officers of the Patriot army as the man to supplant Washington speaks volumes for the low state of morale after the retreat from New York.

I. THE RETREAT TO NEW JERSEY

The fall of Fort Washington left Greene mortified. "I feel mad, vexed, sick, and sorry," *he wrote Henry Knox on November 17 from across the river at Fort Lee.* "Happy should I be to see you. This is a most terrible event: its consequences are justly to be dreaded." *In a sober report to Congress written the previous day, Washington summed it up:* "The loss of such a number of officers and men, many of whom have been trained with more than common attention, will I fear be severely felt. But when that of the arms and accoutrements is added, much more so, and must be a farther incentive to procure as considerable a supply as possible for the new troops, as soon as it can be done."

On the stormy night of November 19, 1776, six thousand men under

Cornwallis crossed the Hudson, and by morning had dragged their artillery to the top of the Palisades. Fort Lee was hurriedly evacuated. Greene had no time to remove the stores, only to save the gunpowder. Washington, who had brought over some of his troops from White Plains, ordered a retreat through flat country, though the army might be trapped between the Hackensack and Passaic rivers. Commented one British officer, "On the appearance of our troops, the rebels fled like scared rabbits. . . . They have left some poor pork, a few greasy proclamations, and some of that scoundrel Common Sense man's letters, which we can read at our leisure, now that we have got one of the 'impregnable redoubts' of Mr. Washington's to quarter in." Other British officers were equally jubilant, while the Americans realized that Philadelphia and the control of the Delaware seemed to be the new objective of Sir William. Were the British to move against Philadelphia, General Mifflin wrote Robert Morris on November 21, that city would "in a few hours after it shake to her centre."

The British advance soon bogged down. "As we go forward into the country the rebels fly before us," one British officer observed, "and when we come back they always follow us. 'Tis almost impossible to catch them. They will neither fight, nor totally run away, but they keep at such a distance that we are always a day's march from them. We seem to be playing at bo peep." The British and Hessian advance was accompanied by scenes of pillaging and criminal acts. "They to the disgrace of civilised nations ravish the fair sex, from the age of ten to seventy," one correspondent wrote Jefferson in December. Patriot morale seemed to one British traveler, Nicholas Cresswell, to be on the verge of collapse. "The politicians (or rather timid Whigs) give up all for lost," he commented, "and the Tories begin to exult. I am convinced that if General Howe will push to Philadelphia the day is his own."

1. The Fall of Fort Lee: "Their Army Is Broken to Pieces"

Probably from Francis, Lord Rawdon, to Robert Auchmuty.

November 25, 1776

. . . This grand point [Fort Washington] being gained, by which York Island and a great part of the province was cleared from the rebels, General Howe, I think on the morning of the 20th instant, landed 5,000 men under the command of Lord Cornwallis up the North River on the Jersey shore, a few miles above the other famous fortification, called Fort Constitution or Fort Lee. His Lordship immediately marched to attack this place, and got to it by 1 o'clock the same day, but found it had been evacuated by the rebels so precipitately that the pots were left absolutely boiling on the fire, and the tables spread for dinner of some of their officers. In the fort they found but twelve men, who were all dead drunk. There were forty or fifty pieces of cannon found loaded, with two large iron sea mortars and one brass one, with a vast quantity of ammunition, provision and stores, with all their tents standing.

His Lordship, finding this, pressed forward as quick as he could toward Hackinsack new bridge. But the people belonging to the fort had the heels of him. However, on the road he met with 3 or 4,000 fresh hands coming from Newark to assist in garrisoning the forts. To these gentry the troops distributed a couple of rounds, and set them a scampering, leaving behind them several brass field pieces and their baggage; and as they marched along, found the roads thick strewed with muskets, knapsacks, etc. But the number of cattle taken in the Hackinsack meadows, which had been driven from Pensylvania and some parts of the Jerseys for the use of the grand rebel army, is truly astonishing, and amount to many thousands.

His Lordship's face seems to be set towards Philadelphia, where he will meet with no kind of opposition. I hope he will be at Amboy or Brunswick to-morrow or next day, if it will leave off raining. You see, my dear sir, that I have not been mistaken in my judgement of this people. The southern people will no more fight than the Yankees. The fact is that their army is broken all to pieces, and the spirits of their leaders and their abettors is also broken. However, I think one may venture to pronounce that it is well nigh over with them.

—Gr. Brit. Hist. Mss. Comm., *Hastings Manuscripts,* III, 190-192.

2. "I Am in Great Fear for Our Political Salvation"

Ebenezer Huntington, Captain in the Continental Army, to his grandfather, Jabez Huntington.

Peeks Kill, November 25, 1776

This comes by Mr Grover, who can better tell you news from this post than myself. The anxiety I am in for raising of a new army is not small but to parents I think I have an undoubted right to write freely. The present appearance is very gloomy, the British troops making head whereever they attempt. Our people, instead of behaving like brave men, behave like rascalls, and to add to that, it seems that the British troops had gone into the Jersies, only to receive the submission of the whole country. People join them almost in captains' companies to take the oath of allegiance. Besides, those of the Militia who have been sent for our assistance leave us the minute their times are out and would not stay tho' their eternal salvation was to be forfeited if they went home. The persuasion of a Cisero would not any more effect their tarry than the Niagara Falls would the kindling of a fire. Besides the slow progress of a new army, it seems as though the few that remain till the first of January are to fall a sacrafice to the British savages.

Dear Father, no man unless on the spott can have a tolerable idea of it. Our stores lost without an exchange of a shott. A Hell itself could not furnish worse beings than subsist in the world where our army are now posted.

I am, Dear Sir, in Great Fear for our political salvation while I subscribe myself your dutiful son.

—Huntington, *Letters Written During the Revolution,* p. 53.

3. "An Indecisive Mind Is One of the Greatest Misfortunes to an Army"

A. adjutant general joseph reed to general charles lee

Hackensack, November 21, 1776

The letter you will receive with this contains my sentiments with respect to your present station. But besides this I have some additional reasons for most earnestly wishing to have you where the principal scene of action is laid.

I do not mean to flatter, nor praise you at the expence of any other, but I confess I do think that it is entirely owing to you that this army and the liberties of America so far as they are dependant on it are not totally cut off. You have decision, a quality often wanting in minds otherwise valuable, and I ascribe to this an escape from York Island—from Kingsbridge and the Plains —and I have no doubt had you been here the garrison at Mount Washington would now have composed a part of this army. Under all these circumstances I confess I ardently wish to see you removed from a place where I think there will be little call for your judgment and experience to the place where they are like to be so necessary. Nor am I singular in my opinion—every gentleman of the family, the officers and soldiers generally have a confidence in you—the enemy constantly inquire where you are, and seem to me to be less confident when you are present.

Col. Cadwallader, thro a special indulgence on account of some civilities shewn by his family to Gen. Prescott, has been liberated from New-York without any parole. He informs that the enemy have a southern expedition in view—that they hold us very cheap in consequence of the late affair at Mount Washington where both the plan of defence and execution were contemptible—if a real defence of the lines was intended the number was too few; if the fort only, the garrison was too numerous by half. General Washington's own judgment, seconded by representations from us, would I believe have saved the men and their arms, but unluckily General Greene's judgment was contrary; this kept the general's mind in a state of suspense till the stroke was struck. Oh! General—an indecisive mind is one of the greatest misfortunes that can befall an army—how often have I lamented it this campaign.

All circumstances considered we are in a very awful and alarming state, one that requires the utmost wisdom and firmness of mind. As soon as the season will admit I think yourself and some others should go to Congress and form the plan of the new army—point out their defects to them and if possible prevail on them to bind their whole attention to this great object—even to the exclusion of every other. If they will not or cannot do this, I fear all our exertions will be vain in this part of the world. Foreign assistance is soliciting but we cannot expect they will fight the whole battle—but artillery and artillerists must be had, if possible.

I intended to have said more but the express is waiting—and I must conclude with my clear and explicit opinion that your presence is of the last importance.

—REED, "Letter," *N. Y. Hist. Soc. Coll.*, V, 293-294.

B. GENERAL CHARLES LEE TO JOSEPH REED.

Camp, November 24, 1776

I received your most obliging, flattering letter—lament with you that fatal indecision of mind which in war is a much greater disqualification than stupidity or even want of personal courage. Accident may put a decisive blunderer in the right—but eternal defeat and miscarriage must attend the man of the best parts if cursed with indecision. The General recommends in so pressing a manner as almost to amount to an order to bring over the Continental troops under my command—which recommendation or order throws me into the greatest dilemma from sev'ral considerations. Part of the troops are so ill furnished with shoes and stockings, blankets, etc., that they must inevitably perish in this wretched weather. Part of 'em are to be dismissed on Saturday next and this part is the best accoutred for service.

What shelter we are to find on the other side the river is a serious consideration: but these considerations should not sway me; my reason for not having marched already is that we have just received intelligence that Rogers's corps, the Light Horse, part of the Highlanders and another brigade lye in so exposed a situation as to give the fairest opportunity of being carried off. I should have attempted it last night but the rain was too violent, and when our pieces are wet you know our troops are *hors de combat*. This night I hope will be better.

If we succeed we shall be well compensated for the delay. We shall likewise be able in our return to clear the country of all the articles wanted by the enemy. In every view therefore the expedition must answer. . . . I only wait myself for this business I mention of Rogers and Co. being over—shall then fly to you—for to confess a truth I really think our Chief will do better with me than without me.

—CHARLES LEE, "Letter," *N. Y. Hist. Soc. Coll.*, V, 305-306.

4. "By Retreating I Shall Lull Them into Security"

George Washington to General Charles Lee, an intercepted letter found among the archives at Marburg, Germany.

Brunswick, 30th of November, 1776

The movements of the enemy are, since I wrote you from Newark, of such a nature, as things stand at present, sincerely to be wished for. I have feared that they would take Newark, Elizabeth Town and Amboy for their winter quarters in order to undertake from these places early in the spring an attack on Philadelphia and at the same time having a favourable season ahead that they would make a diversion on the Delaware river with their fleet. The advantages they have gained over us in the past have made them so proud and sure of success that they are determined to go to Philadelphia this winter. I have positive information that this is a fact and because the term of service of the light troops of Jersey and Maryland are ended they anticipate the weakness of our army. Should they now really risk this undertaking then there is a great probability that they will pay dearly for it for I shall continue to retreat before them so as to lull them into security.

—STRYKER, *Battles of Trenton and Princeton*, pp. 326-327.

5. The Flight of Congress to Baltimore

General Oliver Wolcott, delegate to Congress from Connecticut, to his wife.

Philadelphia, December 13, 1776

The 11th in the evening a detachment of the enemy took possession of Burlington, about 20 miles from this city on the Jersey shore. The rest of their army are at Trenton, and upon the banks of the river above it; their numbers are uncertain, but are computed about twelve thousand, and as their designs are undoubtedly to gain possession of this city, the Congress, upon the advice of Genls Putnam and Mifflin (who are now here to provide for the protection of the place) as well as the result of their own opinion, have adjourned themselves to Baltimore in Maryland, about 110 miles from this city, as it was judged that the Council of America ought not to sit in a place liable to be interrupted by the rude disorder of arms, so that I am at this moment going forward for that place. Whether the army will succeed in their cruel designs against this city must be left to time to discover. Congress have ordered the General to defend it to the last extremity, and God grant that he may be successful in his exertions!

Whatever event may take place, the American cause will be supported to the last, and I trust in God that it will succeed. The Grecian, Roman and Dutch States were in their infancy reduced to the greatest distress, infinitely beyond what we have yet experienced. The God who governs the universe and who holds empires in His hand, can with the least effort of His will, grant us all that security, opulence and power which they have enjoyed. . . .

Gen. Howe has lately published a proclamation abusing the Congress as having sinister designs upon the people and has offered, to such as will accept of pardon upon an unlimited submission, "Royal Forgiveness." But who is base enough to wish to have a precarious care dependent upon the caprice of power, unrestrained by any law and governed by the dangerous thirst of avarice and ambition?

My best love to my children and friends. May the Almighty ever have you and them in His protection!

—JOHNSTON, *Campaign of 1776*, II, 147-148.

6. "A Certain Great Man Is Most Damnably Deficient"

General Charles Lee to General Horatio Gates, written the day of Lee's capture.

Basking Ridge, N. J., December 13, 1776

The ingenious manoeuvre of Fort Washington has unhinged the goodly fabrick we had been building. There never was so damned a stroke. *Entre nous*, a certain great man is most damnably deficient. He has thrown me into a situation where I have my choice of difficulties. If I stay in this Province I risk myself and army, and if I do not stay the Province is lost for ever. I have neither guides, cavalry, medicines, money, shoes or stockings. I must act with the greatest circumspection. Tories are in my front, rear and on my flanks. The mass of the people is strangely contaminated.

In short unless something which I do not expect turns up we are lost. Our counsels have been weak to the last degree. As to what relates to yourself, if you think you can be in time to aid the General I would have you by all means go. You will at least save your army. It is said that the Whigs are determined to set fire to Philadelphia. If they strike this decisive stroke the day will be our own, but unless it is done all chance of liberty in any part of the globe is forever vanished.

Adieu, my dear friend. God bless you!

—CHARLES LEE, "Letter," *N. Y. Hist. Soc. Coll.*, V, 348.

7. The Capture of General Charles Lee

A. "a most miraculous event"

Banastre Tarleton to his mother.

Prince's Town, December 18, 1776

My dear Madam

Our correspondence is totally stopt, so few ships go to and come from England on acct. of the quantity of American privateers that this continent seems utterly secluded from Great Britain.

You will with pleasure, if you receive it, read this letter. Lieutenant General Earl Cornwallis, under whose command the King's army has penetrated into the Jerseys as far as the River Delaware, being ignorant of General Lee's motions and situation, gave orders on the 11th inst. for a party of the Queen's Light Dragoons, consisting of a captain, 2 subalterns and 25 privates, to be ready to march in expedition order the next morning. Colonel Harcourt who was with the regiment received his private orders from Lord Cornwallis, together with Captain Eustace, his Lordship's aid de camp, who attended us on this expedition.

Our first day's march was 18 miles, but barren of incidents. We took up our quarters at night at Hillsborough upon the River Millstone. A battalion of the 71st covered us at that place. Our house caught fire at 1 o'clock in the morning and burnt to the ground. We escaped without loss or damage— we bedded ourselves in straw till 5 o'clock. We then received orders to march. Col. Harcourt gave me the advanced guard, consisting of 6 men: a circumstance I ever shall esteem as one of the most fortunate of my life. We marched by different and cross roads towards Maurice Town. We had not proceeded above 14 miles before the advanced guard discovered some and took one Rebel in arms. We marched 2 miles forward, then Colonel Harcourt found by some people that General Lee was not above 4 or 5 miles distant from the detachment, and at the same time heard that our retreat was cut off by the road we had come. He detached Captain Nash with 4 dragoons back to prove the truth of the last information. Colonel Harcourt then ordered me to advance. We trotted on about 3 miles when my advanced guard seized 2 sentrys without firing a gun.

The dread of instant death obliged these fellows to inform me, to the best of my knowledge, of the situation of General Lee. They told us he was about a mile off, that his guard was not very large and that he was about half a mile in the rear of his army. These men were so confused that they gave us but an imperfect idea where General Lee was. Colonel Harcourt immediately detached me with 2 men only to the top of an eminence in the road, to get what intelligence I could, and if much fired upon, immediately to retreat upon him. In going quick to the ground I observed a Yankee light-horseman, at whom I rushed and made prisoner. I brought him in to Colonel Harcourt; the fear of the sabre extorted great intelligence, and he told us he had just left General Lee from whom he had an express to carry to General Sullivan at Pukamin. He could not satisfy me exactly as to the strength of General Lee's guard, but confirmed the account of the other 2 prisoners as to his situation.

He said he thought his guard did not consist of above 30 men. He pointed out to us the house where he had left General Lee and mentioned that he was going to move directly.

Colonel Harcourt called to Eustace, to know whether he thought we were strong enough. Eustace replyed in the affirmative. Without further consultation I was ordered to lead on my advanced guard which consisted of only 5 men as quick as possible. I went on at full speed, when perceiving two sentrys at a door and a loaded waggon I pushed at them, making all the noise I could. The sentrys were struck with a panic, dropped their arms and fled. I ordered my men to fire into the house thro' every window and door, and cut up as many of the guard as they could. An old woman upon her knees begged for life and told me General Lee was in the house.

This assurance gave me pleasure. I carried on my attack with all possible spirit and surrounded the house, tho' fired upon in front, flank and rear. General Lee's aid de camp, 2 French colonels and some of the guard kept up a fire for about 8 minutes, which we silenced. I fired twice through the door of the house and then addressed myself to this effect: "I knew Genl. Lee was in the house, that if he would surrender himself, he and his attendants should be safe, but if my summons was not complied with immediately, the house should be burnt and every persòn without exception should be put to the sword."

At this instant I was called by one of my men to the back door, my attention being directly engaged by his saying that Genl. Lee was escaping that way and I galloped to the spot. The French colonels, one of the aid de camp (the other being shot) and some of the guard attempted to retreat sword in hand. We took one colonel prisoner, the rest were killed or wounded. Genl. Lee surrendered himself to the sentry I had placed at the front door, whilst we were employed as above. The prisoner was led to Col. Harcourt, who was silencing the fires in my rear and flanks whilst I carried on the attack upon Genl. Lee's quarters with the advanced guard only. Col. Harcourt placed his noble prisoner upon a horse and led him off by a different road from that which we had come with all possible expedition.

The bugle horn was then sounded. I brought up the rear of the men and the French colonel. This attack which continued in the whole about 15 minutes proved fatal to none of the officers or dragoons. One horse's leg which was slightly grazed and one saddle which was shot through the pommel were the only damages we sustained. We retreated afterwards 13 miles thro' an enemys country without any accident. We then forded a river, approached Hillsborough and gave each other congratulations with every symptom of joy.

Captain Nash whom I mentioned being detached did not join us again till Genl. Lee was our prisoner. He was beat back from the place where we had passed in the morning and where they meant to cut off our retreat. He lost a servant and a horse. The party returned safe.

This is a most miraculous event—it appears like a dream. We conducted Genl. Lee and the French col. to Lord Cornwallis at Penning. Our day's march only exceeded 60 miles.

Genl. Lee is sent prisoner to Brunswick. Colonel Harcourt's whole conduct was masterly—it deserves every applause. Present my love, comps., etc. (I shall tire you if I write any more).

I forgot to tell you that this coup de main has put an end to the campaign. We have not yet crossed the Delaware. The Queen's Regt. of Lt. Dragoons are cantoned off Princes Town and Brunswick; at the former exists one who will always be proud to subscribe himself

Your affectionate son
BANASTRE TARLETON
—BASS, The Green Dragoon, pp. 20-22.

B. "HERE IS THE GENERAL. HE HAS SURRENDERED"

Memoirs of Captain James Wilkinson of the Continental Army.

General Lee wasted the morning in altercation with certain militia corps who were of his command, particularly the Connecticut light horse, several of whom appeared in large full-bottomed perukes, and were treated very irreverently; the call of the adjutant general for orders also occupied some of his time, and we did not sit down to breakfast before 10 o'clock. General Lee was engaged in answering General Gates's letter, and I had risen from the table and was looking out of an end window down a lane about one hundred yards in length which led to the house from the main road, when I discovered a party of British dragoons turn a corner of the avenue at a full charge.

Startled at this unexpected spectacle, I exclaimed, "Here, Sir, are the British cavalry!"

"*Where?*" replied the general, who had signed his letter in the instant.

"Around the house;" for they had opened files and encompassed the building.

General Lee appeared alarmed, yet collected, and his second observation marked his self-possession: "Where is the guard?—damn the guard, why don't they fire?" and after a momentary pause, he turned to me and said, "Do, Sir, see what has become of the guard."

The women of the house at this moment entered the room and proposed to him to conceal himself in a bed, which he rejected with evident disgust. I caught up my pistols which lay on the table, thrust the letter he had been writing into my pocket, and passed into a room at the opposite end of the house, where I had seen the guard in the morning. Here I discovered their arms; but the men were absent. I stepped out of the door and perceived the dragoons chasing them in different directions, and receiving a very uncivil salutation, I returned into the house.

Too inexperienced immediately to penetrate the motives of this enterprize, I considered the *rencontre* accidental, and from the terrific tales spread over the country of the violence and barbarity of the enemy, I believed it to be a wanton murdering party, and determined not to die without company. I accordingly sought a position where I could not be approached by more than one person at a time, and with a pistol in each hand I awaited the expected search, resolved to shoot the first and the second person who might appear, and then to appeal to my sword. I did not remain long in this unpleasant situation, but was apprised of the object of the incursion by the very audible declaration, *"If the general does not surrender in five minutes, I will set fire to the house;"* which after a short pause was repeated with a solemn oath; and within two minutes I heard it proclaimed, *"Here is the general. He has surrendered."* A general shout ensued, the trumpet sounded the assembly, and the unfortunate Lee mounted on my horse, which stood ready at the door, was hurried off in triumph, bareheaded, in his slippers and blanket coat, his collar open, and his shirt very much soiled from several days' use.

—WILKINSON, *Memoirs of My Own Times,* I, 105-106.

8. THE LOW EBB OF THE AMERICAN CAUSE

George Washington to Lund Washington.

Ten miles above the Falls [of the Delaware],
December 17, 1776

I have since [his letter of Dec. 10] moved up to this place, to be more convenient to our great and extensive defences of this river. Hitherto, by our destruction of the boats, and vigilance in watching the fords of the river above the falls (which are now rather high), we have prevented them from crossing; but how long we shall be able to do it God only knows, as they are still hovering about the river. And if every thing else fails, will wait till the 1st of January, when there will be no other men to oppose them but militia, none of which but those from Philadelphia . . . are yet come (although I am told some are expected from the back countries). When I say none but militia, I am to except the Virginia regiments and the shattered remains of Smallwood's, which, by fatigue, want of clothes, etc., are reduced to nothing —Weedon's, which was the strongest, not having more than between one hundred and thirty to one hundred and forty men fit for duty, the rest being in the hospitals.

The unhappy policy of short enlistments and a dependence upon militia will, I fear, prove the downfall of our cause, though early pointed out with an almost prophetic spirit! Our cause has also received a severe blow in the captivity of Gen. Lee. Unhappy man! Taken by his own imprudence, going three or four miles from his own camp, and within twenty of the enemy, notice of which by a rascally Tory was given a party of light horse, seized him in the morning after travelling all night, and carried him off in high triumph and with every mark of indignity, not even suffering him to get his hat or surtout coat. The troops that were under his command are not yet come up with us, though they, I think, may be expected to-morrow.

A large part of the Jerseys have given every proof of disaffection that they can do, and this part of Pennsylvania are equally inimical. In short, your imagination can scarce extend to a situation more distressing than mine. Our only dependence now is upon the speedy enlistment of a new army. If this fails, I think the game will be pretty well up, as, from disaffection and want of spirit and fortitude, the inhabitants, instead of resistance, are offering submission and taking protection from Gen. Howe in Jersey.

—FITZPATRICK, ed., *Writings of Washington,* VI, 346-347.

9. "THESE ARE THE TIMES THAT TRY MEN'S SOULS"

Joining the Patriot army, Tom Paine took part in the retreat across New Jersey. At Newark he wrote the first of his Crisis *papers, according to tradition with a drumhead for a desk and a flickering campfire for light. Ordered read to the troops, the pamphlet resolved by its eloquent patriotism the hesitation of many in and out of the army. The* Crisis *papers continued to be written down to 1783. Paine therein proposed that the property of Loyalists be confiscated to provide a base for Continental currency, advocated effective fiscal measures, the imposing of oaths to the new government, and a strong federal union. Here are the opening paragraphs of the first of Thomas Paine's pamphlets collectively entitled* The American Crisis, *published on December 19, 1776.*

These are the times that try men's souls. The summer soldier and the sunshine patriot will, in this crisis, shrink from the service of their country; but he that stands it *now* deserves the love and thanks of man and woman. Tyranny, like hell, is not easily conquered; yet we have this consolation with us, that the harder the conflict, the more glorious the triumph. What we obtain too cheap, we esteem too lightly: it is dearness only that gives every thing its value. Heaven knows how to put a proper price upon its goods; and it would be strange indeed if so celestial an article as FREEDOM should not be highly rated. Britain, with an army to enforce her tyranny, has declared that she has a right (*not only to* TAX) but "to BIND *us in* ALL CASES WHATSOEVER," and if being *bound in that manner* is not slavery, then is there not such a thing as slavery upon earth. Even the expression is impious; for so unlimited a power can belong only to God.

Whether the independence of the continent was declared too soon, or delayed too long, I will not now enter into as an argument; my own simple opinion is that had it been eight months earlier, it would have been much better. We did not make a proper use of last winter, neither could we, while we were in a dependent state. However, the fault, if it were one, was all our own; we have none to blame but ourselves. But no great deal is lost yet. All that Howe has been doing for this month past is rather a ravage than a conquest, which the spirit of the Jerseys, a year ago, would have quickly repulsed, and which time and a little resolution will soon recover.

I have as little superstition in me as any man living, but my secret opinion has ever been, and still is, that God Almighty will not give up a people to military destruction, or leave them unsupportedly to perish, who have so earnestly and so repeatedly sought to avoid the calamities of war by every decent method which wisdom could invent. Neither have I so much of the infidel in me as to suppose that He has relinquished the government of the world and given us up to the care of devils; and as I do not, I cannot see on what grounds the king of Britain can look up to heaven for help against us: a common murderer, a highwayman or a house-breaker has as good a pretence as he.

'Tis surprising to see how rapidly a panic will sometimes run through a country. All nations and ages have been subject to them: Britain has trembled like an ague at the report of a French fleet of flat-bottomed boats; and in the fourteenth century the whole English army, after ravaging the kingdom of France, was driven back like men petrified with fear; and this brave exploit was performed by a few broken forces collected and headed by a woman, Joan of Arc. Would that heaven might inspire some Jersey maid to spirit up her countrymen and save her fair fellow sufferers from ravage and ravishment! Yet panics, in some cases, have their uses; they produce as much good as hurt. Their duration is always short; the mind soon grows through them and acquires a firmer habit than before. But their peculiar advantage is that they are the touchstones of sincerity and hypocrisy, and bring things and men to light which might otherwise have lain forever undiscovered. In fact, they have the same effect on secret traitors which an imaginary apparition would have upon a private murderer. They sift out the hidden thoughts of man and hold them up in public to the world. Many a disguised tory has lately shown his head, that shall penitentially solemnize with curses the day on which Howe arrived upon the Delaware.

As I was with the troops at Fort Lee and marched with them to the edge of Pennsylvania, I am well acquainted with many circumstances which those who live at a distance know but little or nothing of. Our situation there was exceedingly cramped, the place being a narrow neck of land between the North River and the Hackensack. Our force was inconsiderable, being not one fourth so great as Howe could bring against us. We had no army at hand to have relieved the garrison, had we shut ourselves up and stood on our defence. Our ammunition, light artillery and the best part of our stores had been removed, on the apprehension that Howe would endeavor to penetrate the Jerseys, in which case Fort Lee could be of no use to us; for it must occur to every thinking man, whether in the army or not, that these kind of field forts are only for temporary purposes, and last in use no longer than the enemy directs his force against the particular object which such forts are raised to defend.

Such was our situation and condition at Fort Lee on the morning of the 20th of November, when an officer arrived with information that the enemy with 200 boats had landed about seven miles above. Major General Green, who commanded the garrison, immediately ordered them under arms, and sent express to General Washington at the town of Hackensack, distant by way of the ferry six miles.

Our first object was to secure the bridge over the Hackensack, which laid up the river between the enemy and us, about six miles from us, and three from them. General Washington arrived in about three quarters of an hour, and marched at the head of the troops towards the bridge, which place I expected we should have a brush for; however, they did not choose to dispute it with us, and the greatest part of our troops went over the bridge, the rest over the ferry, except some which passed at a mill on a small creek, between the bridge and the ferry, and made their way through some marshy grounds up to the town of Hackensack, and there passed the river. We brought off as much baggage as the wagons could contain, the rest was lost. The simple object was to bring off the garrison and march them on till they could be strengthened by the Jersey or Pennsylvania militia, so as to be enabled to make a stand. We staid four days at Newark, collected our outposts with some of the Jersey militia, and marched out twice to meet the enemy, on being informed that they were advancing, though our numbers were greatly inferior to theirs.

Howe, in my little opinion, committed a great error in generalship in not throwing a body of forces off from Staten Island through Amboy, by which means he might have seized all our stores at Brunswick and intercepted our march into Pennsylvania; but if we believe the power of hell to be limited, we must likewise believe that their agents are under some providential controul.

I shall not now attempt to give all the particulars of our retreat to the Delaware; suffice it for the present to say that both officers and men, though greatly harassed and fatigued, frequently without rest, covering or provision, the inevitable consequences of a long retreat, bore it with a manly and martial spirit. All their wishes centred in one, which was that the country would turn out and help them to drive the enemy back.

Voltaire has remarked that King William never appeared to full advantage but in difficulties and in action; the same remark may be made on General Washington, for the character fits him. There is a natural firmness in some minds which cannot be unlocked by trifles, but which, when unlocked, discovers a cabinet of fortitude; and I reckon it among those kind of public blessings, which we do not immediately see, that God hath blessed him with uninterrupted health, and given him a mind that can even flourish upon care.

—CONWAY, ed., *Complete Writings of Paine*, I, 170-173.

II. COUNTERATTACK: THE VICTORY AT TRENTON

Since the troops sent from New York to reinforce him had in most cases not re-enlisted and their service would expire the first of the year, Washington in desperation realized that a blow must be struck at once. By mid-December the British had gone into winter quarters. Howe's forces had spread themselves very thin, extending from Perth Amboy and New Brunswick as far south as Burlington and Mount Holly. General Grant, in command of the British forces in New Jersey, saw little danger from the American army which had retreated across the Delaware to Pennsylvania. Writing on December 21 to Lieutenant Colonel Rall in command of the Hessian garrison at Trenton, he stated that the American army was "almost naked, dying of cold, without blankets, and very ill supplied with provisions." On this east side of the Delaware "they have not three hundred men."

This optimistic note left the nervous Rall ill-prepared for the blow that followed. Washington decided on a surprise attack at Trenton.

He proposed to cross the Delaware above Trenton with about one half of his command, while General Ewing and Colonel Cadwalader should cross opposite Trenton and Bristol, cut Rall's line of retreat and prevent Colonel Carl von Donop, Rall's superior in command of the forces in Southern Jersey, from bringing reinforcements up from Mount Holly. Because of the snow and ice Cadwalader found he could not move his artillery to the other side of the river and abandoned his part of the attack.

Jagged cakes of ice, strong winds and snow and sleet made the Christmas night crossing of the Delaware a trying operation. No episode of the war is perhaps so familiar to Americans, in large part owing to the industry of Emmanuel Leutze, who put the story down on canvas at Düsseldorf on the Rhine some 60 years after the event and managed to capture the spirit of 'seventy-six even though he was inaccurate in his details. Glover's Marbleheaders, again at the oars as they had been in the retreat from Long Island, got the troops safely across the river. Sullivan entered Trenton from the northwest, Greene from the north. Advancing early in the morning of the twenty-sixth through a violent snow and hailstorm, both forces attacked virtually simultaneously. The Hessians were caught by surprise. Hand's riflemen kept them from crossing the bridge over the Assanpink Creek. Rall was mortally wounded and his command quickly surrendered. Almost a thousand prisoners were taken in fighting that lasted three quarters of an hour. The Americans suffered five casualties—two men frozen to death on the march, two officers and one private wounded. One of the officers was a future President, Lieutenant James Monroe.

For the Americans Trenton was like an eleventh-hour reprieve. The Patriot cause, which had seemed desperate, now took on new life and hope. As Thomas Rodney wrote, a few days after Trenton, "Never were men in higher spirits than our whole army is." Washington had seized the offensive, and was to hold it for some time; the murmurings against his Fabian tactics died down.

1. The British Are Buoyed by Favorable Intelligence

Intelligence by Mr. Hovenden, who left Bucks County December 20, 1776.

That the main body of the rebel army lies at Beaumonts between Telits and Bakers Ferry about 11 miles above Trenton Ferry commanded by General Washington and Lord Stirling. That a party of about 3000 men under Gen. Sulivan had joined Gen. Washington and it was said they were immediately to march and make their quarters at Newtown. That of this number near 200 sick and invalids were arrived at the hospital at Newtown. A party [of] 200 or 300 men are stationed at Robinsons Ferry about 7 miles above Beaumonts. Don't know of any other party higher up the river. That General Washington had with him 6 eight-pounders but were removed from thence, know not where. There are opposite to Slacks Island about 5 miles below Beaumonts 4 eight-pounders. That below Slack's Island and at Yardley's are about 600 men, commanded by Gen. Dickinson with two pieces of cannon. Gen. Mercer was there but often shifts his quarters. That upon the most diligent inquiry and best intelligence he could procure, General Washington's whole army did not consist of more than 8000 men. That General Sulivan went to Philadelphia on the 15th inst from Washington's quarters. That General Gates had not passed the river on Thursday last, but was informed, he was coming forward with about 500 men.

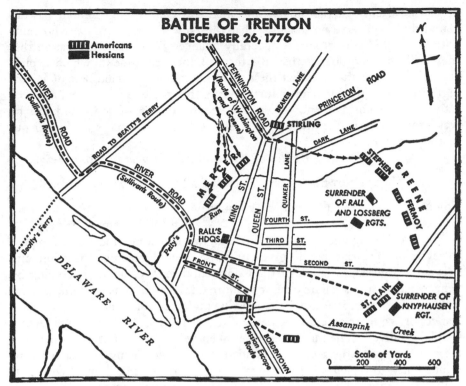

BATTLE OF TRENTON
DECEMBER 26, 1776

From The Encyclopedia of American History   *Courtesy of Harper & Brothers*
by Richard B. Morris

Intelligence by Mr. Haines, a Burlington County Loyalist.

Bazilla Haines, sent out to procure intelligence on the 21st of Dec., 1776, arrived at Mount Holly in the night and lodged in the Rebel camp there. Was informed they had only two field pieces, which he thinks were three-pounders as he perceived them at the church. That all the troops were drawn up in his view, that he walked round them and thinks there were not above eight hundred, near one half boys and all of them militia, a very few Pennsylvanians excepted. That he knew a great many of them, who came from Gloucester, Egg Harbour, Penns Neck and Cohansey. They were commanded by Col. Griffin.

Intelligence by Samuel Brown, who left Bucks County on December 22, 1776.

That the troops opposite to Trenton and Bordentown are in number about 600 men commanded by General Ewing. Of these men there is a guard of 25 men opposite Mr. Field's, about 50 at Mr. Riche's opposite to Bordenton, about half a mile nearer Trenton about thirty; the rest lay above between Riche's and Trenton, and over against Trenton there are two pieces of cannon. That Gen. Washingtons whole army does not consist of more than 8000 men, about 5000 of them troops formerly enlisted, partly brought from Jersey to Washington and partly by Sulivan; the rest are new raised militia. That the time of enlistment of Ewing's brigade of 600 men all expire the first of Jan. next and that the officers and men and Gen. Ewing himself has declared they will serve no longer. That the New England troops who came with General Washington it is generally believed from their declaration that they will not serve longer than the term of their enlistment, which expires also the first of Jan'y next; that these troops compose the main part of Washington's army. Mr. Hovenden further says that there are four regiments or rather the remains of them, whose time expires the 1st of Jan'y and that he was informed by their principal officers that they would serve no longer out of their own Province.

—STRYKER, *Battles of Trenton and Princeton*, pp. 336-338.

2. "WILL IT NOT BE POSSIBLE TO MAKE A DIVERSION AT TRENTON?"

Colonel Joseph Reed to George Washington.

Bristol, December 22, 1776

We are all of opinion, my dear General, that something must be attempted to revive our expiring credit, give our cause some degree of reputation, and prevent a total depreciation of the Continental money, which is coming on very fast; that even a failure cannot be more fatal than to remain in our present situation; in short, some enterprise must be undertaken in our present circumstances or we must give up the cause. In a little time the Continental Army will be dissolved. The militia must be taken before their spirits and patience are exhausted; and the scattered, divided state of the enemy affords us a fair opportunity to trying what our men will do when called to an offensive attack. Will it not be possible, my dear General, for your troops, or such part of them as can act with advantage, to make a diversion, or something more, at or about Trenton? The greater the alarm, the more likely the success will attend the attacks. If we could possess ourselves again of New Jersey, or any considerable part of it, the effects would be greater than if we had never left it.

Allow me to hope that you will consult your own good judgment and spirit, and not let the goodness of your heart subject you to the influence of opinions from men in every respect your inferiors. Something must be attempted before the sixty days expire which the commissioners have allowed; for, however many affect to despise it, it is evident that a very serious attention is paid to it, and I am confident that unless some more favourable appearance attends our arms and cause before that time, a very large number of the militia officers here will follow the example of those of Jersey and take benefit from it. I will not disguise my own sentiments, that our cause is desperate and hopeless if we do not take the opportunity of the collection of troops at present to strike some stroke. Our affairs are hastening fast to ruin if we do not retrieve them by some happy event. Delay with us is now equal to a total defeat. Be not deceived, my dear General, with small, flattering appearances; we must not suffer ourselves to be lulled into security and inaction because the enemy does not cross the river. It is but a reprieve; the execution is the more certain, for I am very clear that they can and will cross the river in spite of any opposition we can give them.

Pardon the freedom I have used. The love of my country, a wife and four children in the enemy's hands, the respect and attachment I have to you, the ruin and poverty that must attend me and thousands of others will plead my excuse for so much freedom.

Your obedient and affectionate humble servant
JOSEPH REED

—FITZPATRICK, ed., *Writings of Washington*, VI, 426n-427n.

3. "CHRISTMAS NIGHT IS THE TIME FIXED UPON"

George Washington to Joseph Reed "or, in his absence, to John Cadwalader, Esq., only, at Bristol."

23 December 1776

The bearer is sent down to know whether your plan was attempted last night and if not to inform you, that Christmas-day at night, one hour before day is the time fixed upon for our attempt on Trenton. For Heaven's sake keep this to yourself, as the discovery of it may prove fatal to us, our numbers, sorry am I to say, being less than I had any conception of: but necessity, dire necessity, will, nay must, justify an attempt. Prepare, and, in concert with Griffin, attack as many of their posts as you possibly can with a prospect of success: the more we can attack at the same instant, the more confusion we shall spread and greater good will result from it. If I had not been fully convinced before of the enemy's designs, I have now ample testimony of their intentions to attack Philadelphia, so soon as the ice will afford the means of conveyance. . . .

We could not ripen matters for our attack before the time mentioned in the first part of this letter: so much out of sorts and so much in want of everything are the troops under Sullivan, etc. Let me know by a careful express the plan you are to pursue. The letter herewith sent, forward on to Philadelphia: I could wish it to be in time for the Southern post's departure, which will be I believe by eleven o'clock tomorrow.

I am, dear Sir, Your obedient servant
GEO. WASHINGTON

P.S.—I have ordered our men to be provided with three days' provisions ready cooked, with which and their blankets they are to march: for if we are successful, which Heaven grant and the circumstances favor, we may push on. I shall direct every ferry and ford to be well guarded, and not a soul suffered to pass without an officer's going down with the permit. Do the same with you.

—STRYKER, *Battles of Trenton and Princeton*, pp. 342-343.

4. "FOR GOD'S SAKE, KEEP BY YOUR OFFICERS!"

Memoirs of Elisha Bostwick of the Seventh Connecticut Regiment.

[O]ur army passed through Bethleham and Moravian town and so on to the Delaware which we crossed 9 miles north of Trenton and encamped on the Pennsylvania side and there remain to the 24th December. [O]ur whole army was then set on motion and toward evining began to recross the Delaware but by obstructions of ice in the river did not all get across till quite late in the evening, and all the time a constant fall of snow with some rain, and finally our march began with the torches of our field pieces stuck in the exhalters. [They] sparkled and blazed in the storm all night and about day light a halt was made, at which time his Excellency and aids came near to front on the side of the path where the soldiers stood.

I heard his Excellency as he was comeing on speaking to and encourageing the soldiers. The words he spoke as he passed by where I stood and in my hearing were these:

"Soldiers, keep by your officers. For God's sake, keep by your officers!" Spoke in a deep and solemn voice.

While passing a slanting, slippery bank his Excellencys horse's hind feet both slipped from under him, and he siezed his horse's mane and the horse recovered. Our horses were then unharnessed and the artillery men prepared. We marched on and it was not long before we heard the out centries of the enemy both on the road we were in and the eastern road, and their out gards retreated fireing, and our army, then with a quick step pushing on upon both roads, at the same time entered the town. Their artilery taken, they resigned with little opposition, about nine hundred all Hessians, with 4 brass field pieces; the remainder crossing the bridge at the lower end of the town escaped. . . .

Marched the next day with our prisoners back to an encampment. I will here make a few remarks as to the personal appearance of the Hessians. They are of a moderate stature, rather broad shoulders, their limbs not of equal proportion, light complexion with a b[l]ueish tinge, hair cued as tight to the head as possible, sticking straight back like the handle of an iron skillet. Their uniform blue with black facings, brass drums which made a tinkling sound, their flag or standard of the richest black silk and the devices upon it and the lettering in gold leaf. . . .

When crossing the Delaware with the prisoners in flat bottom boats the ice continually stuck to the boats, driving them down stream; the boatmen endevering to clear off the ice pounded the boat, and stamping with their feet, beconed to the prisoners to do the same, and they all set to jumping at once with their cues flying up and down, soon shook off the ice from the boats, and the next day recrossed the Delaware again and returned back to Trenton, and there on the first of January 1777 our yeers service expired, and then by the pressing solicitation of his Excellency a part of those whose time was out consented on a ten dollar bounty to stay six weeks longer, and altho desirous as others to return home, I engaged to stay that time and made every exertion in my power to make as many of the soldiers stay with me as I could, and quite a number did engage with me who otherwise would have went home. . . .

—Bostwick, *Memoirs.*

5. "Providence Seemed to Have Smiled upon This Enterprise"

Henry Knox to his wife.

Delaware River, near Trenton, December 28, 1776

. . . Trenton is an open town, situated nearly on the banks of the Delaware, accessible on all sides. Our army was scattered along the river for nearly twenty-five miles. Our intelligence agreed that the force of the enemy in Trenton was from two to three thousand, with about six field cannon, and that they were pretty secure in their situation, and that they were Hessians— no British troops. A hardy design was formed of attacking the town by storm. Accordingly a part of the army, consisting of about 2,500 or 3,000, passed the river on Christmas night, with almost infinite difficulty, with eighteen field-pieces. The floating ice in the river made the labor almost incredible. However, perseverance accomplished what at first seemed impossible. About two o'clock the troops were all on the Jersey side; we then were about nine miles from the object. The night was cold and stormy; it hailed with great violence; the troops marched with the most profound silence and good order.

They arrived by two routes at the same time, about half an hour after daylight, within one mile of the town. The storm continued with great violence, but was in our backs, and consequently in the faces of our enemy. About half a mile from the town was an advanced guard on each road, consisting of a captain's guard. These we forced, and entered the town with them pell-mell; and here succeeded a scene of war of which I had often conceived, but never saw before.

The hurry, fright and confusion of the enemy was [not] unlike that which will be when the last trump shall sound. They endeavored to form in streets, the heads of which we had previously the possession of with cannon and howitzers; these, in the twinkling of an eye, cleared the streets. The backs of the houses were resorted to for shelter. These proved ineffectual: the musketry soon dislodged them. Finally they were driven through the town into an open plain beyond. Here they formed in an instant.

During the contest in the streets measures were taken for putting an entire stop to their retreat by posting troops and cannon in such passes and roads as it was possible for them to get away by. The poor fellows after they were formed on the plain saw themselves completely surrounded; the only resource left was to force their way through numbers unknown to them. The Hessians lost part of their cannon in the town: they did not relish the project of forcing, and were obliged to surrender upon the spot, with all their artillery, six brass pieces, army colors, etc. A Colonel Rawle commanded, who was wounded. The number of prisoners was above 1,200, including officers —all Hessians. There were few killed or wounded on either side. After having marched off the prisoners and secured the cannon, stores, etc., we returned to the place, nine miles distant, where we had embarked.

Providence seemed to have smiled upon every part of this enterprise. Great advantages may be gained from it if we take the proper steps. At another post we have pushed over the river 2,000 men, to-day another body, and to-morrow the whole army will follow. It must give a sensible pleasure to every friend of the rights of man to think with how much intrepidity our people pushed the enemy and prevented their forming in the town.

—DRAKE, *Henry Knox*, pp. 36-37.

6. "THE ENEMY HAVE FLED BEFORE US IN THE GREATEST PANIC"

Thomas Rodney to Caesar Rodney.

Allen's Town, in Jersey, December 30, 1776

. . . On the 25th inst. in the evening, we received orders to be at Shamony ferry as soon as possible. We were there according to orders in two hours, and met the rifle-men, who were the first from Bristol; we were ordered from thence to Dunk's Ferry, on the Delaware, and the whole army of about 2000 men followed as soon as the artillery got up. The three companies of Philadelphia infantry and mine were formed into a body, under the command of Captain Henry (myself second in command), which were embarked immediately to cover the landing of the other troops.

We landed with great difficulty through the ice, and formed on the ferry shore, about 200 yards from the river. It was as severe a night as ever I saw, and after two battalions were landed, the storm increased so much, and the river was so full of ice, that it was impossible to get the artillery over; for we had to walk 100 yards on the ice to get on shore. Gen. Cadwallader therefore ordered the whole to retreat again, and we had to stand at least six hours under arms—first to cover the landing and till all the rest had retreated again—and, by this time, the storm of wind, hail, rain and snow, with the ice, was so bad that some of the infantry could not get back till next day. This design was to have surprised the enemy at Black Horse and Mount Holley, at the same time that Washington surprised them at Trenton; and had we succeeded in getting over, we should have finished all our troubles. Washington took 910 prisoners, with 6 pieces of fine artillery, and all their baggage in Trenton.

The next night I received orders to be in Bristol before day; we were there accordingly, and about 9 o'clock began to embark one mile above Bristol, and about 3 o'clock in the afternoon got all our troops and artillery over, consisting of about 3000 men and began our march to Burlington—the infantry, flanked by the rifle-men, making the advanced guard. We got there about 9 o'clock and took possession of the town, but found the enemy had made precipitate retreat the day before, bad as the weather was, in a great panic. The whole infantry and rifle-men were then ordered to set out that night and make a forced march to Bordentown (which was about 11 miles), which they did, and took possession of the town about 9 o'clock, with a large quantity of the enemy's stores, which they had not time to carry off. We stayed there till the army came up; and the general, finding the enemy were but a few miles ahead, ordered the infantry to proceed to a town called Croswick's, four miles from Bordentown, and they were followed by one of the Philadelphia and one of the New England battalions. We got there about 8 o'clock, and at about 10 (after we were all in quarters) were informed that the enemy's baggage was about 16 miles from us, under a guard of 300 men.

Some of the militia colonels applied to the infantry to make a forced march that night and overhaul them. *We had then been on duty four nights and days, making forced marches, without six hours sleep in the whole time;* whereupon the infantry officers of all the companies unanimously declared it was madness to attempt, for that it would knock up all our brave men, not one of whom had yet gave out, but every one will suppose were much fatigued. . . .

The enemy have fled before us in the greatest panic that ever was known; we heard this moment that they have fled from Princeton, and that they were hard pressed by Washington. Never were men in higher spirits than our whole army is; none are sick, and all are determined to extirpate them from the Jersey, but I believe the enemy's fears will do it before we get up with them. The Hessians, from the general to the common soldier, curse and imprecate the war, and swear they were sent here to be slaughtered; that they never will leave New-York again till they sail for Europe. Jersey will be the most whiggish colony on the continent: the very Quakers declare for taking up arms. You cannot imagine the distress of this country. They have stripped every body almost without distinction—even of all their cloths, and have beat and abused men, women and children in the most cruel manner ever heard of.

We have taken a number of prisoners in our route, Hessians and British, to the amount of about twenty. It seems likely through the blessing of Providence that we shall retake Jersey again without the loss of a man, except one Gen. Washington lost at Trenton. The enemy seem to be bending their way to Amboy with all speed, but I hope we shall come up with the Princeton baggage yet, and also get a share of their large stores at Brunswick. I hope, if I live, to see the conquest of Jersey, and set off home again in two weeks. Some of my men have complained a little, but not to say sick; they are all now well here.

—NILES, *Principles and Acts of the Revolution*, pp. 248-249.

7. BATTLE OF TRENTON
[1776]

On Christmas day in seventy-six
Our ragged troops with bayonets fixed
   For Trenton marched away.
The Delaware see! the boats below!
The light obscured by hail and snow!
   But no signs of dismay.

Our object was the Hessian band
That dared invade fair freedom's land
   And quarter in that place.
Great Washington he led us on,
Whose streaming flag, in storm or sun,
   Had never known disgrace.

In silent march we passed the night,
Each soldier panting for the fight,
   Though quite benumbed with frost.
Greene, on the left, at six began.
The right was led by Sullivan,
   Who ne'er a moment lost.

Their pickets stormed, the alarm was spread
That rebels risen from the dead
   Were marching into town.
Some scampered here, some scampered there,
And some for action did prepare,
   But soon their arms laid down.

Twelve hundred servile miscreants,
With all their colors, guns and tents,
   Were trophies of the day.
The frolic o'er, the bright canteen
In centre, front and rear was seen
   Driving fatigue away.

Now, brothers of the patriot bands,
Let's sing deliverance from the hands
   Of arbitrary sway.
And as our life is but a span,
Let's touch the tankard while we can,
   In memory of that day.
     —MOORE, ed., *Songs and Ballads*, pp. 150-152.

8. AFTERMATH: A HESSIAN COURT-MARTIAL CONVICTS A DEAD MAN

"A most unfortunate business" was the comment of British General Grant. "Why could not Rall have continued to retreat across the bridge to Bordentown?" he asked. From his new quarters at Allentown, Donop wrote Knyphausen:

> *Whether this affair was an accident or whether a mistake had been made could not be determined from the stories told by the fugitives. All agree, however, that if Colonel Rall with his brigade had retreated over the bridge and then destroyed it he could have saved his command instead of fighting for an hour against such heavy odds. Nevertheless it certainly proves his splendid courage and that of his regiments, and this at least is greatly to their honor. Even the two regiments, the von Lossberg and his own, could have been saved. The death of Colonel Rall has therefore avoided a painful investigation, for he would have had to answer for his grave responsibility.*

The Hessian court-martial formally exonerated everyone but the dead Rall, and Howe in his dispatch to Germain took the same position. Perhaps a young Hessian lieutenant had the last word with this epitaph:

Hier liegt der Oberst Rall.
Mit ihm ist alles all!

For the British as well as the Americans, Trenton meant a bitter and te-dious winter. Writing on January 8 from New Brunswick to Lord George Germain, Cornwallis summed up the Battle of Trenton: "The unlucky affair of Raal's brigade has given me a winter campaign."

Finding of Hessian Court Martial

January 11, 1782

The President and the members of the Court were then sworn:—

They gave their decision according to their respective rank after they had been cautioned to keep the same secret:—

The Ensigns. They agree that the disaster at Trenton was due to the neglect of Colonel Rall in not making the necessary preparations in case of retreat. Also that he was to blame for attacking the town instead of retreating, thereby causing the confusion in the Rall and Von Lossberg regiments.

They think that Lieutenant Colonel Scheffer in the situation in which he was when he took command of the regiments, against a superior force, would have found it impossible to have effected a retreat; that he and all his officers did all in their power to encourage their men and preserve order and that the testimony shows no censure should be placed on them.

In the matter of the pickets there could be nothing said against them as they were too weak in number to resist so strong an enemy and they were not guilty of making a premature retreat.

Lieutenant Fischer according to the testimony remained with the Von Lossberg regiment and Lieutenant Engelhardt could not save the cannon of the Rall regiment; therefore the Ensigns judge that no blame can be attached to the Artillery detachment of the brigade.

The minutes show in the case of the Von Knyphausen regiment that the command marched into the low ground on a positive order; therefore the regiment could not be held responsible for it. They also think that it was impossible for Captain von Biesenrodt, who took command when the Von Knyphausen regiment already stood in the low ground, to force the bridge with his small regiment, and there was no way for him to make them cross the creek, and that he had taken the necessary steps in this matter, first to have the creek sounded, second to place an officer and forty men to protect the ford, and third to assume charge himself of the rear guard. Captain von Loewenstein had not then shown him where the water was only knee-deep and therefore no lack of resolution or want of bravery can be charged to him. That he finally surrendered himself and his men he could not be censured for, because first the other regiments were already captured, second the situation of the Von Knyphausen regiment was already known to the enemy from Major von Dechow's movements, and third the enemy put its whole force now against the regiment Von Knyphausen, and this regiment could not successfully resist after having the cannon stuck in the swamp and only numbering then 276 men.

We also find that Captain Schimmelpfennig, Lieutenant now Captain Baum, Lieutenant now Captain Vaupell and Lieutenant von Geyso did not go through the creek until the whole regiment had orders from Captain von Biesenrodt, and took the men across according to the statement already made.

So the Ensigns believe Captain von Biesenrodt as well as the officers, the non-commissioned officers and the privates of the Von Knyphausen regiment are free from blame and ought to be acquitted.

H. G. D. MOLDE

A. VON PAPPENHEIM

F. KUESTER

Verdict. On the surprise at Trenton of the regiments Von Lossberg, Von Knyphausen and Rall, now D'Angelelli, and their capture.

The Court-Martial resolves after thoroughly examining all the testimony and all the facts that by a unanimous vote they judge that the regiments Von Lossberg, Von Knyphausen and Rall, now D'Angelelli, cannot be blamed for any want of courage, premature retreat or insubordination at the surprise at Trenton, and they believe that the commanders of the regiments, the other officers, the regiments themselves, the guards and pickets, the watch at the bridge under Sergeant Mueller, and the detachment of artillery all did their duty....

—STRYKER, *Battles of Trenton and Princeton*, pp. 411-412, 418-419.

III. PRINCETON

After his stunning victory at Trenton, Washington retired across the Delaware into Pennsylvania; a few days later he recrossed the river. Meantime, Cornwallis, who had been about to sail for England to see his ailing wife, was ordered back to the Jerseys with heavy reinforcements. When he reached Trenton on January 2, Cornwallis rejected the advice of his officers to attack Washington at once, observing that he could just as well "bag the fox" the next morning. His quartermaster general retorted: "My Lord, if you trust those people tonight, you will see nothing of them in the morning."

Leaving his campfires burning and muffling his artillery wheels, Washington staged a night march to Princeton with the idea of smashing the relatively small garrison forces stationed there and of obtaining desperately needed stores. After driving back the British reinforcements under Lt. Col. Charles Mawhood that had been coming up to join Cornwallis, Washington entered the town. There Artillery Captain Alexander Hamilton's cannon were brought to bear on Nassau Hall and he gave the order to fire when the British troops who had sought refuge inside the building refused to surrender. On learning that the main British army under Cornwallis was coming up, Washington withdrew his weary troops to the northeast, first destroying the bridge over Stony Brook. Shortly after, he went into winter quarters in the hills around Morristown.

In the engagement at Princeton British casualties amounted to 273, the American half that number, but the Patriots lost such gallant figures as General Mercer and Colonel Haslet. Trenton and Princeton cleared all but east-

ernmost New Jersey of the enemy and had an incalculable effect in restoring the shattered Patriot morale.

The British traveler, Nicholas Cresswell, attributed to the double victory of Trenton and Princeton the fact that "volunteer companies are collecting in every county on the continent and in a few months the rascals will be stronger than ever. Even the parsons, some of them, have turned out as volunteers and pulpit drums or thunder, which you please to call it, summoning all to arms in this cursed babble. Damn them all."

British officers were now impelled to reappraise their leadership and battle strategy. Many of them agreed with the emotional verdict of Cresswell that "it is the damned Hessians that has caused this." As one British officer at New York put it, "The English and Hessian did not coalesce into one corps." General Archibald Robertson of the Royal Engineers blamed the British failure on "imprudently separating our small army of 6,000 men by far too much." The lesson as he saw it: "Never despise any enemy too much."

1. "THE GROUND WAS MARKED WITH THE BLOOD OF SOLDIERS' FEET"

An account by Sergeant R——.

[March 24, 1832]

Three or four days after the victory at Trenton, the American army recrossed the Delaware into New Jersey. At this time our troops were in a destitute and deplorable condition. The horses attached to our cannon were without shoes, and when passing over the ice they would slide in every direction and could advance only by the assistance of the soldiers. Our men, too, were without shoes or other comfortable clothing; and as traces of our march towards Princeton, the ground was literally marked with the blood of the soldiers' feet. Though my own feet did not bleed, they were so sore that their condition was little better. While we were at Trenton, on the last of December, 1776, the time for which I and most of my regiment had enlisted expired. At this trying time General Washington, having now but a little handful of men and many of them new recruits in which he could place but little confidence, ordered our regiment to be paraded, and personally addressed us, urging that we should stay a month longer. He alluded to our recent victory at Trenton; told us that our services were greatly needed, and that we could now do more for our country than we ever could at any future period; and in the most affectionate manner entreated us to stay. The drums beat for volunteers, but not a man turned out. The soldiers, worn down with fatigue and privations, had their hearts fixed on home and the comforts of the domestic circle, and it was hard to forego the anticipated pleasures of the society of our dearest friends.

The General wheeled his horse about, rode in front of the regiment and addressing us again said, "My brave fellows, you have done all I asked you to do, and more than could be reasonably expected; but your country is at stake, your wives, your houses and all that you hold dear. You have worn yourselves out with fatigues and hardships, but we know not how to spare you. If you will consent to stay only one month longer, you will render that service to the cause of liberty and to your country which you probably never can do under any other circumstances."

A few stepped forth, and their example was immediately followed by nearly all who were fit for duty in the regiment, amounting to about two hundred volunteers. (About half of these volunteers were killed in the battle of Princeton or died of the small pox soon after.) An officer enquired of the General if these men should be enrolled. He replied: "No! men who will volunteer in such a case as this need no enrolment to keep them to their duty."

Leaving our fires kindled to deceive the enemy, we decamped that night and by a circuitous route took up our line of march for Princeton. General Mercer commanded the front guard of which the two hundred volunteers composed a part. About sunrise of the 3rd January, 1777, reaching the summit of a hill near Princeton, we observed a light-horseman looking towards us, as we view an object when the sun shines directly in our faces. Gen. Mercer, observing him, gave orders to the riflemen who were posted on the right to pick him off. Several made ready, but at that instant he wheeled about and was out of their reach. Soon after this as we were descending a hill through an orchard, a party of the enemy who were entrenched behind a bank and fence rose and fired upon us. Their first shot passed over our heads, cutting the limbs of the trees under which we were marching. . . . Our fire was most destructive; their ranks grew thin and the victory seemed nearly complete when the British were reinforced. Many of our brave men had fallen, and we were unable to withstand such superior numbers of fresh troops.

I soon heard Gen. Mercer command in a tone of distress, "Retreat!" He was mortally wounded and died shortly after. I looked about for the main body of the army which I could not discover, discharged my musket at part of the enemy, and ran for a piece of wood at a little distance where I thought I might shelter. At this moment Washington appeared in front of the American army, riding towards those of us who were retreating, and exclaimed, "Parade with us, my brave fellows! There is but a handful of the enemy, and we will have them directly." I immediately joined the main body, and marched over the ground again.

. . . The British were unable to resist this attack, and retreated into the College, where they thought themselves safe. Our army was there in an instant, and cannon were planted before the door, and after two or three discharges a white flag appeared at the window, and the British surrendered. They were a haughty, crabbed set of men, as they fully exhibited while prisoners on their march to the country. In this battle my pack, which was made fast by leather strings, was shot from my back, and with it went what little clothing I had. It was, however, soon replaced by one which had belonged to a British officer and was well furnished. It was not mine long, for it was stolen shortly afterwards. . . .

      —R——, "Account of Princeton," *Penn. Mag. of Hist. and Biog.*,
        XX, 515-519.

2. Princeton Changes Masters Three Times in a Day

An account of the Battle of Princeton completed on April 18, 1777, by an 85-year-old resident, name unknown.

Genl Washintons army took all the Regulars in town prissoners, and discharged their Continental prissoners that they had confined in the Colledge to the number of ——, among whom [as it is said] was about 30 of our country people that were accused either of being rebels or aiding and assisting them. They took their stores in which [it is said] was a very large number of new blankets. They took all the enemys cannon in town and was oblidged to leave two of them for want of carriage to take them of[f]. One gun they threw into a well, and then they marcht on with their prissoners and plunder to Summerset Court House that day, and left some of the prissoners, and [some] of their own men to care of the sick and wounded men on both sides.

Genl Washinton, as [soon] as the [batt]le was over, ordered some of [his] men to be pl[a]ced near the [bri]dge over Stoney Brook on the main road to hinder the Regulars pasing over and to pull up the bridge, which was scarcely done when the Regulars apeared, which caused a second fireing about three quarters of an hour appart from the first in which there was no execution done that I heard of. In a little time our men retreated and the Regulars were oblidged to cross the brook at the ford with their artillery almost middle deep in water (the back waters of the mill being then up) and formed on this side the brook, and towards night (when they knew that the other army was gone) marcht into Princetown. Thus that poor and almost wholly desolate town of al its late inhabitants had change of masters two if not three times on that day, for they had the Regulars in the morning, the Continentals at noon, the Regulars again at night, who left them to the Continentals that night again and have not yet returned to assume their conquest. So unconstant is the state of war and so certain and sure are the mischiefs and miserys attending it that it is a wonder that wise men should ever depend on it. . . .

The battle was plainly seen from our door. Before any gun was heard a man was seen to fall and immediately the report and smoke of a gun was seen and heard, and the guns went of[f] so quick and many together that they could not be numbered. We presently went down into the cellar to keep out of the way of the shot. There was a neighbour woman down in the cellar with us that was so affrighted that she imagined that the field was covered with blood, and when we came out of the cellar she called earnestly to us to look out and see how all the field was quit[e] red with blood, when none was to be seen at that distance. This I mention only to show into what strange mistakes sudden frights with the fear of death may put us into.

Almost as soon as the firing was over our house was filled and surrounded with Genl Washington's men, and himself on horseback at the door. They brought in with them on their shoulders two wounded Regulars; one of them was shot in at his hip and the bullet lodged in his groin, and the other was shot through his body just below his short ribs. He was in very great pain and bled much out of both sides, and often desired to be removed from one place to another, which was done accordingly, and he dyed about three o' [clock in the] afternoon. ...

Immediately after the battle Genl Washingtons men came into our house. Though they were bo[th] hungry and thirsty some of them [were] laughing out right, others smileing, and not a man among them but showed joy in his countenance. It really animated my old blood with love to those men that but a few minutes before had been couragiously looking death in the face in ravages of a bold and dareing enemy. By the joy that I felt myself I cannot help but be of the opinion that the most strict of them all against bearing arms in our own defence (if they have any love for their bleeding country) must in some degree or other rejoice with the rest of their neighbours and others for that days happy relief that it pleased God to bless us with.

—ANONYMOUS, *Brief Narrative of the British and Hessians at Princeton*, pp. 32-39.

3. WASHINGTON WITHDRAWS FROM PRINCETON

Journal of Captain Thomas Rodney.

January 3, 1777—As soon as the enemy's main army heard our cannon at Princeton (and not 'til then) they discovered our manoeuvre and pushed after us with all speed, and we had not been above an hour in possession of the town before the enemy's light horse and advanced parties attacked our party at the bridge, but our people by a very heavy fire kept the pass until our army left the town.

Just as our army began our march through Princeton with all their prisoners and spoils, the van of the British army we had left at Trenton came in sight and entered the town about an hour after we left it, but made no stay and pushed on towards Brunswick for fear we should get there before him, which was indeed the course our General intended to pursue had he not been detained too long in collecting the baggage and artillery which the enemy had left behind him.

Our army marched on to Kingston, then wheeled to the left and went down the Millstone, keeping that river on our left; the main body of the British followed, but kept on through Kingston to Brunswick; but one division or a strong party of horse took the road on the left of the Millstone and arrived on the hill, at the bridge on that road just as the van of the American army arrived on the opposite side.

I was again commanding the van of our army, and General Washington, seeing the enemy, rode forward and ordered me to halt and take down a number of carpenters which he had ordered forward and break up the bridge, which was done and the enemy were obliged to return.

We then marched on to a little village called Stone Brook or Summerset Court House about 15 miles from Princeton where we arrived just at dusk. About an hour before we arrived here 150 of the enemy from Princeton and 50 which were stationed in this town went off with 20 wagons laden with clothing and linen, and 400 of the Jersey militia who surrounded them were afraid to fire on them and let them go off unmolested, and there were no troops in our army fresh enough to pursue them, or the whole might have been taken in a few hours.

Our army was now extremely fatigued, not having had refreshment since yesterday morning, and our baggage had all been sent away the morning of the action at Trenton; yet they are in good health and in high spirits.

—RODNEY, "Diary," *Del. Hist. Soc. Papers*, VIII, 32-38.

4. HOWE IS SURROUNDED BY "A GREAT PARCEL OF OLD WOMEN"

Lieutenant Colonel Allan Maclean to Alexander Cummings.

New York, February 19, 1777

Poor devils as the Rebel generals are, they out-generaled us more than once, even since I have been here, which is only six weeks, and it is no less certain that with a tolerable degree of common sense, and some ability in our commanders, the rebellion would now be near ended.

Indeed, I find our mistakes in the campaign were many and some very capital ones; but I know I am writing to a friend who has some prudence and will not expose me, tho' I write real truths. . . .

After what I said it would be unjust not to say that General Howe is a very honest man, and I believe a very disinterested one. Brave he certainly is and would make a very good executive officer under another's command, but he is not by any means equal to a C. in C. I do not know any employment that requires so many great qualifications either natural or acquired as the Commander in Chief of an Army. He has, moreover, got none but very silly fellows about him—a great parcel of old women—most of them improper for American service. I could be very ludicrous on this occasion, but it is truly too serious a matter that brave men's lives should be sacrificed to be commanded by such generals.

For excepting Earl Percy, Lord Cornwallis, both Lt. Generals, and the Brigadier Generals Leslie and Sir William Erskine, the rest are useless. Lord Percy is greatly distinguished with Gen. Howe; Lord Cornwallis is, I believe, a brave man, but he allowed himself to be fairly out-generalled by Washington, the 4th Jan. last at Trenton, and missed a glorious opportunity when he let Washington slip away in the night.

Men of real genius cannot long agree with Howe; he is too dull to encourage great military merit—and our great men at home seem to be as little anxious about encouraging true military abilities as our commanders here.

You will say I am too severe, but upon my soul I would be sorry to judge rashly, and I would rather praise any man than condemn him; I am not afraid that the judicious few, who are real judges, will think me wrong in saying that Gen. Howe is by no means equal to his present command. I also find Gen. Carleton is not thought much of at home. I will not pretend to vindicate him; his conduct deserves censure, but I assure you he is a much better general than Howe. But God knows that neither of them merited Stars, or Ribands—and to you, my friend, I can say that had I not been in Canada he would never have got his Red Riband, for Quebec would have been lost, and he would be a prisoner amongst the Rebels—yet poor me have got nothing, not so much as the King's thanks! I am indeed the single man that has been forgot. This will not alter my conduct during this rascally Rebellion; on the contrary, I shall exert myself more to serve my King and Country. . . .

                    —Wortley, ed., *Correspondence of Bute and Stuart*, pp. 105-106.

5. "They Are Now Become a Formidable Enemy"

Colonel William Harcourt to his father Earl Harcourt.

                                        Brunswick, March 17th, 1777

The public papers have hitherto given you a fair account enough of our operations; in what light they may state the affairs of Trenton and PrinceTown I cannot so easily guess, for, however we may blame the scandalous negligence and cowardice of the Hessian brigade, there certainly was a fault in the original arrangement of the winter quarters, which were much too extensive for an army of our numbers, and the position of Trenton in itself extremely faulty.

. . . However Government may have been flattered by the representations of a few interested individuals, you may depend upon it, as a fact, that we have not yet met with ten, I believe I have said two, disinterested friends to the supremacy of Great Britain; that from the want of intelligence we frequently, nay generally, lose the favourable opportunity for striking a decisive stroke, that in general we ought to avoid attacking any considerable body of them (suppose two or three hundred), unless we can pursue our advantage, or at least take post; for though we may carry our point, nevertheless, whenever we attempt to return to our quarters we may be assured of their harassing us upon our retreat; that detached corps should never march without artillery, of which the rebels are extremely apprehensive; lastly, that, though they seem to be ignorant of the precision and order, and even of the principles, by which large bodies are moved, yet they possess some of the requisites for making good troops, such as extreme cunning, great industry in moving ground and felling of wood, activity and a spirit of enterprise upon any advantage.

Having said thus much, I have no occasion to add that, though it was once the fashion of this army to treat them in the most contemptible light, they are now become a formidable enemy. Formidable, however, as they may be, I flatter myself we are a good deal more so, and I have therefore little doubt that, provided affairs continue quiet in Europe, and the expected reinforcements arrive in good time, we shall soon bring this business to a happy conclusion.

                        —Harcourt, ed., *Harcourt Papers*, II, 207-209.

IV. PILLAGING AND ATROCITIES

The British and Hessian campaigns in New York and New Jersey quickly gave rise to repeated charges of plunder, rape, the shooting of prisoners and civilians, and other war atrocities committed by the enemy. One venerable resident of Princeton told how the British burned all the firewood the inhabitants had stored up for the winter, even ripped the boards off houses, burned the fences, cut down the apple and other fruit trees and burned them, too. In the vicinity of Princeton they set fire to grist and fulling mills, killed sheep, and even had milch cows skinned, leaving the skin and hides and taking away the meat. The homes of those who were reported to the British by informers as being sympathetic to the rebellion were maliciously plundered and gutted.

On January 16, 1777, Congress named a committee to inquire into the conduct of the British and Hessian armies. It included two Jerseyites, John Witherspoon and Abraham Clark, and, in addition, Samuel Chase, Francis Lewis, George Ross, Thomas Heyward and William Smith. They made their report in April.

The British themselves conceded that there was a great deal of plundering, but placed the blame on the Hessians. As late as the summer of 1778, a Hessian officer admitted that "there was much plundering" in New Jersey, to Sir Henry Clinton's chagrin. "It has made the country people all the more embittered rebels," he added. Despite Washington's stern injunctions the Patriot record was certainly not spotless either.

1. Washington Forbids Plundering

Trenton, January 1, 1777

His Excellency General Washington strictly forbids all the officers and soldiers of the Continental army, of the militia and all recruiting parties, plundering any person whatsoever, whether Tories or others. The effects of such persons will be applied to public uses in a regular manner, and it is expected that humanity and tenderness to women and children will distinguish brave Americans, contending for liberty, from infamous mercenary ravagers, whether British or Hessians.

G. Washington

—Fitzpatrick, ed., *Writings of Washington*, VI, 466.

2. "The Track of the British Is Marked with Desolation"

April 18, 1777

The committee appointed by Congress some time ago to inquire into the conduct of the British troops in their different marches through New York and New Jersey, have to-day reported:—That in every place where the enemy has been, there are heavy complaints of oppression, injury and insult suffered by the inhabitants from officers, soldiers and Americans disaffected to their country's cause.

The committee found these complaints so greatly diversified that as it was impossible to enumerate them, so it appeared exceedingly difficult to give a distinct and comprehensive view of them, or such an account as would not appear extremely defective when read by unhappy sufferers or the country in general. In order, however, in some degree to answer the design of their appointment, they determined to divide the object of their inquiry into the following parts, and briefly state what they found to be the truth upon each.

First:—*The wanton and oppressive devastation of the country and destruction of property.*

The whole track of the British army is marked with desolation and a wanton destruction of property, particularly through Westchester County, in the State of New York, the towns of Newark, Elizabethtown, Woodbridge, Brunswick, Kingston, Princeton and Trenton, in New Jersey. The fences destroyed, houses deserted, pulled in pieces or consumed by fire, and the general face of waste and devastation spread over a rich and once well-cultivated and well-inhabited country, would affect the most unfeeling with compassion for the unhappy sufferers, and with indignation and resentment against the barbarous ravagers.

It deserves notice that, though there are many instances of rage and vengeance against particular persons, yet the destruction was very general and often undistinguished; those who submitted and took protections, and some who were known to favor them, having frequently suffered in the common ruin. Places and things, which from their public nature and general utility should have been spared by civilized people, have been destroyed or plundered, or both. But above all, places of worship, ministers and other religious persons of some particular Protestant denominations seem to have been treated with the most rancorous hatred, and at the same time with the highest contempt.

Second:—*The inhuman treatment of those who were so unfortunate as to become prisoners.*

The prisoners, instead of that humane treatment which those taken by the United States experienced, were in general treated with the greatest barbarity. Many of them were kept near four days without food altogether. When they received a supply, it was insufficient in quantity, and often of the worst kind. They suffered the utmost distress from cold, nakedness and close confinement. Freemen and men of substance suffered all that a generous mind could suffer from the contempt and mockery of British and foreign mercenaries. Multitudes died in prison. When they were sent out, several died in being carried from the boats on shore, or upon the road attempting to go home. The committee, in the course of their inquiry, learned that sometimes the common soldiers expressed sympathy with the prisoners, and the foreigners more than the English. But this was seldom or never the case with the officers; nor have they been able to hear of any charitable assistance given them by the inhabitants who remained in or resorted to the city of New York, which neglect, if universal, they believe was never known to happen in any similar case in a Christian country.

Third:—*The savage butchery of those who had submitted and were incapable of resistance.*

The committee found it to be the general opinion of the people in the neighborhood of Trenton and Princeton that the British, the day before the battle of Princeton, had determined to give no quarter. They did not, however, obtain any clear proof that there were general orders for that purpose, but the treatment of several particular persons at and since that time has been of the most shocking kind, and gives too much countenance to the opposition. Officers wounded and disabled, some of them of the first rank, were barbarously mangled or put to death. A minister of the gospel, who neither was nor had been in arms, was massacred in cold blood at Trenton, though humbly supplicating for mercy.

Fourth:—*The lust and brutality of the soldiers in abusing women.*

The committee had authentic information of many instances of the most indecent treatment and actual ravishment of married and single women; but such is the nature of that most irreparable injury that the persons suffering it, though perfectly innocent, look upon it as a kind of reproach to have the facts related and their names known. Some complaints were made to the commanding officers on this subject, and one affidavit made before a justice of the peace, but the committee could not learn that any satisfaction was ever given, or punishment inflicted, except that one soldier in Pennington was kept in custody for part of a day.

On the whole, the committee are sorry to say that the cry of barbarity and cruelty is but too well founded; and as in conversation those who are cool to the American cause have nothing to oppose to the facts but their being incredible and not like what they are pleased to style the generosity and clemency of the English nation, the committee beg leave to observe that one of the circumstances most frequently occurring in the inquiry was the opprobrious, disdainful names given to the Americans. These do not need any proof, as they occur so frequently in the newspapers printed under their direction, and in the intercepted letters of those who are officers and call themselves gentlemen. It is easy, therefore, to see what must be the conduct of a soldiery greedy of prey towards a people whom they have been taught to look upon, not as freemen defending their rights on principle, but as desperadoes and profligates, who have risen up against law and order in general and wish the subversion of society itself. This is the most charitable and candid manner in which the committee can account for the melancholy truths which they have been obliged to report. Indeed, the same deluding principle seems to govern persons and bodies of the highest rank in Britain; for it is worthy of notice that not pamphleteers only, but King and Parliament, constantly call those acts *lenity*, which on their first publication filled this whole continent with resentment and horror.

—MOORE, *Diary of the American Revolution*, I, 419-422.

3. "THERE WAS A GREAT DEAL OF PLUNDERING"

The Examination of Witnesses in the House of Commons on the Conduct of Lord Howe and Sir William Howe, 1779.
From the examination of General [James] Robertson:
Q. Did the troops plunder the inhabitants as they passed through that country?
A. There was a great deal of plundering.
Q. What effect had this on the minds of the people?
A. Naturally it would lose you friends and gain you enemies.
Q. Would it have been possible to have prevented the troops from plundering?
A. The commander in chief gave orders against it repeatedly. A number of officers who lately came into the country, and entertained a notion that Americans were enemies, perhaps did not take enough care to prevent soldiers from gratifying themselves at the expence of the people, so that plundering was very frequent.
Q. You have said there was a great deal of plundering; will you ascertain where and when?
A. The places where I first saw the effect of it was on Long Island; the next on New-York Island.

Q. Do you know of a great deal of plundering in any other part of the country?
A. It has been observed that these are the only two places in which I accompanied the army; I have heard that in other places there has been a good deal of plunder committed.
Q. Will you explain the degree of plunder, within your own knowledge, on Long Island and York Island?
A. When I landed first, I found in all the farms, the poultry, cows, and farm stocked; when I passed sometime afterwards, I found nothing alive: these were some reasons that appeared publicly to me: I saw some men hanged, by Sir William Howe's orders, for plundering; and I have heard that after Mr. Washington took the Hessians at Trenton, he restored to the inhabitants twenty-one waggon-loads of plunder he had found among their baggage.
Q. Did you ever hear of any orders from the convention of New-York for the inhabitants to drive off their cattle and stock?
A. I have seen such a publication.
Q. Did not Sir William Howe give repeated orders to prevent plundering?
A. I have said so.
Q. Do you know, or ever hear, that the Hessian troops were encouraged to go to America by the hopes of plunder?
A. I have heard say that the Hessians before they went away were told that they were going to a country where they would have great plunder; but I don't say that any Hessian officer ever made use of expressions of that sort.
Q. Do you believe that the Hessians looked on America as an enemy's country?
A. I believe so: the Hessians were ignorant of the people; when they saw these people in arms, it was natural for them, who did not know the people, to think they were enemies; people better informed too much adopted the notion.
Q. From your experience of war in Europe, did you observe that there was more plundering in America than there would have been by an army in an enemy's country in Europe?
A. The practice of armies in Europe is very different; some people in Europe would not let their army plunder, even in an enemy's country.
Q. Are you of opinion that Sir William Howe took every proper means to prevent plundering in his power?
A. I dare say, by Sir William Howe's orders, and by what I know of them, he wished to prevent it; and, I dare say, he took the means that occurred to him to do it.
Q. You have said, "A number of officers lately come into the country, and who entertained a notion that Americans were enemies, perhaps did not take enough of care to prevent soldiers from gratifying themselves at the expense of the people, so that plundering was very frequent":—you will therefore explain what officers you meant, and what particular facts you alluded to?
A. I had been asked if I stopped plundering; I answered, "Yes": in order to account for that not happening in every other brigade, I said that the officers who had lately come into the country had not the same sense that I had of the merits and dispositions of the people; and that it was from this want that the commander in chief's orders were not carried into execution in every other brigade; the reflection was general and did not allude to any particular fact.

Q. Do you know of any particular instance where the orders you allude to were disobeyed?

A. As often as plunder was committed the order was disobeyed.

Question repeated.

A. I don't know any other answer I can give; I should wish to satisfy every question that is asked; I don't know how to satisfy it more.

—ADAMS, "Contemporary Opinion on the Howes,"
Mass. Hist. Soc. Proc., XLIV, 118-120.

4. THE PENNSYLVANIA MILITIA DESECRATE A CHURCH

From the Journal of the Reverend Dr. Muhlenberg.

Saturday, Sept. 27, 1777. To-day I was requested to bury the child of one of our vestrymen at Augustus church. When I arrived there, found to my sorrow that a regiment of the Pennsylvania militia had taken possession of the church and schoolhouse. The church was filled with officers and men and their arms; the organ gallery was also full; one was playing on the organ and another singing an accompaniment; the floor was filled with straw and dirt, and on the altar they had their victuals. In short, I saw in miniature the horror of destruction in holy places.

I went in but did not think it prudent to say anything to the crowd, as they began to mock, and some of the officers called out to the one playing on the organ to play a Hessian march. I sought Colonel Dunlap and asked him if this was the promised protection to religious and civil freedom. He excused himself by saying that it was difficult to keep up strict discipline with the militia, who were composed of men of all nations. The schoolmaster complained with tears that they had destroyed his buckwheat patch, now ripe, and plundered and trodden down his garden vegetables. I could give him no assistance, for I was served in the same manner. My lot of three acres near the church, which was full of buckwheat in blossom, and from which I had hoped a frugal supply for the winter, had twenty head of horses and oxen in it, eating it off and treading it down. If one says a word about it, one is called a tory and threatened with burning of house and stable. The other side calls us rebels.

I went home and left a message with the schoolmaster for the parents of the dead child, when they arrived, that in such circumstances I could not attend the funeral or hold a discourse in the church for their consolation. The view of the church made me melancholy.

—MUHLENBERG, "Journal," *Penn. Hist. Soc. Coll.*, I, 168-169.

V. STALEMATE

While Howe's New Jersey campaign was grinding to a standstill American and British forces exchanged light jabs in New York and Connecticut. The first of these was a futile American attempt to capture Fort Independence, situated just north of Spuyten Duyvil. The objective of this ill-planned foray was to alarm the enemy and prevent their reinforcing the army in Jersey. Timothy Pickering's severe judgment that in the opinion of discerning men General Heath, who commanded the expedition, had "acquired nought but disgrace," *was seconded by Washington. In a blistering letter the American commander wrote Heath:*

> *Your conduct is censured (and by men of sense and judgment who were with you on the expedition to Fort Independence) as being fraught with too much caution by which the Army has been disappointed, and in some degree disgraced. Your summons, as you did not attempt to fulfill your threats, was not only idle but farcical, and will not fail of turning the laugh exceedingly upon us.*

Laugh the British did, and uproariously. Ambrose Serle's comment: "One Heath, once a butcher, now a rebel general, has left the army in disgust, on account of some reflections thrown upon him by Washington for not attacking Fort Independence. He blamed his men, and his men, him; villains and cowards altogether!"

A countermove by the British was the raid on Danbury, led by Lord Tryon, the Tory governor of New York. Apparently Howe sought to create the impression that Burgoyne planned to descend upon Connecticut. In counterattacking Tryon's forces, General Wooster was killed, but Benedict Arnold survived to fight at Saratoga. The raid, which, aside from burning some twenty houses and destroying stores, accomplished little, inspired a humorously satirical skit.

As the spring of '77 came to an end, Howe, with other plans in mind which were not clear to Washington, pulled his forces out of all of Jersey except Amboy. General Samuel Parsons commented to his wife: "This State is once more delivered from those pests of society. Who will next be infected with them is uncertain, but we are in high spirits, and ready to march to any part of the country."

1. Heath Muddles the Fort Independence Expedition

Journal of Colonel Timothy Pickering.

Friday, January 24th [*1777*]. The snow fell last night about three or four inches deep, and this morning it rained hard, by which the soldiers were generally wet, in their huts, through to their skins. General Lincoln sent Major Popkin, one of his aides-de-camp, to General Heath, for orders relative to the removing the troops, it being impossible for them to continue in their present situation, either with comfort and a possibility of preserving their health, or safety, for their arms were wet and their ammunition would soon be spoiled.

Major Popkin was gone four hours, being detained that General Heath might get intelligence from his advanced posts, and in endeavoring to persuade him to consent that General Lincoln's division might retire to their old quarters at Tarrytown and Dobbs's Ferry, to shift and dry their clothes and refresh themselves after their fatigues; but General Heath would consent only that they should retire about two and three miles to the nearest houses. But, notwithstanding, General Lincoln, upon considering the uncomfortable condition of his troops, and uselessness of their arms and ammunition from their being so much wet, consented that we should proceed towards our old quarters, and in the mean time went to General Heath to induce him also to consent, saying, as he left me, that, if General Heath would not consent to a necessity so urgent, he must send an express to stop us.

We accordingly began our march; but such had been the fatigues and distress of the men from cold and want of cover for the week past that the impatience of great numbers carried them off without orders, and it was not without much difficulty that I could collect any to form a body capable of action, to secure our retreat. Indeed, the arms and ammunition in general were so damaged by the rain that we could have made but a feeble resistance, had the enemy sallied. 'Tis true the storm rendered a sally improbable; besides, we moved off in silence.

On the march, about half way between our late camp and Tarrytown, the Brigade-Major, Burnham, brought me General Heath's positive orders to march to Mile Square. But it was absolutely impracticable to execute them. A large proportion of the men had by this time arrived at their quarters, and full three fourths of my regiment were ahead of me, and I on foot, with my pack and large blanket at my back (which I chose to carry, that I might know what soldiers endured, and to make *them* more easy, seeing I endured the same fatigues).

Besides, had my regiment been then embodied and under command, I should hardly have attempted to turn them about, to face, in the afternoon, a driving south-east storm of rain, when they had been wet to their skins many hours, and, for the reasons already mentioned, they could have yielded little assistance to General Heath, had we obeyed his orders. Indeed, it appeared to me to be downright cruelty to order them there, especially as no important advantage was held up to view to compensate the soldier's fatigue, nor, indeed, any reason mentioned but the saving General Heath and his division the trouble of turning out of the houses they at that time occupied, and retiring to others a little more remote from the enemy; for, as to the enemy's taking possession of the ground he and we quitted, it was ridiculous to urge that as a reason for our tarrying; for, if we could not drive them from the naked hills, how could he expect to take Fort Independence and destroy Kingsbridge that is open to the fort? against which that he might try his twenty-four-pounder and howitz, General Heath also urged us to stay.

These were his reasons for the orders he gave for our staying in our miserable huts, in cold and rain and snow, or of retiring only two or three miles to houses where we had neither clothes to shift ourselves nor any refreshment save beef and flour; for, when we left Tarrytown, a week before, we had orders to take only our blankets and axes, and the two days' provisions we had cooked, General Lincoln expecting but a short expedition. We did not even take our camp-kettles; and the troops, being detained, suffered a good deal from the want of them, eating their beef roasted (many without salt) on the coals, or held in the fire at the end of a stick sharpened and run through the slices. Indeed, we were so lucky at this time as to get hard bread, a quantity of which had been prepared for the expedition; but this was soon gone, and for two thirds of the week flour was dealt out, which the soldiers made, some into cakes, and some into dumplings, boiled with their meat; for we at length had sent for our camp-kettles.

We continued our route to our old quarters at Tarrytown and Dobbs's Ferry.

Thus ended our week's expedition. After enduring a variety of hardships, we returned, doing nothing and getting nothing but the paltry booty of a few blankets—about forty—a box of candles, a parcel of Osnaburgs, and about forty small arms, all not making a single wagon-load.

The expedition was disgraceful. We were to take Fort Independence, not by storm, for the whole army was militia, and the work was ditched, fraised, and surrounded by an *abatis;* not by regular approaches, for we had not a single intrenching tool; not by cannonade, for we had only three six-pounders. And yet, on the first morning we arrived, General Heath, with ridiculous parade and groundless, vain expectation, sent in a summons, demanding the surrender of the fort! The garrison must have been fools and arrant cowards to have regarded it. They did not regard it. After arriving at Morristown, I understood that part of the plan was to have taken New York itself. . . .

It seems the design of the expedition was, if possible, to take Fort Independence, destroy Kingsbridge, carry off forage and alarm the enemy, so as to draw off from or prevent their reënforcing their army in the Jerseys. But Fort Independence is not taken; Kingsbridge is not destroyed; the enemy has been but little alarmed, for it is now pretty clear they have not lessened their forces in the Jerseys, nor increased them at Fort Independence or Kingsbridge; at the latter they have been induced to throw up a little redoubt. We have, as before mentioned, carried off some forage.

—PICKERING, *Life of Timothy Pickering,* I, 101-104.

2. THE EXPEDITION TO DANBURY

A "royal attack and feat," under the command of General
Tryon, to destroy the stores of beef, pork and rum.

SCENE—NEW YORK.

Without wit, without wisdom, half stupid and drunk,
And rolling along arm in arm with his punk,
The gallant Sir William, who fights all by proxy,
Thus spoke to his soldiers, held up by his doxy:

"My boys, I'm a-going to send you with Tryon,
To a place where you'll all get as groggy as I am;
And the wounded, when well, shall receive a full gill,
But the slain be allowed just as much as they will.
By a Tory from Danbury I've just been informed
That there's *nobody there, so the place shall be stormed.*"

TRYON.

If there's nobody *there,* sir, and nobody *near it,*
Two thousand will conquer the *whole,* never fear it.

JOE GALLOP-AWAY, *a refugee Tory, with several others.*

JOE.

Good soldiers, go fight, that we all may get rich.

SOLDIERS.

Go get you a halter. . . .
Get out, and go live in the woods upon nuts,
Or I'll give you my bayonet plump in your ———
D'ye think, you contemptible thief-looking crew,
That we fight to get beef for such rascals as you?

TRYON.

Come on, my brave boys, now as bold as a lion,
And march for the honor of General Tryon;
My lads, there's no danger, for this you may know,
That I'd let it alone if I thought it was so.

SCENE—CONNECTICUT. TROOPS LANDED.

TRYON.

In cunning and canting, deceit and disguise,
In cheating a friend, and inventing of lies,
I think I'm a match for the best of my species,
But in this undertaking I feel all in pieces;
So I'll fall in the rear, for I'd rather go last;—
Come, march on, my boys, let me see you all past;
For his Majesty's service (so says my commission)
Requires that I *bring up* the whole expedition.

SCENE—DANBURY. TROOPS ARRIVED.

TRYON.

Come, halloo, my lads, for the day is our own,
No rebels are here; not a soul in the town;
So fire all the houses, and when in a blaze,
We'll honor the King with a shout of huzzas.
A noise among the soldiers.

TRYON.

In his Majesty's name, what's this mutinous jargon?

SOLDIERS.

We came to get drunk, sir, for that was the bargain!

IRISH SOLDIER, DRUNK.

Huzza for the Congress—the Congress and toddy!

TRYON.

You scoundrel, I'll run you quite through the body.

SECOND IRISH SOLDIER.

By the head of St. Paddy,
I care not a louse for King George nor his daddy!

THIRD IRISH SOLDIER.

What plenty is here! Oh what eating and drinking!
Who'd stay in New York, to be starving and ———?

FOURTH IRISH SOLDIER.
The rebels, huzza! in a hat full of rum.

FIFTH IRISH SOLDIER.
Come let us drink bumpers, Jack—out of a drum.

SCOTCH SOLDIER.
Laird Bute and his clan are a bundle of thieves.

ENGLISH SOLDIER.
Lord North and his gang are a kennel of slaves.

WELSH SOLDIER.
And a Welshman, prave poys, never harbors with knaves.

ALL.
                              Then let us go over.
Who'd stay to be starved, that might thus live in clover?
                                        They sing.
Let freedom and love be the glee of our song,
Let America flourish—the Congress grow strong,
And brave Washington *conqueror* all the day long!
A consultation of officers. At a distance, houses and stores on fire.

TRYON.
I wish I was back, for I'm woefully scared,
The light will be seen and the noise will be heard,
And the rebels will gather so thick in our way
That whether we run for it or whether we stay,
The fate of the whole will be doubtful—and then——
A sudden alarm; an OFFICER *in a fright gallops about crying:*
To arms, to arms, to arms—ten thousand men
Are pouring from the clouds—ten thousand more
Are got between the army and the shore,
Ten thousand women too.

TRYON.
                    Run, run; stop, stop.
Here, help me on my horse before I drop.

Enter an officer from New York. To Tryon:

OFFICER.
The King hath promised, sir, you shall be *knighted.*

TRYON.
The devil take the King—for I am so frighted——

OFFICER.
But, sir, you must attend to what I've said.

TRYON.
Why, then, the King must knight me when I'm dead.

OFFICER.

But I bring orders, sir, which say "*you must*"——

TRYON.

Aye, *must* or *not*, I'll have a gallop first.

Sets off with the whole after him.

SCENE—THE SHIPPING.

Troops on board. TRYON *surrounded with Surgeons.*

TRYON.

My belly's full of balls—I hear them rattle.

SURGEON.

'Tis only, sir, the echo of the battle.

TRYON.

Do search me over—see where 'tis I'm wounded.

SURGEON.

You are not hurt, sir.

TRYON.

Then I am confounded;
For as I stood, not knowing what to do,
Whether to fight, to fly, or to pursue,
A cannon ball, of two and thirty pound,
Struck me just where Sir Peter got his wound;
Then passing on between my horse's ears—

SURGEON.

Compose yourself, good sir—forget your cares,
You are not slain—you are alive and well.

TRYON.

—Between my horse's ears, and down he fell,
Then getting up again——

SURGEON.

Dear sir, compose,
And try to get yourself into a doze;
The hurt you've got is not so dangerous deep,
But bleeding, shaving, patience, time and sleep,
With blisters, clysters, physic, air and diet,
Will set you up again if you'll be quiet.

TRYON.

So thick, so fast, the balls and bullets flew,
Some hit me here, some there, some thro' and thro'—
And so by thousands did the rebels muster
Under Generals Arnold and old Wooster

That let me, let me, let me, let me but
    Get off alive—*Farewell, Connecticut!*
—"Comus," "Expedition to Danbury," *Penn. Gazette*, May 14, 1777.

3. "The Enemy Are upon the Eve of Evacuating the Jerseys"

Colonel Henry Knox to Henry Jackson.

Camp Middlebrook, June 21, 1777

General Howe on the 14th put his whole army in motion. He had for a long time past been collecting his force from Rhode Island, New York, Staten Island, etc. The boats upon which he designed to cross the Delaware as a bridge were fixed on wagons, besides which he had a large number [of] flat-bottom boats fixed on wagons to transport to the Delaware. These boats with the necessary apparatus, wagons to convey the baggage and the ammunition wagons, etc., swelled the number of his wagons to perhaps 1,000 or 1,100, a great incumbrance to an army not very numerous. . . .

Our position was exceeding good, and while we continued on it the passage to the Delaware would be rendered extremely precarious, and to attack us in camp was an event much to be wished. However, something was to be done.

General Sullivan was posted at Princeton, with a force pretty respectable in itself, but not sufficient to stop General Howe's army; and he might by a forced march push a column between Princeton and us, and cut off General Sullivan's communications at least; but, our intelligence being pretty good, the general directed Sullivan to take post about four miles from Princeton in such a manner that the surrounding him would be impracticable. We also had a party at Milstone, as a cover for the ammunition at Princeton. This was a dangerous post from its proximity to the enemy, but rendered less so by the extreme vigilance which we recommended, and which the officer commanding particularly obeyed.

Matters were thus situated on the morning of the 14th, when we discovered that the party at Milstone was attacked. Support was immediately sent to cover the retreat of the party, when it was discovered to be the enemy's main body, as the same body of observation posted there were obliged to retreat "*pretty quick.*" The enemy took position. Our whole army was immediately ordered under arms, ready to be put in motion; but the conduct of the enemy rendered it unnecessary, for instead of immediately pushing for the Delaware, distant about twenty-five miles, or attacking General Sullivan, he set down on the ground and instantly began to fortify in a very strong position; but it was not till the next day that we discovered their works.

Their conduct was perplexing. It was unaccountable that people who the day before gave out in very gasconading terms that they would be in Philadelphia in six days should stop short when they had gone only nine miles. The intelligence was pretty good with respect to their designs, yet it was too imperfect with respect to their numbers to warrant an attack on troops so well disciplined, and posted as they were. We also in the course of a day or two discovered that they had not moved with any baggage, even tents and the most necessary, but had come out with an intention of drawing us into the plain; had left their immense number of wagons behind them, but even in this kind of ostentatious challenge they omitted not one precaution for their own safety. They had Brunswick and the Raritan River on their right, secured by eight or ten strong redoubts. At Brunswick the Raritan bends and runs a little way north, and then turns nearly west. This they had in their front secured by strong redoubts at Middlebrook. Their left was secured by the River Milstone, which empties itself into the Raritan near Bound Brook: from their right to left was about eight miles.

In this situation they continued until early in the morning of the 19th, continually at work throwing up redoubts. We had a large body of riflemen, under Colonel Morgan, perpetually making inroads upon them, attacking their pickets, killing their light-horse; and beset them in such a manner, assisted by the militia, that Mr. Howe, instead of marching to Philadelphia, found himself almost blockaded in an open flat country. Nothing could exceed the spirit shown on this occasion by the much injured people of the Jerseys. Not an atom of the lethargic spirit that possessed them last winter— all fire, all revenge. The militia of Pennsylvania likewise turned out universally, so that had Sir William put his attempt into execution, we should probably [have] had twenty-five or thirty thousand militia upon his back, besides the most respectable body of Continental troops that ever were in America.

These things being fully represented to General Howe, he thought it proper to take himself and light army back to Brunswick again, and accordingly marched about one o'clock in the morning of the 19th, without beat of drum or sound of fife. When his army had gotten beyond the reach of pursuit, they began to burn, plunder and waste all before them. The desolation they committed was horrid, and served to show the malice which marks their conduct.

The militia, light-horse and riflemen exhibited the greatest marks of valor, frequently taking prisoners within two hundred yards of their encampment. Their loss must be at least one hundred killed and wounded and taken prisoners, among whom are two lieutenants of grenadiers of the 55th and a cornet of light-horse, and a number killed, two sergeants taken. This little march of General Howe's fully proves that no people or country can be permanently conquered where the inhabitants are unanimous in opposition.

What his next manoeuvres may be I can't say, but we suppose the North River; there I believe he will be also disgraced. The motive for belief that the North River will be the scene of his operations is that intelligence is received that Mr. Burgoyne is about crossing the lakes to Ticonderoga, and General Howe must make an attempt to push for a junction. The enemy from all appearances and advices are upon the eve of evacuating the Jerseys. Times are much altered for them from last fall. The people are unanimous in opposing them: just now four thousand marched off to harass the enemy; as many more will go down towards Brunswick this afternoon.

—DRAKE, *Henry Knox*, pp. 43-46.

CHAPTER THIRTEEN

The Burgoyne Campaign

IN THE WINTER *of 1777, General John Burgoyne, known to his troops as "Gentleman Johnny," returned to London after playing a negligible role in the Boston and New York campaigns. Having advanced his social position by his marriage (an elopement) with the daughter of the Earl of Derby, he had distinguished himself in the campaigns in Portugal during the latter part of the Seven Years' War, and won something of a reputation as a moderate by his stand in Parliament on the American question. The playwright-soldier had now worked out a grand strategy to bring the war to a speedy conclusion. This grand strategy was not entirely original in conception. Back in 1776 Carleton had a similar notion, but a combination of stubborn resistance on the part of Benedict Arnold and procrastination on the part of Sir William Howe doomed to failure the previous attempt to capture and divide the state of New York. Burgoyne's plan was more imaginative than any yet proposed and on paper seemed foolproof.*

His three-pronged attack to isolate New England provided for a main army to push southward down Lake Champlain and the upper Hudson, an auxiliary force to operate from Oswego through the Mohawk Valley, and a strong force to be dispatched by Howe up the Hudson. King George's comment, in a manuscript in his own hand in the British Museum, that "the force from Canada must join him [Howe] at Albany," reveals that the monarch originally favored Burgoyne's co-ordinated knockout blow. So did Germain at first. That incompetent head of the Colonial Department approved the plan and gave the command of the expedition to Burgoyne instead of to General Carleton, who, as commander of British forces in Canada, outranked him. But on March 3 Germain also approved Howe's plan for an attack on Philadelphia, in the impractical belief that Howe could complete his mission in time to return and effect a juncture with Burgoyne. Before leaving Canada, Burgoyne saw Howe's letter to Carleton stating that, unless Washington attempted to join the northern American army, he could give Burgoyne no help. At that stage there is no indication that Burgoyne was perturbed. Even as late as August 23 it is clear from a letter of Germain that Howe had been given a free hand.

The documents, then, explode the myth that Howe did not go north to relieve Burgoyne because Germain forgot to tell him about the plan. As that story was subsequently told by William Knox, undersecretary for the Colonial Department:

> *Lord Sackville [Germain] came down to the office on his way to Stoneland, when I observed to him that there was no letter to Howe to acquaint him with the plan or what was expected of him in consequence of it. His Lordship stared and D'Oyly started, but said he would in a moment write a few lines. "So," says Lord Sackville, "my poor horses must stand in the street all the time, and I shan't be to my time anywhere." D'Oyly then said he had better go, and he would write from himself to Howe and include copies of Burgoyne's instructions which would tell him all that he would want to know, and with this his Lordship was satisfied, as it enabled him to keep his time, for he would never bear delay or disappointment.*

Germain was not a man to keep his horses waiting.

Had Burgoyne's plan succeeded it would have been a grave blow to the Patriot cause. But it failed, and with this failure an entire British army vanished. Burgoyne's disaster may properly be considered a turning point of the war. True, six more years lay ahead until peace was made, but it was now apparent that the capture and holding of the interior of the American continent would involve an effort beyond the resources of the British to achieve. This was clearly the case once France entered the war, an involvement undoubtedly precipitated by the collapse of Burgoyne's grand design.

I. THE PLAN FOR A THREE-PRONGED ATTACK ON NEW YORK

1. "THOUGHTS FOR CONDUCTING THE WAR FROM THE SIDE OF CANADA"

Submitted by General Burgoyne to Lord George Germain, February 28, 1777.

I humbly conceive the operating army (I mean exclusively of the troops left for the security of Canada) ought not to consist of less than eight thousand regulars, rank and file. The artillery required in the memorandums of General Carleton, a corps of watermen, two thousand Canadians, including hatchet-men and other workmen, and one thousand or more savages.

It is to be hoped that the reinforcement and the victualling-ships may all be ready to sail from the Channel and from Corke on the last day of March; I am persuaded that to part with a fleet of transports earlier is to subject government to loss and disappointment. It may reasonably be expected that they will reach Quebec before the 20th of May, a period in full time for opening the campaign. The roads, and the rivers and lakes, by the melting and running off of the snows, are in common years impracticable sooner.

But as the weather, long before that time, will probably have admitted of labour in the docks, I will take for granted that the fleet of last year, as well batteaux as armed vessels, will be found repaired, augmented and fit for immediate service. The magazines that remain of provision (I believe them not to be abundant) will probably be formed at Montreal, Sorel and Chamblée.

I conceive the first business for those entrusted with the chief powers should be to select and post the troops destined to remain in Canada; to

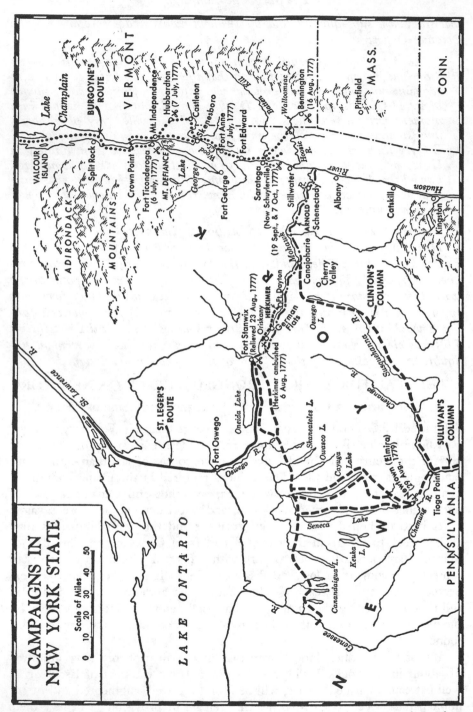

CAMPAIGNS IN
NEW YORK STATE

Scale of Miles
0   10 20 30 40 50

From The Encyclopedia of American History
by Richard B. Morris

Courtesy of Harper & Brothers

throw up the military stores and provision with all possible dispatch, in which service the above-mentioned troops, if properly posted, will greatly assist; and to draw the army destined for operation to cantonments within as few days march of St. John's as conveniently may be. . . .

I must beg leave to state the expeditious conveyance of provision and stores from Quebec and the several other depositaries, in order to form ample magazines at Crown-Point, as one of the most important operations of the campaign, because it is upon that which most of the rest will depend. . . .

The navigation of Lake Champlain secured by the superiority of our naval force, and the arrangements for forming proper magazines so established as to make the execution certain, I would not lose a day to take possession of Crown-Point with Brigadier Fraser's corps, a large body of Savages, a body of Canadians, both for scouts and works, and the best of our engineers and artificers well supplied with intrenching tools.

The brigade would be sufficient to prevent insult during the time necessary for collecting the stores, forming magazines and fortifying the posts; all which should be done, to a certain degree, previous to proceeding in force to Ticonderoga; to such a degree I mean as may be supposed to be effected in time of transporting artillery, preparing fascines and other necessaries for artillery operations; and, by keeping the rest of the army back during that period, the transport of provisions will be lessened, and the soldiers made of use in forwarding the convoys.

But though there would be only one brigade at Crown-Point at that time, it does not follow that the enemy should remain in a state of tranquillity. Corps of savages, supported by detachments of light regulars, should be continually on foot to keep them in alarm and within their works, to cover the reconnoitering of general officers and engineers, and to obtain the best intelligence of their strength, position and design.

If due exertion is made in the preparations stated above, it may be hoped that Ticonderoga will be reduced early in the summer, and it will then become a more proper place for arms than Crown-Point.

The next measure must depend on those taken by the enemy, and upon the general plan of the campaign as concerted at home. If it be determined that General Howe's whole forces should act upon Hudson's-River, and to the southward of it, and that the only object of the Canada army be to effect a junction with that force, the immediate possession of Lake George would be of great consequence, as the most expeditious and most commodious route to Albany; and, should the enemy be in force upon that lake, which is very probable, every effort should be tried, by throwing savages and light troops round it, to oblige them to quit it without waiting for naval preparations. Should these efforts fail, the route by South-Bay and Skenesborough might be attempted; but considerable difficulties may be expected, as the narrow parts of the river may be easily choked up and rendered impassible; and, at best, there will be necessity for a great deal of land-carriage for the artillery, provision, etc., which can only be supported from Canada. In case of success also by that route, and the enemy not removed from Lake George, it will be necessary to leave a chain of posts as the army proceeds, for the securities of your communications, which may too much weaken so small an army.

Lest all their attempts should unavoidably fail, and it becomes indispensably necessary to attack the enemy by water upon Lake George, the army, at the out-set, should be provided with carriages, implements and artificers for conveying armed vessels from Ticonderoga to the lake.

These ideas are formed upon the supposition that it be the sole purpose of the Canada army to effect a junction with General Howe; or, after co-operating so far as to get possession of Albany and open the communication to New-York, to remain upon the Hudson's-River, and thereby enable that general to act with his whole force to the southward. . . .

To avoid breaking in upon other matter, I omitted in the beginning of these papers to state the idea of an expedition at the out-set of the campaign by the Lake Ontario and Oswego to the Mohawk River; which, as a diversion to facilitate every proposed operation, would be highly desirable, provided the army should be reinforced sufficiently to afford it.

It may at first appear, from a view of the present strength of the army, that it may bear the sort of detachment proposed by myself last year for this purpose; but it is to be considered that at that time the utmost object of the campaign, from the advanced season and unavoidable delay of preparation for the lakes, being the reduction of Crown-Point and Ticonderoga, unless the success of my expedition had opened the road to Albany, no greater numbers were necessary than for those first operations. The case in the present year differs; because the season of the year affords a prospect of very extensive operation, and consequently the establishment of many posts, patroles, etc., will become necessary. The army ought to be in a state of numbers to bear those drains and still remain sufficient to attack any thing that probably can be opposed to it.

Nor, to argue from probability, is so much force necessary for this diversion this year as was required for the last; because we then knew that General Schuyler with a thousand men was fortified upon the Mohawk. When the different situations of things are considered, viz. the progress of General Howe, the early invasion from Canada, the threatening of the Connecticut from Rhode-Island, etc., it is not to be imagined that any detachment of such forces as that of Schuyler can be supplied by the enemy for the Mohawk. I would not therefore propose it of more (and I have great diffidence whether so much can be prudently afforded) than Sir John Johnson's corps, a hundred British from the Second Brigade and a hundred more from the 8th Regiment, with four pieces of the lightest artillery and a body of savages; Sir John Johnson to be with a detachment in person, and an able field-officer to command it. I should wish Lieutenant-Colonel St. Leger for that employment.

—BURGOYNE, *A State of the Expedition from Canada*, pp. iii-vi.

2. GEORGE III AGREES THAT HOWE MUST JOIN BURGOYNE AT ALBANY

Remarks on Burgoyne's plan in the handwriting of King George, from a manuscript in the British Museum.

The outlines of the plan seem to be on a proper foundation. The rank and file of the army in Canada (including the 11th of British, McClean's [Maclean's] corps, the Brunswicks and Hanover) amount to 10,527; add the eleven additional companies and 400 Hanover Chasseurs, the total will be 11,443.

As sickness and other contingencies must be expected, I should think not above 7,000 effectives can be spared over Lake Champlain, for it would be highly imprudent to run any risk in Canada.

The fixing of stations of those left in the province may not be quite right, though the plan proposed may be recommended. Indians must be employed, and this measure must be avowedly directed. . . .

As Sir William Howe does not think of acting from Rhode Island into Massachusetts, the force from Canada must join him at Albany.

The diversion on the Mohawk River ought, at least, to be strengthened by the addition of 400 Hanover Chasseurs.

The provisions ought to be calculated for a third more than the effective soldiery, and the General ordered to avoid delivering these when the army can be subsisted from the country.

Burgoyne certainly greatly undervalues the German recruits.

The idea of carrying the army by sea to Sir William Howe would certainly require the leaving a much larger part of it in Canada, as in that case the rebel army would divide that province from the immense one under Sir W. Howe. I greatly dislike that idea.

—DE FONBLANQUE, *Political and Military Episodes*, pp. 486-487.

3. THE STRATEGIC MISUNDERSTANDING BETWEEN HOWE AND BURGOYNE

A. GENERAL HOWE TO SIR GUY CARLETON

New York, April 2, 1777

Having but little expectation that I shall be able, from the want of sufficient strength in this army, to detach a corps in the beginning of the campaign to act up Hudson's River consistent with the operations already determined upon, the force your Excellency may deem expedient to advance beyond your frontiers after taking Ticonderoga will, I fear, have little assistance from hence to facilitate their approach, and as I shall probably be in Pennsylvania when that corps is ready to advance into this province, it will not be in my power to communicate with the officer commanding it so soon as I could wish; he must therefore pursue such measures as may from circumstances be judged most conducive to the advancement of his Majesty's service consistently with your Excellency's orders for his conduct.

The possession of Ticonderoga will naturally be the first object, and without presuming to point out to your Excellency the advantages that must arise by securing Albany and the adjacent country, I conclude they will engage the next attention, but, omitting others, give me leave to suggest that this situation will open a free intercourse with the Indians, without which we are to expect little assistance from them on this side.

The further progress of this corps, depending so much upon the enemy's movements, cannot be foreseen at this distance of time; still I flatter myself and have reason to expect the friends of Government in that part of the country will be found so numerous and so ready to give every aid and assistance in their power that it will prove no difficult task to reduce the more rebellious parts of the province. In the mean while I shall endeavour to have a corps upon the lower part of Hudson's River sufficient to open the communication for shipping thro' the Highlands, at present obstructed by several forts erected by the rebels for that purpose, which corps may afterwards act in favour of the northern army.

—GR. BRIT. HIST. MSS. COMM., *Stopford-Sackville Manuscripts*, II, 64-65.

B. GENERAL HOWE TO LORD GEORGE GERMAIN

Philadelphia, October 22, 1777

I was surprized to find the General's [Burgoyne's] declaration, in his message to Sir H. Clinton by Captain Campbell, "that he would not have given up his communication with Ticonderoga had he not expected a co-operating army at Albany," since in my letter to Sir Guy Carleton, a copy of which was transmitted to your Lordship in my dispatch of 2nd April, 1777, No. 47, and of which his Majesty was pleased to approve, I positively mentioned that no direct assistance could be given by the southern army. This letter I am assured was received by Sir Guy Carleton and carried by him to Montreal before General Burgoyne's departure from thence.

—GR. BRIT. HIST. MSS. COMM., *Stopford-Sackville Manuscripts*, II, 80.

II. FIRST ROUND: A WAR OF WORDS

On June 17, 1777, Burgoyne moved south from St. Johns to Lake Champlain with a mixed force of British and German infantrymen numbering some 7,000, a small force of British and Hesse-Hanau artillerymen, 400 Indians, a handful of Canadians and Tories, along with a huge baggage train of 138 guns. Available to his expedition for transportation on the lake was the navy used by Carleton in the Champlain campaign of the previous year, including ships captured from Arnold after Valcour Bay.

The campaign started off in a cloud of oratory and rhetoric released by Gentleman Johnny. On June 23 he made a speech to his Indian allies and issued a bombastic proclamation. In the speech he cautioned the Indians to conduct humane warfare. Edmund Burke promptly ridiculed this appeal in a debate in the House of Commons, exclaiming:

> *Suppose there was a riot on Tower Hill. What would the keeper of his Majesty's lions do? Would he not fling open the dens of the wild beasts and then address them thus: "My gentle lions—my humane bears— my tenderhearted hyenas, go forth! But I exhort you, as you are Christians and members of civil society, to take care not to hurt any man, woman or child."*

But it was Burgoyne's proclamation commending the justice and clemency of the King, but warning that he would execute "the vengeance of the state against the wilful outcasts," that was greeted with especially shrill cat-calls both in London and America. Most widely publicized of all the satirical

retorts was the parody and counterblast attributed to the Pennsylvania poet,
Francis Hopkinson. Burgoyne soon dropped the quill and plunged ahead with
his lumbering baggage train into the forest.

1. Gentleman Johnny Inflames the Indians

Letter of Thomas Anburey, Lieutenant in the British Army.

Camp at River Bouquet, upon Lake Champlain, June 24, 1777

. . . When the assembly were met, the General thus addressed them, by
means of an interpreter:

"Chiefs and Warriors,

"The great King, our common father and the patron of all who seek and
deserve his protection, has considered with satisfaction the general conduct
of the Indian tribes from the beginning of the troubles in America. Too sagacious and too faithful to be deluded or corrupted, they have observed the
violated rights of the parental power they love, and burned to vindicate them.
A few individuals alone, the refuse of a small tribe, at the first were led
astray: and the misrepresentations, the specious allurements, the insidious
promises and diversified plots in which the rebels are exercised, and all of
which they employed for that effect, have served only in the end to enhance
the honor of the tribes in general by demonstrating to the world how few
and how contemptible are the apostates! It is a truth known to you all [that],
these pitiful examples excepted (and they have probably, before this day,
hid their faces in shame), the collective voices and hands of the Indian tribes
over this vast continent are on the side of justice, of law, and the King. . . .

"The clemency of your father has been abused, the offers of his mercy
have been despised, and his farther patience would, in his eyes, become culpable, in as much as it would with-hold redress from the most grievous oppressions in the provinces that ever disgraced the history of mankind. It therefore remains for me, the General of one of his Majesty's armies and in this
council his representative, to release you from those bonds which your obedience imposed. Warriors, you are free—go forth in might and valour of
your cause—strike at the common enemies of Great Britain and America, dis-
turbers of public order, peace and happiness, destroyers of commerce, parri-
cides of state."

The General, then directing their attentions by pointing to the officers,
both German and British, that attended this meeting, proceeded:

"The circle round you, the chiefs of his Majesty's European forces and
of the Princes his allies, esteem you as brothers in the war; emulous in glory
and in friendship, we will endeavour reciprocally to give and to receive
examples; we know how to value, and we will strive to imitate your perseverance in enterprize, and your constancy to resist hunger, weariness and
pain. Be it our task, from the dictates of our religion, the laws of our warfare and the principles and interest of our policy, to regulate your passions
when they overbear, to point out where it is nobler to spare than to revenge,
to discriminate degrees of guilt, to suspend the uplifted stroke, to chastise and
not destroy.

"This war to you, my friends, is new. Upon all former occasions, in taking the field, you held yourselves authorized to destroy wherever you came, because every where you found an enemy. The case is now very different.

"The King has many faithful subjects dispersed in the provinces; consequently you have many brothers there, and these people are more to be pitied that they are persecuted or imprisoned wherever they are discovered or suspected, and to dissemble, to a generous mind, is a yet more grievous punishment.

"Persuaded that your magnanimity of character, joined to your principles of affection to the King, will give me fuller controul over your minds than the military rank with which I am invested, I enjoin your most serious attention to the rules which I hereby proclaim for your invariable observation during the campaign."

After answering, *"Etow! Etow!"* in their language signifying approbation, they appeared to pay very great attention to the interpreter, eager to catch the General's instructions.

"I positively forbid bloodshed, when you are not opposed in arms.

"Aged men, women, children and prisoners must be held sacred from the knife or hatchet, even in the time of actual conflict.

"You shall receive compensation for the prisoners you take, but you shall be called to account for scalps.

"In conformity and indulgence of your customs, which have affixed an idea of honor to such badges of victory, you shall be allowed to take the scalps of the dead when killed by your fire and in fair opposition; but on no account, or pretence, or subtilty, or prevarication, are they to be taken from the wounded or even dying; and still less pardonable, if possible, will it be held to kill men in that condition on purpose, and upon a supposition that this protection to the wounded would be thereby evaded.

"Base, lurking assassins, incendiaries, ravagers and plunderers of the country, to whatever army they may belong, shall be treated with less reserve; but the latitude must be given you by order, and I must be the judge on the occasion.

"Should the enemy, on their parts, dare to countenance acts of barbarity towards those who may fall into their hands, it shall be yours also to retaliate; but till this severity be thus compelled, bear immoveable in your hearts this solid maxim (it cannot be too deeply impressed): that the great essential reward, the worthy service of your alliance, the sincerity of your zeal to the King, your father and never-failing protector, will be examined and judged upon the test only of your steady and uniform adherence to the orders and counsels of those to whom his Majesty has entrusted the direction and honor of his arms."

After the General had finished his speech, they all of them, cried out, *"Etow! Etow! Etow!"* and after remaining some time in consultation, an old Chief of the Iroquois rose up and made the following answer:

"I stand up, in the name of all the nations present, to assure our father that we have attentively listened to his discourse. We receive you as our father, because when you speak we hear the voice of our great father beyond the great lake.

"We rejoice in the approbation you have expressed of our behaviour.

"We have been tried and tempted by the Bostonians; but we have loved our father, and our hatchets have been sharpened upon our affections.

"In proof of the sincerity of our professions, our whole villages able to go to war are come forth. The old and infirm, our infants and wives, alone remain at home.

"With one common assent we promise a constant obedience to all you have ordered and all you shall order, and may the father of days give you many, and success!"

After the Chief of the Iroquois had finished, they all, as before, cried out, "*Etow! Etow! Etow!*" and the meeting broke up.

—ANBUREY, *Travels through the Interior Parts of America*, I, 248-257.

2. BURGOYNE THREATENS DEVASTATION, FAMINE AND HORROR

Proclamation

By John Burgoyne, Esq; etc. etc. Lieut. General of his Majesty's Forces in America, Colonel of the Queen's Regiment of Light Dragoons, Governor of Fort-William in North-Britain, one of the Representatives of the Commons of Great-Britain in Parliament, and commanding an Army and Fleet in an Expedition from Canada etc. etc. etc.

The Forces entrusted to my Command are designed to act in concert, and upon a common Principle, with the numerous Armies and Fleets which already display, in every Quarter of America, the Power, the Justice, and, when properly sought, the Mercy of the King.

The Cause in which the British Arms are thus exerted, applies to the most affecting Interest of the human Heart: And the Military Servants of the Crown, at first called for the sole Purpose of restoring the Rights of the Constitution, now combine with the Love of their Country, and Duty to their Sovereign, the other extensive Incitements, which spring from a due Sense of the general Privileges of Mankind. To the Eyes and Ears of the temperate Part of the Public, and to the Breasts of suffering Thousands in the Provinces, be the melancholy Appeal—Whether the present unnatural Rebellion has not been made the Foundation of the compleatest System of Tyranny that ever God, in his Displeasure, suffered, for a Time, to be exercised over a froward and stubborn Generation.

Arbitrary Imprisonments, Confiscation of Property, Persecution and Torture, unprecedented in the Inquisitions of the Romish Church, are among the palpable Enormities that verify the Affirmative: These are inflicted by Assemblies and Committees, who dare to profess themselves Friends of Liberty, upon the most quiet Subject, without Distinction of Age or Sex, for the sole Crime, often the sole Suspicion, of having adhered in Principle to the Government under which they were born, and to which, by every Tie divine and human, they owe Allegiance. To consummate these shocking Proceedings the Profanation of Religion is added to the most profligate Prostitution of common Reason! The Consciences of Men are set at naught, and the Multitudes are compelled not only to bear Arms, but also to swear Subjection to an Usurpation they abhor.

Animated by these Considerations, at the Head of Troops in the full Powers of Health, Discipline and Valour, determined to strike where necessary, and anxious to save where possible, I, by these Presents, invite and exhort all Persons, in all Places where the Progress of this Army may point, and by the Blessing of God I will extend it FAR, to maintain such a Conduct as may justify me in protecting their Lands, Habitations, and Families. . . .

If notwithstanding these Endeavors and sincere Inclination to assist them, the Phrenzy of Hostility should remain, I trust I shall stand acquitted in the Eyes of God and Men in denouncing and executing the Vengeance of the State against the wilful Outcast. The Messengers of Justice and of Wrath await them in the Field, and Devastation, Famine, and every concomitant Horror that a reluctant but indispensible Prosecution of Military Duty must occasion, will bar the Way to their Return.

J. BURGOYNE

Camp at the River Bongrett [Bouquet] June 23rd. 1777.
By order of his Excellency the Lieutenant General
    —BURGOYNE, "Proclamation," *Mass. Hist. Soc. Proc.*, XII, 89-90.

3. "I ISSUE THIS MY MANIFESTO"

(Attributed to Francis Hopkinson.)

By John Burgoyne and Burgoyne, John, Esq.,
And graced with titles still more higher,
For I'm Lieutenant-general, too,
Of George's troops both red and blue,
On this extensive continent;
And of Queen Charlotte's regiment
Of light dragoons the Colonel;
And Governor eke of Castle Wil—
And furthermore, when I am there,
In House of Commons I appear
(Hoping ere long to be a Peer),
Being a member of that virtuous band
Who always vote at North's command;
Directing too the fleet and troops
From Canada as thick as hops;
And all my titles to display,
I'll end with thrice et cetera.
    The troops consigned to my command
Like Hercules to purge the land
Intend to act in combination
With th' other forces of the nation,
Displaying wide thro' every quarter
What Britain's justice would be after. . . .
Your ears and eyes have heard and seen
How causeless this revolt has been;
And what a dust your leaders kick up

In this rebellious civil hickup,
And how, upon this cursed foundation,
Was reared the system of vexation
Over a stubborn generation.
  But now inspired with patriot love
I come th' oppression to remove;
To free you from the heavy clog
Of every tyrant demogogue,
Who for the most romantic story
Claps into limbo loyal Tory,
All hurly burly, hot and hasty,
Without a writ to hold him fast by; ...
In short, the vilest generation
Which in vindicative indignation
Almighty vengeance ever hurled
From this to the infernal world. ...
To petticoats alike and breeches
Their cruel domination stretches,
For the sole crime, or sole suspicion
(What worse is done by th' inquisition?)
Of still adhering to the crown,
Their tyrants striving to kick down,
Who, by perverting law and reason,
Allegiance construe into treason. ...
  By such important views there pres't to,
I issue this my manifesto.
I, the great knight of de la Mancha,
Without 'Squire Carleton, my Sancho,
Will tear you limb from limb asunder
With cannon, blunderbuss and thunder;
And spoil your feathering and your tarring;
And cagg you up for pickled herring.
In front of troops as spruce as beaux
And ready to lay on their blows,
I'll spread destruction far and near;
And where I cannot kill, I'll spare,
Inviting, by these presents, all,
Both young and old, and great and small,
And rich and poor, and Whig and Tory,
In cellar deep or lofty story;
Where'er my troops at my command
Shall swarm like locusts o'er the land
(And they shall march from the North Pole
As far, at least, as Pensacole)
To break off their communications,
That I can save their habitations;
For, finding that Sir William's plunders

Prove in the event apparent blunders,
It is my full determination
To check all kinds of depredation;
But when I've got you in my power,
Favored is he I last devour.

    From him who loves a quiet life
And keeps at home to kiss his wife, . . .
I will not defalcate a groat,
Nor force his wife to cut his throat;
But with his doxy he may stay
And live to fight another day; . . .

    With the most Christian spirit fired,
And by true soldiership inspired,
I speak as men do in a passion
To give my speech the more impression.
If any should so hardened be
As to expect impunity,
Because *procul a fulmine*,
I will let loose the dogs of Hell,
Ten thousand Indians, who shall yell
And foam and tear, and grin and roar,
And drench their moccasins in gore;
To these I'll give full scope and play
From Ticonderog to Florida;
They'll scalp your heads, and kick your shins,
And rip your ——, and flay your skins,
And of your ears be nimble croppers,
And make your thumbs tobacco-stoppers.
If after all these loving warnings,
My wishes and my bowels' yearnings,
You shall remain as deaf as adder,
Or grow with hostile rage the madder,
I swear by George and by St. Paul
I will exterminate you all.

    Subscribéd with my manual sign,
    To test these presents, John Burgoyne.
—"A New Jerseyman," *New York Journal*, September 8, 1777.

III. THE FALL OF TICONDEROGA

Burgoyne began his campaign with an easy victory. His first objective was the strategic fortress of Ticonderoga on the western shores of Lake Champlain and commanding fleet movements both north and south on that lake. Despite frantic moves to fortify it, Ticonderoga quickly became indefensible when Burgoyne's men hauled their guns to the top of Mount Defiance, a 750-foot height that enfiladed the whole position. Through a combination of carelessness and a shortage of man power it had been left unde-

*fended. General Arthur St. Clair then evacuated both Fort Ticonderoga
and Mount Independence, across the lake. His rear guard was routed by the
British forces at Hubbardton. On the twelfth of July, St. Clair joined General Schuyler at Fort Edward.*

*St. Clair explained in a letter to James Bowdoin of July 9 that the loss of
the post was infinitely preferable to the loss of the army. This was good
logic, but did not satisfy the politicians. Schuyler, chief of the Northern
Department, was the immediate scapegoat. But he himself had realized that
he did not have enough at hand to defend Ticonderoga. On a visit to the
fort before Burgoyne's action he reported that it was seriously undermanned and that many of the raw militia in its garrison were "mere boys,
and one third of the whole force unfit for duty." Charged by Congress with
"neglect of duty" at Ticonderoga, Schuyler was acquitted by a court-martial
"with the highest honors."*

*The effect of the fall of Ticonderoga on Patriot morale was crushing.
As Alexander Hamilton put it in a letter to John Jay of July 13:*

> *All is mystery and dark beyond conjecture. But we must not be dis-
> couraged at a misfortune. We must rather exert ourselves the more vigor-
> ously to remedy the ill consequences of it. If the army gets off safe, we
> shall soon be able to recover the face of affairs. I am in hope that Bur-
> goigne's success will precipitate him into measures that will prove his
> ruin. The enterprising spirit he has credit for, I suspect, may easily be
> fanned by his vanity into rashness. (Jay Papers, Columbia Univ. Lib.)*

How accurate a prophet Hamilton was, military events would soon reveal.

1. "In This Cruel Situation What Can Be Done?"

Colonel James Wilkinson of the Continental Army to General Horatio
Gates.

Ticonderoga, June 25, 1777

The enemy by gradual movements, which have been duly transmitted to
General Schuyler, last evening arrived at Crown Point with some vessels and
a part of their army, who have encamped on Chimney Point. We are induced to believe from a morning gun, which was repeated down the lake,
that their whole force is at hand, and as they have lately taken several prisoners, and the neighboring inhabitants have had free access to this camp, I am
persuaded they will obtain a true state of our weakness, which will indubitably precipitate their operations: in which case the post is inevitably lost, for
if we risk a battle the inferiority of our numbers (without a miracle, which
we sinners have no right to expect) will subject us to defeat and captivity;
and if we retire to Mount Independence, the scantiness of our provisions will
subject us to reduction by famine, as the enemy, when in possession of this
side of the lake, can easily remove the obstructions up the south bay, and by
their fleet cut off our communications from Skenesborough.

The militia are at our command, but should we call them in, immediate
starvation is the consequence, as General Schuyler has lately assured us that
we have no right or reason to expect more than three hundred barrels of

meat in addition, and we can not subsist our present small garrison longer than seven weeks with what is on the ground. The distance from whence our supplies are derived, and the difficulty of transportation, both tend to embarrass us.

In this cruel situation, what can be done? The most laudable measure, in my opinion, would be to remove our heavy artillery and stores, and the convalescents and invalids of the army, to Fort George. Being then light and unincumbered, we might, if hard pushed, effect a retreat to that post, which would enable us to check the enemy's progress; on the contrary, should we attempt to support this place in our present deficient situation, we lose *all*, and leave the country defenseless and exposed. What, then, will there be to obstruct their favorite scheme—a junction by the North River? Nothing that I can discern.

You remember the state of arms I transmitted you on my first arrival here; I am sorry to inform you that they are not now better in quality, or superior in number. Our men are harassed to extreme weakness by fatigue, and the strong guards which we are now obliged to establish will in a little time quite break up their spirits and constitutions. If fortitude, if enterprise, if perseverance or temerity could avail, I would not complain; but, in the name of Heaven, what can be expected from a naked, undisciplined, badly armed, unaccoutered body of men, when opposed to a vast superiority of British troops?

What can be done, the great St. Clair will effect; but such is the weakness of our numbers that he can not form any plan of defense. Of the two, I prefer death to captivity; but be the event as it will, I shall not disgrace my acquaintance.

General Schuyler has been here a few days, but is now in Albany.

—SMITH, *St. Clair Papers*, I, 407-408.

2. "One of the Most Pleasing Spectacles I Ever Beheld"

Letter of Thomas Anburey, Lieutenant in the British Army.

Camp at Crown Point, June 30, 1777

We are now within sight of the enemy, and their watch-boats are continually rowing about, but beyond the reach of cannon shot. Before I proceed farther, let me just relate in what manner the army passed the lake, which was by brigades, generally advancing from seventeen to twenty miles a day, and regulated in such a manner that the second brigade should take the encampment of the first, and so on successively, for each brigade to fill the ground the other quitted; the time for departure was always at daybreak.

One thing appeared to me very singular, which I am not philosopher enough to account for: in sailing up the lake, on all the islands and points of land, the water seemed to separate the trees from the land, and to pass in a manner through them, having the appearance of small brush wood at a very little heighth from the water; nor do the trees appear to come in contact with the land till you approach within two or three miles of the object, when they show themselves to be distinctly joined.

I cannot forbear picturing to your imagination one of the most pleasing spectacles I ever beheld. When we were in the widest part of the lake, whose beauty and extent I have already described, it was remarkably fine and clear, not a breeze stirring, when the whole army appeared at one view in such perfect regularity as to form the most compleat and splendid regatta you can possibly conceive. A sight so novel and pleasing could not fail of fixing the admiration and attention of every one present.

In the front, the Indians went with their birch canoes, containing twenty or thirty in each; then the advanced corps in a regular line, with the gunboats; then followed the *Royal George* and *Inflexible*, towing large booms, which are to be thrown across two points of land, with the other brigs and sloops following; after them the first brigade in a regular line; then the Generals Burgoyne, Phillips and Riedesel in their pinnaces; next to them were the second brigade, followed by the German brigades; and the rear was brought up with the sutlers and followers of the army.

Upon the appearance of so formidable a fleet, you may imagine they were not a little dismayed at Ticonderoga, for they were not apprized of our advance, as we every day could see their watch-boats. We had, it is certain, a very strong naval force, but yet it might have been greatly in the power of the Americans to have prevented our passing the lake so rapidly as we have done, especially as there are certain parts of it where a few armed vessels might have stopped us for some time: but it is an invariable maxim with the Americans, of which there are numberless instances in the last campaign, never to face an enemy but with very superior advantages and the most evident signs and prospects of success.

—ANBUREY, *Travels through the Interior Parts of America*, I, 268-271.

3. THE AMERICANS GIVE UP TICONDEROGA

Journal of Lieutenant William Digby of the Shropshire Regiment.

[*July*] 4th. Before day light, we shifted our camp farther back a small way from the range of their shot, until our 12-pounders could come up to play on them in return; by their not throwing shells, we supposed they had none, which from our camp being on a rocky eminence would have raked us much; as to their balls we did not much mind them being at too great a distance to suffer from any point blank shot from their cannon.

About noon we took possession of Sugar Loaf Hill [Fort Defiance] on which a battery was immediately ordered to be raised. It was a post of great consequence, as it commanded a great part of the works of Ticonderoga, all their vessels, and likewise afforded us the means of cutting off their communication with Fort Independent, a place also of great strength and the works very extensive. But here the commanding officer was reckoned guilty of a great oversight in lighting fires on that post, tho I am informed it was done by the Indians, the smoak of which was soon perceived by the enemy in the fort; as he should have remained undiscovered till night, when he was to have got two 12-pounders up, tho their getting there was almost a perpendicular ascent, and drawn up by most of the cattle belonging to the Army.

They no sooner perceived us in possession of a post which they thought quite impossible to bring cannon up to, than all their pretended boastings of holding out to the last, and choosing rather to die in their works than give them up, failed them, and on the night of the 5th they set fire to several parts of the garrison, kept a constant fire of great guns the whole night, and under the protection of that fire and clouds of smoke they evacuated the garrison, leaving all their cannon, amunition and a great quantity of stores. They embarked what baggage they could during the night in their battows, and sent them up to Skeensborough under the protection of five schooners, which Captain Carter of the Artillery with our gun boats followed and destroyed with all their baggage and provisions.

As I happened to be one of the lieutenants of the Grenadiers piquet that night, when we perceived the great fires in the fort, the general was immediately made acquainted with it and our suspicion of their abandoning the place, who with many other good officers imagined it was all a feint in them to induce us to make an attack, and seemingly with a great reason of probability, tho to me, who could be but a very poor judge, it seemed quite the contrary, as I never before saw such great fires.

About 12 o'clock we were very near committing a most dreadful mistake. At that hour of the night, as I was going my rounds to observe if all the sentrys were alert on their different posts, one sentry challenged a party of men passing under his post, which was situated on the summit of a ravine or gully, and also heard carriages dragging in the same place, who answered friends, but on his demanding the countersign, they did not give it, and by their hesitating appeared at a loss; when the fellow would have instantly fired upon them according to his orders, had not I come up at the time, on which I caused him to challenge them again; they not answering, I called to the piquet to turn out and stand to their arms, still lothe to fire. Just at the time, Captain Walker came up in great haste and told me it was a party of his Artillery with two 12-pounders going to take post on Sugar Loaf Hill, and his orders to them was to cause it to be kept as secret as possible, which by their too strictly attending to in not answering our challenge, which could never be the intention of their orders, was near involving us all in a scene of the greatest confusion, which must have arose from our piquet firing on them. I own I was somewhat alarmed, still thinking the great fires in their lines a feint and their coming to attack us with more security, imagineing we gave in to that feint.

[*July*] *6th.* At the first dawn of light, 3 deserters came in and informed that the enemy were retreating the other side of Mount Independent. The general was, without loss of time, made acquainted with it and the picquets of the army were ordered to march and take possession of the garrison and hoist the King's colors, which was immediately done, and the Grenadiers and Light Infantry were moved under the command [of] Brigadier General Frazier, if possible to come up with them with the greatest expedition. From the fort we were obliged to cross over a boom of boats between that place and Mount Independent, which they, in their hurry, attempted to burn without effect, as the water quenched it, though in some places we could go but one abreast, and had they placed one gun so as the grape shot [could] take the range of the bridge—and which surprised us they did not, as two men could have fired it, and then made off—they would, in all probability, have destroyed all or most of us on the boom. We continued the pursuit the whole day without any sort of provisions, and, indeed, I may say, we had very little or none, excepting one cow we happened to kill in the woods, which, without bread, was next to nothing among so many for two days after; a few hours rest at night in the woods was absolutely necessary.

—BAXTER, *British Invasion from the North*, pp. 204-209.

4. THE AMERICAN RETREAT TO FORT EDWARD

Journal of Dr. James Thacher, a doctor serving with the Continental Army.

[*July*] *14th.*—By reason of an extraordinary and unexpected event, the course of my Journal has been interrupted for several days. At about 12 o'clock, in the night of the 5th instant, I was urgently called from sleep, and informed that our army was in motion, and was instantly to abandon Ticonderoga and Mount Independence. I could scarcely believe that my informant was in earnest, but the confusion and bustle soon convinced me that it was really true, and that the short time allowed demanded my utmost industry. It was enjoined on me immediately to collect the sick and wounded, and as much of the hospital stores as possible, and assist in embarking them on board the batteaux and boats at the shore.

Having with all possible despatch completed our embarkation, at 3 o'clock in the morning of the 6th, we commenced our voyage up the South bay to Skeenesborough, about 30 miles. Our fleet consisted of five armed gallies and two hundred batteaux and boats deeply laden with cannon, tents, provisions, invalids and women. We were accompanied by a guard of six hundred men, commanded by Colonel Long, of New Hampshire. The night was moon light and pleasant, the sun burst forth in the morning with uncommon lustre, the day was fine, the water's surface serene and unruffled. The shore on each side exhibited a variegated view of huge rocks, caverns and clifts, and the whole was bounded by a thick, impenetrable wilderness. My pen would fail in the attempt to describe a scene so enchantingly sublime. The occasion was peculiarly interesting, and we could but look back with regret, and forward with apprehension. We availed ourselves, however, of the means of enlivening our spirits. The drum and fife afforded us a favorite music; among the hospital stores we found many dozens of choice wine, and we cheered our hearts with the nectareous contents.

At 3 o'clock in the afternoon, we reached our destined port at Skeenesborough, being the head of navigation for our gallies. Here we were unsuspicious of danger, but behold! Burgoyne himself was at our heels. In less than two hours we were struck with surprise and consternation by a discharge of cannon from the enemy's fleet on our gallies and batteaux lying at the wharf. By uncommon efforts and industry they had broken through the bridge, boom and chain, which cost our people such immense labor, and had almost overtaken us on the lake, and horridly disastrous indeed would have been our fate. It was not long before it was perceived that a number of their troops and savages had landed and were rapidly advancing towards our little party.

The officers of our guard now attempted to rally the men and form them in battle array; but this was found impossible, every effort proved unavailing, and in the utmost panic they were seen to fly in every direction for personal safety. In this desperate condition, I perceived our officers scampering for their baggage; I ran to the batteau, seized my chest, carried it a short distance, took from it a few articles, and instantly followed in the train of our retreating party. We took the route to Fort Ann through a narrow defile in the woods, and were so closely pressed by the pursuing enemy that we frequently heard calls from the rear to "march on, the Indians are at our heels." Having marched all night, we reached Fort Ann at 5 o'clock in the morning, where we found provisions for our refreshment. A small rivulet called Wood Creek is navigable from Skeenesborough to Fort Ann, by which means some of our invalids and baggage made their escape; but all our cannon [and] provisions and the bulk of our baggage, with several invalids, fell into the enemy's hands.

On the 7th instant, we received a small reenforcement from Fort Edward by order of Major General Schuyler, and on discovering that a detachment of the enemy under command of Colonel Hill had arrived in our vicinity, a party from our fort was ordered to attack them in their covert in the woods. The two parties were soon engaged in a smart skirmish, which continued for several hours and resulted greatly to our honor and advantage; the enemy, being almost surrounded, were on the point of surrendering, when our ammunition being expended, and a party of Indians arriving and setting up the war whoop, this being followed by three cheers from their friends the English, the Americans were induced to give way and retreat. One surgeon, with a wounded captain and twelve or fifteen privates, were taken and brought into our fort. The surgeon informed me that he was in possession of books, etc., taken from my chest at Skeensborough, and, singular to relate, some of the British prisoners obtained in the same manner, and had in their pockets, a number of *private letters* which I had received from a friend in Massachusetts, and which were now returned to me.

Fort Ann being a small picket fort of no importance, orders were given to set it on fire, and on the 8th we departed for Fort Edward, situated about 30 miles southward on the banks of the Hudson River.

General St. Clair, with his main army from Ticonderoga, took a circuitous route through the woods to Hubbardtown and Castleton, in the New Hampshire Grants, and being pursued by a strong detachment from Burgoyne's army, his rear guard, commanded by Colonel Francis, was overtaken, and on the 7th instant a very close and severe engagement took place, in which bloody conflict the brave Colonel Francis fell with other valuable officers, while fighting with distinguished gallantry. The Americans made an honorable defence, and finally a secure retreat. We lost in this action about three hundred, in killed, wounded and prisoners. The enemy, according to estimation, about two hundred. On the 12th, General St. Clair arrived here [Fort Edward] with the remains of his army, greatly distressed and worn down by fatigue.

General Schuyler is commander at this post; he has a small army of continentals and militia, and is making every possible exertion, by taking up bridges, throwing obstructions in the roads and passes by fallen trees, etc., to impede the march of Burgoyne's army towards Albany. He has also issued a spirited proclamation to counteract the effects of that from General Burgoyne.

The abandonment of Ticonderoga and Mount Independence has occasioned the greatest surprise and alarm. No event could be more unexpected nor more severely felt throughout our army and country. This disaster has given to our cause a dark and gloomy aspect, but our affairs are not desperate, and our exertions ought to be in proportion to our misfortunes and our exigencies. The conduct of General St. Clair on this occasion has rendered him very unpopular, and subjected him to general censure and reproach; there are some, indeed, who even accuse him of treachery; but time and calm investigation must decide whether he can vindicate himself as a judicious and prudent commander. There is much reason to suppose that neither the strength of Burgoyne's army nor the weakness of our garrison were properly considered or generally understood. It must be universally conceded that when the enemy had effected their great object by hoisting cannon from tree to tree till they reached the summit of Sugar-Loaf Hill, the situation of our garrison had become perilous in the extreme. General Schuyler is not altogether free from public reprehension, alleging that he ought in duty to have been present at Ticonderoga during the critical period.

It is predicted by some of our well informed and respectable characters that this event, apparently so calamitous, will ultimately prove advantageous, by drawing the British army into the heart of our country, and thereby place them more immediately within our power.

—THACHER, *Military Journal*, pp. 83-86.

IV. BURGOYNE'S FIRST SERIOUS BLUNDER

In his eagerness to catch up with the American forces at Fort Edward, Burgoyne plowed his way to Skenesborough, where he was induced by the Tory land proprietor, Philip Skene, to continue south on an overland route rather than return to Ticonderoga and approach Fort Edward by way of Lake George. His stores and heavy cannon were sent, however, by water. Perhaps Skene's advice was not unmotivated by his interest in having the British army build a road which would link his undeveloped property with the settlement to the south.

This was Burgoyne's first serious blunder. His march of 23 miles from Skenesborough to Ford Edward lay through a trackless wilderness, thick woods interspersed with streams and boggy marshland. Schuyler's woodmen contributed to stalling the British war machine by felling trees along the route. Burgoyne did not reach Fort Edward until July 30. It took him 24 days to travel 23 miles.

THE BRITISH FIND THAT NOT ALL THE REBELS ARE POLTROONS

Journal of Lieutenant James M. Hadden of the Royal Artillery.

July 12th. Brig. Gen'l Frazer and the corps detached at Castleton, etc., joined the army at Skeensborough. One German and one British regiment were left in garrison at Mount Independence and Tyconderoga. Governor Skeene was appointed to act as Commissioner and to administer the oaths of allegiance, and grant certificates to such inhabitants as sue properly for the same, and regulate all other matters relative to the supplies and assistances required from the country or voluntarily brought in. It was determined by Gen'l Burgoyne that all the provisions and stores, artillery, etc. (except one Light Brigade) should be passed over Lake George to the right, under the escort of one regiment and the corps of Royal Artillery; as the enemy had vessels on this lake, a sufficient number of the gun boats were kept armed and clear for action; the rest were loaded with stores and provisions. The army was to pass by Fort Anne carrying with them through Wood Creek as many batteaux as would be necessary to transport their provisions down the Hudsons River.

After the action at or near Fort Anne, the 9th Regiment were withdrawn and, joining the army at Skeensborough, no other detachment was sent out, and the enemy, though not victorious, were the real gainers by this affair; the advantage they made of it was to fell large trees across Wood Creek and the road leading by the side of it to Fort Anne, the clearing of which cost the army much labour and time, and gave the enemy spirrits and leisure to wait those reinforcements which enabled them to retire deliberately, always keeping near enough to prevent our sending out small detachments: a large corps advanced to Fort Anne (in place of the 9th Regiment) would have encreased the enemies fears and prevented these delays. The proper corps for this purpose had taken another route (General Frazer's), and whatever footing the general might wish to put the action near Huberton upon, that corps certainly discovered that neither they were invincible nor the Rebels all poltroons. On the contrary many of them acknowledged the enemy behaved well, and looked upon General Reidesel's fortunate arrival as a matter absolutely necessary.

This *éclaircissement* should have taken place when something more than honor was to be gained. We were now at Skeensborough, having lost near 200 men, and this post was gained with the loss of one officer and one volunteer, all our other posts being relinquished, and the communications in front to be repaired before we could proceed.

—HADDEN, *Journal*, pp. 93-95.

V. THE JENNY McCREA ATROCITY

A few days before Burgoyne's army took over abandoned Fort Edward an atrocity was committed that did more to arouse the whole North Country against Burgoyne than any other incident of the campaign. A young woman named Jane McCrea was captured by some of Burgoyne's Indians, shot, scalped, and the clothing stripped from her body. Her murderer, reputed to be an Indian appropriately named Wyandot Panther, took the scalp to the British camp. Fearful that his Indians would desert were he to execute the culprit as he originally had intended, Burgoyne pardoned Wyandot. The fact that there were many other atrocities, involving whole families of set-

tlers, that Jane McCrea was a Tory sympathizer, and that she was affianced
to an officer of Burgoyne's Tory contingent, did not in the least abate the
indignation of the Patriots.

Upon relieving Schuyler of command, Gates filed a formal protest with
Burgoyne. This was one of Gates's best efforts in the whole campaign and
he was pleased with his handiwork. I "gave him [Burgoyne] a Tickler upon
Scalping," he wrote Governor Trumbull on September 4. Burgoyne's dis-
avowals were ineffectual. Washington saw to it that the story of Jenny Mc-
Crea was kept alive. He wrote urging the Massachusetts and Connecticut
militia to "repel an enemy from your borders, who, not content with hiring
mercenaries to lay waste your country, have now brought savages, with the
avowed and expressed intention of adding murder to desolation."

1. A BRITISH OFFICER LAMENTS THE MURDER OF JENNY MCCREA

Journal of Lieutenant William Digby of the Shropshire Regiment.

July 24th. We marched from Skeensborough, and tho but 15 miles to
Fort Anne, were two days going it, as the enemy had felled large trees over
the river, which there turned so narrow as not to allow more than one battow
abreast, from whence we were obliged to cut a road through the wood, which
was attended with great fatigue and labour, for our wagons and artillery.
Our heavy cannon went over Lake George, as it was impossible to bring them
[over] the road we made, and were to join us near Fort Edward, in case the
enemy were to stand us at that place, it being a good road for cannon and
about 16 miles. Fort Anne is a place of no great strength, having only a block
house, which though strong against small arms is not proof against cannon.

We saw many of their dead unburied, since the action of the 8th, which
caused a violent stench. One officer of the 9th regiment, Lieut Westrop, was
then unburied, and from the smell we could only cover him with leaves. At
that action, the 9th took their colours, which were intended as a present to
their Colonel Lord Ligonier. They were very handsome, a flag of the United
States, 13 stripes alternate red and white, [with thirteen stars] in a blue field
representing a new constellation.

In the evening, our Indians brought in two scalps, one of them an officer's
which they danced about in their usual manner. Indeed, the cruelties committed by them were too shocking to relate, particularly the melancholy
catastrophe of the unfortunate Miss McCrea, which affected the general and
the whole army with the sincerest regret and concern for her untimely fate.
This young lady was about 18, had a pleasing person, her family were loyal
to the King, and she engaged to be married to a provincial officer in our army
before the war broke out. Our Indians (I may well now call them Savages)
were detached on scouting parties, both in our front and on our flanks, and
came to the house where she resided; but the scene is too tragic for my pen.
She fell a sacrifice to the savage passions of these blood thirsty monsters, for
the particulars of which I shall refer the reader to General Burgoyne's letter,
dated 3rd September, to General Gates. . . .

I make no doubt but the censorious world, who seldom judge but by outward appearances, will be apt to censure Gen Burgoyne for the cruelties

committed by his Indians, and imagine he countenanced them in so acting. On the contrary, I am pretty certain it was always against his desire to give any assistance to the savages.

—Baxter, *British Invasion from the North*, pp. 233-237.

2. Gates and Burgoyne Debate the Responsibility for Her Fate

A. general horatio gates to burgoyne

U. S. Headquarters, September 2, 1777

Last Night I had the honor to receive Your Excellencys letter of the 1st instant. I am astonished you should mention inhumanity, or threaten retaliation; nothing happened in the action at Bennington but what is common when works are carried by assault.

That the savages of America should in their warfare mangle and scalp the unhappy prisoners who fall into their hands, is neither new nor extraordinary; but that the famous Lieutenant General Burgoyne, in whom the fine Gentleman is united with the Soldier and the Scholar, should hire the savages of America to scalp Europeans and the descendants of Europeans, nay more, that he should pay a price for each scalp so barbarously taken, is more than will be believed in Europe, untill authenticated facts shall, in every Gazette, convince mankind of the truth of the horrid fate.

Miss McCrea, a young lady lovely to the sight, of virtuous character and amiable disposition, engaged to be married to an officer in your Army, was with other women and children taken out of a house near Fort-Edward, carried into the woods, and there scalped and mangled in a most shocking manner. Two parents, with their six children, were all treated with the same inhumanity, while quietly residing in their once happy and peaceful dwelling. The miserable fate of Miss McCrea was particularly aggravated by her being dressed to receive her promised husband, but met her murderer employed by you. Upwards of one hundred men, women and children have perished by the hands of the ruffians to whom it is asserted you have paid the price of blood. [The next sentence, crossed out but still clearly legible, reads: "The law of retaliation is a just law, and you must expect to feel its force."]

Inclosed are letters from your wounded officers, prisoners in my hands. By them you will be informed of the generosity of their conquerors. Such money, cloathing, attendants and others necessaries which your Excy pleases to send to the prisoners, shall be faithfully delivered. The late Colonel Baulm's servant is at Benington and would have come to Your Excellency's camp, but when I offered him a flagg, he was affraid to run the risque of being scalped, and declined going. When I know what surgeon and attendants Your Excellency is desirous of sending to Benington, I shall despatch an officer to your lines to conduct them to my camp.

—Gates Papers, N.Y. Hist. Soc., Box XIXb.

B. general burgoyne to gates

September 6, 1777

I received your letter of the 2: instant and in consequence of your compliance with my proposal of sending a surgeon to visit the wounded officers in your hands, and some servants to carry money and necessaries to their masters and to remain with them, I have now to desire the favor of you to dispatch the officer you design with a drum. . . .

It has happened that all my transactions with the Indian Nations, last year and this, have been open; clearly heard; distinctly understood; accurately minuted by very numerous and, in many part, very unprejudiced audiences. So diametrically opposite to truth is your assertion that I have paid a price for scalps that one of the first regulations established by me at the great Council in May, and repeated and enforced and invariably adhered to since, was that the Indians should receive compensation for prisoners because it would prevent cruelty, and that not only such compensation should be withheld, but a strict Account demanded, for scalps—those pledges of conquest, for such you well know they will ever esteem them—were solemnly and peremptorily prohibited to be taken from the wounded and even the dying, and the persons of aged men, women, children and prisoners were pronounced sacred even in assaults.

In regard to Miss McCrea, her fate wanted not of the tragic display you have labored to give it to make it as sincerely abhorred and lamented by me as it can be by the tenderest of her friends. The fact was no premeditated barbarity. On the contrary two chiefs who had brought her off for the purposes of security, not of violence to her person, disputed which should be her guard; and in a fit of savage passion in the one from whose hands she was snatched, the unhappy woman became the victim. Upon the first intelligence of this event I obliged the Indians to deliver the murderer into my hands; and tho to have punished him by our laws or principles of justice would have been perhaps unprecedented, he certainly should have suffered an ignominious death had I not been convinced by circumstances and observation, beyond the possibility of a doubt, that a pardon, under the forms which I prescribed and they accepted, would be more efficacious than an execution to prevent similar mischiefs.

The above instance excepted, your intelligence respecting cruelties of the Indians is false.

—Gates Papers, Box VII, No. 223, N.Y. Hist. Soc.

VI. THE ROUT OF ST. LEGER

While Burgoyne's ponderous war machine was lumbering southward through the forests, a mixed force of some 1,800 men, mostly Tories and Indians, under Colonel Barry St. Leger pushed eastward from Fort Oswego on Lake Ontario to rendezvous with Burgoyne in Albany. On the third of August St. Leger reached Fort Stanwix (renamed Fort Schuyler) on the Mohawk River, the present site of Rome, New York. The fall of that fortress would have opened the gates to Albany some 110 miles away and trapped the American army in between the two British expeditions.

Here St. Leger encountered his first serious resistance. He had not reckoned on the fighting spirit of Colonel Peter Gansevoort and the 750 men who manned the stronghold, nor on the caution and restlessness of his Indian allies. On August 6 General Nicholas Herkimer, with some 800 militiamen march-

ing to the fort's relief, was caught in an ambush at Oriskany by a force of Indians and Tories led by the Mohawk chief Joseph Brant. Suffering at the outset of the battle a wound that was to prove fatal, Herkimer drew his men together on high ground and fought back fiercely. Total disaster was averted when the Indians, alarmed by firing from Fort Schuyler where the garrison had made a sortie against the British camp, broke off the engagement. The Indians, as the account of Lieutenant Bird reveals, had already proved restless and unreliable. Herkimer managed to retreat eastward with less than half his original strength.

Schuyler now dispatched Benedict Arnold from Stillwater with a force of 1,000 volunteers to relieve the desperately besieged garrison. Even though his men never caught up with the British expedition, Arnold was able to raise the siege and rout St. Leger. It so happened that an eccentric, half-mad inhabitant of the Mohawk Valley named Hon Yost Schuyler, whose father was a cousin of General Schuyler and whose mother was Herkimer's sister, was captured by Arnold's men while attempting a recruiting rally behind American lines. Sentenced to death as a spy, Hon Yost was let off on condition that he use his special powers among the red men (his notorious ravings had given him the status of a prophet) to make St. Leger's Indians desert. Hon Yost's deception came in the nick of time, for the British were close enough to the fort to begin digging a tunnel to place mines beneath the wall. Our old friend James Thacher tells the incredible story.

1. A "Continental Flag" Defiantly Floats over Fort Schuyler

Journal of William Colbraith, a soldier in Colonel Gansevoort's regiment at Fort Schuyler.

Aug. 1st.—Three Oneida Indians came express from their castle informing us that they had seen three strange Indians, who told them that there were 100 more at the Royal Block House, and that they were to march for this place. Supposing them to be a party sent to cut off communications, the Colonel detached 100 men under command of Captain Benschoten and three subalterns to meet the bateaux that were hourly expected, in order to reinforce the guard sent with them from Fort Dayton.

Aug. 2d.—Four bateaux arrived, being those the party went to meet, having a guard of 100 men of Colonel Weston's regiment from Fort Dayton, under the command of Lieut. Col. Mellon of that regiment. The lading being brought safe into the fort, guard marched in, when our sentinels on the southwest bastion discovered the enemy's fires in the woods near Fort Newport, upon which the troops ran to their respective alarm posts; at this time we discovered some men running from the landing toward the garrison. On their coming they informed us that the bateaux men who had staid behind when the guard marched into the fort had been fired on by the enemy at the landing, that two of them were wounded, the master of the bateaux taken prisoner, and one man missing.

Aug. 3d.—Early this morning a Continental flag, made by the officers of Colonel Gansevoort's regiment, was hoisted and a cannon leveled at the enemy's camp was fired on the occasion. A small party was sent to the landing to see if the enemy had destroyed any of our bateaux last night. This party found the bateaux man that was missing, wounded through the brain, stabbed in the right breast and scalped. He was alive when found and brought to the garrison, but died shortly after. The bateaux lay at the landing no ways damaged. About 3 o'clock this afternoon the enemy showed themselves to the garrison on all sides, carried off some hay from a field near the garrison, at which a flag brought by Captain Tice came into the fort with a proffer of protection if the garrison would surrender, which was rejected with disdain.

Aug. 4th.—A continual firing of small arms was this day kept up by the enemy's Indians, who advanced within gunshot of the fort, in small parties under cover of bushes, weeds and potatoes in the garden. Colonel Mellon and his party of 100 men, who came from Fort Dayton as a guard to the bateaux, was to have returned this day, but we were now besieged and all communication cut off for the present. The firing ended with the close of the day, we having one man killed and six wounded. This night we sent out a party and brought 27 stacks of hay into the trench and set a barn and house on fire belonging to Mr. Roof.

Aug. 5th.—A continual firing was kept up by the savages. One of our men was shot dead on the northeast bastion. The enemy set fire to the new barracks standing about 100 yards from this fort, between four and five o'clock this afternoon.

Aug. 6th.—This morning the Indians were seen going off from around the garrison towards the landing; as they withdrew we had not much firing. Being uneasy lest the Tories should report that the enemy had taken the fort, Lieut. Diefendorf was ordered to get ready to set off for Albany this evening to inform General Schuyler of our situation, but between nine and ten this morning three militia men arrived here with a letter from General Harkeman [Herkimer] wherein he writes that he had arrived at Orisco [Oriskany] with 1,000 militia, in order to relieve the garrison and open communication, which was then entirely blocked up, and that if the colonel should hear a firing of small arms, desired he would send a party from the garrison to reinforce him. General Harkeman desired that the colonel would fire three cannon, if the three men got safe into the fort with his letter, which was done and followed by three cheers by the whole garrison.

According to General Harkeman's request the colonel detached two hundred men and one field piece under command of Lieut. Col. Willett with orders to proceed down the road to meet the General's party; having marched half a mile, they came upon an encampment of the enemy which they totally routed, and plundered them of as much baggage as the soldiers could carry. Their loss is supposed to be between fifteen and twenty killed. The number of wounded, who got off, is unknown. They took four prisoners, three of whom were wounded, and Mr. Singleton of Montreal, who says he is a lieutenant, without the loss of one man killed or wounded.

Our party returned immediately and brought in a number of blankets, brass kettles, powder and ball, a variety of clothes and Indian trinkets and hard cash, together with four scalps the Indians had lately taken, being entirely fresh and left in their camp. *Two of the scalps taken are supposed to be those of the girls, being neatly dressed and the hair plaited.* A bundle of letters was found in the enemy's camp, which had been sent by one Luke Cassidy for this garrison, who it is supposed is either killed or taken; the letters were not broke open. Four colours were also taken and immediately hoisted on our flagstaff under the Continental flag, as trophies of victory.

By our prisoners we learn that the enemy are 1210 strong, 250 British regulars, that they are all arrived and have with them two six-pounders, two three-pounders and four royals. We also learn that they were attacked by our militia on this side of Orisco, that they drove the militia back, killed some and took several prisoners, but the enemy had many killed.

—REID, *Story of Old Fort Johnson*, pp. 89-92.

2. HERKIMER'S RELIEF FORCE IS ROUTED AT ORISKANY

Lieutenant Colonel Barry St. Leger to General Burgoyne.

Oswego, August 27, 1777

On the 5th [of August], in the evening, intelligence arrived by my discovering parties on the Mohawk River, that a reinforcement of eight hundred militia, conducted by General Herkimer, were on their march to relieve the garrison, and were actually at that instant at Oriṡka, an Indian settlement twelve miles from the fort. The garrison being apprised of their march by four men, who were seen to enter the fort in the morning through what was thought an impenetrable swamp, I did not think it prudent to wait for them and thereby subject myself to be attacked by a sally from the garrison in the rear, while the reinforcement employed me in front. I therefore determined to attack them on the march, either openly or covertly, as circumstances should offer. At this time I had not two hundred and fifty of the King's troops in camp, the various and extensive operations I was under an absolute necessity of entering into having employed the rest; and therefore could not send above eighty white men, rangers and troops included, with the whole corps of Indians.

Sir John Johnson put himself at the head of this party, and began his march that evening at five o'clock, and met the rebel corps at the same hour next morning. The impetuosity of the Indians is not to be described; on the sight of the enemy (forgetting the judicious disposition formed by Sir John, and agreed to by themselves, which was to suffer the attack to begin with the troops in front, while they should be on both flanks and rear), they rushed in, hatchet in hand, and thereby gave the enemy's rear an opportunity to escape.

In relation to the victory, it was equally complete as if the whole had fallen; nay, more so, as the two hundred who escaped only served to spread the panic wider; but it was not so with the Indians; their loss was great (I must be understood Indian computation, being only about thirty killed, and the like number wounded, and in that number some of their favorite chiefs and confidential warriors were slain). On the enemy's side, almost all their principal leaders were slain. General Herkimer has since died of his wounds.

It is proper to mention that the four men detached with intelligence of the march of the reinforcement set out the evening before the action, and consequently the enemy could have no account of the defeat, and were in possession only of the time appointed for their arrival; at which, as I suspected, they made a sally with two hundred and fifty men towards Lieutenant Bird's post, to facilitate the entrance of the relieving corps, or bring on a general engagement, with every advantage they could wish.

Captain Hoyes was immediately detached to cut in upon their rear, while they engaged the lieutenant. Immediately upon the departure of Captain Hoyes, having learned that Lieutenant Bird, misled by the information of a cowardly Indian that Sir John was pressed, had quitted his post to march to his assistance, I marched the detachment of the King's Regiment in support of Captain Hoyes by a road in sight of the garrison, which, with executive fire from his party, immediately drove the enemy into the fort, without any farther advantage than frightening some squaws and pilfering the packs of the warriors which they left behind them.

After this affair was over, orders were immediately given to compleat a two-gun battery and mortar beds, with three strong redoubts in their rear, to enable me, in case of another attempt to relieve the garrison by their regimented troops, to march out a larger body of the King's troops.

—BURGOYNE, A *State of the Expedition from Canada,* pp. xliv-xlv.

3. THE COUNTERATTACK TO RELIEVE HERKIMER

Narrative of Colonel Marinus Willett, Gansevoort's second in command.

German Flatts, August 11, 1777

About eleven o'clock [Wednesday, August 6th] three men got into the fort [Schuyler], who brought a letter from General Harkaman of the Tryon County militia, advising us that he was at Eriska (8 miles off) with part of his militia, and proposed to force his way to the fort for our relief. In order to render him what service we could in his march, it was agreed that I should make a sally from the fort with 250 men, consisting of one half Gansevoort's, one half Massachusetts ditto, and one field piece (an iron three-pounder).

. . . Nothing could be more fortunate than this enterprise. We totally routed two of the enemy's encampments, destroyed all the provisions that were in them, brought off upwards of 50 brass kettles and more than 100 blankets (two articles which were much needed), with a quantity of muskets, tomahawks, spears, ammunition, clothing, deerskins, a variety of Indian affairs and 5 colours. . . . The Indians took chiefly to the woods, the rest of the troops then at their posts to the river. . . . I was happy in preventing the men from scalping even the Indians, being desirous, if possible, to teach even the savages humanity; but the men were much better employed, and kept in excellent order. . . .

From these prisoners [some Oneida Indians] we received the first accounts of General Harkaman's militia being ambushed on their march, and of a severe battle they had with them about two hours before, which gave reason to think they had for the present given up their design of marching to the fort.

—WILLETT, *Narrative of Col. Marinus Willett,* pp. 131-133.

4. "WE WILL DEFEND THE FORT TO THE LAST EXTREMITY"

Journal of William Colbraith.

Aug. 8th.—The enemy threw some shells at us to-day, but did no damage, and in order to return the compliment, they were saluted with a few balls from our cannon. About 5 o'clock this evening Colonel Butler, with a British captain and a doctor from the enemy, came to the garrison with a flag, whose message from Gen. St. Leger was that the Indians, having lost some of their chiefs in a skirmish with our party that sallied out on the 6th inst., were determined to go down the Mohawk River and destroy the women and children; also that they would kill every man in the garrison when they got in; that Gen. St. Leger had held a council with them for two days in order to prevent them, but all to no purpose, unless we would surrender. The general therefore, as an act of humanity, and to prevent the effusion of blood, begged we would deliver up the fort, and promised if we did, not a hair of our heads should be hurt. A letter also came by them (as they say) from Mr. Fry and Colonel Bellinger, whom they took in the fray with the militia, begging us to surrender, telling us our communication was cut off, that the enemy had a large parcel of fine troops and an excellent park of artillery, and further, that they expected General Burgoyne was in Albany, and could see no hopes of our having any succor, as the militia had many killed and taken.

The answer to the general's tender and compassioned (?) letter was deferred until to-morrow morning at 9 o'clock, and a cessation of arms agreed to by both parties till then. Late this evening a party was sent to get water for the garrison, with a guard. One of the guards deserted from us, but left his firelock behind. One of our sentinels fired at him but missed him. Our guard heard the enemy's sentinels challenge him twice and fire on him. Colonel Willett and Lieutenant Stockwell went out of the garrison at one o'clock in the morning on a secret expedition.

Aug. 9th.—Agreeable to the proposals of yesterday between Colonel Gansevoort and Brigadier General St. Leger, a flag was sent out to him requesting him to send his demand in writing and the Colonel would send him an answer, which request he agreed to. The demands in writing was the same in substance with that verbally delivered yesterday by Colonel Butler, to which the Colonel returned for answer: That he was determined to defend the fort in favor of the United States to the last extremity.*

Upon receiving the answer hostilities again commenced by a number of shot and small arms on their side which were not suffered with impunity on ours. This day the Colonel ordered all the provisions to be brought upon the parade for fear of shells setting fire to the barracks and destroying it; also all the public papers and money in the hands of Mr. Hansen and the papers in the hands of Mr. Van Veghten belonging to the paymaster to be lodged in the bombproof in the S. W. bastion. The enemy began to bombard us at half past ten this evening and continued till daylight; their shells were very well

---

* Gansevoort's exact words: "I have only to say that it is my determined resolution, with the forces under my command, to defend this fort, at every hazard, to the last extremity, in behalf of the United American States, who have placed me here to defend it against all their enemies."—W. W. Campbell. *Annals of Tryon County*, p. 80.

directed. They killed one man and wounded another, both of our regiment. None killed or wounded through the day.

—REID, *Story of Old Fort Johnson*, pp. 92-94.

5. THE INDIANS LEAVE THEIR ALLY IN THE LURCH

Journal of James Thacher, doctor with the Continental Army.

[*August, 1777*]. An object which cannot be accomplished by force is often obtained by means of stratagem. Lieutenant Colonel John Brooks, an intelligent officer from Massachusetts, being in advance [of Arnold's party marching to relieve Fort Schuyler] with a small detachment, fortunately found one Major Butler, a noted officer among the Indians, endeavoring to influence the inhabitants in their favor, and he was immediately secured. A man also by the name of Cuyler [Hon Yost Schuyler], who was proprietor of a handsome estate in the vicinity, was taken up as a spy.

Colonel Brooks proposed that he should be employed as a deceptive messenger to spread the alarm and induce the enemy to retreat. General Arnold soon after arrived and approved the scheme of Colonel Brooks; it was accordingly agreed that Cuyler should be liberated and his estate secured to him on the condition that he would return to the enemy and make such exaggerated report of General Arnold's force as to alarm and put them to flight. Several friendly Indians being present, one of their head men advised that Cuyler's coat should be shot through in two or three places to add credibility to his story.

Matters being thus adjusted, the impostor proceeded directly to the Indian camp, where he was well known, and informed their warriors that Major Butler was taken, and that himself narrowly escaped, several shots having passed through his coat, and that General Arnold with a vast force was advancing rapidly towards them. In aid of the project, a friendly Indian followed and arrived about an hour after with a confirmation of Cuyler's report.

This stratagem was successful: the Indians instantly determined to quit their ground and make their escape, nor was it in the power of St. Leger and Sir John [Johnson] with all their art of persuasion to prevent it. When St. Leger remonstrated with them, the reply of the chiefs was, "When we marched down, you told us there would be no fighting for us Indians; we might go down and smoke our pipes; but now a number of our warriors have been killed, and you mean to sacrifice us." The consequence was that St. Leger, finding himself deserted by his Indians, to the number of seven or eight hundred, deemed his situation so hazardous that he decamped in the greatest hurry and confusion, leaving his tents with most of his artillery and stores in the field. General Arnold with his detachment was now at liberty to return to the main army at Stillwater; and thus have we clipped the right wing of General Burgoyne.

In the evening, while on their retreat, St. Leger and Sir John got into a warm altercation, criminating each other for the ill success of their expedition. Two Sachems, observing this, resolved to have a laugh at their expense. In their front was a bog of clay and mud; they directed a young warrior to loiter in the rear, and then on a sudden run as if alarmed, calling out, "*They are coming, they are coming.*" On hearing this, the two commanders in a fright took to their heels, rushing into the bog, frequently falling and sticking in the mud, and the men threw away their packs and hurried off. This and other jokes were several times repeated during the night for many miles.

—THACHER, *Military Journal,* pp. 89-91.

VII. THE HESSIAN DISASTER AT BENNINGTON

As Burgoyne's lines of communication lengthened, the obstacles which Schuyler's men had placed in the way of the British advance and the scorched-earth policy which the Yorker had put into effect began to yield rich dividends but before he could enjoy the fruits of his victory, Schuyler was removed from command largely as a result of dissatisfaction with him on the part of New Englanders in Congress and not a little as a result of the intrigues of Horatio Gates, who now replaced him. In a letter to his friend Gouverneur Morris, member of the Council of Safety, Schuyler compared his treatment at the hands of Congress with that of "a young Jewess" before the Spanish Inquisition.

Meantime Burgoyne's supply problem had become alarming. Learning that the Americans had collected horses at the village of Bennington in near-by Vermont, Burgoyne dispatched some 700 men, mostly Hessians and Indians, under the command of Lieutenant Colonel Friedrich Baum, to capture them, particularly to seize horses for the footsore Hessian dragoons. Burgoyne had not reckoned on the appearance of a new American military luminary, General John Stark, nor on the gullibility of his Hessian commander. Fortunately, as events turned out, Stark, who regarded his New Hampshire brigade as an independent force, had flatly refused to march his troops to reinforce Schuyler. Now they were available where they could do the most damage.

The battle, brilliantly described by a Hessian officer, was disastrous to Burgoyne, as virtually Baum's entire force, save for the Indians who fled, were killed or captured. Reinforcements for Baum under Lieutenant Colonel Breymann came up too late. They in turn were attacked by Stark, now reinforced by Seth Warner, leading 400 veteran Massachusetts troops. With the loss of a third of his 650 men, Breymann fell back on Burgoyne.

An aged veteran of the Battle of Bennington described how the provincial New England soldiers must have looked to the smartly dressed Hessian horseless dragoons:

To a man, they wore small-clothes, coming down and fastening just below the knee, and long stockings with cowhide shoes ornamented by large buckles, while not a pair of boots graced the company. The coats and waistcoats were loose and of huge dimensions, with colors as various as the barks of oak, sumach and other trees of our hills and swamps could make them, and their shirts were all made of flax and, like every other part of the dress, were homespun. On their heads was worn a large round-top and broad-brimmed hat. Their arms were as various as their costume. Here an old soldier carried a heavy Queen's Arm, with which he had done service at the conquest of Canada twenty years previous, while by his side walked a stripling boy, with a Spanish fusee not half its weight or calibre, which his grandfather may have taken at the Havana, while not a few had old French pieces that dated back to the reduction of Louisburg. Instead of the cartridge box, a large powder horn was slung under the arm, and occasionally a bayonet might be seen bristling in the ranks. Some of the swords of the officers had been made by our Province blacksmiths, perhaps from some farming utensil; they looked serviceable, but heavy and uncouth. [Frederic Kidder, *History of New Ipswich*, p. 95.]

An odd ensemble, indeed, but to the surprised Hessians the effect was lethal. As an unnamed American correspondent, reported in Almon's Remembrancer, *put it, Saturday August 16 was a "memorable" day in American military annals, and "General Starke will be endeared to us forever." After rain had intervened to prevent any more than skirmishing on the fifteenth, the Yankee leader was reputed to have declared he would beat the invader or "before night Molly Stark would be a widow." The pledge was kept.*

1. "My Crime Consists in Not Being a New England Man"

General Philip Schuyler to Gouverneur Morris.

Albany, September 7, 1777

The day before yesterday I was favored with yours of the 24th August. I thank you for sympathizing with me on my removal from the command in this department at a time when our affairs were at the worst and when no change could happen but what must be for the best. Congress I find faults me for painting in strong colours the situation we were in, and yet I dare say if I had not done it and any capital misfortune had happened they would have asked why they had not been truly informed. But my crime consists in not being a New England man in principle, and unless they alter theirs I hope I never shall be. Gen. Gates is their idol because he is at their direction.

If an enquiry into my conduct had not been ordered I should have resigned the moment Gates relieved me, but as soon as that has taken place I shall certainly quit. Of this I have advised Congress. I believe a certain set will wish that they had not urged for an enquiry. I shall make my defense in such a manner as that the public may see what has been my conduct, and what that of others, and then they may judge for themselves, and I trust they will easily discover that the cause of our misfortunes in this department has originated where they perhaps little expect it did.

When Gen. Gates took the command I informed him that I had advised Congress that I should remain some time in the department to afford him any assistance in my power and intreated he would call upon whomever he thought proper. He has however not done it. He sent for Gen. Ten Broeck from town to a council of war but not for me. After that I could not with propriety give him my opinion of what ground he ought to possess if Burgoyne should retreat. What I intended to have done had I remained in the command and [been] reinforced I fully communicated to him, and shewed the order I had given Generals Lincoln and Arnold. Hitherto he has not, as

I am informed, made any other disposition with the force he has which daily increases. He may certainly immediately oblige General Burgoyne to retire or oblige him to fight with great disadvantage, but Gates is totally ignorant of the country, and altho he may get people that can give him the best information, yet it falls vastly short of being personally well acquainted with the passes and profiles, of which every country has more or less. From this defect I fear every advantage will not be taken that might be. . . .

I am just now informed that Burgoyne has drawn all his troops from Skenesborough and Fort Ann. This with the bridge he has thrown over Hudson's River indicates that he means to attack our army. If Lincoln is within a day's march of Saratoga and is ordered that way, I wish Burgoyne may advance, and Gates too. If the latter takes post at Stillwater Lincoln might be [in] the rear of Burgoyne before he could attack Gates, in which case the British army must be totally ruined. Nor need we apprehend a want of provisions should Burgoyne be so posted as to render it imprudent to attack him, for there are means of sending on the supplies. If they escape the attention of Gates I will point them out.

—Gouverneur Morris Papers, Columbia Univ. Lib.

2. BURGOYNE DISPATCHES HIS HESSIANS TO BENNINGTON

Account of the expedition by a Hessian officer named Glich.

August 16, 1777

That these advantages [resulting from St. Leger's advance], trifling as they were, might not be wholly wasted, it became incumbent on Gen. Burgoyne to advance without delay; whilst the deplorable deficiency in the means of transport, under which he labored, seemed to render all attempts at moving the army fruitless. Though our troops had toiled without intermission during three whole weeks, there was in camp no greater stock of provisions than sufficed for four days consumption; and to move forward with a supply so slender into a desert country appeared to a leader of the old school little better than insanity.

I have called it a desert country, not only with reference to its natural sterility—and heaven knows it was sterile enough—but because of the pains which were taken, and unfortunately with too great success, to sweep its few cultivated spots of all articles likely to benefit the invaders. In doing this the enemy showed no decency either to friend or foe. All the fields of standing corn were laid waste, the cattle were driven away, and every particle of grain, as well as morsel of grass, carefully removed; so that we could depend for subsistence, both for men and horses, only upon the magazines which we might ourselves establish. But our draft animals were so inadequate to the conveyance of stores that no magazine had as yet been formed farther in advance than Fort George; and Fort George was too much in the rear to be of service as a base of operations, after we should have quitted the position which we now occupied.

I have said that the American army retreated as we advanced, cutting up the roads and devastating the face of the country over which they passed. They were now, according to the best accounts which we could receive, at

Saratoga, a hamlet, or rather farm, on the left bank of the Hudson and about half way between Fort Edward and the Mohawk. It seemed advisable to General Burgoyne to threaten them there; for if they wished an action, he had no apprehension as to the result; if they retired, Col. St. Ledger would be in their rear; and should they succeed in escaping both divisions, then was the road to Albany thrown open, and the principal design of the inroad attained. Increased exertions were accordingly used to bring a flotilla from the lakes to the nearest navigable point in the river; and so unremitting were they that before the close of the first week in August a considerable number of boats and barges, laden with such stores as could be forwarded, were launched upon the stream and ready to accompany the army.

Whilst these projects were in contemplation, and the above means adopted for bringing them to an issue, a piece of information was obtained at head-quarters which promised to bring about the happiest results, by relieving us at once from all the embarrassments attendant upon meagre supplies and inadequate means of transport. About twenty miles to the eastward of the Hudson lies the obscure village of Bennington, a cluster of poor cottages situated in a wild country between the forks of the Hosac. Here the enemy had gathered together a considerable depot of cattle, cows, horses and wheel carriages, most of which were drawn across the Connecticut River from the provinces of New England; and as it was understood to be guarded by a party of militia only, an attempt to surprise it seemed by no means unjustifiable. It is true that between Fort Edward and Bennington the means of communication were exceedingly defective. One prodigious forest, bottomed in swamps and morasses, covered the whole face of the country, through which no body of men, unless accustomed to such expeditions, could hope to make their way, at all events with celerity. But the necessities of the army were pressing; the state of the campaign was a critical one; and the risk, though doubtless great, was considered by no means to outweigh the advantages to be derived from success. General Burgoyne determined to incur it; and a few hours sufficed for the final arrangement of his plan and drawing up of his instructions.

There were attached to our little army two hundred German dragoons, men of tried valor and enterprise, but destitute of horses. These the General selected as part of the force to be employed in the surprise of Bennington, not only because he entertained the most perfect confidence in their steadiness, but because he conceived that, in the country which they were about to penetrate, they might be able to pick up a sufficient number of horses for their own use. In addition to these, the Canadian rangers, a detachment of provincials, about one hundred Indians and Capt. Fraser's marksmen, with two pieces of small cannon, were allotted to their service; and the whole, amounting to five hundred men, were placed under the orders of Lieut. Col. Baume. The latter officer received special instructions to proceed with extreme caution. He was particularly enjoined to keep his dragoons together, and feel his way, foot by foot, with his light troops alone; and whilst it was broadly hinted that he might look for recruits among the well-disposed inhabitants, the greatest care was taken to impress him with the conviction that they were not to be implicitly trusted. It would have been well, both for himself and his followers, had these advices been somewhat more carefully remembered. But there was a fatality attending all our measures which soon began to develop itself; and perhaps the fate of the present expedition ought to have been taken as a fair warning of the destiny which awaited the army at large. —GLICH, "Account," *Vt. Hist. Soc. Coll.,* I, 212-214.

3. How a "Little Army" of Farmers Beat Professional Troops

General John Stark to General Horatio Gates.

Bennington, August 22, 1777

. . . I shall now give Your Honour a short and brief account of the action on the 13th inst. I was informed that there was a party of Indians in Cambridge on their march to this place. I sent Lieut. Colonel Greg of my brigade to stop them with 200 men. In the night I was informed by express that there was a large body of the enemy on their march in the rear of the Indians. I rallied all my brigade and what Militia was at this place in order to stop their proceedings. Likewise sent to Manchester to Colonel Warner's regiment that was stationed there; also sent expresses for the Militia to come in with all speed to our assistance, which was punctually obeyed. I then marched in company with Colonels Warner, Williams, Herrick and Brush, with all the men that were present. About 5 miles from this place I met Colonel Greg on his retreat and the enemy in close pursuit after him.

I drew up my little army in order of battle, but when the enemy hove in sight, they halted on a very advantageous hill or piece of ground. I sent out small parties in their front to skirmish with them, which scheme had a good effect. They killed and wounded thirty of the enemy without any loss on our side, but the ground that I was upon did [not] suit for a general action. I marched back about one mile and incamped. Called a counsel, and it was agreed that we should send two detachments in their rear, while the others attacked them in front. But the 15th it rained all day; therefore, had to lay by, could do nothing but skirmish with them.

On the 16th in the morning was joined by Colonel Simons with some Militia from Berkshire County. I pursued my plan, detached Colonel Nichols with 200 men to attack them in the rear. I also sent Colonel Herrick with 300 men in the rear of their right, both to join, and when joined to attack their rear. I likewise sent the Colonels Hubbard and Whitney with 200 men on their right, and sent 100 men in their front, to draw away their attention that way, and about 3 o'clock we got all ready for the attack. Colonel Nichols began the same, which was followed by all the rest. The remainder of my little army I pushed up in the front, and in a few minutes the action began. In general it lasted 2 hours, the hotest I ever saw in my life. It represented one continued clap of thunder. However the enemy was obliged to give way, and leave their field pieces and all their baggage behind them. They were all invironed within two breastworks, with their artillery. But our martial courage proved too hard for them.

I then gave orders to rally again, in order to secure the victory, but in a few minutes was informed that there was a large reinforcement on their march within two miles of us. Lucky for us, that moment Colonel Warner's regiment came up fresh, who marched on and began the attack afresh. I pushed forward as many of the men as I could to their assistance. The battle continued obstinate on both sides till sunset. The enemy was obliged to retreat. We pursued them till dark. But had daylight lasted one hour longer, we should have taken the whole body of them. We recovered 4 pieces of brass cannon, some hundred stands of arms, 8 brass barrells, drums, several Hessian swords, about seven hundred prisoners. 207 dead on the spot. The number of wounded is as yet unknown. That part of the enemy that made their escape marched all night, and we returned to our camp.

Too much honor cannot be given to the brave officers and soldiers for gallant behaviour. They fought through the midst of fire and smoke, mounted two breastworks that was well fortified and supported with cannon. I can't particularize any officer as they all behaved with the greatest spirit and bravery.

Colonel Warner's superior skill in the action was of extraordinary service to me. I would be glad he and his men could be recommended by Congress.

As I promised in my orders that the soldiers should have all the plunder taken in the enemy's camp, would be glad your Honour would send me word what the value of the cannon and the other artillery stores above described may be. Our loss was inconsiderable, about 40 wounded and thirty killed. I lost my horse, bridle and saddle in the action.

–Gates Papers, N.Y. Hist Soc., Box VII, No. 33.

4. A Hessian Officer Tells Why They Lost the Battle

The Hessian Glich resumes his story of Bennington.

[August 16, 1777]. . . . The morning of the sixteenth rose beautifully serene; and it is not to the operation of the elements alone that my expression applies. All was perfectly quiet at the outposts, not an enemy having been seen nor an alarming sound heard for several hours previous to sunrise. So peaceable, indeed, was the aspect which matters bore that our leaders felt warmly disposed to resume the offensive without waiting the arrival of the additional corps for which they had applied; and orders were already issued for the men to eat their breakfasts, preparatory to more active operations. But the arms were scarcely piled and the haversacks unslung when symptoms of a state of affairs different from that which had been anticipated began to show themselves, and our people were recalled to their ranks in all haste, almost as soon as they had quitted them. From more than one quarter scouts came in to report that columns of armed men were approaching—though whether with friendly or hostile intention, neither their appearance nor actions enabled our informants to ascertain.

It has been stated that during the last day's march our little corps was joined by many of the country people, most of whom demanded and obtained arms, as persons friendly to the royal cause. How Colonel Baume became so completely duped as to place reliance on these men, I know not; but having listened with complacency to their previous assurances that in Bennington a large majority of the populace were our friends, he was somehow or other persuaded to believe that the armed bands, of whose approach he was warned, were loyalists on their way to make tender of their services to the leader of the king's troops. Filled with this idea, he dispatched positive orders to the outposts that no molestations should be offered to the advancing columns, but that the pickets retiring before them should join the main body, where every disposition was made to receive either friend or foe. Unfortunately for us, these orders were but too faithfully obeyed. About half past nine o'clock, I, who was not in the secret, beheld, to my utter amazement, our advanced parties withdraw without firing a shot from thickets which might have been maintained for hours against any superiority of numbers; and the same thickets occupied by men whose whole demeanor, as well as their dress and style of equipment, plainly and incontestably pointed them out as Americans.

I cannot pretend to describe the state of excitation and alarm into which our little band was now thrown. With the solitary exception of our leader, there was not a man among us who appeared otherwise than satisfied that those to whom he had listened were traitors, and that unless some prompt and vigorous measures were adopted, their treachery would be crowned with its full reward. . . .

We might have stood about half an hour under arms, watching the proceedings of a column of four or five hundred men, who, after dislodging the pickets, had halted just at the edge of the open country, when a sudden trampling of feet in the forest on our right, followed by the report of several muskets, attracted our attention. A patrol was instantly sent in the direction of the sound, but before the party composing it had proceeded many yards from the lines, a loud shout, followed by a rapid though straggling fire of musketry, warned us to prepare for a meeting the reverse of friendly. Instantly the Indians came pouring in, carrying dismay and confusion in their countenances and gestures. We were surrounded on all sides; columns were advancing everywhere against us, and those whom we had hitherto trusted as friends had only waited till the arrival of their support might justify them in advancing.

There was no falsehood in these reports, though made by men who spoke rather from their fears than their knowledge. The column in our front no sooner heard the shout than they replied cordially and loudly to it; then, firing a volley with deliberate and murderous aim, rushed furiously towards us. Now then, at length, our leader's dreams of security were dispelled. He found himself attacked in front and flanked by thrice his number, who pressed forward with the confidence which our late proceedings were calculated to produce, whilst the very persons in whom he had trusted, and to whom he had given arms, lost no time in turning them against him. These followers no sooner heard their comrades' cry than they deliberately discharged their muskets among Reidesel's dragoons and, dispersing before any steps could be taken to seize them, escaped, excepting one or two, to their friends.

If Col. Baume had permitted himself to be duped into a great error, it is no more than justice to confess that he exerted himself manfully to remedy the evil and avert its consequences. Our little band, which had hitherto remained in column, was instantly ordered to extend, and the troops lining the breast-works replied to the fire of the Americans with extreme celerity and considerable effect. So close and destructive, indeed, was our first volley that the assailants recoiled before it, and would have retreated, in all probability, within the woods; but ere we could take advantage of the confusion produced, fresh attacks developed themselves, and we were warmly engaged on every side and from all quarters. It became evident that each of our detached posts were about to be assailed at the same instant. No one of our dispositions had been concealed from the enemy, who, on the contrary, seemed to be aware of the exact number of men stationed at each point, and they were one and all threatened with a force perfectly adequate to bear down opposition, and yet by no means disproportionately large or such as to render the main body inefficient. All, moreover, was done with the sagacity and coolness of veterans, who perfectly understood the nature of the resistance to be expected and the difficulties to be overcome, and who, having well considered and matured their plans, were resolved to carry them into execution at all hazards and at every expense of life.

It was at this moment, when the heads of columns began to show themselves in rear of our right and left, that the Indians, who had hitherto acted with spirit and something like order, lost all confidence and fled. Alarmed at the prospect of having their retreat cut off, they stole away, after their own fashion, in single files, in spite of the strenuous remonstrances of Baume and of their own officers, leaving us more than ever exposed by the abandonment of that angle of the intrenchments which they had been appointed to maintain. But even this spectacle, distressing as it doubtless was, failed in affecting our people with a feeling at all akin to despair.

The vacancy which the retreat of the savages occasioned was promptly filled up by one of our two field pieces, whilst the other poured destruction among the enemy in front, as often as they showed themselves in the open country or threatened to advance. In this state of things we continued upwards of three quarters of an hour. Tho' repeatedly assailed in front, flank and rear, we maintained ourselves with so much obstinacy as to inspire a hope that the enemy might even yet be kept at bay till the arrival of Breyman's corps, now momentarily expected; when an accident occurred, which at once put an end to this expectation and exposed us, almost defenceless, to our fate.

The solitary tumbril which contained the whole of our spare ammunition became ignited and blew up with a violence which shook the very ground under our feet and caused a momentary cessation in firing, both on our side and that of the enemy. But the cessation was only for a moment. The American officers, guessing the extent of our calamity, cheered their men to fresh exertions. They rushed up the ascent with redoubled ardor, in spite of the heavy volley which we poured in to check them, and, finding our guns silent, they sprang over the parapet and dashed within our works.

For a few seconds the scene which ensued defies all power of language to describe. The bayonet, the butt of the rifle, the sabre, the pike, were in full play, and men fell, as they rarely fall in modern war, under the direct blows of their enemies. But such a struggle could not, in the nature of things, be of long continuance. Outnumbered, broken and somewhat disheartened by late events, our people wavered and fell back, or fought singly and unconnectedly, till they were either cut down at their posts, obstinately defending themselves, or compelled to surrender. Of Reidesel's dismounted dragoons, few survived to tell how nobly they had behaved; Col. Baume, shot through the body by a rifle ball, fell mortally wounded; and all order and discipline being lost, flight or submission was alone thought of.

For my own part, whether the feeling arose from desperation or accident I cannot tell, but I resolved not to be taken. As yet I had escaped almost unhurt, a slight flesh wound in the left arm having alone fallen to my share; and gathering around me about thirty of my comrades, we made a rush where the enemy's ranks appeared weakest, and burst through. This done, each man made haste to shift for himself without pausing to consider the fate of his neighbor; and losing one third of our number from the enemy's fire, the remainder took refuge, in groups of two or three, within the forest.

　　　　　—GLICH, "Account," *Vt. Hist. Soc. Coll.*, I, 219-223.

VIII. SARATOGA: THE FIRST PHASE: FREEMAN'S FARM

On July 17 Howe wrote Burgoyne: "My intention is for Pennsylvania, where I expect to meet Washington, but if he goes to the northward contrary to my expectations, and you can keep him at bay, be assured I shall soon be after him to relieve you." The day the letter was written Howe had already embarked his troops for the Chesapeake, and by the time it reached Burgoyne, Howe's fleet was south of the Delaware capes. Although Burgoyne kept his own counsel, he recognized his situation as desperate. Feeling that his orders left him no alternative but to push southward to Albany, he determined to cross to the west side of the Hudson River. There his path was blocked by Gates's army which held a commanding position at Bemis Heights, where fortifications had been erected and trenches dug under the direction of the Polish engineer Kosciusko. Pausing for reinforcements of guns, stores and provisions from Lake George, Burgoyne, once they had reached him, crossed the Hudson to Saratoga on September 13.

Burgoyne's thrust south was blocked by Gates's army on the plateau of Bemis Heights. On September 18 the British seized the heights to the north. Burgoyne's plan was to get into the rear of the American left by a flanking movement. For this purpose he sent his right column under Fraser, supported by Breymann's Hessian riflemen and covered by a mixed force of Indians, Loyalists and Canadians. Meanwhile the British general personally led the center in a frontal attack, supported on his left by the Hessian Baron Friederich von Riedesel and Major General William Phillips.

The "old midwife," as Burgoyne called Gates, was strangely inert, trusting to his fortified position rather than taking the initiative and splitting up Burgoyne's widely spaced forces. Arnold, on the other hand, anticipated the movement to turn the American left, and argued vehemently with Gates, who finally dispatched Morgan's riflemen and Dearborn's light infantry to check it. There the battle ebbed and flowed until sundown, while Arnold fell upon the enemy's center with the view to separating Burgoyne and Fraser.

From one point of view Freeman's Farm was a drawn battle. Neither side gained ground. The American suffered some 300 casualties, the British double that number. But the American, rapidly being reinforced, could afford the losses; Burgoyne could not. For him time was running out. His retreat was virtually cut off by Patriot forces in his rear, and the early winter in the north country would have made a withdrawal extremely hazardous under any conditions. With proper reinforcements Arnold might have broken the enemy's line and gained the complete victory. "I trust we have convinced the British butchers that the 'cowardly' Yankees can, and when there is a call for it, will fight," observed Major Henry Dearborn, one of the participants in the Battle of Freeman's Farm.

Freeman's Farm set off a furious quarrel between Arnold and Gates. The latter, in his report to Congress, failed to mention Arnold's personal participation in the battle. Some historians, drawing on pro-Gates and anti-Arnold contemporaries such as the unreliable Wilkinson and the scandalmongering Gordon, have contended that Arnold was not in the battle at all. But the overwhelming evidence is the other way.

The immediate effect of the breach was serious. Arnold was relieved of his command and barred from headquarters.

1. Burgoyne Realizes His Peril, but Germain Does Not

A. GENERAL BURGOYNE TO LORD GEORGE GERMAIN

Camp near Saratoga, August 20, 1777

The consequences of this affair [the Battle of Bennington], my Lord, have little effect upon the strength or spirits of the army; but the prospect of the campaign in other respects is far less prosperous than when I wrote last. In spite of St. Leger's victory, Fort Stanwix holds out obstinately.

I am afraid the expectations of Sir J. Johnson greatly fail in the rising of the country. On this side I find daily reason to doubt the sincerity of the resolution of the professing Loyalists. I have about 400 (but not half of them armed) who may be depended upon; the rest are trimmers, merely actuated by interest. The great bulk of the country is undoubtedly with the Congress, in principle and in zeal; and their measures are executed with a secrecy and dispatch that are not to be equalled. Wherever the King's forces point, militia, to the amount of three or four thousand, assemble in twenty-four hours; they bring with them their subsistence, etc., and, the alarm over, they return to their farms. The Hampshire Grants in particular, a country unpeopled and almost unknown in the last war, now abounds in the most active and most rebellious race of the continent, and hangs like a gathering storm upon my left. In all parts the industry and management in driving cattle and removing corn are indefatigable and certain; and it becomes impracticable to move without portable magazines.

Another most embarrassing circumstance is the want of communication with Sir William Howe; of the messengers I have sent, I know of two being hanged, and am ignorant whether any of the rest arrived. The same fate has

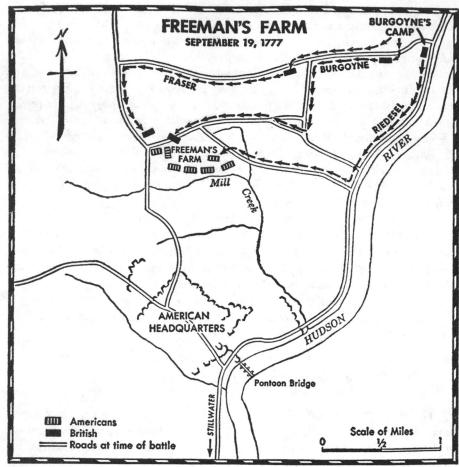

FREEMAN'S FARM
SEPTEMBER 19, 1777

BURGOYNE'S CAMP

FRASER

BURGOYNE

RIEDESEL

RIVER

FREEMAN'S FARM

Mill Creek

AMERICAN HEADQUARTERS

HUDSON

Pontoon Bridge

STILLWATER

Americans
British
Roads at time of battle

Scale of Miles
0   ½   1

From The American Revolution   *Courtesy of Harper & Brothers*
by John Richard Alden

probably attended those dispatched by Sir William Howe, for only one letter is come to hand, informing me that his intention is for Pennsylvania; that Washington has detached Sullivan, with 2500 men, to Albany; that Putnam is in the Highlands with 4000 men; that after my arrival at Albany the movements of the enemy must guide mine; but that he wished the enemy might be driven out of the province before any operation took place against the Connecticut; that Sir Henry Clinton remained in the command in the neighbourhood of New-York, and would act as occurrences might direct.

No operation, my Lord, has yet been undertaken in my favour: the Highlands have not been threatened. The consequence is that Putnam has detached two brigades to Mr. Gates, who is now strongly posted near the mouth of the Mohawk-River, with an army superior to mine in troops of the Congress and as many militia as he pleases. He is likewise far from being deficient in artillery, having received all the pieces that were landed from the French ships which got into Boston.

Had I a latitude in my orders, I should think it my duty to wait in this position, or perhaps as far back as Fort Edward, where my communication with Lake George would be perfectly secure, till some event happened to assist my movement forward; but my orders being positive to "force a junction with Sir William Howe," I apprehend I am not at liberty to remain inactive longer than shall be necessary to collect twenty-five days provision, and to receive the reinforcement of the additional companies, the German drafts and recruits now (and unfortunately only now) on Lake Champlain. The waiting the arrival of this reinforcement is of indispensable necessity, because from the hour I pass the Hudson's River and proceed towards Albany, all safety of communication ceases. I must expect a large body of the enemy from my left will take post behind me.

I have put out of the question the waiting longer than the time necessary for the foregoing purposes, because the attempt, then critical, depending on adventure and the fortune that often accompanies it, and hardly justifiable but by orders from the state, would afterwards be consummately desperate. I mean, my Lord, that by moving soon, though I should meet with insurmountable difficulties to my progress, I shall at least have the chance of fighting my way back to Ticonderoga, but the season a little further advanced, the distance increased, and the march unavoidably tardy because surrounded by enemies, a retreat might be shut in by impenetrable bars of the elements, and at the same time no possible means of existence remain in the country.

When I wrote more confidently, I little foresaw that I was to be left to pursue my way through such a tract of country and hosts of foes, without any co-operation from New-York; nor did I then think the garrison of Ticonderoga would fall to my share alone; a dangerous experiment would it be to leave that post in weakness, and too heavy a drain it is upon the life-blood of my force to give it due strength.

I yet do not despond. Should I succeed in forcing my way to Albany, and find that country in a state to subsist my army, I shall think no more of a retreat, but at the worst fortify there and await Sir W. Howe's operations.

Whatever may be my fate, my Lord, I submit my actions to the breast of the King, and to the candid judgment of my profession, when all the motives become public; and I rest in the confidence that, whatever decision may be passed upon my conduct, my good intent will not be questioned.

I cannot close so serious a letter without expressing my fullest satisfaction in the behaviour and countenance of the troops, and my compleat confidence that in all trials they will do whatever can be expected from men devoted to their King and country.

—BURGOYNE, *A State of the Expedition from Canada*, pp. xxv-xxvi.

B. GERMAIN TO WILLIAM KNOX, UNDERSECRETARY OF STATE FOR THE COLONIES

September 29, 1777

I am sorry the Canada army will be disappointed in the junction they expect with Sir William Howe, but the more honour for Burgoyne if he does the business without any assistance from New York.

—GR. BRIT. HIST. MSS. COMM., *Manuscripts in Various Collections*, VI, 139.

C. GERMAIN TO KNOX

October 31, 1777

I am sorry to find that Burgoyne's campaign is so totally ruined; the best wish I can form is that he may have returned to Ticonderoga without much loss. His private letter to me, being dated the 20th of August, contains nothing material about the affair near Bennington but military reasoning about the propriety of that attack; but what alarms me most is that he thinks his orders to go to Albany to force a junction with Sir William Howe are so positive that he must attempt at all events the obeying them, tho' at the same time he acquaints me that Sir William Howe has sent him word that he has gone to Philadelphia, and indeed nothing that Sir William says could give him reason to hope that any effort would be made in his favor.

—GR. BRIT. HIST. MSS. COMM., *Manuscripts in Various Collections*, VI, 140.

2. MORGAN'S SHARPSHOOTERS PICK OFF THE BRITISH OFFICERS

Journal of Lieutenant William Digby of the Shropshire Regiment.

[*September*] *19th.* At day break intelligence was received that Colonel Morgan, with the advance party of the enemy consisting of a corps of rifle men, were strong about 3 miles from us; their main body amounting to great numbers encamped on a very strong post about half a mile in their rear; and about 9 o'clock we began our march, every man prepared with 60 rounds of cartridge and ready for instant action. We moved in 3 columns, ours to the right on the heights and farthest from the river in thick woods. A little after 12 our advanced picquets came up with Colonel Morgan and engaged, but from the great superiority of fire received from him—his numbers being much greater—they were obliged to fall back, every officer being either killed or wounded except one, when the line came up to their support and obliged Morgan in his turn to retreat with loss.

About half past one, the fire seemed to slacken a little; but it was only to come on with double force, as between 2 and 3 the action became general on their side. From the situation of the ground, and their being perfectly acquainted with it, the whole of our troops could not be brought to engage together, which was a very material disadvantage, though everything possible was tried to remedy that inconvenience, but to no effect. Such an explosion of fire I never had any idea of before, and the heavy artillery joining in concert like great peals of thunder, assisted by the echoes of the woods, almost deafened us with the noise. To an unconcerned spectator, it must have had the most awful and glorious appearance, the different battalions moving to relieve each other, some being pressed and almost broke by their superior numbers. The crash of cannon and musketry never ceased till darkness parted us, when they retired to their camp, leaving us masters of the field; but it was a dear-bought victory if I can give it that name, as we lost many brave men. The 62nd had scarce 10 men a company left, and other regiments suffered much, and no very great advantage, honor excepted, was gained by the day.

On its turning dusk we were near firing on a body of our Germans, mistaking their dark clothing for that of the enemy. General Burgoyne was every where and did every thing [that] could be expected from a brave officer, and Brig. Gen. Frazier gained great honour by exposing himself to every danger. During the night we remained in our ranks, and tho we heard the groans of our wounded and dying at a small distance, yet could not assist them till morning, not knowing the position of the enemy, and expecting the action would be renewed at day break. Sleep was a stranger to us, but we were all in good spirits and ready to obey with cheerfulness any orders the general might issue before morning dawned.

—BAXTER, *The British Invasion from the North*, pp. 270-274.

3. "Nothing Could Exceed the Bravery of Arnold on This Day"

Recollections of Captain E. Wakefield of the American Army.

A persistent effort has been made from the day of the battle to rob Arnold of the glory. Being attached to Dearborn's Light Infantry, which had a conspicuous part in the battles of the 19th of September and the 7th of October, I had the opportunity of witnessing the principal movements of both, and therefore speak from personal knowledge.

I shall never forget the opening scene of the first day's conflict. The riflemen and light infantry were ordered to clear the woods of the Indians. Arnold rode up, and with his sword pointing to the enemy emerging from the woods into an opening partially cleared, covered with stumps and fallen timber, addressing Morgan, he said, "Colonel Morgan, you and I have seen too many redskins to be deceived by that garb of paint and feathers; they are asses in lions' skins, Canadians and Tories; let your riflemen cure them of their borrowed plumes."

And so they did; for in less than fifteen minutes the "Wagon Boy," with his Virginia riflemen, sent the painted devils with a howl back to the British lines. Morgan was in his glory, catching the inspiration of Arnold, as he thrilled his men; when he hurled them against the enemy, he astonished the English and Germans with the deadly fire of his rifles.

Nothing could exceed the bravery of Arnold on this day; he seemed the very genius of war. Infuriated by the conflict and maddened by Gates' refusal to send reinforcements, which he repeatedly called for, and knowing he was meeting the brunt of the battle, he seemed inspired with the fury of a demon.

—GUILD, *Chaplain Smith and the Baptists*, p. 213.

4. The Break Between Arnold and Gates

A. general arnold to general gates

Camp at Stillwater, September 22, 1777

When I joined the army at Vanschaak's Island the first inst. you were pleased to order me to Londons Ferry to take the command of Generals Poor and Learned's Brigades and Colonel Morgan's battalion of rifle men and light infantry. Your command was immediately obeyed. I have repeatedly since received your orders respecting those corps as belonging to my division, which has often been mentioned in General Orders, and the gentlemen commanding those corps have understood themselves as in my division. On the 9th inst. you desired me to anex the New York and Connecticut Militia to such brigades as I thought proper in my division, which I accordingly did and ordered the New York Militia to join Genl. Poor's brigade, and the Connecticut Militia General Learned's. The next day, I was surprised to observe in General Orders the New York Militia anexed to General Glover's brigade, which placed me in the ridiculous light of presuming to give orders I had no right to do, and having them publickly contradicted, which I mentioned to you as I thought it a mistake of the Dep'y Adjutant General. You then observed the mistake your own and that it should be mentioned as such in the ensuing orders, which has never been done.

On the 19th inst. when advice was received that the enemy were approaching, I took the liberty to give it as my opinion that we ought to march out and attack them. You desired me to send Colonel Morgan and the light infantry and support them. I obeyed your orders, and before the action was over, I found it necessary to send out the whole of my division to support the attack. No other troops were engaged that day except Colonel Marshall's regiment of General Pattison's brigade.

I have been informed that in the returns transmitted to Congress of the killed and wounded in the action the troops were mentioned as a detachment from the army, and in the orders of this day I observe it is mentioned that Colonel Morgan's corps not being in any brigade or division of this army are to make returns and reports only to head quarters, from whence they are alone to receive orders, altho it is notorious to the whole army they have been in and done duty with my division for some time past.

When I mentioned these matters to you this day you were pleased to say, in contradiction to your repeated orders, you did not know I was a Major General or had any command in the army. I have ever supposed a Major General's command of four thousand men a proper division and no detachment, when composed of whole brigades forming one wing of the army, and that the general and troops if guilty of misconduct or cowardly behaviour in time of action were justly chargable as a division, and that if, on the other hand, they behave with spirit and firmness in action they were justly initiated to the applause due to a brave division, not detachment, of the army. Had my division behaved ill the other divisions of the army would have thought it extremely hard to have been amenable for their conduct. I mentioned these matters as I wish justice due to the division, as well as particular regiments or persons.

From what reason I know not, as I am conscious of no offence or neglect of duty, but I have lately observed little or no attention paid to any proposals I have thought it my duty to make for the public service, and when a measure I have proposed has been agreed to it has immediately been contradicted. I have been received with the greatest coolness at head quarters, and often treated in such a manner as must mortify a person with less pride than I have, and in my station in the army. You observed you expected General Lincoln in a day or two when I should have no command of a division, that you thought me of little consequence to the army, and that you would with all your heart give me a pass to leave it whenever I thought proper. As I find your observation very just that I am not, or that you wish me of little consequence in the army, and as I have the interest and safety of my country at heart, I wish to be where I can be of the most service to them. I therefore, as General Lincoln is arrived, have to request your pass to Philadelphia with my two aid de camps and three servants, where I propose to join General Washington, and may possibly have it in my power to serve my country, tho I am thought of no consequence in this Department.

—Gates Papers, Box VII, No. 195.

B. GATES TO ARNOLD

Headquarters, September 23, 1777

You wrote me nothing last Night but what had been sufficiently alter-cated between us in the Evening. I then gave such Answers to all your Objections as I think were satisfactory. I know not what you mean by insult or Indignity. I made you such replys only as I conceived proper. As to the Opened Letter I sent you to Mr Hancock, it was the Civilest method I could devise of acquainting Congress with your leaving The Army, and is to all intents and purposes as full a pass as can be desired. I sent it unsealed, as being the more complaisant to You and is what is commonly done upon such Occasions. That not being so agreeable to you as a common pass, I send You one enclosed.

—Gates Papers, N.Y. Hist. Soc., Box XIXb.

5. "TO ARNOLD ALONE IS DUE THE HONOUR OF OUR VICTORY"

A. COLONEL HENRY BROCKHOLST LIVINGSTON OF THE CONTINENTAL ARMY TO GENERAL SCHUYLER

Camp on Behmus Heights, September 23, 1777

I am much distressed at Gen. Arnold's determination to retire from the army at this important crisis. His presence was never more necessary. He is the life and soul of the troops. Believe me, Sir, to him and to him alone is due the honor of our late victory. Whatever share his superiours may claim they are entitled to none. He enjoys the confidence and affection of officers and soldiers. They would, to a man, follow him to conquest or death. His absence will dishearten them to such a degree as to render them of but little service.

The difference between him and Mr Gates has arisen to too great a height to admit of a compromise. I have, for some time past, observed the great coolness and, in many instances, even disrespect with which Gen. Arnold has been treated at Head Quarters. His proposals have been rejected with marks of indignity, his own orders have frequently been contravened, and himself set in a ridiculous light by those of the Commander in Chief. His remonstrances, on those occasions, have been termed presumptuous. In short he has pocketed many insults for the sake of his country, which a man of less pride would have resented.

The repeated indignities he received at length roused his spirit and determined him again to remonstrate. He waited on Mr Gates in person last evening. Matters were altercated in a very high strain. Both were warm, the latter rather passionate and very assuming. Towards the end of the debate Mr Gates told Arnold, "He did not know of his being a Major General. He had sent his resignation to Congress. He had never given him the command of any division of the army. Genl. Lincoln would be here in a day or two, that then he should have no occasion for him, and would give him a pass to go to Philadelphia, whenever he chose it."

Arnold's spirit could not brook this usage. He returned to his quarters, represented what had passed in a letter to Mr Gates and requested his permission to go to Philadelphia. This morning, in answer to his letter, he received a permit, by way of a letter directed to Mr Hancock. He sent this back and requested one in proper form, which was complied with. Tomorrow he will set out for Albany.

The reason of the present disagreement between two old cronies is simply this—*Arnold is your friend.* I shall attend the general down. Chagrining as it may be for me to leave the army at a time when an opportunity is offering for every young fellow to distinguish himself, I can no longer submit to the command of a man whom I abhor from my very soul. This conduct is disgusting to every one but his flatterers and dependents, among whom are some who profess to be your friends. A cloud is gathering and may ere long burst on his head.

—Schuyler Papers, N.Y. Public Lib., Box 33, No. 1191.

B. LIVINGSTON TO SCHUYLER

September 24, 1777

Gen. Arnold's intention to quit this department is made public and has caused great uneasiness among the soldiery. To induce him to stay, General Poor proposed an Address from the general officers and colonels of his division, returning him thanks for his past service and particularly for his conduct during the late action and requesting his stay. The Address was framed, and consented to by Poor's officers. Those of Gen. Learned refused. They acquiesced in the propriety of the measure, but were afraid of giving umbrage to General Gates.

—Schuyler Papers, N.Y. Public Lib., Box 33, No. 1192.

C. COLONEL RICHARD VARICK TO SCHUYLER

Camp Still Water, September 22, 1777

This I am certain of, that Arnold has all the credit of the action on the 19th, for he was ordering out troops to it, while the other [Gates] was in Dr. Pott's tent backbiting his neighbours.

—Schuyler Papers, N.Y. Public Lib., Box 33, No. 2334.

6. THE INDIANS AND TORIES FADE AWAY

[1811]

Memoirs of R. Lamb, Sergeant of the Welsh Fusiliers.

Taking all the results of this battle, if we had reason to boast of it, our advantages from it were few indeed. In fact, difficulty and danger appeared to grow out of it. The intricacy of the ground before us increased at every step. Our scouting, reconnoitring and foraging parties encountered perils uncalculated and unseen before. Our enemy, being at home, was well used to the places, and thus possessed of every local advantage that favours an army.

To procure provisions and forage, without sending out large parties or bodies of soldiers, became impossible, and, therefore, the Indians themselves, who were attached to march with and reinforce us, began to desert. Plunder and free-booting was greatly their object, and to be debarred from that, as they found themselves, they turned away from privations and regular warfare, which they were disused to maintain. Of this we had evidence, for as a party of our troops posted near a wood were severely galled on the right of our line by the fire of the enemy, the Indians who accompanied us seemed to hold a consultation among themselves, precipitately retreated, and abandoned the army altogether.

In this circumstance of our military affairs, the Canadians and Colonists reinforcing us afforded no effectual assistance; they evidently betrayed their wishes of withdrawing from our forces, not being previously made up in mind for the severity and hardships of war, in the inveterate and wasting progress of its continuance, which, instead of favouring them with comfortable prospects of a returning tranquillity, assumed day by day a more ferocious and unpromising aspect. Such then being the gloomy face of affairs in the great cause at issue, and the Colonial armies becoming daily stronger and more formidable opponents to us, it was not surprising that the tribes of Indians and the corps of loyal Colonists along with us should feel disheartened and relax their efforts in his Majesty's service.

—LAMB, *Memoir of His Own Life*, pp. 194-195.

IX. SIR HENRY CLINTON'S RELIEF EXPEDITION

It was now increasingly clear that if Burgoyne were to get out of his entrapment he would have to get aid from Howe's forces. Howe had other ideas, however, and had already embarked on his expedition to conquer Pennsylvania, leaving in command of the garrison in New York a reticent, inhibited, inordinately touchy personality, Sir Henry Clinton, who accurately described himself as "a shy bitch," and, he might have added, an excessively cautious one, too. Clinton had the faculty of never getting along with his commander and never working in harmony with his principal subordinate officer.

Now the great decision to relieve Burgoyne was up to him, and his self-defeating caution greatly contributed to the collapse of Burgoyne's flamboyant campaign. Late in July or early August, Clinton wrote an undated letter to Burgoyne describing Howe's move on Philadelphia. When it is covered by an hourglass-shaped mask, which was sent by separate messenger, it reads as follows:

Sir W. Howe is gone to the Cheasapeak Bay with the greatest part of *the army. I hear he is landed but am not certain. I am left to command here with too small a force to make any effectual diversion in your favour. I shall try something at any rate. It may be of use to you. I own to you I think Sir W.'s move just at this time the worst he could take.*

That small diversion was the best Clinton could do. Fearing that Washington would attack New York he kept the larger part of his forces tied down to the defense of the city. Finally, on October 3 when Burgoyne's situation was desperate if not already hopeless, he dispatched a force of 3,000 men on an expedition up the Hudson River. Fort Montgomery fell to his men easily. Fort Clinton fell after bitter resistance, and on the east bank of the river Tryon forced the abandonment of Fort Constitution. Clinton was momentarily buoyant. "Nous y voici," he wrote Burgoyne, "and nothing now between us but Gates." Burgoyne had asked him whether he should proceed to Albany or retreat, pointing out that he could not stay longer than October 12, if he were to do the latter. Unfortunately for Burgoyne, Clinton's messenger was captured by the Patriots, who forced him to vomit up the silver bullet containing the message. Just at this time Howe called upon Clinton for reinforcements. Clinton stopped his advance and soon afterward abandoned the forts. If Burgoyne had any hope of relief, it was cruelly dissipated by Sir Henry's letter to him of October 6, in which Clinton stated that "he thinks it impossible General Burgoyne could really suppose Sir Henry Clinton had any idea of penetrating to Albany with the small force he mentioned to him in his letter of the 11th September."

Having under his command a force of some 7,000, he could have launched a full-scale rescue expedition had he been willing to take the risks which a commander must be expected to assume. But Clinton, as was his wont, put the blame on someone else, in this case on Howe.

1. The Fall of Forts Clinton and Montgomery

Governor George Clinton to the Council of New York.

New Windsor, October 7, 1777

The extreme fatigue I have undergone this three days past and the want of rest for an equal number of nights renders me unfit to write you matters of so serious consequence to this State as I have to communicate. I am able only briefly to inform you that yesterday about ten o'clock A.M. an advanced party was attacked by the enemy at Doodle Town about 2½ miles from Fort Montgomery. They consisted of about 30 men; the enemy, by appearance and accounts after received, of 5000. They received the Enemys fire, returned it and retreated to Fort Clinton.

Soon after [I] received intelligence that the enemy were advancing on the west side of the mountain with design to attack us in rear. Upon this I ordered out Lieut. Colo. Brown and McClaghey with upwards of 1900 men towards Doodle Town, and a brass field piece with a detachment of 60 men to a very advantageous post in the road to the furnace. They were not long out before they were both attacked by the enemy with their whole force. Our people behaved with spirit and must have made great slaughter of the enemy. I strengthened the party in the furnace road to upwards of 100 but they were obliged to give way to so superior a force as the enemy brought against them. They kept their field piece in full play at them till the men who worked it were drove with fix bayonets, then spiked it and retreated with great good order to a 12-pounder which I had ordered to cover them and from thence in the fort. I immediately posted my men in the most advantageous manner for the defence of the post and it was not many minutes before as well our post as Fort Clinton were invaded on all sides and in a most incessant fire kept up till night and even after dusk, when the enemy forced our lines and redoubts at both posts, and the garrisons were obliged to fight their way out—as many as could as were determined not to surrender—and many have escaped.

I was summoned sun an hour high to surrender in five minutes and thereby prevent the effusion of blood. I sent Lieut. Colo. Livingston to receive the flag, who informed them that he [had] no orders to treat with them except to receive their proposals if they meant to surrender themselves prisoners of war in which case he was impowered to assure them good usage. About 10 minutes after they made a general and desperate attack on both posts which was resisted with great spirit, but we were at length overpowered by numbers and they gained possession of both posts. Officers and men behaved with great spirit, as well Continental troops as Militia. Our loss in slain cannot be great considering the length of the action. My brother Genl. Clinton is wounded and I believe made prisoner. This is the case with Major Logan. The number of missing I cannot ascertain. The ships are both burnt and Fort Constitution demolished by our people without my orders but I can't as yet condemn the measure. The officers all say it was right. I am clear it was as to the fort after removing artillery and stores which has not been done. The ships I hoped might have been saved.

Genl. Putnam will retreat to near Capt. Haights about 3 miles from Mr Van Wyck and I mean to rally my broken but brave forces and advance tomorrow on Butter Hill. Genl. Putnam is to send Colo. Webb's regiment to join me.

I begg you will give the substance of this account to Genl. Gates in answer to his letter to me. I have only to add that I greatly respect the loss of these posts but I am consoled with the full perswasion that they have bought them dear and that I have done the most in my power to save them.

—Gates Papers, N.Y. Historical Soc., Box VIII, No. 40.

2. THE SILVER BULLET AND THE INTERCEPTED MESSAGE

Journal of Dr. James Thacher, serving with the Continental Army.

October 14, 1777: It is the prevalent opinion here [at Albany] that by taking advantage of wind and tide, it is in the power of Sir Henry Clinton to convey his forces to this city within the space of five or six hours, and having arrived here, a march of about twenty miles will carry him without opposition to Stillwater, which must involve General Gates in inexpressible embarrassment and difficulty by placing him between two armies, and thereby extricating Burgoyne from his perilous situation.

We have been trembling alive to this menacing prospect, but our fears are in a measure allayed by the following singular incident. After the capture of Fort Montgomery, Sir Henry Clinton despatched a messenger by the name of Daniel Taylor to Burgoyne with the intelligence; fortunately he was taken on his way as a spy, and finding himself in danger, he was seen to turn aside and take something from his pocket and swallow it. General George Clinton, into whose hands he had fallen, ordered a severe dose of emetic tartar to be administered. This produced the happiest effect as respects the prescriber; but it proved fatal to the patient. He discharged a small silver bullet, which being unscrewed, was found to enclose a letter from Sir Henry Clinton to Burgoyne. "Out of thine own mouth thou shalt be condemned." The spy was tried, convicted and executed. The following is an exact copy of the letter inclosed:

"Fort Montgomery, October 8th, 1777.

"*Nous voici*—and nothing between us but Gates. I sincerely hope this *little* success of ours may facilitate your operations. In answer to your letter of the 28th of September by C. C. I shall only say, I cannot presume to order, or even advise, for reasons obvious. I heartily wish you success.

"Faithfully yours,

"H. Clinton

"*To General Burgoyne.*"

—Thacher, *Military Journal*, pp. 105-106.

3. Sir Henry Clinton Comes to the End of the Line

There not being now a gun left in the Highlands, all the rebel craft on the river destroyed, and a fair prospect opening of our being able to remove every obstruction as far as Albany, I began to extend my views beyond the limits they were at first confined to. However, the small number of men which would remain to me for further operations after garrisoning the extensive posts I had taken—which I was obliged either to defend or dismantle—and securing my communications with New York, precluded every idea for the present of penetrating to Albany, especially as my total ignorance of the situation and strength of Mr. Washington's army prevented my forming a judgment how far it might be practicable for him to detach in force to Stony Point and thereby force me down the river. Therefore, to obviate the latter, I lost no time in ordering the engineer to carefully examine that ground, that with the Commodore's assistance measures might be taken for securing it. And as a remedy for the former I took the precaution, by dismantling Fort Montgomery and strengthening Fort Clinton, so to reduce our defenses in the Highlands as to be able to hold this strong position with a few men. I proposed likewise to leave General Vaughan with a sufficient corps at Verplanck's or on the Croton, from whence he might readily either succor the Highlands or fall back to King's Bridge, as emergencies should require.

But, happening to receive a letter about this time from General Pigot informing me he could spare 1000 men from the defense of Rhode Island, I began to entertain hopes that I should even be able to support General Burgoyne, should he incline to force his way to Albany. Therefore, while Sir James Wallace was employed in exploring a passage through the *chevaux-*

de-frise and removing the booms across the river, I went back to Kings Bridge to make some arrangements respecting the command there which required my presence. [Nobody but drunken General Schmidt to trust the foreposts to; I therefore determined to return myself.—Memoranda] And, availing myself of General Pigot's offer by requesting him to send 1000 men to New York, I ordered the Second Battalion of Anspach, Koeler's Grenadiers and the Forty-fifth Regiment to proceed from thence to the Highlands, and six months' provisions for five thousand men to be directly put on board vessels of proper draft for running up the river to Albany. After making this arrangement I immediately returned, and detached General Vaughan with nearly 2000 men under the escort of Sir James Wallace with the galleys up the Hudson, giving him orders to feel his way to General Burgoyne and do his utmost to assist his operations, or even join him if required.

This little armament got up to Esopus [Kingston] on the 15th; and General Vaughan informed me he judged it proper to stop and destroy the place, lest the works and troops there might interrupt his communication with Fort Clinton or harass him on his return. He afterward proceeded to Livingston's Manor, about forty-five miles from Albany, where the vessels were obliged to come to anchor by the pilots' absolutely refusing to take charge of them further. From hence the General sent me information that he had not been able to communicate with General Burgoyne, as Putnam with 5000 men had taken posts on his right and Parsons with 1500 on his left, but that all accounts agreed in representing his situation as desperate.

Though this intelligence destroyed all my hopes of being in the least serviceable to the northern army, whose fate I now feared was inevitable, it yet was very much my wish to be able to retain the footing we were now possessed of in the Highlands. Every view of that sort was, however, dissipated by my next dispatches from the Commander in Chief, as I was thereby ordered to send him "*without delay* the Seventh, Twenty-sixth and Sixty-third Regiments, two battalions of Anspach and [the] Seventeenth Dragoons, together with all the recruits and recovered men belonging to the southern army and the Jägers and artillerymen which came by the English fleet—*even notwithstanding I might be gone up the North River, agreeable to the intimation I had given him of my intentions in my letter of the 29th of September*—except I should be on the eve of accomplishing some very material and essential stroke, being left at liberty *in that case* to proceed upon it *provided I judged it might be executed in a few days after the receipt of his letters.*"

These orders being too explicit to be misunderstood or obedience to them *even delayed*, and several of the corps with General Vaughan being particularized in them, I wrote to that general officer on the 22d of October to direct him to return with all speed. And, receiving soon afterward another order from Sir William Howe to dismantle Fort Clinton, I was under the mortifying necessity of relinquishing the Highlands and all the other passes over the Hudson, to be reoccupied by the rebels whenever they saw proper. For, even had General Burgoyne been fortunately in a situation to have availed himself of my success and been tempted to trust to my support at the time I received these orders, I believe there is no military man who will not allow that I should have had no small difficulty in reconciling the delay an effort of that consequence must have necessarily occasioned with the obedience I owed to so explicit and pressing an order from my Commander in Chief.

—CLINTON, *The American Rebellion*, pp. 78-81.

X. SARATOGA: THE LAST PHASE: BEMIS HEIGHTS

The climactic phase of the battle of Saratoga occurred on October 7. Burgoyne could no longer afford to await the result of Clinton's push northward. In the meantime detachments of Lincoln's forces operating from Vermont in Burgoyne's rear had seriously threatened the British army's line of retreat and Stark had taken Ft. Edward. While Burgoyne had used the time after the Battle of Freeman's Farm to construct extensive entrenchments and redoubts, Gates's forces were strengthened by the arrival of Lincoln's army and by militiamen who, singly or in groups, were now flocking to Bemis Heights. By the seventh Gates's forces numbered 11,000; Burgoyne's were down to 5,000.

The battle started with a reconnaissance in force by 1,650 of Burgoyne's troops, the right led by Lord Balcarres, the center by the Hessian General von Riedesel, and the left under Major Acland. In a countermove Gates dispatched Morgan to attack the British right and Poor the enemy's left. While Poor's men rushed the grenadiers and took the wounded Acland prisoner, Morgan, who had made a wide circuit around the enemy's right to get into the woods on the flank and the rear of the British, poured a deadly fire on Balcarres' troops and forced them to retreat to their own lines.

What James Wilkinson curiously omits from his narrative is the role of Arnold. When the enemy retreated to the shelter of their breastworks, Arnold, in disgrace and without command that day, led some of Paterson's and Glover's men against the works held by Balcarres, and when Learned's men appeared off to the left, marching toward the extreme British right, Arnold galloped straight across the line of fire, took charge of Learned's men and led a frontal assault on Breymann's redoubt. There his horse was shot down and he himself received a bullet in his leg. The fortifications had now been breached and that night Burgoyne retired to the protection of redoubts on the bluffs along the river's edge; then, fearing an attack on his rear, he withdrew his shattered army the next evening to the heights of Saratoga. He had lost 600 men, many of them officers, four times the casualties suffered by the Americans.

1. "ORDER ON MORGAN TO BEGIN THE GAME"

Memoirs of Colonel James Wilkinson of the Continental Army.

On the afternoon of the 7th October, the advanced guard of the centre beat to arms; the alarm was repeated throughout the line, and the troops repaired to their alarm posts. I was at head quarters when this happened, and with the approbation of the General mounted my horse to inquire the cause;

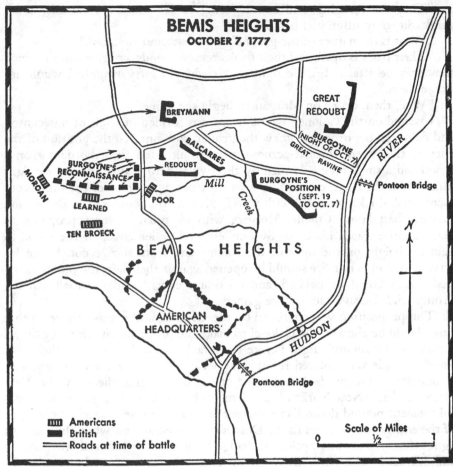

BEMIS HEIGHTS
OCTOBER 7, 1777

From The American Revolution
by John Richard Alden

Courtesy of Harper & Brothers

but on reaching the guard where the beat commenced, I could obtain no other satisfaction but that some person had reported the enemy to be advancing against our left. I proceeded over open ground, and ascending a gentle acclivity in front of the guard, I perceived, about half a mile from the line of our encampment, several columns of the enemy, 60 or 70 rods from me, entering a wheat field which had not been cut and was separated from me by a small rivulet; and without my glass I could distinctly mark their every movement. After entering the field, they displayed, formed the line, and sat down in double ranks with their arms between their legs. Foragers then proceeded to cut the wheat or standing straw, and I soon after observed several officers, mounted on the top of a cabin, from whence with their glasses they were endeavouring to reconnoitre our left, which was concealed from their view by intervening woods.

Having satisfied myself, after fifteen minutes attentive observation, that no attack was meditated, I returned and reported to the General, who asked me what appeared to be the intentions of the enemy.

"They are foraging, and endeavouring to reconnoitre your left; and I think, Sir, they offer you battle."

"What is the nature of the ground, and what your opinion?"

"Their front is open, and their flanks rest on woods, under cover of which they may be attacked; their right is skirted by a lofty height. I would indulge them."

"Well, then, order on Morgan to begin the game."

I waited on the Colonel, whose corps was formed in front of our centre, and delivered the order; he knew the ground and inquired the position of the enemy: they were formed across a newly cultivated field, bordering on a wood and a small ravine formed by the rivulet before alluded to; their light infantry on the right, covered by a worm fence at the foot of the hill before mentioned, thickly covered with wood; their centre composed of British and German battalions. Colonel Morgan, with his usual sagacity, proposed to make a circuit with his corps by our left, and under cover of the wood to gain the height on the right of the enemy, and from thence commence his attack, so soon as our fire should be opened against their left; the plan was the best which could be devised, and no doubt contributed essentially to the prompt and decisive victory we gained.

This proposition was approved by the General, and it was concerted that time should be allowed the Colonel to make the proposed circuit and gain his station on the enemy's right before the attack should be made on their left; Poor's brigade was ordered for this service, and the attack was commenced in due season on the flank and front of the British grenadiers, by the New Hampshire and New York troops. True to his purpose, Morgan at this critical moment poured down like a torrent from the hill, and attacked the right of the enemy in front and flank. Dearborn, at the moment when the enemy's light infantry were attempting to change front, pressed forward with ardour and delivered a close fire; then leapt the fence, shouted, charged and gallantly forced them to retire in disorder. Yet, headed by that intrepid soldier the Earl of Balcarras, they were immediately rallied and reformed behind a fence in rear of their first position; but being now attacked with great audacity in front and flanks by superior numbers, resistance became vain, and the whole line, commanded by Burgoyne in person, gave way and made a precipitate and disorderly retreat to his camp, leaving two twelve and six six-pounders on the field with the loss of more than 400 officers and men killed, wounded and captured, and among them the flower of his officers, viz. Brigadier-general Frazer, Major Ackland commanding the grenadiers, Sir Francis Clark, his first aid-de-camp, Major Williams commanding officer of the artillery, Captain Money, deputy quartermaster general, and many others.

After delivering the order to General Poor and directing him to the point of attack, I was peremptorily commanded to repair to the rear and order up Ten Broeck's brigade of York militia 3000 strong; I performed this service, and regained the field of battle at the moment the enemy had turned their backs, fifty-two minutes after the first shot was fired.

The ground which had been occupied by the British grenadiers presented a scene of complicated horror and exultation. In the square space of twelve or fifteen yards lay eighteen grenadiers in the agonies of death, and three officers propped up against stumps of trees, two of them mortally wounded, bleeding and almost speechless; what a spectacle for one whose bosom glowed with philanthropy, and how vehement the impulse which can excite men of sensibility to seek such scenes of barbarism!

I found the courageous Colonel Cilley astraddle on a brass twelve-pounder and exulting in the capture—whilst a surgeon, a man of great worth who was dressing one of the officers, raising his blood-besmeared hands in a frenzy of patriotism, exclaimed, "Wilkinson, I have dipt my hands in British blood!" He received a sharp rebuke for his brutality, and with the troops I pursued the hard-pressed flying enemy, passing over killed and wounded until I heard one exclaim, "Protect me, Sir, against this boy."

Turning my eyes, it was my fortune to arrest the purpose of a lad, thirteen or fourteen years old, in the act of taking aim at a wounded officer who lay in the angle of a worm fence. Inquiring his rank, he answered, "I had the honour to command the grenadiers." Of course, I knew him to be Major Ackland, who had been brought from the field to this place on the back of a Captain Shrimpton of his own corps, under a heavy fire, and was here deposited, to save the lives of both. I dismounted, took him by the hand and expressed hopes that he was not badly wounded.

"Not badly," replied this gallant officer and accomplished gentleman, "but very inconveniently. I am shot through both legs. Will you, Sir, have the goodness to have me conveyed to your camp?"

I directed my servant to alight, and we lifted Ackland into his seat, and ordered him to be conducted to head-quarters.

—WILKINSON, *Memoirs of My Own Times*, I, 267-272.

2. MORGAN'S SHARPSHOOTERS PICK OFF THE GALLANT FRASER

Recollections of Samuel Woodruff, a volunteer under Gates.

... Soon after the commencement of the action, General Arnold, knowing the military character and efficiency of General Frazer, and observing his motions in leading and conducting the attack, said to Colonel Morgan, "That officer upon a grey horse is of himself a host, and must be disposed of—direct the attention of some of the sharp-shooters among your riflemen to him."

Morgan nodding his assent to Arnold, repaired to his riflemen, and made known to them the hint given by Arnold. Immediately upon this, the crupper of the grey horse was cut off by a rifle bullet, and within the next minute another passed through the horse's mane a little back of his ears.

An aid of Frazer, noticing this, observed to him, "Sir, it is evident that you are marked out for particular aim; would it not be prudent for you to retire from this place?"

Frazer replied, "My duty forbids me to fly from danger," and immediately received a bullet through his body. A few grenadiers were detached to carry him to the Smith [Taylor] house.

—NEILSON, *Account of Burgoyne's Campaign*, pp. 254-257.

3. ARNOLD ATTACKS BREYMANN'S REDOUBT

Ebenezer Mattoon, a Continental officer, to General Philip Schuyler.

October 7, 1835

... About one o'clock of this day, two signal guns were fired on the left of the British army which indicated a movement. Our troops were immediately put under arms, and the lines manned. At this juncture Gens. Lincoln and Arnold rode with great speed towards the enemy's lines. While they were absent, the picket guards on both sides were engaged near the river. In about half an hour, Generals Lincoln and Arnold returned to headquarters, where many of the officers collected to hear the report, General Gates standing at the door.

Gen. Lincoln says, "Gen. Gates, the firing at the river is merely a feint; their object is your left. A strong force of 1500 men are marching circuitously, to plant themselves on yonder height. That point must be defended, or your camp is in danger."

Gates replied, "I will send Morgan with his riflemen, and Dearborn's infantry."

Arnold says, "That is nothing; you must send a strong force."

Gates replied, "Gen. Arnold, I have nothing for you to do; you have no business here."

Arnold's reply was reproachful and severe.

Gen. Lincoln says, "You must send a strong force to support Morgan and Dearborn, at least three regiments."

Two regiments from Gen. Larned's brigade, and one from Gen. Nixon's, were then ordered to that station and to defend it at all hazards. Generals Lincoln and Arnold immediately left the encampment and proceeded to the enemy's lines.

In a few minutes, Capt. Furnival's company of artillery, in which I was lieutenant, was ordered to march towards the fire, which had now opened upon our picket in front, the picket consisting of about 300 men. While we were marching, the whole line, up to our picket or front, was engaged. We advanced to a height of ground which brought the enemy in view, and opened our fire. But the enemy's guns, eight in number, and much heavier than ours, rendered our position untenable.

We then advanced into the line of infantry. Here Lieutenant M'Lane joined me. In our front there was a field of corn, in which the Hessians were secreted. On our advancing towards the corn field, a number of men rose and fired upon us. M'Lane was severely wounded. While I was removing him from the field, the firing still continued without abatement.

During this time, a tremendous firing was heard on our left. We poured in upon them our canister shot as fast as possible, and the whole line, from left to right, became engaged. The smoke was very dense, and no movements could be seen; but as it soon arose, our infantry appeared to be slowly retreating, and the Hessians slowly advancing, their officers urging them on with their hangers. ...

The troops continuing warmly engaged, Col. Johnson's regiment, coming up, threw in a heavy fire and compelled the Hessians to retreat. Upon this we advanced with a shout of victory. At the same time Auckland's corps gave way. We proceeded but a short distance before we came upon four pieces of brass cannon, closely surrounded with the dead and dying; at a few yards further we came upon two more. Advancing a little further, we were met by a fire from the British infantry, which proved very fatal to one of Col. Johnson's companies, in which were killed one sergeant, one corporal, fourteen privates—and about twenty were wounded.

They advanced with a quick step, firing as they came on. We returned them a brisk fire of canister shot, not allowing ourselves time even to sponge our pieces. In a short time they ceased firing and advanced upon us with trailed arms. At this juncture Arnold came up with a part of Brooks's regiment, and gave them a most deadly fire, which soon caused them to face about and retreat with a quicker step than they advanced.

The firing had now principally ceased on our left, but was brisk in front and on the right. At this moment Arnold says to Col. Brooks (late governor of Massachusetts), "Let us attack Balcarras's works."

Brooks replied, "No. Lord Auckland's detachment has retired there, we can't carry them."

"Well, then, let us attack the Hessian lines."

Brooks replies, "With all my heart."

We all wheeled to the right and advanced. No fire was received, except from the cannon, until we got within about eight rods, when we received a tremendous fire from the whole line. But a few of our men, however, fell. Still advancing, we received a second fire, in which a few men fell, and Gen. Arnold's horse fell under him, and he himself was wounded. He cried out, "Rush on, my brave boys!" After receiving the third fire, Brooks mounted their works, swung his sword, and the men rushed into their works. When we entered the works, we found Col. Bremen dead, surrounded with a number of his companions, dead or wounded. We still pursued slowly, the fire, in the mean time, decreasing. Nightfall now put an end to this day's bloody contest. During the day we had taken eight cannon and broken the centre of the enemy's lines.

We were ordered to rest until relieved from the camps. The gloom of the night, the groans and shrieks of the wounded and dying, and the horrors of the whole scene baffle all description.

—STONE, *Campaign of Burgoyne*, pp. 371-375.

4. "ALL OF THE INFANTRY HAD GONE TO THE DEVIL OR RUN AWAY"

Journal of Captain Georg Pausch of the Hanau Artillery.

[*October* 7, *1777*] At this junction, our left wing retreated in the greatest possible disorder, thereby causing a similar rout among our German command, which was stationed behind the fence in line of battle. They retreated —or to speak more plainly—they left their position without informing me, although I was but fifty paces in advance of them. Each man for himself, they made for the bushes. Without knowing it, I kept back the enemy for a while with my unprotected cannon loaded with shells. How long before this the infantry had left its position, I cannot tell, but I saw a great number advance towards our now open left wing within a distance of about 300 paces. I looked back towards the position still held, as I supposed, by our German infantry, under whose protection I, too, intended to retreat—but not a man was to be seen. They had all run across the road into the field and thence into the bushes, and had taken refuge behind the trees. Their right wing was thus in front of the house I have so often mentioned, but all was in disorder, though they still fought the enemy which continued to advance.

In the mean time, on our right wing, there was stubborn fighting on both sides, our rear, meanwhile, being covered by a dense forest, which, just before, had protected our right flank. The road by which we were to retreat lay through the woods and was already in the hands of the enemy, who accordingly intercepted us. Finding myself, therefore, finally in my first mentioned position—alone, isolated, and almost surrounded by the enemy, and with no way open but the one leading to the house where the two 12-pound cannon stood, dismounted and deserted—I had no alternative but to make my way along it with great difficulty if I did not wish to be stuck in a *damned* crooked road.

After safely reaching the house under the protection of a musketry fire —which, however, owing to the bushes, was fully as dangerous to me as if the firing came from the enemy—I presently came across a little earth-work, 18 feet long by 5 feet high. This I at once made use of by posting my two cannon, one on the right, and the other on the left, and began a fire alternately with balls and with shells, without, however, being able to discriminate in favor of our men who were in the bushes; for the enemy, without troubling them, charged savagely upon my cannon, hoping to dismount and silence them. . . .

A brave English Lieutenant of Artillery, by the name of Schmidt, and a sergeant were the only two who were willing to serve the cannon longer. He came to me and asked me to let him have ten artillery-men and one subaltern from my detachment to serve these cannon. But it was impossible for me to grant his request, no matter how well disposed I might have been towards it. Two of my men had been shot dead; three or four were wounded; a number had straggled off, and all of the infantry detailed for that purpose either gone to the devil or run away. Moreover, all I had left, for the serving of each cannon, were four or five men and one subaltern. A six-pound cannon, also, on account of its rapidity in firing, was more effectual than a twelve-pounder, with which only one-third the number of shots could be fired; and furthermore, I had no desire to silence my own cannon, which were still in my possession, and thereby contribute to raise the honors of another corps. Three wagons of ammunition were fired away by my cannon, which became so heated that it was impossible for any man to lay his hands on them. In front, and also to the right and left of my guns, I had conquered, for myself and for those who were in the same *terrain*, a pretty comfortable fort. But this state of things lasted only a short time, the fire behind us coming nearer. Finally, our right wing was repulsed in our rear; its infantry, however, fortunately retreating in better order than our left wing had done.

I still could see, as far as the plain and clearing reached, the road, on which I had marched to this second position, open, and a chance, therefore, to retreat. Accordingly, myself, the artillery-man Hausemann and two other artillery-men, hoping to save one of the cannon, dragged it towards this road. The piece of wood on the cannon made the work for us four men very difficult and, in fact, next to impossible. Finally, a subaltern followed with the other cannon and placed it on the carriage. We now brought up the other carriage, on which I quickly placed the remaining gun, and marched briskly along the road, hoping to meet a body of our Infantry and with them make a stand. But this hope proved delusive and was totally dispelled; for some ran in one, and others in another direction; and by the time that I came within gunshot of the woods, I found the road occupied by the enemy. They came towards us on it; the bushes were full of them; they were hidden behind the trees; and bullets in plenty received us.

Seeing that all was irretrievably lost, and that it was impossible to save anything, I called to the few remaining men to save themselves. I myself took refuge through a fence, in a piece of dense underbrush on the right of the road, with the last ammunition wagon, which, with the help of a gunner, I saved with the horses. Here I met all the different nationalities of our division running pell-mell—among them Capt. Schoel, with whom there was not a single man left of the Hanau Regiment. In this confused retreat all made for our camp and our lines. The entrenchment of Breymann was furiously assailed; the camp in it set on fire and burned, and all the baggage-horses and baggage captured by the enemy. The three 6-pound cannon of my brigade of artillery were also taken, the artillery-men, Wachler and Fintzell, killed, and artillery-man Wall (under whose command were the cannon) severely, and others slightly, wounded. The enemy occupied this entrenchment and remained in it during the night. The approaching darkness put an end to further operations on the part of the Americans.

—PAUSCH, *Journal*, pp. 166-172.

5. THE DECIMATION IN BURGOYNE'S RANKS

Journal of Lieutenant William Digby of the Shropshire Regiment.

[*October* 7, *1777*]. Brigadier General Frazier was mortally wounded, which helped to turn the fate of the day. When General Burgoyne saw him fall, he seemed then to feel in the highest degree our disagreeable situation. He was the only person we could carry off with us. Our cannon were surrounded and taken—the men and horses being all killed—which gave them additional spirits, and they rushed on with loud shouts, when we drove them back a little way with so great loss to ourselves that it evidently appeared a retreat was the only thing left for us.

They still advanced upon our works under a severe fire of grape shot, which in some measure stopped them by the great execution we saw made among their columns; during which another body of the enemy stormed the German lines after meeting with a most shameful resistance, and took possession of all their camp and equipage, baggage, etc., etc., Colo. Bremen fell nobly at the head of the foreigners, and by his death blotted out part of the stain his countrymen so justly merited from that day's behaviour.

On our retreating, which was pretty regular, considering how hard we were pressed by the enemy, General Burgoyne appeared greatly agitated as the danger to which the lines were exposed was of the most serious nature at that particular period. . . . He said but little, well knowing we could defend the lines or fall in the attempt. Darkness interposed (I believe fortunately for us), which put an end to the action.

General Frazier was yet living, but not the least hopes of him. He that night asked if Genl. Burgoyne's army were not all cut to pieces, and being informed to the contrary, appeared for a moment pleased, but spoke no more. Captn. Wight (53rd Grenadiers), my captain, was shot in the bowels early in the action. In him I lost a sincere friend. He lay in that situation between the two fires, and I have been since informed lived till the next day and was brought into their camp. Major Ackland was wounded and taken prisoner with our Quartermaster General and Major Williams of the Artillery. Sir Francis Clerk fell, Aid de camp to the general, with other principal officers. Our grenadier company, out of 20 men going out, left their captain and 16 men on the field.

Some here did not scruple to say General Burgoyne's manner of acting verified the rash stroke hinted at by General Gates in his orders of the 26th; but that was a harsh and severe insinuation, as I have since heard his intended design was to take post on a rising ground, on the left of their camp—the 7th— with the detachment, thinking they would not have acted on the offensive, but stood to their works, and on that night our main body was to move, so as to be prepared to storm their lines by day break of the 8th; and it appears by accounts since that Gen Gates would have acted on the defensive, only for the advice of Brigadier General Arnold, who assured him from his knowledge of the troops a vigorous sally would inspire them with more courage than waiting behind their works for our attack, and also their knowledge of the woods would contribute to ensure the plan he proposed.

During the night we were employed in moving our cannon, baggage, etc., nearer to the river. It was done with silence, and fires were kept lighted to cause them not to suspect we had retired from our works where it was impossible for us to remain, as the German lines commanded them, and were then in possession of the enemy, who were bringing up cannon to bear on ours at day break. It may easily be supposed we had no thought for sleep, and some time before day we retreated nearer to the river. Our design of retreating to Ticonderoga then became public.

—BAXTER, *British Invasion from the North*, pp. 287-292.

XI. THE SURRENDER OF BURGOYNE

Abandoned by his would-be rescuers, cut off in the rear, decimated in numbers and desperately short of provisions, Burgoyne, unanimously supported by his ranking officers, decided to ask for terms. Gates first demanded an unconditional surrender. When Burgoyne rejected that, Gates, in a curi-

*ously craven or strangely conciliatory mood, then accepted the terms vir-
tually dictated by the defeated British general. Apparently fearing that the
small detachment under General Vaughan dispatched by Sir Henry Clinton
might reach Albany and try to effect a juncture with Burgoyne, Gates foolishly made extraordinary concessions.*

*By the terms of the Saratoga Convention of October 16, Burgoyne's
troops were permitted to march out of camp with the honors of war, their
arms "to be piled by word of command of their own officers." "A free passage" to Great Britain was to be granted to Burgoyne's army "on condition
of not serving again in North America during the present contest," and they
were to march to Boston by the most expeditious route and to be quartered
and provisioned in the vicinity of that port until transports came to convey
them home. Burgoyne's army was broadly interpreted to include seamen,
batteaumen, artificers and even camp followers, and special provision was
made for the Canadians, who were to be conducted to Lake George, and
bound by the same conditions as the British army. As Burgoyne put it, in his
letter to Germain of October 20, "I call it saving the army, because if sent
home, the State is thereby enabled to send forth the troops now destined for
her internal defence; if exchanged, they become a force to Sir William Howe,
as effectually as if any other junction had been made." For himself, however,
Burgoyne confessed he was "sunk in mind and body."*

*Two important truths Burgoyne had painfully discovered as a result of
his campaign: first, that "the panic of the rebel troops is confined, and of
short duration; the enthusiasm is extensive and permanent"; second, that no
reliance could be placed on the Loyalists. Subjected to an examination by
Parliament on his return from America, Burgoyne asked his hearers:*

> *Would the Tories have risen? Why did they not rise round Albany
> and below it, at the time they found Mr. Gates's army increasing? ... Why
> did they not rise in that populous and, as supposed, well affected district,
> the German Flats, at the time St. Leger was before Fort Stanwix? A
> critical insurrection from any one point of the compass within distance to
> create a diversion, would probably have secured the success of the cam-
> paign.*

*His demand for a court-martial denied, "Gentleman Johnny" was never
given another command.*

*In a letter to his wife written three days after the surrender Gates summed
up the lesson of Saratoga: "If old England is not by this lesson taught humility, then she is an obstinate old slut, bent upon her ruin."*

1. "The State of Our Army Was Truly Calamitous"

Letter of Thomas Anburey, British lieutenant.

Cambridge, Massachusetts, November 15, 1777

The state and situation of our army was truly calamitous!—worn down by
a series of incessant toils and stubborn actions; abandoned in our utmost distress by the Indians; weakened by the desertion, and disappointed as to the
efficacy of the Canadians and Provincials by their timidity; the regular troops
reduced, by the late heavy losses of many of our best men and distinguished

officers, to only 3500 effective men, of which number there were not quite 2000 British:—in this state of weakness, no possibility of retreat, our provisions nearly exhausted, and invested by an army of four times our number that almost encircled us, who would not attack us from a knowledge of our situation, and whose works could not be assaulted in any part. In this perilous situation the men lay continually upon their arms, the enemy incessantly cannonading us, and their rifle and cannon shot reaching every part of our camp.

True courage submits with great difficulty to despair, and in the midst of all those dangers and arduous trials, the valor and constancy of the British troops were astonishing: they still retained their spirits, in hopes that either the long-expected relief would arrive from New-York, which the army implicitly believed from an order that had been given out at our camp at Still-Water, stating that powerful armies were to act in co-operation with ours, or that the enemy would attack us, which was most fervently wished for, as it would have given us an opportunity of dying gallantly or extricating ourselves with honor.

After waiting the whole of the 13th day of October in anxious expectation of what it would produce, and to which time it had been resolved to endure all extremities in maintaining our ground against the enemy—no prospect of assistance appearing, and no rational ground of hope remaining, it was thought proper, in the evening, to take an exact account of the provisions left, which amounted to no more than three days short allowance.

In this state of distress, a council of war was called, to which all the Generals, Field-officers and commanding officers of corps were summoned, when it was unanimously agreed that in the present circumstances we could do no other than treat with the enemy.

—ANBUREY, *Travels through the Interior Parts of America*, I, 406-411.

2. BARONESS VON RIEDESEL DESCRIBES THE HORRORS OF THE BATTLE

Journal of General Riedesel's wife for the month of October 1777.

Toward evening [of October 9], we at last came to Saratoga, which was only half an hour's march from the place where we had spent the whole day. I was wet through and through by the frequent rains, and was obliged to remain in this condition the entire night, as I had no place whatever where I could change my linen. I, therefore, seated myself before a good fire, and undressed my children; after which, we laid ourselves down together upon some straw. I asked General Phillips, who came up to where we were, why we did not continue our retreat while there was yet time, as my husband had pledged himself to cover it and bring the army through.

"Poor woman," answered he, "I am amazed at you! completely wet through, have you still the courage to wish to go further in this weather! Would that you were only our commanding general! He halts because he is tired, and intends to spend the night here and give us a supper."

In this latter achievement, especially, General Burgoyne was very fond of indulging. He spent half the nights in singing and drinking, and amusing himself with the wife of a commissary, who was his mistress, and who, as well as he, loved champagne.

On the 10th, at seven o'clock in the morning, I drank some tea by way of refreshment; and we now hoped from one moment to another that at last we would again get under way. General Burgoyne, in order to cover our retreat, caused the beautiful houses and mills at Saratoga, belonging to General Schuyler, to be burned. An English officer brought some excellent broth, which he shared with me, as I was not able to refuse his urgent entreaties.

Thereupon we set out upon our march, but only as far as another place not far from where we had started. The greatest misery and the utmost disorder prevailed in the army. The commissaries had forgotten to distribute provisions among the troops. There were cattle enough, but not one had been killed. More than thirty officers came to me, who could endure hunger no longer. I had coffee and tea made for them, and divided among them all the provisions with which my carriage was constantly filled; for we had a cook who, although an arrant knave, was fruitful in all expedients, and often in the night crossed small rivers in order to steal from the country people sheep, poultry and pigs. He would then charge us a high price for them—a circumstance, however, that we only learned a long time afterward. . . .

The whole army clamored for a retreat, and my husband promised to make it possible, provided only that no time was lost. But General Burgoyne, to whom an order had been promised if he brought about a junction with the army of General Howe, could not determine upon this course, and lost every thing by his loitering.

About two o'clock in the afternoon, the firing of cannon and small arms was again heard, and all was alarm and confusion. My husband sent me a message telling me to betake myself forthwith into a house which was not far from there. I seated myself in the calash with my children, and had scarcely driven up to the house when I saw on the opposite side of the Hudson River five or six men with guns, which were aimed at us. Almost involuntarily I threw the children on the bottom of the calash and myself over them. At the same instant the churls fired, and shattered the arm of a poor English soldier behind us, who was already wounded, and was also on the point of retreating into the house.

Immediately after our arrival a frightful cannonade began, principally directed against the house in which we had sought shelter, probably because the enemy believed, from seeing so many people flocking around it, that all the generals made it their headquarters. Alas! it harbored none but wounded soldiers, or women! We were finally obliged to take refuge in a cellar, in which I laid myself down in a corner not far from the door. My children lay down on the earth with their heads upon my lap, and in this manner we passed the entire night. A horrible stench, the cries of the children, and yet more than all this, my own anguish, prevented me from closing my eyes. On the following morning the cannonade again began, but from a different side. I advised all to go out of the cellar for a little while, during which time I would have it cleaned, as otherwise we would all be sick. They followed my suggestion, and I at once set many hands to work, which was in the highest degree necessary; for the women and children, being afraid to venture forth, had soiled the whole cellar.

After they had all gone out and left me alone, I for the first time surveyed our place of refuge. It consisted of three beautiful cellars, splendidly arched. I proposed that the most dangerously wounded of the officers should be brought into one of them; that the women should remain in another; and that all the rest should stay in the third, which was nearest the entrance. I had just given the cellars a good sweeping, and had fumigated them by sprinkling vinegar on burning coals, and each one had found his place prepared for him—when a fresh and terrible cannonade threw us all once more into alarm. Many persons, who had no right to come in, threw themselves against the door. My children were already under the cellar steps, and we would all have been crushed, if God had not given me strength to place myself before the door, and with extended arms prevent all from coming in; otherwise every one of us would have been severely injured.

Eleven cannon balls went through the house, and we could plainly hear them rolling over our heads. One poor soldier, whose leg they were about to amputate, having been laid upon a table for this purpose, had the other leg taken off by another cannon ball, in the very middle of the operation. His comrades all ran off, and when they again came back they found him in one corner of the room, where he had rolled in his anguish, scarcely breathing. I was more dead than alive, though not so much on account of our own danger as for that which enveloped my husband, who, however, frequently sent to see how I was getting along, and to tell me that he was still safe. . . .

Our cook saw to our meals, but we were in want of water; and in order to quench thirst, I was often obliged to drink wine and give it, also, to the children. It was, moreover, the only thing that my husband could take, which fact so worked upon our faithful Rockel that he said to me one day, "I fear that the general drinks so much wine because he dreads falling into captivity, and is therefore weary of life." The continual danger in which my husband was encompassed was a constant source of anxiety to me. I was the only one of all the women whose husband had not been killed or wounded, and I often said to myself—especially since my husband was placed in such great danger day and night—"Shall I be the only fortunate one?" He never came into the tent at night, but lay outside by the watch fires. This alone was sufficient to have caused his death, as the nights were damp and cold.

As the great scarcity of water continued, we at last found a soldier's wife who had the courage to bring water from the river, for no one else would undertake it, as the enemy shot at the head of every man who approached the river. This woman, however, they never molested; and they told us afterward that they spared her on account of her sex.

I endeavored to divert my mind from my troubles by constantly busying myself with the wounded. I made them tea and coffee, and received in return a thousand benedictions. Often, also, I shared my noonday meal with them. One day a Canadian officer came into our cellar who could scarcely stand up. We at last got it out of him that he was almost dead with hunger. I considered myself very fortunate to have it in my power to offer him my mess. This gave him renewed strength, and gained for me his friendship. Afterward, upon our return to Canada, I learned to know his family. One of our greatest annoyances was the stench of the wounds when they began to suppurate. . . .

In this horrible situation we remained six days. Finally, they spoke of capitulating, as by temporizing for so long a time our retreat had been cut off. A cessation of hostilities took place, and my husband, who was thoroughly worn out, was able, for the first time in a long while, to lie down upon a bed. In order that his rest might not be in the least disturbed, I had a good bed made up for him in a little room; while I, with my children and both my maids, lay down in a little parlor close by. But about one o'clock in the night some one came and asked to speak to him. It was with the greatest reluctance that I found myself obliged to awaken him. I observed that the message did not please him, as he immediately sent the man back to headquarters and laid himself down again considerably out of humor.

Soon after this General Burgoyne requested the presence of all the generals and staff officers at a council of war, which was to be held early the next morning; in which he proposed to break the capitulation, already made with the enemy, in consequence of some false information just received. It was, however, finally decided that this was neither practicable nor advisable; and this was fortunate for us, as the Americans said to us afterwards that had the capitulation been broken we all would have been massacred; which they could have done the more easily as we were not over four or five thousand men strong, and had given them time to bring together more than twenty thousand. . . .

At last my husband sent to me a groom with a message that I should come to him with our children. I, therefore, again seated myself in my dear calash; and in the passage through the American camp I observed with great satisfaction that no one cast at us scornful glances. On the contrary, they all greeted me, even showing compassion on their countenances at seeing a mother with her little children in such a situation. I confess that I feared to come into the enemy's camp, as the thing was so entirely new to me.

When I approached the tents, a noble-looking man came toward me, took the children out of the wagon, embraced and kissed them, and then with tears in his eyes helped me also to alight. "You tremble," said he to me. "Fear nothing."

"No," replied I, "for you are so kind, and have been so tender toward my children, that it has inspired me with courage."

He then led me to the tent of General Gates, with whom I found Generals Burgoyne and Phillips, who were upon an extremely friendly footing with him.

Burgoyne said to me, "You may now dismiss all your apprehensions, for your sufferings are at an end."

I answered him that I should certainly be acting very wrongly to have any more anxiety when our chief had none, and especially when I saw him on such friendly footing with General Gates. All the generals remained to dine with General Gates.

The man who had received me so kindly came up and said to me, "It may be embarrassing to you to dine with all these gentlemen; come now with your children into my tent, where I will give you, it is true, a frugal meal, but one that will be accompanied by the best of wishes."

"You are certainly," answered I, "a husband and a father, since you show me so much kindness."

I then learned that he was the American General Schuyler. He entertained me with excellent smoked tongue, beefsteaks, potatoes, good butter and bread. Never have I eaten a better meal. I was content. I saw that all around me were so likewise; but that which rejoiced me more than every thing else was that my husband was out of all danger. As soon as we had finished dinner, he invited me to take up my residence at his house, which was situated in Albany, and told me that General Burgoyne would, also, be there. I sent and asked my husband what I should do. He sent me word to accept the invitation; and as it was two days' journey from where we were, and already five o'clock in the afternoon, he advised me to set out in advance, and to stay over night at a place distant about three hours' ride. General Schuyler was so obliging as to send with me a French officer, who was a very agreeable man and commanded those troops who composed the reconnoitering party of which I have before made mention. As soon as he had escorted me to the house where we were to remain, he went back. . . .

The day after this we arrived at Albany, where we had so often longed to be. But we came not, as we supposed we should, as victors! We were, nevertheless, received in the most friendly manner by the good General Schuyler, and by his wife and daughters, who showed us the most marked courtesy, as, also, General Burgoyne, although he had—without any necessity it was said—caused their magnificently built houses to be burned. But they treated us as people who knew how to forget their own losses in the misfortunes of others.

Even General Burgoyne was deeply moved at their magnanimity and said to General Schuyler, "Is it to *me*, who have done you so much injury, that you show so much kindness!"

"That is the fate of war," replied the brave man; "let us say no more about it."

We remained three days with them, and they acted as if they were very reluctant to let us go.

—RIEDESEL, *Letters and Journals*, pp. 125-137.

3. "Thus Ended All Our Hopes of Victory, Honor, Glory"

Journal of Lieutenant William Digby of the Shropshire Regiment.

[*October*] *17 A day famous in the annals of America.*

Gen. Burgoyne desired a meeting of all the officers early that morning, at which he entered into a detail of his manner of acting since he had the honour of commanding the army; but he was too full to speak; heaven only could tell his feelings at this time. He dwelled much on his orders to make the wished-for junction with General Clinton, and as to how his proceedings had turned out, we must (he said) be as good judges as himself. He then read over the Articles of Convention, and informed us the terms were even easier than we could have expected from our situation, and concluded with assuring us he never would have accepted any terms, had we provisions enough, or the least hopes of our extricating ourselves any other way.

About 10 o'clock we marched out, according to treaty, with drums beating and the honours of war, but the drums seemed to have lost their former inspiriting sounds, and though we beat the Grenadiers march, which not long before was so animating, yet then it seemed by its last feeble effort as if almost ashamed to be heard on such an occasion.

As to my own feelings, I cannot express them. Tears (though unmanly) forced their way, and if alone, I could have burst to give myself vent. I never shall forget the appearance of their troops on our marching past them; a dead silence universally reigned through their numerous columns, and even then they seemed struck with our situation and dare scarce lift up their eyes to view British troops in such a situation. I must say their decent behaviour during the time (to us so greatly fallen) meritted the utmost approbation and praise.

The meeting between Burgoyne and Gates was well worth seeing. He paid Burgoyne almost as much respect as if he was the conqueror; indeed, his noble air, tho prisoner, seemed to command attention and respect from every person. A party of light dragoons were ordered as his guard, rather to protect his person from insults than any other cause.

Thus ended all our hopes of victory, honour, glory, etc. Thus was Burgoyne's Army sacrificed to either the absurd opinions of a blundering ministerial power, the stupid inaction of a general [Howe], who, from his lethargic disposition, neglected every step he might have taken to assist their operations, or lastly, perhaps, his own misconduct in penetrating so far as to be unable to return, and tho I must own my partiality to him is great, yet if he or the army under his command are guilty, let them suffer to the utmost extent, and by an unlimited punishment in part blot out and erase, if possible, the crime charged to their account.

—BAXTER, *British Invasion from the North,* pp. 317-323.

CHAPTER FOURTEEN

Howe Invades Pennsylvania

ALL BRITISH *generals in America were hypnotized by the notion that some place other than where they happened to be located at the moment was the seedbed of loyalism and awaiting deliverance at the hands of the British armed forces. Disappointed in his expectations of the New York campaign, Sir William Howe now considered Pennsylvania to be a major objective of the war. To seize it would be to divide the colonies and to be in control of the leading metropolis of the continent, a center of wealth and culture and a notorious stronghold of loyalism and neutralism.*

Howe's plan for an attack on Philadelphia was approved by Germain as early as March 3, 1777. Howe then decided to invade it by sea rather than by land. The British commander was optimistic that this move would end the war. He was convinced that public opinion in Pennsylvania favored the British cause, that the capture of the province would be easy, and that by drawing Washington into Pennsylvania he would be materially aiding Burgoyne's advance, which was essential to final victory. In guessing Washington's probable moves he was not mistaken, for the American commander might have moved his entire army north, where he could probably have crushed Burgoyne much more quickly than Gates did, and then swung south to meet Howe. Instead, he weakened himself by sending substantial troops to Gates, and for this and other reasons was forced to yield Philadelphia, the main objective of Howe's expedition.

Howe had counted on a quick victory, but as usual his timetable proved his greatest enemy. He had not counted on Washington's keeping the main American army in Pennsylvania nor on the stubborn character of the resistance. In fact, at Brandywine and Germantown it was touch and go. Either side could have won. In both battles faulty intelligence lost the day for Washington. Nevertheless the defenses of the Delaware proved so formidable that it was not until the end of November that the Delaware as far north as Philadelphia was clear for British vessels, more than a month after Burgoyne surrendered his army at Saratoga.

Howe's strategy had failed. He did not destroy Washington's army, but in fact found a second formidable army in the North now arrayed against the British. He did not seize and occupy the interior of the state. He did not move quickly enough to rescue Burgoyne and salvage something from Britain's boldest effort of the war. Since winter campaigns were not fashionable the British bedded down in snug Philadelphia quarters for the season. With spring came word of the French entry into the war. Then it was decided to

606

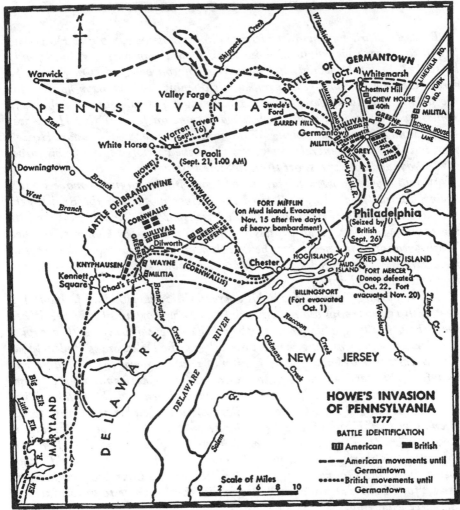

From The American Revolution
by John Richard Alden

Courtesy of Harper & Brothers

abandon Philadelphia and not risk dividing the British forces. Another elaborate campaign had failed, and its failure left thousands of disillusioned Tories to make their peace with a returning Patriot army.

The Pennsylvania campaign revealed, on the one hand, Washington's inadequacies as a battle commander and, on the other, his inspired qualities of courage, candor, and dedication to the cause in the face of overwhelming discouragement. While he was losing Philadelphia, Gates was conquering an entire British army. It was only natural that dissatisfaction with his leadership should arise. Whether the dissatisfaction was conspiratorial or spontaneous is of no consequence. What was important for final victory was Washington's ability to vanquish his enemies in Congress and in the army and to keep his hold upon the affections of his troops.

I. PHILADELPHIA IS THE OBJECTIVE

By early April 1777 word had spread in the Patriot camp that Howe had begun to embark his troops in New York aboard transports. Where would he strike? Strike he would, and soon, Washington believed. On April 3 he wrote General Parsons, "The campaign is opening, and we have no men for the field." Any idea that Howe was planning a frontal attack on the main American army was dissipated when word came on June 21 that Howe was withdrawing from Brunswick. Washington planned to fall upon Howe's rear, but the British general managed to elude the Patriots and move his forces to Amboy, and then transport them to Staten Island.

Would Howe now try to form a junction with Burgoyne or move swiftly against Philadelphia? Logic dictated the former move, but the British general disdained logic. His troops boarded transports at Sandy Hook and on the morning of July 31 an express from the President of Congress reached Washington with the news that the British fleet had appeared off the capes of Delaware Bay the preceding day. Washington quickly put his army in motion toward Philadelphia.

Howe began his operations in his characteristic but plodding fashion. His fleet with 15,000 troops did not embark from New York until July 23. When the British finally got under way, they began the campaign with a capital blunder. Instead of moving the fleet directly up the Delaware to Philadelphia, Howe was persuaded that the navigation of that river was too hazardous and its defenses impressive, and chose to go around Cape Charles and up the Chesapeake, a very long route indeed between New York and the Quaker City. Instead of landing at New Castle, 33 miles from Philadelphia, the British forces disembarked at Head of Elk, 55 miles from their objective. Washington moved down to meet them. His brilliant young aide, Alexander Hamilton, approved this strategy. "I would not only fight them, but I would attack them," he wrote Gouverneur Morris and Robert R. Livingston on September 1, "for I hold it an established maxim that there is three to one in favor of the party attacking."

1. "THIS REBELLION WILL BE CRUSHED IN THE PRESENT CAMPAIGN"

Ambrose Serle to the Earl of Dartmouth.

New York, May 20, 1777

... The army is not yet in motion, though preparing to move. I hear that the want of tents and some other military stores, daily expected, has retarded the commencement of the operations. Your Lordship will perceive by the inclosed papers that there are positive accounts among the Rebels of the Northern Army being at or near Ticonderoga.

The destruction of the late magazines, at this season of the year, has proved a very severe blow to the Rebels: and it has given them the more concern as they know their inability to replace most of the stores and military equipage.

By confirmed intelligence just received from the Rebel-Quarters, we find that Washington's whole force, which is all the force he has been able to collect by every means, does not amount to 7000 men, which are distributed at Bound-brook, Morris Town, Princeton, and all prepared to decamp at a minute's warning; that (as one of the parties learnt by an immediate communication from one of Washington's own family) he himself is frequently shut up-from all company, looks extremely dejected, and is sometimes surprized in tears; that the New England Provinces have sent him few or no men, of which he has made very particular complaints; that his reinforcements and succors from the southward have been very slow and very small; that the Rebels, among themselves, confess that they are unable to defend Philadelphia; that all the necessaries of life, and especially salt, are advanced to an extravagant price; and that the country in general is groaning under the tyranny and difficulties brought upon them, and longing for deliverance and peace. I have examined minutely into these general circumstances from several informants, and find them consistent with or rather corroborating each other.

This being the case, in addition to their numerous losses by sea, we may venture to think that, by the blessing of Providence, this ungrateful rebellion will be crushed in the course of the present campaign. But the Northern Army must descend—descend in force too, and perhaps with force of every kind. There needs no cruelty in that event, but there must be determination and vigor. Afterwards, in their proper place, there will be room for the exercise of compassion and mercy.

—*Stevens Facsimiles*, Doc. No. 2060.

2. The British Land at Head of Elk

Journal of Captain John Montresor of the Royal Engineers.

Sunday 25th. This day August 25th, 1777, landed at head of Elk. This morning at ½ past 9 the van of the fleet came to an anchor opposite Cecil Court House and Elk Ferry, and in half an hour after the flat bottomed boats made good their landing at the ferry house called Elk Ferry in the Province of Maryland, the rebels, consisting only of 4 companies militia under a Colonel Rumsey, fled without firing a shot. The troops hutted with rails and Indian corn stocks, no baggage or camp equipage admitted. Came on about 10 this night a heavy storm of rain, lightning and thunder. The wind being southerly brought up the fleet a short time after the landing. The army surprisingly healthy after so long a voyage and in such a climate—the return of the sick are about four to each battalion, very little fresh stock collected, and imperfect accounts of the situation of the enemy. Inhabitants in numbers and well dressed at Cecil Court House Point. Troops landed with sixty rounds per man.

26th. No motion—no inhabitants having deserted their houses and drove off their stock. Orders this evening for the troops to march to-morrow morning at 3 o'clock. A very heavy storm all this night of thunder, lightning and rain at north east. The shoalness of the Elk convinced the Rebels that our fleet would never navigate it, but through the great abilities of our naval officers it was happily effected as the bottom was muddy and the ships on it were cutting channels through it for each other. . . .

28th. The army moved between 3 and 4 this morning. The weather extremely fine which dried the roads, which would have been otherwise impassible; the medium 12-pounders proved to be most difficult to pass through the sloughs. Two houses got on fire after quitting the quarters but appeared to me to have been done on purpose. About 9 o'clock this morning our army arrived at the town of Elk consisting of about 40 well built brick and stone houses; our march hither about 7½ miles. Very few shots exchanged this day with the enemy. One thousand men under a Colonel Paterson and the Philadelphia Light Horse fled from this town on our approach, part to Gray's hill 2½ miles beyond the town, which the rebels likewise quitted; as we reached the summit we could observe them but not within cannon shot.
—MONTRESOR, "Journal," *N. Y. Hist. Soc. Coll.*, XIV, 442-443.

3. WASHINGTON ADVANCES TO MEET THE BRITISH

Captain Walter Stewart of the Continental Army to General Gates.
New Port, September 2, 1777

We arrived about two miles below this place, the day after the enemy had effected a landing for about four thousand men at a place called Charles Town; from which they the day after pushed for and took possession of Gray's Hill, at the distance of about seven miles in a strait line to Philadelphia; at this place contrary to our expectations they have since remained, as they have had orders at two different times to march at three in the morning; they will now however find it a difficult matter to advance as Genl. Washington has pushed down a light corps, consisting of about three thousand men mostly with rifles, together with the Malitia and Light Horse, to a post about a mile from them, called Iron Hill; here the country is, one would imagine, formed by Nature for defence, having a great quantity of woods, large morasses they must pass through, and many commanding hills, which the Malitia may take post upon.

Shortly after their landing we got a good many prisoners, generally twenty each day, but they are now grown vastly more cautious, and tis very hard to meet with any of them; their pickets are not farther distant from the main body than three hundred yards; indeed all their actions tend to make us imagine they are much afraid of us.

From the best accounts we can gather they consist of about 9000 men, in general very healthy; only 140 of the horses brought with them (as light horse) now exist, having lost 150 the day after they landed by turning them into a corn field, where they were so very voracious that they eat until they dropt dead in the field: this we have from eight or ten people, who were eye witnesses of the matter.

Our army are in amazing high spirits, and very healthy. Wishing earnestly for their approach we were drawn here in order to support the Malitia who are all pushed down between the enemy and us, but believe the General will soon have the greatest part of the army down on Iron Hill, as he has this morning ordered another detachment to join the Light Corps, and I imagine will still be stealing them on in this manner.

We are throwing up a few works at Wilmington, where Wayne is like a mad bear, it falling to his brigade; I believe he heartily wishes all engineers at the devil.

I do assure you, your successes to the northward add vastly to our spirits.
—Gates Papers, Box VII, No. 107.

II. BRANDYWINE

The British moved cautiously up both sides of the Elk. Washington had Brigadier General William Maxwell post his men on the upper waters of the Christina River, a tributary to the Delaware. The British began their forward move on September 2, when they forced back Maxwell's men. To meet a flanking move around his right and rear, Washington then withdrew his forces to Chad's Ford on the Brandywine. Brandywine Creek was a logical place to stop the enemy. Unless he was checked there, there were no obstacles in his way until he reached the Schuylkill. By the tenth the British army had been assembled at Kennett Square, just across Delaware's border in Pennsylvania.

Brandywine was an extraordinary repeat performance of the battle of Long Island. The British advanced their forces toward Chad's Ford on the morning of September 11 and tried to cross the creek under fire from Maxwell's men, but were forced back. Here they seemed to be reinforcing their position on the west bank, and both sides engaged in a furious artillery barrage. About 11 o'clock report came from Colonel Moses Hazen upstream that the British were moving to the forks of the creek to turn the American right flank. Then Sullivan reported to Washington that he had contrary intelligence "so that Colonel Hazen's information must be wrong." Washington, who had intended an offensive at Chad's Ford against what was in fact the weakest link in the British line, hesitated while precious time was lost. Early in the afternoon a farmer rode up to Washington's headquarters to tell the general that unless the army moved immediately it would be surrounded. This was confirmed by Colonel Bland. Sullivan was ordered to march at once to meet the column advancing on his rear. Washington waited impatiently, and finally had a guide take him to the scene of the firing. When he came up he saw that Sullivan had made a faulty disposition of his troops and that the whole line was beginning to break. Washington and Lafayette tried to rally the fleeing army, and among the whistling bullets one lodged in Lafayette's leg. The troops in withdrawal were horribly tangled up and it took until nearly midnight to get them into a semblance of order. The Americans suffered a thousand casualties, the British only half that number.

The defeat must be attributed to a lack of knowledge of the ground and inadequate reconnaissance. Sullivan was the chief scapegoat, but the truth is that Washington himself did not operate on the battlefield that day with his

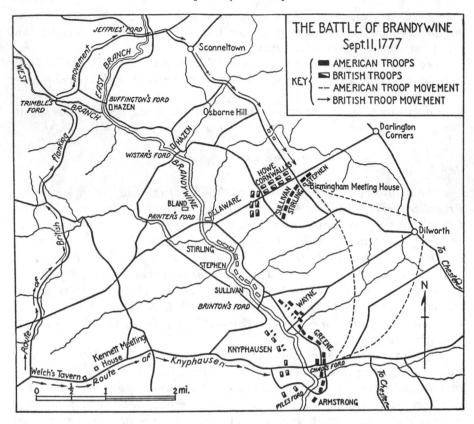

customary alertness and had signally failed to use his cavalry on the right flank. These mistakes opened the back door to Philadelphia.

1. Chad's Ford: "The Event Fell Little Short of the Project"

Journal of Major John André, Adjutant General in the British Army.

Sept. 10th and 11th. The army marched in two columns under Lord Cornwallis and General Knyphausen (Sir William Howe was with the former) and proceeded to the forks of Brandywine, crossed the ford there and by a circuit of about fifteen miles came upon the enemy's right flank, near Birmingham Meeting House. The latter took the straight road to Chad's Ford, opposite to which the Rebel army lay.

The design, it seemed, was that General Knyphausen, taking post at Chad's Ford, should begin early to cannonade the enemy on the opposite side, thereby to take up his attention and make him presume an attack was then intended with the whole army, whilst the other column should be performing the *détour*. Lord Cornwallis's wing being engaged was to be the signal for the troops under General Knyphausen to cross the ford when they were to push their advantage.

The event fell little short of the project. General Knyphausen posted himself early in the day on the heights opposite the Rebel army. This was distributed on all the most advantageous eminences overlooking the ford which lay beneath. On one of these hills they had thrown up a small breastwork with two guns, one a 12-pounder, and beneath this, flanking the ford and road, another battery of three guns and a howitzer. Felled trees obstructed the passage at other fords near this place. It was not without some opposition that General Knyphausen took up his ground, and whilst he was there a body of 2000 men crossed the river and came upon his right. They were driven back by one or two regiments.

On the left, Sir William Howe, drawing near Birmingham, found the Rebels posted on the heights to oppose him. Washington had drawn part of his army here about two hours before, on receiving the first intimation of General Howe's approach. At about 4 o'clock the attack began near the Meeting House. The Guards were formed upon the right, the British Grenadiers in the centre, and the Light Infantry and Chasseurs on the left. The Hessian Grenadiers supported the Guards and British Grenadiers, and the 4th Brigade supported the Light Infantry and the left of the Grenadiers. The 3d Brigade under General Grey was the reserve. The Guards met with very little resistance and penetrated to the very height overlooking the 4-gun battery of the Rebels at Chad's Ford, just as General Knyphausen had crossed. The Hessian Grenadiers were to their left and not so far advanced. The British Grenadiers divided after passing Birmingham Meeting House, the 1st Battalion inclining to the right and the 2d pushing about a mile beyond the village of Dilworth. The Light Infantry and Chasseurs inclined to the left, and by this means left an interval which was filled up by part of the 4th Brigade. The Light Infantry met with the chief resistance at a hill on which the Rebels had four pieces of cannon. At the end of the day the 2d Battalion Grenadiers received a very heavy fire; the 64th Regiment, which was near them, was engaged at the same time. The Rebels were driven back by the superior fire of the troops, but these were too much exhausted to be able to charge or pursue. The reserve moved centrically in the rear of the whole and inclined successively to the parts most engaged.

General Knyphausen, as was preconcerted, passed the ford upon hearing the other column engaged, and the troops under him pushed the enemy with equal success. Night and the fatigue the soldiers had undergone prevented any pursuit. It is remarkable that after reconnoitering after the action, the right of General Howe's camp was found close on General Knyphausen's left, and nearly in a line, and in forming the general camp next day scarce any alteration was made.

—ANDRÉ, *Journal*, pp. 45-47.

2. "It Was Fortunate That the Night Came On"

Journal of Colonel Timothy Pickering of Massachusetts.

September 11th.—This morning a cannonade took place, the enemy having advanced to the heights opposite to those occupied by us, on the other side of the ford. A hot skirmish took place between our light troops, under Maxwell, and a party of Hessians, in which the latter were chiefly killed and wounded, not thirty running away, it being judged by Maxwell that three hundred of them were killed and wounded. The enemy made no attempt to cross at this place. The cannonade was mutual; theirs did us no harm, save killing one man.

The enemy remaining paraded on the distant heights, and continuing the cannonade, induced me to think they did not intend to cross at Chad's Ford, but only to amuse us while their main army crossed at some other place. The event proved the conjecture right. The enemy's main body crossed the Brandywine six or eight miles above, on our right. The General had intelligence of this by some messengers; but it was contradicted by others; and, the information remaining a long time surprisingly uncertain, it was late before a disposition was made to receive the enemy on that quarter. The consequence was that the divisions first engaged, being too far distant to be supported by others, were repulsed; and this laid the foundation for a final defeat. Nevertheless, Weedon's brigade, which got up a little before night, fought bravely and checked the pursuit of the enemy, and gave more time for the others to retreat. This engagement on the right began about half after three P.M., or four, and lasted till night.

When the battle raged most on the right, and the Continental troops were all, save Wayne's division, drawn off to the right, the enemy opposite Chad's Ford began a most furious cannonade, which was as warmly returned from the park of artillery. But at length the enemy pushed over, and, after an obstinate engagement with our artillery and Wayne's division, the latter retreated.

The whole army this night retired to Chester. It was fortunate for us that the night came on, for under its cover the fatigued stragglers and some wounded made their escape.

—PICKERING, *Life of Timothy Pickering*, I, 154-156.

3. A PRINCETON BOY REPORTS, "OUR ARMY WAS SOMETHING BROKE"

Diary of Joseph Clark.

Sept. 11, [1777]. The cannonading began in the morning. At the upper ford the enemy sent a great part of their force about noon. Three divisions of our army were sent immediately to oppose them, viz: Sterling's, Sullivan's and Stephens'; but as there were no heights at this ford, on our side, to prevent their landing by cannon from batteries, we were obliged to oppose them after they had crossed; but as their number was larger than was expected, they stretched their line beyond ours and flanked our right wing shortly after the action began.

This occasioned the line to break, to prevent being surrounded, though the firing, while the action lasted, was the warmest, I believe, that has been in America since the war began; and, as our men on the left of the line were pretty well stationed, they swept off great numbers of the enemy before they retreated, and from the best accounts I could collect from the officers in the action, the enemy must have suffered very much from our people before they broke, though, indeed, our people suffered much in this action, and would have suffered more if Gen'l Green had not been detached to their assistance, by whose timely aid they made a safe retreat of the men, though we lost some pieces of artillery; he, however, got up too late to form in a proper line and give our party that was broken time to recover. Notwithstanding this repulse, which was the most severe upon the 3d Virginia Regiment, who, through mistake, was fired upon by our own men, our whole body got off with but an inconsiderable loss in men, though something considerable in artillery.

When the action began at the upper ford, the batteries at the middle ford opened upon each other with such fury as if the elements had been in convulsions; the valley was filled with smoke, and now I grew seriously anxious for the event. For an hour and a half this horrid sport continued, and about sunset I saw a column of the enemy advance to one of our batteries and take it. Under cover of their cannon they had crossed at the ford, and were advancing in a large body. What we lost at our batteries I have not yet heard. As all our militia were at the lower ford, where was no action, and Gen'l Green sent to reinforce at the upper ford, we had not a very large party to oppose the enemy at the middle ford. The body stationed across the valley drew off to the right, and formed farther back on an eminence, when an engagement began with musketry, and the enemy gave way; but, as night was spreading its dusky shade through the gloomy valley, and our army was something broke, it was necessary to leave the field of action and take care of the troops.

Accordingly, after sunset, the party at the middle ford drew off and marched down to Chester, where the whole army, by appointment, met. The sun was set when I left the hill from whence I saw the fate of the day. His Excellency I saw within 200 yards of the enemy, with but a small party about him, and they drawing off from their station, our army broke at the right, and night coming on, adding a gloom to our misfortunes, amidst the noise of cannon, the hurry of people, and wagons driving in confusion from the field, I came off with a heart full of distress. In painful anxiety I took with hasty step the gloomy path from the field, and travelled 15 miles to Chester, where I slept two hours upon a couple of chairs. . . .

—CLARK, "Diary," *N. J. Hist. Soc. Proc.*, VII, 96, 98-99.

4. AN ELDERLY FARMER WARNS WASHINGTON OF HIS PERIL

William Darlington to Thomas Wharton, Jr.

November 29, 1845

. . . General Washington's headquarters were at Benjamin Ring's tavern, about three quarters of a mile east of Chadd's ford. He was there, and there about, all the fore part of the day of the battle. When he ascertained that the main body of the enemy were at Birmingham Meeting House and engaged our troops, he was anxious to proceed thither by the shortest and speediest route. He found a resident of the neighborhood, named Joseph Brown, and asked him to go as a guide. Brown was an elderly man, and extremely loth to undertake that duty. He made many excuses, but the occasion was too urgent for ceremony. One of Washington's suite dismounted from a fine charger, and told Brown if he did not instantly get on his horse and conduct the General by the nearest and best route to the place of action, he would run him through on the spot.

Brown thereupon mounted and steered his course direct towards Birmingham Meeting House with all speed—the General and his attendants being close at his heels. He said the horse leapt all the fences without difficulty, and was followed in like manner by the others. The head of Gen. Washington's horse, he said, was constantly at the flank of the one on which he was mounted; and the General was continually repeating to him, *"Push along, old man—Push along, old man."* When they reached the road, about half a mile west of Dilworthstown, Brown said the bullets were flying so thick that he felt very uncomfortable; and as Washington now no longer required nor paid attention to his guide, the latter embraced the first opportunity to dismount and make his escape.

—DARLINGTON, "Letter," *Hist. Soc. of Penn. Bulletin,* I, 58-59.

5. WASHINGTON LAYS THE DEFEAT TO CONTRADICTORY INTELLIGENCE

George Washington to the President of Congress.

At Midnight, Chester, September 11, 1777

Sir: I am sorry to inform you, that in this day's engagement, we have been obliged to leave the enemy masters of the field.

Unfortunately the intelligence received of the enemy's advancing up the Brandywine, and crossing at a ford about six miles above us, was uncertain and contradictory, notwithstanding all my pains to get the best. This prevented my making a disposition, adequate to the force with which the Enemy attacked us on the right; in consequence of which the troops first engaged, were obliged to retire before they could be reinforced. In the midst of the attack on the right, that body of the Enemy which remained on the other side of Chad's Ford, crossed it, and attacked the division there under the command of General Wayne and the light troops under General Maxwell who, after a severe conflict, also retired. The Militia under the command of Major Genl. Armstrong, being posted at a ford, about two miles below Chad's, had no opportunity of engaging.

But though we fought under many disadvantages, and were from the causes, above mentioned obliged to retire, yet our loss of men is not, I am persuaded, very considerable, I believe much less than the enemy's. We have also lost about seven or eight pieces of cannon, according to the best information I can at present obtain. The baggage having been previously moved off, is all secure, saving the men's Blankets, which being at their backs, many of them doubtless are lost.

I have directed all the Troops to Assemble behind Chester, where they are now arranging for this Night. Notwithstanding the misfortune of the day, I am happy to find the troops in good spirits; and I hope another time we shall compensate for the losses now sustained.

The Marquis La Fayette was wounded in the leg, and Gen. Woodford in the hand. Divers other Officers were wounded and some Slain, but the number of either cannot now be ascertained.

—FITZPATRICK, ed., *Writings of Washington*, IX, 207-208.

6. GENERAL SULLIVAN, "WHOSE EVIL CONDUCT WAS FOREVER PRODUCTIVE OF MISFORTUNES"

Thomas Burke, member of the Congress from North Carolina, to General Sullivan.

York, Pennsylvania, October 12, 1777

I was present at the action of Brandiwine and saw and heard enough to convince me that the fortune of the day was injured by miscarriages where you commanded.

I understood you were several days posted with the command on the right wing, that you were cautioned by the Commander in Chief early in the day to be particularly attentive to the enemys' motions who he supposed would attempt to cross higher up the creek and attack your flank, that you were furnished with proper troops for reconnotring, and yet you were so ill informed of the enemy's motions that they came up at a time and by a rout which you did not expect. That you conveyed intelligence to the Commander in Chief which occasioned his countermanding the dispositions he had made for encountering them on the rout by which it afterwards appeared they were actually advancing. That when at length the mistake was discovered you brought up your own division by an unnecessary circuit of two miles, and in the greatest disorder, from which they never recovered, but fled from the fire of the enemy without resistance. That the miscarriages on that wing made it necessary to draw off a great part of the strength from the center which exposed General Wayne to the superiority of the enemy.

I heard officers on the field lamenting in the bitterest terms that they were cursed with such a commander and I overheard numbers during the retreat complain of you as an officer whose evil conduct was forever productive of misfortunes to the army.

From these facts I concluded that your duty as a general was not well performed. Otherwise the enemy's motions on the wing where you particularly commanded would not have been unknown to you during great part of the day of action, nor could they have advanced by an unknown and unexpected rout, for you ought to have made yourself well acquainted with the ground. Nor would you have brought up your troops by an unnecessary circuit and in disorder, which exposed them to be surprised and broken.

I also concluded that the troops under your command had no confidence in your conduct, and from the many accounts I had officially received of your miscarriages, I conceived, and am still possessed of an opinion, that you have not sufficient tallents for your rank and office, tho I believe you have strong dispositions to discharge your duty well.

I consider it as one essential part of my duty to attend to the appointments of the army, and where I perceive that any person so unqualified as I deem you to be has got into a command where incompetence may be productive of disasters and disgrace, it is my duty to endeavour at removing him. In discharge of this I gave to Congress all the information I was able, carefully distinguishing what I saw, what I heard, and from whom, as far as I was acquainted with persons. I urged your recall with all the force I could, and thought it, and still do think it, necessary for the public good because, in all your enterprises and in every part of your conduct, even as represented by yourself, you seem to be void of judgement and foresight in concerting, of deliberate vigor in executing, and of presence of mind under accidents and emergencies—and from these defects seem to me to arise your repeated ill success.

These seem to me to form the great essentials of a military character—nor do I think you the only officer in our army who is deficient in them. Nor were my endeavours to free the army from insufficient officers intended to be confined to you. I scarcely know your person, and was not conscious of any injury from you. For a particular reason I should have had great pleasure in justly forming a better opinion of you, but no reason can induce me to overlook the defects of officers on whom so much depends. Nor will any thing deter me from pursuing the measures suggested by my own judgement.

I have now related every thing which I acted with relation to you in Congress together with my motives. I have set down every intelligence, and the opinion I gave concerning you. What hills you struggled for, what fires you sustained, I neither saw or heard of. Your personal courage I meddled not with. I had no knowledge of it, and I was cautious to say nothing unjust or unnecessary. My objection to you is want of sufficient tallents, and I consider it as your misfortune, not fault. It is my duty, as far as I can, to prevent its being the misfortune of my country.

—HAMMOND, ed., *Letters and Papers of Sullivan*, I, 534-537.

III. THE FALL OF PHILADELPHIA

Washington was now in retreat toward Chester. Near White Horse Tavern, twenty miles from Philadelphia, he made a sally against the British, on September 16, but heavy rains which drenched his ammunition prevented a full-scale engagement. Washington withdrew across the Schuylkill, but dispatched Anthony Wayne to the neighborhood of Warren Tavern to be in a position to attack the enemy's rear guard and baggage train. Wayne took up a post near Paoli in secrecy, but his whereabouts were quickly discovered by the Tories. Shortly after midnight of September 21, Wayne's camp was surprised by a detachment under Major General Grey. Leaping forward with unloaded rifles, Grey's men used the bayonet at close quarters; the Patriot defenders drawn up by the light of the campfires were standing targets for the British. The Americans suffered several hundred wounded, and some seventy taken prisoner, the British a mere six or seven casualties. Known as the "Paoli Massacre," the incident led to Wayne's court-martial, from which he was exonerated with the highest honor.

Now free to move as he wished, Howe turned north and crossed the Schuylkill at Swede's Ford, driving a wedge between Washington and the capital city. Congress, heeding Alexander Hamilton's warning, fled to Lancaster, conferring upon Washington dictatorial powers. Washington encamped his army temporarily at Germantown, and on September 26 Cornwallis, with a detachment of British and Hessian grenadiers, entered Philadelphia with bands playing.

Philadelphia had fallen. Most military men were resigned to the event, although some Patriots were disheartened. Not so Franklin in Paris, who, when informed that Howe had taken Philadelphia, rejoined, "No, Philadelphia has captured Howe!"

1. A VIOLENT RAIN DRENCHES THE PATRIOT AMMUNITION

Colonel Henry Knox to his wife.

Pottsgrove, September 24, 1777

I wrote you on the 13th. The same day we crossed the Schuylkill, in order to try the issue of another appeal to *Him who directs all human events.* After some days' manoeuvring, we came in sight of the enemy, and drew up in order of battle, which the enemy declined; but a most violent rain coming on obliged us to change our position, in the course of which nearly all the musket cartridges of the army that had been delivered to the men were damaged, consisting of about 400,000. This was a most terrible stroke to us, and owing entirely to the badness of the cartouch-boxes which had been provided for the army.

This unfortunate event obliged us to retire, in order to get supplied with so essential an article as cartridges, after which we forded the Schuylkill, in order to be opposite to the enemy; accordingly we took post at a place called Flatland Ford.

A defensive war is the most difficult to guard against, because one is always obliged to attend to the feints of the enemy. To defend an extensive river when it is unfordable is almost impossible; but when fordable in every part, it becomes impracticable. On the afternoon of the 21st the enemy made a most rapid march of ten or twelve miles to our right: this obliged us to follow them. They kindled large fires, and in the next night marched as rapidly back and crossed at a place where we had few guards, and pushed towards Philadelphia, and will this morning enter the city without opposition. We fought one battle for it, and it was no deficiency in bravery that lost us the day. Philadelphia, it seems, has been their favorite object. Their shipping has not joined them there. They will first have to raise the *chevaux de frise* in the Delaware, and defeat the naval force there, which is considerable.

The troops in this excursion of ten days without baggage suffered excessive hardships—without tents in the rain, several marches of all night, and often without sufficient provision. This they endured with the perseverance and patience of good soldiers. Generals Smallwood, Wayne, McDougall, and a considerable body of militia, will join us to-day and to-morrow. This day we shall move towards Philadelphia, in order to try the fortune of another battle, in which we devoutly hope the blessing of Heaven. I consider the loss of Philadelphia as only temporary—to be recovered when expedient. It is no more than the loss of Boston, nor, in my opinion, half so much, when the present trade of the latter be considered. It is situated on a point of land formed by the rivers Delaware and Schuylkill, so that it would [have] been highly improper to have thrown ourselves into it.

If the enemy do not get their shipping up soon, and go into Philadelphia, they will be in a very ineligible situation. I do not in the present circumstances consider Philadelphia of so much consequence as the loss of reputation to our arms; but I trust in God we shall soon make up that matter. Billy is well, and undergoes the hardships of the campaign surprisingly well, and they are neither few nor small.

—DRAKE, *Henry Knox,* pp. 50-51.

2. THE HARDSHIPS OF THE RETREAT ACROSS THE SCHUYLKILL

Captain Enoch Anderson of Delaware to his nephew.

May 27, 1819

[After the Battle of Brandywine] we marched from Chester to the heights of Darby, seven miles from old Chester, and here our dispersed army made a gathering to collect its forces. Our army then marched on towards Philadelphia—came within three miles of the city—turned to the left (keeping on the west bank of the River Schuylkill)—and with a veering to the left and some miles from the river we encamped at night, perhaps twenty miles from the battleground. Our loss was greater than that of the British, though the loss in our regiment was small, considering the heavy firing we had come through. It was supposed this was due to the British having shot too high.

I was this night ordered on duty here with one hundred and fifty men—mostly of the Maryland line—with three captains, and the suitable number of subalterns. I, being the eldest captain, had the command. . . .

After dark we began our march and by daybreak we reached Darby [Creek] and a little after sunrise came to old Chester. Here I planted my own sentinels, separate from the Germans. They also did the same, separate from mine. Soon after this was done, the British drums beat about a mile west from us. We were certainly in a dangerous situation—on the bank of the Delaware, the enemy close by, and we were in the land of the Tories. The British were on the march, bearing northwardly. We marched on all this day, keeping near the British army. When they marched, we marched; when they stopped, we stopped. Our guide was the beating of the drums. Night came on, there was no house we dare go into; we had no tents. I had no blanket even and must make no fire. Some had blankets however. The night was very cold. I kept myself tolerably comfortable by walking about, but was very sleepy and could not sleep for the cold.

The British drums beat by daybreak and we were off again. A little before sundown we saw the British in a body coming through a meadow ahead of us. At about twelve o'clock at night we made a short cut to the left, but the next day by sunrise we were again near the British Army. We had heavy rains, were exposed to them all, were wet to the skin but we walked, nay marched, ourselves dry! We continued in this way for several days longer— near the British through the day—in the leaves and bushes at night.

On the seventh day from the commencement of the march of the detachment, I learned that our army had crossed over to the east bank of the Schuylkill. I inquired for the best ford on the river in that neighborhood as the late rains had raised the waters. We entered the river in platoons—the river was about two hundred yards wide. I now gave orders to link arm in arm, to keep close and in a compact form, and to go slow, keeping their ranks. We moved on—we found the river breast deep—it was now night as we gained the eastern shore all wet, but in safety. We got some fire from a neighboring cottage— made a fire in the woods—turned our feet to the fire—slept comfortably and found our clothes on our backs all dry in the morning.

This day—I think about the twenty-sixth of September, 1777—brought us safe to headquarters, being nine days out, during which time we never had our clothes off, lodged in no house, in a manner on half allowance of provisions and had to beg on the road.

—ANDERSON, "Personal Recollections," *Hist. Soc. of Del. Papers,* XVI, 38-40.

3. PAOLI: "WE STABBED GREAT NUMBERS"

Journal of Major John André.

[*Sept.*] *20th.* Intelligence having been received of the situation of General Wayne and his design of attacking our rear, a plan was concerted for surprising him, and the execution entrusted to Major General Grey. The troops for this service were the 40th and 55th Regiments, under Colonel Musgrave, and the 2d Battalion Light Infantry, the 42d and 44th Regiments under General Grey. General Grey's detachment marched at 10 o'clock at night, that under Colonel Musgrave at 11.

No soldier of either was suffered to load; those who could not draw their pieces took out the flints. We knew nearly the spot where the Rebel corps lay, but nothing of the disposition of their camp. It was represented to the men that firing discovered us to the enemy, hid them from us, killed our friends and produced a confusion favorable to the escape of the Rebels and perhaps productive of disgrace to ourselves. On the other hand, by not firing we knew the foe to be wherever fire appeared and a charge ensured his destruction; that amongst the enemy those in the rear would direct their fire against whoever fired in front, and they would destroy each other.

General Grey's detachment marched by the road leading to White Horse, and took every inhabitant with them as they passed along. About three miles from camp they turned to the left and proceeded to the Admiral Warren, where, having forced intelligence from a blacksmith, they came in upon the out sentries, piquet and camp of the Rebels. The sentries fired and ran off to the number of four at different intervals. The piquet was surprised and most of them killed in endeavoring to retreat. On approaching the right of the camp we perceived the line of fires, and the Light Infantry being ordered to form to the front, rushed along the line putting to the bayonet all they came up with, and overtaking the main herd of the fugitives, stabbed great numbers and pressed on their rear till it was thought prudent to order them to desist.

Near 200 must have been killed, and a great number wounded. Seventy-one prisoners were brought off; forty of them badly wounded were left at different houses on the road. A major, a captain and two lieutenants were amongst the prisoners. We lost Captain Wolfe killed and one or two private men; four or five were wounded, one an officer, Lieut. Hunter of the 52d Light Company.

It was about 1 o'clock in the morning when the attack was made, and the Rebels were then assembling to move towards us, with the design of attacking our baggage.

—André, *Journal*, pp. 49-50.

4. The "Paoli Massacre": "A Scene of Butchery"

Major Samuel Hay of the Continental Army to Colonel William Irvine.
                              Camp at Trappe, September 29, 1777

Since I had the pleasure of seeing you, the division under the command of General Wayne has been surprised by the enemy, with considerable loss. We were ordered by his Excellency to march from the Yellow Springs down to where the enemy lay, near the Admiral Warren, there to annoy their rear. We marched early on the 17th instant, and got below the Paoli that night. On the next day fixed on a place for our camp.

We lay the 18th and 19th undisturbed, but, on the 20th, at 12 o'clock at night, the enemy marched out, and so unguarded was our camp that they were amongst us before we either formed in any manner for our safety, or attempted to retreat, notwithstanding the General had full intelligence of their designs two hours before they came out.

I will inform you in a few words of what happened. The annals of the age cannot produce such a scene of butchery. All was confusion. The enemy amongst us, and your regiment the most exposed, as the enemy came on the right wing. The 1st Regiment (which always takes the right) was taken off and posted in a strip of woods, stood only one fire and retreated. Then we were next the enemy, and, as we were amongst our fires, they had great advantage of us. I need not go on to give the particulars, but the enemy rushed on with fixed bayonets and made the use of them they intended. So you may figure to yourself what followed.

The party lost 300 privates in killed, wounded and missing, besides commissioned and non-commissioned officers. Our loss is Col. Grier, Captain Wilson and Lieutenant Irvine wounded (but none of them dangerously) and

61 non-commissioned and privates killed and wounded, which was just half the men we had on the ground fit for duty.

The 22d, I went to the ground to see the wounded. The scene was shocking—the poor men groaning under their wounds, which were all by stabs of bayonets and cuts of Light-Horsemen's swords. Col. Grier is wounded in the side by a bayonet, superficially slanting to the breast bone. Captain Wilson's stabbed in the side, but not dangerous, and it did not take the guts or belly. He got also a bad stroke on the head with the cock nail of the locks of a musket. Andrew Irvine was ran through the fleshy part of the thigh with a bayonet. They are all lying near David Jones' tavern. I left Captain McDowell with them to dress and take care of them, and they all are in a fair way of recovery. Major La Mar, of the 4th Regiment, was killed, and some other inferior officers. The enemy lost Captain Wolf, killed, and four or five Light-Horsemen, and about 20 privates, besides a number wounded.

—HAY, "Letter," *Pennsylvania Archives*, 2nd Series, I, 598-599.

5. "A Sorrowful Day in Philadelphia"

Journal of Mrs. Henry Drinker of Philadelphia.

September 25, 1777.—This has been a day of great confusion in the city. Enoch Story was the first to inform us that the English were within 4 or 5 miles of us. We have since heard they were by John Dickinson's place and are expected to-night. Most of our warm people have gone off. G. Napper brings word that he spoke with Galloway, who told him that the inhabitants must take care of the city tonight, and they would be in in the morning. As it rained, they fixed their camp within 2 miles of the city. Numbers met at the State House since 8 o'clock to form themselves into different companies to watch the city.

Sept. 26.—Well! here are the English in earnest! About 2 or 300 came in through Second Street without opposition. Cornwallis came with the troops. Gen. Howe has not arrived.

Sept. 27.—About 9 o'clock this morning the *Province* and *Delaware* frigates, with several gondollas, came up the river with a design to fire on the city, but they were attacked by a battery which the English had erected at the lower end of the city. The engagement lasted about half an hour. Many shots were exchanged; one house struck, but not much damaged, and no body that I have heard, hurt on shore. The cook on the *Delaware*, 'tis said, had his head shot off, and a man wounded. She ran aground, and by some means took fire, which occasioned her to strike her colors. The English boarded her and the others drew off. Admiral Alexander and his men were taken prisoners. Part of this scene we witnessed from the little window in our loft.

Sept. 29.—Some officers are going about this day numbering the houses with chalk on the doors. A number of the citizens taken up and imprisoned, among them are John Hall, Jacob Bright, Tom Leech, Jacob Douché and William Moulder.

Oct. 1.—Several fire-rafts which were sent down the river in order to annoy the fleet, ran ashore and were burnt.

Oct. 4.—Before I arose this morning I heard cannon firing; understood from inquiry that a part of Washington's army had attacked the English picket guards near Chestnut Hill. This has been a sorrowful day in Philadelphia, and much more so at Germantown and thereabouts. It was reported in the forenoon that 1000 of the English were slain, but Chalkley James told us that he had been as far as B. Chew's place and could not learn of more than 30 of the English being killed, though a great number were wounded and brought to the city. He counted 18 of the Americans lying dead in the lane from the road to Chew's house, and the house is very much damaged as a few of the English troops had taken shelter there and were fired upon from the road. The last accounts towards evening was that the English were pursuing Washington's troops, who were numerous, and that they were flying before them. The Americans are divided into three divisions, one over Schuykill, another near Germantown, and the third I know not where, so that the army with us are chiefly called off, and a double guard this night is thought necessary. Washington is said to be wounded in the thigh.

Oct. 6.—The heaviest firing I think I ever heard was this evening for upwards of two hours; supposed to be the English troops engaged with Mud Island battery. An officer called this afternoon to ask if we could take in a sick or wounded captain, but I put him off by saying that as my husband was from me, I should be pleased if he could obtain some other place. Two of the Presbyterian meeting-houses are made hospitals of for the wounded soldiers, of which there are great numbers.

—DRINKER, "Journal," *Penn. Mag. of Hist. and Biog.*, XIII, 298-299.

IV. GERMANTOWN

Early in October Washington received intelligence that a British detachment was proceeding to Billingsport, New Jersey, on the Delaware River to aid Britain's navy in the attempt to open up that waterway. Howe's main army was encamped at or near Germantown. Washington's officers unanimously favored attacking Howe's camp.

Washington planned the Germantown battle after the model of Cannae, the classic ancient victory of Scipio Africanus over Hannibal. It was to be a great pincers movement of four converging forces. The main British force was to be smashed by Greene and Sullivan, while Armstrong and Smallwood were to close in on its right and left wings and crumble the whole line on itself. And it was to be a surprise on a grand scale.

As so often, well-laid plans miscarried. Despite the early-morning fog the British pickets were not entirely surprised and were soon reinforced by light infantry. Washington's right had begun the engagement, but the left was curiously silent. Sullivan's men pushed forward through the heavy fog as the British gave way. At one point the British held out, and that was at the Chew House, where Washington yielded to Henry Knox's counsel that the quasi-fortress must be reduced instead of by-passing it. Here precious time was lost.

Still Howe's defeat seemed inevitable. As George Weedon later put it, "the great cause was ... in one quarter of an hour of being settled." Suddenly, confused firing broke out between Adam Stephen's and Anthony

*Wayne's men. Panic struck the right wing as rumors spread that the enemy
was in the rear. Turning tail, the men jammed the roads and fields in a shameful retreat. Had Greene come up in time, the story might have been different,
but he had encountered unexpected resistance.*

*Again there was a scapegoat. This time Stephen was charged with being
drunk and with giving the order to retreat. Convicted of "unofficerlike behavior" and drunkenness, he was dismissed from the army. Again, the American casualties far exceeded the British, 700 to 534, with 400 taken prisoner.
But the strange mixed-up battle and unaccountable defeat left military morale
unimpaired. The news of Saratoga had provided a needed elixir. As Washington put it in his dispatch to Congress, "the day was unfortunate rather
than injurious."*

*For this confusing battle we are indebted to various chroniclers: to Sir
Martin Hunter, then a young lieutenant in the 52nd Foot, many years later to
hold the rank of general in the British army; to Timothy Pickering, an able
military figure from New England who had served as adjutant general, later
as quartermaster general, and, as Secretary of State under John Adams, was
to be the stormy petrel of that administration; and to John Armstrong, an aide
of General Gates, later to gain dubious fame as author of the first of the "New-
burg Addresses."*

1. "The First Time We Retreated from the Americans"

Diary of Lieutenant Sir Martin Hunter.

General Wayne commanded the advance, and fully expected to be re-
venged for the surprise we had given him. When the first shots were fired at
our pickets, so much had we all Wayne's affair in remembrance that the
battalion was out and under arms in a minute. At this time the day had just
broke; but it was a very foggy morning and so dark we could not see a hundred yards before us. Just as the battalion had formed, the pickets came in
and said the enemy were advancing in force.

They had hardly joined the battalion, when we heard a loud cry of
"Have at the bloodhounds! Revenge Wayne's affair!" and they immediately
fired a volley. We gave them one in return, cheered, and charged. As it was
near the end of the campaign, it was very weak; it did not consist of more
than three hundred men, and we had no support nearer than Germantown,
a mile in our rear. On our charging, they gave way on all sides, but again
and again renewed the attack with fresh troops and greater force. We
charged them twice, till the battalion was so reduced by killed and wounded
that the bugle was sounded to retreat; indeed had we not retreated at the very
time we did, we should all have been taken or killed, as two columns of the
enemy had nearly got round our flank. But this was the first time we had
retreated from the Americans, and it was with great difficulty we could get
our men to obey our orders.

The enemy were kept so long in check that the two brigades had advanced
to the entrance of Biggenstown when they met our battalion retreating. By
this time General Howe had come up, and seeing the battalion retreating, all
broken, he got into a passion and exclaimed: "For shame, Light Infantry!

I never saw you retreat before. Form! form! it's only a scouting party." However, he was soon convinced it was more than a scouting party, as the heads of the enemy's columns soon appeared. One coming through Biggenstown, with three pieces of cannon in their front, immediately fired with grape at the crowd that was standing with General Howe under a large chestnut-tree. I think I never saw people enjoy a discharge of grape before; but we really all felt pleased to see the enemy make such an appearance, and to hear the grape rattle about the commander-in-chief's ears, after he had accused the battalion of having run away from a scouting party. He rode off immediately, full speed, and we joined the two brigades that were now formed a little way in our rear; but it was not possible for them to make any stand against Washington's whole army, and they all retreated to Germantown, except Colonel Musgrave, who, with the 40th Regiment, nobly defended Howe's house till we were reinforced from Philadelphia.

—HUNTER, "Journal," *Historical Magazine*, IV, 346-347.

2. "The Fog Blinded the Enemy as Well as Ourselves"

Journal of Colonel Timothy Pickering.

October 3d [*1777*].—The troops were got ready for marching, it being intended to make an attack upon the enemy the next morning. In the evening, about eight o'clock, the troops were on the march, in the following disposition: General Sullivan, commanding the right wing, was to move down, with his and Wayne's divisions, on the direct road to Germantown, preceded by Conway's brigade, which was to take off the enemy's picket, file off to the right, and fall upon the enemy's left flank and rear, while Sullivan's and Wayne's divisions attacked them in front. Maxwell's and the North Carolina brigades were to form a second line in rear of Sullivan and Wayne. General Greene, with the left wing, was to move down the North Wales road to attack the enemy's right, the front line of this wing being composed of Greene's and McDougall's divisions, and the second line, of Stephen's; while Smallwood, with his Maryland, and Forman, with his Jersey militia, were to attack them on their right flank and rear. At the same time General Armstrong, with his division of Pennsylvania militia, was to move down the old Egypt or Schuylkill road, and take off a Hessian picket posted there, and attack the enemy's left wing and rear. The attack was to begin upon every quarter at five in the morning.

This disposition appears to have been well made; but to execute such a plan requires great exactness in the officers conducting the columns, as well as punctuality in commencing the march, to bring the whole to the point of action at once; and for this end it is absolutely necessary that the length and quality of the roads be perfectly ascertained, the time it will take to march them accurately calculated, and guides chosen who are perfectly acquainted with the roads. It is also necessary to assign proper halting-places, if either column would arrive before the appointed hour. All these points, I believe, were attended to in the present case; but yet I understood that the guide of the left wing mistook the way, so that, although the right wing halted a considerable time, yet it attacked first, though later than was intended; that halt being occasioned by information from a prisoner that half a battalion of the enemy's light infantry had the preceding evening advanced on the same road a considerable way beyond their picket. It was necessary, therefore, to make a disposition to secure that party of light infantry, that their opposition might not frustrate the principal design. Such a disposition was in fact made; but the enemy had retired about midnight to their camp.

General Conway's brigade formed the advanced guard, and in the morning, October 4th, attacked and drove the enemy's picket at Beggarstown (which is the upper end of Germantown). The rest of the right wing followed to support Conway. In a little time the whole got engaged, save the North Carolina brigade, which was not brought on to the attack at all. The other brigades drove the enemy before them a mile or two to the very centre of Germantown. All this time we could not hear of the left wing's being engaged, for the smoke and fog prevented our seeing them, and our own fire drowned theirs. (General Washington went with the right wing, attended by his aides-de-camp and myself.) But the left wing had engaged, and both wings met almost in the same point, which was at Mr. Chew's house, into which the enemy had thrown a party (we since find them to have been six companies, with a colonel to command them) that annoyed us prodigiously and absolutely stopped our pursuit—not necessarily, but we mistook our true interest; we ought to have pushed our advantage, leaving a party to watch the enemy in that house. But our stop here gave the enemy time to recollect themselves and get reënforced, and eventually to oblige us to retreat; for this period was all suspense, and the brigades not well collected and formed in the mean time. Indeed, this would have been, perhaps, impracticable, for the troops were greatly broken and scattered, great numbers having left their corps to help off the wounded, others being broken by other means, or by carelessness; for officers and men got much separated from each other, neither (in numerous instances) knowing where to find their own.

This house of Chew's was a strong stone building and exceedingly commodious, having windows on every side, so that you could not approach it without being exposed to a severe fire; which, in fact, was well directed and killed and wounded a great many of our officers and men. Several of our pieces, six-pounders, were brought up within musket-shot of it, and fired round balls at it, but in vain: the enemy, I imagine, were very little hurt; they still kept possession. It was proposed (for our advanced brigades had driven the enemy some way beyond it) to send a flag to summon the enemy posted there to surrender, it being urged as dangerous to leave them in our rear. A proposal was made to leave a party to watch them, and for the rest of the army to push on. But a flag was sent, Lieutenant-Colonel Smith, Deputy Adjutant-General, offering himself to carry it. I did not expect to see him return alive. I imagined they would pay no respect to the flag, they being well posted, and the battle far enough from being decided. The event justified my apprehensions: in a few minutes Mr. Smith was brought back with his leg broken and shattered by a musket-ball fired from the house.

During this time there was a cessation of firing; but soon the enemy advanced, and our troops gave way on all sides and retired with precipitation.

This retreat surprised every body (all supposing victory was nearly secured in our favor); but I think the facts before mentioned will tolerably well account for that event. Another circumstance also contributed to it: the foggy, still morning (the air moving very little, but what there was bringing the smoke and fog in our faces) and the body of smoke from the firing absolutely prevented our seeing the enemy till they had advanced close upon us. This also prevented the two wings, and even the different brigades of the same wing, from seeing each other and coöperating in the best manner; nay, I am persuaded they sometimes fired on each other, particularly at Chew's house, where the left wing supposed the cannon-balls fired by the right at the house came from the enemy. In a word, our disaster was imputed chiefly to the fog and the smoke, which, from the stillness of the air, remained a long time, hanging low and undissipated. But, on the other hand, it must be remembered that the fog blinded the enemy as well as ourselves, though it certainly injured us most.

—PICKERING, *Life of Timothy Pickering*, I, 166-170.

3. "A Glorious Victory Was Shamefully Lost"

General John Armstrong to General Gates.

Camp, October 9, 1777

Three days ago I wrote you at greater length than at present I can do, but find thro' hurry in the night I have sent your letter to some other gentleman. On the fourth inst General Washington attacked the enemy, marching his troops by various routes about fifteen miles the preceding night. The British troops were encamped chiefly at German Town, the foreigners principally betwixt the Falls of Scuilkill and John Vandurings mill. We could not take off (as was designed) but beat in the enemies pickquets, so that the surprize was not total but partial.

At the head of German Town the Continental troops attacked with vigour, and drove the British who frequently rallied and were drove again and again about the space of two miles, when some unhappy spirit of information seized our troops almost universally whereby they began to retreat and fled in wild disorder unknown to the General—that is, without his orders and beyond his power to prevent. So that a victory, a glorious victory fought for and eight tenths won, was shamefully but mysteriously lost, for to this moment no one man can or at least will give any good reason for the flight. The conjectures are these: The morning was foggy and so far unfavourable. It's said ours took the manuvres of part of our own people for large reinforcements of the enemy and thereby took fright at themselves or at one another. Some unhappy officer is said to have called out: "We are surrounded, we are surrounded!"

The enemy also in their flight—I mean part of them—took into a church, and a larger body into Mr Chews Germantown house where on our part our ill judged delay was made and the troops impeded in their warm pursuit. There a flag was sent in, insulted and the bearer wounded, where also a number of our people fell by the wall pieces and musquetry from the house which proved too strong for the metal of our field pieces. . . .

My destiny was against the foreigners, rather to divert than with the militia fight their superior body; however, we attempted both, until the General, seeing his men retreat, sent for me with the division. [I] follered a slow cannonade several miles but found him not, fell in with the rear of the enemy, still supposing them a vanquished party and that we had victory tho' the firing was then countered. We gave them a brush, but their artillery, so well directed, soon obliged us to file off, near two hours after our troops had left the field. I lost but thirty-nine wounded.

On the other hand every intelligence from town assures us that the Continental troops in the morning gave the enemy a severe drubing: Genl. Agnew killed, Grant and Erskin wounded, with some colonels in the hospital and some churches crowded with their wounded, the triumphing Tories again shook at the center, the drooping spirits of the Whigs a little relieved—thus God supports our otherwise sinking spirits which were also animated by your northern success.

—Gates Papers, N.Y. Hist. Soc., Box VIII, No. 51.

4. "We Had Gained a Victory Had We Known It"

T. Will Heth, a Continental officer, to Colonel John Lamb.

Camp Parcaoman, October 12, 1777

Before this reaches you, the news of our late action at German Town, no doubt will have come to hand. It was a grand enterprize, an inimitable plan, which nothing but its God-like author could equal. Had the execution of it been equal to its formation, it must have been attended with the most happy success. The following are the outlines of the orders, and the assault, which had nearly completed the total ruin of the British army. In fact, we had gained a victory, had we known it.

On Friday evening the 3d inst. the whole army marched from their encampment (about 11 miles from the enemys), disposed of in such a manner as to march by several ranks, so as to arrive at the enemys picquets by 2 o'c[lock] —there wait till the hour of 3, and then to advance with charged bayonets upon their front, flank and rear, but from short marches and frequent halts it was near 6 before the first volley of small arms were heard, when Genls. Green and Stephen's divisions, who were to oppose the enemys right, were then, from some mismanagement, only forming at more than a mile's distance. However our troops who made the attack were successful. They drove the enemy from field to field, and through part of German Town.

In the mean time [ou]r wing, by another piece of bad conduct, attempted to march in line of battle, till that order was found impracticable, which from the great number of post and rail fences, thickets and in short [ev]ery thing that could obstruct our march, threw us frequently into the greatest disorder, and as the heavy fire before us urged us on to a dog trot, we were nearly exhausted before we came to the first field of action, when unfortunately a strong stone house, in which the enemy had taken post, drew the attention of ten times the number that would have been sufficient to have kept them snug, and from which we received considerable damage. And after we had brought some artillery to play upon opposite parts of the house, each party took [the] other for the enemy. About this time an opinion prevailed among some general officers that the house was occupied by our own men, when part of our troops were accordingly ordered off. The heavy smoke, added to a thick fog, was of vast injury to us. It undoubtedly increased the fear of some to fancy themselves flanked and surrounded, wh[ich] like an electrical shock seized some thousands, who fled in confusion, without the appearance of an enemy.

What makes this inglorious retreat more grating is that we now know the enemy had orders to retreat and rendevouz at Chester, and that upwards of 2000 Hessians had actually crossed the Schuylkill for that purpose; that the Torys were in the utmost distress and moveing out of the city; that our friends confined in the New-Gaol made it ring with shouts of joy; that we passed, in pursuing them, upwards of twenty pieces of cannon, their tents standing filled with that choicest baggage. In fine, everything was as we could wish, when the above flight took place.

Tho we gave away a complete victory, we have learned this valuable truth: [that we are able] to beat them by vigorous exertion, and that we are far superior [in] point of swiftness. We are in high spirits. Every action [gives] our troops fresh vigor and a greater opinion of their own strength. Another bout or two must make their [the British] situation very disagreeable.

—Lamb Papers, N.Y. Hist. Soc., Box I, No. 217.

V. THE STRUGGLE FOR CONTROL OF THE DELAWARE

Howe's obvious move after Germantown was to reduce the American forts on the Delaware in order to clear his supply route to Philadelphia. These defenses proved formidable. There were two forts, Mifflin on the Pennsylvania side and Mercer on the Jersey side, with a spiked barricade, or chevaux de frise, blocking movements up the channel at various points. The first British attack was a failure. The defenders of Fort Mercer, commanded by Colonel Christopher Greene, a cousin of Nathanael Greene, threw back an overwhelming force of Hessians under Donop on October 22. Donop was mortally wounded, "finishing," to use his reported own words, "a noble career early." The next day two British ships that had run aground were bombarded by the Americans. The magazine of the man-of-war Augusta exploded and the sloop Merlin was set afire by her own officers and destroyed.

Now realizing the seriousness as well as the importance of the task, Howe withdrew his forces from Germantown to Philadelphia, and erected a number of batteries on the Pennsylvania shore from which Fort Mifflin could be bombarded. The main British bombardment of that fort started at 7:30 in the morning of November 10. According to the British Chief Engineer, Captain John Montresor, the British artillery employed two 32-pounders, six 24-pounders, one 18-pounder, two 8-inch howitzers, and one 13-inch mortar. The British suffered some damaging hits in return, but kept their batteries shelling the rebel fort throughout the twelfth and thirteenth, on which day the Patriots were still firing from one gun, an 18-pounder. On the fourteenth a floating battery with two 32-pounders was sent over to within

500 yards of the fort, but was finally silenced. At last, on the fifteenth, after one of the most stubborn and heroic defenses of the entire war, the Patriots set fire to the fort and, under the command of Major Simeon Thayer of Rhode Island who succeeded Lieutenant Colonel Samuel Smith when the latter's wound required that he be removed to the Jersey shore, evacuated the garrison by night across the river to Red Bank. The story of that gallant defense is told from the point of view of Major Fleury, the French artillery engineer inside the fort, and of a private in the ranks. Even the British paid reluctant tribute. Said Ambrose Serle, "They certainly defended it [Mifflin] with a spirit they have shewn no where else to an equal degree during the war."

Fort Mercer in turn had to be abandoned against overwhelming enemy forces. On November 23 a British vessel came up the Delaware to Philadelphia, signalizing the passage of control of that waterway from the Cape to Philadelphia from Patriot to British hands.

Early in January of 1778 the Patriots employed David Bushnell, the inventor of the American torpedo and other submarine machinery, to prepare a number of floating combustibles, or "infernals," as the British called them, and set them afloat in the Delaware River a few miles above Philadelphia, with the objective of destroying or impeding British shipping which then lay off that town. Bushnell's machines were constructed of kegs, charged with powder and arranged to explode on coming in contact with an object. Their appearance alarmed the British. Wild rumors spread that the kegs "were filled with armed rebels, who were to issue forth in the dead of the night, as did the Grecians of old from their wooden horse at the siege of Troy, and take the city by surprise." Seamen and troops manned ships and wharves and discharged small arms and cannon at any object seen floating in the river during ebb tide. The failure of the Patriot effort inspired Francis Hopkinson's witty "Ballad of the Kegs," which was extremely popular with the American army.

1. THE BRITISH VIEW THE FORMIDABLE AMERICAN DEFENSES

Anonymous diary recording Howe's military operations in 1777.

September 26, 1777—The rebels have endeavoured with vast labour and expence to stop up the navigation of the Delaware River by sinking several ranges of a kind of chevaux de frise across the channel, to prevent our fleet from geting up to the city. A number of small islands that extend from the mouths of the Schuylkill favoured this design very much. The first range runs from little Tennicomb Island (about ten miles below the city) across to the Jersey shore, where there is a large battery to protect it, called Billens fort. The second range is about two miles higher up, nine hundred yards below Mud Island, where the rebels have a considerable work called Mifflens fort. But afterwards thinking this as too great a distance, they sunk a couple of piers nearer to the fort including that part of the channel and fixed a boom across, besides having another range of chevaux de frise ready to sink occationally.

This kind of chevaux de frise consists of large timbers, like the main mast of a ship at the top of which are three branches armed and pointed with iron, spreading out fanwise . . . fifteen feet asunder. The main beam is fixt at an elevation to the frame of a float or stage, composed of vast logs, bound together as fast as possible; then covered with plank to top, and calked. When this machine is towed to its place, it is loaded with about thirty tuns of stones, secured in cases, which, by takeing the plugs out of the deck to admit the water into the float, sinks it down and keeps it firm and steady . . . the points of the branches about six or seven feet under the surface of the water; and they spread in front thirty feet. A row of these chevaux de frise are sunk sixty feet asunder from each other and another row behind in their intervals, to form a range.

Near to Mud Island, and just above the upper chevaux de frise, the rebel fleet are lying, and consist of the *Delaware* frigate of twenty-eight guns, 12 and 9-pounders; the *Province* ship, of eighteen 9-pounders; two large briggs, of ten and eight guns; two Zebic's of ten guns each; eight smaller armed vessels; thirteen gallies, each one 18-pounder on board; two floating batteries, of ten and nine 18-pounders, seventeen fire vessels, besides a great number of fire rafts.

High up the river near Burlington, they have two large new frigates, the *Effingham* and *Washington*; but neither of them are manned or compleat with guns.

—ANONYMOUS, "Contemporary British Account," *American Antiquarian Soc. Proc.*, New Series, XL, 83-84.

2. "Two Glorious Days"—the Defense of Fort Mercer

Colonel William Bradford of the Continental Army to President Wharton of the Pennsylvania Executive Council.

October 27, 1777

I have been absent from this place for some time up to Burlington, Borden Town and Trenton, after necessaries for the fleet and to hurry the commissaries in their duty. Last Monday evening was returning but when I got within two miles of Cooper's Ferry, I was informed the enemy had just landed a number of troops, which obliged me to return, by which I lost, by all accounts, one of the finest sights ever saw in these parts. My absence prevented me sending your Excellency an account of the action, but shall mention something of it now.

The 22d instant about 4 o'clock, the enemy to the number of about 1500 appeared before the fort at Red Bank, and immediately began a most furious cannonade, for about 15 minutes, when they rushed on with great resolution to storm the fort, and got into the upper part of the old works which were not finished, and gave three cheers, thinking all was their own, but were received so warmly that they were glad to get out. They endeavoured to force thro' the abettes that were before the fort, and some even got over the ditch and were killed within the pickets; after about 40 minutes action they took to their heels and ran off with great precipitation. The enemy had about 100 killed on the field, among which were one Lieut. Colonel and four Captains. They left about 80 wounded, among which were Count Donope their commander, who lays at Red Bank with his thigh broke; and his Brigade Major wounded in three places—near thirty of their wounded are since dead. We had in the fort at Red Bank two regiments of Rhode Island troops under the command of Col. Green, consisting of about 600 men and officers. We are informed the enemy carried over to Philadelphia not less than 300 wounded. The inhabitants that saw the enemy march down say they had 14 pieces of cannon with them and returned with six. If this should be the case they must have thrown them into Timber Creek, as we have taken none.

The next day the 23d the *Augusta* of 64 guns, the *Roebuck* of 44, two frigates and the *Merlin* of 18 guns came up as near as they dare to the upper chevaux de frize, when a most furious engagement ensued between the galleys and floating batters, with the enemys ships; the fire was so incessant that by all accounts the elements seemed to be in flames; about 12 o'clock the *Augusta* blew up, whether by accident or from our shot is unknown, having taken fire some time before. Here presented a glorious sight before she blew, she laying broadside-to aground, and the flames issuing thro every port she had. The action still continued with the other ships and at three o'clock the *Merlin* took fire and blew up also, being aground, and then the fire soon ceased. Thus ended two glorious days.

—BRADFORD, "Letter," *Penn. Archives*, 1st Series, V, 707-709.

3. A FRENCH ENGINEER DIRECTS THE DEFENSE OF FORT MIFFLIN

Journal of Major André-Arsène de Rosset, Vicomte de Fleury.

Nov. 9th at night. The enemy appearing ready to open their batteries, we raised the bank which covers our palisades on the west front, against which the whole fire of the enemy is directed, and which will be the point of attack in a case of their storming the fort. I have some fascines making at Red-bank, but shall want a great number.

10—The 24 and 18-pound shot from the Batteries No. 16 and 17 broke some of our palisades this morning, but this does not make us uneasy—they save us the trouble of cutting them to the height of a man—which we should do, as the fire of loop-holes is in itself not very dangerous, and our loop-holes in particular are so badly contrived as to leave two-thirds of the glacis unraked.

It is probable that the enemy will undertake to carry this place by storm, and I should not fear them if we could fix the floating chain . . . it would cover the front which is likely to be attacked, and by delivering us from our uneasiness for this side, would enable us to post the men destined for its defence, at the wall of masonry which is ten feet high and is not out of the reach of an escalade, notwithstanding the ditches, pits and stakes, etc., with which we have endeavored to surround it.

The commodore, master of the *incomparable* chain in question, proposes to stretch it by means of buoys between our island and Province Island. I believe this obstacle to the communication between the enemy's fleet and army will be of little consequence, and if he would spare us the chain, the enemy would pay dear for their hardiness if they dared attack us. Colonel Smith wrote this morning to ask this favour, but I am afraid that public interest will suffer by private misunderstandings. I am interrupted by the bombs and balls which fall thick.

10 at noon. The firing increases but not the effect—our barracks alone suffer.

At 2 o'clock. The direction of the fire is changed—our palisades suffer—a dozen of them are broke down. One of our cannon is damaged near the muzzle—I am afraid it will not fire streight.

11 at night. The enemy keep up a firing of cannon every half hour. Genl. Varnum promised us fascines and palisades, but they are not arrived—and they are absolutely necessary.

The commodore has promised the chain. Our garrison diminishes, our soldiers are overwhelmed with fatigue—they spend nights in watching and labour without doing much on account of their weakness.

Nov. 13th at night.—The enemy have kept up a firing part of the night—their shells greatly disturb our workmen, and as the moon rises opposite to us, her light discovers to the enemy where we are. As long as my workmen would remain with me, I employed them in covering the two western block-houses with joist within and without and filling the interstices with rammed earth. I have closed the breaches made in our palisades with planks, centry-boxes, rafters, and strengthed the whole with earth. General Varnum has sent me neither ax, fascine, gabion nor palisade, altho he promised me all these articles; I suppose it has not been in his power. It is impossible however with watry mud alone to make works capable of resisting the enemys 32-pounders.

14. Day light discovers to us a floating battery of the enemy, placed a little above their grand battery, and near the shore; it seems to be a bomb-battery.

Fort Mifflin is certainly capable of defence if the means be furnished—if they supply us from Red-bank with tools, fascines, palisades, etc., all which they may do in abundance. The fire of the enemy will never take the fort; it may kill us men but this is the fortune of war. And all their bullets will never render them masters of the island, if we have courage enough to remain on it —but they are removing our cannon from the grand battery under pretext that it is necessary to raise a battery on the Jersey side to keep the enemys shipping at a distance—but what signifies it whether their fleet be at the point of Hog Island or a quarter of a mile lower? Will they not by taking this fort have the channel of Province Island open for their small sloops and the other light vessels? Will they not drive the gallies from the river? Fort Mifflin is the important object; it must be maintained and furnished with means of defence—men, earth and fascines to cover them. Our new garrison consists of 450 men—what can they do in a circumference of works so extensive as ours? . . .

We must have men to defend the ruins of the fort. Our ruins will serve us as breast-works, we will defend the ground inch by inch, and the enemy shall pay dearly for every step—but we want a commanding officer; ours is absent and forms projects for our defence at a distance.

P.S.—As the light becomes clearer, I perceive the enemys floating battery not to be a mortar battery but that it contains two 32-pounders. We are going to raise a counter battery of two eighteen-pounders taken out of our river battery, which will now have no more than 7 guns, the wheels of two of which have been disabled by the enemy's cannon. We are so much neglected that we have been 7 days without wood, and at present have only cartridges of eighteen-pounders for a piece of 32 which does considerable mischief to the enemy.

14th at 7 o'clock. The enemy keep up a great fire from their floating battery and the shore.

I repeat it, our commanding officer issues orders from Woodberry—if he were nearer he would be a better judge of our situation.

Our blockhouses are in a pitiful condition, but with fascines I hope to cover two pieces in each lower story which will be sufficient to flank us. I say again the enemys fire will not take our fort. If they attempt a storm we shall still have a little parapet to oppose to them, but we must have men to defend it.

November 14th at noon. We have silenced the enemy's floating battery. I know not whether we have dismounted her cannon, or whether her present station exposes her too much, but the firing from her has ceased. I suspect that she is destined to land men on this island.

Their grand battery is in little better condition than our block-houses. We have opened an embrasure at the corner of the battery, and two pieces here joined to two others on the left, which we have reinstated, throw the enemy into disorder.

I repeat it—their fire will kill us men, because we have no cover, but it will never take the fort, if we have sufficient courage to keep our ground—but a stronger garrison is indispensably necessary. We are not secured against storm. If the enemy attempt it, I fear they will succeed in penetrating a circumference of 1200 paces defended only by 450 men and half ruined palisades. A boat which this day deserted from the fleet will have given the enemy sufficient intimation of our weakness—they will probably attack us or attempt a lodgment on the island which we cannot prevent with our present strength.

Tonight an attempt is to be made on the floating battery of the enemy.
—FORD, *Defences of Philadelphia*, 106-108, 123-125.

4. BUSHNELL'S "INFERNALS" ROUSE SIR BILLY FROM A SNUG BED

The Battle of the Kegs
Francis Hopkinson, 1778.

Gallants, attend, and hear a friend
    Trill forth harmonious ditty.
Strange things I'll tell, which late befell
    In Philadelphia city.

'Twas early day, as poets say,
    Just when the sun was rising.
A soldier stood on a log of wood
    And saw a thing surprising.

As in amaze he stood to gaze—
    The truth can't be denied, sir—
He spied a score of kegs or more
    Come floating down the tide, sir.

A sailor, too, in jerkin blue,
    This strange appearance viewing,
First damned his eyes, in great surprise,
    Then said, "Some mischief's brewing.

"These kegs, I'm told, the rebels hold,
    Packed up like pickled herring,
And they're come down t'attack the town
    In this new way of ferrying."

The soldier flew, the sailor too,
    And scared almost to death, sir,
Wore out their shoes to spread the news,
    And ran till out of breath, sir. . . .

Sir William, he, snug as a flea,
    Lay all this time a-snoring;
Nor dreamed of harm, as he lay warm
    In bed with Mrs. [Loring].

Now in a fright, he starts upright,
    Awaked by such a clatter;
He rubs his eyes and boldly cries,
    "For God's sake, what's the matter?"

At his bedside, he then espied
    Sir Erskine at command, sir;
Upon one foot he had one boot,
    And t'other in his hand, sir.

"Arise! arise!" Sir Erskine cries.
    "The rebels—more's the pity—
Without a boat are all afloat
    And ranged before the city.

"The motley crew, in vessels new,
    With Satan for their guide, sir,
Packed up in bags, or wooden kegs,
    Come driving down the tide, sir.

"Therefore prepare for bloody war;
    These kegs must all be routed,
Or surely we despised shall be,
    And British courage doubted."

The royal band now ready stand,
    All ranged in dread array, sir,
With stomach stout, to see it out
    And make a bloody day, sir.

The cannons roar from shore to shore,
    The small arms make a rattle;
Since wars began, I'm sure no man
    Ere saw so strange a battle. . . .

The kegs, 'tis said, though strongly made
    Of rebel staves and hoops, sir,
Could not oppose their powerful foes,
    The conquering British troops, sir.

From morn till night, these men of might
    Displayed amazing courage;
And when the sun was fairly down,
    Retired to sup their porridge.

An hundred men, with each a pen,
    Or more, upon my word, sir,
It is most true would be too few
    Their valor to record, sir.

Such feats did they perform that day
    Against those wicked kegs, sir,
That years to come, if they get home,
    They'll make their boasts and brags, sir.
        —Moore, ed., *Songs and Ballads*, pp. 209-216.

VI. VALLEY FORGE

A week before Christmas·of '77 Washington's army took up winter quarters at Valley Forge on the west side of the Schuylkill. Although the general's choice of location was sharply criticized, the site he had selected was central and easily defended. Then came a cruel race with time to get huts erected before the soldiers, barefoot and half naked, froze to death. Hundreds of horses did in fact starve to death, and for the army starvation was a mortal danger. "No meat, no meat!" was the constant wail. Improvements came about after Nathanael Greene assumed the duties of quartermaster general on March 23.

Yet, despite the ever-present fear of mutiny, no real disaffection occurred. As Hessian Major Baurmeister conceded, the army was kept from disintegrating by "the spirit of liberty." Men and officers accepted their tragic plight with a sense of humor and extraordinary forbearance, but it was an ordeal that no army could be expected to undergo for long. Nathanael Greene wrote to General Washington, "God grant we may never be brought to such a wretched condition again!"

Valley Forge has become a national symbol of courage and disinterested patriotism. It was not the coldest winter of the war. A severer one was to follow in 1779-80. Nor was morale as low as it was right before Trenton and Princeton. Washington's army was famished, naked, ill, but miraculously still in being. But the toll to mismanagement, graft and speculation was great. Perhaps 2,500 soldiers perished during the six months in camp, yet instead of dissolving as might have been expected, the army under Washington's leadership came out of Valley Forge a better fighting force than ever.

The improvement in the army's effectiveness must be credited in no small part to the sensible training administered by the popular Prussian drillmaster, Baron Friedrich von Steuben, a former staff officer under Frederick the Great. Other European officers had joined the American army, among them the engineers Louis Duportail of France and Thaddeus Kosciusko of Poland, the latter responsible for the defenses of West Point. A compatriot, the cavalry commander Count Casimir Pulaski, was to lose his life at Savannah in 1779. One of Washington's critics at Valley Forge, the self-styled baron, Johann de Kalb, a Bavarian in the French service, also lost his life in action in the war.

Washington's favorite among the foreign officers was young Marquis de Lafayette. Coming to America a callow youth and stanch monarchist, he had by the end of the war matured in his political thinking and proved his mettle any number of times on the field of battle. Washington's affection for him was like that of a father for a son. Once when discouraged by the incessant importunities of rank-hungry foreign officers, Washington wrote: "I do most devoutly wish that we had not a single foreigner among us, except the Marquis de Lafayette, who acts upon very different principles from those which govern the rest."

1. Should the Army Go into Winter Quarters?

Colonel John Laurens of the Continental Army to his father Henry Laurens, President of Congress.

December 3, 1777

We have received several accounts from outposts within a few days past intimating that an attack upon us was meditated. We have in consequence prepared ourselves, paraded our men so as to make them acquainted with the ground and its advantages; but the enemy have remained within their works. Many are of opinion that Sir William Howe will not suffer any thing but mere necessity, or a very tempting prospect of decisive success, to call him from good winter quarters. Others say that from past experience he knows the vicinity of the Continental army to be exceedingly troublesome, and that it is his interest to drive us to a more respectable distance. In the mean time the season advances in which armies in general are forced to repair to more substantial shelter than tents, and whose inclemency is more particularly grievous to our ill-clothed soldiers.

The question is whether we are to go into remote winter quarters, and form a chain of cantonments in the interior part of the country; leaving a vast extent of territory exposed to the devastation of an enraged unsparing enemy; leaving inhabitants who will be partly seduced by the expectation of gold, or more generally compelled to fill the traitorous provincial corps now raising; leaving plentiful granaries and large stocks of cattle, ample means for subsisting the troops and Tory citizens in Philadelphia, and for victualling transports that may carry home Mr. Burgoyne and his army; leaving the well-affected to fall a sacrifice, and deplore our abandonment of them and the country; or whether we shall take a position more honourable, more military, more republican, more consonant to the popular wish—in a proper situation for covering the country, or at least so much of it as circumstances will permit—and for distressing and annoying the enemy?

Winter campaigns, it is said, are ominous to the best appointed and best disciplined armies. The misery incident to them occasions desertion and sickness which waste their numbers.

Our army in particular requires exemption from fatigue in order to compensate for their want of clothing; relaxation from the duties of a campaign, in order to allow them an opportunity of being disciplined and instructed; warm quarters, that it may appear in the spring with undiminished numbers and in the full prowess of health, etc. Besides it is urged that the hardships which our soldiers undergo discourage men from enlisting.

The answers that might be given in our particular circumstances to these general objections against winter campaigns are only for your private ear, and not to be trusted in a letter to the possibility of miscarriage; besides, we may take a position which will not absolutely expose us to a winter campaign, but furnish us excellent quarters for men at the same time that it leaves us within distance for taking considerable advantages of the enemy, and cover a valuable and extensive country.

—LAURENS, *Army Correspondence*, pp. 90-92.

2. "THE ARMY NOW BEGINS TO GROW SICKLY"

Diary of Surgeon Albigence Waldo of the Connecticut Line.

December 11, [1777].—At four o'clock the whole army were ordered to march to Swedes Ford on the River Schuylkill, about 9 miles N. W. of Chestnut Hill, and 6 from White Marsh, our present encampment. At sun an hour high the whole were moved from the lines and on their march with baggage. This night encamped in a semi circle nigh the ford. The enemy had marched up the west side of Schuylkill—Potter's brigade of Pennsylvania Militia were already there and had several skirmishes with them with some loss on his side and considerable on the enemies. . . .

I am prodigious sick and cannot get any thing comfortable. What in the name of Providence am I to do with a fit of sickness in this place where nothing appears pleasing to the sickened eye and nausiating stomach? But I doubt not Providence will find out a way for my relief. But I cannot eat beef if I starve, for my stomach positively refuses to entertain such company, and how can I help that?

December 12.—A bridge of waggons made across the Schuylkill last night consisting of 36 waggons, with a bridge of rails between each. Some skirmishing over the river. Militia and dragoons brought into camp several prisoners. Sun set—We were ordered to march over the river—It snows—I'm sick—eat nothing—no whiskey—no forage—Lord—Lord—Lord. The army were till sun rise crossing the river—some at the waggon bridge and some at the raft bridge below. Cold and uncomfortable.

December 13.—The army marched three miles from the west side the river and encamped near a place called the Gulph and not an improper name neither, for this Gulph seems well adapted by its situation to keep us from the pleasures and enjoyments of this world, or being conversant with any body in it. It is an excellent place to raise the ideas of a philosopher beyond the glutted thoughts and reflexions of an Epicurian. His reflexions will be as different from the common reflexions of mankind as if he were unconnected with the world and only conversant with immaterial beings. It cannot be that our superiors are about to hold consultations with spirits infinitely beneath their order, by bringing us into these utmost regions of the terraqueous sphere.

No, it is, upon consideration, for many good purposes since we are to winter here: 1st, there is plenty of wood and water. 2ndly, there are but few families for the soldiery to steal from—tho' far be it from a soldier to steal. 4ly [*sic*], there are warm sides of hills to erect huts on. 5ly, they will be heavenly minded like Jonah when in the belly of a great fish. 6ly, they will not become home sick as is sometimes the case when men live in the open world—since the reflections which will naturally arise from their present habitation will lead them to the more noble thoughts of employing their leisure hours in filling their knapsacks with such materials as may be necessary on the Journey to another Home.

December 14.—Prisoners and deserters are continually coming in. The army, which has been surprisingly healthy hitherto, now begins to grow sickly from the continued fatigues they have suffered this campaign. Yet they still show a spirit of alacrity and contentment not to be expected from so young troops. I am sick—discontented—and out of humour. Poor food—hard lodging—cold weather—fatigue—nasty cloathes—nasty cookery—vomit half my time—smoaked out of my senses—the Devil's in't—I can't endure it—Why are we sent here to starve and freeze?—What sweet felicities have I left at home: A charming wife—pretty children—good beds—good food—good cookery—all agreeable—all harmonious! Here all confusion—smoke and cold—hunger and filthyness—a pox on my bad luck! There comes a bowl of beef soup, full of burnt leaves and dirt, sickish enough to make a Hector spue—away with it, boys!—I'll live like the chameleon upon air.

Poh! Poh! crys Patience within me, you talk like a fool. Your being sick covers your mind with a melancholic gloom, which makes everything about you appear gloomy. See the poor soldier when in health—with what cheerfulness he meets his foes and encounters every hardship. If barefoot, he labours thro' the mud and cold with a song in his mouth extolling War and Washington. If his food be bad, he eats it notwithstanding with seeming content—blesses God for a good stomach and whistles it into digestion.

But harkee, Patience, a moment. There comes a soldier; his bare feet are seen thro' his worn out shoes, his legs nearly naked from the tattered remains of an only pair of stockings, his breeches not sufficient to cover his nakedness, his shirt hanging in strings, his hair dishevelled, his face meagre; his whole appearance pictures a person forsaken and discouraged. He comes, and crys with an air of wretchedness and despair, I am sick, my feet lame, my legs are sore, my body covered with this tormenting itch. My cloaths are worn out, my constitution is broken, my former activity is exhausted by fatigue, hunger and cold. I fail fast, I shall soon be no more! and all the reward I shall get will be: "Poor Will is dead."

People who live at home in luxury and ease, quietly possessing their habitations, enjoying their wives and families in peace, have but a very faint idea of the unpleasing sensations and continual anxiety the man endures who is in a camp, and is the husband and parent of an agreeable family. These same people are willing we should suffer every thing for their benefit and advantage, and yet are the first to condemn us for not doing more!!

December 15.—Quiet. Eat pessimmens, found myself better for their lenient opperation. Went to a house, poor and small, but good food within—eat too much from being so long abstemious, thro' want of palatables. Mankind are never truly thankfull for the benefits of life until they have experienced the want of them. The man who has seen misery knows best how to enjoy good. He who is always at ease and has enough of the blessings of common life is an impotent judge of the feelings of the unfortunate. . . .

December 16.—Cold rainy day. Baggage ordered over the Gulph of our division, which were to march at ten, but the baggage was ordered back and for the first time since we have been here the tents were pitched, to keep the men more comfortable.

"Good morning, Brother Soldier," says one to another, "how are you?"

"All wet I thank'e, hope you are so," says the other.

The enemy have been at Chestnut Hill opposite to us near our last encampment the other side Schuylkill, made some ravages, killed two of our horsemen, taken some prisoners. We have done the like by them. . . .

December 21.—[Valley Forge.] Preparations made for hutts. Provisions scarce. Mr. Ellis went homeward—sent a letter to my wife. Heartily wish myself at home. My skin and eyes are almost spoiled with continual smoke. A general cry thro' the camp this evening among the soldiers, "No meat! No meat!" The distant vales echoed back the melancholly sound—"No meat! No meat!" Immitating the noise of crows and owls, also, made a part of the confused musick.

What have you for your dinners, boys? "Nothing but fire cake and water, Sir." At night: "Gentlemen, the supper is ready." What is your supper, lads? "Fire cake and water, Sir."

Very poor beef has been drawn in our camp the greater part of this season. A butcher bringing a quarter of this kind of beef into camp one day who had white buttons on the knees of his breeches, a soldier cries out: "There, there, Tom, is some more of your fat beef. By my soul I can see the butcher's breeches buttons through it."

December 22.—Lay excessive cold and uncomfortable last night. My eyes are started out from their orbits like a rabbit's eyes, occasioned by a great cold and smoke.

What have you got for breakfast, lads? "Fire cake and water, Sir." The Lord send that our Commissary of Purchases may live [on] fire cake and water till their glutted gutts are turned to pasteboard.

Our division are under marching orders this morning. I am ashamed to say it, but I am tempted to steal fowls if I could find them, or even a whole hog, for I feel as if I could eat one. But the impoverished country about us affords but little matter to employ a thief, or keep a clever fellow in good humour. But why do I talk of hunger and hard usage, when so many in the world have not even fire cake and water to eat?

> —WALDO, "Valley Forge, 1777-1778," *Penn. Mag. of Hist. and Biog.*, XXI, 305-310.

3. A CONNECTICUT PRIVATE STARVES AND SHIVERS AT VALLEY FORGE

Narrative attributed to James Sullivan Martin.

Soon after the British had quit their position on Chestnut-hill, we left this place, and after marching and countermarching back and forward some days, we crossed the Schuylkill in a cold, rainy and snowy night, upon a bridge of wagons set end to end and joined together by boards and planks; and after a few days more manoeuvering, we at last settled down at a place called "the Gulf" (so named on account of a remarkable chasm in the hills); and here we encamped some time, and here we had liked to have encamped forever—for starvation here *rioted* in its glory. But, lest the reader should be disgusted at hearing so much said about "starvation," I will give him something that, perhaps, may in some measure alleviate his ill humour.

While we lay here there was a Continental thanksgiving ordered by Congress; and as the army had all the cause in the world to be particularly thankful, if not for being well off, at least that it was no worse, we were ordered to participate in it. We had nothing to eat for two or three days previous, except what the trees of the fields and forests afforded us. But we must now have what Congress said—a sumptuous thanksgiving to close the year of high living we had now nearly seen brought to a close. Well—to add something extraordinary to our present stock of provisions—our country, ever mindful of its suffering army, opened her sympathizing heart so wide, upon this occasion, as to give us something to make the world stare. And what do you think it was, reader?—Guess.—You cannot guess, be you as much of a Yankee as you will. I will tell you: it gave each and every man *half a gill* of rice, and a *table spoon full* of vinegar!!

After we had made sure of this extraordinary superabundant donation, we were ordered out to attend a meeting and hear a sermon delivered upon the occasion. We accordingly went, for we could not help it. I heard a sermon, a "thanksgiving sermon," what sort of one I do not know now, nor did I at the time I heard it. I had something else to think upon; my belly put me in remembrance of the fine thanksgiving dinner I was to partake of when I—could get it. I remember the text, like an attentive lad at church; I can *still* remember that; it was this: "And the soldiers said unto him, And what shall we do? And he said unto them, Do violence to no man, nor accuse any one falsely."

The preacher ought to have added the remainder of the sentence to have made it complete: "And be content with your wages." But that would not do, it would be too appropos; however, he heard it as soon as the service was over; it was shouted from a hundred tongues.

Well—we had got through the services of the day and had nothing to do but to return in good order to our tents and fare as we could. As we returned to our camp, we passed by our Commissary's quarters; all his stores, consisting of a barrel about two thirds full of hocks of fresh beef, stood directly in our way, but there was a sentinel guarding even that; however, one of my messmates purloined a piece of it, four or five pounds perhaps. I was exceeding glad to see him take it; I thought it might help to eke out our thanksgiving supper; but, alas! how soon my expectations were blasted! The sentinel saw him have it as soon as I did and obliged him to return it to the barrel again. So I had nothing else to do but to go home and make out my supper as usual, upon a leg of nothing and no turnips.

The army was now not only starved but naked; the greatest part were not only shirtless and barefoot, but destitute of all other clothing, especially blankets. I procured a small piece of raw cowhide and made myself a pair of moccasons, which kept my feet (while they lasted) from the frozen ground, although, as I well remember, the hard edges so galled my ancles, while on a march, that it was with much difficulty and pain that I could wear them afterwards; but the only alternative I had was to endure this inconvenience or to go barefoot, as hundreds of my companions had to, till they might be tracked by their blood upon the rough frozen ground. But hunger, nakedness and sore shins were not the only difficulties we had at that time to encounter; we had hard duty to perform and little or no strength to perform it with.

The army continued at and near the Gulf for some days, after which we marched for the Valley Forge in order to take up our winter-quarters. We were now in a truly forlorn condition—no clothing, no provisions and as disheartened as need be. We arrived, however, at our destination a few days before Christmas. Our prospect was indeed dreary. In our miserable condition, to go into the wild woods and build us habitations to *stay* (not to *live*) in, in such a weak, starved and naked condition, was appaling in the highest degree, especially to New-Englanders, unaccustomed to such kind of hardships at home. . . .

We arrived at the Valley Forge in the evening; it was dark; there was no water to be found, and I was perishing with thirst. I searched for water till I was weary, and came to my tent without finding any; fatigue and thirst, joined with hunger, almost made me desperate. I felt at that instant as if I would have taken victuals or drink from the best friend I had on earth by force. I am not writing fiction; all are sober realities. Just after I arrived at my tent, two soldiers, whom I did not know, passed by; they had some water in their canteens which they told me they had found a good distance off, but could not direct me to the place as it was very dark. I tried to beg a draught of water from them but they were as rigid as Arabs. At length I persuaded them to sell me a drink for three pence, Pennsylvania currency, which was every cent of property I could then call my own, so great was the necessity I was then reduced to.

—MARTIN(?), *Narrative*, pp. 73-76.

4. WASHINGTON: "WHAT IS TO BECOME OF THE ARMY THIS WINTER?"

George Washington to the President of Congress.

Valley Forge, December 23, 1777

Sir: Full as I was in my representation of matters in the Commys. departmt. yesterday, fresh, and more powerful reasons oblige me to add, that I am now convinced, beyond a doubt that unless some great and capital change suddenly takes place in that line, this Army must inevitably be reduced to one or other of these three things. Starve, dissolve, or disperse, in order to obtain subsistence in the best manner they can; rest assured Sir this is not an exaggerated picture, but that I have abundant reason to support what I say.

Yesterday afternoon receiving information that the Enemy, in force, had left the City, and were advancing towards Derby with apparent design to forage, and draw Subsistance from that part of the Country, I order'd the Troops to be in readiness, that I might give every opposition in my power; when, behold! to my great mortification, I was not only informed, but convinced, that the Men were unable to stir on Acct. of Provision, and that a dangerous Mutiny begun the Night before, and [which] with difficulty was suppressed by the spirited exertion's of some officers was still much to be apprehended on acct. of their want of this Article.

This brought forth the only Comy, in the purchasing Line, in this Camp; and, with him, this Melancholy and alarming truth; that he had not a single hoof of any kind to Slaughter, and not more than 25. Barls. of Flour! From hence form an opinion of our Situation when I add, that, he could not tell when to expect any.

All I could do under these circumstances was, to send out a few light Parties to watch and harrass the Enemy, whilst other Parties were instantly detached different ways to collect, if possible, as much Provision as would satisfy the present pressing wants of the Soldiery. But will this answer? No Sir: three or four days bad weather would prove our destruction.

What then is to become of the Army this Winter? and if we are as often without Provisions now, as with it, what is to become of us in the Spring, when our force will be collected, with the aid perhaps of Militia, to take advantage of an early campaign before the Enemy can be reinforced? These are considerations of great magnitude, meriting the closest attention, and will, when my own reputation is so intimately connected, and to be affected by the event, justifie my saying that the present Commissaries are by no means equal to the execution [of the Office] or that the disaffection of the People is past all belief. The misfortune however does in my opinion, proceed from both causes, and tho' I have been tender heretofore of giving any opinion, or lodging complaints, as the change in that departmt. took place contrary to my judgment, and the consequences thereof were predicted; yet, finding that the inactivity of the Army, whether for want of provisions,

Cloaths, or other essentials, is charged to my Acct., not only by the common vulgar, but those in power, it is time to speak plain in exculpation of myself; with truth then I can declare that, no Man, in my opinion, ever had his measures more impeded than I have, by every department of the Army.

Since the Month of July, we have had no assistance from the Quarter Master Genl. and to want of assistance from this department, the Commissary Genl. charges great part of his deficiency; to this I am to add, that notwithstanding it is a standing order (and often repeated) that the Troops shall always have two days Provisions by them, that they may be ready at any sudden call, yet no oppertunity has scarce ever yet happened of taking advantage of the Enemy that has not been totally obstructed or greatly impeded on this Acct., and this tho' the great and crying evil is not all. Soap, Vinegar and other Articles allowed by Congress we see none of nor have [we] seen I believe since the battle of brandywine; the first indeed we have now little occasion of few men having more than one Shirt, many only the Moiety of one, and Some none at all; in addition to which as a proof of the little benefit received from a Cloathier Genl., and at the same time as a further proof of the inability of an Army under the circumstances of this, to perform the common duties of Soldiers (besides a number of Men confind to Hospitals for want of Shoes, and others in farmers Houses on the same Acct.) we have, by a field return this day made no less than 2898 Men now in Camp unfit for duty because they are bare foot and otherwise naked and by the same return it appears that our whole strength in continental Troops (Including the Eastern Brigades which have joined us since the surrender of Genl. Burgoyne) exclusive of the Maryland Troops sent to Wilmington amount to no more than 8200 In Camp fit for duty. Notwithstanding which, and that, since the 4th Instt. our Numbers fit for duty from the hardships and exposures they have undergone, particularly on Acct. of Blankets (numbers being obliged and do set up all Night by fires, instead of taking comfortable rest in a natural way) have decreased near 2000 Men.

We find Gentlemen without knowing whether the Army was really going into Winter Quarters or not . . . reprobating the measure as much as if they thought Men were made of Stocks or Stones and equally insensible of frost and Snow and moreover, as if they conceived it practicable for an inferior Army under the disadvantages I have describ'd our's to be wch. is by no means exagerated to confine a superior one (in all respects well appointed, and provide for a Winters Campaign) within the City of Phila., and cover from depredation and waste the States of Pensa., Jersey, &ca. but what makes this matter still more extraordinary in my eye is, that these very Gentn. who were well apprized of the nakedness of the Troops, from occular demonstration thought their own Soldiers worse clad than others, and advised me, near a Month ago, to postpone the execution of a Plan, I was about to adopt (in consequence of a resolve of Congress) for seizing Cloaths, under strong assurances that an ample supply would be collected in ten days agreeably to a decree of the State, not one Article of wch., by the bye, is yet come to hand, should think a Winters Campaign and the covering these States from the Invasion of an Enemy so easy a business. I can assure those

Gentlemen that it is a much easier and less distressing thing to draw remonstrances in a comfortable room by a good fire side than to occupy a cold bleak hill and sleep under frost and Snow without Cloaths or Blankets; however, although they seem to have little feeling for the naked, and distressed Soldier, I feel superabundantly for them, and from my Soul pity those miseries, wch. it is neither in my power to relieve or prevent.

It is for these reasons therefore I have dwelt upon the Subject, and it adds not a little to my other difficulties, and distress, to find that much more is expected of me than is possible to be performed, and that upon the ground of safety and policy, I am obliged to conceal the true State of the Army from Public view and therby expose myself to detraction and Calumny.

—FITZPATRICK, ed., *Writings of Washington*, X, 192-196.

5. "EVERYTHING SEEMS TO CONTRIBUTE TO THE RUIN OF OUR CAUSE"

General Johann de Kalb to Count Charles Francis de Broglie.

Valley Forge, December 25, 1777

On the 19th instant, the army reached this wooded wilderness, certainly one of the poorest districts of Pennsylvania; the soil thin, uncultivated and almost uninhabited, without forage and without provisions! Here we are to go into winter-quarters, *i. e.*, to lie in shanties, generals and privates, to enable the army, it is said, to recover from its privations, to recruit, to re-equip, and to prepare for the opening of the coming campaign, while protecting the country against hostile inroads. The matter has been the subject of long debates in the council of war. It was discussed in all its length and breadth—a bad practice to which they are addicted here—and good advice was not taken. The idea of wintering in this desert can only have been put into the head of the commanding general by an interested speculator or a disaffected man. Means were found of implicating Congress, which body has the foible of interfering with matters which it neither understands nor can understand, being entirely ignorant of the locality. It is unfortunate that Washington is so easily led. He is the bravest and truest of men, has the best intentions and a sound judgment. I am convinced that he would accomplish substantial results if he would only act more upon his own responsibility; but it is a pity that he is so weak, and has the worst of advisers in the men who enjoy his confidence. If they are not traitors, they are certainly gross ignoramuses.

I am satisfied that our present position, if retained, will offer none of the advantages expected from it. On the contrary, the army will be kept in continual alarms from being too near the enemy, and too feeble, for our whole effective force hardly amounts to six thousand men. To use them for the protection of the country excludes every idea of rest. It might have been expected that a camp would have been formed in a secure position, and compact in its design, corresponding to the small number of the army; and that it would have been strongly intrenched, so as to resist any attack. Instead of this the divisions are encamped so far asunder that we are practically split up into a number of petty detachments, isolated so as to be unable to support each other, and helplessly exposed to every assault. Who knows whether we shall not receive a severe blow this winter?

Unless Congress will speedily throw off their present vacillation, and adopt energetic measures for completing the regiments and compelling the militia to serve for three years (a step I have been daily advocating for a long time), a time will come when the General will not be able to calculate upon having twenty men to command next morning. The men are drafted in classes, and are only called upon to pledge themselves for a service of two months. After the expiration of that time no man can compel them to remain another day. This state of things is a burthen to the State and to the citizen; there is no end to the drilling of raw recruits, from which the service derives no manner of benefit. This system of militia service will yet prove the destruction of the cause. The devil himself could not have made a worse arrangement. . . .

I do not know what is done in the clothing department; but it is certain that half the army are half naked, and almost the whole army go barefoot. As to patrolling the country round, it is not even carried so far as to keep the road from Lancaster to Erie, and from Erie to the Delaware, in our control. A number of officers have joined me in urging this measure. But it was objected that by so doing we should expose the banks of the Delaware, the eastern part of Maryland, and several counties of Pennsylvania. But do we not expose them now, and all the more? The whole difference would be that such a disposition would enable us to live on what now constitute the supplies of the enemy.

Our men are also infected with the itch, a matter which attracts very little attention either at the hospitals or in camp. I have seen the poor fellows covered over and over with scab. I have caused my seven regiments to put up barracks large enough to hold all these unfortunates, so that they can be subjected to medical treatment away from the others.

All things seem to contribute to the ruin of our cause. If it is sustained, it can only be by a special interposition of Providence. The army contractors have been consulted as to the best place for going into winter-quarters, and have declared that the present location is the most convenient for them. This, by-the-bye, was done contrary to my advice. Now we have hardly been here six days, and are already suffering for want of everything. The men have had neither meat nor bread for four days, and our horses are often left for days without any fodder. What will be done when the roads grow worse, and the season more severe? Strong detachments ought to be sent out at once, to get in provisions. . . .

My blacksmith is a captain! The very numerous assistant-quartermasters are for the most part men of no military education whatever, in many cases ordinary hucksters, but always colonels. The same rank is held by the contractors-general and their agents *(fournisseur général et facteur général)*. It is safe to accost every man as a colonel who talks to me with familiarity; the officers of a lower grade are invariably more modest. In a word, the army teems with colonels.

The quartermasters-general provide quarters for the commander-in-chief and for themselves, but for nobody else. The other generals, even some of the officers, take their quarters where and as they please and can. For this purpose thousands are often to be seen hastening on in advance of the army. In the rear of it nobody thinks of the distance. Luckily we have an enemy to deal with as clumsy as ourselves. If any one you have occasion to look for is to be found, it is only to be accomplished by good luck or indefatigable perambulations. Plans of quarters are unknown. It is necessary to live a long time in every camp before you can find your way.

All my remonstrances against this abuse were of no avail. I have abandoned the practice of suggesting improvements in the service and in organization. I have had the greatest trouble in making them understand the necessity of strong patrols for visiting the posts. . . .

> —KAPP, *Life of Kalb*, pp. 137-143.

6. THE ILL-CLAD OFFICERS AT VALLEY FORGE CALLED *Sans Culottes*

Pierre Etienne du Ponceau to Robert Walsh, a Philadelphia journalist.

> Philadelphia 13th June 1836

I remember seeing the soldiers popping their heads out of their miserable huts and calling out in an undertone ,"No bread, no soldier." Their condition was truly pitiful and their courage and perseverance beyond all praise.

We who lived in good quarters did not feel the misery of the times so much as the common soldiers and the subaltern officers, yet we had more than once to share our rations with the sentry at our door. We put the best face we could upon the matter. Once with the Baron's permission, his aids invited a number of young officers to dine at our quarters, on condition that none should be admitted that had on a whole pair of breeches. This was understood of course as *pars pro toto*, but torn clothes were an indispensable requisite for admission and in this the guests were very sure not to fail. The dinner took place; the guests clubbed their rations, and we feasted sumptuously on tough beefsteaks and potatoes with hickory nuts for our dessert. In lieu of wine, we had some kind of spirits with which we made *Salamanders;* that is to say, after filling our glasses, we set the liquor on fire, and drank it up flame and all. Such a set of ragged and, at the same time, merry fellows were never before brought together.

The Baron [von Steuben] loved to speak of that dinner, and of his *sans culottes*, as he called us. Thus the denomination was first invented in America, and applied to the brave officers and soldiers of our revolutionary army, at a time when it could not be foreseen that the name which honoured the followers of Washington would afterwards be assumed by the sattelites of a Marat and a Robespierre.

> —DU PONCEAU, "Autobiography," *Penn. Mag. of Hist. and Biog.*,
> LXIII, 208.

7. "NOTHING BUT VIRTUE HAS KEPT OUR ARMY TOGETHER"

Colonel John Brooks of Massachusetts to a friend.

> Camp near Valley Forge, Jany 5th, 1778

You make me smile when you observe that you are not so sanguine about matters in this quarter at present as you were. My dear friend, what ever made you sanguine? Could How's marching through a vast extent of country—a country very well formed for defence; could the action at Brandywine, at which time Genl. Washington's army was entirely routed for that day, with as great loss, at least, as ever was published; could the Germantown affair, in which our army were again broke, dispersed, and persued for more than ten miles from the place of the first attack, with the loss of more than one thousand men; in short, could a large superiority of numbers on the side of Mr. How through the whole campaign, and in consequence thereof his being able to go to what point he pleased—I ask could any of these make you sanguine? Even now, since the northern troops have joined, How's army is the largest, which is now some above ten thousand, ours not eight thousand.

With respect to the clothing, etc., etc., of our army, believe it, Sir, to be bad enough. Ever since our march from Albany our men have been suffering all the inconveniences of an inclement season and a want of cloathing. For a week past we have had snow, and as cold weather as I almost ever knew at home. To see our poor brave fellows living in tents, bare-footed, bare-legged, bare-breeched, etc., etc., in snow, in rain, on marches, in camp, and on duty, without being able to supply their wants is really distressing. Where the fault is I know not, but am rather inclined to think our General Court has not done every thing that might be expected of them. If it be for want of foresight in our rulers, the Lord pity us! But if it be through negligence or design, "is there not some chosen curse" reserved for those who are cause of so much misery?

Another thing which has been the occasion of much complaint is the unequal distribution and scanty allowance of provisions. For the former of these the Commissary's are accountable. The cursed Quakers and other inhabitants are the cause of the latter. But those difficulties are at an end. Large supplies of provisions from N. England (which on account of the critical situation of affairs has been stopped till now) are now coming into camp. Another ground of uneasiness among our troops (the northern) is the want of money. Our regiment has never received but two months pay for twelve months past. This difficulty I hope will soon be over.

I have mentioned these particulars not to sink your spirits, but just to give you a small idea of a soldier's life. Under all those disadvantages no men ever shew more spirit or prudence than ours. In my opinion nothing but virtue has kept our army together through this campaign. There has been that great principle, the love of our country, which first called us into the field, and that only to influence us. But this will not last always: Some other motives must cooperate with this in order to keep an army together any length of time. Upon the same principle that we love our country we love ourselves. It must be for private interest of officers, at least, to continue in the service any considerable time: and without having an experienced you cannot have a respectable army; and without a respectable you cannot have a good army. I know of no reason why one part of the community should sacrifice their all for the good of it, while the rest are filling their coffers. We have this consolation, however, that it cannot be said that we are bought or bribed into the service. Those officers who can keep out of debt, especially who have considerable families, this year may with propriety be called good husbands.

The above intelligence with respect to How's and the American army will help you to account for the loss of Philadelphia, the forts on the Delaware, etc., etc. I assure you those events have not been lost for want of spirit, but numbers. As to my observations with respect to the situation of the army at present, and their future prospects, I have made them at your desire and for your speculation. As to another campaign, I can form no judgment about it. How Congress will augment their force is not public. By the inactivity of the States it seems as if they chose to prolong the war.

The States of Pennsylvania and Maryland do not seem to have any more idea of liberty than a savage has of civilization. In general they have not been able to feel themselves interested in this controversey. They have ever supposed (till wofull experience taught them otherwise) that the King's troops were as kind, mercifull and just as they represented themselves to be. But now the tone is altering fast. Even some of the Thees and Thous, who have had their wives ravished, houses plundered and burned, are now ready, on any party's making a sally from the city, to take their arms and oppose them. Last winter How made the Jersey's the best of Whigs. I hope all will be converted in these States this [winter]; and that next summer the whole continent will feel their importance and exert that small part of her strength which, when duly applied, will be sufficient to hurl all the How's in the universe into atoms.

What would have been the situation of New England at this moment had they shown the same disposition towards Genl. Burgoyne which the cringing, non-resisting, ass-like fools of this State have done towards How? The chains of British slavery would have been unalterably fixed: and instead of adressing you at this time as a freeman, I should have expressed my friendship to a slave. Oh! horrid thought! To be a slave! Oh! base idea first conceived in hell!

> "Do thou, great Liberty! inspire our souls,
> And make our lives in thy possession happy,
> Or our deaths glorious in thy just defence!"

P.S.—Notwithstanding my prolixity, I must congratulate you on the success of Gen. Smallwood. A few days since a brig, as she was going from N. York to Philadelphia up the Delaware, was met with a body of ice which drove her ashore, which the Gen. observing sent his division with 4 light field-pieces, and upon receiving two shot surrendered. Exclusive of the crew, 75 troops and 32 officers' wives, alias whores, she had on board large quantities of spirits, wine, porter, officers' baggage, 1800 suits of cloaths, 1500 stand arms, linnens, etc., etc. Several other vessells have shared the same fate. Yesterday one laden with 300 barrells provisions was captured the same way. Gen. Smallwood with his two brigades are stationed at and near Wilmington, below Philadelphia.

—BROOKS, "Letter," *Mass. Hist. Soc. Proc.*, XIII, 243-245.

8. "In All Human Probability the Army Must Soon Dissolve"

Brigadier General James Mitchell Varnum to Nathanael Greene.

Valley Forge, February 12, 1778

The situation of the camp is such that in all human probability the army must soon dissolve. Many of the troops are destitute of meat, and are several days in arrear. The horses are dying for want of forage. The country in the

vicinity of the camp is exhausted. There cannot be a moral certainty of better-
ing our circumstances while we continue here. What consequences have we
rationally to expect? Our desertions are astonishingly great; the love of freedom, which once animated the breasts of those born in the country, is controlled by hunger, the keenest of necessities. If we consider the relation in
which we stand to the troops, we cannot reconcile their sufferings to the sentiments of honest men. No political consideration can justify the measure. There
is no local object of so much moment as to conceal the obligations which bind
us to them. Should a blind attachment to a preconcerted plan fatally disaffect,
and in the end force the army to mutiny, then will the same country, which
now applauds our hermitage, curse our insensibility.

I have from the beginning viewed this situation with horror! It is unparal-
lelled in the history of mankind to establish winter quarters in a country wasted,
and without a single magazine. We now only feel some of the effects which
reason from the beginning taught us to expect as inevitable. My freedom upon
this occasion may be offensive; I should be unhappy, but duty obliges me to
speak without reserve. My own conscience will approve the deed, when some
may perhaps look back with regret to the time when the evil in extreme might
have been prevented. There is no alternative but immediately to remove the
army to places where they can be supplied, unless effectual remedies can be
supplied upon the spot, which I believe every gentleman of the army thinks
impracticable.

—Washington Papers, Lib. of Congress.

VII. THE "CONWAY CABAL"

Washington's disappointing achievements on the field of battle at Brandy-
wine and Germantown stood out in stark contrast to the victory at Saratoga
for which Horatio Gates claimed credit. Critics of the commander in chief
felt that he should be replaced by Gates. Such critics could be found in the
Lee-Adams faction, and included James Lovell of Massachusetts, Samuel
Adams, Thomas Mifflin and Richard Henry Lee. This group were critical of
the handling of foreign affairs by Silas Deane and Benjamin Franklin abroad
and of military operations at home. Most outspoken of Washington's critics
was Dr. Benjamin Rush, once but no longer a member of Congress. John
Adams shared Rush's views. "I am sick of Fabian systems in all quarters!" he
exclaimed.

Congressional enemies of Washington moved to clip his wings when, on
November 27, Gates was named president of the Board of War, and General
Thomas Conway, an Irish-born officer in the French Army, for whom Wash-
ington had little but contempt, was made inspector general on December 14.
Conway, in a letter to Gates, had already expressed his feelings in favor of sub-
stituting Gates for Washington, and the fact of this communication was ap-
parently disclosed by Gates's aide, James Wilkinson, while drunk. A fantastic
personality whose reputation for veracity and loyalty was never high, Wil-
kinson later held a top post in the postwar army and was implicated in Aaron
Burr's western intrigues.

Among the Continental officers there was a solid bloc of influential figures who were thoroughly devoted to Washington. They included Nathanael Greene, Lord Stirling, Lafayette, Hamilton and John Laurens. Washington himself, probably aided and abetted by that master controversialist Alexander Hamilton, took the offensive in a series of devastating letters, and the project to supplant him withered away. Conway was challenged and seriously wounded in a duel by General John Cadwalader, and, in a letter written in expectation of death, apologized to Washington. The fact is that the so-called "Conway Cabal" represented no real "plot" against Washington, and that his opponents did not co-ordinate their moves to displace him.

1. GENERAL CONWAY'S IMAGINARY MERIT

George Washington to Richard Henry Lee.

Matuchen Hill, Phila. City, Oct. 17, 1777

If there is any truth in a report which has been handed to me, Vizt., that Congress hath appointed, or, as others say, are about to appoint, Brigadier Conway a Major General in this Army, it will be as unfortunate a measure as ever was adopted. I may add (and I think with truth) that it will give a fatal blow to the existence of the Army.

Upon so interesting a subject, I must speak plain: The duty I owe my Country; the Ardent desire I have to promote its true Interests, and justice to Individuals requires this of me. General Conway's merit, then, as an Officer, and his importance in this Army, exists more in his own imagination, than in reality: For it is a maxim with him, to leave no service of his own untold, nor to want any thing which is to be obtained by importunity: But, as I do not mean to detract from him any merit he possesses, and only wish to have the matter taken up upon its true Ground, after allowing him every thing that his warmest Friends will contend for, I would ask, why the Youngest Brigadier in the service (for I believe he is so) should be put over the heads of all the Eldest? and thereby take Rank, and Command Gentlemen, who but Yesterday, were his Seniors; Gentlemen, who, I will be bold to say (in behalf of some of them at least) of sound judgment and unquestionable Bravery? If there was a degree of conspicuous merit in General Conway, unpossessed by any of his Seniors, the confusion which might be occasioned by it would stand warranted upon the principles of sound policy; for I do readily agree that this is no time for trifling; But, at the same time, I cannot subscribe to the fact, this truth I am very well assured of . . . that they will not serve under him. I leave you to guess, therefore, at the situation this Army would be in at so important a Crisis, if this event should take place. These Gentlemen have feelings as Officers, and though they do not dispute the Authority of Congress to make Appointments, they will judge of the propriety of acting under them. In a Word, the service is so difficult, and every necessary so expensive, that almost all our Officers are tired out: Do not, therefore, afford them good pretexts for retiring: No day passes over my head without application for leave to resign. . . .

To Sum up the whole, I have been a Slave to the service: I have undergone more than most Men are aware of, to harmonize so many discordant parts;

but it will be impossible for me to be of any further service, if such insuper-able difficulties are thrown in my way. . . .

— FITZPATRICK, ed., *Writings of Washington*, IX, 387-389.

2. WASHINGTON CONFRONTS CONWAY WITH EVIDENCE OF DISLOYALTY

George Washington to General Thomas Conway.

November 9, 1777

Sir:

A Letter which I receivd last Night, containd the following paragraph.

In a Letter from Genl. Conway to Genl. Gates he says: "Heaven has been determind to save your Country; or a weak General and bad Councellors would have ruind it."

I am Sir Yr. Hble Servt.

GEORGE WASHINGTON

— FITZPATRICK, ed., *Writings of Washington,* X, 29.

3. GATES ASSUMES A TONE OF INJURED INNOCENCE

General Gates to George Washington.

November [probably December] 8, 1777

I shall not attempt to describe what, as a private Gentlemen, I cannot help feeling on representing to my Mind the disagreeable Situation which confi-dential Letters, when exposed to public Inspection, may place an unsuspect-ing Correspondent to; but, as a public Officer, I conjure your Excellency to give me all the Assistance you can in tracing out the Author of the Infidelity which put Extracts from General Conway's Letters to me into your Hands. Those Letters have been Stealingly copied; but, of them, when, or by whom is to me, as yet, an unfathomable Search.

There is not one Officer in my Suite, nor amongst those who have a free Access to me, upon whom I would, with the least Justification to myself, fix the Suspicion; and yet my Uneasiness may deprive me of the Usefulness of the worthiest Men. It is, I believe, in your Excellency's Power to do me, and the United States, a very important Service by detecting a Wretch who may betray me and capitally injure the very Operations under your immediate Direction. For this Reason, Sir, I beg your Excellency will favour me with the Proofs you can procure to that Effect. But, the Crime being eventually so important that the least Loss of Time may be attended with the worst Consequences, and it being unknown to me whether the Letter came to you from a Member of Congress or from an Officer, I shall have the Honour of transmitting a Copy of this to the President, that the Congress may, in Con-cert with your Excellency, obtain, as soon as possible, a Discovery which so deeply Affects the Safety of the States. Crimes of that Magnitude ought not to remain unpunished.

— Gates Papers, Box VIII, No. 209, N.Y. Historical Soc.

4. WASHINGTON PUTS GATES IN HIS PLACE

Valley Forge, January 4, 1778

Sir: Your Letter of the 8th. Ulto. come to my hands a few days ago; and, to my great surprize informed me, that a Copy of it had been sent to Congress, for what reason, I find myself unable to acct.; but, as some end doubtless was intended to be answered by it, I am laid under the disagreeable necessity of returning my answer through the same channel, lest any Member of that honble. body, should harbour an unfavourable suspicion of my having practiced some indirect means, to come at the contents of the confidential Letters between you and General Conway.

I am to inform you then, that Colo. Wilkenson, in his way to Congress in the Month of Octobr. last, fell in with Lord Stirling at Reading, and, not in confidence that I ever understood, inform'd his Aid de Camp Majr. McWilliams that General Conway had written thus to you,

"Heaven has been determined to save your Country; or a weak General and bad Councellors* would have ruined it."

Lord Stirling from motives of friendship, transmitted the acct. with this remark.

"The inclosed was communicated by Colonl. Wilkinson to Majr. McWilliams, such wicked duplicity of conduct I shall always think it my duty to detect."

In consequence of this information, and without having any thing more in view than merely to shew that Gentn. that I was not unapprized of his intrieguing disposition, I wrote him a Letter in these Words.

"Sir. A Letter which I received last night contained the following paragraph.

In a Letter from Genl. Conway to Genl. Gates he says, "Heaven has been determined to save your Country; or a weak General and bad Councellors would have ruined it."

I am Sir &ca."

Neither this Letter, nor the information which occasioned it, was ever, directly, or indirectly communicated by me to a single Officer in this Army (out of my own family) excepting the Marquis de la Fayette, who, having been spoken to on the Subject by Genl. Conway, applied for, and saw, under injunctions of secrecy, the Letter which contained Wilkenson's information; so desirous was I, of concealing every matter that could, in its consequences, give the smallest Interruption to the tranquility of this Army, or afford a gleam of hope to the enemy by dissentions therein.

Thus Sir, with an openess and candour which I hope will ever characterize and mark my conduct have I complied with your request; the only concern I feel upon the occasion (finding how matters stand) is, that in doing this, I have necessarily been obliged to name a Gentn. whom I am perswaded (although I never exchanged a word with him upon the Subject) thought he was rather doing an act of Justice, than committing an act of infidility; and sure I am, that, till Lord Stirlings Letter came to my hands, I never knew that General Conway (who I viewed in the light of a stranger to you) was a corrispondant of yours, much less did I suspect that I was the subject of your confidential Letters; pardon me then for adding, that so far from conceiving that the safety of the States can be affected, or in the smallest degree injured,

---

* Washington starred this word "Councellors" and wrote at the bottom of the page: "One of whom, by the by, he was."

by a discovery of this kind, or, that I should be called upon in such solemn terms to point out the author, that I considered the information as coming from yourself; and given with a friendly view to forewarn, and consequently forearm me, against a secret enemy; or, in other words, a dangerous incendiary; in which character, sooner or later, this Country will know Genl. Conway. But, in this, as in other matters of late, I have found myself mistaken. I am, etc.

—FITZPATRICK, ed., *Writings of Washington*, X, 263-265.

5. "PUT A GATES, LEE OR CONWAY AT THE HEAD OF OUR ARMIES!"

The following was an anonymous letter which Patrick Henry forwarded to Washington. The handwriting unquestionably is that of Dr. Benjamin Rush, then one of the medical directors of the army. Its disclosure ruined his army career.

Benjamin Rush to Patrick Henry.

York town, January 12, 1778

The common danger of our country first brought you and me together. I recollect with pleasure the influence of your conversation and eloquence upon the opinions of this country in the beginning of the present controversy. You first taught us to shake off our idolatrous attachment to royalty, and to oppose its encroachments upon our liberties with our very lives. By these means you saved us from ruin. The independence of America is the offspring of that liberal spirit of thinking and acting which followed the destruction of the specters of kings and the mighty power of Great Britain.

But, sir, we have only passed the Red Sea. A dreary wilderness is still before us, and unless a Moses or a Joshua are raised up in our behalf, we must perish before we reach the promised land. We have nothing to fear from our enemies on the way. General Howe, it is true, has taken Philadelphia; but he has only changed his prison. His dominions are bounded on all sides by his outsentries. America can only be undone by herself. She looks up to her councils and arms for protection, but alas! what are they? Her representation in Congress dwindled to only twenty-one members. Her Adams, her Wilson, her Henry, are no more among them. Her counsels weak, and partial remedies applied constantly for universal diseases. Her army—what is it? A major general belonging to it called it a few days ago in my hearing a *mob*. Discipline unknown, or *wholly* neglected. The quartermaster's and commissaries' departments filled with idleness and ignorance and peculation. Our hospitals crowded with 6000 sick but half provided with necessaries or accommodations, and more dying in them in one month than perished in the field during the whole of the last campaign. The money depreciating without any effectual measures being taken to raise it. The country distracted with the Don Quixote attempts to regulate the prices of provision; and *artificial* famine created by it and a *real* one dreaded from it. The spirit of the people failing through a more intimate acquaintance with the causes of our misfortunes—many submitting daily to General Howe, and more wishing to do it only to avoid the calamities which threaten our country.

But is our case desperate? By no means. We have wisdom, virtue and strength *enough* to save us if they could be called into action. The northern army has shown us what Americans are capable of doing with a GENERAL at their head. The spirit of the southern army is no ways inferior to the spirit of the northern. A Gates, a Lee, or a Conway would in a few weeks render them an irresistible body of men. The last of the above officers has accepted of the new office of inspector general of our army in order to reform abuses. But this remedy is only a palliative one. In one of his letters to a friend he says, "A great and good God hath decreed America to be free, or the —— —— and weak counselors would have ruined her long ago." You may rest assured of *each* of the facts related in this letter. The author of it is one of your Philadelphia friends. A hint of his name, if found out by the handwriting, must not be mentioned to your most intimate friend. Even the letter *must* be thrown in the fire. But some of its contents ought to [be] made public in order to awaken, enlighten, and alarm our country. I rely upon your prudence and am, dear sir, with my usual attachment to *you* and to our beloved independence, yours sincerely.

—BUTTERFIELD, ed., *Letters of Benjamin Rush*, I, 182-183.

VIII. THE BRITISH ABANDON PHILADELPHIA

Anyone who had predicted that the American army, freezing and starving at Valley Forge, would soon again become masters of the metropolis of America, and that without firing a shot, would have been regarded as the victim of delusions. The British army found Philadelphia a snug and hospitable retreat for the winter of '77-'78. The city was teeming with friendly Loyalists, and many Quakers, incensed that some of their leaders had been arrested and banished to the western part of Virginia, looked on the red-coats as their deliverers. While foraging parties from both sides desolated the countryside, the city of Philadelphia was a scene of war prosperity. Theaters were crowded, and military companies performed plays for which the talented Major André painted the scenery.

Howe did not move against Washington and the attempts to recruit Loyalist regiments were only partial successes. Finally, the British government, dissatisfied with the way Howe had managed his campaigns, decided on his recall. His successor was his subordinate, Sir Henry Clinton, who arrived in Philadelphia on the eighth of May. Before Howe's departure an elaborate fete was given in his honor, known as the "Mischianza," a regatta, mock tournament and ball; more sober residents felt this levity was in bad taste.

News of the French alliance affected the opposing armies in quite opposite ways. To the Patriots it was the occasion of a great celebration. To the British it meant that they could not continue to keep their lines extended. Clinton brought with him orders to evacuate Philadelphia. This news was a great shock to the Tories, who felt that the British had no moral right to abandon them to reprisals by the Patriots. The leading Loyalist spokesman, Joseph Galloway, who was superintendent of police, argued in vain for a reversal of this decision. On June 18 the British, having dismantled their defenses and loaded their stores on ships in the harbor, embarked their troops on boats and took them over to Gloucester on the Jersey coast. There were no parades, no public farewells. It all happened very quietly. As one resident put it, "They did not go away, they vanished."

1. NEWS OF THE FRENCH ALLIANCE MAKES "A DAY OF REJOYSING"

Diary of George Ewing, a Continental soldier.

May 6th, 1778. This day we fired a grand fue de joy on account of the news brought by Mr. Simeon Dean in the *La Sensible* from our Plenepotentiary at the Court of France the purport of which was that the Courts of France and Spain had declard the U States of America to be free and independant States and had ceded to us all the teritories on the continent of America which formerly belonged to the Crown of Great Britain, and also the Island of Bermuda, and also to assist us in carrying on this just and necessary war with no other conditions on our part but that we should not in any treaty of peace with England give up our independancy.

In consequence of this intelligence this day was set apart for a day of rejoysing throuout the whole army. Accordingly at ten o'clock A M a cannon was fired as a signal for the whole to parade, and after a discourse suited to the subject by the chaplains of each brigade a second cannon fired a signal for each brigade to repair to their respective post. Thirteen six-pounders were drove to a height in the rear of Conway's brigade. After the troops were posted the flag on the fort was dropt and the third cannon fired at the park when the 13 cannon fired on the height, after which a fire of musquetry began on the right of the front line and proceeded to the left of the same and then instantly beginning on the left of the rear line proceeded to the right of the same. After this firing was over a fourth cannon from the park was the signal for three cheers and "Long live the King of France," after this thirteen more cannon and musquetry as aforesaid the signal and three cheers and a shout of "God save the friendly powers of Europe." The third cannon and mus[i]que as aforesaid signal and cheers and a shout of "God Save the American States." As soon as this was concluded the troops marched to their respective quarters. No accident happened during this day. After the fue de joy was over and the troops dismised his Excellency invited the officers of the army to assemble under a booth that was prepared for the purpose and partake of a cold collation which was prepared for them where he did us the honour [to] eat and drink with us where many patriotic toasts were drank and the [celebration] concluded with harmless mirth and jollity.

This day was a general releasement of prisoners.

—EWING, *George Ewing*, pp. 48-51.

2. "THE MOST SPLENDID ENTERTAINMENT GIVEN TO A GENERAL"

Major John André to someone in London, on the Mischianza.

Philadelphia, May 23, 1778

[In honor of Sir William Howe two pavilions were erected on either side of a square prepared for a tournament. Seated in the front were seven young ladies wearing dazzling Turkish costumes, and attached to their turbans were the favors they intended to reward the knights who were to contest in their honor. A band of knights dressed in habits of white and red silk and mounted on gray horses, richly caparisoned in trappings of the same colors, entered the lists.]

After they had made the circuit of the square, and saluted the Ladies as they passed before the pavilions, they ranged themselves in a line with that in which were the Ladies of their device; and their Herald (Mr. Beaumont) advancing into the centre of the square, after a flourish of trumpets, proclaimed the following challenge:

"The Knights of the Blended Rose, by me their Herald, proclaim and assert that the Ladies of the Blended Rose excel in wit, beauty and every accomplishment those of the *whole world;* and should any Knight or Knights be so hardy as to dispute or deny it, they are ready to enter the lists with them and maintain their assertions by deeds of arms, according to the laws of ancient chivalry."

At the third repetition of the challenge the sound of trumpets was heard from the opposite side of the square; and another Herald, with four Trumpeters, dressed in black and orange, galloped into the lists. He was met by the Herald of the Blended Rose, and after a short parley they both advanced in front of the pavilions, when the Black Herald (Lieut. More) ordered his trumpets to sound, and then proclaimed defiance to the challenge in the following words:

"The Knights of the Burning Mountain present themselves here, not to contest by words, but to disprove by deeds, the vain-glorious assertions of the Knights of the Blended Rose, and enter these lists to maintain that the Ladies of the Burning Mountain are not excelled in beauty, virtue or accomplishments by any in the universe."

He then returned to the part of the barrier through which he had entered; and shortly after the Black Knights, attended by their Squires, rode into the lists in the following order:

Four Trumpeters preceding the Herald, on whose tunic was represented a mountain, sending forth flames—Motto, *I burn for ever. . . .*

After they had rode round the lists and made their obeisance to the Ladies, they drew up fronting the White Knights; and the Chief of these having thrown down his gauntlet, the Chief of the Black Knights directed his Esquire to take it up. The Knights then received their lances from their Esquires, fixed their shields on their left arms, and making a general salute to each other by a very graceful movement of their lances, turned round to take their career, and, encountering in full gallop, shivered their spears. In the second and third encounter they discharged their pistols. In the fourth they fought with their swords.

At length the two Chiefs, spurring forward into the centre, engaged furiously in single combat, till the Marshal of the Field (Major Gwyne) rushed in between the Chiefs, and declared that the Fair Damsels of the Blended Rose and Burning Mountain were perfectly satisfied with the proofs of love and the signal feats of valour given by their respective Knights; and commanded them, as they prized the future favours of the Mistresses, that they would instantly desist from further combat.

Obedience being paid by the Chiefs to this order, they joined their respective bands. The White Knights and their attendants filed off to the left, the Black Knights to the right; and, after passing each other at the lower side of the quadrangle, moved up alternately, till they approached the pavilions of the Ladies, when they gave a general salute.

A passage being now opened between the two pavilions, the Knights, preceded by their Squires and the bands of music, rode through the first triumphal arch and arranged themselves to the right and left. This arch was erected in honour of Lord Howe. It presented two fronts, in the Tuscan order; the pediment was adorned with various naval trophies, and at top was the figure of Neptune, with a trident in his right hand. In a nich, on each side, stood a Sailor with a drawn cutlass. Three Plumes of Feathers were placed on the summit of each wing, and in the entablature was this inscription: *Laus illi debetur, et alme gratia major*. The interval between the two arches was an avenue 300 feet long, and 34 broad. It was lined on each side with a file of troops; and the colours of all the army, planted at proper distances, had a beautiful effect in diversifying the scene. Between these colours the Knights and Squires took their stations.

The bands continued to play several pieces of martial music. The company moved forward in procession, with the Ladies in the Turkish habits in front; as these passed, they were saluted by their Knights, who then dismounted and joined them: and in this order we were all conducted to a garden that fronted the house, through the second triumphal arch, dedicated to the General. This arch was also built in the Tuscan order. On the interior part of the pediment was painted a Plume of Feathers, and various military trophies. At top stood the figure of Fame. . . . On the right-hand pillar was placed a bomb-shell, and on the left a flaming heart. The front next the house was adorned with preparations for a fire-work.

From the garden we ascended a flight of steps, covered with carpets, which led into a spacious hall; the pannels, painted in imitation of Sienna marble, enclosing festoons of white marble: the surbase, and all below, was black. In this hall, and in the adjoining apartments, were prepared tea, lemonade and other cooling liquors, to which the company seated themselves; during which time the Knights came in, and on the knee received their favours from their respective Ladies. One of these rooms was afterwards appropriated for the use of the Pharaoh table; as you entered it you saw, on a panel over the chimney, a Cornucopia, exuberantly filled with flowers of the richest colours; over the door, as you went out, another presented itself, shrunk, reversed and emptied.

From these apartments we were conducted up to a ball-room, decorated in a light elegant stile of painting. The ground was a pale blue, pannelled with a small gold bead, and in the interior filled with dropping festoons of flowers in their natural colours. Below the surbase the ground was of rose-pink, with drapery festooned in blue. These decorations were heightened by 85 mirrors, decked with rose-pink silk ribbands and artificial flowers; and in the intermediate spaces were 34 branches with wax-lights, ornamented in a similar manner.

On the same floor were four drawing-rooms, with side boards of refreshments, decorated and lighted in the same stile and taste as the ball-room. The ball was opened by the Knights and their Ladies; and the dances continued till ten o'clock, when the windows were thrown open, and a magnificent bouquet of rockets began the fire-works. These were planned by Capt. Montresor, the chief engineer, and consisted of twenty different exhibitions, displayed under his direction with the happiest success and in the highest stile of beauty. Towards the conclusion, the interior part of the triumphal arch was illuminated amidst an uninterrupted flight of rockets and bursting of baloons. The military trophies on each side assumed a variety of transparent colours. The shell and flaming heart on the wings sent forth Chinese fountains, succeeded by fire-pots. Fame appeared at top, spangled with stars, and from her trumpet blowing the following device in letters of light, *Tes Lauriers sont immortels*. A *sauteur* of rockets, bursting from the pediment, concluded the *feu d'artifice*.

At twelve supper was announced, and large folding doors, hitherto artfully concealed, being suddenly thrown open, discovered a magnificent saloon of 210 feet by 40, and 22 feet in height, with three alcoves on each side, which served for side-boards. The cieling was the segment of a circle, and the sides were painted of a light straw-colour, with vine leaves and festoon flowers, some in a bright, some in a darkish green. Fifty-six large pier-glasses, ornamented with green silk artificial flowers and ribbands; 100 branches with three lights in each, trimmed in the same manner as the mirrours; 18 lustres, each with 24 lights, suspended from the cieling and ornamented as the branches; 300 wax tapers, disposed along the supper-tables; 430 covers, 1200 dishes; 24 black slaves, in oriental dresses, with silver collars and bracelets, ranged in two lines and bending to the ground as the General and Admiral approached the saloon: all there, forming together the most brilliant assemblage of gay objects, and appearing at once as we entered by an easy descent, exhibited a *coup d'oeil* beyond description magnificent.

Towards the end of supper, the Herald of the Blended Rose, in his habit of ceremony, attended by his trumpets, entered the saloon and proclaimed the King's health, the Queen, and Royal Family, the Army and Navy, with their respective Commanders, the Knights and their Ladies, the Ladies in general: each of these toasts was followed by a flourish of music. After supper we returned to the ball-room, and continued to dance till four o'clock.

Such, my dear friend, is the description, though a very faint one, of the most splendid entertainment, I believe, ever given by an army to their General. But what must be most grateful to Sir W. Howe is the spirit and motives from which it was given. He goes from this place to-morrow; but, as I understand he means to stay a day or two with his brother on board the *Eagle* at Billingsport, I shall not seal this letter till I see him depart from Philadelphia.

—*Annual Register for 1778*, pp. 267-270.

3. THE BRITISH DECIDE TO LEAVE PHILADELPHIA AND THE LOYALISTS

Journal of Ambrose Serle.

Thursday, 21st May, 1778. Very uneasy this morning on the information by Mr. G[alloway] of a conversation which passed between Genl. H[owe] and one of the first magistrates (Schumacher) in this city, who waited to take leave of him. Upon representing the uneasiness which prevailed among the loyal subjects on account of the Rebels, the Genl. [Howe] advised him "to make his peace with the States, who, he supposed, would not treat them harshly; for that it was probable, on account of the French War, the troops would be withdrawn." This was soon circulated about the town, and filled all our friends with melancholy on the apprehension of being speedily deserted, now a rope was (as it were) about their necks, and all their property subject to confiscation. The information chilled me with horror, and with some indignation when I reflected upon the miserable circumstances of the Rebels, etc.

Friday 22d. A confirmation of the sad intelligence of yesterday was communicated to Mr. Galloway by Sir Wm. Erskine from Sir Wm. Howe and Sir H. Clinton. It filled my poor friend, as might be expected, with horror and melancholy on the view of his deplorable situation: exposed to the rage of his bitter enemies, deprived of a fortune of about £70,000, and now left to wander like Cain upon the earth without home and without property. Many others are involved in the like dismal case for the same reason—attachment to their King and country, and opposition to a set of daring Rebels who might soon be crushed by spirited exertions. I now look upon the contest as at an end. No man can be expected to declare for us when he cannot be assured of a fortnight's protection. Every man, on the contrary, whatever might have been his primary inclinations, will find it his interest to oppose and drive us out of the country. I endeavored to console, as well as to advise my friend. I felt for him and with him. Nothing remains for him but to attempt reconciliation with (what I may now venture to call) the United States of America; which probably may not succeed, as they have attainted him in body and goods by an Act of the Legislature of Pennsylvania. O Thou righteous GOD, where will all this villainy end!

Mr G[alloway] summoned the magistrates of the town and imparted the sad news, which filled many an honest and loyal heart with grief and despair. . . .

Sunday, 24th May. This day the Genl. Sir Wm. Howe departed from Philadelphia, and the command devolved upon Sir H. Clinton, who presently afterwards sent a message by Col. Innes to my friend Mr. G[alloway], expressing his desire to see him. This was what I expected, and mentioned before to him, as a necessary object upon his assuming the command. So many reasons and circumstances occur against the abandonment of the town that, notwithstanding appearances, some of the most sensible cannot credit it. Their fortifying the principal redoubt, Bomb Proof, is certainly very remarkable. I sat down in the evening, and suggested in writing 13 (as I think) cogent reasons for Mr. G[alloway] to use with Sir Henry against the abandonment of this central province, which appeared so convincing to us that we received a gleam of hope that this terrible measure may be averted. . . .

Tuesday, 26th. Sir Wm. Erskine called upon Mr. G[alloway] and Mr. G[alloway] afterwards upon Sir H. Clinton. The result was, that it appears that the K[ing] under his sign man[ual] has ordered the abandonment of Philadelphia and the march of the army northwards, to co-operate with Sir

Guy Carleton. This damped our spirits. Many people come in who assert that nine tenths of the people are weary of the rebellion and the tyrannical oppression of their new governors, and would take up arms in our behalf if they had them; that the Indians and others are driving all before them in the backcountry; that Washington has sent off his heavy baggage from his present camp, from which he is ready to run, his people being almost ever under arms; that he has sent to the Jersies, apprehending we mean to pass through them, to raise the militia to annoy us; that the Rebels are in high spirits upon the occasion, and mean to throw in a body of the militia as soon as we have left the town, etc. Had much discourse with Mr. G[alloway] upon all these and other matters, and particularly upon the settlement of a correspondence between us. We talked over the idea, suggested to him by some friends, of presenting a memorial of consideration to Administration to be backed by Sir W. H[owe], which we thought it best for the present to delay for several reasons.

The town in great distress was occupied in preparing for our departure.

—Serle, *American Journal*, pp. 295-299.

CHAPTER FIFTEEN

France Comes In

For ALMOST *a century the nations of Europe had been engaged in an intermittent conflict spread over a world stage. Generally called the Second Hundred Years' War, that conflict had turned on dynastic rivalries, colonial interests, and the maintenance of the balance of power. In the four great wars which had ended in 1763 England and France were always on opposing sides, and in each war the North American continent was a theater of operations. The last of these four wars, called in America the French and Indian, saw France stripped of her major possessions in North America and the neat balance of power upon which statesmen had rested their hopes for peace temporarily destroyed.*

Would the American Revolution turn into a world war? Would France again take sides against her ancient enemy? Would the European absolute monarchies support a revolution against a king? Both Britain and her rebellious colonies were keenly aware that aid from the uncommitted foreign powers could tip the scales. Although Great Britain tried desperately to keep the Revolution from turning into a world conflict, she acted precipitately in securing military assistance from various German states. The American Congress in turn looked at once to France for aid short of war, then for a full-scale military alliance.

The diplomats with whom the American commissioners came in contact were experts in the techniques of secret diplomacy, procrastination, evasion and duplicity. But the inexperienced Americans did not behave precisely like innocents abroad. They themselves could be shrewd, subtle and suspicious—unfortunately of each other as well as of foreign chancelleries—and when American interest dictated, they could be forthright and moralistic. They soon learned that national interest governed the decisions of the major European powers and the extent of their involvement in the American conflict.

The story of the war on the diplomatic front, involving transparent subterfuge, plots and counterplots, espionage and counterespionage, and most of all a grand public-relations effort, is told in several chapters in this volume. It introduces America's greatest diplomat, the scientist-philosopher Benjamin Franklin, with the "universal reputation"; the underestimated and traduced Silas Deane, whose early services were indispensable to the cause of inde-

pendence; and brings to the fore two hard-headed and first-rate negotiators, John Jay and John Adams.

I. AMERICA SEEKS FOREIGN AID WITHOUT ENTANGLING ALLIANCES

To win the war against Great Britain the Patriot leaders quickly accepted the need for foreign aid in some form, but at the start many of them were wary of European alliances. On July 7, 1775, Franklin wrote Priestley: "We have not yet applied to any foreign power for assistance, nor offered our commerce for their friendship. Perhaps we never may; yet it is natural to think of it, if we are pressed." In his Common Sense *Tom Paine insisted that independence would free the former colonies from being dragged at the heels of England into European wars that were no concern of theirs.*

No Patriot expressed this view more forthrightly and consistently than did America's stalwart isolationist, John Adams. Arguing in the fall of 1775 that France was bound to come into the war anyhow, he warned that America must avoid alliances which would entangle her in future European wars. "When I first made these observations in Congress," wrote Adams with characteristic complacency, "I never saw a greater impression made upon that assembly or any other."

By the end of November of '75 Congress was ready to make cautious advances to the European powers. Their petition to the King had been disregarded, Americans were proclaimed rebels, and word had come that German troops were to be hired to crush the rebellion. On November 29 Congress set up a five-man secret Committee of Correspondence to get in touch with "our friends" abroad. One of the members, Benjamin Franklin, began almost at once to put out feelers as to the possibility of foreign aid or even an alliance.

By June of 1776 Franklin's position was taken for granted by Richard Henry Lee, who insisted that only by a declaration of independence could a foreign alliance be obtained, and that an alliance with a despotic power would not damage America's interests. As Robert Morris saw it, the issue was not so much that of avoiding entanglements as in dragging all Europe into war to help the cause of the Revolution. "Can this be morally right?" he asked John Jay in September 1776, "or have morality and polity nothing to do with each other?" America's diplomatic representatives abroad found varying answers to this question.

1. Avoid Alliances "Which Would Entangle Us," John Adams Warns

From the Autobiography.

[September 1775]

Some gentlemen doubted of the sentiments of France; thought she would frown upon us as rebels, and be afraid to countenance the example. I replied to those gentlemen that I apprehended they had not attended to the relative situation of France and England; that it was the unquestionable interest of France that the British Continental Colonies should be independent; that Britain, by the conquest of Canada and her naval triumphs during the last war, and by her vast possessions in America and the East Indies, was exalted to the height of power and pre-eminence that France must envy and could not endure.

But there was much more than pride and jealousy in the case. Her rank, her consideration in Europe and even her safety and independence were at stake. The Navy of Great Britain was now mistress of the seas, all over the globe. The Navy of France almost annihilated, its inferiority was so great and obvious that all the dominions of France, in the West Indies and in the East Indies, lay at the mercy of Great Britain, and must remain so as long as North America belonged to Great Britain, and afforded them so many harbors abounding with naval stores and resources of all kinds, and so many men and seamen ready to assist them and man their ships; that interest could not lie; that the interest of France was so obvious, and her motives so cogent, that nothing but a judicial infatuation of her councils could restrain her from embracing us; that our negotiations with France ought, however, to be conducted with great caution, and with all the foresight we could possibly obtain; that we ought not to enter into any alliance with her which should entangle us in any future wars in Europe; that we ought to lay it down as a first principle and a maxim never to be forgotten, to maintain an entire neutrality in all future European wars; that it never could be our interest to unite with France in the destruction of England, or in any measures to break her spirit or reduce her to a situation in which she could not support her independence.

On the other hand, it could never be our duty to unite with Britain in too great a humiliation of France; that our real, if not our nominal, independence would consist in our neutrality. If we united with either nation in any future war, we must become too subordinate and dependent on the nation, and should be involved in all European wars, as we had been hitherto; that foreign powers would find means to corrupt our people, to influence our councils, and, in fine, we should be little better than puppets, danced on the wires of the cabinets of Europe. We should be the sport of European intrigues and politics; that, therefore, in preparing treaties to be proposed to foreign powers, and in the instructions to be given to our ministers, we ought to confine ourselves strictly to a treaty of commerce; that such a treaty would be an ample compensation to France for all the aid we should want from her. The opening of American trade to her would be a vast resource for her commerce and naval power, and a great assistance to her in protecting her East and West India possessions, as well as her fisheries; but that the bare dismemberment of the British empire would be to her an incalculable security and benefit, worth more than all the exertions we should require of her, even if it should draw her into another eight or ten years' war.

—ADAMS, ed., *Works of John Adams*, II, 504-506.

2. FRANKLIN PUTS OUT FEELERS FOR ALLIANCES

Benjamin Franklin to his friend Charles William Dumas, at The Hague.

Philadelphia, December 9, 1775

... We are threatened from England with a very powerful force to come next year against us. We are making all the provision in our power here to prevent that force, and we hope we shall be able to defend ourselves. But as the events of war are always uncertain, possibly after another campaign we may find it necessary to ask aid of some foreign power. It gives us great pleasure to learn from you that "all Europe wishes us the best success in the maintenance of our liberty." But we wish to know whether any one of them, from principles of humanity, is disposed magnanimously to step in for the relief of an oppressed people, or whether if, as it seems likely to happen, we should be obliged to break off all connection with Britain and declare ourselves an independent people, there is any state or power in Europe who would be willing to enter into an alliance with us for the benefit of our commerce, which amounted, before the war, to near seven millions sterling per annum, and must continually increase, as our people increase most rapidly.

Confiding, my dear friend, in your good will to us and our cause, and in your sagacity and abilities for business, the committee of Congress, appointed for the purpose of establishing and conducting a correspondence with our friends in Europe, of which committee I have the honor to be a member, have directed me to request of you that, as you are situated at The Hague, where ambassadors from all courts reside, you would make use of the opportunity which that situation affords you of discovering, if possible, the disposition of the several courts with respect to such assistance or alliance, if we should apply for the one or propose for the other. As it may possibly be necessary, in particular instances, that you should, for this purpose, confer directly with some great ministers, and show them this letter as your credential, we only recommend it to your discretion that you proceed therein with such caution as to keep the same from the knowledge of the English ambassador, and prevent any public appearance, at present, of your being employed in any such business, as thereby, we imagine, many inconveniences may be avoided, and your means of rendering us service increased. . . .

We have hitherto applied to no foreign power. We are using the utmost industry in endeavoring to make saltpeter, and with daily increasing success. Our artificers are also everywhere busy in fabricating small arms, casting cannon, etc. Yet both arms and ammunition are much wanted. Any merchants who would venture to send ships laden with those articles might make great profit; such is the demand in every colony, and such generous prices are, and will be, given, of which, and of the manner of conducting such a voyage, the bearer, Mr. Story, can more fully inform you. And whoever brings in those articles is allowed to carry off the value in provisions to our West Indies, where they will fetch a very high price, the general exportation from North America being stopped. This you will see more particularly in a printed resolution of the Congress.

We are in great want of good engineers and wish you could engage and send us two able ones in time for the next campaign, one acquainted with field service, sieges, etc., and the other with fortifying sea ports. They will, if well recommended, be made very welcome and have honorable appointments, besides the expenses of their voyage hither, in which Mr. Story can also advise them. As what we now request of you, besides taking up your time, may put you to some expense, we send you, for the present, inclosed a bill for one hundred pounds sterling to defray such expenses, and desire you to be assured that your services will be considered and honorably rewarded by the Congress. . . .

—WHARTON, *Revolutionary Diplomatic Correspondence*, II, 64-67.

II. FRANCE GIVES AID SHORT OF WAR

The Seven Years' War, a crushing defeat for France, impelled her statesmen to reassess her diplomatic position and to consider anew ways of weakening Great Britain. In 1767 the Duc de Choiseul, France's foreign minister, dispatched Johann de Kalb, later to serve in the Patriot army, to report on the state of discontent in the American colonies. His report was negative and disappointing to his superiors. Thenceforth it became a cardinal point in French foreign policy that disaffection in America would weaken British power. A successful revolt might well restore the balance of power so rudely upset by the overwhelming British victory in 1763. By calling into existence the New World, France would "redress the balance of the Old."

Thus reasoned that prudent diplomat, the Comte de Vergennes, who became France's foreign minister when Louis XVI ascended the throne in 1774. His views were supported, probably in some measure shaped, by an extraordinary adventurer and master of backstairs intrigue, the talented playwright Pierre Augustin Caron, who wrote Figaro and other plays under the pseudonym of Beaumarchais. The playwright had a talent for publicity, both good and bad. At the time the Revolution began he was under a sentence of the Parlement of Paris, which deprived him of his civil rights for attempting to bribe a judge. The American cause aroused his enthusiasm and challenged his audacity. The result was a practical plan for aiding America.

The curtain for the first act rose in London in September 1775, when Beaumarchais dispatched to his King an exaggerated account of the Patriots' will to resist. ("I say, Sire, that such a nation must be invincible.") On his next visit to England he prepared a second paper for the King, which went through Vergennes's hands. In it he advocated assistance short of war. Beaumarchais discussed his plans with Arthur Lee, the Virginian then resident in England who had been authorized to collect information for the Congress as to the disposition of foreign powers, but who was without power to negotiate. On June 12 the Frenchman wrote Lee that he was setting up a private company to "send help to your friend in the shape of powder and ammunition in exchange for tobacco." This company was to conduct its operations under the name of Roderigue Hortalez et Compagnie.

In July 1776, Silas Deane arrived in Paris in the guise of a businessman. The Connecticut merchant Patriot had been commissioned by the secret Committee of Correspondence to buy military and other supplies and to probe the possibilities of securing more extensive assistance on the part of France. Deane was indefatigable in procuring needed supplies and recruiting officers abroad for the American army, perhaps overly generous in recognizing the rank and talents of some of the European applicants.

In September Congress appointed a diplomatic mission composed of Frank-

lin, Arthur Lee, and Deane himself to secure additional material aid from France, the recognition of independence, and treaties of commerce and alliance. Dr. Bancroft will appear repeatedly.

1. THE AUTHOR OF *Figaro* COMES TO THE RESCUE OF THE COLONIES

Pierre Augustin Caron de Beaumarchais to Louis XVI alone (given unclosed to M. de Vergennes).

February 29, 1776

Sire,—The famous quarrel between America and England, which will soon divide the world and change the system of Europe, imposes upon each power the necessity of examining well in what manner the event of this separation can influence it, and either serve it or injure it. . . .

At present, when a violent crisis is approaching with great rapidity, I am obliged to warn Your Majesty that the preservation of our possessions in America, and the peace which Your Majesty appears to desire so much, depend solely upon this one proposition: *the Americans must be assisted.* I will now demonstrate it.

The King of England, the ministers of the Parliament, the opposition, the nation, the English people, all the parties, in fine, who are tearing this state asunder, agree that they ought no longer to hope to regain the Americans, and that not even the great efforts which are being now made to subject them can ever reduce them with success. Thence, sire, these violent debates between the ministry and the opposition, this flux and reflux of opinions admitted or rejected, which, as they do not advance matters, only serve to put the question in a plainer and a clearer light. . . .

Let us submit all possible hypotheses, and let us reason.

What follows is very important.

Either England will have the most complete success in America during the campaign;

Or the Americans will repel the English with loss.

Either England will come to the determination already adopted by the king of abandoning the colonies to themselves, or parting from them in a friendly manner;

Or the opposition, in taking possession of the government, will answer for the submission of the colonies on condition of their being restored to the position they were in in 1763.

Here are all the possibilities collected together. Is there a single one of them which does not instantly give you the war you wish to avoid? Sire, in the name of God, deign to examine the matter with me.

First, if England triumphs over America, she can only do so by an enormous expenditure of men and money. Now the only compensation the English propose to themselves for so many losses is to take possession on their return of the French islands, and thus make themselves the exclusive vendors of the valuable supply of sugar, which can alone repair all the injuries done to their commerce, and this capture would also render them forever the absolute possessors of the advantages derived from the contraband commerce carried on by the Continent with these islands.

Then, Sire, there would remain to you nothing but the option of commencing at a later period an unprofitable war, or of sacrificing to the most shameful of inactive peaces all your American colonies, and of losing 280 millions of capital, and more than 30 millions of revenue.

2. If the Americans are victorious, they instantly become free, and the English, in despair at seeing their existence diminished by three quarters, will only be the more anxious, the more eager to seek a compensation, which will have become indispensable, in the easy capture of our American possessions; and we may be certain that they will not fail to do so.

3. If the English consider themselves forced to abandon the colonies to themselves without striking a blow, as it is the secret wish of the king they should do, the loss being the same for their existence, and their commerce being equally ruined, the result for us would be similar to the preceeding one, except that the English, less weakened by this amicable surrender than by a bloody and ruinous campaign, would only derive from it more means and facilities for gaining possession of our islands, which they would then be unable to do without if they wished to preserve their own and to keep any footing in America.

4. If the opposition takes possession of the government and concludes a treaty of reunion with the colonies, the Americans, indignant with France, whose refusal will alone have caused them to submit to the mother country, threaten us from the present moment to unite all their forces with England in order to take possession of our islands. They will, indeed, only reunite with the mother country on this condition, and Heaven knows with what joy the ministry, composed of Lords Chatham, Shelburne and Rockingham, whose dispositions toward us are publicly known, would adopt the resentment of the Americans, and carry on against you without cessation the most obstinate and cruel war.

What, then, is to be done in this extremity, so as to have peace and preserve our islands?

You will only preserve the peace you desire, Sire, by preventing it at all price from being made between England and America, and in preventing one from completely triumphing over the other; and the only means of attaining this end is by giving assistance to the Americans which will put their forces on an equality with those of England, but nothing beyond. And believe me, Sire, that the economy of a few millions at present may, before long, cost a great deal of blood and money to France.

—De Lomenie, *Beaumarchais*, III, 117-123.

2. Congress Instructs Deane in the Negotiation with France

The Committee of Secret Correspondence to Silas Deane.

Philadelphia, March 3, 1776

On your arrival in France, you will for some time be engaged in the business of providing goods for the Indian trade. This will give good countenance to your appearing in the character of a merchant, which we wish you continually to retain among the French, in general, it being probable that the court of France may not like it should be known publicly that any agent from the Colonies is in that country. When you come to Paris, by delivering Dr. Franklin's letter to Monsieur Le Roy at the Louvre, and M. Dubourg, you will be introduced to a set of acquaintances, all friends to the Americans. By conversing with them, you will have a good opportunity of acquiring Parisian French, and you will find in M. Dubourg a man prudent, faithful, secret, intelligent in affairs, and capable of giving you very sage advice.

It is scarce necessary to pretend any other business at Paris than the gratifying of that curiosity which draws numbers thither yearly, merely to see so famous a city. With the assistance of Monsieur Dubourg, who understands English, you will be able to make immediate application to Monsieur de Vergennes, *Ministre des Affaires Etrangères*, either personally or by letter, if M. Dubourg adopts that method, acquainting him that you are in France upon business of the American Congress, in the character of a merchant, having something to communicate to him that may be mutually beneficial to France and the North American Colonies; that you request an audience of him, and that he would be pleased to appoint the time and place.

At this audience if agreed to, it may be well to show him first your letter of credence, and then acquaint him that, the Congress finding that in the common course of commerce it was not practicable to furnish the continent of America with the quantity of arms and ammunition necessary for its defence (the Ministry of Great Britain having been extremely industrious to prevent it), you had been despatched by their authority to apply to some European power for a supply. That France had been pitched on for the first application, from an opinion that if we should, as there is a great appearance we shall, come to a total separation from Great Britain, France would be looked upon as the power whose friendship it would be fittest for us to obtain and cultivate. That the commercial advantages Britain has enjoyed with the Colonies had contributed greatly to her late wealth and importance. That it is likely great part of our commerce will naturally fall to the share of France; especially if she favors us in this application, as that will be a means of gaining and securing the friendship of the Colonies; and that as our trade was rapidly increasing with our increase of people, and in a greater proportion, her part of it will be extremely valuable. That the supply we at present want is clothing and arms for twenty-five thousand men with a suitable quantity of ammunition, and one hundred field pieces. That we mean to pay for the same by remittances to France or through Spain, Portugal or the French Islands, as soon as our navigation can be protected by ourselves or friends; and that we besides want great quantities of linens and woollens, with other articles for the Indian trade, which you are now actually purchasing, and for which you ask no credit, and that the whole, if France should grant the other supplies, would make a cargo which it might be well to secure by a convoy of two or three ships of war.

If you should find M. de Vergennes reserved and not inclined to enter into free conversation with you, it may be well to shorten your visit, request him to consider what you have proposed, acquaint him with your place of lodging, that you may yet stay some time at Paris, and that knowing how precious his time is, you do not presume to ask another audience, but that if he should have any commands for you, you will upon the least notice immediately wait upon him.

If at a future conference he should be more free, and you find a disposition to favor the Colonies, it may be proper to acquaint him that they must necessarily be anxious to know the disposition of France on certain points, which, with his permission, you would mention, such as whether if the Colonies should be forced to form themselves into an independent state, France would probably acknowledge them as such, receive their ambassadors, enter into any treaty or alliance with them, for commerce or defence, or both? If so, on what principal conditions? Intimating that you shall speedily have an opportunity of sending to America, if you do not immediately return, and that he may be assured of your fidelity and secrecy in transmitting carefully any thing he would wish conveyed to the Congress on that subject.

In subsequent conversations you may, as you find it convenient, enlarge on these topics that have been the subjects of our conferences with you, to which you may occasionally add the well-known substantial answers we usually give to the several calumnies thrown out against us. If these supplies on the credit of the Congress should be refused, you are then to endeavor the obtaining a permission of purchasing those articles, or as much of them as you can find credit for. . . .

You will endeavor to procure a meeting with Mr. Bancroft by writing a letter to him, under cover to Mr. Griffiths at Turnham Green, near London, and desiring him to come over to you, in France or Holland, on the score of old acquaintance. From him you may obtain a good deal of information of what is now going forward in England, and settle a mode of continuing a correspondence. It may be well to remit him a small bill to defray his expenses in coming to you, and avoid all political matters in your letter to him. You will also endeavor to correspond with Mr. Arthur Lee, agent of the Colonies in London. . . .

—DEANE, "Correspondence," *Conn. Hist. Soc. Coll.*, II, 365-368.

3. "I Am About to Enter on the Great Stage of Europe"

Silas Deane to Mrs. Deane.

March 3, 1776

You will not imagine I am unfeeling on this occasion—but to what purpose would it be to let my tender passions govern, except to distress you? I shall take every precaution, and if I fall into the enemie's hands, doubt not of good usage, as their sending Commissioners will be a security to me; but I am prepared even for the worst, not wishing to survive my country's fate, and confident, while that is safe, I shall be happy in almost any situation.

I have, in one of the most solemn acts of my life, committed my son and what I have to your care and the care of my brother, confident you will be to him a real mother, which you ever have been, and for my sake, as well as from the truly maternal affection you have ever borne for him, guard his youth from any thing dangerous or dishonorable. I can but feel for the pain I must give you by this adventure, but on all occasions you will have this satisfaction, that let what will happen, you have in every situation discharged your duty as one of the best of partners and wives, while on my part, by a peculiar fatality attending me from my first entrance into public life, I have ever been involved in one scheme and adventure after another, so as to keep my mind in constant agitation and my attention fixed on other objects than my own immediate interests.

The present object is great. I am about to enter on the great stage of Europe, and the consideration of the importance of quitting myself well weighs me down, without the addition of more tender scenes; but I am

> "Safe in the hand of that protecting Power,
> Who ruled my natal, and must fix my mortal hour."

It matters but little, my dear, what part we act, or where, if we act it well. I wish as much as any man for the enjoyments of domestic ease, peace and society, but am forbid expecting them soon; indeed, must be criminal in my own eyes, did I balance them one moment in opposition to the public good and the calls of my country.

I do not recollect any thing to add; it is a late hour, and to-morrow will be a busy day with me, as I hope to sail on Tuesday. May God Almighty protect you safe thro' the vicissitudes of times!

Yours, thro' life and all its scenes,

S. D.

P.S. Confident this letter will go safe, I venture to say that a concern, different from my contract, is to support me. I have agreed that all expenses of every kind shall be paid, and referred my salary to be determined hereafter, in consequence of which it is agreed that I have five hundred pounds sterling to carry with me for that purpose, and the same sum is to be remitted to me at the end of six months.

Should any accident happen to me, you will find this entered on the Committee of Secret Correspondence's books. The members are: Dr. Franklin, Mr. Dickinson, Mr. Jay, Mr. Morris, Col. Harrison, and Mr. Johnson. But you must not communicate this to any one except to my brother. This will explain my saying that I have a commission of two thousand pounds free of charge, as my charge will be amply provided for by the other way. And now, my dear, are not the ways of Providence dark and inscrutable to us, short-sighted mortals? Surely they are. My enemies thought to triumph over me and bring me down, yet all they did has been turned to the opening a door for the greatest and most extensive usefulness, if I succeed; but if I fail—why then the cause I am engaged in, and the important part I have undertaken, will justify my adventuring. . . .

—DEANE, "Correspondence," *Conn. Hist. Soc. Coll.*, II, 362-363.

4. BEAUMARCHAIS EXPLAINS HIS SECRET SUPPLY SYSTEM

To the Committee of Secret Correspondence of the Continental Congress.

Paris, August 18, 1776

The respectful esteem that I bear towards that brave people who so well defend their liberty under your conduct has induced me to form a plan concurring in this great work, by establishing an extensive commercial house, solely for the purpose of serving you in Europe, there to supply you with necessaries of every sort, to furnish you expeditiously and certainly with all articles—clothes, linens, powder, ammunition, muskets, cannon, or even gold for the payment of your troops, and in general every thing that can be useful for the honorable war in which you are engaged. Your deputies, gentlemen, will find in me a sure friend, an asylum in my house, money in my coffers, and every means of facilitating their operations, whether of a public or secret nature. I will, if possible, remove all obstacles that may oppose your wishes from the politics of Europe.

At this very time, and without waiting for any answer from you, I have procured for you about two hundred pieces of brass cannon, four-pounders, which will be sent to you by the nearest way, two hundred thousand pounds of cannon powder, twenty thousand excellent fusils, some brass mortars, bombs, cannon balls, bayonets, platines, clothes, linens, etc., for the clothing of your troops, and lead for musket balls. An officer* of the greatest merit for artillery and genius, accompanied by lieutenants, officers, artillerists, cannoniers, etc., whom we think necessary for the service, will go for Philadelphia even before you have received my first despatches. This gentlemen is one of the greatest presents that my attachment can offer you. Your deputy, Mr. Deane, agrees with me in the treatment which he thinks suitable to his office; and I have found the power of this deputy sufficient that I should prevail with this officer to depart under the sole engagement of the deputy respecting him, the terms of which I have not the least doubt but Congress will comply with.

The secrecy necessary in some part of the operation which I have undertaken for your service requires also, on your part, a formal resolution that all the vessels and their demands should be constantly directed to our house alone, in order that there may be no idle chattering or time lost—two things that are the ruin of affairs. You will advise me what the vessels contain which you shall send into our ports. I shall choose so much of their loading, in return for what I have sent, as shall be suitable to me when I have not been able beforehand to inform you of the cargoes which I wish. I shall facilitate to you the loading, sale and disposal of the rest.

For instance, five American vessels have just arrived in the port of Bordeaux, laden with salt fish. Though this merchandise, coming from strangers, is prohibited in our ports, yet as soon as your deputy had told me that these vessels were sent to him by you to raise money from the sale for aiding him in his purchases in Europe, I took so much care that I secretly obtained from the Farmers-General an order for landing it without any notice being taken of it. I could even, if the case had so happened, have taken on my own account these cargoes of salted fish, though it is no way useful to me, and charged myself with its sale and disposal, to simplify the operation and lessen the embarrassments of the merchants and of your deputy.

I shall have a correspondent in each of our seaport towns who, on the

---

* Charles Tronson du Coudray, who caused Washington embarrassment by insisting that he be given command of the artillery, superseding Knox. He was drowned in the Schuylkill, whether accidentally or by suicide has never been determined.

arrival of your vessels, shall wait on the captains and offer every service in my power. He will receive their letters, bills of lading, and transmit the whole to me. Even things which you may wish to arrive safely in any country in Europe, after having conferred about them with your deputy, I shall cause to be kept in some secure place. Even the answers shall go with great punctuality through me, and this way will save much anxiety and many delays. I request of you, gentlemen, to send me next spring, if it is possible for you, ten or twelve thousand hogsheads, or more if you can, of tobacco from Virginia of the best quality. . . .

Notwithstanding the open opposition which the King of France, his ministers and the agents of administration show, and ought to show, to everything that carries the least appearance of violating foreign treaties and the internal ordinances of the kingdom, I dare promise to you, gentlemen, that my indefatigable zeal shall never be wanting to clear up difficulties, soften prohibitions, and, in short, facilitate all operations of a commerce which my advantage, much less than yours, has made me undertake with you. What I have just informed you of is only a general sketch, subject to all the augmentations and restrictions which events may point out to us.

One thing can never vary or diminish: it is the avowed and ardent desire I have of serving you to the utmost of my power. You will recollect my signature, that one of your friends in London, some time ago, informed you of my favorable disposition towards you and my attachment to your interest. Look upon my house, then, gentlemen, from henceforward as the chief of all useful operations to you in Europe, and my person as one of the most zealous partisans of your cause. . . .

—WHARTON, *Revolutionary Diplomatic Correspondence*, II, 129-131.

5. BEAUMARCHAIS AND THE MYSTERY OF THE "LOST MILLION"

Shrouded in mystery are the operations of the colorful and devious Beaumarchais. In furnishing arms and supplies to the American cause through his dummy firm, Beaumarchais was not entirely forthright as to whether the supplies were a gift for which nominal payments in produce were made to disguise the transactions as commercial, or whether Congress was expected to pay for them. On the basis of early conversations with Beaumarchais in London, Arthur Lee was to insist that the supplies were a gift. On the other hand, Deane acted on the assumption that America was expected to pay, and was so instructed by Congress. Beaumarchais entered into a business agreement with Deane according to which Congress was required to pay for the arms and other supplies in produce or money at a date not fixed.

What complicates the whole transaction is the fact that Beaumarchais received a secret subsidy from the Kings of France and Spain in 1776 amounting to two million livres (the livre was replaced by the franc at the time of the French Revolution), and another million the following year. After the war Beaumarchais claimed that the United States government owed him 3,600,000 livres, but payment was put off when it was discovered that the American commissioners at Paris had given receipts to the French government for one million livres more than they had received. The million livres had been given to Beaumarchais by the French government and the United States insisted on the right to set it off against Beaumarchais's claim.

Beaumarchais's accounts were reviewed several times. His arch-foe, Arthur Lee, reported that he owed the United States 1,800,000 livres. Hamilton, when Secretary of the Treasury, restored a balance in his favor, but the French Revolutionary regime failed to support his claim. Beaumarchais's heirs in 1835 received 800,000 francs out of monies due to the United States for spoliations committed in the Napoleonic period in accordance with the treaty of 1831.

A. BEAUMARCHAIS SIGNS A RECEIPT FOR THE MILLION LIVRES

Vergennes refused the request of the United States to give up Beaumarchais's receipt, but after the French Revolution, on application of Gouverneur Morris, then minister to France, a copy of the receipt was turned over, and it is reproduced here in original and translation.

[1776]

J'ai reçu de Monsieur Du Vergier,—Conformément aux ordres de Monsieur le Comte de Vergennes en date du 5. courant que je lui ai remis. La somme d'un million, dont je rendrai compte à monditsieur Comte de Vergennes à Paris ce 10. juin 1776.

Signé: CARON DE BEAUMARCHAIS. Bon pour un million de livres tournois. Pour copie conforme.

Le commissaire de relations Extérieures.

BUCHOT

TRANSLATION: I have received from M. Du Vergier, in conformity with the instructions from the Count de Vergennes under date of the 5th current, which I have remitted to him. The sum of one million, for which I will give an accounting to the Count de Vergennes. At Paris the 10th June 1776.

Signed: Caron de Beaumarchais. For one million livres, Tours currency. [Worth about 10 d.]

A true copy.

The commissioner of foreign affairs.

—Gouverneur Morris Collection.

B. "AMERICANS, I DIE YOUR CREDITOR"

Beaumarchais to the American people.

Hamburg, April 10, 1795

Americans, I have served you with unwearied zeal; I have received during my life nothing but bitterness for my recompense, and I die your creditor. Suffer me, then, in dying, to bequeath to you my daughter to endow with a portion of what you owe me. Perhaps, after me, through the injustice of other persons, from which I shall no longer be able to defend myself, there will remain nothing in the world for her; and perhaps Providence has wished to procure for her, through your delay in paying me, a resource after my death against complete misfortune. Adopt her as a worthy child of the state!

Her mother—equally unhappy, and my widow—her mother will conduct her to you. Let her be looked upon among you as the daughter of a citizen.

But if, after this last effort, after all I have just said, contrary to all that seems possible, I could fear you would again reject my petition—if I could fear that to me or to my heirs you would refuse arbitrators, desperate, ruined as I am, as much through Europe as through you, and as your country is the only one where I can, without shame, extend my hand to the inhabitants, what remains for me to do except to supplicate Heaven to restore me for a short time to health, so as to permit me to travel to America? Arrived in the midst of you, with mind and body weakened, unable to maintain my rights, would it be necessary then that, with my proofs in my hand, I should be carried on a stool to the entrance of your national assemblies, and that, holding out to all the cap of liberty, with which no man has helped more than myself to decorate your heads, I should exclaim to you, "Americans, bestow alms on your friend, whose accumulated services have received but this reward? *Date obolum Belisario!*"

—De Lomenie, *Beaumarchais*, III, 217-218.

III. FRANCE ENTERS THE WAR

Three circumstances conspired to bring France into the war as an ally of America. First of all, there was Franklin's enormous prestige and popularity, a universal reputation to which even John Adams paid grudging tribute. This esteem is illustrated by two different accounts of a celebrated meeting between Franklin and Voltaire. The fur-capped Philadelphian epitomized all the virtues of an eighteenth-century Cincinnatus. His New World prestige was buttressed by Old World diplomatic skill and by his unique talents as a propagandist. Second came the victory at Saratoga, which made it clear that France could now get into the war on the winning side. Thirdly, the British efforts at conciliation with the colonies frightened France into taking hasty action without waiting upon her major ally, Spain.

After Saratoga, Vergennes was alarmed that he might miss the boat. "The power that will first recognize the independence of the Americans will be the one that will reap the fruits of this war," he wrote, paraphrasing Beaumarchais. Pressed by the American commissioners, who were receiving peace feelers from England, and in spite of Spain's refusal to join such an alliance, a French royal council on January 7, 1778, declared unanimously for a treaty of amity and commerce with the United States and then for a treaty of alliance on February 6.

The treaty of alliance had as its avowed end the "absolute and unlimited independence of the United States." It bound each of the allies to guarantee to the other the American possessions that it might hold at the end of the war. Hence, France was bound to defend American territory in North America, and the United States to come to the defense of the French West Indies. The treaty further provided that neither party should sign a treaty of peace with the common enemy without the consent of the other.

The treaty of amity and commerce defined the privileges to be enjoyed

*by the ships and commerce of both countries during a war in which one was
neutral while the other was belligerent. The ships of the neutral should be
free to carry noncontraband merchandise not only to the unblockaded ports
of an enemy but from one enemy port to another. Free ships were to make
free goods. Contraband was narrowly defined to consist almost entirely of
arms and ammunition. All else was noncontraband. In addition, armed ships
of the belligerent ally were to be allowed special privileges in the ports of the
neutral, while they were to be denied to the ships of the opposing belligerent.
This included the belligerent's right to bring prizes into the ports of the
neutral and to depart with them without interference. These provisions were
to plague the Federalist administration of Washington in the years ahead.*

*If to Vergennes France's entry into the war was sweet revenge, his coun-
terpart in the negotiations, Benjamin Franklin, must have nursed emotions
not unsimilar. Bancroft, the British secret agent and Franklin's secretary,
later told the story that at the signing ceremony the Philadelphian wore the
same suit of Manchester velvet that he had worn in London on that day in
1774 when he was subject to the savage examination of Attorney General
Wedderburn for having made public certain letters of Governor Hutchinson—an event which was followed by Franklin's dismissal from his office of
deputy postmaster general in America. Franklin never wore these clothes
again. They had served their purpose.*

1. The Reputation and Influence of Benjamin Franklin

A. solon and sophocles embrace

The diary of John Adams.

April 29, 1778. After dinner we went to the Academy of Sciences and
heard M. d'Alembert, as perpetual secretary, pronounce eulogies on several
of their members, lately deceased. Voltaire and Franklin were both present,
and there presently arose a general cry that M. Voltaire and M. Franklin
should be introduced to each other. This was done, and they bowed and
spoke to each other. This was no satisfaction; there must be something more.
Neither of our philosophers seemed to divine what was wished or expected;
they, however, took each other by the hand. But this was not enough; the
clamor continued, until the explanation came out. *"Il faut s'embrasser, à la
Française."* The two aged actors upon this great theatre of philosophy and
frivolity then embraced each other, by hugging one another in their arms,
kissing each other's cheeks, and then the tumult subsided. And the cry immediately spread through the whole kingdom, and, I suppose, over all Europe,
"Qu'il était charmant de voir embrasser Solon et Sophocle!" . . .

—Adams, ed., *Works of John Adams,* III, 147.

B. condorcet recounts the meeting of franklin and voltaire

They then went to a public meeting of the Academy of Sciences. The
scene was a moving one: Placed side by side, these two men, born in different
worlds, venerated for their years, their reputations, the things they had done
with their lives, and both delighting in the influence they had exerted in
their age.

They embraced each other amid shouts of approval. Some one said that Solon was embracing Sophocles. But the French Sophocles had demolished error and advanced the reign of reason, while the Solon from Philadelphia, resting the constitution of his country on the unshakable foundation of the rights of man, had no occasion to fear that he would see during his lifetime doubtful laws fashioning chains for his country and opening the door to tyranny.

—Condorcet, "Vie de Voltaire," *Oeuvres de Voltaire*, I, 290.

C. "more universal than newton, frederick or voltaire, but——"

John Adams writes in May 1811 about Franklin's reputation.

Mr. Jefferson has said that Dr. Franklin was an honor to human nature. And so, indeed, he was. Had he been an ordinary man, I should never have taken the trouble to expose the turpitude of his intrigues, or to vindicate my reputation against his vilifications and calumnies. But the temple of human nature has two great apartments: the intellectual and the moral. If there is not a mutual friendship and strict alliance between these, degradation to the whole building must be the consequence. There may be blots on the disk of the most refulgent luminary, almost sufficient to eclipse it. And it is of great importance to the rising generation in this country that they be put upon their guard against being dazzled by the surrounding blaze into an idolatry to the spots. If the affable archangel understood the standard of merit, that

> "Great or bright infers not excellence,"

Franklin's character can neither be applauded nor condemned, without discrimination and many limitations.

To all those talents and qualities for the foundation of a great and lasting character, which were held up to the view of the whole world by the University of Oxford, the Royal Society of London and the Royal Academy of Sciences in Paris, were added, it is believed, more artificial modes of diffusing, celebrating and exaggerating his reputation than were ever before or since practiced in favor of any individual.

His reputation was more universal than that of Leibnitz or Newton, Frederick or Voltaire, and his character more beloved and esteemed than any or all of them. Newton had astonished perhaps forty or fifty men in Europe; for not more than that number, probably, at any one time had read him and understood him by his discoveries and demonstrations. And these being held in admiration in their respective countries as at the head of the philosophers, had spread among scientific people a mysterious wonder at the genius of this perhaps the greatest man that ever lived. But this fame was confined to men of letters. The common people knew little and cared nothing about such a recluse philosopher. Leibnitz's name was more confined still. Frederick was hated by more than half of Europe as much as Louis XIV was, and as Napoleon is. Voltaire, whose name was more universal than any of those before mentioned, was considered as a vain, profligate wit, and not much esteemed or beloved by anybody, though admired by all who knew his works.

But Franklin's fame was universal. His name was familiar to government and people, to kings, courtiers, nobility, clergy and philosophers, as well as plebeians, to such a degree that there was scarcely a peasant or a citizen, a *valet de chambre,* coachman or footman, a lady's chambermaid or a scullion in a kitchen who was not familiar with it, and who did not consider him as a friend to human kind. When they spoke of him, they seemed to think he was to restore the golden age. They seemed enraptured enough to exclaim

> *Aspice, venturo laetentur ut omnia saeclo.*

To develop that complication of causes which conspired to produce so singular a phenomenon is far beyond my means or forces. Perhaps it can never be done without a complete history of the philosophy and politics of the eighteenth century. Such a work would be one of the most important that ever was written; much more interesting to this and future ages than the *Decline and Fall of the Roman Empire,* splendid and useful as that is. . . . He [Franklin] was considered as a citizen of the world, a friend to all men and an enemy to none. His rigorous taciturnity was very favorable to this singular felicity. He conversed only with individuals, and freely only with confidential friends. In company he was totally silent. . . .

Franklin had a great genius, original, sagacious and inventive, capable of discoveries in science no less than of improvements in the fine arts and the mechanic arts. He had a vast imagination, equal to the comprehension of the greatest objects, and capable of a steady and cool comprehension of them. He had wit at will. He had humor that, when he pleased, was delicate and delightful. He had a satire that was good-natured or caustic, Horace or Juvenal, Swift or Rabelais, at his pleasure. He had talents for irony, allegory and fable that he could adapt with great skill to the promotion of moral and political truth. He was master of that infantine simplicity which the French call *naïveté,* which never fails to charm, in *Phaedrus* and La Fontaine, from the cradle to the grave. Had he been blessed with the same advantages of scholastic education in his early youth, and pursued a course of studies as unembarrassed with occupations of public and private life, as Sir Isaac Newton, he might have emulated the first philosopher. Although I am not ignorant that most of his positions and hypotheses have been controverted, I cannot but think he has added much to the mass of natural knowledge, and contributed largely to the progress of the human mind, both by his own writings and by the controversies and experiments he has excited in all parts of Europe. . . .

—Adams, ed., *Works of John Adams,* I, 659-661, 663-664.

2. Saratoga Works a Revolution in the French Attitude

Journal of Arthur Lee.

27 Nov. [*1777*]. The commissioners met to consult on their despatches to Congress. Mr. D[eane] began the discourse; he remarked upon the proceedings of this court, with a good deal of ill-humour and discontent, said he thought it was our duty to state the whole to Congress, that things seem to be going very bad in America, they would be less provided for next campaign, and more pressed than ever. He therefore was of opinion we should lay before this court such a statement as would produce a categorical answer to the proposition of an alliance, or satisfy them that without an immediate inter-position, we must accommodate with Great Britain.

Dr. F[ranklin] was of a different opinion; he could not consent to state that we must give up the contest without their interposition, because the effect of such a declaration upon them was uncertain. It might be taken as a menace. It might make them abandon us in despair or in anger. Besides he did not think it true. He was clearly of opinion that we could maintain the contest, and successfully too, without any European assistance; he was satisfied, as he had said formerly, that the less commerce or dependence we had upon Europe, the better, for that we should do better without any connexion with it.

Mr. Lee was against any such declaration, lest it might deprive them of the assistance they now received instead of increasing it. He thought this court had acted uniformly and consistently with their declarations; that the violent things done were of necessity, and compelled by the bad conduct of our people; that we ought to instruct those who were going to America to avoid speaking with bitterness against this country, but rather to soften the resentment of others, arising from considering the injuries and not the benefits we had received from France; he was of opinion that if the credit of their funds was maintained, all would go well. . . .

[*Dec.*] *6th.* Mons. Gérard, first secretary to Count Vergennes, met the commissioners at Passy. He said he came from the counts Maurepas* and Vergennes, to congratulate the commissioners upon the news [of the American victory at Saratoga], to assure them of the great pleasure it gave at Versailles, and to desire on the part of the king any farther particulars they might have. He was informed that extracts were making from all the papers, which should be sent the moment it was finished; and Mr. L. promised to send extracts from his brother's letter, which contained some farther particulars. Mr. Gérard said they might depend on three millions of livres also from Spain, but he believed it would be through the Havannah and New-Orleans. He said as there now appeared no doubt of the ability and resolution of the states to maintain their independency, he could assure them it was wished they would reassume their former proposition of an alliance, or any new one they might have, and that it could not be done too soon; that the court of Spain must be consulted, that they might act in harmony, and prepare for war in a few months.

—R. H. LEE, *Life of Arthur Lee*, I, 354-355, 357-358.

3. NEGOTIATING AN ALLIANCE WITH VERGENNES

Journal of Arthur Lee.

Dec. 12th, [1777]. My colleagues did not reach Versailles till half after eleven o'clock, when, upon sending notice by a servant to Mr. Girard, his servant came with a hackney coach and carried us to a house about half a mile from Versailles, where we found Count Vergennes and his secretary. . . .

The minister took our last memorial from his secretary and read it. He then desired we would give him the information it promised, and any thing

---

* Count Jean Frédéric de Maurepas, Principal Minister in the Cabinet of Louis XVI.

we had new to offer. Dr. F[ranklin] said that the entering into the treaty proposed was the object, and that if there were any objections to it, we were ready to consider them. The count said that it was the resolution of his court to take no advantage of our situation, to desire no terms of which we might afterwards repent and endeavour to retract; but to found whatever they did so much upon the basis of mutual interest as to make it last as long as human institutions would endure. He said that entering into a treaty with us would be declaring our independency, and necessarily draw on a war. In this, therefore, Spain must be consulted, without whose concurrence nothing could be done. . . .

The next objection was that Spain would not be satisfied with the indeterminate boundary between their dominions and the United States, for that the state of Virginia, being supposed to run to the South Sea, might trench upon California. It was answered that the line drawn by the last treaty of peace with England, the Mississippi, would be adopted and would prevent all disputes. For that, though its source was not yet known, yet it might be agreed that a line drawn straight from its source, when found, should continue the boundary. This was admitted, as adjusting the matter properly. . . . It was, too, a first principle with us that fishing was free to all.

The conference ended with the count's observing that we must consider our independence as yet in the womb, and must not endeavour to hasten its birth immaturely. That he would despatch a courier to Spain, and it would be three weeks before his return. That the order for presenting clearances for the United States was recalled, and he would speak with Mons. de Sartine [Minister of Marine] about giving us a convoy for our supplies.

—R. H. Lee, *Life of Arthur Lee*, I, 360-362.

4. It Is Now or Never If France and Spain Are to Profit

Comte de Vergennes to Comte Armand de Montmorin, French Ambassador at Madrid.

Versailles, December 13, 1777

. . . You will understand, Monsieur le Comte, that what I send today . . . must be communicated to the Minister. . . . I shall not recall here either the outlines or the reflections which you will find scattered there; I am sure you will seize in a masterly way the whole state of affairs, and add to the force they so naturally present. There are, however, some considerations I did not wish to insert, which I have reserved for you, and which you will appropriate if you think them worth the trouble.

The first is that Spain's interest in this matter is at least ten times as much as ours; our islands are little likely to tempt the cupidity of the English, who have enough of them themselves. They want treasure, and it is only on the mainland that they can gather it. That being the case, it is easy to estimate, on the one hand, the infinite advantage to Spain of the absolute separation of new and old England, and the safety and peace which would be procured by the guarantee of the former; and, on the other hand, the incessantly arising uneasiness and dangers with which she would be threatened by too close a political coalition between the two nations.

A second reflection may bear on the fresh advantages which Spain may obtain. Perhaps she regrets the loss of Florida, which gives too easy access to the Gulf of Mexico, and would see that province with as much pain in the hands of the United States of America as in those of England. I do not know what the Americans may think on this subject; I have not taken measures to find out; but it is natural to suppose that they cannot care much about a thing which they do not yet possess, and which does not even seem of major importance to them. They are still too young to have ambitious views about opening up an interloping trade for themselves; being without any manufactures suitable for the use of the West Indies, they cannot aspire to carry their goods to lands which would be in a position to furnish them with the same.

A third reflection, which seems a natural consequence of the preceding ones, is that the interest for separating the English Colonies from their mother country and preventing them from ever being re-identified in any manner whatever is so important that even if it had to be purchased at the price of a somewhat disadvantageous war, if the two Crowns brought about that separation, it seems that they should not regret that war, whatever the issue may be.

The King our master is fully convinced, Sir, of these truths; they are so impressed on his mind that although exempt from that cruel ambition which causes the unhappiness of a country, having no views of conquest whatever, His Majesty would not hesitate to declare himself openly and be beforehand with the English, if his extreme delicacy and his warm attachment to the King his uncle did not cause his own interests to give way to the deference which he professes in his heart for that Prince whose enlightenment he admires and whose experience he reveres.

Take for your device, Monsieur le Comte, and cause it to be adopted where you are, *aut nunc aut nunquam* [now or never]. Events have surprised us; they have marched more rapidly than we could have expected. The time lost, if any, is not entirely our fault, but there is no more to be lost. I am pleased to think that no breach has yet been committed, and that if Spain will be good enough to tell us her decision, and the right one, we shall be beforehand with the English, or at least shall cross them: if, against all expectation, we disdain or neglect the most important conjuncture which Heaven could offer, the reproaches of the present generation and those of posterity will for ever accuse our culpable indifference.

—*Stevens' Facsimiles*, No. 1775.

5. Vergennes Agrees to a Treaty of Alliance

Narrative of Conrad Gérard, Secretary to Vergennes, of a conference with the American commissioners.

January 9, 1778

Count de Maurepas and Count de Vergennes having been good enough to commission me to announce to the American Deputies the resolutions taken by the King in adopting the memorandum intended for Spain, . . . we agreed to meet yesterday evening at six o'clock at Mr. Deane's house in Paris. . . .

I opened the conference by announcing that I was charged with a message which would begin to realise the hopes and the assurances which the King and his Ministry had caused to be given them, . . . but [as] in so important a matter most absolute secrecy should be observed, I must before all things beg them to be good enough to promise that, whatever might be the result of our conference and of the whole negotiation, they would not confide my message to anyone soever. . . .

I was allowed to continue to hold forth in this strain, Mr. Deane sometimes supporting my reasoning, and I then formally repeated my proposal. Dr. Franklin finally said, "I promise," and Mr. Lee and Mr. Deane repeated the same formula. Considering the distrust entertained of the Doctor's views, I think I gained a very important point.

Then I declared that, being now able to speak to them without reserve, I would announce to them that the King, being henceforth persuaded that the United States were resolved to maintain their independence, had decided to co-operate efficaciously to uphold it and to cause it to be firmly established; that the very deliberation which His Majesty had observed in coming to this decision, guaranteed the sincerity of his disposition and the firmness which he would bring to the carrying out of his resolutions; that they were exempt from all views of ambition and aggrandisement; that he only desired to bring about irrevocably and completely the independence of the United States; that he would find therein his essential interest in the weakening of his natural enemy, and that this important and permanent interest would render the American cause in future common to France; that His Majesty could not yet take nor announce a decisive course, which depended on combinations personal to himself, and on matters which he could not concert with the Deputies; but that I hoped that the specific and positive assurances I was authorised to give them would cause the most entire confidence in His Majesty's sentiments and in the disposition of His Ministry; that I consequently expected that the Deputies would in future unreservedly disclose their views; that we must at the present moment consider in this way two things which might be distinct: 1st, the decisive means for ending this great quarrel, the examination and employment of which would require time and would depend on events; and 2nd, the necessity of immediately preventing the effect of all the traps and manoeuvres which England employs to seduce the Deputies, and perhaps Congress, by the bait of a false peace and a mutilated or precarious independence; that they must not be mistaken; that England felt that the Americans were really in possession of their independence and would strive to allow only the shadow of it to exist, and that it would perhaps be limited to exclusive commercial advantages; but that it would suffice her to preserve some sort of thread of dependence and obligation, in order to put afterwards the liberty and tranquillity of the Colonies in danger; that they must not deceive themselves; and that the most clear-sighted people had felt, from the beginning of the troubles, that it was a commercial war, and that the least advantage saved for the mother country would decide the contest in her favour. . . .

Mr. Franklin briefly took up my speech, and spoke in a sense which inferred an immediate war.

As soon as I saw him bear on that idea, I stopped him, and stated that the immediate declaration of war did not enter into the present policy of the

King, and that amongst the means we sought, that one must be absolutely excluded. . . . I thought right to press him by telling him that the most urgent point depended on them—the Deputies—since it was a question of knowing what they, as zealous and enlightened citizens, would consider sufficient to reject all the proposals of England which did not include the recognition of full and absolute independence both in politics and trade, and that my second question was—what would they consider equally necessary to produce the same effect on Congress, and on the American people?

Mr. Franklin again spoke of war, and said afterwards that my two questions presented great difficulties, which would require time to settle, and he wished to defer giving me his reply to another day. I told him that I did not know when I could return, but that it seemed to me he might at least answer me as to their personal views. . . .

The Doctor . . . said that he would like to be able to settle the reply together. I . . . said that it was for me to leave them to deliberate without restraint, that I would go away and return. . . . It was agreed that I should return in an hour.

On my return, I found Mr. Franklin writing; he told me they were agreed as to the first point of my request, but that they had not yet come to a decision on the second. I was going to withdraw again, but Mr. Deane stopped me, saying that the manner in which I should explain the first point might facilitate their agreement on the second. I consequently proposed to the Doctor that he should read their first decision. He . . . read an article to the effect that *the immediate conclusion of a treaty of commerce and alliance would induce the Deputies to close their ears to any proposal which should not have as its basis entire liberty and independence, both political and commercial.*

I then declared that the King and his Ministry having presumed that such would be the desire of the Deputies, I had been authorised to tell them that whenever they should judge that treaty to be necessary His Majesty was resolved to conclude it at once, and that it would be begun as soon as they wished.

The Doctor, already softened by this resolution, which he did not appear to expect, observed that this was what they had proposed and solicited vainly for a year past. . . .

I . . . explained to him that two treaties might be concluded: the first, of peace, friendship and commerce, and the second, of eventual alliance; that the first would only contain clauses tending to regulate and confirm good feeling and commerce, that it would be permanent, would only contain harmless clauses, but that it would involve the recognition of independence. . . .

I added that the King, not wishing to make a war of ambition did not think he ought to require the United States to procure him any advantages or any increase of dominion; that the strengthening of the independence forming the principal object of his efforts, everything else would be accessory only; and that the compensation which France might justly claim would depend on events, without embarrassing the alliance with clauses the nonfulfillment of which (often impossible to carry out) only leads to dissatisfaction; that if nevertheless plans were formed on both sides they could agree as to the help to be furnished mutually as well as the advantages destined to form the compensation; that good policy would perhaps demand that they should agree not to cease war until the English were expelled from the continent of North America; that I did not know whether the King would make this a condition, or whether the States themselves would consider themselves in a position to carry out an enterprise on which their security and tranquillity appeared to depend.

The Deputies applauded this recital with a sort of transport. . . .

—*Stevens' Facsimiles*, No. 1831.

CHAPTER SIXTEEN

England Seeks Reconciliation

ALTHOUGH BY THE *end of 1774 George III was determined that blows would decide the issue, conciliatory moves were nonetheless attempted before the actual outbreak of hostilities. They were initiated both in the colonies and in England. We have already seen how the Plan of Union, offered by the Loyalist Joseph Galloway and based substantially upon Franklin's plan of 1754, was barely defeated in the First Continental Congress. Galloway's proposal would have set up a subordinate legislature in America, in effect creating a dominion status for the colonies. In February 1775, Chatham offered a bill legalizing the forthcoming meeting of the Second Continental Congress and denying Parliament's right to tax the colonies for revenue purposes, but nothing came of it. Instead, Lord North's own plan of reconciliation was endorsed by the Commons; by its terms Parliament would "forbear" to lay any but regulatory taxes upon any American colony. Since this proposal was coupled with legislation restraining New Englanders in trading and fishing, it was hardly issued in a conciliatory spirit. Still, despite the bloodshed at Lexington and Bunker's Hill, Congress in July of '75 adopted the Olive Branch Petition professing the attachment of the American people to George III, but that monarch refused even to receive it and issued instead his Proclamation of Rebellion.*

Having spurned Congress' original offer of conciliation, the North ministry suffered a change of heart and sent the olive branch to America on two separate occasions. The Howe mission, as we have already seen, was launched unpropitiously after the Declaration of Independence had been adopted. Its offer of conciliation was backed by what then seemed to be overwhelming force, and still it was rejected. The next occasion upon which the British formally presented conciliation terms was when the prospects of France's entry into the war on the side of the colonies seemed imminent. Since any proposal short of independence was not acceptable in the summer of '76, it should have seemed futile to even the most obtuse British cabinet officer to propose reconciliation when the Patriots had shown unexpected power on the battlefield and considerable success in securing foreign aid. True, the liberal terms which the Carlisle Commission was prepared to offer would have resolved all the major issues leading to the Revolution had they been proposed back in '74, but now it was too late. This chapter deals with Britain's persistent efforts to end the conflict by negotiation, intrigue or bribery.

I. THE ATTEMPT TO WOO FRANKLIN

The same desperate urgency that characterized French overtures to America after Saratoga marked British efforts both on the continent and in America to bring about reconciliation in order to prevent the alliance, and, when that was a fait accompli, to split the allies. In January 1778, James Hutton, an English Moravian, approached Franklin with peace feelers, but was quickly rebuked. Another Englishman, William Pulteney, followed suit. Franklin in March of '78 reminded him: "I see by the propositions you have communicated to me that the ministers cannot yet divest themselves of the idea that the power of Parliament over us is constitutionally absolute and unlimited." Acknowledgment of independence, he reminded Pulteney, was a sine qua non for ending hostilities. Finally, on July 1, he contemptuously rejected the proposals contained in a letter from "Charles de Weissenstein," believed by Franklin to be from King George, and containing peace proposals. It contained the suggestion that the American leaders might be bought with promises of peerages and substantial pensions. Franklin's reply was never sent, but instead was deposited at the French Foreign Office. Apprised that "M. Weissenstein" might show up at Notre Dame Cathedral to receive Franklin's answer, the French secret service reported seeing a mysterious stranger who lurked about the church for two hours and then disappeared.

1. FRANKLIN SPURNS PEACE FEELERS

A. JAMES HUTTON TO BENJAMIN FRANKLIN

London, January 27, 1778

I got to my own house in seventy-three hours from Paris. I shall never forget your kindness to me and your kind intention to serve my Brethren. The sensation I had of the certain miseries of war, that would attend all parties embarked in it, caused my heart almost to break. I always thought it a sad misfortune that there was such a thing as war upon earth.

When I left England I fancied that you and Mr. Deane could treat about peace. I wished it ardently; but having no commission, nor anything to offer, I was sorry to hear nothing of your side that I could mention as ground to treat upon, to such as I fancied could give it weight. I was a loving volunteer, loving both people with common ardour; a friend of peace; a hater of discord, with horror at all bloodshed, wishing you secure in your liberties, and guarded forever against all apprehensions. I did before I set out, and I do now still at this moment, and I think on better grounds, believe that anything short of absolute independency would almost be practicable, and could take place. There is such a spirit and temper now in the nation that I cannot think independency could be successfully proposed. If you and Mr. Deane could give me a hint of anything practicable, you considering not only your own case but ours, I would venture to try what could be done.

I know your hand writing as well as I do your heart. Direct your answer to me Queen's Row, Pimlico, Westminister, under the cover to M. Count de Gebelin, Rue Pompei, Paris, who will put a cover over it, and my friend Mr. Fullerton will without examination forward it to me in the packet of Mr. Stormont.

B. BENJAMIN FRANKLIN TO JAMES HUTTON

Passy, February 1, 1778

My Dear Old Friend,

You desired that if I had no proposition to make, I would at least give my advice. I think it is Ariosto who says that all things lost on earth are to be found in the moon; on which somebody remarked that there must be a great deal of good advice in the moon. If so, there is a good deal of mine, formerly given and lost in this business. I will, however, at your request, give a little more, but without the least expectation that it will be followed; for none but God can at the same time give good counsel and wisdom to make use of it.

You have lost by this mad war, and the barbarity with which it has been carried on, not only the Government and commerce of America, and the public revenues and private wealth arising from that commerce; but what is more, you have lost the esteem, respect, friendship and affection of all that great and growing people, who consider you at present, and whose posterity will consider you, as the worst and wickedest nation upon earth. A peace you may undoubtedly obtain by dropping all your pretensions to govern us; and to your superior skill in huckstering negociations, you may possibly make such an apparently advantageous bargain as shall be applauded in your Parliament; but if you cannot, with the peace, recover the affections of that people, it will not be a lasting nor a profitable one, nor will it afford you any part of that strength which you once had by your union with them, and might (if you had been wise enough to take advice) have still retained.

To recover their respect and affection, you must tread back the steps you have taken. Instead of honouring and rewarding the . . . advisers and promoters of this war, you should disgrace them, with all those who have influenced the nation against America by their malicious writings, and all the ministers and generals who have prosecuted the war with such inhumanity. This would show a national change of disposition and a disapprobation of what had passed.

In proposing terms, you should not only grant such as the necessity of your affairs may evidently oblige you to grant, but such additional ones as may shew your generosity, and thereby demonstrate your good will. For instance, perhaps you might by your treaty, retain all Canada, Nova Scotia and the Floridas. But if you would have a really friendly, as well as able ally in America, and avoid all occasion of future discord, which will otherwise be continually arising on your American frontiers, you should throw in those countries. And you may call it, if you please, an indemnification for the burning of their towns, which indemnification will, otherwise, be some time or other demanded.

I know your people will not see the utility of such measures and will never follow them, and even call it insolence and impudence in me to mention them. I have, however, complied with your desire.

—HUTTON, "Account of Hutton's Visit to Franklin,"
Penn. Mag. of Hist. and Biog., XXXII, 228-230.

2. FRANKLIN SCORNS AN ATTEMPT TO WIN PEACE BY BRIBERY

Benjamin Franklin to "Charles de Weissenstein."

Passy, July 1, 1778

I received your letter, dated at Brussels the 16th past. My vanity might possibly be flattered by your expressions of compliment to my understanding, if your *proposals* did not more clearly manifest a mean opinion of it.

You conjure me, in the name of the omniscient and just God before whom I must appear, and by my hopes of future fame, to consider if some expedient cannot be found to put a stop to the desolation of America, and prevent the miseries of a general war. As I am conscious of having taken every step in my power to prevent the breach, and no one to widen it, I can appear cheerfully before that God, fearing nothing from his justice in this particular though I have much occasion for his mercy in many others. As to my future fame, I am content to rest it on my past and present conduct, without seeking an addition to it in the crooked, dark paths you propose to me, where I should most certainly lose it. This your solemn address would therefore have been more properly made to your sovereign and his venal Parliament. He and they, who wickedly began, and madly continue, a war for the desolation of America, are alone accountable for the consequences. . . .

You think we flatter ourselves and are deceived into an opinion that England *must* acknowledge our independency. We, on the other hand, think you flatter yourselves in imagining such an acknowledgement a vast boon, which we strongly desire, and which you may gain some great advantage by granting or withholding. We have never asked it of you; we only tell you that you can have no treaty with us but as an independent state; and you may please yourselves and your children with the rattle of your right to govern us, as long as you have done with that of your King's being King of France, without giving us the least concern if you do not attempt to exercise it. That this pretended right is indisputable, as you say, we utterly deny. Your Parliament never had a right to govern us, and your King has forfeited it by his bloody tyranny. But I thank you for letting me know a little of your mind, that, even if the Parliament should acknowledge our independency, the act would not be binding to posterity, and that your nation would resume and prosecute the claim as soon as they found it convenient from the influence of your passions, and your present malice against us. We suspected before that you would not be actually bound by your conciliatory acts longer than till they had served their purpose of inducing us to disband our forces; but we were not certain that you were knaves by principle, and that we ought not to have the least confidence in your offers, promises, or treaties, though confirmed by Parliament. . . .

One main drift of your letter seems to be to impress me with an idea of your own impartiality, by just censures of your ministers and measures, and to draw from me propositions of peace, or approbations of those you have inclosed to me, which you intimate may by your means be conveyed to the King directly, without the intervention of those ministers. You would have me give them to, or drop them for, a stranger, whom I may find next Monday in the church of Notre Dame, to be known by a rose in his hat. You yourself, Sir, are quite unknown to me; you have not trusted me with your true name. Our taking the least step towards a treaty with England through you, might, if you are an enemy, be made use of to ruin us with our new and good friends. I may be indiscreet enough in many things; but certainly, if I were disposed to make propositions (which I cannot do, having none committed to me to make), I should never think of delivering them to the Lord knows who, to be carried to the Lord knows where, to serve no one knows what purposes. Being at this time one of the most remarkable figures in Paris, even my appearance in the church of Notre Dame, where I cannot have any conceivable business, and especially being seen to leave or drop any letter to any person there, would be a matter of some speculation, and might, from the suspicions it must naturally give, have very mischievous consequences to our credit here. . . .

This proposition of delivering ourselves, bound and gagged, ready for hanging, without even a right to complain, and without a friend to be found afterwards among all mankind, you would have us embrace upon the faith of an act of Parliament! Good God! An act of your Parliament! This demonstrates that you do not yet know us, and that you fancy we do not know you; but it is not merely this flimsy faith that we are to act upon; you offer us *hope*, the hope of PLACES, PENSIONS and PEERAGES. These, judging from yourselves, you think are motives irresistible. This offer to corrupt us, Sir, is with me your credential, and convinces me that you are not a private volunteer in your application. It bears the stamp of British Court character. It is even the signature of your King. But think for a moment in what light it must be viewed in America. By PLACES, you mean places among us, for you take care by a special article to secure your own to yourselves. We must then pay the salaries in order to enrich ourselves with these places. But you will give us PENSIONS, probably to be paid too out of your expected American revenue, and which none of us can accept without deserving, and perhaps obtaining, a SUS-*pension*. PEERAGES! alas! Sir, our long observation of the vast servile majority of your peers, voting constantly for every measure proposed by a minister, however weak or wicked, leaves us small respect for that title. We consider it as a sort of *tar-and-feather* honour, or a mixture of foulness and folly, which every man among us who should accept it from your King would be obliged to renounce, or exchange for that conferred by the mobs of their own country, or wear it with everlasting infamy.

—SMYTH, ed., Writings of Franklin, VII, 166-172.

II. THE CARLISLE COMMISSION

Failing to thwart the American commissioners in Paris, the British deemed more direct overtures immediately required. On February 17, 1778, before the existence of the Franco-American treaty had been announced to the British court, although its actuality had already leaked out, Lord North introduced in the House of Commons his proposals for conciliation. There followed a memorable scene which Horace Walpole caustically describes. An important bloc in the opposition ranks led by Rockingham would have given America her freedom and ended the contest. But not so Chatham, who in his last speech melodramatically opposed renouncing the sovereignty of America, collapsed, and was borne from the House a dying man. Notwithstanding strong opposition the well-trained cohorts of Lord North accepted this plan for reconciliation and he promptly dispatched a commission to go to America.

The Carlisle Commission took its name from one of its members, Frederick, Earl of Carlisle. To Horace Walpole, Carlisle cut a ridiculous figure. He described him as "a young man of pleasure and fashion, fond of dress and gaming, by which he had greatly hurt his fortune, as totally unacquainted with business, and though not void of ambition, [one who] had but moderate parts, and less application." The originator of the conciliation move was another member of the Commission, William Eden, who drafted North's legislation. The third member of the team was George Johnstone, onetime governor of Florida, a man innocent alike of abilities and of real integrity.

No intimation was given to the Commission of the military or naval plans afoot, although Germain did tell Carlisle to go to New York instead of Philadelphia. "Perhaps that city may not by your arrival be in our hands," he intimated. This was a slip, but the Commission reached Philadelphia in June 1778, just as Sir Henry Clinton was evacuating the city. Loyalist morale and British prestige were at their nadir in that area. Carlisle in a letter to his wife written from his ship, the Trident, *on the Delaware River conceded that the position of the Commission was already "desperate." "As long as we had the army to back us," he explained, "we had hopes of success; but this turning our backs upon Mr. Washington will certainly make them reject offers that perhaps the fear of what that army could have done would have made them listen to."*

Carlisle proved himself a better prophet than a negotiator. Congress refused to appoint commissioners to confer with the British, and the Commission itself made the fatal error of trying to bribe prominent Americans, and then of appealing over the head of the Congress to the people. The mission failed because it came too late, offered too little, and conducted itself in a pompous and even an offensive manner. What is perhaps most astonishing is that British officials deluded themselves that men like Washington, Franklin and Joseph Reed were susceptible to bribery, and that their peace overtures would be "gladly embraced" by the American people.

The British offer was—by British standards—farsighted and liberal; had it been proposed in 1775 or 1776 it would doubtless have satisfied all but the most extreme of the Patriots. Under its terms Britain agreed to keep no stand-

ing army in the colonies in time of peace, to make no change in colonial char-
ters save at the request of the assemblies concerned, to appoint judges during
good behavior, to consider American representation in Parliament or—if
Americans preferred—to recognize the American Congress as a permanent
institution. These concessions would have transformed the British Empire
into something very much like a commonwealth.

1. "An Unequalled Confession of Criminality in the Ministers"

The Journal of Horace Walpole.

Feb. 17, 1778. Disappointed, defeated, disgraced, alarmed, but still depending on a majority in both Houses, and on the blindness and indifference
of the nation, the Administration ventured on taking the very opposite part
to all they had been doing; and as if there was no shame but in losing their
places, presumed to tell the three Kingdoms that they must abandon all the
high views with which they had been lulled, and must stoop to beg peace of
America *at any rate*.

This was the substance of Lord North's opening his plan, which the very
night before had not been fixed, or not fully opened to a meeting of the principal Members at Lord North's—yet even then it had given disgust. The
Attorney-General Thurlow had protested he would take no part in it—and
did at last take but a very cold one. Lord North, who seldom shone when he
could not jest, made a sorry figure except in assurance. He declared he would
treat with the Congress, with anybody—*would even allow the independence
of the Colonies—not verbally, yet virtually*. He owned all his disappointments
—yet recurred to his usual defence, that every act had been the Act of the
Parliament. All the comfort he gave the country gentlemen was some hopes
that America might be persuaded to contribute some pecuniary assistance. He
allowed till the following June twelvemonth for the duration of the negotiation. . . .

The astonishment of a great part of the House at such extensive offers
precluded all expression. The Opposition felt honestly that they could not
decently disapprove a pacification they had so much recommended; and
during the course of the bill the Ministers had the satisfaction of finding this
integrity operate on some of the most upright but least clear-sighted, as Lord
George Cavendish and Frederick Montague pressed the Ministers not to lose
a moment in passing the bills—an instance of more virtue than judgement; for
the duplicity of the Court ought to have made them suspect fraud, and to
weigh every tittle of bills which were likely to be insidious, and the more concise the more capable of sinister interpretations.

The Tories, who could not like concessions so inadequate to their hopes,
and so repugnant to their high-flown attachment to the Prerogative, seeing
the intemperate zeal of the Opposition, were ashamed to mark themselves as
an obstinate and weak party, which they would be if they separated from the
Court when approved by the Opposition. Burke and Charles Fox yielded to
and seconded the torrent; but the latter threw a bomb that much disconcerted
though it did not disappoint the Minister. My cousin Thomas Walpole had

acquainted me that the treaty with France was signed. We agreed to inform Charles Fox; but as we both distrusted Burke, and feared the childish fluctuations of Lord Rockingham, we determined that Fox should know nothing of the secret till an hour or two before the House met. Accordingly, T. Walpole communicated the notice of the treaty to the Duke of Grafton on the 16th, and engaged him to acquaint Charles Fox, but just before the House should meet the next day. This was done most exactly, and Burke knew nothing of the matter till he came into the House.

As soon as Lord North had opened his two bills, Charles Fox rose, and after pluming himself on having sat there till he had brought the noble Lord to concur in sentiments with him and his friends, he astonished his Lordship with asking him whether a commercial treaty with France had not been signed by the American agents at Paris within the last ten days! If so, said he, the Administration is beaten by ten days—a situation so threatening that in such a time of danger the whole House must concur with the propositions, though probably now they would have no effect. Lord North was thunderstruck, and would not rise. . . .

George Grenville, with more sagacity than the rest, showed he felt the ignominious posture of his country in such humiliating concessions. He spoke with energy and weight, said he had been deceived by Administration, and the country had been so too. He would worship any man as the saviour of his country who could make peace; but he did not think these propositions would have that effect. He had seen an extract of a letter from Dr. Franklin, which asserted the treaty as a fact:—what then would be our situation with France? Were these our triumphs?—this the dignity of Parliament? *He felt the humiliating blush that must spread the cheek of his Sovereign when he should be called to give his assent to these bills.* He thought the Parliament had not been to bend, but to assert.

Gilbert, an agent of Lord Gower, proposed rather to tax placemen to carry on the war.

Burke maintained that Lord North had taken precisely the plan that he (Burke) had offered two years before; and he called on his Lordship to answer to the fact of the treaty.

Still the Minister was silent; till George Saville rose and told him it would be criminal to withhold a reply, and a matter of impeachment, and ended with crying, "An answer! an answer! an answer!"

Lord North, thus forced up, owned he had heard the report of a treaty, but desired to give no answer to the House at that moment. He had no official intelligence on that subject. The report might be vague. Some time ago the Ministers of France had denied it.

Such evasive answers rather convinced everybody of the truth. (Three days after this, Lord Mansfield, at Lady Gower's, said openly that the Ministers did not speak truth if they denied the treaty, for it was certainly signed!) Leave was then given, *nemine contradicente*, for the two bills to be brought in.

Such an avowal, in effect, of criminality, ignorance, and incapacity in the Ministers had never been equalled—nor, since King John surrendered his

Crown at the Nuncio's feet, could a more ignominious instance of the debasement of a great monarch be quoted. The Ministers had stigmatized the whole body of colonists as cowards, and boasted they could traverse the whole continent of America with 5000 men; and in four years stooped to offer terms infinitely beyond what would have glutted the most sanguine or presumptuous wishes of the insurgents but two years ago! No matter whether sincere their offers or not: *if insincere, it was but another infamy.* But how could England but fall into disgrace and contempt, when Ministers, by turns so audacious, so criminal, and so mean, remained yet undisturbed in their posts? Their cruelty, injustice, defeats had revolted few. Few showed either joy or indignation at their recantation. The Scots at first inveighed against the pacific spirit, but soon grew so silent that no doubt they were let into the secret of the insincerity of the Court—and both the King and the Scots enjoyed any ignominy that fell on the Parliament.

　　　　　　　　　　　—WALPOLE, *Journal*, II, 200 *et seq.*

2. SIR JOHN DALRYMPLE SUGGESTS A DUKEDOM FOR WASHINGTON

　　　　　　　　　　　　　　　　　[*c.* March 1778]
　　"Thoughts on instructions to the American Commissioners."
... 4thly, America will desire that the laws be repealed which cramp her internal manufactures for the advantages of the British manufactures. It is also full time for England to recover her dream on this head. These laws are of no use to England, because they are not executable in America. They are unpopular, in their eyes they are unjust, and therefore the juries on whom the execution of them depends never did and never will give effect to them.

　　5thly, America will ask that the laws be repealed which have interfered in their internal police; for example, which have declared that a tender of paper payment shall not be a legal tender. It is the busy, meddling, officious, practmatical [*sic*]—I had almost said Parliamentary—turn of England which has brought the present mischief upon us; is it worth our while to maintain a war to prevent the Americans from cheating each other, or even a few of ourselves, in their modes of payments? If our merchants are cheated, they will stop giving credits to the cheaters and then the cheaters will grow honest to recover their credits with our merchants. ...

　　I presume to suggest another thing. From all accounts of General Washington's character there is a resemblance between his character and General Monk's, for he is silent, keeps his mind to himself, has plain understanding, and is a man of principle. Besides this, he has no son, daughter, brother or sister, so that his ambition must be limited to himself. Charles the II owed his kingdom to his personal application to Monk, delivered by one of Monk's own friends. Might not the Ministers treating by the King's command or the King himself write a private letter to Washington to remind him of the similarity between his situation and Monk's, desiring him to ask terms for America fair and just, and they should be granted, and that the terms for himself should be the dukedom that was given to Monk, and a revenue to support it in order to give dignity to the man who generously gave up his own power to save his country?

If the Minister has not a man he can trust with such a commission, I can find one. I mean Mr. Lloyd Delany, the bosom friend of General Washington, a man of fortune in Maryland, now in London; two of whose family are now with General Howe, and who has given proofs of his secrecy, as he was one of those who knew of a scheme of mine relating to the paper money of America.

—Gr. Brit. Hist. Mss. Comm., *Stopford-Sackville Manuscripts,*
II, 103-104.

3. "The Generous Terms Now Held Out Will Be Gladly Embraced"

Lord George Germain to Sir Henry Clinton—"Most Secret."

Whitehall, March 8, 1778

In my last letter I informed you that the command resigned by Sir William Howe had, by the King's wish, been delivered over to yourself, which shows in the highest degree the great confidence felt by his Majesty in your abilities. My circular letter of this day's date will inform you of what has been done by the King and Parliament towards opening the way for the return of peace, and if that be true which has been so repeatedly declared by the Colony Assemblies, and is still asserted by many persons who pretend to be well informed of the dispositions of the inhabitants, that the generality of the people desire nothing more than a full security for the enjoyment of all their rights and liberties under the British Constitution, there can be no room to doubt that the generous terms now held out to them will be gladly embraced, and that a negociation will immediately take place upon the arrival of the New Commission, and be so far advanced before the season will admit of military operations as to supersede the necessity of another campaign. So speedy and happy a termination of the war could not fail to give the greatest pleasure to the King, as the peace, prosperity, and happiness of all his subjects has ever been the most ardent wish of his royal breast....

—Gr. Brit. Hist. Mss. Comm., *Stopford-SackvilleManuscripts,*
II, 94-95.

4. Chatham:"If We Must Fall, Let Us Fall like Men!"

Chatham's last appeal, in the House of Lords, April 7, 1778.
Earl of Chatham. His Lordship began by lamenting that his bodily infirmities had so long, and especially at so important a crisis, prevented his attendance on the duties of Parliament. He declared that he had made an effort almost beyond the powers of his constitution to come down to the House on this day (perhaps the last time he should ever be able to enter its walls) to express the indignation he felt at an idea which he understood was gone forth, of yielding up the sovereignty of America!

My Lords, continued he, I rejoice that the grave has not closed upon me; that I am still alive to lift up my voice against the dismemberment of this ancient and most noble monarchy! Pressed down as I am by the hand of infirmity, I am little able to assist my country in this most perilous conjuncture; but, my Lords, while I have sense and memory, I will never consent to deprive the royal offspring of the House of Brunswick, the heirs of the Princess

Sophia, of their fairest inheritance. Where is the man that will dare to advise such a measure? My Lords, his Majesty succeeded to an empire as great in extent as its reputation was unsullied. Shall we tarnish the lustre of this nation by an ignominious surrender of its rights and fairest possessions? Shall this great kingdom, that has survived whole and entire the Danish depredations, the Scottish inroads, and the Norman conquest, that has stood the threatened invasion of the Spanish Armada, now fall prostrate before the House of Bourbon? Surely, my Lords, this nation is no longer what it was! Shall a people that seventeen years ago was the terror of the world, now stoop so low as to tell its ancient inveterate enemy, Take all we have only give us peace? It is impossible!

I wage war with no man, or set of men. I wish for none of their employments; nor would I co-operate with men who still persist in unretracted error; or who, instead of acting on a firm decisive line of conduct, halt between two opinions, where there is no middle path. In God's name, if it is absolutely necessary to declare either for peace or war, and the former cannot be preserved with honour, why is not the latter commenced without hesitation? I am not, I confess, well informed of the resources of this kingdom; but I trust it has still sufficient to maintain its just rights, tho' I know them not. But, my Lords, any state is better than despair. Let us at least make one effort; and if we must fall, let us fall like men!

—ALMON, *Parliamentary Register*, X, 369-370.

5. THE PEACE COMMISSIONERS SUBMIT THEIR PROPOSALS

The Earl of Carlisle, W. Eden, G. Johnstone, to his excellency Henry Laurens, the President, and other Members of Congress.

June 13, 1778

Gentlemen, With an earnest desire to stop the further effusion of blood and the calamities of war, we communicate to you, with the least possible delay after our arrival in this city, a copy of the communication with which his Majesty is pleased to honour us, as also the acts of parliament on which it is founded; and at the same time that we assure you of our most earnest desire to re-establish, on the basis of equal freedom and mutual safety, the tranquillity of this once happy empire, you will observe that we are vested with powers equal to the purpose, and such as are even unprecedented in the annals of our history. . . .

More effectually to demonstrate our good intentions, we think proper to declare, even in this our first communication, that we are disposed to concur in every satisfactory and just arrangement towards the following among other purposes:

To consent to a cessation of hostilities, both by sea and land. To restore free intercourse, to revive mutual affection, and restore the common benefits of naturalisation through the several parts of this empire. To extend every freedom to trade that our respective interests can require. To agree that no military force shall be kept up in the different states of North America, without the consent of the general congress, or particular assemblies. To concur in measures calculated to discharge the debts of America, and raise the value and credit of the paper circulation.

To perpetuate our union by a reciprocal deputation of an agent or agents from the different states, who shall have the privilege of a seat and voice in the parliament of Great Britain; or, if sent from Britain, to have in that case a seat and voice in the assemblies of the different states to which they may be deputed respectively, in order to attend to the several interests of those by whom they are deputed.

In short, to establish the power of the respective legislatures in each particular state, to settle its revenue, its civil and military establishment, and to exercise a perfect freedom of legislation and internal government, so that the British states throughout North America, acting with us in peace and war, under our common sovereign, may have the irrevocable enjoyment of every privilege that is short of a total separation of interest, or consistent with that union of force on which the safety of our common religion and liberty depends.

In our anxiety for preserving those sacred and essential interests, we cannot help taking notice of the insidious interposition of a power which has from the first settlement of these colonies been actuated with enmity to us both. And notwithstanding the pretended date, or present form, of the French offers to America, yet it is notorious that these were made in consequence of the plans of accommodation previously concerted in Great Britain, and with a view to prevent our reconciliation, and to prolong this destructive war.

But we trust that the inhabitants of North-America, connected with us by the nearest ties of consanguinity, speaking the same language, interested in the preservation of similar institutions, remembering the former happy intercourse of good offices, and forgetting recent animosities, will shrink from the thought of becoming an accession of force to our late mutual enemy, and will prefer a firm, free and perpetual coalition with the parent state to an insincere and unnatural foreign alliance. . . .

If after the time that may be necessary to consider of this communication and transmit your answer, the horrors and devastations of war should continue, we call God and the world to witness that the evils which must follow are not to be imputed to Great Britain; and we cannot without the most real sorrow anticipate the prospect of calamities which we feel the most ardent desire to prevent. We are, with perfect respect, Gentlemen, your most obedient and most humble servants.

—Annual Register for 1778, pp. 327-329.

6. The British Peace Proposals: Too Little and Too Late

Henry Laurens of the Continental Congress to General Horatio Gates.

York, Pennsylvania, June 17, 1778

. . . If all the fine things now offered had been tendered some time ago, admitting their solidity, there can be no doubt but that the people of America would joyfully have embraced the proposition, but now what answer can be given but that which was returned to the foolish Virgins?—"the door is shut"—More especially when we reflect that there is no solidity, because all is to be transmitted to Parliament for ratification, "and until such ratification no such regulation, matter or thing shall have any other force or effect or be carried further into execution than is hereafter mentioned." Here a boy's card house [is] tumbled down by a breath.

"If," say Lord Carlisle, William Eden and Geo. Johnstone, Esquires, "after the time that may be necessary to consider this communication and transmit your answer, the horrors and devastations of war should continue, we call God and the world to witness that the evils which must follow are not to be imputed to Great Britain." To whom are the past to be imputed? But are they not now, in the very moment of pretended attempts to establish peace, burning, ravaging and murdering?

They seem to mistake our understanding as once they did our resolution.
—BURNETT, *Letters of Members of the Continental Congress*, III, 298-299.

7. CONGRESS REJECTS THE CARLISLE PROPOSALS

Henry Laurens to the Earl of Carlisle and the other British commissioners.

June 17, 1778

I have received the letter from your excellencies of the 9th instant, with the enclosures, and laid them before Congress. Nothing but an earnest desire to spare the further effusion of human blood could have induced them to read a paper containing expressions so disrespectful to his most Christian majesty, the good and great ally of these states, or to consider propositions so derogatory to the honor of an independent nation.

The acts of the British parliament, the commission from your sovereign, and your letter suppose the people of these states to be subjects of the crown of Great Britain, and are founded on the idea of dependence, which is utterly inadmissible.

I am further directed to inform your excellencies that Congress are inclined to peace, notwithstanding the unjust claims from which this war originated and the savage manner in which it hath been conducted. They will, therefore, be ready to enter upon the consideration of a treaty of peace and commerce not inconsistent with treaties already subsisting, when the king of Great Britain shall demonstrate a sincere disposition for that purpose. The only solid proof of this disposition will be an explicit acknowledgment of the independence of these states, or the withdrawing his fleets and armies.
—*Journals of the Continental Congress*, XI, 615.

8. "WE CAN FIND NO SAFETY BUT IN BRITAIN'S RUIN"

Patrick Henry to Richard Henry Lee.

Williamsburg, June 18, 1778

I look at the past condition of America as at a dreadful precipice from which we have escaped by means of the generous French, to whom I will be everlastingly bound by the most heartfelt gratitude. But I must mistake matters, if some of those men who traduce you do not prefer the offers of Britain. You will have a different game to play now with the commissioners. How comes Governor Johnstone there? I do not see how it comports with his past life. Surely Congress will never recede from our French friends. Salvation to America depends upon our holding fast our attachment to them. I shall date our ruin from the moment that it is exchanged for anything Great Britain can say or do. She can never be cordial with us. Baffled, defeated, disgraced by her colonies, she will ever meditate revenge. We can find no safety but in her ruin, or at least in her extreme humiliation, which has not happened, and cannot happen until she is deluged with blood, or thoroughly purged by a revolution, which shall wipe from existence the present king with his connexions, and the present system, with those who aid and abet it. For God's sake, my dear sir, quit not the councils of your country until you see us forever disjointed from Great Britain. *The old leaven still works. The flesh pots of Egypt are still savoury to degenerate palates.* Again, we are undone if the French alliance is not religiously observed.

Excuse my freedom. I know your love to our country, and this is my motive. May heaven give you health and prosperity.

—Wirt, *Life of Henry*, I, 564-565.

9. Joseph Reed Spurns a Bribe from the King

On the 18th of June [1778], the city of Philadelphia was evacuated by the British troops, and I came to town the same day, having sent Governor Johnstone's letter to me to the Congress, then sitting at York-Town. On Sunday the 21st of June, at General Arnold's quarters, I received the following letter from Mrs. [Elizabeth] Ferguson, a lady of family and reputation, and who had, before the war, married a gentleman attached to the British interests, and then a commissary of prisoners in their army:

"Having occasion, on particular business, to go to Lancaster, I purpose setting off Monday morning from this place. It would afford me considerable satisfaction, could I be favoured with an hour's conversation with you, Sir, previous to my being at Lancaster. In order to effect this, I propose going near the camp, where, if you will be good enough to meet me at any place you will name, within a mile or two of Valley-Forge, it would vastly oblige me. I should have been at Lancaster last week, but being in the city to take leave of my husband, I was refused a pass on the day I purposed leaving the town. I enclose a letter Col. Boudinot had from General Roberdeau, pointing out the necessity of being soon at Lancaster. I also enclose a letter Mr. Stockton has wrote, relative to Mr. Ferguson's proscription, which I must beg the favour of you to consider and give your advice on when we meet.

"At all events, I would wish much to see you before I go. If one day would suit you better than another, I would postpone or forward a day, in order to see you, though Monday is the time proposed. The Valley-Forge is about twenty-four miles from this, so that if I set off from this in the morning, I shall be able to see you in the afternoon. Be so obliging as to appoint the place; but I would wish to avoid passing through the camp; but any little cottage or farm-house would be agreeable to me to see you in. However it may affect my own private concerns, I cannot avoid sincerely congratulating you, Sir, on the prospect of your entering once more your own house in the city....

"P. S. Since writing the above, I hear the camp is moved; therefore, if this should reach you, I beg you will be so good as to point out where I shall see you, as writing will not do."

I enquired of the servant who delivered me the letter where Mrs. Ferguson was, and was informed she had come to town that morning; upon which I wrote a short billet, mentioning that being engaged to dinner, I could not come so early as she seemed to wish, but would certainly wait on her in the evening, when I left the company with whom I dined. I accordingly did so, and found her in all appearance waiting for me. She opened the conversation by relating the difficulties and perplexities in which she found herself, what advice had been given her respecting Mr. Ferguson, and what her intentions had been. The particulars I did not recollect when I first committed this transaction to writing, nor have I since, as it seemed to be only introductory; or, perhaps, the subsequent conversation being more interesting, the other did not make the usual impression.

From this subject, we imperceptibly slid into that of the British Commissioners, their business and characters, when Mrs. Ferguson mentioned Governor Johnstone's lodging in that very house with her, and that she had frequently conversed with him on public affairs. She described him as a gentleman of great abilities and address, and possessed of many amiable qualities; that he had sketched out a plan of settlement of our disputes, on his passage, which he had permitted her to see, and that she had made some extracts from it, which she gave me expectations she would communicate to me on another occasion. She then added that he had expressed the most favourable sentiments of me, and the part I had acted in this great contest. Upon which I mentioned my having received a letter from him at the Valley-Forge, and acknowledged his civility in sending my packets with unbroken seals.

Mrs. Ferguson then went on to say that Governor Johnstone expressed great anxiety to see me, and particularly wished to engage my interest to promote the object of their commission, *viz.* a reunion between the two countries, if it was consistent with my principles and judgment; and in such case, it could not be deemed improper or unbecoming in Government to take a favourable notice of such conduct; and in this instance I might have £10,000 sterling and any office in the colonies in his Majesty's gift.

I found an answer was expected, and gave one: "That I was not worth purchasing, but·such as I was, the King of Great-Britain was not rich enough to do it." By this time the evening was pretty far advanced, and no reply being made, I rose to take my leave, which I did, after expressing my concern for her private misfortunes, and left the house, with a mind much agitated with this new and unexpected scene.

At this time I had not seen Governor Johnstone's letters to Mr. Morris and Mr. Dana, which would probably have determined me sooner as to the part I ought to act: besides which, the Congress was yet at York-Town, the Executive Council at Lancaster, I was about to join the army again; the battle of

Monmouth and other important events succeeded, which engrossed the public attention and my own, and prevented my return to Congress till the month of July. In the mean time I was deliberating what steps I ought to pursue: On the one hand, the duty I owed to my country seemed to demand a full disclosure; on the other, a reluctance to expose the lady to a criminal prosecution, or popular resentment, and myself to the imputation of vanity and ostentatious integrity, kept me silent, except to General Washington and two or three other gentlemen. But the more I reflected upon the nature of the proposition, and the danger of negotiation in such hands, private considerations gave way to public duty, and on the 18th of July I made a full disclosure of the whole transaction to Congress, only concealing the name of the lady.

—REED, *Remarks on Johnstone's Speech*, pp. 16-22.

10. LORD CARLISLE CONCLUDES HIS MISSION IS RIDICULOUS

To Lady Carlisle.

New York, July 21, 1778

The arrival of this [French] fleet makes every hope of success in our business ridiculous; the address by proclamation to the people ought and has been tried; a certain time will show its effects, but in truth the compliance with our instructions in this particular is the mere obedience to a form. The leaders on the enemy's side are too powerful; the common people hate us in their hearts, notwithstanding all that is said of their secret attachment to the mother country. I cannot give you a better proof of their unanimity against us than in our last march; in the whole country there was not found one single man capable of bearing arms at home; they left their dwellings unprotected, and after having cut all the ropes of the wells had fled to Gen. Washinton. Formerly, when things went better for us, there was an appearance of friendship by their coming in for pardons, that might have deceived even those who have been the most acquainted with them. But no sooner our situation was the least altered for the worse, but these friends were the first to fire upon us, and many were taken with the pardons in our [their] pockets. Beat Gen. Washinton, drive away Monsr. d'Estaing, and we should have friends enough in this country; but in our present condition the only friends we have, or are likely to have, are those who are absolutely ruined for us, and in such distress I leave you to judge what possible use they can be to us.

But don't you say now—if all this is as hopeless as you represent, what is the use of remaining? To tell you fairly, I think none; but as everybody in the world will not be ruled perhaps by my opinions, we must stay till there is not a possibility of doubt upon that subject. God knows what may happen in the course of the next month; we must regulate our conduct by circumstances; the necessity of the times may impel us to steps we at present have not in idea....

—GR. BRIT. HIST. MSS. COMM., *Fifteenth Report*, Appendix, VI, 356-357.

III. FORLORN HOPES OF PEACE

Despite the ridiculous bungling of the Carlisle Commission some Englishmen still felt that peace could be made with America. The Dean of Glou-

cester had the absurd notion that America could be divided into fragments, and Admiral Rodney was so remote from American public opinion as to venture the suggestion that Benedict Arnold, whom he assumed had retained his immense popularity with the American troops despite his treasonable behavior, should be given an important command, and that Washington could still be bought.

1. The Dean of Gloucester Proposes to Fragmentize America

John Adams to the President of the Congress.

Paris, May 9th, 1780

I have the honor to enclose to Congress proposals for a general pacification, by the Dean of Gloucester.

"Proposals to the English, Americans, French, and Spaniards, now at war.

"First. That Great Britain shall retain Newfoundland, with the desert coasts of Labradore; also Canada, Nova Scotia, and the country bordering on the Bay of Fundy, as far as the bay and river of Penobscot.

"Secondly. That all the country from the Penobscot River to the River Connecticut, containing almost all the four populous Provinces of New England, shall be ceded to the Americans.

"Thirdly. That all the country from the Connecticut to the River Delaware, containing the whole of New York, Long Island and the Jerseys, with some parts of two other Provinces indenting with them, shall return to Great Britain.

"Fourthly. That all the country from the Delaware to the northern boundary of South Carolina, containing the greatest part of Pennsylvania, all Maryland, Virginia and North Carolina, shall be ceded to the Americans.

"Fifthly. That all the country from the northern boundary of South Carolina to the extreme point of the eastern Florida, containing three whole Provinces, shall be retained by Great Britain.

"Sixthly. That West Florida, chiefly barren sand, and the Fortress of Gibraltar (totally useless) shall be ceded to Spain, in order to satisfy the punctilio of that nation, and that the Spaniards shall give Porto Rico in exchange, an island on which they seem to set no value, and which indeed is of no use to them, though large in itself, stored with good ports, well situated, and capable (in the hands of the English) of great improvements.

"Seventhly. Lastly, that the English shall give up the conquests they have made on the French in the East Indies, who shall do the like to the English in the West Indies."

I shall make no remarks upon this plan, but there is no Englishman who thinks of a wiser, or at least who dares propose one. All who talk of propositions throw out something as absurd and idle as this, which will convince Congress that we shall have no peace for some time.

The French armament, which sailed from Brest the 2d of May, under the command of M. de Rochambeau, of the troops, and M. de Ternay, of the fleet, and the armament from Cadiz, of twelve ships of the line, besides frigates and other armed vessels, with eleven thousand five hundred land forces, with a fine train of artillery, which were to sail about the same time, or earlier, both destined for America, as it is supposed, will I hope bring the English to think of some plan a little more rational.

—SPARKS, *Diplomatic History of the Revolution*, V, 84-86.

2. ADMIRAL RODNEY STILL THINKS WASHINGTON CAN BE BOUGHT!

Sir George Rodney to Lord George Germain—"Private."

Sandwich, St. Lucia, December 22, 1780

Believe me, my dear Lord, you must not expect an end of the American war till you can find a general of active spirit, and who hates the Americans from principle. Such a man with the sword of war and justice on his side will do wonders, for in this war I am convinced the sword should cut deep. Nothing but making the Americans feel every calamity their perfidy deserves can bring them to their senses. . . .

The war in America is now turned to a war of posts, and, unhappily for England, when they have taken posts of infinite advantage, they have been unaccountably evacuated without one good reason assigned. Such was the Highlands up Hudson's River, and which cut off all communication between the southern and northern provinces, and which with little difficulty might have opened a passage from Canada. This is the post Arnold was to have betrayed, and which he assured me, as he did the General, he would answer with his head should be taken in ten days. But, to my infinite surprize, cold water was immediately thrown upon it, notwithstanding it had but a few days before the arrival of Arnold been told me that it was of infinite consequence, and if taken would ruin the rebels.

Believe me, my Lord, this man Arnold, with whom I had many conferences, will do more towards the suppressing the rebellion than all our generals put together. He perfectly knows every inch of the country, is greatly beloved by the American troops, and if entrusted with a body of what is called Royalists will induce great part of [the] rebels to desert. I am perfectly of his opinion that upon a certainty of their being paid their arrears and a portion of land given after the war, Washington would soon have no army. Jealousy, my Lord, unless commands from home signifies his Majesty's pleasure, will prevent Arnold being employed to advantage. He certainly may be trusted, as the Americans never forgive, and the Congress to a man are his personal enemies. Give him but a command and thousands will join him who are sick of the war and have a great opinion of his generalship. . . .

Thus, my Lord, have I endeavoured to make you truly acquainted with affairs at present in America, but believe me the acting in North Carolina will only prolong the war. The Northern Colonies should feel the fatal results of their treason. There and there only the war must be finished. I cannot conclude without being of opinion that a new Commission with the same powers of Lord Carlisle's, taking care the majority of Commissioners are not *military men*, may have such effect as to bring about a peace. Washington is certainly to be bought—honours will do it.

—GR. BRIT. HIST. MSS. COMM., *Stopford-Sackville Manuscripts*, II, 192-194.

CHAPTER SEVENTEEN

The Patriots Seize the Initiative in the Middle States

WITH THE WITHDRAWAL *in June of '78 of British troops from Philadelphia, a story related toward the close of our first volume, the initiative in the Middle States passed from the British to the Patriots. Not that the Patriots had been entirely inert before that time, but their activities had been largely defensive actions or sporadic raids to throw the enemy off balance, destroy stores, or pick off key personnel. One such raid, holding a larger significance for a later full-scale engagement, was staged near Newport in midsummer of '77, when Major General Richard Prescott, commander of the British troops in Rhode Island, was caught in bed in embarrassing circumstances. His seizure made it possible to effect an exchange of an American prisoner of equal rank, Major General Charles Lee.*

Even before the British evacuation of Philadelphia, Congress, without consultation with Washington, embarked on "one of the maddest of all mad projects," another ill-planned invasion of Canada. This expedition was to be placed under the command of Lafayette, with the trouble-maker Conway as his immediate subordinate. After a midwinter journey to Albany, the young Frenchman found that the troops which were promised him were not at hand. In bitter disillusionment he called off the enterprise. "I am sure I will be very ridiculous and laughed at," he confessed.

When Clinton withdrew his forces across Jersey, Washington pursued him in what proved a futile effort to trap him and cut the British army to pieces. Subsequently, in midsummer of '78, an ill-starred Franco-American amphibious operation was launched against Newport, Rhode Island. The British hold on the lower Hudson was shaken by the Patriots' temporary recapture of Stony Point and the Paulus Hook raid. In January of 1780 Stirling staged what he hoped would be a surprise attack on a British camp on Staten Island, but the enemy was not surprised, and the Patriots withdrew with little or no net profit.

The British in turn threw counterpunches at the Americans. Banastre Tarleton struck at Poundridge, near Bedford, against militia operating in Westchester County and put a church and other buildings to the torch. In New Jersey a British-Hessian force moved from Staten Island and struck in strength at the American army, but was hurled back at Springfield. Raids were staged on New Haven and Norwalk, and the turncoat, Benedict Ar-

nold, made an especially savage raid on New London that outraged the Patriots.

The effect of these offensive and counteroffensive moves was to tie a huge British army down to New York City, while the decisive operations of the war were being determined in the Southern theater.

I. GENERAL PRESCOTT IS CAPTURED

Prescott's capture amused two continents. The London Chronicle *for September 27-30, 1777, spoke of the general as having been carried off "naked, unanointed, unanealed," and put in rhyme some of the gossip that was not reported in the American newspaper account:*

> *What various lures there are to ruin man;*
> *Woman, the first and foremost, all bewitches!*
> *A nymph once spoiled a General's mighty plan,*
> *And gave him to the foe—without his breeches.*

Elias Boudinot, in charge of prisoner exchanges, negotiated the swap of Prescott for Lee. His Journal records a significant conversation with Lee, who, following his capture, was outspoken about the folly of Congress' hoping to withstand the British troops, criticized Washington as "ignorant," and had the ridiculous plan of assembling civilians—the wealthy, the elderly and children—inside a fortress to be built at Pittsburgh. Boudinot had strong reservations about Lee. "Whenever anything on a very large scale struck him," he remarked in his Journal, "a partial lunacy took place." Unfortunately Washington was not aware of the strange indecision and doubtful loyalty of which Lee's mind was a curious compound, nor did he learn that on June 4, 1778, two weeks after rejoining the Patriot army, Lee wrote a letter to Sir Henry Clinton congratulating him on his promotion to succeed Howe!

1. THE BRITISH SOUND THE ALARM AFTER "THE BIRD HAS FLED"

Providence, July 12, 1777: Thursday evening last a party of 38 men, of the troops belonging to this State, under the command of Lieut. Col. William Barton, of this town, accompanied by Major Adams of the Train, Capt. Philips, Lieutenants Potter and Badcock, and Ensigns Stanton and Wilcocks, went in five boats from Warwick-Neck, with a view to take Major-General Prescot, Commander in Chief of the British and foreign troops on Rhode Island, whose headquarters were then at a house about four miles from Newport. The colonel and his party, after passing the enemy's ships and guard boats, landed about twelve at night, and with *"infinite address and gallantry"* got to Prescot's quarters undiscovered. A centinel at the door hailed, but was immediately secured, and the party, instantly breaking the doors and entering the house, took the general in bed. His aid-de-camp leaped from a window in his shirt and attempted to escape, but was taken a few rods from the house.

The party soon after returned to their boats with the prisoners, and some time after they had put off the enemy fired rockets from their several posts as signals for an alarm, but *too late—the bird had fled.* The prisoners were safely landed about day-break at Warwick-Neck. On receiving intelligence here, a coach was immediately sent, and the general with his aid-de-camp, attended by Col. Barton and some other officers, arrived in town at twelve o'clock.

This bold and important enterprize must reflect the highest honor on Col. Barton and his little party. A lieut. col. of Horse, with at least 70 Light Dragoons, took Major General Lee (betrayed by a Tory) five miles from his troops. A lieutenant colonel of Foot, with only 38 privates and 6 officers, has taken a Chief Commander, when almost incircled by an army and navy.

—*Continental Journal and Weekly Advertiser*, July 17, 1777.

2. Lee's Triumphal Return with "a Miserable Dirty Hussy"

Journal of Elias Boudinot.

Dec. 1778: I endeavoured to negotiate his [General Lee's] exchange, and it was agreed (hypothetically) that it should take place for Major Genl Prescott, subject to Genl Howe's approbation. Genl Howe objected, and ordered Genl Lee round by sea to Philadelphia, that he might be exchanged under his own eye. Genl Lee (abhoring the sea) applied to me by letter and most earnestly requested that he might be permitted to go thro' New Jersey, under the care of a British officer, to which Genl Washington consented, and he accordingly went to Philadelphia, but no consent was obtained to the exchange.

In the spring of 1778 a proposition was made by both parties for a partial exchange of prisoners, and I was ordered to Germantown to meet the British commissory to attempt the business. When I was setting off from camp, Genl Washington called me into his room and in the most earnest manner intreated of me, if I wished to gratify him, that I would obtain the exchange of Genl Lee, for he never was more wanted by him than at the present moment, and desired that I would not suffer trifles to prevent it. I accordingly went, and made a pretty considerable exchange of prisoners, but quite new propositions were made for the exchange of Genl Lee, which neither the General or myself had ever thought of; after reducing the terms to as favourable a scale as I thought right, I agreed to it on condition that if General Washington was not pleased with the new plan and notice was given of his refusal within 24 hours, the exchange was to be void, without any charge of failure on my part.

I arrived at head quarters about 6 o'clock P. M. and going in to the General began to tell him of my success. When he interrupted me with much eagerness and asked me if I had exchanged Genl Lee, I informed him of what had been done; he replied, "Sit down at this table and write a letter informing of my confirmation of the exchange and send one of my horse guards immediately to the enemies lines with it." I assured him that next day would be time enough, but he insisted on its being immediately done, and I sent him accordingly, fixing the next day but one for Genl Lee's coming out to us.

When the day arrived the greatest preparations were made for his reception. All the principal officers of the army were drawn up in two lines, advanced of the camp about 2 miles towards the enemy. Then the troops with the inferior officers formed a line quite to head quarters. All the music of the army attended. The General, with a great number of principal officers and their suites, rode about four miles on the road towards Philadelphia and waited till Genl Lee appeared. Gen Washington dismounted and received Gen Lee as if he had been his brother. He passed thro' the lines of officers and the army, who all paid him the highest military honors, to head quarters, where Mrs Washington was, and there he was entertained with an elegant dinner, and the music playing the whole time. A room was assigned him back of Mrs Washington's sitting room, and all his baggage was stowed in it.

The next morning he lay very late, and breakfast was detained for him. When he came out, he looked as dirty as if he had been in the street all night. Soon after I discovered that he had brought a miserable dirty hussy with him from Philadelphia (a British sergeant's wife) and had actually taken her into his room by a back door and she had slept with him that night.

—BOUDINOT, *Journal or Historical Recollections*, pp. 76-78.

II. LAFAYETTE'S ABORTIVE EXPEDITION TO CANADA

Memoirs of the Marquis de Lafayette.

The 22nd of January [1778], Congress resolved that Canada should be entered, and the choice fell upon M. de Lafayette. The Generals Conway and Stark were placed under him. Hoping to intoxicate and govern so young a commander, the war-office, without consulting the commander-in-chief, wrote to him to go and await his further instructions at Albany. But after having won over by his arguments the committee which Congress had sent to the camp, M. de Lafayette hastened to Yorktown, and declared there "that he required circumstantial orders, a statement of the means to be employed, the certainty of not deceiving the Canadians, an augmentation of generals, and rank for several Frenchmen, fully impressed," he added, "with the various duties and advantages they derived from their name; but the first condition he demanded was, not to be made, like Gates, independent of General Washington." At Gates's own house he braved the whole party, and threw them into confusion by making them drink the health of their general. In Congress he was supported by President Laurens, and he obtained all that he demanded.

His instructions from the war-office promised that 2500 men should be assembled at Albany, and a large corps of militia at Co[h]o[e]s; that he should have two millions in paper money, some hard specie, and all means supplied for crossing Lake Champlain upon the ice, whence, after having burnt the English flotilla, he was to proceed to Montreal and act there as circumstances might require.

Repassing then, not without some danger, the Susquehannah, which was filled with floating masses of ice, M. de Lafayette set out for Albany, and, in spite of the obstacles offered by ice and snow, rapidly traversed an extent of four hundred miles. . . .

M. de Lafayette, on arriving at Albany, experienced some disappointments. Instead of 2500 men, there were not 1200. Stark's militia had not even received a summons. Clothes, provisions, magazines, sledges, all were insufficient for that glacial expedition. By making better preparations and appointing the general earlier, success would probably have been secured. Several Canadians began to make a movement, and from that moment they testified great interest in M. de Lafayette; but two months were requisite to collect all that was necessary, and towards the middle of March the lakes began to thaw. M. de Lafayette, general, at twenty years of age, of a small army, charged with an important and very difficult operation, authorized by the orders of Congress, animated by the expectations now felt in America and which, he knew, would ere long be felt likewise in Europe, had many motives for becoming adventurous; but, on the other hand, his resources were slender, the time allowed him was short, the enemy was in a good position, and Lieutenant-General Carleton was preparing for him another Saratoga. Forced to take a decisive step immediately, he wrote a calm letter to Congress, and with a heavy sigh abandoned the enterprise. . . .

—LAFAYETTE, *Memoirs, Correspondence and Manuscripts*, pp. 38-41.

III. MONMOUTH

On June 17, 1778, Washington called a council of war at Valley Forge in which he informed the officers of Clinton's evident intention of evacuating Philadelphia and asked advice as to the course he should pursue. In the march across Jersey Clinton seemed to be heading for Sandy Hook, whence he could embark his troops to New York. This meant taking a northeasterly route to New Brunswick, and then cutting across to Monmouth Courthouse, a short distance from the coast. Major General Lee opposed bringing on a full-scale action as "criminal," and won a majority of the leading officers over to his views. It was voted to strengthen Maxwell's and Dickinson's forces hanging on Clinton's left flank, but to avoid a general engagement with the main army. Hamilton, who kept the minutes of the council, observed that the results of their deliberations "would have done honor to the most honorable society of midwives, and to them only." Nathanael Greene also dissented from the decision. "People expect something from us and our strength demands it," he wrote Washington.

The American commander decided to dispatch an advance guard to establish contact with the enemy and to place it under the command of someone who favored the offensive. He named Lafayette. Lee agreed to the choice, then reasserted his command, then wavered again, and at the moment of contact with the enemy took over the reins once more. When, early in the morning of June 28, word came to Washington that the British were preparing to leave Monmouth Courthouse, Washington determined to strike. Lee was ordered to fall upon the rear of the enemy, but reports coming in indicated that, oddly enough, Lee was falling back. The British, who had received intelligence from an American deserter of Washington's intent to hit their rear, wheeled about and attacked first. Washington put spurs to his horse, and soon came upon the retreating troops. He confronted Lee, demanded to know the reason for the situation, and received a lame explanation. Whether or not he called Lee "a damned poltroon" as tradition would have it, he was in a towering rage and reputedly swore "till the leaves shook on the trees." Taking command of the situation himself, he ordered the soldiers to take cover behind a hedgerow, and Wayne's brigade was placed where it could hold off the

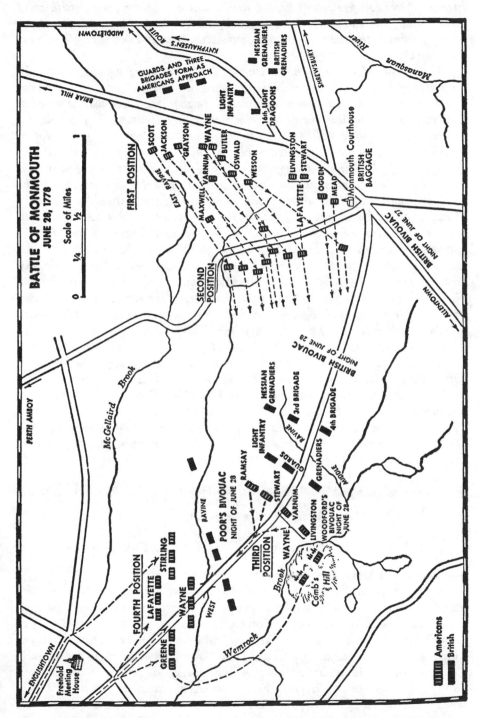

BATTLE OF MONMOUTH
JUNE 28, 1778

Scale of Miles

From The American Revolution
by John Richard Alden

Courtesy of Harper & Brothers

enemy. American fire swept back a British cavalry charge, the British were driven back, but a counterstroke was halted because, as Major Henry Dearborn explained, the men were "beat out with heat and fatigue." The next morning the enemy was gone.

At the end of the day most American officers were agreed with John Laurens, who wrote his father Henry, then President of Congress: "General Lee, I think, must be tried for misconduct." In that letter Lee was depicted as paralyzed by indecision, his orders constantly countermanded, and "all this disgraceful retreating passed without the firing of a musket, over ground which might have been disputed inch by inch." Washington moved fast against Lee. In his letter to Congress of July 1, reporting the battle, he singled out Wayne for commendation, but as regards Lee he commented: "The peculiar situation of General Lee at this time requires that I should say nothing of his conduct. He is now in arrest. The charges against him, with such sentence as the court-martial may decree in his case, shall be transmitted, for the approbation or disapprobation of Congress, as soon as it shall be passed." Although Hamilton believed that Lee's friends would see to it that he was cleared, this was not to be the case. Lee was found guilty and suspended from his command for one year, and then dropped from the army. A repercussion of the affair was a duel between Hamilton's bosom friend, John Laurens, Washington's aide, and Lee, who had made disparaging remarks about the general. Lee received a slight wound, and the affair of honor was terminated.

One colorful incident during that torrid day was the appearance on the battlefield of Molly Hays, a Pennsylvania Dutch girl, who accompanied her husband John, an artilleryman, and brought pitcher after pitcher of water to the parched troops. When John fell wounded, Molly grasped the rammer staff from his hands, swabbed and loaded it, and stood at her post under fire. Her feat is commemorated on the Monmouth battle monument, and artillerymen still offer a toast

> *... Drunk in a beverage richer*
> *And stronger than was poured that day*
> *From Molly Pitcher's pitcher.*

1. Lee Urges "a Bridge of Gold" to Let the Enemy Escape

Memoirs of the Marquis de Lafayette.

On the 17th of June [1778], Philadelphia was evacuated. The invalids, magazines and heavy ammunition of the British were embarked with the general; the commissioners of conciliation alone remained behind. Passing over to Gloucester, the army marched, in two columns, each consisting of seven thousand men, commanded by Clinton and Knyphausen, towards New York. The army of the United States, which was of nearly equal force, directed itself from Valley Forge to Coryell's Ferry, and from thence to King's Town, within a march of the enemy; it was thus left at the option of the Americans, either to follow on their track or to repair to White Plains.

In a council held on this subject, Lee very eloquently endeavoured to prove that it was necessary to erect a bridge of gold for the enemy; that while on the very point of forming an alliance with them, every thing ought not to be placed at hazard; that the English army had never been so excellent and so well disciplined; he declared himself to be for White Plains: his speech influenced the opinion of Lord Stirling and of the brigadiers-general.

M. de Lafayette, placed on the other side, spoke late, and asserted that it would be disgraceful for the chiefs, and humiliating for the troops, to allow the enemy to traverse the Jerseys tranquilly; that, without running any improper risk, the rear guard might be attacked; that it was necessary to follow the English, manoeuvre with prudence, take advantage of a temporary separation, and, in short, seize the most favourable opportunities and situations. This advice was approved by many of the council, and above all by M. du Portail, chief of the engineers, and a very distinguished officer. The majority were, however, in favour of Lee; but M. de Lafayette spoke again to the general on this subject in the evening, and was seconded by Hamilton, and by Greene, who had been lately named quarter-master in place of Mifflin.

Several of the general officers changed their opinion; and the troops having already begun their march, they were halted in order to form a detachment. When united, there were 3,000 continentalists and 1,200 militia; the command fell to the share of Lee, but, by the express desire of the general, M. de Lafayette succeeded in obtaining it. Everything was going on extremely well, when Lee changed his mind and chose to command the troops himself; having again yielded this point, he rechanged once more; and as the general wished him to adhere to his first decision—"It is my fortune and honour," said Lee to M. de Lafayette, "that I place in your hands; you are too generous to cause the loss of both!" This tone succeeded better, and M. de Lafayette promised to ask for him the next day.

The enemy, unfortunately, continued their march; M. de Lafayette was delayed by want of provisions; and it was not until the 26th, at a quarter to twelve at night, that he could ask for Lee, who was sent with a detachment of one thousand men to Englishtown on the left side of the enemy. The first corps had advanced upon their right; and M. de Lafayette, by Lee's especial order, joined him at midday, within reach of the enemy, from whom he fortunately succeeded in concealing this movement. The two columns of the English army had united together at Monmouth Courthouse, from whence they departed on the morning of the 28th.

—LAFAYETTE, *Memoirs, Correspondence, and Manuscripts*, pp. 50-52.

2. "BY GOD! THEY ARE FLYING FROM A SHADOW!"

Testimony of Lieutenant Colonel Richard Harrison of the Continental Army at the court-martial of General Lee.

On the 28th of June, as one of His Excellency's [General Washington's] suite, I marched with him till we passed the Meetinghouse near Monmouth. . . . When we came to where the roads forked, His Excellency made a halt for a few minutes, in order to direct a disposition of the army. The wing under General Greene was then ordered to go to the right to prevent the enemy's turning our right flank.

After order was given in this matter, and His Excellency was proceeding down the road, we met a fifer, who appeared to be a good deal frighted. The General asked him whether he was a soldier belonging to the army, and the cause of his returning that way; he answered that he was a soldier, and that the Continental troops that had been advanced were retreating. On this answer the General seemed to be exceedingly surprized, and rather more exasperated, appearing to discredit the account, and threatened the man, if he mentioned a thing of the sort, he would have him whipped.

We then moved on a few paces forward (perhaps about fifty yards) where we met two or three persons more on that road; one was, I think, in the habit of a soldier. The General asked them from whence they came, and whether they belonged to the army; one of them replied that he did, and that all the troops that had been advanced, the whole of them, were retreating. His Excellency still appeared to discredit the account, having not heard any firing except a few cannon a considerable time before. However, the General, or some gentleman in company, observed that, as the report came by different persons, it might be well not wholly to disregard it.

Upon this I offered my services to the General to go forward and to bring him a true account of the situation of matters, and requested that Colonel Fitzgerald might go with me. After riding a very short distance, at the bridge in front of the line that was afterwards formed on the heights, I met part of Colonel Grayson's regiment, as I took it, from some of the officers that I knew. As I was in pursuit of information, I addressed myself to Captain Jones of that regiment and asked him the cause of the retreat, whether it was general, or whether it was only a particular part of the troops that were coming off. I do not precisely recollect the answer that he gave me; but I think, to the best of my knowledge, he said, "Yonder are a great many more troops in the same situation."

I proceeded and fell in with Lieutenant-Colonel Parke. These troops were rather disordered. The next officer that I was acquainted with was Lieutenant-Colonel William Smith. I addressed myself to Colonel Smith and asked him what was the cause of the troops retreating, as I had come to gain information? who replied that he could not tell, that they had lost but one man. I then proceeded down the line, determined to go to the rear of the retreating troops, and met with Colonel Ogden. I asked him the same question, whether he could assign the cause or give me any information why the troops retreated. He appeared to be exceedingly exasperated and said, "By God! they are flying from a shadow."

I fell in immediately after with Captain Mercer, who is aid-de-camp to Major-General Lee, and, expecting to derive some information from him, I put the same question to him. Captain Mercer seemed, by the manner of his answer (as I addressed myself to him, saying, "For God's sake, what is the cause of this retreat?"), to be displeased; his answer was, "If you will proceed, you will see the cause; you will see several columns of foot and horse." I replied to Captain Mercer that I presumed that the enemy was not in greater force than when they left Philadelphia, and we came to that field to meet columns of foot and horse.

The next field-officer I met was Lieutenant-Colonel Rhea, of New Jersey, who appeared to be conducting a regiment. I asked him uniformly the same question for information, and he appeared to be very much agitated, expressed his disapprobation of the retreat, and seemed to be equally concerned (or perhaps more) that he had no place assigned to go where the troops were to halt.

About this time I met with General Maxwell; and, agreeable to the General's direction to get intelligence, I asked him the cause. He appeared to be as much at a loss as Lieutenant-Colonel Rhea or any other officer I had met with; and intimated that he had received no orders upon the occasion and was totally in the dark what line of conduct to pursue.

I think nearly opposite to the point of wood where the first stand was made, I saw General Lee. I do not recollect that anything passed between us, but General Lee's asking me where General Washington was, and my telling him that he was in the rear advancing.

I then went to the extreme of the retreating troops, which were formed of Colonel Stewart's regiment, and found them in the field where the enemy retreated to, just beyond the defile. I addressed myself to General Wayne, General Scott and, I believe, to Colonel Stewart, and to several other officers who were there; and asked General Wayne the cause of the retreat, who seemed no otherwise concerned than at the retreat itself, told me he believed it was impossible to tell the cause; and while we were standing together, which I supposed might be three or four minutes, the enemy's light infantry and grenadiers came issuing out of the wood, pressing very hard upon us at about two or three or four hundred yards distance. The troops that had been halted were put in motion.

I had some conversation with General Wayne relative to a disposition of the troops, if nothing could be done to check the advance of the enemy, who seemed to consider the matter exceedingly practicable, provided any effort or exertion was made for the purpose, alledging that a very select body of men had been that day drawn off from a body far inferior in number. General Wayne then told me that as General Washington might not be perfectly well acquainted with the country, it might be well to advise him of a road, if I met him, that led by Taylor's Tavern, on which it would be necessary to throw a body of troops, in case the enemy should attempt to turn our right flank.

I, upon this, left General Wayne and galloped down the line to meet General Washington, to report to him the state of our troops and the progress of the enemy. I met General Washington at the point of wood, or near it, where the first stand was made, and reported to him what I had seen, adding that the enemy was pressing hard and would be upon him in a march of fifteen minutes; which (I have since understood) was the first information he received of the enemy being so close upon our retreating troops. We remained there a few minutes until the extreme rear of our retreating troops got up.

—HARRISON, Testimony, *N. Y. Hist. Soc. Coll.*, VI, 71-75.

3. LEE'S RETREAT ROUSES WASHINGTON TO FURY

Narrative attributed to James Sullivan Martin.

After all things were put in order, we marched, but halted a few minutes in the village, where we were joined by a few other troops and then proceeded on. We now heard a few reports of cannon ahead; we went in a road running through a deep narrow valley, which was for a considerable way covered with thick wood; we were some time in passing this defile. While in the wood we heard a volley or two of musketry, and upon inquiry we found it to be a party of our troops who had fired upon a party of British horse; but there was no fear of horse in the place in which we then were.

It was ten or eleven o'clock before we got through these woods and came into the open fields. The first cleared land we came to was an Indian corn-field, surrounded on the east, west and north sides by thick tall trees; the sun shining full upon the field, the soil of which was sandy, the mouth of a heated oven seemed to me to be but a trifle hotter than this ploughed field; it was almost impossible to breathe. We had to fall back again as soon as we could, into the woods; by the time we had got under the shade of the trees, and had taken breath, of which we had been almost deprived, we received orders to re-treat, as all the left wing of the army (that part being under the command of Gen. Lee) were retreating. Grating as this order was to our feelings, we were obliged to comply.

We had not retreated far before we came to a defile, a muddy sloughy brook; while the artillery were passing this place, we sat down by the road side;—in a few minutes the Commander-in-chief and suit crossed the road just where we were sitting. I heard him ask our officers, "by whose order the troops were retreating," and being answered, "by Gen. Lee's," he said some-thing, but as he was moving forward all the time this was passing, he was too far off for me to hear it distinctly; those that were nearer to him said that his words were—"D—n him"; whether he did thus express himself or not I do not know; it was certainly very unlike him, but he seemed at the instant to be in a great passion; his looks if not his words seemed to indicate as much.

After passing us, he rode on to the plain field and took an observation of the advancing enemy; he remained there some time upon his old English charger, while the shot from the British artillery were rending up the earth all around him. After he had taken a view of the enemy, he returned and ordered the two Connecticut brigades to make a stand at a fence, in order to keep the enemy in check while the artillery and other troops crossed the before-men-tioned defile.

—MARTIN(?), *Narrative of a Revolutionary Soldier*, pp. 91-95.

4. "MOLLY PITCHER" MANS A GUN AT MONMOUTH

Narrative attributed to Joseph P. Martin.

One little incident happened during the heat of the cannonade, which I was eye-witness to, and which I think would be unpardonable not to men-tion. A woman whose husband belonged to the Artillery, and who was then attached to a piece in the engagement, attended with her husband at the piece the whole time. While in the act of reaching a cartridge and having one of her feet as far before the other as she could step, a cannon shot from the enemy passed directly between her legs without doing any other damage than carry-ing away all the lower part of her petticoat. Looking at it with apparent unconcern, she observed that it was lucky it did not pass a little higher, for in that case it might have carried away something else, and continued her occupation.

—MARTIN(?), *Narrative of a Revolutionary Soldier*, pp. 96-97.

IV. THE RHODE ISLAND CAMPAIGN OF 1778

A French fleet under Count d'Estaing arrived before New York too late to prevent Lord Howe from ferrying Clinton's forces across to Manhattan. A naval attack against New York seemed hazardous because D'Estaing's huge ships of war drew too much water to take them into the bay as the channel across Sandy Hook bar was not dredged until modern times. Not knowing where the French fleet or Washington's army might strike, the British seemed temporarily paralyzed. As Captain Mackenzie of the Royal Welsh Fusiliers commented somewhat inaccurately in his diary:

> So extraordinary an event as the present certainly never before occurred in the history of Britain! An army of 50,000 men, and a fleet of nearly 100 ships and armed vessels, are prevented from acting offensively by the appearance on the American coast of a French squadron of 12 sail of the line and 4 frigates, without troops. Some unpardonable faults have been committed somewhere; and those whose duty it is to watch the motions of the enemy in every quarter should answer with their heads for risquing the fate of so large a portion of the national force by their supineness and total want of intelligence.

The most feasible place to use this amphibious force (4,000 French soldiers were transported with the fleet), it was soon decided, was to be against the British in Rhode Island, in a joint operation with American troops under General Sullivan. Sullivan's army, divided between Greene and Lafayette, with the New Hampshireman in supreme command, marched to a rendezvous with the French some miles north of Newport. But New England militia reinforcements failed to arrive until some ten days after D'Estaing appeared off Newport. By that time Clinton had sent an expeditionary force in Lord Howe's fleet to the relief of General Pigot, commanding the Newport defenses.

The Franco-American campaign was marked at the start by maladroit moves, bad luck and lack of co-operation. When the British fleet appeared off Newport, D'Estaing, in order to keep his front together and drive off the enemy, re-embarked the French troops over Sullivan's protest. But the naval engagement never took place, for a violent storm on the night of August 11 scattered both squadrons and forced Sullivan to abandon his ground attack. Howe put back to New York for repairs. D'Estaing sailed to Boston to refit.

Sullivan's temper, which he always had such difficulty in controlling, now got out of hand. The American general published an order condemning the French move. The lowered Patriot morale, to which both commanders had contributed in different ways, caused some five thousand militiamen to go back home. Now that Sullivan's forces were weakened, Pigot attacked, but the Patriot troops refused to give ground. Under cover of night Sullivan ferried his men over to Tiverton and Bristol.

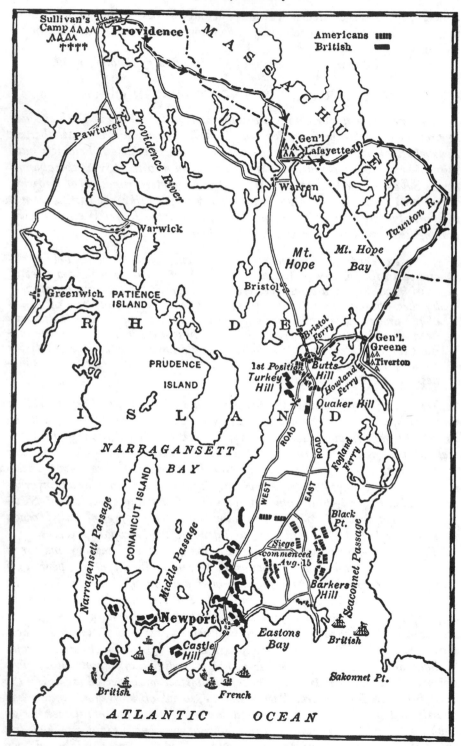

SIEGE OF NEWPORT

In the Newport venture both sides suffered equally, about two hundred and fifty casualties apiece, but for the grand alliance it was an inauspicious start. An anti-French riot broke out in Boston, and it took the combined arts of John Hancock, Nathanael Greene and Alexander Hamilton to heal the wounds to Gallic pride. Lafayette was temporarily embittered. Writing a friend at this time, he declared: "I begin to see that, seduced by a false enthusiasm, I made a mistake to leave everything and run to America. But it would be a greater one to return. My cup is filled; I must drink it to the dregs, but the dregs can already be tasted."

The Newport fiasco set off fierce polemics. Writing to a critic, the Rhode Island merchant John Brown, on September 6, Greene contraverted Brown's assertion that the expedition had been "the worst concerted and executed of the war." The plan of attack had been to land on the northern part of the island to lull the enemy into a belief that the Americans intended to storm the garrison by regular approaches. But Greene pointed out that they really intended to re-embark the troops and land on the southern part of the island, and he maintained this would have been successful "had our strength been sufficient and the disembarkation covered by the fleet." Defending Sullivan's conduct, Greene held that "an attack with militia, in an open country where they could retire after defeat, might be very prudent, which would be very rash and unwarrantable upon an island." This was probably a judicious analysis. The risks had become too great, and Sullivan did the best he could in extricating his forces from disaster.

1. THE FRENCH ADMIRAL SENDS EFFUSIVE GREETINGS

Count d'Estaing to General Washington.

At sea, July 8, 1778

I have the honor of imparting to Your Excellency the arrival of the King's fleet, charged by His Majesty with the glorious task of giving his allies, the United States of America, the most striking proofs of his affection. Nothing will be wanting to my happiness, if I can succeed in it. It is augmented by the consideration of concerting my operations with a general such as Your Excellency. The talents and great actions of General Washington have insured him, in the eyes of all Europe, the title, truly sublime, of Deliverer of America. Accept, Sir, the homage that every man, that every military man, owes you; and be not displeased that I solicit, even in the first moment of intercourse, with military and maritime frankness, a friendship so flattering as yours. I will try to render myself worthy of it by my respectful devotion for your country. It is prescribed to me by orders, and my heart inspires it. . . .

—SPARKS, *Correspondence of the American Revolution*, II, 155-156.

2. "ALL OUR HOPES OF ASSISTANCE ARE AT AN END"

General John Sullivan to George Washington.

Head Quarters on Rhode Island, August 13, 1778

In my last I had the honor to inform your Excellency of my being in possession of the enemies works on the north part of Rhode Island, and of the arrival of the British fleet the moment we had landed, as also of the sailing of Count Destaing in quest of them. As this unfortunate circumstance deprived us of the assistance we promised ourselves from the French troops, I found it necessary to wait on the ground till the tenth at night; when, finding my own troops numbers had increased sufficiently to warrant my advancing to the town without waiting the return of the fleet, I issued orders for the army to march the 11th at six in the morning, but Fortune, still determined to sport longer with us, brought on a storm so violent that it last night blew down, tore and almost ruined all the tents I had. The arms of course were rendered useless, and almost the whole of our ammunition ruined. The much greater part of the army have no kind of covering, nor would tents if they had them prove a sufficient security against the severity of the storm. My men are mostly lying under the fences, half covered with water, without ammunition, and arms rendered useless; the communication between us and the main cut off by the violence of the wind which will scarcely permit a whale boat to pass. Should the enemy come out to attack us our dependance must be upon the superiority of our numbers and the point of the bayonet. How our militia may behave on such an occasion I am unable to determine. To retreat is impossible; therefore we must conquer or perish.

Perhaps under these circumstances an attack upon us might be of great advantage. Several men have perished with the severity of the weather and I expect more will as I see no probability of the storm ceasing. All our hopes of assistance from the French fleet are at an end as this storm must have driven them far off from this port and, I am very apprehensive, quite far off the coast.

To combat all these misfortunes and to surmount all those difficulties requires a degree of temper and persevering fortitude which I could never boast of, and which few possess in so ample a manner. Your Excellency, I will however endeavour by emulating the example to rise superior to the malevolence of Fortune and my present lamentable situation as quick as possible and, if Heaven will cease to frown, endeavor to gratify your Excellencys desires. . . .

—HAMMOND, ed., *Letters and Papers of Sullivan*, II, 205-207.

3. "EVERY VOICE IS RAISED AGAINST THE FRENCH NATION"

General Sullivan to Henry Laurens.

> Camp before Newport, August 16th, 1778

My dear Sir: I have been honoured with your Excellency's favour of the 8th inst., with the gazette inclosed. I most sincerely thank you for the licence you have given me to communicate intelligence to your Excellency by private letter, and also for your promise to retaliate in kind. My letters to General Washington, copies of which he is to convey to Congress from time to time, must have informed you of the return of the French fleet, the loss it sustained in the storm, and their sudden departure for Boston. This movement has raised every voice against the French nation, revived all those ancient prejudices against the faith and sincerity of that people, and inclines them most heartily to curse the new alliance. These are only the first sallies of passion, which will in a few days subside.

I confess that I do most cordially resent the conduct of the Count, or rather the conduct of his officers, who have, it seems, compelled him to go to Boston and leave us on an island without any certain means of retreat; and what surprises me exceedingly is that the Count could be persuaded that it was necessary for ten sail of the line to lay in the harbour to attend one which is refitting.

I begged the Count to remain only twenty-four hours, and I would agree to dismiss him, but in vain. He well knew that the original plan was for him to land his own troops with a large detachment of mine within their lines, under fire of some of his ships, while with the rest I made an attack in front, but his departure has reduced me to the necessity of attacking their works in front or of doing nothing. They have double lines across the island in two places, at near quarter of a mile distance. The outer line is covered in front by redoubts within musket-shot of each other; the second in the same manner by redoubts thrown up between the lines. Besides this there is an inaccessible pond which covers more than half of the first line. A strong fortress on Tomminy Hill overlooks and commands the whole adjacent country.

The enemy have about six thousand men within these works. I have eight thousand one hundred and seventy-four. With this force I am to carry their lines or retire with disgrace. Near seven thousand of my men are militia, unaccustomed to the noise of arms. Should I throw my men by strategem within these lines it must be my best troops. Should they be defeated the want of ships will render their retreat impracticable, and most of the army must be sacrificed. You will, therefore, judge of my feelings, and of the situation which my inconstant ally and coadjutor has thrown me into. My feelings as a man press me to make the desperate attempt. My feelings as an officer cause me to hesitate.

I have submitted the considerations to my officers; how they will declare I know not. I feel disgrace will attend this fatal expedition, though it gave at first the most pleasing presages of success.

—HAMMOND, ed., *Letters and Papers of Sullivan*, II, 218-220.

4. "WE SOON PUT THE ENEMY TO ROUT"

Nathanael Greene to George Washington.

Camp Tiverton, August 31, 1778

On the evening of the 29th the army fell back to the north end of the island [Rhode Island]. The next morning the enemy advanced upon us in two columns upon the east and west road. Our light troops, commanded by Colonel Livingston and Colonel Laurens, attacked the heads of the columns about seven o'clock in the morning but were beat back; they were reinforced with a regiment upon each road. The enemy still proved too strong. General Sullivan formed the army in order of battle, and resolved to wait their approach upon the ground we were encamped on, and sent orders to the light troops to fall back. The enemy came up and formed upon Quaker Hill, a very strong piece of ground within about one mile and a quarter of our line. We were well posted with strong works in our rear, and a strong redoubt in front, partly upon the right of the line.

In this position a warm cannonade commenced and lasted for several hours, with continual skirmishes in front of both lines. About two o'clock the enemy began to advance in force upon our right, as if they intended to dislodge us from the advanced redoubt. I had the command of the right wing. After advancing four regiments and finding the enemy still gaining ground, I advanced with two more regiments of regular troops and a brigade of militia, and at the same time General Sullivan ordered Colonel Livingston, with the light troops under his command, to advance. We soon put the enemy to the rout, and I had the pleasure to see them run in worse disorder than they did at the battle of Monmouth. Our troops behaved with great spirit; and the brigade of militia under the command of General Lovell advanced with great resolution and in good order, and stood the fire of the enemy with great firmness. Lieutenant-colonel Livingston, Colonel Jackson and Colonel Henry B. Livingston did themselves great honor in the transactions of the day, but it's not in my power to do justice to Colonel Laurens who acted both the general and partisan. His command of regular troops was small, but he did everything possible to be done by their numbers; he had two most excellent officers with him—Lieutenant-colonel Henry and Major Talbot.

The enemy fell back to their strong ground, and the day terminated with a cannonade and skirmishes. Both armies continued in their position all day yesterday, cannonading each other every now and then. Last night we effected a very good retreat without the loss of men or stores.

We have not collected an account of the killed and wounded, but we judge our loss amounts to between two and three hundred, and that of the enemy to much more.

We are going to be posted all round the shores as guard upon them, and in that state to wait for the return of the fleet, which, by the way, I think will not be in a hurry.

It is reported that Lord Howe arrived last night with his fleet and the reinforcement mentioned in your Excellency's letter to General Sullivan. If the report is true we got off the island in very good season.

—GREENE, *Life of Nathanael Greene*, II, 130-132.

5. Boston Riots Against the French Fleet

Petersfield, February, 1784

A most violent affray, in which numbers on both sides were engaged and the French seem to have been very roughly treated, happened on the 17th of September, 1778, at night, in Boston. Some of the French were said to have been killed, and several were certainly wounded; among whom were some officers, and one particularly of considerable distinction. As both D'Estaing and the government of Boston were eager to accommodate matters in such a manner as that no sting should remain behind on either side, a great reserve was observed with respect to the particulars of the riot, as well as of the circumstances which led to it; and the cursory imperfect sketches that were published showed evidently that they were not to be relied upon.

A proclamation was issued by the council of state on the following day, strictly urging the magistrates to use their utmost endeavours for bringing the offenders to justice, and offering a reward of 300 dollars for the discovery of any of the parties concerned in the riot. And to remove the impression of its arising from any popular animosity to the French, the Boston prints laboured to fix it upon some unknown captured British seamen and deserters from Burgoyne's army, who had enlisted in their privateers. D'Estaing had the address to give into this idea, and to appear thoroughly satisfied with the satisfaction he received. The high reward produced no manner of discovery.

The same spirit operated just about the same time and in the same manner, but much more violent in degree, and fatal in consequence between the American and French seamen, in the city and port of Charlestown, South Carolina. The quarrel there began, as at Boston, ashore and at night, and ended in the last extreme of hostility, an open fight with cannon and small arms; the French firing from their ships, whither they had been hastily driven from the town, and Americans from the adjoining wharfs and shore. Several lives were acknowledged to be lost, and a much greater number were, of course, wounded. . . .

—Universal Magazine, LXXIV, 87.

6. Yankee Doodle's Expedition to Rhode Island

A Tory Satire
From Lewis, Monsieur Gérard came,
  To Congress in this town, sir,
They bowed to him, and he to them,
  And then they all sat down, sir.

Begar, said Monsieur, one grand coup
  You shall bientot behold, sir;
This was believed as gospel true,
  And Jonathan felt bold, sir.

So Yankee Doodle did forget
  The sound of British drum, sir,
How oft it made him quake and sweat,
  In spite of Yankee rum, sir.

He took his wallet on his back,
  His rifle on his shoulder,
And veowed Rhode Island to attack
  Before he was much older.

In dread array their tattered crew
  Advanced with colors spread, sir.
Their fifes played Yankee doodle, doo,
  King Hancock at their head, sir. . . .

They swore they'd make bold Pigot squeak,
  So did their good ally, sir,
And take him prisoner in a week,
  But that was all my eye, sir.

As Jonathan so much desired
  To shine in martial story,
D'Estaing with politesse retired,
  To leave him all the glory.

He left him what was better yet,
  At least it was more use, sir,
He left him for a quick retreat,
  A very good excuse, sir. . . .

Another cause with these combined,
  To throw him in the dumps, sir,
For Clinton's name alarmed his mind
  And made him stir his stumps, sir.
        —Rivington's *Royal Gazette*, October 3, 1778.

V. STONY POINT

Stony Point, on the west side of the Hudson, and Verplanck's Point across the river were likened by Washington to the Pillars of Hercules. He considered them "the key to the Continent." But before the Patriots had completed fortifying these approaches to West Point, they were seized by Clinton in the spring of 1779. The British immediately set about erecting formidable fortifications. Washington asked Anthony Wayne to get a trustworthy officer into the British works to find out whatever he could about them. The man selected was Allen McLane, and the way in which he got inside the fort at Stony Point is told in his manuscript journal. After further reconnaissance of the area, Washington designated Anthony Wayne to attack with a force of 1,350 men. They were to use bayonets, and, except in one battalion, not a musket was loaded. It was to be Paoli in reverse. The plan was skillfully executed, and the fort was taken. The British losses: 63 killed, 70 or more wounded, 543 captured, along with artillery and military equipment. The Americans lost 15 killed, 80 wounded.

Believing that "it would require more men to maintain it than we can afford," Washington had the fort dismantled, and Clinton moved in again. The effects, then, of Stony Point were largely psychological. With the bayonet alone, the Americans had successfully attacked British regulars in a fortified position, and by that achievement won new respect from their enemy.

1. A Spy Gets Inside British-Held Stony Point

Journal of Captain Allen McLane of Pennsylvania.

Friday the 2 July [*1779*].—By Genl. Washington's orders went in with a flag to conduct Mrs. Smith to see her sons. [Elsewhere in the Journal appears the following memorandum: "McLane discovered the unfinished situation of the works on Stony Point while accompanying Mrs. Smith with a flag and communicated his observations to head quarter, which discovery determined Genl. Washington to carry it by storm on the night of the 17th July, 1779."]

Saturday, 3d of July.—Took post at the short clove, nothing occurring this day. At 8 o'clock moved down towards Stony Point—lay close to the works. All quiet this night.

Tuesday, July 6th.—Lay on the line all this day. His Exclly. Genl. Washington reconnoitred the enemy's works.

Wednesday, July 14.—Moved down to the hills in front of Stony Point—took the widow Calhoon and another widow going to the enemy with chickens and greens—drove off 20 head of horned cattle from the enemy's pasture, the property of John Deinke, Saml. Calhoon and Jacob Rose—gave them their cattle.

Lay in the woods this night near Captain Hutchinsons.

Thursday, July 15th.—This morning mustered my company at Hutchins' house—at ten o'clock rode with Majors Posey and Lee to reconnoitre the enemy's lines. Genl. Waine moved down from the forest to the ground near the lines. At 8 o'clock at night moved my company close to the enemy's sentrys in order to intersept intelligence. At 30 minutes past 12 o'clock the light infantry began the attack on the lines, Genl. Waine at their head. They rushed on with fixed bayonets and carried the lines in 25 minutes—killed one capt., 21 privates, wounded 4 subalterns, 66 privates, took one colonel, 4 captains, 15 subalterns, 468 men. At the same time a feint was made against Verplank's Point.

—McLane Papers, Lib. II, N.Y. Hist. Soc.

2. WAYNE'S TROOPS TAKE THE FORT AT BAYONET POINT

Nathanael Greene to Colonel Cox.

Stoney-Point, King's Ferry, July 17, 1779

I wrote you a hasty account yesterday morning of a surprize Gen. Wayne had effected upon the garrison at this place. He marched about two o'clock in the afternoon from Fort Montgomery with part of the light infantry of the army, amounting to about 1,400 men. The garrison consisted of between 5 and 600 men, including officers. The attack was made about midnight and conducted with great spirit and enterprise, the troops marching up in the face of an exceeding heavy fire with cannon and musketry, without discharging a gun. This is thought to be the perfection of discipline and will for ever immortalize Gen. Wayne, as it would do honor to the first general in Europe. The place is as difficult of access as any you ever saw, strongly fortified with lines and secured with a double row of abatis. The post actually looks more formidable on the ground than it can be made by description, and, contrary to almost all other events of this nature, increases our surprize by viewing the place and the circumstances.

The darkness of the night favoured the attack and made our loss much less than might have been expected. The whole business was done with fixed bayonets. Our loss in killed and wounded amounted to 90 men, including officers—eight only of which were killed. Gen. Wayne got a slight wound (upon the side of his head) and three or four other officers—among the number is Lieut. Col. Hay, of Pennsylvania—but they are all in a fair way of recovery.

The enemy's loss is not certainly known, neither have we any certain account of the number of prisoners, as they were sent away in the dark and in a hurry, but it is said they amount to 440; about 30 or 40 were left behind unable to march, and upwards of 30 were buried.

The enemy made little resistance after our people got into the works; their cry was, "Mercy, mercy, dear, dear Americans!"

—JOHNSTON, *Storming of Stony Point*, pp. 174-175.

3. "THE ENTERPRISE WAS REALLY A GALLANT ONE"

Journal of Commodore George Collier.

A very disagreeable event, however, put a stop to the favourite expedition against New London; and this was the surprisal (in the night) of the strong post of Stony Point, in the North River, which was carried by the rebels with very little loss and the garrison all made prisoners or killed. The enterprise was really a gallant one, and as bravely executed. The rebel troops, under a General Wayne, formed two attacks with fixed bayonets and unloaded arms during the darkness and silence of the night; it was said that they had taken the precaution to kill every dog two days before that was within some miles round the post, to prevent their approach being discovered by their barking. They began to march from their camp, eleven miles off, soon after dusk, proceeding with celerity and silence; and soon after midnight fell in with the British piquets, whom they surprised and bayonetted a number of them; the rest hastily retreated, keeping up a straggling fire, though to very little purpose, for the rebels followed close at their heels. Their forlorn hope consisted of forty men, and were followed by a party with hooks on long poles, to pull aside the abattis and thereby give an entrance to the column behind. The works of Stony Point were not half completed; and as one part of its strength at that time consisted in the abattis, the rebels found no great difficulty in getting into the body of a work which was quite open, though on an eminence.

A young man of the name of Johnson, who was Lieut.-Colonel of the 17th Regiment, was left with the charge of this important post; he was reckoned a brave and good officer for his years, but the force was certainly inadequate to its defence. On the first alarm from the piquets he ran down with the main guard to defend the abattis and support them. The rebel column was stopped for a few minutes, and a brisk firing took place on both sides; but to Colonel Johnson's grief and surprise, he heard a cry of "Victory" on the heights above him and the "Fort's our own" (which was the rebel watchword). He very soon learned by some of his officers that the enemy were in full possession of the body of the place. It was certainly so. The column which was destined for making the other attack took a short detour around, and climbed up the perpendicular height, which being over the river, nobody expected an enemy on that side; and the surprise of the King's troops at seeing them in possession of the works was extreme.

The laws of war give a right to the assailants of putting all to death who are found in arms; justice is certainly due to all men, and commendation should be given where it is deserved. The rebels had made the attack with a bravery they never before exhibited, and they showed at this moment a generosity and clemency which during the course of the rebellion had no parallel. There was light sufficient after getting up the heights to show them many of the British troops with arms in their hands; instead of putting them to death, they called to them "to throw their arms down if they expected any quarter." It was too late then to resist; they submitted, and the strong post of Stony Point fell again into possession of the rebels.

The loss of the King's troops, considering the place was taken by storm, was very small, Captain Tew being the only officer killed and thirty-two men; forty-three were wounded, and the rest were made prisoners. The enemy found here many brass mortars, many pieces of large cannon, together with the ammunition necessary for them—an unlucky piece of business and fatal to the reputation of a gallant young man, who was certainly left with a force very inadequate to the purpose for which he was placed at Stony Point. . . .

On the receipt of this disagreeable news, the Commodore sent orders to discontinue the blockade of the harbour at New London, and immediately proceeded back to New York with all the men-of-war and transports, getting through that most dangerous pass called Hell Gates, luckily without losing any of the ships. . . .

The fleet was no sooner descried from Stony Point than the rebels set fire to everything there that would burn, and went off with their usual alertness; they had conveyed away some of the cannon and mortars, but the greatest part of them were loaded on a galley, with which they proposed going up the river to their strong post at West Point; but as the galley was beginning to move she was luckily sunk. . . .

—JOHNSTON, *Storming of Stony Point*, pp. 134-136.

VI. PAULUS HOOK

In his letter of July 27, 1779, to Washington reporting on the capture of Stony Point, Wayne omitted mentioning the role of Allen McLane. Nor did he single out for special commendation Major Henry Lee ("Light-Horse Harry"), whose corps had played a minor role in that engagement. So high-spirited an officer as Lee was certain to make his own bid for glory. As Washington Irving later put it, "Stony Point had piqued his emulation."

Lee's objective was Paulus Hook, a fort directly opposite New York City at what is now Jersey City. McLane scouted the territory, reported that the garrison numbered little over 200, and guided Lee's men through the complex approaches to the fort. Time was of the essence, as the fort was protected by a deep ditch which could be crossed only at low tide. Lee's offensive moves began on the morning of August 18, but a defection of Virginians reduced his forces, and it was four o'clock of the following morning before he approached the marshlands leading to the ditch. A rising tide would soon make it impassable. The Americans staged a gallant bayonet attack and took the fort in a few minutes, with only two killed and three wounded. But alarm guns on the New York side were arousing the British, and Lee had to pull out with some 158 prisoners.

After Paulus Hook, Lee was charged with having taken precedence over officers senior in rank, but a court-martial exonerated him. Hamilton's comment on the charges is worth noting. In a letter to John Laurens, dated September 11, 1779, he wrote:

> The Philadelphia papers will tell you of a handsome stroke by Lee at Powle's Hook. Some folks in the Virginia line, jealous of his glory, had the folly to get him arrested. He has been tried and acquitted with the highest honor. Lee unfolds himself more and more to be an officer of great capacity, and if he had not a little spice of the Julius Caesar or Cromwell in him, he would be a very clever fellow.

1. ALLEN McLANE RECONNOITERS PAULUS HOOK

Monday, August 16. Moved toward Powles Hook to reconeter. Took two prisoners on Hobuck. . . . Returned with the party to Hackinsack. This night lay at Storms house.

Tusday, 17 Aug. Drew four days' provisions. Detached two sergeants [?] with 12 men eatch to lay in Bergain Woods. This night lay near the liberty pole.

Wensday, 18 August. This morning received orders from Maj. Lee to take post in the wood near Bargan in order to intercept the communication between Powles Hook and the [?] and to join him at a sertain place in the woods near the Three Pidgeons in order to conduct him to attack Powles Hook. Met him and after some deficalty arrived at the works half past three in morning. Stormed them without more loss than two men killed and five wounded who killed about fifty, took 150 prisoner, 9 officers

Thursday 19, 1779 August. and then retired to the new bridge the distance of 22 miles. . . .

—McLane Papers, Lib. II, N.Y. Historical Soc.

2. A PATRIOT VIEW: "THE GREATEST ENTERPRISE EVER UNDERTAKEN"

Captain Levin Handy to George Handy.

Paramus, 22 August, 1779

Before this reaches you, I doubt not but you have heard of our success at Powles Hook, where the enemy had a very strong fort, within one and a quarter miles from New York. We started from this place on Wednesday last half after ten o'clock, taking our route by a place called New Bridge on Hackensac River, where my two companies were joined by three hundred Virginians and a company of dismounted Dragoons, commanded by Captain McLane. We took up our line of march about 5 o'clock in the evening from the bridge, the nearest route with safety, to Powles, distant then about twenty miles, with my detachment in front, the whole under command of the gallant Major Lee. The works were to be carried by storm—the whole to advance in three columns, one of which I had the honour to command.

The attack was to commence at one half after 12 o'clock, but having been greatly embarrassed on our march, and having a number of difficulties to surmount, did not arrive at the point of attack till after four o'clock in the morning, when, after a small fire from them, we gained their works and put about fifty of them to the bayonet, took one hundred and fifty-seven prison-ers, exclusive of seven commanding officers; this was completed in less than thirty minutes, and a retreat ordered, as we had every reason to suppose unless timely it would be cut off. Our situation was so difficult that we could not bring off any stores. We had a morass to pass of upwards two miles, the greatest part of which we were obliged to pass by files, and several canals to ford up to our breast in water. We advanced with bayonets, pans open, cocks fallen, to prevent any fire from our side; and believe me when I assure you we did not fire a musket.

You will see a more particular account of it in the papers than it is in my power to give you at present. It is thought to be the greatest enterprise ever undertaken in America. Our loss is so inconsiderable that I do not mention it.

—REED, *Life and Correspondence of Reed*, II, 125-126.

3. A TORY VIEW: THE PATRIOTS FAILED TO EXPLOIT THEIR VICTORY

Nearly half an hour after two, the Rebels in three divisions (exceeding 400 men) passed the ditch in front of the abatis, about 20 yards from the abatis, where they were fired upon by a few centries, but having seized immediately on the block house guards (who, in place of defending their post, ran out to see what was the matter) they proceeded to the work, which they soon became masters of, with the cannon, etc. But they were so con-fused and alarmed, they neither spiked the cannon nor damaged the barracks, or made any other use of their victory than carrying off about 100 prisoners, among whom there are about ten Hessians (whose loss is much regretted) and four officers of Colonel Buskirk's battalion, and plundering a few women.

This panic (amongst them) was occasioned by an incessant fire kept on them from a small redoubt into which Major Sutherland threw himself with a captain subaltern and 25 gallant Hessians on the first alarm. The Rebels repeatedly challenged the redoubt to surrender, or they would bayonet them, to which they received a fire and "No," for answer. About half after 8 o'clock Major Sutherland was joined by one Light Infantry company of the Guards, under the command of Captain Dundass, with which he immediately marched, and Captain Maynard was shortly after ordered to follow Major Sutherland by Colonel Gordon, on which Major Sutherland marched both companies in order to succour Colonel Buskirk, and after going about 15 miles, he found that Colonel Buskirk had a smart engagement with the Rebels some time before and had returned. There were a few prisoners made, amongst whom is a Captain Meale, who was found asleep from the great fatigue he underwent; and surely unless he had been a Livingston, Laurens or Adams, he could not in that situation forfeit his claim to British valor and humanity. The Light Infantry rested here for an hour, during which Dr. Gordon gallantly charged two Rebels, who had fired at him, and took one of them.

Major Sutherland, finding one object of his march answered by Colonel Buskirk's being safe, and 100 men not sufficient to answer his other intentions, returned, this charming body of men having made a march of about 30 miles in less than 10 hours.

—*New York Gazette and Mercury*, August 23, 1779.

VII. SPRINGFIELD

In the spring of 1780 the British had evidence that there was much discontent in the Patriot ranks. Civilian morale was depreciating along with the Continental currency. Washington found that his half-starved army stationed at Morristown was increasingly reluctant to re-enlist. Among the Headquarters Papers in the Clements Library is an undated memorandum from Knyphausen to Clinton:

> *Having received intelligence that Washington's army was very discontented, that many of them wished to have an opportunity given them of coming in to join the royal army, and that he had detached the York Brigade towards Albany to oppose the incursions of the Indians—these reasons induced General Knyphausen to make a move into Jersey with 6,000 men.*

Knyphausen's force crossed over from Staten Island to Elizabethtown and marched to the village of Connecticut Farms, burned the church and other buildings and accidentally killed the wife of the Reverend James Caldwell. To Knyphausen's surprise the militia turned out and disputed his crossing of the Rahway River. That story is told by Sylvanus Seeley, a colonel in the New Jersey state militia, who proved especially useful to Washington in transmitting intelligence regarding British troop and ship movements around New York harbor. With the militia reinforced by Continental troops, Knyphausen faced about and retired to Elizabethtown.

To save face he decided to try once again. On June 23 his forces marched to the Jersey town of Springfield, but were obstinately resisted by Patriot troops under Nathanael Greene. After seizing the town, Knyphausen pushed a column to the American left, threatening Greene's rear. The American general withdrew his troops to higher ground and stopped the British column cold. Outnumbered five or six to one, the Americans had fought the British and Hessian troops to a standstill. The burning and looting of Springfield, following hard on the atrocities at Connecticut Farms, roused the countryside against the British, who attempted no further operations in New Jersey.

1. The Preliminary Battle of Connecticut Farms

Diary of Colonel Sylvanus Seeley, of the New Jersey militia.

7th June 1780: Had an alarm and the enemy came out as far as Springfield Bridge. The Militia colected fast and joining Maxwells brigade stopt the enemy and after sum fire at long shot the enemy retired to a breast work they had threw up on an advantagious pice of ground on this side the farm meeting hous. About 3 this aftarnoon they set fire to about 30 buildings, one of which is the meeting hous. We have had about 15 killed and 40 wounded, among the latter my brother Saml, slightly. I had orders and marched my regiment to Thompsons Mills whare we lay all night.

8th: This morning about ½ after 12 the rear of the enemy left the ground. About 8 o'clock received orders to follow them and on ower march receive[d] inteligence that the enemy are going, but when we got to town find a guard in the woods back of Decon Ogdens hous and at the forks of the road. Aftar sum time here and being joined by Lord Stirlings troopes he orders us to advance in three colloms, one on the main road, the Continental troops of Col. Cortland on the left, myself in the centor. We advanced, and the troop under my command behaved exceading well, altho at a certain time one platoon fell back a little, but after being ordered to com up came up and stood thare ground well. We took about 20 prisoners and advance through the woods whare the enemy open upon us with a number of field pieces, and finding they ware true [too?] heavy for us General Hand ordered a retreat, which was performed in good order. I had one man killed and three wounded. After retiring about half a mile we lay on ower armes untill evening and then returned to the north end of town and staid all night.

22d. [23d]: This day the enemy came out and burnt Springfield and returned about 3 o'clock P.M., pursewed by ower people. The enemies loss this day is thought to be considerable. Owers is about 15 killed and 40 wounded. I got home about 10 at night.

    —SEELEY, Diary, Morristown National Historical Park.

2. "THE ENEMY WERE OBSTINATELY OPPOSED"

Lieutenant Colonel Lewis Morris, Jr., to his father, Brigadier General Lewis Morris.

                              Springfield, June 24th, 1780

My Dear Sir,

    I have only time to inform you that I got neither wound or bruise in the conflict of yesterday. The enemy advanced with their whole force about sunrise in two columns, one upon the Vauxhall road, the other upon the Springfield road. Genl. Greene, who was left here for the security of the post and protection of the country with two brigades and the militia, formed his little army judiciously and to the best advantage at the bridge leading into town. The enemy were obstinately opposed and several times repulsed, but after a fire of forty minutes, both artillery and musquetry, our brave fellows were obliged to yield to superior numbers.

    To cover this retreat the General had posted Col. Smith with a regiment in an orchard about the center of the town and thrown a small party into a stone house upon his left flank. Here the enemy met with a second check and lost a considerable number of men About a quarter of a mile from this the troops rallied and the artillery being posted upon commanding ground, a warm cannonade commenced, but the enemy would not advance near enough for our musquetry. The troops being greatly exposed in this position to the fire of their artillery, the general thought it most prudent to retire to an eminence about three hundred yards in the rear, where we continued spectators to the melancholy, general conflagration of Springfield, till they retreated, and then followed them into Elizabeth Town. About twelve at night they crossed their bridge, cut it away and are now secure upon Staten Island.

    I will not recapitulate the scene of destruction and distress which I have been witness to. I dont wish to wound your humanity—happy I am that your family has never fallen in the track of such barbarians. It is a sweet consolation to me that they paid so dearly for their conquest. You may depend upon it that they lost a considerable number of both officers and men—I will not pretend to say how many, but from the numbers engaged you may rate them great. Let my friends in Philadelphia know this as I am in haste and cannot write. My love to you and God bless you also.

—LEWIS MORRIS, JR., Ms. Letter, Morristown National Historical Park.

VIII. BENEDICT ARNOLD FIRES NEW LONDON

When it was known that Washington's army was heading southward to trap Cornwallis, Benedict Arnold, rewarded for his treason with a commission as brigadier general, proposed an expedition against Connecticut in order to force Washington to leave some of his forces in the North. The raid was as ferocious as any conducted by British and Tories in the entire war. Arnold's forces landed on the morning of September 6, 1781, one division on each side of the harbor, and drove the defenders from Fort Trumbull on the west side of the Thames River. Fort Griswold on the opposite bank was valiantly defended by Lieutenant Colonel William Ledyard, who finally surrendered to overwhelming numbers, only to be bayoneted by Lieutenant Colonel Van Buskirk of the New Jersey Volunteers. Tories, Hessians and British joined in indiscriminate slaughter of the garrison after it had surrendered. Before embarking his troops for New York, Arnold put the town to the torch, in all some 143 buildings, with an estimated loss of a half-million dollars. It is said that Arnold stood in the church belfry and watched the conflagration with as much satisfaction as Nero. This was Arnold's last act of spite against his own people and his native land. He had been born in Norwich, a dozen miles away.

1. COLONEL LEDYARD IS BAYONETED WHILE SURRENDERING

Memoirs of Major General William Heath.

September 10, 1781

Intelligence was received from Governor Trumbull that the enemy had made a descent on New London, on the [morning] of the 6th with about two thousand infantry and three hundred light horse. Their fleet consisted of about forty sail of ships-of-war and transports; they plundered the inhabitants of property to a large amount, and burnt a great part of the town. The militia behaved very gallantly, and a number of very valuable citizens were killed; among others Col. Ledyard, Captains Saltonstall and Richards. The enemy in three assaults on the fort on Groton side of the river were repulsed, but on the fourth attempt carried it. . . .

In Governor Trumbull's letter, the enemy were charged with behaving in a wanton and barbarous manner; and that of between seventy and eighty men who were killed, three only were killed before the enemy entered the fort and the garrison had submitted; that on Col. Ledyard's delivering his sword reversed to the commanding officer who entered the fort, the officer immediately plunged it into the colonel's body, on which several soldiers bayoneted him. It is also asserted that upon the foregoing taking place, an

American officer, who stood near to Col. Ledyard, instantly stabbed the British officer who stabbed the colonel; on which the British indiscriminately bayoneted a great number of Americans. . . .

Arnold himself continued on the New London side and, while his troops were plundering and burning, was said to have been at a house where he was treated very politely; that while he was sitting with the gentleman [Christopher Christophers] regaling himself, the latter observed that he hoped his house and property would be safe; he was answered that while he [Arnold] was there it would not be touched; but the house, except the room in which they were, was soon plundered and found to be on fire.

During the plunder of the town, the British . . . were in great confusion, setting their arms against trees and fences while they were collecting and carrying off their plunder; in this situation they might easily have been defeated. . . .

—HEATH, *Memoirs*, pp. 282-284.

2. ARNOLD CLAIMS THAT THE BURNING OF THE TOWN WAS ACCIDENTAL

Benedict Arnold to Sir Henry Clinton.

Sound, off Plumb Island, September 8, 1781

. . . At one o'clock the next morning, we arrived off the harbour [New London], when the wind suddenly shifted to the northward, and it was nine o'clock before the transports could beat in. At ten o'clock, the troops in two divisions, and in four debarkations, were landed: one on each side the harbour, about three miles from New London.

. . . Lieutenant Col. Eyre had sent Captain Beckwith with a flag to demand a surrender of the fort, which was peremptorily refused, and the attack had commenced. After a most obstinate defense of near forty minutes, the fort was carried by the superior bravery and perseverance of the assailants. The attack was judicious and spirited and reflects the highest honor on the officers and troops engaged, who seemed to vie with each other in being first in danger. The troops approached on three sides of the work, which was a square with flanks, made a lodgment in the ditch and under a heavy fire, which they kept up on the works, effected a second lodgment on the friezing, which was attended with great difficulty, as only a few pickets could be forced out or broken in a place, and was so high that the soldiers could not ascend without assisting each other. Here the coolness and bravery of the troops were very conspicuous, as the first who ascended the frieze were obliged to silence a nine-pounder, which infiladed the place on which they stood, until a sufficient body had collected to enter the works, which was done with fixed bayonets through the embrazures, where they were opposed with great obstinacy by the garrison with long spears. . . .

Our loss, though very considerable, is very short of the enemy's who lost most of their officers, among whom was their commander, Col. Ledyard. Eighty-five men were found dead in Fort Griswold, and 60 wounded, most of them mortally; their loss on the opposite side must have been considerable, but cannot be ascertained. I believe we have about 70 prisoners, besides the wounded, who were left paroled.

Ten or twelve of the enemy's ships were burned, . . . one loaded with naval stores. An immense quantity of European and West India goods were found in the stores, . . . the whole of which was burnt with the stores, which proved to contain a large quantity of powder, unknown to us; the explosion of the powder and change of wind soon after the stores were fired, communicated the flames to a part of the town, which was, notwithstanding every effort to prevent it, unfortunately destroyed.

—ARNOLD, *Life of Benedict Arnold*, pp. 349-351.

CHAPTER EIGHTEEN

Spies, Treason and Mutiny

As we have already observed in connection with the British background to the American war, and the position of the Loyalists, the American Revolution was a rather special kind of war, one in which we cannot glibly apply the familiar standards of wars between nations. In the first place it was very difficult to know at just what point the conflict between colonies and mother country became a war between America and Britain, and at what point, therefore, lack of enthusiasm for separation, or for war, became treason. Galloway, for example, remained Loyalist too long; Dickinson, who was almost as lukewarm in the beginning, changed in the nick of time. Second, the Revolution was still an eighteenth-century war, one which attracted mercenaries, adventurers and soldiers of fortune, men like Charles Lee and General von Steuben and even the beloved Montgomery and—on the other side—Dr. Church and Dr. Bancroft. Were these men guilty of treason, or were they merely following accepted practices of the day? Were the Hessians who left the British Army deserters, or were they free of any obligations to the foreign masters who had hired their services from their princes? Third, and most pervasive, the circumstances of the war were such as to make it difficult to know just what constituted comfort to the enemy, and what constituted aid, even more difficult to hold comfort or aid treasonable, and almost impossible to punish it as treason. It was, indeed, a very mixed-up war: one in which participants flowed in and out, as it were; one in which absence without leave and desertion were hopelessly blended; one in which it was almost impossible for civilians to escape involvement with whatever army happened to be in the vicinity and to levy on provisions, shelter and information.

Espionage, treason and mutiny—these things had meanings and connotations different from those which we attach to them today. By modern standards men like Charles Lee and Silas Deane were subversives if not traitors, but then so, too, were Fox, Camden, Barré, Wilkes and others who championed the American cause in Parliament. By modern standards armies that melted away after battles (or sometimes before them) were guilty of desertion. By modern standards refusal to obey officers, refusal to abide by rules, refusal to fight except after approval by military town meetings as it were—these things were all mutinous. But it is best to put aside modern standards, and take the Revolution on its own terms.

Recent wars have depended much on intelligence and counterintelligence, espionage and counterespionage, security, underground movements and so

733

forth, but there was little of this in the American Revolution, which was, in a sense, a much less sophisticated war. Where thousands of Loyalists were prepared to tell what they knew, why hire spies? Where tens of thousands of Americans were prepared to inform on the invaders, why build up an espionage system? There were spies, there was an espionage system, but these never mattered very much. Almost the only place where espionage was important was Europe, and London and Paris swarmed with spies and informers in the best cloak-and-dagger tradition.

What of treason? Here Benedict Arnold looms up in lonely and awful infamy. There were, in fact, other traitors—Benjamin Thompson, for example, or Dr. Church—but Arnold alone is remembered and execrated. Washington was right when he said that "this is the first instance of treason of this kind" and that "nothing is so high an ornament to the characters of the American soldiers as their withstanding all the arts and seductions of an insidious enemy." Arnold almost cost Americans their Revolution—it was a close thing—yet we cannot but be wryly grateful for our only genuine villain; what, after all, would we do without him?

Not only was treason rare, but mutiny, too. The American soldiers were not professionals and they clung, many of them, to their amateur standing. They were oftentimes required to serve far longer than they had bargained for, and often, too, without pay, or with pay in worthless currency; they were exposed to danger and to harsh discipline, to summer heat and winter blizzards, to starvation and nakedness, to misery and disease. Yet there were few mutinies, and those that did occur—chiefly in 1781—were merely desperate protests against conditions that had become intolerable, not shifts of allegiance to the British cause.

We give, in this chapter, a few indications of espionage and of plots and counterplots; a more circumstantial account of the most notorious treason in our history, and with it the touching story of John André; and finally some accounts of the famous mutiny in January 1781 and its peaceful outcome.

I. DR. CHURCH GOES OVER TO THE ENEMY

Colonel Benjamin Church was the hero of King Philip's War, and one of the notable figures in the history of the Plymouth Colony; something of his fame was transmitted to his grandson, Benjamin Church of Rhode Island, who managed to tarnish it. A graduate of Harvard College, Church studied medicine in London, and returned to Massachusetts to an established position and a handsome practice. One of the inner circle of Patriot leaders, he had been appointed to the First Continental Congress and then made director and chief physician to the American army outside Boston. Yet from the beginning his conduct had been a bit ambiguous, and Paul Revere, for one, suspected that his patriotism was by no means pure. For reasons never wholly explained Dr. Church entered into questionable—if not treasonable—correspondence with General Gage. A cipher letter giving information on American military arrangements was intercepted by Henry Ward of Rhode Island. Unable to explain it away, Dr. Church was condemned by a court-martial to imprison-

ment, then released on parole. The next year he sailed for the West Indies in search of health, and was lost at sea; his family was pensioned by George III.

1. "An Event Which Gives Me Much Uneasiness"

James Warren to John Adams.

Watertown, October 1, 1775

An event has lately taken place here which makes much noise, and gives me much uneasiness, not only as it affects the character, and may prove the ruin of a man who I used to have a tolerable opinion of, but as it may be the cause of many suspicions and jealousies, and what is still worse, have a tendency to discredit the recommendations of my friends at the Congress. Dr. Church has been detected in a correspondence with the enemy, at least so far that a letter wrote by him in curious cypher and directed to Major Cane (who is an officer in the Royal army and one of Gage's family) has been intercepted.

The history of the whole matter is this. The Doctor, having formed an infamous connection with an infamous hussey to the disgrace of his own reputation, and probable ruin of his family, wrote this letter last July, and sent it by her to Newport with orders to give it to Wallace, or Dudley to deliver to Wallace, for conveyance to Boston. She, not finding an opportunity very readily, trusted it with a friend of hers to perform the orders, and came away and left it in his hands. He kept it some time and, having some suspicions of wickedness, had some qualms of conscience about executing his commissions, after some time consulted his friend. One result was to open the letter, which was done. The appearance of the letter increasing their suspicions, the next question after determining not to send it to Boston was, what should be done with it. After various conferences at divers times, they concluded to deliver it to General Washington.

Accordingly the man came with it last Thursday. After collecting many circumstances, the man was employed to draw from the girl, by using the confidence she had in him, the whole secret, but without success. She is a subtle, shrewd jade. She was then taken into custody and brought to the General's quarters that night. It was not till the next day that anything could be got from her. She then confessed that the Doctor wrote and sent her with the letter as above.

Upon this, the General sent a note desiring Major Hawley and me to come immediately to Cambridge. We all thought the suspicion quite sufficient to justify an arrest of him and his papers, which was done, and he is now under a guard. He owns the writing and sending the letter, says it was for Flemming in answer to one he wrote to him, and is calculated by magnifying the numbers of the army, their regularity, their provisions and ammunition, etc., to do great service to us. He declares his conduct tho' indiscreet was not wicked. There are, however, many circumstances, new and old, which time won't permit me to mention, that are much against him. The letter, I suppose, is now decyphering, and when done will either condemn, or in some measure excuse him. Thus much for this long story.

—*Warren-Adams Letters*, I, 121-122.

2. "What Punishment Can Equal Such Horrid Crimes!"

Governor Samuel Ward of Rhode Island to Henry Ward.

Philadelphia 11th October 1775

Dear Brother

I received yours of 3rd inst. and very readily allow it to ballance our literary accounts to that time.

Dr. Church, who could have thought or even suspected it, a man who seemed to be all animation in the cause of his country, highly connected, employed in several very honorable and lucrative departments, and in full possession of the confidence of his country—what a complication of madness and wickedness must a soul be filled with to be capable of such perfidy, what punishment can equal such horrid crimes! I communicated the affair to the Massachusetts delegates; they could hardly conceive it possible. They soon after received some account of the matter themselves. A letter from Mr. Secretary Read says upon searching his papers nothing amiss was found in them; his friends from thence would infer his innocence; he pretends that the letters sent through [Captain James] Wallace were wrote to his brother in law Fleming (late partner with Mein) and contained accounts favourable to our cause; such letters as these might have been sent in every week without interruption; of course there could be no occasion for that expensive roundabout and suspicious way of conveyance which he took.

I am obliged to you for the circumstantial account of the matter as it throws light on the subject. How happy it is that he is discovered before he had done us any considerable mischief! The greatest that I am apprehensive of is that it may induce suspicions and lessen that confidence which is necessary to a cordial union and our mutual support; this ought carefully to be guarded against as fatal, and at the same time the utmost vigilance is necessary least we should be betrayed. . . .

—Ward, *Correspondence*, pp. 99-100.

II. ARSON IN AMERICA AND ENGLAND

The Revolution had its quota of plots and counterplots, some of them sensible enough, some melodramatic, some the products of a fevered imagination. The first of these was known as the Hickey Plot after the ringleader, Thomas Hickey, one of Washington's guards, who was hanged in June 1776. Its purported objective was the assassination of the general. Another is the orgy of arson attributed to "John the Painter" in England. The accused claimed that Silas Deane encouraged him during the early months of his Paris residence to set on fire the Portsmouth dockyard. Deane's complicity has never been proved.

1. "A Most Barbarous and Infernal Plot among the Tories"

Extract of a letter.

New York, June 24, 1776

My last to you was by Friday's post, since which a most barbarous and infernal plot has been discovered among our Tories, the particulars of which

I cannot give you, as the Committee of Examination consists of but three, who are sworn to secrecy. Two of Washington's guards are concerned; the third they tempted to join them made the first discovery. The general report of their design is as follows: Upon the arrival of the troops they were to murder all the staff officers, blow up the magazines, and secure the passes of the town. Gilbert Forbes, gunsmith in the Broadway, was taken between two and three o'clock on Saturday morning, and carried before our Provincial Congress, who were then sitting, but refusing to make any discovery, he was sent to jail and put in irons. Young Mr. Livingstone went to see him early in the morning, and told him he was sorry to find he had been concerned, and, as his time was very short, not having above three days to live, advised him to prepare himself. This had the desired effect; he asked to be carried before Congress again, and he would discover all he knew. Several have been since taken (between twenty and thirty), among them our Mayor, who are all now under confinement. It is said their party consisted of about five hundred.

I have just heard the Mayor has confessed bringing money from Tryon to pay for rifle-guns that Forbes had made. Burgoyne is arrived at Quebeck with his fleet.

—FORCE, *American Archives*, 4th Series, VI, 1054.

2. JOHN THE PAINTER TRIES TO BURN PORTSMOUTH AND BRISTOL

Towards the close of the year [1776], and in the beginning of the ensuing, much confusion, apprehension, and suspicion was excited by the machinery of a wretched enthusiast and incendiary, since well known by the appellation of John the Painter, but whose real name was James Aitken. This man, who was born in Edinburgh, and bred a painter, possessing an extraordinary spirit of rambling, with a strong propensity to vice, had passed in the course of a few years thro' an uncommon variety of those scenes which attend the most profligate and abandoned state of a vagabond life—a kind of life for which a manual trade, however followed, affords the most perfect opportunity and cover.

Among his other exploits, he had passed through several marching regiments of foot, from each of which he deserted as soon as opportunity served, after receiving the bounty money. In his various peregrinations through the different parts of England, he alternately committed highway robberies, burglaries, petty thefts, rapes, and worked at his trade, as occasion invited, villainy prompted, or fear or necessity operated. Whether it proceeded from the apprehension of punishment, or that the original bent of his genius led him to new scenes of action, whatever was the operative motive, he shipped himself off for America, where he continued for two or three years. His being of a melancholy solitary nature, which neither sought for associates in crimes, nor admitted of partners in pleasure, as it contributed much to his preservation for so long a time from the justice of those laws which he was constantly breaking, served equally to throw in utter darkness all those parts of his life which he did not himself think fitting or necessary to communicate. His transactions in America are accordingly unknown, any further than that he traversed, and worked at his trade in, several of the colonies.

As his pilgrimage on that continent was in the beginning, and during the progress, of the present troubles, it may well be imagined that the violence of the language and sentiments held in political matters by that order of the people with whom he lived and conversed gave birth to that madness of enthusiasm in him which afterwards became so dangerous. He accordingly returned to England with the most deadly antipathy to the government and nation, and soon after, if not originally, adopted the design of subverting, in his own single person, that power which he so much abhorred.

The scheme was as detestable as could even be expected from the villainous character of the framer. It was to destroy the maritime force of this country, as well as its internal strength and riches, by setting fire to the royal dockyards, and burning the principal trading cities and towns, with their shipping, of whatever sort, so far as it could possibly be done. In the prosecution of this atrocious design, he traversed the kingdom to discover the state of the several docks, and the nature of the watch by which they were guarded, which he in general found to be as lax and insufficient as he could have wished. He also took wonderful pains in the construction of fireworks, machines and combustibles for the purpose, but was strangely unsuccessful in all his attempts of this nature.

It was owing to this unaccountable failure in his machines that the nation was saved from receiving some dreadful, if not irretrievable shock. One of them, which extinguished of its own accord, without any human interference, was found, several weeks after it had been laid, in the center of a prodigious quantity of one of the most combustible substances, in the great hemp house at Portsmouth. He, however, succeeded in setting fire to the rope house in that yard, and had an opportunity, for several miles in his flight to London, to feast the malignity of his nature in the contemplation of that dreadful conflagration which he had excited, and which from its prodigious appearance he imagined had spread to all the magazines, buildings and docks. The fire was happily subdued, with no other loss than that of the rope house and its contents.

The incendiary still pursued his design, but failed in his attempts upon the royal docks, and narrowly escaped being taken at Plymouth. The city of Bristol was at that time greatly divided between the two numerous parties of Tories and Whigs, as they were called, the former of which eagerly supported, and the latter as highly detested, the present court measures against America. The former carried up an address of congratulation upon the late successes of his Majesty's arms, which the latter condemned in the strongest terms, representing it as an act highly indecent, unchristian and impious to exhibit any marks of triumph and rejoicing in the slaughter and destruction of their fellow-subjects.

In this state of party and political disunion among the inhabitants, John the Painter, in the month of January 1777, attempted first to burn the shipping, and afterwards the city itself. A deep and narrow chasm, which is nearly dry when the tide is out, fronts a great part of the quay in Bristol, which is generally crowded with a prodigious number of vessels, all lying so close together, and so free from water in that season, that the first thing which strikes the attention of a stranger is a surprize how they could be so lodged, and the second, a conviction of the fatal and irremediable consequences both to the shipping and the city, which a fire must inevitably produce. The incendiary, failing in his attempt to set two or three of those vessels on fire, found so strict a watch kept afterwards that he was obliged to change his mode of operation, and to secure the destruction of the ships by beginning with the houses. After some failures in his attempts this way, in which, as in all others, the findings of his ineffective apparatus afforded full evidence of the atrociousness of the design, he at length succeeded so far as to set fire to some warehouses in the vicinity of the quay, six or seven of which were consumed.

These facts and circumstances afforded a full scope to all the rage and virulence of party to blaze out in their utmost violence. The most bigotted and furious, and consequently the most ignorant, on the one side, attributed them to the disaffection, the republican and American principles, of the other; whilst those on an equal scale of understanding and prejudice on that, were fully convinced that they were malicious acts or inventions of the Tories, merely for the purpose of calumniating and blackening their adversaries.

The reign of the incendiary was not much longer. He was taken up soon after his departure from Bristol, upon some suspicious circumstances, and behaved with great boldness, art and an uncommon government in point of speech upon his several examinations, refusing peremptorily to answer any questions which admitted even of a doubt in the remotest tendency that the answer could by any construction be wrested to his own crimination; nor was he at all disconcerted or embarrassed by the appearance, or the questions proposed to him, by some of the Lords and other principal officers of the admiralty. . . .

The news of his commitment was soon spread; and it having been reported that he had been in America, and had worked there as a painter, Earl Temple desired one Baldwin, a painter who had likewise been in America and had done business there, to attend his examination before Sir John Fielding, to see if he could recollect him. But Baldwin, upon looking at the man and being asked the question, frankly declared that he had never before seen him in his life.

This open declaration, after others, as he said, had borne false witness against him, prejudiced the prisoner in favour of Baldwin, and he expressed a strong desire to cultivate an acquaintance with him, which Baldwin did not decline, being encouraged to visit him as often as opportunity offered, in order, if possible, to bring him to confession. This had the desired effect, and brought the whole scene of iniquity to light.

After a regular attendance on him for 15 days, sometimes once a day and sometimes twice, the prisoner at length began to trust him and to speak openly. He told him he had been in France; that he had there seen Silas Deane; that Silas Deane had given him some money; had encouraged him to set fire to the dock-yards at Portsmouth, Plymouth, Woolwich, etc. as the best means of distressing Great-Britain; that he had promised to reward him according to the service he should do to the American cause; and that, as an earnest of what should follow, he had given him a recommendation to, and bills upon, a merchant in London to the amount of 300 *l.*, which, however, he had found it necessary to burn, to prevent a discovery; that, in consequence of this encouragement, he procured a passport from the French king; which passport he lamented that he had left at Portsmouth, with other things, in a bundle. That from France he came to Canterbury, where he devised the machine which had been found in the hemp house, and had it there constructed; that before he left Canterbury he had a quarrel with a dragoon; and that when he removed from thence he directed his course to Portsmouth, where he prepared the combustibles with which he afterwards set the place on fire; that he disclosed to him (Baldwin) the secret of making the composition, and the manner of his applying it; told him the circumstance of his being locked in the rope-house; of his quarreling with his landlady on account of the interruption she gave him in his operations; of her forcibly turning him out of her house; of his taking another lodging; of the difficulty he had in lighting his matches; of his purchasing other matches; of his flight from Portsmouth in a woman's cart; with many other particulars, all of which were confirmed on his trial by the testimony of the persons, respectively, who were any ways employed by him, or with whom he had any thing to do in the business. The boy who made the cannister, the dragoon with whom he quarrelled at Canterbury, the woman at whose house he lodged at Portsmouth, the man who let him out of the rope-house, the persons who saw him in the dock-yard, the woman who sold him the matches, the woman who took him up in her cart in his flight from Portsmouth, and last of all the bundle in which was his passport from France, with the identical articles in it which he had specifically mentioned to Baldwin; all these were produced against him, and, as the judge observed, in summing up the evidence, that from a chain of circumstances attentively put together, such a body of evidence may be drawn as would be abundantly stronger than where two or three witnesses swear to a positive fact.

It is no wonder, therefore, that the jury, without going out of court, pronounced the prisoner GUILTY; and he being asked in the usual form what he had to say, why sentence of death should not be passed upon him, replied *he had nothing to say.*

—*Annual Register for 1777, pp. 28-31, 246-247.*

III. A REGIUS PROFESSOR REMAINS LOYAL TO HIS KING

John Vardill, rector of Trinity Church and professor at King's College, was—so it would seem—loyal to his King because he was so deeply loyal to the Anglican Church. He had gone to England in 1774 and remained there throughout the war, spying on American sympathizers and, on one occasion, arranging for the theft of the whole of Silas Deane's correspondence with the French Court. He was well paid for these activities, but thought that he ought to have his various American salaries as well.

The Memorial of John Vardill.

                                                        November 16, 1783

Sheweth:

That he is a native of New York, and was late Professor of Natural Law and Moral Philosophy in King's College, and Assistant Preacher and Lecturer in the Episcopal Churches and Chapels in that city. He has been long obnoxious to the Rebels from his uniform opposition to their measures. . . .

In consequence of these and such like services and to give the Loyalists at New York a proof of the attention and rewards which would follow their zeal and loyalty, Administration were pleased to appoint him Regius Professor of Divinity at King's College, and he was ordered to acquaint the President of the College with this instance of royal patronage, and that the establishment of the professorship and his appointment should make a clause in the Charter then to be granted. The intelligence was accordingly inserted in the New York *Gazette* of 1775, but the national disappointments which ensued have prevented the grant of that Charter.

In 1775 the Rebels having gained the ascendancy at New York, and being much incensed by letters against him from London, and by their knowledge of his character and conduct in general, he could not return to New York with any safety, and Government was therefore pleased to give him his present allowance of £200 per annum with the most direct and explicit promise that he should be no loser by his loyalty and services, and that the allowance should be other ways provided for, or [he be] able to return to New York with honour and advantage to them and himself. Relying on this, instead of returning into the country or employing himself in the line of his profession, he devoted his time, from 1775 to 1781, to the service of government: and not to mention various periodical pieces and pamphlets which he wrote, or furnished materials for, as well as intelligence supplied from an extensive American correspondence; waiving these and hoping that the necessity will apologize for this free communication:

In 1777 your Memorialist detected a gentleman in London employed by Dr. Franklin, among other purposes, to purchase cutters for packet boats, in which he and a Capt. Nicholson were to sail from France to America. Your Memorialist perswaded him to unbosom himself, and at the desire of the late Lord Suffolk went down with Col. Smith after him to Dover; where, after obtaining a full discovery, the Captain was engaged to proceed to France, to furnish all the intelligence he could collect and to deliver the letters from time to time committed to him. This he faithfully did for two years, whereby many vessels bound to America were taken and much useful information obtained. A gentleman of distinction was also sent over to him to direct and receive information and he proceeded (thro the Captain) very far in a negotiation for peace with Dr. Franklin; but the capture of Burgoyne blasted it.

Your Memorialist having also discovered that a mistress of Dr. Bancroft, Secy. to Dr. Franklin, was about to leave London for Paris, he formed an acquaintance with her, and found, as he suspected, that she had letters to convey from the factions in this country, on which he proposed a plan, and procured a person to accompany her to Brighthelmston who there obtained a coppy of the most material contents of the letters, for the use of Government.

Hearing about the same time that an American vessel was taken and brought into Portsmouth by a mutiny of the sailors, and finding that the Captain was an acquaintance, your Memorialist invited him to his house, and led him to confess that he was bound to Amsterdam, that he had a number of letters (come from the Board of War at Boston) to people in Holland, France and England. These he delivered to your Memorialist who gave them to Mr. Eden, by which means, among other particulars, Government was informed of the articles most wanted by Congress, of the houses and persons with whom they corresponded and of the ships employed for the purpose.

In 1777 your Memorialist also met accidentally in London with an American fellow student, a gentleman of birth, fortune and considerable confidence with Dr. Franklin, who, after much perswasion and promise, confessed that he was here on Congress business, had brought letters from Dr. Franklin and others at Paris, and was about to return with some from hence; he was prevailed on by your Memorialist to disclose them and for a certain reward to continue his residence at Paris and to give all the information he could to Lord Stormont, occasionally visiting this country to convey letters to and from Paris. This gentleman often dined with Dr. Franklin and was intimate with all the American leaders. He among other things informed Government of the fict[it]ious titles and directions under which the Rebel correspondents have received their letters.

These services were not without expence to your Memorialist and in one instance endangered his life and drew on him the hatred of many of his countrymen, especially the trimmers and false Loyalists. As a reward for these and other services, Government was pleased to give him an immediate appointment, by warrant in 1777 (the Charter being unavoidably postponed), to the Regius Professorship of Divinity with a full promise and purpose of granting him at the same time a direct, certain and permanent provision for life, by annexing to it a salary of £200 per annum. But thro' the changes and misfortunes of the times, this engagement has not yet been fulfilled.

In 1778 at the request of one of the commissioners then embarking for America, he drew up an account of the characters of the leading Rebels and Loyalists and supplied him with letters of introduction to Messrs. Jay, Livingston, Duane and Morris, of the Congress; and to Messrs. Benson, Harper, Jones and Custis, who had great influence in the Rebel states.

In 1779 he went down to Yorkshire and opposed the Association in a series of papers called "The Alarm" and signed *Cassandra*, which he caused to be printed and circulated thro' the counties. For these he had the thanks of the nobility and gentlemen of the county, and a letter of high approbation from a distinguished person in Administration.

In 1780 he also published a pamphlet against the Associations, and assisted in writing another entitled "The Declaration and Address, from the Loyalists to the People of America," which was extensively circulated thro' the Colonies; not to mention that for three years he supplied (without reward) a morning paper with paragraphs and essays in support of Government.

Your Memorialist has lost, by his loyalty, by the services above recited and others of the same nature, and by the unfortunate issue of the war, his income as Professor of Natural Law and Moral Philosophy at King's College, £100 stg., exclusively of fees for private pupils, which from his station and established character would have been numerous, and the use of chambers, a cellar, yard and garden; the salary as assistant minister and lecturer in the church at New York £200 stg., not to mention that he was next in order to the Rector, and would have succeeded (as was the established rule) on his death or removal; the salary which Government engaged to annex to his Regius Professorship £200 stg. . . .

Having thus briefly stated his services and losses, your Memorialist therefore prays that his case may be taken into your consideration in order that your Memorialist may be enabled, under your report, to receive such aid and relief as his services and loses may be found to deserve.

—American Loyalist Audit Office Transcripts, Vol. 42, pp. 37-46, N. Y. Public Lib.

IV. DR. BANCROFT GIVES THE HISTORY OF HIS CAREER AS A SPY

Dr. Edward Bancroft was not only a spy but a double spy, and a highly accomplished one at that. A Massachusetts Yankee, he had, like Dr. Church, studied medicine in England; unlike Church he decided to settle down in England and there pursue his scientific and literary interests. There he made the acquaintance of Franklin, and it was on this acquaintance that he later capitalized. When Franklin went to France, Bancroft arranged to act as his spy; later he made the same arrangements with Silas Deane, to whom he had been commended by the Committee of Secret Correspondence and with whom he became on terms of intimacy. Meantime Bancroft had been appointed agent for the British government—at the handsome salary of £1,000 per year—and a most successful agent he was. Just to add to his interests—and rewards—he speculated heavily on the secret information which he obtained through espionage. To top it, Bancroft had himself appointed secretary of the American Peace Commission which negotiated the final settlement with England! After the war Bancroft devoted himself for many years—he lived until 1821—to scientific and literary pursuits. His espionage was not suspected until a century after his death.

Letter from Edward Bancroft, "British-American spy," to the Marquis of Carmarthen, British Foreign Secretary.

Duke Street, London, September 17, 1784

In the month of June 1776, Mr. Silas Deane arrived in France, and pursuant to an instruction given him by the Secret Committee of Congress, wrote to me in London, requesting an interview in Paris, where I accordingly went early in July and was made acquainted with the purposes of his mission and with everything which passed between him and the French Ministry. After staying two or three weeks there, I returned to England, convinced that the Government of France would endeavour to promote an absolute separation of the then United Colonies from Great Britain, unless a speedy termination of the revolt, by reconciliation or conquest, should frustrate this project.

I had then resided near ten years, and expected to reside the rest of my life, in England; and all my views, interests and inclinations were adverse to the independancy of the Colonies, though I had advocated some of their claims from a persuasion of their being founded in justice. I therefore wished that the Government of this country might be informed of the danger of French interference, though I could not resolve to become the informant. But Mr. Paul Wentworth having gained some general knowledge of my journey to France and of my intercourse with Mr. Deane, and having induced me to believe that the British Ministry were likewise informed on this subject, I at length consented to meet the then Secretaries of State, Lords Weymouth and Suffolk, and give them all the information in my power; which I did with the most disinterested views, for I not only did not ask, but expressly rejected, every idea of any reward.

The Declaration of Independancy was not then known in Europe, and I hoped that Government, thus informed of the danger, would prevent it by some accomodation with the Colonies, or by other means. It had been my original intention to stop after this first communication; but having given the first notice of a beginning intercourse between France and the United Colonies, I was urged on to watch and disclose the progress of it; for which purpose I made several journeys to Paris and maintained a regular correspondence with Mr. Deane through the couriers of the French Government. And in this way I became *entangled* and obliged to proceed in a kind of business as repugnant to my feelings as it had been to my original intentions.

Being thus devoted to the service of Government, I consented, like others, to accept such emoluments as my situation indeed required. And in Feb'y 1777, Lord Suffolk, to whom by Lord Weymouth's consent my communications were then made, formally promised me, in the King's name, a pension for life of £200 per annum, to commence from the Christmas preceeding. This was for services *then rendered;* and as an inducement for me to go over and reside in France and continue my services there until the revolt should terminate or an open rupture with that nation ensue, his Lordship farther promised that when either of these events should happen, my permanent pension of £200 per annum should be increased to £500 *at least.*

Confiding in this promise, I went to Paris, and during the first year resided in the same house with Dr. Franklin, Mr. Deane, etc., and regularly informed this Government of every transaction of the American Commissioners; of every step and vessel taken to supply the revolted Colonies with artillery, arms, etc.; of every part of their intercourse with the French and other European courts; of the powers and instructions given by Congress to the Commissioners, and their correspondence with the Secret Committees, etc.; and when the Government of France at length determined openly to support the revolted Colonies, I gave notice of this determination, and of the progress made in forming the two Treaties of Alliance and Commerce, and when these were signed, on the evening of the 6th of Feb'y, I at my own expence, by a special messenger and with unexampled dispatch conveyed this intelligence to this city, and to the King's Ministers, within 42 hours from the instant of their signature, a piece of information for which many individuals here would, for purposes of speculation, have given me more than all that I have received from Government. Afterwards, when that decisive measure of sending Count d'Estaing with the fleet from Toulon to commence hostilities at the Delaware and New York was adopted, I sent intelligence of the direct object and plan of the expedition. . . .

—BANCROFT, "Letter," *American Historical Review*, XXIX, 493-494.

V. THE TREASON OF BENEDICT ARNOLD

Benedict Arnold has the distinction of being the one villain of American history whose villainy is universally recognized and conceded. He is not, to be sure, our only traitor, nor the only American soldier or official who took money from foreign governments; his villainy did not seriously injure the American cause; he had, before his day of infamy, contributed greatly to the American cause. What, then, is the explanation of his singular notoriety? It is in part because the stakes were so high and it was so near a thing—had he succeeded the American cause might well have been lost. It is in part because his betrayal was so cold-blooded and calculated; in part because it involved such cherished institutions as West Point (not yet an Academy) and Washington; in part because he was not punished for his perfidy, but richly rewarded. But beyond all this there is a happier reason that, as Washington himself observed, villainy and treason were rare in the Revolution and have remained rare in our history. Arnold, in short, has no very serious competitors, none, certainly, who played so melodramatically for such high stakes.

The story of Arnold's treason is too familiar for elaboration; its essentials are told in our letters and documents. Arnold is, in any event, already a familiar figure: we have seen him sharing in the capture of Ticonderoga, fighting his way through the Maine wilderness, leading a desperate attack on Quebec, engaged in furious combat on Lake Champlain, emerging out of arrest to win victory at Saratoga. No wonder Washington thought highly of him; he might have said, as Lincoln said of Grant, "he fights." He was given command of Philadelphia; he asked for and obtained command at West Point; there was nothing, it seemed, that he could not have.

Why, then, did he go over to the enemy? His own explanation—that he was outraged by the French alliance and in despair over the American cause—cannot be accepted; it came too late. Aside from this rationalization there were two motives or pressures to which Arnold responded: resentment against real and imagined slights by the Congress and by the authorities of Pennsylvania; reckless extravagance and a desperate need for money. A court-martial had only just reprimanded him for improper conduct bordering on corruption. Yet all American generals who felt slighted and who needed money did not turn traitor; in fact none did but Arnold. Clearly the ultimate explanation is to be found in the mysterious realm of personality. Arnold was a man without principles or convictions, a gambler, hot-blooded, reckless, arrogant and ambitious.

We know that treason is heinous and should be punished, and that such treason as Arnold's should bring odium and remorse. There is no evidence that it did. Arnold was extremely well paid for his betrayal—much too well paid considering how little the British got out of it; he saw to it, too, that his wife and his sons were amply taken care of by the British government. Legend has him suffering the agonies of the damned and, on his deathbed, calling for his old uniform, but the legend is baseless. The virtue of many of Arnold's companions in arms was its own reward, but Arnold's treason was handsomely rewarded.

The documents which we present here tell their own story, and need neither explanation nor elaboration, nor do their authors need further introduction: André, Clinton, Wayne, Lafayette—these are old familiars. Joseph Stansbury, Loyalist poet and halfhearted spy, was sufficiently involved in the treason to be arrested by the Americans but not sufficiently involved to be rewarded by the British. When, after the war, he claimed compensation for his services, his claims were disallowed with the nasty observation that "however you may like the treason it is impossible to approve the traitor." Andrew Elliot, another British agent, was uncle to William Eden of the Carlisle Commission. The "Mr. Moore" referred to in a letter is Arnold himself, and "John Anderson" is of course André, as Elliot explains.

1. Arnold and André Complete Their Business Arrangements

A. DRAFT OF A LETTER FROM MAJOR JOHN ANDRÉ TO JOSEPH STANSBURY, BRITISH AGENT IN PHILADELPHIA

May 10, 1779

Altho I think we understood each other clearly this morning and nothing was omitted which I could have to say on the subject, it is, or may be, of too much importance not to take further pains that all may be perfectly well comprehended.

On our part we meet ["ArnGen" deleted] Monk's ouvertures with full reliance on his honourable intentions and disclose to him with the strongest assurances of our sincerity that no thought is entertained of abandoning the point we have in view. That on the contrary powerfull means are expected for accomplishing our end. We likewise assure him that in the very first instance of receiving the tidings or good offices we expect from him, our liberality will be evinced; that in case any partial but important blow should by his means be struck or aimed, upon the strength of just and pointed information and cooperation, rewards equal at least to what such service can be estimated at will be given, but should the abilities and zeal of that able and enterprizing gentleman amount to the seizing an obnoxious band of men, to the delivering into our power or enabling us to attack to advantage and by judicious assistance compleately to defeat ["our Enemy" deleted] a numerous body, then would the generosity of the nation exceed even his own most sanguine hopes, and in the expectation of this he may rely on that *honour* he now trusts in his present advances. Should his manifest efforts be foiled and after every zealous attempt flight be at length necessary, the cause in which he suffers will hold itself bound to indemnify him for his losses and receive him with the honour his conduct deserves. His own judgment will point out the services required, but for his satisfaction we give the following hints. . . .

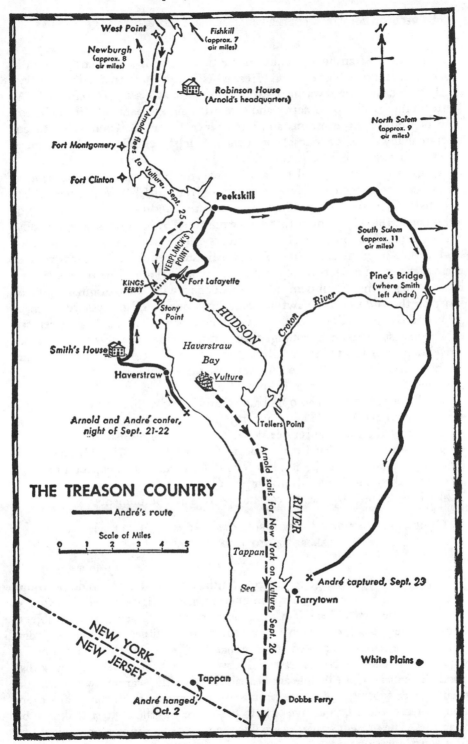

West Point

Fishkill
(approx. 7
air miles)

Newburgh
(approx. 8
air miles)

N

Robinson House
(Arnold's headquarters)

North Salem
(approx. 9
air miles)

Fort Montgomery

Fort Clinton

Peekskill

South Salem
(approx. 11
air miles)

VERPLANCK'S POINT

Fort Lafayette

Pine's Bridge
(where Smith
left André)

KINGS FERRY

HUDSON

Stony Point

Croton   River

Smith's House

Haverstraw
Bay

Vulture

Haverstraw

Tellers Point

Arnold and André confer,
night of Sept. 21-22

THE TREASON COUNTRY

Arnold sails for New York on Vulture, Sept. 26

— André's route

RIVER

Scale of Miles

0   1   2   3   4   5

Tappan

× André captured, Sept. 23

Sea

Tarrytown

NEW YORK
NEW JERSEY

White Plains

Tappan

André hanged,
Oct. 2

Dobbs Ferry

From Traitorous Hero
by Willard M. Wallace

Courtesy of Willard M. Wallace

B. DECODED COPY OF A LETTER FROM GENERAL ARNOLD TO MAJOR ANDRÉ

May 23, 1779

Our friend S[tansbury] acquaints me that the proposals made by him in my name are agreeable to S[ir] H[enry] C[linton], and that S[ir] H[enry] engages to answer my warmest expectations for any services rendered. As I esteem the interest of America and Great Britain inseparable S[ir] H[enry] may depend on my exertions and intelligence. It will be impossible to co-operate unless there is a mutual confidence. S[ir] H[enry] shall be convinced on every occasion that his is not misplaced.

Gen. W[ashington] and the army move to the North River as soon as forage can be obtained. C[ongress] have given up Ch[arle]s Town if attempted. They are in want of arms, ammunition and men to defend it. 3 or 4 thousand Militia is the most that can be mustered to fight on any emergency. Seizing papers is impossible. Their contents can be known from a Member of Congress. 4 months since, the French Minister required Congress to vest their agents with powers to negotiate peace with Britain. The time is elapsed in disputing if they shall demand independency with their original terms or insist on the addition of Newfoundland. No decision, no measure taken to prevent the depreciation of money; no foreign loan obtained. France refused to become surety; no encouragement from Spain. The French fleet has co[nditional] orders to return to this continent. They depend on great part of their provision from hence. A transport originally a 64 and a foreign 28 guns and daily expected here for provision.

I will cooperate when an opportunity offers, and as life and every thing is at stake I will expect some certainty, my property here secure and a revenue equivalent to the risk and service done. I cannot promise success; I will deserve it. Inform me what I may expect. Could I know S[ir] H[enry's] intentions he should never be at a loss for intelligence. I shall expect a particular answer thro our friend S[tansbur]y.

Madam Ar[nold] presents you her particular compliments.

C. DECODED COPY OF A LETTER FROM GENERAL ARNOLD TO MAJOR ANDRÉ,
ADDRESSED TO JOHN ANDERSON

July 12, 1780

... General W[ashington] expects on the arrival of the F[rench] troops to collect 30,000 troops to act in conjunction; if not disappointed, N. York is fixed on as the first object; if his numbers are not sufficient for that object, Can-a- is the second; of which I can inform you in time, as well as of every other design. I have accepted the command at W[est] P[oint] as a post in which I can render the most essential services, and which will be in my disposal. The mass of the people are heartily tired of the war and wish to be on their former footing. They are promised great events from this year's exertion. If disappointed, you have only to persevere and the contest will soon be at an end. The present struggles are like the pangs of a dying man, violent but of a short duration.

As life and fortune are risked by serving His Majesty, it is necessary that the latter shall be secured as well as the emoluments I give up, and a compensation for services agreed on, and a sum advanced for that purpose—which I have mentioned in a letter which accompanies this, which Sir Henry will not, I believe, think unreasonable.

P. S. I have great confidence in the bearer, but beg Sir Henry will threaten him with his resentment in case he abuses the confidence placed in him, which will bring certain ruin on me. The bearer will bring me 20 guineas, and pay the remainder to Captain A—— who is requested to receive the deposit for Mr. Moore.

D. DECODED COPY OF A LETTER FROM GENERAL ARNOLD TO MAJOR ANDRÉ

July 15, 1780

Two days since I received a letter without date or signature, informing me that S[ir] Henry —— was obliged to me for the intelligence communicated, and that he placed a full confidence in the sincerity of my intentions, etc., etc. On the 13th instant I addressed a letter to you expressing my sentiments and expectations, viz, that the following preliminaries be settled previous to cooperating. First, that S[ir] Henry secure to me my property, valued at ten thousand pounds sterling, to be paid to me or my heirs in case of loss; and, as soon as that shall happen, —— hundred pounds per annum to be secured to me for life, in lieu of the pay and emoluments I give up, for my services as they shall deserve. If I point out a plan of cooperation by which S[ir] H[enry] shall possess himself of West Point, the garrison, etc., etc., etc., twenty thousand pounds sterling I think will be a cheap purchase for an object of so much importance. At the same time I request a thousand pounds to be paid my agent. I expect a full and explicit answer. The 20th I set off for West Point. A personal interview with an officer that you can confide in is absolutely necessary to plan matters. In the mean time I shall communicate to our mutual friend S[tansbur]y all the intelligence in my power, until I have the pleasure of your answer.

—VAN DOREN, *Secret History of the Revolution*, 439-440, 441-442, 463-464, 464-465.

2. CLINTON EMBRACES "A PLAN OF SUCH INFINITE EFFECT"

Sir Henry Clinton to Lord George Germain.

New York, October 11, 1780

About eighteen months since, I had some reason to conceive that the American Major General Arnold was desirous of quitting the rebel service and joining the cause of Great Britain. A secret correspondence which I conceived to be from this officer, which expressed a displeasure at the alliance between America and France, engaged me to pursue every means of ascertaining the identity of the person who was thus opening himself to me, and from whom I had on every occasion received, during the whole of our correspondence, most material intelligence. . . .

The correspondence was continued up to July, 1780, when Major General Arnold obtained the command of all the rebel forts in the Highlands, garrisoned with near 4000 men. And it seemed to me, by the correspondence in question, that it was certainly that officer who made the offers under the description I have given. The getting possession of these posts with their garrisons, cannon, stores, vessels, gunboats, etc., etc., appeared to me an object of the highest importance, which must be attended with the best consequences to His Majesty's service—among others that of opening the navigation of the North River and the communication, in a certain degree, with Albany, as appears by the enclosed copy of a letter from G[eneral] Haldimand to me.

The very particular situation of the campaign at this period will mark of what great import such an event would prove. A French fleet and a considerable land force had arrived at Rhode Island. Mr. Washington had very much augmented his army, and was drawing additional strength to it daily by every strained exertion upon the country and the militia of it. There was great reason, from information, to suppose that an attempt was intended upon New York, that Mr. Washington with his army was to have moved upon Kings Bridge and Morrisania while a corps threatened—perhaps attacked—Staten Island, at the same time that the French would have invaded Long Island and have moved upon New York by that inroad. To have pursued these plans large magazines of every nature must have been formed by the rebels, and it is beyond doubt that the principal rebel depot must have been made at West Point and its dependent forts.

From this description, which I have reason to believe just, will be seen of what great consequence would be the encouraging and closing in with a plan of such infinite effect, if carried into execution, toward the success of the campaign, and that it was to be pursued at every risk and at every expense. . . .

Many projects for a meeting were formed, and in consequence several appointments made, in all which General Arnold seemed extremely desirous that some person who had my particular confidence might be sent to him—some man, as he described in writing, of *his own mensuration*. I had thought of a person under this immediate description, who would have cheerfully undertaken it but that his peculiar situation at the time (from which I could not then release him) precluded him from engaging in it [ed. note—"Maj. Gen. William Phillips, who had been captured at Saratoga and was on parole in New York"]. General Arnold finally insisted that the person sent to confer with him should be the Adjutant General, Major André, who indeed had been the person on my part who managed and carried on the secret correspondence.

—CLINTON, *The American Rebellion*, pp. 462-465.

3. ARNOLD'S PLANS GO AWRY

Extract from an intelligence report of Andrew Elliot of New York, October 4-5, 1780.

. . . General Arnold with whom a secret correspondence has been carrying on for a considerable time without the least suspicion, about three months ago got the command of the forts and troops up the North River. His head quarters was at Colonel Robinsons house on this side the North River, which is near West Point, and about twelve miles above Stoney Point.

A meeting with the French generals was appointed by General Washington at Hartford, which took place near three weeks ago. When Washington set off, General Arnold had the sole command. He in consequence of his correspondence and intentions appointed a meeting with Colonel Robinson and Major André, now Adjutant General; it was to take place first on this side the river a little above Tarry Town, or on the water near the *Vulture* sloop of war that generally lays at Spitendevil, but as there was no trusting the secret with any body, unfortunately the *Vulture* had sent her boats up the river the very night of the intended meeting. Colonel Robinson and André got to the place appointed and waited many hours; they got safe back.

Arnold . . . immediately proposed by letter a meeting at Haverstraw near Mr. William Smiths home. Colonel Robinson and Major André went on board the *Vulture;* she proceeded by way of a cruise up the river; on the night appointed Mr. Joseph Smith, brother to William Smith, came to the *Vulture* with a flag of truce from General Arnold, and a pass for Mr. John Anderson to go up the river to meet him (John Anderson was the name André had corresponded under for some time past). Colonel Robinson unfortunately was not mentioned in the pass, so staid on board the *Vulture.*

John Anderson left the *Vulture* about one o'clock on Thursday morning, met General Arnold on the shore within three miles of Smiths house, the conversation passed, but it was thought necessary that John Anderson should bring down plans of the forts, the grounds that commanded them, the approaches, etc. These done in General Arnolds own hand were lodged at Smiths house; there they went. General Arnold *says* he thought it would be dangerous for John Anderson to return by water, as they had spyboats always plying on the river when our armed vessels were advanced from their usual station (but if Anderson had been taken by them he would have been brought directly to Arnold, and as papers were *necessary* to be sent, they could have easily been sunk). Whether it was a desire of doing too much or *fate*, it was therefore determined that André, still as John Anderson, should pass the river and go by land to Kingsbridge, with a pass from General Arnold, Mr. Smith (who all this time Arnold declares knew nothing of his plan) to conduct him and pass him over the new bridge on Croton River and there leave him, all which was happily effected, and Smith returned.

André, before he set out by land, had at the express desire of General Arnold changed his cloaths, left his uniform at Smiths, was there furnished with other cloaths, and a horse and saddle from Arnold. The day after André parted with Smith, he was met by a party of militia near Tarry Town, stopt, suspected, taken, searched, the papers found under his stockings; he [was] sent up the country, and the papers dispatched to Washington who was expected back from Hartford at Robinsons home Sunday the 24th September.

Fryday André was taken, Washington was delayed. We know not how or when he got Andrés papers, but on Monday the 25th two of Washingtons aid de camps came to Arnold at Robinsons house at breakfast time, and told the general that Washington would dine there. Arnold had then heard nothing of André, but just as the aid de camps set down to breakfast Arnold went out of the room to give some orders. He was met by an officer with a letter from the commander of the militia who had taken André, telling him the event and of his having sent the papers to Washington as they were of so dangerous a nature (this officer must have been Arnolds friend as he must know his hand).

Arnold desired the messenger to stay for an answer, ran out and ordered an horse saddled, and sent a servant down the hill to order his barge's crew to man the boat (they were just returned from buying a suit of new sails). He then went to Mrs. Arnold (formerly Miss Peggy Shippen of Philadelphia). The two aid de camps had just left her to get peaches. He told her he must fly to save his life without having time to explain (she was ignorant of all). He jumped on his horse and, as he turned the stable, met four Light Horse men who told him His Excellency was just coming up the road. Arnold told them to put up their horses, and then galloped down almost a precipice (the short road), threw his saddle with his pistols into the boat, and desired the men to pull away as he was obliged to go to Stoney Point and was anxious to return to meet his Excellency.

Just as he set off an armed boat from West Point came to the landing (supposed to be ordered by Washington to carry off Arnold). General Arnold called to them to go up to the house to get refreshment and tell his Excellency when he arrived that he would be back before dinner. He was not three hundred yards from the wharf when he saw the armed vessel put off after him, but having new sails got soon from them. When he was as far as Stoney Point he told his men particular business from His Excellency to the Captain of the *Vulture* obliged him to go on board. He promised them two gallons of rum and they rowed on, but never were men so surprised when they found their general was to stay, and that they were prisoners.

Col. Robinson was on board the *Vulture* waiting for André, ignorant of his fate. Arnolds arrival unfolded all. Arnold sent back his boatswain with a letter to Washington assuring him his wife and aid de camps and all his family were ignorant of his proceedings and intentions, that he would soon make his reasons public (which will be done this week; the printers here have been *prevented* saying any thing till Arnold wrote his own sentiments). He also declared that André at his desire came in a flag from the *Vulture* with his pass, under the name he had desired him to assume, that at his desire he had at Smiths house changed his uniform for other cloaths, and set off with his pass, his guide and horse and saddle for Kingsbridge, that as he was then Commanding Officer he had a right to do all this, and André every reason in the world to depend on such protection and to act as he did as it was by his orders.

Robinson and Arnold arrived to the amazement of all here on Tuesday the twenty sixth. The General was thrown into the greatest distress from the failure of so well concerted a plan, so near ending the rebellion, as it would have given us all the forts, half the army, and cut off all communication with the Southern and Eastern Provinces as also the French. Andrés situation gives the General great distress. He immediately wrote Washington, enclosed another letter from Arnold to the same purpose as above, and demanded his Adjutant General.

—Stevens' Facsimiles, No. 739.

4. Benedict Arnold Is Conscious of His Own Rectitude

Arnold to Washington.

Vulture, September 25, 1780

Sir: The heart which is conscious of its own rectitude cannot attempt to palliate a step which the world may censure as wrong; I have ever acted from a principle of love to my country since the commencement of the present unhappy contest between Great-Britain and the Colonies; the same principle of love to my country actuates my present conduct, however it may appear inconsistent to the world, who very seldom judge right of any man's actions.

I have no favour to ask for myself. I have too often experienced the ingratitude of my country to attempt it; but from the known humanity of your Excellency, I am induced to ask your protection for Mrs. Arnold from every insult and injury that the mistaken vengeance of my country may expose her to. It ought to fall only on me; she is as good and as innocent as an angel, and is incapable of doing wrong. I beg she may be permitted to return to her friends in Philadelphia, or to come to me as she may choose; from your Excellency I have no fears on her account, but she may suffer from the mistaken fury of the country.

I have to request that the inclosed letter may be delivered to Mrs. Arnold, and she be permitted to write to me.

I have also to ask that my cloaths and baggage, which are of little consequence, may be sent to me; if required their value shall be paid in money.

　　　　　　　　　　　　　　　　—André, *Papers*, pp. 26-27.

5. Wayne's Veterans Hurry to the Defense of West Point

General Anthony Wayne to H. A. Sheel.

Haverstraw near Stoney Point, October 2, 1780

I am confident that the perfidy of Gen. Arnold will astonish the multitude. . . . The dirty, dirty acts which he has been capable of committing beggar all description, and are of such a nature as would cause the *Infernals to blush* were they accused with the invention or execution of them.

The detached and debilitated state of the garrison of West Point insured success to the assailants. The enemy were all in perfect readiness for the enterprize, and the discovery of the treason only prevented an immediate attempt by open force to carry those works which perfidy would have effected the fall of by a slower and less sanguine mode. Our army was out of protecting distance, the troops in the possession of the works of a spiritless miserable *Vulgus* in whose hands the fate of America seemed suspended. In this situation his Excellency (in imitation of Caesar and his Tenth Legion) called for his *veterans;* the summons arrived at one o'clock in the morning, and we took up our line of march at 2 and by sunrise arrived at this place distant from our former camp 16 miles, the whole performed in four hours in a dark night, without a single halt or a man left behind.

When our approach was announced to the General he thought it fabulous, but when convinced of the reality he received us like a god, and retiring to take a short repose exclaimed, "All is safe, and I again am happy." May he long, very long, continue so!

—STILLÉ, *Wayne and the Pennsylvania Line*, pp. 236-237.

6. LaFayette Asks: What Will the French Officers Say?

LaFayette to the Chevalier de la Luzerne.

West Point, 25 September 1780

When I left you yesterday morning, M. le Chevalier, to come here to take breakfast with General Arnold, we were very far from thinking of the event which I am now about to announce to you. You will shudder at the danger we have run. You will be astonished at the miraculous chain of accidents and circumstances by which we have been saved. But you will be still more greatly surprised when you learn by what instrument this conspiracy was being carried on. West Point was sold, and it was sold by Arnold! That same man who had covered himself with glory by rendering valuable services to his country, had lately formed a horrid compact with the enemy. And, but for the chance which brought us here at a certain time, but for the chance which, by a combination of accidents, caused the Adjutant General of the English army to fall into the hands of some countrymen, beyond the line of our own posts, West Point and the North River would probably be in the possession of our enemies.

When we left Fishkill we were preceded by one of my aides-de-camp and General Knox's aide, who found General and Mrs. Arnold at table and who sat down to breakfast with them. During that time two letters were brought to General Arnold giving him information of the capture of the spy. He ordered a horse saddled, went to his wife's room and told her that he was lost, and directed one of his aides-de-camp to say to General Washington that he had gone to West Point and should return in an hour.

Upon our arrival here, we crossed the river and went to look at the works. Judge of our astonishment when, upon our return, we were informed that the captured spy was Major André, the Adjutant General of the English army, and that among the papers found upon him was a copy of a very important council of war, a statement of the strength of the garrison and of the works, and certain observations upon the methods of attack and defence, all in General Arnold's handwriting. The English Adjutant-General wrote also to the General, admitting his rank and his name. A search was made for Arnold, but he had escaped in a boat on board the sloop of war *Vulture*, and, as nobody suspected his flight, no sentry could have thought of arresting him. Colonel Hamilton, . . . who had gone in quest of Arnold, received soon afterward a flag of truce with a letter from Arnold for the General, in which he made no effort to justify his treason, and a letter from the English Commandant, Robertson [Robinson], who in a most insolent manner demanded the surrender of the Adjutant-General, upon the ground that he had been acting under the permission of General Arnold.

The first care of General Washington was to return to West Point the troops whom Arnold had dispersed under various pretexts. We remained here to insure the safety of a fort which the English would value less if they knew it better. The Continental troops are being brought here, and, as tne advice of Arnold may induce Clinton to make a sudden movement, orders have been given to the army to hold itself in readiness to march at a moment's notice.

I cannot describe to you, M. le Chevalier, to what degree I am astounded by this piece of news. In the course of a revolution such as ours it is natural that a few traitors should be found, and every conflict which resembles a civil war of the first order . . . must necessarily bring to light some great virtues and some great crimes. Our struggles have brought forward some heroes (General Washington for instance) who would otherwise have been merely private citizens. They have also developed some great scoundrels who would otherwise have remained merely obscure rogues. But that an Arnold, a man who, although not so highly esteemed as has been supposed in Europe, had nevertheless given proof of talent, of patriotism, and especially of the most brilliant courage, should at once destroy his very existence and should sell his country to the tyrants whom he had fought against with glory, is an event, M. le Chevalier, which confounds and distresses me, and, if I must confess it, humiliates me to a degree that I cannot express. I would give anything in the world if Arnold had not shared our labors with us, and if this man, whom it still pains me to call a scoundrel, had not shed his blood in the American cause. My knowledge of his personal courage led me to expect that he would decide to blow his brains out (this was my first hope); at all events, it is probable that he will do so when he reaches New York, whither the English sloop proceeded immediately upon receiving Arnold on board. That vessel had come up the river in connection with this despicable conspiracy, and the house of the Chevalier Smith, which is in our possession, was the place of rendezvous. . . .

Unaccustomed as they are to the convulsions of a revolution, what will the officers of the French army say when they see a general abandon and basely sell his country after having defended it so well! You can bear witness, M. le Chevalier, that this is the first atrocity that has been heard of in our army. . . .

—TOWER, *La Fayette in the American Revolution*, II, 164-167.

7. "TREASON OF THE BLACKEST DYE"

Nathanael Greene's Order of the Day, September 26, 1780.

Treason of the blackest dye was yesterday discovered. General Arnold, who commanded at West Point, lost to every sentiment of honor, of public and private obligation, was about to deliver up that important fort into the hands of the enemy. Such an event must have given the American cause a deadly wound if not a fatal stab. Happily the scheme was timely discovered to prevent the final misfortune. The providential train of circumstances which led to it affords the most convincing proofs that the liberties of America are the object of divine protection. At the same time the treason is so regretted the General cannot help congratulating the army on the happy discovery.

Our enemies, despairing of carrying their point by force, are practising every base art to effect, by bribery and corruption, what they cannot accomplish in a manly way. Great honor is due to the American army that this is the first instance of treason of this kind, where many were to be expected from the nature of the dispute, and nothing is so high an ornament to the characters of the American soldiers as their withstanding all the arts and seductions of an insidious enemy.

Arnold the traitor has made his escape to the enemy, but Mr. André, Adjutant-General to the British army, who came out as a spy to negotiate the business, is our prisoner.

His Excellency the Commander-in-Chief has arrived at West Point from Hartford, and is now doubtless taking proper steps to unravel fully so hellish a plot.

—MOORE, *Diary of the American Revolution*, II, 323.

8. WASHINGTON RECALLS THE HISTORY OF ARNOLD'S TREASON

Diary of Tobias Lear, private secretary to Washington.

Oct. 23, 1786. Mr. Drayton and Mr. Izard here all day. After dinner General Washington was, in the course of conversation, led to speak of Arnold's treachery, when he gave the following account of it, which I shall put in his own words, thus:

"I confess I had a good opinion of Arnold before his treachery was brought to light; had that not been the case, I should have had some reason to suspect him sooner, for when he commanded in Philadelphia, the Marquis la Fayette brought accounts from France of the armament which was to be sent to co-operate with us in the ensuing campaign. Soon after this was known, Arnold pretended to have some private business to transact in Connecticut, and on his way there he called at my quarters, and in the course of conversation expressed a desire of quitting Philadelphia and joining the army the ensuing campaign. I told him that it was probable we should have a very active one, and that if his wound and state of health would permit, I should be extremely glad of his services with the army. He replied that he did not think his wound would permit him to take a very active part; but still he persisted in his desire of being with the army.

"He went on to Connecticut, and on his return called again upon me. He renewed his request of being with me next campaign, and I made him the same answer I had done before. He again repeated that he did not think his wound would permit him to do active duty, and intimated a desire to have the command at West Point. I told him I did not think that would suit him, as I should leave none in the garrison but invalids, because it would be entirely covered by the main army. The subject was dropt at that time, and he returned to Philadelphia. It then appeared somewhat strange to me that a man of Arnold's known activity and enterprise should be desirous of taking so inactive a part. I however thought no more of the matter.

"When the French troops arrived at Rhode Island, I had intelligence from New York that General Clinton intended to make an attack upon them before they could get themselves settled and fortified. In consequence of that, I was determined to attack New York, which would be left much exposed by his drawing off the British troops; and accordingly formed my line of battle, and moved down with the whole army to King's Ferry, which we passed. Arnold came to camp at that time, and having no command, and consequently no quarters (all the houses thereabouts being occupied by the army), he was obliged to seek lodgings at some distance from the camp. While the army was crossing at King's Ferry, I was going to see the last detachment over and met Arnold, who asked me if I had thought of anything for him. I told him that he was to have the command of the light troops, which was a post of honor, and which his rank indeed entitled him to. Upon this information his countenance changed, and he appeared to be quite fallen; and instead of thanking me, or expressing any pleasure at the appointment, never opened his mouth. I desired him to go on to my quarters and get something to refresh himself, and I would meet him there soon. He did so.

"Upon his arrival there, he found Col. Tilghman, whom he took a-one side, and mentioning what I had told him, seemed to express great uneasiness at it—as his leg, he said, would not permit him to be long on horse-back; and intimated a great desire to have the command at West Point. When I returned to my quarters, Col. Tilghman informed me of what had passed. I made no reply to it—but his behavior struck me as strange and unaccountable. In the course of that night, however, I received information from New York that General Clinton had altered his plan and was debarking his troops. This information obliged me likewise to alter my disposition and return to my former station, where I could better cover the country. I then determined to comply with Arnold's desire, and accordingly gave him the command of the garrison at West Point.

"Things remained in this situation about a fortnight, when I wrote to the Count Rochambeau desiring to meet him at some intermediate place (as we could neither of us be long enough from our respective commands to visit the other), in order to lay the plan for the siege of Yorktown, and proposed Hartford, where I accordingly went and met the Count. On my return I met the Chevalier Luzerne towards evening, within about 15 miles of West Point (on his way to join the Count at Rhode Island), which I intended to reach that night, but he insisted upon turning back with me to the next public house; where, in politeness to him, I could not but stay all night, determining, however, to get to West Point to breakfast very early. I sent off my baggage, and desired Colonel Hamilton to go forward and inform General Arnold that I would breakfast with him.

"Soon after he arrived at Arnold's quarters, a letter was delivered to Arnold which threw him into the greatest confusion. He told Colonel Hamilton that something required his immediate attendance at the garrison, which was on the opposite side of the river to his quarters; and immediately ordered a horse to take him to the river, and the barge, which he kept to cross, to be ready; and desired Major Franks, his aid, to inform me when I should arrive that he was gone over the river and would return immediately.

"When I got to his quarters and did not find him there, I desired Major Franks to order me some breakfast; and as I intended to visit the fortifications I would see General Arnold there. After I had breakfasted, I went over the river, and inquiring for Arnold, the commanding officer told me that he had not been there. I likewise inquired at the several redoubts, but no one could give me any information where he was. The impropriety of his conduct when he knew I was to be there, struck me very forcibly, and my mind misgave me; but I had not the least idea of the real cause.

"When I returned to Arnold's quarters about two hours after and told Colonel Hamilton that I had not seen him, he gave me a packet which had just arrived for me from Col. Jemmison, which immediately brought the matter to light. I ordered Colonel Hamilton to mount his horse and proceed with the greatest despatch to a post on the river about eight miles below, in order to stop the barge if she had not passed; but it was too late.

"It seems that the letter Arnold received which threw him in such confusion was from Col. Jemmison, informing him that André was taken and that the papers found upon him were in his possession. Col. Jemmison, when André was taken with these papers, could not believe that Arnold was a traitor, but rather thought it was an imposition of the British in order to destroy our confidence in Arnold. He, however, immediately on their being taken, despatched an express after me, ordering him to ride night and day till he came up with me. The express went the lower road, which was the road by which I had gone to Connecticut, expecting that I would return by the same route, and that he would meet me; but before he had proceeded far, he was informed that I was returning by the upper road. He then cut across the country and followed in my track till I arrived at West Point. He arrived about two hours after and brought the above packet.

"When Arnold got down to the barge, he ordered his men, who were very clever fellows and some of the better sort of soldiery, to proceed immediately on board the *Vulture* sloop of war, as a flag, which was lying down the river; saying that they must be very expeditious, as he must return in a short time to meet me, and promised them two gallons of rum if they would exert themselves. They did accordingly; but when they got on board the *Vulture*, instead of their two gallons of rum, he ordered the coxswain to be called down into the cabin and informed him that he and the men must consider themselves as prisoners. The coxswain was very much astonished and told him that they came on board under the sanction of a flag. He answered that that was nothing to the purpose; they were prisoners. But the Captain of the *Vulture* had more generosity than this pitiful scoundrel and told the coxswain that he would take his parole for going on shore to get clothes and whatever else was wanted for himself and his companions. He accordingly came, got his clothes and returned on board. When they got to New York, General Clinton, ashamed of so low and mean an action, set them all at liberty."

—RICHARD RUSH, *Occasional Productions*, pp. 79-85.

VI. THE CAPTURE AND EXECUTION OF ANDRÉ

Dramatically André is, of course, the foil to Arnold. All that Arnold was not, André was—or seemed to be. Young, handsome, brilliant, charming, loyal, high-minded, he was to be the sacrifice to evil, or to fate, that mythology demands. He is, indeed, so nearly legendary a character that had he not existed, legend must inevitably have created him. Born in London, the son of a Genevese merchant, educated in Geneva, he was something of a soldier of fortune.

He was, in addition, a minor poet, a dramatist and actor, and an amateur artist.
General Clinton loved him; his fellow officers regarded him with admiration
and affection. He won the respect of all the Americans who came to know
him, not least young Alexander Hamilton, who wrote a secret letter to Clinton
urging the exchange of André for Arnold.

Should Washington have pardoned him, or allowed him a soldier's death?
Certainly these would have been the easier decisions, and may have been the
right ones. But it is worth quoting the conclusion of R. E. Graves, author of
the article on André in the (English) Dictionary of National Biography, *on*
this vexatious question: "Washington has been unreasonably censured for not
having granted him a more honourable death. To have done so would have
implied a doubt as to the justice of his conviction. . . . Washington and André
deserve equal honour: André for having accepted a terrible risk for his country and borne the consequences of failure with unshrinking courage; and
Washington for having performed his duty to his own country at a great
sacrifice of his feelings."

1. Colonel Hamilton Describes the Capture of André

Alexander Hamilton to John Laurens.

October 1780

Arnold employed one Smith to go on board the *Vulture* on the night of the
twenty-second, to bring André on shore with a pass for Mr. John Anderson.
André came ashore accordingly, and was conducted within a picket of ours to
the house of Smith, where Arnold and he remained together in close conference all that night and the day following.

At daylight in the morning, the commanding officer at King's Ferry, without the privity of Arnold, moved a couple of pieces of cannon to a point
opposite to where the *Vulture* lay, and obliged her to take a more remote station. This event, or some lurking distrust, made the boatmen refuse to convey
the two passengers back, and disconcerted Arnold so much that, by one of
those strokes of infatuation which often confound the schemes of men conscious of guilt, he insisted on André's exchanging his uniform for a disguise,
and returning in a mode different from that in which he came. André, who
had been undesignedly brought within our posts in the first instance, remonstrated warmly against this new and dangerous expedient. But Arnold persisting in declaring it impossible for him to return as he came, he at length
reluctantly yielded to his direction and consented to change his dress and take
the route he recommended. Smith furnished the disguise, and in the evening
passed King's Ferry with him and proceeded to Crompond, where they
stopped the remainder of the night, at the instance of a militia officer, to avoid
being suspected by him.

The next morning they resumed their journey, Smith accompanying André a little beyond Pine's Bridge, where he left him. He had reached Tarrytown when he was taken up by three militiamen, who rushed out of the woods
and seized his horse.

At this critical moment his presence of mind forsook him. Instead of producing his pass, which would have extricated him from our parties and could have done him no harm with his own, he asked the militiamen if they were of the *upper* or *lower* party—descriptive appellations known among the enemy's refugee corps. The militiamen replied they were of the lower party, upon which he told them he was a British officer and pressed them not to detain him, as he was upon urgent business. This confession removed all doubts, and it was in vain he afterwards produced his pass.

He was instantly forced off to a place of greater security, where, after a careful search, there were found concealed in the feet of his stockings several papers of importance, delivered to him by Arnold! Among these were a plan of the fortifications of West Point; a memorial from the engineer on the attack and defence of the place; returns of the garrison, cannon and stores; copy of the minutes of a council of war held by General Washington a few weeks before.

The prisoner at first was inadvertently ordered to Arnold, but on recollection, while still on the way, he was countermanded and sent to Old Salem. The papers were enclosed in a letter to General Washington, which, having taken a route different from that by which he returned, made a circuit that afforded leisure for another letter, through an ill-judged delicacy, written to Arnold with information of Anderson's capture, to get to him an hour before General Washington arrived at his quarters; time enough to elude the fate that awaited him. He went down the river on his barge to the *Vulture* with such precipitate confusion that he did not take with him a single paper useful to the enemy. On the first notice of the affair he was pursued but much too late to be overtaken.

—LODGE, ed., *Works of Hamilton*, IX, 210 ff.

2. "BETRAYED INTO THE VILE CONDITION OF AN ENEMY IN DISGUISE"

John André to George Washington.

Salem, September 24, 1780

I beg your Excellency will be persuaded that no alteration in the temper of my mind, or apprehension for my safety, induces me to take the step of addressing you, but that it is to secure myself from an imputation of having assumed a mean character for treacherous purposes or self interest, a conduct incompatible with the principles that actuated me, as well as with my condition in life.

It is to vindicate my fame that I speak and not to solicit security.

The person in your possession is Major John André, Adjutant General to the British army.

The influence of one commander in the army of his adversary is an advantage taken in war. A correspondence for this purpose I held, as confidential (in the present instance) with his Excellency Sir Henry Clinton.

To favor it, I agreed to meet, upon ground not within posts of either army, a person who was to give me intelligence; I came up in the *Vulture* man of war for this effect, and was fetched by a boat from the shore to the beach. Being there I was told that the approach of day would prevent my return, and that I must be concealed until the next night. I was in my regimentals and had fairly risked my person.

Against my stipulation, my intention and without my knowledge before hand, I was conducted within one of your posts. Your Excellency may conceive my sensation on this occasion and will imagine how much more I must have been affected by a refusal to reconduct me back the next night as I had been brought. Thus become a prisoner I had to concert my escape. *I quitted my uniform* and was passed another way in the night without the American posts to neutral ground, and informed I was beyond all armed parties and left to press for New-York. I was taken at Tarry Town by some volunteers.

Thus as I have had the honor to relate was I betrayed (being Adjutant General of the British army) into the vile condition of an enemy in disguise within your posts.

Having avowed myself a British officer I have nothing to reveal but what relates to myself, which is true on the honor of an officer and a gentleman.

The request I have to make your Excellency, and I am conscious I address myself well, is, that in any rigor policy may dictate, a decency of conduct towards me may mark that though unfortunate I am branded with nothing dishonourable, as no motive could be mine but the service of my king and as I was involuntarily an imposter. . . .

—ANDRÉ, *Papers*, pp. 20-22.

3. "YOUR EXCELLENCY WILL DIRECT THIS OFFICER TO RETURN!"

Sir Henry Clinton to George Washington.

New York, September 26, 1780

Being informed that the King's Adjutant General in America has been stopt, under Major General Arnold's passports, and is detained a prisoner in your Excellency's army, I have the honour to inform you, Sir, that I permitted Major André to go to Major General Arnold at the particular request of that general officer. You will perceive, Sir, by the inclosed paper, that a flag of truce was sent to receive Major André, and passports granted for his return. I therefore can have no doubt but your Excellency will immediately direct that this officer has permission to return to my orders at New-York.

—ANDRÉ, *Papers*, pp. 27-28.

4. "MAJOR ANDRÉ . . . OUGHT TO BE CONSIDERED AS A SPY"

George Washington to Sir Henry Clinton.

Head Quarters, September 30, 1780

In answer to Your Excellency's Letter of the 26th Instant, which I had the honor to receive, I am to inform You, that Major André was taken under such circumstances as would have justified the most summary proceedings against him. I determined however to refer his case to the examination and decision of a Board of General Officers, who have reported, on his free and voluntary confession and Letters; "That he came on Shore from the *Vulture* Sloop of war in the night of the Twenty first of September Instant on an interview with General Arnold in a private and secret manner. Secondly that he changed his dress within our lines, and under a feigned name and in a disguised habit passed our Works at Stoney and Verplanks points the Evening of the Twenty second of September Instant, at Tarry Town, in a disguised habit, being then on his way to New York, and when taken he had in his possession Several papers which contained intelligence for the Enemy. The Board having maturely considered these Facts do also report to His Excellency General Washington, that Major André Adjutant General to the British Army ought to be considered as a Spy from the Enemy, and that agreable to the Law and usage of Nations it is their opinion he ought to suffer death."

From these proceedings it is evident Major André was employed in the execution of measures very foreign to the Objects of Flags of truce and such as they were never meant to authorise or countenance in the most distant degree; and this Gentleman confessed with the greatest candor in the course of his examination, "that it was impossible for him to suppose he came on shore under the sanction of a Flag."

—FITZPATRICK, ed., *Writings of Washington*, XX, 103-104.

5. "I SHALL THINK MYSELF BOUND TO RETALIATE"

Arnold to George Washington.

New York, October 1, 1780

If after this just and candid representation of Major André's case the board of general officers adhere to their former opinion, I shall suppose it dictated by passion and resentment. And if that gentleman should suffer the severity of their sentence, I shall think myself bound by every tie of duty and honour to retaliate on such unhappy persons of your army as may fall within my power—that the respect due to flags and to the law of nations may be better understood and observed.

I have further to observe that forty of the principal inhabitants of South Carolina have justly forfeited their lives, which have hitherto been spared by the clemency of His Excellency Sir Henry Clinton. Sir Henry could not in justice extend his mercy to them any longer, if Major André suffers; which in all probability will open a scene of blood at which humanity will revolt.

Suffer me to entreat your Excellency, for your own and the honour of humanity, and the love you have of justice, that you suffer not an unjust sentence to touch the life of Major André. But if this warning should be disregarded, and he should suffer, I call heaven and earth to witness that your Excellency will be justly answerable for the torrent of blood that may be spilt in consequence.

—VAN DOREN, *Secret History of the Revolution*, pp. 369-370.

6. "ADOPT MY DEATH TO THE FEELINGS OF A MAN OF HONOUR"

John André to George Washington.

Tappan, October 1, 1780

Buoyed above the terror of death by the consciousness of a life devoted to honourable pursuits, and stained with no action that can give me remorse, I trust that the request I make to your Excellency at this serious period, and which is to soften my last moments, will not be rejected.

Sympathy towards a soldier will surely induce your Excellency and a military tribunal to adopt the mode of my death to the feelings of a man of honour.

Let me hope, Sir, that if aught in my character impresses you with esteem towards me, if aught in my misfortunes marks me as the victim of policy and not of resentment, ·I shall experience the operation of these feelings in your breast, by being informed that I am not to die on a gibbet.

—ANDRÉ, *Papers*, p. 40.

7. REMORSELESS WASHINGTON!

A Monody on the Death of André
by Ann Seward
Oh Washington! I thought thee great and good,
Nor knew thy Nero thirst for guiltless blood:
Severe to use the power that fortune gave,
Thou cool determined murderer of the brave.
Remorseless Washington! the day shall come
Of deep repentance for this barbarous doom;
When injured André's mem'ry shall inspire
A kindling army with resistless fire,
Each falchion sharpen that the Britons wield,
And lead their fiercest lion to the field;
Then, when each hope of thine shall end in night,
When dubious dread and unavailing flight
Impel your haste, thy guilt-upbraided soul
Shall wish, untouched, the precious life you stole;
And when thy heart, appalled and vanquished pride,
Shall vainly ask the mercy you denied,
With horror shalt thou meet the fate thou gave,
Nor pity gild the darkness of thy grave.

—NILES, ed., *Principles and Acts*, p. 497.

8. NEVER WAS DEATH SUFFERED WITH MORE JUSTICE OR LESS DESERT

Alexander Hamilton to John Laurens.

October 1780

André was, without loss of time, conducted to the headquarters of the army, where he was immediately brought before a board of general officers to prevent all possibility of misrepresentation, or cavil on the part of the enemy. The board reported that he ought to be considered as a spy, and, according to the laws of nations, to suffer death, which was executed two days after.

Never, perhaps, did a man suffer death with more justice, or deserve it less. The first step he took after his capture was to write a letter to General Washington, conceived in terms of dignity without insolence, and apology without meanness. The scope of it was to vindicate himself from the imputation of having assumed a mean character for treacherous or interested purposes; asserting that he had been involuntarily an imposter; that contrary to his intention, which was to meet a person for intelligence on neutral ground, he had been betrayed within our posts, and forced into the vile condition of an enemy in disguise; soliciting only that, to whatever rigor policy might devote him, a decency of treatment might be observed, due to a person who, though unfortunate, had been guilty of nothing dishonorable. His request was granted in its full extent; for, in the whole progress of the affair, he was treated with the most scrupulous delicacy. When brought before the board of officers he met with every mark of indulgence, and was required to answer no interrogatory which could even embarrass his feelings. On his part, while he carefully concealed every thing that might involve others, he frankly confessed all the facts relating to himself; and, upon his confession, without the trouble of examining a witness, the board made their report. The members of it were not more impressed with the candor and firmness, mixed with a becoming sensibility, which he displayed, than he was penetrated with their liberality and politeness. He acknowledged the generosity of the behavior towards him in every respect, but particularly in this, in the strongest terms of manly gratitude. In a conversation with a gentleman who visited him after his trial, he said he flattered himself he had never been illiberal; but if there were any remains of prejudice in his mind, his present experience must obliterate them.

In one of the visits I made to him (and I saw him several times during his confinement), he begged me to be the bearer of a request to the General, for permission to send an open letter to Sir Henry Clinton. "I foresee my fate," said he, "and though I pretend not to play the hero, or to be indifferent about life, yet I am reconciled to whatever may happen, conscious that misfortune, not guilt, has brought it upon me. There is only one thing that disturbs my tranquillity. Sir Henry Clinton has been too good to me; he has been lavish of his kindness. I am bound to him by too many obligations, and love him too well, to bear the thought that he should reproach himself, or that others should reproach him, on the supposition of my having conceived myself obliged by his instructions to run the risk I did. I would not for the world leave a sting in his mind that should imbitter his future days." He could scarce finish the sentence, bursting into tears in spite of his efforts to suppress them, and with difficulty collected himself enough afterwards to add, "I wish to be permitted to assure him I did not act under this impression, but submitted to a necessity imposed upon me, as contrary to my own inclination as by his orders." His request was readily complied with, and he wrote the letter annexed, with which I dare say you will be as much pleased as I am, both for the diction and sentiment.

When his sentence was announced to him he remarked that since it was his lot to die, there was still a choice in the mode, which would make a material difference in his feelings, and he would be happy, if possible, to be indulged with a professional death. He made a second application, by letter, in concise but persuasive terms. It was thought this indulgence, being incompatible with the customs of war, could not be granted, and it was therefore determined, in both cases, to evade an answer, to spare him the sensations which a certain knowledge of the intended mode would inflict.

In going to the place of execution, he bowed familiarly as he went along to all those with whom he had been acquainted in his confinement. A smile of complacency expressed the serene fortitude of his mind. Arrived at the fatal spot, he asked, with some emotion, "Must I then die in this manner?" He was told that it had been unavoidable. "I am reconciled to my fate," said he, "but not to the mode." Soon, however, recollecting himself, he added: "It will be but a momentary pang," and, springing upon the cart, performed the last offices to himself with a composure that excited the admiration and melted the hearts of the beholders. Upon being told that the final moment was at hand, and asked if he had anything to say, he answered: "Nothing but to request you will witness to the world that I die like a brave man." Among the extraordinary circumstances that attended him, in the midst of his enemies, he died universally esteemed and universally regretted.

There was something singularly interesting in the character and fortunes of André. To an excellent understanding, well improved by education and travel, he united a peculiar elegance of mind and manners, and the advantage of a pleasing person. 'Tis said he possessed a pretty taste for the fine arts, and had himself attained some proficiency in poetry, music and painting. His knowledge appeared without ostentation, and embellished by a diffidence that rarely accompanies so many talents and accomplishments: which left you to suppose more than appeared. His sentiments were elevated, and inspired esteem: they had a softness that conciliated affection. His elocution was handsome; his address easy, polite and insinuating. By his merit he had acquired the unlimited confidence of his general, and was making a rapid progress in military rank and reputation. But in the height of his career, flushed with new hopes from the execution of a project the most beneficial to his party that could be devised, he was at once precipitated from the summit of prosperity and saw all the expectations of his ambition blasted, and himself ruined.

—LODGE, ed., *Works of Hamilton*, IX, 216 ff.

9. "MELANCHOLY AND GLOOM AFFECTED ALL RANKS"

Journal of Dr. James Thacher.

October 2d, 1780.—Major André is no more among the living. I have just witnessed his exit. It was a tragical scene of the deepest interest. During his confinement and trial, he exhibited those proud and elevated sensibilities which designate greatness and dignity of mind. Not a murmur or a sigh ever escaped him, and the civilities and attentions bestowed on him were politely acknowledged. Having left a mother and two sisters in England, he was heard to mention them in terms of the tenderest affection, and in his letter to Sir Henry Clinton he recommended them to his particular attention.

The principal guard officer, who was constantly in the room with the prisoner, relates that when the hour of his execution was announced to him in the morning, he received it without emotion, and while all present were affected with silent gloom, he retained a firm countenance, with calmness and composure of mind. Observing his servant enter the room in tears, he exclaimed, "Leave me till you can show yourself more manly!" His breakfast being sent to him from the table of General Washington, which had been done every day of his confinement, he partook of it as usual, and having shaved and dressed himself, he placed his hat on the table and cheerfully said to the guard officers, "I am ready at any moment, gentlemen, to wait on you."

The fatal hour having arrived, a large detachment of troops was paraded, and an immense concourse of people assembled; almost all our general and field officers, excepting His Excellency and his staff, were present on horseback; melancholy and gloom pervaded all ranks, and the scene was affectingly awful. I was so near during the solemn march to the fateful spot as to observe every movement and participate in every emotion which the melancholy scene was calculated to produce. Major André walked from the stone house, in which he had been confined, between two of our subaltern officers, arm in arm. The eyes of the immense multitude were fixed on him, who, rising superior to the fears of death, appeared as if conscious of the dignified deportment which he displayed. He betrayed no want of fortitude, but retained a complacent smile on his countenance, and politely bowed to several gentlemen whom he knew, which was respectfully returned.

It was his earnest desire to be shot, as being the mode of death most conformable to the feelings of a military man, and he had indulged the hope that his request would be granted. At the moment, therefore, when suddenly he came in view of the gallows, he involuntarily started backward and made a pause.

"Why this emotion, sir?" said an officer by his side.

Instantly recovering his composure, he said, "I am reconciled to my death, but I detest the mode."

While waiting and standing near the gallows, I observed some degree of trepidation: placing his foot on a stone and rolling it over, and choking in his throat as if attempting to swallow. So soon, however, as he perceived that things were in readiness, he stepped quickly into the wagon, and at this moment he appeared to shrink, but instantly elevating his head with firmness, he said, "It will be but a momentary pang," and taking from his pocket two white handkerchiefs, the provost-marshal, with one, loosely pinioned his arms, and with the other, the victim, after taking off his hat and stock, bandaged his own eyes with perfect firmness, which melted the hearts and moistened the cheeks, not only of his servant, but of the throng of spectators.

The rope being appended to the gallows, he slipped the noose over his head and adjusted it to his neck, without the assistance of the awkward executioner. Colonel Scammel now informed him that he had an opportunity to speak, if he desired it. He raised the handkerchief from his eyes, and said, "I pray you to bear me witness that I meet my fate like a brave man." The wagon being now removed from under him, he was suspended, and instantly expired; it proved indeed "but a momentary pang." He was dressed in his royal regiments and boots, and his remains, in the same dress, were placed in an ordinary coffin and interred at the foot of the gallows; and the spot was consecrated by the tears of thousands.

Thus died, in the bloom of life, the accomplished Major André, the pride of the Royal Army, and the valued friend of Sir Henry Clinton. He was about twenty-nine years of age, in his person well proportioned, tall, genteel and graceful. His mien respectable and dignified. His countenance mild, expressive and prepossessing, indicative of an intelligent and amiable mind. His talents are said to have been of a superior cast, and, being cultivated in early life, he had made very considerable proficiency in literary attainments. . . . Military glory was the mainspring of his actions and the sole object of his pursuits, and he was advancing rapidly in the gratification of his ambitious views till by a misguided zeal he became a devoted victim.

—THACHER, Military Journal, pp. 226-231.

VII. MUTINY

The year of Arnold's treason was also one of mutinies and dissension. There had been a minor mutiny in Washington's army at Morristown in May 1780, when two Connecticut regiments had defied their officers and demanded their back pay; they were disarmed by Pennsylvania troops. Next January it was the turn of the Pennsylvania Line. These soldiers had genuine grievances. They had gone for months without pay; they were in rags; they were reduced to dry bread and cold water. Worst of all many of them who had enlisted for "three years or the duration of the war" found, to their indignation, that this meant the longer rather than the shorter of the two periods. The particular occasion of their mutiny, the night of January 1, 1781, was the appearance in camp of recruiting agents offering $25 in specie for new recruits! Some 2,400 men were involved in this mutiny—a formidable force. On January 3 they made camp at Princeton and chose spokesmen to present their case to Congress. Pennsylvania's President Reed ended the mutiny by acceding to most of their terms. Meantime word of the outbreak had reached Clinton, who promptly sent two spies to seduce the Americans from their allegiance; these were seized by the men themselves and promptly hanged.

A few weeks later three New Jersey regiments mutinied; this time Washington acted promptly and harshly. The mutiny was put down by arms, and the ringleaders executed. Again in June—after the war was over—some three hundred troops demonstrated in front of Independence Hall in Philadelphia; Congress promptly escaped to Princeton.

The most astonishing aspect of this whole matter is that there were, over the years, so few mutinies, and that so many soldiers—nonprofessionals—endured so much for so long.

1. THE SUFFERINGS AND GRIEVANCES OF THE PENNSYLVANIA LINE

Anthony Wayne to President Joseph Reed.

Mount Kemble, N. J., December 16, 1780

. . . I don't mean to cast any reflection upon the conduct of your Excellency or the Honourable Council; on the contrary, I am but too well convinced that nothing on your part was omitted to render the situation of the officers and soldiers as comfortable as the exhausted state of the treasury and other circumstances would admit of; and although they were not equal to your wishes or their merits and expectations, yet they have been such as afforded great relief to both officers and soldiers. But those comforts being for some time totally consumed, we are reduced to dry bread and beef for our food, and to cold water for our drink. Neither officers or soldiers have received a single drop of spirituous liquors from the public magazines since the 10th of October last, except one gill per man some time in November; this, together with the old worn out coats and tattered linen overalls, and what was once a poor substitute for a blanket (now divided among three soldiers), is but very wretched living and shelter against the winter's piercing cold, drifting snows and chilling sleets.

Our soldiery are not devoid of reasoning faculties, nor are they callous to the first feelings of nature; they have now served their country with fidelity for near five years, poorly clothed, badly fed and worse paid; of the last article, trifling as it is, they have not seen a paper dollar in the way of pay for near *twelve months*.

In this situation the enemy began to work upon their passions and have found means to circulate some proclamations among them. Capt. Zeigler will be able to inform your Excellency of matters which I don't choose to commit to paper. However, I don't despair of being able to restore harmony and content, and to defeat every machination of the public foe and the more dangerous lurking incendiary, if aided by your Excellency in a timely supply of stores and clothing. But what will insure success is the immediate passing of the act for making good the depreciation. Give your soldiery a landed property, make their interest and the interest of America reciprocal, and I will answer for their bleeding to *death*, drop by drop, to establish the independency of this country. On the contrary, should we neglect rewarding their past services, and not do justice to their more than Roman virtue, have we nothing to apprehend from their defection? Believe me, my dear sir, that if something is not immediately done to give them a local attachment to this country and to quiet their minds, we have not yet seen the worst side of the picture.

The officers in general, as well as myself, find it necessary to stand for hours every day, exposed to wind and weather, among the poor naked fellows, while they are working at their huts and redoubts, often assisting with our own hands, in order to produce a conviction to their minds that we share and more than share every vicissitude in common with them, sometimes asking to participate of their bread or water. The good effect this conduct has is very conspicuous and prevents them murmuring in public; but the delicate mind and eye of humanity are hurt, very much hurt, at their visible distress and private complainings. Be assured, sir, that we depend much upon your interest (and we flatter ourselves that that dependence is well founded) to remove those difficulties and alleviate the distresses they now experience.

An immediate supply of hard cash to pay the bounty to the recruits we have enlisted for the war out of the seven months' men is absolutely necessary; I think the number is already about one hundred. We could have retained every man we wished, had we been furnished with specie in time. I fear it is now too late; the mode of recruiting will probably be by classing the inhabitants, and obliging those classes to furnish a given number of men for the war by a certain day, which I wish the earliest possible, to the end that we may have it in our power to reduce them to some degree of discipline before the opening of the campaign, as we shall probably take the field in conjunction with the first corps of France.

—REED, *Life and Correspondence of Reed*, II, 315-317.

2. MUTINY IN JANUARY

Lieutenant Enos Reeves of the Pennsylvania Line.

Mount Kemble, N. J., January 2, 1781

Yesterday being the last time we (the officers of the regiment) expected to be together, as the arrangement was to take place this day, we had an elegant regimental dinner and entertainment, at which all the field and other officers were present, with a few from the German regiment, who had arrived with the men of their regiment that belong to the Penna. Line. We spent the day very pleasantly and the evening till about ten o'clock as cheerfully as we could wish, when we were disturbed by the huzzas of the soldiers upon the Right Division, answered by those on the Left.

I went on the Parade and found numbers in small groups whispering and busily running up and down the line. In a short time a gun was fired upon the right and answered by one on the right of the Second Brigade, and a skyrocket thrown from the center of the first, which was accompanied by a general huzza throughout the line, and the soldiers running out with their arms, accoutrements and knapsacks.

I immediately found it was a mutiny, and that the guns and skyrocket were the signals. The officers in general exerted themselves to keep the men quiet, and keep them from turning out. We each applied himself to his own company, endeavored to keep them in their huts and lay by their arms, which they would do while we were present, but the moment we left one hut to go to another, they would be out again. Their excuse was they thought it was an alarm and the enemy coming on.

Next they began to move in crowds to the Parade, going up to the right, which was the place appointed for their rendezvous. Lieut. White of our regiment, in endeavoring to stop one of those crowds, was shot through the thigh, and Capt. Samuel Tolbert in opposing another party was shot through the body, of which he is very ill. They continued huzzaing and fireing in a riotous manner, so that it soon became dangerous for an officer to oppose them by force. We then left them to go their own way.

Hearing a confused noise to the right, between the line of huts and Mrs. Wicks, curiosity led me that way, and it being dark in the orchard I mixed among the crowd and found they had broken open the magazine and were preparing to take off the cannon.

In taking possession of the cannon they forced the sentinel from his post and placed one of their own men. One of the mutineers coming officiously up to force him away (thinking him to be one of our sentinels) received a ball through the head and died instantly.

A dispute arose among the mutineers about firing the alarms with the cannon, and continued for a considerable time—one party aledging that it would arouse the timid soldiery, the other objected because it would alarm the inhabitants. For a while I expected the dispute would be decided by the bayonet, but the gunner in the meantime slipped up to the piece and put a match to it, which ended the affair. Every discharge of the cannon was accompanied by a confused huzza and a general discharge of musketry.

About this time Gen. Wayne and several field officers (mounted) arrived. Gen. Wayne and Col. Richard Butler spoke to them for a considerable time, but it had no effect. Their answer was, they had been wronged and were determined to see themselves righted. He replied that he would right them as far as in his power. They rejoined, it was out of his power; their business was not with the officers, but with Congress and the Governor and Council of the State; 'twas they had wronged and they must right. With that, several platoons fired over the General's head. The General called out, "If you mean to kill me, shoot me at once—here's my breast!" opening his coat. They replied that it was not their intention to hurt or disturb an officer of the Line (two or three individuals excepted); that they had nothing against their officers, and they would oppose any person that would attempt anything of the kind.

A part of the Fourth Regiment was paraded and led on by Capt. Campbell, to recapture the cannon; they were ordered to charge and rush on. They charged but would not advance, then dispersed and left the officer alone. Soon after a soldier from the mob made a charge upon Lieut. Col. William Butler, who was obliged to retreat between the huts to save his life. He went around one hut and the soldier around another to head him, met Capt. Bettin who was coming down the alley, who seeing a man coming towards him on a charge, charged his espontoon to oppose him, when the fellow fired his piece and shot the captain through the body and he died two hours later.

About twelve o'clock they sent parties to relieve or seize the old camp guard, and posted sentinels all round the camp. At one o'clock they moved off towards the left of the line with the cannon and when they reached the centre they fired a shot. As they came down the line, they turned the soldiers out of every hut, and those who would not go with them were obliged to hide till they were gone. They continued huzzaing and a disorderly firing till they went off, about two o'clock, with drums and fifes playing, under command of the sergeants, in regular platoons, with a front and rear guard.

Gen. Wayne met them as they were marching off and endeavored to persuade them back, but to no purpose; he then inquired which way they were going, and they replied either to Trenton or Philadelphia. He begged them not to attempt to go to the enemy. They declared it was not their intention, and that they would hang any man who would attempt it, and for that, if the enemy should come out in consequence of this revolt, they would turn back and fight them. "If that is your sentiments," said the General, "I'll not leave you, and if you wont allow me to march in your front, I'll follow in your rear."

This day Col. Stewart and Richard Butler joined Gen. Wayne in hopes they could turn them when they grew cooler, being much agitated with liquor when they went off; it being New Years Day, they had drawn half a pint per man. The men have continued going off in small parties all day. About one o'clock one hundred head of cattle came in from the eastward, which they drove off to their main body, which lay in a wood near Vealtown, leaving a few behind for the use of the officers.

When we came to draw provisions and State stores this day, we found that near half of the men of our regiment had remained.

The men went off very civilly last night to what might have been expected from such a mob. They did not attempt to plunder our officers' huts or insult them in the least, except those who were obstinate in opposing them. They did not attempt to take with them any part of the State stores, which appears to me a little extraordinary, for men when they get but little want more.

The militia are called out—they are to assemble at Chatham—in order to oppose the enemy if they come out, or the mutineers if they attempt going to them.

—REEVES, "Extracts," *Penn. Mag. of Hist. and Biog.*, XXI, 72-75.

3. THE BRITISH PLAN TO PROFIT BY THE MUTINY

Diary of Captain Frederick Mackenzie of the Royal Welsh Fusiliers.

January 4, 1781. Thick weather, and heavy rain from 5 this evening.

Undoubted intelligence received that the whole Pennsylvania Line have mutinied. They began on Monday the 1st instant by seizing all the artillery, military stores and provisions, and marched that evening from their huts at Morristown to an advantageous piece of ground about 7 miles from thence, where they took post. In moving off, they passed General Waynes quarters, where they huzzaed for officers and soldiers without pay, clothing or provisions; then for Thirteen Kings without breeches. Wayne desired to know what they would have, and what they intended; they said they were determined to go to the Congress at Philadelphia, to demand their arrears of pay, clothing and provisions, and their dismission.

On Tuesday they marched on to Middlebrook, and yesterday to Brunswick. They amount to about 1200 men. Two companies of riflemen from Bottle Hill marched off to join them, without the militia daring to molest them. All the boats on the Delaware have been secured so as to prevent the mutineers from making use of them to pass the river to Philadelphia. The country is in great confusion, and the persons in authority under Congress dread the effects of this revolt, as the people in general are tired of the oppression and difficulties they suffer and earnestly wish for a return of peace and the old Government.

In consequence of this information the Commander in Chief has ordered the British Grenadiers and Light Infantry, three battalions of Hessian Grenadiers, and the Jagers, to march at day break tomorrow towards Denyces Ferry, from whence if there is occasion he intends to go with them to South Amboy, in Jersey, to favor the revolt and keep the militia back.

A person has been sent to them to assure the mutineers that in this struggle for their just rights and liberties, they will be assisted by a body of British troops; that if they will lay down their arms they shall be pardoned all past offences, be paid all the pay due them by Congress, and not be required to serve unless they chuse it. They are desired to send Commissioners to Amboy to treat for them, to whom safe conduct shall be given, and to whom the sincerity of these proposals shall be explained. They are advised to move and take post behind South River, in which situation nothing can approach them, and where they can be immediately supported from hence. They are desired to consider the total inability of Congress to satisfy their just demands, even if they were inclined to grant them, and they are warned of the severity with which numbers of them will be punished, if they suffer themselves to be satisfied with the promises of Congress, and return to their service.

This letter is addressed, "To the persons chosen by the Pennsylvania Line to head them in their struggle for their rights."

'Tis said they have chosen a British serjeant (a deserter) for their leader, and have given him the rank of Major General.

—MACKENZIE, *Diary*, II, 442-444.

4."THIS SURPRIZING AFFAIR HAS BEEN BROUGHT TO A HAPPY ISSUE"

General John Sullivan to the French minister.

Trenton, N. J., January 13, 1781

The soldiers in general shew no disposition to injure their officers though some who were intoxicated with liquors discharged their muskets, killed one officer and wounded three or four. Part of the division moved a few miles that evening [January 1], and the remainder followed them the next morning, when the whole assumed a military order under the command of their sergeants, and marched without offering the least insult to the inhabitants, except in one instance for which the culprit was immediately apprehended and delivered over to the civil power. The inhabitants say that on their march they never suffered the soldiers to enter their houses even for water, nor was any article taken from them during their march.

Upon their taking post at Princeton it began to be suspected that their intentions were to join the enemy, but they persevered in declaring their detestation of the British and their attachment to the cause of their country. They said they were only seeking a redress of grievances, which when obtained they would cheerfully return to their duty. And if the enemy appeared in the interim they would fight them with desperation.

This however was not fully credited untill they seized and brought to Gen. Waine, who with Col. Butler and Stewart remained among them without command, two British emissaries from Sir Henry Clinton with a written invitation promising them great rewards if they would march to South River about 20 miles distant from Princeton where he would cover them with a body of British troops. The spies were delivered over to Gen. Waine and, after Governor Reeds arrival, to him, but afterwards by their request returned to them. The board of sergeants, who had assumed the command, issued orders next morning, stating the facts and declaring that the Pennsylvania Line dispised a treachery and meanness like that of Benedict Arnold, that their views were honorable and their attachment to the cause of their country unalterable, and they were only seeking redress of grievances from men of honor. When Governor Reed came to Princeton they received him with every mark of respect and esteem. They mentioned to him the grounds of their complaints which were principally the two first mentioned.

He made them some proposals and communications from the Committee of Congress which were readily accepted. They were then requested to march to Trenton, which they agreed to, and delivered to the Committee of Congress the two spies sent from Sir Henry Clinton, who were tried by a board of officers, condemned and executed on the 11th instant. The Committee of Congress have appointed Commissioners to determine respecting their inlistments, to discharge such as are entitled thereto, and to give them the necessary certificates. This seems to be perfectly satisfactory to them; many of those discharged are now offering to reinlist upon having a furlough for a short time.

Thus, Sir, has this surprizing affair been brought to a happy issue. Perhaps history does not furnish an instance of so large a body of troops revolting from the command of their officers, marching in such exact order, without doing the least injury to individuals, and remaining in this situation for such a length of time, without division or confusion among themselves, and then returning to their duty as soon as their reasonable demands were complied with. This conduct ought to convince the British how much they mistake the disposition of the Americans at large when they assert that they would willingly join them if not overawed by their tyrannic rulers. Here was a large body composed as well of foreigners as natives, having no officer to command them and no force to prevent their joining the enemy for which they had repeated invitations, yet, though they well knew they were liable to the severest punishment for their revolt, they disdained the British offers with a firmness that would have done honor to the antient Romans, and through the whole have shown the greatest respect to the Committee of Congress, to the Governor and members of the Council for the State of Pensylvania, and expressed the highest confidence in the justice of their civil rulers and have not through the whole deviated from that order and regularity which upon other occasions must have done honor to military discipline.

P. S. One circumstance ought not to be omitted which in my opinion does the insurgents much honor. When they delivered up the British emissaries Governor Reed offered them a hundred gold guineas, which they refused, saying that what they did was only a duty they owed that country, and that they neither received nor would receive any reward but the approbation of that country for which they had so often fought and bled.

—HAMMOND, ed., *Letters and Papers of Sullivan*, XV, 263-265.

5. WASHINGTON DEALS FIRMLY WITH THE JERSEY MUTINEERS

George Washington to the Commission for Redressing the Grievances of the New Jersey Line.

Ringwood, January 27, 1781

Gentlemen: The fatal tendency of that spirit which has shown itself in the Pensylvania and Jersey lines, and which derived so much encouragement from impunity in the case of the former determined me at all events to pursue a different conduct with respect to the latter. For this purpose I detached a body of troops under Major Genl. Howe with orders to compel the mutineers to unconditional submission and execute on the spot a few of the principal incendiaries. This has been effected this morning; and we have reason to believe the mutinous disposition of the troops is now completely subdued and suceeded by a genuine penitence.

But having punished guilt and supported authority, it now becomes proper to do justice. I therefore wish the Commissioners, as soon as convenient to enter upon the objects for which they have been appointed. But I think it my duty to observe to them the necessity of the greatest caution in discussing one article, the terms of the inlistments of the troops. In transacting this with the Pensylvanians for want of proper care, the greatest part of the line has been dismissed, though only a small proportion was intitled to a dismission. Authentic and unequivocal proofs have been since found, that a majority of the discharged men were fairly and explicitly inlisted for the war. This evil arose from admitting the oaths of the individuals themselves, before the vouchers could be assembled. From the temper of the soldiery who will scruple no means of getting rid of the service it becomes necessary to admit none but the most unsuspicious evidence in their favour. Generally on investigation the complaints on this head have appeared ill founded, and as the presumption is strong against the soldier, the proofs of an unfair detention ought to be equally strong. Men are extremely wanted, it is at an infinite expence they are procured and they ought not lightly to be released from their engagements.

Whenever a complaint has been made to me, I have invariably directed an inquiry, for I have ever considered it as not less impolitic than unjust in our service to use fraud in engaging or retaining men; but as I mentioned above, the complaint has much oftner. been found to originate in the levity of the soldier than in truth. I have the honor etc.

—FITZPATRICK, ed., *Writings of Washington*, XXI, 147-148.

CHAPTER NINETEEN

The Home Front in the War

IT DID NOT *take long for the Patriot leaders to realize that there was much more to winning the war than ambushing Redcoats. The war had to be fought on the home front as well as on the battlefield. Committees of safety, state governments, and the Continental Congress had not only to raise men for the army, but to supply them with arms, powder, equipment, medicines, food, clothing and a hundred other necessities. To keep the armies properly supplied without a central fiscal system, or an effective machinery of taxation, required heroic exertions. Desperate efforts were made on various levels, local, state and interstate, to hold the price and wage line in the face of printing-press inflation, for military and civilian leaders alike recognized that unless prices and wages were brought under control, the cost of fighting the war would be prohibitive. At the same time speculation, profiteering, cornering the market and hoarding posed heavy problems for the military who, from time to time, had to impress the goods and services of civilians.*

Central to the problem was the lack of a taxing power by Congress, which had merely the power to levy requisitions; when the states proved delinquent in meeting these—as they all did—paper currency seemed the only way out. Inevitably it depreciated, and eventually the phrase "not worth a Continental" became a part of the American vocabulary. Foreign loans helped stave off total bankruptcy, but inflation and repudiation left ugly scars. Yet in the perspective of history paper money seems not only the inevitable solution, but probably that one which spread the costs of the war most equitably over the population at large.

I. MUNITIONS, SUPPLIES AND IMPRESSMENT

From the first, the Patriot leaders were concerned with the desperate need for gunpowder, of which saltpeter (potassium nitrate) was a major component, and for arms. Pennsylvania, a center for arms manufacturing, rushed production as soon as hostilities began. But as prices for materials and parts mounted, arms makers found it necessary to seek an upward revision of their contracts. As a result of higher domestic costs muskets made under contract in Pennsylvania averaged $12 apiece as against 24 livres or about five dollars for those imported from France. Fortunately for the Patriot army the cheaper French arms were quickly made available; well over 100,000 French arms were imported during the Revolution for the use of the Continental forces.

From time to time it was necessary to impress supplies, provisions, wagons and horses for carrying on the war. But the Patriot authorities, reluctant to antagonize civilians or jeopardize property rights, trod softly. Washington told the Continental Congress in December 1777, "I confess I have felt myself greatly embarrassed with respect to a vigorous exercise of military power. An ill-placed humanity perhaps and a reluctance to give distress may have restrained me too far." In 1780 he justified impressment on the ground that "Our affairs are in so deplorable a condition (on the score of provisions) as to fill the mind with the most anxious fears. . . . Men half-starved, imperfectly cloathed, riotous, and robbing the country people of their subsistence from shear necessity."

During his campaign in the South, Nathanael Greene found it necessary to seize wagons when wagoners proved unco-operative. But the most desperate need was for horses. After Guilford Courthouse, Cornwallis began his retreat to the North Carolina coast on March 18, 1781. A month later he headed north for Virginia, having seized swift-blooded horses to mount the dragoons of Tarleton. Greene was handicapped in his pursuit as he found that Marion and his partisans were impressing horses for themselves rather than turning them over to the regular army. In desperation Greene's officers began to seize horses wherever they could locate them. On March 24, 1781, Governor Jefferson wrote Greene complaining that his officers had made illegal impressments, and on April 1 enclosed a set of resolutions of the Virginia legislature demanding restitution. Greene sent back a stinging rebuke.

1. "I AM DETERMINED NEVER TO HAVE SALT PETRE OUT OF MY MIND"

John Adams to James Warren.

October 21, 1775

We must bend our attention to salt petre. We must make it. While Britain is Mistress of the Sea and has so much influence with foreign courts we cannot depend upon a supply from abroad.

It is certain that it can be made here, because it is certain that it has been formerly and more latterly. Dr. Graham, of White Plains in the Colony of New York, told me that he has made some thousands of pounds weight many years ago, by means of a German servant whom he bought and found to be good for nothing else.

Messrs. De Witts—one of Windham, the other of Norwich—have made a considerable quantity, a sample of which has been shewn me by Col. Dyer, and they have made a large collection of materials for making more.

Mr. Wisner of New York informs me that his son has made a quantity of very good, also by the method published by the Continental Congress.

Two persons belonging to York Town in this Colony have made one hundred and twenty weight, have received the premium and are making more.

A gentleman in Maryland made some last June from tobacco house earth.

Mr. Randolph, our venerable President, affirms to me that every planter almost in that Colony has made it from tobacco house earth. That the process is so simple that a child can make it. It consists in nothing but making a lixivium from the earth which is impregnated with it, and then evaporating the lixivium. That there is certainly discovered in Virginia a vast quantity of the rocks of salt petre. That there are salt petre rocks, he says, all chemists and naturalists who have written agree, and that he was informed by many gentlemen in Virginia, cautious, incredulous men, of strict honour and veracity, that they have been to see the rocks and tryed them and found them by experiment to be the very rock of salt petre.

The old gentleman, in short, who is not credulous nor inthusiastical but very steady, solid and grave, is as sanguine and confident as you can conceive, that it is the easiest thing in the world to make it, and that the tobacco colonies alone are sufficient to supply the Continent forever.

Every Colony, my friend, must set up works at the public expense.

I am determined never to have salt petre out of mind, but to insert some stoke or other about it in every letter for the future. It must be had.
—*Warren-Adams Letters*, I, 158-159.

2. Prices and Wages Add to Gunsmiths' Difficulties

[December 1776]

The Gunlock Makers to the Honorable the Committee of Safety.

The humble address and petition of James Walsh and Samuel Kinder, gunlock makers of the City of Philadelphia, sheweth:

That your Petitioners, from many unforeseen difficulties attending their business, and the extravagant advance on the necessities of life, have been obliged to solicit your honorable board for redress.

At the commencement they had materials to procure which were new and uncommon; hands to instruct who were strangers and unlearned, and even those to purchase at double their value; steel to provide, in which article their loss is manifest to their acquaintance. Still hoping that their perseverance would surmount every difficulty, they continued with labour and assiduity. Notwithstanding which, they now find it impossible to subsist, as their most painful endeavors bear no proportion to the present rate of things. Files are now double what they have been, and some treble; vices, double; steel, scarce any to be found good; thirty to forty shillings advance on one hundred bushels of coal; journeymen's wages still rising; your Petitioners limited; and the enormous price of every other necessity too well known to trouble your Honors with a repetition.

Your Petitioners humbly beg your Honors to take their case into consideration and act therein as to your Honors shall seem meet, and your Petitioners, as in duty bound, etc.

JAMES WALSH
SAMUEL KINDER
—Archives, Pennsylvania Historical Commission.

3. "Are Horses Dearer Than the Liberties of the People?"

Nathanael Greene to Governor Thomas Jefferson.

April 28, 1781

. . . I was very particular in giving my orders to guard against the evils complained of . . . and I have no wish to screen a single officer who has wantonly invaded the property of the people or offered any insult to the inhabitants; but I wish the improper conduct of a few officers may not be made to operate as a punishment upon the whole army. Particular situations and particular circumstances often make measures necessary that have the specious show of oppression, because they carry with them consequences pointed and distressing to individuals. It is to be lamented that this is the case; but pressing circumstances make it political and sometimes unavoidable.

When we retired over the Dan, our force was too small to stop the progress of the enemy, or mark the limits of their approach. We appealed to the only means left us to save your country and prevent the destruction of a virtuous little army. Men were called for; they turned out with a spirit that did honor to themselves and their country. Horses were wanted to mount our dragoons; they could not be procured but by virtue of impress warrants. You was convinced of the fact, and therefore furnished me with the warrants for the purpose. I took the most advisable and, as I thought, most effectual means to have the business conducted with propriety; and I cannot but think the gentlemen generally who were intrusted with the execution of my orders were governed entirely by a principle of public good. Some mistakes and several abuses appear to have happened in impressing stud-horses instead of geldings; but those mistakes arose from the necessity of mounting our dragoons in such a manner as to give us an immediate superiority over the enemy, as well as in the quality of the horses as their number. The people complained; I was ready to redress their grievances; some of the most valuable horses were returned; and I shall direct some others to be restored, notwithstanding the great inconvenience which must inevitably attend this army by it. The Assembly of your State appear to have taken up the matter from a principle acknowledged to be virtuous, but from its tendency must be allowed to be impolitic.

The rights of individuals are as dear to me as to any man; but the safety of a community I have ever considered as an object more valuable. In politics, as well as in everything else, a received and established maxim is, that greater evils should, in every instance, give way to lesser misfortunes. In war it is often impossible to conform to all the ceremonies of law and equal justice; and to attempt it would be productive of greater misfortunes to the public from the delay than all the inconveniences which individuals may suffer.

Your Excellency must be sensible of the innumerable inconveniences I had to labor under at the time, and the variety of difficulties that still surround us. Nothing but light-horse can enable us, with the little army we have, to appear in the field; and nothing but a superiority in cavalry can prevent the enemy from cutting to pieces every detachment coming to join the army or employed in collecting supplies. From the open state of this country their services are particularly necessary, and unless we can keep up the corps of cavalry, and constantly support a superiority, it will be out of our power to act or to prevent the enemy from overrunning the country and commanding all its resources.

The Assembly, I fear, by their resolves have destroyed my hopes and expectations on this head. Under the law as it at present stands, it is certain nothing can be done. By limiting dragoon horses to the narrow price of five thousand pounds, it amounts only to a prohibition, and cuts off the prospect of any future supplies. At this moment the enemy are greatly superior to us; and unless Virginia will spring immediately to the most generous exertions, they will indubitably continue so. It is in vain to expect protection from an army which is not supported, or make feeble efforts upon narrow principles of prudence or economy; they only serve to procrastinate the war, and tire out the patience of the people. Already have we experienced, in many instances, the ill consequences of neglecting the army when surrounded with difficulties and threatened with ruin. Great expense of blood and treasure have attended this policy; and to redress the grievances of a few individuals when it will entail a calamity on the community, will be neither political or just. If horses are dearer to the inhabitants than the lives of subjects, or the liberties of the people, there will be no doubt of the Assembly persevering in their late resolution; otherwise I hope they will reconsider the matter, and not oblige me to take a measure which cannot fail to bring ruin upon the army, and fresh misfortunes upon the country.

—Greene, *Life of Nathanael Greene*, III, 288-290.

II. HOLDING THE PRICE AND WAGES LINE

On the verge of hostilities Congress not only imposed nonimportation regulations but fixed schedules to restrain the increase in the prices of articles already imported. Alexander Hamilton, the fiery young Patriot, applauded Congress' action in his treatise A Full Vindication *(December 1774). Nonetheless the war years were marked by a rapid rise in the cost of living, an astonishing decline in the value of Continental paper money, and an orgy of profiteering and black-marketeering. To meet this threat the New England states sent delegates to a convention at Providence toward the close of 1776, where a formula was adopted for curbing wages and prices. This action was defended on the ground that something had to be done to sustain the morale of the armed forces, increasingly resentful of profiteering back home by farmer, merchant and laborer. The resentment of the soldier to high prices and profiteering was expressed by Nathanael Greene early in the war.*

1. "The Farmers Are Extortionate"

Nathanael Greene to Governor Samuel Ward of Rhode Island.

Camp on Prospect Hill, December 31, 1775

. . . You misunderstood me, Dear Sir, or I wrote what I did not mean. It was not the lower class of people that I meant to complain of, but the merchants and wealthy planters, who I think does not exert themselves as they ought. This is no time for giting riches but to secure what we have got. Every shadow of oppresseon and extortion ought to disappear, but instead of that we find many articles of merchandise multiplied four fold their original value, and most cent per cent [100%]. The farmers are extortionate where ever their situation furnishes them with an opportunity. These are the people that I complain mostly of; they are wounding the cause.

When people are in distress its natural for them to try every thing and every where to get relief, and to find oppresseon instead of relief from these two orders of men will go near to driving the poorer sort to desperation. It will be good policey in the United Colonies to render the poorer sort of people as easy and happy under their present circumstances as possible, for they are creatures of a day, and present gain and gratification, tho small, has more weight with them than such greater advantagies at a distance. A good politician must and will consider the temper of the times and the prejudices of the people he has to deal with, when he takes his measures to execute any great design. The current sentiment in the New England Colonies greatly favors the opposition, but if the distresses of the people are multiplied their oppinions may change. They naturally look back upon their former happy situation and contrast that with their present wretched condition, and conclude that the source of all their misery originates in the despute with Great Britain. . . .

We have suffered prodigiously for want of wood; many regiments has been obliged to eat their provision raw for want of fireing to cook, and notwithstanding we have burnt up all the fences and cut down all the trees for a mile round the camp, our suffering has been inconceivable. The barracks has been greatly delayed for want of stuff; many of the troops are yet in their tents and will be for some time, especially the officers. The fatigues of the campaign, the suffering for want of wood and cloathing, has made abundance of the soldiers heartily sick of service.

The Connecticut troops went off in spite of all that could be done to prevent it; but they met with such an unfavorable reception at home that many are returning to camp again already. The people upon the roads exprest so much abhorrence at their conduct for quiting the army that it was with difficulty they got provisions. I wish all the troops now going home may meet with the same contempt.

—Greene Papers.

2. Wage and Price Regulation by the Providence Convention

December 31, 1776

This Committee taking into consideration the unbounded avarice of many persons, by daily adding to the now most intollerable exhorbitant price of every necessary and convenient article of life, and also the most extravagant price of labour in general, which at this time of distress, unless a speedy and effectual stop be put thereto, will be attended with the most fatal and pernicious consequences, as it not only disheartens and disaffects the soldiers who have nobly entered into service, for the best of causes, by obliging them to give such unreasonable prices for those things that are absolutely needful for their very existence that their pay is not sufficient to subsist them, but it is also very detrimental to the country in general.

Wherefore it is recommended by this Committee, that the rates and prices hereafter enumerated be affixed and settled within the respective states in New England, to wit:

Farming Labour in the summer season shall not exceed three shillings and four pence per diem, and so in the usual proportion at other seasons of the year, and the labour of mechanics and tradesmen and other labour to be computed according to the usages and customs that have heretofore been adopted and practised in different parts of the several states compared with farming labour. . . .

—CONVENTION OF THE NEW ENGLAND STATES, Journals.

The states represented at the meeting acted with commendable speed. New Hampshire, Massachusetts, Connecticut and Rhode Island almost immediately enacted legislation incorporating the wage and price schedule recommended by the Providence Convention. In addition to fixing the scale of wages for farm labor Rhode Island set maximum wages as follows:

[1777]
per diem

Teaming work, the teamster finding himself and cattle, for one hand
    with cart or waggon, one yoke of oxen, and a good draught-horse,
    or two yoke of oxen . . . . 13s.
Teaming to and from sea port markets and for the army per ton per
    mile, if not more than one mile 4s. For every mile after the first
    mile out 1s. 6d.
Horse-keeping, at sea port towns per night or 24 hours, 2s. 6d.
Horse-shoeing all round, with steel corks, heel and toe, 6s.
Ox-shoeing and other blacksmith's work in the same proportion.
Ships iron-work—weight-work at 3d. per lb. and all light work in the
    same proportion, excepting cast iron.
House-carpenters, finding themselves . . . . 5s.
Ship carpenters, finding themselves . . . . 6s.
Caulkers, finding themselves . . . . 7s.
Masons, finding themselves . . . . 6s. 6d.
Taylors making a plain suit of best broadcloth cloths, 24s. and their
    daily wage, the employer finding them at . . . . 3s.
Trucking, 1s. 6d. per hogshead, and other things in proportion
Best beaver hats at 42s. best felt hats at 8s.
Coopers, finding themselves . . . . 5s.
    setting and finding hogshead hoops, 3d. each
    setting and finding barrel hoops, 2d. each
Barbers for shaving, 3d.

—Rhode Island Records, 1772-1777, pp. 641 *et seq.*,
State Archives, Providence.

3. A LEARNED DOCTOR OPPOSES PRICE CONTROLS

The proceedings of the Providence Convention were laid before Congress on January 28, 1777, and evoked a spirited debate. On February 4, a resolution of the Committee of the Whole was debated setting forth the opinion of the committee

    that the peculiar situation of the New England states, whose communication with Congress was in a great measure cut off, and who were invaded or threatened with an immediate invasion by the enemy, rendered the appointment and meetings of the Committee proper and necessary, and consequently worthy of the approbation of Congress.

The motion was carried that day, but, on reconsideration, was defeated by one vote, only to be reopened on February 14. The debates of that day were carefully preserved in the diary of one of the chief participants, Dr. Benjamin Rush, whom we have already met on several occasions. They were strikingly parallel to the arguments following the close of World War II between those who favored continuing price controls and rationing and those who maintained that artificial price controls were ineffective so long as bank credit was permitted to expand at a disturbing rate.

From the Diary of Dr. Benjamin Rush.

February 14, 1777

Upon the question whether the Congress should recommend to the States to adopt the plan for reducing and regulating the price of labor, manufactures, imports, and provisions which had been adopted in the four New England states:

It was said in the negative by *Mr. James Smith*, that such a recommendation would interfere with the domestic policies of each State, which were of too delicate a nature to be touched by the Congress.

Dr. Rush: I am against the whole of the resolution. It is founded in the contrary of justice, policy and necessity as has been declared in the resolution. The wisdom and power of government have been employed in all ages to regulate the price of necessaries to no purpose. It was attempted in England in the reign of Edward II by the English parliament, but without effect. The laws for limiting the price of everything were repealed, and Mr. Hume who mentions this fact records even the very attempt as a monument of human folly.

The Congress with all its authority has failed in a former instance of regulating the price of goods. You have limited Bohea tea to ¾ of a dollar, and yet it is daily sold before your eyes for 30s. The Committee of Philadelphia limited the price of West India goods about a year ago. But what was the consequence? The merchants, it is true, sold their rum, sugar and molasses at the price limited by the committee, but they charged a heavy profit upon the barrel, or the paper which contained the rum or the sugar.

Consider, Sir, the danger of failing in this experiment. The salvation of this continent depends upon the authority of this Congress being held as sacred as the cause of liberty itself. Suppose we should fail of producing the effects we wish for by the resolution before you. Have we any character to spare? Have we committed no mistakes in the management of the public affairs of America? We have, Sir. It becomes us therefore to be careful of the remains of our authority and character.

It is a common thing to cry aloud of the rapacity and extortion in every branch of business, etc., among every class of men. This has led some people to decry the *public virtue* of this country. We estimate our virtue by a false barometer when we measure it by the price of goods. The extortion we complain of arises only from the excessive quantity of our money. Now, Sir, a failure in this attempt to regulate the price of goods will encrease the clamors against the rapacity of dealers, and thus depreciate our public virtue.

Consider, Sir, the consequence of measuring our virtue by this false standard. You will add weight to the arguments used at St. James's to explode patriotism altogether, and by denying its existence in this country destroy it forever. Persuade a woman that there is no such thing as chastity, and, if there is, that she does not possess it, and she may be easily seduced if she was as chaste as Diana. Sir, the price of goods may be compared to a number of light substances in a bason of water. The hand may keep them down for a while, but nothing can detain them on the bottom of the bason but an abstraction of the water. The continent labours under a universal malady. From the crown of her head to the sole of her feet she is full of disorders. She requires the most powerful tonic medicines. The resolution before you is nothing but an opiate. It may compose the continent for a night, but she will soon awaken again to a fresh sense of her pain and misery.

Colonel Richard Lee, in the affirmative. Mr. President, the learned Doctor has mistook the disorder of the continent. She labours under a spasm, and spasms, he knows, require *palliative* medicine. I look upon the resolution before you only as a temporary remedy. But it is absolutely necessary. It is true the regulations formerly recommended by Congress were not faithfully carried into execution, but this was owing to the want of regular government. New and regular governments have been instituted in every part of America, and these will enable all classes of people to carry the resolution into execution.

Mr. Samuel Chase, in the affirmative. Mr. President, this is a necessary resolution. It is true it failed formerly in Philadelphia because it abounded with Tories. But it succeeded in Maryland. It must be done. The mines of Peru would not support a war at the present high price of the necessaries of life. Your soldiers cannot live on their pay. It must be raised unless we limit the price of the clothing and other articles necessary for them.

Mr. Seargant, Negative. The price of goods cannot be regulated while the quantity of our money and the articles of life are allowed to fluctuate.

Colonel James Wilson, Negative. There are certain things, Sir, which absolute power cannot do. The whole power of the Roman emperors could not add a single letter to the alphabet. Augustus could not compel old bachelors to marry. He found out his error, and wisely repealed his edict lest he should bring his authority into contempt. Let us recommend the resolution to the *consideration* of the States only without giving our opinion on it, that they may discuss it with unbiassed minds.

Dr. Witherspoon, Negative. Sir, it is a wise maxim to avoid those things which our enemies wish us to practise. Now I find that our enemies have published the act of the assembly of Connecticut for regulating the price of necessaries in the New York paper in order to show our distress from that quarter. Remember, laws are not almighty. It is beyond the power of despotic princes to regulate the price of goods. I fear if we fail in this measure we shall weaken the authority of Congress. We shall do mischief by teaching the continent to *rest* upon it. If we limit *one* article, we must limit *every* thing, and this is impossible.

Mr. John Adams, Negative. Perhaps I may here speak against the sense of my constituents, but I cannot help it. I much doubt the justice, policy and necessity of the resolution. The high price of many articles arises from their scarcity. If we regulate the price of imports we shall immediately put a stop to them forever.

Dr. Rush. Sir, it has been said that the high price of goods in Philadelphia arose from the monopolies and extortion of the Tories. Here I must say the Tories are blamed without cause. A similar spirit of speculation prevails among the Whigs in Philadelphia. They are disposed to realise their money in lands or goods. But this is not owing to any timidity or disaffection among them. They fear the further depreciation of your money by future emissions. Stop your emissions of money and you will stop speculation. I am not apt to reply to *words*, much less to *play* upon them. The gentleman from Virginia has miscalled the malady of the continent. It is not a spasm, but a dropsy. I beg leave to prescribe two remedies for it. (1) Raising the interest of the money we borrow to six per cent. This, like a cold bath, will give an immediate *spring* to our affairs; and (2) *taxation*. This, like *tapping*, will diminish the quantity of our money, and give a proper value to what remains.

The resolution was amended. The plan of the four New England States was *referred* only to the other States, to act as they thought proper.

—RUSH, Diary. Library Company of Philadelphia, Ridgeway Branch.

III. FURTHER EFFORTS TO HOLD THE PRICE LINE

In November 1777, after the New England states had found it expedient to scuttle their price and wage codes, Congress recommended a broad scheme of price and wage regulations. A call for three regional conventions was issued. Of these, only one was held and set schedules for labor and commodities—a Northern and Middle States convention at New Haven. "Why do we complain of a partial infringement of liberty manifestly tending to the preservation of the whole?" the convention asked. "Must the lunatick run uncontrouled to the destruction of himself and neighbours merely because he is under the operation of medicines which may in time work his cure?"

The problem was exigent and demanded the attention of Congress, of interstate conventions, of state legislatures and of town conventions, as well as of theoreticians. The delicate balance between prices and wages was carefully analyzed by one writer in the New Jersey Gazette. *Conceding that in general "trade can best regulate its own prices," this writer contended that on extraordinary occasions legislative intervention was justifiable. Such schedules, he urged, should bear equitably on all groups in the community and should favor the production of necessaries.*

In addition to state laws and town regulations, local courts, Revolutionary committees and self-appointed vigilante groups sought to enforce price and wage controls, and to punish profiteers and monopolizers. At Fishkill, New York, a group of housewives took the law into their own hands, weighed out their own purchases, and remitted the money to the Dutchess County Com-

mittee. A Schenectady weaver was denounced for charging too much for weaving linen, and a Boston hatter who exceeded the regulated price was named "an enemy of his country." In Boston five "Tory villains" were punished for profiteering by a vigilante group under the leadership of a masked man called "Joyce Junior," a veteran agitator, and a new order of "female mobility" disciplined the Boston merchant, Thomas Boylston.

1. Joyce Junior Rides Again

Letter of Abigail Adams.

April 20, 1777

About eleven o'clock yesterday William Jackson, Dick Green, Harry Perkins and Sargent, of Cape Ann, and A. Carry, of Charlestown, were carted out of Boston under the direction of Joice junior, who was mounted on horseback with a red coat, a white wig and a drawn sword, with drum and fife following. A concourse of people to the amount of five hundred followed. They proceeded as far as Roxbury, when he ordered the cart to be tipped up, then told them if they were ever caught in town again it should be at the expense of their lives. He then ordered his gang to return, which they did immediately without any disturbance.

Monday, 21st

Have now learned the crime of the carted Tories. It seems they have refused to take paper money, and offered their goods lower for silver than for paper; bought up articles at a dear rate and then would not part with them for paper.

—Adams, *Familiar Letters*, pp. 262-263.

2. "Trade Can Best Regulate Its Own Prices"

From the *New Jersey Gazette*, March 11, 1778.

... in order to find out how to proportion the limitations duly, it may be necessary to have recourse to calculation.

By the law lately passed for regulating prices, the legislature seem to have aimed at fixing most of the articles of internal produce at double the former prices. This may perhaps be a proper standard for some articles; but when the matter is fairly considered, it will be found that the same reasons which require the prices of some things to be doubled, will call for a similar advance on some others, and on others again a much greater. Of the latter kind are such articles as derive their value chiefly from labour, and require the use of some commodity, either imported from abroad or which, from its scarcity, cannot be obtained but at a very high price. To explain my meaning I shall subjoin a few calculations.

I. As to farmers. Let us suppose a farm, the annual produce of which is for sale, exclusive of what was necessary for the consumption of such parts of the family as do not labour, would sell in former time for £300.0.0

It is said to be a large allowance to admit that one half of this value is paid for labour, supposing the whole to be done on hire . . . 150.0.0

Annual profit remaining 150.0.0

Supposing the price of labour to be doubled, the labour on the same
farm will be worth 300.0.0
The consumption of the family will be the same, and allow the same
annual profit as formerly 150.0.0
The extraordinary price of salt may be 15.0.0
Allow, moreover, the use of as much rum, tea, sugar and other luxuries that will cost extra 35.0.0
                                                                 —————
                                                              £500.0.0

The farmer ought therefore to have for his produce on an average
now 5*s.* for what he would formerly have sold for 3*s.*, or 1*s.* 8 now
for 1*s.* formerly.

II. As to labourers. Let us suppose a labourer, finding his own provisions and cloathing, formerly earned per annum 45.0.0

That his provisions cost him 20.0.0
And his cloathing 10.0.0
Profit toward maintenance of his family 15.0.0
                                                                 —————
                                                                 45.0.0

Provisions at double price will be 40.0.0
Cloathing will cost at least three times the old price 30.0.0
His profit for the use of his family ought to be at least double as they
must purchase all they consume 30.0.0
                                                                 —————
                                                              £100.0.0

His wages therefore ought to be increased to 10*s.* for every 4*s.*6 he
would formerly have received; or 1*s.*8 now for 9*d.* formerly.

The same proportion will be requisite for mechanicks, handicraftsmen,
lawyers, clerks, etc., so far as their several productions derive their value from
labour; making the proper additions or deductions for what the prices of their
respective materials may exceed or fall short of that proportion.

It will be observed that I have stated the price of labour at double the
former price to the farmer, though I have shewn it must cost more to others;
and that I have stated provisions at double to labourers, etc., though I have said
the farmer ought to sell them at a lower rate. A little reflection will justify
these diversities. As to the first, the farmer, having the advantage of feeding
and, in a great measure, clothing and paying his labourers from his own produce without purchase (to say nothing of the advantage he may derive from
the labour of his children and servants), can always procure at a much cheaper
rate than a person of any other class. And as to the second—suppose the price
of the common articles of provisions should be fixed at the rate of 5*s.* now, for
3*s.* formerly, as above stated, if we move but a small allowance for the extraordinary prices of salt, sugar, tea, rum, etc. . . . we shall find the average price of
provisions to labourers, mechanicks, etc., will not be less than doubled. I have
heard it remarked that a great majority of the members of the legislature being
farmers, their limitations are calculated greatly in favour of that class of men.
If there is any truth in the remark, I am persuaded it must arise from their want

of proper information, as I cannot suppose they would designedly oppress others for their own emolument. As faithful representatives of the people, I should suppose they would be particularly watchful that no just ground should be given for a suspicion of this kind. . . .

—*New Jersey Gazette*, March 11, 1778.

3. THE LADIES OF BOSTON STAGE A BOSTON COFFEE PARTY

Abigail to John Adams.

Boston, July 31 [1777]

I have nothing new to entertain you with, unless it is an account of a new set of mobility, which has lately taken the lead in Boston. You must know that there is a great scarcity of sugar and coffee, articles which the female part of the state is very loath to give up, especially whilst they consider the scarcity occasioned by the merchants having secreted a large quantity. There had been much rout and noise in the town for several weeks. Some stores had been opened by a number of people, and the coffee and sugar carried into the market and dealt out by pounds. It was rumored that an eminent, wealthy, stingy merchant (who is a bachelor) had a hogshead of coffee in his store, which he refused to sell to the committee under six shillings per pound.

A number of females, some say a hundred, some say more, assembled with a cart and trucks, marched down to the warehouse and demanded the keys, which he refused to deliver. Upon which, one of them seized him by his neck and tossed him into the cart. Upon his finding no quarter, he delivered the keys, when they tipped up the cart and discharged him; then opened the warehouse, hoisted out the coffee themselves, put it into the truck and drove off.

It was reported that he had personal chastisement among them; but this, I believe, was not true. A large concourse of men stood amazed, silent spectators of the whole transaction. . . .

—ADAMS, ed., *Letters of Mrs. Adams*, I, 109-110.

IV. THE ISSUANCE AND CONTROL OF THE CURRENCY

Lacking the power to tax, dependent on the states for requisitions which they grudgingly met in only small part, and rescued from total bankruptcy by timely foreign loans, Congress found it necessary to turn to the printing presses to finance the war. As the contest proved long and increasingly costly, the government issued twice as much Continental money in the year 1778 as in the three preceding years, and the year 1779 saw that figure increased another two-and-a-half-fold. In addition the states issued around $210 million in paper notes, the overwhelming portion by the Southern states. The indebtedness of the United States government was estimated by a committee of Congress in 1783, and the cost of operating the war by Hamilton in a report to Congress in 1790.

Since currency depreciation set in almost at once, the Patriot authorities, federal, state and local, sought to make paper money legal tender in business transactions. Wherever they could, farmers and merchants tried to get specie, like the brazen tavern keeper for whose story we are indebted to Joseph White, an orderly sergeant in an artillery regiment, who participated in the battles of Trenton and Princeton and received an enlisted man's eight-dollar-a-month pension in 1819. It goes without saying that price and wage controls could not hold up, were people to demand more in paper than in specie, and those who did were held to be enemies of their country, at times punished criminally, and at other times denounced publicly. The unequal struggle to maintain the paper standard in the early period of depreciation is reported by Robert Morton, son of a Philadelphia merchant, who kept a diary during the British occupation of Philadelphia. At the time of these entries he was just seventeen years of age. Newspaper accounts ranged from satirical Tory and British stories ridiculing the effort to maintain the worthless paper, to serious proposals by Patriots for stabilizing the economy.

1. DEBTS AND INFLATION

A. ESTIMATE OF THE DEBT OF THE UNITED STATES, 1783

As reported by the Grand Committee of Congress, April 8, 1783.

Foreign Debt

To the Farmers General of France . . Livres	1,000,000	
To Beaumarchais	3,000,000	
To the King of France, to the end of 1782 . . .	28,000,000	
To ditto for 1783	6,000,000	
Livres	38,000,000 =	$7,037,037
Received on loan in Holland, 1,678,000 florins		671,200
Borrowed in Spain by Mr. Jay		150,000
Interest on Dutch one year, at 4 per cent		26,848
Total foreign debt		$7,885,085

Domestic Debt

Loan Office	$11,463,802	
Interest unpaid for 1781	190,000	
Ditto 1782	687,828	
Credit to sundry persons on Treasurey books	638,042	
Army debt to 31 December 1782 . . .	5,635,618	
Unliquidated ditto	8,000,000	
Deficiencies in 1783	2,000,000	
Total domestic debt		$28,615,290
Aggregate debt		$36,500,375

Interest

On foreign debt, 7,885,085, at 4 per cent	315,403
On domestic debt, 28,615,290, at 6 per cent	1,716,917
On commutation of half-pay, estimated at 5,000,000 at 6 per cent	300,000
Bounty to be paid, estimated at 5,000,000 at 6 per cent . .	30,000
Aggregate of interest	$2,362,320

—HUNT, ed., *Writings of Madison*, I, 443.

B. ALEXANDER HAMILTON'S ESTIMATE OF THE COST OF THE WAR (1790)

Transactions of the Treasury

	Bills of credit	New emissions	Total specie value
1775 and 1776	$ 20,964,666	. . . .	$20,064,666
1777	26,426,333	. . . .	24,986,646
1778	66,965,269	. . . .	24,289,438
1779	149,703,856	. . . .	10,794,620
1780	82,908,320	$ 891,236	3,000,000
1781*	11,408,095	1,179,249	1,942,465
1782	. . . .	. . . .	3,632,745
1783	. . . .	. . . .	3,226,583
Total	$357,476,541	$2,070,485	$91,937,168

Total Expenditures

Expenditures at the treasury	$ 91,937,168
Outstanding certificates of indebtedness	16,708,009
Expended in Europe	5,000,000
State debts	21,000,000
Total cost of war	$134,645,177

—BULLOCK, *Finances of the U. S.*, pp. 174-175.

C. PRICES RISE FANTASTICALLY AS PAPER MONEY SHRINKS IN VALUE

Quantity of Certain Staples That Could Be Purchased in Pennsylvania for £100 in paper currency.

April	Flour cwt.	Sugar cwt.	Iron cwt.	Beef bbl.
1774	105.9	36.4	76.9	36.4
1775	133.3	39.5	77.9	33.3
1776	143.3	30.8	74.8	26.7
1777	83.8	8.89	40.0	10.5
1778	63.2	2.75	11.8	9.78
1779	6.67	0.84	2.65	1.82
1780	1.15	0.30	0.88	0.22
1781	0.71	0.21	0.52	0.11

cwt. = 112 lbs.; bbl. = 225 lbs.

—BEZANSON, *Prices and Inflation during the Revolution*, p. 321.

2. THE DEPRECIATION OF THE CURRENCY THREATENS TOTAL RUIN

Robert Morris to the Commissioners in France.

Philadelphia, December 21, 1776

Gentlemen: . . . I must add to this gloomy picture one circumstance, more distressing than all the rest, because it threatens instant and total ruin to the

---

* In the year 1781 the finances were restored to a specie basis.

American cause, unless some radical cure is applied, and that speedily; I mean the depreciation of the Continental currency. The enormous pay of our Army, the immense expenses at which they are supplied with provisions, clothing and other necessaries, and, in short, the extravagance that has prevailed in most departments of the publick service, have called forth prodigious emissions of paper money, both Continental and Colonial. Our internal enemies, who, alas! are numerous and rich, have always been undermining its value by various artifices, and now that our distresses are wrought to a pitch by the success and near approach of the enemy, they speak plainer and many peremptorily refuse to take it at any rate. Those that do receive it, do it with fear and trembling; and you may judge of its value, even amongst those, when I tell you that £250 Continental money, or 666 2-3 dollars, is given for a bill of exchange of £100 sterling, sixteen dollars for a half-johannes, two paper dollars for one of silver, three dollars for a pair of shoes, twelve dollars for a hat, and so on; a common labourer asks two dollars a day for his work and idles half his time.

All this amounts to real depreciation of the money. The war must be carried on at an expense proportioned to this value, which must inevitably call for immense emissions, and, of course, still further depreciations must ensue. This can only be prevented by borrowing in the money now in circulation. The attempt is made, and I hope will succeed by loan or lottery. The present troubles interrupt those measures here, and as yet I am not informed how they go on in other States, but something more is necessary; force must be inevitably employed, and I fear to see that day. We have already calamities sufficient for any country, and the measure will be full when one part of the American people is obliged to dragoon another, at the same time that they are opposing a most powerful external foe. . . .

—FORCE, *American Archives,* 5th Series, III, 1334.

3. "I Do Not Like Your Rebel Money"

Narrative of Joseph White, sergeant of artillery in the Continental Army.

[December, 1776]

After crossing the [Delaware] river, we were put into the back part of a tavern; the tavernkeeper refused to take rebel money, as he called it. I went to General Putnam and told him that he had everything he wanted, "but he will not take paper money. He calls it rebel money."

"You go and tell him, from me, that if he refuses to take our money, take what you want without any pay."

I went and told the man what the General said.

"Your Yankee general dare not give such orders," said he.

I placed two men at the cellar door, as centries. "Let nobody whatever go down," I said. I called for a light, and two men to go down cellar with me. We found it full of good things, a large pile of cheeses, hams of bacon, a large tub of honey, barrels of cider, and 1 barrel marked cider-royal, which was very strong; also, all kinds of spirit. The owner went to the General to complain.

"The sergeant told me," said the General, "that you refused to take paper money."

"So I did," said he. "I do not like your rebel money."

The General flew round like a top. He called for a file of men. A corporal and four men came. "Take this Tory rascal to the main guard house."

I sent a ham of bacon, one large cheese and a bucket full of cider-royal to General Putnam. He asked who sent them. He told him the sergeant that he gave leave to take them.

"Tell him I thank him," said he.

—WHITE, *Narrative.*

4. "MORE TO FEAR FROM PAPER MONEY THAN FROM BRITISH GENERALS"

Joseph Eggleston, Jr., to Joseph Eggleston, Amelia County, Virginia.

State of Delaware, September 2, 1777

I sit down to answer your letter by Mr. Ellison which he delivered to me this day. He tells me he came from Philadelphia for that purpose, and seems to be pleased with the thoughts of having it in his power to return your favor of lending him the horse to ride to Richmond. I have written twice in answer to those letters which Peter Berry brought out; in those letters I informed Messrs. Cocke and Hardaway that Old Figure was on Staten Island and in possession of the enemy, and therefore not to be purchased by any person among us. I should have been much pleased if it had been in my power to have assisted Berry in purchasing any firm horse for them, but it would have been impracticable if I had seen him.

The horse you mentioned called Bay Richmond could not be had for less than £1500. The prices of every kind of article here would astonish you. You desire I would procure you a good beaver hatt and some other articles. In answer to which part of your letter I would inform you that goods are 200 per cent dearer than they were in Virginia when I left it. I was obliged to buy a hat a few days past, and paid 18 dollars for one of an inferior kind. Boots sell for the *moderate* price of 21 dollars; broad cloth £12 a yard. Rum is 20/ the quart; whiskey 10/. Every other article bears a proportionate price.

But I turn from this prospect to one that can be contemplated with much greater pleasure. I mean our military affairs; for it is my fixed opinion that America has much more to fear from the effects of the large quantities of paper money than from the operations of Howe and all the British generals. Burgoyne has been defeated by General Arnold, has lost his tents, baggage, etc., and is retreating with his broken forces towards Ticonderoga. We are this moment alarmed with some movements of the enemy which the Light Horse must attend to and therefore my letter will be much shorter than it would have been. I will just inform you that the whole army, from General Washington downwards, are in high spirits and make no doubt of keeping the enemy from Philadelphia. . . .

—EGGLESTON, Letter, Morgan Library.

5. THE BANEFUL INFLUENCE OF PAPER MONEY

From the diary of Robert Morton of Philadelphia.

Nov. 27th, 28th, 29th, 30th [*1777*].—These 4 days the fleet [has been] coming up in great numbers. Some part of the army have marched over

Schuylkill, and reports are prevalent that the main part of the army will soon move off. The Americans are moving off their heavy cannon. Gen'l Washington, it is said, is going to Virginia in a few weeks, and the command [is] to devolve upon Gen'l Gates. Great exertions are making, both by the men and women of this city, to support the credit of the paper money legally issued. The women are determined to purchase no goods with hard money. Some of those who agreed to receive paper money have refused it for their goods, and among the rest some of our Society [of Friends].

Dec. 1st, 2nd, 3rd.—Numbers of the fleet [are] daily arriving. None of the large ships have yet come up. A contest has subsisted in this city since the arrival of the fleet, concerning the legal paper currency. The English merchants that came in the fleet will not dispose of their goods without hard money, alleging that no bills are to be bought, no produce to be obtained, and no method can be adopted by which they can send remittances. Numbers of the most respectable inhabitants are using all their influence to support it, and numbers of others who have no regard for the public good are giving out the hard money for what they want for immediate use, thus purchasing momentary gratifications at the expense of the public, for if the circulation of this money should be stopt, many who have no legal money but paper and have no means of obtaining gold and silver, will be reduced to beggary and want, and those who are so lost to every sense of honor, to the happiness of their fellow citizens, and eventually their own good, as to give out their hard money, either for the goods of those who are newcomers, or in the public market where it is now exacted for provisions, will, by their evil example, oblige those who possess hard money, to advance it and ruin the credit of the other money for the present. The consequence of which must be that we shall be shortly drained of our hard cash, the other money rendered useless, no trade by which we can get a fresh supply; our ruin must therefore be certain and inevitable.

This depreciation of the paper currency will not only extend its baneful influence over this city, but over all the continent, as the friends of government and others have been collecting this legal tender for several months past, expecting that in those places in the possession of the British Army it will be of equal value with gold and silver. But from the enemies of the British constitution among ourselves, who give out their hard money for goods, from the almost universal preference of private interest to the public good, and from a deficiency of public virtue, it is highly probable the paper money will fall, and those newcomers, having extracted all our hard money, will leave us in a situation not long to survive our ruin. . . .

—Morton, "Diary," *Penn. Mag. of Hist. and Biog.*, I, 31-33.

V. AN END TO DEPRECIATION: THE FORTY-TO-ONE FORMULA

By 1779 the depreciation of the Continental currency had become alarming, rising from 8 to 1 in January to 38½ to 1 by November. But besides the "Continentals" additional millions were outstanding in quartermaster certificates, which were receipts given in payment by the Army for supplies it requisitioned, in loan-office certificates, and in certificates given soldiers for back pay. Repudiation of the paper had long been urged. Congress finally decided to face reality, which in fact meant repudiation or bankruptcy. On March 18, 1780, it retired the bills in circulation by accepting them in payments due it from the states at one-fortieth of their face value. This wiped the federal-currency slate clean. A timely subsidy from France in May 1781, and French backing for a large loan from the Netherlands forthcoming in November, enabled Robert Morris to make some progress toward returning the country to a specie basis before the war came to an end.

1. Repudiation "to Save Our Estates and Liberties"

March 12, 1778

To the Inhabitants of the United States, from "A Naturalized American."

The hopes of our enemies are now built upon the expences they are putting us to. The question is no more who are poltroons? but whose resources will fail soonest? We must put the trial upon this issue. . . .

The debt of America, though much larger than it need to have been had honesty, economy and good sense prevailed in every department, is not in itself alarming. The Continent, from its different climates and being so well cultivated, hath those internal advantages that most of the necessaries wanted may be furnished out of its own produce; and were patriotic societies to be formed in every State for encouraging the most *useful* arts and manufactures, within a few years it might support itself without going to any foreign market whatsoever.

But, it will be inquired, how are the high prices of things to be reduced in the mean while, without which the war cannot be carried on much longer? This brings me to the main source of our present difficulties—the depreciation of the currency—which must be remedied or we are undone. I doubt not to assert that the *grand* occasion of such depreciation hath been a *redundancy* through the amazing quantities that have been emitted. New emissions must decrease its value yet more. Borrowing what hath been emitted upon loan-office tickets, bearing interest, and then circulating it afresh, continues the evil while it increases our debt.

The only sovereign remedy that can produce a radical cure is the lessening of the currency till there is barely sufficient for circulation—all others are mere temporary palliatives. It is to be feared that the currency exceeds the quantity wanted for circulation by two-thirds, if not four-fifths. Let the Continent agree then to sink the redundancy—or that will sink the Continent. We shall be no losers; the remainder will be worth the whole nominal sum. Can an individual with a single dollar purchase after the proposed diminution what he must otherwise give five for; and with equal ease can he procure the one as the five; he is no real sufferer by the diminution, while the public is a great gainer, for the *fluctuating* value of the currency is cured.

But how is this diminution to be fairly brought about? I humbly apprehend, gentlemen, it may be done as follows, viz. Let one or more, or all the emissions of the *United Colonies*, after certain days, be no longer legal tenders through the Continent—let the bills be paid by every holder to his town collector, as a part of his tax for the current year, or, if more, for future ones, till the whole is exhausted (whatever may be advanced not to be taxed as a part of his estate, and in case of his death to be accounted for in like mode to his successors)—let the bills thus collected be paid to the respective Treasurer of each State, to be by him defaced, and then to be put into the hands of the Continental Treasurer, who shall credit the State for the same as its quota for past, present or future taxes. There would be still in circulation all the emissions of the *United States*, which, if not sufficient, would leave room for all that might be further necessary. . . .

The scheme, gentlemen, is practicable, have we but spirit but to adopt it, for we have *all* the paper among us, the circulation being confined to ourselves. The matter is near a crisis: we have our choice either to part with our paper and so to save our estates and liberties, or to retain it and so doing lose all. We must either submit to the necessity of the day and tax ourselves voluntarily, or we must submit to the parliament of Great-Britain and be taxed for the little property they may leave us, just as their *omnipotence* shall direct. . . .

—*Independent Chronicle*, March 12, 1778.

2. The Stampede to Pay Off Debts in Paper—An English View

November 6, 1780.—A writer in London says:—The incredible fall of continental currency in America may be understood from the following notorious fact, viz.: Ten thousand pounds Maryland currency *was* worth six thousand sterling; ten thousand pounds continental money *is* worth one hundred pounds. The difference makes a loss of five thousand nine hundred pounds sterling, being as sixty to one.

This was the exchange at Philadelphia in June last, and as they had not then heard of Gates's defeat*, it must be now lower. Actions commenced for considerable sums by creditors have been obliged to be withdrawn, or a non-suit suffered; a lawyer of eminence not opening his mouth in a trial of consequence, under a fee of *one thousand pounds*, though the legal fee is about forty, and the debt, if recovered, being paid in continental money, dollar for dollar, worth now but a penny, the difference between a penny and 4*s*. 6*d*. sterling, is lost to the receiver. The Congress having called in the former emissions, forty dollars for one, and giving that *one* in paper, cut off every hope it will hereafter *appreciate*. The freight of a hogshead of tobacco is three hundred pounds, or one hogshead for the carriage of another; instead of the creditor pursuing the debtor with an arrest, the debtor pursues the creditor with a *tender* of continental money and forces the bond out of his hand.

Hence it appears what the best fortunes in that country are reduced to; an unpleasing reflection it must be! for time, which lightens all other losses, aggravates the loss of fortune. Every day we feel it more, because we stand more in want of the conveniences we have been used to. On the other hand, new fortunes are made on the ruin of old ones.

---

* At Camden, August 16, 1780.

War, which keeps the spirits in motion, has diffused a taste for gayety and dissipation. The French Resident at Philadelphia gives a rout twice a week to the ladies of that city, amongst whom French hair-dressers, milliners and dances are all the *ton*. The Virginia jig has given place to the cotillon, and minuet-de-la-cour.

The Congress are fallen into general contempt, for their want of credit and power; the army is absolute and has declared it will not submit to a peace made by Congress; the people grumble, but are obliged to surrender one piece of furniture after another, even to their beds, to pay their taxes.

After all, a power drawn from such distant and dissonant parts cannot form a permanent union. The force of this kingdom, moving uniformly from one centre, must in all human probability ultimately prevail; or an accident may produce, in an instant, what the most powerful efforts require time and perseverance to accomplish.

—MOORE, *Diary of the American Revolution*, II, 343-344.

3. A TORY EXULTS: "THE CONGRESS IS FINALLY BANKRUPT!"

From Rivington's *Royal Gazette* for May 12, 1781.

May 7, [1781]—The Congress is finally bankrupt! Last Saturday a large body of the inhabitants with paper dollars in their hats by way of cockades paraded the streets of Philadelphia, carrying colors flying, with a DOG TARRED, and instead of the usual appendage and ornament of feathers, his back was covered with the Congress' paper dollars. This example of disaffection, immediately under the eyes of the rulers of the revolted provinces, in solemn session at the State House assembled, was directly followed by the jailer, who refused accepting the bills in purchase of a glass of rum, and afterwards by the traders of the city, who shut up their shops, declining to sell any more goods but for gold or silver. It was declared also by the popular voice that if the opposition to Great Britain was not in future carried on by solid money instead of paper bills, all further assistance to the mother country were vain and must be given up.

—MOORE, *Diary of the American Revolution*, II, 425-426.

4. "WE HAVE PURSUED OUR PAPER PROJECTS AS FAR AS IS PRUDENT"

James Madison, the writer of this letter, was already gaining a reputation as a leading Nationalist in Congress. His addressee was to be the author of an early history of the United States.

James Madison to Philip Mazzei, a European intellectual.

Philadelphia, July 7, 1781

The vicissitudes which our finances have undergone are as great as those of the war, the depreciation of the old continental bills having arrived at forty, fifty and sixty for one. Congress, on the 18th of March, 1780, resolved to displace them entirely from circulation, and substitute another currency, to be issued on better funds, and redeemable at a shorter period. For this purpose they fixed the relative value of paper and specie at forty for one; directed the States to sink by taxes the whole two hundred millions in one year, and to provide proper funds for sinking in six years a new currency which was not

to exceed ten millions of dollars, which was redeemable within that period
and to bear an interest of five per cent., payable in bills of exchange on Europe
or hard money. The loan-office certificates granted by Congress are to be
discharged at the value of the money at the time of the loan, a scale of depreciation being fixed by Congress for that purpose.

This scheme has not yet been carried into full execution. The old bills are
still unredeemed, in part, in some of the States, where they have depreciated
to two, three and four hundred for one. The new bills, which were to be issued only as the old ones were taken in, are consequently in a great degree
still unissued; and the depreciation which they have already suffered has determined Congress and the States to issue as few more of them as possible.

We seem to have pursued our paper projects as far as prudence will warrant. Our medium in future will be principally specie. The States are already
levying taxes in it. As the paper disappears, the hard money comes forward
into circulation. This revolution will also be greatly facilitated by the influx
of Spanish dollars from the Havannah, where the Spanish forces employed
against the Floridas consume immense quantities of our flour and remit their
dollars in payment. We also receive considerable assistance from the direct
aids of our ally and from the money expended among us by his auxiliary
troops.

These advantages, as they have been and are likely to be improved by the
skill of Mr. Robert Morris, whom we have constituted minister of our finances, afford a more flattering prospect in this department of our affairs than
has existed at any period of the war.

—HUNT, ed., *Writings of Madison*, I, 144-145.

VI. THE BANK AND THE FINANCIER

*In the closing years of the Revolution the government was heading for a
financial crisis. Various proposals were made to expedite raising money for
the war. One of the earliest, and certainly the most thoroughgoing, was
the series of proposals drawn up by Washington's aide, Alexander Hamilton.
We give here a portion of an undated letter, probably written by Hamilton
some time in 1780, and addressed "To a Member of Congress." Although
some historians have named Robert Morris as the addressee, he was not in
Congress at this time. Hamilton's letter takes on deeper significance in view of
his later plan for a national bank, which he proposed when he became Secretary of the Treasury, and his later efforts to attach the financial and commercial interests to the new nation on the basis of self-interest. His two bank plans
had a common end, but the later was less grandiose and at the same time more
clearly under private control than that envisioned in the earlier proposal.*

*In the following letter Hamilton suggests that a foreign loan be procured
that would be convertible into merchandise and imported on public account.
To obtain the full support of the moneyed men behind the government he
recommended that a national bank be set up, the ownership of which was to
be evenly divided between the government and private capital. When on*

February 20, 1781, Robert Morris was named by Congress to the post of Super-
intendent of Finance, Hamilton pressed the matter once more. But Morris was
less venturesome and instead pushed through Congress a charter for the Bank
of North America, which was to perform the functions of discount and de-
posit. In addition, Hamilton's bank would have coined money, issued paper
currency, and have charge of contracts for supplying the armed forces.

When, in June 1781 Robert Morris entered upon his duties as Superin-
tendent of Finance, his only available resources were bills of exchange that
Congress from time to time drew on foreign envoys, optimistically assuming
that funds existed in Europe for meeting the bills. Almost immediately Morris
was called upon by Washington to finance the Yorktown campaign. The
financier managed to provide the army with transportation from the head of
the Chesapeake, to advance a month's pay to the soldiers, and to forward
needed supplies. The arrival in August of almost a half million dollars in specie
from France eased his burdens. Nonetheless, Morris seems to have personally
advanced $12,000 toward the expenses of the Yorktown campaign.

Following the suggestions of Hamilton, Gouverneur Morris and others,
Robert Morris secured the consent of Congress to establishing a bank. Incor-
porated in 1782 both by Congress and the State of Pennsylvania, the Bank of
North America rendered valuable assistance to the government, lending the
United States $1,249,000 during Morris' regime.

Morris employed his personal credit to secure the notes issued to the army
at the time of its disbanding. As his letter to Washington reveals, the army's
demands constituted merely a small part of his fiscal problems. Needless to
say he—and his policies—encountered heavy criticism. Finding it impossible
to carry through his program, he resigned in despair. We include some letters
of his supporters and one written by a puzzled critic.

1. Hamilton Enlists "the Interest of the Moneyed Men"

Alexander Hamilton to "a Member of Congress."

[1780]

The present conjuncture is by all allowed to be peculiarly critical. . . . The
object of principal concern is the state of our currency. In my opinion, all
our speculations on this head have been founded in error. Most people think
that the depreciation might have been avoided by provident arrangements in
the beginning without [any aid] from abroad; and a great many of our
[sanguine] politicians, till very lately, imagined the [money] might still be
restored by expedients with [in our] selves. Hence the delay in attempting [to
procure] a foreign loan.

This idea proceeded from [an igno]rance of the real extent of our resources. The war, particularly in the first periods, [required] exertions beyond our strength, to which [neither] our population nor riches were
equal. . . .

The public expenditures, from the dearness of everything, necessarily became immense; great[er] in proportion than in other countries; and much
beyond any revenues which the best concerted scheme of finance could have

extracted from the natural funds of the State. No taxes, which the people were capable of bearing, on that quantity of money which is deemed a proper medium for this country (had it been gold instead of paper), would have been sufficient for the current exigencies of government.

The most opulent states of Europe, in a war of any duration, are commonly obliged to have recourse to foreign loans or subsidies. [Here Hamilton cited the huge debts of foreign nations.] How, then, could we expect to do without them, and not augment the quantity of our artificial wealth beyond those bounds which were proper to preserve its credit? The idea was chimerical. . . .

Could a loan have been obtained, and judiciously applied, assisted by a vigorous system of taxation, we might have avoided that excess of emissions which has ruined the paper. The credit of such a fund would have procured loans from the moneyed and trading men within ourselves; because it might have been so directed as to have been beneficial to them in their commercial transactions abroad. (This will appear from the plan which will be proposed.)

The necessity for a foreign loan is now greater than ever. Nothing else will retrieve our affairs. . . .

How this loan is to be employed is now the question; and its difficulty equal to its importance. Two plans have been proposed: one, to purchase up at once, in specie or sterling bills, all superfluous paper; and to endeavor, by taxes, loans and economy, to hinder its returning into circulation. The remainder, it is supposed, would then recover its value. This, it is said, will reduce our public debt to the sterling cost of the paper. . . .

The other plan proposed is to convert the loan into merchandise and import it on public account. This plan is incomparably better than the former. Instead of losing on the sale of its specie or bills, the public would gain a considerable profit on the commodities imported. The loan would go much further this way towards supplying the expenses of the war; and a large stock of valuable commodities, useful to the army and to the country, would be introduced. This would affect the prices of things in general and assist the currency. But the arts of monopolizers would prevent its having so extensive and durable an influence as it ought to have.

A great impediment to the success of this, as well as the former scheme, will be the vast sums requisite for the current expenses. . . .

The only plan that can preserve the currency is one that will make it the *immediate* interest of the moneyed men to cooperate with government in its support. . . .

The plan I would propose is that of an American bank, instituted by authority of Congress for ten years, under the denomination of The Bank of the United States. . . .

I give one half of the whole property of the bank to the United States, because it is not only just but desirable to both parties. The United States contribute a great part of the stock; their authority is essential to the existence of the bank; their credit is pledged for its support. The plan would ultimately fail if the terms were too favorable to the company and too hard upon government. It might be encumbered with a debt which it could never pay and be obliged to take refuge in a bankruptcy. The share which the State has in the profits will induce it to grant more ample privileges, without which the trade of the company might often be under restrictions injurious to its success. . . .

It may be objected that this plan will be prejudicial to trade by making the government a party with a trading company; which may be a temptation to arrogate exclusive privileges and thereby fetter that spirit of enterprise and competition on which the prosperity of commerce depends. But Congress may satisfy the jealousies on this head by a solemn resolution not to grant exclusive privileges, which alone can make the objection valid. . . .

—Hamilton Papers, 1st Series, Lib. of Congress.

2. MORRIS AND THE "ART MAGICK"—SOME WASHINGTON COMMENTS

George Washington to Robert Morris.

New Windsor, June 4, 1781

The present conveyance is sudden and unexpected; I have only time therefore to acknowledge the receipt of your favors of the 29th. Ulto. and to assure you, that I felt a most sensible pleasure, when I heard of your acceptance of the late appointment of Congress to regulate the Finances of this Country. My hand and heart shall be with you, and as far as my assistance will, or can go, command it.

Washington to John Mathews.

New Windsor, June 7, 1781

. . . I have great expectations from the appointment of Mr. Morris, but they are not unreasonable ones; for I do not suppose that by Art magick, he can do more than recover us, by degrees, from the labyrinth into which our finance is plunged.

Washington to the Chevalier de la Luzerne.

New Windsor, June 8, 1781

I presage the happiest Consequences from the Appointment of a Gentleman of Mr. Morris's Character and Abilities to the Superintendance of our Finance. I wait impatiently for his making me the Visit which he proposes, as many very essential Matters in the Operations of the Campaign will depend upon the Assistance which he will be able to afford us.

—FITZPATRICK, *Writings of Washington*, XXII, 159, 177, 181.

3. JOSEPH REED CALLS MORRIS "A PECUNIARY DICTATOR"

Joseph Reed to Nathanael Greene.

November 1, 1781

. . . It would add too much to this already tedious letter to enter into a detail of the events which have put us into our present state, but in brief it may be ascribed to the failure of public credit, the non-production of taxes, and consequent poverty of Congress, which was, indeed, truly abject and distressing; in this wretched extremity, it became necessary to appoint what I may properly call a pecuniary dictator. The qualities required were ability of mind, some money in hand, and a private credit for more. I believe I ought to have put the latter qualities first, for if Sully had been here without them, he would not have been thought of.

Mr. Morris, who had been long pursuing a gainful traffic from which others were excluded by embargo and restrictions, . . . naturally presented himself as combining the necessary qualities; but his terms were high, and at first blush inadmissible. He claimed a right of continuing in private trade, of dismissing all Continental officers, handling public money at pleasure, with many lesser privileges amounting to little less than an engrossment of all those powers of Congress which had been deemed incommunicable, and which we have sometimes thought they exercised with rather too much hauteur. However, Mr. Morris was inexorable, Congress at mercy, and, finally, the appointment made with little relaxation in the original conditions, since which the business of that august body has been extremely simplified, Mr. Morris having relieved them from all business of deliberation or executive difficulty with which money is in any respect connected.

—REED, *Life and Correspondence of Reed*, II, 374-375.

4. MORRIS IS "CONCILIATING FAST THE SUPPORT OF MONEYED MEN"

Alexander Hamilton to Marquis de Noailles.

[1782]

There has been no material change in our internal situation since you left us. The capital successes we have had have served rather to increase the hopes than the exertions of the particular States. But in one respect we are in a mending way. Our financier has hitherto conducted himself with great ability, has acquired an entire personal confidence, revived in some measure the public credit, and is conciliating fast the support of the moneyed men. His operations have hitherto hinged chiefly on the seasonable aids from your country; but he is urging the establishment of permanent funds among ourselves; and though, from the nature and temper of our governments, his applications will meet with a dilatory compliance, it is to be hoped they will by degrees succeed. . . .

Upon the whole, however, if the war continues another year, it will be necessary that Congress should again recur to the generosity of France for pecuniary assistance. The plans of the financier cannot be so matured as to enable us by any possibility to dispense with this; and if he should fail for want of support, we must replunge into that confusion and distress which had liked to have proved fatal to us, and out of which we are slowly emerging. The cure, on a relapse, would be infinitely more difficult than ever.

—J. C. HAMILTON, ed., *Writings of Hamilton*, I, 314-317.

5. "NO OTHER MAN COULD HAVE KEPT THE MONEY MACHINE A-GOING"

Alexander Hamilton to George Washington.

April [9,] 1783

As to Mr. Morris, I will give your Excellency a true explanation of his conduct. He had been for some time pressing Congress to endeavor to obtain funds, and had found a great backwardness in the business. He found the taxes unproductive in the different States; he found the loans in Europe making a very slow progress; he found himself pressed on all hands for supplies; he found himself, in short, reduced to this alternative: either of making engagements which he could not fulfill, or declaring his resignation in case funds were not established by a given time. Had he followed the first course, the bubble must soon have burst; he must have sacrificed his credit and his character, and public credit, already in a ruinous condition, would have lost its last support.

He wisely judged it better to resign. This might increase the embarrassments of the moment; but the necessity of the case, it was to be hoped, would produce the proper measures; and he might then resume the direction of the machine with advantage and success.

He also had some hope that his resignation would prove a stimulus to Congress.

He was, however, ill advised in the publication of his letters of resignation. This was an imprudent step and has given a handle to his personal enemies, who, by playing upon the passions of others, have drawn some well-meaning men into the cry against him. But Mr. Morris certainly deserves a great deal from his country. I believe no man in this country but himself could have kept the money machine a-going during the period he has been in office. From every thing that appears, his administration has been upright as well as able.

The truth is, the old leaven of Deane and Lee is, at this day, working against Mr. Morris. He happened, in that dispute, to have been on the side of Deane; and certain men can never forgive him. A man whom I once esteemed, and whom I will rather suppose *duped* than wicked, is the second actor in this business.

—Hamilton Papers, 1st Series, Lib. of Congress.

Robert Morris to George Washington.

The Office of Finance, November 26, 1783

I have been honored with the receipt of your Excellency's letter of the eighteenth instant and in consequence shall send this to the City of New York which I hope and expect is now in our possession. It is unnecessary to assure you, Sir, how pleasing it would be to comply with the wishes of the officers now in service, as expressed in their memorial of the seventeenth instant: because I am sure both you and they must be convinced of my disposition to render justice to every part of the Army. But alas, Sir, the good will is all which I have in my power. The means of making payment is not, on the contrary. I am constantly involved in scenes of distress to keep pace with those engagements which I have already taken for the subsistence and pay which the Army have heretofore received.

Those engagements, which I dreaded at the time, were taken under various considerations. The relief of the Army then to be discharged—your Excellency's earnest desire—the orders of Congress and in particular the urgency of the committee appointed to treat with me on that subject and my own desire to render service to the Army—these were amongst the motives which induced me to hazard an anticipation of above a million of dollars on the public account. My solicitude to fulfill those engagements is extreme, but my calls for help are disregarded, and under such circumstances it cannot be expected that I shall make new engagements—and there is not any money in the Treasury. I lament the situation of the officers and am truly sorry that the States are so inattentive to the finances of the Union.

—Robert Morris Papers.

VII. PROFITEERS AND PROFITEERING

1. The Operations of "the Tribe of Profiteers"

The American Revolution brought to the fore a handful of dedicated leaders of unimpeachable integrity, and it disclosed, too, devotion and integrity in the people at large. But as in all wars there were "patrioteers" who profited while their fellow men fought and sacrificed. If the Revolution as a whole were to be judged in moral terms, it would appear a triumph of character over venality. But the venality was there, it was pervasive, it was continuous. We give here some of the innumerable protests against that "spirit of avarice" which threatened the liberties of the young nation.

A. "monopolizers are our worst oppressors"

"P.W." on monopolies.

Needham, Massachusetts, October 29, 1776

If the traders in this town and land had managed their commerical business with any tolerable regard to the good of the publick, as they might have done in consistency with seeking their own profit so far as it was fit and proper they should, being members of one and the same political body, we should have been at this day in happy circumstances, compared with what we now are. Our traders, considered in general, are, in the view of all considerate persons, as grand oppressors, and as truly and extensively so, in proportion to the sphere in which they move, as our ministerial oppressors in England; and unless they are soon restrained, either from a virtuous principle within or from some extensive power, they will be the destroyers of the poor, the widow, the fatherless, and all others whose situation in life is such as renders it impossible for them to do justice to themselves. To what can it be attributed but the excessive love traders have to their own precious selves, that they put such an extravagant price upon the commodities they have to sell?

And what an unspeakable damage has this been to the publick! It has occasioned the undue rise of everything we depend upon for the support and comfort of life. Farmers, manufacturers in their several occupations, and labourers in all their kinds, excuse their high demands for what is wanted in their way from the still higher demands of traders for what they have to sell. In very truth, our traders, both in town and country, are the real cause of the monstrously high price of every thing; and the love of their own interest, in opposition to the interest of all others and to the subversion of it, if they may get by it, is that shameful principle by which they are governed in this whole affair.

Monopolizers in this day of common calamity are our worst oppressors. Those among them, in special, are so, who, not content with the thousands they are righteously entitled to, in consequence of the prizes the commissioned vessels they own have brought in, have been unduly influenced, from an avaricious disposition, to make a monopoly of as much of the effects of those prizes as their cunning would enable them to do, that, by an excessively enhanced price they might by and by get that from others, however poor and destitute, which both reason and revelation unite in calling the gain of oppression. These extortioners are not only sordidly unjust, but basely wanting in gratitude to that Providence which has distinguished them from most others in this day of general distress; and they ought to be restrained by Government within the limits of what is right and fit; and unless some measures are soon authoritatively come into to effect so righteous and valuable an end, it may be feared whether undesirable consequences will not take place, as a general clamour begins to be loudly heard.

–FORCE, *American Archives*, 5th Series, II, 1288-1289.

B. THAT "PERNICIOUS PRACTICE" OF ENGROSSING

John Penn to Governor Richard Caswell of North Carolina.

Philadelphia, June 25th, 1777

In my way to this place I was informed that salt sold in Maryland for 20 dollars a bushill. There are a considerable number of merchants in this and that State that make it their business to buy up all the necessaries of life in order to fix what price they please afterwards.

I suspect some of that tribe will be soon in N. Carolina to ingross all our salt and other things. Would it not be proper to keep a look out and prevent if possible such a pernicious practice? . . .

–Emmett Collection, Facsimile 3933, N. Y. Public Lib.

C. THE SPIRIT OF AVARICE THREATENS THE LIBERTIES OF AMERICA

John Harvie to Thomas Jefferson.

York Town, December the 29th, 1777

. . . If the late generous spirit of Virginia in their Act of cloathing and measures for preventing of forestalling does not inspire the other States with a virtuous emulation, the avarice of individuals will be more fatal to the liberties of America than the sword of the enemy. I have a great while past shuddered at the rapid strides of this monster in society, but lately he has broke through every feeble fort opposed to him, and threatens us with inevitable destruction unless his carrier [career] is immediatly checked by the joint efforts of the United States. In short the avarice and disaffection of the people here is so great that they refuse any price that we can give for the necessary provisions for the army, and the General's last letter, couched in terms strong and pathetic, holds out a probability of the army desolveing unless they are more fully and constantly supplied.

You would execrate this State if you were in it. The supporters of this government are a set of weak men without any weight of character. No kind of respect is paid by the people either to their laws or advice, and instead of checking they in many instances countenance the exactions of their constituents, being otherwise fearful of looseing their present shadow of power. Two thirds of the State of Delaware are notoriously known in their hearts to be with our enemys. They have not at present the shadow of government amongst them, and their representation to Congress has been withdrawn a considerable time before I had a seat in it. From this you must foresee that these execrable States clogg the operations of the Continent in an alarming degree.

Then what is to be done? Are we with this conviction upon our minds to suffer them, for the want of virtue and vigour in their governments, to involve the whole in the worst of calamitys or will not Congress be justifyable (from the necessity of the case as guardians to the sacred rights of the people at large) in pursueing such measures as will eventually save this Continent from perdition? The feelings of my own heart tells me they will. Yet I revere the sovereignty of the States and civil rights of the people as much as any man liveing who is not capable of more refined and deeper reflections than myself. Such I acknowledge see things of this delicate nature in a more enlarged comprehensive point of view and by such I ardently wish to be instructed.

Indeed, my honored friend, for such I esteem you, the present state and condition of this Continent, oweing to the alarming disaffection in this quarter, an almost universal discontent in the army, a reformation therein meditated by Congress to commence and be carryed into effect this winter, with numberless other matters that I am not at liberty to disclose even to you, requires the wisdom of the first characters amongst us to give them weight and efficacy.

—Boyd, ed., *Writings of Thomas Jefferson*, II, 125-126.

D. WASHINGTON: "HUNT THEM DOWN AS PESTS OF SOCIETY"

George Washington to Joseph Reed.

December 12, 1778

It gives me very sincere pleasure to find that there is likely to be a coalition of the Whigs in your State (a few only excepted) and that the assembly of it, are so well disposed to second your endeavours in bringing those murderers of our cause (the monopolizers, forestallers, and engrossers) to condign punishment. It is much to be lamented that each State long ere this has not hunted them down as the pests of society, and the greatest Enemys we have to the happiness of America. I would to God that one of the most attrocious of each State was hung in Gibbets upon a gallows five times as high as the one prepared by Haman. No punishment in my opinion is too great for the Man who can build his greatness upon his Country's ruin.

—Fitzpatrick, ed., *Writings of Washington*, XIII, 383.

E. "AMERICANS SEEM TO HAVE LOST THEIR OLD NOBLE PRINCIPLES"

Samuel Shaw to Francis and Mary Shaw.

28th of June, 1779

I wish, seriously, that the ensuing campaign may terminate the war. The people of America seem to have lost sight entirely of the noble principle which animated them at the commencement of it. That patriotic ardor which then inspired each breast; that glorious, I had almost said godlike, enthusiasm—has given place to avarice, and every rascally practice which tends to the gratification of that sordid and most disgraceful passion. I don't know as it would be too bold an assertion to say that its depreciation is equal to that of the currency—*thirty for one*. You may perhaps charitably think that I strain the matter, but I do not. I speak *feelingly*. By the arts of monopolizers and extortioners, and the little, the very little, attention by authority to counteract them, our currency is reduced to a mere name.

Pernicious soever as this is to the community at large, its baneful effect is more immediately experienced by the *poor* soldier. I am myself an instance of it. For my services I receive a nominal sum, —— dollars at *eight* shillings, in a country where they pass at the utmost for *fourpence* only. If it did not look too much like self-applause, I might say that I engaged in the cause of my country from the purest motives. However, be this as it may, my continuance in it has brought me to poverty and rags; and, had I fortune of my own, I should glory in persevering, though it should occasion a sacrifice of the last penny. But, when I consider my situation—my pay inadequate to my support, though within the line of the strictest economy; no private purse of my own—and reflect that the best of parents, who, I am persuaded, have the tenderest affection for their son and wish to support him in character, have not the means of doing it, and may, perhaps, be pressed themselves—when these considerations occur to my mind, as they frequantly do, they make me serious; more so than my natural disposition would lead me to be. The loss of my horse, by any accident whatever (unless he was actually killed in battle, and then I should be entitled only to about one third of his value), would plunge me in inextricable misfortune; two years' pay and subsistence would not replace him. Yet the nature of my office renders it indispensable that I should keep a horse. These are some of the emoluments annexed to a military station. I hardly thought there were so many before I began the detail; but I find several more might be added, though I think I have mentioned full enough.

Believe me, my dear and honored parents, that I have not enumerated these matters with a view to render you uneasy. Nothing would give me more pain, should they have that effect; but I think communicating one's difficulties always lessens, and, of course, makes them more tolerable; and I fancy it has already had some influence on me. I feel much easier than when I began to write, and more reconciled to my lot. It is true I shall see many persons grown rich at the end of the war, who at the commencement of it had no more than myself; but I shall not envy them.

I must, notwithstanding, repeat my wish that this campaign may put an end to the war, for I much doubt the virtue of the people at large for carrying it on another year. Had the same spirit which glowed in the breast of every true American at the beginning of the controversy been properly cherished, the country, long ere now, had been in full enjoyment of the object of our warfare—"peace, liberty, and safety." But, as matters are at present circumstanced, it is to be feared these blessings are yet at a distance. Much remains to be done for the attainment of them. The recommendations of Congress, in their late address to the inhabitants of the States, should be in good earnest attended to. We are not to stand still and wait for salvation, but we must exert ourselves—be industrious in the use and application of those means with which Heaven has furnished us, and then we may reasonably hope for success.

—SHAW, *Journals*, pp. 58-60.

2. SPECULATION IN HIGH PLACES

That distinction which now, in principle at least, obtains between public and private interest was at best dimly perceived in the era of the Revolution. Robert Morris, who conducted the major business operations for the Congress, engaged, too, in extensive business operations on his own, especially with Silas Deane, American agent in Paris. Congressman Samuel Chase of Maryland, who had earlier favored price and wage controls, took advantage of inside information to make a secret purchase of grain for the French fleet—conduct which aroused young Hamilton to a public denunciation of the transaction. Officers of the Army trafficked with the enemy, and General Greene himself engaged in wartime speculations—with the brother of Silas Deane. It is some satisfaction to recall that few of the speculators came out ahead in their dubious ventures.

A. ROBERT MORRIS ADVISES DEANE NOT TO MISS A CHANCE FOR A KILLING

Philadelphia, February 27, 1777

You will receive herewith copy of a letter I wrote you the 11th January on commercial matters, also copy of one dated 31st January respecting my brother; the contents of both are hereby confirmed, and I am sorry it is not in my power to own receipt of any fresh letters from you or him. The state of suspense I am left in makes me very uneasy, especially on his account; however, I must wait with patience to have my doubts cleared up, and hope it will be done more to my satisfaction than my present fears suggest.

I have not received any goods from you or him. Neither have I heard of any being sent by you either for this place or the West Indies. If you have, from any cause that I am unacquainted with, neglected doing it, you may have leisure to repent hereafter that you missed so fine an opportunity of making a fortune. The prices of all imported articles have been enormously high. I could have sold any quantity of European manufactures for 500 to 700 per cent and bought tobacco for 25s. to 30s. per ct. It is not too late, but goods are becoming rather more plenty and tobacco is rising, but there is plenty of room to make as much money as you please, and if insurance could be obtained in Europe it might be reduced to a certainty even if you gave a premium of 50 per cent, which, however, is vastly too high. I think some good hand might be found to go over to London and manage such insurances there. They love high premiums and will insure anything for money, but this really would be to their advantage, as I don't think we have lost above one fourth or at most one third of our inward-bound vessells.

I am sorry to inform you that there are now two or three British men of war in Chesapeak Bay. They have taken the ship *Farmer*, Captain Dashiel, which had on board 500 hhds. of tobacco on the public account and 50 hhds.

on my account; was bound for Nantes, consigned to Messrs. Pliarne Penet & Co. They have for the present blocked up several others there, but we shall get them away by and by. . . .

—DEANE, *Papers*, XX, 14-15.

B. YOUNG HAMILTON DENOUNCES THE WAR PROFITEERS

Alexander Hamilton to John Holt, Printer.

Poughkeepsie, October 19, 1778

SIR:—While every method is taken to bring to justice those men whose principles and practices have been hostile to the present revolution, it is to be lamented that the conduct of another class, equally criminal, and, if possible, more mischievous, has hitherto passed with impunity, and almost without notice. I mean that tribe who, taking advantage of the times, have carried the spirit of monopoly and extortion to an excess which scarcely admits of a parallel. Emboldened by the success of progressive impositions, it has extended to all the necessaries of life. The exorbitant price of every article, and the depreciation upon our currency, are evils derived essentially from this source. When avarice takes the lead in a state, it is commonly the forerunner of its fall. How shocking is it to discover among ourselves, even at this early period, the strongest symptoms of this fatal disease! . . .

When a man appointed to be the guardian of the state and the depositary of the happiness and morals of the people, forgetful of the solemn relation in which he stands, descends to the dishonest artifices of a mercantile projector and sacrifices his conscience and his trust to pecuniary motives, there is no strain of abhorrence of which the human mind is capable, no punishment the vengeance of the people can inflict, which may not be applied to him with justice. If it should have happened that a member of C——ss had been this degenerate character, and has been known to turn the knowledge of secrets to which his office gave him access to the purposes of private profit, by employing emissaries to engross an article of immediate necessity to the public service, he ought to feel the utmost rigor of public resentment and be detested as a traitor of the worst and most dangerous kind.

October 26, 1778

SIR:— . . . When you resolved to avail yourself of the extraordinary demand for the article of flour which the wants of the French fleet must produce, and which your official situation early impressed on your attention, to form connections for monopolizing that article, and raising the price upon the public more than an hundred per cent; when by your intrigues and studied delays you protracted the determination of the C—tt—e of C——ss on the proposals made by Mr W—sw—th, C—s—y G—n—l [Jeremiah Wadsworth, Commissary General], for procuring the necessary supplies for the public use, to give your agents time to complete their purchases;—I say when you were doing all this, and engaging in a traffic infamous in itself, repugnant to your station, and ruinous to your country, did you pause and allow yourself a moment's reflection on the consequences? Were you infatuated enough to imagine you would be able to conceal the part you were acting? Or had you conceived a thorough contempt of reputation, and a total indifference to the opinion of the world? Enveloped in the promised gratifications of your avarice, you probably forgot to consult your understanding and lost sight of every consideration that ought to have regulated the man, the citizen or the statesman. . . .

—*New York Journal and General Advertiser*, Oct. 19 and Oct. 26, 1778.

C. GREENE INSISTS HIS BUSINESS PARTNERSHIP BE KEPT SECRET

Nathanael Greene to Colonel Jeremiah Wadsworth.

Camp, April 30th, 1779

You may remember I wrote you sometime since that I was desirous that this copartnership between Mr. Dean, you and myself should be kept a secret. I must beg leave to impress this matter upon you again; and to request you to enjoin it upon Mr Dean. The nearest friend I have in the world shall not know it from me; and it is my wish that no mortal should be acquainted with the persons forming the Company except us three. I would not wish Mr Dean even to let his brother know it. Not that I apprehend any injury from him, but he may inadvertently let it out into the broad world, and then I am persuaded it would work us a public injury.

While we continue in the offices which we hold, I think it is prudent to appear as little in trade as possible. For however just and upright our conduct may be, the world will have suspicions to our disadvantage.

By keeping the affair a secret I am confident we shall have it more in our power to serve the commercial connection than by publishing it.

I have wrote to my brother Jacob Greene to pay you £5000 without informing him for what purpose or on what account. If you could advance the other 5000 until you come to Camp, it would be very agreeable to me. If not I must take some other way of sending it. . . .

Camp, April 30th, 1779

I have received your two last letters with the inclosed alphabet of figures to correspond with. The plan is very agreeable which is proposed. But in addition to it will it not be best to take upon us a fictitious name? This will draw another shade of obscurity over the business and render it impossible to find out the connection. The busy world will be prying into the connection and nature of the business; and more especially as a letter of Mr Deane's has lately been intercepted in which it is pretended great things are discovered and dangerous combinations formed. Whether there has been any letter intercepted and if there has whether it contains anything of the kind that is represented, I am by no means certain. It is said he is forming one of the greatest commercial houses in the world; and has a plan for land jobing of equal extent. I know not what it all means; but believe it is the effects of malice and detraction; which I can assure you was never more prevalent. . . .

Morristown, 11th of April, 1780

...How stands our 298.37 [company affair] with B. D. [Barnabas Deane]? Let me know as particularly as you can. Send the information in one letter and what you say upon it in another.

Yours

You Know Who

—GREENE, "Letters," *Penn. Mag. of Hist. and Biog.*, XXII, 211-216.

D. AMERICAN OFFICERS TRAFFIC WITH THE ENEMY

Governor William Livingston of New Jersey to General John Sullivan.

Morris Town, August 19, 1779

I have sufficient evidence to believe that constant communication and commercial intercourse has for a considerable time past been held by many of the County of Essex; that those communications have been principally supported by means of flaggs and passports obtained from divers officers of the Army belonging to the United States, who for some time past have been stationed at Elizabeth Town, Newark and other places in that neighbourhood.

Under colour of their flaggs, which from their frequency must be supposed (to use the softest term) to have been imprudently granted, great mischiefs have arisen to those parts of the country—mischiefs, I imagine, greatly superior to the advantages that may be pretended to be derived from any intelligence that can be gained thereby. Persons of dubious political characters, as I am informed, have been sent over; provisions for the aid and comfort of the British troops furnished; a pernicious and unlawful traffic carried on; the little specie left among us collected with the greatest avidity to maintain this execrable trade; and the Continental currency by that means further depreciated; opportunities afforded the enemy for circulating their counterfeit bills, and the disaffected of conveying to them intelligence of every movement and designed operation of our troops; the confidence of the people in the integrity of our officers diminished, and a universal murmuring excited among the friends of the common cause.

It is made capital by an Act of our legislature for any subject of this state to go into the enemy's lines with a passport from any officer under the rank of a Brigadier General of the Continental Army or of our militia, or of the Governor of this state.

To prevent the further abuse of those flags by the officers of our militia, I have given the strictest orders and issued a proclamation for the purpose. I have also represented the matter to his Excellency General Washington, that he may take such measure to discountenance the practice in the officers under his command as he shall think best calculated to answer the end.

I am credibly informed that no person is guilty of a greater prostitution of passports than Doctor Barnet, a captain of horse, who is not a little suspected of disaffection. He is at all events a very improper person to be trusted with blank flaggs (as I am told he is), being much addicted to strong drink, and having very little discretion when sober.

If he has any of those blanks from you, I hope you will caution him against using them for the future but upon the most important occasion, and indeed I believe it was not the intent of our law that the person thereby authorized to grant passports should delegate that power to any other, it being a personal trust reposed in them who from their stations the law presumed would always use it with prudence.

I do not pretend that our legislature supposed that the officers of the Army of the United States wanted any authority from them to grant flaggs, but they have made it felony for the subjects of this state to go with any other than the Act has appointed, which they had a right to do, and consequently any inferior officer granting them thereby deludes the person into a capital crime.

You will excuse my earnestness on this subject as I am a daily witness of the inexpressible mischiefs resulting from the abuse I complain of.

—HAMMOND, ed., *Letters and Papers of Sullivan*, XIII, 433-435.

3. WAR ON THE PROFITEERS: THE ATTACK ON "FORT WILSON"

The radical party in Pennsylvania sought in vain to have Congress halt the depreciation of Continental money by reducing emissions, imposing additional taxes, and obtaining new loans. Congress took no effective action, and soaring prices and scarcities caused widespread discontent. A mass meeting in the Statehouse yard authorized a new committee to fix a schedule of prices, and to discipline merchants and financiers who failed to co-operate.

During the summer and fall of '79 popular feeling against the speculators ran high. On October 4 a mob attacked the residence of James Wilson, the lawyer who had incurred the special animosity of the radicals by serving as counsel for the Penn family in their suit against the state, and by defending merchants before price-control committees. Wilson's own speculative propensities were notorious; even later, when he had become justice of the Supreme Court, he was deeply involved in land speculation and on the run from creditors. A number of merchants, war speculators and conservatives sought refuge from the mob in Wilson's house, which was then dubbed "Fort Wilson"; they were joined there by Wilson's friend General Mifflin.

We give two eyewitness accounts of the attack on "Fort Wilson"—one by the distinguished artist, Charles Willson Peale; the other by the dashing hero of Stony Point, Allen McLane.

A. "THE MILITIA WOULD HAVE KILLED EVERY ONE ASSEMBLED"

Statement of Charles Willson Peale.

The rapidity of the depreciation of the Continental money was at this period such that those who retained it a few days could not purchase near the value which they had given for it.

This being a grievance greatly felt by those who had been most active in favour of the Revolution, and among them those who had on every occasion rendered their personal service in the militia, many of whom thought that this continual depreciation of their favourite paper was brought about by the machinations of their internal enemies. Very few indeed could trace the real or principal cause to its true source, viz. that of too great a quantity being issued and put into circulation. Taxation being too slow to obtain the necessary supply for the support of an army, Congress were continually obliged to be issuing more, although there was already so much in use as to have totally banished gold and silver in common dealings.

At the meeting of the militia of Philadelphia on the commons in 1779, a number of those active Whigs whose zeal would carry them any length in their favourite cause, and whose tempers had now become soured by the many insults they had met with from the Tories, assembled at Burns' tavern, and after they had come to some resolutions, more passionate than judicious, that of sending away the wives and children of those men who had gone with the British, or were within the British lines, was adopted.

After these zealots had formed this design, they then began to devise the mode of carrying it into execution, and proposed to put themselves under some commander, and accordingly sent a messenger to request Captain Peale to attend them. But so soon as he was made acquainted with the business, he told them that he could not approve of the measure, as it would in the practice be found a difficult and dangerous undertaking; that the taking of women and children from their homes would cause much affliction and grief; that, when seen, the humanity of their fellow-citizens would be roused into an opposition to such a measure; that such attempts must of course fail. But all his arguments were in vain; they could not see these difficulties with a *determined* band. He then told them that the danger in case of a failure in such an attempt would be imminent to the commander of such a party. The reply was that General Washington could not take his command without running some risks, and that they in this undertaking would sacrifice their lives or effect it.

Captain Peale was at last obliged to refuse, and made the excuse that he was applied to by some of his friends to stand as a candidate at the then approaching election for members of the General Assembly; after which all further entreaty ceased, and he left them, and did not hear anything further of their proceedings until the Thursday following, when he received a notice that desired him, with Col. Bull, Major Boyd and Dr. Hutchinson, to meet the militia on the Monday following at Mrs. Burns' tavern on the common. Those persons so noticed having consulted together, all of them disapproved of the violent proceedings of the militia. Dr. Hutchinson said he would not attend the meeting; Peale and the other gentlemen conceived that they as good citizens were in duty bound to go and use their best endeavours to restrain, as far as they might be able, any violent and improper proceedings, and, in duty to themselves, at least to remonstrate in a public manner against having any part in the business.

After further consideration, Dr. Hutchinson agreed to meet them; Col. Bull, being dangerously ill, could not attend.

Accordingly, on that memorable Monday Dr. Hutchinson, Major Boyd and Captain Peale went to Mrs. Burns' tavern (where great numbers of the militia had already asembled), and they did use every argument in their power to prevent any further proceedings in that vain and dangerous undertaking. They represented the difficulty of selecting such characters as all could agree to be obnoxious amongst such a body of the people; that in such an attempt they must infallibly differ as to the object—of course no good purpose could be answered.

Among the militia were many Germans, whose attachment to the American cause was such that they disregarded every danger, and whose resentment at this time was most violently inveterate against all Tories. They only looked straight forward, regardless of consequences. In short, to reason with a multitude of devoted patriots assembled on such an occasion was in vain; and after Peale found all that could be said availed nought, he left them and went to his home, and afterwards to the President's, General Reed, whom he found was preparing to go out in order to prevent mischief, which he said was to be feared from the tidings then brought him. Captain Peale immediately returned to his home, where he had not long been before he heard the firing of small arms. He then began to think that he ought to prepare himself by getting his fire-arms in order, in case he should be under the necessity of making use of them; for no man could now know where the affair would end; and finding his wife and family very uneasy, he determined to stay within his own doors for the present time.

Shortly that tragical scene was ended, and very fortunately no more lives were lost.

The militia having taken two men who they conceived were inimical to the American cause, they were parading them up Walnut Street, and when they had got opposite James Wilson, Esq.'s house at the corner of Third Street, where a considerable number of gentlemen to the number of about thirty had collected and had armed themselves, amongst them Captain Campbell, commander of an invalid corps, this unfortunate person hoisted a window with a pistol in his hand, and some conversation having passed between him and the passing militia, a firing began, and poor Campbell was killed; a Negro boy at some distance from the house was also killed, and four or five persons badly wounded. The militia had now become highly exasperated, and had just broke into the house, and most probably would have killed every one assembled within those walls; but, very fortunately for them, General Reed with a number of the light horse appeared at this fortunate juncture and dispersed the militia. Numbers of them were taken and committed to the common jail, and a guard placed to prevent a rescue.

The next morning the officers of the militia and numbers of the people assembled at the Court House in Market Street, and the minds of the citizens generally seemed to be much distressed.

The militia of Germantown were beginning to assemble, and General Reed had sent Mr. Matlack, the Secretary of Council, to the officers of the militia, then assembled in Market Street, as above mentioned, to endeavour to keep them waiting until he could address the militia of Germantown, after which he would be with them.

Peale, hearing of this meeting at the Court House, went there, and found that the officers were exceedingly warm and full of resentment that any of the militia should be kept in durance in the jail; they appeared to be ripe for undertaking the release of the prisoners, and all Mr. Matlack's arguments, perhaps, would have been insufficient to keep them much longer from being active.

Several of the magistrates were present, and Peale whispered Mr. Matlack to know if he did not think it would be prudent to propose the taking bail for the persons and let them be released by the magistrates then present. This opinion was approved of as the most certain means to prevent disorder and perhaps a further shedding of blood. This measure being offered to the officers of the militia, they readily entered security for the personal appearance of the militia then confined at any future time for trial, and, in consequence, the prisoners were released by the magistrates' orders.

General Reed, having succeeded in preventing the Germantown militia from entering the city, came expecting to find things in the situation he had left them, and was not a little mortified to find that Mr. Matlack could not do as he had ordered. The people were assembled at the State House, and he publicly harangued them, after which, amongst a number of the officers and his particular acquaintance, he was blaming Mr. Matlack for not doing as he had requested him. Peale then told the General that Mr. Matlack ought not to suffer blame, for if the measure was wrong, that he was the unlucky person who had proposed that measure, which he then conceived was the best expedient, as it had the appearance of being a judicial act.

C.W.P.

—REED, *Life and Correspondence of Reed*, II, 423-426.

B. "THE LABORING PART OF THE CITY HAD BECOME DESPERATE"

Journal of Allen McLane.

I was standing on the front steps of my house in Walnut Street and observed Colonel Grayson beckoning to me from the door of the War Office. I went to him, and he told me he was glad I had not left the city, for that he had great apprehensions that several of our most respectable citizens, then assembled at Mr. Wilson's house, would be massacred, as they were determined to defend themselves against the armed mob that had assembled on the Commons this morning and were moving down Second Street, expecting to find Mr. Wilson and his friends at the City Tavern, but they were within pistol shot of the War Office. I listened to the sound of the drum and fife, could distinctly hear the sound in Second Street, and in a few minutes observed the front of those in arms appeared in Walnut Street, moving up the street; by this time the front of the mob was near Dock Street, in Walnut Street.

The colonel asked me if I knew those in front of the armed men; I answered I thought the leader was Captain Faulkner, a militia officer. The colonel proposed that we should meet and persuade them to turn up Dock to Third Street, which we did attempt. I introduced Colonel Grayson to Captain Faulkner, as a member of the Board of War. Grayson addressed him and expressed his fears as to the consequence of attacking Mr. Wilson in his house. Faulkner observed, they had no intention to meddle with Mr. Wilson or his house; their object was to support the constitution, the laws and the Committee of Trade. The labouring part of the City had become desperate from the high price of the necessaries of life.

The halt in front brought a great press from the rear; two men, Pickering and Bonham, ran up to the front, armed with muskets and bayonets fixed, and inquired the cause of the halt, at the same time ordered Faulkner to move up Walnut Street. Grayson addressed Bonham, and I addressed Pickering, who answered me with the threat of a bayonet, sometimes bringing himself in the attitude of a charge from trailed arms. Captain Faulkner and Mr. John Haverstadt interfered, to pacify Pickering and Bonham. Then word was given to pass up Walnut Street. By this time the press of the mob was so great that it was difficult to keep our feet, and we were crowded among the citizen prisoners, which they had taken into custody in their march through the city. Colonel Grayson and myself linked arms and determined to clear ourselves from the press when we reached the War Office.

As we passed my house, I saw my wife and Mrs. Forrest at the window of the second story. The moment she saw me in the crowd she screamed out and fainted. It was impossible then to escape. We were then within pistol-shot of Wilson's house. I saw Captain Campbell, of Colonel Hazen's regiment of the Continental Army, at one of the upper windows at Wilson's house; heard him distinctly call out to those in arms to pass on. Musketry was immediately discharged from the street and from the house, the mob gave way and fled in all directions, and left Grayson and myself under the eaves of the house in Third Street, exposed to the fire of those in the street at a distance. We concluded we would run into Wilson's garden, but there we found ourselves exposed to the fire of both the mob in the neighbours' yards, as well as those of Wilson's friends in the house.

In a few minutes we were discovered by General Mifflin, who recognised us as officers of the Continental Army, and ordered one of the doors of the back building to be opened; at this moment several persons in the house became much alarmed, and jumped out of the second-story windows. The back door of the house was immediately opened, and we entered. General Mifflin and Thompson met us on the lower floor, and requested us to follow them up stairs, observing that Mr. Wilson and his friends were about retiring to the upper rooms, which we did. When I reached the third story, I looked out of one of the windows in Third Street, looked up Third Street, could see no person in the street nearer than Dock Street, where the mob had dragged a field-piece. I looked down Third Street and saw a number of desperate-looking men in their shirt sleeves coming out of Pear Street, moving towards Wilson's house, armed with bars of iron and large hammers, and in a minute reached the house and began to force the doors and windows; they presently made a breach in Third Street, but on entering the house, they received a fire from the staircases and cellar windows, which dropped several of them; the others broke and dispersed, leaving their wounded in the house. Some of Wilson's friends ran down stairs, shut the doors and barricaded them. . . .

In a few minutes, Governor Reed, with a detachment of the first troop of City Horse, appeared. Wilson and his friends in the house sallied out. I moved with them, and the first person I recognised in the street was Governor Reed, who called upon me, by name, to aid in seizing the rioters.

—McLane Journal, N. Y. Historical Soc.

CHAPTER TWENTY

Health, Hospitals and Medicine

JOHN ADAMS *and Benjamin Rush did not always see eye to eye, but on one subject they were in agreement. "Disease," wrote Adams, "has destroyed ten men for us where the sword of the enemy has killed one." And Rush said that "hospitals are the sinks of human life in an army. They robbed the United States of more citizens than the sword." Unfortunately we do not have reliable statistics by which to test the accuracy of these generalizations, but it is reasonably clear that even Adams was not exaggerating. That the battlefield was safer than the hospital was an accepted fact in eighteenth-century warfare, and even in nineteenth-century. In the course of the Seven Years' War, for example, the British lost 1512 killed in battle and 134,000 from disease; even in our own Civil War deaths in action in the Union armies came to 67,000 while 224,000 died from disease.*

The explanation of the heavy mortality in the Revolutionary armies is to be found partly in the condition of medicine in the eighteenth century generally, partly in the situation that obtained in the American states during the war. Medicine was still more medieval than modern; there was no understanding of infection or knowledge of asepsis; only a primitive form of inoculation against smallpox; no proper safeguards against typhus, diphtheria, malaria or even scurvy; surgery was primitive, and anesthetics were unknown. As for the American situation, most of the soldiers were young and strong, and conditions of army life were, on the whole, healthy; soldiers lived mostly outdoors, managed generally to get enough vegetables; and were not so exposed to venereal diseases as were soldiers in the armies of the Old World. On the other hand the American states boasted very few well-trained doctors, almost no hospital facilities, and a desperate want of medicines, surgical instruments, bandages, bedding and other necessities.

Congress undertook early to provide some kind of medical establishment, but lacked understanding of the nature or dimensions of the problem. The original plan was shockingly inadequate; here, as elsewhere, Congress was trying to wage a cheap war. Charles Lee denounced the "little, narrow dirty economy in all things relating to the hospitals," and even Washington, who served without compensation, exclaimed that the pay of physicians was so low that "no man, sustaining the Character of a Gentleman . . . can think of accepting it." Not only were the rates of pay for physicians, nurses, orderlies and other medical personnel scandalously low, but arrangements for hospitals, food, clothing, bedding and medicines were likewise niggardly.

Congress was unfortunate, too, in its choice of director-generals. The first choice was Dr. Benjamin Church, who shortly went over to the enemy. As his successor Congress appointed Dr. John Morgan. He had studied at that seat of medical learning, Edinburgh, and on the continent; held membership in many professional and scientific societies; helped found the Philadelphia College of Medicine; and was generally regarded as the first doctor in the country. But within a year Dr. Morgan had fallen victim to a combination of professional jealousy and impossible conditions of work, and was cavalierly dismissed. His successor was the almost equally famous Dr. William Shippen, also of Philadelphia, also a graduate of Edinburgh, and also a professor at the new medical school. Though he lasted longer, he too, in the end, fell victim to the unavoidable difficulties of his position, and to the vindictiveness of his professional rivals, notably the third member of the Philadelphia fraternity, Dr. Benjamin Rush. Shippen was succeeded by Dr. Cochran of New Jersey, who was happily divorced from the internecine bickering of the Philadelphia medicos and survived the war.

Of the many other doctors who served as "physician-in-chief" for the various departments, the most famous was undoubtedly Benjamin Rush, doctor, teacher, reformer, educator, politician, signer of the Declaration, friend and patron of Tom Paine, critic of Washington, proponent of a new system of medicine, and the most articulate of all the doctors of the Revolution.

It is to Rush that we owe the most comprehensive and the most perspicacious commentary on medicine during the Revolution. Some of the other doctors were ready enough with the pen, but used it either to defend themselves against what they thought scurrilous attacks upon their integrity, or to display the breadth of their interests. Thus Dr. Morgan devoted a good deal of energy to presenting his defense against Shippen; thus Dr. James Thacher left a substantial "Military Journal" which says next to nothing about health, hospitals or medical practices. Surprisingly enough we do not have a single good comprehensive printed journal, diary, memoir or autobiography from the pen of a doctor active in the war. By all odds our best source is the correspondence of Benjamin Rush, and some of his official and semiofficial papers, and on these we have relied heavily.

In the beginning Congress provided only for medical departments of New England and the North; only very late in the war did it get around to organizing a Southern department. All of the director-generals came from the North—Church from New England, Morgan and Shippen from Pennsylvania, and Cochran from New Jersey—and so did most of the physicians-in-chief. The story of health and hospitals is therefore very largely that of the Northern campaigns—particularly the ill-omened Canadian campaign.

We present our fragmentary material here largely in chronological sequence—which is also the sequence of the military campaigns.

I. SETTING UP A MEDICAL ESTABLISHMENT

Congress wrestled with the medical problem throughout the war, but never very energetically and never successfully. From time to time it pro-

vided elaborate medical establishments, but almost always on paper. Appropriations for medical services were parsimonious; the wages provided for in the resolution of July 27 could scarcely be expected to attract talent, and though these wages—it would be improper to call them salaries—were from time to time increased, they never remotely approached what might be called a living wage. Thus as late as July 1782—when Continental money had depreciated heavily—the director of the hospital was given a salary of $122 a month, hospital surgeons $96 a month, and stewards $30 a month.

Nor were efforts to insure skillful and experienced medical help more successful. There was provision for examinations for appointment to the position of physician, but there simply were not enough trained doctors to go around, and as for assistants, stewards and nurses, it was pretty much a matter of making out with what came along. The British medical services, it should be noted, were not much better; there was no examination for appointment to army physician, and many officers, and even sergeants (like the famous Sergeant Lamb), wholly without any medical training, nevertheless performed medical duties.

1. Congress Makes Provision

July 27, 1775

The Congress took into consideration the report of the committee on establishing an hospital, and the same being debated, was agreed to as follows:

That for the establishment of an hospital for an army consisting of 20,000 men, the following officers and other attendants be appointed, with the following allowance or pay, viz.:

One director general and chief physician, his pay per day, 4 dollars.

Four surgeons, per diem each, one and one third of a dollar.

One apothecary, one and one third of a dollar.

Twenty [surgeons'] mates, each, two thirds of a dollar.

Two storekeepers, each four dollars per month.

One nurse to every 10 sick, one fifteenth of a dollar per day, or 2 dollars per month.

Labourers occasionally.

The duty of the above officers: viz.:

Director to furnish medicines, bedding and all other necessaries, to pay for the same, superintend the whole, and make his report to, and receive orders from the commander in chief.

Surgeons, apothecary and mates: to visit and attend the sick, and the mates to obey apothecary and the orders of the physicians, surgeons and apothecary.

Matron: to superintend the nurses, bedding, etc.

Nurses: to attend the sick and obey the matron's orders.

Clerk: to keep accounts for the director and storekeepers.

Storekeeper: to receive and deliver the bedding and other necessaries by order of the director. . . .

—*Journals of the Continental Congress*, II, 207-208.

2. Appointing Surgeons for the Revolutionary Army

Diary of Dr. James Thacher.

July 1775. On the day appointed, the medical candidates, sixteen in number, were summoned before the board for examination. This business occupied about four hours; the subjects were anatomy, physiology, surgery and medicine. It was not long after that I was happily relieved from suspense by receiving the sanction and acceptance of the board, with some acceptable instructions relative to the faithful discharge of duty, and the humane treatment of those soldiers who may have the misfortune to require my assistance. Six of our number were privately rejected as being found unqualified. The examination was in a considerable degree close and severe, which occasioned not a little agitation in our ranks. But it was on another occason, as I am told, that a candidate under examination was agitated into a state of perspiration, and being required to describe the mode of treatment in rheumatism, among other remedies he would promote a sweat, and being asked how he would effect this with his patient, after some hesitation he replied, "I would have him examined by a medical committee."

I was so fortunate as to obtain the office of surgeon's mate in the provincial hospital at Cambridge, Dr. John Warren being the senior surgeon. He was the brother and pupil of the gallant General Joseph Warren, who was slain in the memorable battle on Breed's Hill. This gentleman has acquired great reputation in his profession, and is distinguished for his humanity and attention to the sick and wounded soldiers, and for his amiable disposition. Having received my appointment by the Provincial Congress, I commenced my duty in the hospital July 15th. Several private but commodious houses in Cambridge are occupied for hospitals, and a considerable number of soldiers who were wounded at Breed's Hill, and a greater number of sick of various diseases, require all our attention. Dr. Isaac Foster, late of Charlestown, is also appointed a senior hospital surgeon; and his student, Mr. Josiah Bartlet, officiates as his mate; Dr. Benjamin Church is director-general of the hospital. . . .

—Thacher, *Military Journal*, pp. 28-29.

II. THE RAVAGES OF SMALLPOX ON THE EXPEDITION AGAINST CANADA

Smallpox, wrote John Adams, was "ten times more terrible than Britons, Canadians and Indians together." It was, in all probability, the worst killer during the Revolution. It was still almost a quarter of a century to Edward Jenner's discovery of inoculation with cowpox, but the practice of inoculation with smallpox itself was widespread—and sometimes successful. The worst ravages of the smallpox were on the Canadian campaign, and after. Dr. Lewis Beebe, from whose journal we take this account of that campaign, was a Massachusetts Jack-of-all-trades; for a time a doctor, he shifted later to the ministry, and ended up keeping a liquor shop in New York City.

"Nothing to Be Heard but 'Doctor! Doctor! Doctor!'"

Sunday 19th of May [*1776*]: In the afternoon was entertained with a sermon by one of the chaplains; midling morallity.

On Thursday, general orders were given by Gen. Arnold for innoculation; accordingly Col. Porters regiment was innoculated. On Fryday Gen. Thomas arrived at head quarters from Quebeck and gave counter orders: that it should be death for any person to innoculate, and that every person innoculated should be sent immediately to Montreal. . . . General Thomas this day is under great indisposition of body.

Monday 20th: General Thomas remained poorly, with many symptoms of the small pox. Early this morning 2 privates received the lash for desertion. Express orders were sent early this morning to the Three Rivers for all there to repair immediately to Sorrell. This day an express arrived to Gen. Thomas from Gen. Schuyler informing of 4000 Hanoverians laying of[f] Boston, 1000 more being gone to New York. Also another express from Maj. Sherburn who went with 140 men of Colo. Pattersons regiment from Montreal to reinforce Colo. Beadle, informing that Capt. Bliss was taken prisoner by a party of 100 regulars, 1000 savages, but received the most humane treatment, contrary to the expectation of all. . . .

Saturday 25: This day Colo. Poor arrived from Sorrell, and marched the same immediately for St. Johns. He gave me an invitation to join his regiment as surgeons mate, of which I accepted, etc.

Sunday 26: Parts of different regiments arrived from Sorrell, all being ignorant of their destination, but very few general orders, and they usually countermanded within few hours after given. Yesterday and today I have been much unwell, troubled with the quick step, attended with severe gripings. If ever I had a compassionate feeling for my fellow creatures who were objects in distress, I think it was this day; to see large barns filled with men in the very heighth of the small pox and not the least thing to make them comfortable, was almost sufficient to excite the pity of brutes. . . .

Sunday 2d. June: This morning a little after the first dawnings of the day Gen. Thomas expired; this was the 13th day after the eruption first appeared.

> Thomas is dead, that pious man,
> Where all our hopes were laid.
> Had it been one, now in command,
> My heart should not be grieved. . . .

Tuesday 4th: One of our regiment died this morning very suddenly, and was intered in the afternoon without so much as a coffin and with little or no ceremony. Among hundreds of men it was difficult to procure 8 or 10 to bear the corps about 15 rods. Death is a subject not to be attended to by soldiers; Hell and Damnation is in allmost every ones mouth from the time they awake till they fall asleep again; the stupidity of mankind in this situation is beyond all description. This day Majr. Brewer, Majr. Thomas and Majr. Sedgwick left this place for New England.

Wednesday 5th: For 10 days past I have been greatly troubled with the dysentery, and for three days it has been very severe. Took physic in the morning. Hope for some relief. In the afternoon went across the river to visit Col. Reed who I found to have the disorder very light. The number of sick with the pekot on this side is about 300, the greater part of which have it by innoculation and like to do well. I accidentally met, near night, a little, great, proud, self-conceited, foppish quack; the coxcomb appeared very haughty and insolent, but after some time in a stiff, starched and a most exalted manner says, "How do you do, Mr. Beebe." After a few complements had passed between us, I asked if he could let me have a little physic; says he, "I have plenty of physic but God damn my soul if I let you have an atom!" Here our conversation ended. . . .

Friday 7: Last evening one died of the small pox, and early this morning one of the colic; at 10 A.M. one of the nervous fever. Here in the hospital is to be seen at the same time some dead, some dying, others at the point of death, some whistling, some singing and many cursing and swearing. This is a strange composition and its chief intention has not as yet been discovered; however it appears very plain that it is wonderfully calculated for a campaign, and, if applied properly and in time, is very efficatious to prevent anything that is serious or concerning futurity. Visited many of the sick in the hospital —was moved with a compassionate feeling for poor distressed soldiers, [who,] when they are taken sick, are thrown into this dirty, stinking place and left to take care of themselves. No attendance, no provision made, but what must be loathed and abhorred by all both well and sick. . . .

Monday 10th: This day died two in Colo. Pattersons regiment with the small pox. No intelligence of importance comes to hand this day, except orders, from the great Mr. Brigadier Gen. Arnold, for Colo. Poor with his regiment to proceed to Sorrell immediately. Is not this a politick plan, especially since there is not ten men in the regiment but what has either now got the small pox or taken the infection? Some men love to command, however ridiculous their orders may appear. But I am apt to think we shall remain in this garrison for the present. It is enough to confuse and distract a rational man to be surgeon to a regiment. Nothing to be heard from morning to night but "Doctor! Doctor! Doctor!" from every side till one is deaf, dumb and blind, and almost dead; add to all this, we have nothing to eat; thus poor soldiers live sometimes better, but never worse. . . .

Thursday 13th: Arose this morning at the revilee beat, put on my morning dress, walked abroad and found the camp in a most profound silence, the whole being buried in sleep, but it was not long before the whole camp echoed with execrations upon the musketoes; was not a little pleased to hear the characters of particular persons handled in the most familiar manner, and thought many observations which were made upon particular persons were very pertinent and just. Extracted one tooth a little after sunrise, which caused one hearty "O! Dear." About 10 A.M. extracted another tooth. Bought a fowl and some fresh butter, with which we had a very good dinner. The great Gen. Arnold arrived here yesterday and began to give his inconsistent orders today for his great pity and concern for the sick; in the first place gave particular orders that every sick man, together with everyone returned not fit for duty, should draw but half allowance. In this order is discovered that superior wisdom which is necessary for a man in his exalted station in life to be possessed of. . . .

Monday 17: This morning had Colo. Poors orders to repair to Isle aux Naux to take care of the sick there; accordingly sailed in a batteau, and arrived there about 3 P.M. Was struck with amazement upon my arrival to see the vast crowds of poor distressed creatures. Language cannot describe nor imagination paint the scenes of misery and distress the soldiery endure. Scarcely a tent upon this isle but what contains one or more in distress and continually groaning and calling for relief, but in vain! Requests of this nature are as little regarded as the singing of crickets in a summers evening. The most shocking of all spectacles was to see a large barn crowded full of men with this disorder, many of which could not see, speak or walk. One—nay two —had large maggots, an inch long, crawl out of their ears, were on almost every part of the body. No mortal will ever believe what these suffered unless they were eye witnesses. Fuller appeared to be near his end. Gen. Sullivan set fire to all the armed vessels, 3 gundalows and fort at Chambly, and at evening came all his army, with all the stores and baggage, to St. Johns. . . .

Wednesday 26: The regiment is in a most deplorable situation, between 4 and 500 now in the height of the small pox. Death is now become a daily visitant in the camps, but as little regarded as the singing of birds. It appears, and really is so, that one great lesson to be learnt from Death is wholly forgot: (viz) that therein we discover our own picture; we have here pointed out our own mortality in the most lively colours. Strange that the frequent instances of so solemn a scene as this should have such an effect that it should harden, and render us stupid, and make us wholly insensible of the great importance of so serious a matter, but herein is discovered the amazing blindness and stupidity which naturally possess our minds. 40 to 50 batteaus sailed this morning for Isle aux Naux, to bring the remainder of the army; having a fair wind they cut a pretty figure. This day had intelligence that the Congress had agreed to raise an army of 72 thousand men for the year 1777. Visited many of the sick, see many curious cases, find in general that I can effect greater cures by words than by medicine.

Thursday 27: Buried two of our regiment this day. The hot weather proves very unfriendly to those who have the small pox. A large schooner arrived from Isle aux Naux, deeply loaded with stores. One thing, by the way, is somewhat remarkable, that a regiment so distressed with sickness as ours is should be so engaged in fatigue and doing duty that they can by no means find time to attend prayers night and morning or even preaching upon the Sabbath; the regiments are generally supplied with chaplains, who are as destitute of employ in their way as a parson who is dismissed from his people for the most scandalous of crimes. . . .

Saturday 29th: Buried 4 this day, 3 belonging to our regiment on the other side; they generally lose more than double to what we do here. Alas! What will become of our distressed army? Death reigns triumphant. God seems to be greatly angry with us; He appears to be incensed against us for our abominable wickedness—and in all probability will sweep away a great part of our army to destruction.

'Tis enough to make humane nature shudder only to hear the army in general blaspheme the holy name of God. This sin alone is sufficient to draw down the vengeance of an angry God upon a guilty and wicked army. But what is still melancholy, and to be greatly lamented is, amidst all the tokens of Gods holy displeasure, we remain insensible of our danger, and grow harder and harder in wickedness, and are ripening fast for utter destruction.

Sunday 30: I hardly know what to say. I have visited many of the sick. We have a great variety of sore arms and abscesses forming in all parts of the body, proceeding from the small pox, occasioned by the want of physic to cleanse the patients from the disorder. However we had none so bad as yet but what we have been able to cure, except the disorder otherwise was too obstinate. Buried two today. No preaching or praying as usual. The small pox rather abates in the regiments. A number are employed the other side almost the whole of the day to dig graves and bury the dead. . . .

Wednesday 3d. [*July, 1776*]: Had prayer last evening and this morning; hope the regiment will take a new turn of mind and for the future give steady attendance. Buried 3 this day. How strange it is that we have death sent into our camp so repeatedly, every day! And we take so little notice of it! Nay, it will not prevent cursing and swearing in the same tent with the corps. Several were confined the other side for quarreling; some of their party came to relieve them, which they effected by pulling down the guard house; upon which Gen. Sullivan paraded the whole army. Confined a number of offenders under a guard of every 4th man in the regiment. A special court is ordered to sit to-morrow. Since I have been writing, one more of our men has made his exit. Death visits us every hour. . . .

Friday 12: Felt some better as to my health. Walked to visit some of the sick in the neighborhood. Dined at Colo. Strongs with Colo. Gilman and others. Returned soon to camp. Notwithstanding the regiment as a body are on the gaining hand, yet found 6 or 8 in the most deplorable situation that ever mortals were in; it is in vain to pretend to give any just description of their unhappy circumstances, as language cannot describe, nor imagination paint, their distresses. It is impossible for [a] person that has any feeling for humane nature to enter their tents without droping a tear of pity over them.

Saturday 13: Buried 3 yesterday and 2 today—a number more lay at the point of death. Last evening heard of the death of Colo. Williams. He left this place about 10 days past for Ruport, to regain his health, being much troubled with the dysentery. He arrived at Skenesboro and grew so ill that he was unable to proceed any further, and there died July 10th, 1776, half after one in mane [morning?]. General orders for all the sick to be removed to-morrow morning to Ticonderoga. . . .

Friday 19: Last evening we had one of the most severe showers of rain ever known; it continued almost the whole night, with unremitted violence; many of their tents were ancle deep in water. Many of the sick lay their whole lengths in the water, with one blankett only to cover them. One man having the small pox bad, and unable to help himself, and being in a tent alone, which was on ground descending, the current of water came thro his tent in such plenty that it covered his head, by which means he drowned. This is the care that officers take of their sick. Such attention is paid to the distrest, who are destitute of friends. Buried two yesterday, and two more today. Cursing and damning to be heard, and idleness to be seen throughout the army as usual. . . .

Tuesday October 1st: After breakfast and waiting upon the hospital as usual, crossed to head quarters, took a view of the gundolas and rowgallies, two of which were just going to sail, in order to join the fleet; in which goes Gen. Waterbury. In the afternoon it made my heart ache to visit the hospital, to see the dysentery rage with unabated fury among many of them when I had not one article calculated for their assistance; one with this disorder, and two with the scurvey, were on the brink of the grave. Doctor Mingo is much as was a few days past, his disorder rather abates. Mr. Coxcomb is a little poorly. I almost wish sometimes that he was a good deal so, but this I know does not discover a good disposition. . . .

—BEEBE, "Journal," *Penn. Mag. of Hist. and Biog.*, LIX, 328-350.

III. THE BREAKDOWN OF HOSPITAL SERVICES

In time Congress was to establish a series of hospitals—some on paper, and some real—but at first the regional directors had to improvise hospitals as best they could. For the first few years of the war these hospitals were notoriously lacking in the most elementary necessities. Sometimes they were without heat; sometimes without food; sometimes without bedding for the sick. There were never enough doctors or nurses or orderlies, and rarely enough medicines and bandages. Eventually the French made good American deficiencies, but to the end of the war the hospitals were a cause for discontentment. The conditions described here cannot, therefore, be blamed on the doctors in charge of the medical services of the Northern Department. Actually both Dr. Stringer and Dr. Potts were professionally competent, and both were honest and well intentioned. But they had placed on them an intolerable burden of tending to the victims of the unfortunate Canadian campaign, and, a little later, of the Long Island and New York campaign. Dr. Stringer was dismissed along with Dr. Morgan; Potts succeeded him and managed the Department until after Saratoga.

1. DR. STRINGER FAILS THE NORTHERN ARMY

A. "IN THE NAME OF GOD WHAT SHALL WE DO WITH THE SICK?"

Samuel Stringer to Horatio Gates.

Fort George, July 24, 1776

Sir: . . . On my return yesterday evening I found Major Stewart's letter on the 18th, also one from Colonel Trumbull of the same date, requesting a return of the sick, etc., who I find are greatly increased, insomuch that we are in the utmost distress for both assistants and medicines. . . .

At the same time that I wrote to General Washington, I requested an augmentation of the hospital surgeons and mates, and sent a list for such a supply of medicines as I thought necessary for the campaign; and, from a letter I received from Mr. Giles, Apothecary-General, before I departed, I expected the medicines to be forwarded immediately; but, to my great mortification, except a few that Dr. Potts brought with him, none are arrived, not even a quantity that the doctor informed me were to come from Philadelphia, under the care of Mr. McHenry. What we are to do, under these shocking circumstances, I know not; I say shocking, because nothing can appear more so than our present situation—men dying for want of assistance that we are not empowered to give. Besides a want of surgeons, I am not furnished with clerks or stewards; one clerk, that I took upon myself to appoint, with General Schuyler's concurrence, is not now capable of going through the business he is obliged to take charge of. As our men's lives are thus wasted, would it be improper (as writing answers no end) that I should leave the care of the sick to Dr. Potts, and go to York myself, and see the medicines forthwith forwarded by land, until they can be safely conveyed by water, and from thence wait on Congress in person, lay our situation before them, and endeavour to have my powers enlarged, or at least get their consent to provide the number of assistants that are requisite? If, sir, you should approve of such a step, I should be much obliged to you for a letter enforcing the necessity of the application. I should not, at this time of distress, hesitate to engage surgeons, had not General Schuyler received an answer in the winter to the purport of my letter above mentioned, which was contained in a fresh resolve, "that the resolve (now enclosed) was sufficient." . . .

Dr. Potts informed me that there were twenty half-chests of medicines, already put up at York, to be sent off by the first sloop, for ten battalions in this department. I made at Albany the strictest inquiry about them, and find they are not come. Whence such a dilatoriness arises, I cannot account; but there certainly is a remissness somewhere that ought to be removed, if possible.

Just now Lieutenant Diffendorff arrived, and acquaints us that a large number of sick are coming, in addition to what we already have (about fifteen hundred). In the name of *God*, what shall we do with them all, my dear General?

—FORCE, *American Archives*, 5th Series, I, 651-652.

B. "NONE OF THE TEN CHESTS OF MEDICINE HAS EVER BEEN RECEIVED"

Horatio Gates to Egbert Benson.

Tyconderoga, August 22, 1776

Dear Sir: The 29th ultimo I granted Doctor Stringer, at his earnest request, a permission to go to New York with all expedition, to procure medicines for the General Hospital and Army in this department. He made me a solemn promise he would not delay an instant in returning to his duty with the medicinal stores so much wanted, and which the troops here are almost ready to mutiny to obtain. I am this day informed that Doctor Stringer, instead of fulfilling his promises and returning with all imaginable despatch to his duty, is gone a preferment hunting to the Congress at Philadelphia, while the troops here are suffering inexpressible distress for want of medicines.

I entreat, sir, you will instantly lay this letter before General Washington, and receive his commands for sending a supply of medicines to Doctor Potts at Lake George. Not one of the ten chests of medicines, which you told me at New York were sent to the ten regiments that marched in the spring from thence, have ever been received by either of those regiments; therefore be sure you send the supply now demanded by some person whose particular duty it will be to see it delivered to Doctor Potts. Many of the regimental surgeons here have not any medicines, nor do I believe there is a pound of bark in the whole camp.

I cannot be long answerable for the consequences of the shameful neglect of the Army in this department. The United States expect the same good service from their troops here as everywhere else. This they cannot have unless they command the same attention to be paid the health of their soldiers here as elsewhere.

–FORCE, *American Archives*, 5th Series, I, 1114.

2. "THE SITUATION OF THE SICK IS NOT TO BE DESCRIBED"

Dr. Jonathan Potts to Dr. John Morgan.

Fort George, August 10, 1776

... The distressed situation of the sick here is not to be described: without clothing, without bedding or a shelter sufficient to screen them from the weather.

I am sure your known humanity will be affected when I tell you we have at present upwards of one thousand sick crowded into sheds and laboring under the various and cruel disorders of dysenteries, bilious putrid fevers and the effects of a confluent smallpox; to attend this large number we have four seniors and four mates, exclusive of myself, and our little shop does not afford a grain of jalap, ipecac, bark, salt, opium and sundry other capital articles and nothing of the kind to be had in this quarter; in this dilemma our inventions are exhausted for substitutes, but we shall go on doing the best we can in hopes of speedy supply. . . .

–GIBSON, *Dr. Otto and the Medical Background of the Revolution*, p. 107.

3. "IT WOULD MELT A HEART OF STONE TO HEAR THE MOANS"

Samuel Wigglesworth to the New Hampshire Committee of Safety.

Mount Independence, opposite Ticonderoga, September 27, 1776

Gentlemen: When I waited upon you to receive a commission for Doctor Mooers, if I am not mistaken Colonel Thornton informed me that there would be a supply of medicines proper for the campaign without fail. In hopes that it would be so I appeased the troops at Number-Four, but alas! how have we found ourselves mistaken. Gentlemen, I wish you could transport yourselves to this place for a moment, to see the distressed situation of these troops, and no medicines. Near half of this regiment is entirely incapable of any service, some dying almost every day. Colonel Wymans regiment in the same unhappy situation. There are no medicines of any avail in the Continental chest; such as are there are in their native state, unprepared; no emetic nor cathartic; no mercurial or antimonial remedy; no opiate or elixir tincture, nor even any capital medicine. It would make a heart of stone melt to hear the moans and see the distresses of the sick and dying. I scarce pass a tent but I hear men solemnly declaring that they will never engage another campaign without being assured of a better supply of medicines.

The above, gentlemen, is this real state of this army. Now, sirs, think how much more unhappy and distressed the condition of these troops must be, should the enemy attack our lines. Numbers of wounded, which is the never failing consequences of obstinate battles, and nothing suitable wherewith to dress their wounds.

Gentlemen, you will excuse the freedom I have used in transmitting to you the state of this army in the above respect, and thought it my duty to acquaint you therewith.

I am, gentlemen, with great respect, your humble servant,

SAMUEL WIGGLESWORTH

—FORCE, *American Archives*, 5th Series, II, 574.

4. THE HOSPITALS AT TICONDEROGA

Report of the Committee sent to the Northern Department.

November 27, 1776

. . . Your Committee . . . beg leave further to report that they have visited the General Hospital for the Northern Army, situated at Fort George; that there is a range of buildings erected convenient for the purpose, which . . . contained about four hundred sick, including those wounded and sent from General Arnold's fleet; that they were sufficiently supplied with fresh mutton and Indian meal, but wanted vegetables; that the Director-General in that department obtained a large supply of medicines, but that the sick suffered much for want of good female nurses and comfortable bedding; many of those poor creatures being obliged to lay upon the bare boards. Your Committee endeavored to secure straw as the best temporary expedient; but they earnestly recommended it to the attention of Congress that a quantity of bedding be speedily furnished. . . .

A hospital, in the opinion of your committee, should be continued at Fort George for the reception of persons infected with contagious disorders; but your Committee are clearly of the opinion that the General Hospital for the army stationed at Tyconderoga ought to be erected on the opposite grounds, called Mount Independence, Fort George being at much too great a distance. Your Committee recommended that a quantity of vegetables be sent to Tyconderoga without delay. . . . Your Committee cannot omit mentioning, under this head, the complaints which they have received from persons of all ranks, in and out of the army, respecting the neglect and ill-treatment of the sick. It is shocking to the feelings of humanity, as well as ruinous to the publick service, that so deadly an evil hath been so long without a remedy. . . .

—FORCE, *American Archives*, 5th Series, III, 1584.

5. SMALLWOOD COMPLAINS OF THE INHUMAN NEGLECT OF THE SICK

Colonel William Smallwood to the Maryland Council of Safety.

Philips's Heights, [New York,] October, 1776

. . . We want medicine much; none can be had here. Our sick have and are now suffering extremely. The number you'll observe from the list is very considerable, owing in a great measure to the bad provision made for and care taken of them, the men being often moved, and have been exposed to lie on the cold ground ever since they came here; often lying without their tents for several nights, as is now the case, having been five nights and days without them, being ever since the enemy landed up here. . . .

Our next greatest suffering proceeds from the great neglect of the sick; and his [Washington's] orders . . . are most salutary, were they to be duly attended to; but here, too, there is not only a shameful but even an inhuman neglect daily exhibited. The Directors of the General Hospitals supply and provide for the sick, who are extremely remiss and inattentive to the well-being and comfort of these unhappy men; out of this train they cannot be taken. I have withdrawn all mine long ago, and had them placed in a comfortable house in the country, and supplied with only the common rations; even this is preferable to the fare of a General Hospital. Two of these Regimental Hospitals, after I have had them put in order, one has been taken away by the Directors for a General Hospital, and my people turned out of doors, and the other would have been taken in the same manner, had I not have applied to General Washington, who told me to keep it. The misfortune is that every supply to the Regimental Hospital of necessaries suitable for the sick must come from an order from these Directors, and is very seldom obtained. I have more than once applied that my Quartermaster might furnish and make a charge for what was supplied, by which means I could have rendered the situation of the sick much more comfortable, at a less expense, but could not be allowed. I wish this could be obtained.

I foresee the evils arising from the shameful neglect in this department. One good-seasoned and well-trained soldier, recovered to health, is worth a dozen new recruits, and is often easier recovered than to get a recruit, exclusive of which this neglect is very discouraging to the soldiery and must injure the service upon the new inlistments after the troops go into winter quarters.
—FORCE, *American Archives*, 5th Series, II, 1099-1100.

6. DR. MORGAN REFUSES MEDICINES TO THE MARYLAND TROOPS

John Pine to James Tighlman, Esq.

Camp at White-Plains, November 7th, 1776

Dear Sir: I arrived here on Monday, the 28th of last month, about four in the afternoon, while our people were engaged in a very hot battle, the particulars of which I suppose you'll hear before this comes to hand. Colonel Smallwood's battalion suffered a good deal; the Colonel himself wounded in two places; the number of killed and wounded, as the report is in the camp, amounts only to about ninety, but from the wounded I saw myself in the hospital and adjacent houses, there must at least be an hundred and twenty or thirty wounded; the number of killed I don't know.

The day after I came here I waited on Doctor Morgan, Director General of the hospitals here, for medicines, etc. He told me he had nothing to say to the Maryland troops, and that it was not his business to supply the regimental surgeons with medicines, and that it must have been a mistake of the Convention or Council of Safety of Maryland to send their surgeons here without them and think they were to be supplied here. Upon this, I went to Colonel Smallwood, who is about fifteen miles from this, near the hospital, and told him the case, and what condition I found the sick in, both the Regular and Flying-Camp, Maryland troops, without the least morsel of physick of any sort, although a great many of them in a very pitiable condition, upon which the Colonel gave me a letter to Doctor Morgan. The doctor then told me I might have some few things if I could go to New York for them, which is about eighty miles from this. I told him by the time I went there and got back, that the time of most of the Maryland troops would be expired. He told me he could not help it, and that medicines were very hard to be got.

I should be glad this matter was communicated to the Council of Safety. Since I came here I have been of what service I could to the Maryland troops; all their surgeons are over in the Jerseys with their sick, and a great number are still sick here.

—Force, *American Archives*, 5th Series, III, 836-837.

7. "Our Hospital Beggars Description and Shocks Humanity"

Anthony Wayne to Horatio Gates.

Ticonderoga, 1 December, 1776

I must take the liberty to remind you that the term for which the Pennsylvanians are engaged expires the 5th of next month; no time is therefore to be lost in relieving them. We shall be hard set to get the sick away; our hospital, or rather house of carnage, beggars all description, and shocks humanity to visit. The cause is obvious: no medicine or regimen on the ground suitable for the sick; no beds or straw to lay on; no covering to keep them warm, other than their own thin wretched clothing. We can't send them to Fort George as usual, the hospital being removed from thence to Albany, and the weather is so intensely cold that before they would reach there they would perish. It lays much in your power, by a proper representation to Congress, to have these defects supplied, and many other abuses redressed that tend to render the service almost intolerable to men and officers. But as you are a much better judge of those matters than me, I shall say no more on the subject.

—Force, *American Archives*, 5th Series, III, 1031.

8. "They Went, and Found No Hospital"

Court-Martial of Caleb Green.

Tavern near Peekskill, 25 December, 1776

Caleb Green, a soldier in Colonel Thomas's regiment and my company, confined for desertion: Samuel Townsend, Captain, to the officer of the main guard. Peekskill, 9th December, 1776.

The prisoner to the crime pleads not guilty.

Abraham Egburt, on oath, testifies that himself and the prisoner had liberty to go to the hospital, to recover their health. They went, and found no doctor, nor any body to assist them; from the hospital the prisoner went to his own home, about two miles, and that he has not seen him since, till he returned to his own company, the 8th of December.

William Brown, on oath, testifies that he was sent to order the prisoner to camp, but on being informed by his neighbours that he was unable to go to camp, never went to him. I was sent to him a second time, about the beginning of this month. I forwarded the order by the prisoner's brother, and the prisoner made no delay in coming.

Nathan Merrit testifies that he agrees with William Brown, and further saith that about the 25th of last November he was at the prisoner's house, and that he appeared very unwell.

Daniel Lewis, on oath, agrees with Nathan Merrit respecting the prisoner's health.

The Court, having heard the evidence offered, do unanimously adjudge the prisoner not guilty of the crime laid to his charge.

SAM'L WYLLYS, *President*

W. HEATH. I do hereby approve the sentence.

—FORCE, *American Archives*, 5th Series, III, 1421.

IV. DR. SHIPPEN AND DR. RUSH TRY TO BRING ORDER OUT OF CHAOS

In October 1776 Dr. Shippen was promoted to the post of Director-General of the hospitals west of the Hudson. Shocked by the conditions that he discovered, he promptly wrote his friend, R. H. Lee, a proposal for the reorganization of the medical services; this proposal contained, implicitly, criticism of his superior, Dr. Morgan. The following spring Shippen submitted to the Congress a formal plan for a general reorganization of the medical services of the Army; Congress adopted the plan and appointed its author to be Director-General of all the hospitals.

Meantime a new star was rising on the medical horizon. Benjamin Rush was younger than Dr. Morgan or Dr. Shippen, but did not suffer his youthfulness to embarrass him. Professor of Chemistry at the College of Philadelphia, he counted medicine merely one of his many interests. He was a leader in the Patriot cause; as we have seen, he sponsored Thomas Paine and limned the Founding Fathers; he signed the Declaration of Independence; he wrote antislavery pamphlets; he championed popular education, and even education for girls; he tried a variety of religious faiths; he was, in short, a universal genius. He was, in addition, ambitious and vindictive. In April 1777 he was appointed Surgeon General of the armies of the Middle Department, and signalized his appointment by producing an eminently sensible manual for preserving the health of soldiers. No less disturbed by incompetence than Shippen had been, he now blamed Shippen for the distressing condition of army medical services, and lodged a formal complaint against his superior. Congress investigated, sustained Dr. Shippen, and Rush resigned, returning to teaching, private practice and politics.

We give here extracts from some of the many letters of accusation and complaint—letters which, for all their querulousness and partisanship, provide us with authentic information.

1. Dr. Shippen Proposes a Plan of Reorganization

Dr. William Shippen, Jr., to Richard Henry Lee.

Bethlehem, Tuesday, December 17, 1776

From a tedious experience I have learned what is necessary in a military hospital, and I think it my duty to give my opinion thereon to my friends in Congress. I have attended to this matter more carefully, because I saw on my first entering the Army that many more brave Americans fell a sacrifice to neglect and iniquity in the medical department than fell by the sword of the enemy. I saw Directors, but no direction; physicians and surgeons, but too much about their business, and the care of the sick committed to young boys in the character of mates, quite ignorant, and, as I am informed, hired at half price, etc., etc., etc. Some I found honestly doing the duty of their stations.

How far my own department has been better filled does not become me to say, and I am not ashamed to own that I am conscious of many imperfections, but flatter myself that none of them have arisen from want of care and integrity in the Director, or skill and industry in his physicians, surgeons and mates; all the latter, he can with pleasure declare, have done more than their duty cheerfully. Some have arisen from my inexperience, some from the scarcity of many articles necessary for the sick, and some from the distracted, flying state of the army. All these causes, I persuade myself, will in a great measure be removed in the next campaign, if our cruel enemies risk another.

I would humbly propose the following arrangements as necessary and, I hope, adequate to making the sick soldiery comfortable and happy: Suppose three armies, a Northern, Middle and Southern; to each of these the following officers:

 1 Director and Surgeon General
 3 Sub or Assistant Directors
 10 Surgeons or Physicians
 20 Mates
 1 Apothecary General
 4 Mates
 1 to act as Quartermaster General
  and Commissary General
 3 Deputies, or one to every hundred sick
 1 Steward to every hundred sick
 1 Matron to . . . ditto . . .
 1 Ward-Master to ditto . . .
 1 Nurse to every fifteen sick,
 1 to act as Secretary and Storekeeper
  to every hospital

The Directors-General and Sub-Directors to be chosen by the Congress; the Physicians and Surgeons, after a strict examination; all other officers by the Directors.

Not less than this, in my opinion, will induce men properly qualified to engage; and any others will be dear at any price.

—Force, *American Archives*, 5th Series, III, 1259.

2. DR. RUSH CONTRASTS BRITISH AND AMERICAN ESTABLISHMENTS

A. BENJAMIN RUSH TO JOHN ADAMS

Trenton, October 1st, 1777

Dear Sir:

They [the British] pay a supreme regard to the cleanliness and health of their men. After the battle on the 11th of last month, the soldiers were strictly forbidden to touch any of the blankets belonging to the dead or wounded of our army lest they should contract the "rebel distempers." One of their officers, a subaltern, observed to me that his soldiers were infants that required constant attendance, and said as a proof of it that although they had blankets tied to their backs, yet such was their laziness that they would sleep in the dew and cold without them rather than have the trouble of untying and opening them. He said his business every night before he slept was to see that no soldier in his company laid down without a blanket.

Great pains were taken to procure vegetables for the army, and I observed everywhere a great quantity of them about the soldiers' tents. The deputy quartermasters and deputy commissaries in Howe's army are composed chiefly of old and reputable officers, and not of the vagrants and bankrupts of the country.

There is the utmost order and contentment in their hospitals. The wounded whom we brought off from the field were not half so well treated as those whom we left in General Howe's hands. Our officers and soldiers spoke with gratitude and affection of their surgeons. An orderly man was allotted to every ten of our wounded, and British officers called every morning upon our officers to know whether their surgeons did their duty. You must not attribute this to their humanity. They hate us in every shape we appear to them. Their care of our wounded was entirely the effect of the perfection of their medical establishment, which mechanically forced happiness and satisfaction upon our countrymen perhaps without a single wish in the officers of the hospital to make their situation comfortable.

It would take a volume to tell you of the many things I saw and heard which tend to show the extreme regard that our enemies pay to discipline, order, economy and cleanliness among their soldiers.

In my way to this place I passed through General Washington's army. To my great mortification I arrived at the headquarters of a general on an outpost without being challenged by a single sentry. . . . Our hospital opened a continuation of the confused scenes I had beheld in the army. The waste, the peculation, the unnecessary officers, etc. (all the effects of *our* medical establishment), are enough to sink our country without the weights which oppress it from other quarters. It is now universally said that the system was formed for the Director General and not for the benefit of the sick and wounded. Such unlimited powers and no checks would have suited an angel. The sick suffer, but no redress can be had for them. Upwards of 100 of them were drunk last night. We have no guards to prevent this evil. In Howe's army a captain's guard mounts over every 200 sick. Besides keeping their men from contracting and prolonging distempers by rambling, drinking, and whoring,

guards keep up at all times in the minds of the sick a sense of military subordination. A soldier should never forget for a single hour that he has a
master. One month in our hospitals would undo all the discipline of a year,
provided our soldiers brought it with them from the army.

I know it is common to blame our subalterns for all these vices. But we
must investigate their source in the higher departments of the army. . . .

The present management of our army would depopulate America if men
grew among us as speedily and spontaneously as blades of grass. The "wealth
of worlds" could not support the expense of the medical department alone
above two or three years. . . .

B. BENJAMIN RUSH TO JOHN ADAMS

Reading, October 21, 1777

My dear Friend:
. . . Our hospital affairs grow worse and worse. There are several hundred
wounded soldiers in this place who would have perished had they not been
supported by the voluntary and benevolent contributions of some pious whigs.
The fault is both in the establishment and in the Director General. He is both
ignorant and *negligent* of his duty. There is but *one* right system for a military hospital, and that is the one made use of by the British army. It was once
introduced by Dr. Church at Cambridge, and Dr. McKnight informs me that
he never has seen order, economy or happiness in a hospital since it was banished by Dr. Morgan and his successor. My heart is almost broken at seeing
the distresses of my countrymen without a power to remedy them. Dr. S.
never sets his foot in a hospital. Tell me, are there any hopes of our plan being
mended? Dr. Brown and every medical officer in the hospital execrate it. If it
cannot be altered, and that soon, I shall trouble you with my resignation, and
my reasons shall afterwards be given to the public for it. The British system
would save half a million a year to the continent, and what is more, would
produce perfect satisfaction and happiness.

A surgeon general is wanted in the northern department. Give me leave to
recommend Dr. McKnight, a senior surgeon in the flying hospital, for that
office. He has skill, industry and humanity, and has served with unequaled
reputation since the beginning of the war. . . .

C. BENJAMIN RUSH TO WILLIAM DUER, DELEGATE TO CONGRESS FROM NEW YORK

Princeton, December 8th, 1777

Dear Sir,
I beg leave to trouble you for a few minutes with some remarks upon the
medical establishment, which in spite of the munificence and good intentions
of the Congress has not produced that happiness which was expected. The
reason of it appears from experience to be owing to your having deviated from
the plans used in all European armies, and in particular from that most excellent one which is now in use in the British army. It is as follows:

1. There is an inspector general and chief physician, whose only business
it is to visit all the hospitals, to examine into the quantity and quality of the
medicines, stores, instruments, etc., and to receive and deliver reports of the
number of sick and wounded to the commander in chief.

2. There is a purveyor general, whose business it is to provide hospitals, medicines, stores, beds, blankets, straw, and necessaries of all kinds for the sick and wounded. He is allowed as many deputies as there are hospitals. He has nothing to do with the care of the sick.

3. There are physicians and surgeons general, whose business it is to administer the stores provided by the purveyor general and to direct everything necessary for the recovery, the convenience and happiness of the sick. The purveyor is subject to all their orders, which are always made in writing to serve as vouchers for the expenditures of the purveyor. As an additional check upon the purveyor, none of his accounts are passed until they are certified by the physicians and surgeons general. This renders it impossible to defraud the sick of anything prescribed or purchased for them. The physicians and surgeons general have their deputies under them who are called *seniors* and *mates*.

This is a short account of the outlines of the British system, which is said to be the most perfect in the world. I shall now compare it with the establishment now in use in the American hospitals.

The director general possesses all the powers of the above officers. He is chief physician, inspector general, purveyor or commissary general, physician and surgeon general. All reports come through his hands, by which means the number of sick, wounded and dead may always be proportioned to his expenditures and to his fears of alarming Congress with accounts of the mortality of diseases. He can be present only in one place at a time but is supposed to be acquainted with all the wants of his hospitals. This is impossible. The sick therefore must suffer, for the surgeons of hospitals have no right to *demand* supplies for them, the director general being the only judge of their wants. Lastly, his accounts are *not* certified by the physicians and surgeons general, so that the sick have no security for the stores and medicines intended for them. A director general may sell them to the amount of a million a year without a possibility of being detected by your present establishment. All that the Congress requires of him are receipts for the purchase of the articles intended for the sick.

These ample and *incompatible* powers thus lodged in the hands of *one* man appear to be absurd as if General Washington had been made quartermaster, commissary and adjutant general of your whole army. And your having invested him with a power to direct the physicians and surgeons in anything while he acts as purveyor is as absurd as it would be to give the commissary general a power to command your commander in chief. To do the duty of purveyor general *only*, requires a share of industry and a capacity for business which falls to the lot of few men in the world. What can be expected then from one who, added to that office, is responsible for every life in the army?

D. BENJAMIN RUSH TO WILLIAM DUER

Princeton, December 13, 1777

Dear Sir,

In my letter to you a few days ago I informed you that we had 3000 patients in our hospitals. Since the dating of that letter I have discovered that they now amount to 5000. They consist chiefly of southern army, and amount to near one half of the number of troops which composed that army during the last campaign.

I have heard with great pleasure that you are about to new-model the army. For God's sake, do not forget to take the medical system under your consideration. It is a mass of corruption and tyranny and has wholly disappointed the benevolence and munificence of the Congress. It would take up a volume to unfold all the disorders and miseries of the hospitals. What do you think of 5000 being supported with stores, hospital furniture, etc., sufficient for only 1500 men? What do you think of 600 men in a village without a single officer to mount a guard over them or punish irregularities? This is the case at this time in Princetown, and the consequences are: Old disorders are prolonged, new ones are contracted, the discipline of the soldiers (contracted at camp) is destroyed, the inhabitants are plundered, and the blankets, clothes, shoes, etc., of the soldiers are stolen or exchanged in every tavern and hut for spiritous liquors.

I have witnessed these things for these six months and have complained of them to the Director General, to the Congress, and to the generals of the army to no effect. What do you think of 400 sick being crowded into a house large enough (according to the calculations of Pringle, Monroe and Dr. Jones, who have all written upon military hospitals) for only 150? This has been done in one place, and the consequences of it was a putrid fever was generated which carried off 12 soldiers in three days (who all came into the hospital with other diseases) and many more in the space of two weeks. Upon my complaining to the Director General that he had crowded too many sick into one house, he told me "he was the *only* judge of that, and that my *only* business was to take care of all he sent there." Your system justified his making me this answer, although it does not oblige him ever to go *inside* of a hospital or to expose himself to the least danger of being infected by a fever. Six surgeons have died since last spring of fevers contracted in our hospitals, and there is scarcely one who has not been ill in a greater or lesser degree with it.

Nothing like this has happened in the northern department. The reasons of which are these. Dr. Potts has confined himself *solely* to the purveying business, and Dr. Treat, who served as a surgeon in the British hospitals last war, has introduced the British system in its *most minute parts* into the hospitals under his direction.

I wish some members of Congress (not related to Dr. S——n) would visit our hospitals and converse with the principal surgeons in them. Although Dr. S——n has taken great pains to extort the power of appointing them out of the physician and surgeon generals' hands, and has made some of them dependent upon his will, yet I believe you will not find more than *one* man among them who does not reprobate our system and who will not ring peals of distress and villainy in your ears much louder than anything you have heard from me.

I bequeath you these broken hints as a legacy, being determined, as soon as I can with honor and a clear conscience leave my present charge, to send you my commission. I beg leave to repeat my solicitation in favor of Dr.

Jones (of New York) being appointed *inspector general* of your hospitals. He will save you millions of dollars, and what are more estimable, thousands of lives in a year. I would rather serve as a mate in a hospital under him with the British system than share with the present Director General in all his power and glory. . . .

—BUTTERFIELD, ed., *Letters of Benjamin Rush*, I, 154-176 *passim*.

V. THE IMPACT OF THE WAR ON MEDICINE

War tends to specialize and restrict science, but does provide doctors with clinical facilities in a highly concentrated form, and some opportunity for medical experimentation. The American Revolution stimulated both thinking and writing in the field of medicine. At its outset Dr. John Jones of New York published a useful volume on the treatment of wounds and fractures; the Baron Van Swieten's The Diseases Incident to Armies *was published in Philadelphia; a Dr. William Brown of Virginia published a pharmacopoeia; and the chief physician for Rochambeau's army, Jean Coste, brought out a pharmacopoeia for the use of the French hospitals; Dr. Morgan wrote on inoculation against the smallpox and so did Benjamin Rush; and a Dr. Barnabas Binney studied a "Remarkable Case of a Gun-Shot Wound"—the remarkable thing being that the patient recovered.*

We give here four examples of the impact of war on medical thought and practice. The first is by Dr. Ebenezer Beardsley, who thought he found the cause, if not the cure, for dysentery, and submitted his findings (after the war) to the newly organized American Academy of Arts and Sciences. The second is from the indefatigable pen of Dr. Rush: Directions for Preserving the Health of Soldiers; *it has some claim to being considered the most important of his medical writings. Third are two brief extracts from Dr. James Thacher's often disappointing* Journal of the American Revolution: *an account of Saratoga as a clinical laboratory, and a description of wholesale inoculation against the dread smallpox. And last a letter to the Earl of Sandwich, First Lord of the Admiralty, tells us some of the measures taken in the British Navy to overcome scurvy.*

1. AN AMERICAN DOCTOR TRIES TO FIND THE CAUSE OF DYSENTERY

[1783]

By Dr. Ebenezer Beardsley.

About the beginning of April 1776, the American army, under the command of his Excellency General Washington, marched from Boston for New York, at which place they arrived near the middle of the month. The sick and invalids having been left behind, the whole army were in perfect health. They took up their quarters in the barracks and houses of the citizens till about the first of May, when they all went into tents, except the 22nd Regiment, under the command of Colonel William Wyllys, who for want of tents continued in their quarters in Smith Street. This regiment was very healthy until about the middle of the month, when upwards of one hundred of the men were taken down with the dysentery in the space of one week.

Such a sudden invasion of this formidable disease alarmed me greatly. As I found upon inquiry that there was not a single dysenteric patient besides in the whole army, I concluded that the disease arose from some cause peculiar to the city; but after a careful inquiry, I could not find that there was a single inhabitant in the whole city that was sick with the distemper. Those who lived in the same street, and many of them in the same houses with us, were entirely free from this, or indeed any other disease.

For several days I was much perplexed and greatly at a loss as to the cause. At length I observed that not only the citizens with whom we lived were free from the disease, but that some whole companies of the same regiment had nothing of it. This led me to consider more minutely the situation and circumstances of those who were sick; all of whom, I found, lived either in low underground rooms, or else in garrets, so situated as not to admit of a free circulation of air. The rooms were also considerably less in proportion to the number of men than usual. Struck with these discoveries, I concluded at once that the difference arose from a confined stagnant air, deprived by this means of its natural elacticity, and loaded with putrid effluvia from the bodies of the unhappy people who lived in it.

Having communicated my discoveries to the Colonel, I requested that the men (both sick and well) might be removed out of those rooms into such as were more airy and capacious. This measure was attended with the most salutary consequences. Those who were sick recovered in a short time, except one or two that died; and no more being seized with the disease, in a few weeks the regiment became entirely healthy. . . .

The discovery of this singular instance of the pernicious effects of confined stagnant air was of great use to me in the course of the campaign. In the months of July and August, the dysentery, bilious and other fevers of the putrid kind became very rife both in the army and the country. Great pains were taken to procure for our men who were sick with any of those disorders, large rooms, and to have them well ventilated. Yet, under these circumstances, I frequently observed that the sick who lay in and near the corners of the rooms were handled much more severely than those which lay in the middle of them.

—BEARDSLEY, "Effects of Stagnant Air," *Memoirs of Academy of Arts and Sciences*, I, 542.

2. DR. RUSH INSTRUCTS OFFICERS IN SOLDIERS' HEALTH

To the Officers in the Army of the United American States: Directions for Preserving the Health of Soldiers.

April 22d, 1777

. . . The art of preserving the health of a soldier consists in attending to the following particulars: I. Dress. II. Diet. III. Cleanliness. And IV. Encampments.

I. *The Dress* of a soldier has a great influence upon his health. It is to be lamented that the peculiar situation of our country, from the infancy of our foreign trade and domestic manufactures, has obliged us to clothe our soldiers chiefly in linen. It is a well-known fact that the perspiration of the body, by attaching itself to linen and afterwards by mixing with rain, is disposed to form miasmata which produce fevers. Upon this account I could wish the rifle shirt was banished from our army. Besides accumulating putrid miasmata, it conceals filth and prevents a due regard being paid to cleanliness. The Roman soldiers wore flannel shirts next to their skins. This was one among other causes of the healthiness of the Roman armies. During the last war in America, Gen. (then Col.) Gage obliged the soldiers of his regiment to wear flannel shirts from an accidental want of linen, and it was remarkable during a sickly campaign on the Lakes not a single soldier belonging to the said regiment was ever seen in any of the military hospitals. I have known several instances where the yearly visits of the intermitting fever have stayed in the State of Pennsylvania, in places most subject to the disorder, by nothing else but the use of flannel shirts.

The hair by being long uncombed is apt to accumulate the perspiration of the head, which by becoming putrid sometimes produces diseases. There are two methods of guarding against this evil: the first is by combing and dressing the hair every day; the second is by wearing it thin and short in the neck. The former is attended with delays often incompatible with the duty of a soldier, and therefore the latter is to be preferred to it. This easy mode of wearing the hair is strongly recommended by Count Saxe and by all modern writers on the military art.

II. *The Diet* of soldiers should consist *chiefly* of vegetables. The nature of their duty, as well as their former habits of life, require it. If every tree on the continent of America produced Jesuits bark, it would not be sufficient to preserve or restore the health of soldiers who eat two or three pounds of flesh in a day. Their vegetables should be well cooked. It is of the last consequence that damaged flour should not be used in the camp. It is the seed of many disorders. It is of equal consequence that good flour should not be rendered unwholesome by an error in making it into bread. Perhaps it was the danger to which flour was always exposed of being damaged in a camp, or being rendered unwholesome from the manner of baking it, that led the Roman generals to use wheat instead of flour for the daily food of their soldiers. Caesar fed his troops with wheat only, in his expedition into Gaul. It was prepared by being well boiled, and was eaten with spoons in the room of bread. If a little sugar or molasses is added to wheat prepared in this manner, it forms not only a most wholesome food but a most agreeable repast.

What shall I say to the custom of drinking spirituous liquors which prevails so generally in our army? I am aware of the prejudices in favor of it. It requires an arm more powerful than mine—the arm of a Hercules—to encounter them. The common apology for the use of rum in our army is that it is necessary to guard against the effects of heat and cold. But I maintain that in no case whatever does rum abate the effects of either of them upon the constitution. On the contrary, I believe it always increases them. The temporary elevation of spirits in summer and the temporary generation of warmth in winter produced by rum always leaves the body languid and more liable to be affected with heat and cold afterwards. Happy would it be for our soldiers if the evil ended here! The use of rum, by gradually wearing away the powers of the system, lays the foundation of fevers, fluxes, jaundices, and all the train of diseases which occur in military hospitals. It is a vulgar error to suppose that the fatigue arising from violent exercise or hard labor is relieved by the use of spirituous liquors. The principles of animal life are the same in a horse as in a man, and horses, we find, undergo the severest labor with no other liquor than cool water. There are many instances where even reapers have been forced to acknowledge that plentiful draughts of milk and water have enabled them to go through the fatigues of harvest with more pleasure and fewer inconveniences to their health than ever they experienced from the use of a mixture of rum and water.

Spirituous liquors were unknown to the armies of ancient Rome. The canteen of every soldier was filled with nothing but vinegar, and it was by frequently drinking a small quantity of this wholesome liquor mixed with water that the Roman soldiers were enabled to sustain tedious marches through scorching sands without being subject to sickness of any kind. The vinegar effectually resists that tendency to putrefaction to which heat and labor dispose the fluids. It moreover calms the inordinate action of the solids which is created by hard duty. It would be foreign to my purpose, or I might show that the abstraction of rum from our soldiers would contribute greatly to promote discipline and a faithful discharge of duty among them. Gen. Wolfe, who was a philosopher as well as a general, never suffered a drop of spirits to be drank by his soldiers except when they served as sentries or upon fatigue duty in rainy weather. Perhaps these are the only cases in which a small quantity of rum may be useful. It will be of the most essential service if it be mixed with three or four times its quantity of water.

III. Too much cannot be said in favor of *Cleanliness*. If it were possible to convert every blade of grass on the continent into an American soldier, the want of cleanliness would reduce them in two or three campaigns to a handful of men. It should extend 1. To the *body* of a soldier. He should be obliged to wash his hands and face at least once every day, and his whole body twice or three times a week, especially in summer. The cold bath was part of the military discipline of the Roman soldiers and contributed much to preserve their health. 2. It should extend to the *clothes* of a soldier. Frequent changes of linen are indispensably necessary, and unless a strict regard is paid to this article, all our pains to preserve the health of our soldiers will be to no purpose. 3. It should extend to the *food* of a soldier. Great care should be taken that the vessels in which he cooks his victuals should be carefully washed after each time of their being used.

Too many soldiers should not be allowed on any pretense whatever to crowd into the same tent or quarter. The jail fever is the offspring of the perspiration and respiration of human bodies brought into a compass too narrow to be diluted and rendered inert by a mixture with the atmosphere.

The straw or hay which composes the bed of a soldier should be often changed, and his blanket should be exposed every day to the sun. This will prevent the perspiration from becoming morbid and dangerous by accumulating upon it.

The commanding officer should take the utmost care never to suffer a soldier to sleep or even to sit down in his tent with wet clothes, nor to lie down in a wet blanket or upon damp straw. The utmost vigilance will be necessary to guard against this fruitful source of disorders among soldiers.

The environs of each tent and of the camp in general should be kept perfectly clean of the offals of animals and of filth of all kinds. They should be buried or carefully removed every day beyond the neighborhood of the camp.

IV. The formation of an *Encampment* is of the utmost importance to the health of an army. It is to no purpose to seek for security from an enemy in the wisest disposition of troops in a country where marshes and millponds let loose intermitting fevers upon them. Sometimes it may be necessary to encamp an army upon the side of a river. Previous to this step, it is the duty of the quartermaster to inquire from what quarter the winds come at the season of his encampment. If they pass across the river before they reach his army, they will probably bring with them the seeds of bilious and intermitting fevers, and this will more especially be the case in the fall of the year. The British troops at Pensacola, by shifting their quarters every year so as to avoid the winds that come over a river in the neighborhood of the town at a certain season, have preserved their health in a manner scarcely to be paralleled in so warm a climate.

It is the duty of the commanding officer of a division or detachment of the army to avoid as much as possible exposing his troops to *unnecessary* fatigue or watchfulness. The daily exercises of the manual and maneuvers (which contribute to the health of soldiers), as also all marches, should be performed in the cool of the morning and evening in summer. Sentries should always be provided with watch coats, and they should be *often* relieved in very hot, cold, and rainy weather.

The fire and smoke of wood, as also the burning of sulphur and the explosion of gunpowder, have a singular efficacy in preserving and restoring the purity of the air. There was an instance in the last war between Britain and France of a ship in Sir Edward Hawke's fleet that had above one hundred men on board ill with a putrid fever. This ship was obliged to bear her part in the well-known battle between Sir Edward and Monsieur Conflans. A few days after the engagement, every man on board this ship recovered, and an entire stop was put to the progress of the disorder. This extraordinary event was thought to be occasioned by the explosion and effluvia of the gunpowder.

I shall conclude these directions by suggesting two hints which appear to be worthy of the attention of the gentlemen of the army. Consider in the first place that the principal study of an officer in the time of war should be to save the blood of his men. An heroic exploit is admired most when it has been performed with the loss of a few lives. But if it be meritorious to save the lives of soldiers by skill and attention in the field, why should it be thought less so to preserve them by skill and attention of another kind, in a march or an encampment? And on the contrary, if it be criminal in an officer to sacrifice the lives of thousands by his temerity in a battle, why should it be thought less so to sacrifice twice their number in a hospital by his negligence? Consider in the second place that an attention to the health of your soldiers is absolutely necessary to form a *great* military character.

Had it not been for this eminent quality, Xenophon would never have led ten thousand Greeks for sixteen months through a cold and most inhospitable country, nor would Fabius have kept that army together without it which conquered Hannibal and delivered Rome. . . .

—BUTTERFIELD, ed., *Letters of Benjamin Rush*, I, 141-145.

3. DR. THACHER FINDS SARATOGA A GOOD CLINICAL LABORATORY

October 24th, 1777.—This hospital is now crowded with officers and soldiers from the field of battle; those belonging to the British and Hessian troops are accommodated in the same hospital with our own men, and receive equal care and attention. The foreigners are under the care and management of their own surgeons. I have been present at some of their capital operations, and remarked that the English surgeons perform with skill and dexterity, but the Germans, with a few exceptions, do no credit to their profession; some of them are the most uncouth and clumsy operators I ever witnessed, and appear to be destitute of all sympathy and tenderness towards the suffering patient. Not less than one thousand wounded and sick are now in this city; the Dutch church and several private houses are occupied as hospitals. We have about thirty surgeons and mates; and all are constantly employed. I am obliged to devote the whole of my time, from eight o'clock in the morning to a late hour in the evening, to the care of our patients.

Here is a fine field for professional improvement. Amputating limbs, trepanning fractured skulls, and dressing the most formidable wounds, have familiarized my mind to scenes of woe. A military hospital is peculiarly calculated to afford example for profitable contemplation, and to interest our sympathy and commiseration. If I turn from beholding mutilated bodies, mangled limbs, and bleeding, incurable wounds, a spectacle no less revolting is presented, of miserable objects languishing under afflicting diseases of every description—here, are those in a mournful state of despair, exhibiting the awful harbingers of approaching dissolution—there, are those with emaciated bodies and ghastly visage, who begin to triumph over grim disease and just lift their feeble heads from the pillow of sorrow. . . .

It is my lot to have twenty wounded men committed to my care by Dr. Potts, our surgeon-general; one of whom, a young man, received a musket-ball through his cheeks, cutting its way through the teeth on each side and the substance of the tongue; his sufferings have been great, but he now begins to articulate tolerably well. Another had the whole side of his face torn off by a cannon-ball, laying his mouth and throat open to view. A brave soldier received a musket-ball in his forehead; observing that it did not penetrate deep, it was imagined that the ball rebounded and fell out; but after several days, on examination, I detected the ball laying flat on the bone, and spread under the skin, which I removed. No one can doubt but he received his wound while facing the enemy, and it is fortunate for the brave fellow that his skull proved too thick for the ball to penetrate. But in another instance, a soldier's wound was not so honorable; he received a ball in the bottom of his foot, which could not have happened unless when in the act of running from the enemy. This poor fellow is held in derision by his comrades, and is made a subject of their wit for having the mark of a coward. . . .

—THACHER, *Military Journal,* pp. 112-114.

4. How the Army Inoculated Against Smallpox

April 20th (1781). All the soldiers, with the women and children, who have not had the small-pox, are now under inoculation. Of our regiment, one hundred and eighty seven were subjects of the disease. The old practice of previous preparation by a course of mercury and low diet has not been adopted on this occasion; a single dose of jalap and calomel, or the extract of butternut, *juglans cinerea,* is in general administered previous to the appearance of the symptoms. As to diet, we are so unfortunate as to be destitute of the necessary comfortable articles of food, and they subsist principally on their common rations of beef, bread, and salt pork. A small quantity of rice, sugar or molasses, and tea, are procured for those who are dangerously sick. Some instances have occurred of putrid fever supervening, either at the first onset or at the approach of the secondary stage, and a few cases have terminated fatally.

Many of our patients were improper subjects for the disease, but we were under the necessity of inoculating all, without exception, whatever might be their condition as to health. Of five hundred who have been inoculated, four only have died, but in other instances the proportion of deaths is much more considerable.

The extract of butternut is made by boiling down the inner bark of the tree; the discovery of this article is highly important, and it may be considered as a valuable acquisition to our materia medica. The country people have for some time been in the practice of using it, and Dr. Rush . . . has recommended the employment of it among our patients, as a mild yet sufficiently active cathartic, and a valuable and economical substitute for jalap. It operates without creating heat or irritation, and is found to be efficacious in cases of dysentery and bilious complaints. As the butternut tree abounds in our country, we may obtain at a very little expense a valuable domestic article of medicine. . . .

—THACHER, *Military Journal,* pp. 257-258.

5. A Naval Surgeon Prescribes Citrus Fruits for Scurvy

Mr. Northcote, Surgeon, to the Earl of Sandwich.

Prudent, Sandy Hook, New York, August 19, 1781

I should not presume to address your Lordship was I not persuaded that whatever contributes to promote the health and happiness of so valuable a life as that of a British sailor cannot fail of meeting your Lordship's most gracious acceptance, which I flatter myself will in some measure apologize for the liberty I have taken, and that the justness of my intentions will excuse the freedom.

As the scurvy, my Lord, is the most prevalent and most destructive disease incident to seamen, and lemon and orange juice the grand specific in that most terrible malady, I humbly beg leave to recommend it to your Lordship's consideration whether it would not be of infinite more service to the Navy if the surgeons of his Majesty's ships were to be largely supplied with those most salutary vegetable acids instead of the present mineral acid (elixir of vitriol), which is of little or no use.

Two thirds of our seamen die of the scurvy and other diseases which take their rise from putrefaction, and for which the Peruvian bark, lemon and orange juice are the great and peculiar antiseptics. Therefore, if our seamen could be preserved free from those diseases, they would seldom be endangered by any other.

I beg to recall to your Lordship's memory that, by the returns made to the House of Commons in December 1760, out of 185,000 men raised for the sea service during the last war, above 130,000 died by diseases, and two thirds of those of the putrid kind.

If the seizures of tobacco (instead of being burnt) were always sent to the dockyards to supply the ships destined for foreign service, it would be of infinite service to fumigate the ships frequently therewith, whenever there was a contagious disorder on board, and this without any additional expense to the Government.

The vinegar supplied the Navy at present is good for little or nothing; it should always be the strongest that can be procured.

Good, sound, rough cyder would also be of infinite use to scorbutics; and every ship should be supplied with some for their use only. Essence of malt and sour khrout are also of great use. These and many other articles (which would be a means of saving the lives and preserving the health of our seamen, if put in execution), I recommended some years ago in an appendix to the *Marine Practice of Physic and Surgery*, to which I beg leave to refer your Lordship; and as the subject of this letter is a great national concern, I have the vanity to hope that it will not be disregarded.

—BARNES & OWENS, eds., *Private Papers of Earl of Sandwich*, IV, 178-179.

6. THE HESSIAN DOCTOR

In May 1780, Philip Freneau quit the New Jersey militia, where he had served briefly, and shipped on the cargo ship Aurora, *bound for St. Eustatius. On May 25 she was captured by an enemy sloop; Freneau was sentenced to imprisonment on the notorious prison ship* Scorpion *in the Hudson River. Falling ill, he was transferred to the hospital ship* Hunter, *more a charnal house than a prison. We give here some embittered lines on the Hessian doctor whose duty it was to care for the sick.*

> From Brooklyn heights a Hessian doctor came,
> Nor great his skill, nor greater much his fame:
> Fair Science never called the wretch her son,
> And Art disdained the stupid man to own. . . .
> He on his charge the healing work begun
> With antinomial mixtures by the tun:
> Ten minutes was the time he deigned to stay,
> The time of grace allotted once a day:

He drenched us well with bitter draughts, 'tis true,
Nostrums from hell, and cortex from Peru:
Some with his pills he sent to Pluto's reign,
And some he blistered with his flies of Spain.
His Tartar doses walked their deadly round,
Till the lean patient at the potion frowned,
And swore that hemlock, death, or what you will,
Were nonsense to the drugs that stuffed his bill.
On those refusing he bestowed a kick,
Or menaced vengeance with his walking stick:
Here uncontrolled he exercised his trade,
And grew experienced by the deaths he made. . . .
Knave though he was, yet candor must confess
Not chief physician was this man of Hesse:
One master o'er the murdering tribe was placed,
By him the rest were honored or disgraced.
Once, and but once, by some strange fortune led,
He came to see the dying and the dead.
He came, but anger so inflamed his eye,
And such a faulchion glittered on his thigh,
And such a gloom his visage darkened o'er,
And two such pistols in his hands he bore,
That, by the gods, with such a load of steel,
We thought he came to murder, not to heal.
Rage in his heart, and mischief in his head,
He gloomed destruction, and had smote us dead
Had he so dared, but fear withheld his hand,
He came, blasphemed, and turned again to land.
　　　　　　　　　—Freneau, *Poems*, pp. 48-49.

CHAPTER TWENTY-ONE

Prisons and Escapes

WE HAVE *a great many hardship and atrocity stories from prisoners, both American and British, but few facts and almost no reliable statistics. Just as neither the Americans nor the British were prepared to care for the sick and the wounded, so they were unprepared to care for prisoners; these elementary and familiar accompaniments of war seemed to take both sides by surprise. It cannot be said that either side ever got over its surprise; at the very close of the war both the British Cabinet and the Congress were playing fast and loose with their prisoners. Nor did either army, at any time during the war, make really adequate preparation for the care of prisoners, or for their orderly exchange or release.*

A miasmic air of incompetence, spite and brutality hangs over the whole story of Revolutionary War prisoners. From the beginning to the end of the war there was confusion on both sides about the status of prisoners. Because the British did not at first—or for a long time—concede the de jure *existence of the United States, they adopted the logical but untenable position that American prisoners were not in fact prisoners of war, but traitors in rebellion against their lawful sovereign. The circumstances of war, and the threat of retaliation, persuaded them not to insist on this position, or on its consequences; yet to the very end they refused to concede diplomatic immunity to Henry Laurens, who languished in the Tower until 1782. Americans were almost equally shortsighted toward the Loyalists who had the bad luck to be captured; they insisted that these were not ordinary prisoners, subject to exchange, but criminals who should be turned over to their states for punishment. To make the situation worse, neither side trusted the other. Thus some of the British officers held that they were not, in any event, bound by agreements with rebels, and that they could violate their parole with impunity. The Americans, in turn, dishonored General Gates's agreement with Burgoyne on the disposition of the so-called "Convention" troops.*

We simply do not know how many prisoners were taken by the rival armies, but there is some reason to believe that these numbers may have run about even. The Americans made three major hauls during the war: Trenton, Saratoga and Yorktown. Trenton accounted for 900 or 1,000 prisoners, Saratoga for about 6,000, and Yorktown for perhaps 8,000. The British captured not far from 4,000 in the fighting around New York City, and over 5,000 at Charleston, and British captures of American fishermen and seamen were substantial—over 1,000 of these were still held in English prisons at the close of the war. British and American captures in the hard-fought campaigns in the Carolinas, and along the far-flung frontiers, probably canceled out; in any event the inclination here was not to be bothered with prisoners, but to dispose of them in the speediest and most convenient way.

Neither side had made adequate provision for their prisoners. The Americans were constantly on the move and did not want to carry prisoners with them, and the few cities which they did hold with any degree of assurance were not prepared to take over responsibility for large numbers. The British had a firm base only in New York—or Quebec and Halifax—and did not have facilities there to take care of their large prisoner hauls. The obvious solution was an exchange, but insuperable difficulties obstructed this—not least that the British had more to gain by exchange than the Americans. Another solution was release on parole, but this was complicated by deep-seated mutual distrust. Indeed in a country as large as America, and with armies so unorganized and records so haphazardly kept, there were no satisfactory means of enforcing paroles.

Both sides therefore fell back on hastily improvised prisons: local jails, barracks, warehouses, churches, underground mines, ships—whatever was at hand. Conditions in these were almost always wretched and sometimes, as in the prison ships or the abandoned copper mines, barbarous. But it is sobering to remember that conditions in prisons were just as barbarous eighty years later, at Andersonville, Libby and Elmira. On the whole the lot of the prisoner in the Revolution was almost as desperate as the lot of the wounded; it is estimated that 7,000 Americans perished on the notorious prison ships in the Hudson.

Prison and escape narratives are often exciting individually but they tend to be monotonous collectively, for on horror stories the law of diminishing returns sets in very speedily. One imprisonment, after all, tends to be very much like another, and the bitterness and invective of the imprisoned, too, forms a pattern. We have tried here to present a variety of prison experiences rather than a large number of prison or escape narratives. We give a lively story of imprisonment in Boston during the siege. There are a handful of narratives from New York; a few descriptions of conditions on the terrible prison ships; some glimpses into the experience of the "Convention" troops from Saratoga to Charlottesville; some samples of British and Loyalist prison narratives; Henry Laurens' own story of his sufferings in the Tower; and, at the end, the dramatic story of Captain Asgill which moved two continents to tears.

I. STORMONT REJECTS FRANKLIN'S PLEA FOR MERCY TO PRISONERS

We begin with a document that illuminates the peculiar difficulties of prisoner exchange—the stiff-necked refusal of some British officials and officers to recognize the rebels even for purposes of negotiation: Franklin's proposal to the British Ambassador to France, Lord Stormont, for an exchange of prisoners, and Stormont's fatuous rejection of the overture. Franklin never forgave the British their ungenerous attitude toward American prisoners, and at one time he undertook to prepare a little illustrated book with 35 engravings, "each expressing one or more of the horrid facts to be inserted in the book, in order to impress the minds of children and posterity with a deep sense of your bloody and insatiable malice and wickedness." Perhaps happily for the future of Anglo-American relations no such book was ever published.

Paris, April 2, 1777

My Lord:—We did ourselves the honor of writing some time ago to your lordship on the subject of exchanging prisoners. You did not condescend to give us any answer, and therefore we expect none to this. We, however, take the liberty of sending you copies of certain depositions, which we shall transmit to Congress, whereby it will be known to your court that the United States are not unacquainted with the barbarous treatment their people receive, when they have the misfortune of being your prisoners here in Europe; and that, if your conduct towards us is not altered, it is not unlikely that severe reprisals may be thought justifiable, from the necessity of putting some check to such abominable practices.

For the sake of humanity, it is to be wished that men would endeavor to alleviate, as much as possible, the unavoidable miseries attending a state of war. It has been said that, among the civilized nations of Europe, the ancient horrors of that state are much diminished; but the compelling men by chains, stripes and famine to fight against their friends and relations is a new mode of barbarity which your nation alone had the honor of inventing; and the sending American prisoners of war to Africa and Asia, remote from all probability of exchange, and where they can scarce hope ever to hear from their families, even if the unwholesomeness of the climate does not put a speedy end to their lives, is a manner of treating captives that you can justify by no other precedent of custom, except that of the black savages of Guinea. We are your lordship's most obedient, humble servants,

B. Franklin, S. Deane

Paris, 3 April, 1777

My Lord:—In answer to a letter, which concerns some of the most material interests of humanity, and of the two nations, Great Britain and the United States of America, now at war, we received the enclosed *indecent* paper, as coming from your lordship, which we return for your lordship's most mature consideration.

B. Franklin, S. Deane

Lord Stormont's letter said:

"The King's Ambassador receives no applications from rebels, unless they come to implore his Majesty's mercy."

—Bigelow, *Works of Franklin*, VII, 394n-395n.

II. JOHN LEACH AND HIS COMPANIONS SUFFER IN A BOSTON PRISON

The British did not bother to imprison many American civilians during their brief occupation of Boston. One of their victims was the remarkable

John Leach, accused, vaguely, of "being a spy and taking plans." Born in England, Leach had early gone to sea, and had circumnavigated the globe no less than three times. This experience suggested to him the propriety of conducting a school of navigation—probably the only one of its kind in Boston. His prison diary is as interesting for what it tells of the moral standards of stout Bostonians as for what it tells of the prisons.

A Journal kept in Boston Gaol, in 1775.

From Sunday, July 2d, to Monday, 17th. From the 2d July to the 17th a complicated scene of oaths, curses, debauchery and the most horrid blasphemy, committed by the Provost Marshal, his deputy and soldiers, who were our guard, soldier prisoners, and sundry soldier women, confined for thefts, etc. We had some of the vilest women for our neighbors; some placed over our heads, and some in rooms each side of us; they acted such scenes as was shocking to nature, and used language horrible to hear, as if it came from the very suburbs of Hell. When our wives, children and friends came to see us (which was seldom they were permitted), we seemed to want them gone, notwithstanding we were so desirous of their company, as they were exposed to hear the most abandoned language, as was grating to the ears of all sober persons.

Friday, July 7th, my wife came to see me. She has attempted it since, but was denied sundry times, and I did not see her again till the 28th July. We are very close confined, having the doors open for air sometimes one hour in 24, and sometimes not at all.

Monday 17th, my son Tileston died, whom I left well in my house; I was not permitted to attend the funeral, notwithstanding my letter to the general this morning requesting the same, or dismission, or trial. This evening the Provost informed us there was to be held a garrison court of enquiry at Concert Hall to-morrow, in consequence of my letter. We were desirous to prepare for trial.

Wednesday, 19th. Escorted from gaol again, with the additional company of 3 sailors, thieves and house-breakers; surrounded by soldiers, we made a curious medley; the fly blowers examined, and the 3 sailors. Mr. Hunt, Mr. Edes and Mr. Starr were asked who prosecuted them, and one Capt. Symmes, of the Regulars, was summoned by Major Moncreif as an evidence against Mr. Lovell and myself. Till this time we did not know our crimes, on what account we were committed, but now we found Mr. Lovell was charged with "being a spy, and giving intelligence to the rebels," and my charge, "being a spy, and suspected of taking plans." When Capt. Symmes appeared, he knew so little of us that he called me "Mr. Lovell"; he knew so little of us that instead of being a just evidence, he appeared ashamed and confounded, and went off. At 2 o'clock we were sent back to our stone edifice under a strong guard.

Thursday, 20th. Our 5 room companions were escorted as before with one Carpenter, a barber, who swam to Cambridge and back again. The said Carpenter and Mr. Hunt were examined. We were all sent back to gaol again under a strong guard. This makes 3 days we were carried out to trial,

4 hours each time (and nothing asked us) under all the disgrace and contempt they could contrive.

August 4. Mr. Gill, printer, was brought to prison and put in our room. He is charged with printing sedition, treason and rebellion.

August 9. Some small liberty of the yard. A poor painter, an inhabitant, was put in the dungeon and very ill used by the Provost and his deputy, Samuel Dyer; the then Provost turned him out and made him get down on his knees in the yard and say, "God bless the King!"

August 11. Close confined; the Provost would not suffer the doors to be opened to put our victuals in, but made us take it through the bars; and we . . . are daily treated with fresh insults and abuses. To day Amos Fisk died; he was a Charlestown prisoner, and the Provost uttered the most horrid speeches of what would become of his soul and body. This afternoon my wife came and tarried some time in the gaol house before she was admitted, in which time the Provost insulted her by saying I was a damned rebel, and my family the damnest rebel family in the country. She was admitted into our room a few minutes, and a sergeant sent in with her to hear the conversation. The Provost told her she must not come again.

Sunday, 13th [*August*]. Close shut up; much swearing and blasphemy close under our window the whole day by the Provost, his deputy and our guard of soldiers. It seems to be done on purpose, as they knew it was grating to us to hear such language. This morning my wife sent me a note in the foot of a stocking rolled up. We are obliged to act with secrecy, as our victuals, cloaths and every thing are constantly searched for letters and papers. This note informed me that my friend and relation, Mrs. B——, was got well of the small pox in the country.

Tuesday, 15th. Close confined, the weather hot. Died, Capt. Walker, a country prisoner from Charlestown. Swearing began at 3 this morning, and held all day: the place seems to be an emblem of Hell. At 9 at night most horrid swearing and blasphemy; the worst man of war that ever I knew was nothing to compare with this diabolical place. Poor Mr. Lovell began to droop; he is very weakly. It gives us all great concern, as we were all more afraid of sickness in this dreadful place than anything else, but God wonderfully preserved our healths and spirits. I did not think we could possibly survive such treatment but our help was from above. They sometimes gave us water in the pail in the morning, and by the heat of the weather and our cell it grew very warm, and they would not change it, and damned us, saying we must have that or none. This night I watched with Mr. Lovell.

Thursday, 17th [*August*]. Kept close all day. One Mr. French, an inhabitant, confined in the dungeon all day, and at night let out, and was obliged to fall down on his knees to the Provost in the yard, and say, "God bless the King!" Today, Phineas Nevers, a Charlestown prisoner, died. James Dickey discharged, and to pay a dollar fees; he paid a pistareen and left his silver broach in pawn for 4 more; the Provost kept the broach and give Dyer the pistareen. Also 3 dollars was demanded of Dorrington, and the Provost kept his bed and bedding 6 days and then delivered them up. The old Dutchman who was discharged the 25th July, was confined for complaining of the soldiers robbing his garden, which was his whole living, and because he had not a dollar to pay his fees, the soldiers on guard were ordered, each, to give him a kick as he went away.

Saturday, 19th. Close confined; dreadful language from morning to night; Mr. Lovell continues poorlye. This afternoon my wife came to ask my advice about signing for buying meat, as none were to have it but friends of Government. I told her to sign nothing and trust to Providence, and ask no favours from such wretches. The poor sick and wounded prisoners fare very hard, are many days without the comforts of life. Doctor Brown complained to Mr. Lovell and me that they had no bread all that day and the day before. He spoke to the Provost, as he had the charge of serving the bread; he replied, they might eat the nail heads and gnaw the plank and be damned. The comforts that are sent us by our friends we are obliged to impart to these poor suffering friends, and see the soldiers and others with rum to carry it them by stealth, when we are close confined and cannot get to them. . . . Some of the limbs which have been taken off, it was said, were in a state of putrification; not one survived amputation.

Wednesday, 23d. This morning, when my son brought my breakfast, the Provost said to the soldiers on guard, "God damn that dog (meaning my child)! Don't let him come up the yard. That dog deserves to be shot." In the afternoon Serjeant Neal and Corporal Royal were confined prisoners by the Provost for giving us air and fresh water in his absence. They told him we were almost suffocated with heat; he replied, "God damn them, if they are dead and rotten, my orders to you is to keep them close."

Friday, 25th. Last night Thomas Forakers, boatbuilder, and his servant John Bouve were brought to gaol on suspicion of concealing a man that swam over from Chelsea, upon false information of a very wicked woman; and this morning the boy John Bouve (about 16 years of age) was put in irons, in the dungeon, as he had nothing to confess; he was examined by Major Sheriff and Major Rooke, and then hand cuffed and put in the dungeon again. We fed the boy from our room, and encouraged him to keep up his spirits by telling him they were a pack of cowardly scoundrels and dare not hurt the hair of his head. While his irons were putting on, close by our cell door, the Provost said to him, he was a man under sentence of death, and might choose his minister to come and see him, for he was to be hanged in the afternoon. At 5 in the afternoon, finding they could make nothing of him, they took his irons off and put him in a room next to ours, among some soldiers, thieves, etc. The weather very hot and we close confined all day.

—LEACH, "Journal," *New England Genealogical Register,* XIX, 255 ff.

III. THE SUFFERINGS OF AMERICAN PRISONERS IN NEW YORK

We give here three narratives of imprisonment in New York, headquarters of British prisons.

The accounts of Jonathan Gillett and Thomas Stone need little introduction. Both were from Connecticut; both were captured on Long Island, Gillett by the Hessians, Stone in the course of a raid on one of the British posts.

Both suffered imprisonment on the Jersey prison ship before being trans-
ferred to the equally notorious Sugar House in New York. Their narratives
serve as an introduction to the story of the prison ships. Shocking conditions
among Patriot prisoners in New York and the benevolence of a courageous
Quaker lady are the subjects of the touching story told by Robert Keith,
chaplain aboard the ship that carried John Jay to Spain on his frustrating
mission for Congress. Jay had Chaplain Keith's statement entered in his
letter book.

1. CAPTURED BY THE HESSIANS!

Jonathan Gillett to Eliza Gillett at West Hartford.

New York, December 2nd, 1776

My Friends,

No doubt my misfortunes have reached your ears. Sad as it is, it is true
as sad. I was made prisoner the 27th day of August past by a people called
Heshens, and by a party called Yagers, the most inhuman of all mortals. I cant
give room to picture them here but thus much——I at first resolved not to be
taken, but by the impertunity of the seven taken with me, and being surrounded on all sides, I unhappily surendered; would to God I never had! Then
I should never [have] known there unmerciful cruelties; they first disarmed
me, then plundered me of all I had, watch, buckles, money and sum clothing,
after which they abused me by bruising my flesh with the butts of there
[guns]. They knocked me down; I got up and they [kept on] beating me
almost all the way to there [camp] where I got shot of them. The next thing
was I was allmost starved to death by them. I was kept here 8 days and then
sent on board a ship, where I continued 39 days, and by [them was treated]
much worse than when on shore.

After I was set on [shore] at New York, [I was] confined [under] a strong
guard till the 20th day of November, after which I have had my liberty to
walk part over the city between sun and sun. Notwithstanding there generous
allowance of food I must inevitably have perished with hunger had not sum
friends in this [city] relieved my extreme necessity, but I cant expect they can
always do it. What I shall do next I know not, being naked for clothes and
void of money, and winter present, and provisions very skerce; fresh meat one
shilling per pound, butter three shillings per pound, cheese two shillings, turnips and potatoes at a shilling a half peck, milk 15 coppers per quart, bread
equally as dear; and the General says he cant find us fuel thro' the winter, tho'
at present we receive sum cole.

I was after put on board siezed violently with the disentarry. It followed
me hard upwards of six weeks—after that a slow fever, but now am vastly
better. . . . my sincere love to you and my children. May God keep and preserve you at all times from sin, sickness, and death! . . .

I will endeavor to faintly lead you into the poor ciuation the soldiers are
in, espechally those taken at Long Island where I was. In fact these cases are
deplorable and they are real objects of pitty. They are still confined and in
houses where there is no fire—poor mortals, with little or no clothes—perish-

ing with hunger, offering eight dollars in paper for one in silver to relieve there distressing hunger, occasioned for want of food. There natures are broke and gone, some almost loose there voices and some there hearing. They are crouded into churches and there guarded night and day. I cant paint the horable appearance they make. It is shocking to human nature to behold them. Could I draw the curtain from before you, there expose to your view a lean jawed mortal, hunger laid his skinny hand [upon him] and whet to keenest edge his stomach cravings, sorounded with tattred garments, rotten rags, close beset with unwelcome vermin—could I do this, I say, possable I might in some [small] manner fix your idea with what appearance sum hundreds of these poor creatures make in houses where once people attempted to implore God's blessings, etc. But I must say no more of there calamities. God be merciful to them—I cant afford them no relief. If I had money I soon would do it, but I have none for myself.

I wrote to you by Mr. Wells to see if some one would help me to hard money under my present necessity. I write no more; if I had the General would not allow it to go out, and if ever you write to me write very short or else I will never see it. What the Heshens robbed me of that day amounted to the value of seventy two dollars at least. . . .

—DANDRIDGE, *American Prisoners of the Revolution,* pp. 28-31.

2. THOMAS STONE CHARGES THAT PRISONERS WERE POISONED

Recollections of Thomas Stone.

About the 25th of Jan., 1778, we were taken from the ships to the Sugar House, which during the inclement season was more intolerable than the ships.

We left the floating Hell with joy, but alas, our joy was of short duration. Cold and famine were now our destiny. Not a pane of glass, nor even a board to a single window in the house, and no fire but once in three days to cook our small allowance of provision. There was a scene that truly tried body and soul. Old shoes were bought and eaten with as much relish as a pig or a turkey; a beef bone of four or five ounces, after it was picked clean, was sold by the British guard for as many coppers.

In the spring our misery increased; frozen feet began to mortify; by the first of April, death took from our numbers, and, I hope, from their misery, from seven to ten a day; and by the first of May out of sixty-nine taken with me only fifteen were alive, and eight out of that number unable to work.

Death stared the living in the face: we were now attacked by a fever which threatened to clear our walls of its miserable inhabitants.

About the 20th of July I made my escape from the prison-yard. Just before the lamps were lighted I got safely out of the city, passed all the guards, was often fired at, but still safe as to any injury done me; arrived at Harlem River eastward of King's Bridge.

Hope and fear were now in full exercise. The alarm was struck by the sentinels keeping firing at me. I arrived at the banks of Harlem—five men met me with their bayonets at my heart; to resist was instant death, and to give up, little better.

I was conducted to the main guard, kept there until morning, then started for New York with waiters with bayonets at my back, arrived at my old habitation about 1 o'clock P.M.; was introduced to the prison keeper who threatened me with instant death, gave me two heavy blows with his cane; I caught his arm and the guard interfered. Was driven to the provost, thrust into a dungeon—a stone floor, not a blanket, not a board, not a straw to rest on. Next day was visited by a refugee lieutenant, offered to enlist me, offered a bounty—I declined. Next day renewed the visit, made further offers, told me the general was determined I should starve to death where I was unless I would enter their service. I told him his general dare not do it. (I shall here omit the imprecations I gave him in charge.)

The third day I was visited by two British officers, offered me a sergeant's post, threatened me with death as before in case I refused.

I replied, "Death if they dare!"

In about ten minutes the door was opened, a guard took me to my old habitation the Sugar House, it being about the same time of day I left my cell that I entered it, being three days and nights without a morsel of food or a drop of water—all this for the crime of getting out of prison. When in the dungeon reflecting upon my situation, I thought if ever mortal could be justified in praying for the destruction of his enemies, I am the man.

After my escape the guard was augmented, and about this time a new prison keeper was appointed. Our situation became more tolerable.

The 16th of July was exchanged. Language would fail me to describe the joy of that hour; but it was transitory. On the morning of the 16th, some friends, or what is still more odious, some refugees, cast into the prison yard a quantity of warm bread, and it was devoured with greediness. The prison gate was opened, we marched out about the number of 250. Those belonging to the North and Eastern States were conducted to the North River and driven on board the flag ship, and landed at Elizabethtown, New Jersey. Those who ate of the bread soon sickened; there was death in the bread they had eaten. Some began to complain in about half an hour after eating the bread; one was taken sick after another in quick succession and the cry was, "Poison, poison!" I was taken sick about an hour after eating. When we landed, some could walk, and some could not. I walked to town about two miles, being led most of the way by two men. About one half of our number did not eat of the bread, as a report had been brought into the prison *that the prisoners taken at Fort Washington had been poisoned in the same way.*

The sick were conveyed in wagons to White Plains, where I expected to meet my regiment, but they had been on the march to Rhode Island, I believe, about a week. I was now in a real dilemma; I had not the vestige of a shirt to my body, was moneyless and friendless. What to do I knew not. Unable to walk, a gentleman—I think his name was Allen—offered to carry me to New Haven, which he did. The next day I was conveyed to Guilford, the place of my birth, but no near relative to help me. Here I learned that my father had died in the service the spring before. I was taken in by a hospitable uncle, but in moderate circumstances. Dr. Readfield attended me for about four months. I was salivated twice, but it had no good effect. They sent me 30 miles to Dr.

Little of East Haddam, who under kind Providence restored me to such a state of health that I joined my regiment in the spring following.

—DANDRIDGE, *American Prisoners of the Revolution*, pp. 133-136.

3. A NEW YORK WIDOW BRAVES PERSECUTION TO SUCCOR PRISONERS

Statement of Robert Keith, chaplain to the *Confederacy*.

On board the *Confederacy* at Martinico, 19th December, 1779

Mrs. Sarah Smith, widow of Mr. John Smith, cabinet maker, late of New York, being an elderly lady of a benevolent Christian disposition, was remarkably charitable and very serviceable to the American prisoners in the years 1776 and '77, to my certain knowledge. I, being one of that unfortunate number captivated at Fort Washington, was brought with the rest of my fellow sufferers to New York. In our approach to the city this good lady met us with her bounty and followed us to the several places of confinement with refreshments, which were very acceptable to us who had been three days destitute of the necessary supports of life.

When the officers had their parole of the city, she invited those whom she met with to come to her house and partake of such as she could afford them; and desired them to invite their acquaintance also to come and partake with them. Her house was kept open, and her table spread, almost constantly for several weeks. She bestowed both food and raiment with so hearty good will that relieving the distressed appeared to be her greatest satisfaction.

She greatly alleviated my misfortune by receiving me into her family as a boarder, where I had the best opportunity of being acquainted with her conduct. Her extraordinary liberality induced me sometimes to express my concern lest she would bring herself to poverty and distress:—to which she replied, she espoused the same cause in which they were suffering; therefore, while she had any thing to give, they should be welcome to share with her; and when it was out of her power to relieve them, she was willing to suffer with them. She not only entertained those who could come to her house, but also daily visited those who were kept in close confinement.

As she was comforting the disconsolate one day in the Provost, she bid them be of good cheer, the scale might turn, and the day might come when they would guard, in the same Provost, those who were now guarding them there. The guard, overhearing this address, shut her immediately in another room, saying that was the fittest place for such a d——d rebel.

After she got out of the gaol, she was likely to suffer for want of bread, and sent to see if I could procure her some flour on Long Island, where I was then upon parole. As I could procure but little, I wrote to Mr. Pintard, our agent there, to supply her out of the flour sent by Congress for the use of the American prisoners, which request he was kind enough to comply with. Her personal distresses did not yet make her forget the poor prisoners; but for their relief she went thro' the city, craving alms from the well disposed people of her acquaintance. This coming to the ears of the mayor and aldermen, they sent for her and examined her concerning it. She honestly confessed the fact, and they asked by what authority she acted.

She replied, "By the authority of the word of God."

Not being able to manage her, they turned her over to the general who also examined her, and received for answer as above. To prevent her future usefulness in this way, he ordered her not only to leave the city, but withdraw out of their lines, permitting her to take with her only one bed and her wearing apparel. When she had disposed of her property which she had not given away, she could not think of going out of the lines without visiting the prisoners on the island and inquiring into their necessities. Nor did she come empty handed, but dealt liberally both clothes and money to those who might never have opportunity to make her restitution. She left New York the latter part of '77, went up the North River to Clark's-town near Tappan Bay, where she was spending the remains of her small living when I had the last account from her.

—Jay, Letter Book, II (appendix), Columbia University Lib.

IV. THE HORRORS OF THE BRITISH PRISON SHIPS

We come now to the most harrowing chapter in the history of Revolutionary prisons, and perhaps in the history of the Revolution itself. What Andersonville was to the Civil War, the British prison ships were to the Revolution. Lacking adequate prisons in their one permanent headquarters, New York City, the British hit on the idea of using ships moored in the Hudson as prisons. This would, presumably, have a double advantage: the ships would be hard to escape from, and they would be clean and healthy. Both of these assumptions proved wrong. As for their presumed safety, prisoners who could swim could escape from them more easily than from a prison on land— if they had enough strength left to swim to shore. And as for their healthful character—they proved to be the most fatally unhealthful prisons ever devised. The fault here was not, to be sure, in the ships, but in the administration. Wretched food, or no food at all; frightful overcrowding in the fetid holds; a complete lack of medical care—these things condemned literally thousands of American prisoners to death. In the end the British prison ships probably killed more American soldiers than British rifles: the total estimate runs to 7,000 or 8,000.

We give here narratives by William Slade and Thomas Dring: Slade's is a contemporary narrative; the other was written up later and strains for literary effect. A Connecticut boy, William Slade had been captured at Fort Washington in November 1776, and imprisoned on the first of the prison ships, the Grosvenor; *he introduces us to what is to be the familiar picture of smallpox, starvation and mistreatment. Thomas Dring was a sailor who passed from one prison ship to another; forty years later he set down his recollections of his dreadful experiences—with the help of one Albert Greene, who was doubtless responsible for the "literary" touches.*

The suffering of American prisoners in New York was notorious, and late in 1777 Washington arranged to send his old friend and associate, Elias Boudinot, then commissary general of prisoners, to New York to investigate conditions. General Clinton gave Boudinot permission to see whatever was to be seen, and early in February he arrived "to inquire and find out the real state of our unfortunate bretheren." On his return to Valley Forge he pre-

pared a report for General Washington. We have taken an excerpt from that report, and added to it a somewhat more systematic statement from Boudinot's later journal. Boudinot himself had a long and distinguished career in American public life: member and President of the Continental Congress; member of the first three United States Congresses; Director of the Mint; lawyer before the United States Supreme Court; and author of many theological tracts.

1. WILLIAM SLADE RECORDS LIFE AND DEATH ON THE PRISON SHIP

Fort Washington, the 16th day November, A. D. 1776. This day I, William Slade, was taken with 2,800 more. We was allowed honours of war. We then marched to Harlem under guard, where we were turned into a barn. We got little rest that night, being verry much crowded, as some trouble [illegible]. . . .

Sunday 17th. Such a Sabbath I never saw. We spent it in sorrow and hunger, having no mercy showed.

Munday 18th. We were called out while it was still dark, but was soon marched to New York, four deep, verry much frowned upon by all we saw. We was called Yankey Rebbels a-going to the gallows. We got to York at 9 o'clock, were paraded, counted off and marched to the North Church, where we were confined under guard.

Tuesday 19th. Still confined without provisions till almost night, when we got a little mouldy bisd [biscuit], about four per man. These four days we spent in hunger and sorrow being derided by everry one and calld Rebs.

Wednesday, 20th. We was reinforsd by 300 more. We had 500 before. This caused a continual noise and verry big huddle. Jest at night drawed 6 oz of pork per man. This we eat alone and raw.

Thursday, 21st. We passed the day in sorrow haveing nothing to eat or drink but pump water.

Friday, 22nd. We drawed ¾ lb of pork, ¾ lb of bisd, one gil of peas, a little rice and some kittels to cook in. Wet and cold.

Saturday, 23rd. We had camps stews plenty, it being all we had. We had now spent one week under confinement. Sad condition. . . .

Wednesday, 27th. Was spent in hunger. We are now dirty as hogs, lying any and every whare. Joys gone, sorrows increase. . . .

Sunday, 1st of Decembere, 1776. About 300 men was took out and carried on board the shipping. Sunday spent in vain.

Munday, 2nd. Early in the morning we was called out and stood in the cold, about one hour and then marched to the North River and went on board the *Grovnor* transport ship. Their was now 500 men on board; this made much confusion. We had to go to bed without supper. This night was verry long, hunger prevailed much. Sorrow more.

Saturday, 7th. We drawed 4 lb of bisd at noon, a piece of meat and rice. This day drawed 2 bisd per man for back allowance, (viz) for last Saturday at the church. This day the ships crew weighed anchor and fell down the river below Govnors Island and sailed up the East River to Turcle Bay [Turtle Bay is at the foot of 23rd Street], and cast anchor for winter months.

Sunday, 8th. This day we were almost discouraged, but considered that would not do. Cast off such thoughts. We drawed our bread and eat with sadness. At noon drawed meat and peas. We spent the day reading and in meditation, hopeing for good news. . . .

Thursday, 12th. We drawed bisd. This morning is the first time we see snow. At noon drawed a little meat and pea broth. Verry thin. We almost despair of being exchanged.

Friday, 13th. of Decr. 1776. We drawed bisd and butter. A little water broth. We now see nothing but the mercy of God to intercede for us. Sorrowful times, all faces look pale, discouraged, discouraged.

Saturday, 14th. We drawed bisd. Times look dark. Deaths prevail among us, also hunger and naked. We almost conclude [that we will have] to stay all winter. At noon drawed meat and rice. Cold increases. At night suffer with cold and hunger. Nights verry long and tiresome, weakness prevails.

Sunday, 15th. Drawed bisd. Paleness attends all faces. The melancholyst day I ever saw. At noon drawed meat and peas. Sunday gone and comfort. As sorrowfull times as I ever saw.

Munday, 16th of Decr. 1776. Drawed bisd and butter at noon. Burgo poor. Sorrow increases. The tender mercys of men are cruelty.

Tuesday, 17th. Drawed bisd. At noon meat and rice. No fire. Suffer with cold and hunger. We are treated worse than cattle and hogs. . . .

Saturday, 21st. Drawed bisd. Last night one of our regiment got on shore, but got catched. Troubles come on, comfort gone. At noon drawed meat and rice. Verry cold. Soldiers and sailors verry cross. Such melancholy times I never saw.

Sunday, 22nd. Last night nothing but grones all night of sick and dying. Men amazeing to behold. Such hardness, sickness prevails fast. Deaths multiply. Drawed bisd. At noon meat and peas. Weather cold. Sunday gone and no comfort. Had nothing but sorrow and sadness. All faces sad.

Munday, 23rd. Drawed bisd and butter. This morning Sergt Kieth, Job March and several others broke out with the small pox. About 20 gone from here today that listed in the King's service. Times look verry dark. But we are in hopes of an exchange. One dies almost every day. Cold but pleasant. Burgo for dinner. People gone bad with the pox.

Tuesday, 24th. Last night verry long and tiresome. Bisd. At noon rice and cornmeal. About 30 sick. [They] were carried to town. Cold but pleasant. No news. All faces gro pale and sad.

Wednesday, 25th. Last night was a sorrowful night. Nothing but grones and cries all night. Drawed bisd and butter. At noon peas. Capt. Benedict, Leiut Clark and Ensn Smith come on board and brought money for the prisoners. Sad times.

Thursday, 26th. Last night was spent in dying grones and cries. I now gro poorly. Terrible storm as ever I saw. High wind. Drawed bisd. At noon meat and peas. Verry cold and stormey.

Friday, 27th. Three men of our battalion died last night. The most melancholyest night I ever saw. Small pox increases fast. This day I was blooded. Drawed bisd and butter. Stomach all gone. At noon, burgo. Basset is verry sick. Not like to live I think.

Saturday, 28th. Drawed bisd. This morning about 10 o'clock Josiah Basset died. Ensn Smith come here about noon with orders to take me a shore. We got to shore about sunset. I now feel glad. Coffee and bread and cheese. . . .

Thursday, 2nd. Ensn Smith looked about and got something to ly on and in. A good deal poorly, but I endeavourd to keep up a good heart, considering that I should have it [the small pox] light, for it was verry thin and almost full. . . .

—DANDRIDGE, *American Prisoners of the Revolution,* pp. 494-499.

2. HEAT, STARVATION, VERMIN AND SMALLPOX ON THE *Jersey*

[1819]

Thomas Dring's narrative.

The First Night on Board

We had now reached the accommodation-ladder, which led to the gangway on the larboard side of the *Jersey*, and my station in the boat, as she hauled alongside, was exactly opposite to one of the air-ports in the side of the ship. From this aperture proceeded a strong current of foul vapor, of a kind to which I had been before accustomed while confined on board the *Good Hope;* the peculiarly disgusting smell of which I then recollected, after a lapse of three years. This was, however, far more foul and loathsome than anything which I had ever met with on board that ship; and it produced a sensation of nausea far beyond my powers of description.

Here, while waiting for orders to ascend on board, we were addressed by some of the prisoners, from the air-ports. We could not, however, discern their features, as it had now become so dark that we could not distinctly see any object in the interior of the ship. After some questions whence we came and respecting the manner of our capture, one of the prisoners said to me that it was "a lamentable thing to see so many young men in full strength, with the flush of health upon their countenances, about to enter that infernal place of abode." He then added in a tone and manner but little fitted to afford us much consolation: "Death has no relish for such skeleton carcasses as we are, but he will now have a feast upon you fresh-comers."

After lanterns had been lighted on board, for our examination, we ascended the accommodation-ladder to the upper deck, and passed through the barricade door, where we were examined and our bags of clothes inspected. These we were permitted to retain, provided they contained no money or weapons of any kind.

After each man had given his name and the capacity in which he had served on board the vessel in which he was captured, and the same had been duly registered, we were directed to pass through the other barricade door, on the starboard side, down the ladder leading to the main hatchway. I was detained but a short time with the examination, and was permitted to take my bag of clothes with me below; and passing down the hatchway, which was still open, through a guard of soldiers, I found myself among the wretched and disgusting multitude, a prisoner on board the *Jersey*.

The gratings were soon after placed over the hatchways and fastened down for the night; and I seated myself on the deck, holding my bag with a firm grasp, fearful of losing it among the crowd. I had now ample time to reflect on the horrors of the scene, and to consider the prospect before me. It was impossible to find one of my former shipmates in the darkness; and I had, of course, no one with whom to speak during the long hours of that dreadful night—surrounded by I knew not whom, except that they were beings as wretched as myself; with dismal sounds meeting my ears from every direction; a nauseous and putrid atmosphere filling my lungs at every breath; and a stifling and suffocating heat, which almost deprived me of sense, and even of life. . . .

The thought of sleep did not enter my mind. At length, discovering a glimmering of light through the iron gratings of one of the air-ports, I felt that it would be indeed a luxury if I could but obtain a situation near that place, in order to gain one breath of the exterior air. Clenching my hand firmly around my bag, which I dared not leave, I began to advance towards the side of the ship, but was soon greeted with the curses and imprecations of those who were lying on the deck, and whom I had disturbed in attempting to pass over them. I, however, persevered and at length arrived near the desired spot, but found it already occupied, and no persuasion would induce a single individual to relinquish his place for a moment.

Thus i passed the first dreadful night, waiting with sorrowful forebodings for the coming day. The dawn at length appeared, but came only to present new scenes of wretchedness, disease and woe. I found myself surrounded by a crowd of strange and unknown forms, with the lines of death and famine upon their faces. My former shipmates were all lost and mingled among the multitude, and it was not until we were permitted to ascend the deck, at eight o'clock, that I could discern a single individual whom I had ever seen before. Pale and meager, the throng came upon deck to view, for a few moments, the morning sun, and then to descend again, to pass another day of misery and wretchedness.

The First Day

After passing the weary and tedious night, to whose accumulated horrors I have but slightly alluded, I was permitted to ascend to the upper deck, where other objects, even more disgusting and loathsome, met my view. I found myself surrounded by a motley crew of wretches, with tattered garments and pallid visages, who had hurried from below for the luxury of a little fresh air. Among them I saw one ruddy and healthful countenance, and recognized the features of one of my late fellow-prisoners on board the *Belisarius*. But how different did he appear from the group around him, who had here been doomed to combat with disease and death! Men who, shrunken and decayed as they stood around him, had been but a short time before as strong, as healthful, and as vigorous as himself—men who had breathed the pure breezes of the ocean, or danced lightly in the flower-scented air of the meadow and the hill, and had from thence been hurried into the pent-up air of a crowded prison ship, pregnant with putrid fever, foul with deadly contagion; here to linger out the tedious and weary day, the disturbed and anxious night; to count over the days and weeks and months of a wearying and degrading captivity, unvaried but by new scenes of painful suffering, and new inflictions of remorseless cruelty—their brightest hope and their daily prayer, that death would not long delay to release them from their torments.

In the wretched groups around me, I saw but too faithful a picture of our own almost certain fate; and found that all which we had been taught to fear of this terrible place of abode was more than realized.

During the night, in addition to my other sufferings, I had been tormented with what I supposed to be vermin; and on coming upon deck, I found that a black silk handkerchief, which I wore around my neck, was completely spotted with them. Although this had often been mentioned as one of the miseries of the place, yet, as I had never before been in a situation to witness anything of the kind, the sight made me shudder; as I knew, at once, that so long as I should remain on board, these loathsome creatures would be my constant companions and unceasing tormentors.

The next disgusting object which met my sight was a man suffering with the smallpox; and in a few minutes I found myself surrounded by many others laboring under the same disease, in every stage of its progress.

As I had never had the smallpox, it became necessary that I should be inoculated; and there being no proper person on board to perform the operation, I concluded to act as my own physician. On looking about me, I soon found a man in the proper stage of the disease, and desired him to favor me with some of the matter for the purpose. He readily complied, observing that it was a necessary precaution on my part, and that my situation was an excellent one in regard to *diet*, as I might depend upon finding that *extremely moderate*. The only instrument which I could procure, for the purpose of inoculation, was a common pin. With this, having scarified the skin of my hand, between the thumb and forefinger, I applied the matter and bound up my hand. The next morning I found that the wound had begun to fester; a sure symptom that the application had taken effect.

Many of my former shipmates took the same precaution and were inoculated during the day. In my case the disorder came on but lightly, and its progress was favorable; and without the least medical advice or attention, by the blessing of Divine Providence, I soon recovered. . . .

In the course of the day, after the regulations of the ship had been made known to us, we divided ourselves into messes of six men each; and on the next morning we drew our scanty pittance of food with the rest of our companions.

The Fourth of July

A few days before the fourth of July, we had made such preparations as our circumstances would admit, for an observance of the anniversary of American Independence. We had procured some supplies wherewith to make ourselves merry on the occasion, and intended to spend the day in such innocent pastime and amusement as our situation would afford, not dreaming that our proceedings would give umbrage to our keepers, as it was far from our intention to trouble or insult them. We thought that, although prisoners, we had a right, on that day at least, to sing and be merry. As soon as we were permitted to go on deck in the morning, thirteen little national flags were displayed in a row upon the booms. We were soon ordered by the guard to take them away; and as we neglected to obey the command, they triumphantly demolished, and trampled them underfoot.

Unfortunately for us, our guards at that time were Scotchmen, who, next to the refugees, were the objects of our greatest hatred; but their destruction of our flags was merely viewed in silence, with the contempt which it merited.

During the time we remained on deck, several patriotic songs were sung, and choruses were repeated; but not a word was intentionally spoken to give offense to our guards. They were, nevertheless, evidently dissatisfied with our proceedings, as will soon appear. Their moroseness was a prelude to what was to follow. We were, in a short time, forbidden to pass along the common gangways, and every attempt to do so was repelled by the bayonet. Although thus incommoded, our mirth still continued. Songs were still sung, accompanied with occasional cheers. Things thus proceeded until about four o'clock, when the guards were turned out, and we received orders to descend between decks, where we were immediately driven at the point of the bayonet.

After being thus sent below in the greatest confusion, at that early and unusual hour, and having heard the gratings closed and fastened above us, we suposed that the barbarous resentment of our guards was fully satisfied; but we were mistaken, for they had further vengeance in store, and merely waited for an opportunity to make us feel its weight.

The prisoners continued their singing between decks, and were, of course, more noisy than usual, but forbore, even under their existing temptations, to utter any insulting or aggravating expressions. At least, I heard nothing of the kind, unless our patriotic songs could be so construed.

In the course of the evening, we were ordered to desist from making any further noise. This order not being fully complied with, at about nine o'clock the gratings were removed, and the guards descended among us, with lanterns and drawn cutlasses in their hands. The poor, helpless prisoners retreated from the hatchways, as far as their crowded situation would permit; while their cowardly assailants followed as far as they dared, cutting and wounding everyone within their reach, and then ascended to the upper deck, exulting in the gratification of their revenge.

Many of the prisoners were wounded; but, from the total darkness, neither their number nor their situation could be ascertained; and if this had been possible, it was not in the power of their companions to afford them the least relief. During the whole of that tragical night, their groans and lamentations were dreadful in the extreme. Being in the gun-room, I was at some distance from the immediate scene of this bloody outrage; but the distance was by no means far enough to prevent my hearing their continual cries from the extremity of pain, their applications for assistance, and their curses upon the heads of their brutal assailants.

It had been the usual custom for each prisoner to carry below, when he descended at sunset, a pint of water, to quench his thirst during the night. But, on this occasion, we had thus been driven to our dungeons three hours before the setting of the sun, and without our usual supply of water.

Of this night I cannot describe the horrors. The day had been very sultry, and the heat was extreme throughout the ship. The unusual number of hours during which we had been crowded together between decks; the foul atmosphere and sickening heat; the additional excitement and restlessness caused by the wanton attack which had been made; above all the want of water, not a drop of which could we obtain during the whole night, to cool our parched tongues; the imprecations of those who were half distracted with their burning thirst; the shrieks and wailings of the wounded; the struggles and groans of the dying—together formed a combination of horrors which no pen can describe.

In the agonies of their suffering the prisoners invited, and even challenged, their inhuman guards to descend once more among them; but this they were prudent enough not to attempt.

Their cries and supplications for water were terrible, and were, of themselves, sufficient to render sleep impossible. Oppressed with the heat, I found my way to the grating of the main hatchway, where on former nights I had frequently passed some time, for the benefit of the little current of air which circulated through the bars. I obtained a place on the larboard side of the hatchway, where I stood facing the East, and endeavored, as much as possible, to draw my attention from the terrific sounds below me, by watching through the grating the progress of the stars. I there spent hour after hour in following with my eye the motion of a particular star as it rose and ascended, until it passed over beyond my sight.

How I longed for the day to dawn! At length the morning light began to appear, but still our torments were increasing every moment. As the usual hour for us to ascend to the upper deck approached, the working-party were mustered near the hatchway, and we were all anxiously waiting for the opportunity to cool our weary frames, to breathe for a while the pure air, and, above all, to procure water to quench our intolerable thirst. The time arrived, but still the gratings were not removed. Hour after hour passed on, and still we were not released. Our minds were at length seized with the horrible suspicion that our tyrants had determined to make a finishing stroke of their cruelty, and rid themselves of us altogether.

It was not until ten o'clock in the forenoon that the gratings were at length removed. We hurried on deck, and thronged to the water-cask, which was completely exhausted before our thirst was allayed. So great was the struggle around the cask that the guards were again turned out to disperse the crowd.

In a few hours, however, we received a new supply of water, but it seemed impossible to allay our thirst, and the applications at the cask were incessant until sunset.

Our rations were delivered to us, but, of course, not until long after the usual hour. During the whole day, however, no fire was kindled for cooking in the galley. All the food which we consumed that day we were obliged to swallow raw. Every thing, indeed, had been entirely deranged by the events of the past night, and several days elapsed before order was restored. This was at length obtained by a change of the guard, who, to our great joy, were relieved by a party of Hessians.

The average number who died on board during the period of twenty-four hours was about five; but on the morning of the fifth of July, eight or ten corpses were found below. Many had been badly wounded, to whom, in the total darkness of the night, it was impossible for their companions to render any assistance; and even during the next day they received no attention, except that which was afforded by their fellow prisoners, who had nothing to administer to their comfort, not even bandages for their wounds.

—DRING, *Recollections of the Jersey Prison Ship*, pp. 28-36, 89-94.

3. ELIAS BOUDINOT REPORTS TO WASHINGTON ON CONDITIONS IN NEW YORK

Draft of his report to George Washington.

Camp, March 2, 1778

Having been detained in New York on the business committed to me by your Excellency much longer than could have been expected, [I] think it my duty to take the earliest opportunity of communicating a report of my proceedings and the reasons of my conduct.

On my arrival in Jersey I wrote to Sir Henry Clinton for permission to pass to New York, for the purpose of visiting our prisoners . . . and received an answer through Mr. Loring [Commissary General of Prisoners, whose wife had been General Howe's mistress]. When arrived at the city, [I] was received with great politeness and civility and put under no other restraint than being informed that they trusted to my prudence for a proper behaviour.

My business here being to inquire and find out the real state of our unfortunate bretheren, and not to negotiate any general principles, I thought it prudent, in the first place, to make it a point to know the tempers and characters of the particular persons I had to do with, and then endeavour to improve it to the advantage of our miserable prisoners.

Having for several days visited the different places of their confinement, and made every inquiry in my power, I beg leave to report to your Excellency the results of the whole: That I found the hospitals in tollerable good order, neat and clean and the sick much better taken care of than I expected. That the Sugar House appeared comfortable and warm, having a stove in each story and shutters to the windows. The prisoners also, being well cloathed and each of them having a good blanket, may stand through the winter very well, especially as they are not crowded, being now reduced in the whole to about 400, two hundred of whom are in the Sugar House; the rest being in the different hospitals. Some of the privates appear to be a sett of sad villains, who rob each other of their cloaths and blanketts, and many of them sell their own shoes, blanketts and even shirts for rum. . . .

That in the Provoost I was greatly distressed with the wretched situation of so many of the human species. That on meeting all the prisoners of war together in a room, in company with Mr. Loring, I heard their complaints and took notes of the accusations on which they were severally confined in order to found a representation to Major General Robertson [James Robertson was commandant of New York City] in their favour. They repeated to me instances of the most shocking barbarity in presence of the keeper of the Provoost, whom they charged as the author: as the beating and knocking down officers of rank and distinction on the most triffling occasion, locking them up in dark, damp dungeons, for asking more water than usual in warm weather; or for not going to bed immediately on being order[ed] by the serjeant [Sergeant Keefe]. Officers have been locked up in the dungeon for examination, and left there without farther inquiry or any charge brought against them for many months. That besides prisoners of war, there are many inhabitants here, as Committee Men, Commissioners, Oppressors of the Friends of Government, etc., etc., who are wretched beyond description. That inhabitants and persons in civil departments when taken are sent to the Provoost without distinction, and at present there seems to be no redemption for them.

That on stating the case of each of these unhappy men . . . and delivering it to General Robertson, he very humanely agreed to the discharge of all the officers (except seven) on their parole; and gave me the strongest assurances that he would not allow of such a power on the serjeant of the Provoost, but would put a stop to it immediately. That the officers on Long Island are boarded out amongst the inhabitants in the most convenient manner, and appear to be very comfortable and healthy. They amount to about 250. . . .

That to answer the pressing necessities of our prisoners I have been obliged to stretch my credit to the utmost. That not being able to obtain the least aid from the State of Jersey, [I] have been put to the greatest difficulty to make remittances, not being able to procure above 300 barrells of flour for want of means of transportation; and although I have employed the best men I could meet with for the purpose, can get nothing done effectually without my personal attendance. . . .

That although the above appears now to be the state of the prisoners in New York, from my personal observation while visiting the several departments, yet I think it my duty nevertheless to add to this report [that] which I received from the unanimous representation of both officers and privates, viz. that this alteration has taken place within a short time past, in a great measure by the industry and attention of Mr. Pintard [Louis Pintard, a brother-in-law of Elias Boudinot], our agent in New York, who has employed special nurses in the hospitals, added to the supplies for the sick, and done every thing in his power for the relief of the unhappy sufferers. . . . But Mr. Pintard being forbid going to the Provoost, his care cannot extend to those confined there, except as to sending them provisions and fire wood. . . .

That after finishing the business of the military prisoners, I waited on Commodore [William] Hotham, and informed him that Mr. Pintard, having obtained provisions and cloathing for the sea prisoners, had been refused the liberty of sending them on board of the prison ships notwithstanding the pressing necessities of those suffering people. He informed me that he could not know Mr. Pintard, or any other person but his own Commissary, and that he would not suffer any cloaths purchased in New York to go on board without Lord Howe's express orders, but that any provisions sent to the Commissary appointed by him should be distributed. I applied then for the enlargement of the sea officers on parole, but he answered that this could not be done, as no sea prisoners were ever admitted to that indulgence. . . .

There are 58 officers and 62 sea men on board the prison ships, who suffer greatly and die daily. . . .

P. S. I had almost forgot to mention that, having receiving the fullest assurances from our officers that a poor woman* had saved the lives of a number of our prisoners by exerting herself in serving them at far beyond her abilities, and that she was now in a suffering condition for want of provision, I thought it prudent to send her a present of 5 barrels of flour.

—Boudinot, "Report," *William & Mary Quarterly*, 3rd ser., XIII, 379-387.

4. Elias Boudinot Finds British Prisons Worse Than Reported

February 4, 1778

. . . I waited on the General [Robertson] at breakfast. He behaved as before with the greatest civility and good humor. After breakfast he asked a great many questions about the news in our lines, and conversed on common topicks, but said nothing about my conduct while in the city, on which I at last introduced the business on which I had come: that I was a stranger to military rule; I knew that I was in a garrisoned town, and therefor wished to know what line of conduct it was expected that I should pursue.

The General answered me that he knew we had heard strange stories within our lines of their conduct to our prisoners; that he rejoiced that General Washington had taken the measure of sending me in to examine for ourselves, for that he was sure that we should find them a parcel of damned lies; that he had ordered every place I should choose to visit to be freely opened to me, and that as I was a gentleman, all that he expected was that I should behave as such, and that I might use my own pleasure and go where I pleased.

I confess I was surprised at this generous conduct, and immediately replied that I could not accept the gentlemanly offer. That I had come on a fair and open business. That I had no secrets to communicate and would not receive any from any person whatever. That I could not put myself so far in their power as after my departure to render it possible for them to charge me with improper behavior unworthy my character, by communicating or receiving secret intelligence to or from our officers. That my intentions were not only to be convinced myself of the truth of the treatment the prisoners had received, but if it had been cruel, that the General should be convinced of the fact also, as necessary towards their relief. That therefor I should not see a prisoner or have any communication with one but in the presence of a British officer, who I hoped he would oblige me by appointing to attend me.

The General expressed himself well pleased with the proposal, and appointed one accordingly, observing again that he was sure I should find the reports we had heard totally false.

Accordingly I went to the Provost with the officer, where we found near 30 officers, from colonels downwards, in close confinement in the gaol in New York. After some conversation with late Ethan Allen, I told him my errand, on which he was very free in his abuse of the British on account of

---

* Very possibly a Mrs. Deborah Franklin, banished from New York in November 1780 for her aid to American prisoners.

the cruel treatment he had received during —— months close confinement. We then proceeded up stairs to the room of their confinement. I had the officers drawn up in a ring and informed them of my mission: that I was determined to hear nothing in secret. That I therefore hoped they would each of them in their turn report to me faithfully and candidly the treatment they severally had received. That my design was to obtain them the proper redress, but if they kept back anything from an improper fear of their keepers, they would have themselves only to blame for their want of immediate redress. That for the purpose of their deliverance the British officer attended that the British General should be also well informed of facts.

On this after some little hesitation from a dread of their keeper, the Provost Martial, one of them began and informed us that they had been confined on the most frivolous pretenses: some for having been oppressors of the friends of Government—for taking refugees' property, while officers under command and in obedience to orders—for being out of their bounds of parole, the week after their return—some confined in the dungeon for a night to wait the censure of General to examine them, and forgot for months—for being Committee Men, etc., etc. That they had received the most cruel treatment from the Provost Martial, being locked up in the dungeon on the most trifling pretenses, such as asking for more water for drinking on a hotter day than usual—for sitting up a little longer in the evening than orders allowed—for writing a letter to the General making their complaints of ill usage and throwing out of the windows. That some of them were kept 10, 12 and 14 weeks in the dungeon on these trifling pretenses.

A Captain Vandyke had been confined 18 months for being concerned in setting fire to the city when, on my calling for the Provost books, it appeared that he had been made prisoner and closely confined in the Provost 4 days before the fire happened.

A Major Paine had been confined 11 months for killing a Capt. Campbell in the engagement when he was taken prisoner, when, on examination, it appeared that the captain had been killed in another part of the action. The charge was that Major Paine when taken had no commission tho' acknowledged by us as a major.

Captain —— was confined for breaking a soldier's thigh with the but of his gun after he was shot down, when the British surgeon on examination acknowledged that the thigh was broken by a ball, etc., etc., etc.

Most of the cases examined into turned out wholly false or too trifling to be regarded. It also appeared by the declaration of some of the gentlemen that their water would be sometimes, as the caprice of the Provost Martial led him, brought up to them in the tubs they used in their rooms, and when the weather was so hot that they must drink or perish.

On hearing a number of these instances of cruelty, I asked who was the author of them. They answered "the provost keeper." I desired the officer to call him up that we might have him face to face. He accordingly came in, and on being informed of what had passed, he was asked if the complaints were true. He with great insolence answered that every word was true—on which the British officer, abusing him very much, asked him how he dared to treat gentlemen in that cruel manner. He, insolently putting his hands to his side, swore that he was as absolute there as Gen'l Howe was at the head of his army. I observed to the officer that now there could be no dispute about facts as the fellow had acknowledged every word to be true.

I stated all the facts in substance and waited again on Gen'l Robertson, who hoped I was quite satisfied of the falsity of the reports I had heard. I then stated to him the facts and assured him that they turned out worse than anything we had heard. On his hesitating as to the truth of this assertion, I observed to him the propriety of having an officer with me, to whom I now appealed for the truth of the facts. He being present confirmed them—on which the General expressed great dissatisfaction, and promised that the author of them should be punished.

—Boudinot, *Journal or Historical Recollections*, pp. 13-17.

V. CONGRESS KEEPS THE "CONVENTION" TROOPS IN AMERICA

Article IV of the Convention (not Capitulation) between Generals Gates and Burgoyne provided that British troops (many of them Hessians) might march to the nearest port and there embark for Britain on the promise that they would not fight again in North America. Under this agreement there was nothing to prevent them from fighting elsewhere, in exchange for troops who could fight in America. No wonder Burgoyne boasted that he had dictated the terms, and that they did not constitute a surrender! The Congress was so delighted at the victory of Saratoga that at first it hastened to congratulate Gates on a "surrender upon terms honorable and advantageous to these states." Upon reflection, however, Congress changed its mind, and sought ways to qualify or evade the arrangements that Gates had made. A Committee of Congress promptly discovered several technicalities which appeared to justify delay. First, Burgoyne had failed to surrender all his arms. Second, he had complained that Congress had violated the terms of the Convention; the Committee argued that this complaint constituted a denunciation of the Convention. Third, there was no evidence that the King had ratified the Convention; when evidence was produced the Committee said that it might all be a forgery! Thus the Committee took refuge in subterfuges not creditable to their honor.

The "Convention" troops were marched to Boston, and encamped in near-by towns, and General Heath was informed that embarkation had been indefinitely postponed. General Burgoyne, however, was permitted to return to England, where he denounced what he rightly considered the violation of the terms of the Convention. In January and February the prisoners were marched south to barracks prepared for them near Charlottesville, Virginia; most of the Hessians melted away during their progress through Pennsylvania, which was just what the Americans wanted.

We give here three accounts of the experiences of the Convention troops. The first, from the lively pen of Hannah Winthrop—wife of the famous Harvard astronomer—to the equally lively Mercy Warren, tells of the arrival of the troops in Cambridge. The second, a long complaint about mistreatment, is written by Lieutenant Colonel Thomas Anburey who later published a volume of Travels Through the Interior Parts of America. *From the Baroness Riedesel, wife of the commander of the Hessian troops at Saratoga and best of all the women chroniclers of the Revolution, comes the story of the long march to Virginia.*

1. The "Convention" Troops March Through Cambridge

Hannah Winthrop to Mercy Warren.

Cambridge, November 11, 1777

Last Thursday, which was a very stormy day, a large number of British troops came softly thro the town via Watertown to Prospect Hill. On Friday we heard the Hessians were to make a procession in the same rout; we thought we should have nothing to do with them but view them as they passt. To be sure, the sight was truly astonishing. I never had the least idea that the Creation produced such a sordid set of creatures in human figure—poor, dirty, emaciated men, great numbers of women, who seemed to be the beasts of burthen, having a bushel basket on their back, by which they were bent double—the contents seemed to be pots and kettles, various sorts of furniture— children peeping thro' gridirons and other utensils, some very young infants who were born on the road; the women [with] bare feet, cloathed in dirty rags—such effluvia filled the air while they were passing, had they not been smoking all the time, I should have been apprehensive of being contaminated.

After a noble looking advanced guard Gen. J. Burgoyne headed this terrible group on horseback. The other general also, cloathed in blue cloaks. Hessians, Anspachers, Brunswickers, etc., etc., followed on. The Hessian general gave us a polite bow as they passed. Not so the British. Their baggage waggons [were] drawn by poor half starved horses. But to bring up the rear, another fine noble looking guard of American brawny victorious yeomanry, who assisted in bringing these sons of slavery to terms. Some of our waggons drawn by fat oxen, driven by joyous looking Yankees, closed the cavalcade.

The generals and other officers went to Bradishs, where they quarter at present. The privates trudged thro thick and thin to the hills, where we thought they were to be confined, but what was our surprise when in the morning we beheld an inundation of those disagreeable objects filling our streets! How mortifying is it—they in a manner demanding our houses and colleges for their genteel accommodations. Did the brave General Gates ever mean this? Did our legislature ever intend the military should prevail above the civil? Is there not a degree of unkindness in loading poor Cambridge, almost ruined before this great army seemed to be let loose upon us? And what will be the consequence time will discover.

Some polite ones say, we ought not to look on them as prisoners; they are persons of distinguished rank. Perhaps too we must not view them in the light of enemys. I fear this distinction will be soon lost. Surpriseing that our general or any of our colonels should insist on the first University in America being disbanded for their more genteel accomodation, and we poor oppressed people seek an asylum in the woods against a piercing winter! . . . It is said we shall have not less than seven thousand persons to feed in Cambridge and its environs, more than its inhabitants. Two hundred and fifty cord of wood will not serve them a week. Think then how we must be distresst. Wood is risen to £5.10 pr. cord and but little to be purchased. I never thought I could lie down to sleep surrounded by these enemies, but we strangely become enured to those things which appear difficult when distant.

—Warren-Adams Letters, II, 451-452.

2. "Stupid Fools, They Might Perceive That We Were Officers!"

Letters from Lieutenant Colonel Thomas Anburey.

December 7, 1777

We are anxiously expecting the vessels, as our situation is not only very unpleasant but dangerous, both to officers and soldiers; the latter of whom are in continual broils with the American guards, which are composed of militia, who, not being under very great discipline, not only infringe their orders, which perhaps they do not comprehend, or else use their authority as they think proper. They have received orders not to let any officer pass without his side arms, and as many of them left their baggage in Canada, others lost them with their baggage during the campaign, this ignorant people will not let any one pass without a sword, drawling out, "I swear now you shan't pass, because you have not got a sword." At the same time, stupid fools, they might perceive by our cloaths and bayonets that we were officers. Much altercation has ensued, to remedy which the officers had passports signed by General Heath, but this did not avail, as very few of the centinels could read. At last it was ordered that any officer who wanted to pass the centinels was to go to the American guard, where the officer should send a soldier to pass him; this did not altogether remedy the evil, as many of the officers could not make out the passport.

When I describe to you the troops, you will not so much wonder at these embarrassments. In marching the party to relief, you will see an old man of sixty and a boy of sixteen; a black and an old decrepid man limping by his side; most of them wear great bushy wigs; in short, they would be a subject for the pencil of Hogarth; but, egad, they are ready enough in presenting their pieces, and if a soldier comes the least near them they level at him and say, "I swear now, if you attempt to pass, I'll blaze at you." . . .

January 19, 1778

It is impossible to describe with what a dejected mind I sit down to write, as not only the flattering hopes of shortly seeing my friend is done away, and every prospect vanished, but some years, perhaps, may elapse before the termination of this unhappy contest.

What was intended as an accommodation to the troops relative to their embarking at Rhode Island, has proved a most unfortunate circumstance indeed; for the Congress have not only denied that request, but have put a stop to any embarkation till the convention is ratified at home by the King and Parliament, an event that can never happen, as it would be allowing the authority of the Congress and the independence of the Americans. What renders our situation more distressing is that had the transports came round to Boston, the Council would have consented to our embarkation. . . .

Judge, my dear friend, what must be the feelings of every one, and how exasperated we must be at this treatment! We have no other hopes left but an exchange of prisoners, which, considering our numbers, will be some time before the whole can be effected. Our situation now becomes every day more and more mortifying, for, exclusive of the insults we continually meet with from the American soldiery, the officers, no doubt stimulated by this resolve of Congress, behave very tauntingly; and Colonel Henley, who commands the troops, has been guilty of great cruelty to the soldiers. That you may form an idea as to the natural ferocity of disposition in this man, and how deliberate he is in his barbarities, I shall state a few of them.

On the 19th of last month, he went up to the American barracks to release some of our soldiers; after calling over their names, he addressed himself to a Corporal Reeves, of the 9th Regiment, and told him "he had been confined for insulting a provincial officer."

Reeves made answer, "He was sorry for it; that he was in liquor, and would not have acted so had he known him to have been an officer, and was ready to ask his pardon."

Colonel Henley said, "By God, Sir, had you served me so, I would have run you through the body, and I believe you to be a great rascal."

Reeves made answer, "I am no rascal, but a good soldier, and my officers know it." Colonel Henley then demanded silence. Reeves repeated nearly the same words, adding, "That he hoped soon to carry arms under General Howe and fight for his King and country."

The colonel then replied, "Damn your King and country! When you had arms, you were willing enough to lay them down." Colonel Henley then ordered silence. Reeves repeating nearly the same words, the colonel ordered one of the guard to run him through for a scoundrel. The men of the guard not obeying his orders, he dismounted from his horse and, seizing a firelock with a fixed bayonet from one of the guard, stabbed Corporal Reeves in the left breast, and whilst he had the bayonet at his bosom, the colonel told him, "If he said another word, he would have it through his body."

Reeves then told him, "He did not care, he would stand by King and his country till he died."

Colonel Henley then made a second dart at him with the firelock and fixed bayonet, which two of the other prisoners threw up, and it passed over Reeves' shoulder. At the same time one of the men said to Colonel Henley, "That the man was his prisoner, that he had better not take his life, as he could do with him as with the other men who were in his custody."

Colonel Henley then returned the firelock and ordered him back into the guard-room, dismissing the rest of the prisoners. . . .

Do not be surprised after this if you should hear of a general massacre of all the British troops! But what more fully stamps the character of this most sanguinary man, and his ferocious disposition, is a most unaccountable expression he made to some soldiers without any provocation.

Our passes are renewable every month, for which purpose the quartermaster-serjeants of the different regiments attend at the American Deputy Adjutant-General's office; on the 16th of last month, as the serjeants attended at the office to apply for passes, Serjeant Fleming, of the 47th Regiment, not being acquainted with Colonel Henley, took him for Colonel Keith, the Deputy Adjutant-General, saluted him cap in hand, and was going to address him when Colonel Henley extended his arm towards him with his fist clenched, and said, "You rascals, I'll make damnation fly out of ye; for I will myself, one of these nights, go the rounds, and if I hear the least word or noise in your barracks, I'll put shot amongst you and make flames of Hell jump out of ye, and turn your barracks inside out"; declaring, if he was a centinel and any British soldiers looked sulky at him, he would blow their brains out!

Such glaring conduct could not escape the notice of General Burgoyne, who applied to General Heath for redress, and he instituted a Court of Enquiry to investigate the grounds of complaint, and reported it would be for the *honor* of Colonel Henley, as well as for the satisfaction of all interested, that the judgement of a court-martial should be taken on his conduct during his command at Cambridge, which court-martial is to sit to-morrow.

—ANBUREY, *Travels Through the Interior Parts of America,* II, 72-86.

3. BARONESS RIEDESEL TAKES THE LONG ROAD TO VIRGINIA

Before we passed the so-called Blue Mountains, we were forced to make a still further halt of eight days, that our troops might have time to collect together again. In the mean time such a great quantity of snow fell that four of our servants were obliged to go before my wagon on horseback, in order to make a path for it. We passed through a picturesque portion of the country, which, however, by reason of its wildness, inspired us with terror. Often we were in danger of our lives while going along these break-neck roads; and more than all this we suffered from cold and, what was still worse, from a lack of provisions.

When we arrived in Virginia and were only a day's journey from the place of our destination, we had actually nothing more remaining but our tea, and none of us could obtain any thing but bread and butter. A countryman whom we met on the way gave me only a hand full of acrid fruits. At noon we came to a dwelling where I begged for something to eat. They refused me with hard words, saying that there was nothing for dogs of Royalists. Seeing some Turkish [Indian] meal lying around, I begged for a couple of hands full, that I might mix it with water and make bread.

The woman answered me, "No, that is for our Negroes, who work for us, but you have wished to kill us." Captain Edmonston offered her from me two guineas for it, as my children were so hungry. But she said, "Not for a hundred would I give you any; and should you all die of hunger, it will be so much the better."

At this reply, the captain became so provoked that he wished to take it by force. I, however, entreated him, in order to prevent disturbance, to keep quiet, as we, perhaps, would soon come across better disposed people. But alas that did not happen! We did not once meet with even a hut. The roads were horrible, the horses completely tired out, my three children exhausted by hunger, very wan, and I for the first time was thoroughly disheartened. Captain Edmonston, exceedingly touched at this sight, went from man to man to see if he could not obtain something to eat. At last he received from one of the drivers of our baggage-wagons a piece of old bread, a quarter of a pound's weight, which had been considerably gnawed at, since, on account of its hardness, no one could bite off the smallest piece.

The instant he brought it to us, joy sparkled in the eyes of the children. I was about to give the first piece to Caroline as the youngest. "No," said the kind child, "my sisters are more hungry than I." Gustava and Frederica also refused to take it, wishing to leave it for their little sister. I therefore divided it and gave it to all three to eat. Tears ran down both my cheeks; and the good Edmonston was so affected that he was unable longer to endure the sight.

If I had at any time refused a piece of bread to the poor, I should have thought that God wished now to punish me for it. The kind driver, who had so willingly given us his last piece of bread, received a guinea from Captain Edmonston, and, on our arrival at the place of our destination, a large stock of bread for his return journey.

The place of our destination was Colle in Virginia, where my husband, who had gone ahead with our troops, awaited us with impatient longing. We arrived here about the middle of February, 1779, having, on our journey, passed through the provinces of Connecticut, New York, New Jersey, Pennsylvania and Maryland, and having traveled in twelve weeks six hundred and seventy-eight English miles. The house in which we lived and the entire estate belonged to an Italian, who, as he was to be absent for some time, gave it up to us. We looked forward longingly to the departure of himself, wife and daughter, for not only was the house small, but, more than all, the scarcity of provisions seemed to trouble them—a circumstance which caused the husband to exercise a kind of guardianship over us. Thus, when he had a ram killed, he gave us on the first day nothing more than the head, the neck and the giblets, although I represented to him that more than twenty persons were to make a meal off them. He assured me that a right good soup might be made of these articles, and gave us, besides, two heads of cabbage, with which, and half of a putrid ham, we were obliged to be satisfied.

The troops had been expected earlier, and accordingly many oxen and swine had been killed for food; and, as salt was very scarce, they cut the meat into quarters, placed it in a vault in the earth, and scattered between the pieces ashes instead of salt which answered equally as well. But as in this part of the country the sun, even in January, often shines out very warm, all the top layers were spoiled. The meat was brought to us on a wheel-barrow; but we were often obliged to throw the whole of it away, although sometimes we could wash it, in which case we salted and hung it up in smoke.

The day of our arrival, when I had scarcely enough for dinner to satisfy us alone, I saw, with tears, eight of our officers ride up just before dinner. What could we do but share with them the little we had?

The troops were stationed at Charlottesville, two hours ride from us. To reach them we were obliged to go through a very beautiful piece of woods. At first they endured many privations. They occupied block-houses, which, however, were without plaster and destitute of doors and windows, so that they were very cold inside. They worked, however, with great industry to build themselves better dwellings; and, in a short time, I saw a pretty little town spring up. Behind each barrack they laid out gardens and constructed pretty little inclosures for poultry. Afterwards, when the old provisions were consumed, they received fresh meat and meal enough to make bread. As this latter was Indian meal, it served them for omelets and dumplings; so that now they were in want of nothing but money. Very little of this latter commodity was sent to them by the English, and it was difficult sometimes to obtain credit—a circumstance which oftentimes gave great inconvenience to the common soldiers.

In the middle of the month of February the fruit trees, which were already in blossom, were all killed by the night-frost. As soon as the temperature of the air would allow, we had the garden and the field tilled and planted; and, as our landlord went off three weeks after, we took possession of everything— swine, wild turkeys, etc. Some of the latter weighed over fifty pounds and were perfectly tame; but when spring came, they all flew off to hatch their eggs, which they had laid in the forests. We gave them up for lost, but they all came back and brought with them a great number of young ones.

We had built for us a large house, with a great drawing-room in the centre, and upon each side two rooms, which cost my husband one hundred guineas. It was exceedingly pretty.

Many of the Negroes brought us everything that we needed in the shape of poultry and vegetables. Every week General Phillips and ourselves killed, by turns, an ox and two pigs. Very soon we wanted nothing. But the heat bothered us very much in summer; and we lived in constant terror of rattle-snakes. The fruits were also eaten into by three kinds of ticks. We had, more-over, very heavy thunderstorms, lasting for five or six days at a time, and accompanied by tempests which tore up by the roots more than one hundred trees in our vicinity. The trees stood very loosely, and their roots were lightly covered, as the strong winds blew away from them the earth, which was mostly sand. Besides all this, the Negroes and herdsmen often made fires un-der the trees, for which they cared nothing. By reason of this the trees were more easily blown down. Often whole forests were set on fire and burned down in order to obtain new land.

At night we were obliged to leave our windows open, that we might be able to draw in fresh air and sleep. Thereupon, three or four nasty bats, three times as large as with us, would wake us up, and we were obliged to spend half the night in chasing them around the room. On one occasion a person came in the night to my husband to tell him that the stable, which was a new one, was in danger of being blown down by the wind. Everyone ran out to prop it up, except myself, who was left alone with my children and women serv-ants. The wind continually grew stronger. A great piece of the chimney fell into the room; the whole house rocked; and I remained half the night in the greatest fear of being killed by a fragment. We were often frightened in this manner.

We had no chairs to sit on, only round blocks, which we also used for a table, laying boards upon them. In this manner we lived for three or four months, pretty contentedly.

—RIEDESEL, *Letters and Journals*, pp. 152-156.

VI. THE SUFFERINGS OF LOYALIST AND BRITISH PRISONERS

If British prisoners suffered less than American, it was not because Americans were more humane, but because they had so few facilities for imprisonment, and so little experience in the practice. They could not afford to maintain large bodies of prisoners, nor did they have enough food and fuel for proper maintenance. They made in fact little effort to detain the Hessians, confident that if they escaped it would not be back to their British masters, but to American farmers. Loyalists, on the other hand, fared hard. Some more extreme Patriots took the same attitude toward Loyalists that extreme English patriots took toward the rebels—they were traitors and should suffer the extreme penalty. This was, happily, impractical, and though—especially in the Carolinas—many of them doubtless were killed and not captured, they could console themselves that this procedure was irregular.

We give here the prison experience of one British soldier, and of two Loyalists. Ensign Hughes was an Old Etonian and a gentleman; he had bought an ensigncy in the 53d Regiment, and fought in Canada and New York. Captured at Ticonderoga, he was taken to Pepperell, Massachusetts—as much out of the world as the deserts of Arabia, he found, and inhabited by people "as ignorant as Hottentots." He was, however, allowed the freedom of the town; about the hardest thing he had to endure was that Americans had not "the least idea of a gentleman" and expected servants to sit down at table with their betters. Eventually Ensign Hughes was exchanged and returned to his native land. He died in Canada a few years later.

What the Jersey prison ship was to Americans, the Simsbury copper mines were to Loyalists, with the important difference that only a few Loyalists were imprisoned in the hideous mines. One of them was Joel Stone of Connecticut who escaped from his dungeon to Upper Canada. Escape was not, apparently, too difficult, for Rivington's Royal Gazette gives us many stories of successful prison breaks.

1. ENSIGN HUGHES ENJOYS "RURAL HAPPINESS" AT PEPPERELL

Oct. 12th [*1777*]. To pass off a tedious minute, I shall describe the passing of one day—which will serve for the whole, there being no variety. At 9 o'clock (arouse is the word) we jump up from the floor, and without the trouble of putting on our clothes, being always dressed, we fall to our breakfast, consisting of boiled rice sprinkled with salt and garnished with a few lumps of stinking butter, to prevent its sticking in the throat. This meal finished, we mount the quarter deck, which is almost five paces long; here we amuse ourselves with walking, sitting, and talking about the weather, wind, tide, etc., etc., till one o'clock, when a servant announces the dinner being ready. Our dinners always (like those of the foundation boys at Eaton) consist of one dish, with this trifling difference—theirs consists of mutton, ours salt pork, with ship biscuit. Our apparatus is first the top of a chest of drawers for table (rather the worse for wear); instead of table cloth, about an inch of grease and dirt. Our plates are formed of pieces of wood, our dish a wooden bowl; 3 one-pronged forks and two knives are laid in order (those that have knives to cut for the rest). Our drink is very small beer (generally sour) and water. After dinner one of the drawers receives the meat, which is laid by for supper. Our afternoon is the most tedious part of the day, so that by 8 o'clock we are heartily tired, when we take a slight repast and lay down on the floor of the cabin, thicker than three in a bed.

Oct. 15th. Two of our men made their escape by slipping unobserved into the boat, untying and letting her drive on shore, they laying at the bottom; this exploit was performed during a hard shower.

Oct. 17th. Most of the gentlemen being unwell, Capt. Davies having the fever and ague and myself a violent dysentery, occasioned by our confined situation and bad diet, we wrote to the Council of Boston and desired leave to go into the country on parole.

Oct. 18th. Our request being granted, a commissary brought us a parole for the town of Pepperell—but we are limited to a mile. . . .

Oct. 21st. Arrived at Pepperell, and were delivered over to the Committee of the town, who distributed us about the neighbourhood for this night. I lay at one Gibson's, who was formerly a cornet in the provincial service, the greatest blackguard and the greatest rebel I ever met with.

Oct. 22nd. Procured quarters in a house, in which I have agreed to pay two silver dollars pr week for board, etc., etc. The family are very civil—it consists of Father (who is almost deaf), Mother (a talkative old woman), and two daughters, who are of the order of old maids, confounded ugly, with beards an inch long.

Oct. 25th. This town is quite a new settlement and so little cleared that in some places the houses are a mile distant. We are almost as much out of the world here as if we were in the deserts of Arabia, and the inhabitants as ignorant as the Hottentots. I have been asked how often I have visited Jerusalem and if I did not live close by it, though I told them I lived in England; and then they asked if England was not a fine town. What a life am I to lead? I am sick of their absurdities.

Oct. 26th. I find that the people here have not the least idea of a gentleman. Our servants are treated just like ourselves, and they are surprised to find our men won't eat at the same table with us, to which they are always invited. Two of our gentlemen agreeing with some inhabitant about boarding, the only thing the people objected to was the article of washing. "Oh! if that is the only obstacle," says a Committee man, who went with them, "it is easily removed; send them a tub, and give them a little soap, and they can wash their own clothes."

November 1st. This life being such a one as perhaps I may never see again, I cannot refrain describing it. We have but one room to eat and sit in, which is in common with all the family, master, mistress and servant, and what to call it I know not, as it serves for parlour, kitchen and workroom. About 9 o'clock, Lt. Brown (who lives with me) and myself breakfast, but they all wonder how we can sleep so long. Our breakfast is bread and milk, or boiled Indian corn with butter and treacle spread over it. This is pretty substantial, and after it we generally walk into the woods, to gather chestnuts or throw stones at squirrels.

About 12 o'clock the whole family collects for dinner, which soon after smokes upon the board; and whilst it is cooling, Father shuts his eyes, mutters an unintelligible monstrous long grace, and down we all sit with no other distinction but Brown and me getting pewter plates—whereas the others have wooden platters. Our food is fat salt pork and sauce (the name they give to roots and greens). We never get fresh meat but when a fox or hawk seizes an unfortunate fowl, but, being discovered by the noise we make, is frightened and lets fall the prey, generally with the loss of a leg or wing. The fowl on this disaster is immediately pickt and put into the pot. The dinners are upon that free and easy mode that neither gentleman or lady use any ceremony—all hands in the dish at once—which gives many pretty opportunities for laughter, as two or three of us often catch hold of the same piece.

This meal over, another grace is said, and we all disperse to our different employments, theirs working and ours the best we can find. At night fall a large fire is made on the hearth, and the kitchen (or whatever it is) receives the whole family, which would present an high scene to an unconcerned spectator—Mother, Brown and me round the fire, she knitting and asking us silly questions; our servant at the opposite corner of the chimney from us; at our back two or three women spinning with large noisy wheels, and in the middle of the room sits Father, and one or two apprentice boys shelling Indian corn. We have no candles, but the room is lighted by splinters of pine wood flung into the fire. About 8 o'clock we get bread and milk for supper; a little after Father begins to yawn—upon which we stand up. He says prayers, and we depart to our beds.

Our apartment, or rather the place we lay in, extends over the whole house and is what is commonly called the garret. We have three beds in it—one of which contains Brown and me, in the second sleep our two young ladies, and close at their feet, in the third, rest the servant and apprentice. Our room is not the worse for being a repository of fruit and nuts, as we generally make an attack on the apples before we get up of a morn.

If this is the kind of life the poets say so much of and call Rural Happiness, I wish to my soul that they were here, and I in London.

—Hughes, *Journal*, pp. 22-26.

2. A Connecticut Loyalist Escapes from His Dismal Dungeon

Narrative of Joel Stone.

November 8th, 1784

In the year 1776 I discovered that it was perfectly impracticable any longer to conceal my sentiments from the violent public. The agents of Congress acted with all the cunning and cruelty of inquisitors and peremptorily urged me to declare without further hesitation whether I would immediately take up arms against the British Government or procure a substitute to serve in the general insurrection.

I could no longer withhold any positive reply and unalterable resolution of declining to fulfil their request by joining in an act which I actually detested and which had been repeatedly deemed a rebellion by the public proclamation of General Howe. The leader of the faction then informed me that my conduct in consequence of such refusal would undergo the strictest scrutiny and that I might expect to meet the utmost severity to my person from those in authority and an incensed public.

Thus perpetually perplexed and harassed, I determined in my own mind to withdraw as soon as possible to the City of New York and there by joining his Majesty's forces cast what weight I was able into the opposite scale. But before I could carry my design into execution a warrant by order of the agents of Congress was issued out in order to seize my person. Being apprized of this and hearing that a party of men were actually on their way to my house, I packed up my books and bills, which I delivered to a careful friend to secrete, and left the care of my effects in the house to one of my sisters who had lived with me some time. Before the tumultuous mob which attended the party surrounded the premises, I had the good fortune to get away on horseback and, being in a dark night, happily eluded their search. But my sister, as I was afterwards given to understand, met the resentment of the mob, who from language the most opprobrious proceeded to actual violence, breaking open every lock in the house and seizing all the property they could discover. My goods and chattels thus confiscated they exposed to sale as soon as possible in opposition to the repeated remonstrances of my partner, declaring that the whole estate, real and personal, was become the property of the States.

But I soon found that my person was one principal object of their aim. Being informed to what place I had fled, a party of about twelve armed men with a constable came up and, seizing my horse, were proceeding into the house when I found an opportunity to slip from their hands. [It] was full fourteen days before I was perfectly secure, during which time several parties were detached after me, whom they were taught to consider as a traitor to the United States and unworthy to live. An invincible frenzy appeared to pervade the minds of the country people, and those very men who so recently had held one in the highest esteem became the most implacable enemies. I could not help considering my fate as peculiarly hard in thus being hunted as a common criminal and proscribed without cause in the very country that gave me birth, merely for performing my duty and asserting the rights of the British Constitution.

However, I had the unspeakable happiness to escape the utmost vigilance of my pursuers and at length reached Long Island. There I soon joined the King's army as a volunteer, in company with several gentlemen in the same persecuted situation, who also like myself had missed no opportunity of serving the royal cause but whose exertion had been greatly curbed by the popular party. I remained thus until the 15th April, 1778, when, finding my money just expended amidst so many enormous calls and dreading that the patience of my best friends would not hold out much longer however willing they had been to assist me, I accepted a warrant to raise a company (as stated in my memorial presented to the Right Honorable the Lords Commissioners of His Majesty's Treasury), with a view to be in pay, especially as but little prospect was presented of a speedy termination being put to the unhappy war.

On the night of the 12th of May, 1778, as I was lying at Huntingdon on Long Island in order to carry my purpose of recruiting further into execution, I was surprised whilst asleep by a company of whale boat men who took me prisoner and carried [me] over to Norwalk in Connecticut.

The magistrate before whom I was taken refused to consider me as a prisoner of war, which I claimed as a right, but charging me with the enormous crime of high treason against the States I was committed a close prisoner to Fairfield jail. I was there indicted, threatened with the vengeance of the law and warned solemnly for that death which most certainly would be inflicted upon me.

In a situation so perfectly horrible, perpetually exposed to the most barbarous insults of the populace and even some of the magistrates of the place, it may easily be supposed I would mediate [meditate] a recovery from a captivity so much to be dreaded. For a purpose so truly desirable I resolved to exert every effort of ingenuity that my mind could suggest. By the aid of my brother and other friends in that country I sent a flag to the commander of the king's army at or nigh King's Bridge in New York, soliciting immediate relief. This not producing the desired effect, I petitioned the Governor . . . that I might, agreeable to justice, be deemed a prisoner of war, treated as such and be permitted to appear before himself and Council in person to remove every objection to the late request. I freely offered to defray all the incidental expenses occasioned by my removal across the country. However, he hesitated some time but at last agreed to my proposal. I paid for the strong guard which attended me by the way and entertained some hope of my meeting a favorable reception from the Governor.

The result turned out quite contrary to my wish. My petition was rejected with the utmost disdain and I was reminded to prepare for that approaching fate which was irrevocably fixed, as I was afterwards informed by a decree which could not be thwarted.

On my return the captain and guard buoyed me up by the way with a distant view of clemency, which in a great measure prevented me from an attempt which by the aid of pecuniary means must have freed me from so dreadful a situation, as I discovered that these mercenaries were far from being invulnerable in the respect alluded to. But as that must have cost me a considerable sum, the notion that I should one day be exchanged soothed for the present my perturbed mind and prevented my immediate attempt to escape. But on my return to prison all my sanguine hopes vanished and left my mind in the utmost agitation. I began to renew my contrivances and intrigues in conjunction with my friends and resolved to spare no expense in my power to regain my liberty. Many of my schemes, though they cost large sums, proved unsuccessful, yet I did not despair of gaining my point. The dungeon was truly dismal, the walls strong and the place perpetually guarded, yet being in the prime of life my spirits were warm and my passions violent. I therefore firmly determined to effect an escape if I even should be obliged to sink the last shilling and go out naked into the world.

Communicating my final resolution to Mr. H——, a fellow prisoner, he readily approved of my plan and embraced the offered opportunity of being again free. By the generous aid of my friends and a judicious application of almost all the money I could raise we happily emerged from that place of horror July 23, 1778, and with quick despatch pursued our way into the wilderness of that country to wait the further assistance of our friends.

The whole country being immediately alarmed, a general hue and cry surrounded us, so that all our expected subsistence was cut off for two days and two nights, during which time we lived upon a fruit which grows spontaneously in those parts called Nurtle berries. When the alarm was somewhat subsided we met the help which we expected from our friends. They also instructed us how to proceed in the further completion of our plan. I found my strength much impaired by the close confinement, and so sudden a transition from a warm prison to be exposed to the dews and damps of the wood had like to have been attended with the most fatal consequences to my health. Amidst this sudden sickness we travelled every night, rested sometimes in caves of the rocks and sometimes on the cold ground in wild marshes. At the same time the heart of my companion failed him, and the dread of falling into the hands of the enemy struck him with an unmanly panic. His unparalleled pusilanimity reminded me of the travelling tribes of old who pressed their leader to return them to their late house of bondage. In vain I attempted to arouse his magnanimity, for it was all absorbed in a littleness of soul which rather would have trusted to the clemency of tyrants than improve the auspicious opportunity which fortune had put into our hands. . . .

—STONE, "Narrative," *Loyalist Narratives*, pp. 323-330.

VII. AMERICAN PRISONERS IN ENGLISH GAOLS

In the course of the war the British captured perhaps two thousand American seamen—crews of privateers and fishermen. Those taken in the coastal waters off Long Island were commonly confined in the prison ships; some were carried to Halifax and jailed there; those taken on the high seas were carried to England and imprisoned in Plymouth and elsewhere.

The British authorities—like the Union authorities in 1861—had trouble making up their minds about the status of these captured seamen. Were they pirates? or did they enjoy belligerent rights? Fear of retaliation rather than magnanimity persuaded the British to accord belligerent status to their American prisoners. These endured the usual privations and humiliations in their British gaols, but their lot was ameliorated by the generosity of many friends of the American cause who supplied them with small sums of money and with food. Throughout the war Franklin tried in vain to arrange an exchange between American prisoners in England, and British seamen held in France or in the States.

We do not have a great many prison or escape narratives from England, but those we have are of unusual interest. One of the best is that of the gifted and distinguished Henry Laurens, President of the American Congress, Minister Plenipotentiary to Holland, and member of the American peace cor.mission. That the British were unprepared to accord him diplomatic immunity, and wavered between treating him as a prisoner of war, subject to exchange, and a traitor, guilty of high treason, reveals a great deal about their confused attitude towards the Revolution as late as 1781.

1. A PLEA FOR AMERICAN PRISONERS IN ENGLAND

Benjamin Franklin to David Hartley, M.P.

Passy, 14 October 1777

You in England, if you wish for peace, have at present the opportunity of trying this means with regard to the prisoners now in your gaols. They complain of very severe treatment. They are far from their friends and families, and winter is coming on, in which they must suffer extremely if continued in their present situation: fed scantily on bad provisions, without warm lodging, clothes, or fire, and not suffered to invite or receive visits from their friends, or even from the humane and charitable of their enemies.

I can assure you from my own certain knowledge that your people, prisoners in America, have been treated with great kindness; they have been served with the same rations of wholesome provisions with our own troops, comfortable lodgings have been provided for them, and they have been allowed large bounds of villages in the healthy air, to walk and amuse themselves with on their parole. Where you have thought fit to employ contractors to supply your people, these contractors have been protected and aided in their operations. Some considerable act of kindness towards our people would take off the reproach of inhumanity in that respect from the nation, and leave it where it ought with more certainty to lie, on the conductors of your war in America. This I hint to you, out of some remaining good-will to a nation I once loved sincerely.

—BIGELOW, ed., *Works of Franklin*, VII, 227-228.

2. HENRY LAURENS IS IMPRISONED IN THE TOWER

Henry Laurens was undoubtedly the most distinguished American captured by the British during the war. Charleston's leading merchant, and one of South Carolina's most distinguished statesmen, he had been one of the leaders in the Revolutionary movement in his state, helped write its conservative Constitution, served as member and then as President of the Continental Congress. In 1779 he was appointed to negotiate a commercial agreement with Holland. In August 1780 he sailed on the brig Mercury, *only to be captured by the frigate* Vestal; *the diplomatic pouch which he threw overboard failed to sink, was recovered by an English seaman, and its secret papers used as a pretext for the British declaration of war against the Dutch.*

Laurens was taken first to Dartmouth prison, then on to London where he was examined by a group of High Commissioners, and held "on suspicion of high treason." In October 1780 he was committed to the Tower, and there, notwithstanding his proper claims for diplomatic immunity, and the protests

of Franklin and others, kept in confinement for over a year. During his im-
prisonment he was subjected not only to hardships but to continuous efforts
to seduce him from his allegiance. After Yorktown he was released on parole,
and early in 1782 exchanged for Lord Cornwallis. He proceeded to Paris
where he participated in the final stages of negotiating the treaty of peace with
Britain.

Laurens' narrative, written 1780-1782.

About 11 o'clock at night I was sent under a strong guard, up three pair
of stairs in Scotland Yard, into a very small chamber. Two king's messengers
were placed for the whole night at one door, and a subaltern's guard of soldiers
at the other. As I was, and had been for some days, so ill as to be incapable
of getting into or out of a carriage, or up or down stairs, without help, I looked
upon all this parade to be calculated for intimidation. My spirits were good, and
I smiled inwardly. The next morning, 6th October [1780], from Scotland Yard
I was conducted again under guard to the secretary's office, White Hall, where
were present Lord Hillsborough, Lord Stormont, Lord George Germain, Mr.
Chamberlain, Solicitor of the Treasury, Mr. Knox, Under-Secretary, Mr.
Justice Addington, and others. I was first asked, by Lord Stormont, "If my
name was Henry Laurens?"

"Certainly, my Lord, that is my name."

Capt. Keppel was asked, "If that was Mr. Laurens?" He answered in the
affirmative.

His Lordship then said: "Mr. Laurens, we have a paper here—" holding the
paper up—"purporting to be a commission from Congress to you, to borrow
money in Europe for the use of Congress. It is signed Samuel Huntingdon,
President, and attested by Charles Thomson, Secretary. We have already
proved the handwriting of Charles Thomson."

I replied: "My Lords, your Lordships are in possession of the paper and
will make such use of it as your Lordships shall judge proper." I had not
destroyed this paper, as it would serve to establish the rank and character in
which I was employed by the United States. Another question was asked me,
which I did not rightly understand. I replied: "My Lords, I am determined to
answer no questions but with the strictest truth; wherefore, I trust, your Lordships will ask me no questions which might ensnare me, and which I cannot
with safety and propriety answer." No further questions were demanded.
I was told by Lord Stormont, I was to be committed to the Tower of London
on "suspicion of high treason." I asked, "If I had not a right to a copy of the
commitment?"

Lord Stormont, after a pause said: "He hesitated on the word right," and
the copy was not granted.

Mr. Chamberlain then very kindly said to me: "Mr. Laurens, you are to be
sent to the Tower of London, not to a prison; you must have no idea of a
prison."

I bowed thanks to the gentlemen, and thought of the new hotel, which had
been recommended by my friends in Newfoundland. A commitment was

made out by Mr. Justice Addington, and a warrant by their Lordships to the Lieutenant of the Tower to receive and confine me.

From White Hall, I was conducted in a close hackney coach, under the charge of Col. Williamson, a polite, genteel officer, and two of the illest-looking fellows I had ever seen. The coach was ordered to proceed by the most private ways to the Tower. It had been rumored that a rescue would be attempted. At the Tower the colonel delivered me to Major Gore, the residing Governor, who, as I was afterward well informed, had previously concerted a plan for mortifying me. He ordered rooms for me in the most conspicuous part of the Tower (the parade). The people of the house, particularly the mistress, entreated the Governor not to burthen them with a prisoner. He replied, "It is necessary. I am determined to expose him." This was, however, a lucky determination for me. The people were respectful and kindly attentive to me from the beginning of my confinement to the end; and I contrived, after being told of the Governor's humane declaration, so to garnish my windows by honeysuckles, and a grape-vine running under them, as to conceal myself entirely from the sight of starers, and at the same time to have myself a full view of them. Governor Gore conducted me to my apartments at a warder's house.

As I was entering the house I heard some of the people say: "Poor old gentleman, bowed down with infirmities. He is come to lay his bones here." My reflection was, "I shall not leave a bone with you."

I was very sick, but my spirits were good, and my mind foreboding good from the event of being a prisoner in London. Their Lordships' orders were: "To confine me a close prisoner; to be locked up every night; to be in the custody of two wardens, who were not to suffer me to be out of their sight *one moment*, day or night; to allow me no liberty of speaking to any person, nor to permit any person to speak to me; to deprive me of the use of pen and ink; to suffer no letter to be brought to me, nor any to go from me," etc. As an apology, I presume for their first rigor, the wardens gave me their orders to peruse. . . .

And now I found myself a close prisoner, indeed; shut up in two small rooms, which together made about twenty feet square; a warder my constant companion; and a fixed bayonet under my window; not a friend to converse with, and no prospect of a correspondence.

Next morning, 7th October, Gov. Gore came into my room with a workman and fixed iron bars to my windows; altogether unnecessary. The various guards were enough to secure my person. It was done, as I was informed, either to shake my mind or to mortify me. It had neither effect. I only thought of Mr. Chamberlain's consolation. I asked Mr. Gore, "What provision was to be made for my support?"

He replied, "He had no directions."

I said, "I can very well provide for myself, but I must be allowed means for obtaining money." He gave no answer.

In a word, I discovered I was to pay rent for my little rooms, find my own meat and drink, bedding, coals, candles, etc. This drew from me an observation to the gentleman jailer (the officer who locks up a prisoner every night), who would immediately report it to the Governor: "Whenever I caught a bird in America I found a cage and victuals for it."

What surprised me most was, although the Secretaries of State had seen the ill state of my health and must also have heard of my continuing ill by reports daily made to them, they never ordered, or caused to be provided for me, any medical assistance. The people around me thought, for a considerable time, my life in imminent danger. I was of a different opinion. When the Governor had retired from his iron bars, neither my servant nor baggage being yet arrived, I asked the warder, "If he could lend me a book for amusement?"

He gravely asked: "Will your honor be pleased to have *Drelincourt upon Death?*"

I quickly turned to his wife, who was passing from making up my bed. "Pray, Madam, can you recommend an honest goldsmith who will put a new head to my cane; you see this old head is much worn?"

"Yes, sir, I can."

The people understood me, and nothing more was said of *Drelincourt.* . . .

The 8th, Governor Gore, hypocritically kind, came and told me I had leave to walk about the Tower (he had received the order from General Vernon); but advised, I would only walk the parade before the door; "if you go farther," said he, "there will be such a rabble after you."

I treated his kindness with contempt, and refused to walk. The parade is the very place where he had predetermined to expose me. The order of General Vernon, received by him from the Secretaries of State, was "that I should be permitted to walk the Tower grounds." Mr. Gore attempted to supersede both. The Governor grew uneasy, and asked the wardens why I had not walked. They answered that I was lame with the gout.

Sunday, 12th November, hobbled out; a warder with a sword in his hand at my back; the warder informed me Governor Gore had ordered that I should walk only on the parade; I returned immediately to my little prison.

The 16th, the Governor, more uneasy, jealous and fearful of General Vernon, sent me notice I might walk the broad pavement (115 yards) before the great armory, and within the armory, all arbitrary on his part; but the walk within the building was very agreeable; it would afford sufficient exercise, and viewing the quantity and variety of military stores, etc., etc., was amusing. I visited the place almost every day, till the third December, when, going there, Lord George Gordon, [who] was also a prisoner in the Tower, unluckily met and asked me to walk with him. I declined it and returned instantly to my apartment. The Governor, being informed of this by one of his spies, although the warder explained and proved to him I was in no respect a transgressor, caught hold of the occasion and locked me up. I remained thus closely confined by his arbitrary will forty-seven days; if any, the fault was in Lord George, but the brutal Governor dared not lock him up. . . .

Sunday, 18th, General Vernon, having been fully informed by a friend in the Tower of the Governor's arbitrary locking me up from the third December, called and very kindly enquired if I took my walks abroad as usual.

I replied in the negative and candidly explained what had passed between the Governor and myself. He was exceedingly displeased and said aloud—the people below stairs heard him—"I'll take care to give orders that you may walk when you please and where you please!" He gave orders, not to the Governor, but to Mr. Kinghorn, an inferior officer.

The 22d February, walked abroad, first time since third December. The Governor very angry and much mortified; I must expect the effect of his ill nature in some other way; but I despise him.

Monday, 26th February, Mr. Oswald having solicited the Secretaries of State for my enlargement upon parole and offered to pledge "his whole fortune as surety for my good conduct," sent me the following message, in addition to the above by Mr. Kinghorn, the gentleman jailer: "Their Lordships say, if you will point out anything for the benefit of Great Britain in the present dispute with the Colonies, you shall be enlarged." The first part of the message overwhelmed me with feelings of gratitude, the latter filled me with indignation. I snatched up my pencil, and upon a sudden impulse wrote a note to Mr. Oswald as follows, and sent it by the same Mr. Kinghorn:

"I perceive, my dear friend, from the message you have sent me by Mr. Kinghorn, that if I were a rascal, I might presently get out of the Tower. I am not. You have pledged your word and fortune for my integrity. I will never dishonor you, nor myself. Yes, I could point out, but is this the place? If I had nothing in view but my own interest or convenience, promises and pointings out would be very prompt; but this is not a proper place. I could point out a doctrine, known to every old woman in the kingdom, 'A spoonful of honey will catch more flies than a ton of vinegar.' What I formerly predicted to you, came to pass. I can foresee, now, what will come to pass, *happen to me what may.* I fear no 'possible consequences.' I must have patience and submit to the will of God. I do not change with the times. My conduct has been consistent, and shall be so." . . .

The 7th March, Mr. Oswald visited and was left alone with me. It immediately occurred he had some extraordinary subject from White Hall for conversation, and so it appeared. Mr. Oswald began by saying, "I converse with you this morning not particularly as your friend, but as a friend to Great Britain." I thanked him for his candor. He proceeded: "I have certain propositions to make for obtaining your liberty, which I advise you should take time to consider. I showed the note you lately sent me to Lord Germain, who was at first very angry. He exclaimed, 'Rascals! rascals!—we want no rascals! Honey! honey!! vinegar! They have had too much honey, and too little vinegar! They shall have less honey and more vinegar for the future!'" I said to Mr. Oswald, I should be glad to taste a little of his lordship's vinegar; his lordship's honey had been very unpleasant; but Mr. Oswald said, "That note was written without a moment's deliberation, intended only for myself, and not for the eye of a minister." Mr. Oswald smiled, and said, "It has done you no harm."

I then replied, "I am as ready to give an answer to any proposition which you have to make to me at this moment as I shall be in any given time. An honest man requires no time to give an answer where his honor is concerned.

If the Secretaries of State will enlarge me upon parole, as it seems they can enlarge me if they please, I will strictly conform to my engagement to do nothing, directly or indirectly, to the hurt of this kingdom. I will return to America, or remain in any part of England which may be assigned, and render myself when demanded."

Mr. Oswald answered, "No, you must stay in London, among your friends. The ministers will often have occasion to send for and consult you; but observe, I say all this as from myself, not by particular direction or authority; but I know it will be so. You can write two or three lines to the ministers and barely say, you are sorry for what is past. A pardon will be granted. Every man has been wrong at some time or other of his life, and should not be ashamed to acknowledge it."

I now understood Mr. Oswald and could easily perceive my worthy friend was more than half ashamed of his mission. Without hesitation, I replied, "Sir, I will never subscribe to my own infamy, and to the dishonor of my children." Mr. Oswald then talked of long and painful confinement, which I should suffer, and repeated "possible consequences." "Permit me to repeat, Sir," said I, "I am afraid of no consequences but such as would flow from dishonorable acts."

Mr. Oswald desired "I would take time, weigh the matter properly in my mind, and let him hear from me."

I concluded by assuring him, "he never would hear from me in terms of compliance; if I could be so base, I was sure I should incur his contempt."

Mr. Oswald took leave with such expressions of regard and such a squeeze of the hand as induced me to believe he was not displeased with my determination.

In the course of this conversation, I asked, "Why ministers were so desirous of having me about their persons?"

Mr. Oswald said, "They thought I had great influence in America."

I answered, "I once had some influence in my own country; but it would be in me the highest degree of arrogance to pretend to have a general influence in America. I know but one man of whom this can be said; I mean General Washington. I will suppose, for a moment, the General should come over to your ministers. What would be the effect? He would instantly lose all his influence, and be called a rascal."

"Mr. Duché dreamed that he had an influence even over the General. What was the consequence of his apostasy? Was the course of American proceedings interrupted? By no means. He was execrated, and the Americans went forward." . . .

—Laurens, "Narrative," *S.C. Hist. Soc. Coll.*, I, 24-34.

VIII. CAPTAIN ASGILL IS REPRIEVED AS A COMPLIMENT TO LOUIS XVI

For excitement, pathos and romance, the affaire Asgill ranks with the affaire André; here romance triumphs over pathos because it had a happy ending.

In March 1782 a group of Loyalist irregulars captured an American Pa-triot, one Joshua Huddy. Turned over to General Clinton in New York, Huddy was—at the request of the Associated Loyalists—returned by Clinton to his captors who, for reasons that appeared to them persuasive, promptly strung him up. Pinned on Huddy's breast was a placard reading:

We, the Refugees, having long with grief beheld the cruel murders of our brethren, and finding nothing but such measures daily carried into execu-tion, therefore determined not to suffer without taking vengeance for the numerous cruelties; and thus begin, having made use of Captain Huddy as the first object to present to your view; and we further determine to hang man for man while there is a Refugee existing.

Washington, supported by a council of war, promptly decided on retali-ation, and demanded that General Clinton turn over to him for punishment the officer who commanded at Huddy's execution. Clinton disowned the act of the Loyalists and refused to surrender one of his own officers as a victim. Washington then determined to retaliate on a British prisoner selected by lot, and the choice fell on Captain Charles Asgill, one of the thousands of prisoners surrendered at Yorktown.

The choice could not have been more unfortunate. By the terms of sur-render, these prisoners were exempted from any punishment of this nature. And as for Captain Asgill, he was designed by Nature to excite sympathy: a lad not yet twenty, only son of Sir Charles Asgill—who was once Lord Mayor of London and was a long-time friend to the American cause—and his French Huguenot wife, Thérèse Prativiel. Young Captain Asgill himself had many American friends—he had been at Westminster School with three South Carolinians—and he was to win many more.

Soon the Asgill case became an international cause célèbre. That a charm-ing young aristocrat should suffer death for a crime of which he was innocent, at a time when the war was clearly over, seemed to many, both in America and in Europe, an intolerable outrage. Pressure on General Washington to stay the execution was strong, and though he was adamant on the matter of release, he did yield on a stay. Meantime there were representations from at home and abroad—from General Rochambeau, from Richard Oswald in Paris, from young Alexander Hamilton. Secretary of Foreign Affairs Robert Livingston acknowledged that "the affair of Huddy . . . will need explanation in Europe." It did indeed; it promised to be a serious impediment to the new nation's cam-paign for diplomatic recognition and support.

Salvation—and rescue from a dangerously embarrassing situation—came in the nick of time. Distracted with grief, Lady Asgill had appealed to the French Court for help; Vergennes enlisted the sympathy of the King and Queen, and they in turn instructed him to appeal for mercy directly to Gen-eral Washington. Such an appeal was, of course, irresistible. With deep relief Washington turned the correspondence over to the Congress which voted "that the life of Captain Asgill should be given as a compliment to the King of

France." Secretary Livingston, who was by now alarmed at the potentialities of the affair, wrote to John Adams:

> *The release of Captain Asgill was so exquisite a relief to my feelings that I have not much cared what interposition it was owing to. It would have been a horrid damp to the joys of peace, if we had received a disagreeable account of him.*

Finally, it should be pointed out that the deliberation and humanity manifest in the Asgill case contrasted sharply with the impulsive and vindictive behavior of the British at Charleston. Isaac Hayne, a prominent South Carolinian and a colonel in the militia, was hanged in the summer of 1781 without formal trial by Rawdon and Balfour on the technical charge of breaking his parole after the surrender of Charleston. Greene and Marion both felt that this action called for retaliation, but Greene waited until the Patriot leader Christopher Gadsden and other fellow prisoners were safe within American lines, then formally declared that the first regular British colonel captured should suffer the fate of Colonel Hayne. In fact, the threat was never carried out.

We give here half a dozen letters which tell the story of the Asgill affair, and an excerpt from the reminiscences of Elias Boudinot—he was a member of Congress at the time, and shortly elected to its Presidency.

1. "The Enemy Have Inhumanly Executed Captain Joshua Huddy"

George Washington to Brigadier General Moses Hazen.

Head Quarters, May 3, 1782

Sir: The Enemy, persisting in that barbarous line of Conduct they have pursued during the course of this War, have lately most inhumanly executed Captain Joshua Huddy of the Jersey State Troops, taken Prisoner by them at a Post on Tom's River, and in consequence, I have written to the British Commander in Chief, that unless the Perpetrators of that horrid deed were delivered up I should be under the disagreeable necessity of Retaliating, as the only means left to put a stop to such inhuman proceedings.

You will therefore immediately on receipt of this designate, by Lot for the above purpose, a British Captain who is an unconditional Prisoner, if such a one is in your possession; if not, a Lieutenant under the same circumstances from among the Prisoners at any of the Posts either in Pennsylvania or Maryland. So soon as you have fixed on the Person, you will send him under a safe Guard to Philadelphia, where the Minister of War will order a proper Guard to receive and conduct him to the place of his Destination.

For your information respecting the Officers who are Prisoners in our possession I have ordered the Commisry of Prisoners to furnish you with a List of them; it will be forwarded with this. I need not mention to you that every possible tenderness, that is consistent with the Security of him, should be shewn to the person whose unfortunate Lot it may be to suffer.

—Fitzpatrick, ed., *Writings of Washington*, XXIV, 217-218.

2. "It Is Really a Melancholy Case"

Robert R. Livingston, Secretary for Foreign Affairs, to Benjamin Franklin.

Philadelphia, May 30, 1782

... I enclose a number of letters that have passed between Generals Washington, Clinton, Robinson, and Sir Guy Carleton, chiefly on the subject of Captain Huddy, who, having been taken prisoner and confined some time at New York, was carried by a Captain Lippincott and a party of soldiers to the Jersey shore, and there hanged without the least pretence. You will see an account of the whole transaction in some of the papers I sent. The General, in pursuance of his determination, has ordered the lot to be cast among the British captains. It has fallen upon the honorable Captain Asgill of the Guards, who is now on his way to camp. A friend of his, Captain Ludlow, is gone to New York to see if anything can be done to save him.

It is really a melancholy case, but the repeated cruelties of this kind that have been practiced, have rendered it absolutely necessary to execute the resolution to retaliate, which we have so often taken, and so frequently been prevented by our feelings from carrying into execution.

—Wharton, ed., *Revolutionary Diplomatic Correspondence*, V, 462-463.

3. "Such a Sacrifice Is Repugnant to the Genius of the Age"

Alexander Hamilton to Henry Knox.

Albany, June 7, 1782

We are told that there is a British officer coming on from Cornwallis' army, to be executed by way of retaliation for the murder of Capt. Hudy. As this appears to me clearly to be an ill-timed proceeding, and if persisted in will be derogatory to the national character, I cannot forbear communicating to you my ideas upon the subject.

A sacrifice of this sort is entirely repugnant to the genius of the age we live in, and is without example in modern history, nor can it fail to be considered in Europe as wanton and unnecessary. It appears that the enemy (from necessity, I grant, but the operation is the same) have changed their system and adopted a more humane one; and, therefore, the only justifying motive of retaliation—the preventing a repetition of cruelty—ceases. But if this were not the case, so solemn and deliberate a sacrifice of the innocent for the guilty must be condemned on the present received notions of humanity, and encourage an opinion that we are, in a certain degree, in a state of barbarism.

Our affairs are now in a prosperous train, and so vigorous—I would rather say so violent—a measure would want the plea of necessity. It would argue that at this late stage of the war, in the midst of success, we should suddenly depart from that temper with which we have all along borne with a great and more frequent provocation. The death of André could not have been dispensed with, but it must still be viewed at a distance as an act of *rigid justice*. If we wreak our resentment on an innocent person, it will be suspected that we are too fond of executions. I am persuaded it will have an influence peculiarly unfavorable to the General's character. . . .

—Lodge, ed., *Works of Hamilton*, IX, 256-258.

4. "Nothing I Could Say Would Have the Least Effect"

Benjamin Franklin to Richard Oswald.

Passy, July 28, 1782

... The situation of Captain Asgill and his family afflicts me, but I do not see what can be done by any one here to relieve them. It can not be supposed that General Washington has the least desire of taking the life of that gentleman. His aim is to obtain the punishment of a deliberate murder, committed on a prisoner in cold blood by Captain Lippincott. If the English refuse to deliver up or punish this murderer, it is saying that they choose to preserve him rather than Captain Asgill. It seems to me, therefore, that the application should be made to the English ministers for positive orders directing General Carleton to deliver up Lippincott, which orders being obtained should be despatched immediately by a swift-sailing vessel. I do not think any other means can produce the effect desired.

The cruel murders of this kind, committed by the English on our people since the commencement of the war, are innumerable. The Congress and their generals, to satisfy the people, have often threatened retaliation, but have always hitherto forborne to execute it, and they have been often insultingly told by their enemies that this forbearance did not proceed from humanity but fear. General Greene, though he solemnly and publicly promised it in a proclamation, never made any retaliation for the murder of Colonel Haynes and many others in Carolina, and the people, who now think if he had fulfilled his promise this crime would not have been committed, clamor so loudly that I doubt General Washington can not well refuse what appears to them so just and necessary for their common security.

I am persuaded that nothing I could say to him on the occasion would have the least effect in changing his determination.

—Wharton, ed., *Revolutionary Diplomatic Correspondence*, V, 617-618.

5. "Let Your Feelings Plead for My Inexpressible Misery"

Lady Asgill to Count de Vergennes.

London, July 18, 1782

Sir: If the politeness of the French court will permit an application of a stranger, there can be no doubt but one in which all the tender feelings of an individual can be interested will meet with a favorable reception from a nobleman whose character does honor, not only to his own country, but to human nature. The subject, sir, on which I presume to implore your assistance is too heart-piercing for me to dwell on, and common fame has most probably informed you of it; it therefore renders the painful task unnecessary.

My son (an only son), as dear as he is brave, amiable as he is deserving to be so, only nineteen, a prisoner under the articles of capitulation of Yorktown, is now confined in America, an object of retaliation. Shall an innocent suffer for the guilty? Represent to yourself, sir, the situation of a family under these circumstances; surrounded as I am by objects of distress, distracted with fear and grief, no words can express my feeling or paint the scene: my husband given over by his physicians a few hours before the news arrived, and not in a state to be informed of the misfortune; my daughter seized with a fever and delirium, raving about her brother, and without one interval of reason, save to hear heart-alleviating circumstances.

Let your feelings, sir, suggest and plead for my inexpressible misery. A word from you, like a voice from heaven, will save us from distraction and wretchedness. I am well informed General Washington reveres your character. Say but to him you wish my son to be released, and he will restore him to his distracted family and render him to happiness. My son's virtue and bravery will justify the deed. His honor, sir, carried him to America. He was born to affluence, independence and the happiest prospects. Let me again supplicate your goodness; let me respectfully implore your high influence in behalf of innocence, in the cause of justice, of humanity, that you would, sir, despatch a letter to General Washington from France, and favor me with a copy of it to be sent from hence.

I am sensible of the liberty I have taken in making this request; but I am sensible, whether you comply with it or not, you will pity the distress that suggests it; your humanity will drop a tear on the fault and efface it. I will pray that heaven may grant you may never want the comfort it is in your power to bestow on

ASGILL

—WHARTON, ed., *Revolutionary Diplomatic Correspondence*, V, 635-636.

6. "Their Majesties Desire to Calm the Anxiety of a Mother"

Count de Vergennes to George Washington.

Versailles, July 29, 1782

Sir: it is not in quality of a King, the friend and ally of the United States (though with the knowledge and consent of His Majesty), that I now have the honor to write to Your Excellency. It is as a man of sensibility, and a tender father who feels all the force of paternal love, that I take the liberty to address to Your Excellency my earnest solicitations in favor of a mother and family in tears. Her situation seems the more worthy of notice on our part, as it is to the humanity of a nation at war with her own, that she has recourse for what she ought to receive from the impartial justice of her own generals.

I have the honor to enclose Your Excellency a copy of a letter which Lady Asgill has just wrote me. I am not known to her, nor was I acquainted that her son was the unhappy victim, destined by lot to expiate the odious crime that a formal denial of justice obliges you to revenge.

Your Excellency will not read this letter without being extremely affected; it had that effect upon the King and Queen, to whom I communicated it. The goodness of Their Majesties' hearts induces them to desire that the inquietudes of an unfortunate mother may be calmed, and her tenderness reassured. I felt, sir, that there are cases where humanity itself exacts the most extreme rigor; perhaps the one now in question may be of the number; but allowing reprisals to be just, it is not less horrid to those who are the victims; and the character of Your Excellency is too well known for me not to be persuaded that you desire nothing more than to be able to avoid the disagreeable necessity.

There is one consideration, sir, which, though it is not decisive, may have an influence on your resolution. Captain Asgill is doubtless your prisoner, but he is among those whom the arms of the King contributed to put into your hands at Yorktown. Although this circumstance does not operate as a safeguard, it however justifies the interest I permit myself to take in this affair. If it is in your power, sir, to consider and have regard to it, you will do what is agreeable to Their Majesties; the danger of young Asgill, the tears, the despair of his mother, affect them sensibly; and they will see with pleasure the hope of consolation shine out for those unfortunate people.

In seeking to deliver Mr. Asgill from the fate which threatens him I am far from engaging you to seek another victim; the pardon, to be perfectly satisfactory, must be entire. I do not imagine it can be productive of any bad consequences. If the English general has not been able to punish the horrible crime you complain of in so exemplary a manner as he should, there is reason to think he will take the most efficacious measures to prevent the like in future.

I sincerely wish, sir, that my intercession may meet success; the sentiment which dictates it, and which you have not ceased to manifest on every occasion, assures me that you will not be indifferent to the prayers and to the tears of a family which has recourse to your clemency through me. It is rendering homage to your virtue to implore it.

I have the honor to be, with the most significant consideration, Sir, yours, etc.

VERGENNES

—WHARTON, ed., *Revolutionary Diplomatic Correspondence*, V, 634-635.

7. "THIS LETTER OPERATED LIKE AN ELECTRIC SHOCK"

Reminiscence of Elias Boudinot.

A very large majority of Congress were determined on his execution, and a motion was made for a resolution positively ordering the immediate execution. Mr. Duane and myself, considering the reasons assigned by the Commander in Chief conclusive, made all the opposition in our power. We urged every argument that the peculiarity of the case suggested, and spent three days in warm debate, during which more ill blood appeared in the House than I had seen. Near the close of the third day, when every argument was exhausted, without any appearance of success, the matter was brought to a close by the question being ordered to be taken. . . .

The next morning as soon as the minutes were read, the President announced a letter from the Commander in Chief. On its being read, he stated the receipt of a letter from the King and Queen of France, inclosing one from Mrs. Asgill, the mother of Capt. Asgill, to the Queen, that on the whole was enough to move the heart of a savage. The substance was asking the life of young Asgill.

This operated like an electrical shock—each member looking on his neighbor in surprise, as if saying "here is unfair play." It was suspected to be some scheme of the minority. The President was interrogated. The cover of the letters was called for. The General's signature was examined. In short, it looked so much like something supernatural that even the minority, who were so much pleased with it, could scarcely think it real.

After being fully convinced of the integrity of the transaction a motion was made that the life of Capt. Asgill should be given as a compliment to the King of France. This was unanimously carried, on which it was moved that the Commander in Chief should remand Capt. Asgill to his quarters at Lancaster. To this I objected that as we considered Capt. Asgill's life as forfeited, and we had given him to the King of France, he was now a free man, and therefore I moved that he should be immediately returned into New York, without exchange. This also was unanimously adopted, and thus we got clear of shedding innocent blood by a wonderful interposition of Providence.

—BOUDINOT, *Life and Letters*, I, 249-251.

CHAPTER TWENTY-TWO

Songs and Ballads of the Revolution

THE GENERAL LEVEL of Revolutionary songs and ballads is low, but that is merely a reflection of the melancholy fact that the general level of poetry, both in America and in Britain, was low. In America this pervading mediocrity, to call it nothing worse, did not represent a descent from a lofty Parnassus but, if anything, an ascent; as a matter of fact Freneau, Trumbull, Dwight, Hopkinson and Barlow are an improvement on almost every poet who had gone before except Edward Taylor. In England, on the other hand, the decline from the previous generation was calamitous, and the contrast between the poetry of the period of the American Revolution and that of the next generation was so startling as to suggest something more than fortuity. During the years of the American Revolution England boasted not a single poet of even second rank, unless Cowper be admitted to this dubious category. And although the American poets, such as they were, confessed the inspiration of the war and tried their hands at some vision of Columbus, some tribute to Washington, some invocation of providential blessing, the English poets were apparently not sufficiently interested in the war to write about it at all.

It is not, however, with formal poetry but with ballads and songs that we are concerned in this chapter; to be sure it is not always easy to distinguish the two categories. For all the volume of doggerel that cluttered up the press and filled the broadsides, the war itself produced nothing to compare with the songs of the American Civil War—not one, for example, that we sing today (as we still sing "Dixie" or "The Battle Hymn of the Republic" or "Marching through Georgia") unless it is "Yankee Doodle"—which probably came before the war. Yet here and there we come across a good ballad: "Yankee Doodle" itself, in almost any of its many-forms; "The Volunteer Boys"; best of all, perhaps, the strangely moving "Nathan Hale" which has qualities of a genuine folk-ballad, and which we have given earlier.

One explanation of this is that Americans were not, as yet, a singing people, or a musical. Except among the Germans there was little church music, and no music in the schools, and few musical societies; Billings was trying to remedy that but with little success. The famous painting of "The Spirit of 'Seventy-Six" reminds us that there were drummers and fifers, but no army bands and no band music. For that matter the Revolutionary armies were not marching armies in any serious way, and it is the requirements of the march that produce the best military music. Except for a convivial song, here and there, set to traditional music, one cannot imagine the American soldiers *actually singing the songs we have here: most of them are hothouse products.*

For the most part we have inserted ballads and poems where they appear to belong in these volumes; thus Warren's stirring "Free America" is part of the chapter on the beginning of the Revolution; the beautiful ballad of Nathan Hale is inserted in the melancholy story of his execution; Hopkinson's "Battle of the Kegs" adorns the story of the battle for Philadelphia; and Freneau's "Prison Ship" adds its poetic testimony to the sufferings of hospitalized American prisoners, while Loyalist poetry has been levied upon to illustrate the attitude of the Tories. We include here, in a sense, what is left, and what does not seem to fit in elsewhere: ballads and songs and poems that are general rather than particular, that celebrate some larger cause or sing the praises of some universal hero rather than those that dramatize a particular battle or incident of war.

The songs themselves need little introduction. We have separated the Patriot and the Loyalist (and British) songs, and it is clear—as it is natural—that the Americans were more vocal than their enemies. We have thought it best, on the whole, to present the songs in chronological order, for there is no topical arrangement in poems and songs so few and so general. Where possible we have provided the date and the author, though these are sometimes in dispute, and often unknown.

Some of the poets' names here and elsewhere in the book are familiar and, by our standards, distinguished: Hopkinson, Dickinson, Paine, Trumbull, Freneau—but most of the songs collected by Frank Moore and other students of Revolutionary War poetry are by little-known or unknown men. Many of them have come down to us in altered form; there is no way of knowing what the soldiers actually sang, and we must be content with what is recorded, sometimes at a much later date.

I. PATRIOT

1. YANKEE DOODLE

The history of this, undoubtedly the most famous song of the Revolution, is, like the history of "Dixie," shrouded in obscurity and in controversy. One version was mentioned in the first American opera libretto, Andrew Barton's The Disappointment *(1767); another is attributed to one Dr. Shuckberg, a surgeon in the British Army, who wrote it—so it is alleged—to ridicule the American troops besieging Boston in 1775. If so, it soon got out of his control. No two versions agree, and the number of verses that got themselves added to the original is incalculable. In* The Contrast *Royall Tyler has his Yankee character Jonathan boast that while he knows only 190 of the verses of "Yankee Doodle," his sister Tabitha can sing them all.*

> Father and I went down to camp
> Along with Captain Gooding,
> And there we see the men and boys
> As thick as hasty pudding.

And there we see a thousand men,
As rich as 'Squire David,
And what they wasted every day,
I wish it could be savéd.

The 'lasses they eat every day
Would keep a house a winter.
They have as much that I'll be bound,
They eat it when they're a mind to.

And there we see a swamping gun,
Big as a log of maple,
Upon a deuced little cart,
A load for Father's cattle.

And every time they shoot it off
It takes a horn of powder,
And makes a noise like Father's gun,
Only a nation louder.

I went as nigh to one myself
As Siah's underpinning,
And Father went as nigh again—
I thought the deuce was in him.

Cousin Simon grew so bold
I thought he would have cock't it;
It scared me so, I shrinked it off
And hung by Father's pocket.

And Captain Davis had a gun,
He kind of clapt his hand on't,
And stuck a crooked stabbing iron
Upon the little end on't.

And there I see a pumkin shell
As big as Mothers bason,
And every time they touched it off
They scampered like the nation.

I see a little barrel too,
The heads were made of leather,
They knocked upon't with little clubs,
And called the folks together.

And there was Captain Washington,
And gentlefolks about him.
They say he's grown so tarnal proud
He will not go without 'em.

He got him on his meeting clothes,
    Upon a slapping stallion.
He set the world along in rows,
    In hundreds and in millions.

The flaming ribbons in his hat,
    They look'd so tearing fine ah,
I wanted pockily to get
    To give to my Jemimah.

I see another snarl of men
    A-digging graves, they told me,
So tarnal long, so tarnal deep,
    They 'tended they should hold me—

It scared me so I hooked it off,
    Nor stopt as I remember,
Nor turned about till I got home
    Locked up in Mother's chamber.

—STEDMAN AND HUTCHINSON, *Library of American Literature*, III, 338.

2. LIBERTY TREE

Thomas Paine, 1775
(Tune: "The Gods of Greece")

In a chariot of light, from the regions of day,
    The Goddess of Liberty came,
Ten thousand celestials directed her way,
    And hither conducted the dame.
A fair budding branch from the gardens above,
    Where millions with millions agree,
She brought in her hand as a pledge of her love,
    And the plant she named Liberty Tree. . . .

Beneath this fair tree, like the patriarchs of old,
    Their bread in contentment they ate,
Unvexed with the troubles of silver or gold,
    The cares of the grand and the great.
With timber and tar they Old England supplied,
    And supported her power on the sea:
Her battles they fought, without getting a groat,
    For the honor of Liberty Tree.

But hear, O ye swains ('tis a tale most profane),
    How all the tyrannical powers,
Kings, Commons and Lords, are uniting amain
    To cut down this guardian of ours.

From the East to the West blow the trumpet to arms,
Thro' the land let the sound of it flee:
Let the far and the near all unite with a cheer,
In defense of our Liberty Tree.
—FONER, ed., *Writings of Paine*, II, 1091.

3. BUNKER HILL, OR THE AMERICAN HERO

1775

Nathaniel Niles, who wrote this "Sapphick Ode," called it "The American Hero," but as "Bunker Hill" it was known then, and since. Niles himself was a versatile Connecticut Yankee who had been educated at Harvard and the College of New Jersey, tried preaching, law, medicine and politics, and in the end combined invention and farming, first in Connecticut and then in Vermont where he had a long and notable career. Andrew Law, of Norwich, Connecticut, put "The American Hero" to music; later he had a distinguished career as a composer and musical critic. His Essays on Music *was probably the first book of musical criticism in our literature; it announced, at the outset, that the musician must be "a linguist, an orator, a poet, a painter, a mathematician, a philosopher, an architect, a Christian, a friend to God and man." This song and Billings' "Chester" were among the most widely sung of Revolutionary songs.*

Why should vain mortals tremble at the sight of
Death and destruction in the field of battle,
Where blood and carnage clothe the ground in crimson,
    Sounding with death-groans?

Death will invade us by the means appointed,
And we must all bow to the King of Terrors;
Nor am I anxious, if I am preparéd,
    What shape he comes in.

Infinite goodness teaches us submission;
Bids us be quiet under all His dealings:
Never repining, but forever praising
    God our Creator.

Well may we praise Him, all His ways are perfect;
Though a resplendence infinitely glowing
Dazzles in glory on the sight of mortals,
    Struck blind by lustre!

Good is Jehovah in bestowing sunshine,
Nor less His goodness in the storm and thunder:
Mercies and judgments both proceed from kindness—
    Infinite kindness.

O then exult that God forever reigneth.
Clouds, which around Him hinder our perception,
Bind us the stronger to exalt His name, and
    Shout louder praises!

Then to the wisdom of my Lord and Master
I will commit all that I have or wish for:
Sweetly as babes sleep will I give my life up
    When called to yield it.

Now, Mars, I dare thee, clad in smoky pillars,
Bursting from bomb-shells, roaring from the cannon,
Rattling in grape shot, like a storm of hailstones,
    Torturing Aether!

Up the black heavens, let the spreading flames rise,
Breaking like Aetna through the smoky columns,
Low'ring like Egypt o'er the falling city,
    Wantonly burnt down.

While all their hearts quick palpitate for havock,
Let slip your blood hounds, named the British lyons:
Dauntless as Death stares; nimble as the whirlwind;
    Dreadful as demons!

Let Oceans waft on all your floating castles,
Fraught with destruction, horrible to nature:
Then, with your sails filled by a storm of vengeance,
    Bear down to battle!

From the dire caverns made by ghostly miners,
Let the explosion, dreadful as vulcanoes,
Heave the broad town, with all its wealth and people,
    Quick to destruction!

Still shall the banner of the King of Heaven
Never advance where I'm afraid to follow:
While that precedes me with an open bosom,
    War, I defy thee.

Fame and dear freedom lure me on to battle,
While a fell despot, grimmer than a death's-head,
Stings me with serpents, fiercer than Medusa's,
    To the encounter.

Life, for my country and the cause of freedom,
Is but a trifle for a worm to part with;—
And if preservéd in so great a contest,
    Life is redoubled.

—STEDMAN AND HUTCHINSON, *Library of American Literature*, III, 263-264.

4. THE PENNSYLVANIA MARCH

1775

We are the troops that n'er did stoop
    To wretched slavery,
Nor shall our seed, by our base deed,
    Despiséd vassels be.
Freedom we will bequeath them
    Or we will bravely die;
Our greatest foe ere long shall know
    How much did Sandwich lie.

CHORUS: And all the world shall know
    Americans are free;
Nor slaves nor cowards will we prove,
    Great Britain soon shall see.

We'll not give up our birthright;
    Our foes shall find us men:
As good as they in any shape,
    The British troops shall ken;
Huzza, brave boys, we'll beat them
    On any hostile plain;
For freedom, wives, and children dear,
    The battle we'll maintain.

What? Can those British tyrants think
    Our fathers crossed the main,
And savage foes and danger met,
    To be enslaved by them?
If so, they are mistaken,
    For we will rather die;
And since they have become our foes,
    Their forces we defy.

        —MOORE, *Songs and Ballads*, p. 90.

5. THE AMERICAN PATRIOT'S PRAYER

1776

This patriotic hymn is sometimes ascribed to Thomas Paine; it is unlikely that Paine should have written it, however. A substantial proportion of the songs of the Revolution were written as hymns—the "Soldier's Hymn" which follows, for example, and the famous "Chester."

Parent of all, omnipotent
    In heav'n and earth below,
Thro' all creation's bounds unspent,
    Whose streams of goodness flow,

Teach me to know from whence I rose,
    And unto what designed;
No private aims let me propose,
    Since linked with human kind.

But chief to hear my country's voice,
    May all my thoughts incline,
'Tis reason's law, 'tis virtue's choice,
    'Tis nature's call and thine.

Me from fair freedom's sacred cause,
    Let nothing e'er divide;
Grandeur, nor gold, nor vain applause,
    Nor friendship false misguide.

Let me not faction's partial hate
    Pursue to this land's woe;
Nor grasp the thunder of the state,
    To wound a private foe.

If, for the right, to wish the wrong
    My country shall combine,
Single to serve th' erron'ous throng,
    Spight of themselves, be mine.
        —PAINE, *Large Additions to Common Sense*,
        appended to *Common Sense*, p. 80.

6. THE AMERICAN SOLDIER'S HYMN

'Tis God that girds our armor on,
    And all our just designs fulfills;
Through Him our feet can swiftly run,
    And nimbly climb the steepest hills.

Lessons of war from Him we take,
    And manly weapons learn to wield.
Strong bows of steel with ease we break,
    Forced by our stronger arms to yield.

'Tis God that still supports our right,
    His just revenge our foes pursues;
'Tis He that with resistless might
    Fierce nations to His power subdues.

Our universal safeguard He!
    From Whom our lasting honours flow;
He made us great, and set us free
    From our remorseless bloody foe.

Therefore to celebrate His fame,
    Our grateful voice to Heaven we'll raise;
And nations, strangers to His name,
    Shall thus be taught to sing His praise.
           —MOORE, *Songs and Ballads*, pp. 221-222.

7. WASHINGTON

The apotheosis of Washington began in the Continental Congress and flourished all through the war—and after. It is a tribute to the judgment of the American people that they at once recognized Washington's superiority and did it homage. There are any number of poems about Washington during the war, and most of them are characterized by good judgment rather than by poetic talent. We give here two anonymous poems, and one—"The Toast"— by Francis Hopkinson. Lawyer, statesman, man of letters and poet, Francis Hopkinson was one of the most gifted men of his generation; it is perhaps fitting that his son, Joseph, should have written "Hail, Columbia!" which has some claim to being our first generally accepted national song. "A New Song" was probably composed in 1776, and "Thanksgiving Hymn" at the end of the war.

A. THE TOAST

Francis Hopkinson

'Tis Washington's health—fill a bumper around,
For he is our glory and pride;
Our arms shall in battle with conquest be crowned,
Whilst virtue and he's on our side.

'Tis Washington's health—and cannons should roar,
And trumpets the truth should proclaim;
There cannot be found, search the world all o'er,
His equal in virtue and fame.

'Tis Washington's health—our hero to bless,
May Heav'n look graciously down!
Oh! long may he live our hearts to possess,
And freedom still call him her own.
           —HOPKINSON, *Miscellaneous Essays*, III, 176.

B. A NEW SONG

(Tune: "The British Grenadiers")

Vain Britons, boast no longer with proud indignity
By land your conquering legions, your matchless strength at sea!
Since we your braver sons, incensed, our swords have girded on,
Huzza, huzza, huzza, huzza, for War and Washington!

Urged on by North and Vengeance, these valiant champions came,
And bellowing "Tea and Treason!" and George was all on flame!
As sacrilegious as it seems, we Rebels still live on
And laugh at all your empty puffs, and so does Washington!

Still deaf to mild intreaties, still blind to England's good,
You have for thirty pieces betrayed your country's blood;
Like Aesop's greedy cur, you'll gain a shadow for your bone,
Yet find us fearful shades indeed, inspired by Washington.

Mysterious! unexampled! incomprehensible!
The blundering schemes of Britain, their folly, pride and zeal!
Like lions how ye growl and threat! mere asses have ye shown,
And ye shall share an ass's fate and drudge for Washington!

Your dark, unfathomed councils our weakest heads defeat,
Our children rout your armies, our boats destroy your fleet!
And to compleat the dire disgrace, cooped up within a town,
You live the scorn of all our host, the slaves of Washington!

Great Heaven! is this the nation whose thundering arms were hurled
Thro' Europe, Afric, India? Whose Navy ruled the world?
The lustre of your former deeds—whole ages of renown—
Lost in a moment—or transferred to us and Washington!

Yet think not thirst of glory unsheaths our vengeful swords
To rend your bands asunder and cast away your cords.
'Tis Heaven-born Freedom fires us all and strengthens each brave son,
From him who humbly guides the plough to god-like Washington!

For this, O could our wishes your ancient rage inspire,
Your armies should be doubled in numbers, force and fire!
Then might the glorious conflict prove which best deserved the boon—
America or Albion—a George or Washington!

Fired with the great idea our fathers' shades would rise!
To view the stern contention, the gods desert their skies,
And Wolfe, mid hosts of heroes, superior, bending down,
Cry out with eager transport, "Well done, brave Washington!"

Should George, too choice of Britons, to foreign realms apply
And madly arm half Europe, yet still we would defy
Turk, Russian, Jew and Infidel, or all those powers in one,
While Hancock crowns our Senate—our camp great Washington.

Tho' warlike weapons failed us, disdaining slavish fears,
To swords we'd beat our plough-shares, our pruning hooks to spears,
And rush all desperate on our foe, nor breathe, till battle won;
Then shout and shout, "America and conquering Washington!"

Proud France should view with terror, and haughty Spain should fear,
While every warlike nation would court alliance here—
And George, his minions trembling round, dismounted from his Throne,
Pay homage to America and glorious Washington!

—Columbia Magazine, August 1789.

C. THANKSGIVING HYMN

1783

The Lord above, in tender love,
Hath saved us from our foes;
Through Washington the thing is done,
The war is at a close.

America has won the day,
Through Washington, our chief;
Come, let's rejoice with heart and voice,
And bid adieu to grief.

Now we have peace, and may increase
In number, wealth, and arts;
If every one, like Washington,
Will strive to do their parts.

Then let's agree, since we are free,
All needless things to shun;
And lay aside all pomp and pride,
Like our great Washington.

From present wars and future foes,
And all that we may fear;
While Washington, the great brave one,
Shall as our chief appear.

—MOORE, *Songs and Ballads*, p. 376.

8. COLUMBIA, COLUMBIA, TO GLORY ARISE

1777

This well-known poem was written by Timothy Dwight while he was serving as chaplain of General Parsons' Connecticut Continental Brigade. Young Dwight had already embarked upon that literary career which was to make him the leading figure of the Hartford Wits, and upon his theological and public careers as well. His later work, "Greenfield Hill," reveals the same patriotic enthusiasm for Columbia as is found here.

Columbia, Columbia, to glory arise.
The queen of the world, and the child of the skies!
Thy genius commands thee; with rapture behold,
While ages on ages thy splendors unfold.
Thy reign is the last, and the noblest of time,
Most fruitful thy soil, most inviting thy clime;
Let the crimes of the east ne'er encrimson thy name,
Be freedom, and science, and virtue thy fame.

To conquest and slaughter let Europe aspire;
Whelm nations in blood, and wrap cities in fire;
Thy heroes the rights of mankind shall defend,
And triumph pursue them, and glory attend.

A world is thy realm: for a world be thy laws,
Enlarged as thine empire, and just as thy cause;
On Freedom's broad basis, that empire shall rise,
Extend with the main, and dissolve with the skies.

Fair Science her gates to thy sons shall unbar,
And the east see thy morn hide the beams of her star.
New bards, and new sages, unrivalled shall soar
To fame unextinguished, when time is no more;
To thee, the last refuge of virtue designed,
Shall fly from all nations the best of mankind;
Here, grateful to heaven, with transport shall bring
Their incense, more fragrant than odors of spring.

Nor less shall thy fair ones to glory ascend,
And genius and beauty in harmony blend;
The graces of form shall awake pure desire,
And the charms of the soul ever cherish the fire;
Their sweetness unmingled, their manners refined,
And virtue's bright image, instamped on the mind,
With peace and soft rapture shall teach life to glow,
And light up a smile in the aspect of woe.

Thy fleets to all regions thy power shall display,
The nations admire, and the ocean obey;
Each shore to thy glory its tribute unfold,
And the east and the south yield their spices and gold.
As the day-spring unbounded, thy splendor shall flow,
And earth's little kingdoms before thee shall bow:
While the ensigns of union, in triumph unfurled,
Hush the tumult of war, and give peace to the world.

Thus, as down a lone valley, with cedars o'erspread,
From war's dread confusion I pensively strayed—
The gloom from the face of fair heaven retired;
The winds ceased to murmur; the thunders expired;
Perfumes, as of Eden, flowed sweetly along,
And a voice, as of angels, enchantingly sung:
"Columbia, Columbia, to glory arise,
The queen of the world, and the child of the skies."

—STEDMAN AND HUTCHINSON, *Library of American Literature*, III, 480-481.

9. CHESTER

1778

This solemn hymn, by William Billings, was one of the most widely sung of all Revolutionary songs. Billings himself has some claim to be called the father of American music. Trained as a tanner, he was self-educated in music, and as early as 1770—he was twenty-four at the time—brought out the first of many books of music: The New England Psalm-Singer. As music master, composer and teacher he did much to reform and modernize the singing habits of the American people.

> Let tyrants shake their iron rod,
>   And slavery clank her galling chains;
> We fear them not, we trust in God—
>   New England's God for ever reigns.
>
> Howe and Burgoyne, and Clinton, too,
>   With Prescott and Cornwallis joined;
> Together plot our overthrow,
>   In one infernal league combined.
>
> When God inspired us for the fight,
>   Their ranks were broke, their lines were forced;
> Their ships were shattered in our sight,
>   Or swiftly driven from our coast.
>
> The foe comes on with haughty stride;
>   Our troops advance with martial noise;
> Their veterans flee before our youth,
>   And generals yield to beardless boys.
>
> What grateful offering shall we bring?
>   What shall we render to the Lord?
> Loud hallelujahs let us sing,
>   And praise his name on every chord.
>   —MOORE, ed., *Songs and Ballads*, pp. 241-242.

10. THE VOLUNTEER BOYS

1780

This is one of the best convivial songs produced during the American Revolution. Its authorship is attributed to Henry Archer, a young Scotsman of fortune who came to America in 1778 and enlisted as a volunteer in the Continental Army.

> Hence with the lover who sighs o'er his wine,
> Chloes and Phillises toasting;
> Hence with the slave who will whimper and whine,
> Of ardor and constancy boasting.
> Hence with love's joys,
> Follies and noise,
> The toast that I give is the Volunteer Boys.
>
> Nobles and beauties and such common toasts,
> Those who admire may drink, sir;
> Fill up the glass to the volunteer hosts,
> Who never from danger will shrink, sir.
> Let mirth appear,
> Every heart cheer,
> The toast I give is the brave volunteer.

Here's to the squire who goes to parade,
Here's to the citizen soldier;
Here's to the merchant who fights for his trade,
Whom danger increasing makes bolder.
Let mirth appear,
Union is here,
The toast that I give is the brave volunteer.

Here's to the lawyer, who leaving the bar,
Hastens where honor doth lead, sir,
Changing the gown for the ensigns of war,
The cause of his country to plead, sir.
Freedom appears,
Every heart cheers,
And calls for the health of the law volunteers.

Here's to the soldier, though battered in wars,
And safe to his farm-house retired;
When called by his country, ne'er thinks of his scars,
With ardor to join us inspired.
Bright fame appears,
Trophies uprear,
To veteran chiefs who became volunteers.
                    —Moore, ed., *Songs and Ballads*, p. 285.

11. Two Satirical Ballads

We conclude the American section with two poems, or ballads, which might fit just as well in the English. Both purport to be written by Englishmen; the first, "The Halcyon Days of Old England," was inspired by Burgoyne's defeat, and picked up somehow by Horace Walpole, who transcribed it in his Journal. The second, "Our Commanders," first appeared in a London paper; it might have been written by an American sympathizer, a follower of Wilkes or Grafton, or by a soured Loyalist.

A. THE HALCYON DAYS OF OLD ENGLAND

or
Wisdom of Administration Demonstrated
A Ballad
To the tune of "Ye Medley of Mortals"

1777
Give ear to my song, I'll now tell you a story,
This is the bright era of Old England's glory;
And though some may think us in pitiful plight,
I'll swear they're mistaken, for matters go right!
                    Sing tantarara, wise all, wise all,
                    Sing tantarara, wise all.

Let us laugh at the cavils of weak silly elves!
Our statesmen are wise men—they say so themselves!
And though little mortals may hear it with wonder,
'Tis consummate wisdom that causes each blunder!
      Sing tantarara, wise all, etc.

They now are conducting a glorious war!
(It began about tea, about feathers, and tar!)
With spirit they pushed when they plannéd with sense!
Forty millions they've spent for a tax of threepence!
      Sing tantarara, wise all, etc. . . .

What honours we're gaining by taking their forts,
Destroying batteaux and blocking up ports;
Burgoyne would have worked them—but for a mishap,
By Gates and one Arnold he's caught in a trap!
      Sing tantarara, wise all, etc. . . .

Oh, think us not cruel because our allies
Are savagely scalping men, women and boys!
Maternal affection to this step doth move us—
The more they are scalpéd, the more they will love us!
      Sing tantarara, wise all, etc.

Some folks are uneasy and make a great pother
For the loss of one army and half of another:
But, sirs, next campaign by ten thousands we'll slay them,
If we can but find soldiers and money to pay them!
      Sing tantarara, wise all, etc.

I've sung you my song, now I'll give you a pray'r:
May peace soon succeed to this horrible war!
Again may we live with our brethren in concord!
And the authors of mischief all hang in a strong cord!
      Sing tantarara, wise all, etc.
    —STONE, ed., *Ballads and Poems Relating to the
    Burgoyne Campaign*, p. 69.

B. OUR COMMANDERS

Gage nothing did, and went to pot;
Howe lost one town, another got;
Guy nothing lost, and nothing won;
Dunmore was homewards forced to run;
Clinton was beat and got a garter,
And bouncing Burgoyne catch'd a tartar;
Thus all we gain for millions spent
Is to be laughed at, and repent.
    —STONE, ed., *Ballads and Poems Relating to the
    Burgoyne Campaign*, p. 68.

II. LOYALIST AND BRITISH

The Tory and British songs and poems make a sorry show. Perhaps the best of them is the anonymous "How Happy the Soldier" which was almost as popular with the Americans as with the British, and which reappeared, with new words by Charles Jones, as "The Stars and Stripes," in the second war with Britain. The best of those which can be identified is doubtless Jonathan Odell's drinking song, "The Old Year and the New." It is interesting to note that so many of the British or Tory songs were drinking songs, and so few—none here—were religious.

1. How Happy the Soldier

How happy the soldier who lives on his pay
And spends half a crown out of six-pence a day;
Yet fears neither justices, warrants, nor bums,
But pays all his debts with the roll of his drums.
With row de dow, row de dow, row de dow, dow;
And he pays all his debts with the roll of his drums.

He cares not a marnedy how the world goes;
His King finds his quarters, and money, and clothes;
He laughs at all sorrow whenever it comes,
And rattles away with the roll of his drums,
With row de dow, row de dow, row de dow, dow;
And he pays all his debts with the roll of his drums.

The drum is his glory, his joy and delight,
It leads him to pleasure as well as to fight;
No girl, when she hears it, tho' ever so glum,
But packs up her tatters and follows the drum.
With row de dow, row de dow, row de dow, dow;
And he pays all his debts with the roll of his drums.
—Dolph, *Sound Off.*

2. The Rebels

1778

Captain Smyth, the author of this song, was an officer in Simcoe's Queen's Rangers, who wrote many songs which were published during the war. "The Rebels" first appeared in the Pennsylvania Ledger *as "a new song, to the tune of Black Joke," and later under its present title.*

Ye brave, honest subjects, who dare to be loyal
And have stood the brunt of every trial
   Of hunting-shirts and rifle-guns:
Come listen awhile, and I'll sing you a song;
I'll show you those Yankees are all in the wrong,
Who, with blustering look and most awkward gait,
'Gainst their lawful sovereign dare for to prate,
   With their hunting-shirts and rifle-guns.

The arch-rebels, barefooted tatterdemalions,
In baseness exceed all other rebellions,
    With their hunting-shirts and rifle-guns.
To rend the empire, the most infamous lies
Their mock-patriot Congress do always devise;
Independence, like the first of rebels, they claim,
But their plots will be damned in the annals of fame,
    With their hunting-shirts and rifle-guns.

Forgetting the mercies of Great Britain's king,
Who saved their forefathers' necks from the string;
    With their hunting-shirts and rifle-guns.
They renounce allegiance and take up their arms,
Assemble together like hornets in swarms.
So dirty their backs and so wretched their show
That carrion-crow follows wherever they go,
    With their hunting-shirts and rifle-guns.

With loud peals of laughter, your sides, sirs, would crack
To see General Convict and Colonel Shoe-black,
    With their hunting-shirts and rifle-guns.
See cobblers and quacks, rebel priests and the like,
Pettifoggers and barbers, with sword and with pike,
All strutting, the standard of Satan beside,
And honest names using, their black deeds to hide.
    With their hunting-shirts and rifle-guns.

This perjured banditti now ruin this land,
And o'er its poor people claim lawless command,
    With their hunting-shirts and rifle-guns.
Their pasteboard dollars prove a common curse;
They don't chink like silver and gold in our purse.
With nothing their leaders have paid their debts off;
Their honor's dishonor, and justice they scoff,
    With their hunting-shirts and rifle-guns.

For one lawful ruler, many tyrants we've got,
Who force young and old to their wars, to be shot,
    With their hunting-shirts and rifle-guns.
Our good king, God speed him! never uséd men so;
We then could speak, act, and like freemen could go;
But committees enslave us, our Liberty's gone,
Our trade and church murdered, our country's undone,
    By hunting-shirts and rifle-guns.

Come take up your glasses, each true loyal heart,
And may every rebel meet his due desert,
    With his hunting-shirt and rifle-gun.

May Congress, Conventions, those damn'd inquisitions,
Be fed with hot sulphur, from Lucifer's kitchens,
May commerce and peace again be restored,
And Americans own their true sovereign lord!
    Then oblivion to shirts and rifle-guns.
      God save the King!
        —Moore, ed., *Songs and Ballads*, pp. 196-199.

3. A Convivial Song

1779

"A song written by a refugee on reading the King's Speech, and sung at the Refugee Club in the City of New York."

Here's a bumper, brave boys, to the health of our king,
Long may he live, and long may we sing
In praise of a monarch who boldly defends
The laws of the realm and the cause of his friends.
  Chorus
    Then cheer up, my lads, we have nothing to fear
      While we remain steady
      And always keep ready
    To add to the trophies of this happy year.

The Congress did boast of their mighty ally,
But George doth both France and the Congress defy,
And when Britons unite, there's no force can withstand
Their fleets and their armies, by sea and on land.
  Chorus

Thus supported, our cause we will ever maintain,
And all treaties with rebels will ever disdain;
Till, reduced by our arms, they are forced to confess
While ruled by Great Britain they ne'er knew distress.
  Chorus

Then let us, my boys, Britain's right e'er defend.
Who regards not her rights, we esteem not our friend;
Then, brave boys, we both France and the Congress defy,
And we'll fight for Great Britain and George till we die.
  Chorus
        —Moore, ed., *Songs and Ballads*, p. 253.

4. The Old Year and the New: A Prophecy

Jonathan Odell, 1779-1780

What though last year be past and gone,
    Why should we grieve or mourn about it?
As good a year is now begun,
    And better, too—let no one doubt it.

'Tis New Year's morn; why should we part?
　　Why not enjoy what heaven has sent us?
Let wine expand the social heart,
　　Let friends, and mirth, and wine content us.

War's rude alarms disturbed last year;
　　Our country bled and wept around us;
But this each honest heart shall cheer,
　　And peace and plenty shall surround us. . . .

Last year saw many honest men
　　Torn from each dear and sweet connection;
But this shall see them home again
　　And happy in their king's protection. . . .

Last year rebellion proudly stood,
　　Elate, in her meridian glory;
But this shall quench her pride in blood;
　　George will avenge each martyred Tory. . . .

Then bring us wine, full bumpers bring;
　　Hail this New Year in joyful chorus;
God bless great George our Gracious King
　　And crush rebellion down before us!

'Tis New Year's morn; why should we part?
　　Why not enjoy what heaven has sent us?
Let wine expand the social heart,
　　Let friends, and mirth, and wine content us.

—SARGENT, ed., *Loyalist Poetry of the Revolution*, pp. 99-101.

5. THE VOLUNTEERS OF IRELAND

This song was written for the Loyalist regiment, the Volunteers of Ire-land, and sung on St. Patrick's Day of 1780 at a celebration provided by the colonel of the regiment, Lord Rawdon.

Success to the Shamrock, and all those who wear it;
　　Be honor their portion wherever they go:
May riches attend them, and stores of good claret,
　　For how to employ them sure none better know.
Every foe surveys them with terror,
But every silk petticoat wishes them nearer;
So Yankee keep off, or you'll soon learn your error,
　　For Paddy shall prostrate lay every foe.

This day, but the year I can't rightly determine,
　　St. Patrick the vipers did chase from the land;
Let's see if like him, we can't sweep off the vermin
　　Who dare 'gainst the sons of the shamrock to stand.

Hand in hand! Let's carol the chorus—
As long as the blessings of Ireland hang o'er us,
The crest of Rebellion shall tremble before us,
    Like brothers, while thus we march hand in hand.

St. George and St. Patrick, St. Andrew, St. David,
    Together may laugh at all Europe in arms.
Fair conquest her standard has o'er their heads wavéd,
    And glory has on them conferred all the charms.
War's alarms to us are a pleasure,
Since honour our danger repays in full measure,
And all those who join us shall find we have leisure
    To think of our sport even in war's alarms.
            —MOORE, *Diary of the American Revolution*, II, 261-262.

CHAPTER TWENTY-THREE

Sea Battles and Naval Raids

THE STORY *of the sea battles and naval campaigns of the American Revolution is a nautical version of David and Goliath. The British Navy enjoyed over-whelming superiority over the tiny Continental naval force, except perhaps for that comparatively brief period when the French Navy was effectively committed and boldly directed to advancing the military and amphibious operations of the allied forces in America. No American naval force could cope with the larger vessels and squadrons of the British Navy. The operations of the Continental cruisers were severely restricted to isolated skirmishes, often heroic in character, to providing a small degree of protection to American coastal shipping, and to making war on hostile privateers and smaller men-of-war. To a limited extent the Continental Navy co-operated with Patriot land forces around certain towns. It attacked the enemy's communications and overseas commerce and even raided the coasts of the British Isles and the out-lying parts of the British Empire.*

The Continental and state navies put to sea some hundred ships. The British, in turn, increased their naval forces from 270 ships in 1775 to 468 in 1783, of which 174 carried sixty cannon or more, heavily outgunning the American frigates. Nevertheless, despite this vast superiority over the Americans the British suffered the loss of 200 ships sunk or captured by the Continental or state navies. Although by the end of the war the Continental Navy was virtually eliminated, the naval war was still fought fiercely on the high seas. The explanation is that the most punishing blows to British commerce were inflicted by American privateers, outfitted in huge numbers, readily manned with trained seamen, and easily replaced when sunk or captured. The privateers accounted for another 600 British ships sunk or captured. Paradoxically, then, there never was a period in the war when American naval operations, public and private, did not constitute a nuisance threat to the British merchant marine as they pinned down British squadrons, raised the price of imports to England, and even on occasion brought the war home to the British people.

Before France came into the war the British used their Navy largely in amphibious operations in America—to launch the Northern campaign down

Lake Champlain, to land and evacuate troops at Boston, to attack New York, Charleston, Narragansett Bay and Philadelphia, and to make sporadic raids against seaport towns like Bristol and Falmouth. Once France openly joined America, and then Spain joined France in alliance against England, large naval engagements were inevitable.

Down until the year 1781 French naval operations off North America were largely inconclusive. As a result of the procrastination of the French admiral, Count d'Estaing, the British fleet stationed at the mouth of the Delaware Bay managed to elude him and to get back to the safety of New York, which d'Estaing's larger vessels did not venture to enter. Instead, the French admiral participated in an inglorious amphibious operation against Newport, with General John Sullivan as commander of the land forces, an operation which is treated at length elsewhere in this volume.

In European waters Admiral Keppel's squadron clashed in an indecisive engagement with the French fleet of Admiral the Comte d'Orvilliers off Ushant. Similarly, in the West Indies, early operations were damaging to British naval power but not decisive. The French captured Dominica and Grenada and repulsed Vice-Admiral Byron's attempt to recapture the latter island with severe losses to the British, who in turn seized Martinique.

The French fleet was unable to prevent the British capture of Savannah or to effect its recapture or to prevent the great capitulation of Charleston to the British. The story was different in the year 1781, when the Count de Grasse, as we shall see in a later chapter, succeeded in bottling up the sea approaches to Yorktown. In other areas of naval operations the British were, however, far more successful. Rodney scored a smashing victory over De Grasse in the West Indies on April 12, 1782; Lord Howe successfully relieved Gibraltar; a British expedition captured the Dutch colony on the Cape of Good Hope; and inconclusive naval sparring off the Coromandel Coast of India took place between French and British squadrons. In fact, the ability of the British Navy to rebound in adversity made it possible for the British to stiffen the terms of peace with America and persuaded France and Spain to agree to a termination of the conflict.

As a preliminary to the story of the naval campaigns we give a collection of narratives and documents designed to illuminate the many political and administrative problems that emerged to perplex the Patriots—problems of Admiralty, prize courts, blockade, appointments, and so forth. It is interesting to note that the ubiquitous John Adams is almost as prominent here as in the political arena. The difficulties that confronted the Americans were natural, almost inevitable, in a country without a prior naval establishment, or a naval tradition. That so great a naval power as Great Britain experienced difficulties equally formidable is to be explained in part by the logistics of the war, but in large part by sheer incompetence and corruption.

I. FOUNDING THE AMERICAN NAVY

As might have been expected, the initiative for building a Navy came from seafaring New England, an area acutely conscious of the need for ob-

taining security on the seas. The first proposal was advanced by Rhode Island. The General Assembly, convened at Providence, adopted a resolution of instructions to the Rhode Island delegates to the Continental Congress on August 26, 1775, which included a proposal for establishing an American Navy. On October 3 the Rhode Island delegates to Congress introduced a motion for setting up a Continental naval force. Two days later letters from London were brought to the attention of Congress revealing that two brigs containing arms, powder and other stores had sailed without convoy from England on August 11 bound for Quebec. A motion was thereupon made that a committee of three be appointed to prepare a plan for intercepting the brigs, and a heated debate was set off. John Adams, who served on the enlarged Committee for Fitting Out Armed Vessels formed shortly thereafter, recounts the proceedings in Congress which led to the founding of the Navy.

1. RHODE ISLAND CALLS ON CONGRESS TO BUILD A FLEET

Resolutions of the General Assembly of Rhode Island.

August 26, 1775

Whereas, notwithstanding the humble and dutiful petition of the last Congress to the King, and otherwise pacific measures taken for obtaining a happy reconciliation between Great Britain and the colonies; the ministry, lost to every sentiment of justice, liberty and humanity, continue to send troops and ships of war into America, which destroy our trade, plunder and burn our towns, and murder the good people of these colonies——

It is therefore voted and resolved, that this colony most ardently wish to see the former friendship, harmony and intercourse between Britain and these colonies restored, and a happy and lasting connection established between both countries, upon terms of just and equal liberty; and will concur with the other colonies in all proper measures for obtaining those desirable blessings.

And as every principle, divine and human, require us to obey that great and fundamental law of nature, self-preservation, until peace shall be restored upon constitutional principles, this colony will most heartily exert the whole power of government, in conjunction with the other colonies, for carrying on this just and necessary war, and bringing the same to a happy issue.

And amongst other measures for obtaining this most desirable purpose, this Assembly is persuaded that the building and equipping an American fleet, as soon as possible, would greatly and essentially conduce to the preservation of the lives, liberty and property of the good people of these colonies; and therefore instruct their delegates to use their whole influence, at the ensuing Congress, for building, at the Continental expense, a fleet of sufficient force for the protection of these colonies, and for employing them in such a manner and places as will most effectually annoy our enemies and contribute to the common defence of these colonies.

—Rhode Island Records, VII, 368-369.

2. "The True Origin and Foundation of the American Navy"

From the Autobiography of John Adams.

[1775]

On Thursday, October 5th, 1775, sundry letters from London were laid before Congress and read, and a motion was made that it be

Resolved, That a committee of three be appointed to prepare a plan for intercepting two vessels which are on their way to Canada, laden with arms and powder, and that the committee proceed on this business immediately.

The secretary has omitted to insert the names of this committee on the journals, but as my memory has recorded them, they were Mr. Deane, Mr. Langdon, and myself, three members who had expressed much zeal in favor of the motion.

[*October 13, 1775*]. As a considerable part of my time, in the course of my profession, had been spent upon the sea-coast of Massachusetts, in attending the courts and lawsuits at Plymouth, Barnstable, Martha's Vineyard, to the southward, and in the counties of Essex, York and Cumberland to the eastward, I had conversed much with the gentlemen who conducted our cod and whale fisheries as well as the other navigation of the country, and had heard much of the activity, enterprise, patience, perseverance, and daring intrepidity of our seamen. I had formed a confident opinion that, if they were once let loose upon the ocean, they would contribute greatly to the relief of our wants, as well as to the distress of the enemy. I became therefore at once an ardent advocate for this motion, which we carried, not without great difficulty.

The opposition to it was very loud and vehement. Some of my own colleagues appeared greatly alarmed at it, and Mr. Edward Rutledge never displayed so much eloquence as against it. He never appeared to me to discover so much information and sagacity, which convinced me that he had been instructed out-of-doors by some of the most knowing merchants and statesmen in Philadelphia. It would require too much time and space to give this debate at large, if any memory could attempt it. Mine cannot. It was, however, represented as the most wild, visionary, mad project that ever had been imagined. It was an infant, taking a mad bull by his horns; and what was more profound and remote, it was said it would ruin the character, and corrupt the morals of all our seamen. It would make them selfish, piratical, mercenary, bent wholly upon plunder, etc., etc. These formidable arguments and this terrible rhetoric were answered by us by the best reasons we could allege, and the great advantage of distressing the enemy, supplying ourselves, and beginning a system of maritime and naval operations, were represented in colors as glowing and animating. The vote was carried, the committee went out, returned very soon and brought in the report. . . .

". . . Friday, October 13. The Congress, taking into consideration the report of the committee appointed to propose a plan, etc., after some debate,

"*Resolved,* That a swift sailing vessel, to carry ten carriage guns and a proportionable number of swivels, with eighty men, be fittted with all possible despatch for a cruise of three months, and that the commander be instructed to cruise eastward, for intercepting such transports as may be laden with warlike stores and other supplies for our enemies, and for such other purposes as the Congress shall direct. That a committee of three be appointed to prepare an estimate of the expense, and lay the same before the Congress, and to contract with proper persons to fit out the vessel.

"*Resolved*, That another vessel be fitted out for the same purposes, and that the said committee report their opinion of a proper vessel, and also an estimate of the expense.

"The following members were chosen to compose the committee: Mr. Deane, Mr. Langdon and Mr. Gadsden.

"*Resolved*, That the further consideration of the report be referred to Monday next.

"Monday, October 30. The committee appointed to prepare an estimate and to fit out the vessels, brought in their report, which, being taken into consideration,

"*Resolved*, That the second vessel, ordered to be fitted out on the 13th instant, be of such a size as to carry fourteen guns and a proportionate number of swivels and men.

"*Resolved*, That two more vessels be fitted out with all expedition, the one to carry not exceeding twenty guns, and the other not exceeding thirty-six guns, with a proportionable number of swivels and men, to be employed in such manner, for the protection and defence of the United Colonies, as the Congress shall direct.

"*Resolved*, That four members be chosen and added to the former committee of three, and that these seven be a committee to carry into execution, with all possible expedition, as well the resolutions of Congress, passed the 13th instant, as those passed this day, for fitting out armed vessels.

"The members chosen: Mr. Hopkins, Mr. Hewes, Mr. Richard Henry Lee and Mr. John Adams."

This committee immediately procured a room in a public house in the city and agreed to meet every evening at six o'clock in order to despatch this business with all possible celerity. . . .

On the 17th of November,

"A letter from General Washington, enclosing a letter and journal of Colonel Arnold and sundry papers, being received, the same were read, whereupon,——

"*Resolved*, That a committee of seven be appointed to take into consideration so much of the General's letter as relates to the disposal of such vessels and cargoes belonging to the enemy as shall fall into the hands of, or be taken by, the inhabitants of the United Colonies.

"The members chosen, Mr. Wythe, Mr. E. Rutledge, Mr. J. Adams, Mr. W. Livingston, Dr. Franklin, Mr. Wilson and Mr. Johnson.

"Thursday, November 23. The committee, for fitting out armed vessels, laid before Congress a draught of rules for the government of the American navy, and articles to be signed by the officers and men employed in that service, which were read, and ordered to lie on the table for the perusal of the members.

"Saturday, November 25. Congress resumed the consideration of the report of the committee on General Washington's letter, and the same being debated by paragraphs, was agreed to as follows.

"Whereas, it appears from undoubted information that many vessels which had cleared at the respective custom-houses in these Colonies, agreeable to the regulations established by Acts of the British Parliament, have in a lawless manner, without even the semblance of just authority, been seized by His Majesty's ships of war and carried into the harbor of Boston and other ports, where they have been rifled of their cargoes, by orders of His Majesty's naval and military officers there commanding, without the said vessels having been proceeded against by any form of trial, and without the charge of having offended against any law.

"And whereas orders have been issued in His Majesty's name, to the commanders of his ships of war, 'to proceed as in the case of actual rebellion against such of the seaport towns and places, being accessible to the King's ships, in which any troops shall be raised, or military works erected,' under color of which said orders, the commanders of His Majesty's said ships of war have already burned and destroyed the flourishing and populous town of Falmouth, and have fired upon and much injured several other towns within the United Colonies, and dispersed at a late season of the year hundreds of helpless women and children, with a savage hope that those may perish under the approaching rigors of the season, who may chance to escape destruction from fire and sword; a mode of warfare long exploded among civilized nations.

"And whereas the good people of these Colonies, sensibly affected by the destruction of their property, and other unprovoked injuries, have at last determined to prevent as much as possible a repetition thereof, and to procure some reparation for the same, by fitting out armed vessels and ships of force; in the execution of which commendable designs it is possible that those who have not been instrumental in the unwarrantable violences above mentioned may suffer, unless some laws be made to regulate, and tribunals erected competent to determine the propriety of captures.

"Therefore, *Resolved*,——

"1. That all such ships of war, frigates, sloops, cutters and armed vessels as are or shall be employed in the present cruel and unjust war against the United Colonies, and shall fall into the hands of, or be taken by, the inhabitants thereof, be seized and forfeited to and for the purposes hereinafter mentioned.

"2. That all transport vessels in the same service, having on board any troops, arms, ammunition, clothing, provisions, or military or naval stores, of what kind soever, and all vessels to whomsoever belonging that shall be employed in carrying provisions or other necessaries to the British army or armies or navy, that now are, or shall hereafter be, within any of the United

Colonies, or any goods, wares, or merchandises, for the use of such fleet or army, shall be liable to seizure, and with their cargoes shall be confiscated."

I have been particular in transcribing the proceedings of this day, November 25th, 1775, because they contain the true origin and foundation of the American Navy, and, as I had at least as great a share in producing them as any man living or dead. . . .

On Tuesday, November 28th, the Congress resumed the consideration of the rules and orders for the Navy of the United Colonies, and the same being debated by paragraphs were agreed to. . . . They were drawn up in the marine committee, and by my hand, but examined, discussed and corrected by the committee. In this place I will take the opportunity to observe that the pleasantest part of my labors for the four years I spent in Congress from 1774 to 1778 were in this naval committee. Mr. Lee, Mr. Gadsden were sensible men, and very cheerful, but Governor Hopkins of Rhode Island, about seventy years of age, kept us all alive. Upon business, his experience and judgment were very useful. But when the business of the evening was over, he kept us in conversation till eleven, and sometimes twelve o'clock. His custom was to drink nothing all day, nor till eight o'clock in the evening, and then his beverage was Jamaica spirit and water. It gave him wit, humor, anecdotes, science and learning. He had read Greek, Roman and British history, and was familiar with English poetry, particularly Pope, Thomson and Milton, and the flow of his soul made all his reading our own and seemed to bring to recollection in all of us all we had ever read. I could neither eat nor drink in these days. The other gentlemen were very temperate. Hopkins never drank to excess, but all he drank was immediately not only converted into wit, sense, knowledge and good humor, but inspired us with similar qualities.

This committee soon purchased and fitted five vessels. The first we named *Alfred,* in honor of the founder of the greatest navy that ever existed. The second, *Columbus,* after the discoverer of this quarter of the globe. The third, *Cabot,* for the discoverer of this northern part of the continent. The fourth, *Andrew Doria,* in memory of the great Genoese Admiral, and the fifth, *Providence,* for the town where she was purchased, the residence of Captain Hopkins and his brother Ezek, whom we appointed first captain. We appointed all the officers of all the ships. At the solicitation of Mr. Deane, we appointed his brother-in-law, Captain Saltonstall.

Sometime in December, worn down with long and uninterrupted labor, I asked and obtained leave to visit my State and family. Mr. Langdon did the same. Mr. Deane was left out of the delegation by his State, and some others of the naval committee were dispersed, when Congress appointed a committee of twelve, one from each State, for naval affairs, so that I had no longer any particular charge relative to them; but as long as I continued a member of Congress, I never failed to support all reasonable measures reported by the new committee.

—ADAMS, ed., *Works of John Adams,* III, 7-12.

II. CONGRESS RUNS THE NAVY

The Marine Committee set up by Congress applied itself at once to the conduct of naval affairs. While the rest of the committee were in Baltimore, Robert Morris proposed to Paul Jones a bold plan of attacking the British West Indies, Pensacola and St. Augustine, to draw the British Navy off the American coast. But most of Morris' colleagues were less sure of how to run the Navy and not agreed on the strategy to be employed.

Writing on November 7, 1776, to William Vernon, a member of the Navy Board, William Ellery of the Marine Committee confessed: "The conduct of the affairs of a navy as well as those of an army we are yet to learn." He asked that all knowledge of maritime and naval affairs be thrown "into the common stock," and particularly solicited advice about how the British Navy operated.

One of the first matters attended to by Congress was the setting up of Boards of Admiralty, which were regional naval boards. It was found necessary not to tie the regional boards down by too rigid instructions, but to give them some latitude in directing fleet operations. Washington, whose experience in the front lines had not augmented his stock of admiration for the way Congress handled military matters, felt much the same way about the Navy. This is made explicit in the exchange between the general and John Jay, at that time serving in Congress. The "certain commercial agent in Europe," to whom Jay refers in unflattering terms, was the paranoid Arthur Lee, and the "family compact" doubtless refers to the political alignments of the Virginia Lees, who generally opposed Deane, Franklin and Washington, and lined up on many questions with John Adams and a few of the New England malcontents in Congress.

The remaining letters in this section illustrate other problems confronting Congress or the regional Navy boards in handling naval affairs—running the blockade, protecting merchant ships, fixing on the size of naval vessels, and settling clashes over rank and seniority. John Paul Jones himself was the victim of the seniority system. In the spring of 1781 Congress recommended his promotion to the rank of Rear Admiral, but the action was blocked by rival officers. Captain Nicholson's letter to Captain Barry reveals the fierce jealousy that at times inspired ungenerous acts by America's first naval heroes.

1. John Paul Jones Is Urged to Carry the War to the Enemy

Robert Morris to John Paul Jones.

Philadelphia, February 1, 1777

... Destroying their settlements [the British West Indies and Pensacola], spreading alarms, showing and keeping up a spirit of enterprize that will oblige them to defend their extensive possessions at all points, is of infinitely more consequence to the United States of America than all the plunder that can be taken. If they divide their force we shall have elbow room and, that gained, we shall turn about and play our parts to the best advantage, which we cannot do now being constantly cramped in one part or an other.

It has long been clear to me that our infant fleet cannot protect our own coasts; and the only effectual relief it can afford us is to attack the enemies defenceless places and thereby oblige them to station more of their ships in their own countries, or to keep them employed in following ours, and either way we are relieved so far as they do it.

I do not pretend to give you any account of the coasts and harbours, strength of fortifications or mode of attack, for I cannot doubt your being well acquainted with these things, knowing as I do that you have been a commander in the West India trade, and at any rate your appearance will be unexpected and the enemy unprepared. They have no troops, and the very sound of a great gun will frighten them into submission. Governor Chester [Governor of West Florida] will no doubt know where the brass artillery are deposited and be glad to surrender them as a ransom for himself and his capital. When your business is done at Pensacola you may give them an alarm at St. Augustine, but they have some troops and you must be careful of your men. I think you should carry with you as many marines as possible, for they will be useful and necessary in all your land excursions.

The southern Colonies wish to see part of their Navy, and if you find it convenient and safe you might recruit and refit at Georgia, South or North Carolina, there make sale of such part of your prize goods, etc., as would be useful to them, learn where was the safest port to the northward, and then push along to such place of safety as might be necessary for refitting and re-manning the fleet. Should you prefer going to the coast of Africa you have the consent of the Marine Committee, but in that case I apprehend you only want the two ships and sloop *Providence*. Remember it is a long voyage—that you cannot destroy any English settlements there, and that if you meet any of their men of war in those seas they will be much superior to you in strength, etc. You may, it is true, do them much mischief, but the same may be done by cruizing to windward of Barbadoes as all their Guineamen fall in there. However, you are left to your choice and I am sure will choose for the best. Should there be a difficulty in getting all the vessels fully manned with so many seamen as you may think necessary, take the more Marines and you will get seamen from prizes in the course of your voyage. . . .

—Paullin, *Out-Letters of the Marine Committee*, I, 65-70.

2. Why Does Congress Keep the Continental Frigates in Port?

George Washington to John Jay.

Middlebrook, April, 1779

In one of your former letters you intimate, that a free communication of sentiments will not be displeasing to you. If, under this sanction, I should step beyond the line you would wish to draw, and suggest ideas or ask questions which are improper to be answered, you have only to pass them by in silence. I wish you to be convinced that I do not desire to pry into measures the knowledge of which is not necessary for my government as an executive officer, or the premature discovery of which might be prejudicial to plans in contemplation.

After premising this, I beg leave to ask what are the reasons for keeping the continental frigates in port? If it is because hands cannot be obtained to man them on the present encouragement, some other plan ought to be adopted to make them useful. Had not Congress better lend them to commanders of known bravery and capacity for a limited term, at the expiration of which the vessels, if not taken or lost, to revert to the States—they and their crews, in the mean time, enjoying the exclusive benefit of all captures they make, but acting either singly or conjointly under the direction of Congress? If this or a similar plan could be fallen upon, comprehending the whole number, under some common head, a man of ability and authority commissioned to act as commodore or admiral, I think great advantages might result from it. I am not sure but at this moment, by such a collection of the naval force we have, all the British armed vessels and transports at Georgia might be taken or destroyed, and their troops ruined. Upon the present system, our ships are not only very expensive and totally useless in port, but sometimes require a land force to protect them, as happened lately at New-London. . . .

Will Congress suffer the Bermudian vessels, which are said to have arrived at Delaware and Chesapeake Bays, to exchange their salt for flour, as is reported to be their intention? Will they not rather order them to depart immediately? Indulging them with a supply of provisions at this time will be injurious to us in two respects: it will deprive us of what we really stand in need of for ourselves, and will contribute to the support of that swarm of privateers which resort to Bermuda, from whence they infest our coast, and, in a manner, annihilate our trade. Besides these considerations, by withholding a supply, we throw many additional mouths upon the enemy's magazines, and increase proportionately their distress. They will not and cannot let their people starve.

In the last place, though first in importance, I shall ask, is there any thing doing, or that can be done, to restore the credit of our currency? The depreciation of it is got to so alarming a point that a wagon-load of money will scarcely purchase a wagon-load of provision.

—FITZPATRICK, ed., *Writings of Washington*, XIV, 435-437.

3. THE LEE FAMILY IS BEHIND THE BUNGLING OF NAVAL AFFAIRS

John Jay to George Washington.

Philadelphia, 26th April, 1779

The questions contained in your favour of the — April instant are as important as the manner of introducing them is delicate.

While the maritime affairs of the continent continue under the direction of a committee, they will be exposed to all the consequences of want of system, attention and knowledge. The marine committee consists of a delegate from each State. It fluctuates, new members constantly coming in, and old ones going out. Three or four, indeed, have remained in it from the beginning; and few members understand even the state of our naval affairs, or have time or inclination to attend to them.

But why is not this system changed? It is, in my opinion, convenient to the family compact. The commercial committee was equally useless. A proposition was made to appoint a commercial agent for the States under certain regulations. Opposition was made. The ostensible objections were various.

The true reason was its interfering with a certain commercial agent in Europe and his connections.

You will, if I am not greatly mistaken, find Mr. Gerard disposed to be open and communicative. He has acquired an extensive knowledge of our affairs. I have no reason to believe he will use it to our prejudice. There is as much intrigue in this State-house as in the Vatican, but as little secrecy as in a boarding-school. It mortifies me on this occasion to reflect that the rules of Congress on the subject of secrecy, which are far too general, and perhaps for that reason more frequently violated, restrains me from saying twenty things to you which have ceased to be private.

—JAY, *Correspondence and Public Papers,* I, 209-210.

4. RUNNING THE BLOCKADE

John Deshon (a member) to the Navy Board.

Providence, March 9th, 1778
Saturday evening I got to this place

Gentlemen

Yours of the 3rd and 5th instant are now before me. In ansuer to the former, respecting the ship *Warren,* I am happy she so well succeeded in getting out of this river. Every circumstance combined in her favour that she might [get] clear of the enemy. The night was exceeding dark, and there was but little wind untill the crittecal time of passing the greatest danger, when the wind shifted very suddenly into the N.W. and blowd exceeding hard, so that the enemy could not without the greatest difficulty get under sail and persue.

I was at Warrick Neck and up the most part of the night when the *Warren* passed and am very sure it was imposable for Capt. Hopkins to gain the port of N. London, there being so much wind and the weather so severe cold. There where [were] on board the *Warren* about 170 men, manny of which had not a second shift of cloaths; therefore it will be very difficult as well as teadius for Capt. Hopkins to beat this courst at this severe season. The orders given him by me, you have with you, which gives him not the least encouragement to cruise. Nevertheless, should the ship keep out this three weeks, I shall not be in the least uneasy about her, well knowin[g] the men in no condission to beat a winters courst. We have succeeded b[e]yound expectation in geting her out, and I have not the least doubt but she will in due time return with honor to the commander and his company. . . .

—DESHON, "Letter," *R. I. Hist. Soc. Pub.,* New Series, VIII, 214.

5. A PATRIOT ARGUMENT AGAINST BUILDING BIG WARSHIPS

William Ellery to William Vernon.

York Town, March 16th, 1778

I read that part of your letter respecting the seventy-four at Portsmouth, and a paragraph of one I received about the same time and upon the same subject from Mr. Whipple, to the Marine Committee, and it was agreed to stop the building of her for the present. These huge ships are too costly and unwieldy, and it will require as many men to man one of them as to man three or four frigates. Besides, we cannot with all the naval force we can collect be able to cope with the British Navy. Our great aim should be to destroy the trade of Britain, for which purpose frigates are infinitely better calculated than such large ships.

Mr. Whipple proposes to the Marine Committee to put the timber prepared for the seventy-four into a frigate to mount 30 18-pounders on one deck, and this proposal I believe would be complied with if our finances were not at present very low and the demands of the great departments of war very high. I wish we may be able to finish, man and get to sea, in the course of the next summer, the frigates that are now in hand; but I very much doubt it.

It gave the Marine Committee great satisfaction to find that the *Warren* had got out. We have since heard that she had arrived at Boston, which we hope will prove true. I hope you will get out the *Providence* and *Columbus*. The *Virginia* hath made two fruitless attempts to pass out Chesapeak. She is ordered to make another. There are four or five men of war in that bay; but I cannot think it so difficult to pass by them as it is to pass those in our bay. Our last accounts from Charlestown, So. Carolina, were that Capt. Biddle with three State armed vessels were determined to go over the bar and attack several British vessels of about an equal force with them. I cannot forbear being anxious for the event.

The Marine Committee lately ordered Capt. Barry of the *Effingham* to take the four boats belonging to the frigates which are sunk in the Delaware, and proceed on a cruise upon that river. On the 7th instant two of them—the other two had not then got below the city—joined by five boats, half manned, attacked (near Bombay-hook) and took two of the enemy's transport ships— one mounting six four-pounders, the other two swivels—and also a schooner with eight 4-pounders, twelve 4-pound howitzers and 32 men, properly equipped for an armed vessel. They first boarded the ships, and, learning from them the strength of the schooner, Capt. Barry prudently sent a flag to the schooner, ordering the captain of her to submit, and promising that he and his officers, on compliance, should be allowed their private baggage; whereupon they thought it proper to strike. As the ships were loaded only with forage, Capt. Barry, after stripping, burnt them. The schooner, being a suitable vessel for a cruiser, he is ordered to purchase and employ on the Delaware so long as he thinks it may be safe. She had in [her] a variety of useful and valuable articles.

This gallant action reflects great honour on Capt. Barry, his officers and the crews of those boats. The other two boats have since got down, and in their way took a small sloop, with fresh provisions, bound to the city. I expect every day to hear of their further success. These boats will annoy and injure the enemy more, in my opinion, than both the seventy-fours would, if they were built, equipped and manned—at least upon the Delaware.

—ELLERY, "Letter," *R. I. Hist. Soc. Pub.*, New Series, VIII, 222-224.

6. "Give the Seamen All the Prizes"

John Paul Jones to Robert Morris.

Providence Sloop-of-War,
at Newport, Rhode Island, October 17, 1776

I wrote to you at sea 4th ultimo, by the brigantine *Sea-Nymph*, my second prize. I have taken sixteen sail, manned and sent in eight prizes, and sunk, burned or destroyed the rest. . . .

It is to the last degree distressing to contemplate the state and establishment of our Navy. The common class of mankind are actuated by no nobler principle than that of self-interest. This, and this only, determines all adventurers in privateers, the owners as well as those they employ. And while this is the case, unless the private enrollment of individuals in our Navy is made superior to that in privateers, it never can become respectable, it never will become formidable; and without a respectable Navy, alas America!

In the present critical situation of affairs, human wisdom can suggest no more than one infallible expedient: Inlist the seamen during pleasure and give them all the prizes. What is the paltry emolument of two-thirds of prizes to the finances of this vast continent? If such a poor resource is essential to its independency, in sober sadness we are involved in a woful predicament, and our ruin is fast approaching. The situation of America is new in the annals of mankind; her affairs cry haste, and speed must answer them. Trifles, therefore, ought to be wholly discharged, as being, in the old vulgar proverb, "penny wise and pound foolish." If our enemies, with the best-established and most formidable Navy in the universe, have found it expedient to assign all prizes to the captors, how much more is such policy essential to our infant fleet?

But I need use no arguments to convince you of the necessity of making the emoluments of our Navy equal, if not superior, to theirs. We have had proof that a Navy may be officered almost on any terms; but we are not so sure the officers are equal to their commissions; nor will the Congress ever obtain such certainty until they in their wisdom see proper to appoint a Board of Admiralty competent to determine impartially the respective merits and abilities of their officers, and to superintend, regulate and point out all the motions and operations of the Navy.

—Force, *American Archives*, 5th Series, II, 1105-1106.

7. The Seniority System Blocks Paul Jones's Promotion

Captain James Nicholson to Captain John Barry.

Philadelphia, June 24th 1781

After congratulating you on your safe arrival and success, I shall without any apology relate to you what has been transacting in this quarter relative to rank for this week past. It still hangs over our head and requires every exertion of interest to prevent its taking place. The attempt has been bold and daring and is only equaled by the man who made it.

The Chevalier [John Paul Jones] ever since his arrival in this city has devoted his time, privately, by making personal application to the individual

Members of Congress to give him rank at the head of our Navy, and after interesting (by being an accomplished courtior) every Member who was weak or of his own stamp in his favor, hands into Congress a narrative of his services from the beginning of time, containing the best part of a quire of paper, and attended with a modest petition seting forth the injustice he had done him in the establishment of rank and desire of redress, etc.

This had the desired effect, and he had a committee of Congress, consisting of Gen. Vernon, Mr. Mathews and Mr. Clymer, appointed to enquire into his claim and to make report. They accordingly did and in his favor. Congress was upon the point of taking the report up, and I have too much reason to believe would have gratified the hight of his ambition, had we not by the greatest accident discovered it. This was done by information a Member of Congress gave Mrs. Reade in whose house he lived. He was also on the most familiar terms with myself. So far he had proceeded without the least suspisian on our side.

As soon as I was informed of it, I immediately took my hat and with very little ceremony waited on the President of Congress at his house, and informed what I had heard. He received me politely and told me my suspisians was just. I therefore desired as my right that Congress might delay determining on it untill Capt. Reade and myself, in behalf of our selves and the absent brother officers equally concerned, should have an opportunity of being heard, which he promised me his interest to have done, and that day Capt. Reade and myself threw in our remonstrance to Congress (a copy of mine you have enclosed), the consequence of which was the committee was ordered to reconsider it and to give us notice to attend. We according did and found Capt. Jones without doors in conferance with two of them.

Capt. Jones did not attend. I desired the chairman would send for him. The reason I assigned was that I would say many things in his presence that I would not in his absence. He sent word that he would wait on us, but never came. We found the President and Mr. Mathews predetermined in his favor, but Mr. Clymer otherwise. After pointing out the absurdity of his claim, which proceeded from a brevial from Commodore Hopkins to the command of the sloop *Providence* ... Capts. Whipple, Hallock, yourself and Alexander where [were] captains before him—I say after pointing out this to them, the President appeared to be convinced, but if so in reality I won't pretend to say. We had a good deal of conversation with the committee. Mr Mathews alone seemed his most strenious advocate and in my oppinion behaved obstinate and ungentiel. I said many things pretty severe of the Chevalier's private as well as public carrector, too odious to mention and yet unnoticed.

Upon the whole we acquited ourselves well. It happened five days ago and they have not yet made their report. Should it be in his favor again, I have some reason to believe the honest part, as well as those who had been imposed on from their ignorance about our naval transactions and the method of establishing rank, are now sufficiently alarmed, and should the report be taken up at all, they will not determine in his favor. Your arrival and success came very opportunily and I did not fail to make use of it—I mean outdoors in presence of Capt. Jones and some of his advocated Members, by observing that you had acquit yourself well, which they acknowledged. I then told them they could not do less than make you admiral also. I had not a sentense of reply. It irritated the Chevalier so much that he was obliged to decamp.

I yesterday was informed by a Member of Congress, a friend of mine, that they had received a letter from Bob Morris (the Financier) that he would undertake to fitt out immediately my ship and the seventy-four and if they agreed to it, there would be a necessity for appointing a captain to her immediately, and at the same time asked if I would accept of the command of her. I refused, but at the same time pointed out the necessity of the next senior officer having the offer and so down, and in case none of them would accept untill it came to Chevalier, that then he should have the offer. He seemed convinced from the arguments I made use of of the necessity of this mode as the only one that would give satisfaction and make our Navy of repute. How it will opperate with Congress I cant undertake to determine. . . .
—NICHOLSON, "Letter," *Naval Hist. Soc. Pub.,* I, 125-126.

III. SANDWICH PRESIDES OVER THE MISFORTUNES OF THE BRITISH NAVY

If any one person must shoulder the blame for Britain's unreadiness at sea and the incompetent direction of her naval operations during the Revolution a scapegoat is near at hand. He is the First Lord of the Admiralty in the North ministry, the notorious profligate and rake, John Montagu, Earl of Sandwich. With a mad wife and a spendthrift son, Sandwich might well be pardoned for his long week ends away from home and office.

But all the blame for Britain's naval inadequacies should not be borne by Sandwich. True, he made some bad decisions. From the start of the war he husbanded his naval strength in European waters, fearing war with France, rather than providing full naval support for combined all-out operations that might have smashed the rebellion at the start. Concentrating on military rather than naval operations in America, the British wasted their army in pointless forays into the interior, and failed to use their naval forces to establish a tight blockade on the coast, as Viscount Barrington for one had repeatedly urged. But Lord North was equally to blame. It was Lord North who was so concerned about cutting down the public debt that he was willing to decommission a substantial part of Britain's Navy. Sandwich fought these cuts, but North's economy was bolstered by his and the King's fear of arousing France by building up the Navy to more formidable strength. However, as a symbol of profligacy, corruption and administrative ineptitude the Earl is a far more colorful personage than his cabinet colleague, Lord George Germain, Secretary of State for the American Department, who, despite having been court-martialed for cowardice after the Battle of Minden in the Seven Years' War, was in charge of military operations in North America. Before the war was long under way these two foolish and incompetent directors of operations were at loggerheads.

On April 23, 1779, a motion was put in the House of Lords to remove Sandwich from his direction of the Admiralty. It was defeated, by 78 votes to 39. Lord North had stepped into the breach with the assertion that a vote of censure against one member of the Cabinet involved the whole, and that the entire cabinet accepted responsibility for Admiralty measures.

What is most extraordinary is the fact that the debate over this motion was postponed owing to the murder on April 7 of Martha Ray, who had been Sandwich's mistress for sixteen years and had borne him two sons. She was murdered by James Hackman outside Drury Lane Theatre.

In addition to a few excerpts dealing with Sandwich's private and public affairs, there is included in this section a letter denouncing the scandalous corruption that accompanied the outfitting and supplying of ships.

1. THE EARL OF SANDWICH IS TROUTING AS USUAL

David Hume to William Strahan.

Bath, May 10, 1776

. . . When we passed by Spine Hill near Newbury we found in the inn Lord Denbigh, who was an acquaintance of my fellow traveller. His Lordship informed him that he, Lord Sandwich, Lord Mulgrave, Mr. Banks and two or three ladies of pleasure had passed five or six days there, and intended to pass all this week and the next in the same place; that their chief object was to enjoy the trouting season; that they had been very successful; that Lord Sandwich in particular had caught trouts near twenty inches long, which gave him incredible satisfaction; but that for his part, being a great admirer of sea fish, in which Bath abounded, and hearing that Friday was the great market day for fish, he commissioned my friend to send him up by the London fly a good cargo of soles, John Dories and pipers, which would render their happiness compleat.

I do not remember in all my little or great knowledge of history (according as you and Dr. Johnson can settle between you the degrees of my knowledge) such another instance; and I am sure such a one does not exist: That the First Lord of the Admiralty, who is absolute and uncontrouled master in his department, should, at a time when the fate of the British Empire is in dependance, and in dependance on him, find so much leizure, tranquillity, presence of mind and magnanimity as to have amusement in trouting during three weeks near sixty miles from the scene of business, and during the most critical season of the year. There needs but this single fact to decide the fate of the nation. What an ornament would it be in a future history to open the glorious events of the ensuing year with the narrative of so singular an incident.

—HILL, ed., *Letters of Hume to Strahan*, pp. 324-325.

2. GEORGE III CONSOLES SANDWICH ON THE MURDER OF HIS MISTRESS

April 11, 1779

. . . I am sorry Lord Sandwich has met with any severe blow of a private nature. I flatter myself this world scarcely contains a man so void of feeling as not to compassionate your situation.

—BARNES & OWEN, *Sandwich Papers*, II, 249.

3. Lord North Holds the Cabinet Responsible for the Acts of the Admiralty

Minutes of Debate in the House of Lords.

April 23, 1779

Every expedition, in regard to its destination, object, force and number of ships, is planned by the Cabinet, and is the result of the collective wisdom of all his Majesty's confidential ministers. The First Lord of the Admiralty is only the executive servant of these measures; and if he is not personally a Cabinet minister he is not responsible for the wisdom, the policy, and the propriety of any naval expedition. But if he is in the Cabinet, then he must share in common with the other ministers that proportional division of censure which is attached to him as an individual. In no situation is he more or less responsible to his country than his colleagues from any misconduct which flows from a Cabinet measure.

—Barnes & Owen, *Sandwich Papers*, II, 255-256.

4. "With Such Rapacity, How Can a Nation Support a War?"

Captain W. Young to Charles Middleton, Lord Barham.

Sandwich: Sandy Hook, 15 November, 1780

I have the pleasure to acquaint you that the South Carolina and New York convoys are arrived, and not above one or two missing. This has been the most fortunate supply that has made its appearance since this war took place. I must again recommend it to you to push and urge the admiralty to establish men-of-war for this service; and let them be the uncoppered ships, as the coppered ones are very unfit for convoys to deep-laden victuallers. I most sincerely wish you to attend to this service, as you are the person army and navy look up to, and not the navy board.

I am likewise to acquaint you of the immense neglects of the people at Woolwich Yard in the lading of the storeships for New York. The beds were all stowed in the hatchway, by which means a great part of them are rotten; the whole of the colours destroyed by their putting up the iron cringles for staysails in the casks with them—the iron having been wet when put up has effectually ruined them, so that out of the whole number only a few are serviceable.

The complaints respecting transports are great, and with great justice; those sent out totally unfit for service, the whole under the auspices of Mr. Wilkinson's house. Sir Hugh [Vice-Admiral Sir Hugh Palliser], I do suppose concerned with them as formerly, though you do not perceive it; I find too many proofs here for this information, as well as those which I well knew when in that department myself. While those men interfere and are concerned, the public must be robbed.

Mr. Arbuthnot's secretary follows the example of the great: he loses sight of no opportunity to rob and distress. In my last I gave you an account of such circumstance as the people chose to send me. I am now to inform you of a part of his villainy which I can personally prove, which is the purchase of fresh beef. He is supplied with it at Sandy Hook at 10*d*. York currency per pound, and charges the public 1*s*. sterling per pound; consequently he clears 5*d*. sterling, or near it, on every pound supplied. I have it from captains in Gardener's Bay, where Mr. Arbuthnot has been ever since our arrival here, that he has supplied the squadron with fresh beef, and on the same principle as at Sandy Hook. With the rapacity of this man of this Navy, and others such as this fellow is, and those in the Army of the same kidney, how can it be supposed that a minister and a nation can support a war? Sir, it is not possible. We must bankrupt, or other methods must be adopted.

—BARHAM, *Letters and Papers*, I, 82-83.

IV. THE NAVAL WAR OFF THE NEW ENGLAND COAST

Holding a military base at Boston and a supply base at Halifax, the British government in the year 1775 was concerned with guarding communications to General Gage's troops, with procuring and transporting supplies needed by the army, with sealing off trade between New England and foreign countries (after July 1 by Parliamentary authorization), and with barring New Englanders from the North Atlantic fisheries (after July 20). The activities of the British fleet in Patriot harbors and offshore were bound to be resented, and the earliest naval engagements were more or less spontaneously ignited, lacking any central planning, direction or official sponsorship on the part of the Patriots. We have already read something of this story in the chapter on the battle for Boston—the ineffectual attacks on Bristol and Falmouth and the general dissatisfaction with the conduct of Admiral Graves.

Several months before the Congress took action to organize a Navy, naval warfare flared up along the New England coast. The action off Machias, in the district of Maine, is generally considered the first naval engagement of the Revolution. Closely related to the battle of Lexington, reports of which reached the Maine area around May 9, the action resulted from the firm resolve of the Patriots to keep a British armed schooner, the Margaretta, *from convoying lumber for the use of the King's troops in Boston. A plot was concocted to seize Captain Moore and the other officers of the* Margaretta *as they were attending church on the Sabbath, but the officers jumped out of the window and escaped to their vessel. Moore fired a few shots at the town and then dropped down about four miles below it. When pursued from shore, he anchored in the bay. Then a New York lad named Jeremiah O'Brien, temporarily residing in Machias, joined forces with a local inhabitant, Joseph Wheaton. Together they boarded one of the sloops being convoyed and moved to the attack. It was spontaneous, planned by no formal Patriot organization. For this reason Machias has been appropriately called the "Lexington of the Sea."*

O'Brien's naval career was indeed conspicuously launched. He now fitted out a privateer, captured two armed schooners off the Bay of Fundy, and delivered the prisoners to General Washington at Cambridge. On the general's recommendation O'Brien was appointed by the revolutionary government of Massachusetts to command the two prizes he had seized.

1. The First Naval Hero—Jeremiah O'Brien

Official report of the Machias Committee of Correspondence to the Massachusetts Provincial Congress.

June 14, 1775

. . . On the 2nd instant Capt. Ichabod Jones arrived in the river with two sloops, accompanied with one of the King's tenders. On the 3rd instant a paper was handed about for the people to sign, as a prerequisite to their obtaining any provisions, of which we were in great want. The contents of this paper required the signers to indulge Capt. Jones in carrying lumber to Boston, and to protect him and his property at all events. But, unhappily for him, if not for us, it soon expired after producing effects directly contrary in their nature to those intended.

The next effort, in order to carry those favorite points, was to call a meeting, which was accordingly done. On the 6th the people generally assembled at the place appointed and seemed so averse to the measures proposed that Capt. Jones privately went to the tender and caused her to move up so near the town that her guns would reach the houses, and put springs upon her cables. The people, however, not knowing what was done, and considering themselves nearly as prisoners of war, in the hands of the common enemy (which is our only plea for suffering Capt. Jones to carry any lumber to Boston, since Your Honors conceive it improper), passed a vote that Capt. Jones might proceed in his business as usual without molestation, that they would purchase the provisions he brought into the place and pay him according to contract.

After obtaining this vote Capt. Jones immediately ordered his vessel to the wharf and distributed his provisions among those only who voted in favor of his carrying lumber to Boston. This gave such offence to the aggrieved party that they determined to take Capt. Jones, if possible, and put a final stop to his supplying the King's troops with anything. Accordingly they secretly invited the people of Mispecka and Pleasant River to join them; accordingly a number of them came and, having joined our people in the woods near the settlement, on the 11th they all agreed to take Capt. Jones and Stephen Jones, Esq., in the place of worship, which they attempted, but Capt. Jones made his escape into the woods and does not yet appear. Stephen Jones, Esq., only was taken and remains as yet under guard.

The Captain and Lieutenant of the tender were also in the meeting house and fled to their vessell, hoisted their flag and sent a message on shore to this effect: "That he had express orders to protect Capt. Jones; that he was determined to do his duty whilst he had life; and that if the people presumed to stop Capt. Jones' vessells he would burn the town."

Upon this a party of our men went directly to stripping the sloop that lay at the wharf, and another party went off to take possession of the other sloop which lay below and brought her up nigh a wharf, and anchored in the stream.

The tender did not fire, but weighed her anchors as privately as possible, and in the dusk of the evening fell down and came to within musket shot of the sloop, which obliged our people to slip their cable and run the sloop aground. In the meantime a considerable number of our people went down in boats and canoes, lined the shore directly opposite to the tender, and having demanded her to "surrender to America!" received for answer, "Fire and be damned!" They immediately fired in upon her, which she returned, and a smart engagement ensued. The tender, at last, slipped her cable and fell down to a small sloop, commanded by Capt. Tobey, and lashed herself to her for the remainder of the night.

In the morning of the 12th she took Capt. Tobey out of his vessel for a pilot, and made all the sail they could to get off, as the wind and tide favored; but having carried away her main boom, and meeting with a sloop from the Bay of Fundy, they came to, robbed the sloop of her boom and gaff, took almost all her provisions, together with Mr. Robert Avery of Norwich in Connecticut, and proceeded on their voyage.

Our people, seeing her go off in the morning, determined to follow her. About forty men, armed with guns, swords, axes and pitchforks, went in Capt. Jones's sloop, under the command of Capt. Jeremiah O'Brien; about twenty armed in the same manner, and under the command of Capt. Benj. Foster, went in a small schooner. During the chase our people built them breastworks of pine boards and anything they could find in the vessels that would screen them from the enemy's fire. The tender, upon the first appearance of our people, cut her boats from her stern, and made all the sail she could; but being a very dull sailor, they soon came up with her, and a most obstinate engagement ensued, both sides being determined to conquer or die; but the tender was obliged to yield. Her captain was wounded in the breast with two balls, of which wounds he died next morning. Poor Mr. Avery was killed and one of the marines, and five wounded.

Only one of our men was killed and six wounded, one of which is since dead of his wounds.

The battle was fought at the entrance of our harbour and lasted for near the space of one hour. We have in our possession four double fortifyed three-pounders and fourteen swivels and a number of small arms, which we took with the tender, besides a very small quantity of ammunition, etc.

—Machias Committee of Correspondence, *Maine Hist. Soc. Coll. and Proc.*, 2nd Series, VI, 129-131.

2. The British Raid on Gloucester

The continued depredations of the British Navy off the New England coast aroused the Patriots to acts of self-defense and retaliation. On August 9, 1775, Captain John Linzee of the sloop-of-war Falcon *chased two schooners bound for the West Indies to Salem. One he captured; the other took refuge in Gloucester harbor. When Linzee entered in pursuit the inhabitants rallied to defend the schooner and fired from shore upon the British boarding party. Linzee in retaliation cannonaded the town, but lost both schooners along with two barges to the defenders. He then quit the harbor and headed for the safety of Nantasket Road.*

The emotionally charged newspaper account of the Gloucester correspondent is largely supported by Captain Linzee's own report to Vice-Admiral Graves, dated August 10. Linzee asserted that his attempt to fire the town failed because "an American part of my complement (who had always been active in our cause) set fire to the powder before it was properly placed." One man was blown up, the Americans then deserted, and further attempts to fire the town failed.

From the *Pennsylvania Packet:*

A correspondent at Gloucester, Cape Ann, has sent the following authentic and particular account of an engagement there, viz:

"Gloucester, Aug. 13.

"On the 9th instant, the *Falcon* sloop of war, Capt. Linzee, hove in sight, and seemed to be in quest of two schooners from the West Indies bound to Salem, one of which he soon brought to, the other taking advantage of a fair wind, put into our harbour; but Linzee, having made a prize of the first, pursued the second into our harbour and brought the first with him. He anchored and sent two barges with fifteen men in each, armed with muskets and swivels; these were attended with a whale boat, in which was the lieutenant and six privates; their orders were to seize the loaded schooner and bring her under the *Falcon's* bow.

"The militia and other inhabitants were alarmed at this daring attempt and prepared for a vigorous opposition. The barge-men under the command of the lieutenant boarded the schooner at the cabbin windows, which provoked a smart fire from our people on the shore, by which three of the enemy were killed, and the lieutenant wounded in the thigh, who thereupon returned to the man of war. Upon this Linzee sent the other schooner and a small cutter he had to attend him well armed, with orders to fire on the damned rebels wherever they could see them, and that he would in the mean time cannonade the town. He immediately fired a broadside upon the thickest settlements and stood himself with diabolical pleasure to see what havock his cannon might make.

" 'Now,' said he, '*my boys, we will aim at the damned Presbyterian Church. Well, my brave fellows, one shot more and the house of God will fall before you.*'

"While he was venting his hellish rage and setting himself as it were against Heaven, the Almighty was on our side: not a ball struck or wounded an individual person, although they went through our houses in almost every direction when filled with women and children; under God, our little party at the water side performed wonders, for they soon made themselves masters of both the schooners, the cutter, the two barges, the boat and every man in them. In the action, which lasted several hours, we lost but one man, two others wounded, one of which is since dead, the other very slightly wounded.

We took of the man of war's men thirty five, several were wounded and one since dead; twenty-four sent to headquarters; the remainder, being impressed from this and neighboring towns, were permitted to return to their friends. Next day, Capt. Linzee warped off with but half his men, never a prize, boat nor tender, except a small skiff the wounded lieutenant returned in. . . ."

—*Pennsylvania Packet*, Aug. 28, 1775.

3. THE DEATH OF CAPTAIN MUGFORD OF MARBLEHEAD

Although the main British fleet had quit Boston harbor with the embarkation of the British army from that town in the spring of 1776, a few vessels stayed in the vicinity of Nantasket Road, and naval skirmishes resulted. In June 1776, General Artemas Ward, left in command by Washington, commissioned Captain James Mugford, and subsequently he was recommissioned by Congress. The account of his heroic death by General Ward, contained in a letter to Washington of May 20, 1776, differs from the following excerpt as regards the fatal injury the naval captain suffered. According to Ward, "he was run through with a lance while he was cutting off the hands of the pirates as they were attempting to board him, and it is said that with his own hands he cut off five pairs of theirs." Among the defenders Mugford alone was killed.

Boston, May 20, 1776

Early last Friday morning the *Franklin* schooner, one of the Continental cruisers, commanded by Captain James Mugford, of Marblehead, fell in with one of the enemy's transport ships from Cork, bound directly into this harbour, the captain not knowing that the place had been evacuated by the British fleet and army. Notwithstanding she appeared to be an armed ship and was in sight of the enemy's men of war lying in Nantasket, Captain Mugford resolutely bore down upon her and took her without opposition. She mounted six carriage-guns, a number of swivels, and had on board eighteen men. The *Franklin*, at that time, had only twenty-one men. Captain Mugford determining to bring her into this harbour, the inhabitants, on leaving their respective places of worship after the forenoon's service (it being the day of the Continental fast), had the pleasure of seeing the most valuable prize taken since the commencement of the war entering the harbour. . . .

The enemy, on board the men of war below, intolerably vexed and chagrined that the above ship should be taken and unloaded in their open view, formed a design of wreaking their vengeance on the gallant Captain Mugford, who took her. The Sunday following Captain Mugford, in company with Captain Cunningham in the *Lady Washington*, a small privateer armed with swivels, blunderbusses and muskets, fell down in order to go out in the bay. The enemy observed their sailing and fitted out a fleet of boats for the purpose of surprising and taking them in the night; and the *Franklin's* running aground in the cut gave them a good opportunity for executing their plan.

The _Lady Washington_ came to anchor near Captain Mugford; and between nine and ten o'clock he discovered a number of boats, which he hailed, and received for answer that they were from Boston. He ordered them to keep off, or he would fire upon them. They begged him for God's sake not to fire, for they were going on board him. Captain Mugford instantly fired and was followed by all his men; and cutting his cable, brought his broadside to bear, when he discharged his cannon, loaded with musket-ball, directly in upon them. Before the cannon could be charged a second time, two or three boats were alongside, each of them supposed to have as many men on board as the _Franklin_, which were only twenty-one, including officers.

By the best accounts there were not less than thirteen boats in all, many of them armed with swivels and having on board, at the lowest computation, two hundred men. Captain Mugford and his men plied those alongside so closely with firearms and spears, and with such intrepidity, activity and success that two boats were soon sunk and all the men either killed or drowned. But while the heroick Mugford, with outstretched arms, was righteously dealing death and destruction to our base and unnatural enemies, he received a fatal ball in his body, which in a few minutes put a period to a life from which, had it been spared, his oppressed country would undoubtedly have reaped very eminent advantages.

After our brave men had maintained this unequal contest for about half an hour, the enemy thought proper to retire. The carnage among them must have been great; for, besides the two boat-loads killed and drowned, many were doubtless killed and wounded on board the others. Great execution was done by spears. One man, with that weapon, is positive of having killed nine of the enemy. . . .

—FORCE, _American Archives_, 4th Series, VI, 495-496.

V. A SUBMARINE IN NEW YORK WATERS?

The successful amphibious landing of the British forces on Long Island in August 1776 remains the most brilliant example of joint operations by the British in the entire war. Against the powerful British fleet, the defenders relied on land and island bases, but their artillery proved ineffective. One other resource was called upon to stop the navy—an ingenious submarine which had been invented by David Bushnell in 1775, and was called—from its appearance—the American Turtle. Bushnell was a Connecticut farm boy with a turn for mechanics, who thought up the submarine and worked it out himself. In 1775 he presented his idea to the Governor and Council of Safety of Connecticut and was authorized by them to go ahead with it. The next year it was ready for action; there was nothing wrong with it in principle, but Bushnell was never able to find a man who could operate it satisfactorily. The submarine was tried in New York waters in 1776-77, and in Philadelphia waters a year later, but in vain. Bushnell later settled in the South where in true Jack-of-all-trades style he taught school and practiced medicine. This account, though *written many years after the events it relates, takes on a special authenticity from the fact that the writer was personally acquainted with Ezra Lee, who operated the submarine. The account is addressed to one of the leading American scientists of his generation, Benjamin Silliman, first professor of chemistry and natural history at Yale.*

Charles Griswold to Professor Silliman.

Lyme, Connecticut, February 21st, 1820

It is to be presumed that every person who has paid any attention to the mechanical inventions of this country, or has looked over the history of her Revolutionary War, has heard of the machine invented by David Bushnell for submarine navigation and the destruction of hostile shipping. I have thought that a correct and full account of that novel and original invention would not be unacceptable to the public, and particularly to those devoted to the pursuit of science and the arts.

If the idea of submarine warfare had ever occurred to any one before the epoch of Bushnell's invention, yet it may be safely stated that no ideas but his own ever came to any practical results. To him, I believe, the whole merit of this invention is unanimously agreed to belong.

But such an account as I have mentioned must derive an additional value and an increased interest from the fact that all the information contained in the following pages has been received from the only person in existence possessed of that information, and who was the very same that first embarked in this novel and perilous navigation.

Mr. Ezra Lee, first a sergeant and afterwards an ensign in the Revolutionary Army, a respectable, worthy and elderly citizen of this town, is the person to whom I have alluded. To him was committed the first essay for destroying a hostile ship by submarine explosion, and upon his statement an implicit reliance may be placed.

Considering Bushnell's machine as the first of its kind, I think it will be pronounced to be remarkably complete throughout in its construction, and that such an invention furnishes evidence of those resources and creative powers, which must rank him as a mechanical genius of the first order.

I shall first attend to a description of this machine, and afterwards to a relation of the enterprise in it by Sergeant Lee; confining myself, in each case, strictly to the facts with which he has supplied me.

Bushnell's machine was composed of several pieces of large oak timber, scooped out and fitted together, and its shape my informer compares to that of a round clam. It was bound around thoroughly with iron bands, the seams were corked, and the whole was smeared over with tar, so as to prevent the possibility of the admission of water to the inside.

It was of a capacity to contain one engineer, who might stand or sit, and enjoy sufficient elbow room for its proper management.

The top or head was made of a metallic composition, exactly suited to its body, so as to be water-tight; this opened upon hinges, and formed the entrance to the machine. Six small pieces of thick glass were inserted in this head for the admission of light: in a clear day and clear sea-water, says my informer, he could see to read at the depth of three fathoms. To keep it upright and properly balanced, seven hundred pounds of lead were fastened to its bottom, two hundred pounds of which were so contrived as to be discharged at any moment, to increase the buoyancy of the machine.

But to enable the navigator when under water to rise or sink at pleasure, there were two forcing pumps, by which water could be pressed out at the bottom; and also a spring, by applying the foot to which a passage was formed for the admission of water. If the pumps should get deranged, then resort was had to letting off the lead ballast from the bottom.

The navigator steered by a rudder, the tiller of which passed through the back of the machine at a water joint, and in one side was fixed a small pocket compass, with two pieces of shining wood (sometimes called foxfire) crossed upon its north point, and a single piece upon the last point. In the night when no light entered through the head, this compass thus lighted was all that served to guide the helmsman in his course.

The ingenious inventor also provided a method for determining the depth of water at which the machine might at any time be. This was achieved by means of a glass tube, twelve inches in length and about four in diameter, which was also attached to the side of the machine: this tube enclosed a piece of cork that rose with the descent of the machine and fell with its ascent, and one inch rise of the cork denoted a depth of about one fathom. The principle upon which such a result was produced, and also the mechanical contrivance of this tube, entirely escaped the observation of Mr. Lee, amidst the hurry and constant anxiety attendant upon such a perilous navigation.

But not the least ingenious part of this curious machine was that by which the horizontal motion was communicated to it. This object was effected by means of two oars or paddles, formed precisely like the arms of a wind-mill, which revolved perpendicularly upon an axletree that projected in front; this axletree passed into the machine at a water joint, and was furnished with a crank by which it was turned: the navigator, being seated inside, with one hand laboured at the crank, and with the other steered by the tiller.

The effect of paddles so constructed, and turned in the manner stated by propelling or rather drawing a body after them under water, will readily occur to any one without explanation.

These paddles were but twelve inches long and about four wide. Two smaller paddles of the same description also projected near the head, provided with a crank inside by which the ascent of the machine could be assisted.

By vigorous turning of the crank, says my informer, the machine could be propelled at the rate of about three miles an hour in still water. When beyond the reach of danger, or observation of an enemy, the machine was suffered to float with its head just rising from the water's surface, and while in this situation, air was constantly admitted through three small orifices in the head, which were closed when a descent was commenced.

The efficient part of this engine of devastation, its magazine, remains to be spoken of. This was separate and distinct from the machine. It was shaped like an egg and, like the machine itself, was composed of solid pieces of oak scooped out and in the same manner fitted together, and secured by iron bands, etc. One hundred and thirty pounds of gun powder, a clock, and a gun lock, provided with a good flint that would not miss fire, were the apparatus which it enclosed. This magazine was attached to the back of the machine, a little above the rudder, by means of a screw, one end of which passed quite into the magazine and there operated as a stop upon the movements of the clock, whilst its other end entered the machine. This screw could be withdrawn from the magazine, by which the latter was immediately detached, and the clock commenced going. The clock was set for running twenty or thirty minutes, at the end of which time the lock struck and fired the powder, and in the mean time the adventurer effected his escape.

But the most difficult point of all to be gained was to fasten this magazine to the bottom of a ship. Here a difficulty arose, which, and which alone, as will appear in the ensuing narrative, defeated the successful operations of this warlike apparatus.

Mr. Bushnell's contrivance was this—A very sharp iron screw was made to pass out from the top of the machine, communicating inside by a water joint; it was provided with a crank at its lower end, by which the engineer was to force it into the ship's bottom: this screw was next to be disengaged from the machine, and left adhering to the ship's bottom. A line leading from this screw to the magazine kept the latter in its destined position for blowing up the vessel. . . .

I shall now proceed to the account of the first attempt that was made to destroy a ship of war, all the facts of which, as already stated, I received from the bold adventurer himself.

It was in the month of August 1776, when Admiral Howe lay with a formidable British fleet in New-York bay, a little above the Narrows, and a numerous British force upon Staten Island, commanded by General Howe, threatened annihilation to the troops under Washington, that Mr. Bushnell requested General Parsons of the American army to furnish him with two or three men to learn the navigation of his new machine, with a view of destroying some of the enemy's shipping.

Gen. Parsons immediately sent for Lee, then a sergeant, and two others, who had offered their services to go on board of a fire ship; and on Bushnell's request being made known to them, they enlisted themselves under him for this novel piece of service. The party went up into Long Island Sound with the machine, and made various experiments with it in the different harbors along shore, and after having become pretty thoroughly acquainted with the mode of navigating it, they returned through the Sound; but during their absence, the enemy had got possession of Long Island and Governor's Island. They therefore had the machine conveyed by land across from New-Rochelle to the Hudson River, and afterwards arrived with it at New-York.

The British fleet now lay to the north of Staten-Island, with a large number of transports, and were the objects against which this new mode of warfare was destined to act; the first serene night was fixed upon for the execution of this perilous enterprise, and Sergeant Lee was to be the engineer. After the lapse of a few days, a favorable night arrived, and at 11 o'clock a party embarked in two or three. whale boats, with Bushnell's machine in tow. They rowed down as near the fleet as they dared, when Sergeant Lee entered the machine, was cast off, and the boats returned.

Lee now found the ebb tide rather too strong and, before he was aware, had drifted him down past the men of war. He however immediately *got the machine about*, and by hard labour at the crank for the space of five glasses by the ship's bells, or two and a half hours, he arrived under the stern of one of the ships at about slack water. Day had now dawned, and by the light of the moon he could see the people on board, and heard their conversation. This was the moment for diving: he accordingly closed up overhead, let in water, and descended under the ship's bottom.

He now applied the screw, and did all in his power to make it enter, but owing probably in part to the ship's copper, and the want of an adequate pressure, to enable the screw to get a hold upon the bottom, his attempts all failed; at each essay the machine rebounded from the ship's bottom, not having sufficient power to resist the impulse thus given to it.

He next paddled along to a different part of her bottom, but in this manoeuvre he made a deviation, and instantly arose to the water's surface on the east side of the ship, exposed to the increasing light of the morning, and in imminent hazard of being discovered. He immediately made another descent, with a view of making one more trial, but the fast approach of day, which would expose him to the enemy's boats and render his escape difficult, if not impossible, deterred him; and he concluded that the best generalship would be to commence an immediate retreat.

He now had before him a distance of more than four miles to traverse, but the tide was favourable. At Governor's-Island great danger awaited him, for his compass having got out of order, he was under the necessity of looking out from the top of the machine very frequently to ascertain his course, and at best made a very irregular zigzag track.

The soldiers at Governor's-Island espied the machine, and curiosity drew several hundreds upon the parapet to watch its motions. At last a party came down to the beach, shoved off a barge, and rowed towards it. At that moment, Sergeant Lee thought he saw his certain destruction, and as a last act of defence, let go the magazine, expecting that they would seize that likewise, and thus all would be blown to atoms together.

Providence however otherwise directed it: the enemy, after approaching within fifty or sixty yards of the machine, and seeing the magazine detached, began to suspect a *yankee trick*, took alarm and returned to the island.

Approaching the city, he soon made a signal, the boats came to him and brought him safe and sound to the shore. The magazine in the mean time had drifted past Governor's-Island into the East River, where it exploded with tremendous violence, throwing large columns of water and pieces of wood that composed it high into the air. Gen. Putnam, with many officers, stood on the shore spectators of this explosion.

In a few days the American army evacuated New-York, and the machine was taken up the North River. Another attempt was afterwards made by Lee upon a frigate that lay opposite Bloomingdale. His object now was to fasten the magazine to the stern of the ship, close at the water's edge. But while attempting this, the watch discovered him, raised an alarm and compelled him to abandon his enterprise. He then endeavoured to get under the frigate's bottom, but in this he failed, having descended too deep. This terminated his experiments.

—GRISWOLD, "Letter," *Am. Journal Science and Arts*, II, No. 2, 94-101.

VI. THE NAVAL WAR IN FOREIGN WATERS

Late in 1775 Congress put a little squadron under the command of Esek Hopkins, but it was too weak to operate as a fleet. Hopkins carried out a successful raid on Nassau in March 1776, in which a hundred cannon were captured, but thereafter the United States Navy generally operated in single units whenever a captain could slip out to sea through the British cordon off the American coast. The most damaging blows the American fleet struck were not to the British Navy, however, but to the British merchant marine. In fact, by the end of the war, only two of the seventeen frigates commissioned by Congress remained in service. The others had been burned or captured.

By May 1777, the American Commissioners in France were convinced of the need for stationing American warships in European waters. It was natural that their choice for conducting American naval operations from European ports should fall on Lambert Wickes. As the first captain commissioned by Congress to carry a Continental cruiser across the ocean, Wickes had brought Franklin to France on the Reprisal. *Operating from French bases Wickes raided English shipping. But since war had not yet been declared by France against Great Britain, Vergennes felt constrained to deny Wickes the right to outfit war vessels in French ports on the ground that such acts would constitute a flagrant violation of neutrality. Before Vergennes took that stand Wickes, as the humorous if biased account of a* Reprisal *raid reveals, had caused panic among British merchant shippers.*

1. FRANKLIN AND DEANE: ATTACK THE ENEMY IN HIS HOME PORTS!

American Commissioners in France to Committee of Foreign Affairs of the Continental Congress.

May 26, 1777

We have not the least doubt but that two or three of the Continental frigates sent into the German Ocean, with some lesser swift sailing cruisers, might intercept and seize great part of the Baltic and Northern trade, could they be in those seas by the middle of August, at farthest; and the prizes will consist of articles of the utmost consequence to the States. One frigate would be sufficient to destroy the whole of the Greenland whale fishery, or take the Hudson Bay ships returning. . . .

A blow might be struck that would alarm and shake Great Britain and its credit to the centre. The thought may appear bold and extravagant, yet we have seen as extraordinary events within these two years past as that of carrying the war to our enemy's doors. As it appears extravagant, it would be in consequence unexpected by them, and the more easily executed. The burning or plundering of Liverpool, or Glasgow, would do more essential service than a million of treasure and much blood spent on the continent. It would raise our reputation to the highest pitch, and lessen in the same degree that of our enemy's. We are confident it is practicable, and with very little danger, but times may alter with the arrival of the frigates, yet in that case their cruise on this coast bids fairer to be profitable than any other, and they may at least carry back in safety many of the stores wanted, which is a most capital object, should the other be laid aside.

—WHARTON, ed., *Revolutionary Diplomatic Correspondence*, II, 325-326.

2. LAMBERT WICKES HARRIES BRITISH MERCHANTMEN

Extract of a letter from France, dated March 10, 1777.
Journal of the transactions respecting the Lisbon *packet and four other prizes, after their capture by the* Reprisal, *an American privateer.*

As the curiosity of the public is no doubt a good deal excited to know all that has passed in regard to the five prizes lately brought in by the *Reprisal*, I have endeavoured to procure the most exact information, and the following is an authentic account:

Prizes taken by the Reprisal

Polly and *Nancy*, Kentuluar, from Pool for Cadiz, with about 2000 quintels of dry fish—150 tons.

Hibernia, Jefferson, from Dublin to Lisbon, with wheat and flour—150 tons.

Generous Friends, Duncan, from Orkney to Cadiz, with barley—70 tons.

Swallow packet, with private adventures of the officers, worth 5 or 600 £. (all restored to them)—150 tons.

Betty, Campbell, from Bourdeaux to Londonderry, with 70 tons of wine and brandy—150 tons.

Each captain's private adventure, and all the bedding, cabin furniture, etc., he chose to claim, was restored to him, as were all the seamen's cloaths, except what had been pillaged and stole by the rabble that composed the crew of the *Reprisal*, unknown to Captain Wickes. This must not be attributed to Wickes's own generosity, the captain of the privateer, as I understand his orders from his employers were to that effect. . . .

It is said here (at Paris) that our ambassador, on application at court, was informed that Wickes had been ordered out of port [Port Louis] with his prizes, which (by the bye) he reported as his vessels, forced in by stress of weather; and it is also said, and believed here, that Wickes had found means to elude the orders and was not sailed from L'Orient the 28th ult.

It was also believed that he had found means to make a private sale of all the vessels, and that two of them had actually sailed for L'Orient, but their destination was not known. In case the under-writers should make any objections, on account of the protest not being made out within the limited time, the accounts I have given will show that no time was lost for that purpose. The protests were to be sworn to at the head Admiralty office at Vannes; and the claim to the vessel was to be made then by the captains, after presenting their protests. They all set out for that place the 28th ult. And I have since learned that they arrived the 2d or 3d inst. and part of them are sailed for Jersey, or Guernsey, in their way to England. Captain N—— goes to London and will inform you of any further particulars.

The protests made by the captains of the ships taken and carried into L'Orient by the *Reprisal* mention that vessel as a ship carrying an unknown flag, with thirteen stripes in it and the union at one corner; that when they came on board, they were informed the said vessel was called the *Reprisal*, commanded by Lambert Wickes, who said he had a commission as captain of a man of war from some persons who appear to be a society of people at Philadelphia, calling themselves the Congress; the protests being in French, the words are *une certaine société à Philadelphie, soi-disant le Congrès*.

The packet sailed from Falmouth the 3d of February; she was taken on the 5th, after an engagement of forty minutes. She would by no means have struck so soon, had she not unfortunately taken fire and been for some time in imminent danger of blowing up. The captain and men behaved in the bravest manner; but her force was very unequal, for she carried only eight four-pounders, four two-pounders and some swivels. The privateer carried sixteen six-pounders and ten or twelve swivels, with about three times as many men as the packet. The *Reprisal* had one man killed and two wounded, whereof one was the first lieutenant, who lost an arm. The packet had none killed nor wounded, excepting two sailors scorched with gunpowder, their cartridges having blown up by accident. They were nine days at sea before they could make L'Orient after taking the packet. The passengers and captain of the packet lived in the same manner as Wickes did, and dined at his table. The other captains and inferior officers were also properly treated while on board the privateer.

It appears by another letter that the prizes have been sold at £120,000 French money, the packet excepted, and they are sailed from L'Orient. The privateer is carreening there, but is ordered to depart as soon as possible.

—ALMON, ed., *The Remembrancer for 1776*, Part III, 308-311.

VII. JOHN PAUL JONES

Once war had broken out between France and England the stage was set for far more audacious raids, some of them under the command of that peppery Scotsman John Paul Jones. Paul Jones, as he preferred to be known in America, quickly won a reputation as a ruthless disciplinarian. At least one mutineer was slain by Jones in self-defense, and an incompetent and lazy ship carpenter died when a cat-o'-nine-tails at Jones's direction was too diligently laid on. When, in the course of one of Jones's many cruises, a naval lieutenant named Thomas Simpson "held up to the crew that, being Americans fighting for liberty, the voice of the people should be taken before the captain's orders were obeyed," Jones promptly thrust the exponent of naval democracy into the brig.

Commissioned in December 1775 a lieutenant in the newly organized Continental Navy, Paul Jones quickly distinguished himself by capturing sixteen prizes as commander of the Providence. *By the time of the incident reported below he had already been promoted to a captaincy. This incident occurred on the direct sea lane between the West Indies and London, where Jones had already inflicted punishing blows to British commerce. Next Jones headed for the fishing coast off Nova Scotia, where by the end of a month he was able to report to the Marine Committee of Congress that he had invaded the harbors of Canso and the Island of Madam and effectively destroyed the fisheries at both places, in addition to taking nine ships. "I only left two small schooners and one small brig to convey a number of unfortunate men, not short of three hundred, across the Western Ocean. Had I gone further, I stood chargeable with inhumanity." This expedition was a rehearsal for the daring raids Jones was later to stage along the English coast.*

1. CAPTAIN JOHN PAUL JONES REPORTS ON HIS VICTORIES AT SEA

To Commodore Esek Hopkins.

Providence, at Sea, in N. Lat. 37° 40', and W. Long 54°,
September 4, 1776

. . . And now for my success. I sent in a Nantucket whaler by Captain Grinnell, 27th ultimo. She appeared, by the voluntary testimony of the master, mate, etc., to be the property of rank Tories, who had ordered their oil to be carried to the London market, and the amount of it to be shipped out in English goods to Nantucket. Since that time I have been further to the southward, where I brought to a number of French, Spanish and Danish ships, but saw no Englishmen till the 1st current, when I fell in with five sail. One of them being very large, we took her to be either an old East-Indiaman or a Jamaica three-decker; but she proved to be an English frigate, mounting twenty-six guns upon one deck. She sailed fast and pursued us by the wind till, after four hours' chase, the sea running very cross, she got within musket shot of our lee quarter.

As they had continued firing at us from the first without showing colours, I was angry at this low piece of conduct; therefore, ordered ours to be hoisted and began to fire at them. They then hoisted American colours and fired guns to the leeward. But the bait would not take. Having everything prepared, I bore away across his forefoot and set all our light sails at once, so that before her sails were trimmed and steering sails set, I was almost out of reach of grape and soon after out of reach of cannon shot. Our "hair-bredth 'scape," and the saucy manner of making it, must have mortified him not a little. Had he foreseen this motion and been prepared to counteract it, he might have fired several broadsides while we were within pistol shot. He was a bad marksman and did not hit the *Providence* with one of the many shot which he fired.

I met with no other adventure till last night, when I took the brigantine *Sea-Nymph*, bound from Barbadoes for London with a cargo of two hundred and twenty-seven hogsheads of rum, besides oil, sugar, ginger and Madeira wine.

I understand by this brig that the *Andrew Doria* is off Bermuda, and that

Captain Weeks hath given a trimming to an English sloop-of-war off Martinico. I am much afraid that the storeships come out under convoy; for who would have expected to find a frigate with no more than two ships, a brig and a sloop? . . .

—FORCE, *American Archives*, 5th Series, II, 171-172.

2. JONES CARRIES THE WAR TO ENGLAND

As early as April '78 Paul Jones had been instructed by Franklin to raid the English coast. These instructions he carried out in a sensational manner. Commanding the Ranger, *he struck at Whitehaven on the northwest coast. Although he failed to accomplish his main objective—the destruction of Whitehaven's shipping—he did bring the war home to the British with a vengeance. British newspaper accounts reflected their consternation.*

Whitehaven, April 28, 1778: Late last night or early this morning a number of armed men (to the amount of 30) landed at this place by two boats from an American privateer, as appears from one of the people now in custody. Whether he was left through accident or escaped by design is yet uncertain.

This much has however been proved: that a little after 3 o'clock this morning he rapped at several doors in Marlborough Street (adjoining one of the piers) and informed them that fire had been set to one of the ships in the harbour; matches were laid in several others; the whole world would be soon in a blaze, and the town also destroyed; that he was one belonging to the privateer, but had escaped for the purpose of saving the town and shipping from further destruction.

An alarm was immediately spread, and his account proved too true. The *Thomson*, Captain Richard Johnson, a new vessel and one of the finest ever built here, was aflame. It was low water, consequently all the shipping in the port was in the most imminent danger and the vessel on which they had begun the diabolical work, lying close to one of the steaths, there was the greatest reason to fear that the flames would, from it, soon be communicated to the town. The scene was too horrible to admit of any further description; we shall therefore only add to this part of this alarming story that, by an uncommon exertion, the fire was extinguished before it reached the rigging of the ship, and thus in a providential manner prevented all the dreadful consequences which might have ensued.

The man who remained on shore was examined by the magistrates, merchants, etc., about eight o'clock this morning. The following is the purport of his affadavit:

"*The Ranger* privateer is commanded by John Paul Jones, fitted out at Piscataqua in New England, mounted 18 six-pounders and 6 swivels, but is pierced for twenty guns. She has on board between 140 and 150 men; sailed from Piscataqua for Brest the 1st of November, 1777, arrived at Nantz the 2nd of December. Took in the passage of two brigs, one commanded by Capt. Richards, the other by Capt. Goldfinch.

"Sailed from Nantz for Quiberon Bay, lay there about three weeks ago in which time she has taken one ship from London (having on board General

Irwin's baggage) and sent her to Brest. She also took and sunk a brig loaden with flax-seed, a schooner with barley and oats, and a sloop from Dublin to London in ballast.

"On Sunday or Monday night, from the intelligence she gained by a fishing boat, she sailed into Belfast Lough, with an intent to attack an armed vessel (the *Drake* sloop of war), stood within half gun shot of her, hailed her, and then stood out again."

David Freeman, the person who was examined and gave the above information, says that the name of the commander is John Paul Jones, the First Lieutenant Thompson Simpson, Second Lieutenant Elisha Hall, Sailing-master David Cullen, Lieutenant of Marines Samuel Willingford.

The above John Paul Jones, alias John Paul, it further appears, served his apprenticeship to the sea in a vessel called the *Friendship*, belonging to this port, was afterwards in the employ of some merchants here, latterly had a brig out of Kirkcudbright, and is well known by many people in this town. David Freeman, it is said, has also declared that the said Paul Jones commanded the party which landed here this morning and was himself on shore.

While this infernal business was transacting, the ship laid to with her head to the northward, distant about two miles, until the boats put off to go on board, which was between three and four o'clock. By this time some of the guns at the Half-moon Battery were loaded, two of which were fired at the boats, but without the desired effect. The boats then fired their signal guns and the ship immediately tacked and stood towards them till they got along aside, and then made sail to the north westward.

The incendiaries had spiked most of the guns of both our batteries; several matches were found on board different vessels, and other combustible matter in different parts of the harbour.

It appears that this infernal plan, unprecedented except in the annals of John the Painter,* was laid at Brest, where for a considerable sum of money *Paul* or *Jones* (the latter is only an addition to his name) engaged to burn the shipping and town of Whitehaven; for which purpose he was convoyed through the channel by a French frigate of 38 guns.

A number of expresses have been dispatched to all the capital sea-ports in the kingdom where any depredations are likely to be made; all strangers in this town are, by an order of the magistrate, to be secured and examined: similar notices have been forwarded through the country, etc., and in short, every caution taken that the present alarming affair could suggest.

The privateer is the same ship which chased the *Hussar* cruiser last week, but the cutter or smack did not belong to her.

They took three people away with them, and staid some time in a public house on the Old Quay.

The *Hussar*, Capt. Gurley, and other vessels are sent to different ports in Ireland express with the news.

There has been almost a continual meeting at Haile's coffee-room to-day; a number of men are raising for the defence of the town by subscription, and

---

* The reader has already made the acquaintance of this notorious saboteur.

the forts, guns, etc., it is expected will now be put into proper condition. —*London Morning Post and Daily Advertiser,* April 28, 1778.

3. THE CAPTURE OF THE *Drake*

Following hard upon his daring raid on Whitehaven, Paul Jones crossed the Irish sea and struck on the northern coast of Ireland, capturing the sloop-of-war Drake *inside the harbor of Carrickfergus. In his account to Franklin, Jones reported the action as "warm, close and obstinate," and as lasting an hour and four minutes. The enemy called for quarter after her sails and rigging had been cut to ribbons, her masts shattered, and her hull "very much galled." In prisoners and wounded the British lost some forty men; Jones's* Ranger *suffered three killed and six wounded.*

The chagrined British press attributed the loss of the Drake *to a combination of British naval graft and the fighting spirit of the Americans.*

To the American Commissioners.

May 27, 1778

On the morning of the 24th [April], I was again off Carrickfergus, and would have gone in, had I not seen the *Drake* preparing to come out. It was very moderate, and the *Drake's* boat was sent out to reconnoitre the *Ranger.* As the boat advanced, I kept the ship's stern directly towards her; and though they had a spy-glass in the boat, they came on within hail, and alongside. When the officer came on the quarter deck, he was greatly surprised to find himself a prisoner; although an express had arrived from Whitehaven the night before. I now understood, what I had before imagined, that the *Drake* came out in consequence of this information, with volunteers, against the *Ranger.* The officer told me also, that they had taken up the *Ranger's* anchor. The *Drake* was attended by five small vessels full of people, who were led by curiosity to see an engagement. But when they saw the *Drake's* boat at the *Ranger's* stern, they most wisely put back.

Alarm smokes now appeared in great abundance, extending along on both sides of the channel. The tide was unfavorable, so that the *Drake* worked out but slowly. This obliged me to run down several times, and to lay with courses up, and maintopsail to the mast. At length the *Drake* weathered the point, and having led her out to about mid-channel, I suffered her to come within hail. The *Drake* hoisted English colours, and at the same instant, the American stars were displayed on board the *Ranger.* I expected that preface had been now at an end, but the enemy soon after hailed, demanding what ship it was? I directed the master to answer, "the American Continental ship *Ranger;* that we waited for them and desired that they would come on; the sun was now little more than an hour from setting, it was therefore time to begin." The *Drake* being astern of the *Ranger,* I ordered the helm up, and gave her the first broadside. The action was warm, close and obstinate. It lasted an hour and four minutes, when the enemy called for quarters; her fore and main-topsail yards being both cut away, and down on the cap; the top-gallant yard and mizen-gaff both hanging up and down along the mast; the second ensign which they had hoisted shot away, and hanging on the quarter gallery in the water; the jib shot away, and hanging in the water; her sails and rigging entirely cut to pieces; her masts and yards all wounded, and her hull also very much galled.

I lost only Lieutenant Wallingsford and one seaman, John Dougall, killed, and six wounded; among whom are the gunner, Mr. Falls, and Mr. Powers, a midshipman who lost his arm. One of the wounded, Nathaniel Wills, is since dead; the rest will recover. The loss of the enemy in killed and wounded was far greater. All the prisoners allow that they came out with a number not less than a hundred and sixty men; and many of them affirm that they amounted to a hundred and ninety. The medium may, perhaps, be the most exact account; and by that it will appear that they lost in killed and wounded forty-two men. The captain and lieutenant were among the wounded; the former, having received a musket ball in the head the minute before they called for quarters, lived, and was sensible some time after my people boarded the prize. The lieutenant survived two days. They were buried with the honours due to their rank, and with the respect due to their memory.

The night and almost the whole day after the action being moderate, greatly facilitated the refitting of both ships. A large brigantine was so near the *Drake* in the afternoon that I was obliged to bring her to. She belonged to Whitehaven, and was bound for Norway.

—TAYLOR, *Life and Correspondence of John Paul Jones,* pp. 84-85.

4. THE *Bon Homme Richard* AND THE *Serapis*

The most spectacular episode in the naval annals of the American Revolution was the three-hour battle fought between the old Indiaman, renamed the Bon Homme Richard *in honor of "Poor Richard," the literary pseudonym of the popular American commissioner to France, and the* Serapis, *which occurred on September 23, 1779. After his sensational raids of the spring of that year John Paul Jones put to sea from France in August with a squadron of four vessels, including the* Bon Homme Richard *and the* Alliance, *the latter under the command of the treacherous and unstable French Captain Pierre Landais. Taking a number of prizes, the squadron passed around the north of Scotland, and followed the east coast of England into the North Sea. Jones's crew was motley, his officers were inexperienced Americans. Forced by a gale to postpone a bold plan to seize shipping and extort a ransom from Leith, the port of Edinburgh, Jones made for the open seas and soon sighted a fleet of forty British merchantmen returning from the Baltic under convoy of the* Serapis, *forty-four guns, and the* Countess of Scarborough, *twenty-eight guns. The merchantmen scurried to the safety of the shore batteries, and Paul Jones took on the* Serapis, *although outgunned by forty-four to forty.*

Numerous accounts of that engagement have come down to us, including the reports by both Paul Jones and Captain Richard Pearson, commander of the Serapis. *The two most vivid stories come from the pens of Lieutenant Richard Dale and Midshipman Nathaniel Fanning. The former was stationed on the main deck in command of a battery of 12-pounders and in a comparatively unfavorable position to observe the maneuvers, but he alone reports the immortal reply of Jones to the* Serapis *when asked, "Has your ship struck?" Midshipman Fanning was stationed in the maintop of the ship. The two ac-*

counts supplement each other extraordinarily well. Fanning's is especially full on the latter phases of the action. In addition, Jones put down on paper several accounts of Landais' treachery, which is also corroborated by Lieutenant Henry Lunt in an account originally written in the Serapis' *log after the Americans had taken that ship. In his letter to Franklin, Jones spelled out the charge against Landais. Writing ten days later to Robert Morris, Jones insisted that "the* Alliance *contributed much to the loss of the* Bon Homme Richard *by hitting her between wind and water and under the water." Politics saved Landais from a court-martial at this time, but he was not so fortunate on a later occasion. With the connivance of Arthur Lee and certain French naval officers Landais was left in command of the* Alliance *and made a summer voyage to America in 1780. During that voyage he behaved like a man whose mind was unhinged. He was supplanted in command of the ship after a rising of passengers and officers against him, was court-martialed on reaching Boston, found guilty, and dismissed from the service.*

A. "I HAVE NOT YET BEGUN TO FIGHT!"

Account by Lieutenant Richard Dale.

On the 23d of September, 1779, being below, was roused by an unusual noise upon deck. This induced me to go upon deck when I found the men were swaying up the royal yards, preparatory to making sail for a large fleet under our lee. I asked the coasting pilot what fleet it was?

He answered, "The Baltic fleet under convoy of the *Serapis* of 44 guns and the *Countess of Scarborough* of 20 guns."

A general chase then commenced of the *Bon Homme Richard*, the *Vengeance*, the *Pallas* and the *Alliance*, the latter ship being then in sight after a separation from the squadron of nearly three weeks, but which ship, as usual, disregarded the private signals of the Commodore. At this time our fleet headed to the northward with a light breeze, Flamborough Head being about two leagues distant. At 7 P.M. it was evident the Baltic fleet perceived we were in chace from the signal of the *Serapis* to the merchantmen to stand in shore. At the same time the *Serapis* and *Countess of Scarborough* tacked ship and stood off shore, with the intention of drawing off our attention from the convoy. When these ships had separated from the convoy about two miles, they again tacked and stood in shore after the merchantmen.

At about eight, being within hail, the *Serapis* demanded, "What ship is that?"

He was answered, "I can't hear what you say."

Immediately after, the *Serapis* hailed again, "What ship is that? Answer immediately, or I shall be under the necessity of firing into you."

At this moment I received orders from Commodore Jones to commence the action with a broadside, which indeed appeared to be simultaneous on board both ships. Our position being to windward of the *Serapis* we passed ahead of her, and the *Serapis* coming up on our larboard quarter, the action commenced abreast of each other. The *Serapis* soon passed ahead of the *Bon Homme Richard*, and when he thought he had gained a distance sufficient to go down athwart the fore foot to rake us, found he had not enough distance, and that the *Bon Homme Richard* would be aboard him, put his helm a-lee, which brought the two ships on a line, and the *Bon Homme Richard*, having head way, ran her bows into the stern of the *Serapis*.

We had remained in this situation but a few minutes when we were again hailed by the *Serapis*, "Has your ship struck?"

To which Captain Jones answered, "I have not yet begun to fight!"

As we were unable to bring a single gun to bear upon the *Serapis* our top-sails were backed, while those of the *Serapis* being filled, the ships separated. The *Serapis* bore short round upon her heel, and her jibboom ran into the mizen rigging of the *Bon Homme Richard*. In this situation the ships were made fast together with a hawser, the bowsprit of the *Serapis* to the mizen-mast of the *Bon Homme Richard*, and the action recommenced from the star-board sides of the two ships. With a view of separating the ships, the *Serapis* let go her anchor, which manoeuver brought her head and the stern of the *Bon Homme Richard* to the wind, while the ships lay closely pressed against each other.

A novelty in naval combats was now presented to many witnesses, but to few admirers. The rammers were run into the respective ships to enable the men to load after the lower ports of the *Serapis* had been blown away, to make room for running out their guns, and in this situation the ships remained until between 10 and 11 o'clock P.M., when the engagement terminated by the surrender of the *Serapis*.

From the commencement to the termination of the action there was not a man on board the *Bon Homme Richard* ignorant of the superiority of the *Serapis*, both in weight of metal and in the qualities of the crews. The crew of that ship was picked seamen, and the ship itself had been only a few months off the stocks, whereas the crew of the *Bon Homme Richard* consisted of part Americans, English and French, and a part of Maltese, Portuguese and Ma-lays, these latter contributing by their want of naval skill and knowledge of the English language to depress rather than to elevate a just hope of success in a combat under such circumstances. Neither the consideration of the relative force of the ships, the fact of the blowing up of the gundeck above them by the bursting of two of the 18-pounders, nor the alarm that the ship was sink-ing, could depress the ardor or change the determination of the brave Captain Jones, his officers and men. Neither the repeated broadsides of the *Alliance*, given with the view of sinking or disabling the *Bon Homme Richard*, the fre-quent necessity of suspending the combat to extinguish the flames, which sev-eral times were within a few inches of the magazine, nor the liberation by the master-at-arms of nearly 500 prisoners, could charge or weaken the purpose of the American commander. At the moment of the liberation of the prison-ers, one of them, a commander of a 20-gun ship taken a few days before, passed through the ports on board the *Serapis* and informed Captain Pearson that if he would hold out only a little while longer, the ship alongside would either strike or sink, and that all the prisoners had been released to save their lives. The combat was accordingly continued with renewed ardor by the *Serapis*.

The fire from the tops of the *Bon Homme Richard* was conducted with so much skill and effect as to destroy ultimately every man who appeared upon the quarter deck of the *Serapis,* and induced her commander to order the survivors to go below. Nor even under the shelter of the decks were they more secure. The powder-monkies of the *Serapis,* finding no officer to receive the 18-pound cartridges brought from the magazines, threw them on the main deck and went for more. These cartridges being scattered along the deck and numbers of them broken, it so happened that some of the hand-grenades thrown from the main-yard of the *Bon Homme Richard,* which was directly over the main-hatch of the *Serapis,* fell upon this powder and produced a most awful explosion. The effect was tremendous; more than twenty of the enemy were blown to pieces, and many stood with only the collars of their shirts upon their bodies. In less than an hour afterward, the flag of England, which had been nailed to the mast of the *Serapis,* was struck by Captain Pearson's *own hand,** as none of his people would venture aloft on this duty; and this too when more than 1500 persons were witnessing the conflict, and the humiliating termination of it, from Scarborough and Flamborough Head.

Upon finding that the flag of the *Serapis* had been struck, I went to Captain Jones and asked whether I might board the *Serapis,* to which he consented, and jumping upon the gun-wale, seized the main-brace pennant and swung myself upon her quarter-deck. Midshipman Mayrant followed with a party of men and was immediately run through the thigh with a boarding pike by some of the enemy stationed in the waist, who were not informed of the surrender of their ship.

I found Captain Pearson standing on the leeward side of the quarter-deck and, addressing myself to him, said, "Sir, I have orders to send you on board the ship alongside." The first lieutenant of the *Serapis* coming up at this moment inquired of Captain Pearson whether the ship alongside had struck to him. To which I replied, "No, Sir, the contrary: he has struck to us."

The lieutenant renewed his inquiry, "Have you struck, Sir?"

"Yes, I have."

The lieutenant replied, "I have nothing more to say," and was about to return below when I informed him he must accompany Captain Pearson on board the ship alongside. He said, "If you will permit me to go below, I will silence the firing of the lower-deck guns."

This request was refused, and with Captain Pearson, he was passed over to the deck of the *Bon Homme Richard.* Orders being sent below to cease firing, the engagement terminated, after a most obstinate contest of three hours and a half.

Upon receiving Captain Pearson on board the *Bon Homme Richard,* Captain Jones gave orders to cut loose the lashings, and directed me to follow him with the *Serapis.* Perceiving the *Bon Homme Richard* leaving the *Serapis,* I sent one of the quartermasters to ascertain whether the wheel-ropes were cut away, supposing something extraordinary must be the matter, as the ship

---

* Captain Pearson subsequently stated: "I found it in vain, and indeed impracticable from the situation we were in, to stand out any longer with the least prospect to success. I therefore struck."

would not pay off, although the head sails were aback, and no after sail; the quartermaster, returning, reported that the wheel-ropes were all well, and the helm hard a-port. Excited by this extraordinary circumstance, I jumped off the binnacle, where I had been sitting, and falling upon the deck, found to my astonishment I had the use of only one of my legs. A splinter of one of the guns had struck and badly wounded my leg without my perceiving the injury until this moment. I was replaced upon the binnacle, when the sailing-master of the *Serapis* coming up to me observed that from my orders he judged I must be ignorant of the ship *being at anchor*. Noticing the second lieutenant of the *Bon Homme Richard*, I directed him to go below and cut away the cable, and follow the *Bon Homme Richard* with the *Serapis*. I was then carried on board the *Bon Homme Richard* to have my wound dressed.

—SHERBURNE, *Life and Character of Jones*, pp. 126-129.

B. CAPTAIN PEARSON CRIES OUT, "QUARTERS, FOR GOD'S SAKE!"

Midshipman Nathaniel Fanning's narrative.

... The battle had now continued about three hours, and as we, in fact, had possession of the *Serapis's* top, which commanded her quarter-deck, upper gun-deck and forecastle, we were well assured that the enemy could not hold out much longer, and were momently expecting that they would strike to us, when the following farcical piece was acted on board our ship.

It seems that a report was at this time circulated among our crew between deck, and was credited among them, that Captain Jones and all his principal officers were slain, the gunners were now the commanders of our ship, that the ship had four or five feet of water in her hold, and that she was then sinking. They therefore advised the gunner to go up on deck, together with the carpenter and master at arms, and beg of the enemy quarters, in order, as they said, to save their lives.

These three men, being thus delegated, mounted the quarter-deck, and bawled out as loud as they could, "Quarters, quarters, for God's sake, quarters! Our ship is sinking!" and immediately got upon the ship's poop with a view of hauling down our colours.

Hearing this in the top, I told my men that the enemy had struck and was crying out for quarters, for I actually thought that the voices of these men sounded as if on board of the enemy; but in this I was soon undeceived. The three poltroons, finding the ensign and ensign-staff gone, they proceeded upon the quarter-deck, and were in the act of hauling down our pennant, still bawling for "quarters!" when I heard our commodore say in a loud voice, "What d——d rascals are them?—Shoot them!—Kill them!" He was upon the forecastle when these fellows first made their appearance upon the quarter-deck where he had just discharged his pistols at some of the enemy. The carpenter and the master-at-arms, hearing Jones's voice, sculked below, and the gunner was attempting to do the same when Jones threw both of his pistols at his head, one of which struck him in the head, fractured his skull and knocked him down at the foot of the gang-way ladder, where he lay till the battle was over.

Both ships now took fire again; and on board of our ship it communicated to and set our main top on fire, which threw us into the greatest consternation imaginable for some time, and it was not without some exertions and difficulty that it was overcome. The water which we had in a tub, in the fore part of the top, was expended without extinguishing the fire. We next had recourse to our clothes, by pulling off our coats and jackets, and then throwing them upon the fire and stamping upon them, which in a short time smothered it. Both crews were also now, as before, busily employed in stopping the progress of the flames, and the firing on both sides ceased.

The enemy now demanded of us if we had struck, as they had heard the three poltroons halloo for quarters. "If you have," said they, "why don't you haul down your pendant?" as they saw our ensign was gone.

"Ay, ay," said Jones, "we'll do that when we can fight no longer, but we shall see yours come down the first; for you must know that Yankees do not haul down their colours till they are fairly beaten."

The combat now recommenced again with more fury if possible than before, on the part of both, and continued for a few minutes, when the cry of fire was again heard on board of both ships. The firing ceased, and both crews were once more employed in extinguishing it, which was soon effected, when the battle was renewed with redoubled vigour, with what cannon we could manage, hand grenadoes, stink pots, etc., but principally, towards the closing scene, with lances and boarding pikes. With these the combatants killed each other through the ship's port holes, which were pretty large; and the guns that had been run out at them becoming useless, as before observed, had been removed out of the way.

At three quarters past 11 P.M. the *Alliance* frigate hove in sight, approached within pistol shot of our stern and began a heavy and well-directed fire into us as well as the enemy, which made some of our officers as well as men believe that she was an English man of war. (The moon at this time, as though ashamed to behold this bloody scene any longer, retired behind a dark cloud.) It was in vain that some of our officers hailed her and desired them not to fire any more; it was in vain they were told they had slain a number of our men; it was in vain also that they were told that the enemy was fairly beaten, and that she must strike her colours within a few minutes. The *Alliance*, I say, notwithstanding all this, kept a position either ahead of us or under our stern, and made a great deal of havock and confusion on board of our ship; and she did not cease firing entirely till the signal of recognisance was displayed in full view on board of our ship; which was three lighted lanthorns ranged in a horizontal line about fifteen feet high, upon the fore, main and mizzen shrouds, upon the larboard side. This was done in order to undeceive the *Alliance*, and which had the desired effect, and the firing from her ceased.

And at thirty-five minutes past 12 at night, a single hand grenado having been thrown by one of our men out of the main top of the enemy, designing it to go among the enemy who were huddled together between her gun decks, it on its way struck on one side of the combings of her upper hatchway,* and rebounding from that, it took a direction and fell between their decks, where it communicated to a quantity of loose powder scattered about the enemy's cannon; and the hand grenado bursting at the same time made a dreadful explosion and blew up about twenty of the enemy.

This closed the scene, and the enemy now in their turn (notwithstanding the gasconading of Capt. Parsons [sic]) bawled out "Quarters, quarters, quarters, for God's sake!"

It was, however, some time before the enemy's colours were struck. The captain of the *Serapis* gave repeated orders for one of his crew to ascend the quarter-deck and haul down the English flag, but no one would stir to do it. They told the captain they were afraid of our rifle-men, believing that all our men who were seen with muskets were of that description. The captain of the *Serapis* therefore ascended the quarter-deck, and hauled down the very flag which he had nailed to the flag-staff a little before the commencement of the battle, and which flag he had at that time, in the presence of his principal officers, swore he never would strike to that infamous pirate J. P. Jones.

The enemy's flag being struck, Captain Jones ordered Richard Dale, his first lieutenant, to select out of our crew a number of men and take possession of the prize, which was immediately put in execution. Several of our men (I believe three) were killed by the English on board of the *Serapis* after she had struck to us, for which they afterwards apologized by saying that the men who were guilty of this breach of honour did not know at the time that their own ship had struck her colours.

Thus ended this ever memorable battle, after a continuance of a few minutes more than *four hours*. The officers, headed by the captain of the *Serapis* now came on baord of our ship; the latter (Captain Parsons) enquired for Captain Jones, to whom he was introduced by Mr. Mase, our purser. They met, and the former accosted the latter, in presenting his sword, in this manner: "It is with the greatest reluctance that I am now obliged to resign you this, for it is painful to me, more partciularly at this time, when compelled to deliver up my sword to a man who may be said to fight *with a halter around his neck!*"

Jones, after receiving his sword, made this reply: "Sir, you have fought like a hero, and I make no doubt but your sovereign will reward you in a most ample manner for it."

Captain Parsons then asked Jones what countrymen his crew principally consisted of.

The latter said, "Americans."

"Very well," said the former, "it has been *diamond cut diamond with us.*"

Captain Parsons's officers had, previous to coming on board of our ship,

---

* The hatchways are generally taken off during an action; for this reason, that if anything thrown on board, such as a hand grenado and the like, happens to fall in through the hatchway, it descends down upon the haul-up-deck, where if it bursts it will injure nobody.

delivered their side arms to Lieutenant Dale. Captain Parsons in his conversation with Captain Jones owned that the Americans were equally as brave as the English. The two captains now withdrew into the cabin and there drank a glass or two of wine together. . . .

—FANNING, *Narrative*, pp. 40-45.

C. "FORBEAR FIRING ON THE *Bon Homme Richard!*"

John Paul Jones to Benjamin Franklin.

On Board the Ship *Serapis*, at anchor without the Texel,
in Holland, October 3, 1779

. . . At last, at half-past 9 o'clock, the *Alliance* appeared, and I now thought the battle at an end; but, to my utter astonishment, he discharged a broadside full into the stern of the *Bon Homme Richard*. We called to him: "For God's sake to forbear firing into the *Bon Homme Richard!*" Yet he passed along the off side of the ship and continued firing. There was no possibility of his mistaking the enemy's ship for the *Bon Homme Richard*, there being the most essential difference in their appearance and construction; besides, it was then full moonlight, and the sides of the *Bon Homme Richard* were all black, while the sides of the prizes were yellow. Yet, for the greater security, I shewed the signal of our reconnoissance by putting out three lanthorns, one at the head [bow], another at the stern [quarter], and the third in the middle in a horizontal line. Every tongue cried that he was firing into the wrong ship, but nothing availed. He passed round, firing into the *Bon Homme Richard's* head, stern and broadside; and by one of his volleys killed several of my best men and mortally wounded a good officer on the forecastle.

My situation was really deplorable. The *Bon Homme Richard* received various shots under water from the *Alliance*, the leak gained on the pumps, and the fire increased much on board both ships. Some officers persuaded me to strike, of whose courage and good sense I entertain a high opinion. My treacherous master-at-arms let loose all my prisoners without my knowledge, and my prospect became gloomy indeed. I would not, however, give up the point. The enemy's mid-mast began to shake, their firing decreased, ours rather increased, and the British colors were struck at half an hour past 10 o'clock. . . .

Upon the whole, the captain of the *Alliance* has behaved so very ill in every respect that I must complain loudly of his conduct. He pretends that he is authorized to act independent of my command. I have been taught the contrary; but, supposing it to be so, his conduct has been base and unpardonable. . . . Either Captain Landais or myself is highly criminal, and one or the other must be punished. I forbear to take any steps with him until I have the advice and approbation of your excellency. I have been advised by all the officers of the squadron to put M. Landais under arrest; but, as I have postponed it so long, I will bear with him a little longer until the return of my express.

—SHERBURNE, *Life and Character of Jones*, pp. 116-120.

D. Jones Wins His Greatest Victory Over Again in Lavish Style

[1808]

Midshipman Captain Nathaniel Fanning's narrative.

About the tenth of December [1779] great preparations were made on board of our ship in consequence of a great number of people of the first character in l'Orient—one prince of the blood royal, and three French admirals, with some ladies of the first quality—having had cards of invitation sent them by Captain Jones inviting them on board of his ship the next day to take dinner with him precisely at 3 o'clock in the afternoon, and also informing the company that Captain Jones would, in the evening of that day, on board of his ship exhibit to them a sham sea fight; and that it should in part represent his battle with the *Serapis,* particularly her tops. . . .

First then, all the boats belonging to our ship were busily employed with their respective crews from the time the approaching scene was known on board (which was the day before it was to take place) at ten o'clock in the morning till about twelve at night of the day on which the company were to dine, in passing to, and coming from the shore, bringing off from thence all the articles wanted. And the reader may rest assured that neither cash nor pains were spared in order that the scene every way should appear magnificent.

In a short time our quarter-deck had the appearance of a lady of qualities' drawing room. Overhead was suspended an elegant awning, the edgings of which were cut in scallops and decorated with a variety of silk roses, tassils, etc., from a little below the awnings. At the sides were hung thin canvass lined with pink coloured silk, and which fell down so as to reach the quarter-deck. These sides were hung with a great variety of French pictures and looking glasses; some of the first had been drawn by one of the most finished artists in France, and many of which were quite indecent, especially to meet the eyes of a virtuous woman. However, in these days they were a part of French etiquette on such an occasion. The quarter-deck of our ship was covered with the most elegant carpet. The plate alone which was made use of on this singular occasion was estimated to be worth two thousand guineas. (For my own part I believe it might have been rated at double that sum.)

French cooks and waiters or servants were brought from the shore to assist in this business, and for nearly twenty hours preceeding the serving up of dinner, we were almost suffocated with garlick and onions, besides a great many other stinking vegetables. A French lady (who was said to be a great *connoiseur* in the art of cookery, and in hanging and arranging pictures in a room where the first companies went to dine) was gallanted on board by Captain Jones the evening before the day on which the company were to dine, and was by him directed to take upon herself the superintendance of the approaching feast.

The next day was ushered in by thirteen guns, and the dressing of the ship with the thirteen stripes, and the colours of all nations who were friendly to the United States. Captain Jones and his officers were all dressed in uniform, with their best bib and band on, and we were directed by Captain Jones to conduct ourselves with propriety and to pay implicit obedience to my *lady superintendent* of the ceremonies.

At a quarter before 3 o'clock in the afternoon the ship's boats (three in number, each having a midshipman who acted for this time as coxswain, and the men who rowed the boats were all neatly dressed in blew broad cloth, with the American and French cockades in their hats) were despatched on shore to bring on board the company. Jones received them as they came up the ship's side, and conducted them to their seats on the quarter deck with a great deal of ease, politeness and good nature.

Dinner was served up at half past 3 P.M. The company did not rise from table till a little after the sun set, when Captain Jones ordered his first lieu-tenant to cause all hands to be called to quarters, which was done just as the moon was rising. I of course mounted into the main top, which had always been my station as long as I had served under Jones (of which and the men quartered there, I had the command). Orders were given before we mounted into the tops that we must be well supplied with ammunition, blunder busses, muskets, cowhorns, hand grenadoes, etc., the same as if we were now to en-gage with an enemy; and when the signal was given (which was to be a cannon fired upon the forecastle) . . . the sham fight was to commence.

At 8 o'clock it began, and lasted about an hour and a quarter without any intermission. Such a cracking of great guns, swivels, small arms, cowhorns, blunder busses, etc., such a hissing and popping of hand grenadoes, stink pots, powder flasks was now heard, as they fell into the water alongside, as was never the like in the harbour of l'Orient seen or heard. Some of the ladies were much frightened and the sham fight would have continued longer had it not been that some of them intreated Captain Jones to command the firing to cease. The fight over, a band of music, which had been ordered on board by the commandant, and who had been paraded upon the fore part of the quarter-deck, now played their part, and all was glee and harmony.

At about twelve at night the company took their leave of Captain Jones, and the boats set them safe on shore, in the same order and regularity as they came on board, excepting a few who were landed *half seas over;* these the midshipmen assisted along to their lodgings, and returned on board to give an account to Captain Jones that we saw all the company safe at their respec-tive places of abode.

For several days after this, nothing of any note was to be heard in conver-sation among the French at l'Orient, in their coffee houses and private dwell-ings, but Captain Jones's feast and sham fight. Upon the whole, I believe it must have cost himself, as well as the United States, a vast sum of money. There was certainly a great quantity of powder burnt, and an abundance of wine (besides other liquors) drank. The cost of the whole of this entertain-ment, including the powder, amounted (by an estimate made by the Amer-ican agent's first clerk, and who it seems paid the cash for sundry bills relative to this business) to 3,027 crown at 6s. 8d. each, Massachusetts currency.

Whether Captain Jones charged the whole or any part of the expense of this business to the United States I never learned.

—FANNING, *Memoirs*, pp. 98-100.

VIII. THE *TRUMBULL* AND THE *WATT*

Next to the clash of the Bon Homme Richard *with the* Serapis, *the naval action fought between the Continental frigate* Trumbull, *commanded by Captain James Nicholson, and the British letter of marque* Watt *was probably the severest sea battle of the war, although inconclusive in its results. It took place some two hundred miles north of Bermuda on June 2, 1780. Nicholson wrote his own account on his return to Boston. His adversary, Captain John Coulthard of the British privateer, gave a somewhat different version, but one which in no way reflected on the fighting stamina of either crew. Gilbert Saltonstall, the captain of the marines aboard the* Trumbull, *observed that "there has not been a more close, obstinate, and bloody engagement since the war began. I hope it won't be treason if I don't except Paul Jones. All things considered we may dispute title with him."*

Nicholson was fortunate on this occasion. On August 8, 1781, the Trumbull *on escort duty to a fleet of 28 merchant ships was forced to strike her colors to the British 32-gun frigate* Iris, *formerly the American frigate* Hancock, *captured off Halifax. The* Iris *was supported by two other British ships. The* Trumbull *was badly manned, partly with British prisoners, and most of the crew disobeyed orders at the height of the engagement. Nicholson carried on the fight as long as possible with a crippled ship and a handful of loyal officers and seamen.*

1. A FIERCE ENCOUNTER WITH A BRITISH LETTER OF MARQUE

Account of James Nicholson, captain of the *Trumbull*.

Boston, June 20, 1780

At half past ten in the morning of June 2d, lat. 35. N., long. 64. W. we discovered a sail from the masthead and immediately handed all our sails, in order to keep ourselves undiscovered until she came nearer to us, she being to windward. At eleven we made her to be a large ship from the deck, coming down about three points upon our quarter. At half-past eleven we thought she hauled a point more a-stern of us. We therefore made sail, and hauled upon a wind towards her, upon which she came right down upon our beams. We then took in all our small sails, hauled the courses up, hove the main-top-sail to the mast, got all clear for action, and waited upon her.

At half past eleven we filled the main-top (the ship being then about gunshot to windward of us) in order to try her sailing; also that by her hauling up after us we might have an opportunity of discovering her broadside. She immediately got her main tack out and stood after us. We then observed she had thirteen ports of a side, exclusive of her briddle ports, and eight or ten on her quarter deck and forecastle.

After a very short exhortation to my people they most chearfully agreed to fight her. At twelve we found we greatly outsailed her and got to windward of her. We therefore determined to take that advantage. Upon her observing our intention she edged away, fired three shot at us and hoisted British colours as a challenge. We immediately wore after her and hoisted British colours also. This we did in order to get peaceably alongside of her, upon which she made us a private signal and upon our not answering it she gave us the first broadside, we then being under British colours and about one hundred yards distant. We immediately hoisted the Continental colours and returned her a broadside, then about eighty yards distance; when a furious and close action commenced and continued for five glasses, no time of which we were more than eighty yards asunder and the greater part of the time not above fifty; at one time our yard-arms were almost enlocked. She set us twice on fire with her wads, as we did her once; she had difficulty in extinguishing her's, being obliged to cut all her larboard quarter nettings away.

At the expiration of the above time my first lieutenant (after consulting and agreeing with the second) came aft to me and desired I would observe the situation of our masts and rigging, which were going over the side; therefore begged I would quit her before that happened; otherwise we should certainly be taken. I therefore most unwillingly left her, by standing on the same course we engaged on; I say unwillingly, as I am confident if our masts would have admitted of our laying half an hour longer alongside of her, she would have struck to us, her fire having almost ceased and her pumps both going. Upon our going ahead of her she steered about four points away from us. When about musquet shot asunder, we lost our main and mizen topmast and in spite of all our efforts we continued losing our masts until we had not one left but the foremast and that very badly wounded and sprung. Before night shut in we saw her lose her maintopmast.

I was in hopes when I left her of being able to renew the action after securing my mast, but upon inquiry found so many of my people killed and wounded, and my ship so much of a wreck in her masts and rigging, that it was impossible. We lost eight killed and thirty one wounded; amongst the former was one lieutenant, one midshipman, one serjeant of marines and one quarter gunner; amongst the latter was one lieutenant, since dead, the captain of marines, the purser, the boatswain, two midshipmen, the cockswain and my clerk. The rest were common men, nine of which in the whole are since dead.

No people shewed more true spirit and gallantry than mine did. I had but one hundred and ninety-nine men when the action commenced, almost the whole of which, exclusive of the officers, were green country lads, many of them not clear of their sea-sickness, and I am well persuaded they suffered more in seeing the masts carried away than they did in the engagement. We plainly perceived the enemy throw many of his men overboard in the action, two in particular which were not quite dead; from the frequent cries of his wounded and the appearance of his hull, I am convinced he must have lost many more men than we did and suffered more in his hull. Our damage was most remarkable and unfortunate in our masts and rigging, which I must again say alone saved him; for the last half hour of the action I momently expected to see his colours down, but am of opinion he persevered from the appearance of our masts.

You will perhaps conclude from the above that she was a British man of war, but I beg leave to assure you that it was not then, nor is it now my opinion; she appeared to me like a French East-Indiaman cut down. She fought a greater number of marines and more men in her tops than we did, the whole of which we either killed or drove below. She dismounted two of our guns and silenced two more; she fought four or six and thirty twelve-pounders, we fought twenty-four twelves and six sixes. I beg leave to assure you that let her be what she would, either letter of marque or privateer, I give you my honour that was I to have my choice tomorrow, I would sooner fight any two-and-thirty-gun frigate they have on the coast of America than to fight that ship over again. Not that I mean to degrade the British men of war, far be it from me, but I think she was more formidable and was better manned than they are in general.

—ALMON, ed., *The Remembrancer*, X, 225-227.

2. "MY MEN BEHAVED LIKE TRUE SONS OF OLD ENGLAND"

June 14, 1780

Account of John Coulthard, captain of the *Watt*.

Saw a large ship under the lee bow, bearing N.W. by W., distant about three or four miles; supposed her to be a rebel vessel bound to France and immediately bore down upon her. When she perceived we were standing for her she hauled up her courses and hove to. We then found her to be a frigate of 34 or 36 guns and full of men and immediately hoisted our colours and fired a gun; she at the same time hoisted Saint George's colours and fired a gun to leeward. We then took her for one of his Majesty's cruizing frigates and intended speaking to her, but as soon as she saw we were getting on her weather quarter, they filled their topsails and stood to the eastward. We then fired five guns to bring her to, but she having a clean bottom and we foul and a cargo in, could not come up with her. Therefore, finding it a folly to chace, fired two guns into her and bore ship to the westward; at the same time she fired one gun at us, loaded with grape shot and round, and bore after us. Perceiving this, we immediately hauled up our courses and hove to for her.

She still kept English colours flying till she came within pistol shot on our weather quarter. She then hauled down English colours and hoisted rebel colours, upon which we instantly gave her three cheers and a broadside. She returned it and we came alongside one another and for above seven glasses engaged yard arm and yard arm. My officers and men behaved like true sons of Old England. While our braces were not shot away, we box hauled our ship four different times and raked her through the stern, shot away her main topmast and main yard and shattered her hull, rigging and sails very much. At last all our braces and rigging were shot away and the two ships lay alongside of one another, right before the wind. She then shot a little ahead of us, got her foresail set and run. We gave her t'other broadside and stood after her. She could only return us two guns. Not having a standing shroud, stay or back-stay, our masts wounded through and through, our hull, rigging and sails cut to pieces, and being very leaky from a number of shot under water, only one pump fit to work, the other having been torn to pieces by a twelve-pound shot, after chasing her for eight hours, lost sight and made the best of our way to this port. We had eleven men killed, two more died the next day, and seventy-nine wounded.

—ALMON, ed., The Remembrancer, X, 142-143.

IX. THE *PROTECTOR* AND THE *ADMIRAL DUFF*

In addition to the small and hard-hit Continental Navy, several states raised their own naval forces. These improvised fleets comprised a few deep-sea cruising vessels, but mostly gunboats, barges and other makeshift floating defenses. The chief role of the state forces was to serve as coast defense. An exception to the less formidable ships in the states' naval service was the 26-gun frigate Protector, *launched by Massachusetts in 1779. In one of the fiercest actions of the war the* Protector *on June 9, 1780, sank the 32-gun* Admiral Duff *off the banks of Newfoundland. Luther Little, a midshipman on the Massachusetts frigate, has left a stirring account of this action.*

Narrative of Luther Little.

When the fog lifted, saw large ship to windward under English colors, standing before the wind for us, we being to leeward. Looked as large as a 74. Concluded she was not a frigate. All hands piped to quarters. Hammocks brought and stuffed in the nettings, decks wet and sanded, etc. . . .

We stood on under cruising sail. She tried to go ahead of us and then hove to under fighting sail. We showed English flag. She was preparing for action. We steered down across her stern and hauled up under her lee quarter, breeching our guns aft to bring them to bear. Our first lieutenant hailed from the gangboard. . . .

Our captain [John Foster Williams] ordered broadside and colors changed. She replied with three cheers and a broadside. Being higher, they overshot us, cutting our rigging. A regular fight within pistol range. In a half hour a cannon shot came through our side, killing Mr. Scollay, a midshipman who commanded the fourth 14-pounder from the stern. His brains flew over my face and my gun, which was the third from the stern.

In an hour all their topmen were killed by our marines, sixty in number and all Americans. Our marines killed the man at their wheel, and the ship came down on us, her cat-head staving in our quarter galley. We lashed their jib-boom to our main shrouds. Our marines firing into the port holes kept them from charging. We were ordered to board, but the lashing broke and we were ordered back. Their ship shooting alongside nearly locked our guns and we gave a broadside, which cut away her mizenmast and made great havoc. Saw her sinking and her main topgallant sail on fire, which run down her rigging and caught a hogshead of cartridges under her quarter deck and blew it off.

A charge of grape entered my port hole. One passed between my backbone and windpipe and one through my jaw, lodging in the roof of my mouth and taking off a piece of my tongue, the other through my upper lip, taking away part and all my upper teeth. Was carried to cockpit; my gun was fired only once after. I had fired it nineteen times. Thinking I was mortally wounded, they dressed first those likelier to live. Heard the surgeon say, "He will die."

The *Duff* sunk, on fire, colors flying. Our boats had been injured, but were repaired as well as possible and sent to pick up the swimmers; saved fifty-five, one half wounded. Their first lieutenant confided to me that many were drowned rather than be made captives. Some tried to jump from the boats. Our surgeons amputated limbs of five of them. One was sick with West India fever and had floated out of his hammock between decks. The weather was warm and in less than ten days sixty of our men had it. Among those saved were two American captains and their crews, prisoners on board the *Duff*. One of the American captains told us that Captain [Richard] Stranger [commander of the *Admiral Duff*] had hoped we were a Continental frigate when he first saw us.

—ALLEN, *Naval History of the Revolution*, II, 515-517.

X. THE EXPEDITIONS OF CAPTAIN JOHN BARRY

The Alliance, *which had been under the colorful misdirection of the eccentric Pierre Landais and the legendary John Paul Jones, ended her career with Captain John Barry on the quarter-deck. Barry's most successful cruise started in February 1781, when the* Alliance *sailed from Boston for France, capturing the privateer* Alert *en route. Leaving L'Orient in company with the 40-gun letter of marque* Marquis de Lafayette, *Barry first put down a mutiny ("I believe a ship never put to sea in a worse condition as to seamen," he reported). Then he captured the privateers* Mars *and* Minerva, *and after a hot engagement forced two British brigs, the* Atalanta *and the* Trepassey, *to strike.*

One of the big litigations to clog the docket of the Admiralty Court in Boston and the Court of Appeals in Cases of Capture set up by Congress to handle prize disputes was the issue over the disposition of the captured brig Mars. *A jury in the Boston court awarded the* Alliance *two-thirds of the prize, and gave the remainder to her consort, the French privateer* Marquis de Lafayette. *The French consul insisted on a fifty-fifty split, but this claim was destined to die on appeal. Of special interest in the case are the depositions of the master of the brig* Mars *and of passengers on the* Alliance, *both supporting the claim of Barry and his crew to having played the decisive role in bringing about the capture of the prize.*

To Captain Barry, too, must go the distinction of having fought the last naval action of the war save for some privateering exploits. The Alliance *sailed from L'Orient on December 8, 1782, arrived at Martinique early in January, and found orders to proceed to Havana. Leaving that port in company with the Continental frigate* Duc de Lauzun *he encountered the* Sybille. *John Kessler, mate aboard the* Alliance, *has left us an account of that action.*

1. THE TAKING OF THE PRIZE *Mars*

Deposition of William Ryan, captain of the *Mars*, in *John Barry v. Brig Mars.*

August 25, 1781

I, William Ryan, late sailing master of the brigg *Mars* captured by the *Alliance*, a Continental frigate commanded by John Barry, Esq., do testify and declare that said brigg was British property, and that her owners were some of them in England and some in Guernsey, that she was taken the second day of April, a Domini 1781, being then on a cruise in the Bay of Bisca.

When we struck to the *Alliance*, the French ship, called the *Marquis Fayette,* whom I took to be a merchantman, was in sight, to leward, but not within gun-shot, but making towards us, but did not fire at us till about fifteen minutes after we had struck as afore mentioned, which was as soon as he could bring his guns to bear. I did not see any colours flying on the *Marquis* till after we struck and then saw a white flagg. When the *Marquis* came up with me, by the appearance of the ship I took her to be about thirty guns.

Soon after the *Mars* struck, the *Alliance* threw out a signal, which I supposed was for the *Marquis* to take charge of the *Mars* while the *Alliance* went after another vessel, then in sight, because the *Marquis* on the signal sent a number of hands on board the *Mars,* and the *Alliance* then went after said other vessel. It was about an hour after our striking before the *Marquis's* hands came on board the *Mars,* and about ten of said hands remained on board until her arrival in portage. Then with about eighteen or twenty of the *Alliance's* men there were no officers from the *Marquis.* When the *Marquis's* men came on board the *Mars,* they began to plunder immediately and took from me seven half Jo's, and about forty moidores in a purse from the purser of the *Mars,* broke open chests, took all the slops, spy glasses and wearing apparell, which they carried away from the *Mars;* when they took out the men, being about ninety eight in number, and carried [them] on board the *Marquis.*

It is my opinion that the *Marquis* could not have come up with the *Mars,* unless she had been stopped by the *Alliance,* nor could she have taken the *Mars,* if she had come up with her. The *Mars* mounted twenty twelve, two six and sixteen brass five-pounders and had an hundred and twelve men on board. I did not count the *Marquis's* guns, nor know how many men she had on board. I heard our purser say that she had stores on board to the value of three hundred and fifty pounds sterling.

Deposition of Samuel Bradford in *Barry* v. *Mars.*

I, Samuel Bradford, say that I was a passenger on board the Continental frigate *Alliance;* that a ship called the *Marquiss de la Fayette* loaded with stores for the United States sailed under convoy of said frigate; that on the passage the *Alliance* captured an armed brig called the *Mars,* at which time the *Marquiss de la Fayette* was at the distance of about a mile standing the same course with us; that the *Alliance* hung out a signal for the *Marquiss* to secure the prize, in consequence of which the *Marquiss* came up, took out the prisoners and kept possession of her till Capt. Barry returned, when Capt. B. put on board a prize master, and some sailors belonging to the *Marquiss de la Fayette.* That the *Mars* gave information of having spoke with the preceding day a large ship carrying fifty guns, and that the day after the *Alliance* discovered a large ship. Capt. Barry supposing her to be the ship referred to, ordered the *Marquiss* to haul her wind in order to get out of her way which she readily complied with. Capt. B. then pursued the said ship, which proved to be a Portuguese merchantman. The *Alliance* and *Marquiss* then joined company.

I further testify that the *Alliance* after capturing the *Mars* pursued the brig that was in company with her and captured her likewise. That I heard Mr. Williams of Nantes say that he had chartered the *Marquiss de la Fayette* and in behalf of Dr. Franklin for the United States. That I heard Capt. Barry say when we were bearing down on the Portuguese that should she prove an enemy's ship and superior to himself he would fight her till the *Marquiss* had time to get away. That the *Marquiss* appeared to be mounted with forty guns.

Sworn to in Court August 25, 1781

—Records of the Court of Appeals in Cases of Capture, National Archives.

2. Captain Barry Fights the Last Naval Battle of the War

Account of John Kessler, mate on the *Alliance*.

March 7, 1783

Sailed after taking on board a large quantity of dollars and in company with the Continental ship *Luzerne* of 20 guns, Captain Green, who also had a quantity of dollars on board for Congress. We left the Havana for the United States, after having taken on board between one and two hundred thousand dollars (specie) for Congress.

On the passage one morning when it became light we discovered three frigates right ahead within two leagues of us. The *Alliance* and *Luzerne* hove about and the three frigates gave us chase. The *Alliance* left them and the *Luzerne* fast, and Captain Barry, seeing that they were gaining on the *Luzerne*, we lay by for her to come up. The enemy also immediately lay by. When the *Luzerne* came up Captain Barry told Captain Greene to heave his guns overboard and put before the wind, while the *Alliance* would be kept by the wind that the *Luzerne* might escape. It was not probable that the enemy would attend most to the *Alliance*, and the *Alliance* was out of danger in consequence of her superior sailing. Captain Green threw overboard all his guns but two or three, but instead of bearing away he got on our weather bow. A sail being observed on our weather bow standing towards us, Captain Barry hoisted a signal which was answered, and thereby Captain Barry knew her to be a French 50-gun ship from the Havana, and he concluded to permit the enemy to come up, under the assurance that the French ship would arrive and assist.

Two of the enemy's ships kept at a distance on our weather quarter as if waiting to ascertain about the French ship, while the other was in our wake with topsails only and courses hauled, as was also the case with the *Alliance*. The French ship approaching fast, Captain Barry went from gun to gun on the main deck, cautioning against too much haste and not to fire until the enemy was right abreast. He ordered the main topsail hove to the mast that the enemy (who had already fired a bow gun, the shot of which struck into the cabin of the *Alliance*) might come up as soon as he was abrest, when the action began, and before an half hour her guns were silenced and nothing but musketry was fired from her. She appeared very much injured in her hull. She was of thirty-two guns and appeared very full of men, and after an action of forty-five minutes she sheered off. Our injured was, I think, three killed and eleven wounded (three of whom died of their wounds) and one sail and rigging cut. During all the action the French lay to as well as the enemy's ships.

As soon as the ship which we had engaged hove from us, her consorts joined her and all made sail, after which the French ship came down to us, and Captain Barry asked them why they did not come down during the action. They answered that they thought we might have been taken and the signal known and the action only a sham to decoy him. His foolish idea thus perhaps lost us the three frigates, for Captain Barry's commencing the action was with the full expectation of the French ship joining and thereby not only be able to cope, but in fact subdue part, if not the whole, of them. The French captain proposed, however, giving chase, which was done; but it soon appeared that his ship would not keep up with us, and the chase was given over.

—GRIFFIN, *Commodore John Barry*, pp. 222-224.

CHAPTER TWENTY-FOUR

Privateering

THE REGULAR *Continental Navy never was built up to impressive strength, never engaged in full battle maneuvers, but confined its efforts to convoying ships and to forays upon shipping and single British frigates. These facts, however, do not adequately spell out the offensive power of the Patriots at sea, for the principal naval engagements were fought by privateers, privately owned vessels sailing under licenses (letters of marque) issued by the Continental or state governments. To mount such an offensive was relatively easy. There was a long tradition of privateering in the colonies reaching back to the earliest of the intercolonial wars and burgeoning to impressive strength during the French and Indian War. The fact that fishing off the Great Banks was barred to the Patriots meant that thousands of New England fishermen were unemployed. They preferred privateering to enlisting in the Continental or state naval service, for the rewards were infinitely greater. The profits of privateering went to the owners and the crews, and more than one privateersman became a very rich man as a result of a fortunate cruise. Compared with the rich prizes attainable, the wages of the Continental Navy seemed most unattractive.*

Estimates vary as to the number of ships which were commissioned as privateers, ships often operating but for a single voyage. Congress commissioned some 1,700. But the states probably sent out an even greater number of privateers. Massachusetts alone commissioned 600 vessels, and considerable numbers were commissioned also by Rhode Island, Connecticut, New Hampshire and Delaware, as well as from the Chesapeake and more southerly states. In all, perhaps 2,000 were commissioned by the states. These privateers ranged from under 100 to 500 tons, with as many as 20 guns. The average crew of a privateer was 100 men. Some estimates place the number of seamen engaged in privateering for the Patriots at upwards of 60,000, but these figures doubtless involve a good deal of duplication. Were we to add the total of men aboard privateers to the numbers enlisted in the regular Navy it is probable that the American Navy, public, semipublic and private, drew as many men as the Patriot Army.

As commerce raiders the privateers were far more feared by the British than were the few Continental frigates with their occasional forays. It is estimated that the privateers took in all some 600 prizes worth altogether $18 *million as compared with less than 200 prizes amounting to $6 million credited to the Continental Navy proper. When the Navy dwindled toward the end of the war, privateering expanded in scope and volume.*

It was perhaps not unexpected that Silas Deane and his brother Simeon should have been active in promoting privateering. Shrewd merchants who knew how to combine patriotism and profits, they represented that fraternity of businessmen who combined private interests and public duty. What Simeon Deane wrote about the primacy of Massachusetts was underscored by a letter of James Warren to Samuel Adams of August 15, 1776, in which he wrote:

> *The spirit of privateering prevails here greatly. The success of those that have before engaged in that business has been sufficient to make a whole country privateering mad. Many kinds of West India goods that we used to be told we should suffer for want of, are now plentier and cheaper than I have known them for many years.*

I. BOON OR BANE OF THE REVOLUTIONARY CAUSE?

Privateering offered formidable competition to the Navy, as those responsible for its direction confessed. If seamen were not seduced to join privateering ventures or private voyages, it might be possible, William Vernon of the Eastern Navy Board pointed out to John Adams, to have the Navy make a move in force. Vernon's idea of the ill effects of privateering on the regular Navy were borne out by the letter of William Whipple, New Hampshire's delegate to the Continental Congress, to Josiah Bartlett, a leading New Hampshire Patriot. Some lads like young Andrew Sherburne resisted the lure of privateering and chose the Continental service, but they were a distinct minority in New England.

1. Connecticut Men Ask Congress for Privateering Commissions

Simeon Deane to Silas Deane.

Wethersfield, Connecticut, November 27, 1775

I am desired by a number of gentlemen here to ask, thro' your influence, whether the Congress will grant commission to private adventurers to fit out a privateer or privateers to take British property on this coast, or in the West Indies. I observe that the General Assembly of Massachusetts have commissioned armed vessels on their coast, though we are not told what their limitations (if any) are. In case American privateers are to be allowed to take British property in the West Indies, you are sensible that the first opportunity may be very advantageous, and as well disposed of in this Colony as anywhere, especially as the persons now applying are your good friends and would prosecute the affair immediately.

If you think there is a probability of permission from the Congress, pray attempt it and write me in answer per next post, as those persons desirous of adventuring are very impatient to be informed, and any very considerable delay would perhaps put it out of their power to equip in season. . . .

—Deane, "Correspondence," II, 326.

2. The Lures of Privateering for the Lads of New England

Memoirs of Andrew Sherburne.

... Ships were building, prizes taken from the enemy unloading, privateers fitting out, standards waved on the forts and batteries. The exercising of soldiers, the roar of cannon, the sound of martial music and the call for volunteers so infatuated me that I was filled with anxiety to become an actor in the scene of war. My eldest brother, Thomas, had recently returned from a cruise on board the *General Mifflin,* of Boston, Capt. McNeal. This ship had captured thirteen prizes, some of which, however, being of little value, were burnt, some were sold in France, others reached Boston, and their cargoes were divided among the crew of that ship.

On my brother's return, I became more eager to try my fortune at sea. My father, though a high Whig, disapproved the practice of privateering. Merchant vessels, at this period, which ran safe, made great gains, seamen's wages were consequently very high. Through my father's influence Thomas was induced to enter the merchants' service. Though not yet fourteen years of age, like other boys, I imagined myself almost a man. I had intimated to my sister that if my father would not consent that I should go to sea, I would run away and go on board a privateer. My mind became so infatuated with the subject that I talked of it in my sleep, and was overheard by my mother. She communicated what she had heard to my father. My parents were apprehensive that I might wander off and go on board some vessel without their consent. At this period it was not an uncommon thing for lads to come out of the country, step on board a privateer, make a cruise and return home, their friends remaining in entire ignorance of their fate until they heard it from themselves. Others would pack up their clothes, take a cheese and a loaf of bread and steer off for the army. There was a disposition in commanders of privateers and recruiting officers to encourage this spirit of enterprise in young men and boys. ...

The continental ship of war *Ranger,* of eighteen guns, commanded by Thomas Simpson, Esq., was at this time shipping a crew in Portsmouth. This ship had been ordered to join the *Boston* and *Providence* frigates and the *Queen of France* of twenty guns, upon an expedition directed by Congress. My father, having consented that I should go to sea, preferred the service of Congress to privateering. He was acquainted with Capt. Simpson. On board this ship were my two half uncles, Timothy and James Weymouth. Accompanied by my father, I visited the rendezvous of the *Ranger* and shipped as one of her crew. There were probably thirty boys on board this ship. As most of our principal officers belonged to the town, parents preferred this ship as a station for their sons who were about to enter the naval service. Hence most of these boys were from Portsmouth. As privateering was the order of the day, vessels of every description were employed in the business. Men were not wanting who would hazard themselves in vessels of twenty tons or less, manned by ten or fifteen hands. Placing much dependence on the protection of my uncles, I was much elated with my supposed good fortune, which had at last made me a sailor. ...

Boys were employed in waiting on the officers, but in time of action a boy was quartered to each gun to carry cartridges. I was waiter to Mr. Charles Roberts, the boatswain, and was quartered at the third gun from the bow.
—SHERBURNE, *Memoirs*, pp. 18-20.

3. THE "PERNICIOUS CONSEQUENCES" OF PRIVATEERING

William Whipple to Dr. Josiah Bartlett, both members of the Continental Congress from New Hampshire.

Portsmouth, N. H., July 12, 1778

... As I am happy in agreeing with you in opinion in general, I should be exceedingly glad if there was a coincidence in our sentiments respecting privateering. I agree with you that the privateers have much distressed the trade of our enemies, but had there been no privateers is it not probable there would have been a much larger number of public ships than has been fitted out, which might have distressed the enemy nearly as much and furnished these states with necessaries on much better terms than they have been supplied by privateers?

However, I will not contend with you about the advantages or disadvantages that have been the consequence of that business. All I wish to convince you of is that [it] is *now* attended with the most pernicious consequences, which there would be no need of my undertaking if you were only to pass three months in this or any other town where the spirit for privateering rages with such violence as it does here. No kind of business can so effectually introduce luxury, extravagance and every kind of dissipation that tend to the distraction of the morals of people. Those who are actually engaged in it soon lose every idea of right and wrong and, for want of an opportunity of gratifying their insatiable avarice with the property of the enemies of their country, will, without the least compunction, seize that of her friends.

Thus far I am sure you would agree with me, had you the opportunity before mentioned of making your observations, but perhaps you may say these are evils attendant on this business to society in general. I will allow that to be the case, but then, it must be allowed, they will operate with more violence in this country, in its present unsettled state, than in a country where all the powers of government can be vigorously exercised. But besides these, there are many other mischiefs that attend this business peculiar to these states in our present circumstances. Some of the towns in this state have been obliged to give 400 dollars bounty (per man) to serve three or four months at Rhode Island, exclusive of what is allowed by the state. This is wholly owing to privateering. The farmers cannot hire a laborer for less than 50 or 40 dollars per month, and in the neighbourhood of this town, 3 or 4 dollars per day, and very difficult to be had at that. This naturally raises the price of provision. Indian corn is not to be purchased under 6 dollars per bushel.

There is at this time 5 privateers fitting out here, which I suppose will take 400 men. These must be by far the greater part countrymen, for the seamen are chiefly gone, and most of them in Halifax gaol. Besides all this, you may depend no public ship will ever be manned while there is a privateer fitting out. The reason is plain. Those people who have the most influence with the seamen think it their interest to discourage the public service, because by that they promote their own interest, viz. privateering. In order to do this effectually, every officer in the public service (I mean in the Navy) is treated with general contempt. A man of any feeling cannot bear this; he, therefore, to avoid these indignities, quits the service and is caressed. By this means all the officers that are worth employing will quit the service, and you'll have the Navy (if you think it worth while to keep up that show) officered by tinkers, shoemakers and horse jockeys, and no gentleman worth employing will accept a commission. This you may depend will soon be the case, unless privateering is discouraged, and the business of the Marine in this department more attended to and conducted with more regularity. In short, it would be better to set fire to the ships now in port than to pretend to fit them for sea, for as matters now are (if I am rightly informed and my authority is very good), the public are at an amazing expense to procure men for privateers, for if they (the public ships) get two men one day, they are sure to lose four the next, who take care to carry off with them the advance pay, etc. . . .

—WHIPPLE, "Letter," *Historical Magazine*, VI, pp. 74-75.

4. "THE INFAMOUS PRACTICE OF SEDUCING" SEAMEN OF THE NAVY

William Vernon to John Adams.

Boston, 17th December, 1778

Since my last, we have lost the brig *Resistance* that was given to Capt. Burke. She was sent out as far as Cape-Cod to look for Count de Estaing's fleet that was expected here after the Rhode Island expedition was given up. Missing of them off Cape-Cod, he stood to the southward. The third day, fell in with Lord How's squadron, who captured him.

We have now in this harbour the Continental ships *Warren*, *Providence*, *Boston*, *Queen of France* and *Dean*, the last full manned and ready to sail. The other ships are in great forwardness, may sail in three weeks, if it was possible to get men, which we shall never be able to accomplish unless some method is taken to prevent desertion, and a stopage of private ships sailing until our ships are manned. The infamous practice of seducing our men to leave their ships, and taking them off at an out-port, with many other base methods, will make it impossible ever to get our ships ready to sail in force, or perhaps otherwise than single ships—from which we cannot expect any great matters. Indeed it hath generally proved fatal.

I wish, I hope and pray for [that] an embargo upon all private property, whether armed or merchant ships, may take place through all the United States, until the fleet is compleatly manned. This is the only method, in my opinion, that can be taken. They elude our utmost efforts at present, and at a most enormous expence. It was truly great before you left us, but you can scarsely form an idea of the increase and groath of the extravagance of the people in their demands for labour and every article for sale, etc. Dissipation has no bounds at present. When or where it will stop, or if a reform will take place, I dare not predict.

—VERNON, "Papers," *R. I. Hist. Soc. Pub.*, New Series, VIII, 255-256.

5. "THE WRETCHES LIVE BY PIRACY"

Admiral Rodney to Philip Stephens, Secretary of the Admiralty.

Sandwich off New York, 28th October 1780

The ships I stationed upon the coast have been very successful against the enemy's privateers and ships of war, eleven having been taken since my arrival, and the others obliged to take shelter in their ports.

By the great number of prisoners taken (which amount to upwards of 1400) the rebels will find it extremely difficult to man the Continental ships of war now in the Delaware and at Boston. Their Lordships by the Gazette Extraordinary, which I have the honor to inclose for their perusal, will perceive to what a low state the rebel Navy is reduced, and I am fully persuaded that if their prisoners are not released it will be of the greatest advantage to the commerce of His Majesty's loyal subjects, and the severest blow that can be given to the rebels, whose chief support arises from the piratical captors they make.

The wretches with which their privateers are manned have no principal whatever; they live by piracy and the plunder of their fellow subjects; when they have been released out of humanity to return to their families and live by honest industry, they forget the mercy that has been shown them, and instantly return to renew their acts of piracy.

Since my arrival here I have allowed none of them to be released, and have given notice that till the seven hundred prisoners their Congress owes are liquidated the rebel sailors will be detained in confinement; as with pleasure I can assure their Lordships that very few of the British seamen are in the possession of the rebels.

The great increase of prisoners and the extreme bad condition of the prison ships rendered it necessary to convert the *Jersey* hospital ship into a prison ship, which I hope will meet with their Lordships approbation, more especially as a naval hospital ship (because unfit for that service) [she was] totally useless, and by converting her into a prison ship has saved a considerable expense to Government. . . .

G. B. RODNEY
—RODNEY, *Letter-books*, I, 54-56.

II. SOME PRIVATEERING ADVENTURES

Privateering held all the ordinary risks of a Continental frigate, and one that was extraordinary. There was always the danger that British naval authorities would treat captured privateers as pirates, especially where the vessel seized was commanded by an American who had lately been English or Scot, or where the crew were largely drawn from these nationalities. Seamen switched from the Continental naval service to privateering, then back to Continental or state service, and a considerable number were captured and confined in British prisons.

Some of the risks that privateers took are typified by the engagement of the Yankee Hero, *recounted in the first excerpt below. While making a run from Newburyport to Boston on June 7, 1776, that privateer, with only a*

third of her complement of men, was attacked by an English frigate. Priva-
teersmen often saw the world from the inside of jails. The narrative of Cap-
tain Philip Besom of Marblehead exemplifies the extraordinary risks priva-
teersmen often saw the world from the inside of jails. The narrative of Cap-
Cromwell *chartered out of New London, attests to the fact that Colonel Pres-*
cott's immortal words at Bunker's Hill soon became the common property of
aspiring naval heroes. Joshua Davis, a Boston seaman who was pressed and
served on six ships aboard the British Navy, gives testimony to the iron dis-
cipline imposed by captains of privateers. In this case the captain was a well-
known naval commander, John Manley, who had a series of heartbreaking
adventures of his own and more than his share of hard luck. He had been
obliged to strike the frigate Hancock, *and then lost a privateer, the* Cumberland, *to a British frigate. With other prisoners he escaped from Barbados,*
seized a sloop, and finally reached Boston in April 1779, when the story of the
cruise of the Jason *begins. One of the sensational engagements of the war*
was the capture of the British naval sloop Savage *by Captain George Geddes*
of the Philadelphia privateer Congress. *Captain Charles Stirling, the van-*
quished commander, recounts that episode. The ship he lost was later recap-
tured by the British frigate Solebay.

1. The *Yankee Hero* Strikes to the British Frigate *Melford*

[June 7, 1776]

. . . After some time, the ship thus getting in the wake of the brig, the wind
again came fresh to the westward, upon which the brig hauled to the wind,
in the best angle for the shore. The ship gave chase and in an hour came up
within half a mile, and began to fire her bowchasers, which the brig only
answered with a swivel, Captain Tracy reserving his whole fire until the
ship, keeping a constant fire, came up within pistol-shot upon his lee-quarter,
when the brig gave her the best return they could make from their main and
quarter-deck guns, swivels and small arms, and after that kept up a constant
fire.

The ship was soon up alongside; and with twelve nine-pounders of a side,
upon one deck, besides forecastle and quarter-deck guns, and with her marines overlooking the brig as high as her leading blocks, kept a continual fire.
After some time the ship hauled her wind so close (which obliged the brig to
do the same) that Captain Tracy was unable to fight his lee guns; upon this he
backed under her stern; but the ship, which sailed much faster and worked as
quick, had the advantage, and brought her broadside again upon him, which
he could not evade, and in this manner they lay not a hundred feet from each
other, yawing to and fro, for an hour and twenty minutes, the privateer's men
valiantly maintaining their quarters against such a superior force.

About this time the ship's foremast guns beginning to slack fire, Captain
Tracy slacked under her stern, and, when clear of the smoke and fire, perceived his rigging to be most shockingly cut—yards flying about without
braces, some of his principal sails shot to rags, and half of his men to appearance dying and wounded. Mr. Main, his First Lieutenant, was among the first
wounded, and Mr. Davis, one of the prize-masters, fell in the last attack.

Benjamin Franklin.   Portrait by Duplessis   (*The New York Public Library*)

Robert Morris. Portrait by Charles Willson Peale (*Pennsylvania Academy of the Fine Arts*)

Thomas Paine. Portrait by John Wesley Jarvis (*National Gallery of Art, Washington, D.C.*)

Nathanael Greene. After the original by Charles Willson Peale (*Independence National Historical Park Collection*)

Benjamin Lincoln. After the original by Charles Willson Peale (*Independence National Historical Park Collection*)

Sir Henry Clinton (*The New-York Historical Society*)

Cornwallis. Engraving by G. Stodart from a painting by John Singleton Copley (*Emmet Collection, New York Public Library*)

Tarleton. Engraving by J. R. Smith, after Sir Joshua Reynolds (*The Metropolitan Museum of Art*)

Battle of Germantown: Attack on the Chew House. Engraving by Hinshelwood of painting by Chappel

First Recognition of the American Flag by a Foreign Government. Salute to the U.S.S. *Ranger* in command of John Paul Jones in the harbor of Quiberon, France, February 13, 1778   (*Franklin D. Roosevelt Library*)

The Memorable Engagement of the *Serapis* and the *Bon Homme Richard*. A contemporary engraving by Richard Paten *(Franklin D. Roosevelt Library)*

The Redoubtable John Paul Jones. Captain Jones shoots a sailor who attempted to strike his colors in an engagement. English mezzotint, 1780

Benedict Arnold. Drawn from life
by Du Simetière in Philadelphia

── The Unfortunate DEATH of MAJOR ANDRE ──
(C. Adjutant Generl. to the English Army) at Head Quarters, in New York, Octr. 2.1780.
who was found within the American lines in the character of a Spy.

Engraving by
John Goldar, 1783

The Attack on Fort Moultrie, June 28, 1776 (*Emmet Collection, New York Public Library*)

The Wyoming Massacre. From the painting by Chappel

Storming of Stony Point. "March on, carry me into the Fort, and let me die at the head of the column."—Anthony Wayne. From the original painting by Chappel

Death of Pulaski at Savannah   (*Emmet Collection, New York Public Library*)

Sergeant Jasper Raising the South Carolina Flag on Spring Hill Redoubt, Savannah, October 9, 1779   (*Emmet Collection, New York Public Library*)

Battle of King's Mountain. From the original painting by Chappel

Battle of the Waxhaws (*Emmet Collection, New York Public Library*)

Colonels Washington and Tarleton Clash After the Battle of Cowpens.
From the original painting by Chappel

Marion Crossing the Pedee (*Emmet Collection, New York Public Library*)

The Horse America Throwing His Master. A British cartoon, 1779 (*Library of Congress*)

Surrender at Yorktown. Painting by John Trumbull (*Yale University Art Gallery*)

In this situation they went to work to refit the rigging and to carry the wounded below, the ship having then taken a broad sheer some way off, and none of her guns bearing; but before they could get their yards to rights, which they zealously tried for in hopes still to get clear of the ship, as they were now nearer in shore, or to part from her under the night, she again came up and renewed the attack, which obliged Captain Tracy to have recourse to his guns again, though he still kept some hands aloft to his rigging; but before the brig had again fired two broadsides, Captain Tracy received a wound in his right thigh, and in a few minutes he could not stand. He laid himself over the arm-chest and barricade, determined to keep up the fire, but in a short time, from pain and loss of blood, he was unable to command, growing faint, and they helped him below. As soon as he came to, he found his firing had ceased and his people round him wounded and, not having a surgeon with them, in a most distressed situation, most of them groaning and some expiring.

Struck severely with such a spectacle, Captain Tracy ordered his people to take him up in a chair upon the quarter-deck, and resolved again to attack the ship, which was all this time keeping up her fire; but after getting into the air, he was again so faint that he was for some time unable to speak, and finding no alternative but they must be taken or sunk, for the sake of the brave men that remained he ordered them to strike to the ship (the *Melford,* of twenty-eight guns, John Burr commander).

Thus was this action maintained for upwards of two hours in a low single-decked vessel, with not half the metal the ship had, against an English frigate, whose Navy has been the dread of nations, and by a quarter the number of people in the one as the other. . . .

—FORCE, *American Archives,* 4th Series, VI, 747-748.

2. A MUTINY, A DARING ESCAPE AND THE INSIDE OF A FRENCH JAIL

Captain Philip Besom's narrative of a privateer's life.

In the year 1771, I commenced going to sea, from Marblehead, in the merchant service; and returned from the last voyage, previous to taking any part in the Revolutionary War, immediately after the battle at Concord; at which time, in consequence of an English sloop-of-war being in Marblehead harbor, we proceeded directly to Salem; from which place my father sent the cargo to Andover, where he had removed his family, and left me and one other young man to take care of the vessel. On the 17th of June, 1775, I returned to Marblehead, and, with seventeen more young men, proceeded to Bunker Hill; but, finding it impossible to cross the ferry, returned back to Marblehead.

I then went to Andover and enlisted as a soldier in Captain Abbot's company, which was attached to Colonel Hitchcock's regiment in Roxbury; from which place we were sent to Dorchester Heights, and remained there until the English left Boston.

I then went with my father to Lyndesborough, and remained there until 1777, when I left his house, unknown to any of the family, and went back to Marblehead again, and shipped on board the privateer *Satisfaction* of fourteen guns, Captain John Stevens. We went to sea immediately, and, during that cruise, captured four English ships, one of which carried sixteen guns. On my return from that cruise, I went on board the brig *Fanny*, of fourteen guns, Captain Lee, and captured on the Banks of Newfoundland, after a severe engagement, an English ship of fourteen guns, the captain of which we killed. We destroyed fifteen Newfoundland fishermen, and proceeded to cruise in the channel of England, where we captured a French brig laden with English goods. I was put on board of her as prize-master and succeeded in getting her into Marblehead. The privateer afterwards went on shore in Mount's Bay, and the crew were taken prisoners and sent to Mill Prison.

I then entered on board the ship *Brandywine*, intending to cruise about the shores of Nova Scotia: but, being chased into a harbor by an English sloop-of-war, we were compelled to run our vessel ashore, when one other young man and myself set fire to her and took to the woods in order to make our escape. We travelled about ten miles, then returned to the shore and, finding three whale-boats, took them and succeeded in getting home. I then sailed with Captain St. Barbs from Newburyport for North Carolina. After arriving there, we were blockaded by an English squadron and were obliged to travel home.

I then sailed in the ship *Freemason*, Captain Conway. We captured four vessels. I returned and entered on board the ship *Monmouth* of twenty guns, commanded by Thomas Colyer. We captured four prizes, one of which, loaded with brandy, I was put on board of as prize-master; was taken by an English privateer, and carried to Bristol; from which place I ran away, and succeeded in getting to a town called Kingswood, where I, together with another young man by the name of Thomas Johnson, of Salem, shipped on board an English brig bound to New York. We soon became acquainted with the English sailors, and, after some consultation, agreed to rise upon the officers, take the brig and carry her to Marblehead. When we had sailed as far west as Nantucket Shoals, we did take the brig, and had her in possession two days, when we unfortunately fell in with the English sloop-of-war *Hunter*, bound to New York, with the news of their having destroyed the American squadron at Penobscot. We were retaken, carried to New York in her and put on board a sloop-of-war at Sandy Hook.

News of what we had done was immediately communicated to the commander of the *Russel*, seventy-four—which, together with the Cork fleet, was bound directly to England—[who] gave òrders to have the leaders in the affair brought on board his ship, to be tried for their lives. We were then taken out of irons and went to the boat; viz., myself and an Englishman. We were placed in the stern sheets. The boat's crew consisted of six men, commanded by a lieutenant, assisted by a cockswain. The ship lay at a considerable distance, and the sloop in which we were being to the leeward of them and the wind favorable to our design, as we were going to the seventy-four the Englishman knocked the cockswain overboard; I knocked the lieutenant down, took his pistols and dagger from him and, putting the boat before the wind, made for the shore.

As soon as we landed, we obliged the boat's crew to go before us until we reached a house. We told the man residing there that we were refugees and asked for help. He informed us that Colonel Washington was stationed at Middleton, only four miles' distance, with a regiment. We started off for his quarters, and, on arriving, were taken for spies and placed under guard for three days; after which time, I, together with the young man, w[as] set at liberty and proceeded to Amboy, where Lord Stirling was stationed with a brigade; who generously gave us a good dinner, and forty dollars in money to assist us in getting home.

I then sailed in the ship *Aurora*, of twenty guns, Thomas Colyer, master. We took four prizes; had an engagement with two ships and a brig, in which we lost five or six men, and were obliged to retreat and return home. I then sailed for Guadaloupe, mate of a schooner, and, on returning, was taken and carried to Bermuda, but, in consequence of there being no provisions for us, we had the liberty of going at large. Here we found a ship which we rigged for St. George's, but proceeded to a place about opposite on the same island, called Salt Kettle, where I shipped on board a schooner bound to Turk's Island for a cargo of salt for Halifax. We agreed to take the schooner as soon as we arrived on the coast; but, on our passage to Turk's Island, we were obliged to cut away our masts in a gale of wind in order to save the schooner, and we put for Jamaica. When we arrived off Cape François, we took her and carried her in there; but the governor seized the schooner and caused us to be put in prison, where we remained four days, being obliged to beg of strangers part of a subsistence; when it happened that Colonel Thorndike, having arrived there in a letter of marque, was accidentally passing by. I asked of him some trifle. He inquired the cause of my imprisonment. I informed him; and he, together with some American captains, prevailed on the governor, and we were taken from prison, and sent home in a letter of marque.

I then sailed in the privateer *Montgomery*, of fourteen guns—John Carnes, master—from Salem, to cruise on the West-Indies' coast. We took three prizes, fought a ship of sixteen guns, and had seventeen men killed and wounded; after which we captured a schooner for New York. I came home as prize-master of it.

My next cruise was with the same person, John Carnes, in the ship *Porus*. We captured four prizes. I returned home in one, and proceeded immediately to sea in the letter-of-marque ship *Cato*, Captain John Little, for Virginia. She mounted fourteen guns and had a crew of fifty-seven men and boys. We loaded with tobacco and proceeded to sea; but we had scarcely cleared the capes before we fell in with three English privateers—one of which carried sixteen guns; one, fourteen guns; and a sloop, eight guns. We fought them from two to four, P.M., when they attempted to board us; but, the largest of them having lost a considerable part of their crew, we succeeded—after having our foremast a little below the top, and our mizenmast above the top, cut away—in beating them off; and we continued on our voyage to Nantes, in France, where we arrived without any other trouble. On our return home, we made one prize; but, happening to spring a leak, were compelled to stop at St. Andero [?], in Spain, and repair our vessel. We arrived home in March 1783. . . .

—Besom, "Narrative," *Mass. Hist. Soc. Proc.*, V, 357-360.

3. "Don't Fire Till We Can See the White of Their Eyes"

Timothy Boardman's journal.

April 7th, [*1778*]: The *Defence* had five men broke out with the small pox.

9th: They lost a man with the small pox.

10th: Exersised cannon and musquetry.

11th: Saw a sail. The *Defence* spoke with her. She was a Frenchman from Bourdeaux bound to the West Indies.

13th: Crossed the tropick, shaved and duck about 60 men.

14th: At four oclock afternoon saw a sail bearing E S E. We gave chase to her and came up with her at 8 o'clock. She was a large French ship. We sent the boat on board of her. She informed us of two English ships which she left sight of at the time we saw her.

15th: At day break we saw two sail bareing SE.S distance 2 leagues. We gave chase under a moderate sail. At 9 oclock P. M. came up with them. They at first shew French colours to decoy us. When we came in about half a mile of her they ups with English colours. We had Continental colours flying. We engaged the ship *Admiral Kepple* as follows. When we came in about 20 rods of her we gave her a bow gun. She soon returned us a stern chaise and then a broad side of grape and round shot.

Capt. [Parker] orders not to fire till we can see the white of their eyes. We got close under their larboard quarter. They began another broad side and then we began and held tuff and tuff for about 2 glasses, and then she struck to us. At the same time the *Defence* engaged the *Cyrus,* who, as the *Kepple* struck, wore round under our stern. We wore ship and gave her a stern chase, at which she immediately struck. The loss on our side was one killed and six wounded, one mortally who soon died. Our ship was hulled nine times with six-pound shott, three of which went through our birth, one of which wounded the boatswains yoeman. The loss on their side was two killed and six wounded. Their larbourd quarter was well filled with shott. One nine-pounder went through her main mast. Imployed in the after-noon takeing out the men and maning the prise. The *Kepple* mounted 20 guns, 18 six-pounders and two wooden ditto with about 45 men; the *Cyrus* mounted 16 six-pounders with 35 men: letters of marque bound from Bristol to Jamaica laden with dry goods, paints, etc.

18th: Capt Day died.

19th: Capt Brown of the ship *Admiral Kepple* and Capt Dike of the *Cyrus,* with three ladies and 8 men, sett off in a long boat for St. Kitts on Captains Parker and Smedleys permition.

20th: Imployed in·taking things out of the prize, viz., one chist of Holland, a quantity of hatts and shoes, cheeses, porter and some crockery ware, small arms, pistols, hangers, two brass barrel blunderbusses, a quantity of riggen, etc.

—Boardman, *Log-Book,* pp. 51-53.

4. Captain Manley Finds Privateering as Hazardous as Naval Service

Joshua Davis' narrative.

[1779]

I, Joshua Davis, was born in Boston, in the Commonwealth of Massachusetts, on the 30th of June, 1760. On the 14th of June, 1779, I entered on board of the privateer *Jason*, of 20 guns, commanded by Commodore John Manly, bound on a cruise. About the 25th of the same month, we sailed from Boston to Portsmouth, N. H. in order to take on board Lieutenant Frost and a number of men. We arrived there the next day and, after taking the men on board, put to sea again.

The morning following, the man at the masthead discovered two sail ahead of us. . . . On running nearer them, we supposed them to be enemies, and Lieutenant Thayer advised the captain to heave the ship in stays, to see if they would follow us; to which the captain consented, and we hove the ship about. When they saw this, they hove in stays and gave us chase. We ran back for Portsmouth, and by the time we had got within half a league of the Isle of Shoals, the vessel got within two gun-shot of us.

We perceived a squall coming on to the westward, very fast, and the captain ordered every man to stand by to take in sail. When the squall struck us, it hove us all aback, when we clued down. In ten seconds the wind shifted our sails. In a few seconds more the wind shifted on our starboard quarter and struck us with such force that hove us on our beam ends and carried away our three masts and bowsprit. She immediately righted and the squall went over. The vessels that were in chase of us saw our trouble, hove about, and went off with the squall. We never saw no more of them.

We went to work to strip our masts and to get the sails and rigging on board; when we found one of our men drowned under the foretop-sail. We got up jury-masts and run in between the Isle of Shoals and Portsmouth, where our captain was determined to take our masts in. In a few days Captain Manly went on shore to see to getting the masts on board. While he was gone, Patrick Cruckshanks, our boatswain, Michael Wall, boatswain's mate, and John Graves, captain of the forecastle, went forward and set down on the stump of the bowsprit, and said they would not step the masts in such a wild rodestead, to endanger their lives; but if the ship was taken into the harbour, they would do it with pleasure.

When the captain came on board, he asked Mr. Thayer why the people were not at work, and was told they wished to get into the harbour first.

The captain answered, "I'll harbour them," and stepped up to the sentry at the cabin door, took his cutlass out of his hand, and ran forward, and said, "Boatswain, why do you not go to work?"

He began to tell him the impropriety of getting the masts in where the ship then was, when Captain Manly struck him with the cutlass on the cheek with such force that his teeth were to be seen from the upper part of the jaw to the lower part of the chin.

He next spoke to John Graves, and interrogated, and was answered in a similar manner, when the captain struck him with the cutlass on the head, which cut him so bad that he was obliged ot be sent to the hospital with the boatswain.

The captain then called the other to come down and to go to work. Michael Wall come down to him. The captain made a stroke at him which missed, and while the captain was lifting up the cutlass to strike him again,

Wall gave him a push against the stump of the foremast and ran aft. The captain made after him. Wall ran to the main hatchway and jumped down between decks and hurt himself very much.

The captain then with severe threats ordered the people to go to work. They went to work and stepped the masts, got the topmasts on end, lower yards athwart, top sail yards on the cap, top gallant masts on end, sails bent, running rigging rove, boats on the booms, etc., and all done in the space of 36 hours.

Following the repairs, Manley resumed the cruise. Off Sandy Hook on July 23 the Jason *fell in with two British privateer brigs of sixteen and eighteen guns. Joshua Davis resumes his narrative:*

The enemy hove upon the wind with his larboard tacks on board, run up his courses, hoisted his colours and gave us a broadside. Our captain ordered the sailing master to get the best bower anchor out, so that the bill of it should take into the fore shrouds of the enemy. It was quickly done. The captain ordered the helm hard a-port, which brought us alongside. The anchor caught their fore rigging.

Our captain then said, "Fire away, my boys!"

We then gave them a broadside which tore her off side very much and killed and wounded some of them. The rest all ran below, except their captain who stood on the deck like a man amazed.

Both privateers surrendered and were brought safely into Boston harbor, but off Newfoundland the Jason *was overhauled by a frigate, which cut it to ribbons and forced Manley to take the trumpet and call out for quarters. Manley was sent to Mill Prison, near Plymouth, England, where he remained for more than two years; this was the third and last time he was captured during the war.*

—DAVIS, *Narrative*, pp. 3-12.

5. THE PRIVATEER *Congress* DEFEATS THE NAVAL SLOOP *Savage*

Captain Charles Stirling to Rear Admiral Thomas Graves.

Lancaster, Sept. 23, 1781

It is with the most poignant grief that I acquaint your Excellency of the capture of his Majesty's sloop *Savage*, late under my command, the particulars of which I have the honour to transmit. Early in the morning of the 6th. inst., 10 leagues east of Charles Town, we espied a ship bearing down on us, who, when about four miles distant, hauled her wind to the eastward, shewing, by her appearance, she was an American cruizer. Her force could not be easily distinguished. I therefore gave way to the pleasing idea that she was a privateer, carrying 20 nine-pounders, whom I had intelligence was cruizing off here, and instantly resolved either to bring her to action or oblige her to quit the coast; for which purpose we gave chase, but were prevented continuing it long by her edging down, seemingly determined to engage us.

Conscious of her superiority in sailing and force, this manoeuver coincided with my wishes. I caused the *Savage* to lay by, till we perceived on her nearer approach she was far superior to what we imagined, and that it was necessary to attempt making our escape, without some fortunate shot, in the course of a running fight (which we saw inevitable), admitted our taking advantages and bringing on a more equal conflict. At half past ten she began firing her bow chasers, and at eleven, being close on our quarter, the action commenced with musquetry, which, after a good deal of execution, was followed by a heavy cannonade on both sides.

In an hour's time I had the mortification to see our braces and bowlings shot away, and not a rope left to trim the sail with, notwithstanding every precaution had been taken. However, our fire was so constant and well directed that the enemy did not see our situation, but kept along side of us till accident obliged him to drop astern. The *Savage* was now almost a wreck, her sails, rigging and yards so much cut that it was with the utmost difficulty we could alter our position time enough to avoid being raked, the enemy lying directly athwart our stern for some minutes. This was the only intermission of great guns, but musquetry and pistols still did execution and continued till they opened again, which was not till both ships were almost on board each other, when the battle became more furious than before. Our quarter-deck and forecastle were soon now nearly cleared, scarce a man belonging to either not being killed or wounded, with three guns on our main deck rendered useless.

In this situation, we fought near an hour with only five six-pounders, the fire from each ship's guns scorching the men who opposed them, shot and other implements of war thrown by hand doing execution; when—our mizenmast being shot away by the board; our main mast tottering, with only three shrouds standing; the ship on fire dangerously; only forty men on duty to oppose the foe, who was attempting to board us in three places; no succour in sight, or possibility of making further resistance—I was necessitated at a quarter before 3 P. M. to surrender to the *Congress*, a private ship of war, belonging to Philadelphia, who carried 215 men and mounted 20 twelve-pounders on her main deck and four sixes above, fourteen of which were fought on one side.

She lost during the action eleven men and had nearly thirty wounded, several of them mortally. Her masts, her sails and rigging were so much damaged that she was obliged to return to port, which partly answered my wishes prior to the action, as great part of the Carolina trade was daily expected on the coast, and this privateer we saw sailed remarkably fast. Three days were employed putting her in a condition to make sail, and five for the *Savage*, who was exceedingly shattered. Indeed it is astonishing more damage was not done, as the weather was fine, the water remarkably smooth, and the ships never thirty yards asunder.

The courage, intrepidity and good behaviour of the officers and ship's company I had the honour to command, deserve the highest commendation and my warmest thanks.

—Stirling, "Letter," *Annual Register, 1781,* Appendix.

III. CAPTAIN CONYNGHAM STRIKES AT BRITAIN FROM FRENCH BASES

Some of the most daring and damaging raids upon British shipping were launched by American privateers from French bases. Until her formal entry into the war against Britain, France found these activities a source of some embarrassment. France was willing to aid the United States short of war, but the activities of American privateers operating from her ports was a flagrant violation of her treaty obligation with Great Britain made in 1713 and renewed in 1763, by which she bound herself not to harbor the prizes or privateers of the enemies of Britain, except in real emergencies such as storm or shipwreck, and not to allow private ships of war to be fitted out in her ports. But American privateers, encouraged by Deane and Franklin, constantly fitted out in French ports, and even sold their prizes to French buyers without going through the formality of a condemnation by a French court of admiralty. Vergennes moved to stop these activities only when Lord Stormont, the British ambassador, presented him with a virtual ultimatum. Even then the French embargo was at best temporary. During the year 1777, marine insurance rates in Great Britain rose over twenty per cent, solid testimony to the effectiveness of American privateering. As England stormed and threatened, France backed and filled until she felt the time had come openly to declare war.

The case of Captain Gustavus Conyngham can be technically differentiated from that of Captain Lambert Wickes. The latter had sailed from French ports in a Continental cruiser. The former, though an officer in the Continental Navy, sailed in privateers fitted out in France. His expeditions were partly public and partly private in character. But the British were disinclined to split hairs. Conyngham had been furnished with a blank commission given the American commissioners in France for that purpose and signed by John Hancock as President of Congress. To the British he was not a naval officer but a pirate.

For Conyngham's ventures a lugger was purchased at Dover and sent to Dunkirk, where it was fitted out with armament and crew and named the Surprise. *Conyngham, sailing from Dunkirk, picked up the packet* Prince of Orange *and a brig. His seizures caused an outcry across the Channel. Conyngham was jailed, his lugger confiscated, and his prizes returned. But soon the French ministry, on the intervention of the American commissioners, secured his release. Another vessel, a cutter, was bought and armed for him, partly by private persons, and on the flimsy pretext that he was going on a trading voyage, he sailed on the* Revenge. *This trip was much more successful. Conyngham made several prizes, actually refitted his vessel in an English port, and then eluded the English Navy when his presence became known. Again the British stormed. The French made a characteristic gesture. This time they shipped William Hodge, a Philadelphia merchant and backer of Conyngham, off to the Bastille. After a short time he was released. Silas Deane's account to Congress and Franklin's letter to Ferdinand Grand, a Swiss financier who was close to both the American commissioners and the French government, provide proof, if such were needed, that the American commissioners stood solidly behind Conyngham.*

1. Vergennes Promises the British Ambassador That Privateers Will Not Be Built or Manned in French Ports for Attacks on England

Lord Stormont to Lord Weymouth.

Paris, 16th April, 1777

... I then, my Lord, went to a subject of more importance: I mean the French vessels that are to be manned by French soldiers and commanded by American captains. I told him [M. de Vergennes] that it was more necessary for me to repeat what I had said both to his Excellency and the Monsieur de Maurepas upon this very unpleasant subject, as I found that the number of those vessels increased and that instead of four ships, which my first intelligence mentioned, there would be eight or ten. I added, my Lord, that I did not indeed know the names of these ships nor the ports of France from which they were to sail, but that I did know there was such a design, and was certain that there were several American captains now at Paris who expected the command of those ship and were waiting here till they could be got ready. I likewise informed him, my Lord, that according to my last intelligence those ships are designed not only to cruise in our seas but to insult our coast (I have information which says one of the projects is an attack on Glasgow). I ended with saying that we had, to be sure, little to apprehend from such enterprises, but I begged him to consider what an impression the mere attempt must necessarily make—ships built in France for the use of the rebels, manned with French sailors and commanded by American captains, who sail from the ports of France to insult and attempt to ravage the coast of Great Britain.

I spoke to him, my Lord, very strongly but in the politest and most friendly manner, and went all along upon this supposition: that after the mutual assurances that had passed and the public proofs we meant to give of our pacific intentions, everything that had a contrary tendency must be as disagreeable to this Court as it could be to mine. He readily assented to this, said that if there was any such thing in agitation it should be prevented, *qu'on y mettroit ordre*, and that no such attempt ever should be made from the ports of France, and that they never would suffer their sailors to be so employed.

In a word, my Lord, his promises were as fair as I could wish; but I do not expect the performance to be complete. I see but too plainly that my best endeavours will not prevent these secret succours; but still, my Lord, I shall continue them, as they show we are upon the watch and tend to retard and lessen the evil they cannot remove.

—Barnes and Owen, *Private Papers of the Earl of Sandwich*, I, 221-222.

2. "The French Violate the Laws of Nations"

London, July 4, 1777

The following advertisement appeared in all the daily newspapers:

"New Lloyd's Coffee-house, July 3, 1777.

"the merchants, owners of ships, and insurers, observing that the French, in violation of the laws of nations, have permitted American privateers not

only to bring in British ships and cargoes, but also to sell the same in their
ports in Europe and the West-Indies, many of which privateers, it is well
known, are the property of, and manned by, Frenchmen; and whereas a continuance of such practice must prove ruinous to the commercial interests of
this kingdom, the owners of all such ships and cargoes as have been, or may
be, taken and sold in any of the ports of France or the West Indies are earnestly intreated to send the particulars thereof to Lord Viscount Weymouth,
his Majesty's Secretary of State for the southern department, and also to the
Lords of the Admiralty, in order that Administration may be fully apprised
of the alarming extent of this growing and destructive evil."

For the Remembrancer

The number of our ships taken by the American and French privateers is
truly alarming; and what appears more surprising is that we scarcely ever hear
of any of those privateers being taken, but frequently a number of their trading ships. This circumstance to the intelligent English merchant accounts for
the mystery, viz., in former wars the first object of administration was to
protect our own commerce, then to annoy the enemy's; for which purpose,
besides the proper convoys, a number of our own men of war were ordered
to cruize in the various tracts and latitudes of *our trade*, which effectually
secured it. The residue of our fleet was either employed in squadrons against
the enemy, or in single ships in the latitudes of *their trade*, to destroy it. But
this wise and safe system has been reversed, for the sake of encouraging a few
naval commanders at the expence of the merchants; for our officers are now
at liberty, without any regard to the protection of our trade, to cruize in the
latitudes of the enemy's where they joyfully succeed in taking some prizes.
—ALMON, ed., *The Remembrancer*, (1777), p. 176.

3. THE THAMES IS CROWDED WITH FRENCH SHIPS

Silas Deane's narrative, read before Congress.

[1778 ?]

From Dunkirk, Mr. Hodge fitted out Captain Conyngham in a cutter,
with the design of intercepting a rich packet-boat from Harwich, to destroy
some of the transports carrying over the Hessian troops to England, and to
cruise in the Northern Ocean. Captain Conyngham captured a packet-boat
and, supposing he had intercepted important intelligence, unadvisedly returned into port. He also took a brig on his return. Mr. Hodge came up to
Paris with the letters taken in the packet. Orders were sent from the court
to restore the two prizes, to detain Captain Conyngham's vessel, and to imprison him and his people. These orders were executed; but these expeditions
caused a great sensation to the British commerce; and for the first time since
Britain was a maritime power, the River Thames and others of its ports were
crowded with French and other ships taking in freight, in order to avoid the
risk of having British property captured.

After the alarm had a little subsided, liberty was obtained to send Captain
Conyngham and his people out of France in another vessel. To effect this,
Mr. Carmichael went with Mr. Hodge to Dunkirk, purchased and fitted out a

second vessel well armed against the insults of British cruisers, and ordered Captain Conyngham not to cruise or commit hostilities on the coast of France. Captain Conyngham sailed with the resolution of following his orders, but he had not been long at sea before his people mutinied and obliged him to take prizes. This renewed the alarm in England, occasioned fresh and warm complaints from that side; to silence which, Mr. Hodge was confined in the Bastile for five or six weeks, where he was treated as well as a prisoner could be and suffered in nothing but the confinement, which indeed was sufficiently severe to one of his spirit and feelings.

Captain Conyngham pursued his cruise, sailed round England and Ireland.

—NEESER, *Gustavus Conyngham*, pp. 145-146.

4. CONYNGHAM WILL BE PUNISHED "IF HE HAS BEEN GUILTY OF PIRACY"

Benjamin Franklin to Ferdinand Grand, banker to the American ministers.

Passy, October 14, 1778

I have considered the note you put into my hands containing a complaint of the conduct of Captain Conyngham in the *Revenge* privateer. We have no desire to justify him in any irregularities he may have committed. On the contrary, we are obliged to our friends who give us information of the misconduct of any cruisers, that we may take the occasion of representing the same to our Government, and recommending more effectual provisions for suppressing, punishing, and preventing such practices in future.

By the papers I have the honor to send you enclosed, and which I request you would put into the hands of his excellency Count of Aranda [Spanish Ambassador at Paris], the care of the Congress to avoid giving offense to neutral powers will appear most evident: First, in the commission given to privateers, wherein it appears that sureties are taken of their owners that nothing shall be done by them "inconsistent with the usage and custom of nations," and those sureties are obliged to make good all damages. Courts of admiralty are regularly established in every one of the United States for judging of such matters, to which courts any person injured may apply, and will certainly find redress. Secondly, in the proclamation of Congress, whereby strict orders are given to all officers of armed vessels to pay a sacred regard to the rights of neutral powers and the usage and customs of civilized nations, and a declaration made that if they transgress they shall not be allowed to claim the protection of the States, but shall suffer such punishment as by the usage and custom of nations may be inflicted on them. Lastly, in the particular care taken by Congress to secure the property of some subjects of Portugal (a power that has not been very favorable to us).

All these will show that the States give no countenance to acts of piracy; and if Captain Conyngham has been guilty of that crime he will certainly be punished for it when duly prosecuted, for not only a regard to justice in general, but a strong disposition to cultivate the friendship of Spain, for whose sovereign they have the greatest respect, will induce the Congress to pay great attention to every complaint, public and private, that shall come from thence.

—NEESER, *Gustavus Conyngham*, pp. 146-148.

CHAPTER TWENTY-FIVE

American Diplomats on the Vaunted Scene of Europe

BRINGING FRANCE *into the war was a triumph for American diplomacy, but it was only half the diplomatic battle. American diplomats—never working as a harmonious team—were dispatched to win over Spain, Holland, Prussia and other countries. These countries had stakes in the possible spread of the conflict, and their diplomatic interests did not—as the American plenipotentiaries were to discover to their dismay—coincide with those of the United States. This was notably true of Spain, and, to a varying degree, American diplomats found this to be true in every capital to which they were assigned. As negotiations dragged painfully on, a civil war was metamorphosed into a world war. In 1779 Spain came in on the side of France, rather than on the side of America; the next year England concluded that Holland's violation of neutrality justified a declaration of war. Most of the other nations of Europe formed a League of Armed Neutrality, and England found herself isolated on the diplomatic as on the military front.*

In this chapter we observe the American commissioners in action in Paris, then visit Madrid with Jay, and Amsterdam and Leyden with John Adams. Both diplomats steadfastly defended American interests despite innumerable frustrations. Space does not permit our chronicling the story of Arthur Lee's futile efforts to obtain recognition from the King of Prussia. He received nothing for his pains, but had his confidential papers stolen by the British minister, Hugh Elliott. Arthur's brother, William, was equally unsuccessful in his mission to Vienna. Ralph Izard failed to be received as a commissioner to the Grand Duke of Tuscany, and Francis Dana received no encouragement from Catherine the Great of Russia. Franklin had an apt comment for this futile and humiliating policy of sending missions to countries without any advance indication that such missions would be acceptable. "A virgin state," Franklin dryly observed, "should preserve its virgin character, and not go about suitoring for alliances, but wait with decent dignity for the application of others."

I. THE AMERICAN COMMISSION IS RIDDLED WITH DISSENSION

Unfortunately, the American diplomatic corps was riddled with dissension, and some of the commissioners quickly became the laughingstock of European courts. These indecorous brawls are considered because they had an impact on the course of our diplomacy abroad.

The most notorious of the quarrels was that between Arthur Lee and the hapless Silas Deane. Deane, who came to France in July 1776 as an agent of Congress, was joined in Paris by Arthur Lee and Benjamin Franklin. All three were designated as commissioners to negotiate treaties with European nations. Lee was a trying colleague. Quarrelsome, suspicious, a born trouble-maker, he did not get on with his associates from the start, was disliked intensely and with good reason by the French, and was at least as careless as his colleagues in guarding the secrets of the American mission. Nevertheless, despite his low repute in France, Lee counted on his influential friends in Congress, whom he bombarded with accusations against Deane and Franklin. While Franklin proved invulnerable to attack, Deane was recalled for questioning. The French government, in a gesture of confidence and friendship, sent him back to America on a warship along with the new minister Conrad Gérard. Returning to France in 1780 to adjust his official accounts, Deane deserted the cause of independence and was in communication with Paul Wentworth, a British agent. Letters of Deane advocating peace with Great Britain without independence were published in the New York press, and caused him to be denounced by the Patriots as a renegade. He died abroad, but many years later Congress paid his heirs the sum of $37,000 for expenses incurred by him in carrying out his difficult mission.

Franklin's support of Deane made him the target for attack by Arthur Lee and his faction in Congress. Lee hounded Franklin although he was unable to find anything wrong with his accounts, and made himself a formidable enemy of the French alliance. Arthur Lee's brother William wrote in 1779, "America has struggled to a fine purpose to make a Ben. instead of a Geo. her absolute lord and master."

1. BEAUMARCHAIS EXPLAINS LEE'S HATRED OF DEANE

March 13, 1778

Secret Memoir to the King's Ministers, sent to the Count de Vergennes.

Mr. Arthur Lee, from his character and his ambition, at first was jealous of Mr. Deane. He has ended by becoming his enemy, as always happens in little minds more concerned to supplant their rivals than to surpass them in merit.

Mr. Lee's connections in England and his two brothers in Congress have since made him a prominent and dangerous man. His design has ever been to choose, as between England and France, the power that would most surely promote his fortunes, and he has frequently declared this at his dissolute suppers.

But to succeed, it was first necessary to dispose of a colleague so formidable, because of his intelligence and patriotism, as Mr. Deane. He has succeeded, by rendering him, in many respects, an object of suspicion to Congress.

Having learned that foreign officers demanding commissions were unfavorably regarded by the American Army, he has put the worst construction upon the conduct of his colleagues who sent them, and the behavior of some Frenchmen, slipping over from our (West Indian) islands, justifying perhaps the aversion with which our officers are regarded in America. Mr. Lee has turned these circumstances to his advantage by maintaining to Congress that Mr. Deane, arbitrarily, and in spite of good advice, is responsible for their presence, as costly as it is unprofitable to the Republic.

Moreover, in order to disavow everything that Mr. Deane has done, advantage has been taken of his earlier instructions, which mentioned only commercial matters, and this is today one of the reasons for his recall.

Another reason is the officious zeal displayed by Mr. Lee in continually writing to Congress that all the merchandise and European supplies furnished through the firm of Hortalez were a present from France to America, and that he had been so informed by M. Hortalez himself. Congress, in consequence, has viewed with much mistrust the prices-current, the requests for payment and for purchases to be made, although these were attested and signed by Mr. Deane, as having been entered into with a business firm, and strictly on condition of returns to be sent as soon as possible. Nothing, then, has been easier than for the adroit Lee to blacken the conduct of Mr. Deane, by representing it as the result of underhand measures, contrived to support demands for money in which he expected to share; and this explains the silence, more than astonishing, that Congress has observed in regard to over ten letters of mine full of details.

At present Mr. Deane, overwhelmed with troubles, finds himself rudely and imperatively recalled, and commanded, moreover, to explain his conduct and to vindicate himself from the imputation of numerous faults not mentioned.

Conscious of injustice, Mr. Deane had resolved not to return until Congress should communicate the charges and complaints against him, unwilling, as he said, to deliver himself to his personal enemies without proofs capable of confuting them. But I have persuaded him to change his resolution.

In order fully to understand this recall at a critical moment it is necessary, if I may be permitted to speak frankly, that others should be persuaded, as I am, that England has much to do with the proceedings of Mr. Lee. It is necessary to realize that he has brought his brother, the alderman, from London, that it is through him he maintains his secret correspondence, and that after I had investigated many theories of the means employed by England to keep perfectly informed of everything done in France, I was the more impressed with the idea that Mr. Lee was a two-edged sword, and that within four days of the arrival of letters recalling Mr. Deane and appointing Mr. Adams, Mr. Lee furtively sent his valet de chambre, who set out the day before yesterday, to London.

Why this mysterious message? How does it happen that what passes at Versailles is always so accurately known in London? In what way was the information of the projected treaty instantly conveyed, and with what intent have strenuous efforts been made to corrupt and bribe me to speak, unless, by giving ground for insinuations, to involve me in Mr. Deane's disgrace, and to ruin me at Versailles while he was being ruined at Philadelphia? The expedition of that valet to London upon the news of Mr. Deane's recall explains everything.

Thus it is clear, in my opinion, that while England sends Commissioners to America, and Mr. Lee's relatives and friends exert themselves to render popular a reconciliation between the two countries, there is at the same time an attempt to destroy by slander the influence or the credit of Mr. Deane and myself—the men known to be the most attached to the policy of an alliance between France and America. . . .

—DEANE, *Papers, N.Y. Hist. Soc. Coll.*, XX, 399-406.

2. FRANKLIN TESTIFIES TO DEANE'S PATRIOTISM AND ABILITY

Benjamin Franklin to Henry Laurens, President of Congress.

Passy, near Paris, March 31, 1778

Sir: My colleague, Mr. Deane, being recalled by Congress, and no reasons given that have yet appeared here, it is apprehended to be the effect of some misrepresentations from an enemy or two at Paris and at Nantes. I have no doubt that he will be able clearly to justify himself; but having lived intimately with him now fifteen months, the greatest part of the time in the same house, and being a constant witness of his public conduct, I cannot omit giving this testimony, though unasked, in his behalf, that I esteem him a faithful, active and able Minister, who, to my knowledge, has done, in various ways, great and important services to his country, whose interests I wish may always be, by everyone in her employ, as much and as effectually promoted. . . .

—FRANKLIN, Letter, *N.Y. Hist. Soc. Coll.*, XX, 445.

3. THE AMERICAN NEGOTIATORS TRADE INSULTS

Arthur Lee to Benjamin Franklin.

Chaillot, April 2, 1778

It was with the utmost surprise that I learned yesterday that M. Gerard was to set out in the evening for America in a public character, and that Mr. Deane was to accompany him, without either you or he having condescended to answer my letter of the preceding day. . . .

I trust, Sir, that you will think with me that I have a right to know your reasons for treating me thus. If you have anything to accuse me of, avow it, and I will answer you. If you have not, why do you act so inconsistently with your duty to the public and injuriously to me? Is the present state of Europe of so little moment to our constituents as not to require our joint consideration, and information to them? Is the character of the Court here, and of the person sent to negotiate with our constituents, of no consequence for them to be appraised of? Is this the example, you, in your superior wisdom, think proper to set, of order, decorum, confidence, and justice?

I trust, too, Sir, that you will not treat this letter, as you have done many others, with the indignity of not answering it. Though I have been silent, I have not felt the less the many affronts of this kind which you have thought proper to offer me. . . .

In reply to Lee's letter of April 2, Franklin prepared two drafts. The first he did not send; nor is it clear that he dispatched the second draft, which we reproduce here.

Benjamin Franklin to Arthur Lee.

Passy, April 4th, 1778

Mr. Deane communicated to me his intention of setting out for America immediately as a secret, which he desired I would mention to nobody. I complied with his request. If he did not think fit to communicate it to you also, it is from him you should demand his reasons. . . .

You ask me why I act so inconsistently with my duty to the public. This is a very heavy charge, sir, which I have not deserved. But it is to the public that I am accountable, and not to you. I have been a servant to many publics, through a long life; have served them with fidelity, and have been honored by their approbation. There is not a single instance of my ever being accused before of acting contrary to their interest or my duty. I shall account to the Congress, when called upon, for this my terrible offence of being silent to you about Mr. Deane's and M. Gerard's departure. And I have no doubt of their equity in acquitting me.

It is true that I have omitted answering some of your letters, particularly your angry ones, in which you, with very magisterial airs, schooled and documented me, as if I had been one of your domestics. I saw in the strongest light the importance of our living in decent civility towards each other, while our great affairs were depending here. I saw your jealous, suspicious, malignant and quarrelsome temper, which was daily manifesting itself against Mr. Deane and almost every other person you had any concern with. I, therefore, passed your affronts in silence, did not answer, but burnt your angry letters, and received you, when I next saw you, with the same civility as if you had never written them. Perhaps I may still pursue the same conduct, and not send you these. I believe I shall not, unless exceedingly pressed by you; for, of all things, I hate altercations. . . .

—Bigelow, ed., *Works of Franklin*, VII, 277, 283.

4. Parties and Divisions Have Pernicious Effects

Diary of John Adams.

April 21, 1778 . . . It is with much grief and concern that I have learned, from my first landing in France, the disputes between the Americans in this kingdom: the animosities between Mr. Deane and Mr. Lee; between Dr. Franklin and Mr. Lee; between Mr. Izard and Dr. Franklin; between Dr. Bancroft and Mr. Lee; between Mr. Carmichael and all. It is a rope of sand. I am at present wholly untainted with these prejudices, and will endeavor to keep myself so. Parties and divisions among the Americans here must have disagreeable, if not pernicious, effects. Mr. Deane seems to have made himself agreeable here to persons of importance and influence, and is gone home in such splendor that I fear there will be altercations in America about him. Dr. Franklin, Mr. Deane and Dr. Bancroft are friends. The Lees and Mr. Izard are friends. Sir James Jay insinuated that Mr. Deane had been at least as attentive to his own interest, in dabbling in the English funds and in trade, and in fitting out privateers, as to the public; and said he would give Mr. Deane fifty thousands pounds for his fortune, and said that Dr. Bancroft too had made a fortune. Mr. McCreery insinuated to me that the Lees were selfish, and that this was a family misfortune.

What shall I say? It is said that Mr. Lee has not the confidence of the ministry, nor of the persons of influence here; that he is suspected of too much affection for England, and of too much intimacy with Lord Shelburne; that he has given offence by an unhappy disposition, and by indiscreet speeches before servants and others, concerning the French nation and government—despising and cursing them. I am sorry for these things, but it is no part of my business to quarrel with anybody without cause; it is no part of my duty to differ with one party or another, or to give offence to anybody; but I must do my duty to the public, let it give offence to whom it will.

The public business has never been methodically conducted. There never was, before I came, a minute book, a letter book or an account book; and it is not possible to obtain a clear idea of our affairs.

Mr. Deane lived expensively, and seems not to have had much order in his business, public or private; but he was active, diligent, subtle and successful, having accomplished the great purpose of his mission to advantage.

—ADAMS, ed., *Works of John Adams*, III, 138-140.

5. The New Envoy Takes a Poor View of His Paris Colleagues

John Adams to James Warren, member of the Navy Board for the Eastern Department.

Passy, December 5, 1778

I wish I could unbosom myself to you, without reserve, concerning the state of our affairs here. But you know the danger. The two passions of ambition and avarice, which have been the bane of liberty, and the curse of human kind in all ages and countries, are not without their influence upon our affairs here. But I fancy the last of the two has done the most mischief. Where the carcas is, there the crows will assemble, and you and I have had too much experience of the greediness with which the Continental Treasury has been aimed at by many, to expect that the coffers of the American banker here would not make some mens mouths water. This appetite for the bankers treasures I take to have been the source of most of the altercations and dissentions that have happened here. Your old friend [Arthur Lee] I take to be a man of honor and integrity, yet, to be very frank, he cannot easily govern his temper, and he has some notions of elegance, rank and dignity that may be carried rather too far. He has been of opinion that the public money has been too freely issued here, and has often opposed. The other [Benjamin Franklin] you knew personally, and that he loves his ease, hates to offend, and seldom gives any opinion untill obliged to do it. I know also, and it is necessary you should be informed, that he is overwhelmed with a correspondence from all quarters, most of them upon trifling subjects, and in a mere trifling style; with unmeaning visits from multitudes of people chiefly from the vanity of having it to say they have seen him.

There is another thing which I am obliged to mention. There are so many private families, ladies, and gentlemen that he visits so often and they are so fond of him that he cannot well avoid it, and so much intercourse with accademicians that all these things together keep his mind in such a constant state of dissipation that if he is left alone here, the public business will suffer in a degree beyond description, provided our affairs are continued upon the present footing.

If indeed you take out of his hands the public treasury, and the direction of the frigates and Continental vessells that are sent here, and all commercial affairs, and intrust them to persons to be appointed by Congress, at Nantes and Bourdeaux, I should think it would be best to leave him here alone, with such a secretary as you can confide in.

But if he is left here alone, even with such a secretary, and all maritime and commercial as well as political affairs and money matters are left in his hands, I am persuaded that France and America both will have reason to repent it. He is not only so indolent that business will be neglected; but you know that altho' he has as determined a soul as any man, yet it is his constant policy never to say Yes or No decidedly but when he cannot avoid it, and it is certain in order to preserve the friendship between the two countries the Minister here must upon some occasions speak freely and without reserve, preserving decency and politeness at the same time. Both he and his colleague [Silas Deane], who is or has been lately with you, were, I am sorry to say, in a constant opposition to your old friend, and this misunderstanding was no secret at court, in the city or in the seaport towns, either to French, English or Americans, and this was carried so far that insinuations, I have been told, have been made at Court against your old friend, not by either of his colleagues that I know of, but by somebody or other, emboldened by and taking advantage of the misunderstanding among the three, that he was too friendly to the English, too much attached to Lord Shelburne, and even that he corresponded with his Lordship and communicated intelligence to him. . . .

The other gentleman [Silas Deane], whom you know, I need not say much of. You know his ambition, you know his desire for making a fortune, of promoting his relations; you also know his art and his enterprize. Such characters are often useful, altho always to be carefully watched and controuled, especially in such a government as ours.

There has been so much said among Americans here and in America about his making a fortune by speculating in English funds and by private trade that it is saying nothing new to mention it. Our countrymen will naturally like to know if it is true, and it will be expected of me that I should say something of it. I assure you I know nothing about it. `An intimate friend of his . . . certainly speculated largely in the funds, and some persons suspect that the other was concerned with him. But I know of no proof that he was.

Combinations, associations, copartnerships in trade have been formed here, in which he and his brothers are or have been supposed to be connected, but I know nothing more than you do about them.

But suppposing it was proved that he speculated and traded, the question will arise whether it was justifiable. Neither you nor I should have done it, it is true; but if he did not employ the public money, nor so much of his own time as to neglect the public business, where is the harm? That is the question, and it ought to be remembered that he was here a long time, not as Ambassador, Envoy, Commissioner or Minister, or in any other trust or character from Congress, but merely as an agent for the committees of Commerce and Correspondence. . . .

·This letter is not so free as I wish to write to you, but still it is too free to be used without discretion. You will use it accordingly only for the public good. Knowing the animosity that has been in two against one here, which I believe to have been carried to unwarrantable lengths, knowing the inveteracy of many subaltern and collateral characters, which I think is injurious to the individuals as well as the public, and knowing that you have these things, and will have them, in contemplation and much at heart, I have said thus much of my sentiments upon these subjects, which I hope will do no harm.
—*Warren-Adams Letters*, II, 73-77.

6. Adams Is *Persona Non Grata* to Vergennes

A. Adams: the king did nothing until solicited

John Adams to the Count de Vergennes.

Paris, July 27, 1780

Sir: Since my letter of the 21st, and upon reading over again your Excellency's letter to me of the 20th, I observed one expression which I think it my duty to consider more particularly. The expression I have in view is this: "that the King, without having been solicited by the Congress, had taken measures the most efficacious to sustain the American cause."

Upon this part of your letter, I must entreat your Excellency to recollect that the Congress did as long ago as the year 1776, before Dr. Franklin was sent off for France, instruct him, Mr Deane and Mr Lee to solicit the King for six ships of the line, and I have reason to believe that the Congress have been from that moment to this persuaded that this object has been constantly solicited by their Ministers at this Court. . . .
—Sparks, ed., *Diplomatic Correspondence*, V, 301-302.

B. Vergennes: "i did not expect the animadversion . . ."

Count de Vergennes to John Adams.

Versailles, July 29, 1780

I have received the letter, which you did me the honor to write me on the 27th of this month. When I took upon myself to give you a mark of my confidence by informing you of the destination of Messrs De Ternay and Rochambeau, I did not expect the animadversion which you have thought it your duty to make on a passage of my letter of the 20th of this month. To avoid any further discussions of that sort, I think it my duty to inform you that Mr. Franklin being the sole person who has letters of credence to the King from the United States, it is with him only that I ought and can treat of matters which concern them, and particularly of that which is the subject of your observations.

Besides, Sir, I ought to observe to you that the passage in my letter which you thought it your duty to consider more particularly related only to sending the fleet commanded by the Chevalier de Ternay, and had nothing further in view than to convince you that the King did not stand in need of your solicitations to induce him to interest himself in the affairs of the United States.

—Sparks, ed., *Diplomatic Correspondence*, V, 304-305.

C. Vergennes: Let Congress Judge Whether Adams Is Endowed With a Conciliating Spirit

Count de Vergennes to Benjamin Franklin.

Versailles, July 31, 1780

The character with which you are invested, your wisdom, and the confidence I have in your principles and sentiments, induce me to communicate to you a correspondence which I have had with Mr Adams.

You will find, I think, in the letters of that Plenipotentiary opinions and a turn which do not correspond either with the manner in which I explained myself to him, or with the intimate connexion which subsists between the King and the United States. You will make that use of these pieces which your prudence shall suggest. As to myself, I desire that you will transmit them to Congress, that they may know the line of conduct which Mr Adams pursues with regard to us, and that they may judge whether he is endowed, as Congress no doubt desires, with that conciliating spirit which is necessary for the important and delicate business with which he is intrusted.

—Sparks, ed., *Diplomatic Correspondence*, V, 305-306.

II. MISSION TO SPAIN

Spain felt that France had been too precipitate in allying herself with America. As Charles III's chief minister, Grimaldi, had said earlier in the war, "The rights of all sovereigns to their respective territories ought to be regarded as sacred, and the example of a rebellion is too dangerous to allow of His Majesty's wishing to assist openly." Floridablanca, who succeeded to Grimaldi's post in 1777, distrusted the United States even more than he feared England. Under pressure from Vergennes Spain finally agreed to the secret Convention of Aranjuez of April 12, 1779. Spain was now ready to go to war alongside of France. The bait was Gibraltar, then in British hands. No commitment was made to fight for the independence of the United States. On June 21 Spain, on the pretext that her mediation efforts had been spurned and her territories attacked, declared war against Great Britain.

From time to time Spain had advanced funds to America. In 1776 a million livres were turned over to Beaumarchais to help finance his operations. Small sums were added in the two years that followed. But Spain was understandably anxious about America's objectives which might conflict with her own interests. She feared that America would wrest control of the Mississippi from her and was concerned about the probable southern and western boundaries of the United States. The southern boundary that the Americans wanted clearly conflicted with Spain's claims to Florida, which she had been forced to cede to Great Britain in 1763. Since Spain soon reconquered West Florida the conflict of interest was serious. Spain claimed that the northern boundary of West Florida ran at the latitude of the mouth of the Yazoo River (about 32° 28'), the boundary which Britain had established in 1764. The United States wanted its southern boundary to lie at 31° north latitude. This was a thorny problem in the peace negotiations and in the postwar years.

To secure recognition of the independence of the United States, an effective military alliance, and the concession to America of the right to navigate the Mississippi to the sea, along with a substantial subsidy or loan, John Jay, the New York lawyer Patriot, was sent as diplomatic representative to Madrid.

John Jay was in Spain from January 1780 to May 1782. Except for a small advance of $174,000, which the United States chose to regard as a loan, Jay secured no satisfaction on any of the points at issue between America and France's ally. He refused to barter the Mississippi for a Spanish alliance. He was prepared to yield, at Congress' urging, the right to navigate the lower Mississippi, but withdrew that concession when Spain did not enter into an alliance with America.

To Floridablanca, Jay was disagreeably insistent. As the Spanish minister put it, "His two chief points were: Spain, recognize our independence; Spain, give us more money." Jay's forthright reactions are found in excerpts from some of his own letters written from Madrid.

1. "THE KING AND THE MINISTRY ARE WARM, THE NATION IS COLD"

John Jay to Samuel Huntington, President of Congress.

Madrid, May 26, 1780

The people in this country are in almost total darkness about us. Scarce any American publications have reached them, nor are they informed of the most recent and important events in that country. The affairs of Stony Point, Paulus Hook, etc., etc., had never been heard of here, except perhaps by the great officers of state, and they could scarcely believe that the Roman Catholic religion was even tolerated there.

There are violent prejudices among them against us. Many of them have even serious doubts of our being civilized, and mention a strange story of a ship driven into Virginia by distress, about thirty years ago, that was plundered by the inhabitants, and some of the crew killed in a manner and under circumstances which, if true, certainly indicate barbarity. The King and Ministry are warm, yet I have reason to believe that the bulk of the nation is cold toward us. They appear to me to like the English, hate the French, and to have prejudices against us.

I mention these things to show in a stronger light the necessity of punctuality in sending me from time to time all American intelligence of importance, and observing such conduct towards Spaniards in general as may tend to impress them with more favourable sentiments of us.

—JAY, *Correspondence and Public Papers*, I, 342-343.

2. SPAIN SETS A HIGH PRICE FOR MEAGER AID

John Jay's account of conferences with Don Diego de Gardoqui, financial intermediary between the Spanish Court and the United States, and with

Del Campo, confidential secretary to the Count de Floridablanca, who in turn was official spokesman for the King in the negotiations.

September 3-4, 1780

In the evening M. Gardoqui . . . paid me a visit and pointedly proposed my offering the navigation of the Mississippi as a consideration for aids.

I told him that object could not come in question in a treaty for a loan of one hundred thousand pounds, and Spain should consider that, to render alliances permanent, they should be so formed as to render it the interest of both parties to observe them; that the Americans, almost to a man, believed that God Almighty had made that river a highway for the people of the upper country to go to the sea by; that this country was extensive and fertile; that the General, many officers, and others of distinction and influence in America were deeply interested in it; that it would rapidly settle, and that the inhabitants would not readily be convinced of the justice of being obliged either to live without foreign commodities and lose the surplus of their productions, or be obliged to transport both over rugged mountains and through an immense wilderness, to and from the sea, when they daily saw a fine river flowing before their doors and offering to save them all that trouble and expense, and that without injury to Spain.

He observed that the present generation would not want this navigation, and that we should leave future ones to manage their own affairs, etc.

The next day, that is, the 4th of September, I met M. Gardoqui at M. Del Campo's. After some unconnected conversation, I observed to M. Del Campo that as all the papers between the Minister and myself had passed through his hands, it was unnecessary to give him any information, except what related to the present state of the bills drawn upon me, which I proceeded to state in a short but particular manner.

He replied by making several strictures on the impropriety of drawing bills without previous notice and consent. He remarked that they might with more propriety have been drawn on France, with whom we were allied, and who were richer than they; that the King must first take care of his own people before he could supply us; that Spain had been brought into the war by our quarrel but received no advantage from us; that they had been told of our readiness to assist in taking Pensacola, etc., but instead of aids, he had heard of nothing but demands from us; that our situation was represented as being deplorable, and that the enemy talked of the submission of some of the States, and of negotiations being on foot for that purpose.

Whether this style proceeded from natural arrogance or was intended to affect my temper, I cannot say. In either case, I thought it most prudent to take no notice of it, but proceed calmly and cautiously, and the more so as this was the first time I had ever conversed with this man. I told him in substance, though more at large, that the assurances given Congress of the friendly disposition of Spain by M. Mirales and others had been confided in and had induced Congress to expect the aids in question. That if this application could be called a demand, it was still the first they had made to my knowledge; that men in arms against the enemies of Spain were serving her as well as themselves, and therefore might without impropriety request her aid; that our separation from Britain was an object important to Spain, and that the success with which we had opposed her whole force for six years showed what the power of both, if under one direction, might be capable of; that I knew nothing of Spain's having been drawn into the war by or for us, and that this was not [to] be found among the reasons she had alleged for it; that an attack on Pensacola could not be expected to be made by troops actually employed in repelling the enemy's assaults from their own doors, and that the principles of self-defence would not permit or justify it; that Spain had much to expect in future from our commerce, and that we should be able as well as willing to pay our debts; that the tales told of our despondency and submission resulted from the policy of the enemy, not from fact, and I believed no more of their private negotiations between America and Britain than I did of there being private negotiations between Spain and Britain for a separate peace, which the Minister assured me was not the case. . . .

He . . . then made some reflections on the proposal of a treaty. We agreed perfectly well that mutual interest should be the basis of it, and I added that the good opinion entertained of the King and nation by America was also a pleasing circumstance. He said, however that might be, America did not seem inclined to gratify Spain in the only point in which she was deeply interested. Here followed much common-place reasoning about the navigation of the Mississippi, of which your Excellency has heretofore heard too much to require a repetition. . . .

—JAY, *Correspondence and Public Papers,* I, 394 ff.

3. JAY REFUSES TO SUPPLICATE

John Jay to the President of Congress.

Madrid, November 6, 1780

. . . On Wednesday afternoon, 30th of August, I waited on the [French] ambassador to know the result of the conversation he had promised to have with the minister on our affairs. He did not appear very glad to see me. . . . He said . . . he hoped things would take a more favorable turn; that to his knowledge the minister had been of late much occupied and perplexed with business; that I should continue to conduct the business smoothly, having always in view the importance of Spain, and remembering that we were as yet only rising States, not firmly established or generally acknowledged, etc., and that he would by all means advise me to write the minister another letter *praying* an audience.

I answered that the object of my coming to Spain was to make *propositions,* not *supplications,* and that I should forbear troubling the minister with further letters till he should be more disposed to attend to them. That I considered America as being, and to continue, independent in *fact,* and that her becoming so in *name* was of no further importance than as it concerned the common cause, in the success of which all the parties were interested; and that I did not imagine Congress would agree to purchase from Spain the acknowledgment of an undeniable fact at the price she demanded for it; that I intended to abide patiently the fate of the bills, and should transmit to Congress an account of all matters relative to them; that I should then write the minister another letter on the subject of the treaty, and if that should be treated with like neglect, or if I should be informed that his Catholic majesty declined going into that measure, I should then consider my business at an end, and proceed to take the necessary measures for returning to America; that I knew my constituents were sincerely desirous of a treaty with Spain, and that their respect for the house of Bourbon, the desire of France signified in the secret article, and the favorable opinion they had imbibed of the Spanish nation were the strongest inducements they had to wish it; that the policy of multiplying treaties with European nations was with me questionable, and might be so with others; that for my own part, I was inclined to think it the interest of America to rest content with the treaty with France, and by avoiding alliances with other nations, remain free from the influence of their disputes and politics; that the situation of the United States, in my opinion, dictated this policy; that I knew it to be their interest, and of course their disposition, to be at peace with all the world; and that I knew too it would be in their power, and I hoped in their inclination, always to defend themselves.

The ambassador was at a stand. After a little pause he said he hoped my mission would have a more agreeable issue. . . .

—WHARTON, *Revolutionary Diplomatic Correspondence*, IV, 130-132.

III. JOHN ADAMS DESCENDS UPON THE DUTCH

Looking back upon his mission to the Netherlands, John Adams wrote Jay in July 1782: "I hope in God that your Spanish negotiation has not wrecked your constitution as my Dutch one has mine. I would not undergo again what I have suffered in body and mind for the fee simple of all their Spice Islands. I love them, however, because with all their faults and under all their disadvantages they have at bottom a strong spirit of Liberty, a sincere affection for America, and a kind of religious veneration for her cause."

Unlike the absolute monarchy of France which flamed with enthusiasm for the American cause, the Dutch republic was apathetic, divided, cautious. In the long run French diplomacy and British naval policy created a more favorable climate of opinion in the Netherlands for the cause of the United States. The Amsterdam shippers and merchants, whose highly profitable contraband trade with America via the Dutch island of St. Eustatius in the West Indies was challenged by the British Navy, put the pressure on the Dutch government, which finally decided to convoy their merchant ships. The British regarded this as a violation of old treaty commitments, and declared war late in 1780. The pretext was the seizure of dispatches that Henry Laurens was carrying when he was captured by the British indicating that the Dutch had been negotiating with the United States. The Dutch Navy was not built up rapidly enough to ward off serious blows upon her commerce inflicted by the British fleet, which wiped out the clandestine trade between the United States and St. Eustatius.

The issue of the freedom of the seas and the rights of neutrals impelled Catherine the Great of Russia to organize, in February 1780, a League of Armed Neutrality, which Denmark, Sweden, the Netherlands, Prussia, Portugal, Austria and the Kingdom of the Two Sicilies joined in the next two years.

Great Britain had to reshape her naval activities and was now diplomatically isolated. It was a triumph for Vergennes that John Adams was quick to exploit.

Adams, who had already done some effective propaganda work for the American cause in Holland, arranged a loan of ten million livres which was guaranteed by France, secured recognition as minister plenipotentiary, and negotiated a substantial loan directly with a consortium of Dutch bankers. He topped it off with a treaty of commerce and friendship, which he signed in October 1782. "One thing, thank God, is certain," Adams wrote to his friend James Warren: "I have planted the American standard at the Hague."

1. The Dutch Know Nothing of the American Cause

John Adams to Samuel Huntington.

Amsterdam, September 25, 1780

There are persons in this republic who have been attentive to this war, and who know somewhat of the history of the rise and progress of the United States of America; but it is surprising that the number should be so small. Even in the city of Amsterdam, which is the most attentive to our affairs and the best inclined towards us, there are few persons who do not consider the American resistance as a desultory rage of a few enthusiasts, without order, discipline, law or government. There are scarcely any who have an adequate idea of the numbers, the increasing population or the growing commerce of America.

Upon my arrival here some gentlemen were inquisitive about our governments. I asked if they had seen them in print, and was answered no. Upon this I made it my business to search in all the booksellers' shops for the collection of them which was published in French two or three years ago, but could find only two copies, which I presented to the gentlemen who made the inquiry. Nothing would serve our cause more than having a complete edition of the American constitutions correctly printed in English by order of Congress and sent to Europe, as well as sold in America. The Rhode Island and Connecticut constitutions ought not to be omitted, although they have undergone no alteration; and it would be proper to print the Confederation in the same volume. This work would be read by everybody in Europe who reads English and could obtain it, and some would even learn English for the sake of reading it; it would be translated into every language of Europe, and would fix the opinion of our unconquerability more than anything could, except driving the enemy wholly from the United States.

There has been nobody here of sufficient information and consideration to turn the attention of the public towards our affairs, to communicate from time to time with the public, in a language that is understood, intelligence from America, France, England, etc.; but, on the contrary, there have been persons enough employed and well paid by our enemies to propagate misinformation, misrepresentation and abuse.

The ancient and intimate connection between the houses of Orange and Brunswick, the family alliances and the vast advantages which the princes of Orange have derived from them in erecting, establishing and at last perpetuating the stadtholderate against the inclination of the Republican party, and the reliance which this family still has upon the same connection to support it, have attached the executive power of this government in such a manner to England that nothing but necessity could cause a separation. On the contrary, the Republican party, which has heretofore been conducted by Barnevelt, Grotius, the De Witts and other immortal patriots, have ever leaned towards an alliance with France, because she has ever favored the republican form of government in this nation. All parties, however, agree that England has been ever jealous and envious of the Dutch commerce, and done it great injuries; that this country is more in the power of France, if she were hostile, than of England; and that her trade with France is of vastly greater value than that with England. Yet England has more influence here than France. The Dutch—some of them, at least—now see another commercial and maritime power arising that it is their interest to form an early connection with. All parties here see that it is not their interest that France and Spain should secure too many advantages in America and too great a share of her commerce, and especially in the fisheries in her seas. All parties, too, see that it would be dangerous to the commerce, and even independence, of the United Provinces to have America again under the dominion of England; and the Republicans see, or think they see, that a change in this government and the loss of their liberties would be the consequence of it too.

Amidst all these conflicts of interest and parties and all these speculations the British ambassador, with his swarms of agents, are busily employed in propagating reports, in which they are much assisted by those who are called here stadtholderians, and there has been nobody to contradict or explain anything. This should be the business in part of a minister plenipotentiary. Such a minister, however, would not have it in his power to do it effectually without frequent and constant information from Congress. At present this nation is so ignorant of the strength, resources, commerce and constitution of America; it has so false and exaggerated an imagination of the power of England; it has so many doubts of our final success; so many suspicions of our falling finally into the hands of France and Spain; so many jealousies that France and Spain will abandon us or that we shall abandon them; so many fears of offending the English ministry, the English ambassador, the great mercantile houses that are very profitably employed by both, and, above all, the stadtholder and his friends, that even a loan of money will meet with every obstruction and discouragement possible. These chimeras, and many more, are held up to people here, and influence men's minds and conduct to such a degree that no man dares openly and publicly to disregard them.

—WHARTON, ed., *Revolutionary Diplomatic Correspondence*, IV, 67-69.

2. ADAMS DESCRIBES HIS DIFFICULTIES IN RAISING A DUTCH LOAN

John Adams to the President of Congress.

Leyden, 19 March, 1781

I have experienced since my residence in this republic a great change in the external behavior of several persons of rank, who, upon my first arrival, received me with distinction, but, from the moment of the publication of the papers taken with Mr. Laurens, have been afraid to see me. The nation has indeed been in a violent fermentation and crisis. It is divided in sentiments. There are stadtholderians and republicans; there are proprietors in English funds, and persons immediately engaged in commerce; there are enthusiasts for peace and alliance with France, Spain and America; and there is a third sort who are for adhering in all things to Russia, Sweden and Denmark; some are for acknowledging American independence and entering into treaties of commerce and alliance with her; others start at the idea with horror, as an everlasting impediment to a return to the friendship and alliance with England; some will not augment the Navy without increasing the Army; others will let the Navy be neglected rather than augment the Army.

In this perfect chaos of sentiments and systems, principles and interests, it is no wonder there is a languor, a weakness and irresolution that is vastly dangerous in the present circumstances of affairs. The danger lies not more in the hostile designs and exertions of the English than in the prospect of seditions and commotions among the people, which are every day dreaded and expected. If it were not for a standing Army and troops posted about in several cities, it is probable there would have been popular tumults before now; but everybody that I see appears to me to live in constant fear of mobs and in a great degree of uncertainty whether they will rise in favor of war or against it, in favor of England or against it, in favor of the Prince or of the city of Amsterdam, in favor of America or against it.

I have ventured, in the midst of these critical circumstances, pressed as I am to get money to discharge the bills of exchange which Congress have drawn and I have accepted, to open a loan; but this is looked upon as a very hardy and dangerous measure, which nobody but an American would have risked, and I am obliged to assure Congress that people are as yet so much afraid of being pointed out by the mob or the soldiery as favorers of this loan that I have no hopes at all of succeeding for several months, if ever.

—ADAMS, ed., *Works of John Adams*, VII, 380-381.

CHAPTER TWENTY-SIX

War out of Niagara

THE AMERICAN FRONTIER *of the 1770's stretched in a great broken arc from Maine to Georgia—through northern Vermont, along the borderland of New York, across northern and western Pennsylvania, through Ohio and to Detroit, southward to the Ohio, into the Kentucky country, along the Appalachians down through Virginia and the Carolinas to the frontier of Georgia. It embraced a large part of the American territory, and a substantial part of the American population, and all of it was exposed to Indian depredations. And Indian war was a constant all through the Revolution. Sometimes it was in the background—a threat, a tension, a fear that drove pioneers back to the safety of the settlements; sometimes, as with the Wyoming Valley massacre, it was in the foreground. It began, in a sense, with Lord Dunmore's War in 1774; it did not end until Indians overwhelmed Kentuckians at Blue Licks in August 1782 and Colonel Willett launched an abortive attack on Oswego in February 1783. It played a not unimportant part in the war; it played an important part in the American imagination, in history, story and legend.*

The Indians were everywhere, and most of them were hostile to the Americans. If they were to be involved in the war it was clear that they would fight on the side of the British. The British had the supplies, the articles for trade, the fur-trading posts; the British seemed to be there as their defenders; it was the Americans who were advancing into their hunting grounds. And it was inevitable that the Indians would be caught up in the war. The British could not advance, by land, except through their territory—from Canada, from Niagara, from Detroit, from Georgia—and from the first the two Johnsons and Stuart and General Carleton made use of them.

The use that they made of the Indians, however, was halfhearted, sporadic, and shortsighted. There was no grand strategy; there was no strategy at all. Organized, officered, armed and supplied by the British, the Indians might have been a formidable force; they might even have been a decisive force. It is difficult to see how the Americans could have resisted a co-ordinated series of attacks from the sea and a series of attacks along their frontiers. Had the British struck at Boston, New York and Charleston (as they did) and, at the same time, down the Champlain frontier, the Mohawk frontier, the Susquehanna frontier, the mountainous frontier of the Allegheny-Monongahela, the newly settled frontier of Kentucky, back-country Carolina and Georgia, the impact would have been irresistible. Happily for the Americans the threat of organized Indian warfare never materialized. Some of the Indian tribes were actually friendly to the Americans; others adopted neutrality, at least for a time. And the British had no master plan, nor is there any strong reason to suppose that the Indians would have lent themselves to such a plan.

At that the border warfare went badly for the Americans. There were, to be sure, some bright spots: Clark's conquest of the Northwest, for example, or the punishment of the Cherokee in the South. But most of the news from the frontier was bad news. Tories and Indians wiped out the flourishing settlements along the Susquehanna; ravaged the Mohawk and Schoharie valleys; and made New York borderlands an open wound all through the war. The British reconquered the Northwest; the Indians ravaged Kentucky again and again, and carried the war to the smoking cabins on the Monongahela. At the end of the war the Indians were still unsubdued, and the British controlled most of the territory north of the Ohio.

For all the terror that they spread among the Americans, it is by no means clear that the Indians really helped the British in the war. They were a distraction. They diffused and dissipated British energies. They exacerbated opinion back home and turned many a neutral frontiersman into an implacable enemy. They were not reliable either on a long campaign or in a battle. Properly used they might have changed the fortunes of war; actually all they did was to change the nature of the war, and for the worse.

It is impossible to give here even a sampling of the vast literature dealing with the borderlands during the Revolution. Fighting surged back and forth, winter after winter, on a dozen frontiers; each of these frontier skirmishes took on—in the minds of its participants—a heroic quality, each of them seemed as worthy of annals as the Trojan War or the Crusades. We select for this chapter some accounts that give a history of the most important of the Indian campaigns—the fight for back-country New York. Our next chapter will chronicle the exploits of George Rogers Clark and the battle for Kentucky.

I. BOTH SIDES ENLIST INDIANS

"Everybody" knows that the English were the first to employ Indians. The Great Declaration itself contributes this to history: "He has . . . endeavored to bring on the inhabitants of our frontiers, the merciless Indian Savages, whose known rule of warfare is an undistinguished destruction of all ages, sexes and conditions." Burke denounced the use of Indians, and Chatham exhausted his eloquence in excoriation of so wicked a policy. The consequences that they foresaw were, alas, realized: Wyoming, Cherry Valley, German Flats, Blue Licks were all monuments to the infamy of using the "merciless Indian."

Yet in fact it was the Americans who took the first step in enlisting the Indians. Even before the battle of Lexington the Massachusetts Provincial Congress enlisted the Stockbridge Indians as "minutemen"; not content with this they tried to raise Indian soldiers from Nova Scotia. In May 1775 Congress instructed its Indian commissioners to try to hold the Indians to neu-

trality; if that was not possible, however, they should enlist them on the American side. As we know, it was not possible. Already the two Johnsons— Sir John and Sir Guy—were moving in a gingerly fashion toward using the Indians of the Six Nations, at first for defensive but ultimately for offensive operations. By July 1775 the devout Lord Dartmouth officially sanctioned the employment of Indians; no less than a year later the Continental Congress came out strongly for the same policy. "It is highly expedient," they resolved, "to engage the Indians in the service of the United Colonies," and they even offered bounties for prisoners taken by the Indians.

Both sides, to be sure, tried to tame the savages; both discovered that they could as soon tame the panther or the rattlesnake as tame the Mohawk or the Delaware when he was aroused and on the warpath. Both were to find their Indian allies something of an embarrassment; as the Americans had few Indian allies their embarrassment was ephemeral, but the British suffered severely from an outraged opinion, not only in America but at home as well. We give here, along with some of the letters about enlisting the Indian, Chatham's famous reply to the Earl of Suffolk's speech urging the use of all means "that God and nature had put in our hands."

1. "Induce the Six Nations to Take Up the Hatchet"

The Earl of Dartmouth to Colonel Guy Johnson.

Whitehall, 24. July 1775

I have already in my letter to you of the 5th inst. hinted that the time might possibly come when the King, relying upon the attachment of his faithful allies, the Six Nations of Indians, might be under the necessity of calling upon them for their aid and assistance in the present state of America.

The unnatural rebellion now raging there calls for every effort to suppress it, and the intelligence His Majesty has received of the Rebells having excited the Indians to take a part, and of their having actually engaged a body of them in arms to support their rebellion, justifies the resolution His Majesty has taken of requiring the assistance of his faithful adherents the Six Nations.

It is therefore His Majesty's pleasure that you do lose no time in taking such steps as may induce them to take up the hatchet against His Majesty's rebellious subjects in America, and to engage them in His Majesty's service upon such plan as shall be suggested to you by General Gage to whom this letter is sent accompanied with a large assortement of goods for presents to them upon this important occasion.

Whether the engaging the Six Nations to take up arms in defence of His Majesty's Government is most likely to be effected by separate negociation with the chiefs or in a general council assembled for that purpose, must be left to your judgement, but at all events as it is a service of very great importance, you will not fail to exert every effort that may tend to accomplish it, and to use the utmost diligence and activity in the execution of the orders I have now the honor to transmit to you.

—O'Callaghan, ed., *Documents Relating to Colonial History of New York*, VIII, 596.

2. GERMAIN ENCOURAGES THE USE OF INDIAN WARRIORS

Lord George Germain to John Stuart, Indian Agent.

Whitehall, 6th November, 1776

. . . I expect with some impatience to hear from you of the success of your negociation with the Creeks and the Choctaws and that you have prevailed with them to join the Cherokees who I find have already commenced hostilities against the Rebels in Carolina and Virginia. The Rebel government in the former province have, I also learn, not only offered considerable rewards for the scalps of those Indians but declared their children of a certain age which may be taken prisoners the slaves of the captors, a measure which I am sure must inflame the enmity of that nation to the highest pitch against them and excite the resentment of all the other Indians in so great a degree that I cannot doubt of your being able under such advantageous circumstances to engage them in a general confederacy against the Rebels in defence of those liberties of which they are so exceedingly jealous and in the full enjoyment of which they have always been protected by the King.

At this distance and before the issue of the campaign to the northward can be known here it is impossible to give you any instructions for the employment of the savages. General Howe will no doubt give you full directions when he has formed his plan of operations against the Southern Colonies. In the mean time as the Cherokees have declared for us they must be supported and it will be your duty to procure them all the aid in your power from the other Indian nations and to supply them with arms and ammunition and other necessaries to enable them to carry on the war. I am not without hopes that Governor Sawyer will find means of assisting them with a detachment of his numerous garrison, and if the well affected inhabitants in the back countries could be collected and embodied to conduct and support the Indians, the Rebels on the sea coast would soon feel the distress from the want of the accustomed supplies, the discontent of the people with the new mode of government would increase with that distress, and resentment against the authors of their calamities would be the necessary consequences.

Inclosed I send you by the King's command printed copies of His Majesty's most gracious speech at the opening of the session together with the addresses of both Houses of Parliament to His Majesty in return, which I have the pleasure to acquaint you were passed in both Houses by very great majorities.

—SAUNDERS, ed., *Colonial Records of North Carolina*, X, 893-894.

3. TRYON CALLS FOR BRUTALITY FROM THE INDIANS

Governor William Tryon to William Knox, Secretary of the War Office in London.

New York, 21 April, 1777

I thank you for the favour of your letter of the 14th of January, which gave me much satisfaction in the assurance that my sentiments respecting the present rebellion correspond with those of my superiors. I am exactly of opinion with Colonel La [Corne] St Luc, who says; *Il faut lacher les sauvages contre les misérables Rebels, pour imposer de terreur sur les frontiers; il dit de plus (mais un peu trop pour moi) "qu'il faut brutalizer les affaires"; as-surément, il est bien enragé de la mauvais traitement qu'il a reçu de les aveugles peuples*—but not to blunder longer on in a language I know imperfectly, I shall express his other sentiments in the English dialect.

He assured me that upon the opening of the first assembly with the savages in Canada, his feelings would be too poignant at their first interview, as would impose a perfect silence upon him, while tears would run down his cheeks; and that when he should be able to expatiate on the indignities and injuries he had experienced, they would instantly take up the hatchet and resent his affronts. So reciprocal is the affection between the Father and his Children, for such they style each other respectively, and by whom he is as much cher-ished as was Sir Wm Johnson by the Indians of the Six Nations. These anec-dotes you may esteem worthy to communicate.

His Excellency General Sir William Howe has been pleased to appoint me to command the Provincial Corps within this Province with the rank of Major General of the Provincial Forces. This places me behind all the Majors General in this army, though I am an older Colonel than any of them. How-ever, at this crisis a *passé droit* does not weigh so much with me as an oppor-tunity given me to lend a hand to beat down this republican revolt. . . .

—O'CALLAGHAN, ed., Documents Relating to Colonial History
of New York, VIII, 707-708.

4. CHATHAM: "WE TURN LOOSE THESE SAVAGE HELL-HOUNDS"

Speech of William Pitt, Earl Chatham, delivered in the House of Lords, November 18, 1777.

My lords, I am astonished to hear such principles confessed! I am shocked to hear them avowed in this house, or in this territory! Principles, equally unconstitutional, inhuman, and unchristian!

My lords, I did not intend to have encroached again on your attention; but I cannot repress my indignation. I feel myself impelled by every duty. My lords, we are called upon as members of this house, as men, as Christian men, to protest against such notions standing near the throne, polluting the ear of majesty. "That God and nature put into our hands!" I know not what ideas that lord may entertain of God and nature; but I know that such abom-inable principles are equally abhorrent to religion and humanity.

What! to attribute the sacred sanction of God and nature to the massacres of the Indian scalping knife? to the cannibal savage, torturing, murdering, roasting and eating; literally, my lords, *eating* the mangled victims of his bar-barous battles! Such horrible notions shock every precept of religion, divine or natural, and every generous feeling of humanity. And, my lords, they shock every sentiment of honor; they shock me as a lover of honorable war, and a detester of murderous barbarity.

These abominable principles and this more abominable avowal of them de-mand the most decisive indignation. I call upon that right reverend bench, those holy ministers of the gospel and pious pastors of our church: I conjure them to join in the holy work and vindicate the religion of their God. I appeal to wisdom and the law of this *learned bench* to defend and support the justice of their country. I call upon the bishops to interpose the unsullied sanctity of their *lawn;* upon the learned judges to interpose the purity of their *ermine*, to save us from this pollution. I call upon the honor of your lordships to reverence the dignity of your ancestors, and to maintain your own. I call upon the spirit and humanity of my country to vindicate the national character. I invoke the genius of the constitution.

From the tapestry that adorns these walls, the immortal ancestor of this noble lord frowns with indignation at the disgrace of his country. In vain he led your victorious fleet against the boasted armada of Spain, in vain he defended and established the honor, the liberties, the religion, the protestant religion of this country, against the arbitrary cruelties of popery and the inquisition, if these more than popish cruelties and inquisitorial practices are let loose among us; to turn forth into our settlements, among our ancient connections, friends and relations, the merciless cannibal, thirsting for the blood of man, woman and child! to send forth the infidel savage—against whom?— against your protestant brethren; to lay waste their country; to desolate their dwellings, and extirpate their race and name, with these horrible hell-hounds of savage warfare!

Spain armed herself with blood-hounds to extirpate the wretched natives of America; and we improve on the human example even of Spanish cruelty. We turn loose these savage hell-hounds against our brethren and countrymen in America, of the same language, laws, liberty and religion, endeared to us by every tie that should sanctify humanity.

My lords, this awful subject, so important to our honor, our constitution and our religion, demands the most solemn and effectual inquiry. And I again call upon your lordships and the united power of the state to examine it thoroughly and decisively, and to stamp upon it an indelible stigma of the public abhorrence. And I again implore those holy prelates of our religion to do away these iniquities from among us. Let them perform a lustration; let them purify this house and this country from this sin.

My lords, I am old and weak and at present unable to say more; but my feelings and indignation were too strong to have said less. I could not have slept this night in my bed nor reposed my head upon my pillow without giving this vent to my eternal abhorrence of such preposterous and enormous principles.

—Cobbett, *Parliamentary History of England*, XIX, 368-370.

5. Washington: Employ Indians When Divested of Savage Customs

To the Commissioners of Indian Affairs.

Head Quarters, Valley Forge, March 13, 1778

Gentlemen: You will perceive, by the inclosed Copy of a Resolve of Congress, that I am impowered to employ a body of four hundred Indians, if they can be procured upon proper terms. Divesting them of the Savage customs exercised in their Wars against each other, I think they may be made of excellent use, as scouts and light troops, mixed with our own Parties. I propose to raise about one half the number among the Southern and the remainder

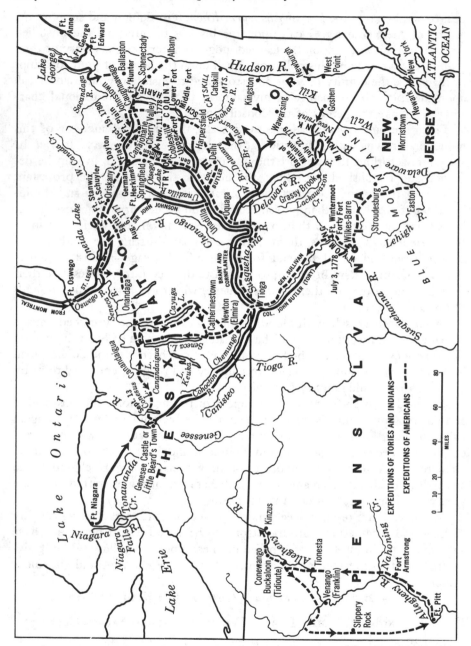

SULLIVAN'S INDIAN CAMPAIGN

among the Northern Indians. I have sent Colo Nathl. Gist, who is well acquainted with the Cherokees and their Allies, to bring as many as he can from thence, and I must depend upon you to employ suitable persons to procure the stipulated number or as near as may be from the Northern tribes. The terms made with them should be such as you think we can comply with, and persons well acquainted with their language, manners and Customs and who have gained an influence over them should accompany them. The Oneidas have manifested the strongest attachment to us throughout this dispute and I therefore suppose, if any can be procured, they will be most numerous. Their Missionary Mr Kirkland seemed to have an uncommon ascendency over that tribe and I should therefore be glad to see him accompany them. If the Indians can be procured, I would choose to have them here by the opening of the Campaign, and therefore they should be engaged as soon as possible as there is not more time between this and the Middle of May than will be necessary to settle the business with them and to March from their Country to the Army. I am not without hopes that this will reach you before the treaty which is to be held, breaks up. If it should, you will have an Opportunity of knowing their sentiments, of which I shall be glad to be informed, as soon as possible. I have the honour, etc.

—FITZPATRICK, ed., *Writings of Washington*, XI, 76-77.

II. WYOMING

A special pathos clings to the Wyoming Massacre, which has been called "the surpassing horror of the Revolution." The Wyoming Valley, along the banks of the beautiful Susquehanna, near present-day Wilkes-Barre, was claimed by the state of Connecticut and had been settled largely from that state. From the time of its original settlement, in 1762, down to the Revolution, these Connecticut Yankees had fought an almost continuous struggle with Indians and Pennsylvanians—and nature—for their cherished lands; even as late as 1775 Pennsylvania militiamen had invaded the valley, only to be driven out. The Wyoming settlements—flourishing towns and farms, with a population of over 2,000—had sent a large portion of their able-bodied men to the Connecticut Line and were all but defenseless. In 1777, after their defeat at Fort Stanwix and Oriskany, Butler's Tory Rangers and their Indian allies planned an attack on these rich settlements. In July 1778 they struck, twelve hundred strong. Against them Colonel Zeb Butler, veteran of the wars with Pennsylvania, could muster only 300 old men and boys. He managed them badly, sallying out from the Forty Fort—which offered some protection—to seek battle in the open. There his forces were ambuscaded and destroyed. Then the Wyoming settlements were put to the torch, and many of the inhabitants killed.

Not long after, the Indian leader Thayendanegea—known as Joseph Brant —struck at the frontier settlement of Cherry Valley, near Otsego Lake, killed or imprisoned most of its inhabitants, including women and children, and burned all its houses. Brant disclaimed responsibility for the barbarities of this massacre, but the frontiersmen held him responsible and regarded him with execration.

We give here two accounts of Wyoming. The first comes from the untutored pen of a carpenter, Richard McGinnis, who fought under the British Colonel John Butler. The second is by the famous American farmer, Hector Saint-John de Crèvecoeur, whose "Letters" are a classic of American literature and history; this essay on the Wyoming Massacre is valuable chiefly for its picture of the refugees from border war.

1. "LOYALTY AND ORDER TRIUMPH OVER CONFUSION AND TREASON"

From the Journal of Richard McGinnis, carpenter.

May 2, [1778]. We set out for Wioming with about 70 white volunteers and about 300 Indians of different tribes, cheifly Senecas and Delawares. With these nations Col. Butler held frequent counsels. The purport of them was cheifly to deter them if possible from murdering the women and innocent, in consequence of which they agreed not to do it on any pretence whatever, and I must say for my part they did not comit any thing of the kind to my certain knowledge.

In our way through the savage country we many a time had very hungry times. I was under the needsesity of giving an hard doller for 4 small Indian cakes and sometime could not get it [at] all. Many a time I have gone into a wigwam a[nd] waited for the hommany kettle with the greatest impatience to get a trifle and was as often disappointed.

When we came to Tioga there was some familys on their [way] to Niagara that had left their places. I remember I gave a woman an excellent white shirt for 4 quarts of rye meal and was glad to get it. In one word, let it suffice to say I went through every species of distress to serve my King and country in the best manner I possibly could.

From the banks of Tioga we proceeded to the Standing Stone on the Susquehannah, and from thence to Wylucing. This place was formerly inhabited by the Moraving people. We stayed one night.

Next day, being the 28 of June, 1778, we came to a mill belonging to the Rebles. The Savages burnt the mill and took 3 prisoners, two white men and a Negro whom they afterward murdered in their own camp.

About this time we were much distrest for provision, having nothing to subsist on except a little parched corn stamped at the mill above mentioned. The savages found 5 barrels of flour, but little good was it to us. I know I was very glad to scrape the moulded husks from out of the barrels and secure it for a rainy day, which happened the day after. But in the midst of our distress kind Providence was indeed very, very favourable to us. June 30th at night two men, Wintermots by name, hearing of our approach and distress for provision, came to our releif with 14 head of fat cattle. The blessed moment they arrived we set to work and butchered and divided severally amongst us.

The men above mentioned had a fort at Wioming of their own name, which immediately surrendered to the arms of His Majesty our Gracious Sovereign, under the command of Col. John Butler.

Upon this success a flag was sent to 40 Fort and another to Jenkins to surrender. Jenkins Fort complyed immediately, but Forty thought proper to se it out, for a Mr Stewart told the flag—to wit Mr Tourney, a Leiutenat of the Rangers, and John Phillips, fifer of the same—that he never would give it over to Tories and savages but stand it out to the last and defend it to the last extremity. Upon which the flag told him that he was very sorry, and was setting of[f] to delever his answer to Col. John Butler. Stewart, however, invited the flag to take some spirits, as he looked on him to be a good fellow, and which he refused. He then told him—to wit, the flag—that as he had refused the offer, he or they then in possession of 40 Fort would give them spirits enough before night. Mr. Fourney and Phillips returning and delivering their message, Col. Butler ordered a number of Indians to watch their mote and to hold ourselves in constant readiness.

July 3, 1778, 5 o'clock, P.M., they left their strong holds and proceeded up to give us battle. The fort called Wintermot's above mentioned we set on fire to decoy the enemy, they thinking by this that we were fled. But they soon found it a mistake to their sorrow, for we immediately treed ourselves and secured every spot that was any way advantageous to our designs. When the enemy came within sight of us they fell a-blackguarding of us, calling out aloud, "Come out, ye villianous Tories! Come out, if ye dare, and show your heads, if ye durst, to the brave Continental Sons of Liberty!" (Remark, I call them Sons of Sedition, Schism and Rebellion.)

But we came out to their confusion indeed—for the Indians on the right under the command of Col. Butler and their King Quirxhta entirely surrounded the enemy, and the white men under the command of Quiskkal . . . on the left drove and defeated the enemy on every quarter. They fled to the river and many of them even there where [were] pursued by the savages and shared the same fate as those on the land.

The prisoners that we took told us there where [were] 450 men in the battle and after we went to the 40 Fort . . . to destroy it, they protested not above 45 returned. The loss on our side was one Indian killed and two white men wounded. One of the white men, Willson by name, died of his wound, it having mortefeid. The other recovered. Thus did loyalty and good order that day triumph over confusion and treason, the goodness of our cause, aided and assisted by the blessing of Divine Providence, in some measure help to restore the ancient constitution of our mother country, governed by the best of kings. This I must say: Every man behaved with uncommon bravery. They vied each other for glory to se who should do most in supporting the injured cause of our excellent constitution.

With the defeat of the rebles followed a total confiscation of all their property, such as oxen, cows, horses, hogs, sheep and every other thing of that kind. Thus did Rebellion get a severe shock. The Rebles begged of us to restore them something back, but "No," we replyed. "Remember how you served the peaceable subjects of his Majesty at Tankennick. Remember how you took their property and converted it to Reble porpesses, and their persons fell in your hands, you immediately sent them of[f] to prison clean into Connetticut and left their numerous familys in the utmost distress. And be contented, Rebles, that your lives are still spared and that you have not shared the same fate with your sedetious brethren."

This was the argument we made use of to the surviving Rebles of Wioming. But on the whole my heart was affected for the women and children, who came after us, crying and beseeching us that we would leave them a few cows, and we told them it was against the orders of Col. Butler. However, privately we let them have 4 or 5 cows. . . .

—McGinnis, Journal, pp. 12-18.

2. Crèvecoeur Reflects on the Tragedy of Wyoming

The assailants formed a body of about eight hundred men who received their arms from Niagara; the whites under the conduct of Colonel Butler, the Indians under that of Brant. After a fatiguing march, they all met at some of the upper towns of the Susquehanna, and while they were refreshing themselves and providing canoes and every other necessary implement, parties were sent out in different parts of the country. Some penetrated to the west branch and did infinite mischief; it was easy to surprise defenceless, isolated families who fell an easy prey to their enemies. Others approached the New England settlements, where the ravages they committed were not less dreadful. Many families were locked up in their houses and consumed with all their furniture. Dreadful scenes were transacted which I know not how to retrace. This was, however, but the prelude of the grand drama. A few weeks afterwards, the whole settlement was alarmed with the news of the main body coming down the river. Many immediately embarked and retired into the more interior parts of Pennsylvania; the rest immediately retired with their wives and children into the stockade they had erected there some time before.

Meanwhile, the enemy landed at Lackawanna or Kingston, the very place where the stockade was erected. Orders were immediately issued by their commanders for the rest of the militia to resort to them. Some of the most contiguous readily obeyed; distance prevented others. Colonel Butler, seeing they had abandoned their dwellings, proposed to them to surrender and quit the country in a limited time. It was refused by the New England people, who resolved to march out and meet them in the open fields. Their number consisted of five hundred and eighty-two. They found the enemy advantageously situated, but much weaker in numbers, as they thought, than had been reported. This encouraged them; they boldly advanced; and the Indians as sagaciously retreated. Thus they were led on to the fatal spot where all at once they found themselves surrounded. Here some of the New England leaders abandoned them to their evil destiny. Surprised as they were at this bad omen, they still kept their ground and vigorously defended themselves until the Indians, sure of their prey, worked up by the appearance of success to that degree of frenzy which they call courage, dropped their guns and rushed on them with the tomahawk and the spear. The cruel treatment they expected to receive from the wrathful Indians and offended countrymen animated them for a while. They received this first onset with the most undaunted courage, but, the enemy falling upon them with a redoubled fury and on all sides, they broke and immediately looked for safety in flight.

Part of them plunged themselves into the river with the hopes of reaching across, and on this element a new scene was exhibited not less terrible than that which had preceded it. The enemy, flushed with the intoxication of success and victory, pursued them with the most astonishing celerity, and, being naked, had very great advantage over a people encumbered with clothes. This, united with their superiority in the art of swimming, enabled them to overtake most of these unfortunate fugitives, who perished in the river pierced with the lances of the Indians. Thirty-three were so happy as to reach the opposite shores, and for a long time afterwards the carcasses of their companions, become offensive, floated and infested the banks of the Susquehanna as low as Shamokin. The other party, who had taken their flight towards their forts, were all either taken or killed. It is said that those who were then made prisoners were tied to small trees and burnt the evening of the same day.

The body of the aged people, the women and children who were enclosed in the stockade, distinctly could hear and see this dreadful onset, the last scenes of which had been transacted close to the very gates. What a situation these unfortunate people were in! Each wife, each father, each mother could easily distinguish each husband and son as they fell. But in so great, so universal a calamity, when each expected to meet the same fate, perhaps they did not feel so keenly for the deplorable end of their friends and relations. Of what powerful materials must the human heart be composed, which could hold together at so awful a crisis! This bloody scene was no sooner over than a new one arose of a very similar nature. They had scarcely finished scalping the numerous victims which lay on the ground when these fierce conquerors demanded the immediate entrance to the fort. It was submissively granted. Above a hundred of them, decorated with all the dreadful ornaments of plumes and colour of war, with fierce animated eyes, presented themselves and rushed with impetuosity into the middle of the area, armed with tomahawks made of brass with an edge of steel. Tears relieved some; involuntary cries disburdened the oppression of others, a general shriek among the women was immediately heard all around.

What a spectacle this would have exhibited to the eyes of humanity: hundreds of women and children, now widows and orphans, in the most humble attitude, with pale, dejected countenances, sitting on the few bundles they had brought with them; keeping their little unconscious children as close to them as possible; hiding by a mechanical instinct the babies of their breasts; numbers of aged fathers oppressed with the unutterable sorrow; all pale, all trembling, and sinking under the deepest consternation, were looking towards the door—that door through which so many of their friends had just passed, alas! never more to return. Everyone at this awful moment measured his future punishment by the degree of revenge which he supposed to animate the breast of his enemy. The self-accusing consciences of some painted to them each approaching minute as replete with the most terrible fate. Many there were who, recollecting how in the hour of oppression they had insulted their countrymen and the natives, bitterly wept with remorse; others were animated with the fiercest rage. What a scene an eminent painter might have copied from that striking exhibition, if it had been a place where a painter could have calmly sat with the palette in his hands! How easily he might have gathered the strongest expressions of sorrow, consternation, despondency, and despair, by taking from each countenance some strong feature of affright, of terror, and dismay, as it appeared delineated on each face! In how many different modes these passions must have painted themselves according as each individual's temper, ardent or phlegmatic habit, hurried or retarded the circulation of the blood, lengthened or contracted the muscles of his physiognomy!

But now a scene of unexpected humanity ensues. . . . Happily these fierce people, satisfied with the death of those who had opposed them in arms, treated the defenceless ones, the woman and children, with a degree of humanity almost hitherto unparalleled.

In the meantime the loud and repeated war-shouts began to be re-echoed from all parts; the flames of conflagrated houses and barns soon announced to the other little towns the certainty of their country's defeat; these were the first marks of the enemies' triumph. A general devastation ensued, but not such as we read of in the Old Testament where we find men, women, children, and cattle equally devoted to the same blind rage. All the stock, horses, sheep, etc., that could be gathered in the space of a week, were driven to the Indian towns by a party which was detached on purpose. The other little stockades, hearing of the surrender of their capital, opened their gates and submitted to the conquerors. They were all immediately ordered to paint their faces with red, this being the symbol established then, which was to preserve peace and tranquillity while the two parties were mingled together.

Thus perished in one fatal day most of the buildings, improvements, mills, bridges, etc., which had been erected there with so much cost and industry. Thus were dissolved the foundations of a settlement begun at such a distance from the metropolis, disputed by a potent province; the beginning of which had been stained with blood shed in their primitive altercations. Thus the ill-judged policy of these ignorant people and the general calamities of the times overtook them and extirpated them even out of that wilderness which they had come twelve years before to possess and embellish. Thus the grand contest entered into by these colonies with the mother-country has spread everywhere, even from the sea-shores to the last cottages of the frontiers. This most diffusive calamity, on this fatal spot in particular, has despoiled of their goods, chattels, and lands, upwards of forty-five hundred souls, among whom not a third part was ever guilty of any national crime. Yet they suffered every extent of punishment as if they had participated in the political iniquity which was attributed to the leaders of this unfortunate settlement. . . .

The complete destruction of these extended settlements was now the next achievement which remained to be done, in order to finish their rude triumph, but it could not be the work of a few days. Houses, barns, mills, grain, everything combustible to conflagrate; cattle, horses, and stock of every kind to gather; this work demanded a considerable time. The collective industry of twelve years could not well be supposed, in so great an extent, to require in its destruction less than twelve days. . . .

For a considerable time the roads through the settled country were full of these unhappy fugitives, each company slowly returning towards those counties from which they had formerly emigrated. Some others, still more unfortunate than others, were wholly left alone with their children, obliged to carry through that long and fatiguing march the infants of their breasts, now no longer replenished as before with an exuberant milk. Some of them were reduced to the cruel necessity of loading the ablest of them with the little food they were permitted to carry. Many of these young victims were seen bare-headed, bare-footed, shedding tears at every step, oppressed with fatigues too great for their tender age to bear; afflicted with every species of misery, with hunger, with bleeding feet, every now and then surrounding their mother as exhausted as themselves. "Mammy, where are we going? Where is Father? Why don't we go home?"

"Poor innocents, don't you know that the King's Indians have killed him and have burnt our house and all we had? Your Uncle Simon will perhaps give us some bread."

Hundreds were seen in this deplorable condition, yet thinking themselves happy that they had safely passed through the great wilderness, the dangers of which had so much increased the misfortunes of their situation. Here you might see a poor starved horse as weak and emaciated as themselves, given them perhaps by the enemy as a last boon. The poor beast was loaded with a scanty feather-bed serving as a saddle which was fastened on him with withes and bark. On it sat a wretched mother with a child at her breast, another on her lap, and two more placed behind her, all broiling in the sun; accompanied in this pilgrimage of tribulation by the rest of the family creeping slowly along; leading at a great distance behind a heifer once wild and frolicsome but now tamed by want and hunger; a cow, perhaps, with hollow flanks and projecting ribs closed the train; these were the scanty remains of greater opulence. Such was the mournful procession, which for a number of weeks announced to the country through which they passed the sad disaster which had befallen them. The generous farmers sent their wagons to collect as many as they could find, and convey them to the neighbouring county, where the same kindness was repeated. Such was their situation, while the carcasses of their friends were left behind to feed the wolves of that wilderness on which they had so long toiled, and which they had come to improve.

—Crèvecoeur, *Sketches of 18th Century America*, pp. 197-206.

III. THE AMERICANS STRIKE BACK: THE SULLIVAN EXPEDITION

The Wyoming and Cherry Valley massacres, together with sporadic attacks on American settlements in the Mohawk and Schoharie valleys, spread terror all through the New York and Pennsylvania borderlands. Unless the Americans were to abandon this hard-won ground to the Tories and their Indian allies—and such an abandonment would have serious military consequences for the Hudson Valley—they would have to mount a counteroffensive against the Six Nations. In the spring of 1779 Washington planned the strategy of such a counteroffensive; when General Gates refused command, it was given to General Sullivan. The plan called for a three-pronged invasion of the Indian country. One column, under Sullivan, was to move up the Susquehanna to the New York border; another, under General James Clinton, was to strike across the Mohawk Valley, down Otsego Lake, and down the Susquehanna; a third, under Colonel Daniel Brodhead, was to advance from Pittsburgh up the Allegheny into the Indian country.

During the summer of 1779 this complicated plan was carried through with qualified success. Clinton—brother to Governor George and father to Governor De Witt Clinton—made his way along the Mohawk, down to Lake Otsego; there he built a dam, then broke it and floated downstream on the swollen waters to join Sullivan, who had come up from Easton, Pennsylvania. Brodhead, as we shall see, invaded from the west but did not join forces with the eastern armies. Altogether Sullivan commanded about 4,000 fighting men, probably the largest of frontier armies during the Revolution. During August he built a fort at Tioga, near the New York boundary. Late that month the combined forces moved out on the offensive; on the twenty-sixth they met an army of Indians and Tories, shattered them, and drove them from the field. They then proceeded systematically to lay waste the country of the Seneca, the Cayuga and the Onondaga, cutting down orchards, burning the standing grain, destroying the Indian "castles." But though the Indians were forced to flee to Niagara and to depend on the bounty of the British, their power was unbroken and they were able to resume the offensive the following year.

Few Revolutionary expeditions were so fully recorded as this one; almost every officer, it seems, kept a journal or a diary. We give here excerpts from three of these journals, and a letter from General Clinton to his brother. Of Lieutenant Barton little is known except that he was from New Jersey. So, too, was Lieutenant—afterwards Major—Erkuries Beatty. Only twenty years old at the time of the Sullivan expedition, he was already a veteran; he had fought at White Plains, Brandywine and Germantown, and suffered through Valley Forge; he was in on the surrender at Yorktown, and stayed on in the army after the war until 1793—one of our earliest professional soldiers. Major Fogg—a graduate of Harvard College and a student in the office of the famous Theophilus Parsons—like Beatty, fought through the whole war; later he achieved some minor prominence in New Hampshire politics.

1. General Sullivan Spreads Terror along the Border

From the Journal of Lieutenant William Barton.

Tuesday, June 8th, 1779.—Took leave of my friends and set out to join the regiment at Wyoming: arrived at Easton the same evening where I found the second and third Jersey regiments and one company of our regiment which was left behind to take care of the baggage belonging to it, and was the next day to proceed with it on horses to Wyoming. . . .

[July] 31st.—The army marched at 12 o'clock, after signals being given by a discharge of cannon from the fort, which were immediately answered from the boats, which carried all the artillery and stores, excepting some kegs of flour, which were carried on horses—Gen. Hand, having previously advanced about one mile, being appointed to the light corps on this expedition. The whole proceeded, only our regiment, which composed the rear guard, having in charge stragglers, cattle, etc., which occasioned us to march very slow. After a tedious march, came to some cleared fields one mile distant from Lackawannah, then 11 P. M. . . . .

[August] 26th.—At half past 12 P.M. began our march with several pieces of cannon, which caused us to move very slowly, as we had formed a hollow

square, in which the pack horses and cattle were all driven together with the cannon. This day received information that Col. Broadhead, with six hundred troops, was within forty miles of the Senakee [Seneca] castle, and had destroyed almost one whole tribe of Indians by strategem; he painted his men like Indians, with cutting their hair, etc. We this day likewise received intelligence of Count De Estaing's victory over the British fleet, and having taken the island of St. Vincents. This day marched about four miles and encamped at 5 P.M. near a large flat, on the north-east side of Cahuga Creek. This day's march through a level land, but very poor, excepting the flats, which are good, grown up with grass of great height.

Sunday, 29th.—Proceeded very slowly two miles, occasioned by the roughness of the way, which we had to clear for the artillery, baggage, etc., to pass. Here we halted for one hour and a half, until the artillery, etc., should raise a difficult height, at which time an advanced party of our riflemen discovered the enemy throwing up some works on the other side of a morass, and a difficult place through which we had to pass. It appears this was intended for an ambuscade, it being on a small height, where some logs, etc., were laid up, covered with green bushes; which extended half a mile. On the right was a small town which they had destroyed themselves, making use of the timber, etc., in the above works. After the ground was well reconnoitered, the artillery was advanced on their left. At the same time Gen'l Poor with his brigade was endeavoring to gain their rear around their left; Gen'l Hand's brigade was following in rear of Poor. Our brigade was kept as a reserve, as also Gen'l Clinton's, until their rear should be gained; but they having a party posted on a very considerable height, over which our right flank had to pass, we were discovered by them.

Previous to this, some shells and round shot were thrown among them in their works, which caused them to give several yells, and doubtless intimidated them much. But at this discovery they gave a most hideous yell and quit their works, endeavoring to prevent Gen'l Poor's ascending the height by a loose scattering fire; but our troops, pressing forward with much vigor, made them give way, leaving their dead behind (amounting to eleven or twelve), which were scalped immediately. We likewise took one white man, who appeared to be dead, and was stripped, when an officer came up and examined him, said he was not wounded, gave him a stroke and bade him get up; he immediately rose up and implored mercy, and was kept a prisoner some time. In the evening a Negro was taken. Their number wounded not known. Two or three of ours killed, and thirty-four or five wounded. Among the latter Major Titcomb, Capt. Cloise, and Lt. Allis.

At half after three the firing ceased, and the army proceeded one mile and a half to a considerable town consisting of about twenty huts. The number of the enemy uncertain, but from the best intelligence from the prisoners, the whites were about two hundred, the Indians five. They were commanded by Butler and Brant, who had been waiting some days for our approach. It appears their expectations were great, from their numbers, situation, etc. The prisoners likewise inform us they had been kept on an allowance of seven ears of corn per day each although there is a very great abundance of corn, beans, potatoes, squashes, etc., for several miles on the creek, upon which our whole army has subsisted for days. We had nevertheless to destroy some hundred bushels. Here was found a deal of plunder of theirs, such as blankets, brass kettles, etc.

Monday [September] 13th.—At half past four, morning, proceeded one mile and a half; came to a considerable town, Canesaah, consisting of from sixteen to twenty huts, and halted for the troops to get some refreshment and to build a bridge across a creek; meantime a party of twenty-six men, commanded by Lt. Boyd, was sent out to a town about six miles for discovery, at which place he arrived without molestation. Here an Indian was killed and scalped by his party. He then dispatched two men to inform us what had happened; after they had gone two miles they saw five Indians. They immediately ran back and told the lieutenant what they had seen, who marched on to the place with all speed, when he discovered some few of them who retreated; he pursued and killed one of them. The men then went to scalp him, which caused some dispute who should have it; at the same instant the enemy rose up from their ambuscade, when the action commenced, but they being much superior in numbers, caused him and one or two others to surrender, though not until the rest were all killed and got off.

About the same time, Capt. Lodge, surveyor of the road, with a small party, was discovered about one mile beyond, where the party was building a bridge. They were fired on by the Indians and one of his men wounded. The rest ran off and were pursued so closely that one of them drew out his tomahawk and was close on the heels of one of our men, when a sentinel from the party at the bridge fired at the Indian, which caused them all to run off. Major Poor immediately pushed on, hearing the firing, and found the knapsacks, etc., of the Indians, who had all run off on his approach.

At two o'clock the bridge being completed, we marched on to a town, Casawavalatetah, where we arrived about dark, in expectation of an attack, and encamped. Land continuing very fertile; at both of these places was a large quantity of corn; at the former we did not destroy all.

Tuesday, 14th.—Early in the morning was ordered to destroy the corn, which we did by throwing the ears into the creek, which runs close to the town and is a branch of the Canisee [Genesee] River, which empties into the Lake Ontario about fourteen miles hence. At 2 P.M. marched and crossed the creek, and forded the main branch of Canisee, and proceeded four miles down to the Chenisee castle, where we arrived about four P.M. At this place was Lieut. Boyd and one soldier found, with their heads cut off; the Lieutenants head lay near his body; his body appeared to have been whipped and pierced in many different places. The others head was not found. A great part of his body was skinned, leaving the ribs bare.

Wednesday, 15th.—The whole army employed until 3 o'clock in gathering the corn, and burning it in their huts, which were in number about eighty or a hundred, and much the largest quantity of corn I have yet seen in any one place since I have been out. Here came in a white woman with a young child, who was almost starved, having made her escape two or three nights before from the enemy. She informs us they were in great confusion, the Indians some times agreeing to treat with us, but it was made void by Butler and Johnson, who promised to supply them with provisions. One of the Indians at this cocked his gun and was about to shoot Johnson, but was prevented. This woman was taken from Wyoming in '77, where her husband was killed. At half past two P.M. we began our march for returning, and proceeded as far as the fording place of the creek, crossed onto, encamping near the town Casawavalatetah. This place very rich and good. Distance from here to Niagaree said to be about eighty miles, whither the Indians carry all their furs, etc., for sale. They go and return in canoes in five or six days.

Thursday, 23rd.—Proceeded to Catharine town, at which place we arrived at twelve o'clock, finding the old squaw here which was left as we went up, with a paper that had many lines of Indian wrote underneath, a protection that was given her by the general, the contents of which I did not hear. We likewise found the corpse of a squaw who appeared to have been shot three or four days, which lay in a mud hole; supposed to have came there since our departure to take care of the old brute. Who killed her I cannot ascertain, but it is generally believed to be three men of ours who were sent up from Tioga express a few days before. At our departure from here the General ordered there should be left a keg of pork and some biscuit, etc., for the old creature to subsist on, although it was so scare an article that no officer under the rank of a field officer had tasted any since leaving Tioga, and a very scant allowance of half a pound of poor beef and a like quantity of flour.

Proceeded at two o'clock about three miles through a swamp of exceeding bad road for the pioneers to repair them and halted for the army's arrival, which was at five o'clock P.M., on a small flat of cleared ground, and encamped. Distance of day's march from 16 to 18 miles. This evening we, the advance guard, had orders to march at reveille for the purpose of having the roads repaired through a most notorious swamp of five miles, and appearance of rain, which would render the swamp almost impassable.

Sunday, 26th.—Still remained at Fort Reed. In the morning there was a detachment of three hundred men ordered to be sent up the river Kihuga [Cayuga] for the purpos of destroying a town or two, but was defered by reason of rain coming. At one in the afternoon the detachment under Col. Durbin, that came down the south of the Kihuga lake, arrived with two squaws, and inform us they burnt three or four towns. They likewise say they found one Indian and one other squaw, the latter so old as not to be able to be brought off; the Indian man young but decrepid to such a degree that he could not walk. I have since heard it said, the Colonel left one house standing for them to stay in, and would not suffer them to be hurt, but some of the soldiers taking an opportunity when not observed set the house on fire, after securing and making the door fast. The troops having got in motion and marched some distance, the house was consumed together with the savages, in spite of all exertions.

Monday, 27th.—The morning clear. The detachment yesterday detained by rain has gone out with an addition of two hundred men more, and divided into two parties, one under the command of Col. Courtland, and the other under Col. D'Hart; one going up the north side, and the other the south of the Kihuga Creek. In the evening the detachments came in, after destroying a considerable quantity of corn, etc.

Tuesday, 28th.—The same detachment again sent out an account of a small party being sent farther up, who say there is a large quantity of corn yet standing on the creek. About ten o'clock A.M. the detachment under Col. Butler came in from the north of Kihuga Lake, who say they have destroyed vast quantities of corn and several very considerable of their towns. . . .

—Cook, ed., *Journals of Expedition of Sullivan*, pp. 3-13.

2. General Sullivan Smashes Brant at Newtown

James Clinton to George Clinton.

New Town 5 miles above Chemung, August 30, 1779

Dear Brother, I have just time to inform you that the army under Genl. Sullivan arrived on this ground yesterday evening, in perfect helth and spirits. On Thursday last the 26th we left Tioga, but being incumbered with a train of artillery and waggons and the roads being very bad, owing to an heavy rain the preceeding day, together with other circumstances attending the first day's movements, we did not march more than three miles and encamped. Friday we proceeded on our march about eight o'clock in the morning, but my brigade, which formed the rear or second line of the army, had not marched from their ground more than two miles before the infantry in front halted at a narrow defile formed by the jutting out of the mountain to the river. This defile which was near half a mile in length and would at first sight have been judged impassible, particularly to artillery, etc., detaind the army so long that it was near ten o'clock at night before the rear of the main body, consisting of Poor's and Maxwell's brigades, had passed. As it was then dark, and as the cattle had not yet passed it, I judged it most proper not to attempt it that night, but marched back about a mile and encamped on tolerable good ground. Saturday I decamped and joined the army at Chemung about twelve o'clock. This town, which is about twelve miles from Tioga, had been destroyed by Genl. Sullivan immediately on his arrival at Tioga, together with a large quantity of corn, beans, etc., preserving only one field, consisting of about forty acres, for the use of the army on their arrival, and which they effectually consumed and destroyed.

Altho we had every reason to expect the enemy would have attempted to prevent our progress and retard our march, from the amaizing advantages Nature had liberally furnished them with, yet they never gave us the least opposition, or ever made their appearance, except a small party who fired upon and killed and wounded a few of Genl. Hand's advanced guard on the former attempt to destroy the settlement.

Sunday the army was put in motion about nine o'clock with the greatest circumspection and caution. Our scouts had brought intelligence the preceeding evening that the enemy were discovered at about five miles distance, supposed to be at or near New Town, and from the magnitude of their fires appeared to be in considerable force; that the sound of their axes were heard distinctly, which induced us to believe they intended either to throw up works or obstruct the march of the army, untill they could form a plan to attack our flanks or rear.

This in fact appeared to be their intention, and if we had proceeded as they expected, in all probability we should have been very severely handled. About ten o'clock a scattering fire commenced between some of their scouts and a few of our rifle men and volunteers, when the former gave way, and the latter proceeded untill they plainly discouvered their works which were very extensive, tho' not impregnable. As our design was not to drive them, but to surround or bring them to a fair open action, the army halted, and a council being called, it was concluded that the artillery, supported by Genl. Hand with the infantry and rifle corps, should commence the action, previously allowing sufficient time for Poor's and my brigade to gain their right flank, while Maxwell's and the covering party under Col. Ogden might gain their left.

About one o'clock Col. Proctor commenced a very warm cannonade upon their works, which continued near two hours, in which time we attempted to compleat our march upon their flanks, but from the very thick swamps and rough country thro' which we were to pass we were in some measure prevented. The enemy, finding their situation in their lines rather uncomfortable and finding we did not intend to storm them, abandoned them some time before the infantry discouvered it, and immediately proceeded to join the remaining half of their force who were posted on a hill, and attack our right flank as we expected. Genl. Poor who was near a quarter of a mile on the left of my front, had assended a considerable mountain about half way, which was very steep, when he discouvered them and received their fire accompanied by the war whoop, but tho' his troops were considerably fatigued with ascending the mountain under their heavy packs, yet they pushed up in the face of their fire, driving them from tree to tree untill they fled with the utmost precipitation, leaving their pack and blankets behind them, etc. in order to take off their dead and wounded, which must be very considerable as they left nine Indians on the field whom they could not carry off. My brigade, which had just reached the foot of the hill when the firing commenced, pushed up with such ardor that many of them almost fainted and fell down with excessive heat and fatigue, for the ground was so steep that no person could ride up.

During the action which lasted from the first to the last near six hours, we had three privates killed and forty wounded, among whom were three officers, Major Titcomb, Capt. Clause and Lt. McCauly, who is since dead of his wounds; there are few of the wounded dangerous.

The enemy's loss must be considerable; nine of them were found dead on the field, and many of them must have been wounded, as they were tracked some three miles by the blood, while others were seen sent off in canoes.

After the action we descended the hill, and encamped on a most beautiful plain, where we refreshed ourselves after the fatigues of the day, which were neither few nor small.

Monday this day, eight hundred men have been employed in destroying all the corn, etc., etc., etc., about the town, which is by far the finest I ever saw in my life; upwards of six thousand bushells have been cut down and piled up, the more effectually to destroy it. And such is the spirit of the troops that they have requested the General to put them upon half allowance of bread and beef, as long as they can supply themselves with corn and beans, in order that they may lengthen out the campaign and the more effectually to compleat the business they were sent upon, so that we have the strongest assurances to hope that under the smiles of Heaven we shall be able to work out a lasting blessing to our country.

I had almost forgot to tell you that we took two prisoners, a Negro and a Torie, one Hoghtailer from the Helder Barrack, who inform us that the enemy's force consisted of about two hundred and fifty white men, comanded by Col. and Capt. Butler, and about five hundred Indians commanded by Brandt; that they had eat nothing but corn for eight days past, except a small proportion of five small cattle; that before the corn was fit to roast they fed upon herbs and roots which they found in the woods.

We shall send off our wounded down to Tioga in boats brought up with provisions, but we have not five sick men in the whole army.

I beg you will receive this scrawl, as rough as the country thro' which we march, without reflecting on the accuracy of my aid de camp, who would have transcribed it, but the express is waiting with the utmost impatience. I am with perfect esteem, dear Brother, Yours sincerely,

James Clinton

—Clinton, *Public Papers*, V, 224-228.

3. "The Nests Are Destroyed but the Birds Are Still on the Wing"

Account of Jeremiah Fogg, major with General Sullivan.

[*September*] *30th, 1779*. Arrived at Tioga about 3 o'clock, where we were saluted by thirteen cannon from the fort. From hence we have water carriage to Wyoming, a most fortunate affair as our horses are worn down and our men are naked.

Although we are, now, one hundred and twenty miles from peaceful inhabitants, yet we consider ourselves at home, and the expedition ended; having fulfilled the expectations of our country by beating the enemies and penetrating and destroying their whole country. The undertaking was great and the task arduous. The multiplicity of disappointments, occasioning a long delay at the beginning, foreboded a partial, if not a total frustration of our design; but the unbounded ambition and perseverance of our commander and army led him to the full execution contrary to our most sanguine expectations.

The army marched from Tioga, with twenty pounds of beef and twenty seven pounds of flour per man, with which they marched twenty days out through an enemy's country yet unexplored with five pieces of artillery; having a road to clear, through swamps and over mountains a hundred and fifty miles; after having marched three hundred from their winter quarters; a cruel, subtle and desultory foe to contend with; void of hospital stores and conveniences for the sick and wounded; scarcely able to move for want of means of transportation. One battle, at the extent of our route, must have been attended with consequences such as nothing but the event itself could ascerain; yet a march of three hundred miles was performed, a battle was fought and a whole country desolated in thirty days.

But let us not arrogate too much, for "The battle is not to the strong" is a proverb fully verified in this expedition; the special hand and smiles of Providence being so apparently manifested that he who views the scene with indifference is worse than an infidel. The dimest eye must observe through the whole a succession of most unfortunate events. The very evils that at first predicted a defeat were a chain of causes in our favor. (I mean our delay.) Had we marched when we wished we could not have had a general engagement; for a great scarcity amounting almost to a famine the preceding year had prevented their embodying until the growth of the present crop, and we must therefore have been harassed daily by small parties much to our disadvantage. The artillery, which at first seemed a clog and totally useless, served a noble purpose. The action being general, their total rout together with the thunder of our artillery impressed them with such a terrific idea of our importance that a universal panic struck both the sachem and the warrior, each finding full employment in removing his little ones from threatening danger.

The place of action was likewise remarkable, having water carriage for our wounded. Not a single gun was fired for eighty miles on our march out, or an Indian seen on our return. Then we expected the greatest harassment—a hundred might have saved half their country by retarding us until our provisions were spent; and a like number hanging on our rear in the return would have occasioned the loss of much baggage and taught us an Indian dance. Their corn and vegetables were half our support, which we should have been deprived of had our march been earlier. And to say no more, the extraordinary continuance of fair weather has infinitely facilitated our expectations, having never been detained a single day, nor has there been an hour's rain since the thirtieth day of August.

The question will naturally arise, What have you to show for your exploits? Where are your prisoners? To which I reply that the rags and emaciated bodies of our soldiers must speak for our fatigue, and when the querist will point out a mode to tame a partridge, or the expediency of hunting wild turkeys with light horse, I will show them our prisoners. The nests are destroyed, but the birds are still on the wing.

—Cook, ed., *Journals of Expedition of Sullivan*, p. 101.

4. The Americans Carry Fire and Sword to the Onondaga

From the Journal of Erkuries Beatty, lieutenant with General Sullivan.

Kanadasgo. Wednesday 8th. This morning came out orders that the men was to remain here all day and for the men to clean their pieces likewise, for all the sick, lame, etc., to return to Tyoga properly officered. After 10 oclock Major Parr with the rifle corps and the cohoun was going up the lake to a little town called Kushay to destroy it. I with a number of others went volunteers and got there about 12 o'clock, found it about 8 miles from camp and the town opposite to where we lay two nights ago. The town consisted of about 15 houses tolerable well built and all together we got here 5 horses and a great number of potatoes, apples, peaches, cucumbers, watermelons, fowls, etc., and found a great quantity of corn here which we went about to destroy, after burning the houses, but our party being to[o] small Major Parr sent for a reinforcement to camp. We all lay under a bark hutt to night or shed. I believe the Indians had left it the same time they left Kanadasago. It lies on the banks of the lake, very prettyly situated, which is 4 miles wide here.

Tuesday 14th. The whole army was under arms this morning an hour before day and remained so till sunrise; about 7 oclock fatigue parties was sent out to destroy corn, which was there in great abundance, and beans. About 12 o'clock we marched, crossed over the branch of the Jinasee River and came upon a very beautiful flat of great extent growing up with wild grass higher in some places than our heads. We marched on this flat 2 mile and crossed the Jinesee River, which is about as big as the Tyoga but very crooked. Left the flats and marched thro the woods 3 mile and arrived at Chenesee Town, which is the largest we have yet seen; it lies in a crook of the river on extraordinary good land, about 70 houses, very compact and very well built, and about the same number of out houses in cornfields, etc. On entering the town we found the body of Lt. Boyd and another rifle man in a most terrible mangled condition. They was both stripped naked and their heads cut off, and the flesh of Lt. Boyds head was intirely taken of[f] and his eyes punched out. The other mans hed was not there. They was stabed, I supose, in 40 diferent places in the body with a spear and great gashes cut in their flesh with knifes, and Lt. Boyds privates was nearly cut of[f] and hanging down, his finger and toe nails was bruised of[f], and the dogs had eat part of their shoulders away; likewise a knife was sticking in Lt. Boyds body. They was imediately buried with the honour of war.

Wensday 15th. The whole army went out this morning 6 oclock to destroy corn and was out till 12 o'clock. There was here the greatest quantity of corn and beans here of any of the towns. Some of it we husked and threw in the river; the rest we carried to the houses and burned; the whole we totally destroyed. About 10 o'clock we received orders to begin our march home, which we did leaving the towns in flames. To day there was a white woman and child came in to us but I believe brought no intelligence of consequence. Marched over the Chenesee River and encamped after dark on the edge of the flats nigh to Cossawauloughly town.

Thursday 16th. The whole army was out this morning cutting corn which we left as we was going. Our brigade crossed the river to cut, which we did, and I believe there was a great quantity destroyed and some houses burnt. Marched of[f] about 10 o'clock in the following line of march: an advance guard of 100 men in front, Genl. Clintons brigade following in 4 columns, the other troops marching as usual, Genl. Hands brigade fetching up the rear, 2 pieces of artillery in the rear of him and the rifle men in the rear of the whole, the cohoun with the advance guard. Capt. Henderson with 60 men went in front of the army to bury the dead, and just as we came up he was a-going to bury 14 bodies in a most terrible mangled condition. They was buryed with the honour of war. Encamped to night at Adjutse. . . .

Tuesday 28th. This morning all the sick was ordered to go down in boats to Tiogo, and the lame to ride down the worst horses. The same detachment that was up the Tyoga yesterday was ordered up again to day and a very large comand was ordered to go down the Tyoga to destroy corn. Just as our detachment paraded Col. Butlers command came in and informed us that they had destroyed on the east side of the Cauga Lake three capital towns and a great number of scattering houses and destroyed a very great quantity of corn. The houses, I am informed, was much larger and better built than any we have yet seen, and it was a very old sittled country as they had great number of apple and peach trees which they likewise cut down. Our detachment marched up the Tyoga 5 miles above where we was yesterday and burnt 2 or 3 houses and destroyed a little corn on each side of the river. A little before night I went up the river about 5 mile farther but found no corn and returned, where we found them encamped in one of the corn fields but had no tents.

—Cook, ed., *Journals of Expedition of Sullivan*, pp. 30-35.

IV. THE AMERICANS STRIKE BACK: THE BRODHEAD EXPEDITION

The western Pennsylvania frontier was the scene of intermittent warfare all through the Revolution. Sparsely settled, it offered no substantial population on which to draw for defense, and a good many men of fighting age had joined the armies of the East, or those which George Rogers Clark from time to time recruited. The Allegheny frontier was exposed to attack by the Seneca from the north, by the Shawnee and the Miami from the west. In 1778 the Scots Highlander, Lachlan McIntosh of Charleston, was given command of the Western Department with headquarters at Pittsburgh. He did little but quarrel with his subordinates, and in the spring of 1779 he was directed to turn the command over to Daniel Brodhead. Brodhead was almost equally quarrelsome, but did display some energy. With some 600 men he advanced up the Allegheny to the New York border, through country "almost impassable by reason of the stupendous heights and frightful declivities," scattered a slight Indian opposition, burned Indian villages and fields of standing grain, and then returned to Fort Pitt—a march of 400 miles in 33 days without the loss of a man, something of a record in the Revolution.

We give here a letter from General McIntosh describing conditions on the Pennsylvania frontier, an account of the Brodhead expedition, and a report of a council meeting with the Wyandots—more commonly known as Hurons —of the Ohio country.

1. "THINGS HAVE TAKEN A TURN MUCH FOR THE WORSE"

General Lachlan McIntosh to George Washington.

March 12, 1779

The emigration down the Ohio from this quarter I fear will depopulate it altogether, unless I have orders to put a timely stop to it immediately. It is thought that near one half of what remain here will go down to Kentucky, the Falls or the Illinois, as they say themselves, this spring. Their design of securing land is so great, notwithstanding the danger of this country, they will go, etc.

I am sorry to inform you that, contrary to my expectations, things have taken a turn here much for the worse since I wrote you the 13th of January. The 30th of that month I received an express from Col. Gibson, informing me that one Simon Girty, a renegade among many others from this place, got a small party of Mingoes, a name by which the Six Nations, or rather Seneca Tribe, is known among the Western Indians, and waylaid Capt. Clark of the 8th Pennsylvania Regiment with a seargent and 14 privates, about three miles this side of Fort Laurens, as they were returning after escorting a few supplies from that post, and made Clark retreat to the fort again after killing two and taking one of his men with his saddle bags and all his letters.

Upon hearing this unexpected intelligence, I immediately sent for Cols. Crawford and Brodhead to advise with them upon the best method of supplying that garrison with provisions, of which it was very short, and we had barely horses enough fit for service to transport a sufficient quantity of flour over the mountains for our daily consumption, and scarce of forage for them, altho' they were most worn down. It was, therefore, thought most eligible upon that and other accounts to send a supply by water up Muskingum River by Maj. Taylor, who was charged with that duty. . . .

The 26th of February a scalping party killed and carried off 18 persons, men, women and children, upon the branches of Turtle Creek, 20 miles east of this, upon the Pennsylvania road, which was the first mischief done in the settlements since I marched for Tuscarawas, and made me apprehensive now that the savages were all inimically inclined, and struck the inhabitants of Westmoreland with such a panick that a great part of them were moving away. While I was endeavoring to rouse the militia, and contriving by their assistance to retaliate and make an excursion to some Mingo Towns upon the branches of Alleghany River who were supposed to have done the mischief, a messenger came to me the 3d of March instant, who slipt out of Fort Laurens in the night of Sunday the 28th February—by whom Col. Gibson would not venture to write—and informed me that on the morning of Tuesday, the 23d February, a waggoner who was sent out of the fort for the horses to draw wood, and 18 men to guard him, were fired upon, and all killed and scalped in sight of the fort, which the messenger left invested and besieged by a number of Wyandotts, Chippewas, Delawares. etc.; and in the last account I had from them, which made me very unhappy, as they were so short of provision, and out of my power to supply them with any quantity, or, if I had it, with men for an escort, since Major Taylor went, who I thought now was inevitably lost; and if I had both, there were no horses to carry it, or forage to feed them, without which they cannot subsist at this season.

In this extreme emergency and difficulty, I earnestly requested the lieutenants of the several countys on this side of the mountains to collect all of the men, horses, provisions and forage they could at any price and repair to Beaver Creek [Fort McIntosh] on Monday next, the 15th instant, in order to march on that or the next day to Tuscarawas; and if they would not be prevailed on to turn out, I was determined with such of the Continental troops as are able [to] march, and all the provisions we have, at all events to go to the relief of Fort Laurens; upon the support of which I think the salvation of this part of the country depends.

I have yet no intelligence from the country that I can depend on. Some say the people will turn out on this occasion with their horses; others, that mischievous persons influenced by our disgusted staff are discouraging them as much as possible. But I am now happily relieved by the arrival of Major Taylor here, who returned with 100 men and 200 kegs of flour. He was six days going up about 20 miles of Musking[um] River, the waters were so high and stream so rapid; and as he had above 130 miles more to go, he judged it impossible to relieve Col. Gibson in time, and therefore returned, having lost two of his men sent to flank him upon the shore, who were killed and scalpt by some warriors coming down Muskingum River, and I have my doubts of our only pretended friends, the Delawares of Cooshocking, as none other are settled upon that water.

I have the honor to enclose you the last return from Col. Brodhead at Beaver Creek. . . .

—KELLOGG, *Frontier Advance*, 240-242.

2. COLONEL BRODHEAD SPREADS DESOLATION ALONG THE ALLEGHENY

Pittsburgh, September 16, 1779

Colonel Brodhead, who commanded a party from Fort Pitt, has penetrated the Indian country, lying on the Alleghany River, one hundred and eighty miles, burnt ten of the Mingo, Munsey and Seneca towns in that quarter, containing one hundred and sixty-five houses, and destroyed all the fields of corn, computed to be five hundred acres, with the only loss on our side three men slightly wounded. Forty-three of their warriors were met by Lieutenant Harding and an advance party of twenty-two men, who attacked the savages and routed them, killed five on the spot and took all their canoes and blankets.

A gentleman who attended Colonel Brodhead, gives the following particular account of the expedition:—The many savage barbarities and horrid depredations committed by the Seneca and Munsey nations upon the western frontiers had determined Colonel Brodhead, as the most effectual way to prevent such hostilities in future, and revenge the past, to carry the war into their own country and strike a decisive blow at their towns.

On the 11th of August, our little army, consisting of only six hundred and five rank and file, marched from Pittsburg with one month's provision. At Mahoning, fifteen miles above the Old Kittanning, we were detained four days by the excessive rains, from whence (leaving the river, which flows in a thousand manners) we proceeded by a blind path leading to Cuscushing, through a country almost impassable by reason of the stupendous heights and frightful declivities, with a continued range of craggy hills, overspread with fallen timber, thorns and underwood; here and there an intervening valley, whose deep, impenetrable gloom has always been impervious to the piercing rays of the warmest sun. As Cuscushing (which is fifteen miles above Venango) we crossed the Alleghany and continued our route upon its banks. But here our march was rendered still more difficult by the mountains, which jutted close upon the river, forming a continued narrow defile, allowing us only the breadth of an Indian path to march upon.

In the midst of these defiles, our advanced party, consisting of fifteen white men and eight Delawares, discovered between thirty and forty warriors land-ing from their canoes, who, having also seen part of our troops, immediately stripped themselves and prepared for action. Lieutenant Harding, who com-manded our advance, disposed his men in a semi-circular form, and began the attack with such irresistible fury, tomahawk in hand, that the savages could not long sustain the charge, but fled with the utmost horror and precipitation, some plunging themselves into the river, and others, favored by the thickness of the bushes, made their escape on the main, leaving five dead on the field, without any loss on our side except three men slightly wounded.

Upon the first alarm, supposing it to be more serious, the army was arranged for fight; both officers and men, enraged at their former cruelties, animated by the calmness, resolution and intrepidity of the commandant, showed the utmost ardor to engage; and had the action been general, we had every pros-pect of the most ample success from a brave commander at the head of brave men.

Continuing our march, we arrived the same day at Buchan, where, leaving our baggage, stores, etc., under a guard, we proceeded to their towns with the utmost despatch, which we found at the distance of about twenty miles further, with extensive cornfields on both sides of the river, and deserted by the inhabitants on our approach. Eight towns we set in flames and committed their pagod and war posts to the river. The corn, amounting in the whole to near six hundred acres, was our next object, which in three days we cut down and piled into heaps, without the least interruption from the enemy.

Upon our return, we several times crossed a creek about ten miles above Venango, remarkable for an oily liquid which oozes from the sides and bottom of the channel and the adjacent springs, much resembling British oil, and if applied to woolen cloth, burns in an instant.

After burning the old towns of Conauwago and Mahusquachinkocken, we arrived at Pittsburg, the fourteenth instant, with the scalps we had taken and three thousand dollars' worth of plunder; having, in the course of thirty-three days, completed a march of near four hundred miles, through a country the Indians had hitherto thought impenetrable by us, and considered as a sufficient barrier for the security of their towns; and, indeed, nothing but the absolute necessity of such a measure and a noble sprit of enterprise could be a sufficient inducement to undertake so arduous a task and encounter those difficulties and obstacles which require the most consummate fortitude to surmount.

—Moore, *Diary of the American Revolution*, II, 216-219.

3. The Wyandot Treat for Peace but Brodhead Is Not Content

A. the wyandots' speech to colonel daniel brodhead,
headquarters, pittsburgh, september 17, 1779

The Speech of Doonyontat, the Wyandot Chief, to Maghingwe Keeshuch:
Brother, listen to me!
Brother, it grieves me to see you with the tears in your eyes. I know it is the fault of the English.

Brother, I wipe away all those tears, and smooth down your hair, which the English and the folly of my young men has ruffled.

Now, *my brother*, I have wiped away all the stains from your clothes, and smoothed them where my young men had ruffled them, so that you may now put on your hat, and sit with that ease and composure which you would desire.

(Four strings of white wampum)

Brother, listen to the Huron Chiefs!

Brother, I see you all bloody by the English and my young men. I now wipe away all those stains and make you clean.

Brother, I see your heart twisted, and neck and throat turned to the one side, with the grief and vexation which my young men have caused, all which disagreeable sensations I now remove, and restore you to your former tranquillity, so that now you may breathe with ease, and enjoy the benefit of your food and nourishment.

Brother, your ears appear to be stopped, so that you cannot listen to your brothers when they talk of friendship. That deafness I now remove, and all stoppage from your ears, that you may listen to the friendly speeches of your brothers, and they may sink deep into your heart.

(Seven strings of white wampum)

Brother, listen to me!

When I look around me, I see the bones of our nephews lie scattered and unburied.

Brother, I gather up the bones of all our young men on both sides, in this dispute, without any distinction of party.

Brother, I have now gathered up all the bones of our relations on both sides, and will bury them in a large deep grave, and smooth it over so that there shall not be the least sign of bones, or any thing to raise any grief or anger in our minds hereafter.

Brother, I have now buried the bones of all our and your relations very deep. You very well know that there are some of your flesh and blood in our hands prisoners: I assure you that you shall see them all safe and well.

(Eight strings of white wampum)

Brother, I now look up to where our Maker is, and think there is still some darkness over our heads, so that God can hardly see us, on account of the evil doings of the King over the great waters. All these thick clouds, which have [been] raised on account of that bad King, I now entirely remove, that God may look and see in our treaty of friendship, and be a witness to the truth and sincerity of our intentions.

(Four strings of white wampum)

Brother, As God puts all our hearts right, I now give thanks to God Almighty, to the chief men of the Americans, to my old father the King of France, and to you, Brother, that we can now talk together on friendly terms, and speak our sentiments without interruption.

(Four strings of black and white wampum)

Brother, you knew me before you saw me and that I had not drawn away my hand from yours, as I sent word last year by Captain White Eyes.

Brother, I look up to Heaven, and call God Almighty to witness to the truth of what I say, and that it really comes from my heart.

Brother, I now tell you that I have forever thrown off my Father the English, and will never give him any assistance; and there are some amongst all the nations that think the same things that I do, and I wish they would all think so. . . .

Brother, I now take a firmer hold of your hand than before, and beg that you will take pity upon other nations who are my friends, and if any of them should incline to take hold of your hand, I request that you would comply and receive them into friendship.

(A black belt of eleven rows)

Brother, listen! I tell you to be cautious, as I think you intend to strike the man near to where I sit [the chief refers to an anticipated attack upon Detroit by the American forces], not to go the nighest way to where he is, lest you frighten the owners of the lands who are living through the country between this and that place.

Brother, you now listen to me, and one favour I beg of you is that when you drive away your enemies you will allow me to continue in possession of my property, which if you grant will rejoice me.

Brother, I would advise you, when you strike the man near where I sit, to go by water, as it will be the easiest and best way.

Brother, if you intend to strike, one way is to go up the Allegheny and by Prisquille; another way is to go down this river and up the Wabash.

Brother, the reason why I mentioned the road up the river is that there will be no danger of your being discovered until you are close upon them, but on the road down the river you will be spied.

Brother, now I have told you the way by Prisquille, and that it is the boundary between us and your enemies; if you go by Wabash your friends will not be surprised.

Brother, you must not think that what I have said is only my own thoughts, but the opinion of all the Huron Chiefs, and I speak in behalf of them all. If you grant what favours I have asked of you, all our friends and relations will be thankful and glad as far as they can hear all round.

Brother, the reason why I have pointed out these two roads is that when we hear you are in one of them we will know your intentions without further notice, and the Huron Chiefs desired me particularly to mention it that they may meet you in your walk, and tell you what they have done, who are your enemies and who are your friends, and I in their name request a pair of colors to shew we have joined in friendship. . . .

(Fourteen strings of black wampum)

B. COLONEL DANIEL BRODHEAD'S SPEECH TO DOONYONTAT,
THE WYANDOT CHIEF, SEPTEMBER 18TH, 1779

Maghingwe Keeshuch to Doonyontat, principal chief of the Wyandots
Brother, yesterday I had the pleasure to hear you speak. But when I had heard

all, and you had taken no notice of what I mentioned to you before against the English, I could not tell what to think.

Brother, the Chiefs of the Wyondats have lived too long with the English to see things as they ought to do. They must have expected when they were councilling that the Chief they sent to this council fire would find the Americans asleep. But the sun which the Great Spirit has set to light this island discovers to me that they are much mistaken.

(Four strings of white and black wampum)

Brother, I will tell you why they are mistaken: they must have thought that it was an easy matter to satisfy us, after doing all the mischief they could. They must have heard that the English were getting weaker and the Americans stronger, and that a few flattering words would, with giving up our prisoners, secure to them their lives, the lives of their women and children, and their lands and the wicked Shawnese who have so often embrued their hands in the blood of the Americans; and that in my military operations they had a right to mark out the road I should march on.

(Six strings of white and black wampum)

Brother, I, however, thank you for wiping away the blood and burying the bones of our young men, and for casting off that bad father the King of Britain over the great lake. . . .

(Three strings of white wampum)

Brother, I will now tell you what I conceive to be right, and I will leave it to all the world to judge it. I think the Nations you mention and wish me to receive into friendship, ought to send hostages to me. As I said before, unless they have killed and taken as many from the English and their allies as they have killed and taken from the Americans, and return whatever they have stolen from their brothers, together with their flesh and blood, and on every occasion join us against their enemies—upon these terms, which are just, they and their posterity may live in peace and enjoy their property without disturbance from their brethren of this island, so long as the sun shines or the waters run.

(A black belt—rows)

Brother, I have now spoke from my heart. I am a warrior as well as a councillor; my words are few, but what I say I will perform. And I must tell you that if the Nations will not do justice, they will not be able, after the English are driven from this island, to enjoy peace or property.

(Four strings black wampum)

Brother, when I go to war, I will take my choice of roads; if I meet my friends I shall be glad to see them, and if I meet my enemies I shall be ready to fight them.

Brother, you told you had not yet spoken to the Shawnese. You likewise say that you had not yet let slip my hand; if so, why did you not speak to them? They have heard their grandfathers the Delawares, and they have heard me. I sent them a good talk, but they threw it into the fire.

Now, *Brother*, I must tell you that I cannot now prevent the Shawnese being struck. Col. Clark, I hear, is gone against them and will strike them before I can send to him to call him back; but if the Shawnese do what is right, as I have told you, they should enjoy peace and property. This belt confirms my words.

> *(A white and black belt—rows)*
> —KELLOGG, ed., *Frontier Retreat*, 67-72.

V. THE FINAL CAMPAIGNS ALONG THE NEW YORK BORDERLANDS

Sullivan's expedition had checked but not defeated the Tories and their Indian allies, and there were still two more years of war along the battered New York frontier. In April 1780 Brant destroyed the little village of Harpersfield and attacked the Schoharie forts. The next month Sir John Johnson came down the Champlain, destroyed Johnstown, and swept on to the Mohawk Valley settlements. The American reaction was feeble, and in August the British renewed their assault, burning Canajoharie, on the Mohawk, and once again ravaging Schoharie. In September Johnson collected a formidable force at Montreal, ferried them across to Oswego, and marched on Unadilla on the upper Susquehanna; here he joined forces with Brant, and together they ravaged at will the Mohawk and Schoharie valleys. Finally the Americans collected a force under General Robert Van Rensselaer, advanced on the enemy and dispersed him, but Van Rensselaer lacked the resolution to pursue the defeated foe, and the campaign was, once again, inconclusive. The following spring, 1781, Brant and Johnson and Walter Butler were once again on the warpath, spreading death and destruction almost at will. Not until the fall did the Americans strike back with any effectiveness. Then Governor Clinton called on that sturdy frontier fighter, Colonel Marinus Willett, to save the border. Willett met the enemy at Johnstown, defeated them, and pursued them relentlessly to the gates of Oswego.

1. AN INCONCLUSIVE FIGHT AT CANAJOHARIE

A. "THE ENEMY HAVE BURNT THE WHOLE OF SCHOHARY"

Lieutenant Colonel V. Veeder to General Robert Van Rensselaer.

> Lower Fort Schoharie, October 17, 1780

Dear Sir, The enemy have burnt the whole of Schohary; the first fire was discovered about the middle fort 8 o'clock this morning; they passed by this post on both sides at 4 o'clock this afternoon; they took the whole of their booty and moved down to Harmen Sitneys; they have fired two swivel shoots thro' the roof of the church. I have sent three scouts to make some discoveries about the middle fort at different times this day, and none have as yet returned; no express has arrived at this post from either fort; by what we have seen of the enemy we suppose their force to be between 5 or 600, mostly regulars and Tories.

> —CLINTON, *Public Papers*, VI, 303.

B. GENERAL VAN RENSSELAER IS APPREHENSIVE

Robert Van Rensselaer to Governor George Clinton.

Canajoharie opposite Frey's, October 18, 1780

Sir, this morning about nine I arrived so near the enemy's rear as to afford me a prospect of engaging them before noon. They have, however, by the celerity of their movements effected their escape to Stone Arabia, part of which is now in flames and the whole will probably share the same fate before I can possibly support the distressed inhabitants. I intend to ford the river immediately and march in quest of them, but harrassed and fatigued as my force is by a long march, I am apprehensive I shall not be able to pursue them with that dispatch which is necessary to overtake them. No exertion, however, shall be wanting on my part to effect it. . . .

—CLINTON, *Public Papers*, VI, 319.

C. "SIR JOHN JOHNSON HAS BEEN PUT TO ROUT"

General Philip Schuyler to Governor George Clinton.

Saratoga, October 20, 1780

Dear Sir: Your Excellency's favor of yesterday morning from Caghnawaga I had the pleasure to receive at five in the afternoon. I am happy to learn that Sir John Johnson has been overtaken and put to rout; when your letter arrived, we had about 150 men at Fort Edward and as many more had arrived here about ten in the morning; those at Fort Edward without any beef, and those here with none but what I could furnish them; all my cattle fit for the knife are already killed and I have sent to try and collect some more, but I fear a supply will arrive too late to push a party in pursuit of the enemy who were at Ballstown. I have, however, sent to Fort Edward on the subject, but with little hopes that any will move from thence. One of the enemies party, who stole into the country and was taken, informs that Major Carlton intended to remain at Tyconderoga and to push for White Creek as soon as the militia should be retired; the prisoner calls himself an ensign and came from New York in August last. Another villain is gone past here, who corroborates the account as some tories advice with whom he lodged.

The panic that has seized the people is incredible; with all my efforts I cannot prevent numbers from deserting their habitations, and I very much apprehend that the whole will move, unless the militia will remain above until a permanent relieve can be procured. I am, D'r Sir, most sincerely your Excellency's Obed: Hu. Serv't.

—CLINTON, *Public Papers*, VI, 324-325.

D. ONCE AGAIN SIR JOHN AND BRANT ESCAPE

Governor George Clinton to George Washington.

Pokeepsie, October 30, 1780

Dear Sir, My last letter was dated at Albany and communicated the disagreeable intelligence of the destruction of Schoharie and part of Balls Town, about 12 miles northeast of Schenectady, since which I have not been able to write to Your Excellency. As I then proposed, I immediately left Albany in order to take the necessary measures for checking further incursions of the enemy. On my arrival at Schenectady I was advised that the different parties of the enemy at Schoharie and Balls Town had left those places, the former moving towards the Mohawk River and the latter shaping their course towards Sacondaga.

Genl. Van Rensselaer, who had arrived at Schenectady before me, at the head of about four or five hundred militia and with orders to act according to emergencies, on receiving this intelligence immediately moved up the river in hopes of being able to gain their front, but this proved impracticable as their route was much shorter and their troops more enured to marching; they reached the river at the confluence of the Schoharie Kill about six miles ahead of him, and recommenced in that fertile country their devastations by burning the houses and with marks of the greatest barbarity destroying every thing in their way.

Under these circumstances I was exceedingly perplexed. The militia under Genl. Rensselaer were inferior in number to that of the enemy. The few I had with me were too far in the rear to sustain them and not much could be expected from the militia of the country through which the enemy passed, their whole attention being engaged in the preservation of their families, and the levies were necessarily very much dispersed at the different posts to cover the frontier settlements against the incursions of small parties. Genl. Rensselaer, however, continued to move on and, being soon after joined by Col. DuBois with between 3 and 400 levies and 60 of the Oneida Indians, pursued the enemy with vigor; he came up with them and attacked them at Fox Mills (26 miles from where the enemy first struck the river) about sunset. After a considerable resistance they gave way and fled with precipitation, leaving behind them their baggage, provisions and a brass three-pounder with its ammunition.

The night came on too soon for us to avail ourselves of all the advantages which we had reason to promise ourselves from this action. The enemy took advantage of passing the river at a ford a little above where they again collected and renewed their march up the river with great celerity, and it became necessary for our troops, who had marched upwards of 30 miles without halting, to retire from the ground to refresh themselves. The pursuit was, however, renewed early in the morning and the enemy so closely pushed as to prevent their doing any farther mischief.

The morning after the action, I arrived with the militia under my immediate command, but they were so beat out with fatigue, having marched at least 50 miles in less than 24 hours, as to be unable to proceed any farther. I, therefore, left them and put myself at the head of the advanced troops and continued the pursuit till within about 15 miles of Oneida, and if we could possibly have procured provission to have enabled us to have persisted one or two days longer, there is little doubt that we might have succeeded, at least so far as to have scattered their main body and made many prisoners, but there was no supplies but such as I was obliged to take from the inhabitants on our route and these was inadequate and the collection of them attended with delay, nor could the pack horses, with the small quantities procured in this disagreeable manner, overtake us in so rapid a march through a perfect wilderness. I was, therefore, obldiged, tho' reluctantly, to return, most of the troops having been near two days utterly destitute and unable to proceed. Sir John, Brandt and Butler, immediately after the action at Fox Mills, left their troops and, with a party of Indians on horseback, struck across the country and went towards Oneida, taking their wounded with them. We discovered where they joined their main body again near the waters of the Susquehanna about six miles on this side where we quitted the pursuit. Brandt was wounded through the foot. . . .

The losses we have sustained by these different incursions of the enemy will be most severely felt; they have destroyed, on a moderate computation, 200 dwellings and 150,000 bushels of wheat, with a proportion of other grain and forage. The enemy to the northward continue in the neighborhood of Crown Point, and the inhabitants, in consequence of their apprehensions of danger, are removing from the northern parts of the state. . . .

—CLINTON, *Public Papers*, VI, 351-354.

2. COLONEL WILLETT DRIVES THE BRITISH FROM NEW YORK

Colonel Marinus Willett to Major General Stirling.

26 October, 1781

Major Ross, commanding officer at Bucks Island, with about 450 men left that place in batteaux and proceeded to Oneida Lake, where they left their boats, some provisions and about 20 lame men to take care of them, and proceeded from thence by the way of Cherry Valley to the Mohawk River, and made their first appearance at the place opposite to Anthony's Nose, from whence they proceeded to Warrens Bush and its vicinity and destroyed upwards of 20 farm houses with out houses, great quantity of grain and killed two persons; after that they crossed the Mohawk River at a fording place about 20 miles above this place and proceeded in order to Sir William's [Johnson] Hall, where they arrived about one quarter of an hour before Col. Willet with his body, who had crossed the river about 6 miles higher and marched also for the same place. Col. Willet commenced an action with the British which was much in his favor, had not some of his troops which covered a field piece gave way, which was the loss of the piece and ammunition cart, which in a little while after he bravely recovered; the enemy had, however, stripped the cart of all its ammunition. The evening coming on put an end to the action; part of Col. Willets men, however, passed the hall all night. The enemy retreated about 6 miles back into the woods, where the last account just now comes leaves them. About thirty British have been taken during the action and in the morning before the action commenced yesterday in the afternoon.

Col. Willett went in pursuit of them this morning with a force about equal to theirs. An account is also come to hand (altho not official) that a party is sent from Fort Herkimer to destroy their boats and provisions. There are 7 of the enemy found dead on the field of action this morning, and 3 of ours; between thirty and 40 wounded on both sides.

—CLINTON, *Public Papers*, VII, 443-444.

3. The Death of Captain Walter Butler

Colonel Marinus Willett to Governor George Clinton.

Fort Rensselaer, 2nd November, 1781

Dear Sir, I am just returned from a most fatiguing pursuit of the enemy, and tho it has not been in my power to take or kill the whole of the detachment that lately made their appearance in this quarter, yet I flatter myself they are little better off, as those that are not among the killed and taken are in a famising situation, scattered throughout the wilderness on the rout to Buck Island, where any of them that may arrive will have tales of horror only to relate.

After the affair at Johnstown, which happened on the 25th ultimo, and which would at once have proved fatal to them had the right wing of the small number of troops I had engaged behaved half as well as the left, the enemy took to the wilderness and, finding it out of their power to pass us so as to get to the Oneida Creek where they had left their boats, they directed their rout towards Buck Island, keeping far back in the wilderness. This determined me to cut across from the German Flatts in order to intercept them on that rout. Accordingly, on the evening of the 28th, having furnished near 400 men and sixty Indians, who had just joined me, with four days and a half provisions, which was all I could procure, I crossed the Mohawk from Fort Herkimer and incamped in the woods.

The 29th we marched north upwards of twenty miles in a snow storm, and at eight oclock A.M. of the 30th we fell in with the enemy, who, without making any resistance worth mentioning, fled from that time until night. We pursued them closely and warmly as possible. Nor did they ever attempt to check us in our advance except at one difficult ford in Canada Creek, where they lost several of their men. Amongst those killed at that place was Walter Butler, the person who commanded the massacre at Cherry Valley in November 1778. He was called Major, but by the commission found in his pocket appears to be no more than a captain.

A number of prisoners have been taken and many were killed in our intercourse with those gentry.

To pursue them any farther was thought improper; many of the troops as well as the Indians had laid aside their blankets and provisions in order to pursue with greater ease. And in the evening we find ourselves at least twenty miles from those packs. The woods was strewed with the packs of the enemy; provision they had none. The few horses they had amongst them when we first fell in with them, they were obliged to leave; except five, which were sent a considerable way in front, with some of their wounded and a few prisoners. Their flight was performed in an Indian file upon a constant trott, and one man's being knocked in the head or falling off into the woods never stoped the progress of his neighbour. Not even the fall of their favorite Butler could attract their attention so much as to induce them to take even the money or anything else out of his pocket, altho he was not dead when found by one of our Indians, who finished his business for him and got a considerable booty.

Strange as it may appear, yet it is true, that notwithstanding the enemy had been four days with only half a pound of horseflesh for each man per day, yet they did not halt from the time we began to pursue them untill they had proceeded more than thirty miles (and they continued their rout a considerable part of the night). In this situation to the compassion of a starving wilderness, we left them in a fair way of receiving a punishment better suited to their merit than a musquet ball, a tomahawk or captivity. . . .

—CLINTON, *Public Papers*, VII, 472-474.

CHAPTER TWENTY-SEVEN

The Conquest of the Old Northwest

MANY OF *the American colonies had claims to lands west of the Appalachians; none of these claims was so well established, or so extensive, as those of Virginia which ran "westward and northward from sea to sea." First the Proclamation Line of 1763 and next the Quebec Act of 1774 challenged colonial claims to the land north of the Ohio. At the time of the outbreak of the war British control over the vast area west of Niagara and south of the Great Lakes was pretty well established. Niagara was one center of British power, Detroit another, and Michilimackinac a third; these were designed to give the British control of the fur trade, of the Indians, and of the water system of the West.*

With the Revolution Virginia—and to a lesser extent other American states—revived their claims to the West. Kentucky had been explored from Virginia as early as the 1750's, but it was not until 1774 that James Harrod planted the first permanent settlement, at Harrodsburg; the next year saw the establishment of Boonesborough and St. Asaph—named after the Anglican bishop so friendly to the American cause.

From the beginning Kentucky was on the defensive, open to raids by the Indians, chiefly those north of the Ohio—and to attack by the British. There is little doubt that the feeble frontier settlements would have been overwhelmed had it not been for the foresight and energy of one man, George Rogers Clark. It was Clark who saved Kentucky; it was Clark who "conquered" the Northwest—that it did not stay conquered was not his fault. No other chapter in the history of the Revolution is so dominated by one man as is this chapter of the struggle for the Northwest. Only 23 when the war broke out, Clark had already had a long experience as surveyor and Indian fighter, and as a leader of those who wanted to see Kentucky part of Virginia, and not a proprietary colony. In 1776 Clark went east to Williamsburg to enlist support for the defense of Kentucky, and was partially successful. During the following year he came to realize that the only effective defense was offense, and conceived the grandiose plan of saving Kentucky by conquering the Northwest—Vincennes, Detroit and Michilimackinac. This plan too he presented to the Virginia authorities, who responded with approval though not with help. Jefferson, for one, saw that a conquest of the Northwest "would have an important bearing ultimately in establishing our western boundary." In any event Clark was commissioned colonel in the Virginia forces, authorized to raise seven companies, and to conquer the northwest—for Virginia.

How Clark carried out this mission is one of the most familiar—and most heroic—chapters in the history of the Revolution; we have given here some of the essential accounts. With less than 200 men he floated down the Ohio to Ft. Massac, below Louisville, marched overland to Kaskaskia and captured it without a struggle. Cahokia surrendered, and so did Vincennes, and the American flag waved over the Northwest. That winter however Governor Hamilton swept down from Detroit with an army of 1,000 Indians and regulars and took over Vincennes. Clark's reconquest of Vincennes, in mid-winter of 1779, remains, with Arnold's march on Quebec, the most heroic episode of the war; unlike Arnold's march it ended not in frustration but in triumph.

Just as the war along the New York border dragged on for two years after Sullivan's expedition, so the war in the Illinois country, Ohio and Kentucky, dragged on to the bitter end. After his victory at Vincennes, Clark was almost continuously on the defensive. He met a British threat to the Spanish outpost in St. Louis in 1780; he hurried back to Kentucky and into Ohio to deal with a serious attack under Colonel Bird; in 1781 he tried to mount an offensive against Detroit but instead was forced to parry a series of attacks on Kentucky. The worst of these attacks came in 1782 while Clark was busy with the defenses at Fort Nelson near the Falls of the Ohio. A band of Pennsylvanians had massacred, in cold blood, the Christian Indians of Gnaddenhütten; this appalling act aroused the Indians of the Ohio country to new energies and new furies. First they defeated a small expedition under Colonel Crawford, subjecting him to fiendish tortures; then in July they invaded Kentucky, besieged Bryant's Station, and, at the battle of Blue Licks (August 19, 1782), inflicted one of the worst defeats of the war on the Kentucky frontiersmen. Clark mounted a counteroffensive into Ohio, with limited success.

Did Clark win the Northwest? This is, in a sense, a trick question. He did conquer the Northwest, but could not hold it. Yet at the close of the war Kentucky was in American hands, and so, too, much of the territory of Ohio and Illinois, while St. Louis was controlled by the Spaniards—who had even thrust one expedition all the way to southern Michigan! Whether the treaty of peace ratified what Clark had achieved, whether it ratified only what he was supposed to have achieved, or whether it recognized merely the inevitable, we are not called on to decide. However clouded the years from 1780 to 1783, nothing can dim Clark's great achievements of 1778 and 1779.

I. KASKASKIA AND VINCENNES: THE FIRST CONQUEST

These three documents tell their own story, and require neither explanation nor elaboration. Two of them are from the vigorous pen of Clark himself—the appeal to Governor Patrick Henry, and the account, written a year later to the Virginian George Mason, of the first conquest of the Illinois country. The third comes from Governor Hamilton. Poor Hamilton had, then and later, a bad reputation. Known as "the hair-buyer" he was execrated throughout the borderlands, and when he was captured and sent to Virginia, Jefferson refused to exchange him or release him on parole because of his reputation for wickedness. He was probably neither better nor worse than other British and American officers dealing with Indians, and it is interesting to note that he himself was horrified at what he regarded as barbarous conduct by Clark!

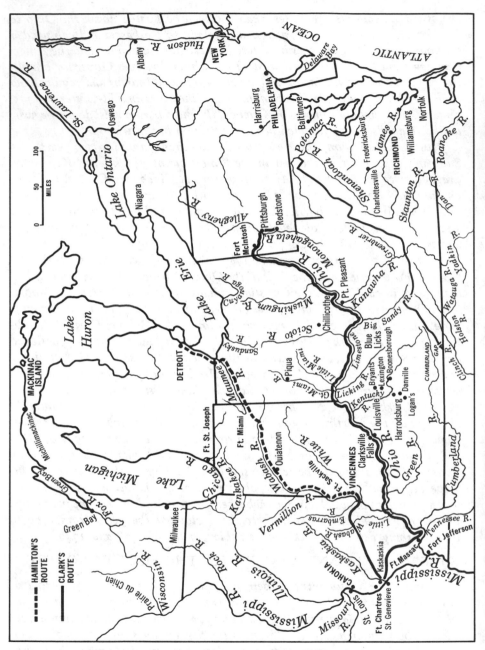

From George Rogers Clark
by James A. James

Courtesy of the University of Chicago Press

THE NORTHWEST

1. Kaskaskia "Would Give Us the Command of the Two Great Rivers"

Colonel George Rogers Clark to Governor Patrick Henry, summer or fall of 1777.

According to promise I haste to give you a description of the town of Kuskuskies, and my plan for taking of it. It is situated 30 leagues above the mouth of the Ohio, on a river of its own name, five miles from its mouth and two miles east of the Mississippi. On the west side of the Mississippi 3 miles from Kuskuskies is the village of Mozier [Misere—Ste. Genevieve] belonging to the Spaniards. The town of Kuskuskies contains about one hundred families of French and English and carry on an extensive trade with the Indians; and they have a considerable number of Negroes that bear arms and are chiefly employed in managing their farms that lay around the town, and send a considerable quantity of flour and other commodities to New Orleans. The houses are framed and very good, with a small but elegant stone fort situated [but a little distance from] the centre of the town. The Mississippi is undermining a part of Fort Chartress; the garrison was removed to this place, which greatly added to its wealth; but on the commencement of the present war, the troops [were] called off to re-inforce Detroit, which is about three hundred miles from it—leaving the fort and all its stores in care of one Roseblack [Rocheblave] as commandant of the place, with instructions to influence as many Indians as possible to invade the Colonies, and to supply Detroit with provisions, a considerable quantity of which goes by the way of the Waubash River, and have but a short land carriage to the waters of the [Maumee].

. . . The fort, which stands a small distance below the town is built of stockading about ten feet high, with blockhouses at each corner, with several pieces of cannon mounted—powder, ball and other necessary stores without [any] guard or a single soldier. Roseblock, who has acted as governor, by large presents engaged the Waubash Indians to invade the frontiers of Kentucky; was daily treating with other nations, giving large presents and offering them great rewards for scalps. The principal inhabitants are entirely against the American cause, and look on us as notorious rebels that ought to be subdued at any rate; but I don't doubt but after being acquainted with the cause they would become good friends to it.

The remote situation of this town on the back of several of the Western Nations; their being well supplied with goods on the Mississippi, enables them to furnish the different nations, and by presents will keep up a strict friendship with the Indians; and undoubtedly will keep all the nations that lay under their influence at war with us during the present contest, without they are induced to submission; they will be able to interrupt any communication that we should want to hold up and down the Mississippi, without a strong guard; having plenty of swivels they might, and I dont doubt but would keep armed boats for the purpose of taking our property. On the contrary, if it was in our possession it would distress the garrison at Detroit for provisions, it would fling the command of the two great rivers into our hands, which would enable us to get supplies of goods from the Spaniards, and to carry on a trade with the Indians. . . .

I am sensible that the case stands thus—that [we must] either take the town of Kuskuskies, or in less than twelve month send an army against the Indians on Wabash, which will cost ten times as much, and not be of half the service.
—CLARK PAPERS, *Ill. State Hist. Lib. Coll.*, VIII, 30-32.

2. THE AMERICANS CAPTURE KASKASKIA

George Rogers Clark to George Mason.

November 19, 1779

I set out from Red Stone the 12th of May, 1778, leaving the country in great confusion, much distressed by the Indians. General Hand, pleased with my intentions, furnished me with every necessary I wanted, and the — of May I arrived at the Canoweay (Kanawha) to the joy of the garrison, as they were very weak and had the day before been attacted by a large body of Indians. Being joined by Capt. Oharrads company on his way to the Osark, after spending a day or two we set out and had a very pleasant voyage to the Falls of Ohio, having sent expresses to the stations on Kentucky from the mouth of the river for Capt. Smith to join me immediately, as I made no doubt but that he was wateing for me. But you may easily guess at my mortification on being informed that he had not arrived; that all his men had been stopt by the incessant labours of the populace, except part of a company that had arrived under the command of one Capt. Delland, some on their march being threatened to be put in prison if they did not return. This information made me as desperate as I was before determined.

Reflecting on the information that I had of some of my greatest opponents censureing the Governour for his conduct, as they thought, ordering me for the protection of Kentucky only; that and some other secret impulses occasioned me in spite of all council to risque the expedition to convince them of their error, until that moment secret to the principal officers I had. I was sensible of the impression it would have on many to be taken near a thousand [miles] from the body of their country to attact a people five times their number, and merciless tribes of Indians, their allies and determined enemies to us.

I knew that my case was desperate, but the more I reflected on my weakness the more I was pleased with the enterprise. Joined by a few of the Kentuckians, under Col. Montgomery, to stop the desertion I knew would ensue on troops knowing their destination, I had encamped on a small island in the middle of the Falls, kept strict guard on the boats, but Lieutenant Hutchings of Dillards Company contrived to make his escape with his party after being refused leave to return. Luckely a few of his men was taken the next day by a party sent after them. On this island I first began to discipline my little army, knowing that to be the most essential point towards success. Most of them determined to follow me. The rest seeing no probability of making their escape, I soon got that subbordination as I could wish for. About twenty families that had followed me much against my inclination I found now to be of service to me in guarding a block house that I had erected on the island to secure my provisions.

I got every thing in readiness on the 26th of June, set off from the Falls, double manned our oars and proceeded day and night until we run into the mouth of the Tenesse River. The fourth day landed on an island to prepare ourselves for a march by land. A few hours after we took a boat of hunters but eight days from Kaskaskias; before I would suffer them to answer any person a question after their taking the oath of allegiance, I examined them particularly. They were Englishmen, and appeared to be in our interest; their intiligence was not favourable; they asked leave to go on the expedition. granted it, . . .

In the evening of the same day I run my boats into a small creek about one mile above the old Fort Missack, reposed ourselves for the night, and in the morning took a rout to the northwest and had a very fatigueing journey for about fifty miles, until we came into those level plains that is frequent throughout this extensive country. As I knew my success depended on secrecy, I was much afraid of being discovered in these meadows, as we might be seen in many places for several miles. Nothing extraordinary happened dureing our route excepting my guide loosing himself and not being able, as we judged by his confusion, of giving a just acccount of himself; it put the whole troops in the greatest confusion.

I never in my life felt such a flow of rage—to be wandering in a country where every nation of Indians could raise three or four times our number, and a certain loss of our enterprise by the enemie's getting timely notice. I could not bear the thoughts of returning; in short every idea of the sort served to put me in that passion that I did not master for some time; but in a short time after our circumstance had a better appearance, for I was in a moment determined to put the guide to death if he did not find his way that evening. He begged that I would not be hard with him, that he could find the path that evening; he accordingly took his course and in two hours got within his knowledge.

On the evening of the 4th of July we got within three miles of the town Kaskaskias, having a river of the same name to cross to the town. After making ourselves ready for anything that might happen, we marched after night to a farm that was on the same side of the river about a mile above the town, took the family prisoners, and found plenty of boats to cross in; and in two hours transported ourselves to the other shore with the greatest silence.

I learned that they had some suspician of being attacted and had made some preparations, keeping out spies, but they, making no discoveries, had got off their guard. I immediately divided my little army into two divisions, ordered one to surround the town, with the other I broke into the fort, secured the Governour Mr. Rochblave, in 15 minutes had every street secured, sent runners through the town ordering the people on the pane of death to keep close to their houses, which they observed and before daylight had the whole disarmed; nothing could excell the confusion these people seemed to be in, being taught to expect nothing but savage treatment from the Americans. Giving all for lost, their lives were all they could dare beg for, which they did with the greatest fervancy; they were willing to be slaves to save their families. I told them it did not suit me to give an answer at that time. They repared to their houses, trembling as if they were led to execution; my principal would not suffer me to distress such a number of people, except through policy it was necessary. A little reflection convinced me that it was my interest to attach them to me, according to my first plan; for the town of Cohos [Cahokia] and St. Vincents [Vincennes] and the numerous tribes of Indians attached to the French was yet to influence, for I was too weak to treat them any other way. . . .

As soon as they were a little moderated they told me that they had always been kept in the dark as to the dispute between America and Britain; that they had never heard any thing before but what was prejuditial and tended to insence them against the Americans, that they were now convinced that it was a cause they ought to espouse; that they should be happy of an oppertunity to convince me of their zeal, and think themselves the happyest people in the world if they were united with the Americans. . . .

The priest that had lately come from Canada had made himself a little acquainted with our dispute; contrary to the principal of his brother in Canada was rather prejudiced in favour of us. He asked if I would give him liberty to perform his duty in his church. I told him that I had nothing to do with churches more than to defend them from insult; that by the laws of the state his religion had as great previledges as any other. This seemed to compleat their happiness. They returned to their families, and in a few minutes the scean of mourning and destress was turned to an excess of joy, nothing else seen nor heard—addorning the streets with flowers and pavilians of different colours, compleating their happiness by singing, etc.

In meantime I prepared a detachment on horseback, under Capt. Bowman, to make a descent on Cohos, about sixty miles up the country. The inhabitants told me that one of their townsmen was enough to put me in possession of that place by carrying the good news that the people would rejoice. However, I did not altogether chuse to trust them, dispatched the captain, attended by a considerable number of the inhabitants, who got into the middle of the town before they were discovered; the French gentlemen calling aloud to the people to submit to their happier fate, which they did with very little hesitation. . . .

—Clark Papers, *Ill. State Hist. Lib. Coll.*, VIII, 117-123.

3. Governor Hamilton and Indian Allies Recapture Vincennes

Report of Lieutenant Governor Henry Hamilton to the British authorities, July 6, 1781.

On the 7th of October, 1778, the various necessaries for a winter movement of 600 miles being provided, by the activity and goodwill of Captains Lernoult and Grant, the latter of whom had attended to everything afloat, and by the assistance of Major Hay and Mr. Fleming, the Commissary, we struck our tents and embarked with one field peece which was all could be spared from the garrison.

One single person, he an Indian, was affected with liquor.

We proceeded a little way down the river and encamped. I should observe, once for all, that camp duty was as strictly attended to as the slender knowledge I possessed would admit, and that the guards, picketts and advanced centries were regularly visited from the setting the watch, which was usually at sunset till broad daylight, that the boats were loaded, manned, and arranged in such a way as to be perfectly secured within our centries every night; that the Indians encamped and decamped as regularly as could be wished, and that among them not a single instance of drunkenness or quarrelling occurred for 72 days, nor the least repining at the fatigues of the journey, or the hardships of the season. Their customs in war, their ceremonies on the way, and what passed in the meetings with various tribes, with the speeches, are entered upon my diary, and may be of service to persons who wish to be acquainted with their forms, without an attention to which no hearty assistance is to be expected from them.

On the 9th a snowstorm having subsided, it was debated whether or not we should hazard the passage of the lake from the mouth of Detroit River to that of the Miamis, but considering the advanced season, and that contrary winds or the freezing of the lake would frustrate our design, I determined to make the push. The traverse is of 36 miles and it was noon before the swell on the lake was fallen sufficiently. . . .

On the 24th we arrived at the Miamis town after the usual fatigues attending such a navigation, the water being remarkably low. Here we met several tribes of the Indians previously summoned to meet here, and held several conferences, made them presents, and dispatched messengers to the Shawanese, as well as the nations on our route, inviting them to join us, or at least watch the motions of the Rebels upon the frontiers; for which purpose I sent them amunition.

Having passed the portage of nine miles, we arrived at one of the sources of the Ouabache called the petite Riviere, . . .

In our progress down the Ouabache difficulties encreased, the setting in of the frost lowered the river, the floating ice cut the men as they worked in the water to haul the boats over shoals and rocks, our batteau were damaged, and to be repeatedly unloaded, calked and payd, 97,000 lbs. of provisions and stores to be carried by the men, in which the Indians assisted chearfully, when the boats were to be lightened. It was sometimes a day's work to get the distance of half a league. It was necessary to stop frequently at the Indian villages, to have conferences with them, furnish them with necessarys, and engage a few to accompany us. At length we got into a good depth of water, a fall of rain having raised the river. This advantage was succeeded by fresh difficultys, the frost becoming so intense as to freeze the river quite across. However by hard labour we made our way, and now approaching within a few days' journey of St. Vincennes, our reconnoitring party brought in a lieutenant and three men, sent from Fort Sackville to gain intelligence.

Major Hay was detached with orders to fall down the river and send to the principal inhabitants of St. Vincennes, acquainting them that unless they quitted the Rebels and laid down their arms, there was no mercy for them. Some chiefs accompanied him to conciliate the Peankashaa Indians residing at St. Vincennes, and to show the French what they might expect if they pretended to resist. Major Hay secured the arms, ammunition and spiritous liquors as soon as the inhabitants laid down their arms, and the officer who commanded in the fort (Captain Helm), being deserted by the officers and men who to the number of 70 had formed his garrison and were in pay of the Congress, surrendered his wretched fort on the very day of our arrival, being the 17th of December 1778. Thus we employed 71 days in coming only six hundred miles, which is to be attributed to the extraordinary difficulties of the way owing to an uncommon drought, the severity of the season, and the inevitable delays at the Indian villages. . . .

—Clark Papers, *Ill. State Hist. Lib. Coll.*, VIII, 178-181.

II. THE CAPTURE OF VINCENNES

Here is the heart of the story, the most splendid chapter in the history of the early West, and one of the illustrious chapters in the history of the Revolution, the subject of more song, story, poetry and painting than almost any other episode except Valley Forge. Once again we draw on Clark's famous letter to George Mason and, for the British side of the story, on the journal kept by Colonel Hamilton.

1. CLARK IS "RESOLVED TO RISQUE THE WHOLE ON A SINGLE BATTLE"

George Rogers Clark to Governor Patrick Henry.

Kaskaskias, February 3, 1779

As it is now near twelve months since I have had the least inteligence from you, I almost despair of any relief sent to me. I have, for many months past, had reports of an army marching against DeTroit, but no certainty.

A late menuver of the famous hair buyer general, Henry Hamilton, Esq., Lieut. Governor of DeTroit, hath allarmed us much. On the 16th of December last he, with a body of six hundred men, composed of regulars, French voluntier and Indians, took possession of St. Vincent on the Waubach, what few men that composed the garison not being able to make the least defence. He is influancing all the Indians he possibly can to join him. I learn that those that have treated with me have as yet refused his offers. I have for some time expected an attact from him. He has blockd up the Ohio River with a party [of] French and Indians.

Yesterday I fortunately got every peace of inteligence that I could wish for, by a Spanish gentleman that made his escape from Mr. Hamilton. No attact to be made on the garison at Kaskaskias until the spring . . . passage is too difficult at present. . . . Both presents and speaches sent to all the nations south of the Ohio amediately to meet at a great council at the mouth of the Tennesse River to lay the best plans for cuting of[f] the Rebels at Illinois and Kentucky, and the Grand Kite and his nation living at Post St Vincent told Mr. Hamilton that he and his people was Big Knives and would not give their hands any more to the English, for he would shortly see his Father that was at Kaskaskias. . . . They are very busy in repairing the fort, which will shortly be very strong; one brass six-pounder, two iron four-pounders and two swivels mounted in the bastians, plenty of amunition and provisions and all kinds of warlike stores, making preparation for the reduction of the Illenois, and has no suspition of a visit from the Americans. This was Mr. Hamilton circumstance when Mr. Vigo left him.

Being sensible that without a reinforcement, which at present I have hardly a right to expect, that I shall be obliged to give up this cuntrey to Mr. Hamilton without a turn of fortune in my favour, I am resolved to take the advantage of his present situation and risque the whole on a single battle. I shall set out in a few days with all the force I can raise of my own troops and a few militia that I can depend on, whole [amounting] to only one hundred, of which —— goes on board a small g[alley sent] out some time ago. . . . This boat is to make her way good if possible and take her station ten leagues below St. Vincens. I shall march across by land my self with the rest of my boys. The principal persons that follow me on this forlorn hope is Capt. Joseph Bowman, John Williams, Edward Worthing[ton], Richard M Carty, and François Charlovielle, Lieuts. Richard Brashears, Abraham Chaplin, John Jerault and John Bayley, and several other brave subalterns.

You must be sensible of the feeling that I have for those brave officers and soldiers that are determined to share my fate, let it be what it will. I know the case is desperate but, Sir, we must either quit the cuntrey or attact mr. Hamilton. No time is to be lost. Was I shoer of a reinforcement I should not attempt it. Who knows what fortune will do for us? Great things have been affected by a few men well conducted. Perhaps we may be fortunate. We have this consolation: that our cause is just, and that our cuntrey will be greatful. . . .

—Clark Papers, *Ill. State Hist. Lib. Coll.*, VIII, 97-100.

2. Clark Describes the Capture of Vincennes

George Rogers Clark to George Mason.

November 19, 1779

By the 4th day of [February] I got every thing compleat and on the 5th I marched, being joined by two volunteer companys of the principal young men of of the Illinois commanded by Capt. McCarthy and Francis Charlaville. Those of the troops was Capts. Bowman and William Worthingtons of the Light Horse. We were conducted out of the town by the inhabitants: and Mr. Jeboth [Gibault] the priest, who, after a very suitable discourse to the purpose, gave us all absolution, and we set out on a forlorn hope indeed; for our whole party with the boats crew consisted of only a little upwards of two hundred. I cannot account for it but I still had inward assurance of success; and never could, when weighing every circumstance, doubt it: but I had some secret check.

We had now a rout before us of two hundred and forty miles in length, through, I suppose, one of the most beautiful country in the world; but at this time in many parts flowing with water and exceading bad marching. My greatest care was to divert the men as much as possible in order to keep up their spirits.

The first obstruction of any consequence that I met with was on the 13th arriveing at the two Little Wabachces. Although three miles asunder they now make but one, the flowed water between them being at least three feet deep, and in many places four, being near five miles to the opposite hills. The shallowest place, except about one hundred yards, was three feet.

This would have been enough to have stopped any set of men that was not in the same temper that we was, but in three days we contrived to cross by building a large canoe, ferried across the two channels, the rest of the way we waded; building scaffolds at each to lodge our baggage on until the horses crossed to take them. It rained nearly a third of our march, but we never halted for it.

In the evening of the 17th we got to the low lands of the River Umbara [Embarras] which we found deep in water, it being nine miles to St. Vincents which stood on the east side of the Wabache and every foot of the way covered with deep water. We marched down the little river in order to gain the banks of the main, which we did in about three leagues, made a small canoe and sent an express to meet the boat and hurry it up. From the spot we now lay on was about ten miles to town, and every foot of the way put together that was not three feet and upwards under water would not have made the length of two miles and a half, and not a mouthful of provision. To have waited for our boat, if possible to avoid it, would have been impolitic.

If I was sensible that you would let no person see this relation, I would give you a detail of our suffering for four days in crossing those waters, and the manner it was done, as I am sure that you would credit it; but it is too incredible for any person to believe except those that are as well acquainted with me as you are, or had experienced something similar to it. I hope you will escuse me until I have the pleasure of seeing you personally.

But to our inexpressible joy in the evening of the 23d we got safe on terra firma within half a league of the fort, covered by a small grove of trees, had a full view of the wished for spot. (I should have crossed at a greater distance from the town but the White River comeing in jest below us we were affraid of getting too near it). We had already taken some prisoners that was coming from the town. Laying in this grove some time to dry our clothes by the sun, we took another prisoner known to be a friend, by which we got all the intiligence we wished for, but would not suffer him to see our troops except a few.

A thousand ideas flashed in my head at this moment. I found that Governor Hamilton was able to defend himself for a considerable time, but knew that he was not able to turn out of the fort; that if the seige continued long a superior number might come against us, as I knew there was a party of English not far above the river, that, if they found out our numbers, might raise the disaffected savages and harass us. I resolved to appear as darring as possible, that the enemy might conceive by our behaviour that we were very numerous and probably discourage them.

I immediately wrote to the inhabitants in general, informing them where I was and what I determined to do, desireing the friends to the States to keep close in their houses, those in the British interest to repair to the fort and fight for their King: otherways there should be no mercy shewn them etc., etc. Sending the compliments of several officers that was known to be expected to reinforce me to several gentlemen of the town, I dispatched the prisoner off with this letter, waiting until near sunset, giving him time to get near the town before we marched.

As it was an open plain from the wood that covered us, I marched time enough to be seen from the town before dark, but, taking advantage of the land, disposed the lines in such a manner that nothing but the pavilions could be seen, having as many of them as would be sufficient for a thousand men, which was observed by the inhabitants, who had just received my letter, counted the different colours and judged our number accordingly. But I was careful to give them no oppertunity of seeing our troops before dark, which it would be before we could arrive. . . .

I detached Lieut. Bayley and party to attact the fort at a certain signal, and took possession of the posts of the town with the main body. The garrison had so little suspicion of what was to happen that they did not believe the fireing was from an enemy until a man was wounded through the ports (which hapned the third or fourth shot), expecting it to be some drunken Indians. The fireing commenced on both sides very warm. A second division joined the first. A considerable number of British Indians made their escape out of town. The Kickepous and Peankeshaws to the amount of about one hundred that was in town immediately armed themselves in our favour and marched to attact the fort. I thanked the chief for his intended service, told him the ill consequence of our people being mingled in the dark; that they might lay in their quarters until light. He approved of it and sent off his troops, appeared to be much elivated himself and staid with me giving all the information he could. (I knew him to be a friend.) The artillery from the fort played briskly but did no execution. The garrisson was intirely surrounded within eighty and a hundred yards behind houses, palings and ditches, etc., etc. . . .

In a few hours I found my prize sure, certain of taking every man that I could have wished for, being the whole of those that incited the Indians to war. All my past sufferings vanished. Never was a man more happy. It wanted no encouragement from any officer to inflame our troops with a martial spirit. The knowledge of the person they attacted and the thoughts of their massecred friends was sufficient. I knew that I could not afford to loose men and took the greatest care of them that I possibly could; at the same time encouraged them to be daring, but prudent. Every place near the fort that could cover them was crowded, and a very heavy firing during the night. Having flung up a considerable intrenchment before the gate where I intended to plant my artillery when arrived. . . . The firing again commenced, a number of the inhabitants joining the troops and behaved exceeding well in general. . . .

About eight o'clock in the morning I ordered the fireing to cease and sent a flag into the garrisson with a hard bill, recommended Mr. Hamilton to surrender his garrisson and severe threats if he should destroy any letters, etc. He returned an answer to this purpose: that the garrisson was not disposed to be awed into any thing unbecomeing British soldiers. The attact was renewed with greater vigour than ever and continued for about two hours. I was determined to listen to no terms whatever until I was in possession of the fort; and only ment to keep them in action with part of my troops, while I was making necessary preparations with the other (neglected calling on any of the inhabitants for assistants although they wished for it).

A flag appeard from the fort with a proposition from Mr. Hamilton for three days cessation—a desire of a conference with me immediately; that if I should make any difficulty of comeing into the fort, he would meet me at the gate. I at first had no notion of listening to any thing he had to say as I could only consider himself and officers as murderers and intended to treat them as such. But after some deliberation I sent Mr. Hamilton my compliments and beged leave to inform him that I should agree to no other terms than his surrendering himself and garrison prisoners at discretion; but if he was desirous of a conference with me I would meet him at the church.

We accordingly met, he offered to surrender, but we could not agree upon terms. He received such treatment on this conference as a man of his known barbarity deserved. I would not come upon terms with him, recommended to him to defend himself with spirit and bravery, that it was the only thing that would induce me to treat him and his garrisson with lenity in case I stormed it, which he might expect. He asked me what more I could require than the offers he had already made. I told him (which was really the truth) that I wanted a sufficient excuse to put all the Indians and partisans to death, as the greatest part of those villians was then with him. All his propositions was refused. He asked me if nothing would do but fighting. I knew of nothing else. He then begged me to stay until he should return to the garrisson and consult his officers. Being indiferent about him and wanted a few moments for my troops to refresh themselves, I told him that the firing should not commence until such an hour, that during that time he was at liberty to pass with safety.

Some time before, a party of warriers sent by Mr. Hamilton against Kentucky had taken two prisoners, [and] was discovered by the Kickebues who gave information of them. A party was immediately detached to meet them, which hapned in the Commons. They conceived our troops to be a party sent by Mr. Hamilton to conduct them in—an honour commonly paid them. I was highly pleased to see each party hooping, hollowing and striking each others breasts as they approached in the open fields. Each seemed to try to out do the other in the greatest signs of joy. The poor devils never discovered their mistake until it was too late for many of them to escape. Six of them was made prisoners, two of them scalped, and the rest so wounded, as we afterwards learnt, but one lived.

I had now a fair oppertunity of making an impression on the Indians that I could have wished for: that of convincing them that Governour Hamilton could not give them that protection that he had made them to belive he could. In some measure to insence the Indians against him for not exerting himself to save their friends, [I] ordered the prisoners to be tomahawked in the face of the garrisson. It had the effect that I expected. Insted of making their friends inviterate against us, they upbraided the English parties in not trying to save their friends, and gave them to understand that they believed them to be liers and no warriers.

A remarkable circumstance hapned that I think worthy our notice: An old

French gentleman of the name of St. Croix, Lieut. of Capt. McCarty's volunteers from Cohos, had but one son, who headed these Indians and was made prisoner. The question was put whether the white man should be saved. I ordered them to put him to death, through indignation which did not extend to the savages. For fear he would make his escape, his father drew his sword and stood by him in order to run him through in case he should stir; being painted could not know him. The wretch, on seeing the executioners tomahawk raise to give the fatal stroke, raised his eyes as if making his last addresses to Heaven, cried out, "O, save me!" The father knew his son's voice. You may easily guess of the adgetation and behaviour of these two persons comeing to the knowledg of each other at so critical a moment. I had so little mercy for such murderers, and so valuable an oppertunity for an example, knowing there would be the greatest selicitations made to save him, that I immediately absconded myself; but by the warmest selicitations from his father who had behaved so exceedingly well in our service, and some of the officers, I granted his life on certain conditions.

Mr. Hamilton and myself again met. He produced certain Articles which was refused; but towards the close of the evening I sent him . . . Articles . . . which was agreed to and fulfilled.

The next day knowing that Governour Hamilton had sent a party of men up the Ouabach to [c]ome for stores that he had left there which must be on the return, I waited about twelve hours for the arival of the galley to intercept them, but, fearing their getting intiligence, dispatched Capt. Helms with a party in armed boats who supprised and made prisoners of forty, among which was Dejeane, Grand Judge of Detroit, with a large packet from Detroit and seven boats load of provisions, Indian goods, etc.

Never was a person more mortified than I was at this time to see so fair an oppertunity to push a victory: Detroit lost for want of a few men.

—Clark Papers, *Ill. State Hist. Lib. Coll.*, VIII, 139-146.

3. HAMILTON OWNS THE MORTIFICATION OF SURRENDER TO CLARK

[*Feb. 22nd, 1779*] Roll calling was just over, when we were surprized by the firing of small arms. This I attributed to some drunken frolic of the inhabitants, but going upon the parade heard the balls sing; still I could not conceive otherways than that some drunken people were amusing themselves.

Shortly after Serjeant Chapman of the King's Regiment was reported to be mortally wounded, but it proved only a contusion, a metal button having saved his life, a shot from a rifled piece having struck him opposite the pit of the stomach. The men had been ordered before this to stand to their arms; they were now sent to occupy the blockhouses and platforms, with orders not to fire till they could be at a certainty of doing it to purpose, and to be very managing of their ammunition.

It was now near dark and the fire increasing we were not at a loss to conclude our opponents were those whose fires had been discovered. In course as three sides of the fort were fired upon, we despaired of our reconnoirting party being able to return to us. The firing continued all night on both sides, but without any effect from us, the enemy having the cover of the church, the churchyard fence, houses, barns, all within muskett shot. We dislodged those at the church by a few discharges of a 3-pounder from the blockhouse, but had little chance of doing any execution against riflemen under cover. It was very practicable to have burned the village, but there were too many reasons against it which I shall take occasion to mention.

The situation of the fort had no one advantage but its neighbourhood to the river.

Our surgeon, who had been in the village when the firing began, finding the fort invested, made a push for the gate and narrowly escaped having several shot fired at him, one of which went thro' his legging. He told us that when the first shots were fired the woman at whose house he was cried out, "There is Colonel Clarke. [He] is arrived from the Ilinois with 500 men."

We had 1 serjt., one matross and 2 men wounded, which were brought into the officers quarters, not being able to bear the cold of the night, for we were obliged to put out the fires in the huts, as the light gave advantage to the riflemen who could see men pass in the fort, and the picketting not being all lined we were much exposed. We worked hard to remedy this defect with what spare picketts and plank we had.

About 4 o'clock in the morning the fire slackened, and a little before sunrise I lay down, when some one came in and told me they were scaling the stockades. Running out hastily and expecting to find the enemy attempting to get over the stockades [I] was agreeably surprized to find Captain La Mothe's party had made a fortunate push, and did actually get over with their arms in their hands, tho the picketts were perpendicular and eleven feet high. . . .

23d. The firing recommenced on both sides after sunrise. We cleared the houses next the fort by a few cannon shot from the blockhouses, but this did not prevent our having two men wounded thro the loopholes, and one walking across the parade. This last was one of La Mothe's, and I could not find that those of his company had acted with spirit from the first. On the contrary the men of the Kings Regiment behaved with the greatest alacrity, and even exposed themselves more than I wished.

At eleven this morning one of the captains of militia of St. Vincennes advanced towards the fort gate with a flag of truce and being admitted delivered me a letter from Colonel Clarke which was expressed in the following terms—

"St. Vincennes Feby. 23d.
"Sir

"I expect you shall immediately surrender yourself with your garrison prisoners at discretion. If any of the stores be destroyed or any letters or papers burned, you may expect no mercy, for by Heavens you shall be treated as a murtherer—

"I am Sir your humble servant
"*Lt. Govr. Hamilton*   GEORGE ROGERS CLARKE"

The following answer was returned—

"Lieutenant Governor Hamilton acquaints Colonel Clarke that neither he or his garrison are to be prevailed on by threats to act in a manner unbecoming the character of British subjects.

"Fort Sackville, 23d Feby., 1779"

Having called the officers together I read them Col. Clarke's letter, with the answer, and told them I was determined if they and the men were of my mind to hold out to the last, rather than to trust to or accept Colonel Clarkes proposition.

They all declared themselves willing to second me.

The men were then assembled on the parade, when I read the letter and answer in English and French, telling them it was the determination of the officers, as well as my own, to defend the Kings colours to the last extremity rather than yield to such ignominious terms.

The English to a man declared they would stand to the last for the honour of their country, and as they expressed it, would stick to me as the shirt on my back.

Then they cried "God save King George!" and gave three huzzas.

The French hung their heads, and their serjeants first turned round and muttered with their men. Some said it was hard they should fight against their own friends and relations who they could see had joined the Americans and fired against the fort.

This was indeed fact, for as I found afterwards Bosseron had secreted powder with which he had supplied Colonel Clarke on his arrival, and made an offer of his services with 75 men of the militia of St. Vincennes.

Finding one half of my little garrison thus indisposed, and that with so small a number as were well affected it would be absurd to think of holding out, that to retain the French was to depend on traitors, and to turn them out must give additional confidence to our Enemies, I determined from that moment to accept honorable terms if I could procure them. I first consulted with the officers and then communicated to the English the necessity of a surrender, assuring them at the same time that no consideration whatever should induce me to accept any but honorable terms.

They seemed very unwilling to listen to anything of the kind, but as it was obvious we were not in a condition to make any essential resistance, that we were 600 miles distant from any relief, that duty must fall too heavy on our small numbers now reduced one half by the treachery or cowardice or both of our Canadian volunteers, that we had already a fifth of our trusty Englishmen wounded, and wretched accommodations for them, they agreed to act as I judged best.

The men having had no rest the preceding night I divided the garrison into two watches, and sent one watch to rest. . . .

About two in the afternoon the party of Indians which had gone towards the Falls of Ohio returned, and advancing over the common to the fort, seeing the English flag flying and not knowing that we were attacked, discharged their pieces. 'Tis usual with them to fire three vollies on their approach to a fort or a town, as a salute; this is practiced also among themselves.

This party was in all but 15 or 16 men, of whom were the two sergeants of Volunteers.

Col. Clarke, being informed of their arrival, sent off 70 men to attack them, who fired on these people unprepared for such a salute, killed one, wounded two and made 5 of the rest prisoners, taking them to the village.

On their arrival, they were placed in the street opposite the Fort Gate, where these poor wretches were to be sacrificed—one of them, a young Indian about 18 years of age, the son of Pontiach, was saved at the intercession of one Macarty, a Captain of Col. Clarkes banditti, who said he had formerly owed his life to the Indian's father.

One of the others was tomahawked either by Clarke or one of his officers. The other three, foreseeing their fate, began to sing their death song, and were butcherd in succession, tho at the very time a flag of truce was hanging out at the fort and the firing had ceased on both sides. A young chief of the Ottawa nation called Macutte Mong, one of these last, having received the fatal stroke of a tomahawk in the head, took it out and gave it again into the hands of his executioner, who repeated the stroke a second and third time, after which the miserable being, not entirely deprived of life, was dragged to the river and thrown in with the rope about his neck, where he ended his life and tortures. This horrid scene was transacted in the open street, and before the door of a house where I afterward was quartered, the master of which related to me the above particulars. The blood of the victims was still visible for days afterwards, a testimony of the courage and humanity of Colonel Clarke.

When the prisoners were brought in, Bosseron, the villain already mentioned, levelled his piece at Serjeant [Sanscrainte], whose father (who had come with Clarke from the Illinois) at that instant stepping up, raised the muzzle and obtained his son's life by applying to Col. Clarke.

Serjeant Robert was saved by his sister's interceding. The flag of truce had been hung out on the occasion of my sending a messenger to Col. Clarke that I would treat with him about the surrender of the fort on honorable terms if he would come to a parly, and that I would talk with him on the subject in the fort, passing my word for his security. He sent word he would talk with me on the parade. We were each to bring a person to be present at our interview.

In consequence I met him on the parade outside the fort. He had just come from his Indian tryumph all bloody and sweating—seated himself on the edge of one of the batteaus that had some rainwater in it, and while he washed his hands and face still reeking from the human sacrifice in which he had acted as chief priest, he told me with great exultation how he had been employed. The soldiers in the fort, having some suspicion of treachery, were got into the blockhouse next to us with their pieces loaded and kept a watchfull eye on us during our conversation. The Colonel proceeded to tell me that it was in vain to think of persisting in the defence of the fort, that his cannon would be up in a few hours, that he knew to a man who of my people I could depend upon, with every other circumstance of my situation, and that if from a spirit of obstinacy I persevered while there was no prospect of relief, and should stand an assault, that not a single man should be spared.

I replyed that tho my numbers were small I could depend on them.

He said he knew the reverse, that there were but 35 or 36 that were really staunch and that I could depend on, and that 'twas folly to think of making a defence against such unequal numbers; that if I surrenderd at discretion and trusted to his generosity, I should have better treatment than if I articled for terms.

My answer was, "Then, Sir, I shall abide the consequences, for I never will take a step so disgracefull and unprecedented while I have ammunition and provision."

"You will" (said he) "be answerable for the lives lost by your obstinacy."

I said my men had declared they would die with arms in their hands rather than surrender at discretion.

The officer who was with him said he wished we should come to some composition rather than that blood should be spilt.

I said that I would accept such terms as should consist with my honor and duty—that as I knew what I might pretend to, it would take but little time to draw up articles.

He said he would think upon it and return in half an hour.

He returned accordingly with Captain Bowman, one of his officers, and I met him with Major Hay. We resumed our conversation. He seemed as determined as before. I then said further discourse was in vain. I would return to the fort, and to prevent mistakes the firing should not recommence till an hour after our parting, that each side might be prepared. I then gave him my hand, saying we might part as gentlemen tho not as friends. I had gone but a little way when Major Hay and Captain Bowman called me back, the subject was resumed, and Colonel Clarke agreed to my sending terms which he should assent to or reject, according as he should find their tenor. They were sent that same evening, C. Clarke made his answer, and I agreed to the conditions, having first assembled the officers and exposed to them the necessity of the step.

The men were next called together and I convinced them that the King's service could not derive any advantage from our holding out. . . .

The poltronnerie and treachery of our French Volunteers who made half our number, with the certainty of the St. Vincennes men having joined Col. Clarke, and the miserable state of our wounded men, all conspired to make me adopt the disagreeable terms of capitulation which are refered to. . . .

The mortification, disappointment and indignation I felt may possibly be conceived if all the considerations are taken together which suggested themselves in turn. Our views of prosecuting any design against the enemy totally overturned—the being captives to an unprincipled motley banditti and the being betrayed and sacrificed by those very people who owed the preservation of their lives and properties to us, and who had so lately at the foot of the altar called God to witness their sincerity and loyalty.

—HAMILTON, *Journal*, pp. 130-139.

III. THE FIGHT FOR ST. LOUIS

From the beginning Spain had made some feeble gestures of aid toward the American cause. As early as 1776 New Orleans was supplying the Westerners with guns, powder, medicines and other supplies—mostly bought by and on the credit of Oliver Pollock, an American merchant in New Orleans. When Bernardo de Gálvez became governor aid to the Americans was increased, and Clark profited greatly by supplies forwarded from New Orleans by Pollock. In the summer of 1779 Spain formally joined the war against Britain. She had little interest in American independence, but a substantial interest in conquering British outposts in the West; in quick succession Baton Rouge, Natchez, Mobile and Pensacola fell to the Spaniards. Far to the north, Governor Sinclair of Michilimackinac decided to counterattack, and launched an expedition whose first objective was St. Louis and whose ultimate objective was New Orleans. British incompetence, the unreliability of Indian allies, the presence of Clark at Kaskaskia, and Spanish resolution frustrated this expedition. The following year the Spaniards launched a counterexpedition towards Detroit which reached Fort St. Joseph in what is now southern Michigan.

1. The Hesse Expedition down the Mississippi Is Launched

Patrick Sinclair to Governor Frederick Haldimand of Canada.

Michilimackinac, 17 February, 1780

Sir,—Since my letter of the 15th instant the arrival of an Indian chief personally acquainted with me, affords me an opportunity, earlier than I expected, of ordering Mr. Hesse, a trader and a man of character (formerly in the 60th Regiment) to assemble the Minomines, Puants, Sacks and Rhenards in the neighborhood and to take post at the portage of the Ouisconsing's and Foxes Rivers, there to collect all the canoes and corn in the country, for his own and for the use of the nations higher up, who will be ordered to join him at the confluence of the Rivers Mississippi and Ouisconseing. Mr. Hesse is ordered not to move from his first stand until I send him instructions by Serjeant [J. F.] Phillips of the 8th Regiment, who will set out from this on the 10th of March with a very noted Chief Machiquawish and his band of Indians. For want of a cypher and to assist the serjeant, I am unwillingly obliged to send a private of the Kings Regiment, a Highlander writing in that language, to the Brigadier.

The reduction of Pencour by surprise, from the easy admission of Indians at that place and from assault from those without, having for its defence, as reported, only 20 men and 20 brass cannon, will be less difficult than holding it afterwards. To gain both these ends the rich furr trade of the Missouri River, the injuries done to the traders who formerly attempted to partake of it, and the large property they may expect in the place will contribute.

The Scious shall go with all dispatch as low down as the Natchez, and as many intermediate attacks as possible shall be made. We will endeavor a system and connection in directing their operations to the service in view.

I have only to add that I am with the greatest respect, Sir, Your Excellency's most obedient and most humble servant

PATK SINCLAIR

Lt Govr of Michilimackinac

—SINCLAIR, "Letter," *Wis. State Hist. Soc. Coll.,* XI, 147-148.

2. THE SPANIARDS REPULSE CAPTAIN HESSE'S ATTACK ON ST. LOUIS

Martin Navarro to José de Galvez, member of the Council of the Indies under Charles III.

August 18, 1780

Your Excellency—While we were under the belief that the English had been falsely charged with the atrocities committed in North America upon persons of all classes in that continent by the hands of the various savage tribes who followed their banners, there was given a most amazing proof of the fact by Captain Esse [Hesse] at the head of three hundred regular troops and nine hundred savages which left not the least doubt that this nation, having forgotten how to make war according to the system practiced in Europe, does not desire to be false in America to the title with which an author of ability has characterized it.

Captain Don Fernando de Leyba of the infantry regiment of Luisiana was commandant at the post of San Luis de Ylinoises; and having received information that a body of one thousand two hundred men, composed partly of savages and partly of troops, was being drawn up for an attack upon the town under the orders of Captain Esse, he fortified it as well as its open situation permitted. He built at the expense of the inhabitants a wooden tower at one of the ends of the town, overlooking it, and placed therein five cannon. In addition to these he had some cannon with which he defended the two intrenchments that he threw up at the other two extreme points. These were manned by twenty-nine veteran soldiers and two hundred and eighty-one countrymen.

The enemy arrived May twenty-sixth at one o'clock in the afternoon, and began the attack upon the post from the north side, expecting to meet no opposition; but they found themselves unexpectedly repulsed by the militia which guarded it. A vigorous fire was kept up on both sides, so that by the service done by the cannon on the tower where the aforesaid commander was, the defenders at least succeeded in keeping off a band of villains who if they had not opportunely been met by this bold opposition on our part would not have left a trace of our settlements. There were also to be heard the confusion and the lamentable cries of the women and children who had been shut up in the house of the commandant, defended by twenty men under the lieutenant of infantry, Don Francisco Cartabona; the dolorous echoes of which seemed to inspire in the besieged an extraordinary valor and spirit, for they urgently demanded to be permitted to make a sally.

The enemy at last, seeing that their force was useless against such resistance, scattered about over the country, where they found several farmers who with their slaves were occupied in the labors of the field. If these hungry wolves had contented themselves with destroying the crops, if they had killed all the cattle which they could not take with them this act would have been looked upon as a consequence of war, but when the learned world [*mundo filosofico*] shall know that this desperate band slaked their thirst in the blood of innocent victims, and sacrificed to their fury all whom they found, cruelly destroying them and committing the greatest atrocities upon some poor people who had no other arms than those of the good faith in which they lived, the English nation from now on may add to its glorious conquests in the present war that of having barbarously inflicted by the hands of the base instruments of cruelty the most bitter torments which tyranny has invented. The number dead, wounded and prisoners is detailed in the report and information is constantly looked for as to the end of the prisoners, which is believed to be as unfortunate as that of their companions, perhaps more so. . . .

—Navarro, "Letter," *Wis. State Hist. Soc. Coll.*, XVIII, 406-408.

IV. KENTUCKY: WAR TO THE BITTER END

The attack on St. Louis was part of a large British plan for the conquest of the trans-Appalachian West. This plan called for an attack on New Orleans out of Pensacola, a drive down the Illinois River, and an invasion of Kentucky from Detroit. Only the last of these materialized. Early in May 1780—just as Hesse was approaching St. Louis—Captain Bird set out from Detroit with a force of some 1,200 Indians and whites, made his way along the Maumee and Miami rivers, and struck into Kentucky. His was the first British expedition to carry artillery, and with this he speedily reduced two Kentucky forts, Ruddle and Martin's Station. Then, laden with plunder, he withdrew. Already Clark had hurried down to Kentucky to organize a counterattack. By August he was ready; with an army of 1,000 men he moved into the Ohio country, burned the Shawnee village of Chillicothe, marched on the Indians at Piqua, on the Big Miami, and defeated them there.

The year 1781 was relatively quiet on the Kentucky frontier, except for attacks by Joseph Brant, veteran of the New York borderland wars. Early in 1782, however, the massacre, by Patriot militia from the Monongahela, of the peaceable Delawares at Gnadenhütten in Ohio set the whole frontier a-flame. The Delawares at once took to the warpath. They joined with the Shawnee and the Wyandots to destroy Colonel Crawford's expedition on the Sandusky. Then a segment of these Indian forces crossed the Ohio, besieged Bryant's Station and, in August, defeated a Kentucky force of some 200 at the battle of Blue Licks. Thereafter the Kentucky frontier was exposed. Clark counterattacked, destroyed Chillicothe for a second time, and gave Kentucky a breathing spell. Happily for the frontiersmen the end of the war put an end to their fighting and their trials.

1. CLARK REPORTS ON HIS CHASTISEMENT OF THE SHAWNEE

Colonel George Rogers Clark to Governor Thomas Jefferson.

Louisville, August 22, 1780

By every possible exertion, and the aid of Col. Slaughter's corps, we completed the number of 1000, with which we crossed the river at the mouth of

Licking on the first day of August, and began our march on the 2d. Having a road to cut for the artillery to pass, for 70 miles, it was the 6th before we reached the first town, which we found vacated, and the greatest part of their effects carried off. The general conduct of the Indians, on our march, and many other corroborating circumstances, proved their design of leading us on to their own ground and time of action. After destroying the crops and buildings of Chillecauthy, we began our march for the Picaway settlements, on the waters of the Big Miami, the Indians keeping runners continually before our advanced guards. At half past two in the evening of the 8th, we arrived in sight of the town and forts, a plain of half a mile in width lying between us. I had an opportunity of viewing the situation and motion of the enemy near their works.

I had scarcely time to make those dispositions necessary before the action commenced on our left wing, and in a few minutes became almost general, with a savage fierceness on both sides. The confidence the enemy had of their own strength and certain victory, or the want of generalship, occasioned several neglects, by which those advantages were taken that proved the ruin of their army, being flanked two or three different times, drove from hill to hill in a circuitous direction for upwards of a mile and a half; at last took shelter in their strongholds and woods adjacent, when the firing ceased for about half an hour, until necessary preparations were made for dislodging them. A heavy firing again commenced, and continued severe until dark, by which time the enemy were totally routed. The cannon playing too briskly on their works they could afford them no shelter. Our loss was about 14 killed and thirteen wounded; theirs at least triple that number. They carried off their dead during the night, except 12 or 14 that lay too near our lines for them to venture. This would have been a decisive stroke to the Indians, if unfortunately the right wing of our army had not been rendered useless for some time by an uncommon chain of rocks that they could not pass, by which means part of the enemy escaped through the ground they were ordered to occupy.

By a French prisoner we got the next morning we learn that the Indians had been preparing for our reception ten days, moving their families and effects: That the morning before our arrival, they were 300 warriors, Shawanese, Mingoes, Wyandots and Delawares. Several reinforcements coming that day, he did not know their numbers; that they were sure of destroying the whole of us; that the greatest part of the prisoners taken by Byrd were carried to Detroit, where there were only 200 regulars, having no provisions except green corn and vegetables. Our whole store at first setting out being only 300 bushels of corn, and 1500 of flour; having done the Shawanese all the mischief in our power, after destroying Picawey settlements, I returned to this post, having marched in the whole 480 miles in 31 days. We destroyed upwards of 800 acres of corn, besides great quantities of vegetables, a considerable proportion of which appear to have been cultivated by white men, I suppose for the purpose of supporting war parties from Detroit. I could wish to have had a small store of provisions to have enabled us to have laid waste part of the Delaware settlements, and falling in at Pittsburg, but the excessive heat and weak diet shew the impropriety of such a step. Nothing could excel the few regulars and Kentuckians, that composed this little army in bravery and implicit obedience to orders; each company vying with the other who should be the most subordinate.

—Clark Papers, *Ill. State Hist. Lib. Coll.*, VIII, 451-453.

2. Gnadenhütten: "They Sang Hymns till the Tomahawks Struck"

Diary of David Zeisberger, Moravian missionary to the Delawares.

March 7, 1782. The militia, some 200 in number, as we hear, came first to Gnadenhütten. A mile from town they met young Schebosh in the bush, whom they at once killed and scalped, and, near the houses, two friendly Indians, not belonging to us, but who had gone there with our people from Sandusky, among whom were several other friends who perished likewise. Our Indians were mostly on the plantations and saw the militia come, but no one thought of fleeing, for they suspected no ill. The militia came to them and bade them come into town, telling them no harm should befall them. They trusted and went, but were all bound, the men being put into one house, the women into another.

The Mohican, Abraham, who for some time had been bad in heart, when he saw that his end was near, made an open confession before his brethren, and said: "Dear brethren, according to appearances we shall all very soon come to the Saviour, for as it seems they have so resolved about us. You know I am a bad man, that I have much troubled the Saviour and the brethren, and have not behaved as becomes a believer, yet to him I belong, bad as I am; he will forgive us all and not reject me; to the end I shall hold fast to him and not leave him."

Then they began to sing hymns and spoke words of encouragement and consolation one to another until they were all slain, and the above mentioned Abraham was the first to be led out, but the others were killed in the house. The sisters also afterwards met the same fate, who also sang hymns together. Christina, the Mohican, who well understood German and English, fell upon her knees before the captain, begging for life, but got for answer that he could not help her. Two well-grown boys, who saw the whole thing and escaped, gave this information. One of these lay under the heaps of slain and was scalped, but finally came to himself and found opportunity to escape. The same did Jacob, Rachel's son, who was wonderfully rescued. For they came close upon him suddenly outside the town, so that he thought they must have seen him, but he crept into a thicket and escaped their hands. . . . He went a long way about and observed what went on.

John Martin went at once to Salem when the militia came, and thus knew nothing about how the brethren in Gnadenhütten fared. He told them there the militia were in Gnadenhütten, whereupon they all resolved not to flee, but John Martin took with himself two brethren and turned back to Gnadenhütten, and told them there were still more Indians in Salem, but he did not know [how] it had gone with them in Gnadenhütten. A part of the militia went there on the 8th with a couple of Indians, who had come to Salem and brought the brethren away, after they had first taken away their arms, and when they came to Gnadenhütten, before they led them over the stream, they bound

them, took even their knives from them. The brethren and the sisters alike were bound, led into town, and slain. They made our Indians bring all their hidden goods out of the bush, and then took them away; they had to tell them where in the bush the bees were, help get the honey out; other things also they had to do for them before they were killed. Prisoners said that the militia themselves acknowledged and confessed they had been good Indians. They prayed and sang until the tomahawks struck into their heads. The boy who was scalped and got away said the blood flowed in streams in the house. They burned the dead bodies, together with the houses, which they set on fire.
—ZEISBERGER, *Diary, Hist. and Phil. Soc. of Ohio Pub.*, New Series, II, 79-81.

3. KENTUCKY IS ONCE AGAIN DRENCHED IN BLOOD

A. THREATENED WITH "ANARCHY, CONFUSION AND DESTRUCTION"

John Floyd to John May.

April 8, 1782

Dear Sir, The savages began their hostilities early in February, and are constantly ravaging the most interior parts of the country, which makes it impossible for any one settlement to assist another. Even the populous parts of Lincoln are infested, and from the number of horses already taken off by them, it is notorious to every capacity that their design is to disable the inhabitants from removing untill their present intended campaign from Detroit against Fort Nelson can be carried into effect. This design is communicated to us thro' three different channels, and so well authenticated that it can not be doubted; and the conduct of the enemy ever since last fall coincides exactly with the information.

One fourth of the militia is called for by Genl Clark for the purpose of fortifying the fort against a siege; but from the immediate danger in which every one conceives his own family, the authority of militia officers at such a distance from Government growing every day weaker and weaker, and the new invented ideas of a separate State, calculated on purpose for disaffection and an evasion of duty, are so many causes to retard this necessary business, and seems to threaten us on all sides with anarchy, confusion, and I may add destruction.

But even to suppose that the works can be completed before the arrival of the enemy, it is then impossible that Genl Clark with the inconsiderable number of troops he now has can defend it; and a dependence on militia scattered over three extensive counties under the circumstances before mentioned, is depending upon a very great uncertainty; especially when the enemy have all the advantages of a heavy current from high up the Miamia to the very place of their destination. They can float from the mouth of that river to the falls in less than thirty hours. And to suppose that our spies should discover their approach as high up as Miamia, it will then take eight days at least before we can be collected if we were under the strictest military subordination. Should no reinforcements arrive in May, and if Genl Clark be obliged to evacuate his post rather than suffer such a quantity of military stores to fall into the hands of the enemy, and the whole Indian army let loose among the scattered inhabitants unprepared to receive them, what must be the consequence? Is it not evident that the whole must fall a sacrifice?

As a means of averting the storm which is gathering against us, and preventing those fatal consequences, your immediate interposition with the legislative body and with the Governor and Council is now called for by every inhabitant of Jefferson County. This is our last effort; and your exertions on this occasion may possibly save our families from the hands of merciless savages.

You are sensible from your own knowledge of this Western country that no place can be better calculated for the purpose of carrying on the Indian war against (if I may use the expression) the interior frontiers of this State than the Falls of the Ohio. Its situation is exactly centrical to the Northern, Southern, and Western tribes. The distance to Holston, Clinch, New River, Green Brier, etc., very trifling. Their supplies already here provided, and the communication to the British posts in Canady very safe and easy. I would further observe that if this country must be laid waste, which nothing but an early reinforcement or an accident can prevent, those settlements above mentioned must once more experience the disadvantages of a savage war, and must contend with more than ten times the number which have heretofore visited their borders. One who is unacquainted with the true situation of this county, and also with me, might probably conclude that those reflections might proceed from timidity. But you are acquainted with both and can judge whether it is so or not.

Our whole strength at this time is three hundred and seventy men, and who, according to the best calculations I can make, have about eight hundred and fifty helpless women and children to take care of, and very generally deprived of every possible means of removing back to the settlement.

This is at present as just a state of this county as I am able to give you, only I omitted to mention that this number of men were exclusive of the small remains of the Illinoise Regement. Who am, Dear Sir, with much respect your very hble Servt.   JN FLOYD

— Clark Papers, *Ill. State Hist. Lib. Coll.*, XIX, 54-56.

B. COLONEL CRAWFORD IS TORTURED TO DEATH

William Croghan to William Davies.

Fort Pitt, July 6th, 1782

Dear Colonel: ... Gen. Irvine commands at this post, where he has so few Continental troops (about 200 for duty) that 'tis not in his power to go from the garrison against the Indians, who are daily committing murders through this country. The Pennsylvania militia formed an expedition against the Indians about three months ago; but instead of going against the enemies of the country, they turned their thoughts on a robbing, plundering, murdering scheme, on our well known friends, the Moravian Indians, all of whom they met in the most cool and deliberate manner (after living with them apparently in a friendly manner for three days), men, women and children, in all ninety three, tomahawked, scalped and burned, except one boy, who after being scalped made his escape to the Delaware Indians (relations of the Moravians) who have ever since been exceeding cruel to all prisoners they have taken.

About six weeks ago, 500 volunteers of this country, commanded by (our old) Colonel William Crawford, went on an expedition against the Indian towns . . . the men behaved amiss (were cowardly) no more than about 100 having fought the Indians, who came out from their towns to meet them . . . the firing continued at long shot with rifles for near two days. . . . The second evening our party broke off and retreated in the most disorderly manner. . . . Colonel Crawford and a few others, finding the men would pay no attention to orders, were going on coolly in the rear, leaving the road in case the Indians should pursue, until the second day when they thought they might venture on the road, but before they had marched two miles, a body of Indians fell in between them and the rear of the party, and took them prisoners.

We had no certainty of this unhappy affair until yesterday, when Doctor Knight, who was taken with Crawford, came into the garrison in the most deplorable condition man could be in and be alive. He says that the second day after they were taken, they were carried to an Indian town, stripped and then blacked, and made to march through the Indians, when men, women and children beat them with clubs, sticks, fists, etc., in the most cruel manner.

Col. Crawford and the Doctor were confined together all night; the next day they were taken out, blacked again, and their hands tied behind their backs, when Col. Crawford was led by a long rope to a high stake, to the top of which the rope about the colonel was tied; all around the stake a great quantity of red hot coals were laid, on which the poor colonel was obliged to walk barefoot, and at the same time the Indians firing squibs of powder at him, while others poked burning sticks on every part of his body; thus they continued torturing him for about two hours, when he begged of Simon Girty, a white renegade who was standing by, to shoot him, when the fellow said, "Don't you see I have no gun?"

Some little time after they scalped him, and struck him on the bare scull several times with sticks. Being now nearly exhausted, he lay down on the burning embers, when the squaws put shovels full of coals on his body, which, dying as he was, made him move and creep a little. The Doctor was obliged to stand by and see the cruelty performed. When the Colonel was scalped, they slapped the scalp over the Doctor's face, saying, "This is your great captain's scalp; to-morrow we will serve you so."

The Doctor was to be served in the same manner in another town some distance off; and on his way to this place of torment he passed by where Col. Crawford's dead body had been dragged and burned, and saw his bones. The Doctor was guarded by but one Indian, who seemed pretty kind to him; on the way the Indian wanted a fire made, and untied the Doctor, ordering him to make it. The Doctor appeared willing to obey, and was collecting wood till he got a good chunk in his hand, with which he gave the Indian so severe a blow as levelled him; the Indian sprang up, but seeing the Doctor seize his gun, he ran away; the Doctor could not get the gun off, otherwise would have shot the Indian. He steered through the woods, and arrived here the twenty first day after he left the Indian, having no clothes. The gun being wood bound, he left it after carrying it a few days.

For the twenty one days, and two or three more while he had been under sentence of death, he never ate anything but such vegetables as the woods afforded. None of the prisoners were put to death but those that fell into the hands of the Delawares, who say they will shew no mercy to any white man, as they would shew none to their friends and relations, the religious Moravians. I believe I have not told you that the whole of the five hundred who went out with Crawford returned, except about fifty. Colonel Harrison and Mr. William Crawford, relatives of Col. Crawford, were likewise taken prisoners, but fortunately fell into the hands of the Shawnees, who did not kill their prisoners.

–Clark Papers, *Ill. State Hist. Lib. Coll.*, XIX, 71-73.

C. "THE DIREFUL CATASTROPHY OF BLUE LICKS"

Andrew Steele to Benjamin Harrison, Governor of Virginia.

August 26, 1782

Sir: Through the continued series of a seven years vicessitude, nothing has happened so alarming, fatal and injurious to the interest of the Kanetuckians of particular and all its votaries in general, as the present concatination of hostilities, wherewith I am now to acquaint your Excellency.

The fifteenth of this inst. Bryan's Station was besieged by a number of Indians, whereof I am not able to form a just estimate. The attack continued warm for about thirty hours, during which period the enemy burned several exterior houses, killed three of our men and made large depredations on the neat stock and crop. They then retired, leaving three of their savage party dead on the ground, besides a number of circumstantially so.

The seventeenth, we were reinforced from Lincoln with one hundred and fifty horse men, commanded by Lieut. Col. Stephen Trigg, and joined by a few of the Fayette commanded by Colo. Jno. Todd, who composed an army of one hundred and eighty two. We followed them to the Lower Blue Licks, where ended the direfull catastrophy—in short we were defeated, with the loss of seventy five men, among whom fell our two commanders with many others officers and soldiers of distinguished bravery. To express the feelings of the inhabitants of both the counties at this ruefull scene of hitherto unparalelled barbarities barre all words and cuts description short.

The twenty fifth, five hundred of the Lincoln Militia commanded by Col. Benjamin Logan (who hitherto had neither been consulted, nor solicited to our assistance) marched to the battle ground in expectation of a second engagement, but the enemy had marched several days before. From the order of their march, with many other accruing circumstances, their number was supposed to be nearly six hundred.

Forty seven of our brave Kanetuckians were found in the field, the matchless massacraed victims of their unprecedented cruelty. We are led to conceive that none were captivated, from the number found at the crossing of the creek tied and butchered with knives and spears.

Labouring under these distressing circumstances we rely on your goodness (actuated from a principle of universal benevolence which is the distinguishing characteristic of the truly great and noble soul) that we will not only become subjects of your commiseration, but of your patronage and protection also. The ballance stands upon an equilibrium and one stroke more will cause it to preponderate to our irretrievable wo, and terminate in the intire break of our country, if your Excellency is not concerned in our immediate safety.

The author of this narrative is a person in a private sphere of life and hopes that your forgiving candour will induce you to not only pardon the intrusion, but the many inaccuracies that may appear through the whole of this illiterate and undigested detail, as it comes from a wel-wisher to Ameriacn liberty and your Excellency's most obed't H'ble Servt.

—Clark Papers, Ill. State Hist. Lib. Coll., XIX, 96-97.

CHAPTER TWENTY-EIGHT

The Redcoats Carry the War to the South

THROUGHOUT *the war the British demonstrated wonderful incapacity to evolve an over-all strategy to crush the rebellion. They first moved against New England, regarded as the prime instigator of sedition. When that move failed, they transferred their main operations to the Middle States. Here again they failed to co-ordinate their efforts in a plan to conquer New York, and frittered away time and expense on a second campaign to subdue Pennsylvania.*

The story of the campaigns in the South reflects the same lack of capacity to evolve a unified plan and to muster all the resources of the empire behind it. Even in the early period of the war the South attracted British military planners because it was regarded as a stronghold of loyalism. There was some justification for this view. The Scottish Highlanders, many of whom were centered in the Cape Fear country of North Carolina, possessed a romantic attachment to the Stuart Pretenders which in the crisis was transmuted into a stanch loyalty to George III. In the back country of North and South Carolina were persons of motley national origins, although mostly Scotch-Irish and German, who had long-standing grievances against local government. Setting themselves up in defiance of the courts, they called themselves Regulators, and forced the royal governor, William Tryon, to defeat them on the field of battle in 1771. Many left North Carolina and went into Tennessee, where they became chiefly Patriots, but those who stayed were more incensed at the seaboard planters and wealthy merchants than at the royal government. Although they were mostly Presbyterians, and the ministry of that denomination was overwhelmingly Patriot, these settlers constituted a stronghold of loyalism.

A checkerboard of sectional divisions made large parts of the lower South a political no man's land. In these areas partisan bands flourished. They were commanded by such inspired leaders as Francis Marion, the "Swamp Fox," who joined lightning action with humane restraint; Thomas Sumter, the "Carolina Game Cock," a bold and imperious fighter who was often too self-centered to fit into the general strategy of larger forces; and Andrew Pickens, a dour but vigorous elder of the Presbyterian Church. The troops they commanded were irregulars and varied in numbers from a handful to hundreds. Sometimes they were ragged and ill-armed. Sometimes they descended upon their foes as uniformed dragoons and acted in concert with the Continental troops. In large measure they kept Patriot resistance alive until substantial Continental forces could be spared for the South.

THE CHARLESTON EXPEDITION

In addition to attempting to put down the Patriot movement in Virginia and North Carolina the British organized an expedition against the Southern colonies generally. An intercepted letter of December 23, 1775, from Lord George Germain to Governor Robert Eden of Maryland, reveals that a fleet and seven regiments were to proceed to North Carolina, and then "either to South Carolina or Virginia as circumstances . . . shall permit." The expedition sailed from Cork on February 13, 1776, under the command of Admiral Sir Peter Parker. The crushing defeat of the Loyalists at Moore's Creek Bridge persuaded the British command to direct the expedition to Charleston, the most important port south of Philadelphia. Early in June two ships of the line and six frigates brought seven regiments of regulars from Britain under Lord Cornwallis, who was joined by Sir Henry Clinton, to command the land operations. Accompanying this force was a regiment made up of units lately evacuated from Boston.

The defense of the harbor was entrusted by the Carolinians to Colonel William Moultrie, whose brother John was an ardent Tory. Breastworks were hurriedly thrown up around the town, but the major effort was devoted to preventing access of the fleet. The entry into the harbor was controlled by fortifications on two islands, Fort Johnson on James Island, which had been seized by provincial troops in September of '75 and held since then, and, opposite it, Sullivan's Island, on whose southern shore the principal fortifications were now constructed. A square redoubt was originally planned, but at the time of the British attack only the front wall toward the sea was completed. The side walls had been built to a height of only seven feet, and the rear was virtually open and undefended. General Charles Lee, who had been given a separate command in the South, arrogantly argued that Sullivan's Island was a "slaughter pen" and should be abandoned. But fortunately Rutledge and Moultrie did not yield.

The defenders were helped by an unforeseeable event—the grounding of three British ships of war on the shoals. Had not this occurred the three ships could have attacked the undefended rear of the fort. The British navy hardly covered itself with glory. Neither did the army. Sullivan's Island could have been taken from the rear by a successful landing from Long Island, a short distance away. There Clinton had put his forces. But when Clinton tried the crossing, the resistance was so furious that his halfhearted efforts at an amphibious operation were abandoned, to the immense annoyance of the British navy and to his own "unspeakable mortification." He discovered that the channel separating the two islands was not a mere eighteen inches, as he had been told, "but nowhere shallower at low water than seven feet." He had neither sufficient boats nor derring-do to accomplish his mission. A battered navy turned tail and headed north to New York.

1. Moultrie and Lee Prepare to Defend Charleston

Memoirs of Colonel William Moultrie of South Carolina.

May 31, 1776, expresses were sent to the President from Christ-church Parish, informing him that a large fleet of British vessels were seen off Dewee's Island, about twenty miles to the northward of the bar; and on the *first of June* they displayed about fifty sail before the town, on the out side of our bar. The sight of these vessels alarmed us very much—all was hurry and confusion, the President with his council busy in sending expresses to every part of the country to hasten down the militia; men running about the town looking for horses, carriages and boats to send their families into the country; and as they were going out through the town gates to go into the country, they met the militia from the country marching into town. Traverses were made in the principal streets; fleches thrown up at every place where troops could land; military works going on every where, the lead taken from the windows of the churches and dwelling houses to cast into musket balls, and every preparation to receive an attack which was expected in a few days.

June 4. General Lee arrived from the northward and took the command of the troops; his presence gave us great spirits, as he was known to be an able, brave and experienced officer, though hasty and rough in his manners, which the officers could not reconcile themselves to at first: it was thought by many that his coming among us was equal to a reinforcement of 1000 men, and I believe it was, because he taught us to think lightly of the enemy, and gave a spur to all our actions. After Gen. Lee had waited upon the President and talked with him upon his plan of defence, he hurried about to view the different works and give orders for such things to be done as he thought necessary. He was every day and every hour of the day on horse back, or in boats viewing our situation and directing small works to be thrown up at different places.

When he came to Sullivan's Island, he did not like that post at all; he said there was no way to retreat, that the garrison would be sacrificed; nay, he called it a "slaughter pen," and wished to withdraw the garrison and give up the post, but President Rutledge insisted that it should not be given up. Then Gen. Lee said it was "absolutely necessary to have a bridge of boats for a retreat"; but boats enough could not be had, the distance over being at least a mile. Then a bridge was constructed of empty hogsheads buoyed at certain distances, and two planks from hogshead to hogshead; but this would not answer, because when Col. Clark was coming over from Haddrell's with a detachment of 200 men, before they were half on it sunk so low that they were obliged to return.

Gen. Lee's whole thoughts were taken up with the post on Sullivan's Island; all his letters to me shew how anxious he was at not having a bridge for a retreat. For my part, I never was uneasy on not having a retreat because I never imagined that the enemy could force me to that necessity; I always considered myself as able to defend that post against the enemy. I had upwards of 300 riflemen, under Col. Thompson, of his regiment, Col. Clark, with 200 North-Carolina regulars, Col. Horry, with 200 South-Carolina, and the Racoon

Company of riflemen, 50 militia at the point of the island behind the sand hills and myrtle bushes; I had also a small battery with one 18-pounder, and one brass field-piece, 6-pounder, at the same place, which entirely commanded the landing and could begin to fire upon them at 7 or 800 yards before they could attempt to land. This would have disconcerted them very much. Besides, had they made their landing good, the riflemen would have hung upon their flanks for three miles as they marched along the beach, and not above fifty yards from them.

Col. Thompson had orders that if they could not stand the enemy they were to throw themselves into the fort, by which I should have had upwards of 1000 men in a large strong fort, and Gen. Armstrong in my rear with 1500 men, not more than one mile and a half off, with a small arm of the sea between us, that he could have crossed a body of men in boats to my assistance. This was exactly my situation. I therefore felt myself perfectly easy because I never calculated upon Sir Henry Clinton's numbers to be more than 3000 men. As to the men-of-war, we should have taken very little notice of them if the army had attacked us.

Gen. Lee one day on a visit to the fort, took me aside and said, "Col. Moultrie, do you think you can maintain this post?"

I answered him, "Yes, I think I can."

That was all that passed on the subject between us.

Another time Capt. Lamperer, a brave and experienced seaman, who had been master of a man-of-war and captain of a very respectable privateer many years ago, visited me at the fort after the British ships came over our bar; while we were walking on the platform looking at the fleet, he said to me: "Well, Colonel, what do you think of it now?"

I replied that "we should beat them."

"Sir," said he, "when those ships" (pointing to the men-of-war) "come to lay along side of your fort, they will knock it down in half an hour," (and that was the opinion of all the sailors).

"Then," I said, "we will lay behind the ruins and prevent their men from landing."

—MOULTRIE, *Memoirs*, I, 140-144.

2. The Batteries of Charleston Repel the British Navy

Letter of a surgeon with the British fleet.

July 9, 1776

We left Cape-Fear on the 27th of May, and anchored the same evening off the bar. The camp was struck at the same time, and the troops embarked the same evening on board the several transports. All our motions were so languid and so innervate that it was the 9th of June before the *Bristol* and *Pigot* passed the bar of Charlestown; the *Bristol* in passing struck, which alarmed us all exceedingly; but, as it wanted two hours of high water, she soon floated again. The *Prince of Piedmont*, a victualling ship, was totally lost on the north breakers of the bar. General Clinton and Lord Cornwallis were both on board when she struck; but as the weather was very fine, they were not in the least danger.

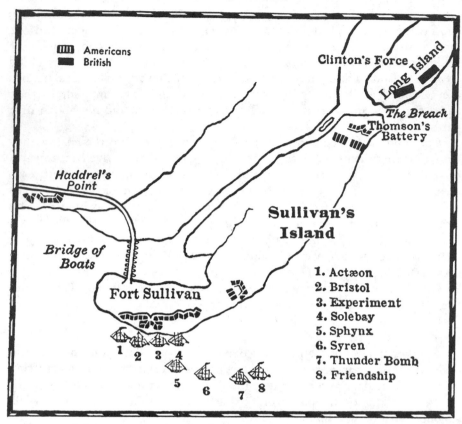

By our delays we gave the people every opportunity they could have asked for to extend their lines, etc.: they were not idle—every hour gave us astonishing proofs of their industry. As we anchored at one league distance from Sullivan's Island, we could see all that was going on with the help of our glasses. The fort of this island is exceedingly strong (or rather the battery); it is built of palm trees and earth, and on it are mounted eighteen of the lower deck guns of the *Foudroyant:* I never could distinguish more than seventeen; others imagined they could see nineteen—however, that is immaterial.

The signal for attacking was made by Sir Peter Parker on the 27th of June; but the wind coming suddenly to the northward, the ships were obliged again to anchor. The troops have been encamped on Long-Island since the 15th, and it was intended that General Clinton should pass the neck that divides Long-Island from Sullivan's Island, and attack by land while Sir Peter attacked by sea. General Lee had made such a disposition of masked batteries, troops, etc., that it is the opinion of all the officers of the Army whom I have heard mention this circumstance, that if our troops had attacked, they must have been cut off; but this assertion does not satisfy the Navy, for they certainly expected great assistance from the Army. Excuse this necessary digression.

On the morning of the 28th, the wind proved favourable; it was a clear fine day, but very sultry. The *Thunder*, bomb, began the attack at half past eleven by throwing shells while the ships were advancing. The ships that advanced to attack the battery were the *Bristol* and *Experiment*, two fifty-gun ships; the *Solebay*, *Active*, *Acteon* and *Syren*, of twenty-eight guns; the *Sphinx*, of twenty, and the *Friendship*, an armed ship of twenty-eight guns. With this force what might not have been expected?

Unfortunately the bomb was placed at such a distance that she was not of the least service. This Colonel James, the principal engineer, immediately perceived; to remedy which inconvenience, an additional quantity of powder was added to each mortar: the consequences were the breaking down the beds and totally disabling her for the rest of the day.

The *Bristol* and *Experiment* have suffered most incredibly: the former very early had the spring of her cable shot away—of course she lay end on to the battery and was raked fore and aft; she lost upwards of one hundred men killed and wounded. Captain Morris, who commanded her, lost his arm; the worthy man, however, died a week after on board the *Pigot*. Perhaps an instance of such slaughter cannot be produced; twice the quarter-deck was cleared of every person except Sir Peter, and he was slightly wounded. She had nine thirty-two-pound shot in her mainmast, which is so much damaged as to be obliged to be shortened; the mizzen had seven thirty-two-pound shot and was obliged, being much shattered, to be entirely cut away.

It is impossible to pretend to describe what our shipping have suffered. Captain Scott, of the *Experiment*, lost his right arm, and the ship suffered exceedingly; she had much the same number killed and wounded as the *Bristol*. Our situation was rendered very disagreeable by the *Acteon*, *Syren* and *Sphinx* running foul of each other, and getting on shore on the middle ground. The *Sphinx* disengaged herself by cutting way her bowsprit; and, as it was not yet flood-tide, the *Sphinx* and *Syren* fortunately warped off. The *Acteon* was burnt next morning by Captain Atkins, to prevent her falling into the hands of the Provincials, as fine a new frigate as I ever saw.

Our ships, after laying nine hours before the battery, were obliged to retire with great loss. The Provincials reserved their fire until the shipping were advanced within point-blank shot; their artillery was surprisingly well served, it is said, under the command of a Mr. Masson and DeBrahm; it was slow, but decisive indeed; they were very cool, and took great care not to fire except their guns were exceedingly well directed. But there was a time when the battery appeared to be silenced for more than an hour; the Navy say, had the troops been ready to land at this time, they could have taken possession. How that is I will not pretend to say. I will rather suppose it; but the fire became exceedingly severe when it was renewed again, and did amazing execution after the battery had been supposed to have beeen silenced.

This will not be believed when it is first reported in England. I can scarcely believe what I myself saw on that day—a day to me one of the most distressing of my life. The Navy, on this occasion, have behaved with the usual coolness and intrepidity; one would have imagined that no battery could have resisted their incessant fire.

—FORCE, ed., *American Archives*, 4th Series, VI, 1209n.-1210n.

3. "NEVER DID MEN FIGHT MORE BRAVELY"

Memoirs of Colonel William Moultrie.

On the morning of the 28th of June [1776], I paid a visit to our advance-guard (on horseback three miles to the eastward of our fort.) While I was there, I saw a number of the enemy's boats in motion, at the back of Long-Island, as if they intended a descent upon our advanced post; at the same time I saw the men-of-war loose their topsails. I hurried back to the fort as fast as possible; when I got there the ships were already under sail. I immediately ordered the long roll to beat, and officers and men to their posts. We had scarcely manned our guns when the following ships of war came sailing up, as if in confidence of victory. As soon as they came within the reach of our guns, we began to fire. They were soon a-breast of the fort . . . let go their anchors, with springs upon their cables, and begun their attack most furiously about 10 o'clock A. M. and continued a brisk fire till about 8 o'clock P. M.

The ships were:

The *Bristol*, of 50 guns, Commodore Sir Peter Parker: the captain had his arm shot off, 44 men killed and 30 wounded.

The *Experiment*, 50 guns: the captain lost his arm, 57 men killed and 30 wounded.

The *Active*, 28 guns: 1 lieutenant killed, 1 man wounded.

The *Sole-Bay*, 28 guns: 2 killed, 3 or 4 wounded.

The *Syren*, 28 guns.

The *Acteon*, 28 guns: burnt; 1 lieutenant killed.

The *Sphinx*, 28 guns: lost her bowsprit.

The *Friendship*, 26 guns; an armed vessel taken into service.

The *Thunder*, bomb, had the beds of her mortar soon disabled; she threw her shells in a very good direction; most of them fell within the fort, but we had a morass in the middle that swallowed them up instantly, and those that fell in the sand and in and about the fort were immediately buried so that very few of them bursted amongst us. At one time the Commodore's ship swung round with her stern to the fort, which drew the fire of all the guns that could bear upon her: we supposed he had had the springs of her cables cut away. The words that passed along the platform by officers and men were: "Mind the Commodore! Mind the two fifty-gun ships!" Most all the attention was paid to the two fifty-gun ships, especially the Commodore, who, I dare say, was not at all obliged to us for our particular attention to him; the killed and wounded on board those two fifty-gun ships confirms what I say.

During the action Gen. Lee paid us a visit through a heavy line of fire and pointed two or three guns himself; then said to me, "Colonel, I see you are doing very well here. You have no occasion for me. I will go up to town again," and left us.

When I received information of Gen. Lee's approach to the fort, I sent Lieut. Marion from off the platform, with 8 or 10 men, to unbar the gateway. Our gate not being finished, the gateway was barricaded with pieces of timber 8 or 10 inches square, which required 3 or 4 men to remove each piece. The men in the ships' tops, seeing those men run from the platform, concluded "we were quitting the fort," as some author mentions. Another says, "We hung up a man in the fort at the time of the action." That action was taken from this circumstance: when the action begun (it being a warm day), some of the men took off their coats and threw them upon the top of the merlons. I saw a shot take one of them and throw it into a small tree behind the platform. It was noticed by our men and they cried out, "Look at the coat!"

Never did men fight more bravely, and never were men more cool; their only distress was the want of powder; we had not more than 28 rounds, for 26 guns, 18 and 26-pounders, when we begun the action; and a little after, 500 pounds from town and 200 pounds from Captain Tufft's schooner lying at the back of the fort.

There cannot be a doubt but that, if we had had as much powder as we could have expended in the time, the men-of-war must have struck their colors or they would certainly have been sunk, because they could not retreat, as the wind and tide were against them; and if they had proceeded up to town, they would have been in a much worse situation. They could not make any impression on our fort, built of palmetto logs and filled in with earth. Our merlons were 16 feet thick and high enough to cover the men from the fire of the tops. The men that we had killed and wounded received their shots mostly through the embrasures.

An author, who published in 1779, says, "The guns were at one time so long silenced that it was thought the fort was abandoned; it seems extraordinary that a detachment of land forces were not in readiness on board of the transports, or boats, to profit of such an occasion."

The guns being so long silent was owing to the scarcity of powder which we had in the fort, and to a report that was brought to me "that the English troops were landed between the advance-guard and the fort." It was upon this information that I ordered the guns to cease firing, or to fire very slow upon the shipping; that we should reserve our powder for the musketry to defend ourselves against the land forces, there being a scarcity of powder at this time.

At one time, 3 or 4 of the men-of-war's broadsides struck the fort at the same instant, which gave the merlons such a tremor that I was apprehensive that a few more such would tumble them down. During the action three of the men-of-war, in going round to our west curtain, got entangled together, by which the *Acteon* frigate went on shore on the middle ground; the *Sphinx* lost her bow-sprit; and the *Syren* cleared herself without any damage; had these three ships effected their purpose, they would have enfiladed us in such a manner as to have driven us from our guns. It being a very hot day, we were served along the platform with grog in fire-buckets, which we partook of very heartily: I never had a more agreeable draught than that which I took out of one of those buckets at the time. It may be very easily conceived what heat and thirst a man must feel in this climate, to be upon a platform on the 28th June, amidst 20 or 30 heavy pieces of cannon in one continual blaze and roar, and clouds of smoke curling over his head for hours together; it was a very honourable situation, but a very unpleasant one.

During the action thousands of our fellow-citizens were looking on with anxious hopes and fears, some of whom had their fathers, brothers and husbands in the battle; whose hearts must have been pierced at every broad-side. After some time our flag was shot away; their hopes were then gone, and they gave up all for lost, supposing that we had struck our flag, and had given up the fort! Sergeant Jasper, perceiving that the flag was shot away and had fallen without the fort, jumped from one of the embrasures and brought it up through a heavy fire, fixed it upon a spunge-staff, and planted it upon the ramparts again. Our flag once more waving in the air revived the drooping spirits of our friends; and they continued looking on till night had closed the scene and hid us from their view; only the appearance of a heavy storm, with continual flashes and peals like thunder. At night when we came to our slow firing (the ammunition being nearly quite gone) we could hear the shot very distinctly strike the ships.

At length the British gave up the conflict. The ships slipt their cables and dropped down with the tide, and out of the reach of our guns. When the firing had ceased, our friends for a time were again in an unhappy suspense, not knowing our fate till they received an account by a dispatch boat, which I sent up to town to acquaint them that the British ships had retired and that we were victorious.

Early the next morning was presented to our view the *Acteon* frigate hard and fast aground at about 400 yards distance. We gave her a few shot, which she returned, but they soon set fire to her and quitted her. Capt. Jacob Milligan and others went in some of our boats, boarded her while she was on fire, and pointed 2 or 3 guns at the Commodore and fired them; then brought off the ship's bell and other articles, and had scarcely left her when she blew up, and from the explosion issued a grand pillar of smoke, which soon expanded itself at the top and, to appearance, formed the figure of a palmetto tree; the ship immediately burst into a great blaze that continued till she burnt down to the water's edge.

—Moultrie, *Memoirs*, I, 174-181.

4. Sergeant Jasper Raises the Flag over Fort Moultrie

Major Barnard Elliott of South Carolina to his wife.

Charleston, June 29, 1776

As soon as I got to my battery after leaving you, we took up several places on the inside of the cabin, upon which were brass screws, all bespattered with blood, and other ornaments of the man-of-war. The firing continued till near 10 o'clock, and I have the pleasure to inform you that we have lost but ten men and twenty-two wounded. Dr. Faysseaux came up this morning with the latter. He tells me that Richard Baker, our nephew, behaved gallantly, as did all the officers and men.

The expression of a Sergeant McDaniel, after a cannon ball had taken off his shoulder and scouped out his stomach, is worth recording in the annals of America: "Fight on, my brave boys; don't let liberty expire with me today!"

Young, the barber, an old artillery man, who lately enlisted as sergeant, has lost a leg. Several arms are shot away. Not an officer is wounded.

My old grenadier, Serj. Jasper, upon the shot carrying away the flag-staff, called out to Col. Moultrie: "Colonel, don't let us fight without our flag!"

"What can you do?" replied the Colonel. "The staff is broke."

"Then, sir," said he, "I'll fix it to a halbert and place it on the merlon of the bastion next to the enemy," which he did, through the thickest fire.

General Lee crossed from Haddrell's to Sullivan's in the heat of the cannonade and was at the fort. His letter to the President says he never saw but one cannonade equal to this, though he has seen many; nor did he ever see officers and men behave better, nor could any in the world exceed them.

A fine sight from our cupola. I wish you and Rinchey were here to look at it, viz.: One of the finest of the enemy's frigates was all in a blaze, and has been burning two hours. She is one of the two that got on shore on the middle ground, which they, not being able to get off, have burnt. A bowsprit was shot away yesterday afternoon; part of her rigging came up with the tide—also, several yards of the masts.

The *Bristol*, of 50 guns, the *Roebuck*, of 44 guns, and the *Syren*, of 28, were the three ships that lay nearest the fort. The distance, though it appeared great from our cupola, did not exceed 400 yards. Six men-of-war engaged. Col. Moultrie has sent up for ammunition. The President told me he had sent to Dorchester for 2000 lbs. The fort was three-quarters of an hour yesterday without powder.

I think you and Rinchey may come down with safety to-day, and if they should renew the attack in the afternoon, you may stay till Johnston's Fort is engaged. Now, my dear wife, let us not forget to whom we are indebted for this success against our enemy. Let us return God thanks for it. It is He that does all for us. He inspires our officers and men with courage, and shields their heads in the day of battle. He is the wonderful God of victory.

—GIBBES, *Documentary History of the American Revolution*, II, 6-7.

5. A REVOLUTIONARY FALSTAFF COMES TO GRIEF

A New War Song
by Sir Peter Parker
1777

(Tune: "Well Met, Brother Tar")

My Lords, with your leave
An account I will give
That deserves to be written in meter;
  For the Rebels and I
  Have been pretty nigh—
Faith! almost too nigh for Sir Peter.

With much labour and toil
Unto Sullivan's Isle
I came fierce as Falstaff or Pistol,
  But the Yankees (od rot 'em)—
  I could not get at 'em—
Most terribly mauled my poor *Bristol*.

Bold Clinton by land
Did quietly stand
While I made a thundering clatter;
But the channel was deep,
So he could only peep
And not venture over the water.

De'il take 'em; their shot
Came so swift and so hot,
And the cowardly dogs stood so stiff, sirs,
That I put ship about
And was glad to get out,
Or they would not have left me a skiff, sirs!

Now bold as a Turk
I proceed to New York
Where with Clinton and Howe you may find me.
I've the wind in my tail,
And am hoisting my sail,
To leave Sullivan's Island behind me.

But, my lords, do not fear
For before the next year,
(Altho' a small island could fret us),
The Continent whole
We shall take, by my soul,
If the cowardly Yankee will let us.
                              —Moore, ed., *Songs and Ballads*, p. 135.

CHAPTER TWENTY-NINE

The Second Campaign to Conquer the South

Following *the withdrawal of the British army from Philadelphia, Clinton was ordered to dispatch troops to Georgia or Florida and to attempt what was optimistically expected to be the "comparatively easy" conquest of South Carolina. That long-drawn-out campaign was a seesaw affair, marked by ups and downs for both sides, advance and retreat, siege and countersiege, the capitulation of towns and garrisons, the disastrous rout of the Patriots in the field, only to be succeeded by a total capitulation of the main British army in the South.*

First the British won Georgia, and despite partisan resistance held it against the Patriots. Then came the fall of Charleston, not only the worst defeat which the Americans suffered in the Revolution, but the worst defeat in American military history until Bataan. Now the Carolinas lay open to Cornwallis; what with the collapse of American finances, and the treason of Arnold, the Patriot cause seemed desperate that summer of 1780. But once again—as in New England and in the Middle States—British plans miscarried. Heat, disease, swamps and space combined with guerrillas and partisans to frustrate and then to defeat the invaders. Loyalists were numerous, but weakened the British by their excesses and their independence. Though the incompetent Gates was disastrously defeated at Camden, partisans and regulars combined to overwhelm the Loyalists at King's Mountain. The British did not know it, but that was the turn of the tide.

I. THE FALL OF SAVANNAH

The campaign against the South was outlined by Germain to Clinton as early as March 8, 1778, but it took time for the fleet and armies to get moving. A force from Florida under Brigadier General Augustine Prevost pushed up north to reinforce the main attack against Savannah, which was assigned to Lieutenant Colonel Archibald Campbell. Campbell's fleet of transports and war vessels arrived at the mouth of the Savannah River at the end of December, 1778.

Campbell's amphibious expedition was opposed by a small American army in the South under General Robert Howe. Against a hard-pressed attack the Savannah defenses proved untenable. A Negro guided Campbell's men through the wooded swamps guarded by Howe's forces and gained their rear. Attacked from front and rear, the Americans broke in confusion. Many were

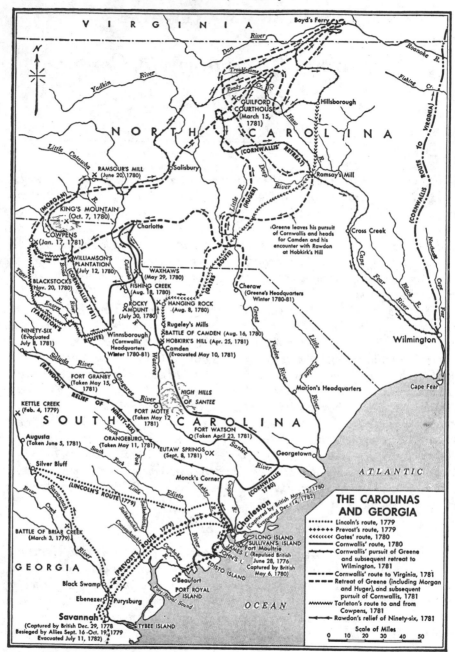

From The American Revolution
by John Richard Alden

Courtesy of Harper & Brothers

*drowned in the rice swamps in their headlong flight. The American losses
were immensely heavy for such small forces—83 killed or drowned, 453
captured, against British casualties of three killed, ten wounded. Following
the fall of Savannah, Sunbury and Augusta were taken, and the royal government, including a royal legislature, re-established. Howe was cleared by a*

court of inquiry, but his reputation was permanently damaged. As "Light-Horse Harry" Lee put it, "never was a victory of such magnitude so completely gained, with so little loss."

1. Britain Launches a New Move in the South

Lord George Germain to Sir Henry Clinton.

March 8, 1778

. . . Could a small corps be detached at the same time to land at Cape Fear and make an impression on North Carolina, it is not doubted that large numbers of the inhabitants would flock to the King's standard, and that His Majesty's Government would be restored in that province also. But your own knowledge of those provinces, and the information you can collect from the naval and military officers that have been upon service there, will enable you to give the officer to whom you may entrust the command better instructions than I can pretend to point out to you at this distance. I will therefore only further observe to you that the conquest of these provinces is considered by the King as an object of great importance in the scale of the war, as their possession might be easily maintained, and thereby a very valuable branch of commerce would be restored to this country and the rebels deprived of a principal resource for the support of their foreign credit, and of paying for the supplies they stand in need of, as the product of these provinces make a considerable part of their remittances to Europe.

While these operations are carrying on, every diversion should be made in the provinces of Virginia and Maryland that the remaining troops which can be spared for the offensive service, in conjunction with the fleet, will admit of. The great number of deep inlets and navigable rivers in these provinces expose them in a peculiar manner to naval attacks, and must require a large force to be kept on foot for their protection, and disable them from giving any assistance to the Carolinas. The seizing or destroying their shipping would also be attended with the important consequence of preventing the Congress from availing themselves, as they have done, of their staple commodity, tobacco, on which, and the rice and indigo of Carolina and Georgia, they entirely depend for making remittances to Europe.

Should the success we may reasonably hope for attend these enterprizes, it might not be too much to expect that all America to the south of the Susquehannah would return to their allegiance, and in the case of so happy an event, the northern provinces might be left to their own feelings and distress to bring them back to their duty, and the operations against them confined to the cutting off all their supplies and blocking up their ports. . . .

—Gr. Brit. Hist. Mss. Comm., *Stopford-Sackville Manuscripts*, II, 99.

2. "Come and Take It!"—Fort Morris Dares the British Invaders

Colonel L. V. Fuser of the British Army to Colonel John McIntosh of the Continental Army, commanding at Fort Morris in Georgia.

November 25, 1778

Sir:—You cannot be ignorant that four armies are in motion to reduce this Province. The one is always under the guns of your fort, and may be joined when I think proper, by Colonel Prevost, who is now at the Medway meeting-house. The resistance you can or intend to make will only bring destruction upon this country. On the contrary, if you will deliver me the fort which you command, lay down your arms, and remain neuter until the fate of America is determined, you shall, as well as all the inhabitants of this parish, remain in peaceable possession of your property. Your answer, which I expect in an hour's time, will determine the fate of this country, whether it is to be laid in ashes, or remain as above proposed.

> I am, sir, your most obedient, etc.,
>
> L. V. FUSER

P.S.—Since this letter was closed, some of your people have been firing scattering shot about the line. I am to inform you that if a stop is not put to such irregular proceedings, I shall burn a house for every shot so fired.

McIntosh's reply.

> Fort Morris, November 25, 1778

Sir:—We acknowledge we are not ignorant that your army is in motion to endeavour to reduce this State. We believe it entirely chimerical that Colonel Prevost is at the meeting-house; but should it be so, we are in no degree apprehensive of danger from a junction of his army with yours. We have no property compared with the object we contend for that we value a rush, and would rather perish in a vigorous defence than accept your proposals. We, sir, are fighting the battles of America, and therefore disdain to remain neutral till its fate is determined. As to surrendering the fort, receive this laconic reply, "*Come and take it!*" Major Lane, whom I send with this letter, is directed to satisfy you with respect to the irregular, loose firing mentioned on the back of your letter.

> I have the honour to be,
>
> Sir, your most obedient serv't,
>
> JOHN McINTOSH,
>
> *Colonel of Continental Troops*
>
> —WHITE, *Historical Collections of Georgia*, pp. 525-526.

3. THE MANEUVER THAT LED TO THE FALL OF SAVANNAH

Lieutenant Colonel Archibald Campbell to Lord George Germain.

> Savannah, January 16, 1779

In consequence of Sir Henry Clinton's orders to proceed to Georgia with His Majesty's Seventy-first Regiment of Foot, two battalions of Hessians, four battalions of Provincials and a detachment of the Royal Artillery, I have the honor to acquaint your lordship of our having sailed from the Hook on the 27th of November, 1778, escorted by a squadron of His Majesty's ships of war under the command of Commodore Parker; and of the arrival of the whole fleet off the island of Tybee on the 23rd of December thereafter, two horse-sloops excepted.

Having no intelligence that could be depended upon with respect to the military force of Georgia or the disposition formed for its defence, Sir James Baird's Highland company of light-infantry, in two flat-boats, with Lieutenant

Clark of the Navy, was dispatched in the night of the 25th to seize any of the inhabitants they might find on the banks of Wilmington Creek. Two men were procured by this means, by whom we learned the most satisfactory intelligence concerning the state of matters at Savannah, and which settled the Commodore and I in the resolution of landing the troops the next evening at the plantation of one Gerridoe, an important post. This post was the first practicable landing-place on the Savannah River; the whole country between it and Tybee being a continued tract of deep marsh, intersected by the creeks of St. Augustine and Tybee, of considerable extent, and other cuts of water, impassable for troops at any time of the tide.

The *Vigilant*, man-of-war, with the *Comet*, galley, the *Keppel*, armed brig, and the *Greenwich*, armed sloop, followed by the transports in the divisions, in the order established for a descent, proceeded up the river with the tide at noon; about 4 o'clock in the evening the *Vigilant* opened the reach to Gerridoe's plantation and was cannonaded by two rebel galleys, who retired before any of their bullets had reached her: a single shot from the *Vigilant* quickened their retreat.

The tide and evening being too far spent, and many of the transports having grounded at the distance of five or six miles below Gerridoe's plantation, the descent was indispensably delayed till next morning. The first division of the troops, consisting of all the light-infantry of the army, the New York Volunteers and first battalion of the Seventy-first under the command of Lieutenant-colonel Maitland, were landed at break of day on the river-dam, in front of Gerridoe's plantation, from whence a narrow causeway of six hundred yards in length, with a ditch on each side, led through a rice-swamp directly to Gerridoe's house, which stood upon a bluff of thirty feet in height above the level of the rice-swamps.

The light-infantry, under Captain Cameron, having first reached the shore, were formed and led briskly forward to the bluff, where a body of fifty rebels were posted, and from whom they received a smart fire of musketry, but the Highlanders, rushing on with their usual impetuosity, gave them no time to repeat it: they drove them instantly to the woods and happily secured a landing for the rest of the army. Captain Cameron, a spirited and most valuable officer, with two Highlanders, were killed on this occasion, and five Highlanders wounded.

Upon the reconnoitering the environs of Gerridoe's plantation, I discovered the rebel army, under Major-general Robert Howe, drawn up about half a mile east of the town of Savannah, with several pieces of cannon in their front. The first division of troops, together with one company of the second battalion of the Seventy-first, the first battalion of Delancey's, the Wellworth, and part of the Weissenbach regiment of Hessians, being landed, I thought it expedient, having the day before me, to go in quest of the enemy rather than give them an opportunity of retiring unmolested.

A company of the second battalion of the Seventy-first, together with the first battalion of Delancey's, were accordingly left to cover the landing-place, and the troops marched for the town of Savannah.

The troops reached the open country near Tatnal's plantation before three o'clock in the evening and halted in the great road about two hundred paces short of the gate leading to Governor Wright's plantation, the light-infantry excepted, who were ordered to form immediately upon our right of the road, along the rails leading to Governor Wright's plantation.

The enemy were drawn up across the road at the distance of eight hundred yards from this gateway. One half, consisting of Thompson's and Eugee's [Huger's] regiments of Carolina troops, were formed under Colonel Eugee, with their left obliquely to the great road leading to Savannah, their right to a wooded swamp, covered by the houses of Tatnal's plantation, in which they had placed some riflemen. The other half of their regular troops, consisting of part of the first, second, third and fourth battalions of the Georgia brigade, was formed under Colonel Elbert, with their right to the road and their left to the rice-swamps of Governor Wright's plantation, with the fort of Savannah Bluff behind their left wing, in the style of second flank; the town of Savannah, round which they had the remains of an old line of intrenchment, covered their rear. One piece of cannon was planted on the right of their line, one upon the left, and two pieces occupied the traverse, across the great road, in the centre of their line. About one hundred paces in front of this traverse, at a critical spot between two swamps, a trench was cut across the road, and about one hundred yards in front of this trench, a marshy rivulet ran almost parallel the whole extent of their front, the bridge of which was burned down to interrupt the passage and retard our progress.

I could discover from the movements of the enemy that they wished and expected an attack upon their left, and I was desirous of cherishing that opinion.

Having accidentally fallen in with a Negro who knew a private path through the wooded swamp upon the enemy's right, I ordered the first battalion of the Seventy-first to form on our right of the road and move up to the rear of the light-infantry, whilst I drew off that corps to the right as if I meant to extend my front to that quarter, where a happy fall of ground favored the concealment of this manoeuvre, and increased the jealousy of the enemy with regard to their left. Sir James Baird had directions to convey the light-infantry in this hollow ground quite to the rear and penetrate the wooded swamp upon our left, with a view to get round by the new barracks into the rear of the enemy's right flank. The New York volunteers, under Colonel Trumbull, were ordered to support him.

During the course of this movement, our artillery were formed in a field on our left of the road, concealed from the enemy by a swell of ground in front, to which I meant to run them up for action when the signal was made to engage, and from whence I could either bear advantageously upon the right of the rebel line, as it was then formed, or cannonade any body of troops in flank which they might detach into the wood to retard the progress of the light-infantry.

The regiment of Wellworth was formed upon the left of the artillery, and the enemy continued to amuse themselves with their cannon without any return upon our part till it was visible that Sir James Baird and the light-infantry had fairly got round upon their rear. On this occasion I commanded the line to move briskly forward. The well-directed artillery of the line, the rapid advance of the Seventy-first Regiment and the forward countenance of the Hessian regiment of Wellworth instantly dispersed the enemy.

A body of the militia of Georgia, posted at the new barracks with some pieces of cannon to cover the road from Great Ogeeche, were at this juncture routed, with the loss of their artillery, by the light-infantry under Sir James Baird, when the scattered troops of the Carolina and Georgia brigades ran across the plain in his front. This officer with his usual gallantry dashed the light-infantry on their flank and terminated the fate of the day with brilliant success.

Thirty-eight officers of different distinctions, and four hundred and fifteen non-commissioned officers and privates, one stand of colors, forty-eight pieces of cannon, twenty-three mortars, ninety-four barrels of powder, the fort with all its stores, agreeable to the inclosed return, and, in short, the capital of Georgia, the shipping in the harbor, with a large quantity of provisions, fell into our possession before it was dark, without any other loss on our side than that of Captain Peter Campbell, a gallant officer of Skinner's light-infantry, and two privates killed, one sergeant and nine privates wounded. Eighty-three of the enemy were found dead on the Common, and eleven wounded. By the accounts received from their prisoners, thirty lost their lives in the swamp, endeavoring to make their escape.

—DAWSON, *Battles of the United States*, I, 477-479.

II. ADVANCE AND REPULSE IN GEORGIA

General Lincoln, dispatched by Congress to take command in the South, pushed down from Charleston toward Savannah. He encamped at Purrysburg opposite Prevost, who was across the river on the Georgia side. Morale was high but the numbers of Patriot soldiers were too few to mount an attack. Nevertheless in quick succession two victories were scored against the British—at Beaufort and at Kettle Creek. Moultrie marched a force from Purrysburg over to Beaufort where they came to grips with the British. The American victory was the more astonishing since the Patriots fought on open ground while the British fought from bushes and swamp which they had quickly seized: a reversal of the usual military pattern of the Revolutionary War.

Kettle Creek was a fight between Tories and militiamen. The former, chiefly Scotsmen, were marching from North Carolina to join up with Tory partisans in back-country Georgia. Colonel Pickens caught the Tories by surprise at Kettle Creek, where they were engaged in slaughtering a herd of stolen cattle. Attacked from both wings and in the center, the British force broke and scattered. Seventy of the prisoners were condemned to death, all but five pardoned. These, the ringleaders, were hanged.

From his camp at Purrysburg Lincoln now seized the initiative. He sent one force to the eastern bank of the Savannah River opposite Augusta, another to the Black Swamp, and a third to Briar Creek south of Augusta. This last force was under the command of General John Ashe and comprised some 1,400 North Carolina militia and a handful of Continentals. As the Patriot

*forces converged on Augusta, Campbell evacuated that frontier town and set
his own troops in motion for the return to Savannah. Ashe followed in pursuit. Campbell crossed Briar Creek and destroyed the bridge over it. Then
Ashe came up and set to work to rebuild it. This encouraged Campbell to send
a detachment under Colonel Mark Prevost, younger brother of the commander, to make a wide turning movement, cross the creek above Ashe's
camp and attack him from the rear. When that attack came, the militia fled.
The Patriots suffered 400 casualties against 16 for the British. Six hundred
others ran home. In all, only 400 ever got back to Lincoln, who had lost one
third of his army. Briar Creek showed that the militia were still not consistently reliable under fire and spelled finis to Lincoln's campaign to recapture Georgia at that time.*

1. "Let Not Economy Border Too Much upon Parsimony"

William Moultrie to C. C. Pinckney, President of the Senate of South
Carolina.

Purisburgh [Purrysburg] January 10, 1779

I challenge you to open a correspondence between Charlestown and our
camp. If you accept I shall expect to hear from you, and shall continue to
write you and give you the earliest and best intelligence that comes in my
way; and shall hope you will answer me accordingly.

We are (I mean the Continentals) encamped at Purisburgh, the N. Carolinians on the road leading to this place, about two miles from us. Our numbers are about 500 privates (Continentals), and the North-Carolinians about
1200 of all ranks. We are all in good spirits and ready to receive the enemy,
but are not strong enough to pay them the first visit. From all the intelligence
we can get, their numbers on the opposite side of the river to us amount to
about 1500 and they occupy all the posts near us over which we could possibly pass; besides our men are undisciplined and many unarmed. I hope
Richardson and others will soon join us. I think we should have 5,000 men
before we cross the river, as we shall get immediately into action.

I hope we shall drive those gentry on board their vessels. We hear their
drums beat every morning from our out posts; nay, hear their sentinels cough.
I have no idea of the enemy coming over to us; their principal aim seems to
be, until they can strengthen themselves from the back parts of these two
southern states, then perhaps they may endeavor to push us from hence. I
hope our countrymen turn out cheerfully; if they do not, I fear the war will
be long and serious and brought into our own state, which will be very unfortunate.

A late instance I have had before my eyes: the poor women and children
and Negroes of Georgia, many thousands of whom I saw on my journey to
this place (a spectacle that even moved the hearts of the soldiers), travelling
to they knew not where.

I fear we have lost Sunberry and two gallies that took shelter under that
battery last Thursday or Friday, as we heard a very heavy cannonade from
that quarter. The officer commanding had about 120 Continentals and some
inhabitants within the fort, refused to evacuate the post; notwithstanding his

receiving positive orders for that purpose, he Don Quixote-like thought he was strong enough to withstand the whole force the British had in Georgia, for which I think he deserved to be hanged.

We have the *Congress* and *Lee*, gallies, a ten-gun sloop and two schooners now lying under this bluff (they pushed up here to get out of the way of the British). They may be of some service to cover our crossing, should it be expedient to land below this place, or to establish any post on the other side of the river. I believe they cannot go much higher than where they now are.

As it is absolutely necessary to keep open the communication between this place and Charlestown, I wish you would think of some way, either legislatively or otherwise, to keep the roads and bridges in good order; they are now wearing away fast, notwithstanding we have had so much dry weather; how will they be when the rains set in, as they seem to begin to day? For God's sake, let not your legislative or executive economy border too much upon parsimony! Be generous to your militia. Allow them every thing necessary to take the field. It is now time to open your purse strings. Our country is in danger. Be more bountiful than you have been hitherto in this present administration. Have the modesty to allow that very few of you have the least idea of what is necessary for an army, and grant what the officers shall ask for that purpose. They are certainly the best judges.

Excuse me for this digression, but I cannot help being warmed, when I think how ill the officers of this state have been treated, in being refused almost every necessary they applied for; and had not Gen. Lincoln arrived here as he did, with the money, we should not have been able to take the field at this time, and our country might have been lost. I shall say no more on this head, as my warmth might carry me too far. . . .

—MOULTRIE, *Memoirs*, I, 258-261.

2. AT BEAUFORT A REVERSAL OF THE USUAL WAY OF FIGHTING

William Moultrie to General Benjamin Lincoln.

Beaufort, February 4, 1779

I wrote you a few days ago from Gen. Bull's, when I was there. The militia requested me to cross the river with them, which I readily consented to. The next morning, after leaving a proper guard to our camp, we began to cross the ferry and got near three hundred over by sun set. We immediately marched off and continued till we got within one mile of Beaufort. Here I rested the troops a few hours and then proceeded to the town which we entered at sun rise next morning.

Having ordered the troops into quarters and reposed myself a little, I rode down to view the fort with Gen. Bull and two or three other gentlemen. We had scarce been a moment there when an express arrived informing that the enemy were in full march for Beaufort and not more than five miles off; upon this I requested Gen. Bull to ride on to town and have the men turned out. I followed immediately and found them all paraded, and had another account that the enemy were coming very fast.

I then moved off the troops in order to meet them and, having marched two miles, was again informed they were within four miles of us. I then proceeded very slowly, looking for a proper piece of ground to form upon. Having soon found a very advantageous spot, I continued there, waiting an hour for the enemy, and was then informed that they had, after halting awhile, altered their march and were going towards our ferry. I followed them and had gone about three miles when I learnt that they were upon their return from the ferry, in full march towards us, and not more than one mile distant. Having sent my aid, Mr. Kinlock, to reconnoitre and bring me a particular account, he soon returned and informed me they were just at hand. I hastened our march to gain a swamp which was near; but finding the enemy had already got possession of the ground I intended to occupy, I halted at about two hundred yards distance from the enemy and drew up the troops to the right and left of the road, with two field-pieces (6-pounders) in the centre, and one small piece (2-pounder) on the right in the wood. On the enemy's near approach, I ordered Capt. Thomas Heyward to begin with the two field-pieces, and advanced my right and left wings nearer the swamp, and then the firing became pretty general.

This action was reversed from the usual way of fighting between the British and Americans: they taking to the bushes and we remaining upon the open ground. After some little time, finding our men too much exposed to the enemy's fire, I ordered them to take trees. About three quarters of an hour after the action began, I heard a general cry through the line of "No more cartridges"; and was also informed by Captains Heyward and Rutledge that the ammunition for the field-pieces was almost expended, after firing about forty rounds from each piece. Upon this I ordered the field-pieces to be drawn off very slowly, and their right and left wings to keep pace with the artillery to cover their flanks, which was done in tolerable order for undisciplined troops. The enemy had beat their retreat before we began to move, but we had little or no ammunition and could not of consequence pursue. They retreated so hastily as to leave an officer, one sergeant and three privates wounded in a house near the action, and their dead lying on the field. . . .

It makes me happy to assure you that our militia have that spirit which they have always been allowed to possess. Nothing but discipline is wanting to make them good troops. The Charlestown artillery behaved gallantly; they stood to their pieces like veterans and served them well, until I was constrained to order them to retire in consequence of their ammunition being nearly expended. I had in the action only nine Continental troops: Capt. De Treville, two officers, and six privates, with one brass two-pounder and only fifteen rounds. I must, in justice to them, say, that they behaved well.
—MOULTRIE, *Memoirs*, I, 291-295.

3. THE DISASTROUS REPULSE AT BRIAR CREEK

General John Ashe of North Carolina to Governor Caswell of North Carolina.
Camp, Zubley's Ferry, March 17, 1779

I should have wrote you long since, had I had time or opportunity, but we have been constantly marching since we left Elizabeth—from thence to

Charlestown, to Purisburg, to Augusta—to prevent the enemies' crossing into this State and making a junction with the disaffected (which are numerous) of this and our State.

The night of our arrival opposite to Augusta, the enemy encamped and made a precipitate retreat down the Savannah River (tho' double our number), from an information that my command amounted to eleven thousand, when in fact it did not exceed twelve hundred. I halted at this place, considering it an important pass to the State of South Carolina, till directed by General Lincoln to cross the river and march down to a place called Bryer Creek, the bridge of which the enemy had burnt down on their retreat. The creek makes out of the Savannah River, on the Georgia side, about sixty miles below Augusta, runs at right angles from the river about half a mile back of the river swamp, and then runs almost parallel with the river, so that forty miles up the river it is but ten miles distant, the swamp of the river being generally three miles wide, and on the creek a deep swamp, eight miles above the bridge a mill, and several fords between the bridge and mill, and also above.

Here we reached on the 27th ulto., and halted till the 3rd instant, expecting to be reinforced with such of the Georgia militia as were well affected, about one hundred and thirty Georgia Continentals, horse and some of the militia from South Carolina, and General Rutherford's brigade—none of which, except two hundred and seven horse from South Carolina, one hundred and fifty only of which were fit for duty, joined us. Genl. Rutherford, with part of his brigade, had reached Matthew's Bluff, about five miles above, with the river between, and Col. Marbury, of the Georgia horse, lay a few miles above on Bryer Creek, so that I had with me only Genl. Bryan's brigade, consisting of nine hundred men; Lieut. Col. Lytle's light infantry of about two hundred fit for duty; about seventy Georgia Continental troops (the South Carolina light horse being sent over the creek to reconnoitre); one four-pound brass field-piece, and two iron two-pound swivels, mounted as field-pieces. From these are to be deducted near a hundred waggoners and carters, which were always returned as soldiers in Gen. Bryan's brigade, with a guard of 50 men that had been sent to guard the baggage across the river, about eight miles above us (which had fortunately been effected a few minutes before the enemy appeared), and fifty on a fatigue party, to make bridges and clear the road (about three miles above us) to the river for General Rutherford's brigade and two brass field-pieces that had been sent from head quarters to Matthews' Bluff.

In this situation, without a possibility of retreat, I had advice of the enemy being about eight miles above, in full march toward us. We immediately beat to arms, formed the troops into two lines and served them with cartridges, which they could not prudently have been served with sooner, as they had several times received cartridges which had been destroyed and lost for want of cartouch boxes. We marched out of lines to meet the enemy, some carrying their cartridges under their arms, others in the bosoms of their shirts, and some tied up in the corners of their hunting shirts. Having advanced about a quarter of a mile from our encampment, I saw the enemy on a quick march, in force amounting, as I have since been informed, to eighteen hundred regulars. Several hundred Georgia and Florida scouts, with four or five hundred horse (by some said to be nine hundred), formed in three columns, with several field-pieces called grasshoppers. When they came within one hundred and fifty yards of us, they then displayed their columns to the right and left to form a line.

It was now that the Georgia Continentals and Col. Perkins' regiment, which formed the right of our first line, began their fire. The Georgia Continentals, under Genl. Elbert who acted as colonel, after two or three rounds advanced without orders a few steps beyond the line and moved to the left in front of the regiment from the district of New Bern, which much impeded their firing. By this movement and that of the Edenton regiment, which had been obliged to move a little to the right, there was a vacancy in the line. At this instant of time the Halifax regiment, which was upon the left of the second line, broke and took to flight without firing a gun. The Wilmington (except a small part under the command of Lieut. Col. Young, who were advancing in their line to the right to prevent being flanked, and fired two or three rounds) and the New Bern regiments followed their example. The Edenton regiment continued for two or three discharges longer, when they gave way and took to flight, just as Lieut. Col. Lytle, with his light infantry and a brass field-piece (which had been posted at the bridge about a mile and a half from the field), came up. As he saw the impossibility of the troops being rallied, and that it would be only exposing his small corps to no purpose, he moved off in order in the rear of the fugitives, reserving his fire. The Georgia Continentals still continued in action some little time longer, till their General surrendered himself a prisoner.

When I found the second line had given way, I rode across from the rear of Perkins' regiment and the Georgians, where I had taken post for a better observation of the movement of the enemy, to the rear of the fugitives, and called to the officers to rally their men, which I was in expectation might be done while there was an opposition made by the first line, but by the time I had wheeled my horse and got a few paces on my return, I saw the Edenton regiment break and take to flight. I then used my utmost exertions to get in front of the fugitives for half a mile or three-quarters, in order to rally them; in which I was assisted by Col. Perkins, Lieut. Cols. Young and Williams, Majors Blount and Doherty, with some few others, who exerted themselves on this occasion, when, finding it impossible, and that if I proceeded much further I must unavoidably fall into the hands of the enemy, I wheeled to the left into the river swamp and made my escape to Matthews' Bluff, which I had crossed on my return from Genl. Lincoln the preceding day—a place unknown to the troops, about four miles up the swamp—accompanied by Majors Pointer and McIlhean and one light horseman, swimming several lagoons on our horses.

I imagined most of the troops would have been either killed or taken, as they had very little further to fly before the broken bridge at Bryer Creek must stop them; but by a lucky halt which the enemy made for a few moments at the place of our encampment, they made their escape down the creek and thro' the river swamp, many of which swam the river, some crossed on rafts which they made, and others were fetched across in canoes, which were ordered down from Matthews' Bluff; so that we have only one hundred and fifty missing, upwards of fifty of which, we hear, crossed the river above and returned into our State. . . .

The little attention paid to orders, both by officers and soldiers, the several mutinies of the Halifax regiment, and desertions from the brigade, and Genl. Bryan's unhappy temper, from my march from Elizabeth to Bryer Creek, have rendered my command very disagreeable; and since the action, his conduct has been such as will forever render him contemptible to me; of which I shall inform you when I have the pleasure of seeing you, which I hope will be ere long. Let it suffice that at present I only add that he has, by himself and his tools, endeavored to propagate a report that I was both a traitor and coward, on which I have procured a court of inquiry to be held. . . .

—*North Carolina State Records*, XIV, 39-43.

III. PREVOST'S CHARLESTON EXPEDITION

Lincoln still kept the initiative despite the reverse at Briar Creek. On April 23 he marched up the Savannah River to cross near Augusta and cut off supplies to the British from the west. He left Moultrie with a thousand men at Purrysburg and Black Swamp to guard Savannah. Realizing Moultrie's weakness, Prevost crossed the Savannah and drove up toward Charleston. Moultrie retreated before him, delaying the advance by rear-guard skirmishes.

When Prevost reached Charleston he found it more formidable than he had anticipated. The neck of land between Charleston and the mainland was now fortified, and the city had received reinforcements under Count Casimir Pulaski. Nevertheless, to hold off the attack, Moultrie, at Governor Rutledge's request, entered into negotiations with the British. To everyone's surprise Rutledge offered to have the state remain neutral, a far cry from the heroic resistance back in '76. Prevost insisted on unconditional surrender. The approach of a relief force under Lincoln persuaded the British commander to pull out while he still had the chance. He withdrew through the islands along the coast, establishing a strong force on the mainland at Stono Ferry, where he could secure the navigation of the Stono River and protect the retreat to Georgia. As the South Carolina militia were beginning to drift homeward and the terms of the Virginia and North Carolina militia would expire in a few days, a Council of War determined to attack the Stono Ferry. A force under Moultrie arrived before the works just after daybreak, but his numbers were inadequate. The Highlanders stood up against a bayonet attack until all but eleven of them had fallen. The British were able to retreat safely to Savannah, hopping from island to island.

The Prevost expedition was accompanied by enormous looting by the British troops. Many of the slaves who flocked to the British army were sold off to the West Indies. But pillage was to become a minor phase of the fratricidal slaughter that now flared up in the Carolinas and Georgia as war's terrors spread throughout the lower South.

MOULTRIE DECIDES: "WE WILL FIGHT IT OUT"

About 3 o'clock in the morning [of May 11, 1779], it being still very dark, I heard some person inquiring for me. I rode up and was then told the governor wanted to see me; upon which I rode up to him. He then took me aside and asked me "whether we had not best have a parly with the enemy, and whether we were able to resist their force"; and asked about our numbers.

I assured him that they were upwards of 2,200 men.

He replied, "he did not think we had more than 1,800 men; and that the enemy's force, as he was informed, was 7 or 8,000 men at least; and should they force the lines, a great number of the citizens would be put to death." He represented to me the horrors of a storm: he told me that the state's engineer (Col. Senf) had represented to him the lines to be in a very weak state. After some conversation, he proposed to me the sending out a flag, to know what terms we could obtain.

I told him I thought we could stand against the enemy, that I did not think they could force the lines, and that I did not chuse to send a flag in my name, but if he chose it and would call the council together, I would send any message. They requested me to send the following, which was delivered by Mr. Kinlock:

"Gen. Moultrie, perceiving from the motions of your army that your intention is to besiege the town, would be glad to know on what terms you would be disposed to grant a capitulation, should he be inclined to capitulate."

About 11 o'clock, A.M., the following letter was sent in from the enemy:

"Sir,

"The humane treatment which the inhabitants of Georgia and this province have hitherto received will, I flatter myself, induce you to accept of the offers of peace and protection which I now make by the orders of Gen. Prevost; the evils and horrors attending the event of a storm (which cannot fail to be successful) are too evident not to induce a man of human feelings to do all in his power to prevent it: you may depend that every attention shall be paid, and every necessary measure be adopted, to prevent disorders; and that such of the inhabitants who may not chuse to receive the generous offers of peace and protection may be received as prisoners of war, and their fate decided by that of the rest of the colonies.

"Four hours shall be allowed for an answer; after which your silence, or the detention of the bearer of this, will be deemed a positive refusal.

"I have the honor to be, etc.,
"J. M. PREVOST,
"Col. commanding the advance,
"Camp at Ashley-Ferry.
"May 11th, 1779
"Brig. Gen. Moultrie, or the commanding officer in Charlestown."

On my receiving this letter, I showed it to the governor, who immediately summoned his council to meet at his own house, and requested I would go with them and bring Count Paulaski with me. Col. Laurens was also sent for. And I sent to Col. Cambray, the engineer, to work upon the left of our lines as fast as possible, because that part was very incomplete, and also ordered the bringing up the ammunition from town to the lines, as a number of the men had not more than three rounds the preceeding night. They had come in but the night before from the country. We scarcely had time to furnish them with arms and ammunition when the enemy were at our gates.

On the meeting of the council, the letter was read to them; they argued the matter of giving up the town amongst themselves. Gen. Count Paulaski and myself advised them not to give up the town, that we had men enough to beat the enemy; and so did Col. Laurens. They then asked me our number, which I gave the governor an account of, corps by corps, and which he took down on the back of the letter sent to me from Col. Prevost. They amounted to 3,180 at the lowest computation. I had mentioned more, in some of the corps, but it would not be allowed me: the governor was sure there must be some mistake in the returns; that he did not think we had more than 2,500 men on the lines. . . .

A gentleman who had been reconnoitreing with a party of horse about Ponpon Bridge and Parker's-ferry was asked his opinion respecting the number of the enemy; he gave them to the governor, corps by corps, according to the information he had received; which account was taken down by the governor on the back of the same letter from Col. Prevost and [totaled 3,620 men]. . . .

The gentleman also said that he was informed that besides those already taken down, there were a great many tories from North and South-Carolina and Georgia that had joined them.

I then replied to him, "that I believed they could not have more than 1,000, at most."

He said, "he could not tell."

During this business at the governor's house Captain Dunbar, of the Second Regiment, came in great haste to acquaint me that Gen. Prevost had observed our working on the lines during the passing of the flags, and that if I did not immediately desist, he would march his troops in. I sent orders to stop the working, and urged the governor and council to conclude upon something, as the time was growing very short, and that I wanted to be at the lines. At length they resolved I should send the following message:

> "Charlestown, May 12th, 1779.
>
> "Sir,
>
> "I cannot possibly agree to so dishonorable a proposal as is contained in your favor of yesterday; but if you will appoint an officer to confer on terms, I will send one to meet him, at such time and place as you fix on.
>
> "I have the honor to be, etc.
> "WILLIAM MOULTRIE.

"Brig. Gen. Prevost."

On my retreat from Black-swamp, Colonel Senf, from the governor's camp, Orangeburgh, joined me at Ponpon Bridge with the Racoon Company, commanded by Captain John Allston, of about fifty men on horseback. I ordered the stores at the borough to be burnt, with a quantity of rice that was in them, to prevent its falling into the enemy's hands, and the bridge to be destroyed; I also ordered Colonel Senf, with his men, to keep in my rear, and to burn all boats and bridges and throw every obstruction in the enemy's way to retard their march. They were the last corps that came into the town before the gates were shut.

When the question was carried for giving up the town upon a neutrality, I will not say who was for the question, but this I well remember, that Mr. John Edwards, one of the privy council, a worthy citizen and a very respectable merchant of Charlestown, was so affected as to weep, and said, "What, are we to give up the town at last?"

The governor and council adjourned to Colonel Beekman's tent on the lines at the gate. I sent for Colonel John Laurens from his house, to request the favor he would carry a message from the governor and council to General Prevost; but when he knew the purport, he begged to be excused from carrying such a message, that it was much against his inclination; that he would do any thing to serve his country; but he could not think of carrying such a message as that.

I then sent for Colonel M'Intosh and requested he would go with Colonel Roger Smith, who was called on by the governor, with the message. They both begged I would excuse them; hoped and requested I would get some other person. I however pressed them into a compliance; which message was as follows:

"To propose a neutrality during the war between Great-Britain and America, and the question whether the state shall belong to Great-Britain or remain one of the United States be determined by the treaty of peace between those two powers."

Colonel Prevost was appointed one of the commissioners to confer with Colonel M'Intosh and Colonel Smith, and they held their conference a quarter of a mile from our gate. We could see them from our lines. Upon the above proposal being made, Colonel Prevost answered, "that they did not come in a legislative capacity, but if Colonel Smith pleased, he would show the proposal to the general." Upon meeting them a second time, at 12 o'clock, Colonel Prevost said, "he had nothing to do with the governor, that his business was with General Moultrie, and as the garrison was in arms, they must surrender prisoners of war." . . .

Upon this the governor and council looked very grave and stedfastly on each other and on me, not knowing what I would say. After a little pause, I said to the governor and council, "Gentlemen, you see how the matter stands. The point is this: Am I to deliver you up prisoners of war or not?"

Some replied "yes."

I then said, "I am determined not to deliver you up prisoners of war. *We will fight it out!*"

Upon my saying this, Colonel Laurens, who was in the tent, jumped up and said, "Thank God! we are upon our legs again"; and as I was coming out of the tent, General Gadsden and Mr. Ferguson, two of the council who were against giving up the town, followed me and said, "Act according to your own judgment, and we will support you."

I immediately ordered the flag to be waved from the gate, which was a signal agreed upon should the conference be at an end. They did not perceive our flag wave; they therefore continued with theirs flying some time longer, upon which I sent out Mr. Kinlock to inform them "that I was very sorry they should be detained so long, that our flag had been waved some time ago, and that all conference was at an end." After which I hurried on in preparing every thing for our defence.

In justice to the citizens, they knew nothing of what was going forward in the council. They all seemed firm, calm, and determined to stand to the lines and defend their country.

The next morning at day-light, to the great joy of the citizens, it was cried out along the line, "The enemy is gone." There is no doubt they must have begun their retreat with their main body immediately after the conference was at an end, leaving some of their light troops to make a show before our lines, to divert us from treading too close upon their rear, and to move themselves off under the cover of the night. Early next morning, not seeing any of them, it was conjectured they were gone; and Count Paulaski went out on horseback and made two or three circuits at full speed; and not discovering any of them, returned in and made his reports, and then collected the cavalry and followed; but they had crossed Ashley River before he got there. I had given orders to him to endeavor to find out where Gen. Lincoln was, with his army. . . .

On the 14th I received the following letter from Gen. Lincoln:

"May 10th, 1779, 4 o'clock, P.M.

"Dear Sir,

"I just now received your favor of the 8th. . . . We are making and shall continue to make every exertion for the relief of Charlestown. The baggage will be left. . . . The inability of the men only will put a period to our daily marches. . . . I am unhappy to inform you that the 1,000 horse you mention are decreased to less than 150, a number scarcely sufficient for our front and flank guards and the other necessary duties of camp. . . . Pray stimulate your people to every exertion for the defence of the town, until the troops here can arrive. Our men are full of spirits; I think they will do honor to themselves, and render service to the public. . . . *Do not give up, or suffer the people to despair.*

"I am, etc.

"B. Lincoln

"Brig. Gen. Moultrie."

A copy of this letter was taken by the British on the 11th near our lines, which we suppose obliged them to retreat so precipitately, as they found Gen. Lincoln was on his march downwards with about 4,000 men, and had they staid two or three days longer on the town-neck, they would have been in a very unpleasant situation between two fires; and if they had retreated the same way back, they would have met Gen. Lincoln's army. They therefore filed off to the left and went on the islands.

—Moultrie, Memoirs, I, 426-437.

IV. THE FRANCO-AMERICAN EXPEDITION
TO RECAPTURE SAVANNAH

The withdrawal of Prevost from the outskirts of Charleston resulted in the initiative once more passing to the Patriots. The operations of Admiral d'Estaing against the British West Indies served to check militant moves by the British in the lower South. Governor Rutledge of South Carolina and General Lincoln were convinced now that, with the co-operation of the French fleet, Georgia might be regained to the Patriot cause. The main body of D'Estaing's fleet, consisting of 22 ships of the line and 11 frigates, arrived off the approaches to Savannah on September 8, 1779. The British sent a call for help by fast ship to Sir Henry Clinton in New York, and planned to employ their own vessels of war either to retire up the river or defend the entry to the harbor. Slave labor was employed to improve the town's fortifications. Two vessels of war and four transports were sunk in the channel, blocking it up. The combined Franco-American attacking forces numbered 5,000, along with General Pulaski's Legion, as against 3,200 defenders.

Savannah was the Charleston story again, but in reverse. D'Estaing called on the garrison to surrender. Prevost stalled for time. Under cover of the truce until the following day Colonel Maitland's forces from Port Royal, after a remarkable march, reached the town in safety, and, thus reinforced, Prevost refused to surrender. Several bombardments did some damage to the town, but not to the British military installations. D'Estaing decided that unless the town could be taken by storm, he would discontinue the siege. The assault took place on October 9, preceded by a heavy bombardment. But plans misfired: some troops got lost in a swamp and were exposed to heavy enemy fire; others, betrayed by a deserter, were hard hit by both direct fire from the redoubt and cross fire from the works on the right and an armed ship in the river. Some of the attackers scaled the ramparts, and a bloody fight ensued, until they were forced to give way and a retreat was ordered. Count Pulaski, having dashed forward to charge the rear of the enemy's line, was struck by a small cannon ball and mortally wounded. The allied casualties exceeded 800; the British were hardly more than 150.

Admiral d'Estaing had had enough. As a French officer put it, "Our situation had become terrible and disheartening." On October 20 the French returned to their fleet, and the ships proceeded to leave on different missions. The Americans recrossed the river. Thus ended the campaign of 1779.

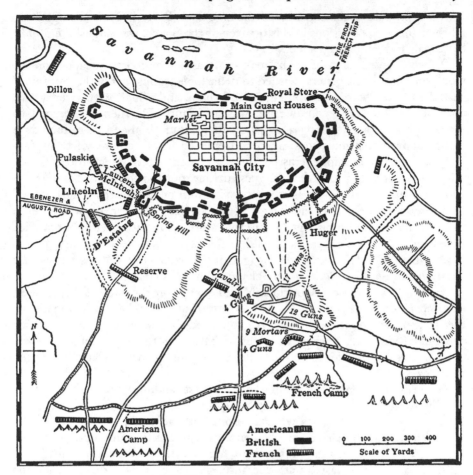

Map labels: Savannah River · Dillon · Royal Store · Main Guard Houses · Market · Savannah City · FIRE FROM FRENCH SHIP · Pulaski · Laurens · McIntosh · Lincoln · EBENEZER & AUGUSTA ROAD · D'Estaing · Spring Hill · Reserve · Cavalry · 4 Guns · 17 Guns · 12 Guns · Huger · 9 Mortars · 4 Guns · French Camp · N · American Camp · American · British · French · Scale of Yards · 0 100 200 300 400

SIEGE OF SAVANNAH

Numerous ironical ballads commemorated the Franco-American rout at Savannah, and British and Tories rejoiced that another allied operation in which D'Estaing played a central role was a fiasco.

> *To Charleston with fear*
> *The rebels repair;*
> *D'Estaing scampers back to his boats, sir,*
> *Each blaming the other,*
> *Each cursing his brother,*
> *And—may they cut each other's throats, sir!*

1. BAD WEATHER DELAYS D'ESTAING'S LANDING OPERATIONS

Journal of an anonymous French naval officer with the fleet.

[September 8-18, 1779].

Wednesday, the eighth of September, we made the coast of Florida [should be Georgia]. That evening the fleet anchored within three leagues of the lighthouse at the entrance of the Savannah River in New Georgia. Of all their former possessions in this quarter of the South, the English held only Savannah and Saint Augustine. . . .

We took possession of such small craft as attempted to escape from us along the coast. The general wished to debark his troops that night, but found that the place where he proposed to land them, and which with twenty-five men he had himself reconnoitered, was an island. He then determined to place all his troops, forming a corps of about four thousand men, including eight hundred free mulattoes taken and enlisted in the colony of Saint Domingo, on board six ships entrusted to the command of M. de la Motte-Piquet, with instructions to proceed six leagues further south to the River Saint Mary, and there disembark. He was to carry with him nearly all the long-boats of the vessels left at the first anchorage. The Chevalier du Rumain was ordered to enter the river with his frigate, and two store ships armed with 18-pounder guns, and as many lighters as possible, and advance as near the city as was practicable. The frigates were engaged in guarding the various passes. *Le Sagittaire* and *le Fier Rodrigue* blockaded Port Royal.

Having made these dispositions M. d'Estaing, on the 11th of September, accompanied the six ships of M. de la Motte-Piquet, leaving the command of the fleet to the Count de Broves. He anchored that evening at the mouth of the Saint Mary and, during the night, debarked with fifteen hundred men, each soldier, in obedience to his orders, carrying provisions and water for three days.

The rowboats having accomplished this first landing were desirous of returning to the ships that they might bring the remainder of the troops. Some of the longboats and canoes which, despite the bad weather, obstinately determined to leave the river in obedience to the positive instructions of the general, who knew not the difficulties which confronted them, perished. . . .

The bad weather lasted until the 18th. It was impossible to continue the disembarkation. Not even a canoe could be sent ashore. Nearly all the vessels, moored on the open coast, were forced to set sail and go far out to sea to escape destruction.

For six days Count d'Estaing remained on shore, with fifteen hundred men having only their guns, some rounds of ammunition and three days rations, destitute of tents and baggage, exposed to a constant rain, and near enough to the enemy to apprehend an attack each instant. Fortunately the enemy was ignorant of the situation of our troops.

At last the weather permitted us to finish the debarkation; and Count d'Estaing, without losing a moment, advanced upon the enemy whom he found entrenched below the city of Savannah. With the few troops under his command he could not attack with hope of success. Many have thought he should, under the circumstances, have then re-embarked. It is certain, had he done so, he would have followed a wiser plan, for his entire fleet was lying exposed upon the coast. But this is judgment after event. M. d'Estaing could rely on the co-operation of the Americans. Major General Prevost seemed inclined to surrender. In a conference he announced that he would, to save his honor, make an apparent defense; but Colonel Meklen [Maitland], who with seven hundred men threw himself into the place by way of Saint Augustine Creek, changed all at once these pacific dispositions.

—JONES, ed., *Siege of Savannah*, pp. 58-60.

2. SAVANNAH'S CIVILIANS BEAR THE BRUNT OF THE BOMBARDMENT

Loyalist Chief Justice Anthony Stokes of Georgia to his wife.

November 9, 1779

The French and Americans had invested the town, and the French had intrenched themselves up to the chin, about two hundred yards from our lines, some time before their artillery and ammunition came up from their ships; and as a slight cannonade had passed over, many began to flatter themselves that the enemy would go away without any further effects. But in this they found themselves much mistaken; for at midnight of the third of October, when all the woman and children were asleep, the French opened a battery of nine mortars and kept up a very heavy bombardment for an hour and a half, in which time those who counted the shells found that they fired one hundred, which were chiefly directed to the town.

I heard one of the shells whistle over my quarters, and presently afterwards I got up and dressed myself; and as our neighborhood seemed to be in the line of fire, I went out with a view to go to the eastward, out of the way; but a shell that seemed to be falling near me, rather puzzled me how to keep clear of it, and I returned to the house not a little alarmed. I then proceeded to the westward, and then the shells seemed to fall all around. There I soon joined a number of gentlemen who had left their houses on account of the bombardment and, like me, were retiring from the line of fire to Yammacraw. Here we stayed till between one and two in the morning, when the bombardment ceased. Fortunately for us, there was no cannonade at the same time, and in the night shells are so discernible that they are more easily avoided than in the day.

Being indisposed, I had not slept a wink from my going to bed at nine till the bombardment began at twelve; and before I returned again, it was near three in the morning, when from fatigue I soon fell asleep; but at five I was awakened with a very heavy cannonade from a French frigate to the north of the town, and with a bombardment which soon hurried me out of bed; and before I could get my clothes on, an eighteen-pounder entered the house, stuck in the middle partition, and drove the plastering all about. We who were in the house now found ourselves in a cross fire; and notwithstanding the rum in the cellar, we thought it less dangerous to descend there than to continue in the house, as the fall of a shell into the cellar was not so probable as the being killed in the house with a cannon ball; for the cellar being under ground, a shot in its usual direction would not reach us.

The cellar was so full of rum and provisions that Mrs. Cooper, the Negroes and myself could hardly creep in; and after we had descended into it, some shot struck the house, and one passed through the kitchen, from which the Negroes had then lately come down; and had they not luckily moved away, it is probable that several of them would have been killed. Whilst we were in the cellar, two shells burst not far from the door, and many others fell in the neighborhood all around us. In this situation a number of us continued in a damp cellar, until the cannonade and bombardment almost ceased, for the French to cool their artillery; and then we ascended to breakfast.

As the cannonade and bombardment were chiefly directed to the town, no mischief was done in the lines that I heard of; but a Mr. Pollard, deputy barrack-master, was killed by a shell in that house on the bay which was formerly inhabited by Mr. Moss; and the daughter of one Thomson was almost shot in two by a cannon ball, at the house next to where Mr. Elliott lived. I am told there were other lives lost, but I have not heard the particulars.

Fortunately for us, after breakfast the town adjutant's wife and myself went over to Captain Knowles, who is agent for the transports, and to whose cellar Mr. Prevost, the general's lady and several gentlemen and ladies had retired for security. This house was directly opposite to my quarters, and about thirty or forty feet distant. The general's lady and Captain Knowles invited us to stay there, which invitation we accepted, and we continued in the cellar, with several others, as agreeably as the situation of matters would admit of, until three o'clock on Tuesday morning.

During the whole of this time the French kept up a brisk cannonade and bombardment, the shot frequently struck near us, and the shells fell on each side of us with so much violence that in their fall they shook the ground, and many of them burst with a great explosion. On Monday night we heard a shot strike my quarters, and in the morning we found an eighteen-pounder had entered the house and fallen near the head of my Negro, Dick, who providentially received no hurt.

The guns seemed to approach on each side, and about three o'clock on Wednesday morning a shell whistled close by Captain Knowles' house. Soon afterwards another came nearer and seemed to strike my quarters, and I thought I heard the cry of people in distress. We all jumped up, and before I could dress myself, my quarters were so much in flames that I could not venture further than the door, for fear of an explosion from the rum. George and Jemmy were over with me in Captain Knowles' cellar; the others were at my quarters. George ran over before me, and fortunately for me drew out of the flames the two black trunks with some of my apparel, etc., that I brought out with me, and then removed them over to Captain Knowles' passage, which was all the property I saved, except a little black trunk that was put into one of the large ones by accident; for I momently expected that the explosion of the rum would blow up the house and kill every one near it; and as soon as the French observed the flames, they kept up a very heavy cannonade and bombardment and pointed their fire to that object to prevent any person approaching to extinguish the flames.

I retired to Captain Knowles', where, in vain, I called out for some Negroes to help me to save my two trunks, for I expected that Captain Knowles' house, and the commodore's next to it, would be destroyed. No Negro came to my assistance, and I was informed that mine, who slept at the quarters, being frightened at the shell, had ran away; but unfortunately that information was not true. Being in the direction of the French fire, I was every moment in danger of being smashed to pieces with a shell, or shot in two with a cannon ball; and as each of the trunks were too large for me to carry off, I thought it safer to abandon them and retire to a place of safety than to run the risk of losing my life as well as my property.

I had some distance to go before I got out of the line of fire, and I did not know the way under Savannah Bluff, where I should have been safe from cannon balls; and, therefore, whenever I came to the opening of a street, I watched the flashes of the mortars and guns, and pushed on until I came under cover of a house; and when I got to the common and heard the whistling of a shot or shell, I fell on my face. But the stopping under cover of a house was no security, for the shot went through many houses; and Thomson's daughter was killed at the side opposite to that where the shot entered. . . .

The appearance of the town afforded a melancholy prospect, for there was hardly a house which had not been shot through, and some of them were almost destroyed. Ambrose, Wright and Stute's, in which we lived, had upwards of fifty shot that went through each of them, as I am informed; and old Mr. Habersham's house, in which Major Prevost lived, was almost destroyed with shot and shells. In the streets and on the common there was a number of large holes made in the ground by the shells, so that it was not without some difficulty the chair got on; and in the church and Mr. Jones' house I observed that the shells came in at the roof and went through to the ground; and a number of other houses suffered by shells. The troops in the lines were much safer from the bombardment than the people in town. . . .

In short, the situation of Savannah was at one time deplorable. A small garrison in an extensive country was surrounded on the land by a powerful enemy, and its seacoast blocked up by one of the strongest fleets that ever visited America. There was not a single spot where the women and children could be put in safety; and the numerous desertions daily weakened that force which was at first inadequate to man such extensive lines; but the situation of the ground would not permit the able engineer to narrow them. However, with the assistance of God, British valor surmounted every difficulty.

—MOORE, *Diary of the American Revolution*, II, 224-228.

3. THE STORMING OF SAVANNAH: PULASKI IS KILLED

Account of Major Thomas Pinckney of the South Carolina militia.

On that day [October 8] we were ordered to parade near the left of the line at 1 o'clock of the next morning, where we were to be joined by the French, and to march to the attack in the following order: The French troops were to be divided into three columns, the American into two, the heads of which were to be posted in a line, with proper intervals at the edge of the wood adjoining the open space of five or six hundred yards between it and the enemy's line, and at 4 o'clock in the morning, a little before daylight, the whole was, on a signal being given, to rush forward and attack the redoubts and batteries opposed to their front. The American column of the right, which adjoined the French, were to be preceded by Pulaski, with his cavalry and the cavalry of South Carolina, and were to follow the French until they approach[ed] the edge of the wood, when they were to break off and take their position. . . .

A faint attack by the South Carolina militia and Georgians, under Brigadier General Huger, was ordered to be made on the enemy's left; but, instead of the French troops being paraded so as to march off at 4 o'clock, it was near four before the head of that column reached our front. The whole army then marched towards the skirt of the wood in one long column and, as they approached the open space, were to break off into the different columns, as ordered for the attack. But by the time the first French column had arrived at the open space, the day had fairly broke, when Count d'Estaing, without waiting until the other columns had arrived at their position, placed himself at the head of his first column and rushed forward to the attack. But this body was so severely galled by the grape-shot from the batteries as they advanced, and by both grape-shot and musketry when they reached the abbatis, that, in spite of the effort of the officers, the column got into confusion and broke away to their left toward the wood in that direction; the second and the third French columns shared successively the same fate, having the additional discouragement of seeing, as they marched to the attack, the repulse and loss of their comrades who had preceded them.

Count Pulaski, who, with the cavalry, preceded the right column of the Americans, proceeded gallantly until stopped by the abbatis, and before he could force through it, received his mortal wound. In the mean time, Colonel Laurens at the head of the light infantry, followed by the 2d South Carolina Regiment and 1st Battalion Charleston Militia, attacked the Spring Hill Redoubt, got into the ditch and planted the colours of the 2d Regiment on the berm, but the parapet was too high for them to scale it under so heavy a fire, and after much slaughter they were driven out of the ditch. When General Pulaski was about to be removed from the field, Colonel D. Horry, to whom the command of the cavalry devolved, asked what were his directions. He answered, "Follow my lancers to whom I have given my order of attack." But the lancers were so severely galled by the enemy's fire that they also inclined off to the left, and were followed by all the cavalry breaking through the American column, who were attacking the Spring Hill Redoubt.

By this time the 2d American column headed by Gen. M'Intosh, to which I was attached, arrived at the foot of the Spring Hill Redoubt, and such a scene of confusion as there appeared is not often equalled. Col. Laurens had been separated from that part of his command that had not entered the Spring Hill ditch by the cavalry, who had borne it before them into the swamp to the left, and when we marched up, inquired *if we had seen them.* Count d'Estaing was wounded in the arm, and endeavouring to rally his men, a few of whom with a drummer he had collected. General M'Intosh did not speak French, but desired me to inform the commander-in-chief that his column was fresh, and that he wished his directions, where, under present circumstances, he should make the attack. The Count ordered that we should move more to the left, and by no means to interfere with the troops he was endeavoring to rally; in pursuing this direction we were thrown too much to the left, and before we could reach Spring Hill Redoubt, we had to pass through Yamacraw Swamp, then wet and boggy, with the galley at the mouth annoying our left flank with grape-shot.

While struggling through this morass, the firing slacked, and it was reported that the whole army had retired. I was sent by General M'Intosh to look out from the Spring Hill, where I found not an assailant standing. On reporting this to the general, he ordered a retreat, which was effected without much loss, notwithstanding the heavy fire of grape-shot with which we were followed.

The loss of both armies in killed and wounded amounted to 637 French and 457 Americans, 1100. The Irish Brigade in the French service and our 2d Regiment particularly distinguished themselves and suffered most. The loss of the British amounted only to fifty-five.

Thus was this fine body of troops sacrificed by the imprudence of the French general, who, being of superior grade, commanded the whole. If the French troops had left their encampment in time for the different corps to have reached their positions, and the whole attacked together, the prospect of success would have been infinitely better, though even then it would have been very doubtful on account of the strength of the enemy's line, which was well supplied by artillery. But if Count d'Estaing had reflected a moment, he must have known that attacking with a single column, before the rest of the army could have reached their position, was exposing the army to be beaten in detail. In fact the enemy, who were to be assailed at once on a considerable part of their front, finding themselves only attacked at one point, very deliberately concentrated their whole fire on the assailing column, and that was repeated as fast as the different corps were brought up to the attack.

General Lincoln had the command of the reserve and covered the retreat; if he had led the attack, I think the event could not have been so disastrous, and I am warranted in this opinion by the attack he made on the enemy's lines at Stono, where, when he found how strongly the enemy were entrenched, although his light infantry, on both flanks, had gained some advantage, withdrew the troops without any considerable loss.

—HOUGH, *Siege of Savannah*, pp. 164-170.

V. THE FALL OF CHARLESTON

The next phase of the British effort to conquer the South revealed that the British had finally learned something from their previous and relatively ineffectual moves. If there was to be a conquest it could be achieved only by a move in force. Sir Henry Clinton, a cautious man at all times, felt that his move against Charleston was being made without sufficient superiority over the combined defenders. But the armada Clinton dispatched was indeed formidable. Having recalled to New York the 3,000 men stationed at Newport, he was able to spare 3,500 British, Hessian and Tory soldiers for the Charleston expedition. Along with crews numbering 5,000, this large force sailed on December 26, 1779, in a fleet of 90 transports under Admiral Arbuthnot's command.

Clinton's expedition almost came to grief on the high seas. The voyage was stormy, horses perished, stores were damaged, and the fleet dispersed. It was not until February 11, 1780, that the fleet finally entered Edisto Inlet and

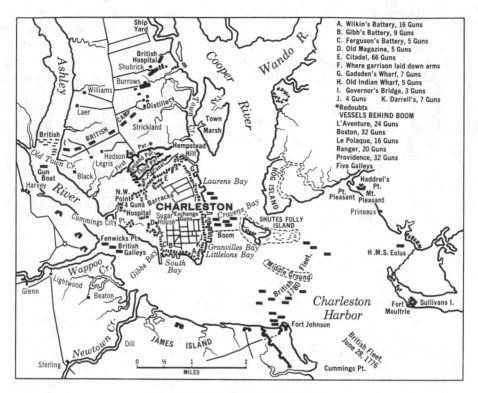

A. Wilkin's Battery, 16 Guns
B. Gibb's Battery, 9 Guns
C. Ferguson's Battery, 5 Guns
D. Old Magazine, 5 Guns
E. Citadel, 66 Guns
F. Where garrison laid down arms
G. Gadsden's Wharf, 7 Guns
H. Old Indian Wharf, 5 Guns
I. Governor's Bridge, 3 Guns
J. 4 Guns   K. Darrell's, 7 Guns
*Redoubts
VESSELS BEHIND BOOM
L'Aventure, 24 Guns
Boston, 32 Guns
Le Polaque, 16 Guns
Ranger, 20 Guns
Providence, 32 Guns
Five Galleys

SIEGE OF CHARLESTON

landed troops on Johns Island, thirty miles south of Charleston. That city's defenses had been allowed to fall into shocking disrepair. The forts on Sullivan's and James islands were no longer tenable and there was no artillery defense against an attacking fleet entering the harbor. The city was connected with the mainland by a narrow isthmus known as the Neck, partially fortified in 1779. Clinton's customary cautious advance gave the Americans time to work on the town's fortifications. The Neck was cut across by a canal, behind which breastworks and redoubts were raised, a redoubt was erected at the town's southern extremity, and a line of small forts hastily put up along the Cooper and Ashley sides.

Charleston was Long Island all over again except that the retreat of the besieged was cut off—an important difference. The disaster which befell the Patriot defenders must be placed at the door of their commander, General Lincoln. Although he stationed cavalry detachments at Monck's Corner near the head of the Cooper River, some thirty miles north of Charleston, to keep open his communication with the northern part of the state, he drew all other available troops into the town, and thus committed his army to a fatal trap. His forces numbering 3,600 were reinforced by 1,500 Virginia and North Carolina Continentals. But Clinton also called on his huge garrison in New York for more men, until he had built up his attacking force, excluding seamen, to 10,000.

In the cavalry sorties in the vicinity of Charleston Southerners came to know and fear a new luminary on the British military horizon, the twenty-five-year-old Lieutenant Colonel Banastre Tarleton, commandant of the green-uniformed British Legion, a Tory cavalry outfit. "Bloody" Tarleton was to become a synonym for ruthless warfare. His surprise attack upon General Huger's cavalry at Moncks' Corner tightened the escape corridor from Charleston. The arrival of reinforcements from New York enabled Clinton to send a force into the last open stretch of ground between the Cooper and the sea. The American army was bottled up.

Lieutenant Governor Christopher Gadsden and his Council pleaded with Lincoln not to abandon the town, yet the longer he stayed on, the more perilous became his position and the greater the danger to the town itself. Finally, the civilians could endure the siege no longer. The capitulation came on May 12 and was the largest single American loss of the war.

Under the British surrender terms, the Continental troops were to be prisoners of war, but the militia and armed civilians were allowed to go home on parole. With colors cased and drums beating a Turkish march—not a British one as Lincoln had requested—the Patriot defenders marched out and piled their arms beside the Citadel, a redoubt in the center of the lines.

For Charleston it was all over, but in the rest of the South the real war was just beginning.

1. THE PERILOUS VOYAGE OF THE BRITISH TRANSPORTS

Diary of Captain Johann Hinrichs of the Hessian Jäger Corps.

Jan. 3, [1780]. Today was no better than yesterday; in fact, it was worse. Left to the fury of wave and wind, we drifted southward with helm lashed and before one sail, the wind being westerly. Of the entire fleet we saw this morning only one man-of-war and seventeen sail. It may be safely said that the most strenuous campaign cannot be as trying as such a voyage; for (1) one cannot prepare a decent meal; (2) one takes every morsel with the greatest difficulty and discomfort; (3) one enjoys not a moment of sleep because of the fearful rolling and noise, which is worse in the cabin than in any other place in the ship. Nevertheless, so far we have all been well and in good spirits, although somewhat weakened.

Jan. 4. Last night was no better than the previous night, nor was the day any better— if anything, it was worse. It was so gloomy and dark that we lost sight of the fleet during the night. Hence, in spite of the abominable weather, we set four sails at eight o'clock in the morning. Toward noon we rejoined the fleet and then lay to again. The wind was NW. and we drifted SW. Of the entire fleet only forty-eight ships were together; but among the missing were the *Russell*, the *Renown* and the *Robust*, which presumably were with the greater part of the missing ships. The absence of the *Renown* allowed us to hope that the *Anna* transport, which was carrying Captain von Hanger's company of chasseurs and had lost her mainmast and mizzenmast in the first storm, was still afloat and the chasseurs alive, for she had been taken in tow by the *Renown* after the first storm.

Jan. 5. This morning we sailed for a few hours, but then the storm began to rage again so violently that toward noon it was necessary to lash the helm again and furl all sails except one. The entire day and night one could see and hear nothing but the flags and shots of ships in distress. However, no one could go to their assistance. At noon our ship, too, sprung a leak below the cabin, near the helm. But it was easily stopped since one could get to it without trouble. The wind was NW. and we stood SW....

Jan. 8. The wind was as violent as before, and from yesterday noon until noon today it was SW. The ship drifted WSW. In the afternoon we caught a shark. It weighed about two hundred pounds and measured nine feet and two and one-half inches from head to tail. I kept a piece of its skin, which is so sharp that it can be used as a fine saw in a mechanic's shop....

Jan 9. Up to midnight last night we had a SW. storm; about twelve o'clock in the night the wind was WSW., and around ten o'clock in the morning it was N. by W. The helm was unlashed, and we made nine miles W. by N. before two in the afternoon. At two o'clock the wind veered to the north and the storm abated. During the night there was a calm.

Jan. 10. At seven o'clock in the morning we again raised the top-yard and set all mainsails. We were fifty-five ships. Around ten o'clock there came a gentle breeze from S. by W., before which we stood W. by N. In a short time the sea had become so calm and looked so innocent that one could almost come to love this treacherous element. We were especially happy because not a single jäger had become ill, and flattered ourselves that we would be able to land within a few days; however, at two o'clock in the afternoon the wind veered to W.

Jan. 11. This morning we had a head wind (SW.), and every inch we moved we went farther from our destinaton. We plied from S. to N. and from N. to S. In the afternoon there was a little mutiny among the crew, who complained to the ship's master about their rations. But everything was adjusted....

Jan. 13. Everything the same! Still a westerly wind! We cruised up and down. Terrible weather! Snow, rain, hail, storm, foaming waves and bitter cold! Toward noon the *Judith* transport, carrying fascines and engineers, hoisted a flag of distress. She had sprung a leak and, furthermore, had lost all her yards. She approached the flagship and obtained assistance. Toward evening it cleared up, but the blue horizon was a foreboding of severe cold. During the night the wind veered somewhat to N., so that it was about NW. We stood WSW. and were hoping for the wind to shift still more to the north. With such hopes we slept fairly well, especially since the ship did not roll as much as usual, for snow and rain had beaten down the waves somewhat.

Jan 14. However, we had hoped in vain; the wind remained the same, backing even more to the westward in the morning. We cruised up and down. The weather was rather good, but there was no indication of any change of wind in spite of the fact that the moon entered the first quarter in the afternoon.

—UHLENDORF, ed., *Siege of Charleston,* pp. 117-125.

2. THE BRITISH AND HESSIANS LAND IN THE REAR OF THE DEFENDERS

Diary of Captain Johann Hinrichs.

Feb. 11. Because of our extremely long voyage and because of severe storms and the scattering of many of our ships, the enemy no longer seriously thought that we would still land in South Carolina. They were, furthermore, confused by our stay at Tybee, by certain orders given publicly at headquarters for the purpose of deceiving them, and by the movements of the regiments under the command of General Paterson, who had already actually advanced toward Purysburg. The enemy were looking for development near Beaufort, their troops having advanced as far as Ponpon. Thus we were able to land unmolested on Johns Island in the enemy's rear.

Feb 11 [*1780*]. This afternoon the light infantry, the British grenadiers and two companies of Hessian grenadiers began the disembarkation. Rain and darkness prevented us from following. . . .

The landing place was Simmons Point on Simmons Island, unmarked by name on any map. It is a part of Johns Island, desolate and salty, and full of cabbage trees. The landing was effected under the direction of Captain Elphinstone of the *Perseus,* who had demolished a battery here two years ago and had roamed all over Johns Island. The Commanding General and Lord Cornwallis were at the head of the light infantry. They advanced as far as Simmons' house and bridge, the generals remaining with the men as they marched through the woods in swamp and rain.

Feb. 12. While we and the rest of the troops were landing, the light infantry advanced as far as Wilson's house and the British grenadiers to within three miles of Simmons' house. The latter was used as headquarters, and the two Hessian grenadier companies remained there. Our landing was effected in good enough time, although we had to go two miles in boats; but the march to headquarters was the more arduous. A column making its way through a wilderness of deep sand, marshland, and impenetrable woods where human feet had never trod! Even Elphinstone, our guide, led us two miles out of our way. Sometimes we had to struggle, singly or two abreast, through marsh and woodland for half a mile. What a land to wage war in! Toward afternoon we arrived at headquarters, advanced another one and one-half miles and made camp on the left of the road, close to the Bohicket River. At our right was the 33rd Regiment, and next to it were the Hessian grenadiers.

We were encamped twenty-two miles from James Chapel, one and one-half miles from Simmons' bridge and twenty-five miles from Charleston.

—UHLENDORF, ed., *Siege of Charleston,* pp. 179-183.

3. THE DESPERATE POSITION OF THE DEFENDERS

Lieutenant-Colonel John Laurens of the Continental Army to George Washington.

Charleston, March 14, 1780

The enemy's present disposition of his force, and all his late operations, indicate a design to attack Charleston by a siege in form. To complete the investiture, he must introduce his ships of war into the harbour. That it is his intention appears from his fixing buoys on the bar, barricading his ships' waists, and anchoring them in a station where they may embrace the first favorable spring tides to enter. His transports and store-ships have removed from Edisto up Stono River, where they lie contiguous to Wappoo Cut, which is the water communication from thence to Ashley River. At a point of the mainland, formed by the issuing of the former in the latter, he raised, in the course of a night, the 11th instant, a battery of six embrasures. This situation, naturally advantageous, he will probably render very strong and establish in it his deposit of military stores and provisions. He then may either force a passage over Ashley River or turn it by a circuitous march, fortify a camp on the Neck and open his trenches. The best communication between his magazines and camp will be across Ashley River, from a bluff marked Bull in your large map.

Your Excellency will have learnt that the Commodore and all his officers renounce the idea of defending the passage of the bar; they declare it impracticable for the frigates to lie in a proper position for that purpose. The government has neglected to provide floating batteries, which might have been stationed there; so that it has been agreed, as the next best plan, to form a line of battle in such a manner as to make a cross-fire with Fort Moultrie, a shoal called the Middle Grounds being on the right of the ships, and the fort advanced on the left. As it would be the enemy's policy, with a leading wind and tide, to pass the fire of the fort and run aboard of our ships, the Commodore is contriving an obstruction which he thinks will check their progress and allow time for the full effect of our fire.

The impracticability of defending the bar, in the first instance, appears to me a great diminution of our means of defence. We must not only have a greater number of shipping below, and consequently withdraw them from flanking the enemy's approaches on the Neck, but are subject to the chances of a combat, which, in the other case, were out of the question. The Commodore has destroyed one set of the enemy's buoys, and I hope he will cut away such as may have been since put down, and order the galleys to give all possible annoyance to the enemy's ships in the act of entering.

The attention of the engineers has been distracted by different demonstrations on the part of the enemy, and they have not perfected the line across Charleston Neck. Henceforward I hope they will confine themselves solely to completing it, and then proceed to the construction of some interior inclosed works, to prolong the defence.

As the enemy is determined to proceed by regular approaches, all his operations are submitted to calculation, and he can determine with mathematical precision that with such and such means, in a given time, he will accomplish his end. Our safety, then, must depend upon the seasonable arrival of such re-enforcements as will oblige him to raise the siege. The Virginia line is much more remote than we could have thought it would have been at this moment. Your Excellency, in person, might rescue us all. Virginia and North Carolina would follow you. The glory of foiling the enemy in his last great effort and terminating the war ought to be reserved for you. Whatever fortune attends us, I shall, to my latest moments, feel that veneration and attachment which I always had for your Excellency.

—SPARKS, *Correspondence of the American Revolution*, II, 413-415.

4. A COUP AT MONCK'S CORNER NARROWS THE ESCAPE OUTLET

Lieutenant-Colonel Banastre Tarleton's account.

The Americans had joined a body of militia to three regiments of Continental cavalry, and the command of the whole was intrusted to Brigadier-General Huger. This corps hold possession of the forks and passes of Cooper River, and maintained a communication with Charles Town, by which supplies of men, arms, ammunition and provision might be conveyed to the garrison during the siege, and by which the Continental troops might escape after the defences were destroyed. Sir Henry Clinton was thoroughly sensible of the inconveniencies that might arise from this situation of the enemy's light troops; and being lately relieved by a detachment of sailors and mariners from the charge of Fort Johnson, he directed his attention to disloge them from their position. As soon as he received intelligence of the arrival of a number of waggons, loaded with arms, ammunition and clothing, from the northward, he selected a detachment of one thousand four hundred men, whom he committed to Lieutenant-Colonel Webster, with orders to counteract the designs of the Americans, and to break in upon the remaining communications of Charles Town.

On the 12th of April, Lieutenant-Colonel Tarleton, being reinforced at the quarter house by Major Ferguson's corps of marksmen, advanced to Goose Creek. Colonel Webster arrived on the following day at the same place, with the 33d and 64th Regiments of infantry. Tarleton again moved on in the evening, with his own and Ferguson's corps, toward Monk's Corner ... in order, if possible, to surprise the Americans encamped at that place.

An attack in the night was judged most advisable, as it would render the superiority of the enemy's cavalry useless, and would, perhaps, present a favourable opportunity of getting possession of Biggin Bridge, on Cooper River, without much loss to the assailants. Profound silence was observed on the march. At some distance from Goose Creek, a Negro was secured by the advanced guard, who discovered him attempting to leave the road. A letter was taken from his pocket, written by an officer in General Huger's camp the afternoon of that day, and which he was charged to convey to the neighbourhood of Charles Town. The contents of the letter, which was opened at a house not far distant, and the Negro's intelligence, purchased for a few dollars, proved lucky incidents at this period.

Lieutenant-Colonel Tarleton's information relative to the situation of the enemy was now complete. It was evident that the American cavalry had posted themselves in front of the Cooper River, and that the militia were placed in a meeting house which commanded the bridge, and were distributed on the opposite bank. At three o'clock in the morning, the advanced guard of dragoons and mounted infantry, supported by the remainder of the legion and Ferguson's corps, approached the American post. A watch word was

immediately communicated to the officers and soldiers, which was closely followed by an order to charge the enemy's grand guard on the main road, there
being no other avenue open, owing to the swamps upon the flanks, and to
pursue them into their camp.

The order was executed with the greatest promptitude and success. The
Americans were completely surprised. Major Vernier, of Pulaski's legion,
and some other officers and men who attempted to defend themselves were
killed or wounded. General Huger, Colonels Washington and Jamieson, with
many officers and men, fled on foot to the swamps close to their encampment,
where, being concealed by the darkness, they effected their escape. Four hundred horses belonging to officers and dragoons, with their arms and appointments (a valuable acquisition for the British cavalry in their present state),
fell into the hands of the victors; about one hundred officers, dragoons and
hussars, together with fifty wagons loaded with arms, clothing and ammunition, shared the same fate.

Without loss of time, Major Cochrane was ordered to force the bridge and
the meeting house with the infantry of the British legion. He charged the
militia with fixed bayonets, got possession of the pass and dispersed every
thing that opposed him.

In the attack at Monk's Corner, and at Biggin Bridge, the British had one
officer and two men wounded, with five horses killed and wounded. This signal instance of military advantage may be partly attributed to the judgement
and address with which this expedition was planned and executed, and partly
to the injudicious conduct of the American commander, who, besides making
a false disposition of his corps by placing his cavalry in front of the bridge
during the night and his infantry in the rear, neglected sending patroles in
front of his videttes; which omission equally enabled the British to make a
surprise and prevented the Americans recovering from the confusion attending an unexpected attack.

When the news of this success reached Colonel Webster, he commenced
his march for Biggin Bridge with the two British regiments under his command, as there were other difficulties to be surmounted before the general's
plan was fully accomplished. On his arrival at Monk's Corner, he detached
Lieutenant-Colonel Tarleton to seize the boats and take possession of Bon-
neau's Ferry—a necessary, but easy operation, whilst the country felt the influence of the late unexpected defeat. This passage over another branch of
Cooper River was secured, and by the subsequent movement of the King's
troops into the district of St. Thomas, Charles Town became completely invested.

—TARLETON, *History of Campaigns in the Southern Provinces*, pp. 15-18.

5. A SCOTTISH OFFICER DESCRIBES THE BOMBARDMENT OF CHARLESTON

Journal of Lieutenant John Peebles of the Royal Highland Regiment.

Thursday, 13th April, 1780. After 12 days work in compleating the first
paralel which stands opposed the enemy line from six to eight hundred yards

distance and which consists of six works numbered from the right and a battery in front of No. 5 and a line of approach advanced from thence. The three batteries opened this morning between 8 and 9 o'clock with above 20 pieces of cannon (mostly 24-pounders), 2 howitzers, a mortar and some cohorns, and kept up a tolerable fire during the day, which brought a warm return from the enemy. We set the town on fire at 3 different times, 2 places with shells carcases or red hot shot, but they soon put it out again, and the General gave orders himself to the artillery officers not to set the town on fire again. This day's firing has dismounted several of the enemy's guns and toward evening they were almost silent. An artillery man lost an arm and an assistant killed by one of our own guns hanging fire and going off when they put in the spunge. A man of the 37th Light Infantry had his backside shot away looking for balls. The working party last night advanced the aproach and made a traverse on it, but the moonlight increasing makes the nights very short for working.

Found five deserters came in last night who say Mr. Lincoln is determined to defend the place to the last. . . .

Sunday, 16th April, fair weather and warm. Went to the trenches last night, and was sent to occupy the intrenchment at the head of the sap with 130 men. A working party came there of 200 and lengthened the trench a good way to the left and carried out the sap about 20 yards in front ending with a traverse. They left off about 3 o'clock in the morning and went home. Soon after 50 Yagers came there who were posted along the banquet before day, ready to take a shot when they could see, and we stood to our arms till near sunrise—firing from both sides in the course of the night as usual. The rebels throw their shells better than we do, but did no harm. The night very light being almost full moon. When it was fair daylight the Yagers began to fire at any body they could see about the enemy's works, which are above 300 yards distant yet. They returned the fire from some marksmen in a trench without their line of works, but to very little purpose on both sides. The Yagers think they killed one, and the rebels killed one of our party, a light infantry man of the 16th shot in the eye.

Our batterys kept up a superior fire all day, the rebels having but a few guns on their left that fire, and only two or three little mortars on their right. The Yagers went off in the evening and I was releived 'tween 8 and 9. A rebel galley came in the afternoon near the hospital and fired a good many shot, one of which went thro' the house, but a small gun was brought down and drove her off. . . .

Monday, 17th April, warm weather and little wind about N.E. A good deal of firing last night, 4 or 5 wounded. The working party carried out another sap in front of No. 2 about as far advanced as that to the left. The fire from the batteries kept up as usual. We sent a dead 13-inch shell into the town yesterday to let them see what we have, but the beds of the 2 large mortars are both insufficient.

I hear the navy have made a battery at the mouth of Wapoo from whence they fire into the town when the fancy strikes them.

Some frigates and armed sloops are ready to come up Cooper River when the wind serves; two flag staffs set up at the foot of the garden at Lord Cornwallis' quarters for signals for them.

Dined with Lordship today, who is always very civil to me.

—PEEBLES, *Journal*, pp. 1-4.

6. CHARLESTON IN ITS EXTREMITY

From General William Moultrie's journal.

Monday, [April] 24th, [1780]. A party composed of three hundred men, Virginians and South-Carolinians, under the command of Lieutenant Colonel Henderson, made a sortie upon the enemy's approaches opposite the advance redoubts at day light. They were completely surprised, and lost about fifteen or twenty men killed with the bayonet, besides twelve persons brought off, seven of whom were wounded. Captain Moultrie killed and two men wounded on our side. The enemy attempted to support their guards from the trenches, but on receiving rounds of grape, made their retreat. The prisoners report their party to have beeen commanded by Major Hall of the 71st Regiment, but no officers were to be found. Colonel Parker killed about eight o'clock, looking over the parapet; two privates killed and seven wounded. The greatest part of the 1st South-Carolina Regiment came into garrison this morning, with Colonel C. Pinckney from Fort Moultrie.

Tuesday, 25th. Between twelve and one this morning, a heavy fire of cannon and musketry commenced from our advanced redoubt and the right of the lines, occasioned, as it was said, by the enemy's advancing in column. It is certain they gave several huzzas, but whether they were out of their trenches it is not clear. They kept up a very heavy and incessant fire with musketry for thirty minutes. The enemy threw several light balls into town. Two o'clock P. M. Lord Cornwallis at Mount-Pleasant.

Wednesday, 26th. The *Lord George Germaine* and a sloop joined the enemy's fleet. The enemy were very quiet all day and last night. We suppose they are bringing cannon into their third parallel. They are strengthening their approaches. Lord Cornwallis took possession of Mount-Pleasant yesterday. Brigadier General du Portail arrived from Philadelphia. The garrison ordered to be served with the usual quantity of provision, a plentiful supply having been received. One killed, Captain Goodwin of the Third South-Carolina Battalion, and one private wounded.

On General du Portail declaring that the works were not tenable, a council was again called upon for an evacuation, and to withdraw privately with the Continental troops. When the citizens were informed upon what the council were deliberating, some of them came into council and expressed themselves very warmly, and declared to General Lincoln that if he attempted to withdraw the troops and leave the citizens, they would cut up his boats and open the gates to the enemy. This put a stop to all thoughts of an evacuation of the troops, and nothing was left for us but to make the best terms we could.

—MOULTRIE, *Memoirs*, II, 78-80.

7. THE LAST AMERICAN SORTIE IS REPULSED

Diary of Captain Johann Hinrichs.

[*April 24, 1780*]. I was ordered by Major General Leslie at three o'clock this morning to take thirty men and occupy the left of the advanced work, while Lieutenant von Winzingeroda with thirty jägers was to proceed to the right. When I arrived at the part thrown up last night, I had my jägers halt, while I myself and two men inspected the work, for I was aware of our light way of building and knew that we were right under the enemy's outer works. There was not a single traverse in a trench four hundred paces long. I went as far as the enemy's gatework. But as day was breaking, the enemy sent two enfilading shots from their left front redoubt into our trench, one of them enfilading *en flanc* down the entire trench as far as the sap, while the other, *en revers*, struck the back of the parapet a hundred paces this side of the gatework.

I had my two jägers halt at the end of the trench to watch the gatework while I ran back to the British grenadiers in the second parallel. I brought one noncommissioned officer and twelve men (of the grenadier company of the 42nd Regiment) and had a traverse made approximately in the center of the trench. General Leslie came and was surprised that no infantry was here yet. He thanked me for my labors. In the meantime I had my jägers fetch sandbags and lay them on the parapet. While in the trench, which was barely six feet deep where I stood, I heard a loud yelling in the center, *i.e.* in the space that was still between the right and the left section of the third parallel. At the same moment the double post I had left standing above fired, and the workmen on the other side of the traverse came running over crying, "D— me, the rebels are there!"

I jumped on the parapet and when I saw the enemy, who were already pressing upon our right wing from a barrier situated at their left-wing front redoubt and were also rushing out of the gatework, I had my workmen seize their muskets, withdrew the two jägers this side of the traverse, and opened a continuous fire along the unoccupied part of the parallel as far as the gatework. The enemy, having penetrated our right wing, were already more than fifty paces behind us, partly between the third and second parallels. I ordered some jägers and Corporal Rübenkönig behind the traverse and had them fire behind the trench across the plain. Now our second parallel began to fire. This made many bullets fall in our rear. But when the second parallel pressed forward on our right wing, the enemy withdrew, leaving twenty muskets behind. But they covered their retreat with so excessive a shower of canisters which were loaded with old burst shells, broken shovels, pickaxes, hatchets, flat-irons, pistol barrels, broken locks, etc., etc. (these pieces we found in our trench), and so enfiladed us at the same time from the front redoubt of their left wing (fifteen balls were embedded in the traverse I had thrown up) that one could hardly hear another close beside him.

It was still dark, and the smoke of the powder was so thick that one could not tell friend from enemy. Since I could not know that the enemy had withdrawn, I jumped on the parapet and had my jägers and grenadiers keep up such a hot fire along the trench and upon their embrasures that after half an hour's cannonade the enemy's batteries were silent. A deserter told us in the evening that Colonel Parker and several artillerymen were killed in an embrasure. I suffered no loss except one Englishman slightly wounded with a bayonet. The entire parapet where I stood with my men was razed more than one foot by the enemy's battery. What luck!

Our right wing, where Lieutenant von Winzingeroda was stationed with thirty jägers and twenty-five light infantry, did not get off so well. One light-infantryman was killed, five wounded; two jägers had bayonet wounds and three, one of whom had a bullet wound in the abdomen, were taken prisoners. They were compelled to repair to the second parallel because through the negligence of the English the enemy was upon them too quickly, and without support they could not make a stand with discharged rifles against bayonets.

From Captain Lawson of the artillery I had borrowed two pieces resembling cohorns, taken on the *Delaware* frigate, which he had changed into swivels. They were made of brass and had a chamber. They served me splendidly today, for my jägers had no more cartridges. (At ten o'clock fifteen fresh men and two companies of light infantry came to support me.) These Lawsons, as I shall call them, threw a hand grenade 1,800 feet. I also fired 100-bullet canisters, 3-pound case shot, and one-half-pound bogy shot, firing in the course of the day 130 shots. The enemy tried to silence me with cannon, a sign that our fire was effective. However, I moved from one place to another with my pieces and sometimes fired three to four 100-bullet canisters into the enemy's embrasures. During the night this part of the parallel, which was pretty well shot to pieces, was repaired again and provided with several traverses. Likewise, a new sap was begun on the left wing of the left section of the third parallel.

The signal that the enemy was making a sortie along the whole line was a threefold "Hurray!" on our side—a fatal signal, indeed! About twenty to thirty of the enemy were seen at the gatework. Our nearest infantry post on guard gave the signal and fired. Everyone repeated the signal; the workmen ran back; the second parallel saw them coming, heard the "Hurray!" believed they were enemies, and fired. Within a short time there was a tremendous fire of musketry, cannon and shell on both sides. It was two o'clock in the morning before everyone realized that it was a mistake. We had an officer killed (71st) and more than fifty [men] killed and wounded. Besides, our working parties could accomplish little or nothing during the night.

—UHLENDORF, ed., *Siege of Charleston*, pp. 259-265.

8. "OUR LAST GREAT EFFORT—IT AVAILED US NOTHING"

Memoirs of General William Moultrie.

"May 9th, 1780

"Sir,

"No other motives but those of forbearance and compassion induced us to renew offers of terms you certainly had no claim to. The alterations you propose are all utterly inadmissable; hostilities will in consequence commence afresh at eight o'clock.

"H. Clinton, M. Arbuthnot

"Maj. Gen. Lincoln"

After receiving the above letter, we remained near an hour silent, all calm and ready, each waiting for the other to begin. At length we fired the first gun and immediately followed a tremendous cannonade, and the mortars from both sides threw out an immense number of shells. It was a glorious sight to see them like meteors crossing each other and bursting in the air; it appeared as if the stars were tumbling down. The fire was incessant almost the whole night; cannon-balls whizzing and shells hissing continually amongst us; ammunition chests and temporary magazines blowing up; great guns bursting, and wounded men groaning along the lines. It was a dreadful night! It was our last great effort, but it availed us nothing. After this our military ardor was much abated. We began to cool, and we cooled gradually, and on the eleventh of May we capitulated, and in the morning of the twelfth we marched out and gave up the town.

"To Sir Henry Clinton.

"Charlestown, May 11th, 1780

"Sir,

"The same motives of humanity which inclined you to propose articles of capitulation to this garrison induced me to offer those I had the honor of sending you on the 8th inst. They then appeared to me such as I might proffer, and you receive, with honor to both parties. Your exceptions to them, as they principally concerned the militia and citizens, I then conceived were such as could not be concurred with; but a recent application from those people, wherein they express a willingness to comply with them, and a wish on my part to lessen as much as may be the distresses of war to individuals, lead me now to offer you my acceptance of them.

"I have the honor to be, etc.

"B. Lincoln."
—Moultrie, *Memoirs*, II, 96-97.

9. Powder Store Blows Up During the Capitulation

Memoirs of General William Moultrie.

About eleven o'clock A.M. on the twelfth of May, we marched out between 1500 and 1600 Continental troops (leaving five or six hundred sick and wounded in the hospitals) without the horn-work, on the left, and piled our arms. The officers marched the men back to the barracks, where a British guard was placed over them. The British then asked where our second division was? They were told these were all the Continentals we had, except the sick and wounded. They were astonished, and said we had made a gallant defence.

Captain Rochfort had marched in with a detachment of the artillery to receive the returns of our artillery stores. While we were in the horn-work together in conversation, he said, "Sir, you have made a gallant defence, but you had a great many rascals among you " (and mentioned names) "who came out every night and gave us information of what was passing in your garrison."

The militia marched out the same day and delivered up their arms at the same place; the Continental officers went into town to their quarters, where they remained a few days to collect their baggage and signed their paroles, then were sent over to Haddrell's Point. The militia remained in Charleston. The next day the militia were ordered to parade near Lynch's pasture and to bring all their arms with them, guns, swords, pistols, etc., and those that did not strictly comply were threatened with having the grenadiers turned in among them. This threat brought out the aged, the timid, the disaffected and the infirm, many of them who had never appeared during the whole siege, which swelled the number of militia prisoners to, at least, three times the number of men we ever had upon duty.

I saw the column march out and was surprised to see it so large; but many of them we had excused from age and infirmities; however, they would do to enrol on a conqueror's list. When the British received their arms, they put them in waggons and carried them to a store-house, where we had deposited our fixed ammunition (about 4,000 pounds) and although they were informed by some of our officers that the arms were loaded, and several of them went off before the explosion took place, yet in taking them out of the waggons they threw them so carelessly into the store that some at last set fire to the powder, which blew up the whole guard of fifty men and many others that were standing by; their carcasses, legs and arms were seen in the air and scattered over several parts of the town. One man was dashed with violence against the steeple of the new independent church, which was at a great distance from the explosion, and left the marks of his body there for several days. The houses in the town received a great shock, and the window sashes rattled as if they would tumble out of the frames. . . .

The British were very much alarmed at the explosion; all the troops were turned out under arms and formed: they could not tell what was the matter. Some of the British and Hessian officers supposed it was designed by us. I was abused and taken up by a Hessian officer (whose guard was at Broughton's battery). He was very angry and said to me, "You, General Moultrie, you rebels have done this on purpose, as they did at New-York"; and ordered his guard to take me a prisoner into a house near, and placed a sentry at the door, where a number of us were confined; but I soon got a note over a back way to General Leslie, acquainting him of my situation, upon which he immediately sent one of his aids to me with an apology, that my confinement was contrary to orders, and ordered the sentry from the doors.

After a little time the alarm subsided. They went back and stopped the progress of the fire.

—MOULTRIE, *Memoirs*, II, 108-111.

VI. THE MASSACRE AT THE WAXHAWS

After the fall of Charleston the British sought to extinguish the flame of insurrection throughout the state. Learning that a force of 300 men from Virginia under the command of Colonel Buford had reversed their course toward Charleston on news of the capitulation, had retired toward Hillsborough, and then had temporarily halted near the Waxhaw Creek, about nine miles from Lancaster Courthouse, Cornwallis detached a mixed force of dragoons, but mainly men from the Loyal Legion under Tarleton, to intercept them. When hot weather proved fatal to his horses, the indomitable Tarleton had others seized in their places and drew close to Buford. Then he sent forth an emissary, enjoining the Americans to surrender and magnifying the numbers of their pursuers. "If you are rash enough to reject the terms," Tarleton informed the Americans, "the blood be upon your head."

"I reject your proposals," Buford wrote, "and shall defend myself to the last extremity."

This literary exchange proved prophetic. Although only 300 yards separated the forces, Tarleton was astonished to hear the American officers shouting to their men to hold their fire until the dragoons were within ten paces. The Americans soon asked for quarter, and Buford hoisted the white flag. However, on the pretext that he was shot at during the negotiations, Tarleton allowed his dragoons to plunge their bayonets into men who had surrendered and to carry out a massacre which for sheer savagery was unmatched in the entire war. From this atrocity was born the American battle cry of "Tarleton's quarter!" As "Light-Horse Harry" Lee put it, "This bloody day only wanted the war dance and the roasting fire to have placed it first in the records of torture and death in the West."

South Carolina was now firmly in British hands. Clinton's work was done, and he returned to New York, leaving the rest of the Southern campaign in the hands of Lord Cornwallis.

1. TARLETON'S DRAGOONS GAVE "THE HORRID YELLS OF DEMONS"

Dr. Robert Brownsfield to William D. James.

. . . In a short time Tarleton's bugle was heard, and a furious attack was made on the rear guard, commanded by Lieut. Pearson. Not a man escaped. Poor Pearson was inhumanely mangled on the face as he lay on his back. His nose and lip were bisected obliquely; several of his teeth were broken out in the upper jaw, and the under completely divided on each side. These wounds were inflicted after he had fallen, with several others on his head, shoulders and arms. As a just tribute to the honour and Job-like patience of poor Pearson, it ought to be mentioned that he lay for five weeks without uttering a single groan. His only nourishment was milk, drawn from a bottle through a quill. During that period he was totally deprived of speech, nor could he articulate distinctly after his wounds were healed.

This attack gave Buford the first confirmation of Tarleton's declaration by his flag. Unfortunately he was then compelled to prepare for action, on ground which presented no impediment to the full action of cavalry. Tarleton, having arranged his infantry in the centre and his cavalry on the wings, advanced to the charge with the horrid yells of infuriated demons. They were received with firmness and completely checked, until the cavalry were gaining the rear.

Buford, now perceiving that further resistance was hopeless, ordered a flag to be hoisted and the arms to be grounded, expecting the usual treatment sanctioned by civilized warfare. This, however, made no part of Tarleton's creed. His ostensible pretext for the relentless barbarity that ensued was that his horse was killed under him just as the flag was raised. He affected to believe that this was done afterwards, and imputed it to treachery on the part of Buford; but, in reality, a safe opportunity was presented to gratify that thirst for blood which marked his character in every conjuncture that promised probable impunity to himself. Ensign Cruit, who advanced the flag, was instantly cut down.

Viewing this as an earnest of what they were to expect, a resumption of their arms was attempted, to sell their lives as dearly as possible; but before this was fully effected, Tarleton with his cruel myrmidons was in the midst of them, when commenced a scene of indiscriminate carnage never surpassed by the ruthless atrocities of the most barbarous savages.

The demand for quarters, seldom refused to a vanquished foe, was at once found to be in vain; not a man was spared, and it was the concurrent testimony of all the survivors that for fifteen minutes after every man was prostrate they went over the ground plunging their bayonets into every one that exhibited any signs of life, and in some instances, where several had fallen one over the other, these monsters were seen to throw off on the point of the bayonet the uppermost, to come at those beneath.

Capt. Carter, who commanded the artillery and who led the van, continued his march without bringing his guns into action; this conduct excited suspicions unfavourable to the character of Carter, and these were strengthened by his being paroled on the ground, and his whole company without insult or injury being made prisoners of war. Whether he was called to account for his conduct, I have never learnt. These excepted, the only survivors of this tragic scene were Capts. Stokes, Lawson and Hoard, Lieuts. Pearson and Jamison, and Ensign Cruit. . . .

Capt. John Stokes . . . received twenty-three wounds, and as he never for a moment lost his recollection, he often repeated to me the manner and order in which they were inflicted.

Early in the sanguinary conflict he was attacked by a dragoon, who aimed many deadly blows at his head, all of which by the dextrous use of the small sword he easily parried; when another on the right, by one stroke, cut off his right hand through the metacarpal bones. He was then assailed by both, and instinctively attempted to defend his head with his left arm until the forefinger was cut off, and the arm hacked in eight or ten places from the wrist to the shoulder. His head was then laid open almost the whole length of the crown to the eye brows. After he fell he received several cuts on the face and shoulders. A soldier, passing on in the work of death, asked if he expected quarters. Stokes answered, "I have not, nor do I mean to ask quarters. Finish me as soon as possible." He then transfixed him twice with his bayonet. Another asked the same question and received the same answer, and he also thrust his bayonet twice through his body.

Stokes had his eye fixed on a wounded British officer sitting at some distance, when a serjeant came up who addressed him with apparent humanity and offered him protection from further injury at the risk of his life.

"All I ask," said Stokes, "is to be laid by that officer that I may die in his presence."

While performing this generous office the humane serjeant was twice obliged to lay him down and stand over him to defend him against the fury of his comrades. Doctor Stapleton, Tarleton's surgeon, . . . was then dressing the wounds of the officer. Stokes, who lay bleeding in every pore, asked him to do something for his wounds, which he scornfully and inhumanely refused until peremptorily ordered by the more humane officer, and even then only filled the wounds with rough tow, the particles of which could not be separated from the brain for several days.

. . . Shortly after the adoption of the constitution of the United States, he [Stokes] was promoted to the bench in the Federal Court—married Miss Pearson—and settled on the Yadkin River, where the county is called Stokes, after his name.

—JAMES, *Marion*, Appendix, 1-7.

2. TARLETON ATTRIBUTES HIS VICTORY TO THE MISTAKES OF BUFORD
[written in 1787]

By pressing horses on the road, the light troops arrived the next day May 28, at Camden, when Lieutenant-Colonel Tarleton gained intelligence that Colonel Buford had quitted Rugely's mills on the 26th, and that he was marching with great diligence to join a corps then upon the road from Salisbury to Charlotte town in North Carolina.

This information strongly manifested that no time was to be lost, and that a vigorous effort was the only resource to prevent the junction of the two American corps. At two o'clock in the morning, the British troops being tolerably refreshed continued their pursuit. They reached Rugeley's by day light, where they learned that the Continentals were retreating above twenty miles in their front, towards the Catawba settlement, to meet their reinforcement. At this period, Tarleton might have contented himself with following them at his leisure to the boundary line of South Carolina, and from thence have returned upon his footsteps to join the main army, satisfied with pursuing the troops of Congress out of the province; but animated by the alacrity which he discovered both in the officers and men to undergo all hardships, he put his detachment in motion, after adopting a stratagem to delay the march of the enemy. Captain Kinlock, of the legion, was employed to carry a summons to the American commander, which, by magnifying the number of the British, might intimidate him into submission, or at least delay him whilst he deliberated on an answer. Colonel Buford, after detaining the flag for some time, without halting his march, returned a defiance. By this time many of the British cavalry and mounted infantry were totally worn out and dropped successively into the rear; the horses of the three-pounder were likewise unable to proceed. In this dilemma, Lieutenant-Colonel Tarleton found himself not far distant from the enemy, and, though not in a suitable condition for action, he determined as soon as possible to attack, there being no other expedient to stop their progress and prevent their being reinforced the next morning. The only circumstance favourable to the British light troops at this hour was the known inferiority of the Continental cavalry, who could not harass their retreat to Earl Cornwallis's army, in case they were repulsed by the infantry.

At three o'clock in the afternoon, on the confines of South Carolina, the advanced guard of the British charged a serjeant and four men of the American light dragoons and made them prisoners in the rear of their infantry. This event happening under the eyes of the two commanders, they respectively prepared their troops for action. Colonel Buford's force consisted of three hundred and eighty Continental infantry of the Virginia line, a detachment of Washington's cavalry, and two six-pounders. He chose his post in an open wood, to the right of the road. He formed his infantry in one line, with a small reserve. He placed his colours in the center, and he ordered his cannon, baggage and waggons to continue their march.

Lieutenant-Colonel Tarleton made his arrangement for the attack with all possible expedition. He confided his right wing, which was composed of sixty dragoons and nearly as many mounted infantry, to Major Cochrane, desiring him to dismount the latter to gall the enemy's flank, before he moved against their front with his cavalry. Captains Corbet and Kinlock were directed, with the 17th Dragoons and part of the legion, to charge the center of the Americans, whilst Lieutenant-Colonel Tarleton, with thirty chosen horse and some infantry, assaulted their right flank and reserve. This particular situation the commanding officer selected for himself, that he might discover the effect of the other attacks. The dragoons, the mounted infantry, and three-pounder in the rear, as they could come up with their tired horses, were ordered to form something like a reserve, opposite to the enemy's center, upon a small eminence that commanded the road; which disposition afforded the British light troops an object to rally to, in case of a repulse, and made no inconsiderable impression on the minds of their opponents.

The disposition being completed without any fire from the enemy, though within three hundred yards of their front, the cavalry advanced to the charge. On their arrival within fifty paces, the Continental infantry presented, when Tarleton was surprised to hear their officers command them to retain their fire till the British cavalry were nearer. This forbearance in not firing before the dragoons were within ten yards of the object of their attack, prevented their falling into confusion on the charge, and likewise deprived the Americans of the farther use of their ammunition. Some officers, men and horses suffered by this fire; but the battalion was totally broken, and slaughter was commenced before Lieutenant-Colonel Tarleton could remount another horse, the one with which he led his dragoons being overturned by the volley.

Thus in a few minutes ended an affair which might have had a very different termination. The British troops had two officers killed, one wounded; three privates killed, thirteen wounded; and thirty-one horses killed and wounded. The loss of officers and men was great on the part of the Americans, owing to the dragoons so effectually breaking the infantry, and to a report amongst the cavalry that they had lost their commanding officer, which stimulated the soldiers to a vindictive asperity not easily restrained. Upwards of one hundred officers and men were killed on the spot; three colours, two six-pounders and above two hundred prisoners, with a number of waggons containing two royals, quantities of new clothing, other military stores and camp equipage, fell into the possession of the victors.

The complete success of this attack may, in great measure, be ascribed to the mistakes committed by the American commander. If he had halted the waggons as soon as he found the British troops pressing his rear, and formed them into a kind of redoubt for the protection of his cannon and infantry against the assault of the cavalry, in all probability he either would not have been attacked or by such a disposition he might have foiled the attempt. The British troops, in both cases, would have been obliged to abandon the pursuit, as the country in the neighborhood could not immediately have supplied them with forage or provisions; and the Continentals might have decamped in the night, to join their reinforcement. Colonel Buford also committed a material error in ordering the infantry to retain their fire till the British dragoons were quite close; which, when given, had little effect either upon the minds or bodies of the assailants, in comparison with the execution that might be expected from a successive fire of platoons or divisions, commenced at the distance of three or four hundred paces.

—TARLETON, *History of Campaigns in the Southern Provinces*, pp. 29-33.

3. SOUTH CAROLINA RESOLVES TO FIGHT ON

President John Rutledge of South Carolina to Governor Abner Nash of North Carolina.

Camden, May 24, 1780

I could not obtain a copy of the Articles of Capitulation at Charles Town untill yesterday. Inclosed you will receive it. Last Saturday the enemy took post, with a considerable force, at Dupree's Ferry on Santee River, which they began to cross that day on their march to George Town, whither they had sent some vessels from Charles Town. They are certainly in possession of George Town, which was not defensible. Genl. Caswell, who lay a little below Lanier's Ferry with the North Carolina Brigade and the Virginia Continentals under Col. Buford, had luckily retreated this way before the enemy got to that ferry, and thereby prevented their cutting off his retreat, which was probably their first scheme.

Those troops are now under command of Brigadier Gen. Huger, about 15 miles below this place, and will be here to-day; his future motions will be directed by the camp and force of the enemy. Sorry I am to say, his force is altogether inadequate to any offensive operations. The enemy, according to advices received last night were, the evening before, at Black Mingo, but whether their intention was to take a circuit by way of the Hanging Rock Road in order to get in the rear of our troops, or to proceed for your state, is as yet uncertain. The next movement they make will demonstrate which of these points is their objects. Parties are gone to reconnoitre; however, I think it advisable not to wait their return, but to give you the foregoing intelligence and what follows as early as possible, especially as I have charged the bearer to collect what intelligence he can as he proceeds, and to communicate it to you

We have no certain account what the force above mentioned is, or by whom commanded, but it is said to be considerable, and under Lord Cornwallis. It is evident that the conquest of North as well as South Carolina is the enemy's plan. The time for which they endeavour to enlist men is untill those countries can be conquered, and a junction with them at Cross Creek will probably be attempted with the body above mentioned, who have with them a large Highland regiment. I have good reason to believe that they will send vessels (some perhaps with troops) to possess your rivers, and the towns on them, and it is probable that they will establish at Brunswick and Wilmington magazines of provisions. They may send hither great quantities of rice from the lower part of our State. They can hardly expect, I apprehend, to penetrate far into your back country unless they depend more than I hope they can with good grounds on the disaffection of your people, but I presume they will extend their camp along, and at some distance from the sea.

I hope, indeed, that their progress will be soon checked, tho' their numbers are really great; but surely Virginia will now be roused, and the forces of your State, in conjunction with the Virginians, and (supported, as I hope you will be, powerfully by Congress) will make the enemy repent of their audacity in attempting a conquest your way. Can't account for the backwardness of the troops ordered hither by Congress and Virginia, and for our want of intelligence respecting them. I still hope, however, that a combination of forces and better fortune than our late experience will soon oblige the enemy to head back their steps, and that, altho' there is no hope of regaining Charles Town except by treaty, the country will be preserved, and North Carolina, and even Georgia, be retained in the Union; for surely our brethren and allies will never give up the independence of either of those States or suffer such valuable territories to be lopped off.

I request the favour of you to forward the inclosed per express immediately to the governor of Virginia. Whether attempts will be made by the enemy on our back country (except by Tories and Indians) is still uncertain. If they send up a regular force, I am convinced they will be joined by numbers, and many will fall a sacrifice to the resentment of our domestic or internal enemies. But if regular troops are not sent up, I think our people will manage the disaffected and keep them from doing any considerable mischief. However, I expect no other service from the militia; they are so apprehensive of their families being killed (and their properties destroyed) by the Tories and Indians, who daily threaten hostilities while they are absent from their districts, that I believe it will be impracticable to keep any number worth mentioning on duty when the army are at any distance from their homes. If I can get them to embody in their own districts and keep the country quiet, it is really as much as I expect they will do at present and until troops arrive from the northward, but even this depends on the enemy's not sending up regular forces to take post in the back parts of the State; for if they do the disaffected will certainly flock to them, and those who are not disaffected will either abscond if they can or, which is more probable, be taken prisoners without arms, in which case they will expect to be treated as others are who have been taken under similar circumstances, in being dismissed on their parole, a piece of policy which the enemy have adopted with respect to our militia for obvious reasons.

This is a melancholy but a faithful representation of our affairs at this period. However, we must not despair. I still hope for great and speedy success from our brethren to animate and support our people and for a reverse of our late bad fortune, but immediate and the greatest exertions of the Northern States are indispensable to prevent the desolation and ruin of this State and Georgia, and the enemy's obtaining (what they flatter themselves with securing shortly) the three southernmost States, too valuable a prize ever to be given up by them.

—*North Carolina State Records*, XIV, 821-824.

VII. PATRIOTS WHIP TORIES AT RAMSOUR'S MILL

Although partisan bands were to render his interior position in South Carolina insecure, Cornwallis felt that his hold on the province was strong enough to justify pushing north into North Carolina, once the hot weather had abated. But a restless Tory in North Carolina jumped the gun. John Moore gathered some 1,300 Tories and encamped them near Ramsour's Mill, in Lincoln County, North Carolina. Colonel Locke and 400 of the North Carolina militia arrived at daybreak of June 20 to within a mile of the enemy. The Tory camp was thrown into disorder by the forward move of the Whig horsemen. Some Tories stood their ground, fired down the hill, and pursued the retreating horsemen, only to fall into a trap as the Whig infantry opened fire. A Patriot move on the Tories' right flank forced them to fall back toward the summit of the hill and over its brow. Hemmed in between two fires, they finally managed to withdraw in small parties. The Whig casualties were unusually heavy, 150 killed and wounded out of the 250 that saw action. The Tories had casualties of 150.

The remarkable fact about Ramsour's Mill is that the Whigs did not act as a unit. The officers made decisions as representatives of the men, and each officer, once the action started, was on his own. The battle proved a crushing loss of face for the Tories in that section of the state.

Account of General Joseph Graham of North Carolina, written in 1820.

The Tories were encamped on a hill three hundred yards east of Ramsour's Mill, and half a mile north of the present flourishing village of Lincolnton. The ridge stretched nearly to the east on the south side of the mill pond, and the road leading to the Tuckasege ford, by the mill, crosses the point of the ridge in a north-western direction. The Tories occupied an excellent position on a summit of the ridge; their right on the road fronting the south. The ridge has a very gentle slope, and was then interspersed with only a few trees, and the fire of the Tories had full rake in front for more than two hundred yards. The foot of the hill was bounded by a glade, the side of which was covered with bushes. The road passed the western end of the glade, at right angles; opposite the centre of the line and on the road a fence extended from the glade to a point opposite the right of the line. The picket guard, twelve in number, were stationed on the road, two hundred and fifty yards south of the glade, and six hundred yards from the encampment.

The companies of Captains Falls, M'Dowell and Brandon being mounted, the other [Whig] troops under Colonel Locke were arranged in the road, two deep, behind them and, without any other organization or orders, they were marched to battle. When the horsemen came within sight of the picket, they plainly perceived that their approach had not been anticipated. The picket fired and fled towards their camp. The horsemen pursued, and turning to the right out of the road, they rode up within thirty steps of the line and fired at the Tories, who, being in confusion, had not completely formed their line; but seeing only a few men assailing them, they quickly recovered from their panic and poured in a destructive fire, which obliged the horsemen to retreat. They retreated in disorder, passing through the infantry, who were advancing; several of the infantry joined them and never came into action. At a convenient distance the greater part of the horsemen rallied and, returning to the fight, exerted themselves with spirit during its continuance. The infantry hurried to keep near the horsemen in pursuit of the picket, and their movements being very irregular, their files were opened six or eight steps, and when the front approached the Tories, the rear was eighty poles back.

The Tories, seeing the effect of their fire, came down the hill a little distance and were in fair view. The infantry of the Whigs kept the road to the point between the glade and the corner of the fence, opposite the centre of the Tories. Here the action was renewed; the front fired several times before the rear came up. The Tories being on their left, they deployed to the right in front of the glade and came into action without order or system. In some places they were crowded together in each other's way; in other places there were none. As the rear came up, they occupied those places, and the line gradually extending, the action became general and obstinate on both sides. In a few minutes the Tories began to retire to their position on the top of the ridge, and soon fell back a little behind the ridge to shelter part of their bodies from the fire of the Whigs who were fairly exposed to their fire. In this situation their fire became very destructive, so that the Whigs fell back to the bushes near the glade, and the Tories, leaving their safe position, pursued them half way down the ridge.

At this moment Capt. Harden led a party of Whigs into the field, and, under cover of the fence, kept up a galling fire on the right flank of the Tories; and some of the Whigs, discovering that the ground on the right was more favorable to protect them from the fire of the Tories, obliqued in that direction towards the east end of the glade. This movement gave their line the proper extension. They continued to oblique until they turned the left flank of the Tories; and the contest being well maintained in the centre, the Tories began to retreat up the ridge. They found part of their position occupied by the Whigs. In that quarter the action became close, and the parties mixed together in two instances, and having no bayonets, they struck at each other with the butts of their guns. In this strange contest, several of the Tories were taken prisoners, and others, divesting themselves of their mark of distinction (which was a twig of green pine top stuck in their hats), intermixed with the Whigs, and all being in their common dress, they escaped unnoticed.

The Tories, finding the left of their position in possession of the Whigs, and their centre being closely pressed, retreated down the ridge toward the mill, exposed to the fire of the centre and of Captain Harden's company behind the fences. The Whigs pursued until they got entire possession of the ridge, when they perceived to their astonishment that the Tories had collected in force on the other side of the creek, beyond the mill. They expected the fight would be renewed and attempted to form a line; but only eighty-six men could be paraded. Some were scattered during the action, others were attending to their wounded friends, and, after repeated efforts, not more than one hundred and ten could be collected.

In this perilous situation of things it was resolved that Major Wilson and Captain William Alexander of Rowan should hasten to General Rutherford and urge him to press forward to their assistance. Rutherford had marched early in the morning and, at the distance of six or seven miles from Ramsour's, was met by Wilson and Alexander. Major Davie's cavalry was started at full gallop, and Colonel Davidson's infantry were ordered to hasten on with all possible speed. At the end of two miles they were met by others from the battle, who informed them that the Tories had retreated. The march was continued, and the troops arrived on the ground two hours after the battle had closed. The dead and most of the wounded were still lying where they fell.

As soon as the action began, those of the Tories who had no arms, and several who had, retreated across the creek. They were joined by others when they were first beaten back up the ridge, and by two hundred that were well-armed, who had arrived two days before from Lower Creek, in Burke County, under Captains Whiston and Murray. Col. Moore and Major Welch soon joined them, and those of the Tories who continued the fight to the last crossed the creek and joined them as soon as the Whigs got possession of the ridge. Believing that they were completely beaten, they formed a stratagem to secure their retreat. About the time that Wilson and Alexander were dispatched to General Rutherford, they sent in a flag under a pretence of proposing a suspension of hostilities, to make arrangements for taking care of the wounded and burying the dead. To prevent the flag-officer from perceiving their small number, Major James Rutherford and another officer were ordered to meet him a short distance from the line. The proposition being made, Maj. Rutherford demanded that the Tories should surrender as prisoners within ten minutes, and then the arrangements should be made that were requested.

In the meantime, Moore and Welsh gave orders that such of their men as were on foot, or had inferior horses, should move off singly as fast as they could; and when the flag returned, not more than fifty returned. They immediately fled. Moore with thirty men reached the British army at Camden, when he was threatened with a trial by a court-martial for disobedience of orders, in attempting to embody the royalists before the time appointed by the commander-in-chief. He was treated with disrespect by the British officers, and held in a state of disagreeable suspense; but it was at length deemed impolitic to order him before a court-martial.

As there was no organization of either party, nor regular returns made after the action, the loss could not be ascertained with correctness. Fifty-six lay dead on the side of the ridge where the heat of the action prevailed; many lay scattered on the flanks and over the ridge toward the mill. It is believed that seventy were killed, and that the loss on each side was equal. About an hundred men on each side were wounded, and fifty Tories were taken prisoners. The men had no uniform and it could not be told to which party many of the dead belonged. Most of the Whigs wore a piece of white paper on their hats in front, and many of the men on each side being excellent riflemen, this paper was a mark at which the Tories often fired, and several of the Whigs were shot in the head. The trees behind which both Whigs and Tories occasionally took shelter were grazed by the balls; and one tree in particular on the left of the Tory line, at the root of which two brothers lay dead, was grazed by three balls on one side and by two on the other.

In this battle neighbors, near relations and personal friends fought against each other, and as the smoke would from time to time blow off, they would recognize each other. In the evening, and on the next day, the relations and friends of the dead and wounded came in, and a scene was witnessed truly afflicting to the feelings of humanity.

After the action commenced, scarcely any orders were given by the officers. They fought like common soldiers and animated their men by their example, and they suffered severely. Captains Fall, Dobon, Smith, Bowman and Armstrong were killed, and Captains Houston and M'Kissick wounded. Of the Tories Captains Cumberland, Murray and Worlick were killed, and Captain Carpenter wounded. Few either of the officers or men had ever been in battle before.

—Murphey, *Papers*, II, 222-226.

VIII. PILLAGE AND CIVIL WAR FLAME IN SOUTH CAROLINA

The British and Tory invaders quickly earned an unenviable reputation for pillage, looting, and disrespect toward women. Patriot ladies whose husbands were prisoners of war or were away with the partisan bands showed remarkable courage in standing up to British and Tory looting parties. In fact, much smuggling of supplies from Charleston to the partisans in the interior was carried on by Patriot ladies.

The main forces on which the South Carolina Patriots counted to keep the British off balance were the partisans under such leaders as Thomas Sumter and Francis Marion. The former moved at the end of July 1780 against a detachment of British troops stationed at Rocky Mount, a high point on the western bank of the Catawba River, thirty miles from Camden. The log-house fortifications were defended by Tories commanded by Lieutenant Colonel Turnbull. Apprised by other Tories of the approach of Sumter, Turnbull was ready. Three times the Americans charged but, lacking artillery, they were unable to penetrate the defenses of felled trees.

About a week later Sumter joined with Major William Davie in an attack on an open camp of the enemy at Hanging Rock, about twelve miles from Rocky Mount. After stout resistance this encampment fell to the attackers, who then proceeded to plunder the stores and get drunk. Seeing the confusion among the victors, the enemy rallied, formed themselves into a square and held off the Patriots until reinforcements forced Sumter with his plunder-laden troops to quit the field. One of the most obstinately fought engagements of the war, Hanging Rock was a fight between Patriots and Tories—not a single British soldier participated. However, on August 18 Tarleton surprised Sumter's encampment at Fishing Creek, about two miles from its junction with the Catawba and forced the surviving defenders to precipitous flight and to abandon the booty gained in previous engagements.

1. The Redcoats Strip Patriot Women of Their Jewels

Letter from Eliza Wilkinson.

Yonge's Island

Well, now comes the day of terror—the 3d of June [1780]. (I shall never love the anniversary of that day.) In the morning, fifteen or sixteen horsemen rode up to the house. We were greatly terrified, thinking them the enemy, but from their behavior were agreeably deceived and found them friends. They sat a while on their horses, talking to us; and then rode off, except two, who tarried a minute or two longer and then followed the rest, who had nearly reached the gate. One of them said two must needs jump a ditch—to show his activity I suppose; for he might as well, and better, have gone in the road. However, he got a sad fall; we saw him, and sent a boy to tell him, if he was hurt, to come up to the house, and we would endeavor to do something for him. He and his companion accordingly came up; he looked very pale and bled much; his gun somehow in the fall had given him a bad wound behind the ear, from whence the blood flowed down his neck and bosom plentifully. We were greatly alarmed on seeing him in this situation, and had gathered around him, some with one thing, some with another, in order to give him assistance.

We were very busy examining the wound when a Negro girl ran in, exclaiming, "O! the King's people are coming! It must be them, for they are all in red!" Upon this cry, the two men that were with us snatched up their guns, mounted their horses and made off, but had not got many yards from the house before the enemy discharged a pistol at them. Terrified almost to death as I was, I was still anxious for my friends' safety. I tremblingly flew to the window, to see if the shot had proved fatal, when, seeing them both safe, "Thank heaven," said I, "they've got off without hurt!"

I'd hardly uttered this when I heard the horses of the inhuman Britons coming in such a furious manner that they seemed to tear up the earth, and the riders at the same time bellowing out the most horrid curses imaginable, oaths and imprecations, which chilled my whole frame. Surely, thought I, such horrid language denotes nothing less than death; but I'd no time for thought. They were up to the house—entered with drawn swords and pistols in their hands. Indeed, they rushed in, in the most furious manner, crying out, "Where're these women rebels?" (pretty language to ladies from the *once famed Britons!*). That was the first salutation!

The moment they espied us, off went our caps (I always heard say none but women pulled caps!). And for what, think you? Why, only to get a paltry stone and wax pin, which kept them on our heads; at the same time uttering the most abusive language imaginable, and making as if they'd hew us to pieces with their swords. But it's not in my power to describe the scene. It was terrible to the last degree; and, what augmented it, they had several armed Negroes with them, who threatened and abused us greatly. They then began to plunder the house of every thing they thought valuable or worth taking; our trunks were split to pieces, and each man, pitiful wretch, crammed his bosom with the contents, which were our apparel, etc., etc., etc.

I ventured to speak to the inhuman monster who had my clothes. I represented to him the times were such we could not replace what they'd taken from us, and begged him to spare me only a suit or two; but I got nothing but a hearty curse for my pains; nay, so far was his callous heart from relenting that, casting his eyes towards my shoes, "I want them buckles," said he, and immediately knelt at my feet to take them out, which, while he was busy about, a brother villain, whose enormous mouth extended from ear to ear, bawled out, "Shares there! I say, shares!" So they divided my buckles between them.

The other wretches were employed in the same manner; they took my sister's ear-rings from her ears; hers, and Miss Samuells's buckles. They demanded her ring from her finger. She pleaded for it, told them it was her wedding ring, and begged they'd let her keep it. But they still demanded it, and, presenting a pistol at her, swore if she did not deliver it immediately, they'd fire. She gave it to them, and, after bundling up all their booty, they mounted their horses. But such despicable figures! Each wretch's bosom stuffed so full they appeared to be all afflicted with some dropsical disorder. Had a party of rebels (as they called us) appeared, we should soon have seen their circumference lessen. . . .

—WILKINSON, *Letters*, pp. 27-30.

2. ROCKY MOUNT AND HANGING ROCK: "NO PRISONERS COULD BE TAKEN"

Recollections of Colonel William R. Davie.

Colonels Sumpter and Neal with a number of the South Carolina Refugees and Col. Irwin with 300 of the Mecklenburg Militia rendezvoused near Major Davie's camp about the last of July, and a council was immediately held by the officers to fix upon a proper object to strike at while this volunteer force was collected. Rocky-Mount and the Hanging-Rock presented themselves as not only the most important at the time but lying within their reach and strength; and it was finally agreed that Col. Sumpter should march with the Refugees and the North Carolinians under Col. Irwin to the attack of Rocky-Mount, while Major Davie made a diversion to engage the attention of the corps at the Hanging-Rock, and their detachments marched the same evening.

The defences of Rocky-Mount consisted of two log houses calculated for defense, and a loop-holed building, the whole secured by a strong abbatis. The situation was considerably elevated, and surrounded with cleared grounds. Col. Sumpter arrived before this place early the next day. Some small parties of rifle men were advanced under the cover of rocks and trees and kept up a fire under the houses. Several corps of this detachment marched repeatedly thro' the old field to the attack with great intrepidity, but were repulsed by the heavy fire of the garrison. Various stratagems were employed in vain to set the buildings on fire, and having no artillery they were obliged to give over the attempt of taking the place. . . . The retreat was effected without interception.

Major Davie's detachment consisted of 40 mounted rifle-men and about that number of dragoons, and considering himself obliged to alarm the enemy in their camp at all events the same day, he approached the Hanging Rock about 1 o'clock, and fortunately while he was reconoitering their position to fix upon the point of attack, he received information that three companies of their mounted infantry, returning from some excursion, had halted at a farmer's house, situated in full view of the camp. The house was placed in the point of a right angle made by a lane of staked and ridered fence, the one end of which opened to the enemy's encampment, the other terminated in the woods. The major advanced on that next to the woods, and as the rifle-men were not distinguishable from the Loyalists, they were sent round to the other end of the lane with orders, on gaining it, to rush forward and fire on the enemy. The dragoons were divided so that one half could occupy the lane while the other half entered the field. This disposition was made with such promptitude that the attention or suspicion of the enemy was never excited. The rifle company . . . passed the camp sentries without being challenged, dismounted in the lane and gave the enemy a well-directed fire.

The astonished Loyalists fled instantly the other way, and were immediately charged by the dragoons in full gallop and driven back in great confusion. On meeting again the fire of the infantry, they all rushed impetuously against the angle of the fence where in a moment they were surrounded by the dragoons who had entered the field and literally cut them to pieces. As this was done under the eye of the whole British camp, no prisoners could be safely taken, which may apologize for the slaughter that took place on this occasion. They took sixty valuable horses with their furniture and one hundred muskets and rifles; the whole camp beat to arms but the business was done and the detachment out of their reach before they recovered from their consternation.

—Davie-Weems Collection, No. 2540.

IX. AT CAMDEN GATES'S NORTHERN LAURELS TURN TO SOUTHERN WILLOWS

Although Nathanael Greene was Washington's personal choice to take command of the Southern troops after Lincoln's capture, and although in fact Major General Johann de Kalb, who fancied the title "Baron de Kalb," was already in the South with a force of Virginia and North Carolina Continentals, Congress had other ideas. It named the victor of Saratoga to that critical post. "Take care lest your Northern laurels turn to Southern willows," Charles Lee warned Gates.

Gates had no illusions about either his army or his situation, but he was shockingly unintelligent in handling his problems. Writing to Governor Jefferson on July 19, he deplored the "multiplied and increasing wants" of his command. Lack of meat and corn "must eventually break up our camp," he asserted. Furthermore, little if any assistance could be expected from the inhabitants, as the area was now swarming with Tories.

Gates's defeat can be laid to a series of inexplicable errors. He ignored well-informed advice to follow a circuitous route from North Carolina to Camden by way of Salisbury and Charlotte, which would have taken his army through fruitful and friendly country, and chose instead a route 50 miles shorter through wilderness and swampland, one of the most belligerently Tory regions in the South. He forced his men, starved and ill though many of them were, to march 18 miles a day. Yet his army was doubled by the addition of 2,000 North Carolina militia, and on paper he had a tremendous numerical superiority over the forces he was opposing. Lord Rawdon of Bunker's Hill fame concentrated his troops at Camden to check the American advance, and called on Cornwallis for reinforcements.

Gates weakened his army by detaching some 400 regulars and sending them to Sumter, and by dispatching Marion on a meaningless mission when in fact he should have held every man and called all the irregulars to his colors. At the least, if he had to spare men it should have been his militia, not his trained troops. To compound his difficulties, Gates tried to send back to Charlotte his heavy baggage and the women and children camp followers, but there was no transportation for the former, and the women and children clung to their protectors.

Then, over the protests of his own staff, he called for a night march. "I will breakfast tomorrow in Camden with Lord Cornwallis at my table," tradition has him say. Not having rum available, he issued a gill of molasses to each man, along with a ration of half-cooked meat and corn meal. The gastronomical disturbances that followed debilitated a substantial part of his troops.

By coincidence, Cornwallis also decided on a night march to surprise the Patriots, and the two armies came upon each other to their mutual surprise. Cornwallis carefully disposed his men and waited until daylight. Then Gates made another mistake. He had his untried militia on the left and center change position just as the armies were on the point of engaging. The British light infantry saw the opportunity and charged. A stampede followed. The militia

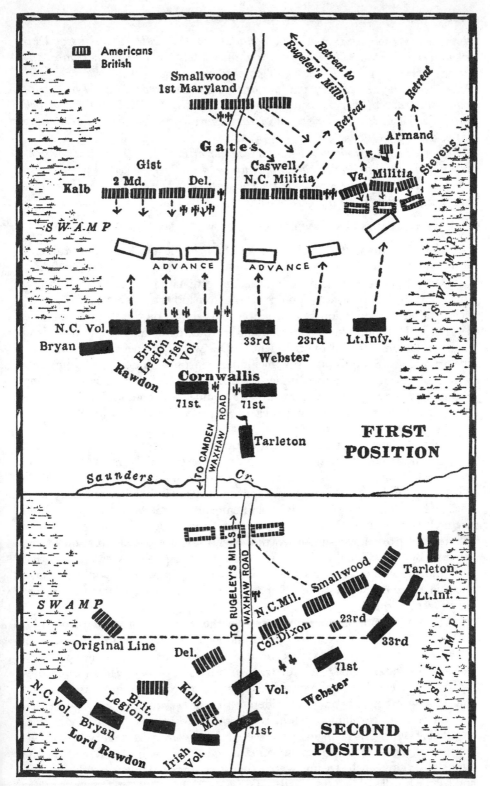

CAMDEN

threw away their arms and fled precipitately. De Kalb gallantly stood his ground and was mortally wounded, and only a handful of regular troops—the stalwart Maryland and Delaware regiments—were left to resist the British. A combined charge of cavalry and foot broke up these last defenses. The Patriot army was routed, dispersed, disintegrated and dissolved. As John Marshall aptly described it, "Never was a victory more complete, or a defeat more total."

Camden spelled finis to the military career of Horatio Gates. But the general did accomplish one remarkable feat that day. Fleeing with his militia on the fastest horse in the army, he did not stop until he reached Charlotte that night, sixty miles from the battlefield.

1. Gates Takes His Starving Army by the Wrong Road to Camden

Narrative of Colonel Otho Williams of the Continental Army, an Adjutant General with Gates's troops.   [1780]

General Gates, who had so fortunately terminated the career of General Burgoyne in the north, was appointed to command the southern army immediately after the reduction of Charleston. His arrival on the 25th of July was a relief to DeKalb, who, condescendingly, took command of the Maryland division, which included the regiment of Delaware. Besides these two corps, the army consisted only of a small legionary corps, which formed a junction with them a few days before, under the command of Colonel Armand, being about sixty cavalry and as many infantry; and Lieutenant Colonel Carrington's detachment of three companies of artillery, which had joined in Virginia.

General Gates was received with respectful ceremony; the baron ordered a Continental salute from the little park of artillery—which was performed on the entrance into camp of his successor, who made his acknowledgments to the baron for his great politeness, approved his standing orders, and, as if actuated by a spirit of great activity and enterprise, ordered the troops to hold themselves in readiness *to march at a moment's warning.* The latter order was a matter of great astonishment to those who knew the real situation of the troops. But all difficulties were removed by the general's assurances that plentiful supplies of *rum* and *rations* were on the route, and would overtake them in a day or two—assurances that certainly were too fallacious, and that never were verified.

All were in motion, however, early in the morning of the 27th of July, and the general took the route over Buffalo Ford, leading towards the enemy's advanced post on Lynch's Creek, on the road to Camden, leaving two brass field-pieces and some baggage for want of horses. Colonel Williams, presuming on the friendship of the general, ventured to expostulate with him upon the seeming precipitate and inconsiderate step he was taking. He represented that the country through which he was about to march was by nature barren, abounding with sandy plains, intersected by swamps, and very thinly inhabited; that the little provisions and forage which were produced on the banks of its few small streams were exhausted, or taken away by the enemy, and by the hordes of banditti (called Tories) which had retired from what they called the persecution of the rebels, and who would certainly distress his army, small as it was, by removing what little might remain out of his way.

On the other hand, the colonel represented that a route about north west would cross the Pee Dee River some where about where it loses the name of Yadkin, and would lead to the little town of Salisbury in the midst of a fertile country and inhabited by a people zealous in the cause of America. That the most active and intelligent officers had contemplated this route with pleasure, not only as it promised a more plentiful supply of provisions, but because the sick, the women and children, and the wounded, in case of disaster, might have an asylum provided for them at Salisbury or Charlotte, where they would remain in security, because the militia of the counties of Mecklenburgh and Roan, in which these villages stand, were staunch friends. The idea of establishing a laboratory for the repair of arms at a secure place was also suggested as necessary—the security of convoys of stores from the northward, by the upper route—the advantage of turning the left of the enemy's out-posts even by a circuitous route—that of approaching the most considerable of these posts (Camden) with the River Wateree on our right, and our friends on our backs—and some other considerations were suggested. And, that they might the more forcibly impress the general's mind, a short note was presented to him, concisely intimating the same opinion and referring to the best informed gentlemen under his command.

General Gates said he would confer with the *general officers* when the troops should halt at noon. Whether any conference took place or not, the writer don't know.

After a short halt at noon, when the men were refreshed upon the *scraps* in their *knapsacks*, the march was resumed. The country exceeded the representation that had been made of it—scarcely had it emerged from a state of sterile nature—the few rude attempts at improvement that were to be found were most of them abandoned by the owners and plundered by the neighbours. Every one, in this uncivilized part of the country, was flying from his home and joining in parties under adventurers who pretended to yield them protection until the British army should appear—which they seemed confidently to expect. The distresses of the soldiery daily increased—they were told that the banks of the Pee Dee River were extremely fertile—and so indeed they were; but the preceding crop of corn (the principal article of produce) was exhausted, and the new grain, although luxuriant and fine, was unfit for use. Many of the soldiery, urged by necessity, plucked the green ears and boiled them with the lean beef, which was collected in the woods, made for themselves a repast, not unpalatable to be sure, but which was attended with painful effects. Green peaches also were substituted for bread and had similar consequences. Some of the officers, aware of the risk of eating such vegetables, and in such a state, with poor fresh beef and without salt, restrained themselves from taking any thing but the beef itself, boiled or roasted. It occurred to some that the hair powder which remained in their bags would thicken soup, and it was actually applied.

The troops, notwithstanding their disappointment in not being overtaken by a supply of *rum* and provisions, were again amused with promises, and gave early proofs of that patient submission, inflexible fortitude and undeviating integrity which they afterwards more eminently displayed.

On the 3d day of August the little army crossed Pee Dee River in batteaus at Mask's Ferry, and were met on the southern bank by Lieutenant Colonel Porterfield, an officer of merit, who, after the disaster at Charleston, retired with a small detachment and found means of subsisting himself and his men in Carolina until the present time.

Colonel Marion, a gentleman of South Carolina, had been with the army a few days, attended by a very few followers, distinguished by small black leather caps and the wretchedness of their attire; their number did not exceed twenty men and boys, some white, some black, and all mounted, but most of them miserably equipped; their appearance was in fact so burlesque that it was with much difficulty the diversion of the regular soldiery was restrained by the officers; and the general himself was glad of an opportunity of detaching Colonel Marion, at his own instance, towards the interior of South Carolina, with orders to watch the motions of the enemy and furnish intelligence.

These trifling circumstances are remembered in these notes to show from what contemptible beginnings a good capacity will rise to distinction. The history of the war in South Carolina will recognize Marion as a brave partisan, if only the actions of the two last year's campaigns are recorded.

The expectation, founded on assurances, of finding a plentiful supply of provisions at May's Mill induced the troops again to obey the order to march with cheerfulness; but being again disappointed, fatigued and almost famished, their patience began to forsake them, their looks began to be vindictive; mutiny was ready to manifest itself, and the most unhappy consequences were to be apprehended; when the regimental officers, by mixing among the men and remonstrating with them, appeased murmurs, for which, unhappily, there was too much cause. The officers, however, by appealing to their own empty canteens and mess cases, satisfied the privates that all suffered alike; and, exhorting them to exercise the same fortitude of which the officers gave them the example, assured them that the best means of extricating them from the present distress should be immediately adopted; that if the supplies expected by the general did not arrive very soon, detachments should go from each corps in all directions to pick up what grain might possibly be found in the country and bring it to the mill.

Fortunately, a small quantity of Indian corn was immediately brought into camp—the mill was set to work, and as soon as a mess of meal was ground it was delivered out to the men; and so, in rotation, they were all served in the course of a few hours—more poor cattle were sacrificed—the camp kettles were all engaged—the men were busy but silent until they had each taken his repast; and then all was again content, cheerfulness and mirth. It was as astonishing as it was pleasing to observe the transition. . . .

Dangerous as deceptions had been, it was still thought expedient to flatter the expectation of the soldiery with an abundance of provisions, so soon as a junction could be formed with the militia; therefore, after collecting all the corn which was to be found in the neighbourhood of May's Mill, and huckstering all the meal that could be spared from our present necessities, the march was resumed towards Camden.

—Johnson, Life of Greene, I, 486-488, 489.

2. The Panic-Stricken Militia Flee Without Firing a Shot

Narrative of Colonel Otho Williams.

It has been observed that the direct march of the American army towards Camden and the prospect of considerable re-enforcements of militia had induced the commanding officer, Lord Rawdon, to collect there all the forces under his direction. And it is certain that the seeming confidence of the American general had inspired him with apprehensions for his principal post. Lord Cornwallis, at Charlestown, was constantly advised of the posture of affairs in the interior of the country; and, confident that Lord Rawdon could not long resist the forces that might, and probably would, be opposed to him, in a very short time resolved to march himself, with a considerable re-enforcement, to Camden. He arrived on [August] 14th and had the discernment at once to perceive that delay would render that situation dangerous, even to his whole force; the disaffection from his late assumed, arbitrary and vindictive power having become general through all the country above General Gates' line of march, as well as to the eastward of Santee and to the westward of Wateree Rivers. He, therefore, took the resolution of attacking the new constituted American army in their open irregular encampment at Clermont. Both armies, ignorant of each other's intentions, moved about the same hour of the same night and, approaching each other, met about half way between their respective encampments at midnight.

The first revelation of this new and unexpected scene was occasioned by a smart, mutual salutation of small arms between the advanced guards. Some of the cavalry of Armand's legion were wounded, retreated and threw the whole corps into disorder; which, recoiling suddenly on the front of the column of infantry, disordered the First Maryland Brigade and occasioned a general consternation through the whole line of the army. The light infantry under Porterfield, however, executed their orders gallantly; and the enemy, no less astonished than ourselves, seemed to acquiesce in a sudden suspension of hostilities.

Some prisoners were taken on both sides. From one of these, the deputy adjutant general of the American army extorted information respecting the situation and numbers of the enemy. He informed that Lord Cornwallis commanded in person about three thousand regular British troops, which were in line of march, about five or six hundred yards in front. Order was soon restored in the corps of infantry in the American army, and the officers were employed in forming a front line of battle when the deputy adjutant general communicated to General Gates the information which he had from the prisoner. The general's astonishment could not be concealed. He ordered the deputy adjutant general to call another council of war. All the general officers immediately assembled in the rear of the line. The unwelcome news was communicated to them.

General Gates said, "Gentlemen, what is best to be done?"

All were mute for a few moments, when the gallant Stevens exclaimed, "Gentlemen, is it not too late *now* to do any thing but fight?"

No other advice was offered, and the general desired the gentlemen would repair to their respective commands.

The Baron de Kalb's opinion may be inferred from the following fact: When the deputy adjutant general went to call him to council, he first told him what had been discovered. "Well," said the baron, "and has the general given you orders to retreat the army?" The baron, however, did not oppose the suggestion of General Stevens, and every measure that ensued was preparatory for action.

Lieutenant Colonel Porterfield, in whose bravery and judicious conduct great dependence was placed, received in the first rencontre a mortal wound (as it long afterwards proved) and was obliged to retire. His infantry bravely kept the ground in front; and the American army were formed in the following order: The Maryland division, including the Delawares, on the right—the North Carolina militia in the center—and the Virginia militia on the left. It happened that each flank was covered by a marsh, so near as to admit the removing of the First Maryland Brigade to form a second line, about two hundred yards in the rear of the first. The artillery was removed from the center of the brigades and placed in the center of the front line; and the North Carolina militia (light infantry) under Major Armstrong, which had retreated at the first rencontre, was ordered to cover a small interval between the left wing and the swampy grounds on that quarter.

Frequent skirmishes happened during the night between the advanced parties—which served to discover the relative situations of the two armies—and as a prelude to what was to take place in the morning.

At dawn of day (on the morning of the 16th of August) the enemy appeared in front, advancing in column. Captain Singleton, who commanded some pieces of artillery, observed to Colonel Williams that he plainly perceived the ground of the British uniform at about two hundred yards in front. The deputy adjutant general immediately ordered Captain Singleton to open his battery, and then rode to the general, who was in the rear of the second line, and informed him of the cause of the firing which he heard. He also observed to the general that the enemy seemed to be displaying their column by the right; the nature of the ground favored this conjecture, for yet nothing was clear.

The general seemed disposed to wait events—he gave no orders. The deputy adjutant general observed that if the enemy, in the act of displaying, were briskly attacked by General Stevens' brigade, which was already in line of battle, the effect might be fortunate, and first impressions were important.

"Sir," said the general, "that's right—let it be done."

This was the last order that the deputy adjutant general received. He hastened to General Stevens, who instantly advanced with his brigade, apparently in fine spirits. The right wing of the enemy was soon discovered *in line* —it was too late to attack them displaying. Nevertheless, the business of the day could no longer be deferred. The deputy adjutant general requested General Stevens to let him have forty or fifty privates, volunteers, who would run forward of the brigade and commence the attack. They were led forward within forty or fifty yards of the enemy, and ordered to take trees and keep up as brisk a fire as possible. The desired effect of this expedient, to extort the enemy's fire at some distance in order to the rendering it less terrible to the militia, was not gained.

General Stevens, observing the enemy to rush on, put his men in mind of their bayonets; but the impetuosity with which they advanced, *firing* and *huzzaing*, threw the whole body of the militia into such a panic that they generally threw down their *loaded* arms and fled in the utmost consternation. The unworthy example of the Virginians was almost instantly followed by the North Carolinians; only a small part of the brigade commanded by Brigadier General Gregory made a short pause. A part of Dixon's regiment of that brigade, next in the line to the Second Maryland Brigade, fired two or three rounds of cartridge. But a great majority of the militia (at least two-thirds of the army) fled without firing a shot. The writer avers it of his own knowledge, having seen and observed every part of the army, from left to right, during the action.

He who has never seen the effect of a panic upon a multitude can have but an imperfect idea of such a thing. The best disciplined troops have been enervated and made cowards by it. Armies have been routed by it, even where no enemy appeared to furnish an excuse. Like electricity, it operates instantaneously—like sympathy, it is irresistible where it touches. But, in the present instance, its action was not universal. The regular troops, who had the keen edge of sensibility rubbed off by strict discipline and hard service, saw the confusion with but little emotion. They engaged seriously in the affair; and, notwithstanding some irregulartiy, which was created by the militia breaking pell mell through the second line, order was restored there—time enough to give the enemy a severe check, which abated the fury of their assault and obliged them to assume a more deliberate manner of acting. The Second Maryland Brigade, including the battalion of Delawares, on the right, were engaged with the enemy's left, which they opposed with very great firmness. They even advanced upon them and had taken a number of prisoners when their companions of the First Brigade (which formed the second line), being greatly outflanked and charged by superior numbers, were obliged to give ground.

At this critical moment the regimental officers of the latter brigade, reluctant to leave the field without orders, inquired for their commanding officer (Brigadier General Smallwood) who, however, was not to be found. Notwithstanding, Colonel Gunby, Major Anderson and a number of other brave officers, assisted by the deputy adjutant general and Major Jones, one of Smallwood's aids, rallied the brigade and renewed the contest. Again they were obliged to give way, and were again rallied. The Second Brigade were still warmly engaged. The distance between the two brigades did not exceed two hundred yards, their opposite flanks being nearly upon a line perpendicular to their front.

At this eventful juncture, the deputy adjutant general, anxious that the communication between them should be preserved, and wishing that, in the almost certain event of a retreat, some order might be sustained by them, hastened from the First to the Second Brigade, which he found precisely in the same circumstances. He called upon his own regiment (the 6th Maryland) not to fly, and was answered by the Lieutenant Colonel, Ford, who said, "They have done all that can be expected of them. We are outnumbered and outflanked. See the enemy charge with bayonets!"

The enemy having collected their corps and directing their whole force against these two devoted brigades, a tremendous fire of musketry was for some time kept up on both sides with equal perseverance and obstinacy, until Lord Cornwallis, perceiving there was no cavalry opposed to him, pushed forward his dragoons, and his infantry charging at the same moment with fixed bayonets put an end to the contest.

His victory was complete. All the artillery and a very great number of prisoners fell into his hands. Many fine fellows lay on the field, and the rout of the remainder was entire. Not even a company retired in any order. Every one escaped as he could. If in this affair the militia fled too soon, the regulars may be thought almost as blamable for remaining too long on the field, especially after all hope of victory must have been despaired of. Let the commandants of the brigades answer for themselves. Allow the same privilege to the officers of the corps comprising those brigades, and they will say that they never received orders to retreat, nor any order from any *general* officer, from the commencement of the action until it became desperate. The brave Major General, the Baron de Kalb, fought on foot with the Second Brigade and fell, mortally wounded, into the hands of the enemy, who stripped him even of his shirt: a fate which probably was avoided by other generals only by an opportune retreat.

The torrent of unarmed militia bore away with it Generals Gates, Caswell and a number of others, who *soon* saw that all was lost. General Gates at first conceived a hope that he might rally, at Clermont, a sufficient number to cover the retreat of the regulars; but the farther they fled the more they were dispersed, and the generals soon found themselves abandoned by all but their aids. Lieutenant Colonel Senf, who had been on the expedition with Colonel Sumpter, returned and, overtaking General Gates, informed him of their complete success—that the enemy's redoubt on Wateree, opposite to Camden, was first reduced, and the convoy of stores, etc., from Charleston was decoyed and became prize to the American party almost without resistance. That upwards of one hundred prisoners and forty loaded waggons were in the hands of the party, who had sustained very little loss; but the general could avail himself nothing of this trifling advantage. The detachment under Sumpter was on the opposite side of the Wateree, marching off as speedily as might be to secure their booty—for the course of the firing in the morning indicated unfavorable news from the army.

The militia, the general saw, were in air, and the regulars, he feared, were no more. The dreadful thunder of artillery and musketry had ceased, and none of his friends appeared. There was no existing corps with which the victorious detachment might unite, and the Americans had no post in the rear. He, therefore, sent orders to Sumpter to retire in the best manner he could; and proceeded himself with General Caswell towards Charlotte, an open village on a plain, about sixty miles from the fatal scene of action. The Virginians, who knew nothing of the country they were in, involuntarily reversed the route they came, and fled, most of them, to Hillsborough. General Stevens pursued them, and halted there as many as were not sufficiently refreshed before his arrival to pursue their way home. Their terms of service, however, being very short, and no prospect presenting itself to afford another proof of their courage, General Stevens soon afterwards discharged them.

The North Carolina militia fled different ways, as their hopes led or their fears drove them. Most of them, preferring the shortest way home, scattered through the wilderness which lies between Wateree and Pee Dee rivers, and thence towards Roanoke. Whatever these might have suffered from the disaffected, they probably were not worse off than those who retired the way they came; wherein they met many of their insidious friends, armed and advancing to join the American army; but, learning its fate from the refugees, they acted decidedly in concert with the victors, and, captivating some, plundering others and maltreating all the fugitives they met, returned, exultingly, home. They even added taunts to their perfidy. One of a party who robbed Brigadier General Butler of his sword consoled him by saying, "You'll have no further use of it."

The regular troops, it has been observed, were the last to quit the field. Every corps was broken and dispersed; even the boggs and brush, which in some measure served to screen them from their furious pursuers, separated them from one another. Major Anderson was the only officer who fortunately rallied, as he retreated, a few men of different companies, and whose prudence and firmness afforded protection to those who joined his party on the rout. . . .

The general order for moving off the heavy baggage, etc., to Waxaws was not put in execution, as directed to be done on the preceding evening. The whole of it, consequently, fell into the hands of the enemy, as well as all that which followed the army except the waggons of the Generals Gates and De Kalb; which, being furnished with the stoutest horses, fortunately escaped under the protection of a small quarter guard. Other waggons also had got out of danger from the enemy; but the cries of the women and the wounded in the rear and the consternation of the flying troops so alarmed some of the waggoners that they cut out their teams and, taking each a horse, left the rest for the next that should come. Others were obliged to give up their horses to assist in carrying off the wounded, and the whole road, for many miles, was strewed with signals of distress, confusion and dismay.

What added not a little to this calamitous scene was the conduct of Armand's Legion. They were principally foreigners, and some of them, probably, not unaccustomed to such scenes. Whether it was owing to the disgust of the colonel at general orders, or the cowardice of his men, is not with the writer to determine; but certain it is, the Legion did not take any part in the action of the 16th. They retired early and in disorder, and were seen plundering the baggage of the army on their retreat. One of them cut Captain Lemar, of the Maryland infantry, over the hand for attempting to reclaim his own portmanteau, which the fellow was taking out of the waggon. Captain Lemar was unarmed, having broke his sword in action, and was obliged to submit both to the loss and to the insult. The tent covers were thrown off the waggons, generally, and the baggage exposed, so that one might take what suited him to carry off. General Caswell's mess waggon afforded the best refreshment; very unexpectedly to the writer, he there found a pipe of good Madeira, broached, and surrounded by a number of soldiers, whose appearance led him to inquire what engaged their attention. He acknowledges that in this instance he shared in the booty and took a draught of wine, which was the only refreshment he had received that day.

—JOHNSON, *Life of Greene*, I, 494-498.

3. "STRAYED, DESERTED, OR STOLEN—A WHOLE ARMY"

September 15, 1780

REWARD

STRAYED, DESERTED, OR STOLEN, from the subscriber, on the 16th of August last, near Camden, in the State of South Carolina, a whole ARMY, consisting of horse, foot and dragoons, to the amount of near TEN THOUSAND (as has been said) with all their baggage, artillery, wagons and camp equipage. The subscriber has very strong suspicions, from information received from his aid de camp, that a certain CHARLES, EARL CORNWALLIS, was principally concerned in carrying off the said ARMY with their baggage, etc. Any person or persons, civil or military, who will give information, whether to the subscriber, or to Charles Thompson, Esq., Secretary to the Continental Congress, where the said ARMY is, so that they may be recovered and rallied again, shall be entitled to demand from the Treasurer of the United States the sum of

THREE MILLION OF PAPER DOLLARS

as soon as they can be spared from the public funds, and

ANOTHER MILLION

for apprehending the person principally concerned in taking the said ARMY off. Proper passes will be granted by the President of the Congress to such persons as incline to go in search of the said ARMY. And as a further encouragement, no deduction will be made from the above reward on account of any of the Militia (who composed the said ARMY) not being found or heard of, as no dependence can be placed on their services, and nothing but the most speedy flight can ever save their Commander.

HORATIO GATES, M. G.
and late Commander in Chief of the Southern Army, August 30, 1780
—Rivington's *Royal Gazette*, Sept. 17, 1780.

4. "For God's Sake, Send Greene!"

Alexander Hamilton to James Duane.

September 6, 1780

... What think you of the conduct of this great man? I am his enemy personally, for unjust and unprovoked attacks upon my charatcer; therefore what I saw of him ought to be received as from an enemy, and have no more weight than as it is consistent with fact and common sense. But did ever any one hear of such a disposition or such a flight? His best troops placed on the side strongest by nature, his worst on that weakest by nature, and his attack made with these. 'Tis impossible to give a more complete picture of military absurdity. It is equally against the maxims of war and common sense. We see the consequences. His left ran away, and left his right uncovered. His right wing turned on the left has in all probability been cut off. Though, in truth, the general seems to have known very little what became of his army. Had he placed his militia on his right, supported by the morass, and his Continental troops on his left, where it seems he was most vulnerable, his right would have been more secure, and his left would have opposed the enemy; and instead of going backward when he ordered to attack, would have gone forward. The reverse of what has happened might have happened.

But was there ever an instance of a general running away, as Gates has done, from his whole army? And was there ever so precipitate a flight? One hundred and eighty miles in three days and a half. It does admirable credit to the activity of a man at his time of life. But it disgraces the general and the soldier. I have always believed him to be very far short of a Hector or a Ulysses. All the world, I think, will begin to agree with me.

But what will be done by Congress? Will he be changed or not? If he is changed, for God's sake overcome prejudice, and send Greene. You know my opinion of him. I stake my reputation on the events, give him but fair play.

But, above all things, let us have, without delay, a vigorous government, and a well constituted army for the war.

—Morris, *Hamilton and the Founding of the Nation*, pp. 38, 39.

X. THE PATRIOT CAUSE LOOKS UP: KING'S MOUNTAIN

Having routed Gates and scattered Sumter's forces, Cornwallis moved from Camden on September 8, 1780, pressing a full-scale invasion into North Carolina. Three parallel forces moved northward—Cornwallis, with the main body of his army; Tarleton at the head of the British Legion and light infantry; and still farther westward, Major Ferguson and his Tory command. Colonel Davie, at the head of such fragments of American troops as he could command, fell back; then on the night of September 20 he surprised the hated British Legion at the plantation of one of his own officers, Captain Wahab, near Charlotte, inflicted severe casualties upon them and retired with his booty. Knowing that Wahab was with the attackers, the enemy burned the plantation to the ground as soon as Davie's forces retired.

If Gates found his route to Camden infested with hostile Tories, the score was evened when Cornwallis made Charlotte, North Carolina, his temporary

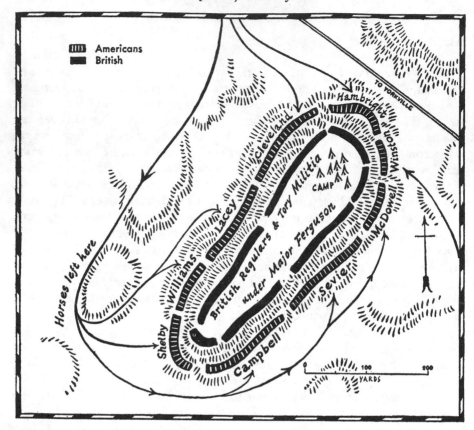

Americans
British

Horses left here

Shelby
Williams
Lacey
Cleveland

British Regulars & Tory Militia
under Major Ferguson

CAMP

Hambright
Winston

TO YORKVILLE

McDowell

Sevier

Campbell

0   100   200
YARDS

KING'S MOUNTAIN

headquarters. That area was a stronghold of die-hard Patriot resistance. Under Davie the Patriots put up a brilliant defense. The British finally took Charlotte with substantial losses in an affair where the British Legion scarcely covered itself with glory. Cornwallis found that communication with Camden was difficult to maintain and that foraging parties ran into crack-shot guerrilla forces that played havoc with morale.

Major Ferguson's Tories were assigned to move along the foothills and cover Cornwallis' left flank. At the suggestion of Colonel Isaac Shelby measures were taken for co-operative action by partisan leaders to cut off Ferguson's forces. Accordingly, forces under Colonels Charles McDowell, John Sevier, Isaac Shelby and William Campbell assembled at Watauga on September 25 and were joined by Colonel Benjamin Cleveland. Learning of the approach of this force, Ferguson first sought to retreat to the Catawba, then was forced to take a stand on King's Mountain, a mile and a half south of the North Carolina boundary line. This narrow stony ridge was about 500 yards in length, some 70 to 120 yards in width, and averaged 100 feet in height above the ravines surrounding it. Atop this level summit Ferguson "defied God Almighty and all the rebels out of Hell to overcome him." The Americans attacked the enemy in front and on his left flank simultaneously, and within *five minutes followed with an attack on the enemy's right flank. It was a complete envelopment. Ferguson was killed after desperate resistance and at the moment when he had cut down the Patriot Colonel Williams. Then the largely Tory force surrendered, with losses of 400 killed and wounded, and 700 captured, to Patriot casualties of 88. Scores of prisoners were shot after they surrendered and a dozen hanged by way of reprisal for the British having executed several deserters who had taken up arms against them.*

For undisciplined and largely inexperienced troops King's Mountain was an exhilarating achievement. It was also a stunning blow to Cornwallis and imperiled his position in North Carolina. He was forced to pull back across the state line to Winnsborough. King's Mountain once and for all destroyed Tory influence in North Carolina.

1. The Hated British Legion Is Surprised at the Waxhaws

Recollections of Colonel William R. Davie.

The camp of Lord Cornwallis extended along the north side of the Waxhaw Creek, and the 71st Regiment was posted in the rear about half a mile on the south side in a parallel line. The Catawba River in some measure covered their left flank and the Loyalists and light troops encamped on their right and already began to spread havoc and destruction.

Throughout the neighbouring country Col. Davie had procured information of their situation and formed a design to attack them; for this purpose he marched [September 20] with his own corps and Major Davidson's rifle men, making together one hundred and fifty men, with intention to fall on their quarters in the night, hoping by these means to check, if not entirely disperse, these lawless marauders. After taking a considerable circuit to avoid the patroles of the enemy, about 2 o'clock in the morning he turned Lord Cornwallis' right flank and approached a plantation where the Tories were said to be encamped; but on examining the ground [it] was found they had changed their position a few days before. Two other places were reconoitered in consequence of advice received in the night from terrified or disaffected people. At the last of these certain information was procured that they had retired within the flanks of the British army to the plantation of a Capt. Wahab, which was overlooked by the camp of the 71st Regiment, and that they might amount to three or four hundred mounted infantry. This partizan [Davie], unwilling to lose his object, reached Wahab's as the sun was rising. The moment was fortunate. The British party were going on command, their sentries were all called in, and about sixty of them with a party of the British Legion were mounted near the house which stood about the middle of a lane, covered on the same side by a corn field cultivated to the very door.

A company of infantry were detached thro' the corn with orders to take possession of the houses and immediately fire on the enemy. The cavalry were sent round the corn field with directions to gain the other end of the lane and charge the foe as soon as the fire commenced at the houses, while the Colonel advanced to receive them with about forty riflemen. The houses were briskly attacked, and the cavalry charged at the same moment. The enemy, being completely surprised, had no time to form and crowded in great disorder to the other end of the lane, when a well-reserved fire from the rifle men drove them back upon the cavalry and infantry who were now drawn up at the houses, and by whom they were instantly attacked. Thus pushed vigorously on all sides, they fluctuated some moments under the impressions of terror and dismay and then bore down the fences and fled in full speed. The Colonel's situation was too hazardous to risque any time in pursuit; the horses and arms were ordered to be collected, and in a few minutes the infantry were all mounted and the surplus horses secured. . . .

The British left fifteen or 20 dead on the field and had about forty wounded; they were surprised, pushed off their reflection and made no resistance, so that only one man of the Americans was wounded and that by mistake; being unwarily separated in the pursuit and having no regimentals, he was not distinguishable from the enemy. The British commanding officer, out of pique or a mistaken and cruel policy, immediately ordered the improvements of the plantation to be set on fire, and the houses, barns and fences were all laid in ashes, although there were three families of women and children living there at the time.

The proprietor, Capt. Wahab, was a volunteer with Colonel Davie and had been exiled some time from his family, and his wife and children were unavoidably in the midst of the action. "These were moments which try men's souls." They gathered round him in tears of joy and distraction, the enemy advanced, and he could only embrace them, and in a few minutes afterwards, turning his eyes back towards his all, as the detachment moved off, he had the mortification to see their only hope of subsistence wrapt in flames. This barbarous practice was uniformly enacted by the British officers in the Southern States. However casual the rencounter might be, when it happened at a plantation, their remaining in possession of the ground was always marked by committing the houses to the flames.

The Colonel, expecting to attack the enemy in the night, had given orders to take no prisoners. These orders in the hurry of the morning were not revoked. This circumstance, the vicinity of the British quarters and the danger of pursuit satisfactorily account for no prisoners being taken. He brought off ninety-six horses with their furniture, and one hundred and twenty stand of arms, and arrived at his camp the same afternoon, having performed a march of sixty miles in less than twenty-four hours, notwithstanding the time employed in seeking and beating the enemy.

—Davie-Weems Collection, No. 2540.

2. Banastre Tarleton Finds Charlotte a Hornets' Nest

Account written in 1787.

Charlotte town afforded some conveniences, blended with great disadvantages. The mills in its neighbourhood were supposed of sufficient consequence to render it for the present an eligible position and, in future, a necessary post when the army advanced. But the aptness of its intermediate situation between Camden and Salisbury and the quantity of its mills did not counterbalance its defects. The town and environs abounded with inveterate enemies. The plantations in the neighbourhood were small and uncultivated;

the roads narrow and crossed in every direction; and the whole face of the country covered with close and thick woods. In addition to these disadvantages, no estimation could be made of the sentiments of half of the inhabitants of North Carolina, whilst the royal army remained at Charlotte town.

It was evident, and it had been frequently mentioned to the King's officers, that the counties of Mecklenburg and Rohan were more hostile to England than any other in America. The vigilance and animosity of these surrounding districts checked the exertions of the well-affected, and totally destroyed all communication between the King's troops and the Loyalists in the other parts of the province. No British commander could obtain any information in that position which would facilitate his designs or guide his future conduct. Every report concerning the measures of the governor and assembly would undoubtedly be ambiguous; accounts of the preparations of the militia could only be vague and uncertain; and all intelligence of the real force and movements of the Continentals must be totally unattainable.

The foraging parties were every day harassed by the inhabitants, who did not remain at home to receive payment for the produce of their plantations, but generally fired from covert places to annoy the British detachments. Ineffectual attempts were made upon convoys coming from Camden and the intermediate post at Blair's mill; but individuals with expresses were frequently murdered. An attack was directed against the picket at Polk's mill, two miles from the town. The Americans were gallantly received by Lieutenant Guyon, of the 23d Regiment; and the fire of his party from a loop-hold building adjoining the mill repulsed the assailants. Notwithstanding the different checks and losses sustained by the militia of the district, they continued their hostilities with unwearied perseverance; and the British troops were so effectually blockaded in their present position that very few, out of a great number of messengers, could reach Charlotte town in the beginning of October, to give intelligence of Ferguson's situation.

—TARLETON, *History of Campaigns in the Southern Provinces*, pp. 162-164.

3. FERGUSON VOWS "HE NEVER WOULD YIELD TO DAMNED BANDITTI"

Account of Colonel Isaac Shelby of North Carolina.

In September 1780 Maj. Ferguson, who was one of the best and most enterprising of the British officers in America, had succeeded in raising a large body of Tories, who, with his own corps of regulars, constituted an effective force of eleven hundred and twenty-five men. With a view of cutting off Col. Clarke, of Georgia, who had recently made a demonstration against Augusta, which was then in the hands of the British, Ferguson had marched near the Blue Ridge and had taken post at Gilbert Town, which is situated but a few miles from the mountains. Whilst there he discharged a Patriot, who had been taken prisoner on his parole, and directed him to tell Col. Shelby (who had become obnoxious to the British and Tories from the affair at Musgrove's Mill) that if Shelby did not surrender he (Ferguson) would come over the mountains and put him to death, and burn his whole county.

It required no further taunt to rouse the patriotic indignation of Col. Shelby. He determined to make an effort to raise a force, in connection with other officers, which should surprise and defeat Ferguson. With this object in view, he went to a horse race near where Jonesborough has since been built, to see Sevier and others. Shelby and Sevier there resolved that if Col. Campbell would join them they would raise all the force they could and attack Ferguson; and if this was not practicable they would co-operate with any corps of the army of the United States with which they might meet. If they failed and the country was overrun and subdued by the British, they would then take water and go down to the Spaniards in Louisiana.

Col. Campbell was notified of their determination, and a place of rendezvous in the mountains appointed east of Jonesborough. At the time appointed, September 25th, Campbell joined them, and their united force numbered about one thousand riflemen. They crossed the mountains on the 27th in a ravine and fell in, accidentally, with Col. Cleveland, of North Carolina, who had under his command about four hundred men.

The force having been raised by officers of equal rank, and being without any higher officer entitled to command the whole corps, there was a general want of organization and arrangement. It was then determined that a board of officers should convene each night and decide on the plan of operations for the next day; and further, that one of the officers should see those orders executed as officer of the day, until they should otherwise conclude. Shelby proposed that Col. Campbell should act as officer of the day. Campbell took him aside and requested Shelby to withdraw his name and consent to serve himself. Shelby replied that he was himself the youngest Colonel present from his State, that he had served that year under several of the officers who were present and who might take offence if he commanded; that Gen. McDowell, who was with them, was too slow an officer for his views and the enterprise in which they were engaged, and added that as he ranked Campbell, yet as Campbell was the only officer from Virginia, if he (Shelby) pressed his appointment no one would object. Col Campbell felt the force of this reasoning and consented to serve, and was appointed to the command as officer of the day.

The force of the detachment was still considered insufficient to attack Ferguson, as his strength was not known. It was agreed that an express be sent to invite Gen. Morgan or Gen. Davidson to take the command. Gen. McDowell tendered his serviecs for this purpose and started on his mission. Before proceeding far he fell in with Col. Williams, of South Carolina, who was at the head of from two to three hundred refugees. Gen. McDowell advised them where the patriot force was encamped. They joined the army and thus made a muster roll of about sixteen hundred men.

The board of officers determined to march upon Ferguson. In the meantime two or three of their men had deserted after their first rendezvous, and had gone to Ferguson and advised him of the intended attack. The army marched to Gilbert Town and found that Ferguson had left it several days before, having taken the route towards Fort Ninety-Six.

Finding that Ferguson was retreating, and learning what was his real strength, it was determined on Thursday night the 5th of October, to make a desperate effort to overtake him before he should reach any British post or receive any further reinforcements. Accordingly, they selected all who had good horses, who numbered about nine hundred and ten, and started the next morning in pursuit of Ferguson as soon as they could see.

Ferguson, after marching a short distance towards Ninety-Six, had filed off to the left toward Cornwallis. His pursuers never stopped until late in the afternoon, when they reached the Cowpens. There they halted, shot down some beeves, ate their suppers and fed their horses. This done, the line of march was resumed and continued through the whole night, amidst an excessively hard rain. In the morning Shelby ascertained that Campbell had taken a wrong road in the night and had separated from him. Men were posted off in all directions and Campbell's corps found and put in the right road. They then crossed Broad River and continued their pursuit until twelve o'clock, the 7th of October. The rain continued to fall so heavily that Campbell, Sevier and Cleveland concluded to halt, and rode up to Shelby to inform him of their determination. Shelby replied: "I will not stop till night, if I follow Ferguson into Cornwallis' lines!" Without replying, the other colonels turned off to their respective commands and continued the march. They had proceeded but a mile when they learned that Ferguson was only seven miles from them at King's Mountain.

Ferguson, finding that he could not elude the rapid pursuit of the mounted mountaineers, had marched to King's Mountain, which he considered a strong post, and which he had reached the night previous. The mountain, or ridge, was a quarter of a mile long, and so confident was Ferguson in the strength of his position that he declared the Almighty could not drive him from it.

When the patriots came near the mountain they halted, tied all their loose baggage to their saddles, fastened their horses and left them under charge of a few men, and then prepared for an immediate attack. About 3 o'clock the patriot force was led to the attack in four columns. Col Campbell commanded the right centre column, Col. Shelby the left centre, Col. Sevier the right flank column, and Col. Cleveland the left flank. As they came to the foot of the mountain, the right centre and right flank columns deployed to the right, and the left centre and left flank columns to the left, and thus surrounding the mountain they marched up, commencing the action on all sides.

Ferguson did all that an officer could do under the circumstances. His men, too, fought bravely. But his position, which he thought impregnable against any force the Patriots could raise, was really a disadvantage to him. The summit was bare, whilst the sides of the mountain was covered with trees. Ferguson's men were drawn up in close column on the summit and thus presented fair marks for the mountaineers, who approached them under cover of the trees. As either column would approach the summit, Ferguson would order out a charge with fixed bayonet, which was always successful, for the riflemen retreated before the charging column slowly, still firing as they retired. When Ferguson's men returned to regain their position on the mountain, the patriots would again rally and pursue them. In one of these charges Shelby's column was considerably broken; he rode back and rallied his men, and when the enemy retired to the summit he pressed on his men and reached the summit whilst Ferguson was directing a charge against Cleveland.

Col. Sevier reached the summit about the same time with Shelby. They united and drove back the enemy to one end of the ridge. Cleveland's and Campbell's columns were still pressing forward and firing as they came up. The slaughter of the enemy was great, and it was evident that further resistance would be unavailing. Still Ferguson's proud heart could not think of surrender. He swore "he never would yield to such a d——d banditti," and rushed from his men, sword in hand, and cut away until his sword was broken and he was shot down. His men, seeing their leader fall, immediately surrendered. The British loss, in killed and prisoners, was eleven hundred and five. Ferguson's morning report showed a force of eleven hundred and twenty-five. A more total defeat was not practicable. Our loss was about forty killed. Amongst them we had to mourn the death of Col. Williams, a most gallant and efficient officer. The battle lasted one hour.

—*North Carolina State Records*, XV, 105-108.

4. The Face of the Mountain Is Strewn with the Bodies of Tories

Account of Ensign Robert Campbell of North Carolina.

Ferguson, finding that he must inevitably be overtaken, chose his ground and waited for the attack on King's Mountain. On the 7th of October, in the afternoon, after a forced march of forty-five miles on that day and the night before, the volunteers came up with him. The forenoon of the day was wet, but they were fortunate enough to come on him undiscovered and took his pickets, they not having it in their power to give an alarm. They were soon formed in such order as to attack the enemy on all sides. The Washington and Sullivan regiments were formed in the front and on the right flank; the North and South Carolina troops, under Cols. Williams, Sevier, Cleveland, Lacey and Brandon, on the left. The two armies being in full view, the centre of the one nearly opposite the centre of the other, the British main guard posted nearly half-way down the mountain, the commanding officer gave the word of command to raise the Indian war-whoop and charge. In a moment King's Mountain resounded with their shouts, and on the first fire the guard retreated, leaving some of their men to crimson the earth. The British beat to arms and immediately formed on top of the mountain behind a chain of rocks that appeared impregnable, and had their wagons drawn up on their flank across the end of the mountain, by which they made a strong breast work.

Thus concealed, the American army advanced to the charge. In ten or fifteen mintues the wings came round, and the action became general.

The enemy annoyed our troops very much from their advantageous position. Col. Shelby, being previously ordered to reconnoitre their position, observing their situation and what a destructive fire was kept up from behind those rocks, ordered Robert Campbell . . . to advance and post themselves opposite to the rocks and near to the enemy, and then return to assist in bringing up the men in order, who had been charged with the bayonet. These orders were punctually obeyed, and they kept up such a galling fire as to compel Ferguson to order a company of regulars to face them, with a view to cover his men that were posted behind the rocks.

At this time a considerable fire was drawn to this side of the mountain by the repulse of those on the other, and the Loyalists not being permitted to leave their post. This scene was not of long duration, for it was the brave Virginia volunteers and those under Col. Shelby, on their attempting rapidly to ascend the mountain, that were charged with the bayonet. They obstinately stood until some of them were thrust through the body, and having nothing but their rifles by which to defend themselves, they were forced to retreat. They were soon rallied by their gallant commanders, Campbell, Shelby and other brave officers, and by a constant and well-directed fire of their rifles drove them back in their turn, strewing the face of the mountain with their assailants, and kept advancing until they drove them from some of their posts.

Ferguson, being heavily pressed on all sides, ordered Capt. DePeyster to reinforce some of the extreme post with a full company of British regulars. He marched, but to his astonishment, when he arrived at the place of destination, he had almost no men, being exposed in that short distance to the constant fire of their rifles. He then ordered his cavalry to mount, but to no purpose. As quick as they were mounted they were taken down by some bold marksman. Being driven to desperation by such a scene of misfortune, Col. Ferguson endeavored to make his escape, and, with two colonels of the Loyalists, mounted his horse and charged on that part of the line which was defended by the party who had been ordered round the mountain by Col. Shelby where it appeared too weak to resist them. But as soon as he got to the line he fell, and the other two officers, attempting to retreat, soon shared the same fate.

It was about this time that Col. Campbell advanced in front of his men and climbed over a steep rock close by the enemy's lines to get a view of their situation, and saw that they were retreating from behind the rocks that were near to him.

As soon as Capt. DePeyster observed that Col. Ferguson was killed, he raised a flag and called for quarters. It was soon taken out of his hand by one of the officers on horse back and raised so high that it could be seen by our line, and the firing immediately ceased. The Loyalists, at the time of their surrender, were driven into a crowd, and being closely surrounded, they could not have made any further resistance.

In this sharp action, one hundred and fifty of Col. Ferguson's party were killed, and something over that number were wounded. Eight hundred and ten, of whom one hundred were British regulars, surrendered themselves prisoners, and one thousand five hundred stand of arms were taken. The loss of the American army on this occasion amounted to thirty killed and something over fifty wounded, among whom were a number of brave officers. Col. Williams, who has been so much lamented, was shot through the body, near the close of the action, in making an attempt to charge upon Ferguson. He lived long enough to hear of the surrender of the British army. He then said, "I die contented, since we have gained the victory," and expired.

—*North Carolina State Records*, XV, 101-103.

5. A Nervous Recruit Describes the Charge in the Center

Account of James P. Collins.

The enemy was posted on a high, steep and rugged ridge—very difficult of access. . . . The plan was to surround the mountain and attack them on all sides, if possible. In order to do this, the left had to march under the fire of the enemy to gain the position assigned to them on the stream on the right of the enemy, while the right was to take possession of the other stream. In doing this they were not exposed, the cliff being so steep as to cover them completely.

Each leader made a short speech in his own way to his men, desiring every coward to be off immediately. Here I confess I would willingly have been excused, for my feelings were not the most pleasant. This may be attributed to my youth, not being quite seventeen years of age—but I could not well swallow the appellation of coward. I looked around. Every man's countenance seemed to change. Well, thought I, fate is fate; every man's fate is before him and he has to run it out. . . .

We were soon in motion, every man throwing four or five balls in his mouth to prevent thirst, also to be in readiness to reload quick. The shot of the enemy soon began to pass over us like hail. The first shock was quickly over, and for my own part, I was soon in profuse sweat. My lot happened to be in the center, where the severest part of the battle was fought. We soon attempted to climb the hill, but were fiercely charged upon and forced to fall back to our first position. We tried a second time, but met the same fate; the fight then seemed to become more furious. Their leader, Ferguson, came in full view, within rifle shot as if to encourage his men, who by this time were falling very fast. He soon disappeared. We took to the hill a third time; the enemy gave way.

When we had gotten near the top, some of our leaders roared out, "Hurrah, my brave fellows! Advance! They are crying for quarter."

By this time, the right and left had gained the top of the cliff; the enemy was completely hemmed in on all sides, and no chance of escaping—besides, their leader had fallen. They soon threw down their arms and surrendered. After the fight was over, the situation of the poor Tories appeared to be really pitiable; the dead lay in heaps on all sides, while the groans of the wounded were heard in every direction. I could not help turning away from the scene before me with horror and, though exulting in victory, could not refrain from shedding tears. . . .

On examining the dead body of their great chief, it appeared that almost fifty rifles must have been leveled at him at the same time; seven rifle balls had passed through his body, both of his arms were broken, and his hat and clothing were literally shot to pieces. Their great elevation above us had proved their ruin. They overshot us altogether, scarce touching a man, except those on horseback, while every rifle from below seemed to have the desired effect. . . .

Next morning, which was Sunday, the scene became really distressing; the wives and children of the poor Tories came in, in great numbers. Their husbands, fathers and brothers lay dead in heaps, while others lay wounded or dying—a melancholy sight indeed! while numbers of the survivors were doomed to abide the sentence of a court martial, and several were actually hanged. . . .

We proceeded to bury the dead, but it was badly done. They were thrown into convenient piles and covered with old logs, the bark of old trees, and rocks; yet not so as to secure them from becoming a prey to the beasts of the forest or the vultures of the air; and the wolves became so plenty that it was dangerous for any one to be out at night, for several miles around; also, the hogs in the neighborhood gathered in to the place to devour the flesh of men, inasmuch as numbers chose to live on little meat rather than eat their hogs, though they were fat. Half of the dogs in the country were said to be mad and were put to death. I saw, myself, in passing the place a few weeks after, all parts of the human frame lying scattered in every direction. . . .

—Collins, *Autobiography of a Revolutionary Soldier*, pp. 259-261.

CHAPTER THIRTY

The Turn of the Tide

On October 14, 1780, *the same day that Shelby and Campbell annihilated the Tories at King's Mountain, General Nathanael Greene was named to succeed Gates in the Southern command. Greene did not reach the field until December. In the meantime Cornwallis' forces in South Carolina were continually and effectively harassed by partisans, notably the small bands skillfully and daringly led by Frances Marion and Thomas Sumter, the latter increasingly independent of direction. More and more Cornwallis counted on Tarleton to cope with the guerrillas. Even the affair at Blackstock's in which Tarleton suffered ten casualties to every one suffered by Sumter was magnified by the Green Dragoon into a victory, and as such was accepted by Cornwallis.*

Outnumbered by Cornwallis three to two, and operating in a theater terribly wracked by war, pillage and discord, Greene wisely concentrated first on guerrilla tactics, developing on a more comprehensive scale the tactics of the Carolina partisans. He detached some of his own forces and placed them under Morgan, one of the few military geniuses the war produced, who had now come out of self-imposed retirement. Morgan was sent to harass the British outposts in the western part of South Carolina, and Greene moved to the north-central part of the state to support the American partisans. The disaster Morgan inflicted upon the British at Cowpens ended the legend of Tarleton's invincibility.

Now Cornwallis became the pursuer. Too late to catch Morgan, he tried to corner Greene, pressing him north into Virginia, only to fall back on Hillsborough for support. Guilford Courthouse was a costly technical victory for Cornwallis, who momentarily kept the field but had his army terribly mauled by Greene's men. The British commander now gave up all thought of capturing Greene, moved to the coast, and finally quit North Carolina for a new theater of action in Virginia, where to all intents and purposes he brought the curtain down on the war.

I. PARTISAN WARFARE TAKES ITS TOLL

1. "Damn It, Boys, You ... You Know What I Mean! Go On!"

Memoirs of Captain Tarleton Brown of South Carolina.

Overtaking General Marion at Kingstree, Black River, S. C., we immediately united with his troops. Marion's route lay then between the Santee and Little Pedee rivers; and being desirous to intercept and defeat Col. Watts, who was then marching at the head of 400 men between Camden and Georgetown, every arrangement and preparation was made to carry into execution his design. All things being now ready, Watts appeared in sight at the head of his large force, and as they marched down the road with great show and magnificence (hoping, no doubt, to terrify and conquer the country), they spied us; at which time, the British horse sallied forth to surround us.

Marion, with his characteristic shrewdness and sagacity, discovered their manoeuvres, anticipated their object and retreated to the woods, some four or five hundred yards, and prepared for them. In a few moments they came dashing up, expecting to find us all in confusion and disorder, but to their astonishment we were ready for the attack, and perceiving this, they called a halt, at which time Marion and Horry ordered a charge. Col. Horry stammered badly, and on this occasion he leaned forward, spurred his horse, waved his sword and ran fifty or sixty yards, endeavoring to utter the word *charge*, and finding he could not, bawled out, *"Damn it, boys, you . . . you know what I mean. Go on!"*

We were then doing what we could, pressing with all rapidity to the strife, and before the British could get back to the main body we slew a goodly number of them. Being eager to do all the damage we could, we pursued the fellows very close to the line of their main body, and as soon as they got in, Watts began to thunder his cannon at us, and to tear down the limbs and branches of the trees, which fell about us like hail, but did no other damage than to wound one of our men, Natt. Hutson, and one horse slightly. Marion, now finding his force, which consisted only of two hundred men (though sterling to a man, brave, fearless and patriotic), was too small to give Watts open battle, guarded the bridges and swamps in his route, and annoyed and killed his men as they passed.

For prudence sake, Marion never encamped over two nights in one place, unless at a safe distance from the enemy. He generally commenced the line of march about sun-set, continuing through the greater part of the night. By this policy he was enabled effectually to defeat the plans of the British and to strengthen his languishing cause. For while the one army was encamping and resting in calm and listless security, not dreaming of danger, the other, taking advantage of opportunity and advancing through the sable curtains of the night unobserved, often effectually vanquished and routed their foes. It was from the craftiness and ingenuity of Marion, the celerity with which he moved from post to post, that his enemies gave to him the significant appellation of the "Swamp Fox." Upon him depended almost solely the success of the provincial army of South Carolina, and the sequel has proven how well he performed the trust reposed in him. His genuine love of country and liberty, and his unwearied vigilance and invincible fortitude, coupled with the eminent success which attended him through his brilliant career, has endeared him to the hearts of his countrymen, and the memory of his deeds of valor shall never slumber so long as there is a Carolinian to speak his panegyric.

The heavy rains which prevailed at this time and inundated the country to a considerable extent, proved very favorable to Marion. He now sent a detachment of seventy men, myself one of the number, across the Santee, to attack the enemy stationed at Scott's Lake and Monk's Corner. We crossed the river at night in a small boat, commanded by Captains James and John Postell, dividing our force into two companies, each consisting of thirty-five men. Capt. James Postell took one company and proceeded to Scott's Lake, but ascertaining the strength of the enemy and finding the place too well fortified to warrant an attack, he abandoned the project and returned again to the river, and awaited the arrival of Capt. John Postell, who, in the meantime, had marched with the other company to Monk's Corner. It was my good fortune to accompany the latter.

Just about the break of day we charged upon the enemy. Our appearance was so sudden and unexpected that they had not time even to fire a single gun. We took thirty-three prisoners, found twenty-odd hogsheads of old spirits and a large supply of provisions. The former we destroyed, but returned with the latter and our prisoners to the army on Santee. The news of our attack on Monk's Corner having reached the enemy at Scott's Lake, they forthwith marched to their assistance, but arrived too late to extend any. We had captured their comrades, bursted their hogsheads of spirits, gathered their provisions and decamped before their arrival. Capt. James Postell, being apprised of their march to assist their friends at Monk's Corner, returned to the fort, set fire to it and burned it level to the ground.

—Brown, *Memoirs*, pp. 34-38.

2. Nathanael Greene Assumes Command in the South

Nathanael Greene to Catherine Greene.

[October, 1780]

My dear Angel

What I have been dreading has come to pass. His Excellency General Washington by an order of Congress has appointed me to the command of the Southern Army, Gen. Gates being recalled to undergo an examination into his conduct. This is so foreign from my wishes that I am distressed exceedingly: especially as I have just received your letter of the 2d of this month where you describe your distress and sufferings in such a feeling manner as melts my soul into the deepest distress.

I have been pleasing my self with the agreeable prospect of spending the winter here with you; and the moment I was appointed to the command I sent off Mr Hubbard to bring you to camp. But alas, before we can have the happiness of meeting, I am ordered away to another quarter. How unfriendly is war to domestic happiness! . . .

—Greene, "Letter," *R. I. Hist. Soc. Coll.*, XX, 106.

3. Only Tarleton Is Able to Cope with the Partisans

Lord Cornwallis to Sir Henry Clinton.

Camp at Wynnesborough, December 3, 1780

Wynnesborough, my present position, is an healthy spot, well situated to protect the greatest part of the northern frontier and to assist Camden and Ninety-Six. The militia of the latter, on which alone we could place the smallest dependence, was so totally disheartened by the defeat of Ferguson that of that whole district we could with difficulty assemble one hundred, and even those, I am convinced, would not have made the smallest resistance if they had been attacked. I determined to remain at this place until an answer arrived from Gen. Leslie, on which my plan for the winter has to depend, and to use every possible means of putting the Province into a state of defence, which I found to be absolutely necessary, whether my campaign was offensive or defensive.

Bad as the state of our affairs was on the northern frontier, the eastern part was much worse. Col. Tynes, who commanded the militia of the High Hills of Santee, and who was posted on Black River, was surprized and taken, and his men lost all their arms. Col. Marion had so wrought on the minds of the people, partly by the terror of his threats and cruelty of his punishments, and partly by the promise of plunder, that there was scarce an inhabitant between the Santee and Pedee that was not in arms against us. Some parties had even crossed the Santee and carried terror to the gates of Charles-town. My first object was to reinstate matters in that quarter, without which Camden could receive no supplies. I therefore sent Tarleton, who pursued Marion for several days, obliged his corps to take to the swamps, and by convincing the inhabitants there was a power superior to Marion who could likewise reward and punish, so far checked the insurrection that the greatest part of them have not dared openly to appear in arms against us since his expedition. . . .

Major Wemyss, who had just passed Broad River at Brierly's Ferry, came to me on the seventh of last month and told me that he had information that Sumpter had moved to Moore's Hill, within five miles of Fishdam Ford and about twenty-five miles from the place where the 63d then lay; that he had accurate accounts of his position and good guides, and that he made no doubt of being able to surprize and rout him. As the defeating of so daring and troublesome a man as Sumpter, and dispersing such a banditti, was a great object, I consented to his making the trial on the 9th at daybreak, and gave him forty of the dragoons which Tarleton had left with me, desiring him, however, neither to put them in the front nor to make any use of them during the night.

Major Wemyss marched so early and so fast on the night of the 8th that he arrived at Moore's Hill soon after midnight. He then had information that Sumpter had marched that evening to Fishdam Ford, where he lay with his rear close to Broad River on a low piece of ground. The Major immediately proceeded to attack him in his new position, and succeeded so well as to get into his camp whilst the men were all sleeping round the fires; but as Major Wemyss rode into the camp at the head of the dragoons and the 63d followed them on horseback, the enemy's arms were not secured, and some of them recovering from the first alarm got their rifles and with the first fire wounded Major Wemyss in several places and put the cavalry into disorder. The 63d then dismounted and killed and wounded about seventy of the rebels, drove several over the river and dispersed the rest. The command, however, devolving on a very young officer who neither knew the ground nor Major Wemyss's plan, nor the strength of the enemy, some few of which kept firing from the wood on our people who remained in the enemy's camp and who were probably discovered by their fires, our troops came away before daybreak, leaving

Major Wemyss and 22 sergeants and rank and file at a house close to the field of action. In the morning those who were left with a flag of truce with the wounded found that the enemy were all gone, but on some of their scouting parties discovering that our people had likewise retired, Sumpter returned and took Major Wemyss's parole for himself and the wounded soldiers. Major Wemyss is gone to Charleston and is in a fair way of recovery.

The enemy on this event cried "Victory," and the whole country came in fast to join Sumpter, who passed the Broad River and joined Branan, Clarke, etc. I detached Major McArthur with the 1st Battalion of the 71st and the 63d Regiment, after having sent my aid-de-camp, Lieut. Money, to take the command of it, to Brierly's Ferry on Broad River, in order to cover our mills and to give some check to the enemy's march to Ninety-Six. At the same time I recalled Lieut. Col. Tarleton from the Low Country. Tarleton was so fortunate as to pass not only the Wateree but the Broad River without Gen. Sumpter's being apprised of it, who, having increased his corps to one thousand, had passed the Ennoree and was on the point of attacking our hundred militia at Williams's house, fifteen miles from Ninety-Six, and where I believe he would not have met with much resistance.

Lt. Col. Tarleton would have surprized him on the south of Ennoree had not a deserter of the 63d given notice of his march. He, however, cut to pieces his rear guard in passing that river, and pursued his main body with such rapidity that he could not safely pass the Tyger and was obliged to halt on a very strong position at a place called Black Stocks, close to it. Tarleton had with him only his cavalry and the 63d mounted, his infantry and 3-pounder being several miles behind. The enemy, not being able to retreat with safety, and being informed of Tarleton's approach and want of infantry by a woman who passed him on the march and contrived by a nearer road to get to them, were encouraged by their great superiority of numbers and began to fire on the 63d, who were dismounted. Lt. Col. Tarleton, to save them from considerable loss, was obliged to attack, altho' at some hazard, and drove the enemy, with loss, over the river. Sumpter was dangerously wounded, three of their colonels killed, and about 120 men killed, wounded or taken. On our side about 50 were killed and wounded. Lieuts. Gibson and Cope, of the 63d, were amongst the former, and my aid-de-camp, Lieut. Money, who was a most promising officer, died of his wounds a few days after.

Lt. Col. Tarleton, as soon as he had taken care of his wounded, pursued and dispersed the remaining part of Sumpter's corps, and then, having assembled some militia under Mr. Cunningham, whom I appointed Brig. General of the Militia of that district, and who has by far the greatest influence in that country, he returned to the Broad River, where he at present remains, as well as Major McArthur, in the neighborhood of Brierley's Ferry.

It is not easy for Lt. Col. Tarleton to add to the reputation he has acquired in this Province, but the defeating 1,000 men posted on very strong ground and occupying log houses with 190 cavalry and 80 infantry is a proof of that spirit and those talents which must render the most essential services to his country. . . .

—*North Carolina State Records*, XV, 303-306.

4. Governor Rutledge Indicts Tarleton for Barbarity

Governor John Rutledge to South Carolina's delegates in the Continental Congress.

December 8, 1780

It is really melancholy to see the desolate condition of Mr. Hill's plantation in the New Acquisition: all his fine iron-works, mills, dwelling-houses and buildings of every kind, even his Negro-houses, reduced to ashes, and his wife and children in a little log hut. I was shocked to see the ragged, shabby condition of our brave and virtuous men, who would not remain in the power of the enemy but have taken to arms.

This, however, is but a faint description of the sufferings of our country, for it is beyond a doubt the enemy have hanged many of our people, who from fear and the impracticability of removing had given paroles, and from attachment to our side joined it. Nay, Tarleton has since the action at Black-stocks hung one Johnson, a magistrate of respectable character. They have also burnt a prodigious number of houses, and turned a vast many women, formerly of affluent and easy fortunes, with their chilldren, almost naked into the woods.

Tarleton, at the house of General Richardson, exceeded his usual barbarity; for, having dined in his house, he not only burnt it afterwards, but having driven into the barns a number of cattle, hogs and poultry, he consumed them, together with the barn and the corn in it, in one general blaze. This was done because he pretended to believe that the poor old general was with the Rebel army, though had he opened his grave before the door, he might have seen the contrary. Colonel Charles Cotesworth Pinckney's family was turned out of his house.

In short, the enemy seem determined, if they can, to break every man's spirit, if they cannot ruin him. Engagements of capitulations and proclamations are no security against their oppressions and cruelties.

—Moultrie, *Memoirs*, II, 239-240.

5. Greene's Troops Are "Wretched Beyond Description"

Nathanael Greene to Joseph Reed of Pennsylvania.

Camp on the Pedee, January 9, 1781

I intended to have written you before, but I have been so employed since I left Philadelphia that I have been obliged to deny myself the pleasure of writing to my friends, to attend to the more immemdiate duties of my department. On my journey I visited the Maryland and Virginia Assemblies and laid before them the state of this army, and urged the necessity of an immediate support. They both promised to do everything in their power, but such was their poverty, even in their capitals, that they could not furnish forage for my horses. I have also written to the States of Delaware and North Carolina, neither of which have taken any measures yet for giving effectual aid to this army. I left General Gist in Maryland, and Baron Steuben in Virginia, to forward the recruits and supplies. Measures are taking in Virginia which promise us some aid, though very trifling to what they ought to give and what our state requires. All the way through the country as I passed, I found the people

engaged in matters of interest and in pursuit of pleasure, almost regardless of
their danger, public credit totally lost, and every man excusing himself from
giving the least aid to Government, from an apprehension that they would
get no return for any advance. This afforded but a dull prospect, nor has it
mended since my arrival.

I overtook the army at Charlotte, to which place General Gates had advanced. The appearance of the troops was wretched beyond description, and
their distress, on account of provisions, was little less than their sufferings for
want of clothing and other necessaries. General Gates had lost the confidence
of the officers, and the troops all their discipline, and [they have been] so
addicted to plundering that they were a terror to the inhabitants. The general
and I met upon very good terms, and parted so. The old gentleman was in
great distress, having but just heard of the death of his son before my
arrival. . . .

The wants of this army are so numerous and various that the shortest way
of telling you is to inform you that we have nothing, as General du Portail
can inform you from his own observation. The great departments of the army
had nobody at the head of them fit to provide in a country like this for a sergeant's party. I have got Colonel Carrington to accept of the Quartermaster-
General's department, and am in hopes of getting a good man at the head of
the commissaries, without which I foresee we must starve. I am endeavouring
to bring everything into order and perfect our arrangements as much as possible, but it is all an up-hill business.

The loss of our army in Charleston and the defeat of General Gates has
been the cause of keeping such vast shoals of militia on foot, who, like the
locusts of Egypt, have eaten up everything, and the expense has beeen so enormous that it has ruined the currency of the State. It is my opinion there is
no one thing upon the Continent that wants regulating so much as the right
which the States exercise of keeping what militia on foot they please at the
Continental expense. I am persuaded North Carolina has militia enough to
swallow up all the revenues of America, especially under their imperfect
arrangements, where every man draws and wastes as much as he pleases.

The country is so extensive and the powers of government so weak that
everybody does as he pleases. The inhabitants are much divided in their political sentiments, and the Whigs and Tories pursue each other with little less
than savage fury. The back-country people are bold and daring in their make,
but the people upon the sea-shore are sickly and but indifferent militia. The
ruin of the State is inevitable if there are such large bodies of militia kept on
foot. No army can subsist in the country long if the ravages continue. Indeed, unless this army is better supported than I see any prospect of, the country is lost beyond redemption, for it is impossible for the people to struggle
much longer under their present difficulties. There appears a foolish pride in
the representation of things from this quarter; the strength and resources of the
country are far overrated, and those who are engaged in this business, to indulge their pride, will sacrifice their country. The inhabitants are beginning
to move off in great bodies, and unless a firmer barrier can be formed, this
quarter will be all depopulated.

We are living upon charity and subsist by daily collections. Indian meal and beef is our common diet, and not a drop of spirits have we had with us since I came to the army. An army naked and subsisted in this manner, and not more than one-third equal to the enemy in numbers, will make but a poor fight, especially as one has beeen accustomed to victory and the other to flight. It is difficult to give spirits to troops that have nothing to animate them.

I have been obliged to take an entire new position with the army. General Morgan is upon Broad River with a little flying army, and Colonel Washington since his arrival there has defeated a party of Tories, the particulars of which I beg leave to refer you to the President of Congress for. This camp I mean as a camp of repose, for the purpose of repairing our wagons, recruiting our horses and disciplining the troops. . . .

—REED, *Life and Correspondence of Reed*, II, 334-336.

II. COWPENS, THE PATRIOTS' BEST-FOUGHT BATTLE

Morgan and Greene were now 140 miles apart, the former in the western part of South Carolina, the latter operating with the guerrillas in the north-central part of the state. Cornwallis detached Tarleton to handle Morgan while he readied himself to take on Greene.

On January 16, 1781, Morgan, with 1,000 men, including reinforcements under Colonel Andrew Pickens, was informed by his scouts that Tarleton, with a mixed force of 1,100 regulars and Tories, was but a day's march away. Should Morgan retreat, he knew his militia would vanish. A withdrawal across the unfordable Broad River meant dangerous delay, as he lacked boats. Should he fight, his troops might panic again as at Camden. He decided to stand and fight.

Morgan made his stand in a level clearing known as the Cowpens, once a pasture for backwoods cattle. The Broad River cut off all retreat for his men. The night before, he went among the militia, for whom he had reserved a conspicuous role, and encouraged them, telling them that "the 'Old Wagoner' would crack his whip over Ben in the morning, as sure as he lived." He exhorted them to fire two volleys, after which they could retire. There was no sleep for Morgan that night.

Morgan acted in a very unorthodox way. In the front line he placed his raw militia. Behind them on slightly rising land were the Continentals and some seasoned Virginia militiamen under Lieutenant Colonel John Eager Howard. They were ordered to hold their ground at all cost. Farther to the rear on a low ridge, sheltered from British fire, he placed his cavalry under Lieutenant Colonel Washington.

To Tarleton Cowpens seemed a perfect setup for the standard tactics of a frontal bayonet attack, before which the militia had always run. When the British approached to within 100 yards of the Americans they were met by the first volleys. The sharpshooting militiamen heeded Morgan's exhortation, "Look for the epaulets! Pick off the epaulets!" They fired twice with lethal effect, then moved around to the American left toward the low ridge in the rear. The British line now lunged forward and attacked the second line. To

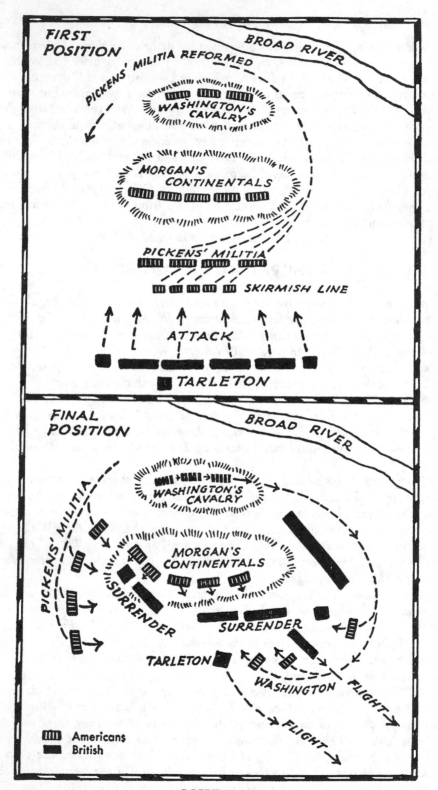

COWPENS

bring the battle to a swift ending Tarleton ordered his reserves to advance on the extreme left of his line, and the cavalry, still farther to the left, to turn the right flank of the American line. To counter this threat, Howard ordered his right flank company to change its front and form at right angles with the main body. Instead, in the confusion the men fell back. Then, Morgan, keeping his head at the most critical moment of the battle, ordered the entire line to pull back, too. Sensing victory, Tarleton's men rushed forward impetuously, wildly, and in complete disorder.

Now was Morgan's great opportunity. He ordered the line to halt and face about. Howard had his men charge the enemy with bayonets, and Washington prevented Tarleton's dragoons from covering his retreat. The British surrendered en masse. Their casualties were 100 killed, 200 wounded, 600 prisoners. The Patriots lost 12 killed, 60 wounded. With a corporal's guard Tarleton escaped, but not before a colorful hand-to-hand saber encounter with Colonel Washington.

Morgan's masterly battle strategy was used by Greene at Guilford Courthouse and Eutaw Springs, but in neither case was the execution so precise nor were the results so successful. The British never forgot Cowpens. "The late affair almost broke my heart," Cornwallis confessed to Lord Rawdon. Tarleton preserved his fiery impetuosity throughout the rest of the campaign, but the ghost of Cowpens continued to haunt him on his return to England. There his most acid critic, Lieutenant Mackenzie of the 71st Regiment of Highlanders, who was wounded at Cowpens, published a series of attacks upon Tarleton's conduct of the battle. Tarleton was charged with putting his troops into battle immediately after a night march and with advancing his line before it had been properly formed. In one of his most savage letters, published in the London Morning Chronicle *on August 9, 1782, Mackenzie asserted:*

> *You got yourself and the party completely ambuscaded, completely surrounded, upon all sides, by Mr. Morgan's rifle men. What was the consequence? The two detachments of British were made prisoners after a great slaughter was made among them, your legion dragoons were so broke by galling fire of rifle shot that your charging was in vain, till prudence, on your side, with about twenty more who were well mounted, made your retreat good, by leaving the remains of the poor blended legion in the hands of Mr. Morgan, who I must say, though an enemy, showed great masterly abilities in this manoever.*
>
> *Thus fell, at one blow, all the Provincial Legion, with about* three hundred veterans!

1. Cornwallis Orders Tarleton to Push Morgan "to the Utmost"

Winnsborough, January 2, 1781

Dear Tarleton: I sent Haldane to you last night to desire you would pass Broad River with the Legion and the first battalion of the 71st as soon as possible. If Morgan is still at Williams's, or any where within your reach, I should wish you to push him to the utmost. I have not heard, except from McArthur, of his having cannon, nor would I believe it, unless he has it from very good authority. It is, however, possible, and Ninety-six is of so much consequence that no time is to be lost.

Yours sincerely,

Cornwallis

Let me know if you think that the moving the whole, or any part, of my corps can be of use.

—Tarleton, *History of Campaigns in the Southern Provinces,* p. 244.

2. Morgan Exults: "One More Fire and the Day Is Ours!"

Account of James P. Collins.

. . . About sunrise on the 17th of January, 1781, the enemy came in full view. The sight, to me at least, seemed somewhat imposing. They halted for a short time, and then advanced rapidly as if certain of victory. The militia under Pickins and Moffitt was posted on the right of the regulars some distance in advance, while Washington's cavalry was stationed in the rear. We gave the enemy one fire; when they charged us with their bayonets, we gave way and retreated for our horses. Tarleton's cavalry pursued us. "Now," thought I, "my hide is in the loft."

Just as we got to our horses, they overtook us and began to make a few hacks at some, however without doing much injury. They, in their haste, had pretty much scattered, perhaps thinking they would have another Fishing Creek frolic, but in a few moments Col. Washington's cavalry was among them like a whirlwind, and the poor fellows began to keel from their horses without being able to remount. The shock was so sudden and violent they could not stand it and immediately betook themselves to flight. There was no time to rally, and they appeared to be as hard to stop as a drove of wild Choctaw steers going to a Pennsylvania market. In a few moments the clashing of swords was out of hearing and quickly out of sight.

By this time both lines of the infantry were warmly engaged and we, being relieved from the pursuit of the enemy, began to rally and prepare to redeem our credit, when Morgan rode up in front and, waving his sword, cried out, "Form, form, my brave fellows! Give them one more fire and the day is ours. Old Morgan was never beaten."

We then advanced briskly and gained the right flank of the enemy, and they, being hard pressed in front by Howard and falling very fast, could not stand it long. They began to throw down their arms and surrender themselves prisoners of war. The whole army, except Tarleton and his horsemen, fell into the hands of Morgan, together with all the baggage. . . .

—Collins, *Autobiography of a Revolutionary Soldier,* pp. 264-265.

3. Howard's Retreating Troops Face About and Charge the Enemy

Lieutenant Colonel John Eager Howard's account.

. . . Seeing my right flank was exposed to the enemy, I attempted to change the front of Wallace's company (Virginia regulars); in doing it, some confusion ensued, and first a part, and then the whole of the company commenced a retreat. The officers along the line seeing this, and supposing that orders had been given for a retreat, faced their men about and moved off. Morgan, who had mostly been with the militia, quickly rode up to me and expressed apprehensions of the event; but I soon removed his fears by pointing to the line and observing that men were not beaten who retreated in that order. He then ordered me to keep with the men until we came to the rising ground near Washington's horse; and he rode forward to fix on the most proper place for us to halt and face about.

In a minute we had a perfect line. The enemy were now very near us. Our men commenced a very destructive fire, which they little expected, and a few rounds occasioned great disorder in their ranks. While in this confusion, I ordered a charge with the bayonet, which order was obeyed with great alacrity. As the line advanced, I observed their artillery a short distance in front and called to Captain Ewing, who was near me, to take it. Captain Anderson (now General Anderson, of Montgomery County, Maryland), hearing the order, also pushed for the same object, and both being emulous for the prize, kept pace until near the first piece, when Anderson, by placing the end of his spontoon forward into the ground, made a long leap which brought him upon the gun and gave him the honor of the prize.

. . . In the pursuit I was led towards the right, in among the 71st, who were broken into squads, and as I called to them to surrender, they laid down their arms, and the officers delivered up their swords. Captain Duncanson, of the 71st Grenadiers, gave me his sword and stood by me. Upon getting on my horse, I found him pulling at my saddle, and he nearly unhorsed me. I expressed my displeasure and asked him what he was about. The explanation was that they had orders to give no quarter, and they did not expect any; and as my men were coming up, he was afraid they would use him ill. I admitted his excuse and put him into the care of a sergeant. . . .

—LEE, *Campaign of 1781 in the Carolinas*, pp. 97n-98n.

4. "AND ALL THEIR MUSIC ARE OURS"—MORGAN SUMS UP COWPENS

General Daniel Morgan to Nathanael Greene.

Camp near Cain Creek, January 19, 1781

The troops I have the honor to command have been so fortunate as to obtain a complete victory over a detachment from the British army, commanded by Lieut. Col. Tarleton. The action happened on the 17th inst., about sunrise, at the Cowpens. It, perhaps, would be well to remark, for the honor of the American arms, that although the progress of this corps was marked with burning and devastation, and although they waged the most cruel warfare, not a man was killed, wounded or even insulted after he surrendered. Had not Britons during this contest received so many lessons of humanity, I should flatter myself that this might teach them a little. But I fear they are incorrigible.

To give you a just idea of our operations, it will be necessary to inform you that on the 14th inst., having received certain intelligence that Lord Cornwallis and Lieut. Col. Tarleton were both in motion, and that their movements clearly indicated their intentions of dislodging me, I abandoned my encampment on Grindall's Ford on the Pacolet, and on the 16th, in the evening, took possession of a post about seven miles from the Cherokee Ford on Broad River. My former position subjected me at once to the operations of Cornwallis and Tarleton, and in case of a defeat, my retreat might easily have been cut off. My situation at the Cowpens enabled me to improve any advantages I might gain, and to provide better for my own security should I be unfortunate. These reasons induced me to take this post, at the risk of its wearing the face of a retreat.

I received regular intelligence of the enemy's movements from the time they were first in motion. On the evening of the 16th inst., they took possession of the ground I had removed from in the morning, distant from the scene of action about twelve miles. An hour before daylight one of my scouts returned and informed me that Lieut. Col. Tarleton had advanced within five miles of our camp. On this information, I hastened to form as good a disposition as circumstances would admit, and from the alacrity of the troops we were soon prepared to receive him.

The light infantry, commanded by Lieut. Col. Howard, and the Virginia militia, under the command of Maj. Triplett, were formed on a rising ground and extended a line in front. The third regiment of dragoons, under Lieut. Col. Washington, were posted at such a distance in their rear as not to be subjected to the line of fire directed at them, and to be so near as to be able to charge the enemy should they be broken. The volunteers of North Carolina, South Carolina and Georgia, under the command of the brave and valuable Col. Pickens, were situated to guard the flanks. Maj. McDowell, of the North Carolina volunteers, was posted on the right flank in front of the line, one hundred and fifty yards; and Maj. Cunningham, of the Georgia volunteers, on the left, at the same distance in front. Cols. Brannon and Thomas, of the South Carolinians, were posted in the right of Maj. McDowell, and Cols. Hays and McCall, of the same corps, on the left of Maj. Cunningham. Capts. Tate and Buchanan, with the Augusta riflemen, to support the right of the line.

The enemy drew up in single line of battle, four hundred yards in front of our advanced corps. The first battalion of the 71st Regiment was opposed to our right, the 7th Regiment to our left, the infantry of the Legion to our centre, the light companies on their flanks. In front moved two pieces of artillery. Lieut. Col. Tarleton, with his cavalry, was posted in the rear of his line.

The disposition of battle being thus formed, small parties of riflemen were detached to skirmish with the enemy, upon which their whole line moved on with the greatest impetuosity, shouting as they advanced. McDowell and Cunningham gave them a heavy and galling fire and retreated to the regiments intended for their support. The whole of Col. Pickens's command then kept up a fire by regiments, retreating agreeably to their orders. When the enemy advanced to our line, they received a well-directed and incessant fire. But their numbers being superior to ours, they gained our flanks, which obliged us to change our position. We retired in good order about fifty paces, formed, advanced on the enemy and gave them a fortunate volley, which threw them into disorder. Lieut. Col. Howard, observing this, gave orders for the line to charge bayonets, which was done with such address that they fled with the utmost precipitation, leaving their fieldpieces in our possession. We pushed our advantage so effectually that they never had an opportunity of rallying, had their intentions been ever so good.

Lieut. Col. Washington, having been informed that Tarleton was cutting down our riflemen on the left, pushed forward and charged them with such firmness that instead of attempting to recover the fate of the day, which one would have expected from an officer of his splendid character, [they] broke and fled.

The enemy's whole force were now bent solely in providing for their safety in flight—the list of their killed, wounded and prisoners will inform you with what effect. Tarleton, with the small remains of his cavalry and a few scattering infantry he had mounted on his wagon-horses, made their escape. He was pursued twenty-four miles, but, owing to our having taken a wrong trail at first, we never could overtake him.

As I was obliged to move off of the field of action in the morning to secure the prisoners, I cannot be so accurate as to the killed and wounded of the enemy as I could wish. From the reports of an officer whom I sent to view the ground, there were one hundred non-commissioned officers and privates and ten commissioned officers killed and two hundred rank and file wounded. We have now in our possession five hundred and two non-commissioned officers and privates prisoners, independent of the wounded, and the militia are taking up stragglers continually. Twenty-nine commissioned officers have fell into our hands.* Their rank, etc., you will see by an enclosed list. The officers I have paroled; the privates I am conveying by the safest route to Salisbury.

Two standards, two fieldpieces, thirty-five wagons, a travelling forge and all their music are ours. Their baggage, which was immense, they have in a great measure destroyed.

Our loss is inconsiderable, which the enclosed return will evince. I have not been able to ascertain Col. Pickens' loss, but know it to be very small.

From our force being composed of such a variety of corps, a wrong judgment may be formed of our numbers. We fought only eight hundred men, two-thirds of which were militia. The British, with their baggage-guard, were not less than one thousand one hundred and fifty, and these veteran troops. Their own officers confess that they fought one thousand and thirty-seven.

Such was the inferiority of our numbers that our success must be attributed to the justice of our cause and the bravery of our troops. My wishes would induce me to mention the name of every sentinel in the corps I have the honor to command. In justice to the bravery and good conduct of the officers, I have taken the liberty to enclose you a list of their names, from a conviction that you will be pleased to introduce such characters to the world. . . .

—GRAHAM, *Life of Morgan*, pp. 467-470.

---

* In a postscript Morgan lists the American losses at 12 killed, 60 wounded; the British killed—10 commissioned officers and over a hundred enlisted men, with 200 British wounded, and 27 officers and more than 500 enlisted men prisoners. In addition to the booty listed in the letter, he adds 800 stand of arms and over 100 dragoon horses.

III. THE HUNTER BECOMES THE HUNTED: GUILFORD COURTHOUSE

Cornwallis now prepared to avenge Cowpens. Having lost his light troops in that battle, he transformed his whole force into light troops by destroying superfluous baggage, most wagons, all his tents, all provisions except what his men could carry, and even had his rum casks stove in. To his soldiers this was the cruelest blow of all. He was now stripped down for sprinting.

Greene, outnumbered three to two, kept ahead of his pursuer, conducting a masterly retreat. He crossed the Catawba, the Yadkin, the Deep River and finally the Dan. As Alexander Hamilton said: "To have effected a retreat in the face of so ardent a pursuit, through so great an extent of country, through a country offering every obstacle, affording scarcely any resource; with troops destitute of every thing, who a great part of the way left the vestiges of their march in their own blood—to have done all this, I say, without loss of any kind, may, without exaggeration, be denominated a masterpiece of military skill and exertion."

In crossing the Dan, Greene took with him all the boats to the farther shore. Cornwallis had lost the race. Having rashly destroyed his supplies, the British commander was now forced to get closer to his supply base. He reversed his course and returned to Hillsboro. Greene, on receiving small reinforcements from Virginia, recrossed the Dan, took post in the vicinity of the British army and harassed their communication with the country. For three weeks Greene eluded the action that Cornwallis sought, and the massacre by Pickens' men of a body of 400 Tories under Colonel John Pyle on their way to the British army ended all hope of Loyalist reinforcements for Cornwallis. The Tories, now indifferent or terror-stricken, were a bitter disappointment to Cornwallis.

When Greene outnumbered the enemy he prepared to give battle. On March 14, 1781, he went into camp near Guilford Courthouse. He planned the battle after the pattern of Cowpens. He put the raw North Carolina militia in the center, and followed Morgan's advice to put picked troops in their rear "to shoot down the first man that runs." The first line was reinforced by a second, 300 yards back, and that in turn by a last line along the courthouse hill back another 550 yards. Greene gave the militia the privilege of withdrawing after firing two rounds. They fired their two volleys and rushed pell-mell to the rear. Still Greene might have destroyed the British had he been willing to throw his cavalry upon the disordered ranks of the enemy, but he was reluctant to risk his whole army on the fate of this attack. Instead, he withdrew after Cornwallis, in a desperate expedient, opened fire with grapeshot which killed both British and Americans. Cornwallis kept the field but he lost one fourth of his army, along with some of his finest officers. In his dispatches home he claimed the victory, but, as Charles James Fox put it, "Another such victory would destroy the British army."

Now the two commanders faced major decisions. Should each go after the other for a final showdown? Cornwallis felt he could not risk a stand in the interior any longer, and three days later pulled up stakes for Wilmington

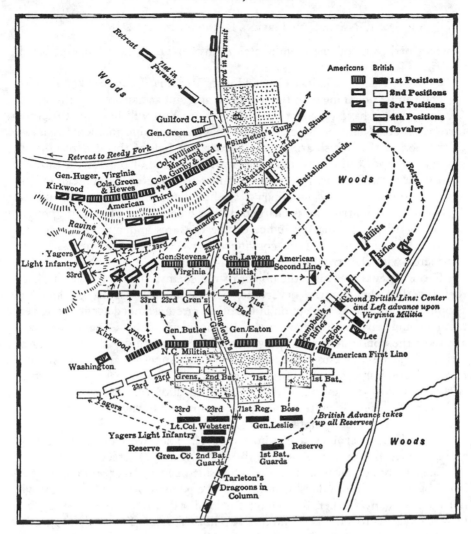

GUILFORD COURTHOUSE

on the coast. Greene might have pursued him, but he prudently recognized that Virginia could look to Washington for military assistance, and therefore made the crucial decision to move southward and reconquer South Carolina and Georgia. Hamilton compared that decision to "Scipio leaving Hannibal in Italy, to overcome him at Carthage!" Cornwallis felt that it would be unwise to pursue him. Writing to Clinton on April 23, 1781, he confessed: "My present undertaking sits heavy on my mind. I have experienced the distresses and dangers of marching some hundreds of miles, in a country chiefly hostile, without one active or useful friend; without intelligence, and without communication with any part of the country." Virginia, and a chance to recoup some of his reverses, beckoned, and he quit the soil of the Carolinas for the last time.

1. NATHANAEL GREENE RETREATS TO THE DAN

Lewis Morris, Jr., of the Continental Army to his father, General Lewis Morris.

Halifax Court House, Virginia, February 19, 1781

You can be no stranger to the weakness and embarrassments of this army. My letters must have long since informed you. You will hear of Tarleton's fortunate defeat, and perhaps conclude in your sanguine moments that the destruction of the British army must follow; but before this can reach you, you will hear of Lord Cornwallis' rapid movement and of our retreat through North Carolina. This will be very alarming to those at a distance, and no doubt censured as a very unmilitary step; but the man who is to defend the liberties of his country, and is charged with the command of an army, ought not to regard the popular prejudice or the censures and opinion of the ignorant and disappointed. I am convinced it was dictated by necessity and conducted with the strictest military propriety.

The army was evidently the object of the enemy, and while we can keep that together the country never can be conquered—disperse it, and the people are subjugated. An action in Carolina, circumstanced as we were, certainly would have involved us in this predicament. The General was well aware of the consequences—to prevent which he was under the necessity of retiring—and he was closely pressed by a much superior army and incumbered with an immense deal of baggage and stores. The retreat was performed without any loss—not even a broken waggon to show that we were hurried—and, what makes it the more brilliant, the enemy had burned all their baggage and pursued us perfectly light.

The militia in Carolina gave us no assistance. They were more intent upon saving their property by flight than by embodying to protect it.

The enemy are encamped on the other side of Dan River and are collecting provisions for a ten days' march. It is the general opinion that they will not pursue us any farther, but file off for Hallifax and Newbern in Carolina. If so we shall recross the Dan and press upon their rear. The army has recovered from its fatigue, and the militia of Virginia are turning out in great numbers. We shall move as light as they are, and may engage them partially without hazarding a general action. We have a superior body of cavalry, and the militia may go on without any apprehension, and if we can but turn the tide against them I am confident a very considerable part of the soldiers will desert.

—MORRIS, "Letters," *N. Y. Hist. Soc. Coll.*, VIII, 480-481.

2. "THE BATTLE WAS LONG, OBSTINATE AND BLOODY"

Nathanael Greene to President Joseph Reed of Pennsylvania.

Camp near the Iron Works, March 18, 1781

. . . Our force was so small and Lord Cornwallis's movements were so rapid that we got no reinforcements of militia, and therefore were obliged to retire out of the State, upon which the spirits of the people sunk, and almost all classes of the inhabitants gave themselves up for lost. They would not believe themselves in danger until they found ruin at their doors. The foolish prejudice of the formidableness of the militia being a sufficient barrier against any attempts of the enemy prevented the Legislature from making any exertions equal to their critical and dangerous situation. Experience has convinced them of their false security.

It is astonishing to me how these people could place such a confidence in a militia scattered over the face of the whole earth, and generally destitute of everything necessary to their own defence. The militia in the back country are formidable, the others are not, and all are very ungovernable and difficult to keep together. As they have generally come out, twenty thousand might be in motion, and not five hundred in the field.

After crossing the Dan and collecting a few Virginia militia, finding the enemy had erected their standard at Hillsborough and the people began to flock to it from all quarters, either for protection or to engage in their service, I determined to recross at all hazards, and it was very fortunate that I did, otherwise Lord Cornwallis would have got several thousand recruits. Seven companies were enlisted in one day. Our situation was desperate at the time we recrossed the Dan; our numbers were much inferior to the enemy, and we were without ammunition, provisions or stores of any kind, the whole having retired over the Stanton River. However, I thought it was best to put on a good face and make the most of appearances. Lieutenant Colonel Lee's falling in with the Tories upon the Haw almost put a total stop to their recruiting service.

Our numbers were, doubtless, greatly magnified, and pushing on boldly towards Hillsborough led Lord Cornwallis into a belief that I meant to attack him wherever I could find him. The case was widely different. It was certain I could not fight him in a general action without almost certain ruin. To skirmish with him was my only chance. Those happened daily, and the enemy suffered considerably; but our militia coming out principally upon the footing of volunteers, they fell off daily after every skirmish and went home to tell the news. In this situation, with an inferior force, I kept constantly in the neighbourhood of Lord Cornwallis until the 6th, when he made a rapid push at our Light Infantry, commanded by Colonel Williams, who very judiciously avoided the blow. This manoeuvre of the enemy obliged me to change my position. Indeed, I rarely ever lay more than two days in a place. The country, being much of a wilderness, obliged the enemy to guard carefully against a surprise and rendered it difficult to surprise us. We had few wagons with us— no baggage, and only tents enough to secure our arms in case of a wasting rain.

Here has been the field for the exercise of genius and an opportunity to practise all the great and little arts of war. Fortunately, we have blundered through without meeting with any capital misfortune. On the 11th of this month I formed a junction, at the High Rock Ford, with a considerable body of Virginia and North Carolina militia, and with a Virginia regiment of eighteen months' men. Our force being now much more considerable than it had been and upon a more permanent footing, I took the determination of

giving the enemy battle without loss of time and made the necessary dispositions accordingly

The battle was fought at or near Guilford Court-House, the very place
from whence we began our retreat after the Light Infantry joined the army
from the Pedee. The battle was long, obstinate and bloody. We were obliged
to give up the ground and lost our artillery, but the enemy have been so
soundly beaten that they dare not move towards us since the action, notwithstanding we lay within ten miles of him for two days. Except the ground and
the artillery, they have gained no advantage. On the contrary, they are little
short of being ruined. The enemy's loss in killed and wounded cannot be less
than between six and seven hundred, perhaps more.

Victory was long doubtful, and had the North Carolina militia done their
duty, it was certain. They had the most advantageous position I ever saw, and
left it without making scarcely the shadow of opposition. Their general and
field officers exerted themselves, but the men would not stand. Many threw
away their arms and fled with the utmost precipitation, even before a gun was
fired at them. The Virginia militia behaved nobly and annoyed the enemy
greatly. The horse, at different times in the course of the day, performed
wonders. Indeed, the horse is our great safeguard, and without them the
militia could not keep the field in this country. . . . Never did an army labour
under so many disadvantages as this; but the fortitude and patience of the
officers and soldiery rise superior to all difficulties. We have little to eat, less
to drink, and lodge in the woods in the midst of smoke. Indeed, our fatigue
is excessive. I was so much overcome night before last that I fainted.

Our army is in good spirits, but the militia are leaving us in great numbers
to return home to kiss their wives and sweethearts.

I have never felt an easy moment since the enemy crossed the Catawba
until since the defeat of the 15th, but now I am perfectly easy, being persuaded it is out of the enemy's power to do us any great injury. Indeed, I
think they will retire as soon as they can get off their wounded. My love to
your family and all friends. . . .

—REED, *Life and Correspondence of Reed*, II, 348-351.

3. "COME ON, BRAVE FUZILEERS!"—WEBSTER RALLIES THE BRITISH

[1809]

Journal of Sergeant R. Lamb of the Royal Welsh Fusiliers.

. . . After the brigade formed across the open ground, the colonel rode
on to the front and gave the word, "*Charge!*" Instantly the movement was
made, in excellent order, in a smart run, with arms charged. When arrived
within forty yards of the enemy's line, it was perceived that their whole force
had their arms presented and resting on a rail fence, the common partitions in
America. They were taking aim with the nicest precision. . . . At this awful
period a general pause took place; both parties surveyed each other for the
moment with the most anxious suspense. . . . Colonel Webster rode forward
in the front of the 23d Regiment and said with more than even his usual
commanding voice (which was well known to his brigade), "Come on, my
brave Fuzileers!" This operated like an inspiring voice; they rushed forward

amidst the enemy's fire; dreadful was the havoc on both sides. At last the Americans gave way, and the brigade advanced to the attack of their second line. Here the conflict became still more fierce. . . .

I saw Lord Cornwallis riding across the clear ground. His Lordship was mounted on a dragoon's horse (his own having been shot); the saddle-bags were under the creature's belly, which much retarded his progress, owing to the vast quantity of underwood that was spread over the ground; His Lordship was evidently unconscious of his danger. I immediately laid hold of the bridle of his horse and turned his head. I then mentioned to him that if His Lordship had pursued the same direction, he would have been surrounded by the enemy and, perhaps, cut to pieces or captured. I continued to run along side of the horse, keeping the bridle in my hand, until His Lordship gained the 23d Regiment, which was at that time drawn up in the skirt of the woods.

—LAMB, *Journal of Occurrences*, pp. 361-362.

4. "LIGHT-HORSE HARRY" LEE ATTEMPTS TO RALLY THE FUGITIVES

Memoirs of Henry Lee.

Lieutenant Colonel Webster took his part with his usual ability, moving upon the Virginia militia, who were not so advantageously posted as their comrades of North Carolina, yet gave every indication of maintaining their ground with obstinacy. Stevens, to give efficacy to this temper, and stung with the recollection of their inglorious flight in the battle of Camden, had placed a line of sentinels in his rear with orders to shoot every man that flinched. When the enemy came within long shot, the American line, by order, began to fire. Undismayed, the British continued to advance and, having reached a proper distance, discharged their pieces and rent the air with shouts.

To our infinite distress and mortification, the North Carolina militia took to flight, a few only of Eaton's brigade excepted, who clung to the militia under Clarke, which, with the legion, manfully maintained their ground. Every effort was made by the Generals Butler and Eaton, assisted by . . . many of the officers of every grade, to stop this unaccountable panic, for not a man of the corps had been killed or even wounded. Lieutenant Colonel Lee joined in the attempt to rally the fugitives, threatening to fall upon them with his cavalry. All was vain—so thoroughly confounded were these unhappy men that, throwing away arms, knapsacks and even canteens, they rushed like a torrent headlong through the woods.

Gunby, being left free by Webster's recession, wheeled to his left upon Stuart, who was pursuing the flying Second Regiment. Here the action was well fought, each corps manfully struggling for victory, when Lieutenant Colonel Washington, who had, upon the discomfiture of the Virginia militia, placed himself upon the flank of the Continentals agreeably to the order of battle, pressed forward with his cavalry.

Stuart beginning to give ground, Washington fell upon him sword in hand, followed by Howard with fixed bayonets, now commanding the regiment in consequence of Gunby being dismounted. This combined operation was irresistible. Stuart fell by the sword of Captain Smith, of the First Regiment, . . . his battalion driven back with slaughter, its remains being saved by the British artillery, which, to stop the ardent pursuit of Washington and Howard, opened upon friends as well as foes; for Cornwallis, seeing the vigorous advance of these two officers, determined to arrest their progress, though every ball levelled at them must pass through the flying guards. Checked by this cannonade, and discovering one regiment passing from the woods on the enemy's right across the road, and another advancing in front, Howard, believing himself to be out of support, retired, followed by Washington. . . .

The night succeeding this day of blood was rainy, dark and cold; the dead unburied, the wounded unsheltered, the groans of the dying and the shrieks of the living shed a deeper shade over the gloom of nature. The victorious troops, without tents and without food, participated in sufferings which they could not believe.*

The ensuing morning was spent in performing the last offices to the dead and in providing comfort for the wounded. In executing these sad duties, the British general regarded with equal attention friends and foes. As soon as this service was over Lord Cornwallis put his army in motion for New Garden, where his rear guard, with his baggage, met him. All his wounded incapable of moving (about seventy in number) he left to the humanity of General Greene.

—LEE, Memoirs, I, 343-359.

5. THE VIRGINIA MILITIA RAN "LIKE A FLOCK OF SHEEP"

Major St. George Tucker of the Virginia militia to his wife.

Laura Town, March 18, 1781

When the cannonade ceased, orders were given for Holcombe's regiment and the regiment on the right of him to advance and annoy the enemy's left flank. While we were advancing to execute this order, the British had advanced, and, having turned the flank of Col. Mumford's regiment—in which Skipwith commanded as major, we discovered them in our rear. This threw the militia into such confusion that, without attending in the least to their officers who endeavored to halt them and make them face about and engage the enemy, Holcombe's regiment and ours instantly broke off without firing a single gun and dispersed like a flock of sheep frightened by dogs. With infinite labor Beverley and myself rallied about sixty or seventy of our men and brought them to the charge. Holcombe was not so successful. He could not rally a man though assisted by John Woodson, who acted very gallantly. With the few men which we had collected we at several times sustained an irregular kind of skirmishing with the British, and were once successful enough to drive a party for a very small distance. On the ground we passed over I think I saw about eight or ten men killed and wounded. During the battle I was forced to ride over a British officer lying at the root of a tree. One of our soldiers gave him a dram as he was expiring and bade him die like a

---

* Having no tents, and the houses being few, many of both armies were necessarily exposed to the deluge of rain, which fell during the night; and it was said that not less than fifty died before morning.

brave man. How different this conduct from that of the barbarians he had commanded! . . .

The Virginia militia had the honor to receive Gen. Greene's thanks for their conduct. Some were undoubtedly entitled to them, while others ought to blush that they were undeservedly included in the number of those who were supposed to have behaved well. . . . I believe the rest of the Virginia militia behaved better than Holcombe's regiment and ours. The surprise at finding the enemy in their rear I believe contributed to the disgraceful manner in which they fled at first. But it is not a little to the honor of those who rallied that they fired away fifteen or eighteen rounds—and some twenty rounds—a man, after being put into such disorder. Such instances of the militia rallying and fighting well are not very common, I am told. Perhaps it is more honorable than making a good stand at first, and then quitting the field in disorder. . . .

> —TUCKER, "The Southern Campaign," *Magazine of American History*, VII, 40-42.

6. "I AM DETERMINED TO CARRY THE WAR INTO SOUTH CAROLINA"

Nathanael Greene to George Washington.

Head-quarters at Colonel Ramsay's, on Deep River, March 29, 1781

The regular troops will be late in the field in the southern States, if they are raised at all. Virginia, from the unequal operation of the law for drafting, is not likely to get many soldiers. Maryland, as late as the 13th of this month, had not got a man, nor is there a man raised in North Carolina, or the least prospect of it. In this situation, remote from reinforcements, inferior to the enemy in number, and no prospect of support, I am at a loss what is best to be done. If the enemy fall down towards Wilmington, they will be in a position where it would be impossible for us to injure them if we had a force.

In this critical and distressing situation, I am determined to carry the war immediately into South Carolina. The enemy will be obliged to follow us or give up their posts in that State. If the former takes place it will draw the war out of this State and give it an opportunity to raise its proportion of men. If they leave their posts to fall, they must lose more than they can gain here. If we continue in this State, the enemy will hold their possessions in both. All things considered, I think the movement is warranted by the soundest reasons, both political and military. The manoeuvre will be critical and dangerous, and the troops exposed to every hardship. But as I share it with them, I hope they will bear up under it with that magnanimity which has already supported them, and for which they deserve everything of their country.

I expect to be ready to march in about five days, and have written to General Sumter to collect the militia to aid the operations. I am persuaded the movement will be unexpected to the enemy, and I intend it shall be as little known as possible. Our baggage and stores not with the army, I shall order by the route of the Saura Towns and Shallow Ford to Charlotte: By having them in the upper country we shall always have a safe retreat, and from those inhabitants we may expect the greatest support. I shall take every measure to avoid a misfortune, but necessity obliges me to commit myself to chance; and I trust my friends will do justice to my reputation if any accident attends me.

—GREENE, *Life of Greene*, III, 213-214.

7. CORNWALLIS PLANS TO MAKE THE CHESAPEAKE "THE SEAT OF WAR"

Lord Cornwallis to Sir Henry Clinton.

Camp near Wilmington, April 10, 1781

The fatigue of the troops and the great number of wounded put it out of my power to pursue beyond the Reedy Fork in the afternoon of the action; and the want of provisions and all kinds of necessaries for the soldiers made it equally impossible to follow the blow next day. I, therefore, issued the inclosed Proclamation, and, having remained two days on the field of battle, marched to Bell's-Mill on Deep-River, near part of the country where the greatest number of our friends were supposed to reside. Many of the inhabitants rode into camp, shook me by the hand, said they were glad to see us and to hear that we had beat Greene, and then rode home again; for I could not get 100 men in all the Regulators' country to stay with us, even as militia.

With a third of my army sick and wounded, which I was obliged to carry in waggons or on horseback, the remainder without shoes and worn down with fatigue, I thought it was time to look for some place of rest and refitment. I, therefore, by easy marches, taking care to pass through all the settlements that had been described to me as most friendly, proceeded to Cross-Creek. On my arrival there, I found, to my great mortification and contrary to all former accounts, that it was impossible to procure any considerable quantity of provisions, and that there was not four days forage within twenty miles. The navigation of Cape Fear River, with the hopes of which I had been flattered, was totally impracticable, the distance from Wilmington by water being 150 miles, the breadth of the river seldom exceeding one hundred yards, the banks generally high, and the inhabitants on each side almost universally hostile. Under these circumstances I determined to move immediately to Wilmington. By this measure the Highlanders have not had so much time as the people of the upper country to prove the sincerity of their former professions of friendship. But, tho' appearances are rather more favourable among them, I confess they are not equal to my expectations. . . .

I am now employed in disposing of the sick and wounded, and in procuring supplies of all kinds, to put the troops into a proper state to take the field. I am, likewise, impatiently looking out for the expected reinforcement from Europe, part of which will be indispensibly necessary to enable me either to act offensively or even to maintain myself in the upper parts of the country, where alone I can hope to preserve the troops from the fatal sickness which so nearly ruined the army last autumn.

I am very anxious to receive Your Excellency's commands, being as yet totally in the dark as to the intended operations of the summer. I cannot help expressing my wishes that the Chesapeak may become the seat of war, even (if necessary) at the expence of abandoning New-York; untill Virginia is in a manner subdued, our hold of the Carolinas must be difficult, if not precarious. The rivers of Virginia are advantageous to an invading army, but North-Carolina is, of all the provinces in America, the most difficult to attack (unless material assistance could be got from the inhabitants, the contrary of which I have suffiicently experienced) on account of its great extent, of the numberless rivers and creeks, and the total want of interior navigation.

—STEVENS, ed., *Clinton-Cornwallis Controversy*, I, 395-399.

IV. THE PARTISAN ROLE IN THE RECONQUEST OF SOUTH CAROLINA

The campaign for regaining South Carolina moved quickly into high gear. In the short space of two months all the interior posts were reduced and the state in large measure brought once more under Patriot control. In that achievement no inconsiderable part was played by Francis Marion, who, in co-operation with "Light-Horse Harry" Lee, began systematically to cut Rawdon's tenuous communication line between Camden and Charleston. The task of investing Augusta and Ninety-Six was assigned to Pickens, and Greene moved directly against Camden.

This was civil war and it was ugly. Each side accused the other of carrying on inhuman warfare. Colonel John Watson of the British Army charged that Sumter's men fired upon prisoners. "The houses of desolate widows have been laid waste," he declared, and "innocent and neutral persons murdered by partisans." But he in turn defended under "the law of nations" the hanging of Patriot militiamen who had been placed on parole after the Charleston capitulation and then had taken up arms once more. The Whig case was presented by Captain Tarleton Brown of South Carolina, who recorded in his Memoirs numerous instances where the Tories killed aged and harmless persons in cold blood.

Both sides were equally guilty. As Andrew Jackson, a youthful participant, later put it, "In the long run, I am afraid the Whigs did not lose many points in the game of hanging, shooting and flogging. They had great provocation, but upon calm reflection I feel bound to say that they took full advantage of it."

But the main objective of each side was to kill fighting men. In this kind of merciless guerrilla warfare Jackson had his first brush with the enemy. He reminisced about his role in the Revolution to a number of his friends. According to one account, he was, along with his brother Robert, a member of a company of some forty Whigs assembled at the Waxhaw meetinghouse. The defenders were deceived by a ruse, as the British surprised the Patriots by placing a body of Tories, wearing the dress of the country, in advance of the Redcoats. Eleven were taken prisoner, the rest scattered. Young Andrew was trapped by Tory intelligence at the home of a Patriot fighter. The dragoons smashed the furnishings to pieces. The British officer in command ordered Jackson to clean his high jackboots.

Jackson replied, "Sir, I am a prisoner of war, and claim to be treated as such."

The officer smashed his sword down on the boy's head, but Andrew broke

*the force of the blow with his left hand. He carried to his grave two wounds
—a deep gash on his head, another on his hand. He would not soon forget
the British.*

1. YOUNG ANDREW JACKSON REFUSES TO CLEAN AN OFFICER'S BOOTS

His experience as a Revolutionary soldier, as reported to Francis P. Blair.

[Spring, 1781]

I witnessed two battles, Hanging Rock and Hobkirk's Hill, but did not
participate in either. I was in one skirmish—that of Sands House—and there
they caught me, along with my brother Robert and my cousin, Tom Crawford. A lieutenant of Tarleton's Light Dragoons tried to make me clean his
boots and cut my arm with his sabre when I refused. After that they kept me
in jail at Camden about two months, starved me nearly to death and gave me
the small-pox. Finally my mother succeeded in persuading them to release
Robert and me on account of our extreme youth and illness. Then Robert
died of the small-pox and I barely escaped death. When it left me I was a
skeleton—not quite six feet long and a little over six inches thick! It took me
all the rest of that year [1781] to recover my strength and get flesh enough to
hide my bones. By that time Cornwallis had surrendered and the war was
practically over in our part of the country.

I was never regularly enlisted, being only fourteen when the war practically ended. Whenever I took the field it was with Colonel Davie, who never
put me in the ranks, but used me as a mounted orderly or messenger, for
which I was well fitted, being a good rider and knowing all the roads in that
region. The only weapons I had were a pistol that Colonel Davie gave me and
a small fowling-piece that my Uncle Crawford lent to me. This was a light
gun and would kick like sixty when loaded with a three-quarter-ounce ball or
with nine buckshot. But it was a smart little gun and would carry the ball
almost as true as a rifle fifteen or twenty rods, and threw the buckshot spite-
fully at close quarters—which was the way I used it in the defence of Captain
Sands's house, where I was captured.

I was as sorry about losing the gun there as about the loss of my own
liberty, because Uncle Crawford set great store by the gun, which he had
brought with him from the old country; and, besides, it was the finest in that
whole region. Not long afterward—while I was still in the Camden jail or
stockade—some of Colonel Davie's men under Lieutenant Curriton captured a
squad of Tories, one of whom had that gun in his possession, together with
my pistol that Colonel Davie had given to me. This Tory's name was Mul-
ford. The gun and pistol cost him his life. Davie's men regarded his possession
of them as prima facie evidence that he had been a member of the party that
captured Captain Sands's house, sacked and burned it and insulted the women-
folks of his family. He pleaded that he was not there; that he had bought the
gun and pistol from another Tory. Davie's men told him it would do him no
good to add lying to his other crimes, hanged him forthwith and afterward
restored the gun and pistol to their proper owners.

The Tories also got the horse I had when captured. He was a three-year-
old colt—fine fellow—belonging to Captain Sands himself. He was hid in the

woods when they attacked the house, but they [the Tories] found him the next morning. This colt was also retaken about six weeks afterward. The Tory who had him was not hanged, because he had been shot through the stomach before he surrendered and was already dying.

Take it altogether, I saw and heard a good deal of war in those days, but did nothing toward it myself worth mention.

—BUELL, *History of Jackson*, I, 51-53.

2. ONE OF MARION'S SWAMP FOXES

Narrative of Paul Hamilton of the South Carolina militia.

Having remained sometime with Marion, I availed myself of an opportunity that offered of returning homeward with Col. Harden, who had fled from the Parish of Prince William to Marion's camp and, assembling about 70 followers, determined to return southward and, by stirring up his friends who had submitted to the enemy, to cover that part of our country. Him I joined as a volunteer, having previously received, while with Marion, a letter from my good mother with a supply of money and clothes, most wonderfully conveyed to me through the country then overrun by the enemy. With Harden I approached Jacksonboro, and hearing that my mother was then at the plantation of my deceased Grandfather Branford, two miles off, I with leave quitted the party, galloped off to the plantation opposite (then Dupont's, now Jacob Walter's), where, finding a small canoe which I ordered a Negro man to enter, I threw thereon my arms, and on my horse swam the river.

Arriving near the house I was informed that my grandfather's widow was then in a most dreadful state with small pox, which I had not had, and that my mother had that morning gone to her house at Wiltown. . . . To avoid the infection of small pox I had remained at the fence of the plantation near the swamp, where I met the best of mothers.

What our meeting was I cannot describe. Neither had for minutes the power of utterance. At length a flood of tears on her part enabled her to break silence, when such affectionate expressions were poured out as I can never forget, nor the warmth of that maternal embrace in which I was clasped to her aching bosom, after an absence of 12 months lacking 6 days, during which she had received but one letter from me and had often heard of my having been killed. I remained with her for two hours. I then left her with her blessing on my head, and an assurance that I would shortly again see her. She presented me with some clothing which she had prepared for me; these she had tied up hastily in a pillow case, and I tucked them behind my saddle, a circumstance which had well nigh cost me my life that very night.

On regaining my party we proceeded southwardly, and at midnight encountered a body of British cavalry near Saltketcher Bridge. The onset was in our favor, but, Harden being but an indifferent commander, we were defeated and in the rout I suffered a hard pursuit, in which my pursuers were guided by the whiteness of the pillow case that contained the clothes behind me. A good horse and some presence of mind at last secured me from pursuit. Our whole party was dispersed, and about 15 severely wounded with the sabre. In two days we were again collected and retorted this defeat by surprising and making prisoners of part of this cavalry at Pocataligo, among them their Colonel Fenwicke and other officers.

This success led to the surrender of the British Fort Balfour, at the above place, under the ramparts almost of which this surprise was made. I must, as I am writing of myself, be allowed to be somewhat particular as to this little, but handsome military exploit. Colonel Harden, knowing that we had some staunch friends who had been compelled to enter and garrison the fort, thought that if he could destroy the cavalry, he might induce a surrender of the remainder of the garrison, which were militia, and perhaps one half of them friendly to the American cause; some of whom were men of considerable influence and weight. He therefore drew near the fort and with the effective force he had remaining formed an ambuscade. Twelve well-mounted young men, of whom I was one, named as Light Horsemen, were selected and ordered to decoy the cavalry out.

With this view we moved on briskly and openly toward Von Bitter's Tavern, which stood almost a quarter of a mile from the fort and in full view. While approaching we discovered that some of the enemy were at the tavern, on which we darted forward and captured as follows: Col Fenwicke, Lieut. Bond, a sergeant and 15 privates of the cavalry with Lieut. Col. Lechmere of the British militia. Lechmere was taken as he ran within 100 yards of the fort, and brought off by one of our young men named Green. Our prisoners had come out on foot to the tavern to regale themselves [and], having only their swords, made no attempt to resist. They were hurried off to the ambuscade and delivered. After which, reinforced by eight more swordsmen, we returned, 20 in number, to the tavern, drew up in the adjoining pasture, offered battle to the British cavalry whose number we had reduced now to about our standard, a part of their force having been previously detached to Charleston immediately after we had been defeated by them at Saltketchie. The cavalry made a show of advancing to the charge, but finding us firm they turned about and were insulted by us as they retired to the fort.

Col. Harden now came up with the remainder of his force. Leaving the servants and baggage just partly in view to keep up the appearance of a reserve, Major Harden, the brother of the colonel, was now sent to summon the fort to surrender with threats of an assault if refused. I accompanied the major. We were met by Major De Veaux (after Col. DeVeaux who took the Bahamas from Spain) at so short a distance from the fort that we could recognize countenances and exchanged an occasional nod with some of the garrison.

At first the answer through Major DeVeaux was a refusal from Col. Kitsall, who commanded the fort, to surrender, on which I was desired by Major Harden to communicate to his brother this answer. The colonel inquired of me if we could distinguish any of our friends in the fort. I replied that Major Harden had recognized Cols. Stafford and Davis and Mr. Thomas Hutson, with none of whom I had any acquaintance, but that I thought that I discovered some confusion and clamour in the fort. On which the colonel, his countenance brightening, formed his men in column and ordered them to prepare for immediate action.

This done, he turned to me and said, "Go to Major Harden and say to him that I allowed ten minutes to Col. Kitsall to consider of a surrender, after which, if he refuses, you are both to return immediately to me and, by God, I will be in the fort!"

The major communicated this to Major De Veaux with whom he had been chatting with great familiarity, being acquaintances and closely related by blood. The latter went in and delivered this last message to Col. Kitsall, who, having discovered a division among his militia, agreed to lay down his arms.

Thus was Fort Balfour, which had for some months completely bridled that part of the country, surrendered without a shot. The garrison consisted of 92 militia, about 25 regulars, cavalry well mounted and equipped and uniformed as Light Dragoons. In the fort we found an abundance of provisions, some muskets and a six-pound cannon, with a good supply of ammunition for it.

—HAMILTON, "Extracts from a Private Manuscript,"
Year Book of Charleston, 1898, pp. 315-320.

3. GREENE PRAISES MARION'S "COURAGE, ADDRESS AND MANAGEMENT"

Nathanael Greene to Francis Marion.

Camp before Camden, April 24, 1781

Your favour of the 21st has just come to hand. When I consider how much you have done and suffered, and under what disadvantages you have maintained your ground, I am at a loss which to admire most, your courage and fortitude or your address and management. Certain it is no man has a better claim to the public thanks or is more generally admired than you are. History affords no instance wherein an officer has kept possession of a country under so many disadvantages as you have. Surrounded on every side with a superior force, hunted from every quarter with veteran troops, you have found means to elude all their attempts, and to keep alive the expiring hopes of an oppressed militia, when all succour seemed to be cut off. To fight the enemy bravely with a prospect of victory is nothing; but to fight with intrepidity under the constant impression of a defeat, and inspire irregular troops to do it, is a talent peculiar to yourself.

Nothing will give me greater pleasure than to do justice to your merit, and I shall miss no opportunity of declaring to Congress, the Commander-in-chief of the American Army and to the world in general the great sense I have of your merit and services.

I thank you for the measures you have taken to furnish us with provisions, and for the intelligence you communicate. A field piece is coming to your assistance, which I hope will enable you and Col. Lee to get possession of the fort [Watson]. With the artillery you will receive 100 lbs. powder and 400 lbs. lead. I wish my present stock would enable me to send you a larger supply, but it will not, having sent you near half we have. I have reason to believe the enemy have evacuated their post upon the Congarees; and if there is no object very important on the other side of the river, it is my wish you should move upon this, in order to enable us to invest Camden to more advantage, the garrison of which, I have good reason to believe, is short of provisions.

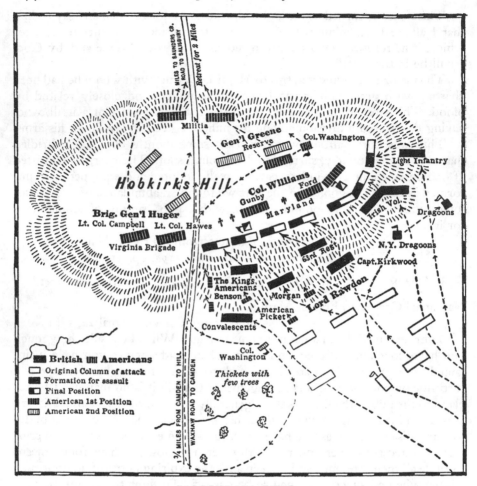

HOBKIRK'S HILL

I have this moment got intelligence that Lord Cornwallis crossed the Cape Fear River last week, in order to begin his march towards this State. I beg you to take measures to discover his route and approach. Col. Horry's attack upon a party of Watson's does him great honour.

—GIBBES, ed., *Documentary History of the Revolution*, III, 58-59.

V. HOBKIRK'S HILL, THE SECOND BATTLE OF CAMDEN

The element of surprise was lacking in Greene's advance on Camden, as Rawdon was informed of his approach. Facing a chain of strong redoubts which protected the town, Greene decided to fall back to Hobkirk's Hill, a high ridge overlooking Camden and about a mile from it. He hoped to lure the enemy out of their fortified position, and his expectations were gratified when, on the morning of April 25, Rawdon sallied from the town at the head of 900 men. Against him Greene could count on 1,400, nearly four fifths of them Continentals.

The battle plan was a modified version of Cowpens. Greene borrowed from Cornwallis' desperate tactics at Guilford Courthouse. When the enemy advanced on a narrow front, Greene had his two center regiments draw aside, uncovered his guns and opened fire with canister and grape, throwing the enemy into momentary confusion. Then the center regiments charged with the bayonet, and the flank regiments tried to effect a double envelopment, with Washington's cavalry sweeping around to get at the British rear.

Unlike Guilford Courthouse, the weak link in Greene's battle plan proved to be not the raw militia but the battle-hardened Continentals, in this case Colonel John Gunby's 1st Maryland Regiment. They paused to fire a volley instead of pushing on with the bayonet. A captain was shot. His men faltered. Confusion spread. Gunby ordered the whole regiment to retire to the foot of the hill and re-form there. The British seized on the opportunity and plunged forward. Then the 5th Maryland broke, and panic hit the 4th Virginia. Now the guns were in danger and they were saved only by the timely arrival of Washington's dragoons. But Washington, in the course of his encirclement, had cluttered up his forces with a horde of noncombatant prisoners, surgeons, commissaries, quartermasters and the like. This made it necessary for him to abandon the attack on the enemy's rear, and he got back just in time to save the artillery. Greene retreated in good order. Washington's cavalry charged the British down the hill and forced them to withdraw into town. Rawdon actually suffered slightly heavier casualties, about 270 to 234 for the Americans.

For this setback Gunby was the scapegoat. "Gunby was the sole cause of the defeat," Greene wrote Joseph Reed. "I found him much more blameable afterwards than I represented him in my public letters." But the quick thinking of Rawdon and the brilliant fighting of the Grenadier Guards had saved the day for the British. Greene took the repulse philosophically. He wrote to Luzerne, the French envoy, "We fight, get beat, rise, and fight again."

1. Defeat Is Snatched from the Jaws of Victory

Nathanael Greene to Samuel Huntington, President of Congress.

April 25, 1781

I had the honour to write to Your Excellency the 2d instant, April, to inform you that we were encamped before Camden, having found it impossible to attempt to storm the town with any hopes of success; and having no other alternative but to take such a position as should induce the enemy to sally from their works. To this end we posted ourselves on an eminence about a mile from the town, near the high road leading to Wacsaws. It was covered with woods, and flanked on the left by an impassable swamp. The ground between this place and the town is covered by a thick wood and shrubbery. In this situation we remained constantly on the watch and ready for action at a moment's warning.

On the morning of the 25th, about eleven o'clock, our advanced pickets received the first fire from the enemy and returned it warmly. The line was formed in an instant. General Huger's brigade to the right; Colonel Williams' Maryland brigade to the left; the artillery in the center; Colonel Read, with some militia, formed a kind of second line; Captain Kirkwood, with the light infantry, was posted in our front, and when the enemy advanced, he was soon engaged with them, and both he and his men behaved with a great deal of bravery; nor did the pickets under Captains Morgan and Benson act with less courage or regularity.

Observing that the enemy advanced with but few men abreast, I ordered Lieut.-Col. Ford, with the 2d Maryland Regiment, to flank them on the left, while Lieut.-Col. Campbell was to do the same on the right. Colonel Gunby, with the 1st Maryland Regiment, and Lieut.-Col. Hawes, with the 2d Virginia Regiment, received orders at the same time to descend from the eminence and attack in front; and I sent Lieut.-Col. Washington at the same time to double the right flank and attack the rear of the enemy.

The whole line was soon in action in the midst of a very smart fire, as well from our small arms as from our artillery, which, under the command of Colonel Harrison, kept playing upon the front of the enemy, who began to give way on all sides, and their left absolutely to retreat; when, unfortunately, two companies on the right of the 1st Maryland Regiment were entirely thrown into disorder; and, by another stroke of fortune, Colonel Gunby ordered the rest of the regiment, which was advancing, to take a new position towards the rear, where the two companies were rallying. This movement gave the whole regiment an idea of a retreat, which soon spread through the 2d Regiment, which retreated accordingly. They both rallied afterwards, but it was too late. The enemy had gained the eminence, silenced the artillery and obliged us to draw it off.

The 2d Virginia Regiment having descended the eminence a little, and having its flank left naked by the retreat of the Marylanders, the enemy immediately doubled upon them and attacked them both on the flank and in front. Colonel Campbell's regiment was thrown into confusion, and had retreated a little. I therefore thought it necessary for Colonel Hawes to retreat also. The troops rallied more than once; but the disorder was too general and had struck too deep for one to think of recovering the fortune of the day, which promised us at the onset the most complete victory; for Colonel Washington, on his way to double and attack in the rear, found the enemy, both horse and foot, retreating with precipitation towards the town, and made upwards of two hundred of them prisoners, together with ten or fifteen officers, before he perceived that our troops had abandoned the field of battle. The colonel, upon this occasion, and indeed his whole corps acquired no inconsiderable share of honour.

We then retreated two or three miles from the scene of action without any loss of artillery, waggons or provisions, having taken the precaution to send away our baggage at the beginning of the action. The enemy have suffered very considerably; our forces were nearly equal in number; but such were the dispositions that I had made that, if we had succeeded, the whole of the enemy's army must have fallen into our hands, as well as the town of Camden....

—TARLETON, *History of Campaigns in the Southern Provinces*, pp. 482-484.

2. "A Single Word Turned the Fate of the Day"

Samuel Mathis to General W. R. Davie.

[Camden], June 26, 1819

The British when they first attacked near the spring pressed directly forward and succeeded in turning our left. Their left had displayed towards our right and under cover of thick woods and could scarcely be seen except by our pickets until they began to rise the hill (which is about 150 or 60 yards from bottom to top). The cavalry had reached the great road and advanced in close order and slow step up the hill directly in front of our cannon which had just arrived and opened on them in the road. A well-directed fire with cannister and grape did great execution and soon cleared the road so that all their doctors were sent to take care of the wounded. Washington's cavalry coming up at this moment completed the route [*sic*] of the York Volunteers, took all the British doctors or surgeons and a great many others (alas! too many) prisoners; more than one third of Washington's men were incumbered with prisoners, who hindered their acting when necessary.

Here the battle was equal or rather in our favor, and only *one* word, a single *word*, and that only because it was spoken out of season, turned the fate of the day.

Our left was somewhat turned or yielding, then our Col. (Ford) was wounded, but the men were neither killed nor prisoners. The left of the British, at least their cavalry, were routed, many killed and many prisoners. Lord Rawdon, hearing the cannon and seeing his horse dispersed, was stunned beyond measure, . . . and, galloping up to the scene of disaster, was quickly surrounded by Washington's horse and his sword demanded. One of his aids received a severe wound from the sword of a dragoon.

Lord Rawdon is a man of uncommon address. This was a critical moment. Altho' our left was giving way, yet Gen. Huger on our right was gaining ground and was beginning to advance upon the enemy and Col. Gunby's regiment of brave soldiers, veterans of the Maryland line, had all got to their arms, were well formed and in good order, but too impatient waiting the word of command. Some of them had begun to fire in violation of orders and, seeing the British infantry coming up the hill in front of them, Col. Gunby suffered them to come up within a few paces and then ordered his men to charge without firing. Those near him, hearing the word, first rushed forward, whereby the regiment was moving forward in the form of a bow. Col. Gunby ordered a "halt" until the wings should become straight: this turned the fate of the day. Previously being ordered not to fire and now ordered to *halt*, while the British were coming up with charged bayonets, before the colonel could be understood and repeat the charge, the enemy were in among them and made them give way.

Lord Rawdon was surrounded near the head of this regiment and saw the scene and also that some of his cavalry had rallied and with infantry were coming to his relief, while he very politely bowed and seemed to acquiesce with the demand of the dragoons around him, pretended that his sword was hard to get out of the scabbard, feigned to endeavor to draw or unhook it for the surrender required, until the party that took him were attacked and had to fly.

. . . The scene was quickly changed. Washington's dragoons were now attacked by horse and foot, and the very prisoners that they had mounted behind them seized the arms of their captors and overcame them. Gen. Green now ordered a retreat and pushed on Washington's cavalry to Saunders' Creek, which lay 4 miles in the rear, to halt the troops and stop the straglers should there be any either from the militia or regulars attempting to make off. In this he succeeded, carrying off with him all the British surgeons and several officers.

As above mentioned the artillery had just come up . . . and now, seeing a general retreat of the American army, attempted to get off through the woods without going out into and along the road. They soon got . . . entangled among the trees and could not get along, but cut their horses and fled, leaving the limbers of both pieces of cannon in the woods where they were found by the British and taken.

Under these circumstances Gen. G[reene] galloped up to Capt. John Smith and ordered him to fall into the rear and save the cannon. Smith instantly came and found the artillery men hauling off the pieces with the dragropes; he and his men laid hold and off they went in a trot, but had not gone far until he discovered that the British cavalry were in pursuit. He formed his men across the road, gave them a full fire at a short distance and fled with the guns as before. This volley checked the horses and threw many of the riders; but they after some time remounted and pushed on again. Smith formed his men, gave them another fire with the same effect, and proceeded as before. This he repeated several times until they had got two or three miles from the field of action. Here one of Smith's men fired or his gun went off by accident before the word was given, which produced a scattering fire, on which the cavalry rushed in among them and cut them all to pieces. They fought like bull-dogs and were all killed or taken. This took up some time, during which the artillery escaped.

—MATHIS, Letter, *American Historical Record*, II, 106-109.

VI. THE FALL OF THE BRITISH OUTPOSTS

Even as the Patriots were repulsed at Hobkirk's Hill the British outposts between Camden and Charleston were beginning to fall. On April 22 Lee and Marion invested Fort Watson near Vance's Ferry in the Sumter District. Since the attackers had neither artillery nor entrenching tools, they worked out an ingenious device of building a wooden tower higher than the walls of the fort. The idea is credited to Colonel Hezekiah Maham of South Carolina and was thereafter known as a "Maham tower." From atop the tower riflemen poured a lethal barrage into the stockade. Meanwhile the troops breached the wall and compelled the garrison to surrender.

A different device was used on May 12 in the siege of Fort Motte, located on the south bank of the Congaree some 33 miles below Columbia. Marion had flaming arrows shot into the main structure of the fort, setting it afire. The day before, Orangeburg fell to Sumter, and Augusta was taken by Lee and Pickens on May 22. Again a Maham tower contributed to the downfall of that post. On the same day Greene began the siege of Ninety-Six, actually 96 miles from the old frontier fort of Prince George on the Keowee River. Its commander was the New York Tory, Lieutenant Colonel John Harris Cruger. Here Kosciusko's parallel approaches, the Maham tower some 40 feet in height, and fire arrows seemed to spell inevitable doom for the stubborn defenders, until Rawdon, who had marched from Charleston in relief, saved the day. The incorrigible and truculent Sumter violated Greene's orders to keep in Rawdon's front and failed to intercept the British commander. As Morgan had discovered earlier, Sumter was now a liability. Again a setback for Greene, and again a scapegoat. But soon after, Georgetown fell to Marion, and on July 3 Ninety-Six was abandoned by the British.

Writing toward the end of July from a camp at "High Hills Santee," Lewis Morris, Jr., reported the evacuation by Cruger of Ninety-Six, the junction of his Tories with Lord Rawdon at Orangeburg, and Rawdon's own return to Charleston, thoroughly worn out from his exertions. "Light-Horse Harry" Lee took prisoners as close as six miles from Charleston, causing panic in that town. "Let me observe," Morris added, "that we are now in full possession of all the upper country in this state as well as Georgia, and that, though the enemy have lately received a reinforcement of at least two thousand men, they have been obliged to act upon the defensive by a little army, scarcely one third of their number."

1. Fort Motte: A Patriot Lady Aids the Burning of Her House

Memoirs of "Light-Horse Harry" Lee.

[*May 6-11, 1781*]. This post [Fort Motte] was the principal depot of the convoys from Charleston to Cambden, and sometimes of those destined for Fort Granby and Ninety-Six. A large new mansion house, belonging to Mrs. Motte, situated on a high and commanding hill, had been selected for this establishment. It was surrounded with a deep trench, along the interior margin of which was raised a strong and lofty parapet. To this post had been regularly assigned an adequate garrison of about one hundred and fifty men, which was now accidentally increased by a small detachment of dragoons. . . . Captain M'Pherson commanded, an officer highly and deservedly respected.

Opposite to Fort Motte, to the north, stood another hill, where Mrs. Motte, having been dismissed from her mansion, resided in the old farmhouse. On this height Lieut. Col. Lee with his corps took post, while Brigadier Marion occupied the eastern declivity of the ridge on which the fort stood.

Very soon the fort was completely invested; and the six-pounder was mounted on a battery erected in Marion's quarter for the purpose of raking the northern face of the enemy's parapet, against which Lee was preparing to advance. M'Pherson was unprovided with artillery and depended for safety upon timely relief, not doubting its arrival before the assailant could push his preparations to maturity.

. . . The works advanced with rapidity. Such was their forwardness on the 10th that it was determined to summon the commandant.

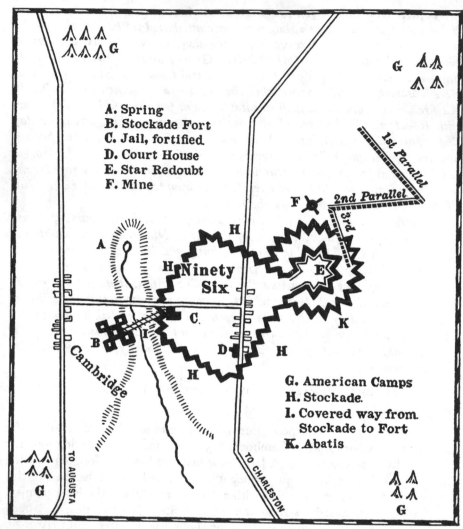

A. Spring
B. Stockade Fort
C. Jail, fortified
D. Court House
E. Star Redoubt
F. Mine

G. American Camps
H. Stockade
I. Covered way from Stockade to Fort
K. Abatis

NINETY-SIX

A flag was accordingly despatched to Captain M'Pherson, stating to him with truth our relative situation. . . . The captain replied that, disregarding consequences, he should continue to resist to the last moment in his power. The retreat of Rawdon was known in the evening to the besiegers; and in the course of the night a courier arrived from General Greene confirming that event, urging redoubled activity. . . .

The large mansion in the centre of the encircling trench left but a few yards of the ground within the enemy's works uncovered: burning the house must force their surrender.

. . . Orders were instantly issued to prepare bows and arrows, with missive combustible matter. This measure was reluctantly adopted, for the destruction of private property was repugnant to the principles which swayed the two commandants.

. . . Taking the first opportunity which offered the next morning, Lieut. Col. Lee imparted to Mrs. Motte the intended measure, lamenting the sad necessity and assuring her of the deep regret which the unavoidable act excited in his and every breast.

With the smile of complacency this exemplary lady listened to the embarrassed officer and gave instant relief to his agitated feelings by declaring that she was gratified with the opportunity of contributing to the good of her country. . . . Shortly after, seeing accidentally the bows and arrows which had been prepared, she sent for the lieutenant colonel, and presenting him with a bow and its apparatus imported from India, she requested his substitution of these, as probably better adapted for the object than those we had provided. . . .

It was now about noon, and the rays of the scorching sun had prepared the shingle roof for the projected conflagration. . . . The first arrow struck and communicated its fire; a second was shot at another quarter of the roof, and a third at a third quarter; this last also took effect, and, like the first, soon kindled a blaze. M'Pherson ordered a party to repair to the loft of the house and by knocking off the shingles to stop the flames. This was soon perceived, and Captain Finley was directed to open his battery, raking the loft from end to end.

The fire of our six-pounder, posted close to one of the gable ends of the house, soon drove the soldiers down; and no other effort to stop the flames being practicable, M'Pherson hung out the white flag.

. . . Powerfully as the present occasion called for punishment, and rightfully as it might have been inflicted, not a drop of blood was shed, nor any part of the enemy's baggage taken. M'Pherson and his officers accompanied their captors to Mrs. Motte's and partook with them in a sumptuous dinner, soothing in the sweets of social intercourse the ire which the preceding conflict had engendered.

–LEE, *Memoirs*, II, 73-80.

2. RAWDON TO THE RESCUE—THE TORY DEFENSE OF NINETY-SIX

Narrative of Roderick Mackenzie of the British Army.

When the advanced corps of the enemy appeared, upon the 21st of May, the works were far from being finished; even the platforms in the Star were not in a condition to receive guns.

The whole American army, amounting to upwards of four thousand men, with a respectable park of field artillery, encamped in a wood within cannon shot of the village. Flushed with success from the reduction of a number of the British posts, they, with a contemptuousness to the garrison of Ninety Six to this day unexplained, in the night between the 21st and 22d threw up two works, at no greater distance than seventy paces from the Star. General Greene did not even condescend to summon the place. Whether he meant to assault and reduce it by a *coup de main*, or designed these works for places of arms, is another point as yet undetermined. It can hardly be conceived that his engineer, Koziusco, a foreign adventurer whom *they* created a Count of Poland, would break ground and begin a sap within so small a distance of a regular fortification, if he had intended its reduction by the common mode of approaches.

By eleven o'clock in the morning of the 22d of May, the platform in the salient angle of the Star nearest to the Americans was completed and mounted with guns to fire *en barbet*. These, with incessant platoons of musquetry, played on the works constructed by the enemy the preceding night, under cover of which thirty men, marching in Indian-file, entered them and put every man they could reach to the bayonet. This party was immediately followed by another of the loyal militia, who, in an instant, levelled those works and loaded a number of Negroes with the entrenching tools of the Americans. Though General Greene put his whole army in motion to support the advanced corps, they were intirely routed before he could effect his design. The handful of brave men that performed this service retired into the Star without any loss, excepting that of the officer who led them, Lieutenant Roney. He was mortally wounded, and died the following night, much esteemed and justly lamented.

From such a check the American commander began to entertain a respectable idea of the troops with whom he had to contend. On the night of the 23d the Americans again broke ground, but at the distance of four hundred paces from the Star and behind a ravine. They here began two saps, erected block batteries to cover them, and appointed two brigades for their support. Sorties by small parties were made during the night to interrupt the enemy and retard their approaches. These were occasionally continued for the rest of the siege, notwithstanding which, by incessant labour and the numbers employed, the besiegers had completed a second parallel by the 3d of June, when, for the first time, they beat the chamade and their adjutant general advanced with a flag of truce, desiring to speak to the commandant.

Lieutenant Stelle, the officer on duty who met him, observed that it was unusual for commanding officers to receive and answer flags of truce in person, but that if he had any thing to communicate to Lieutenant Colonel Cruger, it should be forwarded. The American officer then produced a paper, signed by himself, setting forth, with the highest eulogiums, the invincible gallantry of their troops; enumerating their recent conquests "upon the Congaree, the Wateree and the Santee"; declaring that the garrison had every thing to hope from their generosity, and to fear from their resentment; making the commandant *personally* responsible for a fruitless resistance, and demanding an immediate and unconditional surrender to the army of the United States of America. He farther protested that this summons should not be repeated, nor any flag of truce hereafter received, without it conveyed the preliminary proposals for a capitulation.

The commandant directed an officer to inform the person who brought this extraordinary paper that Ninety Six was committed to his charge, and that both duty and inclination pointed to the propriety of defending it to the last extremity. He added that the promises and threats of General Greene were alike indifferent to him.

The truce therefore ceased; the enemy immediately opened four batteries, commenced a heavy cross fire which enfiladed some of the works, and continued this cannonade at intervals for several days, at the same time pushing a sap against the Star and advancing batteries. One of these constructed of fascines and gabions, at no greater distance than thirty-five paces from the abbatis, was elevated forty feet from the earth; upon it a number of riflemen were stationed, who, as they overlooked the British works, did great execution. The garrison crowned their parapet with sand-bags, leaving apertures through which the loyal militia fired their rifles with good effect. African arrows were thrown by the besiegers on the roofs of the British barracks to set them on fire, but this design was immediately counteracted by Lieut. Col. Cruger, who directed all the buildings to be unroofed, an order which, though it exposed both officers and men to the bad effects of the night air, so pernicious in this climate, was obeyed with an alacrity that nothing but their confidence in him could inspire.

With the intention to burn the rifle battery of the assailants, attempts were made to heat shot, but these were frustrated for want of furnaces. The besieged therefore in the Star being no longer able to continue with the cannon on the platforms in the day time, they were dismounted and used only in the night.

On the 8th of June, the garrison had the mortification to see that of Augusta marched by them prisoners of war. Though the gallantry displayed by Lieutenant Colonel Brown in its defence would have excited admiration in a generous foe, Colonel Lee, by whom they were taken, enjoyed the gratification of a little mind in exhibiting them before Ninety Six, with a British standard reversed, drums beating and fifes playing, to ridicule their situation. This pitiful recourse had an effect quite contrary to that which it was intended to produce. The soldiers were easily convinced by their officers that death was preferable to captivity with such an enemy. Having enjoyed this triumph, Colonel Lee, with his corps called the Legion, next sat down to reduce the stockade upon the left, which preserved a communication with the water; his approaches, however, commenced at a respectful distance, and his advances by sap were conducted with extreme caution, while the operations of General Greene were directed against the Star.

On the evening of the 9th of June, in the apprehension that something extraordinary was carrying on in the enemy's works, two sallies, with strong parties, were made. One of these, entering their trenches upon the right and penetrating to a battery of four guns, were prevented from destroying them for want of spikes and hammers. They here discovered the mouth of a mine, designed to be carried under a curtain of the Star, upon springing of which the breach was to be entered by the American army, sword in hand. The other division that marched upon the left fell in with the covering party of the besiegers, a number of whom were put to the bayonet, and the officer who commanded them brought in prisoner. Both divisions returned to the garrison with little loss, though it was impossible for that of the enemy not to have been considerable. Never did luckless wight receive a more inglorious wound, upon any occasion, than Count Koziusco did on this—it was in that part which Hudibras has constituted the seat of honour, and was given just as this engineer was examining the mine which he had projected!

Colonel Lee continued his approaches to the stockade upon the left, before which his corps suffered greatly. On the 12th of June, in a paroxysm of temerity and folly, he directed a serjeant and six men, at eleven o'clock in the forenoon, to advance with lighted combustibles and set fire to the abbatis of the work which he had invested. Not one of them returned to upbraid him with his rashness, and he was the first to solicit a truce to bury the bodies of the men he had so scandalously sacrificed. Having now redoubled his efforts and mounted a number of cannon which followed him from Augusta, he completely enfiladed this work by a triangular fire and by the 17th of June rendered it untenable. It was evacuated in the night without loss and taken possession of by the enemy.

The sufferings of the garrison were now extreme. With infinite labour a well was dug in the Star, but water was not to be obtained, and the only means of procuring this necessary element in a torrid climate in the month of June was to send out naked Negroes, who brought a scanty supply from within pistol shot of the American pickets, their bodies not being distinguishable in the night from the fallen trees with which the place abounded.

Far from despondence in this extremity, Lieutenant Colonel Cruger encouraged the troops, in the hope of relief from the arrival of an army before the enemy, though already advanced in their third parallel, could possibly reach the ditch. From the treatment of their fellow soldiers captured at Augusta, he painted to them, in the strongest colours, the mortifying consequences of a surrender; but, if they continued their defence, he had not the least doubt of their having the honour of brightening the future prospects of the royal army in those provinces.

Whilst the commandant was using these endeavours, an American Loyalist, in open day, under the fire of the enemy, rode through their pickets and delivered a verbal message from Lord Rawdon: "That he had passed Orangeburg and was in full march to raise the siege." The name of *Rawdon* inflamed every breast with additional vigour. They declared they would wait patiently for the assailants and meet them even in the ditch. How well they kept their word the transactions of the 18th will shew.

On the morning of this day the third parallel of the besiegers was completed; they turned the abbatis, drew out the pickets and brought forward two trenches within six feet of the ditch of the Star. General Greene, well informed of the advance of Lord Rawdon and knowing that the garrison was equally apprised of it, determined upon a general assault, which he commenced at noon.

Their forlorn hopes, in two divisions, made a lodgement in the ditch and were followed by strong parties with grappling hooks to draw down the sandbags, and tools to reduce the parapet. The riflemen, posted upon their elevated battery, picked off every British soldier that appeared, while the Virginian and Maryland lines fired by platoons from their trenches. The right flank of the enemy was exposed to the fire of a three-pounder, as well as to that of the block houses in the village, and Major Green with the troops in the Star waited with coolness to receive them on the parapet with bayonets and spears. The attack continued, but the main body of the Americans could not be brought forward to the assault; they were contented with supporting the parties in the ditch by an incessant fire from the lines.

At length the garrison became impatient. Two parties, under Captain Campbell of the New Jersey Volunteers and Captain French of Delancey's, issued from the sally port in the rear of the Star. They entered the ditch, divided their men and advanced, pushing their bayonets till they met each other. This was an effort of gallantry that the Americans could not have expected. General Greene, from one of the advanced batteries, with astonishment beheld two parties, consisting only of thirty men each, sallying into a ditch, charging and carrying every thing before them, though exposed to the fire of a whole army. It was an exertion of officers leading troops ardent in the cause of their sovereign, and steeled with the remembrance of injuries which they and their connections had so often received from the subverters of law and good government.

The Americans covered their shame in the trenches, nor was it till the next day that they recollected themselves so far as to ask permission to bury their dead. The groans also of their wounded assailed their ears and called aloud for that relief which ought to have been much earlier administered.

General Greene raised the siege upon the evening of the 19th, and on the morning of the 21st the army under Lord Rawdon made its appearance.

—MACKENZIE, *Strictures on Tarleton's History*, pp. 146-160.

VII. EUTAW SPRINGS

The last big battle in the lower South took place at Eutaw Springs, South Carolina, on September 8, 1781; like most of Greene's battles, it was indecisive. Rawdon had left the British army in the field under the command of Lieutenant Colonel Alexander Stewart, who was encamped on the west side of the Congaree near its junction with the Wataree. Greene was 16 miles north in the High Hills of Santee, but the two rivers between them were so flooded as to make it necessary for him to make a wide circuit of 70 miles to get close to Stewart.

Having cut off all intelligence to the enemy, Greene was able to approach Eutaw Springs without Stewart's knowledge. The Americans outnumbered the British 2,400 to 2,000. Each side claimed deserters from the other. As Greene put it, "At the close of the war, we fought the enemy with British soldiers; and they fought us with those of America."

Greene once again used the Cowpens pattern. In the center he placed the North Carolina militia, with the South Carolina militia on either side. He posted cavalry on either flank—on the right under Lee, on the left under Wade Hampton. In the second line he placed his regulars, with Washington's cavalry and Kirkwood's light infantry held in reserve. The militia stood up manfully, firing 17 rounds before showing any signs of weakening. When that happened the second line came up and drove the enemy back, while Lee's infantry wheeled upon the British left and Howard led the Marylanders in hand-to-hand combat with the British right. The British fell back in disorder. Now Stewart called on his grenadiers and light infantry under Major Majoribanks, who had been concealed by a dense thicket of blackjack. Washington

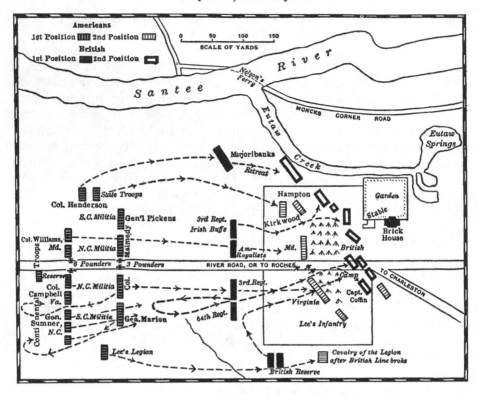

EUTAW SPRINGS

charged Majoribanks, had his own horse shot down, and half of his corps killed or wounded. He himself was captured. But Kirkwood's troops charged into the thicket and forced Majoribanks down into a ravine. The rest of the British army was in full retreat.

Suddenly the discipline of the Virginia and Maryland Continentals cracked. Naked, starved and thirsty, they halted in the British camp, fell upon the spoils of victory and drank themselves into a state of intoxication. Majoribanks, seizing the opportunity, sallied out into the field, swept down upon the disorganized plunderers and drove them into the woods.

Three hours of bloody fighting in intense heat was enough for both sides. Greene withdrew his men to the shelter of the woods. Stewart held the field for the night, but retired toward Monck's Corner the next day. The American casualties were almost one fourth of all who participated, 522 of all ranks; the British, 866, or two fifths of their forces, including Majoribanks, who died of his wounds. With his army decimated, Stewart found it necessary to withdraw to the vicinity of Charleston and the protection of the British warships. Both sides claimed victory.

Otho Williams' fascinating account of the battle was probably written long after the event and contains addenda furnished by other participants. Williams himself, Greene's adjutant general, was a Marylander who had fought

through the entire war from the siege of Boston, Fort Washington and Mon-
mouth to Camden and King's Mountain.

   Greene lost Eutaw Springs as he had numerous other battles, but, save for
Wilmington, N.C., and Charleston and Savannah, he had won the entire lower
South.

1. The Conduct of the Militia "Would Have Graced Veterans"

Account furnished by Colonel Otho Williams of the Continental Army, with
additions by Colonels W. Hampton, Polk, Howard and Watt.

   At about two hundred yards west of the Eutaw Springs, Stewart had
drawn up his troops in one line, extending from the Eutaw Creek beyond the
main Congaree road. The Eutaw Creek effectually covered his right, and his
left, which was, in the military language, in air, was supported by Coffin's
cavalry and a respectable detachment of infantry, held in reserve at a convenient distance in the rear of the left under cover of the wood.

   The ground on which the British army was drawn up was altogether in
wood; but, at a small distance in the rear of this line, was a cleared field extending west, south and east from the dwelling house and bounded north by
the creek formed by the Eutaw Springs, which is bold and has a high bank
thickly bordered with brush and low wood. From the house to this bank
extended a garden enclosed with palisadoes, and the windows of the house,
which was two-stories high with garret rooms, commanded the whole circum-
jacent fields. The house was of brick and abundantly strong to resist small
arms, and surrounded with various offices of wood; one particularly, a barn
of some size, lay to the southeast a small distance from the principal building.
In the open ground, to the south and west of the house, was the British encampment, the tents of which were left standing. . . .

   The superiority of his enemy in cavalry made it necessary that Col.
Stewart should cast his eye to the Eutaw house for retreat and support. To
that, therefore, he directed the attention of Major Sheridan, with orders, upon
the first symptoms of misfortune, to throw himself into it and cover the army
from the upper windows. On his right also, he had made a similar provision
against the possibility of his lines being compelled to give ground. In the
thickets which border the creek, Major Majoribanks, with three hundred of
his best troops, was posted, with instructions to watch the flank of the enemy,
if ever it should be open to attack. This command had assumed a position
having some obliquity to the main line, forming with an obtuse angle. The
artillery of the enemy was also posted in the main road.

   As soon as the skirmishing parties were cleared away from between the
two armies, a steady and desperate conflict ensued. That between the artillery
of the first line and that of the enemy was bloody and obstinate in the extreme;
nor did the American artillery relax for a moment from firing or advancing,
until both pieces were dismounted and disabled. One of the enemy's four-
pounders had shared the same fate, and the carnage on both sides had been
equal and severe.

   Nor had the militia been wanting in gallantry and perseverance. It was
with equal astonishment that both the second line and the enemy contem-

plated these men steadily and without faltering advance with shouts and exhortations into the hottest of the enemy's fire, unaffected by the continual fall of their comrades around them. Gen. Greene, to express his admiration of the firmness exhibited on this occasion by the militia, says of them, in a letter to Steuben, "Such conduct would have graced the veterans of the great king of Prussia." But it was impossible that this could endure long, for these men were, all this time, receiving the fire of double their number; their artillery was demolished, and that of the enemy still vomiting destruction on their ranks. They at length began to hesitate.

Governor Rutledge, who was anxiously attending the event of this battle a few miles in the rear, wrote to the South Carolina delegates that the militia fired seventeen rounds before they retired. That distrust of their own immediate commanders which militia are too apt to be affected with never produced an emotion where Marion and Pickens commanded.

Gen. Sumner was then ordered to support them. This was done with the utmost promptness, and the battle again raged with redoubled fury. In speaking of General Sumner's command, Gen. Greene observes "that he was at a loss which most to admire, the gallantry of the officers or the good conduct of the men."

On the advance of Gen. Sumner's command, Col. Stewart had brought up the infantry of his reserve into line on his left, and the struggle was obstinately maintained between fresh troops on both sides.

From the first commencement of the action, the infantry of the American covering parties, on the right and left, had been steadily engaged. The cavalry of the Legion, by being on the American right, had been enabled to withdraw into the woods and attend on its infantry, without being at all exposed to the enemy's fire. But the State troops under Henderson had been in the most exposed situation on the field. The American right, with the addition of the Legion infantry, had extended beyond the British left. But the American left fell far short of the British right; and the consequence was that the State troops were exposed to the oblique fire of a large proportion of the British right, and particularly of the battalion commanded by Majoribanks.

Never was the constancy of a party of men more severely tried. Henderson solicited permission to charge them and extricate himself from their galling fire, but his protection could not be spared from the artillery or the militia. At length he received a wound which disabled him from keeping his horse, and a momentary hesitation in his troops was produced by the shock. The exertions of Col. Wade Hampton, who succeeded to the command, aided by those of Col. Polk and Middleton, proved successful in restoring them to confidence and order, and they resumed their station in perfect tranquility.

In the mean time things were assuming important changes along the front line. Sumner's brigade, after sustaining for some time a fire superior to their own in the ratio of the greater numbers opposed to them, at length yielded and fell back. The British left, elated at the prospect, sprang forward as to certain conquest, and their line became deranged. This was exactly the incident for which the American commander was anxiously watching, and the next moment produced the movement for availing himself of it. Col. Williams now remained in command of the second line. "Let Williams advance and sweep the field with his bayonets" was the order delivered to a gentleman of medical staff, who acted the surgeon, the aid and the soldier indifferently, as occasion required.

Never was order obeyed with more alacrity. The two brigades received it with a shout. Emulous to wipe away the recollections of Hobkirk's Hill, they advanced with a spirit expressive of the impatience with which they had hitherto been passive spectators of the action. When approached within forty yards of the enemy, the Virginians delivered a destructive fire, and the whole second line, with trailed arms and an animated pace, advanced to the charge. Until this period their progress had been in the midst of showers of grape, and under a stream of fire from the line opposed to them. But eye-witnesses have asserted that the roll of the drum and the shouts which followed it drew every eye upon them alone; and a momentary pause in the action, a suspension by mutual consent, appeared to withdraw both armies from a sense of personal danger to fix their attention upon this impending conflict. It may well be supposed with what breathless expectation the Southern commander hung upon a movement on which all his hopes depended. Had it failed, he must have retired under cover of his cavalry.

Under the approach of the second line, the advanced left of the British army had commenced a retrograde movement in some disorder. This was confirmed by the good conduct of Col. Lee. The Legion infantry had steadily maintained its order in its position on the extreme right; and the advance of the British left having exposed its flank, the Legion infantry were promptly wheeled and poured in upon them a destructive enfilading fire; then joining in the charge, the British left wing was thrown into irretrievable disorder. But their centre and right still remained, greatly outnumbering the assailing party and awaiting the impending charge with unshaken constancy.

If the two lines on this occasion did not actually come to the mutual thrust of the bayonet, it must be acknowledged that no troops ever came nearer. They are said to have been so near that their bayonets clashed and the officers sprang at each other with their swords, before the enemy actually broke away.

But the scales of victory, fortunately for man, are never long in equipoise on these occasions.

In this instance, the left of the British centre appear to have been pressed upon and forced back by their own fugitives, and began to give way from left to right. At that moment, the Marylanders delivered their fire, and along their whole front the enemy yielded.

The shouts of victory resounded through the American line, affording a gleam of consolation to many a brave man bleeding and expiring on the field. Among these was the gallant Campbell, who received a ball in the breast during this onset.

The victory was now deemed certain, but many joined in the shouts of victory who were still destined to bleed. The carnage among the Americans had but commenced; it was in the effort to prevent the enemy from rallying and to cut him off from the brick house, which was all that remained to compel the army to surrender, that their great loss was sustained.

A pursuing army is always impeded by the effort that is necessary to maintain its own order, while, whether from terror, for safety or for rallying, the speed of the fugitive is unrestrained. Hence, cavalry are the military means for rendering disorder irretrievable. It is obvious that at this point of time the Legion cavalry might have been turned upon the British left with very great effect. Their position was highly favorable to such a movement, and their infantry was close up with the enemy to afford support. Why this was not done has never been explained. We can only conjecture that it was prevented by one or both of two causes known to have existed on that day. Col. Lee was generally absent from it during the action and bestowing his attention upon the progress of his infantry; and Captain Coffin was in that quarter, attending on the retreat of the British left. Coffin's force was, probably, superior to that of Lee in cavalry; whether so superior as to justify the latter's not attempting the charge in the presence of the British cavalry, although supported by that of his own infantry, could only have been decided by the attempt.

At this stage of the battle, Majoribanks still stood firm in the thickets that covered him; and, as the British line extended considerably beyond the American left, their extreme right still manifested a reluctance to retire; and as their left had first given way and yielded now without resistance, the two armies performed together a half wheel, which brought them into the open ground towards the front of the house.

Gen. Greene now saw that Majoribanks must be dislodged or the Maryland flank would soon be exposed to his fire and the conflict in that quarter renewed under his protection. Therefore, orders were dispatched to Washington to pass the American left and charge the enemy's right. The order was promptly obeyed and, galloping through the woods, Washington was soon in action. Had he had the good fortune to have taken on Kirkwood's infantry behind his men, all would have gone well; to have been detained by their march would have been inconsistent with his general feeling.

Col. Hampton, at the same time, received orders to co-operate with Col. Washington; and the rapid movement which he made to the creek, in order to fall in upon Washington's left, probably hastened the forward movement of the latter. On reaching the front of Majoribanks, and before Hampton had joined him, Washington attempted a charge, but it was impossible for his cavalry to penetrate the thicket. He then discovered that there was an interval between the British right and the creek, by which he was in hopes to succeed in gaining their rear. With this view, he ordered his troop to wheel by sections to the left, and thus brought nearly all his officers next to the enemy, while he attempted to pass their front. A deadly and well-directed fire, delivered at that instant, wounded or brought to the ground many of his men and horses, and every officer except two.

The field of battle was, at this instant, rich in the dreadful scenery which disfigures such a picture. On the left, Washington's cavalry routed and flying, horses plunging as they died or coursing the field without their riders, while the enemy with poised bayonet issued from the thicket upon the wounded or unhorsed rider. In the fore-ground, Hampton covering and collecting the scattered cavalry, while Kirkwood, with his bayonets, rushed furiously to revenge their fall, and a road strewed with the bodies of men and horses, and the fragments of dismounted artillery. Beyond these, a scene of indescribable confusion, viewed over the whole American line advancing rapidly and in order. And, on the right, Henderson borne off in the arms of his soldiers, and Campbell sustained in his saddle by a brave son, who had sought glory at his father's side.

Nothing could exceed the consternation spread at this time through the British ground of encampment. Every thing was given up for lost; the commissaries destroyed their stores; the numerous retainers of the army, mostly Loyalists and deserters, who dreaded falling into the hands of the Americans, leaping on the first horse they could command, crowded the roads and spread alarm to the very gates of Charleston. The stores on the road were set fire to, and the road itself obstructed by the felling of trees, for miles, across it.

Lieut. Gordon and Cornet Simmons were the only two of Washington's officers who could return into action. The colonel himself had his horse shot under him, and his life saved by the interposition of a British officer. The melancholy group of wounded men and officers, who soon presented themselves to the general's view, convinced him of the severity of his misfortune; but he had not yet been made acquainted with the full extent of it.

The survivors of Washington's command, being rallied, united themselves to Hampton's, and were again led up to the charge upon Majoribanks, but without success. That officer was then retiring before Kirkwood, still holding to the thickets and making for a new position, with his rear to the creek and his left resting on the palisadoed garden. By this time Sheridan had thrown himself into the house, and some of the routed companies from the left had made good their retreat into the picketted garden, from the intervals of which they could direct their fire with security and effect. The whole British line was now flying before the American bayonet. The latter pressed closely upon their heels, made many prisoners, and might have cut off the retreat of the rest, or entered pell-mell with them into the house, but for one of these occurrences which have often snatched victory from the grasp of a pursuing enemy.

The retreat of the British army lay directly through their encampment, where the tents were all standing and presented many objects to tempt a thirsty, naked and fatigued soldiery to acts of insubordination. Nor was the concealment afforded by the tents at this time a trivial consideration, for the fire from the windows of the house was galling and destructive, and no cover from it was anywhere to be found except among the tents or behind the building to the left of the front of the house.

Here it was that the American line got into irretrievable confusion. When their officers had proceeded beyond the encampment, they found themselves nearly abandoned by their soldiers, and the sole marks for the party who now poured their fire from the windows of the house. . . .

Everything now combined to blast the prospects of the American commander. The fire from the house showered down destruction upon the American officers; and the men, unconscious or unmindful of consequences, perhaps thinking the victory secure and, bent on the immediate fruition of its advantages, dispersing among the tents, fastened upon the liquors and refreshments they afforded, and became utterly unmanageable.

Majoribanks and Coffin, watchful of every advantage, now made simultaneous movements—the former from his thicket on the left, and the latter from the wood on the right of the American line. Gen. Greene soon perceived the evil that threatened him, and not doubting but his infantry, whose disorderly conduct he was not yet made acquainted with, would immediately dispose of Majoribanks, dispatched Capt. Pendleton with orders for the Legion cavalry to fall upon Coffin and repulse him. . . .

Major Eggleston . . . made the attack without success. . . .

By this time Gen. Greene, being made acquainted with the extent of his misfortune, ordered a retreat.

Coffin, who certainly proved himself a brave and active officer on this day, had no sooner repulsed the Legion cavalry than he hastened on to charge the rear of the Americans, now dispersed among the tents. Col. Hampton had been ordered up to the road to cover the retreat, at the same time the order was issued to effect it, and now charged upon Coffin with a vigour that was not to be resisted. Coffin met him with firmness, and a sharp conflict, hand to hand, was for a while maintained. But Coffin was obliged to retire, and in the ardour of pursuit the American cavalry approached so near Majoribanks and the picketted garden as to receive from them a fatally destructive fire. Col. Polk, who commanded Hampton's left and was, of consequence, directly under its influence, describes it by declaring "that he thought every man killed but himself." Col. Hampton then rallied his scattered cavalry and resumed his station in the border of the wood. But before this could be effected, Majoribanks had taken advantage of the opening made by his fire to perform another gallant action, which was decisive of the fortune of the day.

The artillery of the second line had followed on, as rapidly as it could, upon the track of the pursuit, and, together with two six-pounders abandoned by the enemy in their flight, had been brought up to batter the houses. Unfortunately, in the ardour to discharge a pressing duty, the pieces had been run into the open field, so near as to be commanded by the fire from the house. The pieces had scarcely opened their fire when the pressing danger which threatened the party in the house and, consequently, the whole army, drew all the fire from the windows upon the artillerists, and it very soon killed or disabled nearly the whole of them. And Majoribanks was no sooner disembarrassed of Hampton's cavalry than he sallied into the field, siezed the pieces and hurried them under the cover of the house. Then being re-inforced by parties from the garden and the house, he charged among the Americans, now dispersed among the tents, and drove them before him. The American army, however, soon rallied, after reaching the cover of the wood, and their enemy was too much crippled to venture beyond the cover of the house. . . .

Both parties claimed, on this occasion, a complete victory; but there is no difficulty in deciding the question between them upon the plainest principles. The British army was chased from the field at the point of the bayonet and took refuge in a fortress; the Americans were repulsed from that fortress. And, but for the demoralizing effect of possessing themselves of the British tents, the cover of the barn presented the means of forcing or firing the house with certainty and reducing the whole to submission.

—GIBBES, ed., *Documentary History of the American Revolution*, III, 147-157.

2. "AT EUTAW SPRINGS THE VALIANT DIED"

TO THE MEMORY OF THE
BRAVE AMERICANS
UNDER GENERAL GREENE, IN SOUTH CAROLINA, WHO
FELL IN THE ACTION OF SEPTEMBER 8, 1781

By Philip Freneau

At Eutaw Springs the valiant died;
    Their limbs with dust are covered o'er—
Weep on, ye springs, your tearful tide;
    How many heroes are no more!

If in this wreck of ruin, they
    Can yet be thought to claim a tear,
O smite your gentle breast and say
    The friends of freedom slumber here!

Thou, who shalt trace this bloody plain,
    If goodness rules thy generous breast,
Sigh for the wasted rural reign;
    Sigh for the shepherds, sunk to rest!

Stranger, their humble graves adorn;
    You too may fall and ask a tear;
'Tis not the beauty of the morn
    That proves the evening shall be clear.

They saw their injured country's woe:
    The flaming town, the wasted field;
Then rushed to meet the insulting foe ;
    They took the spear—but left the shield.

Led by thy conquering genius, Greene,
    The Britons they compelled to fly;
None distant viewed the fatal plain,
    None grieved, in such a cause to die—

But, like the Parthian, famed of old,
    Who, flying, still their arrows threw,
These routed Britons, full as bold,
    Retreated, and retreating slew.

Now rest in peace, our patriot band;
  Though far from nature's limits thrown,
We trust they find a happier land,
  A brighter sunshine of their own.
        —Freneau, *Poems*, II, 70-71.

CHAPTER THIRTY-ONE

Virginia

VIRGINIA ALONE *of Southern states had long been spared the heavy ravages of war. True, Dunmore had left a heritage of hate, and Norfolk had been burned, but, until the spring of '79, the Old Dominion had been relatively free of conflict. Then, in May 1779, a naval expedition under Vice-Admiral Sir George Collier seized Portsmouth without opposition, took a few other coastal towns, looted neighboring plantations, and destroyed or carried away many ships and 3,000 hogsheads of tobacco.*

Among the subjects on which Clinton and Cornwallis could not agree was the importance of Virginia in over-all strategy. Cornwallis felt that Virginia's seizure would end the war. He wanted Clinton to abandon New York and concentrate all his forces there. Ever cautious, and afraid of unknown risks, Clinton refused to do this, but as 1780 came to a close he sent a large detachmen to Virginia under the renegade Benedict Arnold, now a British brigadier general. To Arnold's force he attached Colonels Dundas and Simcoe, and instructed Arnold to be guided by this pair "in every important measure."

Washington had long before warned Governor Jefferson that Virginia must prepare to defend itself. But Jefferson was strangely inert. Virginia was apathetic and its governor had no talent for leadership in a war emergency. The defense was a travesty. Arnold sailed up the James and disembarked his men at Westover, 25 miles below Richmond, marched his forces entirely unopposed to Richmond and entered that town on January 5, 1781.

The defending militiamen fled without firing a shot. Arnold then sent Simcoe and his Tory Rangers up the river to Westham, where they destroyed an iron foundry and gunpowder factory, along with public records sent there for safekeeping. After burning many buildings in Richmond, Arnold returned down-river. En route Von Steuben, who commanded the Patriot forces in Virginia, caught up with him, but what might have been a successful ambush turned into a rout for the Americans, who fled in disorder. After inflicting these damaging blows, Arnold, with few losses of his own men, encamped for the winter at Portsmouth. Jefferson was unable to lay his hands on "this greatest of all traitors." In the spring of '81 Arnold was superseded in command by Major-General William Phillips.

I. GENERAL ARNOLD INVADES VIRGINIA

1. VIRGINIA MUST DEFEND HERSELF

George Washington to Governor Thomas Jefferson.

Headquarters, Ramapo, N. J., June 29, 1780

I have been honored with two of your Excellency's favors both of the 11th inclosing an extract of a letter from Governor Rutlege.

I cannot but feel most sensibly affected by several parts of your Excellency's letter. The successive misfortunes to the Southward, the progress of the enemy, and the great deficiency in military stores give rise to the most serious reflections, while our situation in this quarter precludes every hope of affording you further assistance. What from the system of short inlistments, and [the unfortunate] delays in filling up our battalions the army in this place, is reduced to a mere handful of men, and left as it were at the mercy of a formidable enemy, subject to see the honor and dignity of the States daily insulted without the power either to prevent it or to retaliate. Under these circumstances your Excellency will perceive how utterly impossible it is to go further in succors than what is already sent. To oppose our Southern misfortunes and surmount our difficulties our principal dependence must be on the means we have left us in your quarter. And it is some consolation amidst all our distresses that these are more than adequate to remove them; and to recover what we have lost that it is only necessary these be properly directed.

—FITZPATRICK, ed., *Writings of Washington*, XIX, 97-98.

2. RICHMOND'S FALL AND THE DESTRUCTION OF THE WESTHAM FOUNDRY

Military journal of Lieutenant Colonel J. G. Simcoe of the Queen's Rangers.

The troops under Gen. Arnold being embarked, he issued an order on the 20th of December [1780] against depredations in the country where the expedition was bound to, and in the most forcible terms and strongest manner called upon the officers to second his intentions and the Commander in Chief's orders in this respect. The expedition sailed from Sandy Hook on the 21st of December and arrived in the Chesapeake, but in a dispersed manner, on the 30th: several ships were missing.

General Arnold, without waiting for them, was enabled, by the fortunate capture which the advance frigate under Capt. Evans had made of some small American vessels, to push up the James River, and this was done with incomparable activity and despatch, the whole detachment showing an energy and alacrity that could not be surpassed. The enemy had a battery at Hood's Point, and there was as yet no certainty whether or not it was defended by an enclosed work. The vessels anchored near it late in the evening of the 3d of January; one of them, in which was Capt. Murray of the Queen's Rangers, not perceiving the signal for anchoring, was fired at. Upon the first shot the skipper and his people left the deck; when Capt. Murray seized the helm and, the soldiers assisting him, he passed by the fort without any damage from its fire and anchored above it.

Gen. Arnold ordered Lt. Col. Simcoe to land with one hundred and thirty of the Queen's Rangers and the light infantry and grenadiers of the 80th Regiment: the landing was effected silently and apparently with secrecy about a mile from the battery, and a circuit was made to surprise its garrison. In the mean time the fleet was fired upon, but ineffectually on account of its distance. On the detachment's approach through bypaths to Hood's, the flank companies of the 80th were ordered to file from the rear and to proceed rapidly to the battery, while the Rangers were ready to support them or to receive any enemy who might possibly be on their march from the adjacent country. Major Gordon on his approach found the battery totally abandoned; the concerted signal was made, and the fleet anchored near it. . . . .

On the arrival at Westover, the troops were immediately disembarked. At first, from the reports of the country of the force that was assembling to defend Richmond, Gen. Arnold hesitated whether he should proceed thither or not, his positive injunctions being not to undertake any enterprise that had much risk in it; but Lt. Colonels Dundas and Simcoe concurring that one day's march might be made with perfect security, and that by this means more perfect information might be obtained, the troops were immediately put in motion and proceeded towards Richmond, where the enemy was understood to have very considerable magazines. It was above thirty miles from Westover; several transports had not arrived, and Gen. Arnold's force did not amount to eight hundred men.

On the second day's march, whilst a bridge was replacing over a creek, the advanced guard only having passed over, some of the enemy's militia, who had destroyed it the evening before and were to assemble with others to defend it, were deceived by the dress of the Rangers and came to Lt. Col. Simcoe, who immediately reprimanded them for not coming sooner, held conversation with them and then sent them prisoners to General Arnold.

Within seven miles of Richmond a patrole of the enemy appeared, who, on being discovered, fled at full speed. The Queen's Rangers, whose horses were in a miserable condition from the voyage, could not pursue them.

Soon after Lt. Col. Simcoe halted, having received the clearest information that a road, made passable by wood carts, led through the thickets to the rear of the heights on which the town of Richmond was placed, where they terminated in a plain, although they were almost inaccessible by the common road. On giving this information to Gen. Arnold, he said it was not worth while to quit the road, as the enemy would not fight. On approaching the town, Gen. Arnold ordered the troops to march as open and to make as great an appearance as possible; and the ground was so favourable that a more skilfull enemy than those who were now reconnoitering would have imagined the numbers to have been double.

The enemy at Richmond appeared drawn up on the heights to the number of two or three hundred men. The road passed through a wood at the bottom of these heights, and then ran between them and the river into the lower town. Lt. Col. Simcoe was ordered to dislodge them. He mounted the hill in small bodies, stretching away to the right, so as to threaten the enemy with a design to outflank them; and as they filed off, in appearance to secure their flank, he directly ascended with his cavalry, where it was so steep that they were obliged to dismount and lead their horses. Luckily the enemy made no resistance, nor did they fire, but, on the cavalry's arrival on the summit, retreated to the woods in great confusion.

There was a party of horsemen in the lower town watching the motion of Lt. Col. Dundas, who, the heights being gained, was now entering it. Lt. Col. Simcoe pushed on with the cavalry unnoticed by the enemy in the lower town till such time as he began to descend almost in their rear, when an impassable creek stopped him and gave the enemy time to escape to the top of another hill beyond the town. Having crossed over lower down, he ascended the hill, using such conversation and words towards them as might prevent their inclination to retreat. However, when the Rangers were arrived within twenty yards of the summit, the enemy, greatly superior in numbers, but made up of militia, spectators, some with and some without arms, galloped off. They were immediately pursued, but without the least regularity. . . .

On Lt. Col. Simcoe's return, he met with orders from Gen. Arnold to march to the foundery at Westham, six miles from Richmond, and to destroy it. The flank companies of the 80th, under Major Gordon, were sent as a reinforcement. With these and his corps he proceeded to the foundery. The trunnions of many pieces of iron cannon were struck off, a quantity of small arms and a great variety of military stores were destroyed. Upon consultation with the artillery officer, it was thought better to destroy the magazine than to blow it up. This fatiguing business was effected by carrying the powder down the cliffs and pouring it into the water. The warehouses and mills were then set on fire, and many explosions happened in different parts of the buildings, which might have been hazardous had it been relied on that all the powder was regularly deposited in one magazine; and the foundery, which was a very complete one, was totally destroyed.

It was night before the troops returned to Richmond. The provisions which had been made for them were now to be cooked. Fatigued with the march, the men in general went to sleep. Some of them got into private houses and there obtained rum. . . .

—SIMCOE, *Military Journal*, pp. 159-165.

3. "RATHER THEY HAD BURNT MY HOUSE AND RUINED THE PLANTATION"

One of the embarrassing incidents of the war took place in April 1781, when a British sloop-of-war paid a visit to Washington's plantation and seized 17 Negro slaves, of whom six were later recovered. To prevent further reprisals, Lund Washington, the general's plantation manager, furnished the British with refreshments. When Lafayette, who had been detailed to Virginia, called this to Washington's attention, the latter was quick to repudiate the action.

A. LAFAYETTE TO GEORGE WASHINGTON

Alexandria, Virginia, April 23, 1781

Great happiness is derived from friendship, and I do particularly experience it in the attachment which unites me to you. But friendship has its duties, and the man that likes you the best will be the forwardest in letting you know every thing where you can be concerned.

When the ennemy came to your house many Negroes deserted to them. This piece of news did not affect me much as I little value those concerns but you cannot conceive how unhappy I have been to hear that Mr. Lund Washington went on board the ennemy's vessels and consented to give them provisions. This being done by the gentleman who in some measure represents you at your house will certainly have a bad effect, and contrasts with spirited answers from some neighbours that had their houses burnt accordingly.

You will do what you think proper about it, my dear General, but, as your friend, it was my duty *confidentially* to mention the circumstances.

With the help of some waggons and horses we got in two days from the camp near Baltimore to this place. We halted yesterday, and having made a small bargain for a few shoes are marching to Frederis Burg. No official account from Philips, but I am told they are removing stores from Richmond and Petersburg. I am surprised no body writes to me, and hope soon to receive intelligences.

Our men are in high spirits. Their honor having been interested in this affair, they have made it a point to come with us, and discontents as well as desertion are entirely out of fashion.

Requesting my best respects to be presented to Mrs. Washington and compliments to the family.

—GOTTSCHALK, ed., *Letters of Lafayette to Washington*, pp. 187-188.

B. GEORGE WASHINGTON TO LUND WASHINGTON

New Windsor, April 30, 1781

Your letter of the 18th. came to me by the last Post. I am very sorry to hear of your loss; I am a little sorry to hear of my own; but that which gives me most concern, is, that you should go on board the enemys Vessels, and furnish them with refreshments. It would have been a less painful circumstance to me, to have heard, that in consequence of your non-compliance with their request, they had burnt my House, and laid the Plantation in ruins. You ought to have considered yourself as my representative, and should have reflected on the bad example of communicating with the enemy, and making a voluntary offer of refreshments to them with a view to prevent a conflagration.

It was not in your power, I acknowledge, to prevent them from sending a flag on shore, and you did right to meet it; but you should, in the same instant that the business of it was unfolded, have declared, explicitly, that it was improper for you to yield to the request; after which, if they had proceeded to help themselves, *by force*, you could but have submitted (and being unprovided for defence) this was to be prefered to a feeble opposition which only serves as a pretext to burn and destroy.

I am thoroughly perswaded that you acted from your best judgment; and believe, that your desire to preserve my property, and rescue the buildings from impending danger, were your governing motives. But to go on board their Vessels; carry them refreshments; commune with a parcel of plundering

Scoundrels, and request a favor by asking the surrender of my Negroes, was exceedingly ill-judged, and 'tis to be feared, will be unhappy in its consequences, as it will be a precedent for others, and may become a subject of animadversion.

I have no doubt of the enemys intention to prosecute the plundering plan they have begun. And, unless a stop can be put to it by the arrival of a superior naval force, I have as little doubt of its ending in the loss of all my Negroes, and in the destruction of my Houses; but I am prepared for the event, under the prospect of which, if you could deposit, in safety, at some convenient distance from the Water, the most valuable and least bulky articles, it might be consistent with policy and prudence, and a means of preserving them for use hereafter. Such, and so many things as are necessary for common, and present use must be retained and run their chance through the firy trial of this summer.

Mrs. Washington joins me in best and affectionate regard for you, Mrs. Washington and Milly Posey; and does most sincerely regret your loss. I do not know what Negroes they may have left you; and as I have observed before, I do not know what number they will have left me by the time they have done; but this I am sure of, that you shall never want assistance, while it is in my power to afford it.

—FITZPATRICK, ed., *Writings of Washington*, XXII, 14-15.

II. THE FATEFUL SQUABBLE BETWEEN CLINTON AND CORNWALLIS

The correspondence between the two military rivals, Cornwallis and Clinton, leaves the impression that the former was obsessed with the importance of Virginia in over-all British strategy. He insisted on an all-out campaign to reduce that province. Clinton operated with his customary caution. Fearing an attack in force on New York, Clinton was reluctant to reinforce Cornwallis; in fact, he requested that Cornwallis send back most of his army. If a move away from New York were to be made, Clinton preferred Philadelphia or Rhode Island, neither of which made military sense.

As letters went back and forth between the commanders, Cornwallis, who had quit Wilmington, North Carolina, and reached Virginia shortly after the middle of May, at once engaged in a wild-goose chase after Lafayette. Clinton's compromise proposal that Cornwallis hold a post on the Chesapeake with a small force and send back 3,000 troops to New York was intolerable to the Earl. He at once ordered an evacuation from the province. Clinton, alarmed, countermanded this order and categorically insisted in a letter Cornwallis received on July 8 that the latter take over a post and hold it, with his whole army if necessary. Cornwallis picked Yorktown, but Clinton's failure to throw in more support gave Cornwallis an "out" for his defeat. A postwar battle of words was fought in England between the two generals.

Both British armies were now on the defensive. Each had refused to fortify the other, and as they squabbled the British Navy for the time lost command of the sea. A breakdown of command contributed in no unimportant measure to the British disaster at Yorktown.

1. CORNWALLIS OBJECTS TO BEING KEPT TOTALLY IN THE DARK

To Sir Henry Clinton.

Camp near Wilmington, April 10, 1781

. . . I am very anxious to receive your Excellency's commands, being as yet totally in the dark as to the intended operations of the summer. I cannot help expressing my wishes that the Chesapeak may become the seat of war, even (if necessary) at the expense of abandoning New York. Until Virginia is in a manner subdued, our hold of the Carolinas must be difficult, if not precarious. The rivers in Virginia are advantageous to an invading army; but North Carolina is of all the provinces in America the most difficult to attack (unless material assistance could be got from the inhabitants, the contrary of which I have sufficiently experienced), on account of its great extent, of the numberless rivers and creeks, and the total want of interior navigation.

—Ross, ed., *Correspondence of Cornwallis*, I, 86-87.

2. CORNWALLIS: "I AM QUITE TIRED OF MARCHING ABOUT THE COUNTRY"

To Major General William Phillips.

Camp near Wilmington, April 10, 1781

I have had a most difficult and dangerous campaign and was obliged to fight a battle 200 miles from any communication against an enemy seven times my number. The fate of it was long doubtful. We had not a regiment or corps that did not at some time give way; it ended however happily, in our completely routing the enemy and taking their cannon. The idea of our friends rising in any number and to any purpose totally failed, as I expected, and here I am, getting rid of my wounded and refitting my troops at Wilmington. I last night heard of the naval action,* and your arrival in the Chesapeak. Now, my dear friend, what is our plan? Without one we cannot succeed, and I assure you that I am quite tired of marching about the country in quest of adventures. If we mean an offensive war in America, we must abandon New York and bring our whole force into Virginia; we then have a stake to fight for, and a successful battle may give us America. If our plan is defensive, mixed with desultory expeditions, let us quit the Carolinas (which cannot be held defensively while Virginia can be so easily armed against us) and stick to our salt pork at New York, sending now and then a detachment to steal tobacco, etc.

I daily expect three regiments from Ireland. Leaving one of them at Charlestown, with the addition of the other two and the flank companies I can come by land to you; but whether after we have joined we shall have a sufficient force for a war of conquest, I should think very doubtful. By a war of conquest, I mean, to possess the country sufficiently to overturn the Rebel government, and to establish a militia and some kind of mixed authority of our own. If no reinforcement comes, and that I am obliged to march with my present force to the upper frontiers of South Carolina, my situation will be truly distressing. If I was to embark from hence, the loss of the upper posts

---

* The engagement off the Chesapeake between Arbuthnot and Destouches is discussed in section III following.

in South Carolina would be inevitable. I have as yet received no orders. If the reinforcements arrive, I must move from hence, where the men will be sickly and the horses starved. If I am sure that you are to remain in the Chesapeak, perhaps I may come directly to you.

It is very difficult to get any letters conveyed by land on account of the vigilance and severity of the Rebel government. I believe all mine to General Arnold miscarried, and I did not receive one from him.

—Ross, ed., *Correspondence of Cornwallis*, I, 87-88.

3. Cornwallis Urges a Virginia Offensive and Favors Yorktown

To Sir Henry Clinton.

Byrd's Plantation, North of James River, May 26, 1781

...I shall now proceed to dislodge La Fayette from Richmond, and with my light troops to destroy any magazines or stores in the neighbourhood which may have been collected either for his use or for General Greene's army. From thence I purpose to move to the Neck at Williamsburgh, which is represented as healthy and where some subsistence may be procured, and keep myself unengaged from operations which might interfere with your plan for the campaign, untill I have the satisfaction of hearing from you. I hope I shall then have an opportunity to receive better information than has hitherto been in my power to procure, relative to a proper harbour and place of arms.

At present I am inclined to think well of York. The objections to Portsmouth are that it cannot be made strong without an army to defend it, that it is remarkably unhealthy, and can give no protection to a ship of the line. Wayne has not yet joined La Fayette, nor can I positively learn where he is, nor what is his force. Greene's cavalry are said to be coming this way, but I have no certain accounts of it....

One maxim appears to me to be absolutely necessary for the safe and honourable conduct of this war, which is, that we should have as few posts as possible, and that wherever the King's troops are, they should be in respectable force. By the vigorous exertions of the present governors of America, large bodies of men are soon collected, and I have too often observed that when a storm threatens, our friends disappear....

I shall take the liberty of repeating that if offensive war is intended, Virginia appears to me to be the only Province in which it can be carried on, and in which there is a stake. But to reduce the Province and keep possession of the country, a considerable army would be necessary, for with a small force the business would probably terminate unfavourably, tho' the beginning might be successfull. In case it is thought expedient and a proper army for the attempt can be formed, I hope your Excellency will do me the justice to believe that I neither wish nor expect to have the command of it, leaving you at New York on the defensive. Such sentiments are so far from my heart that I can with great truth assure you that few things could give me greater pleasure than being relieved by your presence from a situation of so much anxiety and responsibility.

—Stevens, ed., *Clinton-Cornwallis Controversy*, I, 488-490.

III. LAFAYETTE TO THE RESCUE

Learning that the British had reinforced Arnold with 2,000 men under General Phillips, Washington dispatched Lafayette and three regiments of light infantry to the defense of Virginia. He was to be reinforced by the French fleet under Admiral Destouches and 1,200 French soldiers. The first part of the project went according to plan. Lafayette marched from Peekskill to the Head of Elk, thence over water to Annapolis. The young French nobleman borrowed from the merchants of Baltimore on his private credit to purchase clothing and other necessities for the army. The second part of the plan did not come off. Admiral Arbuthnot worsted Destouches off the Chesapeake on March 16, and the French fleet returned to Newport.

Lafayette's position was indeed serious, as, in addition to Arnold's force, he now had to face Phillips' reinforcements numbering some 2,600 men. For additional help Lafayette could count merely upon Von Steuben's force of Virginia Continentals and some untrained militia units. Even before Lafayette's arrival, Phillips, after skirmishing with Von Steuben's troops, took Petersburg and destroyed all the vessels lying in the river. One participant, Lieutenant Daniel Trabue, thought the Virginia militia fought surprisingly well in this engagement. But further setbacks faced the defenders. They were forced to scuttle a naval force they had collected on the James with a view to co-operating with the French fleet against Portsmouth. At length the arrival of Lafayette at Richmond caused Phillips to pull his troops down-river.

Meantime, Clinton ordered the British army in Virginia to co-operate with Cornwallis when he began his movement north from Wilmington in April 1781. Arnold attempted now to turn Lafayette's left flank and get into his rear. Lafayette, recognizing that his forces were too small to risk an engagement against the British army, further reinforced on May 20 by Cornwallis' arrival with some 1,500 troops, retired to the interior. Early in June, Tarleton with 250 cavalrymen sped to Charlottesville and caught several members of the state legislature before they could make their escape. Jefferson, whose term of office had expired but who was still acting as governor, pulled out in time, but he did not join the legislature in their flight over the Blue Ridge Mountains to Staunton. Technically Tarleton put an end to Jefferson's term as the state's chief executive. Captain Francis J. Brooke of the Continental Army reports how the American soldiers were panic-stricken on the approach of Tarleton's forces.

In the face of mounting reinforcements for Lafayette, Cornwallis pulled his troops from the interior toward the Chesapeake to establish closer relations with Clinton in New York. Lafayette hung doggedly onto his rear. After some confused skirmishing near Williamsburg, where Cornwallis was encamped, the British general began moving his army across the James to reach Portsmouth. Before the crossing of the river was completed the British were set upon by Anthony Wayne's men, but repulsed the Americans in sharp but inconclusive fighting. Cornwallis, now assuming a defensive posture, failed to counterattack Lafayette's forces, but instead seized Yorktown and Glou-

cester across the York River and proceeded to fortify them. The trap was
soon ready to be sprung.

1. "I Am Determined to Scarmish, but Not to Engage Too Far"

Lafayette to George Washington.

Richmond, May 24, 1781

My official letter, a copy of which I send to Congress, will let you know
the situation of affairs in this quarter. I ardently wish my conduct may meet
with your approbation. Had I followed the first impulsion of my temper, I
would have risked some thing more. But I have been guarding against my own
warmth, and this consideration, that a general defeat, which with such a proportion of militia must be expected, would involve this State and our affairs
into ruin, has rendered me extremely cautious in my movements. Indeed, I am
more embarassed to move, more crippled in my projects than we have been in
the Northern States.

Had the Pennsylvanians arrived before Lord Cornwallis I was determined
to attack the ennemy and have no doubt but what we would have been successfull. Their unaccountable delay cannot be too much lamented, and will make
an immense difference to the fate of this compaign. Should they have arrived
time enough to support me in the reception of Lord Cornwallis's first stroke,
I would still have thought it well enough. But from an answer of General
Waïne received this day and dated the 19th I am affraid that in this moment
they have hardly left York town.

Public stores and private property being removed from Richmond, this
place is a less important object. I don't believe it would be prudent to expose
the troops for the sake of a few houses most of which are empty. But I am
wavering betwen two inconveniences. Was I to fight a battle, I'll be cut to
pieces, the militia dispersed, and the arms lost. Was I to decline fighting, the
country would think herself given up. I am therefore determined to scarmish,
but not to engage too far, and particularly to take care against their immense
and excellent body of horse whom the militia fears like they would so many
wild beasts. . . .

Was I any ways equal to the ennemy, I would be extremely happy in my
present command. But I am not strong enough even to get beaten. Gov-
ernement in this state has no energy, and laws have no force. But I hope this
assembly will put matters up on a better footing. I had great deal of trouble
to put the departements in a tolerable train. Our expenses were enormous,
and yet we can get nothing. Arrangements for the present seem to put on a
better face but for this superiority of the ennemy which will chase us where
they please. They can over run the country, and untill the Pennsylvanians
arrive we are next to nothing in point of opposition to so large a force. This
country begins to be as familiar to me as Tappan and Bergen. Our soldiers
are hitherto very healthy and I have turned doctor to regulate their diet.

Adieu, my dear General. Let me hear some times from you. Your letters
are a great happiness to your affectionate friend.

—GOTTSCHALK, ed., *Letters of Lafayette to Washington*, pp. 197-199.

2. "Cornwallis Is the Scourge"

Richard Henry Lee to Arthur Lee.

Epping Forest, June 4, 1781

... The enemies design seems to be by great distress and much delusion to bring over the minds of the people. It must be confessed that they have the fairest opportunity, for we have no press in the country, we have received next to no assistance from our sister States or from our ally, whilst our veteran regulars have been all sacrificed in the common cause, and a considerable part of our force, being the greatest part of Gen. Green's strength, now in S. Carolina.

The people feel their pressures, find themselves abandoned, and they are exposed to the infinite acts and fraud of our enemies and of our internal Tories. The consequences may be very unpleasing to sound and sensible Whiggism. Shew this to Col. Bland and it will surely rouse him to exert all his powers in Congress to procure us assistance and that which may be effectual. The enemy affect to leave harmless the poor and they take everything from those they call the rich. Tis said that 2 or 3000 Negroes march in their train, that every kind of stock which they cannot remove they destroy—eating up the green wheat and by destroying of the fences expose to destruction the other growing grains. They have burnt a great number of warehouses full of tobacco and they are now pressing on to the large ones on Rappahanock and Potomac rivers and the valuable iron works in our northern parts.

The fine horses on James River have furnished them with a numerous and powerful cavalry—'tis said to consist of 800. I hope that these afflictions are intended to do away some of our overcharge of wickedness, and that we shall be relieved in due season.

Cornwallis is the scourge—and a severe one he is. The doings of more than a year in the South are undoing very fast, whilst they rush to throw ruin into other parts.

I have got your keys from Richmond. Half of our militia is this day to be drafted for the Marquis, but how to get at him I know not, as the enemy are between us and him.

—Ballagh, ed., *Letters of R. H. Lee*, II, 229-231.

3. Tarleton Recalls His Raid on Charlottesville

At this period, the superiority of the army and the great superiority of the light troops were such as to have enabled the British to traverse the country without apprehension or difficulty, either to destroy stores and tobacco in the neighbourhood of the rivers or to undertake more important expeditions. While the main body was in Hanover County and the Marquis de la Fayette lay between them and Fredericksburg, Earl Cornwallis had clear intelligence of the meeting of the governor and assembly at Charlotteville, under the protection of a guard, in order to vote taxes for the exigencies of government, to concert measures for the augmentation of the eighteen-months men, or state troops, and to issue commands for a large draft of militia. At the same time he obtained information that Baron Steuben was gone to Point of Fork, which is situated at the extremity of James River between the Fluvanna and Rivanna, with the eighteen-months men, to cover a Continental store, consisting of cannon, small arms and accoutrements.

To frustrate these intentions, and to distress the Americans by breaking up the assembly at Charlotteville and by taking or destroying the arms and other stores at Point of Fork, his Lordship employed Lieutenant-Colonel Tarleton on the former expedition, as most distant and on that account more within the reach of cavalry, whilst he committed the latter enterprize to the execution of Lieutenant-Colonel Simcoe, with the yagers, the infantry and the hussars of the rangers. It was designed that these blows should, as near as circumstances would permit, be struck at the same moment; that Tarleton, after completing his business, should retire down the Rivanna to give assistance to Simcoe, if he failed in his first attempt, and that both should afterwards join the army, which would in the mean time file to the left through Goochland County and approach the Point of Fork.

Lieutenant-Colonel Tarleton, with one hundred and eighty dragoons, supported by Captain Champagne of the 23d Regiment and seventy mounted infantry, left the army in the beginning of June and proceeded between the North and South Anna. The heat of the weather obliged him to refresh his men and horses in the middle of the day. He pressed forwards in the afternoon, halted at eleven near Louisa Courthouse, and remained on a plentiful plantation till two o'clock in the morning, at which time he again resumed his march. Before dawn he fell in with twelve waggons that were on their journey under a weak guard from the upper parts of Virginia and Maryland, with arms and clothing for the Continental troops in South Carolina. The waggons and stores were burnt, that no time might be lost or diminution of force made by giving them an escort.

Soon after daybreak, some of the principal gentlemen of Virginia, who had fled to the borders of the mountains for security, were taken out of their beds. Part were paroled and left with their families, while others who were suspected to be more hostile in their sentiments were carried off. In the neighbourhood of Dr. Walker's, a member of the Continental Congress was made prisoner, and the British light troops, after a halt of half an hour to refresh the horses, moved on toward Charlotteville. Various were the accounts on the road concerning this place and the force it contained. Lieutenant-Colonel Tarleton imagined that a march of seventy miles in twenty-four hours, with the caution he had used, might, perhaps, give him the advantage of a surprise, and concluded that an additional celerity to the object of his destination would undoubtedly prevent a formidable resistance. He therefore approached the Rivanna, which runs at the foot of the hill on which the town is situated, with all possible expedition. The advanced dragoons reported that the ford was guarded. An attack was nevertheless ordered. The cavalry charged through the water with very little loss and routed the detachment posted at that place.

As soon as one hundred cavalry had passed the water, Lieutenant-Colonel Tarleton directed them to charge into the town, to continue the confusion of the Americans and to apprehend, if possible, the governor and assembly.

Seven members of assembly were secured; a Brigadier-General Scott and several officers and men were killed, wounded or taken. The attempt to secure Mr. Jefferson was ineffectual; he discovered the British dragoons from his house, which stands on the point of a mountain, before they could approach him, and he provided for his personal liberty by a precipitate retreat.

A great quantity of stores were found in Charlotteville and the neighbourhood. One thousand new firelocks that had been manufactured at Fredericksburg were broken. Upwards of four hundred barrels of powder were destroyed. Several hogsheads of tobacco and some Continental clothing and accoutrements shared the same fate. The next morning the British were joined by about twenty men, who, being soldiers of the Saratoga army, had been dispersed throughout the district and allowed to work in the vicinity of the barracks, where they had been originally imprisoned. Many more would probably have joined their countrymen if Lieutenant-Colonel Tarleton had been at liberty to remain at Charlotteville a few days; but his duty pointed out the propriety of returning the same afternoon with his corps and the prisoners down the Rivanna towards the Point of Fork.

The gentlemen taken on this expedition were treated with kindness and liberality. In different conversations with Lieutenant-Colonel Tarleton on the state of public affairs, they generally and separately avowed that if England could prevent the intended co-operation of the French fleet and army with the American forces during the ensuing autumn, both Congress and the country would gladly dissolve the French alliance and enter into treaty with Great Britain. These sentiments were communicated to Earl Cornwallis, who, doubtless, made them known to the commander in chief for the information of the admiral in the West-Indies and the minister in England. The captives of distinction, both civil and military, were restrained by their promise not to quit the camps or line of march of the light troops till they joined the army.
—TARLETON, *History of Campaigns in the Southern Provinces*, pp. 302-306.

4. CORNWALLIS BOASTS, "THE BOY CANNOT ESCAPE ME"

Memoirs of Lafayette.

Lord Cornwallis, when he commenced the pursuit of Lafayette, had written a letter, which was intercepted, in which he made use of this expression: *The boy cannot escape me.* He flattered himself with terminating, by that one blow, the war in the whole southern part of the United States, for it would have been easy for him afterwards to take possession of Baltimore and march towards Philadelphia. He beheld in this manner the failure of the principal part of his plan, and retreated towards Richmond, whilst Lafayette, who had been joined in his new station by a corps of riflemen as well as by some militia, received notice beforehand to proceed forward on a certain day, and followed, step by step, the English general, without, however, risking an engagement with a force so superior to his own. His corps gradually increased. Lord Cornwallis thought proper to evacuate Richmond; Lafayette followed him, and ordered Colonel Butler to attack his rear guard near Williamsburg. Some manoeuvre took place on that side, of which the principal object on Lafayette's part was to convince Lord Cornwallis that his force was more considerable than it was in reality. The English evacuated Williamsburg and passed over James River to James Island.

A warm action took place between the English army and the advance guard, whom Lafayette had ordered to the attack whilst they were crossing the river. Lord Cornwallis had stationed the first troops on the other side, to give the appearance as if the greatest number of the troops had already passed over the river. Although every person was unanimous in asserting that this was the case, Lafayette himself suspected the deception and quitted his detachment to make observations upon a tongue of land from whence he could more easily view the passage of the enemy. A cannon, exposed doubtless intentionally, tempted General Wayne, a brave and enterprising officer.

Lafayette found, on his return, the advance guard engaged in action with a very superior force. He withdrew it, however, (after a short but extremely warm conflict), in good order and without receiving a check. The report was spread that he had had a horse killed under him, but it was merely the one that was led by his aide. The English army pursued its route to Portsmouth; it then returned by water to take its station at Yorktown and Gloucester upon the York River. A garrison still remained at Portsmouth. Lafayette made some demonstrations of attack, and that garrison united itself to the body of the army at Yorktown.

Lafayette was extremely desirous that the English army should unite at that very spot. Such had been the aim of all his movements, ever since a slight increase of force had permitted him to think of any other thing than of retiring without being destroyed and of saving the magazines. He knew that a French fleet was to arrive from the islands upon the American coast. His principal object had been to force Lord Cornwallis to withdraw towards the sea-shore, and then entangle him in such a manner in the rivers that there should remain no possibility of a retreat. The English, on the contrary, fancied themselves in a very good position, as they were possessors of a seaport by which they could receive succours from New York and communicate with the different parts of the coast. An accidental, but a very fortunate circumstance increased their security.

Whilst Lafayette, full of hope, was writing to General Washington that he foresaw he could push Lord Cornwallis into a situation in which it would be easy for him, with some assistance from the navy, to cut off his retreat, the general, who had always thought that Lafayette would be very fortunate if he could save Virginia without being cut up himself, spoke to him of his project of attack against New York, granting him permission to come and take part in it, if he wished it, but representing how useful it was to the Virginian army that he should remain at its head. The two letters passed each other; the one written by Lafayette arrived safely, and Washington prepared beforehand to take advantage of the situation of Lord Cornwallis. Gen. Washington's letter was intercepted, and the English, upon seeing that confidential communication, never doubted for a moment but the real intention of the Americans was to attack New York. Their own security at Yorktown was therefore complete.

—LAFAYETTE, *Memoirs, Correspondence and Manuscripts*, pp. 263-267.

CHAPTER THIRTY-TWO

Yorktown: Washington's Vindication

THE FINAL British disaster of the American Revolution may be attributed to a variety of causes: to Cornwallis' unwise selection of an encampment which could be cut off by superior sea power; to the triangular division of command among Clinton, Cornwallis and Germain, which compounded the confusion; to the timidity of the British naval commanders and the aggressiveness of a French admiral; and, most of all, to the flexibility of Washington's strategy, his ability to seize a grand opportunity when it came within his grasp.

It is hardly necessary to add that without the support of the French land and sea forces the victory at Yorktown could not have been achieved. That support had been long in coming. The bulk of the French army reached Newport in July 1780 after Sir Henry Clinton had evacuated his garrison from Rhode Island. The French forces were commanded by the Comte de Rochambeau, a fifty-five-year-old veteran of the Seven Years' War, tactful, dignified and astute. Without naval support, however, those forces might not have proved decisive. Previous French naval expeditions had been maddeningly futile. Lafayette, who played a central role in the Yorktown campaign, put his finger on the problem when he wrote Vergennes in January 1781 that naval superiority was the key to final victory. In the spring of '81 a powerful fleet commanded by the Comte de Grasse sailed from Brest for the West Indies. A giant of a man, energetic and enthusiastic, De Grasse had been directed to come to the American coast in July and August, relieve the smaller French fleet at Newport, and for a limited period act in co-operation with the French and American armies.

I. WASHINGTON'S STRATEGY LOOKS TO THE CHESAPEAKE

The original plan for combined operations was mapped out by Washington and Rochambeau at a conference held at Wethersfield, Connecticut, on May 21, 1781. There the American commander secured Rochambeau's reluctant consent to a joint attack against New York supported by the French West Indian fleet under De Grasse. Rochambeau left De Grasse free either to sail to New York or to operate against the British army in Virginia. The French army moved from Rhode Island and joined Washington's above New York early in July.

A number of events caused Washington to scrap this plan. Skirmishing at the outposts of New York City revealed that it would be bitterly contested.

Furthermore, De Grasse, taking advantage of the latitude in Rochambeau's instructions, decided to go to the Chesapeake rather than New York. It appears from Allen McLane's unpublished journal that he visited De Grasse in the West Indies and persuaded him of the advantages of sailing to Chesapeake Bay. On August 14 a letter from De Grasse reached Washington with news that he was sailing in force from the West Indies for the Chesapeake and that he could not remain longer than October, at which time it would be necessary for him to be on his station again. This ruled out a New York campaign and suggested to Washington the advisability of sending all the combined Franco-American forces that he could spare to Virginia. On August 17 Washington wrote De Grasse: "It has been judged expedient to turn our attention towards the South."

The new plan was carried out in greatest secrecy not only in order that Clinton would not be apprised of it, but also to prevent Admiral Graves, with his fleet in New York and Newport, from joining Sir Samuel Hood and, by occupying the Chesapeake, keeping open communications between Cornwallis and Clinton. Clinton seems to have assumed that the first movements of Washington's forces were aimed at Staten Island or Sandy Hook to cover the entrance of the French fleet into New York harbor. It was not until the main American army had crossed the Delaware that Washington's real objective became obvious. The Franco-American forces moved southward with speed. At Head of Elk they were brought down to Williamsburg by French transports provided by De Grasse. By September 25 the last detachments arrived on the scene and joined Lafayette's forces. The Franco-Americans now enjoyed an overwhelming military superiority of more than two to one over the defenders. Against Cornwallis' 7,500 troops, and an additional several hundred Loyalists, the combined Franco-American armies besieging Yorktown numbered 5,700 Continentals, 3,100 militia, and 7,000 French troops.

When Admirals Graves and Hood reached the Chesapeake they found that De Grasse had already entered that bay and blockaded the mouths of the James and the York. De Grasse went out and engaged the British fleets, and in his absence Admiral de Barras arrived from Newport with additional French ships. The combined naval forces proved too strong for the timid British fleet, which withdrew to New York. Cornwallis' doom was sealed.

1. Naval Superiority Will Decide the War

Lafayette to the Count de Vergennes.

New Windsor on the North River, January 20, 1781

The first copy of this letter will be delivered to you by Lieutenant-Colonel Laurens, aide-de-camp to General Washington, who is charged by Congress with a private mission. Permit me to recommend to you this officer as a man who, by his integrity, frankness and patriotism, must be extremely acceptable to Government.

According to the instructions of Congress, he will place before you the actual state of our affairs, which demand, I think more than ever, the most serious attention. As to the opinions which I may allow myself to express, sir,

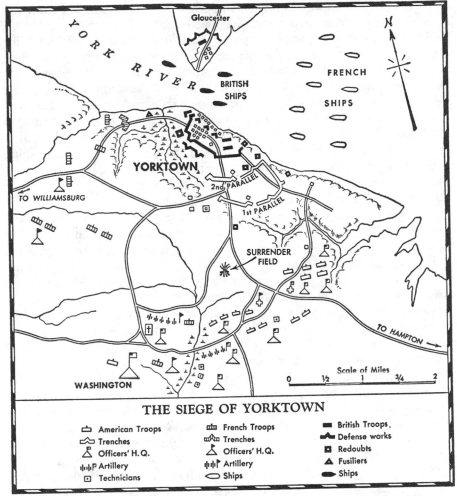

THE SIEGE OF YORKTOWN

American Troops	French Troops	British Troops,		
Trenches	Trenches	Defense works		
Officers' H.Q.	Officers' H.Q.	Redoubts		
Artillery	Artillery	Fusiliers		
Technicians	Ships	Ships		

From The Encyclopedia of American History   *Courtesy of Harper & Brothers*
by Richard B. Morris

they entirely correspond with those I have hitherto expressed, and the very slight alterations observable in them have been occasioned by a change of time, prejudice and circumstances.

With a naval inferiority it is impossible to make war in America. It is that which prevents us from attacking any point that might be carried with two or three thousand men. It is that which reduces us to defensive operations, as dangerous as they are humiliating. The English are conscious of this truth, and all their movements prove how much they desire to retain the empire of the sea. The harbours, the country and all the resources it offers appear to invite us to send thither a naval force. If we had possessed but a maritime superiority this spring, much might have been achieved with the army that M. de Rochambeau brought with him, and it would not have been necessary to have awaited the division he announced to us. If M. de Guichen [the French admiral whose squadron had been in the West Indies] had stopped at Rhode Island on his way to France, Arbuthnot would have been ruined, and not all Rodney's efforts could have prevented our gaining victories.

Since the hour of the arrival of the French, their inferiority has never for one moment ceased, and the English and the Tories have dared to say that France wished to kindle, without extinguishing, the flame. This calumny becomes more dangerous at a period when the English detachments are wasting the South; when, under the protection of some frigates, corps of fifteen hundred men are repairing to Virginia without our being able to get to them. On the whole continent, with the exception of the islands of Newport, it is physically impossible that we should carry on an offensive war without ships, and even on those islands the difficulty of transportation, the scarcity of provisions and many other inconveniences render all attempts too precarious to enable us to form any settled plan of campaign.

The result, sir, of all this is that, the advantage of the United States being the object of the war, and the progress of the enemy on that continent being the true means of prolonging it, and of rendering it, perhaps, even injurious to us, it becomes, in a political and military point of view, necessary to give us, both by vessels sent from France and by a great movement in the fleet in the islands, a decided naval superiority for the next campaign; and also, sir, to give us money enough to place the American forces in a state of activity: fifteen thousand of the regular army and ten thousand or, if we choose it, a still greater number of militia in this part of the country; a Southern army, of which I cannot tell precisely the extent, but which will be formed by the five Southern states, with all means of supporting in this country such a considerable force. Such, sir, are the resources that you may employ against the common enemy. Immense sums of money could not transport resources of equal value from Europe to America, but these, without a succour of money, although established on the very theatre of war, will become useless; and that succour, which was always very important, is now absolutely necessary.

The last campaign took place without a shilling having been spent; all that credit, persuasion and force could achieve has been done—but that can hold out no longer. That miracle, of which I believe no similar example can be found, cannot be renewed, and our exertions having been made to obtain an army for the war, we must depend on you to enable us to make use of it.

From my peculiar situation, sir, and from what it has enabled me to know and see, I think it is my duty to call your attention to the American soldiers, and on the part they must take in the operations of the next campaign. The Continental troops have as much courage and real discipline as those that are opposed to them. They are more inured to privation, more patient than Europeans, who, on these two points, cannot be compared to them. They have several officers of great merit, without mentioning those who have served during the last wars, and from their own talents have acquired knowledge intuitively; they have been formed by the daily experience of several campaigns, in which, the armies being small and the country a rugged one, all the battalions of the line were obliged to serve as advance-guards and light troops. The recruits whom we are expecting, and who only bear, in truth, the name of recruits, have frequently fought battles in the same regiments which they are now re-entering, and have seen more gun-shots than three-fourths of the European soldiers. As to the militia, they are only armed peasants, who have occasionally fought, and who are not deficient in ardour and discipline, but whose services would be most useful in the labours of a siege. . . .

The English having had sufficient time to think of all the naval points, the attacks of next year will be anything rather than surprises, and our forces must increase in proportion to their precautions. I could have wished that there had been some French troops, and my confidence in the decrease of prejudice has been even greater than that of Congress, General Washington or your minister at that time. The advance-guard of the Count de Rochambeau, although inactive itself from want of ships, by its presence alone has rendered an essential service to Amercia: if it had not arrived, the campaign would have been a ruinous one. When I consider the present state of feeling, my notion, as I have had the honour of telling you before, would be to send hither, for the expedition of New York, a division of about ten thousand Frenchmen. . . .

—LAFAYETTE, *Memoirs, Correspondence and Manuscripts*, pp. 373-379.

2. THE AMERICAN PLAN TO ATTACK NEW YORK IS ABANDONED

Diary of George Washington.

[*August 1st, 1781*]. By this date all my Boats were ready, viz—one hundred New ones at Albany (constructed under the direction of Gen. Schuyler) and the like number at Wappings Creek by the Quarter Master General; besides old ones which have been repaired. My heavy Ordnance and Stores from the Eastward had also come on to the North River and every thing would have been in perfect readiness to commence the operation against New York, if the States had furnished their quotas of men agreeably to my requisitions; but so far have they been from complying with these that of the first not more than half the number asked of them have joined the Army, and of 6200 of the latter pointedly and continuously called for to be with the army by the 15th of last Month, only 176 had arrived from Connecticut, independant of about 300 State Troops under the Command of Gen. Waterbury, which had been on the lines before we took the field, and two Companies of York levies (about 80 Man) under similar circumstances.

Thus circumstanced, and having little more than general assurances of getting the succours called for and energetic Laws and Resolves energetically executed, to depend upon, with little appearance of their fulfilment, I could scarce see a ground upon which to continue my preparations against New York; especially as there was much reason to believe that part (at least) of the Troops in Virginia were recalled to reinforce New York, and therefore I turned my views more seriously (than I had before done) to an operation to the Southward and, in consequence, sent to make inquiry, indirectly, of the principal Merchants to the Eastward what number, and what time, Transports could be provided to convey a force to the Southward if it should be found necessary to change our plan and similar application was made in a direct way to Mr. Morris (Financier) to discover what number could be had by the 20th. of this month at Philadelphia, or in Chesapeak bay. At the same time General Knox was requested to turn his thoughts to this business and make every necessary arrangement for it in his own mind, estimating the ordnance and Stores which would be wanting and how many of them could be obtained without a transport of them from the North River. Measures were also taken to deposit the Salt provisions in such places as to be Water-born; more than these, while there remained a hope of Count de Grasse's bringing a land force with him, and that the States might yet put us in circumstances to prosecute the original plan, could not be done without unfolding matters too plainly to the enemy and enabling them thereby to counteract our Schemes.

—FITZPATRICK, ed., *Diaries of Washington*, II, 248-250.

3. "OUR SITUATION REMINDS ME OF SOME THEATRICAL EXHIBITION"

Journal of Dr. James Thacher, attending the Continental Army.

[*Aug. 15th, 1781*]—General orders are now issued for the army to prepare for a movement at a moment's notice. The real object of the allied armies in the present campaign has become a subject of much speculation. Ostensibly an investment of the city of New York is in contemplation—preparations in all quarters for some months past indicate this to be the object of our combined operations. The capture of this place would be a decisive stroke, and from the moment such event takes place, the English must renounce all hopes of subjugating the United States. But New York is well fortified both by land and water and garrisoned by the best troops of Great Britain. The success of a siege must depend entirely on the arrival and coöperation of a superior French fleet. The enemy have a garrison on Staten Island, which is separated from Long Island only by a strait of two miles wide. The capture of this garrison would be a brilliant affair and would essentially facilitate our operations against New York.

General Washington and Count Rochambeau have crossed the North River, and it is supposed for the purpose of reconnoitering the enemy's posts from the Jersey shore. A field for an extensive encampment has been marked out on the Jersey side, and a number of ovens have been erected and fuel provided for the purpose of baking bread for the army. From these combined circumstances we are led to conclude that a part of our besieging force is to occupy that ground. But General Washington possesses a capacious mind, full of resources, and he resolves and matures his great plans and designs under an impenetrable veil of secrecy, and while we repose the fullest confidence in our chief, our own opinions must be founded only on doubtful conjectures. The royal army at New York have received a reinforcement of three thousand Germans from Europe.

20th.—According to orders, we commenced our line of march yesterday, a party of pioneers being sent forward to clear the road towards King's-bridge, and we expected immediately to follow in that direction; but an army is a machine whose motions are directed by its chief. When the troops were paraded for the march, they were ordered to the right about, and, making a retrograde movement up the side of the North River, we have reached King's-ferry and are preparing to cross the Hudson at this ferry. Our allies are in our rear, and it is probable we are destined to occupy the ground on the Jersey side.

21st.—Colonel Laurens has arrived at head-quarters on his way from Boston to Philadelphia. This gentleman is the son of Mr. Henry Laurens, our ambassador to Holland, who is now confined in the Tower of London. We have the pleasing information that he has brought with him from France a large sum of specie for the United States. He reports that the different powers of continental Europe are friendly to the cause in which we are engaged.

Our situation reminds me of some theatrical exhibition, where the interest and expectations of the spectators are continually increasing, and where curiosity is wrought to the highest point. Our destination has been for some time matter of perplexing doubt and uncertainty; bets have run high on one side that we were to occupy the ground marked out on the Jersey shore, to aid in the siege of New York, and on the other, that we are stealing a march on the enemy and are actually destined to Virginia in pursuit of the army under Lord Cornwallis.

We crossed at King's-ferry, 21st instant, and encamped at Haverstraw. A number of batteaux, mounted on carriages, have followed in our train, supposed for the purpose of conveying the troops over to Staten Island.

22d.—Resumed our line of march, passing rapidly through Paramus, Acquackanack, Springfield and Princeton. We have now passed all the enemy's posts and are pursuing our route with increasing rapidity towards Philadelphia; wagons have been prepared to carry the soldiers' packs, that they may press forward with greater facility. Our destination can no longer be a secret. The British army under Lord Cornwallis is unquestionably the object of our present expedition. It is now rumored that a French fleet may soon be expected to arrive in Chesapeake Bay, to coöperate with the allied army in that quarter. The great secret respecting our late preparations and movements can now be explained. It was a judiciously concerted stratagem, calculated to menace and alarm Sir Henry Clinton for the safety of the garrison of New York and induce him to recall a part of his troops from Virginia for his own defence; or, perhaps, keeping an eye on the city, to attempt its capture, provided that by the arrival of a French fleet favorable circumstances should present. The deception has proved completely successful; a part of Cornwallis' troops are reported to have returned to New York. His Excellency General Washington, having succeeded in a masterly piece of *generalship*, has now the satisfaction of leaving his adversary to ruminate on his own mortifying situation, and to anticipate the perilous fate which awaits his friend Lord Cornwallis in a different quarter. Major General Heath is left commander-in-chief of our army in the vicinity of New York and the highlands, and the menacing aspect of an attack on New York will be continued till time and circumstances shall remove the delusive veil from the eyes of Sir Henry Clinton, when it will probably be too late to afford succour to Lord Cornwallis.

To our officers, the inactivity of the royal army in New York is truly unaccountable: they might, without risking a great deal, harass our army on its march and subject us to irreparable injury; but the royalists are more dexterous in availing themselves of treachery and insurrection than in effecting valorous achievements.

In passing through Princeton but little time was allowed me to visit the college. This once celebrated seminary is now destitute of students, and the business of education is entirely suspended in consequence of the constant bustle and vicissitudes of war. The little village of Princeton is beautifully situated, and the college edifice is of stone, four stories high, and lighted by twenty-five windows in front in each story. It has suffered considerable injury in being occupied alternately by the soldiers of the two contending armies.

Trenton, where we are now encamped for the night, is a much more considerable village, and more advantageously situated, on the north-eastern bank of the Delaware, twenty-seven miles above Philadelphia. This is the town which General Washington has rendered famous to the latest times by a victory in which he so happily displayed the resources of his genius in the severe winter of 1776. Great indeed must be the resources of that man who can render himself the most formidable to an enemy when apparently he is the most destitute of power.

General Washington and Count Rochambeau having proceeded to Virginia by land, Major-General Lincoln takes the command of our troops, and the Baron de Viomenil those of the French.

　　　　　　　　　　　　　—THACHER, *Military Journal*, pp. 268-271.

4. THE ADVANCE ON YORKTOWN: "WHAT IS BECOME OF DE GRASSE?"

George Washington to Lafayette.

　　　　　　　　　　Head Quarters, Philadelphia, September 2, 1781

... Calculating upon the regular force under your immediate Orders, the Militia which have already been called for and may be expected in the field; the whole of the French Army, and the American Corps now marching with Major Gen Lincoln from the Northward in addition to the land Forces expected on board the Fleet; I flatter myself we shall not experience any considerable difficulties from the want of Men to carry our most favourite Projects into execution. The means for prosecuting a Seige with rapidity, energy, and success, and of supplying the Troops while they are engaged in that service (as they are more precarious) have been and still continue to be the great objects of my concern and attention.

Heavy Cannon, Ordnance Stores and Ammunition to a pretty large Amount, are now forwarding. General Knox, in whose immediate province these Arrangements are, who knows our whole resources, is making every exertion to furnish a competent supply, and will be on the spot to remedy every deficiency, as far as the circumstances will possibly admit.

Having also, from the first moment, been extremely anxious respecting the *Supplies* of the Army (in which, I comprehended not only Provisions of the Bread and Meat kind etc. but also Forage and the means of transportation) I had written pressingly to the Governors of Maryland and Virginia on that subject previous to the receipt of your favor of the 21st of August. I have since reiterated my Entreaties, and enforced in the strongest terms I was capable of using, the Requisitions for Specific Supplies made by Congress, and now again called for by the Superintendent of Finance from the States of Jersey, Delaware, and Maryland, and as to the supplies of Pennsylvania, we are to look for them, from the Financier himself. I hope and trust the efforts of these States and of Virginia will be uncommonly great and proportionate to the Magnitude of the object before us.

In Order to introduce some kind of System and Method in our Supplies, to know with certainty what may be depended upon, and to put the business in the best possible train of execution, I shall send forward the Heads of Departments as soon as their presence can be dispensed with. I have spoken to the Surgeon General respecting Hospital Stores and Medicines, all that can be done will be done in that department.

As to Cloathing I am sorry to inform you, little is to be expected, except in the Article of Shoes, of which a full supply will be sent on.

In my progress to the Southward, I shall take care, as far as practicable, to make all the Arrangements necessary for the Operation in view, and to impress the Executives, with an idea of the absolute necessity of furnishing their quotas of Supplies regularly, as we have no other resources to rely upon for the support of the Army, and especially, as I am very apprehensive, that a quantity of 1500 Barrels of salted Provisions which I had ordered to be shipped under Convoy of the Count de Barras, did not arrive in time for that purpose.

But my dear Marquis, I am distressed beyond expression, to know what is become of the Count de Grasse, and for fear the English Fleet, by occupying the Chesapeake (towards which my last accounts say they were steering) should frustrate all our flattering prospects in that quarter. I am also not a little solicitous for the Count de Barras, who was to have sailed from Rhode Island on the 23d Ulto. and from whom I have heard nothing since that time. Of many contingencies we will hope for the most propitious events.

Should the retreat of Lord Cornwallis by water, be cut off by the arrival of either of the French Fleets, I am persuaded you will do all in your power to prevent his escape by land. May that great felicity be reserved for you!

You See, how critically important the present Moment is: for my own part I am determined still to persist, with unremitting ardour in my present Plan, unless some inevitable and insuperable obstacles are thrown in our way.

Adieu my Dear Marquis! If you get any thing New from any quarter, send it I pray you *on the Spur of Speed,* for I am almost all impatience and anxiety.

—FITZPATRICK, ed., *Writings of Washington,* XXIII, 75-77.

5. "SUCH A TORRENT OF GOOD NEWS"

Colonel St. George Tucker of the Virginia militia to his wife.

Williamsburg, September 5, 1781

. . . Hear then, my Fanny, from me what perhaps you have not heard yet from good authority. About the middle of last week twenty-nine ships of the line and four frigates arrived in our bay, with four thousand land forces sent to our assistance by Louis the Great. Besides these there are three thousand marines to be landed in case of an emergency. Of the fleet there are ten sixty-fours; eighteen seventy-fours, and one ship of an hundred and ten guns! A fleet of twelve sail of the line has arrived in the West Indies to keep the enemy still employed in that quarter. Of the troops, three thousand five hundred landed at James Town three days ago and are now on their march to this city. Five hundred are left on board to land at York River. The fleet lies from Lynnhaven bay to the mouth of York River, and some, *we are informed*, have proceeded within two or three miles of the town. The British fleet still lies at York, and their land forces are now in the town.

The Count de Grasse, by a flag, declared to the admiral or the commodore of the British fleet that he would put every man to the sword who should fall into his hands if the fleet was destroyed. *This from report*. Lord Rawdon is actually a prisoner on board the French fleet, having been taken on his way to London with all his plunder. Gov. Bull of Charlestown is in the like predicament.

Our troops lie from four miles beyond this town to near James Town; so that Cornwallis is as effectually hemmed in as our troops were in Charlestown. Our force may now be reckoned to be eight thousand men—of which six thousand are regulars—exclusive of the marines whom I mentioned above.

Nor is this all, for, to my great surprise and pleasure, I was this morning informed from undoubted authority that General Washington is at the Head of Elk with five thousand troops, which are to be embarked from thence in transports sent there for that purpose, of which theMarquis last night received official accounts from General Washington in a letter dated at Chatham.

I have not yet done. The French fleet of ten line-of-battle ships, which lay at Rhode Island, are now actually on the way hither, and are daily expected. Whether the Count de Rochambeau, with his troops, is on board, I know not, nor, indeed, is it very material, I conceive.

If after such a torrent of good news I could wish to add another article, it would be that Lord Cornwallis, with his whole army, were in our possession. But this I hope, in that providence to which I prostrate myself with grateful adoration for the present happy aspect of our affairs, will be the subject of some future letter; or that I may, to the happiness of seeing you again, add that of being able to give you the first notice of so important and so happy an event.

My paper would blush to contain matters of lesser moment after what I have written.

　　　　　—TUCKER, "Letter," *Magazine of American History*, VII, 210.

6. "WE HAVE GOT HIM HANDSOMELY IN A PUDDING BAG"

General George Weedon of Virginia to Nathanael Greene.
　　　　　　　　　　Fredericksburg, September 5, 1781

The business with his Lordship in this State will very soon be at an end, for suppose you know e'er this that we have got him handsomly in a pudding bag with 5000 land forces and about 60 ships including transports.

Count de Grasse took possession of Chesapeak the 1st instant. Cornwallis with his whole force is in York. Four 32-gunn ships have entered York River, and others have secured James River. Gen. De St. [illegible] with 3000 men are landing to reinforce the Marquis and 3000 more are on their march from the northward. His Excellency Gen. Washington it is supposed will pay this armament a visit. Precautions are taken to prevent his Lordship from sliping over York River to plague you again, and if our stars dont most wonderfully deceive us, we shall shortly do his business.

You have stood beating like [illegible]. I have often shuddered for you but, knowing a little of your persevering disposition, have frequently said, "Never fear, the more danger the more honor. I will be bound for my old friend Green notwithstanding this little rebuff." And the event shews it. The success of your operations exceeds the most sanguine expectations, and you not coming into Lord Cornwallis's bate by trapsing after him to Virginia but pursueing the serpent in the South was a most masterly stroke. Please to remember I recommended it to you in the worst of our times here; and urged the propriety of leting us suffer rather than not eradicate the poison in that quarter. I well knew the line you would adopt, and only mentioned it to show you that I thought as you did, and nothing has gained you more real eclat than your wise disposition of the troops.

Our new governor is a military man and I promise you nothing will be wanting (that government can satisfy) to facilitate our plans. . . .

. . . Count de Grasse has 27 line-of-battle ships and six frigates besides the Rhode Island fleet, and I think, my dear fellow, there is little risque of our ever being the juniors at sea again. Indeed I hope to see us all set off for South Carolina the moment we do the business here. . . .

I am all on fire. By the Great God of War, I think we may all hand up our swords by the last of the year in perfect peace and security! When I first set down to write intended (if the fever wan't too severe) to have taken you first to the Marquis and Count de Grasse, looking into affairs there, to have whisked you over into the State of New York, nay to have dined you with Gen. W[ashington] and Count Rochambeau; then just touching at the West Indies, to have introduced you to Hyder Alley Khan in the East, and then to have delivered [you] safe over to the guards at High Hills of Santee. But this being a work too much for a sick man, let it suffice to tell you our affairs in all this quarter continue to flourish.

—WEEDON, Letter, Morgan Library.

II. DE GRASSE'S NAVAL VICTORY

On September 1, the day the British became aware of the true objectives of the American march southward, Graves and Hood cleared Sandy Hook to intercept De Grasse's West Indian fleet and Barras's supporting squadron which had left Newport three days earlier. De Grasse won the race to the Chesapeake. French cruisers took up positions in the James River to prevent Cornwallis from crossing and escaping to the south. Others sealed off the mouth of the York. The remainder of the main fleet kept watch at the mouth of the Chesapeake. Contact with the British fleet was made on September 5. Outnumbered by 24 heavy ships of the French to 19 of their own, the British allowed themselves to be hopelessly outmaneuvered as well. With his own fleet running in formation before the wind, Graves might have smashed the French fleet before it cleared Cape Henry, and again when the French van became separated from the center and rear. Graves failed to exploit his opportunities, and according to his junior, Sir Samuel Hood, the defeat of the British was the result of Graves's tactical blunders. The action was indecisive. By the time Graves considered renewing it, De Grasse had been reinforced by Barras, and the combined French fleets blocked passage to Chesapeake Bay. Abandoning the issue, Graves returned to New York and left Cornwallis to his fate. "We cannot succour him, nor venture to keep the sea any longer," Graves wrote Lord Sandwich on September 14.

1. De Grasse Drives Off the English Rescue Fleet

Journal of an anonymous French naval officer with the fleet of Admiral de Grasse.

... On the evening of the same day [September 2, 1781], M. du Portail, a French officer, dispatched by Generals Washington and Rochambeau, announced the departure of the squadron of Count de Barras, escorting the artillery and munitions necessary for the projected siege; he was also directed to ask the assistance of the light vessels of the fleet, to enable the army, on arriving at Baltimore, to come down the Elk by water. The admiral, in the absence of his boats, ordered the vessels of his fleet under 64's to prepare for this service. They were ready to sail September 5th, when the enemy's fleet was signaled.

It had been necessary to post ships-of-the-line at the mouth of the James and York to blockade by sea Lord Cornwallis's army and all the transports attached to his army; these had to be left at their stations; thus the fleet, reduced to twenty-four vessels, had orders to form, at noon, a line in order of swiftness, the tide favoring it at that hour. This movement was executed with such precision and boldness, in spite of the absence of the best-drilled part of the crew, that the enemy, doubtless taken by surprise, at once wore so as to be on the same tack as the French fleet. It had the cape E. and E. N. E.; in this position, being to leeward, it awaited the enemy's attack.

The issue of the expedition, the vacancy left by the crews employed in the debarkation, the fear of getting too far from the mouths of the York and James rivers, and the fear lest the English fleet, by its known superior sailing, should succeed in getting between these mouths and the French fleet, all obliged it to keep on the defensive. The enemy held the weather gage in excess. Their balls did not come near enough to the French to receive a reply. There was no appearance that the combat would become very warm, but the winds ordered otherwise; they shifted till they came to the northeast and forced the English to attack.

The two vans having come so close as to be almost within pistol shot, the fire was long well sustained, and the affair seemed about to be decisive, when Admiral Hood made a signal to the English rear division, which he commanded, to bear down on the French rear. The admiral witnessed this movement with pleasure and prepared to tack his whole fleet together, bearing N. N. W., which would inevitably have thrown the English line into confusion, but Admiral Graves anticipated him and signaled his whole fleet to keep the wind. The heads of the two fleets gradually fell off in consequence of this new order of the English admiral, and the fire ceased at 6½, P. M.

The French fleet passed the night in the presence of the enemy in line of battle, the fires in all the vessels lighted. These signs of victory were not belied in the morning, for we perceived by the sailing of the English that they had suffered greatly; so that during the night of the 9th-10th, they had to blow up the *Terrible*, 64, themselves, and another put into the Hook in a most wretched plight.

The two fleets, in sight of each other, spent the 6th of September in repairing, favored by the calm or rather by the feeble north wind that continued till 4 o'clock. The wind then came from the southwest, and the French availed themselves of it to approach the enemy. It was too late to engage again, and they lay that night as the preceding.

On the 7th of September at daybreak, the French fleet veered and tacked together to attack the head of the enemy's line; he made his van take the opposite tack; as the second English vessel wore, the French van had orders to use all efforts against the enemy; but the English fleet wore and formed a line of battle behind the last vessel. This movement withdrew the English from the French, who, to sail along the enemy's line, were unable to come up except by edging away while the English had studding sails. The variable winds and storms that sprang up in every direction then separated the two fleets.

On the 8th of September the wind was very fresh, and the fleets kept far apart. The English held the north, and it was precisely from this direction that the French expected the squadron of M. de Barras from Newport. It was very essential to gain the weather gage of the enemy, to prevent his revenging himself upon that squadron, composed of only seven ships of the line and one of 50; it escorted all the siege artillery, an object of vital importance. The fleet sailed northward, and at 6 P. M., the enemy lay N. N. W., and N. W. The weather gage thus gained, the French fleet hoped to preserve it to engage in the morning; but the enemy's fleet instantly wore. At 8 P. M., it made signals, and it was thought that they wished to try to get into Chesapeake Bay before us, the more so as on the 6th two frigates detached from the English fleet had entered at full sail.

While the fleets were observing each other, the wind fell during the night, and in the morning, September 9th, a squadron was discovered, though its flag could not be distinguished. The French fleet bore down on it in line of battle, but lost sight of it during the day. It was the squadron of M. de Barras, which anchored on the 10th in Chesapeake Bay. On the same day the French fleet, no longer discovering anything, took its route for the same bay, where it anchored the 11th; two English frigates, the *Iris* and *Richmond*, those detached from the enemy's fleet on the 6th, were taken as they were getting out to rejoin it, by the *Aigrette* and *Diligente*, which were chasing in front of the fleet. They paid dearly for the petty advantage of cutting the buoys which the fleet had left at the anchorage, on hoisting sail September 5.

—Shea, ed., *Operations of the French Fleet*, pp. 154-158.

2. Clinton Is "Prepared to Hear the Worst"

All this time [early in September 1781] I was so confident of our naval strength and Lord Cornwallis' capacity for retaining his post, at least as long as his provisions lasted, that I kept 5000 select troops ready in transports for joining him the instant I should hear that Admiral Graves had cleared the Chesapeake of the enemy's ships and a safe passage was opened for their going thither. For several experienced, sensible officers of rank who had lately left His Lordship at Yorktown were clearly of opinion, which they delivered in council, *that the position he was in might be defended with the troops he then had against twenty thousand assailants for at least three weeks after opened trenches.* And indeed the plans of the ground about Yorktown taken by both English and French officers, which I have since seen, seem strongly to favor this opinion and show that it was not ill founded, as they all represent the exterior position which Lord Cornwallis first occupied to be a space of ground somewhat higher than that round it, between *two impracticable ravines* ascending from the river and not four hundred yards asunder at their extremity, and commanding not only the approaches from the country but, as Mr. Washington expresses it in his letter to Congress, in a near advance all the rest of His Lordship's works in front of the town.

But, when I received the admiral's letter of the 9th of September favoring me with an account of his action on the 5th, I confess my faith in our naval superiority began to waver. However, as I flattered myself (and the admiral still believed it) that Barras' squadron composed part of the French fleet on that day, I was still inclined to hope that Admiral Digby's arrival, which was hourly expected, and the addition of the *Prudent* and the *Robust,* which were now refitted, would soon turn the scale in our favor and enable me to join His Lordship with such a body of troops as might not only dissipate every appearance of danger, but even procure some decisive advantage over the enemy.

This very unpleasant state of doubt, indecision and hope continued until the 23d, when the arrival of Lord Cornwallis' letter of the 16th and 17th of September informed us that Barras' squadron had not been in the action of the 5th, and that his junction with the Count de Grasse augmented the French fleet to thirty-six sail of the line. So unexpected a naval superiority on the side of the enemy—which far exceeded everything we had in prospect—was not a little alarming, and seemed to call for more than common exertion to evade the impending ruin. I consequently solicited an immediate conference in full council with the flag officers of the fleet (which had arrived at Sandy Hook on the 19th), when it was unanimously resolved that above 5000 troops should be embarked in the King's ships as soon as they could be refitted, and every possible effort made to form a junction with the army at Yorktown. A letter was consequently dispatched to Earl Cornwallis, with the approbation of the council, to inform him of their resolution *and that there was every reason to hope we should start from New York about the 5th of October,* to which I had an opportunity of adding that Admiral Digby was just arrived with three ships of the line.

But I must confess that, after I was thus fully apprised of the enemy's strength and informed by the admiral of the crippled condition of his fleet, I should not have been greatly displeased to have heard that Lord Cornwallis had made his escape to Carolina with everything he could take with him. For I could not well comprehend the meaning of His Lordship's declaration in his letter of the 16th that, *if he had no hopes of relief*, he would rather risk an action than defend his half-finished works, but [that], as I said Admiral Digby was hourly expected and *promised every exertion* to assist him, he did not think himself justifiable in putting the fate of the war on so desperate an attempt—as, upon recurring to the letters His Lordship referred to, I could not find that I had promised in them any exertions but *my own*, which I told him must depend upon Admiral Graves' success against De Grasse. But, the admiral's efforts having failed, and it appearing from His Lordship's postscript of the 17th that he knew the French ships of the line then investing his post were at least one-third in number more than we had any probability of even after Admiral Digby should join us, it was manifest His Lordship *could have no hopes of relief*.

Wherefore I was convinced, by his desiring me to *be prepared to hear the worst*, that upon this intelligence His Lordship had resumed his first idea of forcing his way through the enemy before Mr. Washington's junction with Lafayette, and retiring to the southward. But I happened to be single in this opinion, as all the other general officers in council judged the expression *worst* to mean something more serious than *retreat* arising from the unfinished state of His Lordship's works. It was accordingly proposed to their consideration whether a movement into Jersey, threatening Philadelphia, might not be made, provided it could be done without the risk of impeding the principal object we had in view, which was an attempt to join His Lordship in York River. But the general officers were unanimously of opinion that no delay whatsoever should be hazarded as long as we had any reason to expect the fleet would be ready to receive us. And indeed I readily concurred with this opinion, from my being perfectly convinced that nothing but a direct move to the Chesapeake and our being able, after forcing the French fleet, to effect a junction with His Lordship could be now of the least use toward saving the posts of York and Gloucester, or even a part of Lord Cornwallis' army.

—CLINTON, *The American Rebellion,* pp. 337-340.

III. THE SIEGE

Cornwallis occupied Yorktown and Gloucester, on the opposite shore, and pushed through an elaborate system of fortifications. Promptly on their arrival at Williamsburg between September 14 and 24 the allied forces took up siege positions before Yorktown, the Americans moving into a camp on the right and the French on the left, together forming a semicircle around Cornwallis' defenses. Across the river on the Gloucester shore the Duc de Lauzun hemmed in Tarleton. A great artillery barrage opened up on October 9, when Washington touched off the first cannon shot. The climax was reached with the storming by bayonet of two British redoubts near the river, Nos. 9 and 10. The French, under Lieutenant Colonel, the Count Guillaume de Deux-Ponts, were ordered to seize the former redoubt; the American assigned to lead the attack on No. 10 was Alexander Hamilton. Both officers executed their assignments brilliantly, Hamilton with comparatively light casualties.

Cornwallis still had one desperate chance—a night passage of his troops by water to Gloucester and a break-through northward. But a sudden storm forced him to abandon the project. Although he still had considerable ammunition, the British commander felt that there was no way out now but surrender.

It was not until October 17 that Clinton, with his usual timidity and indecision, dispatched a fleet to relieve Cornwallis. Before then Washington was obliged to use powerful arguments to keep De Grasse at his station in the Chesapeake. By the time the British fleet reached Cape Charles a schooner informed the commanders that Cornwallis had surrendered.

1. "Cornwallis May Now Tremble for His Fate"

Colonel St. George Tucker to his wife.

Williamsburg, September 15, 1781

I wrote you yesterday that General Washington had not yet arrived. About four o'clock in the afternoon his approach was announced. He had passed our camp—which is now in the rear of the whole army—before we had time to parade the militia. The French line had just time to form. The Continentals had more leisure. He approached without any pomp or parade, attended only by a few horsemen and his own servants. The Count de Rochambeau and Gen. Hand, with one or two more officers, were with him. I met him as I was endeavoring to get to camp from town in order to parade the brigade; but he had already passed it. To my great surprise he recognized my features and spoke to me immediately by name. Gen. Nelson, the Marquis, etc., rode up immediately after. Never was more joy painted in any countenances than theirs. The Marquis rode up with precipitation, clasped the General in his arms and embraced him with an ardor not easily described.

The whole army and all the town were presently in motion. The General—at the request of the Marquis de St. Simon—rode through the French lines. The troops were paraded for the purpose and cut a most splendid figure. He then visited the Continental line. As he entered the camp the cannon from the park of artillery and from every brigade announced the happy event. His train by this time was much increased; and men, women and children seemed to vie with each other in demonstrations of joy and eagerness to see their beloved countryman. His quarters are at Mr. Wythe's [George Wythe, signer of the Declaration of Independence] house. Aunt Betty has the honor of the Count de Rochambeau to lodge at her house.

We are all alive and so sanguine in our hopes that nothing can be conceived more different than the countenances of the same men at this time and on the first of June.

The troops which were to attend the General are coming down the bay; a part—if not all—being already embarked at the Head of Elk.

Cornwallis may now tremble for his fate, for nothing but some extraordinary interposition of his guardian angels seems capable of saving him and his whole army from captivity. . . .

—Tucker, "The Southern Campaign," *Magazine of American History,*
    VII, 212-213.

2. Washington Begs De Grasse to Stay in the Chesapeake

George Washington to Comte de Grasse.

Williamsburg, September 25, 1781

I cannot conceal from your Excellency the painful anxiety under which I have laboured since the receipt of the letter with which you honored me on the 23d inst.

The naval movements which Your Excellency states there as possible considering the intelligence communicated to you by the baron de Clossen, make it incumbent upon me to represent the consequences that wd arise from them, and to urge a perseverance in the plan already agreed upon. Give me leave in the first place to repeat to Yr Excellency that the enterprise against York under the protection of your Ships is as certain as any military operation can be rendered by a decisive superiority of strength and means; that it is in fact reducible to calculation, and that the surrender of the british Garrison will be so important in itself and its consequences, that it must necessarily go a great way towards terminating the war, and securing the invaluable objects of it to the Allies.

Your Excellency's departure from the Chesapeake by affordg an opening for the succour of York, which the enemy wd instantly avail himself of, would frustrate these brilliant prospects, and the consequence would be not only the disgrace and loss of renouncing an enterprise, upon which the fairest expectations of the Allies have been founded, after the most expensive preparations and uncommon exertions and fatigues; but the disbanding perhaps the whole Army for want of provisions.

The present Theatre of the War is totally deficient in means of land transportation, being intersected by large rivers, and the whole dependance for interior communication being upon small Vessels. The Country has been much exhausted besides by the ravages of the enemy and the subsistence of our own Army; that our supplies can only be drawn from a distance and under cover of a fleet Mistress of the Chesapeake.

I most earnestly entreat Your Excellency farther to consider that if the present opportunity shd be missed; that if you shld withdraw your maritime force from the position agreed upon, that no future day can restore us a similar occasion for striking a decisive blow; that the british will be indefatigable in strengthening their most important maritime points, and that the epoch of an honorable peace will be more remote than ever.

The confidence with which I feel myself inspired by the energy of character and the naval talents which so eminently distinguish Yr Excellency leaves me no doubt that upon a consideration of the consequences which must follow your departure from the Chesapeake, that Yr Excellency will determine upon the possible measure which the dearest interests of the common cause wd dictate.

I had invariably flattered myself from the accounts given me by skilful mariners, that Your Excellys position, moored in the Chesapeake might be made so respectable, as to bid defiance to any attempt on the pt of the british fleet, at the same time that it wd support the operations of a siege, secure the transportation of our supplies by water and oeconomise the most precious time by facilitating the debarkation of our heavy Artillery and stores conveniently to the trenches in York River. It is to be observed that the strength of the enemy's reinforcement announced under Admiral Digby as we have the intelligence from the british, may not only be exaggerated, but altogether a finesse, and supposing the account consistent with truth: their total force it was hoped wd. not put them in condition to attack with any prospect of success.

If the stationary position which had been agreed upon should be found utterly impracticable, there is an alternative which however inferior considered relatively to the support and facility of our land operations would save our affairs from ruin; this is to cruise with Your Excellency's fleet within view of the capes, so as effectually to prevent the entrance of any british Vessels.

Upon the whole, I shd. esteem myself deficient in my duty to the common cause of France and America, if I did not persevere in entreating Yr. Excellency to resume the plans that have been so happily arranged, and if invincible maritime reasons prevent, I depend as a last resource upon Your Excellency's pursuing the alternative above mentioned and rendering the Chesapeake inaccessible to any Enemys Vessel.

However the British Admiral may manoeuvre and endeavour to divert Yr Excellency from the object in view, I can hardly admit a belief that it can be his serious intention to engage in a general action with a Fleet whose force will be superior supposing the most flattering accounts for the British to be true; past experience having taught them to engage with caution even upon equal terms, and forced from them acknowledgements, which prove the respect with which they have been inspired.

Let me add Sir that even a momentary absence of the french fleet may expose us to the loss of the british Garrison at York as in the present state of affairs Ld Cornwallis might effect the evacuation with the loss of his Artillery and baggage and such a sacrifice of men as his object would evidently justify.

The Marquis de la fayette who does me the honor to bear this to Yr Excellency will explain many peculiarities of our situation which could not well be comprised in a letter; his candour and abilities are well known to Yr Excellency and entitle him to the fullest confidence in treating the most important interests. I have earnestly requested him not to proceed any farther than the Cape for fear of accidents shd Yr. Excellency have put to sea; in this case he will dispatch a Letter to Yr Excellency in addition to this. I have the honor etc.

—FITZPATRICK, ed., *Writings of Washington*, XXIII, 136-139.

3. THE DUC DE LAUZUN PROVES THAT TARLETON IS NOT IRRESISTIBLE

Memoirs of Armand-Louis de Gontaut, Duc de Lauzun, French cavalry officer under General de Choisy.

Just as we reached the Gloucester plain [on October 3, 1781] some

Virginia state dragoons came up in great fright and told us that they had seen the English dragoons out and that for fear of accident they had hurried to us at full speed without stopping to see anything more. I went forward to learn what I could. I saw a very pretty woman at the door of a little farmhouse on the high road; I went up to her and questioned her; she told me that Colonel Tarleton had left her house a moment before; that he was very eager to shake hands with the French Duke. I assured her that I had come on purpose to gratify him. She seemed very sorry for me, judging from experience, I suppose, that Tarleton was irresistible; the American troops seemed to be of the same opinion.

I was not a hundred steps from the house when I heard pistol shots from my advance guard. I hurried forward at full speed to find a piece of ground where I could form a line of battle. As I arrived I saw the English cavalry in force three times my own; I charged it without halting; we met hand to hand. Tarleton saw me and rode towards me with pistol raised. We were about to fight single-handed between the two troops when his horse was thrown by one of his own dragoons pursued by one of my lancers. I rode up to him to capture him; a troop of English dragoons rode in between us and covered his retreat; he left his horse with me. He charged me twice without breaking my line; I charged the third time, overthrew a part of his cavalry and drove him within the entrenchment of Gloucester. He lost an officer, some fifty men, and I took quite a number of prisoners.

—LAUZUN, "Memoirs," *Magazine of American History*, VI, 53.

4. THE SIEGE BEGINS

Journal of Colonel Jonathan Trumbull, secretary to George Washington.

[*September*] *28.* A most wonderful and very observable coincidence of favorable circumstances having concentered our various and extended preparations, the army commences its march from Williamsburg and approaches within two miles of York Town. The enemy on our approach make some shew of opposition from their cavalry, but upon our bringing up some field pieces and making a few shot, they retire, and we take a quiet position for the night.

The General and family sleep in the field without any other covering than the canopy of the heavens and the small spreading branches of a tree, which will probably be rendered venerable from this circumstance for a length of time to come. Previous to this movement the enemies post at Glocester on the opposite side of York River had been invested by a body of militia under the command of Gen. Wedon, the French Legion of the Duke de Lauzun, and a body of French troops from the fleet all under the command of Brig. Gen. De Choisey. By the approach of the main body, and lying of the French ships in the mouth of the river, the enemy were now completely invested, except by water above the town, where they are yet open, and their boats are troublesome up the river for some distance. To close them on this side the General has proposed it to the admiral to run some ships above the town and to take their station there.

[*September*] *29.* The American troops take their station in the front of the enemies works, extend from the left of Pigeon Quarter to Moor's Mill on Wormley's Creek, near the river.

The French troops occupy the left of the Americans and extend to the river above the town. No opposition this day except a few shots from the extream works, and small firing from their jagers and our rifle men.

[*September*] *30.* In the morning it is discovered that the enemy have evacuated all their exterior works, and retired to their interior defence near the town. We immediately take possession of Pigeon Quarter and hill, and of the enemies' redoubts, and find ourselves very unexpectedly upon very advantageous ground, commanding their line of works in near approach. Scarce a gun fired this day. At night our troops begin to throw up some works and to take advantage of the enemies' evacuated labours.

Colonel Scammel,* being officer of the day, is cruelly wounded and taken prisoner while reconnoitering.

—TRUMBULL, "Journal," *Mass. Hist. Soc. Proc.*, XIV, 334-335.

5. ADVANCE OF THE SIEGEWORKS

Entries for October 2 and 4-9, 1781, in the journal of Colonel Richard Butler, and for October 3 and 7 in the diary of James Duncan, both of the Pennsylvania Line.

[Butler] *October 2d.*—The fire of the enemy more severe this morning; about 10 o'clock, A.M. they brought up two 18-pounders in addition to what they brought yesterday. They fired severely all day; the shot expended amounted to 351 between sun-rise and sun-set. Wayne's brigade ordered to camp for convenience, but still the covering party till sun-set. The fire of the enemy continued all night. About 10 o'clock, P.M., a heavy firing of the ships in the bay. I reconnoitered the post at Gloster and the shipping, which I compute at 10 sail; the Gloster post not strong—I think, by the size of the camp, 1,000 men; their works not regular, they have one good water battery on the York side; I observed a good work close by the bank with four embrasures, the ground very good for approaches. In general our works go on slow, the heavy artillery hard to get up; not one piece of cannon as yet fired at them. Indeed, I discover very plainly that we are young soldiers in a siege; however, we are determined to benefit ourselves by experience; one virtue we possess, that is perseverance. . . .

[Duncan] *October 3.*—Last night four men of our regiment, detached with the first brigade, were unfortunately killed (on covering party) by one ball; one of the men belonged to my own company (Smith), a loss I shall ever regret, as he was, without exception, one of the finest men in the army. A militia man this day, possessed of more bravery and [*sic*] prudence, stood constantly on the parapet and d——d his soul if he would dodge for the buggers. He had escaped longer than could have been expected, and, growing fool-hardy, brandished his spade at every ball that was fired, till, unfortunately, a ball came and put an end to his capers. . . .

---

* Later information revealed that Alexander Scammell had been shot in the back by a British soldier after he surrendered, and died of his wounds.

[Butler] *October 4th.*—Very little firing all day. Wayne and Colonel Butler went to reconnoiter on the York River side, the enemy very busy forming new works. Two deserters from the enemy, who report that Cornwallis' army is very sickly, to the amount of 2000 men in the hospital, and that the troops had scarce ground to live on, their shipping in a very naked state and their cavalry very scarce of forage. 2000 French marines landed on Gloster side from Count de Grasse at 9 o'clock P.M. A smart firing of small arms, which brought a very heavy cannonade all night.

[Butler] *October 5th.*—Cannonading all morning. Our part increases fast, and things go on well. To-day about 4 o'clock P.M., Corporal Organ, a brave and honest soldier, was unfortunately killed by a cannon shot; a great deal of firing through the night. Pennsylvania and Maryland Militia for gabion making to-morrow. Confirmation of General Green's success came to the Commander-in-Chief.

[Butler] *October 6th.*—Pennsylvania and some other troops went to gabion making; finished a great number and carried them to the right near the York River, 400 paces from the enemy. The first parallel and other works being laid out by the engineer; a body of troops ordered under Generals Lincoln, Wayne and Clinton to break ground and form works, the materials being got ready and brought previously to the spot. The enemy kept up a severe cannonade all night; it began on the left of the allied army, who lost some men killed and one officer and several men wounded; their intention was to possess the enemy's advanced redoubt on the York River, but one of the dragoons having deserted, the enemy discovered the intention, which caused the enemy to keep up an (almost) incessant fire that way through the night; the allied army, finding the enemy too well apprized, contented themselves with going on with their work. The American part of the army on duty made great progress in forming lines and batteries without the loss of a man.

[Butler] *October 7th.*—The whole continued at work, notwithstanding the enemies fire through the whole day and night. About day light, a very sharp fire of small arms commenced, succeeded by artillery; they go on well, and our loss as yet very trifling; indeed the siege appears to be no more than an experimental movement.

[Duncan] *October 7th.*— . . . The trenches were this day to be enlivened with drums beating and colors flying, and this honor was conferred on our division of light infantry. . . . Immediately upon our arrival the colors were planted on the parapet with this motto: *Manus haec inimica tyrannis.* Our next maneuver was rather extraordinary. We were ordered to mount the bank, front the enemy, and there by word of command go through all the ceremony of soldiery, ordering and grounding our arms; and although the enemy had been firing a little before, they did not now give us a single shot. I suppose their astonishment at our conduct must have prevented them, for I can assign no other reason. Colonel Hamilton gave these orders, and although I esteem him one of the first officers in the American army, must beg leave in this instance to think he wantonly exposed the lives of his men. . . .

[Butler] *October 8th, 1781.*—The division of Steuben for the trenches to-day. This is composed of the Virginia, Maryland and Pennsylvania troops.

The enemy continued to cannonade, mounted at 12 o'clock. The enemy kept hard at work, and fired incessantly on our fatigue parties, who really wrought hard and completed one large battery on our extreme right, on the bank of the river, on which three 29-pounders, three 18-pounders, two 10-inch mortars and two 8-inch howitzers were mounted. The Marquis de St. Simon had a battery completed on the extreme left, of eight 18 and 12-pounders, two 10-inch mortars and two 8-inch howitzers, both which batteries were made ready to open at the same instant. A very fine battery of twelve 32, 24, and 18-pounders, six 10-inch mortars and six 8-inch howitzers was forwarded, with small batteries on the right and left of this grand centre battery. The enemy seem embarrassed, confused and indeterminate; their fire seems feeble to what might be expected; their works, too, are not formed on any regular plan, but thrown up in a hurry occasionally, and although we have not as yet fired one shot from a piece of artillery, they are as cautious as if the heaviest fire was kept up.

[Butler] *October 9th.*—Relieved by Major General Lincoln's division. This day, at 3 o'clock, P.M., the batteries of Lamb and the Marquis de St. Simon opened with great elegance and were quickly followed. The Commander-in-Chief paid the allies the compliment of firing first. The shot and shells flew incessantly through the night, dismounted the guns of the enemy and destroyed many of their embrasures.

—BUTLER, "Journal," *Historical Magazine*, VIII, 107-108; DUNCAN, "Diary," *Pennsylvania Archives*, 2d Ser., XV, 748-752.

6. WASHINGTON UP FRONT WITH THE SAPPERS AND MINERS

Narrative of Sergeant James Sullivan Martin, from Connecticut.

We now began to make preparations for laying close siege to the enemy. We had holed him and nothing remained but to dig him out. Accordingly, after taking every precaution to prevent his escape, settled our guards, provided fascines and gabions, made platforms for the batteries, to be laid down when needed, brought on our battering pieces, ammunition, etc., on the fifth of October we began to put our plans into execution.

One third part of all the troops were put in requisition to be employed in opening the trenches. A third part of our sappers and miners were ordered out this night to assist the engineers in laying out the works. It was a very dark and rainy night. However, we repaired to the place and began by following the engineers and laying laths of pine wood end to end upon the line marked out by the officers for the trenches. We had not proceeded far in the business before the engineers ordered us to desist and remain where we were, and be sure not to straggle a foot from the spot while they were absent from us.

In a few minutes after their departure, there came a man alone to us, having on a surtout, as we conjectured (it being exceeding dark), and inquired for the engineers. We now began to be a little jealous for our safety, being alone and without arms, and within forty rods of the British trenches. The stranger inquired what troops we were; talked familiarly with us a few minutes, when, being informed which way the officers had gone, he went off in the same direction, after strictly charging us, in case we should be taken prisoners, not to discover to the enemy what troops we were. We were obliged to him for his kind advice, but we considered ourselves as standing in no great need of it; for we knew as well as he did that sappers and miners were allowed no quarters, at least are entitled to none by the laws of warfare, and of course should take care, if taken and the enemy did not find us out, not to betray our own secret.

In a short time the engineers returned and the aforementioned stranger with them; they discoursed together sometime, when, by the officers often calling him "Your Excellency," we discovered that it was Gen. Washington. Had we dared, we might have cautioned him for exposing himself so carelessly to danger at such a time, and doubtless he would have taken it in good part if we had. But nothing ill happened to either him or ourselves.

It coming on to rain hard, we were ordered back to our tents, and nothing more was done that night. The next night, which was the sixth of October, the same men were ordered to the lines that had been there the night before. We this night completed laying out the works. The troops of the line were there ready with entrenching tools and began to entrench, after General Washington had struck a few blows with a pickaxe, a mere ceremony, that it might be said, "Gen. Washington with his own hands first broke ground at the siege of Yorktown." The ground was sandy and soft, and the men employed that night eat no "idle bread" (and I question if they eat any other), so that by daylight they had covered themselves from danger from the enemy's shot, who, it appeared, never mistrusted that we were so near them the whole night, their attention being directed to another quarter. There was upon the right of their works a marsh; our people had sent to the western side of this marsh a detachment to make a number of fires, by which, and our men often passing before the fires, the British were led to imagine that we were about some secret mischief there, and consquently directed their whole fire to that quarter, while we were entrenching literally under their noses.

As soon as it was day they perceived their mistake and began to fire where they ought to have done sooner. They brought out a fieldpiece or two without their trenches and discharged several shots at the men who were at work erecting a bomb-battery; but their shot had no effect and they soon gave it over. They had a large bull-dog, and every time they fired he would follow their shots across our trenches. Our officers wished to catch him and oblige him to carry a message from them into the town to his masters, but he looked too formidable for any of us to encounter.

I do not remember, exactly, the number of days we were employed before we got our batteries in readiness to open upon the enemy, but think it was not more than two or three. The French, who were upon our left, had completed their batteries a few hours before us, but were not allowed to discharge their pieces till the American batteries were ready. Our commanding battery was on the near bank of the river and contained ten heavy guns; the next was a bomb-battery of three large mortars; and so on through the whole line; the whole number, American and French, was ninety-two cannon, mortars and howitzers. Our flagstaff was in the ten-gun battery, upon the right of the whole.

I was in the trenches the day that the batteries were to be opened; all were upon the tiptoe of expectation and impatience to see the signal given to open the whole line of batteries, which was to be the hoisting of the American flag in the ten-gun battery. About noon the much-wished-for signal went up. I confess I felt a secret pride swell my heart when I saw the "star-spangled banner" waving majestically in the very faces of our implacable adversaries; it appeared like an omen of success to our enterprize, and so it proved in reality. A simultaneous discharge of all the guns in the line followed, the French troops accompanying it with "Huzza for the Americans!"

It was said that the first shell sent from our batteries entered an elegant house, formerly owned or occupied by the Secretary of State under the British government, and burnt directly over a table surrounded by a large party of British officers at dinner, killing and wounding a number of them;—this was a warm day to the British.

—MARTIN(?), *Narrative of a Revolutionary Soldier*, pp. 166-169.

7. AN ARMY SURGEON DESCRIBES THE GREAT CANNONADE

Journal of Dr. James Thacher.

From the 10th to the 15th [of October 1781], a tremendous and incessant firing from the American and French batteries is kept up, and the enemy return the fire, but with little effect. A red-hot shell from the French battery set fire to the *Charon*, a British 44-gun ship, and two or three smaller vessels at anchor in the river, which were consumed in the night. From the bank of the river I had a fine view of this splendid conflagration. The ships were enwrapped in a torrent of fire, which, spreading with vivid brightness among the combustible rigging, and running with amazing rapidity to the tops of the several masts, while all around was thunder and lightning from our numerous cannon and mortars, and in the darkness of night, presented one of the most sublime and magnificient spectacles which can be imagined. Some of our shells, overreaching the town, are seen to fall into the river and, bursting, throw up columns of water like the spouting of the monsters of the deep.

We have now made further approaches to the town by throwing up a second parallel line and batteries within about three hundred yards; this was effected in the night, and at day-light the enemy were roused to the greatest exertions; the engines of war have raged with redoubled fury and destruction on both sides, no cessation day or night. The French had two officers wounded and fifteen men killed and wounded, and among the Americans, two or three were wounded. I assisted in amputating a man's thigh.

The siege is daily becoming more and more formidable and alarming, and his lordship must view his situation as extremely critical, if not desperate. Being in the trenches every other night and day, I have a fine opportunity of witnessing the sublime and stupendous scene which is continually exhibiting. The bombshells from the besiegers and the besieged are incessantly crossing each others' path in the air. They are clearly visible in the form of a black ball in the day, but in the night they appear like a fiery meteor with a blazing tail, most beautifully brilliant, ascending majestically from the mortar to a certain altitude and gradually descending to the spot where they are destined to execute their work of destruction.

It is astonishing with what accuracy an experienced gunner will make his calculations, that a shell shall fall within a few feet of a given point, and burst at the precise time, though at a great distance. When a shell falls, it whirls round, burrows, and excavates the earth to a considerable extent and, bursting, makes dreadful havoc around. I have more than once witnessed fragments of the mangled bodies and limbs of the British soldiers thrown into the air by the bursting of our shells; and by one from the enemy, Captain White, of the Seventh Massachusetts Regiment, and one soldier were killed and another wounded near where I was standing. About twelve or fourteen men have been killed or wounded within twenty-four hours. I attended at the hospital, amputated a man's arm and assisted in dressing a number of wounds.

The enemy having two redoubts, about three hundred yards in front of their principal works, which enfiladed our intrenchment and impeded our approaches, it was resolved to take possession of them both by assault. The one on the left of the British garrison, bordering on the banks of the river, was assigned to our brigade of light-infantry, under the command of the Marquis de la Fayette. The advanced corps was led on by the intrepid Colonel Hamilton, who had commanded a regiment of light-infantry during the campaign, and assisted by Colonel Gimat.

The assault commenced at eight o'clock in the evening, and the assailants bravely entered the fort with the point of the bayonet without firing a single gun. We suffered the loss of eight men killed and about thirty wounded, among whom Colonel Gimat received a slight wound in his foot, and Major Gibbs, of his excellency's guard, and two other officers were slightly wounded. Major Campbell, who commanded in the fort, was wounded and taken prisoner, with about thirty soldiers; the remainder made their escape. I was desired to visit the wounded in the fort even before the balls had ceased whistling about my ears, and saw a sergeant and eight men dead in the ditch. A captain of our infantry, belonging to New Hampshire, threatened to take the life of Major Campbell to avenge the death of his favorite, Colonel Shammel; but Colonel Hamilton interposed, and not a man was killed after he ceased to resist.

During the assault, the British kept up an incessant firing of cannon and musketry from their whole line. His Excellency General Washington, Generals Lincoln and Knox, with their aids, having dismounted, were standing in an exposed situation waiting the result.

Colonel Cobb, one of General Washington's aids, solicitous for his safety, said to His Excellency, "Sir, you are too much exposed here. Had you not better step a little back?"

"Colonel Cobb," replied His Excellency, "if you are afraid, you have liberty to step back."

The other redoubt on the right of the British lines was assaulted at the same time by a detachment of the French, commanded by the gallant Baron de Viomenil. Such was the ardor displayed by the assailants that all resistance was soon overcome, though at the expense of nearly one hundred men killed and wounded. Of the defenders of the redoubt, eighteen were killed, and one captain and two subaltern officers and forty-two rank and file captured.

Our second parallel line was immediately connected with the two redoubts now taken from the enemy, and some new batteries were thrown up in front of our second parallel line, with a covert way and angling work approaching to less than three hundred yards of their principal forts. These will soon be mantled with cannon and mortars, and when their horrid thundering commences, it must convince his lordship that his post is not invincible, and that submission must soon be his only alternative. Our artillery-men, by the exactness of their aim, make every discharge take effect, so that many of the enemy's guns are entirely silenced, and their works are almost in ruins.

—THACHER, *Military Journal*, pp. 283-286.

8. FATAL DELAY OF THE SECOND BRITISH RELIEF EXPEDITION

Rear Admiral Samuel Hood of the British Navy to George Jackson of the Admiralty.

The Barfleur at Sandy Hook, October 14, 1781

On the 24th of last month I attended a consultation of generals and admirals at Sir H. Clinton's, when it was agreed to attempt by the united efforts of army and navy to relieve Lord Cornwallis in the Chesapeake, and I proposed to have three or four fireships immediately prepared, with which the enemy's fleet may possibly be deranged and thrown into some confusion, and thereby give a favourable opening for pushing through it. This was approved, and upwards of 5,000 troops are to be embarked in the King's ships.

While this business was under deliberation, word was brought that Rear-Admiral Digby with the *Canada* and *Lion* were off the Bar. . . . I thank God the disabled ships are now ready, and but for an accident of the *Alcides* driving on board the *Shrewsbury* and carrying away her bowsprit and foreyard, I imagine all the ships would have been here this day; but I hope and trust they will be down tomorrow, and that we shall be moving the day after if the wind will permit. Every moment, my dear Jackson, is precious; and I flattered myself when we came in that we should ere this have been in the Chesapeake, but the repairs of the squadron have gone on unaccountably tedious, which has filled me with apprehension that we shall be too late to give relief to Lord Cornwallis. I pray God grant my fears may prove abortive!

It would, in my humble opinion, have been a most fortunate event had Mr. Graves gone off to Jamaica upon Mr. Digby's arrival as commander-in-chief by commission, and I am persuaded you will think so too, when I relate one circumstance only. On the 7th I received a letter from Mr. Graves, desiring I would meet the flag officers and some captains upon a consultation on board the *London* at ten o'clock the next morning, and acquaint Captain Cornwallis and Captain Reynolds that their company was desired also. Soon after we were assembled, Mr. Graves proposed, and wished to reduce to writing, the following question: "Whether it was practicable to relieve Lord Cornwallis in the Chesapeake?" This astonished me exceedingly, as it seemed plainly to indicate a design of having difficulties started against attempting what the generals and admirals had *most unanimously* agreed to and given under their hands on the 24th of last month, and occasioned my replying immediately that it appeared to me a very unnecessary and improper question, as it had been already maturely discussed and determined upon to be attempted with all the expedition possible; that my opinion had been very strong and pointed (which I was ready to give in writing with my name to it); that an attempt under every risk should be made to force a junction with the troops the commander-in-chief [Sir Thomas Graves] embarks in his Majesty's fleet with the army under General Earl Cornwallis at York; and admitting that junction to be made without much loss, and the provisions landed, I was also of opinion the first favourable opportunity should be embraced of attacking the French fleet, though I own to you I think very meanly of the ability of the present commanding officer. I know he is a *cunning* man, he may be a good theoretical man, but he is certainly a bad practical one, and most clearly proved himself on the 5th of last month to be unequal to the conducting of a great squadron.

If it shall please the Almighty to give success to the arms of his Majesty in the business we are going upon, I think we shall stand a-tiptoe. The *Torbay* and *Prince William* arrived on the 13th, a noble acquisition, and makes my heart bound with joy. Why the *Chatham* is not with us also is matter of astonishment to me.

[P. S.] I trust you will bear in mind that I write to you most *confidentially*. *Desperate* cases require *bold* remedies.

—GRAVES, Papers, pp. 116-118.

9. "THE LAST HOPE OF THE BRITISH ARMY"

By Lieutenant Colonel Banastre Tarleton.

A retreat by Gloucester was the only expedient that now presented itself to avert the mortification of a surrender or the destruction of a storm. Though this plan appeared less practicable than when first proposed, and was adopted at this crisis as the last resource, it yet afforded some hopes of success. In the evening [October 16] Earl Cornwallis sent Lord Chewton to Gloucester, with explicit directions for Lieutenant-Colonel Tarleton to prepare some artillery and other requisites from his garrison to accompany the British troops with which his lordship designed to attack Brigadier de Choisy before daybreak, and afterwards retreat through the country. The guards of cavalry and infantry at Tarleton's post were immediately augmented, and many officers were advanced as sentries, to prevent any intelligence being conveyed to the enemy. All the commanding officers of regiments were afterwards acquainted with the intended project, that their corps might be completely assembled and equipped. The spare horses of the garrison were ordered to parade for the benefit of the infantry, and the necessary artillery and waggons were prepared. A number of sailors and soldiers were dispatched with boats from Gloucester, to assist the troops in passing the river.

Earl Cornwallis sent off the first embarkation before eleven o'clock that night, consisting of the light infantry, great part of the brigade of guards, and the 23d Regiment, and purposed himself to pass with the second, when he had finished a letter to General Washington, calculated to excite the humanity of that officer towards the sick, the wounded and the detachment that would be left to capitulate. Much of the small craft had been damaged during the siege; yet it was computed that three trips would be sufficient to convey over all the troops that were necessary for the expedition.

The whole of the first division arrived before midnight, and part of the second had embarked, when a squall, attended with rain, scattered the boats and impeded their return to Gloucester. About two o'clock in the morning the weather began to moderate, when orders were brought to the commanding officers of the corps that had passed, to re-cross the water. As the boats were all on the York side the river, in order to bring over the troops, it required some time to row them to Gloucester, to carry back the infantry of the first embarkation; but soon after daybreak they returned under the fire of the enemy's batteries to Earl Cornwallis, at York town.

Thus expired the last hope of the British army.

—TARLETON, *History of Campaigns in the Southern Provinces,* pp. 396-400.

10. "I HAVE THE MORTIFICATION TO INFORM YOUR EXCELLENCY"

Lord Cornwallis to Sir Henry Clinton.

Yorktown, October 20, 1781

I have the mortification to inform your Excellency that I have been forced to give up the posts of York and Gloucester, and to surrender the troops under my command, by capitulation on the 19th inst. as prisoners of war to the combined forces of America and France.

I never saw this post in a very favourable light, but when I found I was to be attacked in it in so unprepared a state, by so powerful an army and artillery, nothing but the hopes of relief would have induced me to attempt its defence; for I would either have endeavoured to escape to New-York, by rapid marches from the Gloucester side, immediately on the arrival of General Washington's troops at Williamsburgh, or I would notwithstanding the disparity of numbers have attacked them in the open field, where it might have been just possible that fortune would have favoured the gallantry of the handful of troops under my command. But being assured by your Excellency's letters that every possible means would be tried by the navy and army to relieve us, I could not think myself at liberty to venture upon either of those desperate attempts; therefore, after remaining for two days in a strong position in front of this place, in hopes of being attacked, upon observing that the enemy were taking measures which could not fail of turning my left flank in a short time, and receiving on the second evening your letter of the 24th of September informing that the relief would sail about the 5th of October, I withdrew within the works on the night of the 29th of September, hoping by the labour and firmness of the soldiers to protract the defence until you could arrive. Every thing was to be expected from the spirit of the troops, but every disadvantage attended their labour, as the works were to be continued under the enemy's fire, and our stock of intrenching tools, which did not much exceed four hundred when we began to work in the latter end of August, was now much diminished.

The enemy broke ground on the night of the 30th and constructed on that night, and the two following days and nights, two redoubts, which, with some works that had belonged to our outward position, occupied a gorge between two creeks or ravines, which come from the river on each side of the town.

On the night of the 6th of October they made their first parallel, extending from its right on the river to a deep ravine on the left, nearly opposite to the center of this place and embracing our whole left at the distance of six hundred yards. Having perfected this parallel, their batteries opened on the evening of the 9th against our left, and other batteries fired at the same time against a redoubt advanced over the creek upon our right and defended by about one hundred and twenty men of the 23d Regiment and marines, who maintained that post with uncommon gallantry. The fire continued incessant from heavy cannon and from mortars and howitzes, throwing shells from eight to sixteen inches, until all our guns on the left were silenced, our work much damaged, and our loss of men considerable.

On the night of the 11th they began their second parallel, about three hundred yards nearer to us. The troops being much weakened by sickness as well as by the fire of the besiegers, and observing that the enemy had not only secured their flanks but proceeded in every respect with the utmost regularity and caution, I could not venture so large sorties as to hope from them any considerable effect; but otherwise I did every thing in my power to interrupt this work, by opening new embrazures for guns and keeping up a constant fire with all the howitzes and small mortars that we could man.

On the evening of the 14th, they assaulted and carried two redoubts that had been advanced about three hundred yards for the purpose of delaying their approaches and covering our left flank, and during the night included them in their second parallel, on which they continued to work with the utmost exertion.

Being perfectly sensible that our works could not stand many hours after the opening of the batteries of that parallel, we not only continued a constant fire with all our mortars and every gun that could be brought to bear upon it, but a little before daybreak on the morning of the 16th I ordered a sortie of about three hundred and fifty men under the direction of Lieutenant-Colonel Abercrombie to attack two batteries, which appeared to be in the greatest forwardness, and to spike the guns. A detachment of guards with the Eightieth Company of Grenadiers, under the command of Lieutenant-Colonel Lake attacked the óne, and one of light infantry under the command of Major Armstrong attacked the other, and both succeeded by forcing the redoubts that covered them, spiking eleven guns, and killing or wounding about one hundred of the French troops, who had the guard of that part of the trenches, and with little loss on our side. This action, though extremely honourable to the officers and soldiers who executed it, proved of little public advantage, for the cannon, having been spiked in a hurry, were soon rendered fit for service again, and before dark the whole parallel and batteries appeared to be nearly complete.

At this time we knew that there was no part of the whole front attacked on which we could show a single gun, and our shells were nearly expended; I therefore had only to chuse between preparing to surrender next day or endeavouring to get off with the greatest part of the troops, and I determined to attempt the latter, reflecting that though it should prove unsuccessful in its immediate object, it might at least delay the enemy in the prosecution of further enterprizes. Sixteen large boats were prepared, and upon other pretexts were ordered to be in readiness to receive troops precisely at ten o'clock. With these I hoped to pass the infantry during the night, abandoning our baggage, and leaving a detachment to capitulate for the town's people and the sick and wounded; on which subject a letter was ready to be delivered to General Washington.

After making my arrangements with the utmost secrecy, the light infantry, greatest part of the Guards and part of the Twenty-Third Regiment landed at Gloucester; but at this critical moment the weather, from being moderate and calm, changed to a most violent storm of wind and rain and drove all the boats, some of which had troops on board, down the river. It was soon evident that the intended passage was impracticable, and the absence of the boats rendered it equally impossible to bring back the troops that had passed; which I had ordered about two in the morning. In this situation, with my little force divided, the enemy's batteries opened at daybreak. The passage between this place and Gloucester was much exposed, but the boats having now returned, they were ordered to bring back the troops that had passed during the night, and they joined us in the forenoon without much loss.

Our works in the mean time were going to ruin, and not having been able to strengthen them by abbatis, nor in any other manner but by a slight fraizing which the enemy's artillery were demolishing wherever they fired, my opinion entirely coincided with that of the engineer and principal officers of the army, that they were in many places assailable in the forenoon, and that by the continuence of the same fire for a few hours longer, they would be in such a state as to render it desperate with our numbers to attempt to maintain them. We at that time could not fire a single gun. Only one eight-inch and little more than an hundred cohorn shells remained. A diversion by the French ships of war that lay at the mouth of York River was to be expected. Our numbers had been diminished by the enemy's fire, but particularly by sickness, and the strength and spirits of those in the works were much exhausted by the fatigue of constant watching and unremitting duty.

Under all these circumstances, I thought it would have been wanton and inhuman to the last degree to sacrifice the lives of this small body of gallant soldiers, who had ever behaved with so much fidelity and courage, by exposing them to an assault, which from the numbers and precautions of the enemy could not fail to succeed. I therefore proposed to capitulate.

—STEVENS, ed., *Clinton-Cornwallis Controversy*, II, 205-213.

IV. CORNWALLIS SURRENDERS

Once Cornwallis decided to surrender he had no alternative but to accept Washington's terms. These were, on the whole, both just and generous. The British army was to surrender to the Americans; the navy to the French. Officers were to retain their side arms and private property; soldiers to be kept in

Virginia, Maryland or Pennsylvania; Cornwallis and some other officers per-mitted to return home on parole. The ceremony itself was to take place on October 19:

> *The garrison of York will march out to a place to be appointed in front of the posts, at two o'clock precisely, with shouldered arms, colours cased, and drums beating a British or German march. They are then to ground their arms, and return to their encampments, where they will remain until they are dispatched to the places of their destinations. Two works on the Gloucester side will be delivered at one o'clock to a detachment of French and American troops appointed to possess them. The garrison will march out at three o'clock in the afternoon; the cavalry with their swords drawn, trumpets sounding, and the infantry in the manner prescribed for the gar-rison of York. They are likewise to return to their encampments until they can be finally marched off.*

As Cornwallis was not equal to making his surrender in person, his second in command, General Charles O'Hara, officiated; Washington's second in command, General Lincoln, received O'Hara's sword.

A New Jersey officer reported that "the British officers in general behaved like boys who had been whipped at school. Some bit their lips; some pouted; others cried. Their round, broad-brimmed hats were well-adapted to the oc-casion, hiding those faces they were ashamed to show."

1. "An Ardent Desire to Spare the Further Effusion of Blood"

A. cornwallis to washington, october 17, 1781

I propose a cessation of hostilities for twenty-four hours, and that two officers may be appointed by each side, to meet at Mr. Moore's house, to settle terms for the surrender of the posts of York and Gloucester.

B. washington to cornwallis, october 17

I have had the Honor of receiving Your Lordship's Letter of this Date.

An Ardent Desire to spare the further Effusion of Blood, will readily in-cline me to listen to such Terms for the Surrender of your Posts and Garrisons at York and Gloucester, as are admissible.

I wish previous to the Meeting of Commissioners, that your Lordship's proposals in writing, may be sent to the American Lines: for which Purpose, a Suspension of Hostilities during two Hours from the Delivery of this Letter will be granted.

C. cornwallis to washington, october 17

I have this moment been honoured with your Excellency's letter, dated this day.

The time limited for sending my answer will not admit of entering into the detail of articles; but the basis of my proposals will be, that the garrisons of York and Gloucester shall be prisoners of war, with the customary honours. And, for the conveniency of the individuals which I have the honour to com-mand, that the British shall be sent to Britain, and the Germans to Germany, under engagement not to serve against France, America, or their allies, until released or regularly exchanged. That all arms and public stores shall be delivered up to you; but that the usual indulgence of side-arms to officers, and of retaining private property, shall be granted to officers and soldiers, and that the interest of several individuals, in civil capacities and connected with us, shall be attended to.

If your Excellency thinks that a continuance of the suspensions of hostilities will be necessary, to transmit your answer, I shall have no objection to the hour that you may propose.

D. WASHINGTON TO CORNWALLIS, OCTOBER 18

To avoid unnecessary Discussions and Delays, I shall at Once, in Answer to your Lordship's Letter of Yesterday, declare the general Basis upon which a Definitive Treaty and Capitulation must take place.

The Garrisons of York and Gloucester, including the Seamen, as you propose, will be received Prisoners of War. The Condition annexed, of sending the British and German Troops to the parts of Europe to which they respectively belong, is inadmissible. Instead of this, they will be marched to such parts of the Country as can most conveniently provide for their Subsistence; and the Benevolent Treatment of Prisoners, which is invariably observed by the Americans, will be extended to them. The same honors will be granted to the Surrendering Army as were granted to the Garrison of Charles town.

The Shipping and Boats in the two Harbours, with all their Guns, Stores, Tackling, Furniture and Apparel, shall be delivered in their present State to an Officer of the Navy, appointed to take possession of them.

The Artillery, Arms, Accoutrements, Military Chest and Public Stores of every Denomination, shall be delivered unimpaired to the Heads of Departments, to which they respectively belong.

The Officers shall be indulged in retaining their Side Arms, and the Officers and Soldiers may preserve their Baggage and Effects, with this Reserve, that Property taken in the Country, will be reclaimed.

With Regard to the Individuals in civil Capacities, whose Interests Your Lordship wishes may be attended to, until they are more particularly described, nothing definitive can be settled.

I have to add, that I expect the Sick and Wounded will be supplied with their own Hospital Stores, and be attended by British Surgeons, particularly charged with the Care of them.

Your Lordship will be pleased to signify your Determination either to accept or reject the Proposals now offered, in the Course of Two Hours from the Delivery of this Letter, that Commissioners may be appointed to digest the Articles of Capitulation, or a Renewal of Hostilities may take place.

E. CORNWALLIS TO WASHINGTON, OCTOBER 18

I agree to open a treaty of capitulation upon the basis of the garrisons of York and Gloucester, including seamen, being prisoners of war, without annexing the condition of their being sent to Europe; but I expect to receive a compensation in the articles of capitulation for the surrender of Gloucester in its present state of defence.

I shall, in particular, desire, that the *Bonetta* sloop of war may be left entirely at my disposal, from the hour that the capitulation is signed, to receive an aid-de-camp to carry my dispatches to Sir Henry Clinton. Such soldiers as I may think proper to send as passengers in her, to be manned with fifty men of her own crew, and to be permitted to sail without examination, when my dispatches are ready: engaging, on my part, that the ship shall be brought back and delivered to you, if she escapes the dangers of the sea, that the crew and soldiers shall be accounted for in future exchanges, that she shall carry off no officer without your consent, nor public property of any kind; and I shall likewise desire, that the traders and inhabitants may preserve their property, and that no person may be punished or molested for having joined the British troops.

If you choose to proceed to negociation on these grounds, I shall appoint two field officers of my army to meet two officers from you, at any time and place that you think proper, to digest the articles of capitulation.

—JOHNSTON, *The Yorktown Campaign*, pp. 185-187.

2. "THIS IS TO US A MOST GLORIOUS DAY"

Journal of Dr. James Thacher.

[*October*] *19th.*—This is to us a most glorious day, but to the English, one of bitter chagrin and disappointment. Preparations are now making to receive as captives that vindictive, haughty commander and that victorious army, who, by their robberies and murders, have so long been a scourge to our brethren of the Southern states. Being on horseback, I anticipate a full share of satisfaction in viewing the various movements in the interesting scene.

The stipulated terms of capitulation are similar to those granted to General Lincoln at Charleston the last year. The captive troops are to march out with shouldered arms, colors cased and drums beating a British or German march, and to ground their arms at a place assigned for the purpose. The officers are allowed their side-arms and private property, and the generals and such officers as desire it are to go on parole to England or New York. The marines and seamen of the king's ships are prisoners of war to the navy of France; and the land forces to the United States. All military and artillery stores to be delivered up unimpaired. The royal prisoners to be sent into the interior of Virginia, Maryland and Pennsylvania in regiments, to have rations allowed them equal to the American soldiers, and to have their officers near them. Lord Cornwallis to man and despatch the *Bonetta* sloop-of-war with despatches to Sir Henry Clinton at New York without being searched, the vessel to be returned and the hands accounted for.

At about twelve o'clock, the combined army was arranged and drawn up in two lines extending more than a mile in length. The Americans were drawn up in a line on the right side of the road, and the French occupied the left. At the head of the former, the great American commander, mounted on his noble courser, took his station, attended by his aids. At the head of the latter was posted the excellent Count Rochambeau and his suite. The French troops, in complete uniform, displayed a martial and noble appearance; their bands of music, of which the timbrel formed a part, is a delightful novelty and produced while marching to the ground a most enchanting effect. The Americans, though not all in uniform, nor their dress so neat, yet exhibited an erect, soldierly air, and every countenance beamed with satisfaction and joy. The concourse of spectators from the country was prodigious, in point of numbers was probably equal to the military, but universal silence and order prevailed.

It was about two o'clock when the captive army advanced through the line formed for their reception. Every eye was prepared to gaze on Lord Cornwallis, the object of peculiar interest and solicitude; but he disappointed our anxious expectations; pretending indisposition, he made General O'Hara his substitute as the leader of his army. This officer was followed by the conquered troops in a slow and solemn step, with shouldered arms, colors cased and drums beating a British march. Having arrived at the head of the line, General O'Hara, elegantly mounted, advanced to his excellency the commander-in-chief, taking off his hat, and apologized for the non-appearance of Earl Cornwallis. With his usual dignity and politeness, his excellency pointed to Major-General Lincoln for directions, by whom the British army was conducted into a spacious field, where it was intended they should ground their arms.

The royal troops, while marching through the line formed by the allied army, exhibited a decent and neat appearance, as respects arms and clothing, for their commander opened his store and directed every soldier to be furnished with a new suit complete, prior to the capitulation. But in their line of march we remarked a disorderly and unsoldierly conduct, their step was irregular, and their ranks frequently broken.

But it was in the field, when they came to the last act of the drama, that the spirit and pride of the British soldier was put to the severest test: here their mortification could not be concealed. Some of the platoon officers appeared to be exceedingly chagrined when giving the word "*ground arms,*" and I am a witness that they performed this duty in a very unofficer-like manner; and that many of the soldiers manifested a *sullen temper*, throwing their arms on the pile with violence, as if determined to render them useless. This irregularity, however, was checked by the authority of General Lincoln. After having grounded their arms and divested themselves of their accoutrements, the captive troops were conducted back to Yorktown and guarded by our troops till they could be removed to the place of their destination.

The British troops that were stationed at Gloucester surrendered at the same time and in the same manner to the command of the Duke de Luzerne [Lauzun].

This must be a very interesting and gratifying transaction to General Lincoln, who, having himself been obliged to surrender an army to a haughty foe the last year, has now assigned him the pleasing duty of giving laws to a conquered army in return, and of reflecting that the terms which were imposed on him are adopted as a basis of the surrender in the present instance. It is a very gratifying circumstance that every degree of harmony, confidence and friendly intercourse subsisted between the American and French troops during the campaign—no contest, except an emulous spirit to excel in exploits and enterprise against the common enemy, and a desire to be celebrated in the annals of history for an ardent love of great and heroic actions.

We are not to be surprised that the pride of the British officers is humbled on this occasion, as they have always entertained an exalted opinion of their own miltiary prowess and affected to view the Americans as a contemptible, undisciplined rabble. But there is no display of magnanimity when a great commander shrinks from the inevitable misfortunes of war; and when it is considered that Lord Cornwallis has frequently appeared in splendid triumph at the head of his army, by which he is almost *adored*, we conceive it incumbent on him cheerfully to participate in their misfortunes and degradations, however humiliating; but it is said he gives himself up entirely to vexation and despair.

—THACHER, *Military Journal*, pp. 288-290.

3. LORD NORTH: "OH GOD! IT IS ALL OVER"

Memoirs of Sir Nathaniel Wraxall, who was in London in 1781.

[*November 1781*]. During the whole month of November, the concurring accounts which were transmitted to Government, enumerating Lord Cornwallis's embarrassments and the positions taken by the enemy, augmented the anxiety of the Cabinet. Lord George Germain in particular, conscious that on the prosperous or adverse termination of that expedition must depend the fate of the American contest, his own stay in office, as well as probably the duration of the Ministry, felt, and even expressed to his friends, the strongest uneasiness on the subject. The meeting of Parliament meanwhile stood fixed for the 27th of November.

On Sunday the 25th about noon, official intelligence of the surrender of the British forces at Yorktown arrived from Falmouth at Lord George Germain's house in Pall-Mall. Lord Walsingham, who, previous to his father Sir William de Grey's elevation to the peerage, had been Under-Secretary of State in that department, and who was selected to second the address in the House of Peers on the subsequent Tuesday, happened to be there when the messenger brought the news. Without communicating it to any other person, Lord George, for the purpose of dispatch, immediately got with him into a hackney-coach and drove to Lord Stormont's residence in Portland Place. Having imparted to him the disastrous information and taken him into the carriage, they instantly proceeded to the Chancellor's house in Great Russell Street, Bloomsbury, whom they found at home, when after a short consultation, they determined to lay it themselves in person before Lord North.

He had not received any intimation of the event when they arrived at his door in Downing Street between one and two o'clock. The First Minister's firmness, and even his presence of mind, which had withstood the [Gordon] riots of 1780, gave way for a short time under this awful disaster. I asked Lord George afterwards how he took the communication when made to him. "As he would have taken a ball in his breast," replied Lord George. For he opened his arms, exclaiming wildly, as he paced up and down the apartment during a few minutes, "O God! it is all over!"—words which he repeated many times under emotions of the deepest consternation and distress.

When the first agitation of their minds had subsided, the four Ministers discussed the question whether or not it might be expedient to prorogue Parliament for a few days; but as scarcely an interval of forty-eight hours remained before the appointed time of assembling, and as many members of both Houses were already either arrived in London or on the road, that proposition was abandoned. It became, however, indispensable to alter and almost to model anew the King's speech, which had been already drawn up and completely prepared for delivery from the throne. This alteration was therefore made without delay, and at the same time Lord George Germain, as Secretary for the American Department, sent off a dispatch to his Majesty, who was then at Kew, acquainting him with the melancholy termination of Lord Cornwallis's expedition. Some hours having elapsed before these different but necessary acts of business could take place, the Ministers separated, and Lord George Germain repaired to his office in Whitehall. There he found a confirmation of the intelligence, which arrived about two hours after the first communication, having been transmitted from Dover, to which place it was forwarded from Calais with the French account of the same event.

I dined on that day at Lord George's, and though the information which had reached London in the course of the morning from two different quarters was of a nature not to admit of long concealment, yet it had not been communicated either to me or to any individual of the company (as it might have been through the channel of common report), when I got to Pall-Mall between five and six o'clock. Lord Walsingham, who likewise dined there, was the only guest that had become acquainted with the fact. The party, nine in number, sat down to table. Lord George appeared serious, though he manifested no discomposure. Before the dinner was finished, one of his servants delivered him a letter, brought back by the messenger who had been dispatched to the King.

Lord George opened and perused it, then looking at Lord Walsingham, to whom he exclusively directed his observation, "The King writes," said he, "just as he always does, except that I observe he has omitted to mark the hour and the minute of his writing with his usual precision."

This remark, though calculated to awaken some interest, excited no comment; and while the ladies, Lord George's three daughters, remained in the room we repressed our curiosity. But they had no sooner withdrawn than, Lord George having acquainted us that from Paris information had just arrived of the old Count de Maurepas, First Minister, lying at the point of death, "It would grieve me," said I, "to finish my career, however far advanced in years, were I First Minister of France, before I had witnessed the termination of this great contest between England and America."

"He has survived to witness that event," replied Lord George with some agitation.

Utterly unsuspicious as I was of the fact which had happened beyond the Atlantic, I conceived him to allude to the indecisive naval action fought at the mouth of the Chesapeake early in the preceding month of September between

Admiral Graves and Count de Grasse: an engagement which in its results might prove most injurious to Lord Cornwallis.

Under this impression, "My meaning," said I, "is that if I were the Count de Maurepas, I should wish to live long enough to behold the final issue of the war in Virginia."

"He has survived to witness it completely," answered Lord George. "The army has surrendered, and you may peruse the particulars of the capitulation in that paper," taking at the same time one from his pocket, which he delivered into my hand not without visible emotion.

By his permission I read it aloud, while the company listened in profound silence. We then discussed its contents as affecting the Ministry, the country and the war. It must be confessed that they were calculated to diffuse a gloom over the most convivial society, and that they opened a wide field for political speculation.

After perusing the account of Lord Cornwallis's surrender at Yorktown, it was impossible not to feel a lively curiosity to know how the King had received the intelligence, as well as how he had expressed himself in his note to Lord George Germain on the first communication of so painful an event. He gratified our wish by reading it to us, observing, at the same time, that it did the highest honour to his Majesty's fortitude, firmness and consistency of character. The words made an impression on my memory which the lapse of more than thirty years has not erased, and I shall here commemorate its tenor as serving to show how that prince felt and wrote under one of the most afflicting as well as humiliating occurrences of his reign. The billet ran nearly to this effect:

"I have received with sentiments of the deepest concern the communication which Lord George Germain has made me of the unfortunate result of the operations in Virginia. I particularly lament it on account of the consequences connected with it and the difficulties which it may produce in carrying on the public business or in repairing such a misfortune. But I trust that neither Lord George Germain nor any member of the Cabinet will suppose that it makes the smallest alteration in those principles of my conduct which have directed me in past time and which will always continue to animate me under every event in the prosecution of the present contest."

Not a sentiment of despondency or of despair was to be found in the letter, the very handwriting of which indicated composure of mind. Whatever opinion we may entertain relative to the practicability of reducing America to obedience by force of arms at the end of 1781, we must admit that no sovereign could manifest more calmness, dignity or self-command than George III displayed in this reply.

—WRAXALL, *Historical and Posthumous Memoirs*, II, 137-142.

4. "THE WORLD TURNED UPSIDE DOWN"

One of the minor mysteries of the ceremonies revolves around the particular piece of music the British band played when the troops marched out to surrender. *Under the terms of the capitulation they were not permitted to play an American or French tune but limited to British or German ones. Dr. Thacher and "Light-Horse Harry" Lee say it was a British march. St. George Tucker tells us that the British drummers beat "a slow march," and at retreat the previous evening played the tune of "Welcome, Brother Debtor." There is some evidence that more than drummers participated, that a full band played. That is what John Conrad Doehla reported.*

Not long after Yorktown the tradition became well entrenched that the tune actually played here, as at the very beginning of the war on Colonel Leslie's retreat from Salem Bridge was, appropriately enough, "The World Turned Upside Down, or The Old Woman Taught Wisdom," quite a different version from the earlier English ballad of the same title. Later, when the words were printed on a music sheet, they were adapted to the English tune, Derry Down.

The version which has the strongest support in tradition and which because of its appropriateness we would like to believe was played appeared in the Gentleman's Magazine *of 1766, beginning "Goody Bull and her daughter fell out." But a case has been made for an imaginative but frothy bit, which was more amusing if less pertinent. It ran something like this:*

> *If buttercups buzzed after the bee,*
> *If boats were on land, churches on sea,*
> *If ponies rode men and grass ate the cows,*
> *And cats should be chased to holes by the mouse,*
> *If the mamas sold their babies to the gypsies for half a crown;*
> *Summer were spring and the t'other way round,*
> *Then all the world would be upside down.*

Regardless of which tune the British played, Yorktown inspired one of the most amazing ballads of the Revolution. Throughout the land Americans sang a tune which began thus:

> *Cornwallis led a country dance,*
> *The like was never seen, sir.*
> *Much retrograde and much advance,*
> *And all with General Greene, sir.*

But the dance comes to a surprising finale as the Americans and the French draw their net around their enemy ever tighter:

> *Now hand in hand they circle round*
> *This ever-dancing pair, sir:*
> *Their gentle movements soon confound*
> *The earl as they draw near, sir.*

> *His music soon forgets to play—*
> *His feet can no more move, sir,*
> *And all his bands now curse the day*
> *They jiggéd to our shore, sir.*

> *Now Tories all, what can ye say?*
> *Come—is not this a griper,*
> *That while your hopes are danced away,*
> *'Tis you must pay the piper?*

"THE WORLD TURNED UPSIDE DOWN"

Goody Bull and her daughter together fell out.
Both squabbled, and wrangled, and made a damned rout,
But the cause of the quarrel remains to be told.
Then lend both your ears, and a tale I'll unfold.

The old lady, it seems, took a freak in her head
That her daughter, grown woman, might earn her own bread:
Self-applauding her scheme, she was ready to dance;
But we're often too sanguine in what we advance.

For mark the event: thus by fortune we're crossed,
Nor should people reckon without their good host;
The daughter was sulky, and wouldn't come to,
And pray, what in this case could the old woman do?

In vain did the matron hold forth in the cause
That the young one was able; her duty, the laws;
Ingratitude vile, disobedience far worse;
But she might e'en as well sung psalms to a horse.

Young, froward and sullen, and vain of her beauty,
She tartly replied that she knew well her duty,
That other folks' children were kept by their friends,
And that some folks loved people but for their own ends.

"Zounds, neighbor!" quoth Pitt, "what the devil's the matter?
A man cannot rest in his house for your clatter."
"Alas!" cries the daughter, "here's dainty fine work.
The old woman grown harder than a Jew or than Turk."

"She be damned," says the farmer, and to her he goes,
First roars in her ears, then tweaks her old nose.
"Hallo, Goody, what ails you? Wake! woman, I say;
I am come to make peace in this desperate fray.

"Adzooks, ope thine eyes, what a pother is here!
You've no right to compel her, you have not, I swear;
Be ruled by your friends, kneel down and ask pardon,
You'd be sorry, I'm sure, should she walk Covent Garden."

"Alas!" cries the old woman, "and must I comply?
But I'd rather submit than the huzzy should die."
"Pooh, prithee be quiet, be friends and agree,
You must surely be right, *if you're guided, by me*."

Unwillingly awkward, the mother knelt down,
While the absolute farmer went on with a frown,
"Come, kiss the poor child, there come, kiss and be friends!
There, kiss your poor daughter, and make her amends."

"No thanks to you, Mother," the daughter replied;
"But thanks to my friend here, I've humbled your pride."
     —*Gentleman's Magazine*, XXXVI, 140-141.

CHAPTER THIRTY-THREE

Winning the Peace

THE SUCCESSFUL *negotiation of the treaty of peace with Great Britain still stands as the greatest achievement in the history of American diplomacy. The United States obtained all its principal objectives—independence, adequate continental territory, access to international waterways, and fisheries. That solid achievement is a tribute to the perspicacity and stubbornness of the American peace negotiators—Benjamin Franklin, John Jay and John Adams. The fourth commissioner, Henry Laurens, who had been captured and confined to the Tower of London, was released, but was strangely dilatory in joining his fellow commissioners. He arrived at the very last hour of the negotiations and signed the preliminary articles of peace. At times it seemed as though they were being obstructed by their friends and helped by their enemies. It is an intriguing speculation that had the Americans been less adamant on one point, the insistence on the preliminary acknowledgment of independence, an even more favorable treaty might have been secured. These British-American negotiations were but a fragment of a larger world peace, in which belligerents and neutrals all had a substantial stake. The ability of the American negotiators to hold out against the world for indispensable terms of peace is a dramatic and inspiring story, portions of which are told in the following accounts by the men who made the peace.*

I. FRANCE SEEKS TO DICTATE THE AMERICAN PEACE

Toward the latter part of the American Revolution it was clear that the principal American objective of the war, the recognition of independence, was not an indispensable condition to peace to the Continental powers. Temporary recognition of de facto *independence subject to subsequent readjustments within the British Empire was as much as most of the European powers were ready to demand of England. Spain had sought to mediate the conflict before declaring war on Britain. Then a combined Austro-Russian mediation attempt was made and bogged down. Meantime, Vergennes, who was balancing half a dozen balls on the head of a cane, became concerned about the prolonged and costly character of the war. He was anxious to bring belligerency to an end and willing to compromise to do so. Blocking the road to compromise was American intransigence on the subject of independence, along with her insistence on the navigation of the Mississippi, her territorial ambitions, and her demand to share in the fisheries.*

By February 1781, Vergennes was prepared to end the war between the

United States and Britain on the basis of a long-time truce accepting the actual war map at the beginning of that year. This would have left the British in possession of Maine, New York City, part of the Old Northwest, Charleston and Savannah. In order to carry through a program so objectionable to Americans, Vergennes needed a more pliant peace commission. At that moment it consisted of only one man, the stubborn, independent and irascible John Adams. Vergennes instructed the French minister to America, the Chevalier de la Luzerne, that changes should be made in the peace mission, that Adams should be instructed to take the advice of the King of France, and that the United States should moderate its terms.

As early as December 1775, Bonvouloir, a French agent in America, had boasted of Congress, "I can do what I please with them." Through influence and probably bribery Luzerne was to make substantial headway. For example, Luzerne, according to his own letter to Vergennes, advanced money to General Sullivan, then a member of Congress. Sullivan later insisted that this sum was accepted as a loan, but there is no evidence that he ever paid back a cent of the money.

Luzerne prevailed with Congress. Adams was no longer sole peace commissioner, but was given three colleagues—Franklin, Jay and Laurens (Jefferson did not accept the assignment). Congress on June 15, 1781, instructed the commissioners to be governed in peace-making by the French court. These instructions evoked an eloquent protest from John Jay. Luzerne claimed to have great influence with Robert R. Livingston, Secretary of Foreign Affairs, and to have worked with him on the drafts of instructions which went out from his office. In his instructions of January 7, 1782, Livingston repeated Congress' earlier instruction that the commissioners should in effect be governed by the advice and opinions of their ally, the King of France.

1. "No Step Without the Approbation of His Majesty"

Statement of Chevalier de la Luzerne, minister to the United States.

May 28, 1781

The minister communicated to the committee several observations respecting the conduct of Mr. Adams; and in doing justice to his patriotick character, he gave notice to the committee of several circumstances which proved it necessary that Congress should draw a line of conduct to that minister of which he might not be allowed to lose sight. The minister dwelt especially on a circumstance already known to Congress, namely, the use which Mr. Adams thought he had a right to make of his powers to treat with Great Britain. The minister concluded on this subject that if Congress put any confidence in the king's friendship and benevolence; if they were persuaded of his inviolable attachment to the principle of the alliance, and of his firm resolution constantly to support the cause of the United States, they would be impressed with the necessity of prescribing to their plenipotentiary a perfect and open confidence in the French ministers, and a thorough reliance on the king; and would direct him to take no step without the approbation of his Majesty; and after giving him, in his instructions, the principal and most important outlines for his conduct, they would order him, with respect to the manner of carrying them into execution, to receive his directions from the Count de Vergennes, or from the person who might be charged with the negotiation in the name of the king. The minister observed that this matter is the more important, because, being allied with the United States, it is the business of the king to support their cause with those powers with whom Congress has no connexion, and can have none, until their independence is in a fair train to be acknowledged. That the king would make it a point of prudence and justice to support the minister of Congress; but in case this minister, by aiming at impossible things, forming exorbitant demands which disinterested mediators might think ill-founded, or perhaps by misconstruing his instructions, should put the French negotiators under the necessity of proceeding in the course of the negotiation without a constant connexion with him, this would give rise to an unbecoming contradiction between France and the thirteen United States, which could not but be of very bad effect in the course of the negotiation. . . .

He further observed that whatever might be the resolution of Congress, they would do well to recommend to their plenipotentiary to adopt a line of conduct that would deprive the British of every hope of causing divisions between the allies, and to assume a conciliating character as much as can be consistent with the dignity of his constituents, and to show such a confidence in the plenipotentiary of his Most Christian Majesty as is due to a power so much interested to support the dignity and honour of a nation whose independence they have acknowledged.

—*Journals of the Continental Congress*, XX, 562 ff.

2. CONGRESS AGREES TO BE GOVERNED BY FRENCH ADVICE

Thomas Rodney to Caesar Rodney.

Philadelphia, June 15, 1781

Yesterday I wrote you respecting the Congress of Mediation but when I shall have an opertunity by which I may safely trust the conveyance of such intelligence is uncertain. This important business has chiefly taken up the time of Congress since I last came up and is now completed. It was closed by the decision of an important article in the instructions to our Commissioners which requires them, after having obtained an independence, in all things else to be ultimately governed by the advice of the French Court or Minister. It was moved to reconsider this clause and to strike it out as being too abject and humiliating. It was argued some hours and at last rejected so that the clause stands and the French Court is thereby in possession of full and sufficient power to make a peace, for' there is not the least doubt but the mediating powers will readily consent to our independence provided they may make it as simple as possible and it will be ever the interest of France that they should do this lest we should at a future day form an alliance with Great Britain.

I was against this clause because I think it must convince even the French Court that we are reduced to a weak and abject state and that we have lost all that spirit and dignity which once appeared in the proceedings of Congress. . . .

—BURNETT, *Letters of Members of the Continental Congress*, VI, 121-122.

3. Jay Protests "Casting America into the Arms of France"

John Jay to Thomas McKean, President of Congress.

St. Ildefonso, September 20, 1781

... As an American I feel an interest in the dignity of my country, which renders it difficult for me to reconcile myself to the idea of the sovereign independent States of America submitting, in the persons of their ministers, **to** be absolutely governed by the advice and opinions of the servants of another sovereign, especially in a case of such national importance.

That gratitude and confidence are due to our allies is not to be questioned, and that it will probably be in the power of France almost to dictate the terms of peace for us is but too true. That such an extraordinary extent of confidence may stimulate out allies to the highest efforts of generous friendship in our favor is not to be denied, and that this instruction receives some appearance of policy from this consideration may be admitted.

I must, nevertheless, take the liberty of observing that however our situation may in the opinion of Congress render it necessary to relax their demands on every side, and even to direct their commissioners ultimately to concur (if nothing better could be done) in any peace or truce not subversive of our independence which France determined to accede to, yet that this instruction, besides breathing a degree of complacency not quite republican, puts it out of the power of your ministers to improve those chances and opportunities which in the course of human affairs happens more or less frequently to all men. Nor is it clear that America, thus casting herself into the arms of the King of France, will advance either her interest or reputation with that or other nations. ...

—Wharton, *Revolutionary Diplomatic Correspondence*, IV, 716-717.

II. BRITAIN SUES FOR PEACE

The surrender at Yorktown sealed the doom of the North ministry. During the last few months of his regime Lord North, who had been making futile efforts to relinquish his post ever since Saratoga, repeatedly tendered his resignation to the King. The latter went so far as to prepare a draft of his own abdication. North's action was spurred by a resolution of the Commons of March 4, 1782, to consider as enemies of the King and country all those who should further attempt to carry on the war, and to grant leave to bring in an "Enabling Act" authorizing the King to make a peace or truce with America. Finally, on March 20, the North Ministry resigned. A member of Parliament, Sir Nathaniel Wraxall, has left us a stirring account of the impact on the Commons of North's announcement, which anticipated the passage of a motion of want of confidence in the government.

North was succeeded by Lord Rockingham, a stalwart friend of America. His foreign secretary, Charles James Fox, was a long-time advocate of American independence. Most of the other cabinet posts were given to pro-Americans, but the crucial post of Secretary of Colonial Affairs went to Shelburne, an opponent of independence. William Lee testified to Shelburne's perhaps largely undeserved reputation for duplicity when he declared that "no one will trust for a farthing that knows him, farther than he is bound in black and white." Burke, with the vituperation he customarily reserved for his political adversaries, stigmatized him as "a Catiline or a Borgia in morals."

A fierce rivalry ensued between Fox and Shelburne to control the peace negotiations. Shelburne dispatched Richard Oswald, a retired Scottish merchant and slave trader with family ties in America, to start preliminary talks with Franklin. Fox sent Thomas Grenville to open negotiations with Vergennes. Fox favored the immediate recognition of American independence, as his emissary informed Franklin. Privately he felt that this would split the allies, and, once America was recognized as a foreign power and no longer a colony, it would bring the negotiations entirely into his own hands.

At the start Franklin unlimbered his heaviest artillery and requested the cession of Canada, to which Shelburne was not in the least agreeable. The latter countered with an equally objectionable demand for securing debts due British subjects and the indemnification of the Tories. Then fate determined the issue between the rivals, Fox and Shelburne. On July 1 Rockingham died. Shelburne became Prime Minister. Fox quit the cabinet, leaving his rival in complete control.

Shelburne was taking a calculated risk on negotiating directly with the American commissioners, in whom, he told Oswald, "we have put the greatest confidence," adding, "It is now to be seen how far they or America are to be depended upon." He conceded ruefully, "There never was a greater risk run. I hope the public will be the gainer else our heads must answer for it, and deservedly."

1. LORD NORTH RESIGNS: "GOOD NIGHT, GENTLEMEN"

Memoirs of Sir Nathaniel Wraxall.

... On Tuesday, the 19th of March, [1782,] the First Minister, apprehensive of the event of the debate which was fixed for the ensuing day in the House of Commons, wrote to the King in the most decided terms, resigning his employment; and His Majesty being down at Windsor, Lord North despatched a messenger with the letter. When it arrived, the King was going out to hunt; having perused its contents, for which he was probably not unprepared, he calmly put it into his pocket, made no observation, and mounted his horse. But he had not proceeded more than a few paces when a page came running after him to say that Lord North's messenger had received orders to bring back a reply.

"Tell him," said the King, "that I shall be in town to-morrow morning, and will then give Lord North an answer."

Two noblemen were with him at the time, one of whom was the late Duke of Dorset; the other, Lord Hinchinbrook (afterwards Earl of Sandwich), related to me these particulars. Turning immediately to them, "Lord North," observed His Majesty, "has sent me in his resignation; but I shall not accept it."

If, however, the King was apprised of Lord North's intention or determination to resign, it was by no means known in London, and on the morning of the very day I believe that few individuals of either party entertained a doubt of the continuance of the struggle. Still less did any person conceive that the First Minister would spontaneously lay down his office without giving notice to his friends, and contrary to his own recent professions. He went soon after one o'clock to the Treasury, from whence he was to repair to St. James's, where the King, as usual, had a levee. . . .

It is probable that the conversation which took place between the King and Lord North, on that occasion, was never minutely reported by either to any third person: but we may safely assume that His Majesty endeavoured to prevail on his minister not to abandon him. Robinson profesed himself ignorant of all the particulars, though he entertained no doubt that Lord North, whether from weariness and disgust, or apprehension of the consequences that might accrue to his sovereign, to himself and to the country, had made up his mind as he drove to St. James's to state at once to the King the determination that he had irrevocably embraced of laying down immediately his power, a resolution which he had notified under his hand on the preceding day. It is certain that the interview between them was long, lasting above an hour and a half, without any witness present; at the end of which time the Minister withdrew, in order to attend the House of Commons.

I have rarely witnessed so full an attendance, at so early an hour, as on that day, not less than four hundred members having taken their seats before five o'clock; both parties appearing impatient to proceed to business. The only delay arose from the absence of the First Minister, and he being every instant expected to arrive from St. James's, all eyes were directed towards the door each time that it opened. The members on both sides, who, it was generally understood, would speak in the course of the ensuing debate, were well known; and as the ground of controversy had been so often gone over, as well as on account of many invalids who attended and who were unable to remain long, it was thought that the question would be brought on before midnight.

At length Lord North entering in a full dressed suit, his riband over his coat, proceeded up the House, amidst an incessant cry of "order, and places!" As soon as he had reached the Treasury Bench, he rose and attempted to address the chair, but Lord Surrey, who had given notice of a motion for that day, being consequently in possession of the right to speak first, and having likewise risen, a clamour began from all quarters of the most violent description. It lasted for some moments in defiance of every effort made by the speaker to enforce silence, till in consequence of the earnestness with which the Minister besought a hearing, and some expressions relative to the importance of the communication that he had to make, which pervaded the tumult, the members opposite allowed him the precedence.

He then stated, after a short preface, that "his object was to save the time and trouble of the House, by informing them that the administration was virtually at an end; that His Majesty had determined to change his confidential servants; and that he should propose an adjournment, in order to allow time for the new ministerial arrangements which must take place."

It is not easy to describe the effect which this declaration produced in a popular assembly, scarcely an individual of which did not hear it with lively sentiments of exultation, or of concern, both of which emotions were heightened by surprise. No painter could have done justice to the expression depictured in many countenances. The opposition, without much difficulty, consented to the proposed adjournment; and the members, actuated by very opposite emotions, soon dispersed in all directions, to carry the intelligence through the capital. Not, however, till Burke, assuming the part of a moderator, had endeavoured to temper and restrain the vociferous joy of his friends on so sudden and unexpected an event. But scarcely could he obtain a hearing, amidst the impatience of men who for the first time beheld before their eyes the promised land. Courteney, on the other side of the House, pronounced a panegyric, or more properly, an encomium, on the personal virtues and amiable qualities of the First Minister, which he did not suspend on account of the violent indications of dissatisfaction exhibited from the opposition benches.

A more interesting scene had not been acted within the walls of the House of Commons since February 1743, when Sir Robert Walpole retired from power. Nor did the First Minister of George the Second by any means display in the last moments of his political life the equanimity, suavity and dignity manifested by his successor. Lord North ordered his coach to remain at the House of Commons in waiting on that evening. In consequence of so unexpected an event as his resignation, and the House breaking up at such an early hour, the housekeeper's room became crowded to the greatest degree, few persons having directed their carriages to be ready before midnight. In the midst of this confusion, Lord North's coach drove up to the door, and as he prepared to get into it, he said, turning to those persons near him with that unalterable equanimity and good temper which never forsook him, "Good night, gentlemen, you see what it is to be in the secret."

—WRAXALL, *Historical and Posthumous Memoirs*, pp. 282-284.

2. FRANKLIN PROPOSES THAT BRITAIN CEDE CANADA

Benjamin Franklin to Lord Shelburne.

Passy, April 18, 1782

I have received the letter your Lordship did me the honour of writing to me on the 16th instant. I congratulate you on your new appointment to the honourable and important office you formerly filled so worthily, which must be so far pleasing to you as it affords you more opportunities of doing good, and of serving your country essentially in its great concerns.

I have conversed a good deal with Mr. Oswald and am much pleased with him. He appears to me a wise and honest man. I acquainted him that I was commissioned, with others, to treat of and conclude a Peace. . . .

I leave the rest of the conversation to be related to your Lordship by Mr. Oswald; and, that he might do it more easily and fully than he could by letter, I was of opinion with him that it would be best he should return immediately and do it *viva voce*. Being myself but one of the four persons, now in Europe, commissioned by the Congress to treat of Peace, I can make no propositions of

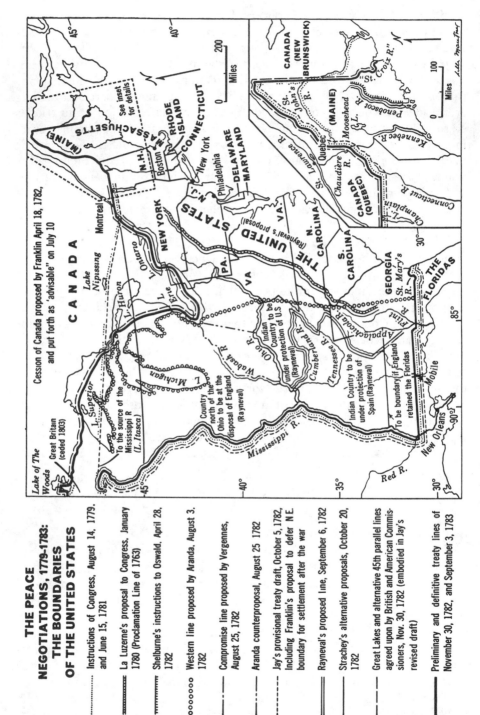

THE PEACE
NEGOTIATIONS, 1779-1783:
THE BOUNDARIES
OF THE UNITED STATES

.... Instructions of Congress, August 14, 1779, and June 15, 1781

▬▬▬ La Luzerne's proposal to Congress, January 1780 (Proclamation Line of 1763)

wwwww Shelburne's instructions to Oswald, April 28, 1782

oooooooo Western line proposed by Aranda, August 3, 1782

—·—· Compromise line proposed by Vergennes, August 25, 1782

— — — Aranda counterproposal, August 25 1782

════ Jay's provisional treaty draft, October 5, 1782, including Franklin's proposal to defer N.E. boundary for settlement after the war

═══ Rayneval's proposed line, September 6, 1782

——— Strachey's alternative proposals, October 20, 1782

– – – Great Lakes and alternative 45th parallel lines agreed upon by British and American Commissioners, Nov. 30, 1782 (embodied in Jay's revised draft)

▬▬▬ Preliminary and definitive treaty lines of November 30, 1782, and September 3, 1783 much importance without them. I can only express my wish that, if Mr. Oswald returns hither, he may bring with him the agreement of your Court to treat for a general Peace, and the proposal of place and time, that I may immediately write to Messrs. Adams, Laurens and Jay. . . . He appeared much struck with my discourse, and as I frequently looked at my paper, he desired to see it. After some little delay, I allowed him to read it; the following is an exact copy:

"NOTES FOR CONVERSATION"

"To make a Peace durable, what may give occasion for future wars should if practicable be removed.

"The territory of the United States and that of Canada, by long extended frontiers, touch each other.

"The settlers on the frontiers of the American Provinces are generally the most disorderly of the people, who, being far removed from the eye and controll of their respective governments, are more bold in committing offences against neighbours, and are for ever occasioning complaints and furnishing matter for fresh differences between their States.

"By the late debates in Parliament, and publick writings, it appears that Britain desires a *reconciliation* with the Americans. It is a sweet word. It means much more than a mere Peace, and what is heartily to be wished for. Nations make a Peace whenever they are both weary of making war. But, if one of them has made war upon the other unjustly, and has wantonly and unnecessarily done it great injuries, and refuses reparation, though there may, for the present, be peace, the resentment of those injuries will remain, and will break out again in vengeance when occasions offer. These occasions will be watched for by one side, feared by the other, and the peace will never be secure; nor can any cordiality subsist between them.

"Many houses and villages have been burnt in America by the English and their allies, the Indians. I do not know that the Americans will insist on reparation; perhaps they may. But would it not be better for England to offer it? Nothing could have a greater tendency to conciliate, and much of the future commerce and returning intercourse between the two countries may depend on the reconciliation. Would not the advantage of reconciliation by such means be greater than the expence?

"If then a way can be proposed which may tend to efface the memory of injuries, at the same time that it takes away the occasions of fresh quarrel and mischief, will it not be worth considering, especially if it can be done, not only without expence, but be a means of saving?

"Britain possesses Canada. Her chief advantage from that possession consists in the trade for peltry. Her expences in governing and defending that settlement must be considerable. It might be humiliating to her to give it up on the demand of America. Perhaps America will not demand it; some of her political rulers may consider the fear of such a neighbour as a means of keeping 13 States more united among themselves, and more attentive to military discipline. But on the minds of the people in general would it not have an excellent effect, if Britain should voluntarily offer to give up this Province; tho' on these conditions, that she shall in all times coming have and enjoy the right of free trade thither, unincumbered with any duties whatsoever; that so much of the vacant lands there shall be sold as will raise a sum sufficient to pay for the houses burnt by the British troops and their Indians; and also to indemnify the royalists for the confiscation of their estates?"

This is mere conversation matter between Mr. O. and Mr. F., as the former is not impowered to make propositions, and the latter cannot make any without the concurrence of his colleagues.

—Smyth, *Writings of Franklin*, VIII, 465-472.

3. Lord Shelburne Does Not Favor Franklin's Suggestions

Memorandum to Mr. Oswald, April 28, 1782.

Remarks on the Private Paper

1st. Why does he [Franklin] say that he does not know of the Americans having any intentions of making claims of indemnification, he and others having full powers. That is not open. No reparation to be thought of. The money spent in America is more than sufficient indemnification for all particular losses. Lord Shelburne has a manuscript of Sir William Petty to send in return for this paper. The title of it is to show that Ireland would have been in a state of poverty and uncivilised savageness if it had not been for the money expended by the English in their wars in that country.

All ideas of a supposed justice in claims of indemnification to be disowned; and if started, to be waived as much as possible.

It is reasonable to expect a free trade, unencumbered with duties, to every part of America.

Make early and strict conditions, not only to secure all debts whatever due to British subjects, but likewise to restore the Loyalists to a full enjoyment of their rights and privileges. And their indemnification to be considered. Lord Shelburne will never give up the Loyalists. The Penn family have been sadly used, and Lord Shelburne is personally interested for them, and thinks it is duty to be so for all.

The private paper desires Canada for three reasons:—

1st. By way of reparation.—Answer. No reparation can be heard of.

2nd. To prevent future wars.—Answer. It is to be hoped that some more friendly method will be found.

3rd. Loyalists as a fund of indemnification to them.—Answer. No independence to be acknowledged without their being taken care of.

A compensation expected for New York, Charlestown and Savannah. Penobscott to be always kept.

—Lewis, *Administrations of Great Britain*, pp. 47-48.

4. The English Look to Franklin to Extricate Them

Benjamin Franklin's Journal of the Negotiation for Peace.

Saturday, June 1st [1782]. Mr. Grenville came according to appointment. Our conversation began by my acquainting him that I had seen the Count de Vergennes, and had perused the copy left him of the power to treat; that after what he, Mr. Grenville, told me of its being to treat with France *and her*

Allies, I was a little surprized to find in it no mention of the Allies, and that it was only to treat with the King of France and his Ministers. . . .

He answered that . . . the greatest part of those instructions related to treating with me. That to convince me of the sincerity of his court respecting us, he would acquaint me with one of his instructions, tho' perhaps the doing it now was premature, and therefore a little inconsistent with the character of a politician, but he had that confidence in me that he should not hesitate to inform me (tho' he wished that at present it should go no further) *he was instructed to acknowledge the independence of America, previous to the commencement of the treaty.*

Mr. Grenville then spoke much of the high opinion the present Ministry had of me, and their great esteem for me, their desire of a perfect reconciliation between the two countries, and the firm and general belief in England that no man was so capable as myself of proposing the proper means of bringing about such a reconciliation; adding that if the old Ministers had formerly been too little attentive to my counsels, the present were very differently disposed, and he hoped that in treating with them, I would totally forget their predecessors. . . .

Mr. G. then discoursed of our resolution not to treat without our Allies. "This," says he, "can properly only relate to France, with whom you have a Treaty of Alliance, but you have none with Spain, you have none with Holland. If Spain and Holland, and even if France should insist on unreasonable terms of advantage to themselves, after you have obtained all you want and are satisfied, can it be right that America should be dragged on in a war for their interests only?" He stated this matter in various lights and pressed it earnestly.

I resolved from various reasons to evade the discussion and therefore answered that the intended treaty not being yet begun, it appeared unnecessary to enter at present into considerations of that kind. The preliminaries being once settled and the treaty commenced, if any of the other powers should make extravagant demands on England, and insist on our continuing the war till those were complyed with, it would then be time enough for us to consider what our obligations were, and how far they extended. . . .

We then spoke of the reconciliation; but his full power not being yet come, I chose to defer entering upon that subject at present. I told him, I had thoughts of putting down in writing the particulars that I judged would conduce to that end, and of adding my reasons, that this required a little time and I had been hindered by accidents; which was true, for I had begun to write, but had postponed it on account of his defective power to treat. But I promised to finish it as soon as possible. He pressed me earnestly to do it, saying an expression of mine in a former conversation, that there still remained *roots of good will* in America towards England, which if properly taken care of might produce a reconciliation, had made a great impression on his mind and given him infinite pleasure, and he hoped I would not neglect furnishing him with the information of what would be necessary to nourish those *roots*, and could assure me, that my advice would be greatly regarded. . . .

On Monday the 3rd, Mr. Oswald came according to appointment. He told me he had seen and had conversation with Lord Shelburne, Lord Rockingham and Mr. Fox. That their desire of peace continued uniformly the same, tho' he thought some of them were a little too much elated with the late victory in the West Indies;* and when observing his coolness, they asked him if he did not think it a very good thing. "Yes," says he, "if you do not rate it too high." He went on with the utmost frankness to tell me that peace was absolutely necessary for them. That the nation had been foolishly involved in four wars, and could no longer raise money to carry them on, so that if they continued, it would be absolutely necessary for them to stop payment of the interest money on the Funds, which would ruin their future credit. He spoke of stopping on all sums above £1000, and continuing to pay on those below, because the great sums belonged to the rich, who could better bear the delay of their interest, and the smaller sums to poorer persons, who would be more hurt and make more clamour, and that the rich might be quieted by promising them interest upon their interest. All this looked as if the matter had been seriously thought on.

Mr. Oswald has an air of great simplicity and honesty, yet I could hardly take this to be merely a weak confession of their deplorable state, and thought it might be rather intended as a kind of intimidation, by showing us they had still that resource in their power, which he said could furnish five millions a year. But he added, our enemies may now do what they please with us—*they have the ball at their foot,* was his expression—and we hope they will show their moderation and their magnanimity. He then repeatedly mentioned the great esteem the Ministers had for me, that they, with all the considerate people of England, looked to and depended on me for the means of extricating the nation from its present desperate situation; that perhaps no single man had ever in his hands an opportunity of doing so much good as I had at this present, with much more to that purpose. . . .

—Smyth, ed., *Writings of Franklin,* VIII, 516-525, *passim.*

III. "THE POINT OF INDEPENDENCE"

Franklin had made it clear to Oswald at the start that there must be a preliminary acknowledgment of American independence before any settlement could be negotiated. But Oswald's commission of August 8 only authorized him to conclude a peace or truce with any commissioner of the "colonies or plantations." Vergennes advised Franklin and Jay to begin negotiations without insisting on preliminary recognition, so long as independence was incorporated in the final treaty. Jay suspected that Vergennes was trying to stall the Anglo-U.S. negotiations until certain objectives of the French and Spanish were obtained, such as the capture of Gibraltar then under siege. Vergennes actually revealed his opposition to the preliminary recognition of American independence in a talk with Alleyne Fitzherbert, British peace commissioner treating with the French government at Versailles.

---

* Rodney's victory over the French fleet, April 12, 1782.

At this point John Jay deliberately ignored Congress' instructions to abide by the advice of the French government and refused to negotiate until the point of independence was settled. John Adams, writing from The Hague, pointed out that American ministers had to make their decisions "amidst all these doublings and windings of European politics." "We ought," he insisted, "have opinions, principles and systems of our own," and Congress should back up its own negotiators. He reached Paris in time to strengthen Jay's hands and save the rights to the fisheries. His suspicions of France confirmed him in his deep-rooted isolationism. "America has been long enough involved in the wars of Europe," he wrote to Livingston on November 11. "She has been a football between contending nations from the beginning, and it is easy to foresee that France and England both will endeavor to involve us in their future wars."

To complicate matters further it was apparent that France also opposed the American annexation of Canada, and that behind the scenes Spain strenuously resisted the territorial demands of the United States to the Mississippi. In fact a Franco-Spanish plan would have left the Mississippi south of the Ohio under exclusive Spanish control and denied to the United States the present states of Kentucky, Tennessee, Mississippi and part of Louisiana, along with Alabama.

To fire Jay's smoldering suspicions the British put into his hands a ciphered dispatch from Barbé-Marbois to Vergennes opposing American claims to fishing off Newfoundland's waters. The young French secretary of legation at Philadelphia denounced the letter as spurious, but a copy is in the French Foreign Archives and Marbois later admitted its authenticity.

Fearing that the United States was on the verge of being sold out by France, Jay, with Franklin's agreement, gave up the demand for immediate recognition of independence and on September 9 asked Oswald to get his commission altered so as to recognize independence constructively by being empowered to treat with the Commissioners of the United States of America. In the negotiations which Jay conducted for a time alone during a period when Franklin was indisposed, the claim to Canada was dropped because Jay was now alarmed that the Franco-Spanish allies would block expansionist aims of the United States to the Mississippi. The fact is that Franklin, by listing Canada among the "advisable" rather than the "necessary" articles of independence in his outline of conditions to Oswald on July 10, had in effect dropped it from serious consideration.

It is hardly likely that Jay lost Canada as a result of his stubborn insistence on the point of independence, but he probably had to settle for a more southerly—though in the long run a more natural and practical—boundary line between Canada and the United States than he might have had if negotiations had not been delayed on this matter of immediate recognition. At the same time the Americans might not have been forced to recognize the debts owing to British creditors or to include the troublesome reference to the Loyalists, had negotiations been carried on at a brisker pace. For on September 30 news reached England of the failure of the attack on Gibraltar. This stiffened the tone of British negotiations thenceforward.

1. Recognition of Independence Is Not a Favor

Richard Oswald to Lord Shelburne.

Paris, July 12, 1782

I will . . . not scruple to give my opinion as things occur to me, viz.:—that the more anxious we appear to be for Peace, the more backward the people here will be, or the harder in their terms, which is much the same thing; and that having fully satisfied this Court of our desire to put an end to the war, as has been done, the more vigorously our exertions are pushed in the interim, we shall come sooner to our purpose, and on better terms.

With respect to the Commissioners for the Colonies, our conduct towards them, I think, ought to be of a style somewhat different; they have shown a desire to treat, and to end with us on a separate footing from the other powers, and I must say, in a more liberal way, or at least with a greater appearance of feeling for the future interests and connections of Great Britain, than I expected. I speak so from the text of the last conversation I had with Mr. Franklin, as mentioned in my letter of yesterday. And therefore we ought to deal with them tenderly, and as supposed conciliated friends, or at least well disposed to conciliation; and not as if we had anything to give them that we can keep from them, or that they are very anxious to have. Even Dr. Franklin himself, as the subject happened to lead that way, as good as told me yesterday, that they were their own masters, and seemed to make no account of the grant of Independence as a favour. I was so much satisfied beforehand of their ideas on that head that I will own to your Lordship I did not read to the Doctor that part of your letter wherein you mention that grant as if it in some shape challenged a return on their part. . . .

I cannot but say I was much pleased, upon the whole, with what passed upon the occasion of this interview. And I really believe the Doctor sincerely wishes for a speedy settlement; and that after the loss of Dependence, we may lose no more; but, on the contrary, that a cordial reconciliation may take place over all that country.

Amongst other things, I was pleased at his showing me a state of the aids they had received from France, as it looked as if he wanted I should see the amount of the obligations to their ally; and as if it was the only foundation of the ties France had over them, excepting gratitude, which the Doctor owned in so many words, but at the same time said the debt would be punctually and easily discharged, France having given to 1788 to pay it. . . .

I should therefore hope it may be possible soon to bring their business near to a final close, and that they will not be any way stiff as to those articles he calls *advisable*, or will drop them altogether. Those he calls necessary will hardly be any obstacle.* I shall be able to make a better guess when I have

---

* This refers to Franklin's outline of conditions of peace. The "necessary" articles were independence, a boundary settlement, a confinement of the boundaries of Canada, and fishing rights off the banks of Newfoundland and elsewhere. The "advisable" articles were an indemnity to those who had suffered by the war, a public acknowledgment of England's error, equality of commercial privileges, and the cession of Canada.

another meeting with him, jointly with Mr. Jay, which I hope to have by the time this courier returns. Allow me, my Lord, to observe that if I continue here any time, I would wish to have a messenger attending. This Potter is a proper man.

—Fox, *Memorials and Correspondence,* IV, 246-252.

2. To Preserve National Dignity John Jay Violates Instructions

Partly decoded letter from John Jay, peace commissioner, to Gouverneur Morris, assistant to the Secretary of Finance. The decoded section is in italics.

Paris, October 13, 1782

Dear Morris

I have received your *festina lente* letter, but wish it had been, at least partly, in cypher; you need not be informed of my reasons for this wish, as by this time you must know that seals are, on this side of the water, rather matters of decoration than of use. It gave me nevertheless great pleasure to receive that letter, it being the first from you that had reached me the Lord knows when. —Except indeed a few lines covering your correspondence with a don. I find you are industrious, and of consequence useful. So much the better for yourself, for the public, and for our friend Morris, whom I consider as the pillar of American credit.

The King of Great Britain, by letters patent under the Great Seal, has authorized Mr. Oswald to treat with the Commissioners of the United States of America. His first Commission litterally pursued the enabling act, and the authority it gave him was expressed in the very terms of that act, viz. to treat with the Colonies, and with any or either of them, and any part of them, and with any description of men in them, and with any person whatsoever, of and concerning Peace, etc.——

Had I not violated the instructions of Congress their dignity would have been in the dust, for the French Minister even took pains not only to persuade us to treat under that commission but to prevent the second by telling Fitzherbert that the first was sufficient. I told the Minister that we neither could nor would treat with any nation in the world on any other than an equal footing.

We may, and we may not, have a peace this winter—act as if the war would certainly continue—keep proper garrisons in your strong posts and preserve your army sufficiently numerous and well appointed until every idea of hostility and surprize shall have compleatly vanished.

I could write you a volume, but my health admits only of short intervals of application.

Present my best wishes to Mr. and Mrs. Morris, Mr. and Mrs. Meredith, and such other of our friends as may ask how we do.

I am, dear Morris, very much
Yours
John Jay

—Gouverneur Morris Papers, Columbia University Lib.

3. ADAMS ARRIVES JUST IN TIME TO STRENGTHEN JAY'S HANDS

John Adams to Robert R. Livingston.

Paris, October 31, 1782

I set off for Paris, where I arrived on Saturday, the 26th of this month, after a tedious journey, the roads being, on account of long-continued rains, in the worst condition I ever knew them.

I waited forthwith on Mr. Jay, and from him learned the state of the conferences. It is not possible at present to enter into details. All I can say is, in general, that I had the utmost satisfaction in finding that he had been all along acting here upon the same principles upon which I had ventured to act in Holland, and that we were perfectly agreed in our sentiments and systems. I can not express it better than in his own words: "to be honest and grateful to our allies, but to think for ourselves." I find a construction put upon one article of our instructions by some persons which, I confess, I never put upon it myself. It is represented by some as subjecting us to the French ministry, as taking away from us all right of judging for ourselves, and obliging us to agree to whatever the French ministers should advise us to do, and to do nothing without their consent. I never supposed this to be the intention of Congress; if I had, I never would have accepted the commission, and if I now thought it their intention I could not continue in it. I can not think it possible to be the design of Congress; if it is I hereby resign my place in the commission, and request that another person may be immediately appointed in my stead.

Yesterday we met Mr. Oswald at his lodgings; Mr. Jay, Dr. Franklin, and myself on one side, and Mr. Oswald, assisted by Mr. Strachey, a gentleman whom I had the honor to meet in company with Lord Howe upon Staten Island in the year 1776, and assisted also by a Mr. Roberts, a clerk in some of the public offices, with books, maps and papers relative to the boundaries.

I arrived in a lucky moment for the boundary of Massachusetts, because I brought with me all the essential documents relative to that object, which are this day to be laid before my colleagues in conference at my house, and afterwards before Mr. Oswald.

It is now apparent, at least to Mr. Jay and myself, that in order to obtain the western lands, the navigation of the Mississippi, and the fisheries, or any of them, we must act with firmness and independence, as well as prudence and delicacy. With these there is little doubt we may obtain them all.

—WHARTON, *Revolutionary Diplomatic Correspondence*, V, 838.

4. "WE HAVE NO DEPENDENCE EXCEPT ON GOD AND OURSELVES"

John Jay to Robert R. Livingston.

Paris, November 17, 1782

... These are critical times, and great necessity there is for prudence and secrecy.

So far, and in such matters as this court [the French government] may think it their interest to support us, they certainly will, but no further, in my opinion.

They are interested in separating us from Great Britain, and on that point we may, I believe, depend upon them; but it is not their interest that we should become a great and formidable people, and therefore they will not help us to become so.

It is not their interest that such a treaty should be formed between us and Britain as would produce cordiality and mutual confidence. They will therefore endeavor to plant such seeds of jealousy, discontent and discord in it as may naturally and perpetually keep our eyes fixed on France for security. This consideration must induce them to wish to render Britain formidable in our neighborhood, and to leave us as few resources of wealth and power as possible.

It is their interest to keep some point or other in contest between us and Britain to the end of the war, to prevent the possibility of our sooner agreeing, and thereby keep us employed in the war, and dependent on them for supplies. Hence they have favored and will continue to favor the British demands as to matters of boundary and the Tories.

The same views will render them desirous to continue the war in our country as long as possible, nor do I believe they will take any measures for our repossession of New York unless the certainty of its evacuation should render such an attempt advisable. The Count de Vergennes lately said that there could be no great use in expeditions to take places which must be given up to us at a peace.

Such being our situation, it appears to me advisable to keep up our army to the end of the war, even if the enemy should evacuate our country; nor does it appear to me prudent to listen to any overtures for carrying a part of it to the West Indies in case of such an event.

I think we have no rational dependence except on God and ourselves, nor can I yet be persuaded that Great Britain has either wisdom, virtue or magnanimity enough to adopt a perfect and liberal system of conciliation. If they again thought they could conquer us, they would again attempt it. . . .

It is not my meaning, and therefore I hope I shall not be understood to mean, that we should deviate in the least from our treaty with France; our honor and our interest are concerned in inviolably adhering to it. I mean only to say that if we lean on her love of liberty, her affection for America, or her disinterested magnanimity, we shall lean on a broken reed, that will sooner or later pierce our hands, and Geneva as well as Corsica justifies this observation. . . .

—WHARTON, *Revolutionary Diplomatic Correspondence*, VI, 45-49.

IV. THE BATTLE FOR THE FISHERIES

As 1782 drew to a close John Adams wrote to Elbridge Gerry, "Thanks be to God that our Tom Cod are safe in spite of the malice of enemies, the finesse of allies, and the mistakes of Congress." Nothing had aroused Adams' lively indignation more than the clear evidence that France opposed granting America the right to fish off the banks of Newfoundland and that a faction in Congress was prepared to sell out the interests of the New England fisher-

men. After much wrangling Adams finally agreed at the last moment, against his better instincts, to have the word "liberty" to fish on the high seas substituted in the treaty for "right." This substitution was to cause a century of controversy.

Diary of John Adams.

[*November*] *25*, [*1782*], *Monday.* Dr. Franklin, Mr. Jay and myself, at eleven, met at Mr. Oswald's lodgings. Mr. Strachey told us he had been to London and waited personally on every one of the King's Cabinet Council, and had communicated the last propositions to them. . . .

They could not admit us to dry on the shores of Nova Scotia, nor to fish within three leagues of the coast, nor within fifteen leagues of the coast of Cape Breton. . . .

I could not help observing that the ideas respecting the fishery appeared to me to come piping hot from Versailles. I quoted to them the words of our treaty with France, in which the indefinite and exclusive right to the fishery on the western side of Newfoundland was secured against us, according to the true construction of the treaties of Utrecht and Paris. I showed them the twelfth and thirteenth articles of the treaty of Utrecht, by which the French were admitted to fish from Cape Bona Vista to Cape Riche. I related to them the manner in which the cod and haddock come into the rivers, harbors, creeks and up to the very wharves, on all the northern coast of America, in the spring, in the month of April, so that you have nothing to do but step into a boat and bring in a parcel of fish in a few hours; but that in May they begin to withdraw; we have a saying at Boston that when the "blossoms fall, the haddock begin to crawl"; that is, to move out into deep water, so that in summer you must go out some distance to fish. At Newfoundland it was the same; the fish, in March or April, were in shore in all the creeks, bays and harbors, that is, within three leagues of the coasts or shores of Newfoundland and Nova Scotia; that neither French nor English could go from Europe and arrive early enough for the first fare; that our vessels could, being so much nearer, an advantage which God and nature had put into our hands; but that this advantage of ours had ever been an advantage to England, because our fish had been sold in Spain and Portugal for gold and silver, and the gold and silver sent to London for manufactures; that this would be the course again; that France foresaw it, and wished to deprive England of it, by persuading her to deprive us of it; that it would be a master stroke of policy if she could succeed, but England must be completely the dupe before she could succeed.

There were three lights in which it might be viewed: 1. as a nursery of seamen; 2. as a source of profit; 3. as a source of contention. As a nursery of seamen, did England consider us as worse enemies than France? Had she rather France should have the seamen than America? The French marine was nearer and more menacing than ours. As a source of profit, had England rather France should supply the markets of Lisbon and Cadiz with fish, and take the gold and silver, than we? France would never spend any of that money in London; we should spend it all very nearly. As a source of contention, how could we restrain our fishermen, the boldest men alive, from fishing in prohibited places? How could our men see the French admitted to fish, and themselves excluded by the English? It would then be a cause of disputes, and such seeds France might wish to sow. That I wished for two hours conversation on the subject with one of the King's council; if I did not convince him he was undesignedly betraying the interests of his sovereign, I was mistaken.

Strachey said, perhaps I would put down some observations in writing upon it.

I said, with all my heart, provided I had the approbation of my colleagues; but I could do nothing of the kind without submitting it to their judgments, and that whatever I had said, or should say, upon the subject, however strongly I might express myself, was always to be understood with submission to my colleagues. . . .

[*November*] *29, Friday*. Met Mr. Fitzherbert, Mr. Oswald, Mr. Franklin, Mr. Jay, Mr. Laurens and Mr. Strachey at Mr. Jay's Hotel d'Orléans, and spent the whole day in discussions about the fishery and the Tories. I proposed a new article concerning the fishery; it was discussed and turned in every light, and multitudes of amendments proposed on each side; and at last the article drawn as it was finally agreed to.

The other English gentlemen being withdrawn upon some occasion, I asked Mr. Oswald if he could consent to leave out the limitation of three leagues from all their shores, and the fifteen from those of Louisburg. He said, in his own opinion he was for it; but his instructions were such that he could not do it. I perceived by this, and by several incidents and little circumstances before, which I had remarked to my colleagues who were much of the same opinion, that Mr. Oswald had an instruction not to settle the articles of the fishery and refugees without the concurrence of Mr. Fitzherbert and Mr. Strachey.

Upon the return of the other gentlemen, Mr. Strachey proposed to leave out the word "right" of fishing, and make it "liberty." Mr. Fitzherbert said the word "right" was an obnoxious expression. Upon this I rose up and said, "Gentlemen, is there or can there be a clearer right? In former treaties—that of Utrecht and that of Paris—France and England have claimed the right, and used the word. When God Almighty made the banks of Newfoundland, at three hundred leagues distance from the people of America, and at six hundred leagues distance from those of France and England, did he not give as good a right to the former as to the latter? If Heaven in the creation gave a right, it is ours at least as much as yours. If occupation, use and possession give a right, we have it as clearly as you. If war, and blood, and treasure give a right, ours is as good as yours. We have been constantly fighting in Canada, Cape Breton and Nova Scotia for the defence of this fishery, and have expended beyond all proportion more than you. If, then, the right cannot be denied, why should it not be acknowledged and put out of dispute? Why should we leave room for illiterate fishermen to wrangle and chicane? . . .

After hearing all this, Mr. Fitzherbert, Mr. Oswald and Mr. Strachey retired for some time; and returning, Mr. Fitzherbert said that, upon consulting together and weighing every thing as maturely as possible, Mr. Strachey and himself had determined to advise Mr. Oswald to strike with us according to the terms we had proposed as our ultimatum respecting the fishery and the Loyalists. Accordingly, we all sat down and read over the whole treaty, and corrected it, and agreed to meet tomorrow, at Mr. Oswald's house, to sign and seal the treaties, which the secretaries were to copy fair in the mean time.

I forgot to mention that, when we were upon the fishery, and Mr. Strachey and Mr. Fitzherbert were urging us to leave out the word "right" and substitute "liberty," I told them at last—in answer to their proposal, to agree upon all other articles, and leave that of the fishery to be adjusted at the definitive treaty—I never could put my hand to any articles without satisfaction about the fishery. . . .

—ADAMS, ed., *Works of John Adams*, III, 327-332, 333-335.

V. THE SETTLEMENT OF THE LOYALIST QUESTION

The American commissioners were to a man united against any restitution to or indemnification of the hated Tories. The British government, anxious to make a quick peace and split the allies, was charged by its critics with being shamelessly indifferent to the cause of the Loyalists. As Lord North put it, "What, are not the claims of those who—in conformity to their allegiance, their cheerful obedience to the voice of Parliament, their confidence in the proclamation of our generals, invited under every assurance of military, parliamentary, political and affectionate protection—espoused with the hazard to their lives and the forfeitures of their properties, the cause of Great Britain!" The Americans finally agreed to a compromise suggested by Oswald that Congress would merely recommend *to the several states that they correct, if necessary, their acts confiscating the estates of British subjects. This in fact gave the Tories little or nothing, as numerous confiscations continued to be carried out in America after the treaty was signed, but it left a vexing question between the two nations in the years to come.*

RESTITUTION TO LOYALISTS IS IMMORAL AND IMPOSSIBLE

Benjamin Franklin to Richard Oswald.

Passy, November 26, 1782

You may well remember that in the beginning of our conferences before the other commissioners arrived, on your mentioning to me a retribution for the Royalists whose estates had been confiscated, I acquainted you that nothing of that kind could be stipulated by us, the confiscation being made by virtue of laws of particular States, which the Congress had no power to contravene or dispense with, and therefore could give us no such authority in our commission. And I gave it as my opinion and advice, honestly and cordially, that, if a reconciliation was intended, no mention should be made in our negotiations of those people; for, they having done infinite mischief to our properties by wantonly burning and destroying farm-houses, villages, towns, if compensation for their losses were insisted on, we should certainly exhibit again such an account of all the ravages they had committed, which would necessarily recall to view scenes of barbarity that must inflame instead of conciliating, and tend to perpetuate an enmity that we all profess a desire of extinguishing. . . . Understanding, however, from you that this was a point your ministry had at heart, I wrote concerning it to Congress, and I have lately received the following resolution, viz:

"By the United States, in Congress assembled

10 September 1782

"Resolved, That the Secretary for Foreign Affairs be . . . directed to obtain, as speedily as possible, authentic returns of the slaves and other property which have been carried off or destroyed in the course of the war by the enemy, and to transmit the same to the ministers plenipotentiary for negotiating peace.

"Resolved, That, in the meantime, the Secretary for Foreign Affairs inform said Ministers that many thousands of slaves, and other property, to a very great amount, have been carried off or destroyed by the enemy; and that, in the opinion of Congress, the great loss of property which the citizens of the United States have sustained by the enemy will be considered by the several States as an insuperable bar to their making restitution or indemnification to the former owners of property, which has been or may be forfeited to, or confiscated by, any of the States."

. . . The mass of evidence, . . . not only of the enormities committed by those people, under the direction of the British generals, but of those committed by the British troops themselves, will form a record that must render the British name odious in America to the latest generations. In that authentic record will be found the burning of the fine towns of Charlestown, near Boston; of Falmouth, just before winter, when the sick, the aged, the women and children were driven to seek shelter where they could hardly find it; of Norfolk, in the midst of winter; of New London, of Fairfield, of Esopus, etc., besides near a hundred and fifty miles of well-settled country laid waste; every house and barn burnt, and many hundreds of farmers, with their wives and children, butchered and scalped.

The present British ministers, when they reflect a little, will certainly be too equitable to suppose that their nation has a right to make an unjust war (which they have always allowed this against us to be) and do all sorts of unnecessary mischief, unjustifiable by the practice of any civilized people, while those they make war with are to suffer without claiming any satisfaction; but that if Britons, or their adherents, are in return deprived of any property it is to be restored to them or they are to be imdemnified. The British troops can never excuse their barbarities. They were unprovoked. The Loyalists may say, in excuse of theirs, that they were exasperated by the loss of their estates, and it was revenge. They have, then, had their revenge. *Is it right they should have both?*

Some of those people may have merit in their regard for Britain, those who espoused her cause from affection; these it may become you to reward. But there are many of them who were waverers and were only determined to engage in it by some occasional circumstance or appearances; these have not much of either merit or demerit. And there are others who have abundance of demerit respecting your country, having by their falsehoods and misrepresentations brought on and encouraged the continuance of the war; these, instead of being recompensed, should be punished.

It is usual among Christian people at war to profess always a desire of peace; but if the ministers of one of the parties choose to insist particularly on a certain article which they have known the others are not and can not be empowered to agree to, what credit can they expect should be given to such professions?

Your ministers require that we should receive again into our bosom those who have been our bitterest enemies, and restore their properties who have destroyed ours; and this while the wounds they have given us are still bleeding! It is many years since your nation expelled the Stuarts and their adherents and confiscated their estates. Much of your resentment against them may by this time be abated, yet, if we should propose it, and insist on it as an article of our treaty with you, that that family should be recalled and the forfeited estates of its friends restored, would you think us serious in our professions of earnestly desiring peace?

I must repeat my opinion that it is best for you to drop all mention of the refugees. We have proposed, indeed, nothing but what we think best for you as well as ourselves. But if you will have them mentioned, let it be in an article in which you may provide that they shall exhibit accounts of their losses to the commissioners, hereafter to be appointed, who should examine the same, together with the accounts now preparing in America of the damages done by them, and state the account, and that if a balance appears in their favor it shall be paid by us to you and by you divided among them as you shall think proper. And if the balance is found due to us, it shall be paid by you.

Give me leave, however, to advise you to prevent the necessity of so dreadful a discussion by dropping the article, that we may write to America and stop the inquiry.

—Wharton, *Revolutionary Diplomatic Correspondence*, VI, 79-80.

VI. THE RECEPTION OF THE PEACE TREATY

The American Commissioners' grand diplomatic achievement in settling the peace evoked mixed reactions. Official French indignation was anticipated. The Commissioners had broken their instructions and signed a separate peace without telling Vergennes until it was all over. The treaty contained a separate secret article stating that in case West Florida should be British at the end of the war, its boundary should be somewhat further north than if it were to remain in the hands of Spain. When, on the day following the signing, Franklin sent a copy of the preliminary articles to Vergennes he prudently omitted including the secret article. "The English buy peace rather than make it," was Vergennes's biting comment on the success of the separate American negotiations. "Their concessions," he added, "exceed all that I could have thought possible." To his secretary, Rayneval, the treaty was a "dream," which had as its object "the defection of the Americans."

Franklin's superb tact prevented an open breach between the allies. In Congress the French party took an even more critical tone than the government at Versailles, but the treaty was ratified none the less. The peace settled, Adams took it upon himself to instruct the British on how to behave to America in the future, and Franklin made some profound comments on the evils of war. While Hamilton and Jefferson were to disagree on many issues, both were united in enthusiastic praise of the treaty. Jefferson paid homage to Jay and his colleagues. "The terms obtained for us are indeed great," he wrote, "and are so deemed by your country, a few ill designing debtors excepted." Hamilton declared that the peace exceeded "in the goodness of its terms the expectations of the most sanguine," and did "the highest honour to those who made it."

Now the Patriots could turn to the work of peace and reconstruction. "We have now happily concluded the great work of independence," Hamilton added in his letter to Jay, "but much remains to be done to reap the fruits of it." To him the solution was a strong central government to replace the inefficient and weak Confederation. "Let us turn our thoughts to what is future," Adams wrote James Warren. "The Union of the states, an affectionate respect and attachment among all their members, the education of the rising generation, the formation of a national system of oeconomy, policy and manners are the great concerns which still lye before us." He cautioned that "we must guard as much as prudence will permit against the contagion of European manners, and that excessive influx of commerce, luxury and inhabitants from abroad which will soon embarrass us."

1. THE TIFF WITH FRANCE

A. "I AM AT A LOSS TO EXPLAIN YOUR CONDUCT"

Comte de Vergennes to Benjamin Franklin.

Versailles, December 15, 1782

I am at a loss, sir, to explain your conduct and that of your colleagues on this occasion. You have concluded your preliminary articles without any communication between us, although the instructions from Congress prescribe that nothing shall be done without the participation of the King. You are about to hold out a certain hope of peace to America without even informing yourself on the state of the negociation on our part.

You are wise and discreet, sir; you perfectly understand what is due to propriety; you have all your life performed your duties. I pray you to consider how you propose to fulfill those which are due to the King. I am not desirous of enlarging these reflections; I commit them to your own integrity. When you shall be pleased to relieve my uncertainty I will entreat the King to enable me to answer your demands.

B. "I HOPE THIS LITTLE MISUNDERSTANDING WILL BE KEPT SECRET"

Benjamin Franklin to Comte de Vergennes.

Passy, December 17, 1782

Nothing has been agreed in the preliminaries contrary to the interests of France; and no peace is to take place between us and England till you have concluded yours. Your observation is, however, apparently just, that in not consulting you before they were signed, we have been guilty of neglecting a point of *bienséance*. But as this was not from want of respect to the King, whom we all love and honor, we hope it will be excused, and that the great work, which has hitherto been so happily conducted, is so nearly brought to perfection, and is so glorious to his reign, will not be ruined by a single indiscretion of ours. And certainly the whole edifice sinks to the ground immediately if you refuse on that account to give us any futher assistance.

We have not yet despatched the ship, and I beg leave to wait upon you on Friday for an answer.

It is not possible for any one to be more sensible than I am of what I and every American owe to the King for the many and great benefits and favors he has bestowed upon us. All my letters to America are proofs of this; all tending to make the same impressions on the minds of my countrymen that I felt in my own. And I believe that no prince was ever more beloved and respected by his own subjects than the King is by the people of the United States. *The English, I just now learn, flatter themselves they have already divided us.* I hope this little misunderstanding will therefore be kept a secret, and that they will find themselves totally mistaken.

—WHARTON, *Revolutionary Diplomatic Correspondence*, VI, 140, 143-144.

2. THE DEBATE IN THE CONGRESS OF CONFEDERATION

A. "THE CONDUCT OF OUR MINISTERS IS A TRAGEDY TO AMERICA"

March 19, 1783 . . . Mr. [John Francis] Mercer said that not meaning to give offence any where he should speak his sentiments freely. He gave it as his clear and decided opinion that the Ministers had insulted Congress by sending them assertions without proof as reasons for violating their instructions and throwing themselves into the confidence of Great Britain. He observed that France in order to make herself equal to the enemy had been obliged to call for aid and had drawn Spain against her interest into the war; that is was not improbable that she had entered into some specific engagements for that purpose; that hence might be deduced the perplexity of her situation, of which advantage had been taken by Great Britain, an advantage in which our Ministers had concurred for sowing jealousies between France and United States and of which further advantage would be taken to alienate the minds of the people of this country from their ally, by presenting him as the obstacle to peace.

The British Court, he said, having gained this point, may easily frustrate the negotiations and renew the war against divided enemies. He approved of the conduct of the Count de Vergennes in promoting a treaty under the 1st Commission to Oswald as preferring the substance to the shadow and proceeding from a desire of peace. The conduct of our Ministers throughout, particularly in giving in writing every thing called for by the British Minister expressive of distrust of France, was a mixture of follies which had no example, was a tragedy to America and a comedy to all the world besides.

He felt inexpressible indignation at their meanly stooping, as it were, to lick the dust from the feet of a nation whose hands were still dyed with the blood of their fellow citizens. He reprobated the chicane and low cunning which marked the journals transmitted to Congress, and contrasted them with the honesty and good faith which became all nations and particularly an infant republic. They proved that America had at once all the follies of youth and all the vices of old age; thinks it would be necessary to recall our Minister; fears that France may be already acquainted with all the transactions of our Ministers, even with the separate article, and may be only waiting the reception given to it by Congress to see how far the hopes of cutting off the right arm of Great Britain by supporting our revolution may have been well founded; and in case of our basely disappointing her, may league with our enemy for our destruction and for a division of the spoils.

He was aware of the risks to which such a league would expose France of finally losing her share, but supposed that the British Islands might be made hostages for her security. He said America was too prone to depreciate political merit and to suspect where there was no danger; that the honor of the King of France was dear to him, that he never would betray or injure us unless he should be provoked and justified by treachery on our part. ...

B. "CENSURE NOT MINISTERS WHO HAVE NEGOTIATED WELL"

Mr. [Arthur] Lee took notice that obligations in national affairs as well as others ought to be reciprocal, and he did not know that France had ever bound herself to like engagements as to concert of negotiations with those into which America had at different times been drawn. He thought it highly improper to censure ministers who had negotiated well; said that it was agreeable to practice, and necessary to the end proposed, for ministers in particular emergencies to swerve from strict instructions. France, he said, wanted to sacrifice our interests to her own, or those of Spain; that the French answer to the British memorial contained a passage which deserved attention on this subject. She answered the reproaches of perfidy contained in that memorial by observing that, obligations being reciprocal, a breach on one side absolved the other. The Count de Vergennes, he was sure, was too much a master of negotiation not to approve the management of our ministers instead of condemning it. No man lamented more than he did any diminution of confidence between this country and France; but if the misfortune should ensue, it could not be denied that it had originated with France, who had endeavored to sacrifice our territorial rights—those very rights which by the treaty she had guaranteed to us.

—HUNT, ed., *Writings of Madison*, I, 411-412.

3. THE BRITISH ARE INSTRUCTED ON THEIR FUTURE POLICY

Diary of John Adams.

Monday [December 9, 1782]. Visited Count Sarsfield, who lent me his Notes upon America. Visited Mr. Jay. Mr. Oswald came in. We slided from one thing to another into a very lively conversation upon politics. He asked me what the conduct of his Court and nation ought to be in relation to America.

I answered, "The alpha and omega of British policy toward America was summed up in this one maxim:

"See that American independence is independent; independent of all the world; independent of yourselves, as well as of France; and independent of both, as well as of the rest of Europe. Depend upon it, you have no chance for salvation but by setting up America very high. Take care to remove from the American mind all cause of fear of you. No other motive but fear of you will ever produce in the Americans any unreasonable attachment to the House of Bourbon."

"Is it possible," said he, "that the people of America should be afraid of us or hate us?"

"One would think, Mr. Oswald," said I, "that you had been out of the world for these twenty years past. Yes, there are three millions of people in America who hate and dread you more than any thing in the world."

"What!" said he. "Now we come to our senses?"

"Your change of system is not yet known in America," said I.

"Well," said he, "what shall we do to remove these fears and jealousies?"

"In one word," said I, "favor and promote the interest, reputation, and dignity of the United States in every thing that is consistent with your own. If you pursue the plan of cramping, clipping and weakening America, on the supposition that she will be a rival to you, you will make her really so; you will make her the natural and perpetual ally of your natural and perpetual enemies."

"But in what instance," said he, "have we discovered such a disposition?"

"In the three leagues from your shores, and the fifteen leagues from Cape Breton," said I, "to which your ministry insisted so earnestly to exclude our fishermen. Here was a point that would have done us great harm, and you no good—on the contrary, harm; so that you would have hurt yourselves to hurt us. This disposition must be guarded against."

"I am fully of your mind about that," said he; "but what else can we do?"

"Send a minister to Congress," said I, "at the peace—a clever fellow who understands himself and will neither set us bad examples nor inter-meddle in our parties. This will show that you are consistent with yourselves; that you are sincere in your acknowledgment of American independence; and that you don't entertain hopes and designs of overturning it. Such a minister will dissipate many fears, and will be of more service to the least obnoxious refugees than any other measure could be. Let the King send a minister to Congress and receive one from that body. This will be acting consistently, and with dignity, in the face of the universe."

—Adams, ed., *Works of John Adams*, III, 344 ff.

4. "There Never Was a Good War or a Bad Peace"

Benjamin Franklin to Joseph Banks.

Passy, July 27, 1783

I join with you most cordially in rejoicing at the return of peace. I hope it will be lasting, and that mankind will at length, as they call themselves reasonable creatures, have reason and sense enough to settle their differences without cutting throats; for, in my opinion, *there never was a good war or a bad peace.* What vast additions to the conveniences and comforts of living might mankind have acquired, if the money spent in wars had been employed in works of public utility! What an extension of agriculture, even to the tops of our mountains; what rivers rendered navigable or joined by canals; what bridges, aqueducts, new roads and other public works, edifices and improvements, rendering England a complete paradise, might have been obtained by spending those millions in doing good which in the last war have been spent in doing mischief; in bringing misery into thousands of families, and destroying the lives of so many thousands of working people, who might have performed the useful labor! . . .

—BIGELOW, ed., *Works of Franklin,* X, 147-148.

CHAPTER THIRTY-FOUR

Closing Scenes

I. IN ENGLAND DEFEAT SHAKES
THE FOUNDATIONS OF MONARCHY

Writing to Lord North in early November 1781 before the news of York-town had reached England, George III stated: "The dye is now cast whether this shall be a great empire or the least significant of European states." And, he might well have added, whether the King should henceforth rule or reign.

As the war dragged on to its humiliating conclusion powerful voices arose in England, not only demanding peace with the former colonies, but insisting on changes in the constitutional relations between the monarch and Parliament. That rigid, moralistic and censorious ruler, George III, had identified his own interests with those of the state. His close attention to his duties and his propensity to meddle in the tasks of his subordinates made it likely that he would have to shoulder a large part of the responsibility for the impending loss of a huge slice of the old British Empire. He had refused to remove Lord North in 1778, and his prime minister was given a new lease on life by the intervention of France in the war. Now George III's prestige was at a new low. So long as the King's party retained the support of the country gentlemen, his ministry could stay in power. But by 1780 he could no longer count on their support.

The passage of the Dunning motion in a Committee of the Commons to the effect that "the power of the Crown has increased, is increasing, and ought to be diminished," was the handwriting on the wall. The news of York-town strengthened the ranks of the opposition. Great public meetings indicated that the people wanted an end to the war with America. It was only a question of time before the ministry would be overthrown in Parliament. The debate in the Commons of December 12, 1781, seventeen days after the fateful news of Yorktown reached England, revealed how the wind was blowing. Resolutions censuring the administration of the Navy were defeated by a slender margin. An address moved by Conway, petitioning the King to stop the American war, was rejected by only a single vote. Finally on March 20, 1782, North, anticipating the move for his dismissal, announced his resignation, a dramatic episode which we have already reported in the previous chapter. "At last," wrote George III, "the fatal day has come." He went so far as to draft a message of abdication, which he never submitted.

In a curious poem called "The Prophecy," Philip Freneau predicted that after 1785 "you hardly shall know that the king is alive." In one sense this turned out to be true, for in 1788 the King went mad. He had had his first attack of insanity back in 1765, and the long years of crisis finally took their toll of his obstinate mind. But politically, despite Yorktown, he had managed to fend off a drastic reform of the monarchy. A few sinecures and plums, by which the King had in the past manipulated Parliament, were cut out, but the changes were by no means of a root-and-branch character. George warded off Fox's ideas of a cabinet virtually independent of the King by allying his forces with William Pitt, son of the Earl of Chatham. In his later years the King was an object of sympathy and respect. Although a Regency was set up in 1812, George III, the man who lost the American colonies, reigned over England until his death in 1820.

1. "The Influence of the Crown Has Increased, Is Increasing, and Ought to Be Diminished"

Debate on Mr. Dunning's motion respecting the Influence of the Crown, April 6, 1780.

Mr. Dunning: It may be asked, are my propositions to be taken from the petitions on the table? Are they to be worded in the language of this or that petition? By no means. Some may be more extensive, others may be more full and specific; it will suffice that my propositions will not differ from any, as to the principle, though copied from none. My first resolution will be, "That it is the opinion of this committee, that it is necessary to declare, that the influence of the crown has increased, is increasing, and ought to be diminished." My second, "That it is competent to this House, to examine into, and to correct, abuses in the expenditure of the civil list revenues, as well as in every other branch of the public revenue, whenever it shall appear expedient to the wisdom of this House so to do."

He then proceeded to argue the question on the ground of notoriety, that the influence of the crown was increased, and ought to be diminished, having first regularly moved it. He supported his argument, not upon proof, which he said it was idle to require, and must be decided by the conscience of those who as a jury were called upon to determine what was or was not within their own knowledge. He quoted Mr. Hume to prove that he foresaw the increasing influence so early as the year 1742; and also quoted Judge Blackstone as an authority for its existence. He cited a passage from Hume's Essays, to show that that able writer had prophesied that arbitrary monarchy would one day or other be the euthanasia of the British constitution. He could affirm upon his own knowledge, and pledge his honour to the truth of the assertion, that he knew upwards of fifty members in that House who voted always in the train of the noble lord in the blue ribbon; that confessed out of the House that the influence of the crown was increased, and dangerously increased.

He adduced several arguments of a similar nature, and sat down, he said, with his consolation that neither the minority of that House, nor the people at large, would be any longer mocked and insulted with this or that management or trick, this or that evasion; for the certain alternative would be that the decision on the question now proposed by him would declare whether the petitions were to be really attended to or finally and totally rejected. . . .

Mr. Thomas Pitt instanced the present possession of office by the noble lord in the blue ribbon, as an indubitable proof of the enormous influence of the crown. He asked whether that noble lord had not lost America? Whether he had not spent millions of public money, and wasted rivers of blood of the subjects of Great Britan? And yet, the noble lord, now that the whole country with one voice cried out against and execrated the American war, held his place. To what was this ascribable but to the increased influence of the crown? The noble lord has sunk and degraded the honour of Great Britain; the name of an Englishman was now no longer a matter to be proud of; the time had been when it was the envy of all the world; it had been the key to universal respect, but the noble lord had contrived to sink it almost beneath contempt. He had rendered his countrymen and their country despicable in the eyes of every other power. He declared the noble lord would not have been so long at the head of administration but for the efforts of the opposition; it was their regular contest against the fatal measures that had marked the noble lord's administration, which had kept the noble lord in office. The whole business of the minister, for a series of years, had been to make excuses, and to devise expedients; to find supplies from year to year, without inventing any method in finance, any scheme of supply, comprehensive or permanent. The people would bear taxes, though enormous, when they heard of victories and an extension of commerce and territory; but were apt to judge of ministers, not from ingenious excuses made for their conduct either by themselves or others, but from the success that followed their measures.

He noticed the silence of ministers on the present question, and concluded with asserting that the influence of the crown was most offensively increased. The people of England, he said, saw it, and were alarmed. They had expressed their sense of it in their petitions, and begged that it might be diminished. To comply with that request was the duty of that House, and if something effectual was not done upon the present occasion, the consequences that might follow would probably be such as the bare thought of made him tremble at. . . .

Mr. Burke rallied Mr. Rigby a good deal upon his curiosity. He also thought the minister a curiosity, but he was more fit for the British Museum than the British House of Commons.*

—Cobbett, *Parliamentary History of England*, XXI, 347-348, 361-367.

2. The House of Commons Passes the Dunning Resolution

Horace Walpole to Sir Horace Mann.

Strawberry Hill, April 8, 1780

. . . On Wednesday, on the question of the new-raised regiments, in which Mr. Fullarton's was comprised, the ministers carried them in the House of Commons by a majority of nearly forty.

---

* Burke's retort to Rigby's observation that "it was one of the curiosities of the present age to see a minister in the minority."

The next day was appointed for consideration of the petitions from the counties and towns; about forty of which, on vast parchments subscribed by thousands of names, were heaped on the table. The opposition had kept secret their intended motions. The very first, made by Mr. Dunning, was a thundering one: the words were "that the influence of the crown has increased, is increasing, and ought to be diminished." The walls could not believe their own ears; they had not heard such language since they had a wainscot. The ministers, as if this winter were at all like the five last, poorly tried that the chairman should leave the chair; but that would not take now. Thomas Pitt, who never spoke so well before, drew a terrible picture of the difference he had felt between his former journey abroad and his last; from what he knew of the dissimilar situations of his country, then so flourishing, now so fallen! and from what he heard foreigners say of it. This apostrophe, addressed very bitterly to Lord North, threw him into a rage against the opposition that produced mighty tumult. The details of all this, and more, you will see in the papers. I have not room for particulars. In short, late at night, Mr. Dunning's motion was carried by 233 to 215, and, as uncommonly, was instantly reported to the House.

The blow seems to me decisive; for this committee is to continue sitting on the petitions, will exclude any other business, will extract from the petitions whatever propositions it pleased, may ground on those what charges it has a mind, and will carry along all those who have already voted on that foundation; so that, if the ministers attempt to make a further stand, nothing seems so probable as their being personally accused. To combat on the same field of battle after being vanquished will, in my opinion, be frenzy. It is to prevent very great mischief that I heartily wish them to retreat before it is too late. The constitution is vigorous enough, when a sudden turn of the tide can, in three months, sweep away a deep-rooted administration. A torrent opposed may damage the foundations of the constitution itself. . . .

—WALPOLE, *Letters*, XI, 151 ff.

3. "BRITAIN SHOWS THE SIGNS OF THE FALL OF A GREAT EMPIRE"

Debate in the Commons on Sir James Lowther's motion for putting an end to the American War, December 12, 1781.

The House was going into a Committee of Supply when *Sir James Lowther* rose to make a previous motion; before the House went into a committee to vote the army supplies, it became them, he said, to enquire whether they were to persevere in this war and feed it with more British blood. It had been obstinately, fatally pursued. The country was drained, exhausted, dejected. Their hearts were against it. They considered it as a struggle against nature, in which every thing was to be hazarded and nothing to be got. The Speech from the Throne had given them a most serious alarm; it shewed them that ministers were determined to persevere in spite of calamity; that they were bigotted to the prosecution of the contest, . . .

They must, if they designed to do their duty, and to discharge their trust to their constituents, come to a specific declaration on the point and put an end to the war by a peremptory resolution. It was for this reason that he recommended to the House to declare "That it is the opinion of this House that the war carried on in the colonies and plantations of North America has proved ineffectual either to the protection of his Majesty's loyal subjects in the said colonies, or for defeating the dangerous designs of our enemies." . . .

Mr. Powys seconded the motion with the most heartfelt satisfaction, for so convinced had he been of the propriety and even necessity of such a resolution that like his hon. friend, from whom on account of his great weight in the county it came with so much more grace, he had determined, unconnected as he was, to have made it himself; for he most sincerely believed that it was the only means left to us, in our present situation, by which we could extricate ourselves from our difficulties and retrieve our rank in Europe.

We had persevered in this war against the voice of reason and wisdom, against experience that ought to teach, against calamity that ought to make us feel. It was the idol of his Majesty's ministers, to which they had sacrificed the interests of the empire and almost half the territories: they bowed before it, they made the nation bow; they said that the resources of the empire were not exhausted; they said so because they themselves found no diminution of income. Their annual incomes arose out of the public purse, and instead of diminishing, they increased with the misfortunes and the impoverishment of the country. The illusion which had filled the minds of some gentlemen with the hope of seeing America reduced to her former obedience to this country was now no more; and though at first it might have betrayed honest men into a determination to support the measures of ministers which had that reduction in view, he could not conceive how it came to pass that now, when the illusion was at an end, when repeated disasters and calamities had proved that the reduction of America by force was impracticable, there could be found a set of honest, independent gentlemen who could persevere in supporting those measures by which the empire had been dismembered and destroyed. That ministers should persevere in the mad plan of pursuing the phantom of conquest in America was not at all surprising to him; on the contrary, it was extremely natural, because to the war they owed their situations and their emoluments, and by a peace they must lose them; but this was not the case of independent gentlemen who supported them; and he was ready to confess that among the friends of administration in that House, he could reckon some gentlemen of independent fortunes; from what motives, or on what principles, such men continued to support the present administration, he was really at a loss to guess. Could it be from experience of their abilities? Alas! the whole history of the American war was one of continued proof that system and abilities were not to be found in the management of our force in the colonies: an army was marched from Canada, and captured at Saratoga: another from Charles-town, and surrendered at York-town.

Was it in the strength and number of our allies that they hoped for success from those measures to which they gave their support? Melancholy reflection! We were left to contend alone with our enemies; abandoned by all the world, we could not find a friend from pole to pole.

There were in this country, at this time, all the signs and tokens of a falling state. The descriptions given of the marks and signs of the decay and fall of a great empire, written by one of the ablest historians of the present age, was so applicable to these times, and to this country, that, if the House would give him leave, he would quote the passage. . . . These were the signs given by the historian of *The Decline and Fall of the Roman Empire*. . . . He called upon gentlemen to recollect that the war in which we were engaged in America was not like a war between two rival or two neighboring states about a barrier or a boundary; a contest which, however it ended, could not detract much from the importance or weight of either. It was a war in which every conclusion was against us; in which we had suffered every thing without gaining any thing. We weakened no enemy by our efforts; we exhausted no rival by distressing ourselves; every point of the war was against us. . . .

He called upon gentlemen to say if there was still any hopes, after the disaster in Virginia; if there was still any disposition in their minds to go on? What ray of hope was not blasted! What prospect had not failed! What object was not abandoned! The country gentlemen, who had been deceived in the beginning, could be deluded no more. There was no idea of drawing a revenue from that country; there was no idea of alleviating the burthens of Britain, by carrying it on; there was no other idea, and there could be no other reason, than to preserve the power, the consequence and the emoluments which flowed from it.

It was time, therefore, for parliament to interfere, and to prevent that total ruin which the measures of administration could not fail to bring on, if they should remain unchecked: the motion that had been just made might prevent that ruin; it did not refuse a supply; it did not clog the wheels of government, nor did it criminate any man or set of men; it had no retrospective tendency; it only asserted a fact which nobody could dispute; of the truth of which the whole world was perfectly well acquainted. It did not encroach upon the prerogatives of the executive power; it did not take away from the crown the right to distribute the forces of the state in whatever manner it should think for the benefit of the people; it went no farther than to say that among the operations of the war, America should not be the theatre. . . .

—COBBETT, *Parliamentary History of England*, XXII, 802-808.

4. GEORGE III DRAFTS HIS ABDICATION

Draft Message from the King.

March 1782

His Majesty during the twenty one years He has sate on the Throne of Great Britain, has had no object so much at heart as the maintenance of the British Constitution, of which the difficulties He has at times met with from His scrupulous attachment to the Rights of Parliament are sufficient proofs.

His Majesty is convinced that the sudden change of Sentiments of one Branch of the Legislature has totally incapacitated Him from either conducting the War with effect, or from obtaining any Peace but on conditions which would prove destructive to the Commerce as well as essential Rights of the British Nation.

His Majesty therefore with much sorrow finds He can be of no further

Utility to His Native Country which drives Him to the painful step of quitting it for ever.

In consequence of which Intention His Majesty resignes the Crown of Great Britain and the Dominions appertaining thereto to His Dearly Beloved Son and lawful Successor, George Prince of Wales, whose endeavours for the Prosperity of the British Empire He hopes may prove more Successful.

—FORTESCUE, ed., *Correspondence of King George*, V, 425.

5. AN ANCIENT PROPHECY

Philip Freneau, 1781

When a certain great king, whose initial is G.
Shall force stamps upon paper, and folks to drink tea;
When these folks burn his tea and stampt paper, like stubble,
You may guess that this king is then coming to trouble.
But when a petition he treads under his feet,
And sends over the ocean an army and fleet;
When that army, half starvéd, and frantic with rage,
Shall be cooped up with a leader whose name rhymes to cage;
When that leader goes home dejected and sad,
You may then be assured the king's prospects are bad.
But when B. and C. with their armies are taken,
This king will do well if he saves his own bacon.
In the year seventeen hundred and eighty and two,
A stroke he shall get that will make him look blue;
In the years eighty-three, eighty-four, eighty-five,
You hardly shall know that the king is alive;
In the year eighty-six the affair will be over,
And he shall eat turnips that grow in Hanover.
The face of the lion shall then become pale,
He shall yield fifteen teeth, and be sheared of his tail.
O king, my dear king, you shall be very sore;
The Stars and the Lily shall run you on shore,
And your Lion shall growl—but never bite more.

—FRENEAU, *Poems*, II, 56.

II. THE ALTERNATIVES OF DICTATORSHIP OR REPUBLICAN GOVERNMENT

In America in the winter of 1783 the chances of a military coup seemed by no means remote. Early in January a delegation of army officers memorialized Congress, pointing out that their pay was seriously in arrears, their food and clothing accounts remained unsettled, and that no provision had been made for the life pension of half pay from the time of their discharge which Congress had promised them in October 1780.

One Congressman, Alexander Hamilton, was thoroughly alarmed. In a letter to Washington of February 7, 1783, he warned the general that the army was prepared to take steps "to procure justice to itself" and urged him to take the lead in advancing the army's claims in order "to keep a complaining and suffering army within the bounds of moderation." Washington ignored Hamilton's advice, and did not sponsor the movement. After Congress had rejected a proposal to give the officers a commutation of their pension for six years' full pay, Major John Armstrong wrote an anonymous address which was circulated in the main camp near Newburgh, New York. Therein he advised the officers to assume a bold tone and "suspect the man who would advise to more moderation and longer forbearance." Armstrong's call for a meeting of officers had the backing of Horatio Gates.

Recognizing the dangers of military dictatorship, Washington quickly blunted the movement's force. On March 11 he issued an order forbidding the unauthorized meeting called for by Armstrong, and proposed instead a regular meeting of the officers for a discussion of grievances on March 15. A second anonymous letter, also written by Armstrong, was issued on March 12, expressing the opinion that Washington's action endorsed (the word "sanctified" was actually used) the claims of the officers. But Washington's unexpected and dramatic appearance at the meeting of the fifteenth quickly disabused the dissident elements. We are indebted to a spectator, Major Samuel Shaw, for an account of Washington's speech, which he read. In his journal the major records that after reading the first paragraph, Washington paused, took out his spectacles, "and begged the indulgence of his audience while he put them on, observing at the same time that he had grown gray in their service, and now found himself growing blind." "There was something so natural, so unaffected, in this appeal," Major Shaw continued, "as rendered it superior to the most studied oratory. It forces its way to the heart, and you might see sensibility moisten every eye."

After Washington withdrew, the officers adopted resolutions, affirming their patriotism, their confidence in Congress, and their disdain of the "infamous propositions . . . in a late anonymous address." Thus, Washington's timely intervention prevented what could have been a military coup. Washington had demonstrated a full measure of courage and a deep sense of public responsibility. "On other occasions," Shaw remarked, Washington "had been supported by the exertions of an Army and the countenance of his friends; but in this he stood single and alone. . . . He appeared, not at the head of his troops, but as it were in opposition to them; and for a dreadful moment the interests of the Army and its General seemed to be in competition! He spoke —every doubt was dispelled, and the tide of patriotism rolled again in its wonted course."

"ONE MORE DISTINGUISHED PROOF OF UNEXAMPLED PATRIOTISM"

Washington addresses the officers of the Army, March 15, 1783.

Gentlemen: By an anonymous summons, an attempt has been made to convene you together; how inconsistent with the rules of propriety! how unmilitary! and how subversive of all order and discipline, let the good sense of the Army decide.

In the moment of this Summons, another anonymous production was sent into circulation, addressed more to the feelings and passions, than to the reason and judgment of the Army. . . . That the Address is drawn with great Art, and is designed to answer the most insidious purposes. That it is calculated to impress the mind, with an idea of premeditated injustice in the Sovereign power of the United States, and rouse all those resentments which must unavoidably flow from such a belief. That the secret mover of this Scheme (whoever he may be) intended to take advantage of the passions, while they were warmed by the recollection of past distresses, without giving time for cool, deliberative thinking, and that composure of Mind which is so necessary to give dignity and stability to measures is rendered too obvious, by the mode of conducting the business, to need other proof than a reference to the proceeding. . . .

It can *scarcely be supposed*, at this late stage of the War, that I am indifferent to its interests. But, how are they to be promoted? The way is plain, says the anonymous Addresser. If War continues, remove into the unsettled Country; there establish yourselves, and leave an ungrateful Country to defend itself. . . . This dreadful alternative, of either deserting our Country in the extremest hour of her distress, or turning our Arms against it, (which is the apparent object, unless Congress can be compelled into instant compliance) has something so shocking in it, that humanity revolts at the idea. My God! what can this writer have in view, by recommending such measures? Can he be a friend to the Army? Can he be a friend to this Country? Rather, is he not an insidious Foe? Some Emissary, perhaps, from New York, plotting the ruin of both, by sowing the seeds of discord and seperation between the Civil and Military powers of the Continent? . . .

For myself . . . a grateful sence of the confidence you have ever placed in me, a recollection of the chearful assistance, and prompt obedience I have experienced from you, under every vicissitude of fortune, and the sincere affection I feel for an Army, I have so long had the honor to Command, will oblige me to declare, in this public and solemn manner, that, in the attainment of compleat justice for all your toils and dangers, and in the gratification of every wish, so far as may be done consistently with the great duty I owe my Country, and those powers we are bound to respect, you may freely command my Services to the utmost of my abilities.

While I give you these assurances, and pledge myself in the most unequivocal manner, to exert whatever ability I am possessed of, in your favor, let me entreat you, Gentlemen, on your part, not to take any measures, which, viewed in the calm light of reason, will lessen the dignity, and sully the glory you have hitherto maintained; let me request you to rely on the plighted faith of your Country, and place a full confidence in the purity of the intentions of Congress; that, previous to your dissolution as an Army they will cause all your Accts. to be fairly liquidated. . . .

And let me conjure you, in the name of our common Country, as you value your own sacred honor, as you respect the rights of humanity, and as you regard the Military and National character of America, to express your utmost horror and detestation of the Man who wishes, under any specious pretences, to overturn the liberties of our Country, and who wickedly attempts to open the flood Gates of Civil discord, and deluge our rising Empire in Blood. By thus determining, and thus acting, you will pursue the plain and direct road to the attainment of your wishes. You will defeat the insidious designs of our Enemies, who are compelled to resort from open force to secret artifice. You will give one more distinguished proof of unexampled patriotism and patient virtue, rising superior to the pressure of the most complicated sufferings; And you will, by the dignity of your Conduct, afford occasion for Posterity to say, when speaking of the glorious example you have exhibited to Mankind, "had this day been wanting, the World had never seen the last stage of perfection to which human nature is capable of attaining."

    —FITZPATRICK, ed., *Writings of Washington*, XXVI, 222-227.

III. WASHINGTON'S PARTING ADVICE TO THE NEW NATION

In several papers and addresses announcing the termination of the war and his own imminent retirement Washington summed up the meaning of the Revolution and the problems facing America in peacetime. The first document included in this section is his "Circular to the States," in which he listed four objectives as "essential to the well being," even to "the very existence" of the United States as "an independent power." They were "an indissoluble union of the states under one Federal Head"; "a sacred regard to public justice"; "the adoption of a proper peace establishment"; and "the prevalence of that pacific and friendly disposition among the people of the United States which will induce them to forget their local prejudices and policies, to make those mutual concessions which are requisite to the general prosperity, and in some instances, to sacrifice their individual advantages to the interest of the community."

The rear guard of the British troops evacuated New York on December 4, 1783. Washington was determined to leave for home as soon as the evacuation was completed, but before departing he had a last meeting with his officers at Fraunces' Tavern. His brief words were reported in Rivington's Tory Gazette. Washington embraced each of his officers in turn, beginning with Knox. "The simple thought," wrote Lieutenant Colonel Benjamin Talmadge, "that we were then about to part from the man who had conducted us through a long and bloody war, and under whose conduct the glory and independence of our country had been achieved, and that we should see his face no more in this world seemed to me utterly insupportable."

Finally, Washington addressed Congress at Annapolis on December 23, and in a few eloquent words submitted his resignation. "The spectators all wept," wrote James McHenry, "and there was hardly a member of Congress who did not drop tears." The preceding evening a ball was given in his honor. "The general," one observer noted, "danced every set, that all the ladies might have the pleasure of dancing with him, or as it has been handsomely expressed, get a touch of him."

1. "WITH OUR FATE WILL THE DESTINY OF MILLIONS BE INVOLVED"

Circular to the States.

                               Head Quarters, Newburgh, June 8, 1783

    Sir: The great object for which I had the honor to hold an appointment in the Service of my Country, being accomplished, I am now preparing to resign it into the hands of Congress, and to return to that domestic retirement, which, it is well known, I left with the greatest reluctance, a Retirement, for which I have never ceased to sigh through a long and painful absence, and in which (remote from the noise and trouble of the World) I meditate to pass the remainder of life in a state of undisturbed repose. But before I carry this resolution into effect, I think it a duty incumbent on me, to make this my last official communication, to congratulate you on the glorious events which Heaven has been pleased to produce in our favor, to offer my sentiments respecting some important subjects, which appear to me, to be intimately connected with the tranquility of the United States, to take my leave of your Excellency as a public Character, and to give my final blessing to that Country, in whose service I have spent the prime of my life, for whose sake I have consumed so many anxious days and watchfull nights, and whose happiness being extremely dear to me, will always constitute no inconsiderable part of my own.

Impressed with the liveliest sensibility on this pleasing occasion, I will claim the indulgence of dilating the more copiously on the subjects of our mutual felicitation. When we consider the magnitude of the prize we contended for, the doubtful nature of the contest, and the favorable manner in which it has terminated, we shall find the greatest possible reason for gratitude and rejoicing; this is a theme that will afford infinite delight to every benevolent and liberal mind, whether the event in contemplation, be considered as the source of present enjoyment or the parent of future happiness; and we shall have equal occasion to felicitate ourselves on the lot which Providence has assigned us, whether we view it in a natural, a political or moral point of light.

The Citizens of America, placed in the most enviable condition, as the sole Lords and Proprietors of a vast Tract of Continent, comprehending all the various soils and climates of the World, and abounding with all the necessaries and conveniences of life, are now by the late satisfactory pacification, acknowledged to be possessed of absolute freedom and Independency; They are, from this period, to be considered as the Actors on a most conspicuous Theatre, which seems to be peculiarly designated by Providence for the display of human greatness and felicity; Here, they are not only surrounded with every thing which can contribute to the completion of private and domestic enjoyment, but Heaven has crowned all its other blessings, by giving a fairer oppertunity for political happiness, than any other Nation has ever been favored with. Nothing can illustrate these observations more forcibly, than a recollection of the happy conjuncture of times and circumstances, under which our Republic assumed its rank among the Nations; The foundation of our Empire was not laid in the gloomy age of Ignorance and Superstition, but at an Epocha when the rights of mankind were better understood and more clearly defined, than at any former period, the researches of the human mind, after social happiness, have been carried to a great extent, the Treasures of knowledge, acquired by the labours of Philosophers, Sages and Legislatures, through a long succession of years, are laid open for our use, and their collected wisdom may be happily applied in the Establishment of our forms of Government; the free cultivation of Letters, the unbounded extension of Commerce, the progressive refinement of Manners, the growing liberality of sentiment, and above all, the pure and benign light of Revelation, have had a meliorating influence on mankind and increased the blessings of Society. At this auspicious period, the United States came into existence as a Nation, and if their Citizens should not be completely free and happy, the fault will be intirely their own.

Such is our situation, and such are our prospects: but notwithstanding the cup of blessing is thus reached out to us, notwithstanding happiness is ours, if we have a disposition to seize the occasion and make it our own; yet, it appears to me there is an option still left to the United States of America, that it is in their choice, and depends upon their conduct, whether they will be respectable and prosperous, or contemptable and miserable as a Nation; This is the time of their political probation, this is the moment when the eyes of the whole World are turned upon them, this is the moment to establish or ruin their national Character forever, this is the favorable moment to give such a tone to our Federal Government, as will enable it to answer the ends of its institution, or this may be the ill-fated moment for relaxing the powers of the Union, annihilating the cement of the Confederation, and exposing us to become the sport of European politics, which may play one State against another to prevent their growing importance, and to serve their own interested purposes. For, according to the system of Policy the States shall adopt at this moment, they will stand or fall, and by their confirmation or lapse, it is yet to be decided, whether the Revolution must ultimately be considered as a blessing or a curse: a blessing or a curse, not to the present age alone, for with out fate will the destiny of unborn Millions be involved.

—FITZPATRICK, ed., *Writings of Washington*, XXVI, 483-486.

2. "I Now Take Leave of You"

Fraunces' Tavern, New York, December 4, 1783. The following report appeared in Rivington's New York *Gazette* of December 6, 1783, and the *Pennsylvania Packet* of December 12, 1783.

His excellency, having filled a glass of wine, thus addressed his brave fellow-soldiers:

"With an heart full of love and gratitude I now take leave of you. I most devoutly wish that your latter days may be as prosperous and happy as your former ones have been glorious and honorable."

These words produced extreme sensibility on both sides; they were answered by warm expressions and fervent wishes from the gentlemen of the army, whose truly pathetic feelings it is not in our power to convey to the reader. Soon after this scene was closed, His Excellency the Governor, the Honorable the Council and citizens of the first distinction waited on the general and in terms most affectionate took their leave.

The corps of light infantry was drawn up in a line. The commander in chief about two o'clock passed through them on his way to Whitehall, where he embarked in his barge for Powles Hook. He is attended by general le baron de Steuben; proposes to make a short stay at Philadelphia; will thence proceed to Annapolis, where he will resign his commission as General of the American Armies into the hands of the Continental Congress, from whom it

was derived, immediately after which His Excellency will set out for his seat named Mount Vernon, in Virginia, emulating the example of his model, the virtuous Roman General, who, victorious, left the tented field, covered with honors, and withdrew from public life, *otium cum dignitate.*
—CLINTON, *Public Papers*, VIII, 306-307.

3. "I RETIRE FROM THE GREAT THEATRE OF ACTION"

Washington's address to Congress resigning his commission.

December 23, 1783

Mr. President:

The great events on which my resignation depended having at length taken place; I have now the honor of offering my sincere Congratulations to Congress and of presenting myself before them to surrender into their hands the trust committed to me, and to claim the indulgence of retiring from the Service of my Country.

Happy in the confirmation of our Independence and Sovereignty, and pleased with the oppertunity afforded the United States of becoming a respectable Nation, I resign with satisfaction the Appointment I accepted with diffidence. A diffidence in my abilities to accomplish so arduous a task, which however was superseded by a confidence in the rectitude of our Cause, the support of the Supreme Power of the Union, and the patronage of Heaven.

The Successful termination of the War has verified the most sanguine expectations, and my gratitude for the interposition of Providence, and the assistance I have received from my Countrymen, encreases with every review of the momentous Contest.

While I repeat my obligations to the Army in general, I should do injustice to my own feelings not to acknowledge in this place the peculiar Services and distinguished merits of the Gentlemen who have been attached to my person during the War. It was impossible the choice of confidential Officers to compose my famliy should have been more fortunate. Permit me Sir, to recommend in particular those, who have continued in Service to the present moment, as worthy of the favorable notice and patronage of Congress.

I consider it an indispensable duty to close this last solemn act of my Official life, by commending the Interests of our dearest Country to the protection of Almighty God, and those who have the superintendence of them, to his holy keeping.

Having now finished the work assigned me, I retire from the great theatre of Action; and bidding an Affectionate farewell to this August body under whose orders I have so long acted, I here offer my Commission, and take my leave of all the employments of public life.
—FITZPATRICK, ed., *Writings of Washington*, XXVII, 284-285.

IV. "PEACE MADE, A NEW SCENE OPENS"

Writing his bosom friend John Laurens on August 15, 1782, Hamilton commented: "Peace made, my dear friend, a new scene opens. The object will be to make our independence a blessing. To do this we must secure our Union on solid foundations—a herculean task—and to effect which mountains of prejudice must be levelled! It requires all the virtue and all the abilities of our country." To Hamilton as to Washington a strong foundation meant a Continental government with power to act. Others reflected the same sentiments. "Say, my friend," Samuel Shaw asked the Reverend Mr. Elliot in February 1783, "is America prepared for the reception of the long wished-for blessing?" There had to be a power vested in some supreme head, he argued. "Thirteen wheels require a steady and powerful regulator to keep them in good order, and prevent the machine from becoming useless. The prospect of peace makes a politician of the soldier. We are thirteen states, and a hoop to the barrel is the prevailing sentiment."

Leaders like Washington and Hamilton were concerned about developing and preserving the American character. "We are placed among the nations of the earth," Washington wrote Lafayette from Newburgh on April 5, 1783, "and have a character to establish, but how we shall acquit ourselves time must discover." The great end was "to form a Constitution that will give consistency, stability and dignity to the Union." Washington would give whatever help he could as a private citizen, "for henceforward my mind shall be unbent; and I will endeavor to glide down the stream of life, till I come to that abyss, from whence no traveller is permitted to return."

In a sermon delivered in 1783 Ezra Stiles expatiated on one essential ingredient of nationalism—a common language. He predicted that "the rough, sonorous diction of the English language may here take its Athenian polish, and receive its Attic urbanity; as it will probably become the vernacular tongue of more numerous millions than ever yet spake one language on earth." He also expressed the belief that travel and communication in the United States would prevent the rise of provincial dialects. It was his expectation that "the English language will grow up with the present American population into great purity and elegance, unmutilated by the foreign dialects of foreign conquests."

This aspect of cultural nationalism was stressed by the distinguished South Carolinian, David Ramsay, physician and historian, in his perceptive appraisal of the social and cultural consequences of the Revolution, first published in 1789, and by Thomas Paine in his last Crisis paper. It is fitting that Paine, whose first Crisis paper evoked that unflinching courage and selfless dedication, which for posterity are epitomized in the "spirit of 'seventy-six," should in these volumes have the last word, and that on the noble prospects of the American nation. Paine notwithstanding, "the times that tried men's souls" were not really over. The American people were still to face other trials in the buildings of the new nation, in the preserving of union, and in the effort to achieve a durable peace, but that unconquerable spirit forged in the crucible of Bunker's Hill and Valley Forge and King's Mountain would sustain the nation through crises that lay ahead.

1. AN AMERICAN NATIONALISM AND AN AMERICAN CHARACTER

[1793]

From Dr. Ramsay's *History of the American Revolution*.

The American Revolution, on the one hand, brought forth great vices; but on the other hand, it called forth many virtues, and gave occasion for the display of abilities which, but for that event, would have been lost to the world.

When the war began, the Americans were a mass of husbandmen, merchants, mechanics and fishermen; but the necessities of the country gave a spring to the active powers of the inhabitants, and set them on thinking, speaking and acting in a line far beyond that to which they had been accustomed.

The difference between nations is not so much owing to nature as to education and circumstances. While the Americans were guided by the leading strings of the mother country, they had no scope nor encouragement for exertion. All the departments of government were established and executed for them, but not by them. In the years 1775 and 1776 the country, being suddenly thrown into a situation that needed the abilities of all its sons, these generally took their places, each according to the bent of his inclination. As they severally pursued their objects with ardour, a vast expansion of the human mind speedily followed. This displayed itself in a variety of ways. It was found that their talents for great stations did not differ in kind, but only in degree, from those which were necessary for the proper discharge of the ordinary business of civil society.

In the bustle that was occasioned by the war, few instances could be produced of any persons who made a figure, or who rendered essential services, but from among those who had given specimens of similar talents in their respective professions. Those who from indolence or dissipation had been of little service to the community in time of peace, were found equally unserviceable in war. A few young men were exceptions to this general rule. Some of these, who had indulged in youthful follies, broke off from their vicious courses and on the pressing call of their country became useful servants of the public; but the great bulk of those who were the active instruments of carrying on the Revolution were self-made, industrious men. These who by their own exertions had established or laid a foundation for establishing personal independence, were most generally trusted and most successfully employed in establishing that of their country. In these times of action, classical education was found of less service than good natural parts, guided by common sense and sound judgment.

Several names could be mentioned of individuals who, without the knowledge of any other language than their mother tongue, wrote not only accurately, but elegantly, on public business. It seemed as if the war not only required, but created talents. Men whose minds were warmed with the love of liberty, and whose abilities were improved by daily exercise, and sharpened with a laudable ambition to serve their distressed country, spoke, wrote and acted with an energy far surpassing all expectations which could be reasonably founded on their previous acquirements.

The Americans knew but little of one another previous to the Revolution. Trade and business had brought the inhabitants of their seaports acquainted with each other, but the bulk of the people in the interior country were unacquainted with their fellow citizens. A Continental Army and a Congress composed of men from all the States by freely mixing together were assimilated into one mass. Individuals of both, mingling with the citizens, disseminated principles of union among men. Local prejudices abated. By frequent collision asperities were worn off, and a foundation was laid for the establishment of a nation out of discordant materials. Intermarriages between men and women of different States were much more common than before the war and became an additional cement to the union. Unreasonable jealousies had existed between the inhabitants of the eastern and the southern states; but on becoming better acquainted with each other, these in a great measure subsided. A wiser policy prevailed. Men of liberal minds led the way in discouraging local distinctions, and the great body of the people, as soon as reason got the better of prejudice, found that their best interests would be most effectually promoted by such practices and sentiments as were favorable to union.

Religious bigotry had broken in upon the peace of various sects before the American war. This was kept up by partial establishments, and by a dread that the Church of England through the power of the mother country would be made to triumph over all other denominations. These apprehensions were done away by the Revolution. The different sects, having nothing to fear from each other, dismissed all religious controversy. A proposal for introducing bishops into America before the war had kindled a flame among the dissenters; but the Revolution was no sooner accomplished than a scheme for that purpose was perfected, with the consent and approbation of all those sects who had previously opposed it. Pulpits which had formerly been shut to worthy men, because their heads had not been consecrated by the imposition of the hands of a bishop or of a presbytery, have since the establishment of independence been reciprocally opened to each other, whensoever the public convenience required it. The world will soon see the result of an experiment in politics, and be able to determine whether the happiness of society is increased by religious establishments, or diminished by the want of them.

Though schools and colleges were generally shut up during the war, yet many of the arts and sciences were promoted by it. The geography of the United States before the Revolution was but little known; but the marches of armies and the operations of war gave birth to many geographical enquiries and discoveries which otherwise would not have been made. A passionate fondness for studies of this kind and the growing importance of the country excited one of its sons, the Reverend Mr. Morse, to travel through every State of the Union and amass a fund of topographical knowledge far exceeding any thing heretofore communicated to the public.

The necessities of the States led to the study of tactics, fortifications, gunnery and a variety of other arts connected with war, and diffused a knowledge of them among a peaceable people who would ohterwise have had no inducement to study them.

The abilities of ingenious men were directed to make farther improvements in the art of destroying an enemy. Among these, David Bushnell of Connecticut invented a machine for submarine navigation, which was found to answer the purpose of rowing horizontally at any given depth under water, and of rising or sinking at pleasure. To this was attached a magazine of powder, and the whole was contrived in such a manner as to make it practicable to blow up vessels by machinary under them. Mr. Bushnell also contrived sundry other curious machines for the annoyance of British shipping, but from accident they only succeeded in part. He destroyed one vessel in charge of Commodore Symonds, and a second one near the shore of Long-Island.

Surgery was one of the arts which was promoted by the war. From the want of hospitals and other aids, the medical men of America had few opportunities of perfecting themselves in this art, the thorough knowledge of which can only be acquired by practice and observation. The melancholy events of battles gave the American students an opportunity of seeing and learning more in one day than they could have acquired in years of peace. It was in the hospitals of the United States that Dr. Rush first discovered the method of curing the lock jaw by bark and wine, added to other invigorating remedies, which has since been adopted with success in Europe, as well as in the United States.

The science of government has been more generally diffused among the Americans by means of the Revolution. The policy of Great Britain in throwing them out of her protection induced a necessity of establishing independent constitutions. This led to reading and reasoning on the subject. The many errors that were at first committed by unexperienced statesmen have been a practical comment on the folly of unbalanced constitutions and injudicious laws. The discussions concerning the new constitutions gave birth to much reasoning on the subject of government, and particularly to a series of letters signed Publius, but really the work of Alexander Hamilton, in which much political knowledge and wisdom were displayed, and which will long remain a monument of the strength and acuteness of the human understanding in investigating truth. . . .

As literature had in the first instance favoured the Revolution, so in its turn the Revolution promoted literature. The study of eloquence and of the belles lettres was more successfully prosecuted in America after the disputes between Great Britain and her colonies began to be serious than it had ever been before. The various orations, addresses, letters, dissertations and other literary performances which the war made necessary, called forth abilities where they were, and excited the rising generation to study arts which brought with them their own reward. Many incidents afforded materials for the favourites of the muses to display their talents. Even burlesquing royal proclamations by parodies and doggerel poetry had great effects on the minds of the people. A celebrated historian has remarked that the song of "Lillibullero" forwarded the revolution of 1688 in England. It may be truly affirmed that similar productions produced similar effects in America. Francis Hopkinson rendered essential service to his country by turning the artillery of wit and ridicule on the enemy. Philip Freneau laboured successfully in the same way. Royal proclamations and other productions which issued from royal printing presses were, by the help of warm imaginations, arrayed in such dresses as rendered them truly ridiculous. Trumbull with a vein of original Hudibrastic humour diverted his countrymen so much with the follies of their enemies that for a time they forgot the calamities of war. Humphries twined the literary with the military laurel by superadding the fame of an elegant poet to that of an accomplished officer. Barlow increased the fame of his country and of the distinguished actors in the Revolution by the bold design of an epic poem ably executed on the idea that Columbus foresaw in vision the great scenes that were to be transacted on the theater of that new world which he had discovered. Dwight struck out in the same line and at an early period of life finished an elegant work entitled *The Conquest of Canaan*, on a plan which has rarely been attempted. The principles of their mother tongue were first unfolded to the Americans since the Revolution by their countryman Webster. Pursuing an unbeaten track, he has made discoveries in the genius and construction of the English language which had escaped the researches of preceding philologists.

These and a group of other literary characters have been brought into view by the Revolution. It is remarkable that of these Connecticut has produced an unusual proportion. In that truly republican state, every thing conspires to adorn human nature with its highest honours.

From the latter periods of the Revolution till the present time, schools, colleges, societies, and institutions for promoting literature, arts, manufactures, agriculture, and for extending human happiness, have been increased far beyond any thing that ever took place before the Declaration of Independence. Every state in the union has done more or less in this way, but Pennsylvania has done the most....

To overset an established government unhinges many of those principles which bind individuals to each other. A long time, and much prudence, will be necessary to reproduce a spirit of union and that reverence for government without which society is a rope of sand. The right of the people to resist their rulers, when invading their liberties, forms the corner stone of the American republics. This principle, though just in itself, is not favourable to the tranquility of present establishments. The maxims and measures which in the years 1774 and 1775 were successfully inculcated and adopted by American patriots for oversetting the established government, will answer a similar purpose when recurrence is had to them by factious demagogues for disturbing the freest governments that were ever devised.

War never fails to injure the morals of the people engaged in it. The American war, in particular, had an unhappy influence of this kind. Being begun without funds or regular establishments, it could not be carried on without violating private rights; and in its progress it involved a necessity for breaking solemn promises and plighted public faith. The failure of national justice, which was in some degree unavoidable, increased the difficulties of performing private engagements, and weakened that sensibility to the obligations of public and private honor which is a security for the punctual performance of contracts.

In consequence of the war, the institutions of religion have been deranged, the public worship of the Deity suspended, and a great number of inhabitants deprived of the ordinary means of obtaining that religious knowledge which tames the fierceness and softens the rudeness of human passions and manners. Many of the temples dedicated to the service of the Most High were destroyed, and these, from a deficiency of ability and inclination, are not yet rebuilt. The clergy were left to suffer without proper support. The depreciation of the paper currency was particularly injurious to them. It reduced their salaries to a pittance, so insufficient for the maintenance that several of them were obliged to lay down their profession and engage in other pursuits. Public preaching, of which many of the inhabitants were thus deprived, seldom fails of rendering essential service to society by civilising the multitude and forming them to union. No class of citizens have contributed more to the Revolution than the clergy, and none have hitherto suffered more in consequence of it. From the diminution of their number and the penury to which they have been subjected, civil government has lost many of the advantages it formerly derived from the public instructions of that useful order of men.

On the whole, the literary, political and military talents of the citizens of the United States have been improved by the Revolution, but their moral character is inferior to what it formerly was. So great is the change for the worse that the friends of public order are loudly called upon to exert their utmost abilities in extirpating the vicious principles and habits which have taken deep root during the late convulsions.

—RAMSAY, *History of the Revolution*, II, 315 *et seq.*

2. "THE TIMES THAT TRIED MEN'S SOULS ARE OVER!": THOMAS PAINE

The *Crisis*, XIII: "Thoughts on the Peace and the Probable Advantages Thereof."

[1783]

"The times that tried men's souls" are over—and the greatest and completest revolution the world ever knew, gloriously and happily accomplished.

But to pass from the extremes of danger to safety, from the tumult of war to the tranquillity of peace, though sweet in contemplation, requires a gradual composure of the senses to receive it. Even calmness has the power of stunning, when it opens too instantly upon us. The long and raging hurricane that should cease in a moment, would leave us in a state rather of wonder than enjoyment; and some moments of recollection must pass, before we could be capable of tasting the felicity of repose. There are but few instances in which the mind is fitted for sudden transitions: it takes in its pleasures by reflection and comparison and those must have time to act, before the relish for new scenes is complete. . . .

To see it in our power to make a world happy—to teach mankind the art of being so—to exhibit on the theatre of the universe a character hitherto unknown—and to have, as it were, a new creation intrusted to our hands, are honors that command reflection and can neither be too highly estimated nor too gratefully received.

In this pause then of recollection, while the storm is ceasing, and the long agitated mind vibrating to a rest, let us look back on the scenes we have passed and learn from experience what is yet to be done.

Never, I say, had a country so many openings to happiness as this. Her setting out in life, like the rising of a fair morning, was unclouded and promising. Her cause was good. Her principles just and liberal. Her temper serene and firm. Her conduct regulated by the nicest steps, and everything about her wore the mark of honor. It is not every country (perhaps there is not another in the world) that can boast so fair an origin. Even the first settlement of America corresponds with the character of the Revolution. Rome, once the proud mistress of the universe, was originally a band of ruffians. Plunder and rapine made her rich, and her oppression of millions made her great. But America need never be ashamed to tell her birth, nor relate the stages by which she rose to empire. . . .

She is now descending to the scenes of quiet and domestic life. Not beneath the cypress shade of disappointment, but to enjoy in her own land, and under her own vine, the sweet of her labors, and the reward of her toil. In this situation, may she never forget that a fair national reputation is of as much importance as independence! That it possesses a charm that wins upon the world, and makes even enemies civil! That it gives a dignity which is often superior to power, and commands reverence where pomp and splendor fail!

It would be a circumstance ever to be lamented and never to be forgotten, were a single blot, from any cause whatever, suffered to fall on a revolution which to the end of time must be an honor to the age that accomplished it; and which has contributed more to enlighten the world, and diffuse a spirit of freedom and liberality among mankind, than any human event (if this may be called one) that ever preceded it. . . .

—CONWAY, ed., *Writings of Paine*, I, 370-375, *passim.*

Thus, almost eight years after the opening shots at Lexington and Concord, Britain acknowledged the independence of the American States, and the war came to an end. The sage Franklin might say that there never was a good war, but he had never for a moment questioned the necessity of this one, nor did he ever doubt that its ultimate consequences were beneficial to mankind. Who now can doubt that John Adams was justified in seeing, "through all the gloom, the rays of ravishing light and glory," or that posterity did indeed "triumph in the transactions of that day" of independence? The American Revolution was costly in lives and in property, and more costly in the terror and the fear and the violence that, as in all wars, fell so disproportionately on the innocent and the weak. Yet by comparison with other wars of comparable magnitude, before and since, the cost was not high. Notwithstanding the ruthlessness and even the ferocity with which it was waged, it did little lasting damage, and left few lasting scars. Population increased all through the war; the movement into the West was scarcely interrupted; and within a few years of peace, the new nation was bursting with prosperity and buoyant with hope. Independence stimulated both material and intellectual enterprise, and five years after the Treaty of Paris Americans brought the Revolution to a triumphant conclusion by writing the first national constitution and setting up the most enduring of national unions.

Of few other wars can it be said that so much was gained at so little lasting cost, either in lives snuffed out, or in a heritage of hatred. As victory did not make Americans ruthless or militaristic, so defeat did not impair British power or undermine British character. In time British statesmen and historians came to look upon the American Revolution as a proud chapter in their own his-

tory, and to rejoice that Washington triumphed over George the Third. The war dramatized for them the necessity of a new and more wholesome relationship between Crown and Parliament; it vindicated seventeenth-century political theories and principles that were to survive and flourish into the nineteenth and twentieth centuries; it foreshadowed a more enlightened relationship between mother country and colony, one that was eventually to evolve into that notable institution, the Commonwealth of Nations.

The United States, born out of the travail of what John Adams called "this mighty Revolution," was the first colony to break away from a mother country and started a process whose end is not yet. It was the first of the new nations of the modern world, and for a long time a model to other new nations. It was the first to realize the great principle that men make government; the first to provide effective limits on government through written constitutions; the first to create a workable federal system; the first to do away with the age-old subordination of colony to mother country and substitute for this a system of equal and co-ordinate states; the first to abolish the interdependence of church and state and institute full religious freedom; the first to encourage and provide for a society without overt class distinctions (except for the tragic one of Negro slavery), and to inaugurate the great experiment of equality in circumstances auspicious to its success.

The Revolution was, therefore, in a very real sense, the first war whose nonmilitary consequences were of significance to the rest of mankind. In the words of Jefferson, Americans undertook "to make a communication of grandeur and freedom" to all the peoples of the globe; it was for this reason that the Great Declaration had asserted the rights not just of Americans or of Englishmen, but of Man. This concern for something more than private and local interests; this sense of obligation to the welfare of mankind, and of posterity, was common to the generation that fought and won the Revolution. Thus Tom Paine thought it was "the opportunity of beginning the world anew and of bringing forward a new system of government in which the rights of all men should be preserved that gave value to independence." Thus Ethan Allen rejoiced that "to see it in our power to make a world happy, to teach mankind the art of being so, to exhibit on the theatre of the universe, a character hitherto unknown, to have . . . a new creation entrusted to our hands, are honors that can neither be too highly estimated nor too greatly received." And thus Washington admonished us that "with our fate will the destiny of unborn millions be involved." The American Revolution was not an event in American history alone, but in world history, and the new nation which came out of it was destined to play on the great stage of history a part more influential than that played by Athens or Rome in the ancient world, by Spain or England in the modern. That this role has been, on the whole, a benevolent one can be explained in part by the principles of conduct laid down at the very beginning by the great good fortune of leadership by men like Washington, Franklin, Jefferson, Hamilton, Adams and Paine, and by the courage and fortitude of thousands of plain men and women who fought and endured that the nation might live.

THE END

Acknowledgments and Bibliography

An enterprise of this character, stretching over many years, naturally incurs many and deep debts and obligations. A number of former Columbia graduate students since distinguished as historians on their own account contributed ideas and findings. Dr. Warren Carroll was notably helpful in the tracking down and transcribing of sources, and we are also appreciative of the assistance in research and verification rendered by Professors Robert Christen of Manhattan College, Jesse Lemisch of the University of Chicago, and Catherine Crary of Finch College. We could not have completed this book without the cheerful help of the staffs of the Columbia University and Amherst College libraries, who endured with good humor continuous raids upon their collections. We are indebted, too, to libraries and librarians elsewhere: the Massachusetts Historical Society; the Houghton Library, Harvard University; the New York Historical Society; the Morristown National Historical Park, and to Mr. Francis Ronalds, its director, as well as to the library of the University of North Carolina; the Manuscript Division of the New York Public Library, and many others.

It is not entirely fortuitous that this one-volume edition should be published coincidentally with the one hundred and fiftieth anniversary of the House of Harper & Row, long committed to publishing significant works in American history. Special acknowledgment must be paid to Mr. Daniel F. Bradley and Mrs. Beulah Hagen of that publishing house for their valued contributions to the production and editorial problems raised by this edition. To the many publishers, historical societies, university presses, government agencies, and private individuals, who, by giving us permission to reproduce material in their possession or their control, displayed the operation of the great community of scholarship, we are deeply grateful. An asterisk (*) before a title indicates that special permission was obtained from the publisher, proprietor, or other copyright owner to use the excerpts published in these volumes. Our mapmaker has sometimes found assistance or reassurance through study of the fine maps in *History of the United States and Its People* by Elroy M. Avery. The map of the peace negotiations, 1779–1783, was especially drawn for use originally in *The Peacemakers* (Harper & Row, 1965). Our wives did not type the manuscript or compile the index or do the other chores so commonly associated with matrimony in academic circles. They did much more: they shared our enjoyment in the undertaking.

HENRY STEELE COMMAGER
RICHARD B. MORRIS

MANUSCRIPTS

American Loyalist Audit Office Transcripts. New York Public Library.
* Baldwin, Loammi. Papers. Houghton Library, Harvard University.
Bancroft Collection. New York Public Library.
Boudinot, Elias. Papers. Library of Congress.

Convention of the New England States with Accompanying Resolutions, 1776-80. Rhode Island State Archives.

*Davie-Weems Collection. University of North Carolina.

Duane, James. Papers. New York Historical Society.

*Eggleston, Joseph, Jr. Letter. The J. Pierpont Morgan Library.

Emmet Collection. New York Public Library.

Gansevoort, Peter, Jr. Military Papers. Lansing-Gansevoort Collection. New York Public Library.

Gates, Horatio. Papers. New York Historical Society.

Greene, Nathanael. Papers. William L. Clements Library.

Hamilton, Alexander. Papers. Library of Congress.

*Hamilton, Lieutenant-Governor Henry. Journal. Houghton Library. Harvard University.

*Howe, Sir William. Orderly Book. Lloyd W. Smith Collection. Morristown National Historical Park.

Jay, John. Papers and Letter Books. Special Collections, Columbia University Library.

Lamb, John. Papers. New York Historical Society.

Lincoln, Benjamin. Papers on the Siege of Savannah. New York Public Library.

McDougall, Alexander. Papers. New York Historical Society.

*McGinnis, Richard. Journal. Privately owned.

McLane, Allen. Papers and Journal. New York Historical Society.

Massachusetts. Town Resolutions, Petitions and Memorials. State Archives, Boston.

Morris, Gouverneur. Papers. Special Collections, Columbia University Library.

Morris, Lewis. Letters. Morristown National Historical Park.

Morris, Robert. Papers. Library of Congress.

Peebles, Captain John, of 42nd or Royal Highland Regiment. Journal, April 13-June 26, 1780, covering siege and capture of Charleston, etc. Cunningham Papers, National Register Office, Edinburgh. Courtesy of Mrs. Inglis Fletcher.

Records of the Court of Appeals in Cases of Capture, 1776-1787. Revolutionary War Prize Cases. National Archives, Washington.

Reed, Joseph. Papers. New York Historical Society.

Rhode Island Records, 1772-1777. State Archives, Providence.

Rush, Benjamin. Diary. Philadelphia Free Library, Ridgeway Branch.

*Schuyler, Philip. Letters. Lloyd W. Smith Collection, Morristown National Historical Park.

———. Papers. New York Public Library.

*Seeley, Sylvanus. Diary. Morristown National Historical Park.

Steuben, Friedrich Wilhelm von. Papers. New York Historical Society.

Stirling, Lord (William Alexander). Papers. New York Historical Society.

*Trumbull, Benjamin. Letters. Lloyd W. Smith Collection, Morristown National Historical Park.

Washington, George. Papers. Library of Congress.
*Weedon, George. Letter of September 5, 1781. "Siege of Yorktown and Surrender of Cornwallis Collection." J. Pierpont Morgan Library.
*Weedon, George. Papers. Chicago Historical Society.

NEWSPAPERS

(Boston) *Continental Journal and Weekly Advertiser*, 1776-1780.
Independent Chronicle and Universal Advertiser, 1776-1783.
·(Kingston, N. Y.) *New York Journal, and the General Advertiser*, 1777.
(London)*Morning Post and Daily Advertiser*, 1778.
New York Gazette and Weekly Mercury, 1776-1782.
(New York) *Royal Gazette*, 1777-1783.
(Philadelphia) *Pennsylvania Evening Post*, 1775-1784.
(Philadelphia) *Pennsylvania Gazette*, 1776-1781.
(Philadelphia) *Pennsylvania Packet*, 1775.
(Poughkeepsie, N. Y.) *New York Journal and General Advertiser*, 1778.
(Trenton) *New Jersey Gazette*, 1778.

BOOKS, PERIODICALS AND HISTORICAL COLLECTIONS

*Adams, Charles Francis. "Contemporary Opinion on the Howes." *Massachusetts Historical Society Proceedings*, XLIV, 118-120.
———, ed. *Familiar Letters of John Adams and His Wife, Abigail Adams, During the Revolution, with a Memoir of Mrs. Adams*. New York: Hurd and Houghton, 1876.
———. ed. *Letters of Mrs. Adams, the Wife of John Adams*. 3rd ed. Boston: C. C. Little and J. Brown, 1841.
———, ed. *The Works of John Adams, Second President of the United States: With a Life of the Author, Notes and Illustrations*. 10 vols. Boston: Little, Brown and Company, 1850-1856.
*Adams, John. "Letter." *Massachusetts Historical Society Proceedings*, VIII, 403-405.
*Ainslee, Thomas. "Journal of the Most Remarkable Occurrences in the Province of Quebec from the Appearance of the Rebels in September 1775 Until Their Retreat on the Sixth of May." *Seventh Series of Historical Documents, 1905*, pp. 11-89. Published by the Literary and Historical Society of Quebec.
Allen, Ethan. "Diary." *Pennsylvania Magazine of History and Biography*, IX, 295-296.
———. *A Narrative of Colonel Ethan Allen's Captivity*. 4th ed. Burlington: 1846.
*Allen, Gardner Weld. *Massachusetts Privateers of the Revolution*. Cambridge: Massachusetts Historical Society, 1927.

——. *Naval History of the American Revolution.* 2 vols. Boston: 1913.

Almon, John, ed. *The Parliamentary Register; or, History of the Debates and Proceedings of the Houses of Lords and Commons.* 17 vols. London: J. Almon, 1775-1780.

——. *The Remembrancer; or Impartial Repository of Public Events.* 17 vols. London: J. Almon, 1775-1784.

Anburey, Thomas. *Travels through the Interior Parts of America; in a Series of Letters. By an Officer.* New ed.; 2 vols. London: W. Lane, 1791.

Anderson, Enoch. *Personal Recollections of Captain Enoch Anderson, an Officer of the Delaware Regiments in the Revolutionary War. Papers of the Historical Society of Delaware, No. XVI.* With notes by Henry Hobart Bellas. Wilmington, Del.: Historical Society of Delaware, 1896.

André, Major John. *Major André's Journal; Operations of the British Army under Lieutenant Generals Sir William Howe and Sir Henry Clinton, June, 1777, to November, 1778, to Which Is Added "The Ethics of Major André's Mission," by C. DeW. Willcox.* Tarrytown, N. Y.: William Abbatt, 1930. Copyright 1904 by the Bibliographical Society.

——. *Papers Concerning the Capture and Detention of Major John André.* Collected by Henry B. Dawson. *The Gazette Series,* I, Henry B. Dawson, ed. Yonkers, N. Y.: 1866.

Andrews, Evangeline McLean, ed., in collaboration with Charles McLean Andrews. *Journal of a Lady of Quality; Being the Narrative of a Journey from Scotland to the West Indies, North Carolina, and Portugal in the Years 1774 to 1776.* New Haven: Yale University Press, 1921.

*Andrews, John. "Letters of John Andrews, Esq., of Boston, 1772-1776." Edited by Winthrop Sargent. *Massachusetts Historical Society Proceedings,* VIII (1866), 316-412.

The Annual Register, or a View of the History, Politics, and Literature for the years 1777, 1778, 1781. London: Printed for J. Dodsley, in Pall-Mall, 1778, 1779, 1782.

*Anonymous. *A Brief Narrative of the Ravages of the British and Hessians at Princeton in 1776-1777—A Contemporary Account of the Battles of Trenton and Princeton.* Edited by Varnum Lansing Collins. Princeton Historical Association, Extra Publications, Number One. Princeton, N. J.: The University Library, 1906.

*Anonymous. "A Contemporary British Account of General Sir William Howe's Military Operations in 1777." Contributed by Robert F. Seybolt. *Proceedings of the American Antiquarian Society,* New Series, XL (1931), 69-92.

Arnold, Benedict. "Letters Written while on an Expedition across the State of Maine to Attack Quebec in 1775." *Maine Historical Society Collections,* I (1831), 341-387.

Arnold, Isaac Newton. *Life of Benedict Arnold.* Chicago: Jansen, McClurg & Co., 1880.

Austin, James Trecothick. *Life of Elbridge Gerry.* 2 vols. Boston: Wells, 1828-1829.

Ballagh, James Curtis, ed. *The Letters of Richard Henry Lee.* 2 vols. New York: The Macmillan Company, 1911-1914.

Bancroft, Edward. "Letter." *American Historical Review*, XXIX, 493-494.

Barham, Lord. *Letters and Papers of Charles, Lord Barham, Admiral of the Red Squadron, 1758-1813.* Edited by Sir Henry Knox Laughton. London: Publications of the Navy Records Society, 1907-1911.

Barnes, G. R., & Owen, J. H., eds. *The Private Papers of John, Earl of Sandwich, First Lord of the Admiralty, 1771-1782.* London: Printed for the Navy Records Society, 1932-1938.

Bartlett, John Russell, ed. *Records of the State of Rhode Island and Providence Plantations in New England.* VII and VIII. Providence: Greene, Jackson & Co., 1863.

*Bass, Robert D. *The Green Dragoon.* New York: Henry Holt, 1957. Courtesy of Mr. Robert D. Bass.

Baxter, James Phinney. *The British Invasion from the North; The Campaigns of Generals Carleton and Burgoyne from Canada, 1776-1777, With the Journal of Lieut. William Digby, of the 53d. or Shropshire Regiment of Foot.* Albany: Joel Munsell's Sons, 1887.

Beardsley, Ebenezer. "Effects of Stagnant Air." *Memoirs of American Academy of Arts and Sciences*, I.

Beebe, Lewis. "Journal." *Pennsylvania Magazine of History and Biography*, LIX, 321-361.

*Bemis, Samuel F. "British Secret Service, and the French-American Alliance." *American Historical Review*, XXIX (1923-1924), 474-495.

*Besom, Philip. "Narrative." *Massachusetts Historical Society Proceedings*, V (1862), 357-360.

Bezanson, Anne, assisted by Blanche Daley, Marjorie C. Denison and Miriam Hussey. *Prices and Inflation During the American Revolution, Pennsylvania, 1770-1790.* Philadelphia: University of Pennsylvania Press, 1951.

Bigelow, John, ed. *Benjamin Franklin, Complete Works.* 10 vols. New York: Putnam, 1887-1889.

Boardman, Rev. Samuel W. *Log-Book of Timothy Boardman . . . also, A Biographical Sketch of the Author.* Albany: Joel Munsell's Sons, 1885.

Bolton, Charles Knowles, ed. *Letters of Hugh, Earl Percy, from Boston and New York, 1774-1776.* Boston: C. E. Goodspeed, 1902.

Boswell, James. *The Life of Samuel Johnson, LL.D., with his correspondence and conversations.* New York: 1872.

Boudinot, Elias. *Journal; or Historical Recollections of American Events During the Revolutionary War, from his own original manuscript.* Philadelphia: Bourquin, 1894.

———. *Life, Public Services, Addresses, and Letters.* Edited by J. J. Boudinot. 2 vols. Boston: Houghton Mifflin, 1896.

*———. "Report on American Prisoners of War in New York." *William & Mary Quarterly*, 3rd Series, XIII (1956), 379-393.

Boyd, Julian P., ed. *The Declaration of Independence; The Evolution of the Text as Shown in Facsimiles of Various Drafts by Its Author.* Issued in conjunction with an exhibit of these drafts at the Library of Congress on the two-hundredth anniversary of the birth of Thomas Jefferson. Washington: Library of Congress, 1943.

*———. *The Papers of Thomas Jefferson.* 10 vols. to date. Princeton, N. J.: Princeton University Press, 1950-1954.

Bradford, William. "Letter." *Pennsylvania Archives,* 1st Series, V (1853), 207-209.

*Brooks, John. "Letter." *Massachusetts Historical Society Proceedings,* XIII (1874), 243-245.

Brooks, Noah. *Henry Knox, A Soldier of the Revolution; Major-General in the Continental Army, Washington's Chief of Artillery, First Secretary of War Under the Constitution, Founder of the Society of the Cincinnati, 1750-1806.* New York and London: G. P. Putnam's Sons, 1900.

Brown, Tarleton. *Memoirs, written by himself.* With a preface and notes by Charles I. Bushnell. New York: Privately printed, 1862.

*Buell, Augustus C. *History of Andrew Jackson.* 2 vols. New York: Charles Scribner's Sons, 1904.

Bullock, Charles Jesse. *Finances of the United States, 1775-89, with Especial Reference to the Budget.* University of Wisconsin Bulletin, Vol. 1, No. 2. Madison: 1895.

Burgoyne, Lieut. Gen. John. *A State of the Expedition from Canada, as Laid Before the House of Commons, by Lieutenant-General Burgoyne, and Verified by Evidence; with a Collection of Authentic Documents, and an Addition of Many Circumstances Which Were Prevented from Appearing Before the House by the Prorogation of Parliament.* London: J. Almon, 1780.

*———. "Proclamation." *Massachusetts Historical Society Proceedings,* XII, 89-90.

Burnett, Edmund C., ed. *Letters of Members of the Continental Congress.* 8 vols. Washington, D. C.: Carnegie Institution of Washington, 1921-1936.

Butler, Colonel Richard. "Journal of the Siege of Yorktown." *Historical Magazine,* VIII, 102 *et seq.*

*Butterfield, L. H., ed. *Letters of Benjamin Rush.* 2 vols. Princeton: Published for the American Philosophical Society by The Princeton University Press, 1951.

Campbell, Mrs. Maria Hull. *Revolutionary Services and Civil Life of General William Hull; Prepared from His Manuscripts, . . . Together with the History of the Campaign of 1812, and Surrender of the Post of Detroit, by James Freeman Clarke.* New York: D. Appleton & Co., 1848.

*Carter, Clarence Edwin, ed. *The Correspondence of General Thomas Gage.* 2 vols. New Haven: Yale University Press, 1931-1933.

Carter, Landon. "Diary." *William & Mary Quarterly*, XVI (1907), 149-152, 258-264.

Chase, Frederick. *A History of Dartmouth College and the Town of Hanover, N. H.* Edited by J. K. Lord. 2 vols. Cambridge: J. Wilson and Son, 1891.

Chastellux, François Jean, Marquis de. *Travels in North America, 1780-82.* Translated by J. Kent. London: 1787; 2 vols, New York: White, 1827.

*Clark, George Rogers. "George Rogers Clark Papers, 1771-1781." *Collections of the Illinois State Historical Library*, VIII (1912); Virginia Series, III, James Alton James, ed.

Clark, Joseph. "Diary." *New Jersey Historical Society Proceedings*, VII (1855), 95-110.

Clinton, George. *Public Papers of George Clinton, First Governor of New York, 1777-1795—1801-1804.* VIII. Edited by Hugh Hastings. Albany: Oliver A. Quayle, State Legislative Printer, 1904.

*Clinton, Sir Henry. *The American Rebellion: Sir Henry Clinton's Narrative of His Campaigns, 1775-1782.* With an Appendix of Original Documents. Edited by William B. Willcox. New Haven: Yale University Press, 1954.

Cobbett, William. *The Parliamentary History of England from the Earliest Period to the Year 1803. . . .* 36 vols. London: Hansard, 1806-1820.

Collier, Sir George. "Extract . . . from the Journal and Papers of Sir George Collier." *Long Island Historical Society, Memoirs*, II (1869), 413-414.

Collins, James. *Autobiography of a Revolutionary Soldier.* Edited by John M. Roberts. Clinton, La.: Feliciana Democrat, 1859.

Columbian Magazine, or Monthly Miscellany. Philadelphia. August, 1789.

Condorcet, Le Marquis de. "Vie de Voltaire." *Oeuvres de Voltaire.* Edited by M. Beuchot. Paris: Chez Lefevre, Libraire, 1834.

Conway, Moncure Daniel, ed. *The Writings of Thomas Paine.* 4 vols. New York: G. P. Putnam's Sons, 1894-1896.

Cook, Frederick, ed. *Journals of the Military Expedition of Major General John Sullivan Against the Six Nations of Indians in 1779 with Records of Centennial Celebrations.* Auburn, N. Y.: Knapp, Peck & Thompson, 1887.

*Corner, George W., ed. *Autobiography of Benjamin Rush; His "Travels Through Life" Together with His Commonplace Book for 1789-1813.* Princeton, N. J.: Published for The American Philosophical Society by Princeton University Press, 1948.

*"Correspondence between a committee of the town of Boston and Contributors of Donations for the Relief of the Sufferers by the Boston Port Bill," *Massachusetts Historical Society Collections*, IV, 4-6, 38-40, 50-52, 71-72, 75-76, 83, 144-145, 251.

*Cresswell, Nicholas. *The Journal of Nicholas Cresswell, 1774-1777.* New York: Dial Press, 1924.

*Crèvecoeur, Hector St. John de. *Sketches of Eighteenth Century America.* New Haven: Yale University Press, 1925.

Curwen, Samuel. *The Journal and Letters of Samuel Curwen, an American in England, from 1775 to 1783*. With an Appendix of Biographical Sketches. By George Atkinson Ward. 4th ed. Boston: Little, Brown and Company, 1864.

Dana, R. H., Jr., ed. "Diary of a British Officer." *Atlantic Monthly*, XXXIX (1877), 394-398.

*Dandridge, Danske. *American Prisoners of the Revolution*. Charlottesville, Va.: The Michie Company, 1911.

Darlington, William. "Letter." *Historical Society of Pennsylvania Bulletin*, I (1845), 58-59.

Davis, Joshua. *A Narrative of Joshua Davis, an American Citizen Who Was Pressed and Served on Board Six Ships of the British Navy*. Boston: 1811.

Dawson, Henry B. *Battles of the United States, by Sea and Land: Embracing Those of the Revolutionary and Indian Wars, the War of 1812, and the Mexican War; with Official Documents, and Biographies of the Most Distinguished Military and Naval Commanders*. 2 vols. New York: Johnson, Fry and Company, 1858.

Deane, Silas. "Correspondence of Silas Deane, Delegate of the First and Second Congress at Philadelphia, 1774-1776." *Connecticut Historical Society Collections*, II. Hartford: 1870.

———. *Silas Deane Papers, 1774-1790*. 5 vols. *New York Historical Society Collections*, "Publication Fund Series," XIX-XXIII. New York: 1887-1891.

De Fonblanque, Edward Barrington. *Political and Military Episodes in the Latter Half of the Eighteenth Century; Derived from the Life and Correspondence of the Right Hon. John Burgoyne, General, Statesman, Dramatist*. London: Macmillan and Co., 1876.

De Lomenie, Louis Leonard. *Beaumarchais and His Times*. Translated by Henry S. Edwards. 4 vols. London: 1856.

Deshon, John. "Letter." *Rhode Island Historical Society Publications*, New Series, VIII (1900), 214-216. Providence: 1900.

Detail and Conduct of the American War, under Generals Gage, Howe, Burgoyne, and Vice-Admiral Lord Howe: With a very Full and Correct State of the Whole of the Evidence, as Given Before a Committee of the House of Commons: And the Celebrated Fugitive Pieces, which are said to have given Rise to that Important Enquiry. The whole Exhibiting a Circumstantial, Connected and Complete History of the Real Causes, Rise, Progress and Present State of the American Rebellion. 3rd. ed. London: Richardson and Urquhart, 1780.

Dexter, Franklin Bowditch, ed. *The Literary Diary of Ezra Stiles, D.D., LL.D., President of Yale College*. New York: Charles Scribner's Sons, 1901.

Dolph, Edward Arthur, ed. *Sound Off, Soldier Songs from Yankee Doodle to Parlez-Vous*. New York: Cosmopolitan Book Corp., 1929.

Donne, W. Bodham, ed. *Correspondence of George III with Lord North, 1768-83*. 2 vols. London: Murray, 1867.

*Douglas, Colonel William. "Revolutionary War Letters of Colonel William Douglas." *The New York Historical Society Quarterly Bulletin,* XIII (1929), 37-40, 79-82, 118-122, 157-163.

Drake, Francis Samuel. *Life and Correspondence of Henry Knox, Major-General in the American Revolutionary Army.* Boston: S. G. Drake, 1873.

Dring, Captain Thomas. *Recollections of the Jersey Prison-Ship; from the Original Manuscripts.* Rewritten by Albert Greene; edited by Henry Dawson. Morrisania, N. Y.: 1865.

Drinker, Mrs. Henry. "Journal." *Pennsylvania Magazine of History and Biography,* XIII (1889), 298-308.

Duncan, James. "Diary of Captain James Duncan, of Colonel Moses Hazen's Regiment, in the Yorktown Campaign, 1781." Edited by William H. Egle. Pennsylvania Archives, 2nd Series, XV. Harrisburg: E. K. Myers, 1890.

Du Ponceau, Pierre. "Autobiography." *Pennsylvania Magazine of History and Biography,* LXIII (1939), 195-227.

Ellery, William. "Letter," *Publications of the Rhode Island Historical Society,* New Series, VIII (1900), 200-201. Providence: 1900.

*Emerson, William. "Diary." In Ralph Waldo Emerson, *Miscellanies.* Boston, New York: Houghton Mifflin & Co., 1863.

Ewing, Thomas. *George Ewing, Gentleman, a Soldier of Valley Forge.* Yonkers, N. Y.: Privately printed by Thomas Ewing, 1928.

Fanning, Nathaniel. *Memoirs of the Life of Captain Nathaniel Fanning, an American Naval Officer. . . .* New York: 1808.

Fanning, Nathaniel. *Narrative of the Adventures of an American Navy Officer.* New York: Printed for author, 1806.

*Farnsworth, Amos. "Diary." Edited by Dr. Samuel A. Greene. *Massachusetts Historical Society Proceedings,* 2nd Series, XII (1899), 74-107.

Field, Edward. *Esek Hopkins, Commander-in-Chief of the Continental Navy. . . .* Providence: 1898.

*Fithian, Philip Vickers. *Journal, 1775-1776, Written on the Virginia-Pennsylvania Frontier in the Army around New York.* Edited by Robert Greenbalgh Albion and Leonidas Dodson. Princeton, N. J.: Princeton University Press, 1934.

Fitzpatrick, John C., ed. *The Writings of George Washington, from the Original Manuscript Sources, 1745-1799.* 39 vols. Washington: United States Government Printing Office, 1931-1944.

*———. *The Diaries of George Washington, 1748-1799.* 4 vols. Boston: Houghton Mifflin Company, 1925. Courtesy of the Mt. Vernon Ladies Association.

Foner, Philip S., ed. *The Complete Writings of Thomas Paine.* 2 vols. Citadel Press, 1945.

Foote, William Henry. *Sketches of Virginia, Historical and Biographical.* Philadelphia: Martier, 1850; 2nd Series, Lippincott, 1855.

Force, Peter, ed. *American Archives: Fourth Series, Containing a Documentary History of the English Colonies in North America from the*

King's Message to Parliament of March 7, 1774, to the Declaration of Independence by the United States. 6 vols. Washington: M. St. Clair Clarke and Peter Force, 1837-1846.

——. *American Archives: Fifth Series, Containing a Documentary History of the United States of America from the Declaration of Independence, July 4, 1776, to the Definitive Treaty of Peace with Great Britain, September 3, 1783.* 3 vols. Washington: M. St. Clair Clarke and Peter Force, 1848-1853.

Ford, Paul Leicester. "Lord Howe's Commission to Pacify the Colonies." *Atlantic Monthly*, LXXVII (1896), 758-766.

——, ed. *Writings of Thomas Jefferson.* 10 vols. New York: Putnam, 1892-1899.

Ford, Worthington Chauncey, ed. *Defences in Philadelphia in 1777.* Brooklyn, N.Y.: Historical Printing Club, 1897.

——. *Letters of Jonathan Boucher to George Washington.* Brooklyn, N.Y.: Historical Printing Club, 1897.

——. *Letters of William Lee, 1766-1783.* 2 vols. Brooklyn, N.Y.: Historical Printing Club, 1892.

*Fortescue, Sir John, ed. *The Correspondence of King George the Third, from 1760 to December 1783.* 6 vols. London: Macmillan and Co., 1927-1928. Courtesy of Librarian, Windsor Castle.

Fox, Charles James. *Memorials and Correspondence of Charles James Fox.* IV. Edited by Lord John Russell. London: R. Bentley, 1857.

*French, Allen. *The First Year of the American Revolution.* Boston: Houghton Mifflin, 1934.

*——. *The Taking of Ticonderoga in 1775: The British Story; A Study of Captors and Captives.* Cambridge, Mass.: Harvard University Press, 1928. Reprinted by permission of the Publishers and the President and Fellows of Harvard College.

Freneau, Philip Morin. *Poems Written and Published During the American Revolutionary War. . . .* 3rd. ed.; 2 vols. Philadelphia: From the Press of Lydia R. Bailey, No. 10, North-Allen, 1809.

Frothingham, Richard. *History of the Siege of Boston and of the Battles of Lexington, Concord, and Bunker Hill. Also, an Account of the Bunker Hill Monument. With illustrative Documents.* 2nd ed. Boston: Charles C. Little and James Brown, 1851.

——. *Rise of the Republic of the United States.* Boston: Little, Brown and Co., 1872.

Gavett, William. "Account of the Affair at North Bridge." *Essex Institute Proceedings*, I (1859), 126-128.

Gentleman's Magazine, XXXVI (March 1776), London.

Gibbes, R. W., ed. *Documentary History of the American Revolution: Consisting of Letters and Papers Relating to the Contest for Liberty, Chiefly in South Carolina, from Originals in the Possession of the Editor, and Other Sources. 1776-1782.* 3 vols. New York: D. Appleton & Company, 1853-1857.

Gibson, James Edgar. *Dr. Bodo Otto and the Medical Background of the American Revolution.* Baltimore: C. C. Thomas, 1937.

Glich, ——. "Account of the Battle of Bennington." *Vermont Historical Society Collections,* I (1870), 211-223.

*Gordon, William. "Letter of Reverend William Gordon, 1776." Edited by Harold Murdock. *Massachusetts Historical Society Proceedings,* LX (1927), 360-366.

Goss, Elbridge Henry. *The Life of Colonel Paul Revere.* I. Boston: Joseph George Cupples, 1891.

*Gottschalk, Louis, ed. *The Letters of Lafayette to Washington, 1777-1779.* New York: Privately printed by Helen F. Hubbard, 1944. Courtesy of Professor Louis Gottschalk.

Graham, James. *The Life of General Daniel Morgan, with Portions of his Correspondence.* New York: 1859.

*Graves, Admiral Lord Thomas. *The Graves Papers and other Documents Relating to the Naval Operations of the Yorktown Campaign, July to October, 1781.* Edited by French Ensor Chadwick. *Publications of the Naval History Society,* VII. New York: The Naval History Society, 1916.

Graydon, Alexander. *Memoirs of His Own Time, with Reminiscences of the Men and Events of the Revolution.* Edited by John Stockton Littrell. Philadelphia: Lindsay & Blakiston, 1846.

Great Britain Historical Manuscripts Commission. *The Manuscript of the Earl of Carlisle, Preserved at Castle Howard, Fifteenth Report, Appendix, Part VI.* London: Eyre and Spottiswoode, 1897.

——. *The Manuscripts of the Earl of Dartmouth.* 3 vols. London: 1887-1896.

——. *Report on the Manuscripts of the Late Reginald Rawdon Hastings.* 4 vols. London: H. M. Stationery Office, 1930-1947.

——. *Report on the Manuscripts of Mrs. Stopford-Sackville.* 2 vols. London: H. M. Stationery Office, 1904-1910.

——. *Manuscripts in Various Collections.*

Greene, George Washington. *The Life of Nathanael Greene, Major-General in the Army of the Revolution.* 3 vols. New York: G. P. Putnam's Sons, 1867-1871.

Greene, Nathanael. "Letter." *Rhode Island Historical Society Collections,* XX (1927), 106-107.

——. "Letters of General Nathanael Greene, to Colonel Jeremiah Wadsworth." *Pennsylvania Magazine of History and Biography,* XXII. Philadelphia: Historical Society of Pennsylvania, 1898.

Griffin, Martin I. J. *Commodore John Barry.* Philadelphia: George W. Gibbens, printer, 1903.

Griswold, Charles. "Letter." *American Journal of Science and Arts,* II, No. 2. (November 1820), 94-101.

Guild, Reuben Aldridge. *Chaplain Smith and the Baptists; or, Life, Journals, Letters, and Addresses of the Rev. Hezekiah Smith, D.D., of Haver-*

hill, *Massachusetts. 1737-1805.* Philadelphia: American Baptist Publication Society, 1885.

Hadden, James M. *A Journal Kept in Canada and Upon Burgoyne's Campaign in 1776 and 1777. Also Orders kept by Him and Issued by Sir Guy Carleton, Lieut. General John Burgoyne and Major General William Phillips in 1776, 1777, and 1778, with an explanatory chapter and notes by Horatio Rogers.* Albany: Joel Munsell's Sons, 1884.

Hamilton, Lieutenant-Governor Henry. "Extracts from a Private Manuscript Written by Governor Paul Hamilton, Sr., During the Period of the Revolutionary War, from 1776-1800." *Year Book—1898, City of Charleston, S. C.,* pp. 299-327.

Hamilton, J. C., ed. *History of the Republic . . . as Traced in the Writings of Alexander Hamilton.* New York: 1857-1864; Boston, 1879.

*Hammond, Otis G., ed. *Letters and Papers of Major-General John Sullivan, Continental Army.* 3 vols. *Collections of the New Hampshire Historical Society.* XIII, XIV, XV. Concord: New Hampshire Historical Society, 1930-1931, 1939.

"Hand Papers." *Pennsylvania Archives,* 2nd Series, X, 308-309.

Harcourt, Edward William, ed. *The Harcourt Papers.* 13 vols. Oxford: Parker, 1880-1905.

Harrison, Richard. "Testimony." *New York Historical Society Collections,* VI (1783), 71-75.

[Hawkes, James, supposed author]. *A Retrospect of the Boston Tea-Party, with a Memoir of George R. T. Hewes, Survivor of the Little Band of Patriots Who Drowned the Tea in Boston Harbour in 1773. By a citizen of New-York. . . .* New York: S. S. Bliss, printer, 1834.

Hay, Samuel. "Letter." *Pennsylvania Archives,* 2nd Series, I (1879), 598-599.

Heath, William. *Memoirs of Major-General William Heath, by Himself, to which is added the Accounts of the Battle of Bunker Hill by Generals Dearborn, Lee and Wilkinson.* Edited by William Abbatt. New York: William Abbatt, 1901.

Hening, William Waller, ed. *The Statutes at Large; Being a Collection of all the Laws of Virginia from the First Session of the Legislature in the Year 1619.* Richmond: 1819-1823.

Henry, John Joseph. *Account of Arnold's Campaign Against Quebec, and of the Hardships and Sufferings of that Band of Heroes who Traversed the Wilderness of Maine from Cambridge to the St. Lawrence, in the Autumn of 1775.* Albany: Joel Munsell, 1877.

Hill, G. Birkbeck, ed. *Letters of David Hume to William Strahan.* Oxford: Clarendon Press, 1888.

Hopkinson, Francis. *The Miscellaneous Essays and Occasional Writings.* III. Philadelphia: 1792.

Hough, Franklin B. *The Siege of Savannah, by the Combined American and French Forces, under the Command of Gen. Lincoln, and the Count d'Estaing, in the Autumn of 1779.* Albany, N. Y.: Joel Munsell, 1866.

Hovey, Alvah. *A Memoir of the Life and Times of the Rev. Isaac Backus, A. M.* Boston: Gould & Lincoln, 1858.

*Hudson, Charles. *History of the Town of Lexington, Middlesex County, Massachusetts, from Its First Settlement to 1868.* I. Boston: Houghton Mifflin Company, 1913. Courtesy of the Lexington Historical Society.

*Hughes, Thomas. *A Journal by Thos. Hughes for his Amusement, and Designed only for his Perusal by the Time he Attains the Age of 50 if he Lives so Long (1778-1789).* Edited by E. A. Benians. Cambridge, England: The University Press, 1947.

*Hulton, Ann. *Letters of a Loyalist Lady; Being the Letters of Ann Hulton, Sister of Henry Hulton, Commissioner of Customs at Boston, 1767-1776.* Cambridge: Harvard University Press, 1927. Reprinted by permission of the publisher and the President and Fellows of Harvard College.

Hunt, Gaillard, ed. *The Writings of James Madison, comprising his public papers and his private correspondence, for the first time printed.* 9 vols. New York: G. P. Putnam's Sons, 1900-1910.

Hunter, Sir Martin. *The Journal of Gen. Sir Martin Hunter, G.C.M.G., G.C.H., and some Letters of his Wife, Lady Hunter.* Edited by Miss Anne Hunter and Miss Bell. Edinburgh: The Edinburgh Press, 1894.

Huntington, Ebenezer. *Letters Written by Ebenezer Huntington During the American Revolution.* Edited by Charles Frederick Heartman. New York: Privately printed, 1914.

Hutchinson, Thomas, ed. *Diary and Letters of Thomas Hutchinson, with an Account of his Administration.* Compiled from the original documents by P. O. Hutchinson. 2 vols. Boston: Houghton, 1884-1886.

———. *The History of Massachusetts-Bay.* . . . Printed by Thomas and John Fleet at the Heart and Crown in Cornhill, 1764-1767.

Hutton, James. "Some Account of James Hutton's Visit to Franklin, in France, in December of 1777." *Pennsylvania Magazine of History and Biography,* XXXII (1908), 223-232.

James, William Dobein. *A Sketch of the Life of Brig. Gen. Francis Marion and a History of His Brigade.* Charleston, S.C.: Gould and Milet, 1821.

Jay, John. *The Correspondence and Public Papers of John Jay, First Chief-Justice of the United States, Member and President of the Continental Congress, Minister to Spain, Member of Commission to Negotiate Treaty of Independence, Envoy to Great Britain, Governor of New York, etc.* Edited by Henry P. Johnson. 4 vols. New York: G. P. Putnam's Sons, 1896.

Jefferson, Thomas. *Notes on the State of Virginia* in *Writings.* Collected and edited by Paul Leicester Ford. III, 68-295. New York: G. P. Putnam's Sons, 1894.

Johnson, Samuel. *Taxation No Tyranny, an answer to the resolutions and address of the American Congress.* 4th ed. London: Printed for T. Cadell, 1775.

Johnson, William. *Sketches of the Life and Correspondence of Nathanael Greene, Major General of the Armies of the United States, in the War of the Revolution.* Compiled Chiefly from Original Materials. 2 vols. Charleston, S. C.: A. E. Miller, 1822.

Johnston, Henry P. *The Battle of Harlem Heights, September 16, 1776, With a Review of the Events of the Campaign.* New York: The Macmillan Company, 1897.

———. *The Campaign of 1776 Around New York and Brooklyn. Including a New and Circumstantial Account of the Battle of Long Island and the Loss of New York, With a Review of Events to the Close of the Year. Memoirs of the Long Island Historical Society,* III. Brooklyn: Long Island Historical Society, 1878.

———. *The Storming of Stony Point on the Hudson, midnight, July 15, 1779; its Importance in the Light of Unpublished Documents.* New York: J. T. White & Co., 1900.

———. *The Yorktown Campaign and the Surrender of Cornwallis, 1781.* New York: Harper & Bros., 1881.

Jones, Charles C., Jr., ed. *The Siege of Savannah in 1779, as Described in Two Contemporaneous Journals of French Officers in the Fleet of Count d'Estaing.* Albany: Joel Munsell, 1874.

Journals of the Continental Congress, 1774-1789. Edited by Gaillard Hunt. 34 vols. Washington: Government Printing Office, 1904-1937.

Kapp, Friedrich. *The Life of John Kalb, Major-General in the Revolutionary Army.* New York: Henry Holt and Company, 1884.

*Kellogg, Louise Phelps, ed. *Frontier Advance on the Upper Ohio. State Historical Society of Wisconsin Collections,* XXIII, Draper Series, IV. Madison: 1916.

*———. *Frontier Retreat on the Upper Ohio. State Historical Society of Wisconsin Collections,* XXIV, Draper Series, V. Madison: 1917.

Kidder, Frederic and Gould, Augustus A. *The History of New Ipswich from Its First Grant in MDCCXXXVI to the Present Time.* Boston: Gould and Lincoln, 1852.

Knox, Major Henry. "Diary." *New England Historical and Genealogical Register,* XXX, 321-326.

Lacey, John. "Memoirs of Brigadier-General John Lacey, of Pennsylvania." *Pennsylvania Magazine of History and Biography,* XXV (1901), 1-13, 191-207, 341-354, 498-515.

Lafayette, Marquis de. *Memoirs, Correspondence and Manuscripts of General Lafayette.* Published by his family. Vol I. New York: Saunders and Otley, 1837.

Lamb, R. *An Original and Authentic Journal of Occurrences During the Late American War from its Commencement to the Year 1783.* Dublin: Wilkinson & Courtney, 1809.

———. *Memoir of His Own Life.* Dublin: J. Jones, 1811.

Laurens, Henry. "Narrative of his Capture, of his Confinement in the Tower of London, etc., 1780, 1781, 1782." *South Carolina Historical Society Collections,* I (1857), 18-83.

Laurens, John. *The Army Correspondence of Colonel John Laurens in the Year 1777-8, Now First Printed from Original Letters Addressed to* his Father, Henry Laurens, President of Congress, with a Memoir by William Gilmore Simms. New York: The Bradford Club, 1867.

Lauzun, Duc de. "Memoirs." *Magazine of American History*, VI (1881), 51-53.

Leach, John. "Journal." *New England Genealogical Register*, XIX (July 1863), 255-263.

Lee, Charles. "The Lee Papers." *New York Historical Society Collections*, V (1872) and VI (1873). The New York Historical Society.

Lee, Henry. *The Campaign of 1781 in the Carolinas*. Philadelphia: E. Littell, 1824.

———. *Memoirs of the War in the Southern Department of the United States*. 2 vols. Philadelphia: Bradford and Inskeep, 1812; 3rd. ed., New York: University Publishing Company, 1869.

Lee, Richard Henry. *Life of Arthur Lee, L.L.D., Joint Commissioner of the United States to the Court of France, and Sole Commissioner to the Courts of Spain and Prussia, During the Revolutionary War. With his Political and Literary Correspondence and his Papers on Diplomatic and Political Subjects, and the Affairs of the United States During the Same Period*. I. Boston: Wells & Lilly, 1829.

Lewis, Sir George Cornewall. *Essays on the Administrations of Great Britain from 1783 to 1830*. Edited by Sir Edmund Head. London: 1864.

*Literary and Historical Society of Quebec. *Manuscripts Relating to the Early History of Canada. Historical Documents*, 2nd Series, V. Quebec: Middleton & Dawson, 1866; reprinted for the Society by T. J. Moore, 1927.

Livesey, Rev. R. *The Prisoners of 1776; a Relic of the Revolution compiled from the Journal of Charles Herbert*. Boston: G. C. Rand, 1854.

Lodge, Henry Cabot, ed. *Complete Works of Alexander Hamilton*. 9 vols. New York: Putnam, 1885-1886.

———. *The Works of Alexander Hamilton*. Constitutional Edition, 12 vols. New York: G. P. Putnam's Sons, n.d.

Lukens, Jesse. "Letter." *American Historical Record*, I, 547-548.

*Lydenberg, Harry Miller, ed. *Diaries and Sketches of Archibald Robertson, 1762-1780*. New York: New York Public Library, 1930.

Lyman, Simeon. "Journal of Simeon Lyman of Sharon, Aug. 10 to Dec. 28, 1775." *Connecticut Historical Society Collections*, VII (1899), 111-133.

Macaulay, Catherine. "Address." *Magazine of History*, Extra No. 114, XXIX, No. 2, 16-18.

Machias Committee of Correspondence. *Maine Historical Society Collections and Proceedings*, 2nd Series, VI (Portland, 1895), 129-131.

*Mackenzie, Frederick. *Diary of Frederick Mackenzie, Giving a Daily Narrative of his Military Service as an Officer of the Regiment of Royal Welsh Fusiliers During the Years 1775-1781 in Massachusetts, Rhode Island and New York*. 2 vols. Cambridge, Mass.: Harvard University Press, 1930. Reprinted by permission of the publishers, and the President and Fellows of Harvard College.

Mackenzie, Roderick. *Strictures on Lt. Col. Tarleton's History "Of the Campaigns of 1780 and 1781, in the Southern Provinces of North America." Wherein Military Characters and Corps are Vindicated From injurious Aspersions, and Several important Transactions placed in their Proper Point of View. In a Series of Letters to a Friend. To Which is added, a Detail of the Siege of Ninety Six, and the Re-Capture of the Island of New-Providence.* London: Privately printed, 1787.

[Martin, Joseph P.] *A Narrative of Some of the Adventures, Dangers and Sufferings of A Revolutionary Soldier.* Hallowell, Me., 1830.

Mathis, Samuel. "Samuel Mathis to General W. R. Davie, June 26, 1819." *American Historical Record.* II. Edited by Benson J. Lossing. Philadelphia: Samuel P. Town, 1873.

Miles, Col. Samuel. "Journal of Col. Samuel Miles, Concerning the Battle of Long Island—1776." *Pennsylvania Archives*, 2nd Series, I (1879), 519-522.

Montresor, John. "The Montresor Journals." Edited by G. D. Scull. *Collections of the New York Historical Society for the year 1881*, XIV. New York: New York Historical Society, 1882.

Moore, Frank, ed. *Diary of the American Revolution. From Newspapers and Original Documents*, 2 vols. New York: Charles Scribner, 1860.

———. *Materials for History, Printed from Original Manuscripts.* 1st Series. New York: Printed for the Zenger Club, 1861.

———. *Songs and Ballads of the American Revolution. With Notes and Illustrations.* New York: D. Appleton & Company, 1855.

Morris, Lewis, Jr. "Letters to General Lewis Morris." *New York Historical Society Collections*, VIII (1875), 433-512.

*Morris, Richard B., ed. *Alexander Hamilton and the Founding of the Nation.* New York: Dial Press, 1957.

"Morris, Robert, Letters to, 1775-1782." *Collections of the New York Historical Society for the Year 1878*, XI, 397-488. New York: New York Historical Society, 1879.

Morton, Robert. "The Diary of Robert Morton. Kept in Philadelphia While that City was Occupied by the British Army in 1777." *Pennsylvania Magazine of History and Biography*, I (1871), 1-39.

Mott, Edward. Journal. *Connecticut Historical Society Collections*, I, 165-172.

Moultrie, William. *Memoirs of the American Revolution, so far as it Related to the States of North and South Carolina, and Georgia. Compiled from the most authentic Materials, the Author's Personal Knowledge of the various Events, and including an Epistolary Correspondence on Public Affairs, with Civil and Military Officers, at that Period.* 2 vols. New York: David Longworth, 1802.

Muhlenberg, Rev. Henry M. "Journal." *Pennsylvania Historical Society Collections*, I (1853), 147-186.

Munro, Wilfred H. *The History of Bristol, Rhode Island: The Story of the Mt. Hope Lands.* Providence: J. A. and R. A. Reid, 1880.

Murphey, Archibald D. *The Papers of Archibald D. Murphey*. Edited by William Henry Hoyt. 2 vols. *Publications of the North Carolina Historical Commission*. Raleigh, N. C.: E. M. Uzzell & Co., State Printers, 1914.

*Navarro, Martin. "Letter." *Wisconsin State Historical Society Collections*, XVIII, 406-408.

*Neeser, Robert Wilden, ed. *Letters and Papers Relating to the Cruises of Gustavus Conyngham, a Captain of the Continental Navy, 1777-1779*. New York: Printed for the Naval History Society by the DeVinne Press, 1915.

Neilson, Charles. *An Original, Compiled and Corrected Account of Burgoyne's Campaign, and the Memorable Battles of Bemis's Heights, Sept. 19, and Oct. 7, 1777, from the most Authentic Sources of Information; Including many Interesting Incidents connected with the Same: and a Map of the Battle Ground*. Albany: J. Munsell, 1844.

*Newell, Timothy. "A Journal Kept During the Time that Boston was Shut Up in 1775-6." *Massachusetts Historical Society Collections*, 4th Series, I (1852), 261-276.

Nicholson, Capt. James. "Letter." *Naval History Society Publications*, I, 125-126. London: 1911.

Niles, Hezekiah, ed. *Centennial Offering. Republication of the Principles and Acts of the Revolution in America*. New York: A. S. Barnes & Co., 1876.

North Carolina (State). *The State Records of North Carolina. Published under the Supervision of the Trustees of the Public Libraries. By Order of the General Assembly*. Edited by Walter Clark. XI-XXVI (1776-1790). Winston, N. C.: M. I. & J. C. Stewart, 1895-1906.

O'Callaghan, E. B., ed. *Documents Relative to the Colonial History of the State of New-York: Procured in Holland, England and France, by John Romeyn Brodhead, Esq*. 9 vols. Albany: Weed, Parsons and Company, 1853-1858.

Onderdonk, Henry. *Revolutionary Incidents of Suffolk and Kings Counties: With an Account of the Battle of Long Island and the British Prisons and Prison-Ships at New-York*. New York: Leavitt & Company, 1849.

Paine, Thomas. *Additions to Common Sense: Addressed to the Inhabitants of America*. Printed in Philadelphia; reprinted in London for J. Almon, 1776.

Paullin, Charles O. *Out-Letters of the Continental Marine Committee and Board of Admiralty August 1776-September 1780*. Publications of the Naval History Society. 2 vols. New York: 1914.

Pausch, Captain Georg. *Journal of Captain Pausch, Chief of the Hanau Artillery During the Burgoyne Campaign*. Translated and annotated by William L. Stone. Albany: Joel Munsell's Sons, 1886.

Pennsylvania (State). *Pennsylvania Archives. Selected and Arranged from original Documents in the office of the Secretary of the Commonwealth, conformably to Acts of the General Assembly, February 15,*

1851 & March 1, 1852, by Samuel Hazard, Commencing 1776, V. Philadelphia: Joseph Severns, 1853.

Pennsylvania Archives. Second Series. "Pennsylvania in the War of the Revolution, Battalions and Line, 1775-1783." Edited by John Blair Linn and William H. Egle. XI, 629-674. 1880.

Pennsylvania Archives. Eighth Series. VIII. 1931-1935.

———. *Statutes at Large, from 1682-1801.* Compiled by J. T. Mitchell and Henry Flanders. 12 vols. Harrisburg: 1896-1908.

Pickering, Octavius. *The Life of Timothy Pickering.* 4 vols. Boston: Little, Brown and Company, 1867.

Price, Richard. *Observations on the Nature of Civil Liberty, the Principles of Government, and the Justice and Policy of the War with America. To which is added an Appendix, containing a State of the National Debt, and Estimate of the money drawn from the Public by the Taxes: and an account of the national Income and Expenditures since the last War.* London: 1776; New York: Reprinted by S. Loudon, 1776.

Proud, R. "On the Violation, etc." *Pennsylvania Magazine of History and Biography*, XX, 515-519.

Ramsay, David. *History of the American Revolution.* 2 vols. London: John Stockdale, 1793.

Reed, Joseph. *Remarks on Governor Johnstone's Speech in Parliament; With a Collection of all the Letters and Authentic Papers, relative to his Propositions to engage the Interest of one of the Delegates of the State of Pennsylvania, in the Congress of the States of America, to Promote the Views of the British Commissioners.* Philadelphia: Francis Barley, 1779.

Reed, William B. *Life and Correspondence of Joseph Reed, Military Secretary of Washington, at Cambridge: Adjutant-General of the Continental Army: Member of the Congress of the United States: and President of the Executive Council of the State of Pennsylvania.* 2 vols. Philadelphia: Lindsay and Blakiston, 1847.

Reeves, Enos. "Extracts from the Letter-Books of Lieutenant Enos Reeves, of the Pennsylvania Line." *Pennsylvania Magazine of History and Biography*, XXI (1897), 72-85, 235-256, 376-391, 466-476 (concluding installment).

*Reid, W. Max. *The Story of Old Fort Johnson.* New York: G. P. Putnam's Sons, 1906.

*Revere, Paul. "Letter of Paul Revere to Dr. Belknap." Edited by Charles Deane. *Proceedings of the Massachusetts Historical Society*, XVI (1879), 370-376.

Riedesel, Baroness Frederike von. *Letters and Journals relating to the War of the American Revolution, and the Capture of the German Troops at Saratoga.* Translated by William L. Stone. Albany: Joel Munsell, 1867.

Robinson, Thomas P., and Leder, Lawrence H., eds. "Governor Livingston and the 'Sunshine Patriots.'" *William & Mary Quarterly*, 3rd Series, XIII (1956), 394-397.

*Rodney, Caesar, and others. *Letters to and from Caesar Rodney, 1756-1784*. Edited by George Herbert Ryden. Philadelphia: University of Pennsylvania Press, 1933.

*Rodney, Sir George. *Letter-Books and Order-Book*. 2 vols. New York: New York Historical Society, 1932.

Rodney, Thomas. *Diary of Captain Thomas Rodney, 1776-1777*. With an Introduction by Caesar A. Rodney. *Papers of the Historical Society of Delaware, No. VIII*. Wilmington, Del.: The Historical Society of Delaware, 1888.

Ross, Charles, ed. *Correspondence of Cornwallis*. 3 vols. London: Murray, 1859.

Rush, Richard. *Occasional Productions, Political, Diplomatic, and Miscellaneous. Including, among others, A Glance at the Court and Government of Louis Philippe and the French Revolution of 1848. While the Author Resided as Envoy Extraordinary and Minister Plenipotentiary from the United States at Paris*. Edited by Rush's executors. Philadelphia: J. B. Lippincott & Company, 1860.

Sargent, Winthrop, ed. *Loyalist Poetry of the Revolution*. Albany, 1860.

———. *The Loyal Verses of Joseph Stansbury and Doctor Jonathan Odell, relating to the American Revolution*. Albany: J. Munsell, 1860.

Saunders, William L., ed. *Colonial Records of North Carolina*. 10 vols. Raleigh: P. M. Hale, 1886-1890.

Scull, G. D., ed. *Memoir and Letters of Captain W. Glanville Evelyn, of the 4th Regiment ("King's Own") From North America, 1774-1776*. Oxford: James Parker and Co., 1879.

Seabury, Reverend Samuel. *Letters of a Westchester Farmer*. Edited by Clarence H. Vance. Published for Westchester County by the Westchester County Historical Society. White Plains, N. Y., 1930.

Senter, Isaac. "The Journal of Isaac Senter, M. D., on a Secret Expedition against Quebec, 1775." *The Magazine of History with Notes and Queries*, Extra No. 42, 1915.

*Serle, Ambrose. *The American Journal of Ambrose Serle, Secretary to Lord Howe, 1776-1778*. Edited by Edward H. Tatum, Jr. San Marino, California: The Huntington Library, 1940.

Shaw, Major Samuel. *The Journals of Major Samuel Shaw, the First American Consul at Canton, With a Life of the Author*, by Joseph Quincy. Boston: Wm. Crosby and H. P. Nichols, 1847.

Shea, J. G., ed. *The Operations of the French Fleet under the Count de Grasse in 1781-2 as Described in two Contemporaneous Journals*. New York: The Bradford Club, 1864.

Sherburne, Andrew. *Memoirs of Andrew Sherburne: A Pensioner of the Navy of the Revolution*. Providence, 1831.

Sherburne, John Henry. *Life and Character of the Chevalier John Paul Jones*. Washington, 1825.

Simcoe, J. G. *Simcoe's Military Journal, A History of the Operations of a Partisan Corps, Called the Queen's Rangers, Commanded by Lieut. Col. J. G. Simcoe, During the War of the American Revolution: Illustrated*

by ten engraved plans of action, etc. Now first Published, with a
Memoir of the Author and other Additions. New York: Bartlett &
Welford, 1844.

*Sinclair, Patrick. "Letter." *Wisconsin State Historical Society Collections*,
XI, 147-148.

Smith, William Henry, ed. *The St. Clair Papers. The Life and Public Services of Arthur St. Clair, Soldier of the Revolutionary War; President
of the Continental Congress; and Governor of the North-Western
Territory, with his Correspondence and other Papers*. 2 vols. Cincinnati: Robert Clarke, 1882.

*Smyth, Albert Henry, ed. *The Writings of Benjamin Franklin*. 10 vols.
New York: The Macmillan Company, 1905-1907.

Sparks, Jared, ed. *Correspondence of the American Revolution: Being
Letters of Eminent Men to George Washington. From the time of
his Taking Command of the Army to the End of his Presidency*.
4 vols. Boston: Little, Brown and Co., 1853.

———. *Diplomatic Correspondence of the American Revolution*. 12 vols.
Boston, 1829-1830.

———. *Life of Gouverneur Morris*. 3 vols. Boston: 1832.

Stedman, Edmund C., and Hutchinson, E. M. *Library of American Literature*. 11 vols. New York: Webster, 1891.

Stevens, Benjamin Franklin. *B. F. Stevens's Facsimiles of Manuscripts in
European Archives Relating to America, 1773-1783*. London: Malby
& Sons, 1889-1895.

———. *The Campaigns in Virginia 1781, An Exact Reprint of Six rare pamphlets on the Clinton-Cornwallis Controversy with very Numerous
Important unpublished manuscript notes by Sir Henry Clinton K. B.
and the Omitted and hitherto unpublished portions of the letters in
their appendixes added from the original manuscripts with a supplement. . . .* 2 vols. London: 1888.

Stillé, Charles J. *Major-General Anthony Wayne and the Pennsylvania
Line in the Continental Army*. Philadelphia: J. B. Lippincott Company, 1893.

Stocking, Abner. "An Interesting Journal of the Expedition Against Quebec, 1775." *The Magazine of History with Notes and Queries*, Extra
No. 75, 1921.

*Stone, Joel. "The Narrative of Joel Stone." *Loyalist Narratives from
Upper Canada*. Edited by James Talmon. Toronto: The Champlain
Society, 1946.

Stone, William Leete, ed. *Ballads and Poems relating to the Burgoyne
Campaign*. Albany: Joel Munsell, 1893.

———. *The Campaign of Lieut. Gen. John Burgoyne, and the Expedition
of Lieut. Col. Barry St. Leger*. Albany: Joel Munsell, 1877.

Story, Joseph. "Account Dictated." *Essex Institute Proceedings*, I, 134-135.

Stryker, William S. *The Battles of Trenton and Princeton*. Boston and
New York: Houghton, Mifflin and Company, 1898.

Tallmadge, Benjamin. *Memoir of Col. Benj. Tallmadge, prepared by himself, at the request of his children.* New York: 1858.

Tarleton, Lt.-Col. Banastre. *A History of the Campaigns of 1780 and 1781, in the Southern Provinces of North America.* Dublin: Colles, Exshaw, et al., 1787.

Taylor, Jeannette. *Life and Correspondence of John Paul Jones, including his Narrative.* New York: 1830.

Thacher, James, M. D. *A Military Journal During the American Revolutionary War, from 1775-1783; Describing interesting events and transactions of this period; With Numerous Historical Facts and Anecdotes, from the original manuscript. To Which is added, an Appendix, Containing Biographical sketches of several general officers.* 2nd ed. Boston: Cottons & Barnard, 1827.

Thacher, Rev. Peter. "Narrative." *Historical Magazine,* 2nd Series, III, 382-384.

Thorpe, Francis Newton, ed. *The Federal and State Constitutions, Colonial Charters, and other organic Laws of the states, territories, and colonies now or heretofore forming the United States of America.* 7 vols. Washington: Government Printing Office, 1909.

Tilghman, Tench. *Memoir of Lieut. Col. Tench Tilghman, Secretary and aide to Washington Together with an appendix containing Revolutionary Journals and Letters Hitherto Unpublished.* Albany, N. Y.: J. Munsell, 1876.

Tower, Charlemagne, Jr. *The Marquis de La Fayette in the American Revolution.* 2 vols. Philadelphia: Lippincott, 1895.

Trumbull, Benjamin. "Benjamin Trumbull's Journal of the Expedition against Canada, 1775." *Connecticut Historical Society Collections,* VII (1899), 137-173.

———. "Journal of the Campaign at New York, 1776-7." *Orderly Books and Journals Kept by Connecticut Men While Taking Part in the American Revolution, 1775-1778,* pp. 177-220. *Collections of the Connecticut Historical Society,* VII. Hartford, Conn.: Connecticut Historical Society, 1899.

Trumbull, John. *The Poetical Works of John Trumbull, LL. D. Containing M'Fingal, A Modern Epic Poem, Revised and corrected with copious explanatory notes: The Progress of Dulness; and a collection of Poems on various subjects written before and during the Revolutionary War.* 2 vols. Hartford: 1820.

*Trumbull, Jonathan. "Minutes of Occurrences Respecting the Siege and Capture of York in Virginia, extracted from the Journal of Colonel Jonathan Trumbull, Secretary to the General, 1781." *Proceedings of the Massachusetts Historical Society,* IV (1876), 331-338.

Tucker, St. George. "The Southern Campaign, 1781, From Guilford Court House to the Siege of York, Narrated in the Letters from Judge St. George Tucker to his Wife." Edited by Charles Washington

Coleman, Jr. *The Magazine of American History with Notes and Queries*, VII (1881), 36-46, 201-216.

*Tyler, J. E., ed. "Account of Lexington." *William & Mary Quarterly*, 3rd Series, X (January 1953), 99-107.

*Uhlendorf, Bernard A., ed. and trans. *The Siege of Charleston, with an Account of the Province of South Carolina: the Von Jungkenn Papers in the William L. Clements Library*. Ann Arbor, Mich.: University of Michigan Press, 1938.

—— and Vosper, Edna, eds. *Letters from Major Baurmeister to Colonel Von Jungkenn Written during the Philadelphia Campaign, 1777-1778*. Philadelphia: The Historical Society of Pennsylvania, 1937.

Universal Magazine of Knowledge and Pleasure. London: 1747-1803.

*Van Doren, Carl. *Secret History of the American Revolution; an Account of the Conspiracies of Benedict Arnold and Numerous Others drawn from the Secret Service Papers of the British Headquarters in North America now for the first time examined and made public*. New York: The Viking Press, 1941.

Van Schaak, Henry Cruger. *Life of Peter Van Schaak*. New York: Appleton, 1842.

Vernon, William. "Papers of William Vernon and the Navy Board, 1776-1794." *Rhode Island Historical Publications*, New Series, VIII (1900), 197-277. Providence: 1900.

Waldo, Albigence. "Valley Forge, 1777-1778. Diary of Surgeon Albigence Waldo, of the Connecticut Line." *Pennsylvania Magazine of History and Biography*, XXI (1897), 299-323.

Walpole, Horace. *Journal of the Reign of George III from 1771 to 1783*. John Doran, ed. 2 vols. London: Bentley, 1859.

——. *The Letters of Horace Walpole*. Arranged and edited by Mrs. Paget Toynbee. Oxford: Clarendon Press, 1903-1905.

——. *The Letters of Horace Walpole, Earl of Oxford, including numerous letters now first published from the original manuscripts*. John Wright, ed. London: R. Bentley, 1840.

*Ward, Samuel. *Correspondence of Governor Samuel Ward, May 1775— March 1776, with a biographical introd., based chiefly on the Ward Papers covering the period 1725-1776*. Edited by Bernhard Knollenberg. Providence: Rhode Island Historical Society, 1952.

Warren-Adams Letters; Being Chiefly a Correspondence among John Adams, Samuel Adams, and James Warren. 2 vols. *Collections of the Massachusetts Historical Society*, Vols. LXXII (1917) and LXXIII (1925).

Watkins, George. *Digest of the Laws of Georgia, from its First Establishment as a British Province down to the Year 1800, inclusive*. . . . Philadelphia: Aitken, 1801.

Webb, Samuel Blachley. *Correspondence and Journals of Samuel Blachley Webb*. Collected and edited by Worthington C. Ford. 3 vols. New York: Burnett, 1894.

Wharton, Francis, ed. *The Revolutionary Diplomatic Correspondence of the United States.* Edited under direction of Congress with Preliminary Index, and Notes Historical and Legal. 6 vols. Washington: Government Printing Office, 1889.

Whipple, William. "Letter." "Stray Leaves from an Autograph Collection: Correspondence of Josiah Bartlett, of N. H. during the American Revolution." *Historical Magazine,* VI (March 1862), 73-78.

White, George. *Historical Collections of Georgia: Containing the Most Interesting Facts, Traditions, Biographical Sketches, Anecdotes, etc. relating to its History and Antiquities, from its First Settlement to the Present Time.* Compiled from Original Records and Official Documents. New York: Pudney & Russell, 1855.

White, John. "Extracts." *Essex Institute Historical Collections,* XLIX (Jan. 1913), 92-94.

White, Joseph. *A Narrative of Events.* Charlestown, Mass.: 1833.

Wilkinson, Eliza. *Letters of Eliza Wilkinson during the Invasion and Possession of Charlestown, S. C. by the British in the Revolutionary War.* Edited by Carolina Gripman. New York: 1839.

Wilkinson, James. *Memoirs of My Own Times.* 3 vols. Philadelphia: A. Small, 1816.

*Willard, Margaret Wheeler, ed. *Letters on the American Revolution, 1774-1776.* Boston: Houghton Mifflin Company, 1925.

Willett, Marinus. *A Narrative of the Military Actions of Colonel Marinus Willett, taken chiefly from his own manuscript.* Prepared by his son, William M. Willett. New York: Carvill, 1831.

Wirt, William. *Sketches of the Life and Character of Patrick Henry.* Philadelphia: Claxton, 1818.

*Wortley, Mrs. E. Stuart, ed. *Correspondence of 3rd Earl of Bute and of Lt. Gen. The Hon. Sir Charles Stuart.* London: John Murray Company, 1923.

Wraxall, Sir Nathaniel William. *The Historical and the Posthumous Memoirs of Sir Nathaniel William Wraxall, 1772-1784.* Edited by Henry B. Wheatley. 5 vols. New York: Scribner and Welford, 1884.

Zeisberger, David. *Diary of David Zeisberger, a Moravian Missionary among the Indians of Ohio.* Translated from the German ms. and edited by Eugene F. Bliss. Historical and Philosophical Society of Ohio Publications, New Series, II, III. Cincinnati: Clarke, 1885.

Index